ISBN 978-0-331-47928-7
PIBN 11086858

1 MONTH OF
FREE
READING

at
www.ForgottenBooks.com

By purchasing this book you are eligible for one month membership to ForgottenBooks.com, giving you unlimited access to our entire collection of over 1,000,000 titles via our web site and mobile apps.

To claim your free month visit:
www.forgottenbooks.com/free1086858

English
Français
Deutsche
Italiano
Español
Português

www.forgottenbooks.com

Mythology Photography **Fiction**
Fishing Christianity **Art** Cooking
Essays Buddhism Freemasonry
Medicine **Biology** Music **Ancient**
Egypt Evolution Carpentry Physics
Dance Geology **Mathematics** Fitness
Shakespeare **Folklore** Yoga Marketing
Confidence Immortality Biographies
Poetry **Psychology** Witchcraft
Electronics Chemistry History **Law**
Accounting **Philosophy** Anthropology
Alchemy Drama Quantum Mechanics
Atheism Sexual Health **Ancient History**
Entrepreneurship Languages Sport
Paleontology Needlework Islam
Metaphysics Investment Archaeology
Parenting Statistics Criminology
Motivational

The
Hispanic American Historical
Review

Volume 4
1 9 2 1

Published Quarterly by the Board of Editors of The
Hispanic American Historical Review

Baltimore
Williams and Wilkins Company
1921

CONTENTS OF VOLUME IV

CONTENTS

The Hispanic American Historical Review

Vol. IV   FEBRUARY, 1921   No. 1

EDITORIAL ANNOUNCEMENTS

THE HISPANIC AMERICAN HISTORICAL REVIEW was founded in 1918, and has since February of that year been published quarterly. With this number, the REVIEW begins its fourth year. During the preliminary stages of organization, some scholars, but only a few, expressed a fear lest there should be a paucity of material of the proper caliber offered for publication. Happily that fear has been groundless as the first three volumes of the REVIEW have shown, and the constantly increasing interest being taken in the REVIEW by scholars, not only of this continent, but of South America and of Europe, proves that there need be no apprehension of a decline in the character of the material to be published in future numbers. Not only have original and valuable historical articles been offered to the readers of this REVIEW, but a great amount of bibliographical material as well, among which are found compilations, serious articles, notes, and lists—in other words tools for the student and worker in the history of Hispanic America. Historical Documents and various notes and comment on many subjects have also been published.

All this material has been given to its readers for the small price of three dollars per annum, or three dollars and fifty cents to countries where domestic rates of postage do not prevail, and this price has not been increased, notwithstanding that the cost of printing and of paper has gone up over a hundred per cent since the first number was issued. The fact is that had this REVIEW not received generous aid from a number of interested persons, it could not have existed one single year. Especially has it had the enthusiastic financial support of a citizen of the United States, who has, indeed, almost entirely assumed the financial burden of the publication. In justice to this gentleman, it can not be expected that he should carry this burden indefinitely. The money that has been received from subscriptions has been a very small part in meeting the expenses of the REVIEW.

There are now between two hundred and fifty and three hundred paid subscriptions. Expenses are confined entirely to the printing and publishing, a very small sum (fifty dollars) paid monthly to the managing editor, and in addition to a few incidental expenses for postage stamps, and other necessary material. The cost for printing the first number of the REVIEW (122 pages) was less than five hundred dollars. The printing of the issue for November, 1920, of double the size, cost over one thousand two hundred dollars. Seven hundred copies are printed of each issue.

The Board of Editors hopes that the REVIEW can become self-sustaining. In order that it may become so, it needs a great many more subscriptions than it has at present. The European War is probably largely responsible for the few subscriptions and the restricted circle of those aiding. This opportunity is being taken to urge the readers of this REVIEW, if they believe in it, if they think that it is serving a useful purpose, if they wish to have it continue, and if they wish to have it reach that goal of excellence that is before it, to use their efforts to increase its circulation. Not only are they requested to suggest to their friends the advantages of subscribing for this REVIEW, but it is also suggested that they may find it advisable to delight their friends by presenting them with a subscription.

It is also suggested that some may find it convenient to become life subscribers to the REVIEW by the payment of one hundred dollars. Also those who wish to aid in a more substantial manner can rest assured that their donations will be used properly.

This REVIEW is not in any sense a money-making project. It can pay no money dividends. It was founded to supply a deficiency that existed prior to its foundation, and the Board of Editors believes that it is fulfilling its end. The friends of the REVIEW are requested to put forth their efforts for its continued existence.

At the meeting of the Board of Editors of THE HISPANIC AMERICAN HISTORICAL REVIEW, held at Washington, on December 28, 1920, Dr. Herbert Ingram Priestley, of the University of California, was unanimously elected to succeed Dr. William Spence Robertson, the retiring member of the Board. In the retirement of Dr. Robertson, who, it will be remembered, was one of the first to propose the foundation of this REVIEW, the Board loses an earnest and serious colleague, whose scholarship and counsel have always been given unstintedly. Both will be needed in the future as in the past. In its new member, the Board welcomes a colleague who is known widely for his work in Mexican history, past and present, and who has given to that study a sympathy of approach and treatment that will go far in the tightening of the intellectual bonds between Mexico and the United States.

Announcement is made also of the unanimous election by the Board of Mr. C. K. Jones as Bibliographer of the REVIEW. Mr. Jones is the author and compiler of *Hispanic American Bibliographies* now appearing in this REVIEW, as well as of other articles that have already appeared in its pages. Mr. Jones, as is well known, is on the staff of the Library of Congress, and has built up to its present excellent condition the department of Hispanoamericana of that institution. He is the foremost authority in this country of that branch of Americana, and is, besides, among other things, a deep student of Rodó and his philosophy.

THE BOARD OF EDITORS.

CAUSES OF THE COLLAPSE OF THE BRAZILIAN EMPIRE

To ex-President Roosevelt has been attributed the statement that there were two revolutions whose motives he had never been able to fathom—the February Revolution which overthrew the government of Louis-Philippe and the Brazilian Revolution of 1889 which brought to an end the only empire in the new world if we except the shortlived monarchy of Maximilian in Mexico. And in truth the causes of the collapse of the imperial regime in Brazil seem at first sight inexplicable. When on November 15, 1889, the world learned that the venerable Emperor Dom Pedro II. had been deposed and a republic declared the news was received with incredulity coupled with a feeling akin to indignation. Outside of South America at least the feeling was all but universal that the Braganza dynasty had become thoroughly acclimated in Brazil; that it was largely due to the wisdom and statesmanship of her ruler that Brazil had enjoyed a half century of almost unbroken peace, accompanied by a material progress which was the admiration and envy of her South American neighbors. Under the liberal and enlightened rule of her emperor, Brazil, the "crowned democracy of America" had apparently solved the difficult problem of wedding the principles of an hereditary monarchy with the political and personal freedom assumed to exist only in a republic. To depose and banish the kindly and genial old emperor, the "grand-son of Marcus Aurelius" as he was somewhat whimsically called by Victor Hugo; to send into exile the aged ruler whose every thought was directed to the welfare of his country, seemed not only unwise but ungrateful. It is the object of this paper to submit to a brief scrutiny the causes of one of the most striking and momentous political transformations in the history of Hispanic America.

It is a historical commonplace that the causes of the great crises in a nation's history, whether it be a civil or foreign war, or as in the case of Brazil, a bloodless revolution, are apt to be complex and strike their roots deep into the nation's past. The explanation ordinarily given for the overthrow of the Braganza dynasty, namely the resentment of the army at the alleged ill-treatment it had suffered at the hands of the imperial government, a resentment culminating in a barrack-room conspiracy and a military pronunciamento of the traditional Spanish American type, is much too simple. If the monarchy tottered and fell at a blow leveled by a few disgruntled regiments garrisoned at Rio de Janeiro, it was because the supports on which the monarchy might be expected to rely were lacking. By 1889, the Brazilian Empire, which to the world at large presented such an imposing front, had in reality become a hollow shell, ready to collapse at the first assault. One by one the foundations on which the stability and persistance of the Empire were based had crumbled.

As a preliminary to our analysis of the causes of the downfall of the Empire stress should be laid on certain peculiar characteristics of the Brazilian monarchy. The history of continental Europe would lead us to believe that if the cause of a monarchy is to become identified with that of the nation certain indispensable conditions must be fulfilled. A monarchy must derive its vitality, and to a certain extent, its sanction, from a national and warlike tradition, a hereditary nobility of which the reigning prince is the chief, a military spirit, incorporated in the prince and finding in him its highest expression, a clergy whose interests are closely identified with those of the crown, and finally a profound conviction in the popular mind of the legitimacy of the privileges and authority claimed by the ruling dynasty. Such a conviction would of course be greatly reënforced by the belief that the sovereign was invested with certain mystical attributes, emanating from the doctrine of the divine right of kings.

In the case of Brazil under Dom Pedro II. these conditions were in considerable part lacking. The Empire possessed a titled aristocracy, to be sure, but it was not hereditary; it enjoyed no political privileges, and the mere possession of a title did not of itself assure any great social prestige.[1] In other words the titles of the swarm of barons, counts, and viscounts whose sonorous names were supplied by the rivers and other geographical features of the Empire were largely honorific distinctions, bestowed by the emperor as a recognition of public service, or for the establishment of a school, hospital, or insane asylum. They were also used, as in England, by the prime minister to pay political debts or to win over possible political opponents. There was little in common, however, between the nobles of Brazil and the aristocracy of England or the noblesse of France under the ancient regime; nor did the court of Rio de Janeiro reflect the pomp and splendor of St. James or Versailles.

As for the emperor himself he was to all outward seeming the exact antithesis of the crowned heads of the late empires of continental Europe. Of the conventional trappings of royalty, he had few if any. Simple, democratic in his tastes, hating all display and ostentation, accessible to even the humblest of his subjects, caring nothing for military pomp, he might inspire respect and esteem, but seldom veneration or awe. By no stretch of the imagination could this kindly, genial, scholarly ruler be regarded as an exemplar of the divine right of kings.[2]

Yet it would be idle to deny that during the greater part of the nineteenth century the Empire enjoyed a real popularity and could count on the support of almost every element of the population. Especially was this true in the '50s, '60s, and '70s, when the influence and prestige of Dom Pedro II. were at their height. The army, the great landowners, the professional classes, the clergy,

---

[1] The Brazilian nobility in 1883 was composed of one duke, 5 counts, 39 viscounts, 268 barons. Widows of the members of the nobility were permitted to keep their titles. Of these noble ladies there were 4 marchionesses, 6 countesses, 7 viscountesses, 41 baronesses. *Almanak administrativo mercantil e industrial do Imperio do Brasil por 1883* (cited by Vicente Quesada, *Mis Memorias diplomaticas, mision ante el gobierno del Bresil,* 2 vols., Buenos Aires, 1907, p. 450). Statistics for 1889 are given by Felisbello Freire, *Historia Constitucional do Brasil,* 3 vols. (Rio de Janeiro, 1895) I. 339.

[2] In Europe and even in Brazil Dom Pedro often declared: "If I were not emperor, I should like to be a school teacher. I know of nothing more noble than to mould the mind of youth, preparing them to be the men of the future." Affonso Celso, *Pourquoi je m'enorgueillis de mon pays* (Paris, 1912), 247.

were all regarded as pillars of the throne. But as the century began to draw to its close one by one these props fell away; the last agony of the Empire found the logical defenders of the dynasty either apathetic or actively hostile. How is this waning of the star of the monarchy to be reconciled with the real and indisputable benefits which the Empire had brought to Brazil?

This change in popular attitude is to be seen most clearly perhaps in the case of the large landowners. This class, comparatively small in number but great in wealth and influence, had always been regarded as one of the pillars of the monarchy. They formed the nearest approach to a landed aristocracy to be found anywhere in South America outside the Republic of Chile. From the great *fazendeiros*, the coffee kings of São Paulo; from the ranchers of Minas Geraes; from the old families of sugar and cotton planters in Bahia and Pernambuco, had been recruited many of the staunchest supporters of the Empire. It was the irony of fate that the loyalty to the throne of this influential class was converted over night into an indifference or hostility as a direct result of the greatest social and humanitarian reform ever consummated in Brazil. On May 13, 1888, Princess Isabella, acting as regent for Dom Pedro who was then in Europe, signed the bill definitely extinguishing slavery in the Empire. That slavery was destined to disappear; that its existence was a standing reproach to the fair name of Brazil, no one undertook to deny. Unlike slavery in the United States, slavery in Brazil, at least in its latter days, had as an institution no defenders. The cleavage in public opinion came between those who favored gradual emancipation and the champions of immediate liberation. Up until 1888 the former had been in the ascendant. In 1871 the Rio Branco bill was passed which, among other provisions, declared that henceforth all children born of slave mothers should be free. In 1885 freedom was granted to all slaves over 60. But the abolitionists were not satisfied. Led by a phalanx of able and enthusiastic young men, of whom the most noted was Joaquim Nabuco,[2] later appointed the first Brazilian ambassador

[2] The relation of Nabuco to the whole abolition movement is graphically described in his two works *O Abolicionismo* (London, 1883) and *Minha Formação* (Rio de Janeiro, 1900).

to the United States, they kept up a ceaseless agitation in press and Parliament and prepared the ground for the final act of 1888. Princess Isabella had become an ardent convert to the abolition cause and threw into the scale all the influence of the monarchy.

The most anomalous and unfortunate aspect of the problem was the question of indemnity.[4] It is probable that the planters would have acquiesced in the situation, even with a certain cheerfulness, had they received some compensation for their slaves. But the abolitionists, who now found themselves in a strategic position, were opposed on principle to any indemnity. This attitude reflected on their part little political acumen or sagacity. The chief wealth of many of the planters was confined to their slaves; to these men emancipation without indemnity seemed to spell financial ruin. Especially was this true in the north where it was hopeless to expect to substitute for slave labor that of European immigrants. But when it became clear that a bill for complete emancipation was certain to be voted by Parliament a curious situation developed. Though the hope of some compensation had in the past been held out to the planters, at the present juncture no one apparently dared to incur the charge or even the odium of pronouncing the word indemnity; this despite the excellent precedent established by England and France in the case of their slaveholding colonies in the Antilles and the Guianas. Even the Brazilian slaveowners themselves, with a delicacy little short of quixotic, seemed loath to mention the fatal word. They feared apparently that they would be accused of placing their opposition on too sordid a basis. The prime-minister, João Alfredo, seemed to have been laboring under the same generous obsession. He made the mistake of assuming that emancipation had become such a national ideal or aspiration that it would be unseemly to tarnish it with financial considerations.

It is true that Princess Isabella had received intimations that abolition, immediate and without compensation, might be fraught

---

[4] The act of May 13 liberated 720,000 slaves (census of 1887) whose value was estimated at some 485,225 contos (something over two hundred million dollars). Duque-Estrada, *A Abolição* (*Esboço historico*) (Rio de Janeiro, 1918), p. 261.

with grave consequences for the Braganza dynasty. Yet some of the most experienced of Isabella's advisors deprecated any such peril. Dantas, the ex-prime minister in reply to Senator Cotegipe who was opposing the act as being too drastic declared: "It were better only to wear the crown a few hours and enjoy the immense happiness of being a fellowworker with a whole people in such a law as this, than to wear the same crown year upon year on the condition of keeping up the accursed institution of slavery. No, there is no danger. From my experience and on my political responsibility I declare from my seat in this house that today we have a new country, that this law is a new constitution."[5]

The popular rejoicings which followed the passage of the emancipation bill awoke few echoes among the great landowners. Following a natural reaction, this influential class ceased to regard its interests as identified with those of the monarchy. While little if any overt opposition was manifest there were evidences of a strong undercurrent of revulsion, to those who could look beneath the surface. It is significant for instance that within a month after the passage of the act of May 13 a number of the larger municipalities of the provinces of Rio de Janeiro, São Paulo and Minas Geraes addressed themselves directly to Parliament demanding not only indemnities for the loss of the former slaves, but what was more ominous, the calling of a constituent assembly to discuss the whole problem of the future government of Brazil.[6] Small wonder therefore that many of the planters joined the ranks of the Republicans or at least looked with complacency or open approval upon their anti-dynastic propaganda. The number of converts to the republican cause was especially strong in the provinces of Rio de Janeiro where the saying was current that since the blacks had been freed it was time the whites should be emancipated likewise.[7]

[5] Quoted in *Anti-Slavery Reporter* (London), ser. 4, VIII. (July–Aug. 1888), p. 125.

[6] Affonso Celso, *Oito annos do parlamento* (Rio de Janeiro, 1901), p. 265.

[7] There are not lacking Brasilian writers who claim that the abolition of slavery had no influence whatever on the collapse of the monarchy. Such a one is Sr. Osorio Duque-Estrada, whose excellent monograph entitled "*A Abolição*

The defection of the great landowners and those financially interested in the maintenance of slavery had been preceded by the loss of another element in the population to which the monarchy should logically have looked for support. Through a chain of mistakes and errors which should never have arisen the Empire had aroused the hostility of the clergy even as it had that of the former slaveowners.

The limits of this article naturally preclude any detailed account of the relations of the church and state under the Braganza dynasty.[8] It may merely be noted that, when Brazil separated from Portugal, the new Empire continued to exercise the jealous and petty supervision over the church that had characterized the Portuguese government since the dignities and prerogatives of the great military orders had been attached to the crown in 1551. This tendency towards an exaggerated regalism was of course accentuated during the despotic rule of Pombal. Of the various prerogatives bequeathed by the mother country to her trans-Atlantic offspring, the most important was perhaps the *patronato*, or right of patronage, a right tolerated, but never recognized by the Holy See.[9] As the nineteenth century wore on the supervision of the state over the church became more minute and vexatious; every important act of the ecclesiastical authorities was subject to inspection and revision.

For a full half century after Brazilian independence this system had evoked no serious opposition from the clergy. The clerical question, in the sense it is understood in Catholic Europe or in such South American countries as Chile had never arisen in Brazil. From the first the Empire had recruited many of its staunchest supporters from the ranks of the clergy. The most striking instance was of course Padre Diogo Feijó who acted as

---

(*Esboço historico*) was published in Rio de Janeiro in 1918. (cf. p. 306 ff.) Yet the consensus of most authorities runs quite to the contrary.

[8] This subject is treated at length from the Catholic point of view in an able article by Padre Julio Maria entitled "A Religão," published in *O Livro do Centenario* (Rio de Janeiro, 1901), pp. 60 ff. An objective and scholarly discussion is given by Joaquim Nabuco, *Um Estadistica do Imperio, Nabuco de Araujo; sua Vida, suas Opinões, su Epoca*, 3 vols. (Rio de Janeiro, 1897), III. *passim*.

[9] *Cf.* J. Burnichon, S.J., *Le Brésil d'aujourd'hui* (Paris, 1910), p. 180.

regent of the Empire during the troublous years 1835–1837. The clergy had full liberty to enter politics and there were repeatedly to be found a number of able and patriotic priests in the Imperial Parliament. If, as has been frequently alleged,[10] the tutelage of the state was but a veiled form of slavery the clergy had willingly acquiesced in this servitude.

In 1873 a change came. The cordial relations hitherto existing between the Empire and the Church were suddenly interrupted by a quarrel of extreme bitterness. The contest which has sometimes, though with scant justification, been styled the Brazilian *Kulturkampf*, was in part but a repercussion of those ultramontane tendencies which during the preceding decade had made such headway in Catholic Europe, particularly in France. As was to be expected the movement was signalized in Brazil by a revival of certain Catholic practices and teachings which had gradually fallen into abeyance.

The relation of the Church to the Masonic Order was the storm-center about which the conflict revolved. It should be kept clearly in mind that the masonic lodges in Brazil had up to this time evinced no antagonism to the Church. Representatives of the clergy were frequently counted among their members. Moreover the lodges had entrenched themselves solidly in public esteem through the conspicuous service many of their members had rendered in public life. A number of the protagonists of Independence had been masons. Dom Pedro himself was a mason; the prime minister, the Baron of Rio Branco was a Grand-Master of the Orient. In many communities the lodge had become a common stamping-ground for monarchists, republicans, Catholics, and free-thinkers.

An institution enjoying wide popularity at this time in Brazil was a kind of religious and benevolent association known as the *irmandade* or brotherhood. Though the members of this organization were almost exclusively laymen it was conducted to a large extent under church auspices and was supposed to be amenable to church discipline. Up until 1873 masons had been freely admitted to membership; their presence in the brotherhoods had

[10] By Padre Julio Maria, for instance (*Livro do Centenario*, I. 60).

not only occasioned no scandal but was regarded as proper and fitting. It was not unusual to find influential Catholics members of both the masonic orders and the *irmandades*.

On which side rests the responsibility for the interruption of these harmonious relations is still a matter of controversy. Certain it is, however, that to the exalted, ultramontane elements among the Brazilian clergy such a situation was regarded as scandalous. The opposition to the masons was led by the Bishop of Olinda, Mgr. Vital de Oliveira, a young, hot-headed[11] prelate, who had been educated in Rome and had been swept into the current of Catholic reaction associated with Pius IX. In December, 1872, Dom Vital, as he was generally called, ordered the *irmandades* of Pernambuco to expel from their organizations all members who were masons unless they should withdraw from this order, "which had repeatedly been the object of condemnation by the Church."

In issuing this command Dom Vital ran directly counter to the laws of the Empire, as the order condemning masonry had been promulgated without the sanction of the government. The *irmandades*, moreover were not only religious but also civil corporations and in the latter capacity did not come under the authority of the Church. The bishop none the less persisted in his course and when the *irmandades* refused to expel the masons their chapels and churches were placed under an interdict.

The *irmandades* in their distress appealed to the imperial government, which in turn laid the matter before the Council of State. In a famous *paracer* or decision, signed by the distinguished Minister of Justice, Nabuco de Araujo, this body declared that the bishop had exceeded his authority in demanding the expulsion of the masons from the *irmandades*.[12] In pursuance of this decision the government ordered the bishop to withdraw within a month the sentence of interdiction. Dom Vital not only refused to obey this injunction but enjoined refusal on his vicars

[11] The epithet was applied by Pius IX. "Que volete? É una testa calda," His Holiness stated to the Brazilian Ambassador Baron Penedo. Penedo, *Missão Especial a Roma* (London, 1881), p. 19.

[12] Joaquim Nabuco, *Um Estadista do Imperio*, III. 375.

under threat of suspension *ex informata conscientia*. He publicly
declared that he refused to abide by the constitution as he recognized no higher authority than that of the Church. The remaining members of the Brazilian episcopate, with the exception of Dom
Antonio de Macedo Costa, Bishop of Pará, took no active part
in the controversy. Dom Antonio, however, late in 1873, endeavored to subject the *irmandades* of Pará to the same discipline
as had been applied by Dom Vital in Pernambuco.

The imperial government took vigorous action to bring to an
end a controversy which was filling northern Brazil with dissension and threatening to envenom the relations between the
Empire and the Church. It determined to attack the Bishop of
Olinda in the most vulnerable point of his defense. In the early
autumn of 1873, it sent a special mission to Rome under Baron
Penedo to secure an official disapproval of his acts. Penedo
carried out his instructions with tact and success. Pius IX.,
through the Secretary of State, Antonelli, wrote a famous letter
to the Bishop of Olinda, formally disapproving his conduct and
containing, according to Penedo, the phrase *gesta tua non lau-
dantur*.[18] The refractory bishop was ordered to restore the broth-

----

[18] This phrase was the occasion of a violent controversy which for years raged
about the so-called "Olinda affair". Penedo explicitly states (*Missão especial a
Roma*, London, 1881, p. 26) that Antonelli read him the phrase from the letter
of disapproval, dated December 18, 1873, and addressed to Dom Vital. On the
order of the Pope, however, this letter was destroyed and its very existence
was denied. But on the occasion of the amnesty of the bishops, Antonelli sent
a copy of the famous document to Brasil. It was not published until 1886 when
the Bishop of Pará made a violent attack on Penedo in a work entitled *A Questão
Religiosa perante à Santa Se* (Maranhão, 1886). The letter, in Latin, appears
on pp. 63–65; the famous phrase beginning *gesta tua* does not appear. Penedo
in the following year replied (*O Bispo da Para e a Missão a Roma*, Lisboa, 1887).
He denied that the letter appearing in the Bishop of Pará's book was the one
read to him by Antonelli, largely owing to the absence of the phrase *gesta tua*.
The Bishop of Pará returned to the charge in his work *O Barão do Penedo e a sua
Missão a Roma* (Rio de Janeiro, 1888). The truth seems to be that the letter
published by the Bishop of Pará in 1886 was a faithful copy of the original letter
minus the phrase *gesta tua*. The mystery has never been satisfactorily cleared
up. In the course of a series of lectures delivered at Harvard in 1916 the well-
known Brazilian historian Dr. Oliveira Lima hazarded the conjecture that we are
to see here a wile of the astute Cardinal Antonelli: the famous passage was
inserted for Penedo's consumption but was omitted when the letter was sent to

erhoods to their former state and to reestablish peace in the Church.

It would have been well for the prestige of the monarchy had the government been content to let this diplomatic triumph close the incident. But in spite of the success of the Penedo mission the government determined to prosecute not only the Bishop of Olinda, but also the Bishop of Pará, who as we have seen had entered the lists in defense of his colleague. Both men were tried and convicted by the Supreme Court at Rio and sentenced to four years of hard labor; Dom Pedro commuted the hard labor and after two years granted pardon to both of the bishops.

It is beyond cavil that the religious controversy of the seventies seriously impaired the prestige of the Empire. The prosecution of the bishops and their four years' sentence won them much sympathy not only in Brazil but also in Europe.[14] Among ultramontane circles they were naturally regarded as martyrs. The Brazilian clergy, though for the most part holding aloof from the controversy, felt keenly the affront suffered by their bishops. This grievance against the Empire, harbored in secret, found passionate expression upon the advent of the Republic. The collective pastoral letter of March 19, 1890, written by the former Bishop of Pará, now Archbishop of Bahia, and signed by the entire Brazilian episcopate declared: "We have just witnessed a spectacle which filled the universe with astonishment; one of those events by which the Almighty, when it is pleasing unto Him, teaches tremendous lessons to peoples and kings; a throne sud-

Dom Vital. On this whole subject, cf., in addition to the works already noted: Nabuco, *Um Estadista do Imperio*, III. 364–415; Padre Julio Maria, *op. cit.* 91 ff.; Padre Raphael M. Galanti, S.J., *Compendio do Historia do Brasil* 5 vols. (São Paulo, 1910), V. 32–37; J. Bournichon, *op. cit.*; Louis de Gonzague, *Une page de l'histoire du Brésil; Mgr. Vital, évêque d'Olinda* (Paris, 1917); Alexandre José Barbosa Lima, "Frei Vital (Bispo de Olinda)" *Revista do Instituto Historico*, 1908, pt. II. 145–152.

[14] During his imprisonment Dom Vital was comfortably installed on the Isla de Cobras (Snake Island) where he was allowed many privileges and permitted freely to see his friends. The French papers of the time—'74, '75—under the reactionary influence of Marshal MacMahon and the dynastic aspirations of the Count of Chambord took up the defense of the prelate and described him as being surrounded by reptiles.

denly precipitated into the abyss which dissolvent principles, flourishing in its very shadow, had during a few years dug for it."[15]

One of the prime factors in the collapse of the Empire was of course the growing sentiment in favor of a republic as the ideal type of government. The very name republic had a certain magical appeal among a people whose political thinking was for the most part immature. That the free soil of America, the continent of liberty, should be the seat of an empire ruled over by the scion of an old world dynasty seemed to such Brazilians illogical and absurd. *O Imperio è planta exotica no continente americano*[16] was a phrase which steadily gained currency in the press and finally was heard even in Parliament. Such ideas found most ready lodgement among the professional classes, especially the lawyers and journalists. Towards the end the officers of the army became inoculated with the republican virus and, for reasons which have already been noted, republican propaganda in the last days of the Empire made rapid headway among the planters and the clergy. *see Boehrer HAHR 1968*

A clear distinction is of course to be made between the republican ideal on the one hand, and the Republican Party, fostered by republican propaganda on the other. While the latter did not make its appearance until 1870 the former antedated the independence of Brazil and harks back in fact to the period of the French Revolution. It is a fact worthy of note that almost every political upheaval in France has had its reverberation in Brazil. In 1789 broke out the ill-starred revolution in Minas Geraes headed by Tiradentes. The July Revolution which brought Louis Philippe to the French throne was not unrelated to the forced abdication and banishment of the dictatorial Dom Pedro I. in 1831. While the Brazilian Empire had by the middle of the century struck its roots too deep to be seriously affected by the proclamation of the Second Republic in France in 1848,[17] the republican spirit was by no means extinct.

[15] Text given in *Livro do Centenario*, I. 108.

[16] "The Empire is an exotic plant on the American continent". Cf. Ernesto Mattoso, *Cousas de meu tempo* (Bordeaux, 1915), p. 12.

[17] It is difficult to establish any direct connection between the February Revolution in France and the so-called "Revolucão Praieira" which broke out in Pernambuco in 1848 and was the last civil war under the Empire.

It was not until 1870, however, that these vague republican aspirations crystallized into a definite political organization, with a program and plan of campaign. Once more the direct impetus came from abroad. The establishment of the Third Republic in France and the temporary overthrow of the Bourbon monarchy in Spain awoke powerful echoes in the only monarchy in the new world.[18] On December 3, 1870, a number of the most enthusiastic of the Brazilian Republicans put forth a Manifesto destined to become famous, as it marked the beginning of a political agitation which finished only with the collapse of the Empire. This document, which was published in the first number of *A Republica*, the official organ of the new party, consists of a "Statement of Motives", followed by an "Historical Retrospect". In the latter we are informed that "the Empire has filched from the Brazilians the glorious conquests sought for by the Wars of Independence in 1822 and 1831. Liberty in appearance, despotism in reality—the form disguising the substance—such is the characteristic of our constitutional system". After a lengthy arraignment of both the spirit and organization of the Empire the Manifesto closes with an eloquent appeal to "American ideals". This document was signed by 57 Brazilians, among whom were a number who sprang into prominence in the overthrow of the Empire.[19]

The extravagant hopes of the signers of the Manifesto proved to be premature and with little foundation in fact. The new party, after being a nine days' wonder, caused scarcely a ripple of

[18] Not inaptly has it been said that Gambetta and Castellar were the godfathers of the Brazilian Republican Party. The former sent a cryptic letter of encouragement without offering any practical suggestions; the latter was much more to the point. He despatched an envoy versed in all the wiles of republican intrigue as practiced in Spain. In initiating the Brazilians into the theories and practices of republican propaganda he pointed out that the all essential thing was "to know how to escape."

[19] *E.g.*, Aristides Lobo, and Quintino Bocayuva, ministers of the interior and foreign affairs, respectively, under the provisional government. The complete list of signers is given in Mattoso, p. 21. Cf. Pereira da Silva, *Memorias de meu tempo* (Rio de Janeiro, 1895) II. 163.

There were a considerable number of defections from the ranks of the Republicans, including their most distinguished representative, Conselheiro Lafayette Rodrigues Pereira, who became prime minister in 1883.

excitement on the placid current of Brazilian political life. The people as a whole were indifferent, the paper *A Republica*, launched with such a flourish of trumpets, died of inanition after a precarious existence of barely four years.[20]

For the next decade and a half the movement grew slowly and adhesions were comparatively few. Its greatest vitality was to be found not in the Capital but in the provinces, particularly in São Paulo and Rio Grande do Sul. Small but active clubs sprang into existence and in São Paulo a number of Republican Congresses were held. In this province the movement was largely under the guidance of two young and able lawyers, Manuel de Campos Salles and Prudente de Moraes Barros, both of whom became presidents of the Republic. It was not until 1884 that the Republican Party entered its candidates for election to Parliament. Although they gained three seats in the parliamentary session of 1885,[21] their candidates were defeated in subsequent elections and it was not until the last year of the Empire that republican deputies were again returned.[22]

The abolition of slavery in 1888 was a turning point in the history of the Republican Party.[23] We have seen that many of the

[20] It is not without interest to note the reaction of the emperor to the new party and its Manifesto. The prime minister, Marquis of São Vicente, informed Dom Pedro on the publication of this document that the imperial government should adopt as an unswerving line of conduct the policy of giving no public office to Republicans. The emperor replied: "Let the country govern itself as it desires and let the best side win (*e de razao a quem tiver*)." The prime minister somewhat scandalized pointed out tlat the monarchy was a dogma of the constitution and was incarnated (*encarnada*) in the person of the emperor. "In that case," replied Dom Pedro with a laugh; "if the Brasilians do not wish me for their emperor, I will go and be a professor." Nabuco, *Um Estadista do Imperio*, III. 192.

[21] The three deputies were Prudente de Moraes and Campos Salles from São Paulo and Alvaro Botelho from Minas. Galanti, V. 95 gives excerpts of Campos Salles' maiden speech in which he makes his profession of faith.

[22] This failure to return Republicans to Parliament was not due entirely to lack of popular support. Almost invariably the Liberals and Conservatives combined forces against the candidates of the new party. The high property qualifications of the electorate and the pressure exerted by the government were also factors in their defeat.

[23] Among the histories of the republican movement in Brasil two may be singled out for special mention. Both were written by partisans of the movement

slaveowners, as well as brokers and others identified with agricultural interests, enrolled in the new party or gave it their moral support. The Republicans in turn were quick to seize upon the occasion and proceeded to capitalize their advantage to the full. Hitherto republican agitation had been carried on sporadically and without system. It was now determined to launch an unremitting propaganda through the length and breadth of the Empire. The number of republican papers, especially in the provinces increased by leaps and bounds until in 1889 they amounted to 88. While few of the metropolitan dailies adopted republicanism as their credo a number were of immense indirect assistance through their unsparing attacks on the government. The Republicans also exploited for their own interest a section of the papers, particularly in the case of the great *Jornal do Commecio*, called *publicacões a pedidos*, open to any type or class of contribution on the payment of a relatively small sum.

Republican agitation was by no means confined to the press. In the last years of the monarchy apostles of the new faith went up and down the land, holding public meetings, and winning proselytes to the cause. Of these itinerant propagandists the most picturesque and important was a young man named Silva Jardim, whose tragic death[24] shortly after the advent of the Republic, helped to invest his exploits with a legendary and heroic character having little warrant in cold fact. This remarkable man, of whose ability and intellectual endowments differing views are held by his own countrymen, seems to have had little appreciation of the common proprieties of life. But he was enflamed

and both show the partisan's impatience with the arguments of their adversaries. Christiano B. Ottoni, *O Advento da Republica no Brasil* (Rio de Janeiro, 1890) is the work of one of signers of the Manifesto of 1871, a distinguished engineer (he was director of the Dom Pedro II. Railroad), and for a number of years member of Parliament. His book, however, is not written *sine ira et studio* and his statements should be checked up by the reply written by the Viscount of Ouro Preto (the last Prime minister of the Empire) in his *Advento da Dictadura Militar no Brasil* (Paris, 1891), 127 ff. *L'Idée républicaine au Brésil*, by Oscar d'Aranjo (Paris, 1893) is an uncritical history of the republican movement.

[24] He lost his life in 1891 through the caving in of the rim of the crater of Mount Vesuvius. Jardim has given an entertaining account of his journeys of propaganda in his *Memorias e Viagens, Campanha de um Propagandista* (Lisboa, 1891).

with the zeal of a fanatic and possessed a certain magnetism which carried his audiences with him. Within a period of little less than two years—from January, 1888 to November 15, 1889— he passed through entire provinces, speaking in hundreds of towns and cities, heartening his coreligionists, converting the undecided and even the hostile. His tour through North Brazil in 1889 when he dogged the heels of the Prince Consort, Count d'Eu, who had undertaken this journey to revive the prestige of the monarchy, is regarded by his admirers as his greatest triumph.

It is difficult accurately to appraise the results of this republican propaganda. While converts were undoubtedly made, their number and importance may easily be exaggerated. Aside from a few zealots like Jardim and a group of able journalists and politicians in the provincial capitals the number of avowed Republicans was comparatively small. Perhaps their most striking success—if success it may be called—was to lower the prestige of the monarchy. The evidence seems to be overwhelming that in political matters the great bulk of the Brazilians were inclined to be apathetic; nowhere, outside of certain restricted circles, was there any insistent or overwhelming demand for the abolition, much less the violent overthrow, of the existing regime.

But the Republicans, even had they been much more numerous, would have been incapable of consummating the overthrow of the monarchy had its supporters rallied vigorously to its defense. Unfortunately many of this class had grown lukewarm in their devotion and loyalty to the Empire;[25] others played directly into the hands of the Republicans through their intemperate, and ofttimes venomous, attacks on the monarchy, attacks frequently motivated by personal pique, thwarted ambition, or merely by the spirit of the *frondeur*.[26] Certain it is that in the late

[25] Yet this feeling of indifference had by no means invaded all monarchical circles. In 1889, Senator Alfred d'Escragnolle Taunay, the distinguished author and abolitionist, made in a series of *Cartas Politicas* a dignified and impressive appeal to the monarchical elements in Brazil to rally to the support of the Empire.

[26] Affonso Celso (the son of the last prime minister of the Empire) then a member of Parliament informs us that the academic belief that a republic was a more perfect form of government than a monarchy was general; usually with the qualification that the country was not prepared for such a change. "At heart

seventies and eighties the star of the monarchy began to wane.[27] There was a growing conviction that the golden days of the Empire were over. Many Brazilians looked back with longing to a generation or even a decade earlier when under the guidance of a galaxy of able and patriotic statesmen chosen by the emperor, Brazil reaped the benefits of what was in many respects a model constitutional government. In the great days of Olinda,[28] Paraná,[29] Zacharias,[30] the Elder Rio Branco,[31] and Nabuco de Araujo,[32] Brazil was a standing refutation of the jibes of such foreign critics as Lastarria and Alberdi that the only American empire had as the maxims of its policy internal despotism and unscrupulous foreign aggression.[33]

One of the most striking indications of the decline of the Empire was the increasing sterility with which the two great political parties seemed to be afflicted, a sterility which was naturally reflected in the labors of Parliament. There was gradually forced home to the thoughtful Brazilian the conviction that the Liberals and Conservatives had abandoned their earlier ideas in favor of a sordid opportunism. The complete volte-face of the Conservative Party in 1888 when it espoused the cause of emancipation, a question whose solution logically devolved upon the Liberals, gave rise to the most cynical commentaries.

Justly or unjustly the emperor was also taxed with the responsibility for the political disintegration which appeared towards the end of his reign. There is reason to believe that the charge harbors at least a kernel of truth. During the waning of the Empire, Dom Pedro was a weary, and for months at a time, a

I am a Republican", affirmed many a higher government functionary. Government offices, learned academies, higher schools contained many such. *Oito Annos do Parlamento*, p. 260.

[27] This point is freely conceded by Nabuco, *Um Estadista do Imperio*, II. 407.
[28] Prime-minister during the periods 1850-1851, 1857-1858, 1862-1864.
[29] Prime minister during the period 1853-1857.
[30] Prime minister during the periods 1862, 1864-1865; 1868.
[31] Prime minister, 1871-1875.
[32] Minister of justice, 1858-1859; 1865.
[33] The attitude of Alberdi towards Brazil is so well known as to make further comment unnecessary. Lastarria's strictures are to be found in his *La América*, 2 vols. (Madrid, n. d.) II. 453 ff.

sick man. Towards the end his attitude in regard to public affairs was colored with a certain scepticism merging into fatalism. He made little effort to stave off the catastrophe with which he must have seen his dynasty was menaced.

The attacks on the emperor which did so much to impair the prestige of the monarchy had as their chief burden the abuse of those prerogatives granted him by the constitution under the designation of the Moderative Power.[34] Under cover of this authority, the emperor was accused of having set up a kind of veiled and irresponsible despotism to which the name of *poder pessoal* was loosely applied. In the appointment of his prime ministers he constantly aimed, it was charged, at maintaining a certain equilibrium between the two political parties in order that the balance of power might always remain in his hands. Though nominally responsible to Parliament, the ministry, critics declared, was really under the control of the emperor. Confronted with a hostile Chamber of Deputies, the ministry was more apt to dissolve Parliament than to go out of office. The electoral system was such that any ministry following dissolution was able to secure a unanimous Chamber and thus remain in office at the good pleasure of the emperor. Dom Pedro was furthermore accused of never allowing his ministers to rise in popular estimation beyond a certain level; nor did he ever accord them his full confidence.

These accusations were by no means confined to zealous Republicans whose stock in trade consisted in disparagement of the Empire. The utterances of a number of Dom Pedro's distinguished ex-ministers have become almost classic. Eusebio de Queiroz,[35] after having been minister for a little over two years, said to his friends: "Who has once been minister of Dom Pedro must put aside all sense of shame to occupy such a post a second time". Senator Silveira Martins[36] stated in Parliament: "The Government is bad; the system is bad. We are living under a disguised absolutism; it is necessary to end it". Ferreira Vi-

---

[34] Constitution of 1824, Tit. V., ch. I.
[35] Minister of Justice in the Olinda Cabinet, 1850–1852.
[36] Minister of finance in 1878.

anna,[37] speaking of the emperor declared: "Forty years of false-hoods, perfidy, domination, usurpation; a caricature of a Caesar; a prince who is a conspirator." But the most celebrated of these indictments was that of the famous novelist José de Alencar.[38] In 1870, possibly as a result of the emperor's refusal to appoint him a member of the Senate, he violently broke with Dom Pedro and in a series of articles contributed to the press of Rio de Janeiro subjected both the emperor and the *poder pessoal* to a scathing arraignment. The sensation caused by these attacks of Alencar was heightened by the fact that less than a decade earlier in a widely-read work entitled "Letters to the Emperor" and signed by "Erasmus" he had depicted Dom Pedro as a model constitutional monarch whose excellent intentions were frequently thwarted by an oligarchy of self-seeking politicians. But in 1870 Alencar entirely recanted his earlier beliefs; the emperor has become a despot while the *poder pessoal* "like a monstrous octopus invades everything from the transcendent questions of high politics to the trifles (*nugas*) of petty administration."[39]

It is now recognized that these attacks on the alleged exercise of despotic power by the emperor are somewhat wide of the mark. Under the social and political conditions then prevailing in Brazil the emperor could hardly have avoided the exercise of the *poder pessoal*, which was thrust upon him by the force of circumstances. There did not exist that indispensable prerequisite to a genuinely representative government—the expression of national opinion by means of a popular vote. We can clearly see now—a fact necessarily obscure to contemporaries—that the smooth functioning of the machinery of government year after year without a serious breakdown was due in large measure to this tireless vigilance of the emperor. Despotic Dom Pedro may have been at times. Not always were the susceptibilities of his ministers duly safe-guarded. But above the interest of parties, of cabinets, of the dynasty itself, was the higher interest of the nation; this was the

[37] Minister of justice in 1888.
[38] Minister of justice in 1868–1870.
[39] A long and sympathetic discussion of the quarrel between Dom Pedro and the author of the *Cartas ao Imperador* is given by Escagnolle Taunay in his *Reminiscencias* (Rio de Janeiro, n. d.). Cf. Freire, *op. cit.*, I. 146.

loadstar by which the actions of the emperor were guided; this the touchstone by which he judged both men and events. In the phrase of the Brazilian historian, Oliveira Lima, "if there was any despotism, it was the despotism of morality."[40]

If despite these attacks the emperor was to the very end of his reign the object of affection and esteem by large classes of the Brazilians, the same could not be said of his daughter Princess Isabella, and the Prince Consort, Count d'Eu. Both were unpopular; both were the victims of charges and calumnies having little basis in fact. More specifically, the princess was accused of being under the control of the church; it was freely declared that on the death of her father the policy of the government would be amenable to clerical influences.[41] As for the prince consort nothing could be alleged against him save his reserved, somewhat formal bearing and the fact that he was a foreigner.[42]

[40] In July 1889, Salvador de Medonça, Brazilian Minister to the United States had an audience with the emperor just before he departed for his post. Dom Pedro said to him: "Study with special care the organization of the Supreme Court of Justice at Washington. I believe that in the function of the Supreme Court is the secret of the successful operation of the American Constitution. When you return we must have a conference on the subject. Between ourselves things do not go well and it seems to me that if we could create here a tribunal of the type of the Supreme Court and transfer to it the attributes of the Moderative Power of our constitution things would do better. Give every attention to this point. Mendonça, *Situação Internacional do Brasil* (Rio de Janeiro, 1913) p. 103.

[41] The popularity won by Princess Isabella through her signature of the Law of May 13 was largely dissipated as the result of an agitation which came to a head later in the year. Largely at the instance of the German colonists in Southern Brazil a bill was introduced into Parliament designed to remove certain legal disabilities under which the Protestants still labored. The bill passed the Senate but was defeated in the Chamber partly as a result of petititon of protest signed by some 14,000 Brazilian women. The princess was accused of having instigated the protest although her name did not appear among the signers. T. H. Fulano, *Der Sturz des Kaiserthrones in Brasilien* (Köln, 1902), p. 91 where the petition is given. Fulano's real name was Pfarrer Esch. He was father confessor of the imperial family and for many years confidant of Dom Pedro II.

[42] The Count d'Eu was the oldest son of the Duke of Nemours, the second son of Louis Philippe. He was born in 1842. The causes of the unpopularity of the Prince Consort have been analyzed at length by Ernesto Mattoso in his *Cousas de Meu Tempo* (Bordeaux, 1916), pp. 141–171. For the most part they were trivial or even frivolous.

In spite of the alienation of the planters and the clergy; in spite of the inroads made by republican propaganda in the ranks of intellectuals and to a certain extent among the mass of the people; in spite of the waning prestige of the dynasty, the Empire might have lasted many years longer had it been able to count on the loyalty of the army. Without the active participation of certain military elements the Republic would not have been declared on November 15, 1889. What were the causes of the disaffection in the army? What plausible reasons could the military leaders advance for their abandonment of the emperor? .

The whole subject of the rôle of the army in the collapse of the Empire is both complicated and controversial. Even now, over a quarter of a century after the event, there exist the sharpest divisions of opinion as to the motives and even honesty of the leaders of the revolt.

Broadly speaking Brazil had been free from the blight of militarism so typical of certain of her Spanish American neighbors. Military dictatorships had been unknown. The higher positions in the government had been filled almost entirely by civilians; it is significant that of the fifty-four ministers of war in the thirty-six cabinets under Dom Pedro II., only eighteen had been officers in the army. While the wellknown pacifist leanings of the emperor were partly responsible for this situation the Brazilian people as a whole were strongly averse to militarism.

The Brazilian army had given a good account of itself in the few foreign conflicts in which the nation had been involved; especially was this true of the Paraguayan War in which both the army and navy added heroic chapters to the annals of Brazilian history. Yet the army, especially in times of peace, had never been a model of discipline. The civil wars and revolutions which had characterized the period of the Regency (1831–1840) and the early years of Dom Pedro's reign had bred a feeling of recklessness and even insolence among the army chiefs. The contact with the Platine Republics during the conflict with the tyrant Rosas and during the Paraguayan War had a deleterious effect. Despite the efforts of President Mitre of Argentina to infuse a new spirit into Argentine institutions only too often the Brazilians found in their southern neighbors a school of despotism and all the evils of *caudillismo*. The chronic disturbance in the Province of Rio Grande do Sul, necessitating the presence of large forces on the Uruguayan frontier, aggravated these evils. Finally the imagination of certain of the Brazilian chieftains was captivated by the sinister but dynamic personalities of Rosas, Rivera, and the younger López.[42]

During the decade of peace following the Paraguayan War the army became increasingly lax in discipline and morale. The type of instruction given in the military schools indirectly fostered this tendency. As a result of a series of reforms in higher education, science, and mathematics were given the places of honor in the curricula.[43] The result was that instruction became theoretical rather than practical; purely military subjects were relegated to a secondary place. Many young officers prized the degree of *bacharel* (bachelor) and *doutor* (doctor) more than their military patents. The lower officers began to find vent for their energies in political discussion in which the terms freedom and equality figured prominently; the higher officers were often more concerned with literature and the vogue of the Positivistic philosophy of Auguste Comte than with military tactics or discipline. The privates, recruited almost exclusively from the lower classes, prone to regard their officers as they would plantation overseers with the additions of gold braid and trappings, were so much malleable material in the hands of their leaders.[44]

All public agitators at the time, republican or otherwise, upheld the doctrine that the members of the army were subject to military discipline only when on duty or in action. At other times they might freely participate in public affairs as "citizens in uniform."

[42] López especially impressed Floriano Peixotto, one of the leading actors in the drama of 1889. "That is the kind of man we need in Brasil", he said to a fellow officer during the Paraguayan War. Tobias Monteiro, *Pesquisas e Despoimentos para a Historia* (Rio de Janeiro, 1913), p. 118.

[43] The educational reforms of the period are admirably characterized by Dr. Oliveira Lima, *Sept Ans de République au Brésil*, in the *Nouvelle Revue*, August 1 and 15, 1896.

[44] Eduardo Prado, *Fastos da Dictadura Militar no Brazil* (Lisbon, 1890), pp. 68-69; Monteiro, p. 123. Prado states that the army was over-officered, the proportion to privates being 1 to 13. *Op. cit.*, p. 5.

In a country like Brazil, in which military discipline is not reenforced by long tradition and in which politics is one of the dominant passions of the race, such a doctrine was especially seductive to those unfamiliar with the problems of government.[46]

Under these circumstances many of the officers began to aspire to a brilliant rôle in politics. This tendency was increased through the absence of any law debarring members of the army from a political career. A number of officers were elected to the Chamber of Deputies and were appointed to life membership in the Senate. Protected by their parliamentary immunities they did not hesitate to attack members of the cabinet including the minister of war. Further possibilities of tension between the military and the government were always present owing to insistence of certain of the officers on their alleged right to ventilate their grievances through the medium of the press.

The historians of the revolt of 1889[47] have succeeded in creating the legend that the army during the last years of the monarchy was the victim of intolerable injustice and vindictive persecution on the part of the government and that it was only when all other means of redress were exhausted that recourse was had to armed rebellion. But when the specific grievances of the army are subjected to a close scrutiny they shrink to pitiable dimensions. For the most part they are either frivolous or based on a palpable misunderstanding. It is possible that the imperial government treated the army with neglect but there is no evidence that this neglect was studied or due to any animus. The unprejudiced investigator is forced to the conclusion that in the final instance the real grievance of the military was the refusal of the government to grant the army a privileged position in the state. Had Brazil possessed a strong military tradition; had the army been content to eschew politics and confine itself purely

[46] Once in power the adherents to this doctrine beginning with the chief of the Provisional Government, Marshal Deodoro da Fonseca, promptly repudiated it. Instances abound during the first few years of the Republic. *Cf.* Monteiro. p. 139.

[47] E. g. Freire, *Historia Constitucional*; Ottoni, *O Advento da Republica no Brazil*; Anfrisio Fialho, *Historia da Fundação da Republica no Bresil* (Rio de Janeiro, 1892).

to its proper rôle of providing for national defense and internal security, it is improbable that any serious issue would ever have arisen.

The first serious clash between the army and the government occurred in 1883. Under the belief that a bill[48] fathered by Senator Paranaguá was a covert attack on the army, a large number of officers of the Military School of Rio de Janeiro formed a *Directorio* whose chief object was to launch a press campaign against the measure. Adhesions from higher officials including a number of generals, and even from students of the Military School poured in. A certain Lieutenant Colonel Senna Madureira, whom we shall meet later, wrote a series of articles for the *Jornal do Commercio* vigorously attacking the bill. Partly as a result of this agitation the obnoxious measure was thrown out by the Senate; at the same time the government called attention to the ministerial *avisos*, repeatedly issued, prohibiting officers of the army from having recourse to the public press without the previous consent of the minister of war.[49]

The year 1883 also witnessed an event which filled the supporters of the monarchy with the gloomiest forebodings and served as a direct encouragement to the unbridled pretension of the army. As is well known the press under the Empire enjoyed a freedom frequently degenerating into a license which did not spare the imperial family itself. Under cover of this toleration a number of disreputable and scurrilous sheets were published in Rio de Janeiro. Such a paper was *O Corsario (The Corsair)*, edited by one Apulcho de Castro. In the fall of 1883 appeared a series of vicious attacks on the reputation and honor of a cavalry officer stationed in the Capital. Rumor had it that the victim of these attacks, together with certain of his brother officers, was

[48] The bill itself was an apparently innocuous measure providing for the organisation by the military of a *Monte Pio*, a kind of loan and insurance association. Details of the measure are given in Freire, I. 181.

[49] The first of these *avisos*, that of October 4, 1859, signed by the minister of war, declared that "every soldier who turned to the press to provoke conflicts or bring disrespect on his superiors, lays himself open to the most severe punishment." An *aviso* of a similar tenor had been issued October 1, 1882. Monteiro, p. 128.

plotting vengeance on the editor of the offensive sheet. Fearing the worst Castro appealed to the police for protection. The chief of police sought the cooperation of the ministry of war. The decision was reached to remove Castro in broad daylight to a distant part of the city where he might be safe from his enemies. To assure him protection a certain Captain Avila was detailed by the ministry of war to accompany him. But the carriage had hardly left the police station before it was beset by a mob in which a number of officers, dressed as civilians, figured prominently. Castro was stabbed to death despite the protests of his escort. In the official investigation which followed no serious effort was made to apprehend or punish the perpetrators of this crime. Both the police department and the ministry of war were held in popular opinion to have been derelict in their duty. The painful impression caused by this outrage was deepened by the fact that while the investigation was still pending the emperor saw fit to visit the quarters of the regiment to which the suspected assassins belonged. Possibly no single event in the later days of the Empire did more to bring the monarchy into disrepute than the unpunished assassination of an obscure and wretched journalist.[50]

The order issued by the minister of war, forbidding officers from ventilating their grievances in the press, was soon disregarded. In 1886 Colonel Cunha Mattos published an attack on one of the deputies who had accused him in the Chamber of conduct in the Paraguayan War unbecoming an officer. The dispute became so acrimonious that the government felt constrained to act. In July, Minister of War Alfredo Chaves formally censured Cunha Mattos, pointing out that he had not only disregarded various ministerial *avisos* but also the order of the adjutant general, which under date of December 20, 1884, had forbidden any officer

[50] *Jornal do Commercio*, October 26, 1883, where a circumstantial account of the assassination, which took place the preceding day, is given. *Cf.* Mattoso, p. 26 ff. for the setting of this drama. The wellknown Brazilian historian, Pereira da Silva, in his *Memorias de meu Tempo* (Rio de Janeiro 1895), II. 262 gives a long but exceedingly inaccurate account of this affair, which he declares occurred not in 1883 but in 1885. Galanti, *Historia do Brasil* (São Paulo, 1910), V. 6-9 falls into the same errors.

from carrying on a discussion in the press, even to vindicate himself from unjust accusations.[51]   He was sentenced to a nominal imprisonment of eight hours in the headquarters of the general staff.

As Cunha Mattos received both the censure and punishment without protest the incident might soon have been forgotten but for the unexpected and intemperate action of Senator Pelotas. The Viscount of Pelotas, General Camara, as one of the heroes of the Paraguayan War, enjoyed general esteem and wielded great influence in military circles.   As a friend and fellow officer of Cunha Mattos he felt called upon to take up his defense. In a lengthy speech, vibrant with suppressed emotion, delivered in the Senate on August 2, 1886 he expressed amazement at the severe punishment inflicted upon the offending officer and declared that the other officers of the army would see in the sufferings of their comrade an offense committed against them all. "The official who is wounded in his military honor has the imprescriptible right to avenge himself."   When one of the Senators interjected, "if the law permits it", Pelotas replied: "I do not say that our laws permit it; I am informing the noble minister of war of what I understand a soldier should do when he is wounded in his honor   .   .   .   and he who is speaking will thus proceed whether or not there is a law to prevent him.   I place my honor above all else".[52]   The effects of this tirade, uttered by an old soldier, a veteran of the Paraguayan War, on the younger officers needs no comment.   The following year when the military question had reached an acute stage the prime minister rightly charged Pelotas with the major responsibility for the crisis.

Meanwhile the government, hoping to strengthen the hands of the minister of war, submitted the whole question of the use of the press by the army to the Supreme Military Council.   This body handed down a decision to the effect that the members of the army, like all other citizens, might according to the constitution, freely have recourse to the public press.   The only excep-

[51] Monteiro, p. 127.
[52] Ibid., p. 129.

tion was questions exclusively between members of the military; these should be forbidden lest discipline suffer. This decision, which played directly into the hands of the radical elements of the army, was naturally regarded as a severe blow to the government. Had it been wise it would have at once recognized that its position in regard to the censures based on the ministerial *avisos*, or even on the order of the adjutant general, was no longer tenable. This it refused to do and as a result soon found itself in a false and even ridiculous position.[53]

While the tension created by the Cunha Mattos episode was still acute, fresh fuel was added to the fire. On August 16, 1886, Lieutenant Colonel Senna Madureira published in a paper in Rio Grande do Sul an article intended to vindicate himself against a slight which he alleged had been cast upon him by a member of the Senate. The article, widely copied in the metropolitan press, aroused much comment. When reprimanded by Minister Alfredo Chaves, unlike Cunha Mattos he refused to accept the rebuke in silence.[54] In November, 1886, he published a vigorous memorial in which he took the ground that no law forbade an officer from defending himself in the press, adding that he for one would refuse to recognize the competency of the minister of war in such matters. He wound up his memorial with the demand that he be granted a trial before a council of war.[55]

This protest of Madureira, coupled with the refusal of Alfredo Chaves to remove the censure or permit a trial before a council of war caused great resentment among the military and won for Madureira much sympathy and admiration among the various elements opposed to the government. The fact that he was known to possess strong republican leanings was an added circumstance in his favor. A new and ominous factor was suddenly injected into the controversy when there rallied to his support perhaps the most popular official in the entire army, General

[53] *Ibid.*, p. 139.

[54] Madureira's reputation for discipline was not of the best. In 1886, at the height of the Paraguayan War, General Caxias said of him: "He is an officer of intelligence and has shown valor but he is very insubordinate." Monteiro, p. 132.

[55] *Ibid*, p. 139.

Deodoro da Fonseca, destined to be the outstanding personality in the Revolution of 1889, the Chief of the Provisional Government, and first President of the Republic. At this time he was the chief military authority in Rio Grande do Sul and was also vice-president of the province. Possessed of but moderate intellectual gifts, headstrong and impulsive, passionately convinced of the justice of any cause he espoused, he was only too often the pliant tool of men more clever or less scrupulous than himself.[56] At the present critical juncture he took up the cause of Madureira and granted permission to a large number of officers stationed at Porto Alegre to hold a meeting of protest against the acts of the minister of war.

The prime minister, Baron Cotegipe, whose cabinet (conservative) had held office since August 20, 1885 fully realized the importance of having Deodoro as a friend rather than an enemy. But when both persuasions and blandishments[57] proved unavailing, he relieved Deodoro from his duties in Rio Grande do Sul and summoned him to Rio de Janeiro. With his own and his brother officers' grievances rankling in his breast[58] the disgruntled general was willing to go to any length to humiliate the cabinet and render its position untenable. On February 2, 1887, was held under his patronage a great meeting of protest in one of the

[56] In an interview granted by Deodoro less than two months before the fall of the Empire the following dialogue took place: "Are you a Conservative?" "I am a Conservative because the Conservative Party protects the army. (At this time the Liberals were in power.) I have had but one protector, Solano Lopes. I owe to him, who provoked the Paraguayan War, my career." Ernesto Senna, *Deodoro, Subsidios para a Historia* (Rio de Janeiro, 1913), p. 19.

[57] The interchange of correspondence between Deodoro and Cotegipe prior to their break is extremely interesting. After pointing out how prejudicial to the discipline of the army and the prestige of the government the conduct of Deodoro was likely to prove the prime minister intimated that Deodoro might, with his assistance, aspire to a seat in the Senate and to a title of nobility, probably that of "Baron of Alagoas." The general thus summarized his reply: "My answer was that the seats in the Senate should be offered to *politicos* . . . and as for titles of nobility I content myself with a nobility of sentiments. I wish to be a simple soldier; therefore I refuse both gifts, preferring to remain at the side of my brothers in arms." A. J. Ribas, *Perfil biographico de Campos Salles* (Rio de Janeiro, 1896), p. 110; *cf.* also Freire, I. 185 ff.; Fialho, p. 65.

[58] In a letter to Cotegipe, Deodoro declared that the wound inflicted upon the army was *forte, cruel e mortal.* Galanti, V. 99.

largest theatres of the Capital. Over two hundred officers were present and the public was admitted to the galleries. From the first it was evident that the purpose of the meeting was to bring pressure to bear upon the government. To the accompaniment of tremendous applause a motion was carried investing Deodoro with full authority to defend before both the government and the emperor the rights of his comrades and his class.[59] In pursuance of this mandate, on February 5, Deodoro sent an open letter to Dom Pedro. Although the writer professed loyalty to the monarchy the burden of the letter was a recital of bitter accusations against the government and insistent demands for justice to the army. It was a frank effort to override and break down the constitutional powers of the government.[60]

In the face of this assault the ministry fell a victim to divided counsels. When energy and unity were essential the cabinet temporized and fell back upon half measures which tended only to aggravate the seriousness of the crisis. There is evidence that the minister of war favored drastic action: Deodoro should be retired from the army and the Military School—rapidly becoming a hotbed of anti-dynastic intrigue—should be closed. But Cotegipe and possibly the emperor opposed these measures and on February 12 Alfredo Chaves tendered his resignation. Once again the belief gained currency that the government had been worsted by the army.[61]

[59] The text of this motion may be found in Monteiro, pp. 137–138.

[60] The text of this and the subsequent letter written by Deodoro to Dom Pedro is given by Ribas, p. 115 ff.

[61] The exact measures proposed by Alfredo Chaves have never been disclosed; that they were far-reaching was admitted by Cotegipe at the opening of Parliament the following May. Cotegipe essayed to defend his temporizing course: "It is very easy to advise 'strike, seize, cut off heads,' but in practice we are often obliged to yield in order not to sacrifice higher interests." (Monteiro, p. 141.) The future was to show that on such fundamental questions compromises were fatal. The perspicacious editor of the *Rio News* wrote, on February 15, à propos of the resignation of Alfredo Chaves: "Whether or not the ministry remains in power this abandonment of their colleague in face of such insubordination will not reflect much credit either on their judgment or their courage. And it must be confessed that the emperor has made a serious mistake in not supporting vigorous measures. We are inclined to think that the worst results of this controversy are yet to be experienced."

On the very day that the minister of war left the cabinet Deodoro wrote another open letter to the emperor in which references to the government were couched in even more violent and minatory terms than in its predecessor. To neither of these letters did Dom Pedro vouchsafe either acknowledgment or reply. Cotegipe declared in this connection that "the cabinet would not remain in power a single hour if it ceased to be the channel through which all communications should pass to his Majesty".[42]

Although Cotegipe had refused to support the minister of war his own course of action was little calculated to allay the growing resentment of the army. On the burning question of the rights of the two officers, Cunha Mattos and Madureira—nominally the pivot about which the whole controversy turned—he yielded to the extent of offering to remove the censures if this were asked for as a favor and not demanded as a right. This compromise the leaders of the army indignantly rejected and on May 14, 1887, was given to the press an energetic and vigorously worded manifesto addressed "to Parliament and to the Nation", and signed by both Deodoro and Pelotas. The gist of this document was the necessity of appealing to the Brazilian people and their representatives for the justice denied the army by the ministry.[43] At the same time Pelotas delivered a speech in the Senate in which he warned the ministry of its dangerous course, ending his address with the covert threat that unless the cabinet reconsidered its action the army might be forced to take independent measures to defend its own interests.[44]

[42] Monteiro, p. 138.

[43] The text of the manifesto is given in Fialho, pp. 80–85. The authorship of the document, according to Cunha Mattos, belonged to Ruy Barbosa, editor of the *Diario de Noticias*, a strong, anti-administration organ. Monteiro, *loc. cit.*

[44] The following excerpt will sufficiently characterize the spirit of Pelotas's address. "I earnestly beg the noble President of the Council (Cotegipe) to reconsider his act, not in order to afford me any personal satisfaction, but for the love of this country. If he refuses to do so we cannot predict what the future may bring forth in spite of the confidence which the noble President of the Council reposes in the armed forces of the nation which he has under his command. The circumstances may be such that they will fail him." Galanti, V. 102.

A way out of the impasse into which the ministry and army chiefs had drifted was at length suggested by Senator Silveira Martins on May 20. The government was invited to declare null and void the censures directed against the two officers, thus bringing the whole episode to a close. After some hesitation this solution was accepted by the cabinet; Cotegipe recognized that it emerged from the controversy "with its dignity somewhat scratched" (*cum alguns arranhões na dignidade*), a phrase which became celebrated.[45]

The heavy atmosphere of suspicion and distrust was only partly clarified by these eleventh hour concessions wrung from the ministry. The military question was suddenly complicated by the emancipation movement, which as we have seen, came to a head in 1888. During the summer and fall of 1887, the slaves, especially in the Province of São Paulo, began to abandon their plantations *en masse*. As the local authorities were quite unable to cope with the situation recourse was had to the army. But the task of chasing run-away slaves was exceedingly repugnant to the soldiery. This sentiment was shared by Deodoro and the powerful Military Club of Rio de Janeiro. In October, 1887, the club sent a petition to Princess Isabella, who was then acting as regent, begging in the name of humanity, that the army be relieved of this odious task. Isabella ignored the petition, while Cotegipe, who was generally regarded as hostile to the abolition movement, refused to act. In practice, however, the soldiery proved a broken reed to the planters, as they rarely if ever captured the slaves whom they were supposed to pursue. None the less the whole episode tended still further to estrange the army from the government.[46]

The Cotegipe cabinet, after having weathered so many storms, was fated tò go down to defeat before the pressure from the army, which on this particular occasion had joined hands with the navy. In the spring of 1888, an officer of the navy, Captain Leite Lobo, while dressed as a civilian, was apprehended by the

[45] Details of the compromise are given in Monteiro, p. 157.

[46] Monteiro, p. 171, where long excerpts of the petition are given. Cf. also Galanti, V. 49 and Duque-Estrada, *A Abolicão* (Rio de Janeiro, 1918), *passim*.

police on pretexts which he regarded as frivolous and subjected to various indignities before his release was effected. The influential Naval Club, vigorously supported by the disaffected elements in the army, raised a great hue and cry, demanding the resignation of the chief of police. Cotegipe refused to yield to this clamor and when Princess Isabella acceded to the demands of the Naval Club and the army, the prime minister resigned (March, 1888).[47] Still another triumph was added to the laurels of the army in its conflict with the government.

The Cotegipe ministry was followed by that of João Alfredo (March 10, 1888), likewise conservative. We have already noted that the energies of the new cabinet were largely absorbed by the solution of the emancipation problem and the great act of May 13. Partly on this account the military question was temporarily relegated to the background. The cabinet showed, however, that it could act with vigor and firmness when occasion demanded. When, at the beginning of 1889, rumor reached Brazil that a conflict was impending between Paraguay and Bolivia the government adopted the bold course of sending to the frontier in distant Matto Grosso two battalions from the Capital under the command of Deodoro, thus removing from Rio de Janeiro the most important leader of the dangerous faction in the army. Had João Alfredo's successor persisted in this course of action the next decade of Brazilian history would have been quite a different story.

On June 7, 1889, came into office the last cabinet of the Empire. It was recruited from the Liberal party and was presided over by Affonso Celso de Assis Figueiredo, Viscount of Ouro Preto. The new prime minister was a man of ripe experience in public affairs. He had held the portfolios of finance and war in 1879 and 1882 respectively and had also served a long apprenticeship in both houses of Parliament and in the Council of State. He was a brilliant lawyer, a formidable debater, and a sincere and devoted supporter of the Empire and the reigning dynasty.[48] As a close

[47] Monteiro, p. 161; Galanti, V. 103.
[48] The monarchical convictions of the prime minister were put to the test on his first appearance before Parliament. One of the Deputies, Padre João Manoel,

student of political and economic problems he fully realized that the maladies from which the Empire was suffering were amenable only to the most drastic and thorough-going remedies. The program which he submitted to Parliament embodied the most comprehensive series of reforms ever sponsored by any of Dom Pedro's ministers. These reforms included extension of the suffrage through the removal of property qualifications, full autonomy of the provinces and the municipalities, election of the presidents of the provinces instead of their appointment, abolition of the life Senate, reorganization of the Council of State, freedom of education and its improvement, reform in agrarian legislation, reduction of export duties, and promotion of credit establishments designed especially to aid the agricultural interests in tiding over the crisis caused by emancipation.[69]

There is some warrant for the belief that Ouro Preto's heroic measures to inject new life into the decrepit institutions of the Empire would have attained a measure of success had they been granted a fair trial. Early in his ministry he won the full confidence of the business circles of the capital; by a stroke of brilliant financiering he converted a portion of Brazil's foreign debt on very favorable terms; foreign exchange, always a barometer of the prosperity of the country for the first time in the history of the

wound up an attack on the government with the phrase "Down with the Monarchy! Long live the Republic!" a cry never before heard in Parliament. Hardly was the seditious but loudly applauded speech finished before Ouro Preto rose to reply. By the testimony of his own enemies he showed himself fully equal to the task. In a voice trembling with indignation he delivered himself of an eloquent and passionate defense of the monarchy. The opening paragraph perhaps deserves to be cited: "Long live the Republic! No! no! a thousand times no! It is under the monarchy that we have won the freedom of which other peoples envy us and we can conserve this liberty with sufficient amplitude to satisfy the most high spirited and freedom-loving nation. Long live the Monarchy! the form of government which the immense majority of the nation embraces and is the only one which can insure its greatness and felicity. Yes! Long live the Brazilian Monarchy! so democratic, so self-sacrificing, so patriotic, that it would be the first to yield to the wishes of the nation and would not oppose the least obstacle to a change in our institutions if the desire were presented through the proper channels." Affonso Celso (son of the prime minister) *Oito Annos de Parlamento*, p. 106.

[69] *Organisacões e programmas ministeraes desde 1822 a 1888* (Rio de Janeiro, 1889), 243.

Empire went above par.[70] His political reforms, could they have been carried out, would have gone far towards neutralizing the propaganda of the Republicans by showing that the monarchy was quite capable of meeting the demands of the Brazilian people for a fuller participation in public affairs. The large' measure of autonomy granted the provinces would have met the justifiable charge that the Empire had fallen victim to an excessive centralization. There were not lacking impartial observers who predicted that under the guidance of Ouro Preto the Empire was about to take on a new lease of life.

Unfortunately the new cabinet in its laudable desire to quicken the economic and political currents of the nation failed to attach sufficient weight to what was after all the gravest menace to the Empire: the grievances and pretensions of the military. To be sure, Ouro Preto had some reason to depreciate the importance of the military question. The army, it would seem, had won all its contentions. The honor of the two aggrieved officers had been fully vindicated; the right of the army to ventilate its grievances in the press had been recognized; the ministry, which had attempted to thwart the wishes of the military, had gone down to defeat. Moreover, the first acts of the Ouro Preto cabinet presaged a policy of conciliation. Probably at the instance of the emperor, two high military and naval officers, Viscount of Maracajú and Baron Ladario were assigned the portfolios of war and marine respectively, thus breaking a long tradition of civilian appointments. The object was probably to allay discontent among the officers by placing them under control of men of their own profession. As a further concession, Ouro Preto recalled from

---

[70] It is hardly necessary to add that Ouro Preto's financial and economic reforms were subjected both during and after his ministry to bitter and at times unfair criticism. Two of the most influential papers of the Capital, *O Paiz*, edited by the avowed Republican Quintino Bocayuva, and *O Diario de Noticias*, edited by the brilliant orator and journalist Ruy Barbosa, kept up an unceasing attack on the cabinet. During the provisional government, Ruy Barbosa as minister of finance drew up a terrific arraignment of Ouro Preto's financial measures especially his plan of aiding the agricultural interests (the so called *auxilios à lavoura*). This attack may be found in Campos Porto, *Apontamentos*. The ex-prime minister met these charges in detail in *A Decada da Republica* (Rio de Janeiro, 2d ed., 1902) I. 3–231.

Matto Grosso General Deodoro da Fonseca. The future was soon to reveal that the prime minister could hardly have committed a worse blunder.

It soon appeared that all attempts on the part of Ouro Preto to bridge the ever-widening breach between the government and the army were fruitless. Of actual grievances against the new cabinet the army leaders had few and these were almost too trivial to merit serious discussion. The punishment of the officer in charge of the treasury guard for a minor dereliction; a clash between the soldiery and police in Minas Geraes; the failure of Ouro Preto to accede to the wishes of the Director of the Military School of Ceará in regard to an appointment: such were the acts of the cabinet, for the most part purely disciplinary in character, which were seized upon by the opposition press and enemies of the Empire as proofs of the injustice of the government towards the military. In the absence of fact the most extravagant rumors were pressed into service. It was declared that the prime minister had nothing less in mind than the total dissolution of the army; as a step in this direction certain of the regiments which were the object of Ouro Preto's special dislike were to be sent to the most distant provinces. The place of the army was to be taken by the police force of the Capital and the National Guard; the latter body according to a plot revealed by the *Diario de Noticias*, was to be armed and placed under the command of the unpopular Count d'Eu. It was even alleged that the government was contemplating the creation of a "Negro Guard" (*Duarda Negra*) to whose special protection the dynasty was to be committed.[71] These charges, capitalized by the hostile press and disseminated by Republican agitators acted as a powerful sol-

[71] These allegations were answered one by one by Ouro Preto in his famous *apologia* published shortly after his banishment. He absolutely denied any intention of disbanding the army; the withdrawal from the Capital of certain infantry battalions was proposed by Adjutant General Floriano Peixoto, one of the chief actors in the drama of November 15; the increase of the police force and the National Guard were fully justified on grounds at which the army could properly take no umbrage; the *Guarda Negra* was a myth pure and simple. "If any accusation is to be leveled at the government it was not oppression but too great condescension." *Advento da Dictadura Militar no Brazil*, 2nd ed. (Paris 1890), 85 ff.

vent to undermine the loyalty of the army and to weaken the monarchical sentiments of the people.[72]

Thus far the disaffected elements in the army, with occasional exceptions, had not made common cause with the Republicans. Opposition had been directed against the government and particularly the ministry in office and not against the dynasty. In this regard the attitude of General Camara, Viscount of Pelotas, one of the signers of the famous Manifesto of May 14, 1887, was typical of that of his class. In a letter written to Ouro Preto in 1890 he declared that he had not considered the possibility of the Republic during the lifetime of the emperor.[73] That the plans and purposes of certain of the recalcitrant officers were directed into frankly revolutionary channels was due in large part to the teachings and machinations of a single individual, Lieutenant-Colonel Benjamin Constant de Botelho Magalhães.

This official, whom the more ardent of the Brazilian Republicans have regarded as not unworthy of the honors of an apotheosis,[74] had for a number of years been professor of mathematics in

[72] A topic deserving of greater attention than is possible in the present article is the rôle played by the press in the last days of the Empire. The assaults of the opposition papers, especially *O Paiz* and *O Diario de Noticias*, on the Ouro Preto cabinet and indirectly on the monarchy were unremitting and at times vindictive. In the appeals to the army rebellion was openly counselled. One or two instances may be noted. On the morning of November 9—less than a week before the revolt—Captain Antonio de Espirito Santo wrote in *O Diario*: "Comrades, the moment is a tragic one. The president of the council (Ouro Preto) intends to annihilate (*aniquilar*) the army. We are under the heel of a daring and ambitious dictator." On the 11th, the same writer thus apostrophised the prime minister: "Tyrannical President of the Council! The oppression (of the army) is a crime. The usurpation of the government is a crime of high treason. Comrades! On your guard in defense of the country!" And finally in a series of leading articles appearing during the first fortnight of November from the pen of Ruy Barbosa, the editor, clear intimations are given that some mysterious and dire catastrophe is impending. (These articles are reprinted in the introduction to Campos Porto under the caption "Prenuncio".) A recent writer (Duque-Estrada, *op. cit.* p. 307) speaks of the Ouro Preto ministry as "Flagellated by the adamantine pen of Ruy Barbosa, who incited and aided the army to overturn the throne, and was thus the real founder of the Republic." It is of interest to note that the preface to this work was written by Ruy Barbosa.

[73] Monteiro, p. 147. Fialho, p. 110, gives similar testimony in regard to Admiral Wandenkolk, who was minister of marine under the provisional government.

[74] He is repeatedly spoken of as the "glorious and immortal founder of the Brazilian Republic", etc. The standard biography of Benjamin Constant is

the Military School of Rio de Janeiro. He was a thorough exponent of that theoretical type of education which, as we have seen, had, in the latter days of the monarchy, made such headway in the Brazilian military academies. The decisive event in his intellectual development was his discovery of the philosophical system of Auguste Comte known as Positivism. The young professor was fascinated with the seductive theories of Comte which seemingly represented the definite integration of all human knowledge; during the remainder of his life he was one of the most ardent champions of Positivism in Brazil. The movement for a time made considerable headway and is regarded by some as one of the factors in the collapse of the Empire.[75] Through the misinterpretation, wilful or otherwise, of Comte's system, the Brazilian Positivists claimed that they found in their master's teaching warrant for the belief that a republic was the ideal type of government. In any event, Benjamin Constant, partly as an outgrowth of his philosophical speculation, became an enthusiastic convert to the republican cause. Inspired with the zeal of a fanatic he did not scruple to inculcate in his students doctrines subversive of their loyalty to the Empire and to Dom Pedro. His keen intelligence, persuasive oratory, and sympathetic personality caused the young officers and cadets to become pliant instruments in his hands. As a consequence the Military School became a veritable hotbed of republican propaganda. It followed as a matter of course that in the controversy between the army and the government he threw the full weight of his influence into the scale in favor of the military. One incident became famous. On October 22, 1889, a group of Chilean naval officers visited the Military School. In the presence of the minister of war and the foreign guests, Benjamin Constant made an impassioned plea in favor of his comrades in arms, protesting against

that of the Positivist R. Teixeira Mendes, *Benjamin Constant, Esboço de una apreciacão sintetica da vida i [sic] da obra do Fundador da Republica Brazileira*, 2 vols., Rio de Janeiro, 1890.

[75] The best account of the Positivist movement in Brazil is that published by Dr. Carlos Rodrigues (for many years the brilliant editor of the *Jornal do Commercio*) entitled "Religões Acatholicas," in vol. II, 110–134 of the *Livro do Centenario* (Rio de Janeiro, 1901).

the "charge of indiscipline, disorder and insubordination leveled by the government", adding that "they would always be armed citizens but never *janizaries*". On the following day his students greeted him with vociferous applause accompanied by a shower of flowers.[76]

The preliminaries of the conspiracy of which Benjamin Constant was the guiding spirit may be passed over rapidly. Unlike the other aggrieved military leaders he was held in check by no dynastic scruples or loyalty to Dom Pedro; to postpone the establishment of the Republic until the death of the emperor would in his opinion play directly into the hands of Ouro Preto and his plan for a monarchical reaction; moreover Princess Isabella and the Count d'Eu, once they were enthroned, might be much more difficult to brush aside than the kindly and peace-loving old emperor. In fine, it was Benjamin Constant's self appointed task to forge the accumulated grievances against the government and more particularly the cabinet of Ouro Preto into a weapon capable of demolishing the monarchy.

Secure in the support of the cadets of the Military School he turned to the powerful Military Club to which many of the prominent officers stationed at Rio de Janeiro belonged. At a secret meeting, held on November 9, and attended by one hundred and fifty-three officers, he was given *carte blanche* to make a final effort to obtain a cessation of the alleged persecutions to which the army was being subjected.[77] Entrusted with this commission he called upon General Deodoro da Fonseca, who, as we have just seen, had been recalled from Matto Grosso, and proposed to him a plan of action not only against the ministry but also against the monarchy. The old soldier was not immediately won over. For a time his loyalty to the emperor, from whom he had received nothing but favors, struggled hard against the passionate pleadings of Benjamin Constant. He finally capitulated: "The Old Emperor (*o Velho*) is no longer the ruler, for if he were there

---

[76] Galanti, V. 109.

[77] Our account of the meeting of the Military Club is derived from an article by Colonel Jacques Ourique who was present on the occasion. "A Revolução de 15 de Novembre," published originally in the *Jornal do Commercio*, and reprinted in Campos Porto, *Apontamentos*, p. 961.

would not be this persecution of the army; nevertheless, now that there is no other remedy, *carry the monarchy by assault.* There is nothing more to be hoped from it. Let the Republic come."[78]

From this moment both set feverishly to work to prepare for the advent of the Republic., Up to this time, with the exception of the editor of the *Diario de Noticias*, Ruy Barbosa, no civilian had been initiated into the plot.[79] On November 11 was held a meeting at Deodoro's house at which in addition to the general and Benjamin Constant were present Ruy Barbosa, Quintino Bocayuva, Aristides Lobo, Francisco Glycerio—all prominent civilian leaders of the Republican party and later members of the provisional government. At this meeting the overthrow of the monarchy was definitely decided upon, in the words of one of the conspirators, "as a measure of urgent necessity for the salvation of the country and the only possible means of restoring the army".[80] The details of the revolt were then worked out; the uprising was scheduled for the evening of November 16 when the emperor would be holding a conference with his ministry. On the 13th the conspirators won another prominent military chieftain to their cause, namely, the adjutant-general of the army, Floriano Peixoto, a warm personal friend of Deodoro, and in due time destined to be the second president of the Republic. The adhesion of Floriano was regarded as an especial piece of good fortune as he enjoyed the entire confidence of the prime minister and the minister of war.[81]

It does not fall within the scope of this article to discuss in detail the actual events of November 15. The military and republican plotters had things practically their own way. Up until almost the last moment the government was strangely

[78] The version of the interview given here is taken from a letter to the *Gazeta de Noticias* (July 17, 1890), written by Captain José Bevilaqua, to whom Benjamin Constant had related the conversation with Deodoro. A somewhat different account of this famous episode is given by Teixeira Mendes (I. 341): "The general hesitated long in replying but finally he rose with the exclamation: 'To the devil with the throne (*Leve o diablo o throno*). I am at your orders.'"

[79] Jacques Ourique, *loc cit.*, states that Ruy Barbosa was apprised of the details of the plot as early as September 18.

[80] *Ibid.*

[81] *Ibid.*

blind to the imminence of the catastrophe. To be sure the prime minister was beset by rumors and anonymous denunciations but he refused to accord them any credence. His suspicions were first aroused when he learned something of the decisions reached at the Military Club on November 9. On November 12, he held a cabinet meeting in which he discussed with the ministers of war and justice the need of precautionary measures. But Minister of War Maracajú scouted even the possibility of a military revolt. "Have no anxiety", he stated to Ouro Preto; "we are on the watch, Floriano and I; nothing will happen".[82] And on the following day this same Floriano Peixoto, who, as we have just seen, was adjutant-general of the army and the recipient of the full confidence of the prime minister wrote to Ouro Preto: "At this hour your Excellency must have observed that plotting is taking place in certain quarters. Attach no importance to it. . . . Trust the loyalty of the military leaders who are on the alert. I thank you once more for the favors you have deigned to bestow upon me."[83]

Despite these assertions Ouro Preto took such eleventh hour precautions as seemed possible. On the 14th, the minister of war was requested to summon Deodoro and if his explanation of his recent conduct was unsatisfactory to remove him from the army; the president of the Province of Rio de Janeiro was ordered to concentrate such troops in the Capital as he had under his command. Finally the minister of justice was instructed to have the police force and national guard ready for any emergency.[84]

The military uprising, scheduled as we have seen for the 16th of November, took place a day earlier as the result of widely

[82] Ouro Preto, *Advento da Dictadura Militar*, p. 45.

[83] *Ibid.* Attempts have been made by apologists of Floriano to exculpate him of the charge of betraying the confidence of Ouro Preto. The effort can hardly be called successful. Colonel Jacques Ourique, later secretary of Deodoro, categorically states that Floriano was fully initiated into the plans of the conspirators as early as the 13th through a long conference which he had with Deodoro. (Campos Porto, *Apontamentos*, p. 961.) This is fully confirmed in an interview which Sr. Tobias Monteiro had with Marshal Hermes da Fonseca, the nephew of Deodoro and later President of Brazil. (Monteiro, *op. cit.*, pp. 242-247.) The republican writer, Fialho (*op. cit.*, p. 134), virtually makes the same admission.

[84] Ouro Preto, pp. 49-51.

scattered rumors, launched on the 14th, to the effect that the government had ordered the imprisonment of Deodoro and Benjamin Constant and the embarcation for the provinces of a battalion of infantry and a regiment of cavalry whose loyalty was suspected. These rumors, utterly without basis of fact, were invented by a certain Major Frederico Solon "as a patriotic stratagem of war"[35] to exacerbate the feelings of the soldiers of the Second Brigade and cause them to precipitate the revolt by taking matters into their own hands. The stratagem was successful. On the night of the 14th, the troops stationed at the imperial palace at Boa Vista in the suburbs of the Capital decided to leave their garrison and fully armed, to march to the Campo da Acclamação, a great park or square in the centre of the city where was located the office of the ministry of war. Learning of this move through Benjamin Constant, General Deodoro rose from his sick bed and hurrying to Boa Vista put himself at the head of the revolting troops.

Through the vigilance of the chief of police, the news of the uprising of the Second Brigade reached the prime minister immediately after the soldiers had left their barracks. At this crisis Ouro Preto displayed both coolness and energy. He sent word to the members of his cabinet to meet him at the marine arsenal, which was immediately placed in a state of defense to repel all attacks. The police force and the municipal firemen were ordered to be ready to march at a moment's notice. The regiments stationed on the Island of Bom Jesus and at the Fortress of Santa Cruz were summoned to the city.

But Ouro Preto was now guilty of a blunder which made the success of the revolt all but inevitable. On his arrival at the marine arsenal, Viscount Maracajú declared that he would return to the war office, which was his post in time of danger. Ouro Preto strongly urged that the entire ministry remain at the marine arsenal, which in case of attack, could be much more easily defended than the war office; moreover, owing to its location on the edge of the harbor, aid and reënforcements could easily be summoned. Maracajú not only did not yield to these arguments but seconded by Floriano Peixoto persuaded the prime minister against

---

[35] *Ibid.* The expression is Solon's own.

his better judgment to accompany him. "The presence of your Excellency," he observed, "is necessary to encourage resistance."[86] This was the type of appeal Ouro Preto found difficult to resist. After receiving assurances from Floriano that everything possible would be done to put down the revolt the prime minister accompanied by several members of his cabinet repaired to the war office.

Here Ouro Preto beheld evidences of both incompetency and treachery. Nothing had been done to put the large fortress-like building with its spacious courtyard in a state of defense nor had any effort been made to intercept the Second Brigade during its long march from Boa Vista to the heart of the city. Surrounded by treacherous friends and evil counsellors the prime minister was caught in a trap from which no escape was possible. Shortly before daylight the revolting brigade with Deodoro da Fonseca at its head reached the park in front of the ministry of war. Orders issued by Ouro Preto and repeated by Maracajú to attack the rebellious troops fell upon deaf ears. When the prime minister reproached Floriano that such a refusal to obey orders hardly became a veteran of the Paraguayan War the adjutant general replied: "Yes, but there we were confronted by enemies; here we are all Brazilians."[87] Shortly afterwards Deodoro rode into the great court yard of the war office amid the *vivas* and acclamations of the troops. The revolt had triumphed.

The immediate results of the pronunciamento whose antecedents and character we have endeavored to sketch are well

[86] In two open letters published respectively in the *Jornal do Commercio* of January 14, 1890, and in the *Gaseta de Noticias* of March 23, 1890, the minister of war challenges this statement of Ouro Preto and accuses him of other inaccuracies. The reply of the prime minister (*Advento da Dictadura Militar*, p. 47 ff.) seems to the present writer to be conclusive.

[87] Ouro Preto, p. 66. Apologists for the pronunciamento of November 15 have cited this reply of Floriano as reflecting credit both on himself and the cause he represented. It is to be noted that on this theory every constituted government should cross its arms and abdicate as soon as it is confronted by rebellious troops. Floriano's own actions when, as chief executive, he was called upon to put down the Revolt of 1893 were hardly consonant with this theory. Not only was the resistance by the government troops of the most sanguinary character but after the revolt was entirely crushed many of the revolutionists were shot.

known. The emperor, summoned by telegraph from his summer residence at Petropolis, made futile efforts on the afternoon of the 15th to form a new cabinet. But even while these deliberations were taking place at the Boa Vista palace the Republic was proclaimed at the Muncipality and the provisional government was organized with Deodoro da Fonseca as its chief and Benjamin Constant as minister of war. At the same time troops were thrown about the palace and the emperor and his family made prisoners. On the 16th, Deodoro formally notified Dom Pedro of his deposition, and banishment from the country within a space of twenty-four hours. The reply of the aged emperor may be quoted:

In view of the representation delivered to me to-day at three o'clock in the afternoon, I resolve, yielding to the force of circumstances, to depart with all my family for Europe to-morrow leaving this country beloved by us all and to which I have striven to give constant proofs of deepseated devotion during almost half a century when I filled the position of chief of the state. In departing therefore I with all my family shall always retain the most tender remembrances of Brazil and offer ardent prayers for her greatness and prosperity.

Before daylight on the morning of November 17, the imperial family was forced to embark on the *Alagoas*, which under convoy of a Brazilian man-of-war set sail directly for Europe. The emperor, already in failing health, died less than two years later in Paris, at the modest Hotel Bedford.

The proximate cause of the collapse of the imperial regime was a barrack-room conspiracy participated in by only a fraction of the Brazilian army whose grievances were skillfully exploited by a small group of determined men bent on the estabblishment of the Republic. The ultimate cause, as we have endeavored to show, was the slow crumbling of the foundations on which the stability of the Empire depended. We have seen that the monarchy had gradually ceased to be identified with the nation in the minds of the majority of the Brazilians. It had become a thing apart, encompassed with a growing isolation, an object of respect but incapable of arousing, save in a small restricted class, any feeling of self-sacrifice or devotion.

Yet the Brazilian people as a whole had neither part nor lot in the Revolution of 1889. Utterly fallacious is the view, assiduously fostered by certain apologists of the revolt, that the overthrow of the Empire represented a great popular reaction against an intolerable despotism. The rejoicings with which the advent of the Republic was hailed were shortlived and in many cases artificial. The populace at large, after the first exuberance had cooled, was almost completely apathetic and regarded the new regime with a mixture of indifference and cynicism. The true character of the revolution was candidly admitted by one of the leading republican propagandists, Aristides Lobo, minister of the interior under the Provisional Government. "I should like to call November 15 the first day of the Republic," he wrote, "but unhappily I cannot do so. What has taken place is one step—perhaps not even that—towards the advent of a great era. What has been done may mean much if the men who are about to assume power possess judgment, patriotism, and a sincere love of liberty. But at present the stamp of the new government is purely that of the military. This is logical. The work was theirs and theirs alone, for the collaboration of the civilian element was almost *nil*. And the people stood by stupefied,[88] dumb-founded, without an inkling of what it all meant. Many honestly believed they were beholding a parade."[89]

Whatever may be the verdict of history on the motives and ideals behind the Revolution of 1889 it is even now reasonably clear that sooner or later the coming of the Republic was inevitable. The Empire touching elbows so to speak with all but one of the Republics of South America was inexorably fated to become more and more of an anachronism. Yet he would be quite wanting in historical perspective who with his eyes fixed only on the remarkable progress and achievements of the Republic would ignore or minimize the beneficent rôle which the Empire played in the national evolution of Brazil. Thanks in large part to the ability, patriotism, and rugged honesty of Dom Pedro II. the monarchy rendered the nation inestimable

[88] The Portuguese is much stronger: *"O povo assistiu bestialisado."*
[89] *Diario Popular de São Paulo*, November 18, 1889.

services. It supplied the cohesive force which prevented Brazil from falling a prey to anarchy and possible dismemberment. Under its aegis Brazil took her place among the most liberal and enlightened countries of Hispanic America. A half century of almost unbroken internal peace made possible a material prosperity which until the spectacular rise of Argentina was unique in South America. Through its intervention in the Platine Republics to aid in the overthrow of the odious tyranny of Rosas and López the Empire won for itself the political preponderance of the continent. Yet after all perhaps the greatest service rendered by the Empire was to afford the Brazilian people, decade after decade, a large and fruitful apprenticeship in the practice of self-government within the spacious confines of a liberal constitutional monarchy. Thus were laid, solid and enduring, the foundations on which the success and prosperity of the Republic had ultimately to depend.[90]

PERCY ALVIN MARTIN.

[90] As an evidence of the respect of the Brasilian people for the memory of their last emperor it may be noted that on the initiative of President Pessoa the Brasilian government has just decreed the transfer of the mortal remains of Dom Pedro and the empress from Lisbon to Rio de Janeiro. Their final resting place will be in the cathedral of Petropolis.

JOSEPH LANCASTER, JAMES THOMSON, AND THE LANCASTERIAN SYSTEM OF MUTUAL INSTRUCTION, WITH SPECIAL REFERENCE TO HISPANIC AMERICA

I. PUBLIC INSTRUCTION IN THE EIGHTEENTH CENTURY

The eighteenth century may be described as a period of mental squalor on both sides of the Atlantic.

In the United States of America the foundations were being laid of some of our oldest universities—as Yale, in 1701, and Princeton in 1746—but the country was yet new and but slight efforts had been made toward the generalization of public instruction outside of the largest centers of population. The means of communication among the different colonies, or states, as they became after the American Revolution, were few and inferior. No community of interests in the public intellectual weal had as yet been aroused. The Revolution and the consequent upheaval of society, incident to the formation of a new government, absorbed the energies of the people during the last quarter of a century and the needs of instruction were, for the time, eclipsed. Even the schools and colleges which had been established were generally broken up and many were unable to reassemble their students when peace had been declared and the new constitution adopted.

In England the century was one of intellectual stagnation. The ancient universities still ministered to the needs of a certain class of society, and the philosophers of the time discussed very learnedly the problems related to education as viewed from their peculiar standpoint. Yet these discussions had to do with theory rather than practice, and no one was found who was capable of applying the philosophical doctrines to a practical solution of the distressing problems of the time. As in France, so in England there was a rising tendency and an increasing desire to replace

49

the monastic and ultramontane education, and to initiate the children of the schools into the study of common and ordinary affairs, of all those subjects which form the conduct of life and the basis of civil society.

The results of this sterile and insipid teaching of the period have been well summed up by a writer of the time. He says:

Most young men know neither the world which they inhabit, the earth which nourishes them, the men who supply their needs, the animals which serve them, nor the workmen and the citizens whom they employ. They do not have even a desire for this kind of knowledge. No advantage is taken of their natural curiosity for the purpose of increasing it. They know not how to admire neither the wonders of nature nor the prodigies of the arts.

Yet, in spite of these conditions, which were recognized and deplored by many thinkers of the day, practical efforts to better the grade of instruction given were but few and sporadic and the children of the proletariat, in particular, received but the scantiest of attention. Instruction, even when given them, was limited to the rudiments of but two or three branches of study and was given under conditions that could not have inspired the pupil to intellectual effort on his own behalf.

A number of "Charity Schools" provided gratuitous instruction for the children of the very poor, but the greater number of schools which pretended to minister to the needs of the children of the working classes were the results of private enterprise. These were of the most meager equipment and would not be tolerated today in any civilized nation, because of their unsanitary, not to say unpedagogical, standards. Those who set up such schools were generally the physically incapacitated of the community who could not, otherwise, gain a livelihood. The lack of pedagogical preparation, or even of intellectual ability, was not, in the mind of the community, a bar to the establishing of a school; and this fact, more than any other, determines the extreme intellectual poverty of the period.

Crabbe, writing in 1780, as quoted by Fitch in his *"Educational Aims and Methods,"* has given us the following vivid description of one of the so-called "Dame Schools" of the time. He says:

Where a deaf, poor, patient widow sits
And awes some thirty infants as she knits.
Her room is small, they can not widely stray;
Her threshold high, they can not run away.
Though deaf, she sees the rebel hearers shout;
Though lame, her white rod nimbly walks about.
With band of yarn she keeps offenders in,
And to her gown the sturdiest rogues can pin.
Aided by these, and spells and tell-tale birds,
Her power they dread and reverence her words.

The same writer gives a description of a Boys' School, of the same period, which is illuminating as to methods and general atmosphere. Evidently the picture is taken from life, and is as follows:

Poor Reuben Dixon has the noisiest school
Of ragged lads that ever bowed to rule,
Low in his price,—the men who heave our coals
And clean our causeways send him boys in shoals.
To see poor Reuben, with his fry, beside
Their half-checked rudeness and his half-scorned pride;
Their room,—the sty in which the assembly meet
In the close lane behind the Northgate street;
To observe his vain efforts to keep the peace,
Till tolls the bell and strife and trouble cease,
Calls for our praise. His lot our praise deserves,
But not our pity. Reuben has no nerves.
Mid noise and dirt and stench and play and prate,
He calmly cuts the pen or views the slate.

In Hispanic America, or all that part of the western continent not included within the present bounds of the United States and Canada, education was in an even more discouraging condition. The universities founded by the representatives of the Spanish crown were in the hands of the clergy and the education given within their halls was monastic and medieval, given according to methods prescribed by the Church in the Old World. It was dogmatic, and its object was to make men submissive to monarchic rule in Church and State. There was no liberty of thought, no free study of history, no practical curricula. To quote another writer:

The instruction was of a pronounced theological character. The object of the universities was to graduate a creole clergy who should keep the principle of the divine right of kings alive and strong in the colonies.

It was not until the opening years of the nineteenth century that the old regime received a rude awakening and by virtue of the revolution against Spain, the creole or common people came to have some voice in the government and the right to demand more and better education for their children. San Martín, Bolívar, O'Higgins, Artigas, and a host of less known leaders were the heralds of the new democracy and it was largely through their help and sympathy that the distressing conditions of the preceding century gave place to an era of progress and it became possible to undertake the education and social uplift of the youth of the hitherto submerged classes.

The principal liberators of Spanish America, as will be seen hereafter, were liberal in sentiment and recognized the urgent need of bettering the condition of the masses through the introduction of free schools and obligatory attendance on their sessions. But the times were troublous and, even after a republican form of government had been established, public instruction remained in a position of secondary importance. Even in this twentieth century, old educational conditions have not been entirely effaced and a free and compulsory system of instruction for the masses has not been universally enforced. The seventy-five per cent of illiterates in Hispanic America considered as a whole speaks eloquently and pitifully of the failure of the mother countries in the matter of education and of the weakness of the republican governments which have in general failed to rise to the height of their opportunities and introduce modern conditions which shall provide the children with at least the rudiments of education.

II. JOSEPH LANCASTER, THE MAN AND HIS WORK

It was in the midst of the distressing period of intellectual poverty noted above that the world had its first glimpse of Joseph Lancaster who was to become the founder of one of the best-known systems of monitorial or mutual instruction of which there is any record in history.

Joseph Lancaster was born in London, in 1778, of the proverbially "poor but pious parents", and his heart was early filled with a desire for service. He was interested, especially, in the education and moral uplift of the poor children who surrounded him, and, while yet a boy, began to gather them together for free instruction. He himself says:

It was my early wish to spend my life to the glory of Him who gave it, and in promoting the happiness of my fellowmen. With this view, I looked forward, at the age of sixteen, to entering the dissenting ministry. But it pleased God to favour me with such a different view of things that I became a frequenter of the religious meetings of the Society of Christians called Quakers, and, ultimately, a member of that Society.

In this connection, he fails to record for our information that, for reasons that must have been satisfactory to them, the members of this same sect afterward expelled him from their membership. Other writers have informed us that such action was taken in view of certain weaknesses of character which were to appear in his later life. Yet, in spite of these defects of character and the fact of his excommunication, he honored the sect as few of its members have done.

At the very close of the century, when just twenty years of age, he made his first attempt at public instruction. A large room was secured for the purpose and he then made the following unusual announcement:

All that will may send their children and have them educated freely; and those who do not wish to have education for nothing may pay for it if they please.

As a result of this extraordinary method of advertising, within a year he found himself surrounded by a thousand children.

"They come to me for education", he said, "like flocks of sheep". Success in his undertaking came faster than he was prepared to meet it, and the burden became almost too heavy for his untried shoulders.

Very soon, however, through the attraction of numbers, some of the most prominent men of the day became interested in his work and they, in turn, enlisted the interest and sympathy of the king, then George III. His interview with the monarch merits full reproduction, since it marks the turning point in Lancaster's career and gave to the Lancasterian system that distinct imprint which makes it worthy of the special consideration of Christian educators of today. This was as follows:

The king:

Lancaster, I have sent for you to give me an account of your system of education, which, I hear, is meeting with opposition. One master teach five hundred pupils at one time? How do you keep them in order?

Lancaster:

Please your majesty, by the same principle thy Majesty's army is kept in order; by the word of command.

The king:

Good, good. It does not require an aged general to give a command. One of younger years can do it.

Lancaster then proceeded to explain his use of monitors and again the king assented and said, "Good". At the conclusion of the interview the king said:

Lancaster, I highly approve of your system and it is my wish that every poor child in my dominions should be taught to read the Bible. I will do anything you wish to promote this object.

Lancaster:

Please thy Majesty, if the system meets thy approbation, I can go through the country and lecture on the system, and I have no doubt but in a few months I shall be able to give thy Majesty an account where ten thousand poor children are being educated and some of my youths instructing them.

The king:

Lancaster, I will subscribe one hundred pounds sterling annually and,—addressing the Queen,—you shall subscribe fifty pounds, Charlotte, and the princesses twenty-five pounds each. You can have the money immediately.

In accordance with this plan, Lancaster at once set about the giving of lectures and the collection of money, and his report for 1810 states that he lectured sixty-seven times during the year to almost twenty-five thousand hearers, that the subscriptions amounted to a total of over three thousand pounds sterling, and that fifty new schools were opened with over fourteen thousand children. This unusual success may be said to have been the cause of the downfall of Lancaster. His head, which had never been strong, was completely turned by the attention shown him by members of the royal house and the influential men of the day, and the possession of so much money by one who had never handled other than small sums soon proved his ruin. He fell into debt, and was even thrown into prison on this charge. He became extravagant, impatient of control, and soon proved himself incapable of working with other people. He was finally compelled to close his schools in London, but the "British and Foreign School Society", which had been organized for the purpose, took charge of them, Lancaster himself went to Ireland where he again met with almost phenomenal success for a time. Here again he soon fell into the same difficulties which he had experienced in London and was finally declared bankrupt and his schools closed.

While his system had been at the height of its popularity and usefulness in London, representatives from both North and South America studied his schools and, as a result, similar institutions were established in the principal centers of the United States and South America.

After his failure in Ireland Lancaster decided to emigrate to the New World and, accordingly, went first to Caracas, Venezuela,[1] where he remained for a short time engaged in the development of the schools which had already been established on his

[1] Then a part of Colombia, but formed into a separate republic in 1845, when its independence was recognised by Spain.

system.   Thence he went to the West Indies and finally reached New York, where he made his headquarters.

The "Society for the Establishment of a Free School", of New York City, after studying the methods in use in other countries, decided to adopt that of Lancaster, and the "Charity Schools" of Philadelphia did the same.   The monitorial system then spread through practically all the eastern states, as far south as Georgia, and as far west as Ohio.   Lancaster in person assisted in the work of the schools of New York City, Brooklyn, and Philadelphia, and his system was generally adopted in the high schools and academies of the region.   The state systems of Maryland and Indiana, which were converted into high schools after the civil war, were originally organized on this basis, and training schools for teachers on the Lancasterian basis also became common.

But this system was, in a sense, a mere makeshift and as soon as the country became sufficiently prosperous to make more generous provision for its educational needs, it fell into disuse and by the middle of the century had been practically abandoned. Its scholastic methods gradually gave way to the more modern and more philosophical conceptions of Pestalozzi, Froebel, and Herbart, but not until it had done a great good to the country in the training of the children of the poor.[2]

Lancaster also went as far north as Montreal, Canada, and succeeded in establishing a number of schools in the Dominion. But his eccentricities of character soon caused him to lose the confidence and support of all with whom he was associated and he was continually obliged to move on to new surroundings. He finally sank into extreme poverty and became a pensioner on the charity of a number of his old friends who remained faithful in spite of his vagaries and failures.   He died in New York in 1838 from a street accident.

Of him, no less an authority than the conservative "Edinburgh Review" said:

Lancaster devised a system and brought it very near perfection, by which education could be placed within the reach of the poorest.   Alge-

---

[2] See Graves's *History of Education*, p. 242.

bra and Geometry, even the sublime theorems of Newton and La Place, may be taught by this method. . . . We do not hesitate to say that it is applicable, or may soon be applied, to the whole circle of human knowledge.

And DeWitt Clinton, President of the "Free School Society of New York City", at the opening of a new free school, in 1806, had said:

I recognize in Lancaster the benefactor of the human race. I consider his system as creating a new era in education.

In spite of a seeming failure, Joseph Lancaster made a deep impression on his own times and set in motion currents of thought and educational reform which reached many distant lands. If his character was defective, it must also be remembered that he had rare gifts which have seldom been equalled among those who have unreservedly dedicated their talents to the education of the young.

III. THE LANCASTERIAN METHOD

A somewhat more detailed description of the methods employed by Joseph Lancaster seems necessary to a full understanding of its remarkable influence on the educational movements of the century in which he lived and its claim to be perpetuated in history. As already seen, his ambition was to educate the children of the very poor. Those whose parents or guardians could not pay were received on equal terms with those who were able to make a small monthly contribution toward the expenses of the school.

The equipment of a Lancasterian school was the most meager. A large rented room sufficed for the number of children who could crowd into it, and the material helps to teaching were the scantiest. Tables in the center of the room and covered with sand served for the classes in writing and arithmetic, while loose leaves torn from a book and passed from hand to hand served for the reading lesson. In view of the king's expressed desire that the children should be taught to read the Bible, selections from this Book were generally used for the lessons in reading, and Lancaster did not fail to make a practical application, too, of the moral lessons thus presented to the pupils. At the head of each table sat a monitor, with the materials for teaching before him, while the head monitors, three or four in number, hovered about the chair of the master, at one end of the room, anxious and ready to carry out his commands.

The children began their work at ten o'clock in the morning, but at half past eight the master met the monitors and gave them the instruction which they, in turn, were to pass on to the pupils. The master from his elevated seat directed the movements of the children by means of a whistle. At a given signal the different groups, each with a monitor at its head, would march from one position to another, as necessity arose for a change of occupation. Inasmuch as this marching and counter-marching was carried on in such small space, the Lancasterian school has often been compared to a man-of-war. The discipline was strictly military and the monitors awaited and executed the orders of the master with as great eagerness and desire for approbation as could be expected of a subaltern officer.

There were different grades of monitors, and to each was given the teaching of that particular branch of study in which he excelled. They also accompanied the children from their homes to the school and again restored them to their parents, thus avoiding loitering in the streets, while they served, at the same time, as a link between the school and the home. Very small children were carefully looked after and it was the continuous duty of the monitors to counsel their pupils on points of morals and conduct.

Corporal punishment was strictly forbidden—a distinct departure from the customs of the times. But the expedients devised for the purpose of punishment, in order to avoid the necessity of striking the child, were too often puerile and, possibly, more mischievous, in the end, than the then prevalent practice of flogging. Refractory pupils were often thrust into a cage and slung up into the roof of the schoolroom by means of a system of pulleys. Others were obliged to kneel or assume other postures which excited the ridicule of their companions. The appeal was made to the sense of shame, only, and such punishments must have hardened some of the coarser children and wounded to the quick many others whose sensibilities were more refined and sensitive.

The instruction given was, necessarily, superficial and was limited to the merest rudiments of the primary branches. Yet, by dint of constant and prolonged repetition, even the dullest made some progress and the great majority learned to read and write and to solve the simpler problems of arithmetic, and to do these few things well.

A yet greater benefit to the unfortunate children of the slums was their rescue from the lives of squalor and evil surroundings for a few hours each day, and their being brought under a kindly discipline and thrown into cheerful association with hundreds of other pupils of their own age. They thus forgot their hunger and lack of proper clothing and secured freedom from parental authority and influence which, it is very probable, were not always helpful.

General conclusions

The Lancasterian system, like all others of its kind, was defective in many respects, even as it excelled in others. In spite of its deficiencies, it awakened a widespread interest in the education of the children of the very poor and the effect of the movement which had its beginning in the influence of this system may be noted in most European countries of today. Had it taken deeper root in the soil of Hispanic America, it is probable that the nations of this part of the western continent would not now have to report that so large a proportion of their population can neither read nor write.

Among the defects of the system, the following may be noted:

1. The monitors, who gave most of the instruction, were young and had received but the scantiest preparation for their work. They came from the same social strata that provided the children for the schools—generally the poorest of the working classes—had the same social deficiences that were to be noted in the character of their small charges, and possessed no education

or culture other than that which they had received in the same school of which they were to become monitors. Moreover, although they might be chosen with the greatest care and given all preparation possible under the practice of the system, it could not be expected that they would have that natural gift for teaching which so distinguished the founder of the system, even from his earliest youth. In Hispanic America, in particular, there was at that time a dearth of suitable material from which to develop efficient monitors, due to the lack of previous instruction in the new communities and the appalling prevalence of analphabetism. To this cause, more than to any other, may be attributed the evanescent influence of the Lancasterian schools of Hispanic America.

2. Although special classes were formed for the instruction of the monitors, the hours were insufficient and the teaching inadequate. Joseph Lancaster, through the genius of his personality, as well as the contagion of his enthusiasm and his unique methods of imparting knowledge, could do much toward the effective preparation of those who were to act as his assistants. But those who endeavored to walk in his footsteps had not the same gifts and could not produce the same results. The monitors learned the mechanism of their office but often without understanding what was to be imparted to others.

3. The giving to young boys an authority beyond their years and attainments must have produced the inevitable result in the development of their own character. They would become domineering and despotic, and would cultivate a certain pride and aloofness which would militate against their success as teachers of children.

4. The attendance of these schools was always large. Hundreds of children were sometimes gathered in a single room. With but one master in charge of this number of pupils, he could not exert that authority nor exercise that discipline which would be necessary, especially among the small children of the poor in whose homes, very often, all discipline had been lacking. Consequently, even with the assistance of monitors, there would be lacking that personal touch between master and pupil which is so essential in all true education.

5. The system was largely military and much time was lost from instruction in the giving and carrying out of commands. No change of occupation or position could be made by a class without the necessary military order, and the marching and evolutions consumed a great deal of time that should have been given to the work of instruction or to study. Furthermore, these exercises were obligatory for all and could not fail to work harm among those who were physically undeveloped or who suffered from weakness or illness due to insufficient nourishment. The smaller and weaker among the pupils would find the military drill a detriment rather than a help, especially when compelled to undergo it in company with older and stronger pupils.

6. The practice of giving badges, offices, and rewards, which was largely developed in the Lancasterian system, tended to develop a utilitarian spirit among the pupils. This would be unfortunate in any school. Moreover, the prizes were given indiscriminately and for acts of insignificant importance. Right was practiced, not because it was right but in order to receive a reward. Such conduct could be but superficial and such teaching could not reach the springs of real character.

7. The crowning pedagogical defect of the system was its inelasticity, its mechanical, repetitious methods, and its lack of a proper psychological basis. It was economical and served admirably the educational needs of a country in the first stages of its intellectual and commercial development. But as soon as it was possible to make greater appropriations for the work of schools, the defects and shortcomings of the Lancasterian system became glaringly apparent and its use was soon discontinued.

The advantages of the system may be summed up, as follows:

1. Owing to the interest awakened by it in the education of poor children, and its phenomenal success in England, primary instruction received a decided impulse in Great Britain and Europe, and elementary schools were established in great numbers. This stimulus persists even now in some countries, and makes possible the unusually favorable showing in the statistics of primary instruction, especially if compared with the countries of Hispanic America where the system did not take deep root.

2. The fact that one master could control such a considerable number of pupils, through his monitors, made it possible to multiply the number of schools. From the standpoint of economy, the system of mutual instruction is vastly superior to that in which individual instruction is given by the master.

3. The system demonstrated the truth of two fundamental principles in pedagogy—a) That children should be grouped in their classes according to their knowledge, and not according to age, size, or the time already spent in the school. b) That simultaneous or group teaching is that which is best adapted to elementary schools, since it gives the stimulus of example and competition and creates a certain degree of animation in the class.

4. One of the greatest recommendations of the system was its absolute freedom from sectarian bias or narrowness. It merely insisted on the use of the Bible as a text-book in the classes of reading, but did not permit religious discussions or comparisons. In this respect it was superior to similar systems of the time— as that of Bell, which was distinctly Anglican—and gained in the estimation of the public and in the efficiency of the work done.

5. Corporal punishment was forbidden. This placed the schools of this system in vivid contrast with other schools of the day, including many of our own century. Force of character, rather than force of arm, was the source of control on the part of the monitor or of the master in the schools of Joseph Lancaster; and, although other punishments, as we have seen, were scarcely less reprehensible, some advance was made in the fact that no one was allowed to strike a pupil.

IV. JAMES THOMSON AND HIS TWO SOCIETIES

"The British and Foreign School Society" took upon itself not only the responsibility in England of the work of the school methods initiated by Lancaster, but, cognizant of the great need for such instruction in other countries, especially in Hispanic America, decided to send its representatives to the western continent for the purpose of establishing schools. In view of the special trend given the instruction in all schools under this system, because of the expressed desire of the king that every pupil should be taught to read the Bible, it is not strange that the above named society should unite its efforts with those of the "British and Foreign Bible Society", and that these two societies should delegate their representation to one and the same man.

James Thomson, a Scotchman, was the man chosen to represent them in Hispanic America, and the success of the Lancasterian system in gaining a foothold among the Spanish speaking nations of the New World was due to him, rather than to the one whose name it bears. Of the man, before he undertook his work in Hispanic America, but little is known. His nationality would suggest that he was a Presbyterian, but of this there seems to be no record. It is also supposed that in addition to the degree of Doctor in Divinity, given him in recognition of his work, he had previously received that of Doctor in Medicine. His own reticence concerning himself, and his complete disregard of personal danger or personal ambition, have thrown a veil over his life before he began the work which has made him worthy a place in history, and there are few sources from which to draw information, other than his own Letters.

The present president of the University of Chile, in a volume which is largely a translation of Thomson's Letters, entitled *The Lancasterian System in Chile and other Countries of South America*,[3] condemns him in unmeasured terms as a hypocrite, since he believes that he endeavored to introduce the Lancasterian system only as a blind to his real work which was the introduction of the Bible into countries that were then, as now, Roman Catholic. In this book it is stated:

To the sound of official trumpets, Thomson founded school and societies in Santiago. How certain of our leading men would have been horrified had they been told that the garments of the schoolmaster concealed a Protestant missionary! And Thomson did not limit his activities to making the Bible known under the form of certain pas-

[3] Domingo Amunátegui Solar, *El Sistema de Láncaster en Chile y en otros países sud-americanos.*

sages in the books which were composed by him for use in the schools. He was, in addition, one of the first among us who insisted on popularizing the reading of the Bible as a whole. And those fervent Catholics, those venerable patriots, gave the use of their names to lend prestige to the work of a heretic!

Summing up the charge against Thomson, as regards his practice of hypocrisy, this author comes to the following conclusions:

The double-faced methods employed by Thomson to diffuse the knowledge of the Bible are, without a doubt, inexcusable; but, in reverence to his memory it must be said that this is the usual method of procedure employed by all missionaries, in general . . . . The opinions of Thomson about the war and the movement toward independence, in general, as well as in regard to certain phases of this movement, reveal a man who is sensible and perspicacious . . . . In a word, when he is not talking about the Bible and the ways of making it known, his observations are always happy. He is something like Don Quijote, whom questions of chivalry made mad, but who thought very reasonably along other lines.

Thomson relates his experiences as Agent of the two Societies in South America in a naïve volume of letters written from different points which he touched on his travels and published under the title *Letters on the Moral and Religious State of South America, written during a residence of nearly seven years in Buenos Aires, Chile, Peru, and Colombia.*[4] In the preface to this little volume, which is now out of print and of which but a very few copies are known to exist, he says:

I am now about to return to that quarter of the world, and trust that the same gracious hand which protected me and guided me in my former wanderings there, will still conduct me and will enable me to sow seed which may spring up to eternal life. Ten days after this date I embark for Mexico, as the Agent of the "*British and Foreign Bible Society.*" I go fraught with a sacred treasure, with some thousands of copies of the Holy Scriptures. Besides circulating these, which are nearly all in the Spanish language, I am commissioned to procure translations of the Scriptures into the native languages of that country, and which are still spoken by some millions of its inhabitants.

[4] Published by James Nisbet, 21 Berners Street, London, 1827.

The success which he had in introducing the Lancasterian schools and the Bible into South America may best be told by following him, by means of his own letters, as well as by references taken from state and other documents, as he journeyed through the continent. Beginning the intellectual and spiritual conquest of South America in the city of Buenos Aires, as José de San Martín, some six years before, had begun the struggle for political liberty, he worked his way westward and then northward, met with an enthusiastic reception from the governments of all the countries visited, and, finally, having traversed the continent from east to west and from south to north, at a time when travel was both difficult and dangerous, he returned to his own land under the mistaken conviction that he had sown seed which would blossom into a bounteous harvest.

His letters give us not only a clear insight into the religious conditions of the time, but, in addition, throw much light on the social and political movements of the period and on the character of the most famous leaders in the liberation of the continent from the power of the Spanish monarch.

In this study we are to notice, especially, his work as the representative of "The British and Foreign School Society", although it is true that he combined this work with that of the Bible Society to such a degree that it is difficult to separate them. The distinguished president of the University of Chile, to whose book reference has already been made, says:

It may seem strange that the two societies should commission one man for work in seemingly diverse occupations. But, if we take into account the fact that the Lancasterian schools used the Bible as a text in the classes for reading, it will the more readily be understood how one person could attend to the interests of both societies. In the light of modern principles, this was the grave defect of the Lancasterian system. The books which compose the Holy Scriptures, are not adapted to the intelligence of a child, either as regards the material which is treated in them nor the age in which they were written. Their adoption, however, is easily explained. It must not be forgotten that the Lancasterian system had its origin in a Protestant country, in which the Bible is the daily bread of the spirit. In England, the principal passages are read daily, in the church by the pastor and in the home by the head of the family. Furthermore, at that time school pedagogy was but slightly developed and all systems of teaching had their faults. For example, it was very common to teach the children to read from some book of mysticism . . . . But the truth is that the Statutes of God, as Thomson calls them, were completely inadequate as a text for reading.

James Thomson reached Buenos Aires on the sixth of October, 1818, and remained in that city and vicinity until about the end of May, 1821. In a work on the *History of Primary Instruction in the Argentine Republic,* we find the following reference to the interest created by the arrival of this representative of a new system of education. The writer of the history says:

The schools from 1810 continued developing their program of studies, very quietly, with no other variation than the occasional change of a teacher, etc., until, at the end of the first decade of the emancipation, they were convulsed by a revolution: the Lancasterian system had reached our shores!

In the same work there are to be found, also, interesting historical references to the arrival of Thomson and the enthusiasm awakened by his efforts on behalf of the new system of education. It will be noted that a priest was chosen as secretary of the "Lancasterian School Society", thus showing how readily even the local Roman Catholic authorities accepted the new system and lent their aid to its adoption and generalization in the different countries which it touched. The following paragraphs are of special interest:

As soon as the Lancasterian system was established in England, and in view of its immediate success, it found itself obliged to enter into a struggle against the influence of the Anglican clergy which was in charge of the greater part of the schools of the country. The struggle was long and obstinate,—so much so that in 1820, the Quaker Lancaster was obliged to emigrate to South America. He established himself in Colombia[5] where, in the prosecution of his apostolate, he began to work for the establishment of the schools according to his

[5] Now Venezuela.

system. . . . Inasmuch as the news of this system extended throughout the civilized world, Buenos Aires had also learned of it but could not put it into practice through the lack of some one who could organize it according to the rules laid down by the founder.

In 1818 the Lancasterian Society designated one of its members, Mr. James Thomson, to visit these countries and set forth the excellencies of the method. Thomson reached Buenos Aires in the same year and met with a chilling reception. But he set to work with his usual enthusiasm and efficiency. On his initiative, a Society was formed for the support of the schools which might be founded and father Bartholomew Muñoz was chosen as its Secretary.

The first meetings were held in the convent of St. Francis. A school for girls was soon founded and came to have an attendance of two hundred and fifty pupils. . . .

Mr. Thomson carried on two classes of propaganda with equal enthusiasm,—the Lancasterian School System and the diffusion of the Bible. His first sale of Bibles reached a total of four hundred copies in 1820. Then he continued his journeys to Montevideo, Patagonia, San Juan, Chile, Peru, Colombia, etc., in the interests of the sale and explanation of the Bible.

However, he did more for schools than for the diffusion of the Bible, in view of the strength of the Roman Catholic Church and the social condition of the countries visited.

In his journeys through South America, which lasted about seven years, Thomson showed himself capable of overcoming obstacles which were almost insurmountable and gave proofs of an energy that is not often seen and that is capable of confronting all trials.

During the period of his stay in Buenos Aires he was so fortunate as to enlist the sympathy and active help of Don Bernardino Rivadavia, who was then an official of the government and, as always, deeply interested in all matters of education. As showing the active participation of this statesman in establishing the Lancasterian system in Argentina, the following decree is copied from the *National Register* of 1823 (folio 1658):

"Buenos Aires, February 24, 1823.

The government has decided and hereby decrees the following:

Article 1. The hospices of the Mercedarian friars, known as San Ramón de las Conchas, and the convent of San Pedro are hereby expropriated for the uses of education.

Article 2. In these centers there shall be educated the children of the towns and territories of the adjacent country districts.

Article 3. The Lancasterian Society, recently established in this country, shall be invited to take charge of the schools of the city and in the country.

Article 4. Said society shall draw up rules for teaching, which shall be submitted to the government for its approbation.

Article 5. Let this decree be transmitted to the proper authorities for putting it into effect and let it be published in the *Official Register*. (Signed) B. RIVADAVIA.

It is interesting to note also that Thomson was warmly supported by Camilo Henriquez, a friar who had been expelled from Chile for political reasons, but who afterward returned to his own country and became one of the most zealous defenders of the Lancasterian system of education in that country. Few names are more widely or more favorably known in the southern half of the continent, in matters of education, than those of Rivadavia and Henriquez, and it is to the credit of Thomson that he was able to enlist the sympathies of such distinguished citizens in his campaign. It was, no doubt, due to the friendly interest of men like Rivadavia that the first society for the extension of the work of the Lancasterian School Society was founded in Buenos Aires. The organization of this society is thus described in the *Ministerial Gazette*, under date of February, 1821, almost three years after the arrival of Thomson in Buenos Aires:

On Monday, the 5th of the present month, there was a general meeting of the Lancasterian Society for the purpose of revising the projected constitution. This was studied and approved and it was voted to send it, with the necessary explanations, to the Honorable Provincial Congress, soliciting its approbation by the body.

There then followed the election of the president, vice-president treasurer, secretary, and counsellors of the society for the present year. The approbation of congress is awaited in order to begin work which is dedicated to the advance of public education—a most worthy task. This is a work that has been neglected because of the thunder of wars and the repeated convulsions of society; but it is so noble, so necessary, that, should it be abandoned, it would be the same as to give up all hope of present and future happiness for the country.

During his residence in Buenos Aires, Thomson was able to found eight schools in that city, and within a few years the local Lancasterian Society reported that there were one hundred with a total matriculation of over five thousand children.

The movement spread to the provinces and a large number of schools were organized. One of these, which merits special attention, was established in Rio Negro, distant more than five hundred miles from Buenos Aires, in what was then a wild territory almost uninhabited by white men. An army officer who had been appointed governor of the district, had attended the Lancasterian school in Buenos Aires and knew something of the system, and, on his departure for his new post carried with him the materials necessary for opening a school. Thomson, in a comment on the conduct of this officer, says:

If all Governors, far and near, were to act in the same manner, we should soon see ignorance turned into knowledge, the world over.

One of the most interesting details of the establishing of the System in Buenos Aires is the step taken by the cabildo in order to secure a school for girls. To this end the following circular was issued:

The Honorable Cabildo Opens a Subscription for the Education of Girls according to the System of Lancaster.

The honorable cabildo, which has put forth every effort, for many years and by every means within its reach, to offer a thorough education to the children of the poor of the vicinity, has spent, in effect, great sums of money in sustaining many schools in different parts of the city, and even in the country districts.

Wishing to put these schools on the best footing possible, in order that instruction and education may be more rapid and efficacious, and, at the same time, more simple, it has been agreed to put all schools under the same plan of mutual instruction as given us by Mr. Lancaster, which, with general approbation, has been adopted in European countries.

To this end, the schools have now been placed under the direction of Mr. James Thomson, who understands the system thoroughly and who has been named general director of them all, both in the city and in the country districts.

The schools which the cabildo has maintained up to the present time are all for boys, and now it desires to establish one for girls under this same system of education.

It had been planned to set aside a sufficient sum of money for this worthy purpose, but the present state of the funds of the cabildo, which are practically exhausted, make it impossible to put into effect such a useful and beneficial resolution.

However, since the cabildo does not wish that the advantages to be gained from such an establishment be entirely lost, it most earnestly begs its fellow-citizens and, in particular, the worthy ladies of the community, that they be kind enough to contribute to the foundation of this useful institution by means of a voluntary subscription, for the collection of which Mr. Thomson himself will act among the foreign population, aided by the probate judge . . . . and by the judge-protector of the poor.

The school or schools which will be established will be under the direction of Mr. Thomson, but, like the other schools for boys, also under the direct supervision of the cabildo.

The above appeal to the community for funds was signed in the office of the cabildo of Buenos Aires and there follows a list of twelve persons who had at once subscribed the sum of about one hundred and fifty pesos for the purpose set forth in the paper.

The provinces of Mendoza and San Juan, on the eastern slope of the Andes, were visited by Thomson, at the urgent request of their authorities. This journey was made from Chile, after he had gone to that country, and necessitated crossing the mountains which, even at the most favorable season of the year was no inconsiderable undertaking. Now the journey is made in a few hours, and in a comfortable train; but Thomson would have had to avail himself of the stage coach or mules, or, what is even more probable, walk a great part of the distance. It is characteristic of him that he makes no mention of the details of this journey. His interest in the work is so great that he enters into no description of the scenery nor of the dangers and difficulties that beset the way.

His first work in these provinces was the establishing of a girls' school, and this was followed by several schools for boys. A branch of the school society was organized and a printing press loaned by the governor of the province of Mendoza for the purpose of publishing a small periodical in the interests of education. In San Juan, Thomson was fortunate in securing the friendship and help of the new governor who, as an evidence of his liberality, had proclaimed freedom of worship throughout his province. A North American, long resident in the city, also favored the establishment of the schools. A meeting was held in which great interest was manifested by the people, and, after providing the new schools with reading matter for the classes, Thomson returned to Chile.

While his headquarters were in Buenos Aires, Thomson visited the neighboring port of Montevideo, then included in Brazil which was under the control of Portugal. The governor of the city was absent at the time of his visit, but the principal clergyman became interested and promised to present the matter of the introduction of the system to the proper authorities. This he did with such good results that Thomson was requested to send a teacher to establish the first school. In a letter addressed to Thomson, this teacher tells of his reception and the introduction of his work, in the following words:

I was cordially received, not only by the Governor but also by the other magistrates. A great room in the Fort was set apart as a school. This room will hold two hundred children. The general gave orders that the carpenters and masons of the Government should arrange this room and I hope to inaugurate the school in about three weeks more. I am doing all possible to organize a School Society which will have our schools of this city and of the Provinces under its direction. I feel sure of being able to do this, for the members of the Government are very well disposed toward the movement.

In a report prepared by the government of the Republic of Uruguay for the International Exposition held in San Francisco in 1915, that portion referring to the development of primary instruction contains the following reference to the school planted by Thomson almost a hundred years before:

During the revolutionary period which began in 1811, the public and private schools suffered from the results of the reigning anarchy, most of them being closed while the remainder continued their work with the inevitable irregularity.

This state of affairs continued until José Artigas, head of the movement to liberate the colony from Spain, in an effort to repair the damage caused society by the lack of educational establishments, founded the "National School." He also authorized the opening of some schools which had been closed, but the Portuguese invasion of 1816 frustrated the noble designs of the Uruguayan deliverer. The patriots were defeated by the invaders during whose domination the "Lancastrian Society" was founded in Montevideo, with a view to extending primary education by the establishment of schools subjected to the system of mutual instruction which, at that time, was very popular in the most advanced countries of Europe.

This was the first evolution of the Uruguayan school, since the empirical and irrational means of teaching till then employed were substituted by better ones, although the mutual system undoubtedly has its defects. Its upholders may have been mistaken with respect to the success of this method of teaching, but its application was the result of a pedagogical plan, which was not the case when the schools were directed by religious orders and laymen who had not the necessary knowledge to appreciate the transcendental mission that was entrusted to them.

So encouraging were the results obtained by the Lancasterian Society that the patriots of the year 1825 adopted the scholastic reform instituted by the Portuguese and, with the hope of extending it throughout the country, decreed the foundation of a normal school. This school had as its special mission the preparation of teachers according to the Lancasterian doctrine. The foundation of primary schools in several of the interior towns was also ordered and Montevideo was endowed with two, one for boys and one for girls.

Children who had not been vaccinated were refused admittance, a Board of Inspectors was established, the use of certificates of aptitude and conduct was also inaugurated for the pupils who terminated their studies in the schools supported by the state, and, finally, a class for the study of Latin was included.

From the correspondence carried on at that time between the Minister of Chile in Buenos Aires and his government, it appears that the authorities of Uruguay made an attempt to secure the permanent services of Thomson himself to direct the schools but recently organized. But the Chilean diplomat presented the attractions and needs of the west coast so convincingly that Thomson signed a contract, by the terms of which he was to give his services to Chile for one year in the establishing of schools and the training of monitors. In payment of these service he was to receive the sum of one hundred *pesos* a month, the *peso* at that time having at least the purchasing power of the dollar. He was also to receive two hundred *pesos* for the payment of his passage around the Horn, but, this amount was not to be paid until after his arrival in the country.

In his last letter written from Buenos Aires he gives an interesting description of the attitude of the people toward him and his work. He says:

I leave all my friends here on the best terms, and I leave the place, in many respects, with regret. I shall never forget all the kindness I have met with in this city, from the magistrates and from all classes with whom I have had intercourse. May God reward them.

When I gave in my resignation, I said that it was my intention to return here next Summer, to visit the schools, and to see how they were coming on. In the kindest manner I was requested not to forget my promise of returning. They were sorry, they said, that it was not in their power to reward me in a pecuniary way, from the lowness of their funds. They begged me to accept of their sincerest thanks for establishing the system of education in the country, from which they said they expected the happiest results in making education general among all classes of people; and they added that, as a mark of respect, they had requested the Government to confer on me the honour of citizenship, which was accordingly done.

The *Ministerial Gazette*, under date of May 30, 1821, contains the following note, in which the request was made in due form:

Most excellent Sir:

The interest with which Mr. James Thomson, on his arrival in these regions, set himself to establish in this country the system of Lancaster for the instruction of the youth; his assiduous dedication to this important establishment; the progress which it has made, due to his influence and skilled administration; the unselfishness with which he has given over a great part of his salary in order to provide a teacher and an assistant; the generous spirit he has shown in helping to extend the System; these are all very helpful services which the cabildo has not been able to forget and they have aroused the gratitude of its members toward this distinguished foreigner and, even in the midst of its scarcity of funds, it has been ordered that Thomson be reimbursed the amounts which he has spent for the provision of a teacher and an assistant in the school.

This is but a slight demonstration, as compared with what has been saved and what the country has gained by the introduction and establishing of this magnificent system of education.

The services which Thomson has rendered this country ought to be considered as extraordinary, and he should be given a commensurate reward.

The cabildo finds no more adequate recompense than that of inscribing Thomson among the number of the citizens of the country and, to that end, approaches your Excellency with the request that he be given the title of citizen, and that he be requested to meet with the cabildo in order that the proper papers may be placed in his hands, manifesting, in this way, our gratitude and making it known that Buenos Aires knows how to appreciate merit and reward services which are rendered the nation. May God keep you many years. Buenos Aires, May 22, 1821.

In reply to this petition, the following action was taken by the government:

Buenos Aires, May 29, 1821.

The government, recognizing the interest and enthusiasm which Mr. James Thomson has shown in establishing the Lancasterian system of instruction in the primary schools of this city and, desiring to give an authentic testimony of the appreciation with which we look on cultured foreigners who are interested in the progress and prosperity of the country, this letter of naturalization is given, as solicited by the illustrious cabildo, to which body this decree will be transmitted together with the letter itself, in order that, in giving them into the hands of the interested party, it may express to him the deep sentiments and the profound consideration which, for the reasons given, he merits from the government.

Chile

The journey to Chile was made in the winter months, and in a sailing-vessel, around Cape Horn. Forty-four days were occupied in this journey which is now made by modern steamship in ten days, through the Straits of Magellan, or by train, across the Andes, in less than forty hours. In regard to his reception by the authorities of the government of Chile, he has the following to say in a letter written soon after his arrival in Santiago:

You know already t hat I was engaged to come here by this Government, and that my passage around the Cape was paid by the same. I therefore looked for a fair and open reception. I have not been disappointed;—or, rather, I should say that I have, for I have met with a reception beyond my expectation, I might say to my wish. I have been introduced to the Director and the Ministers of Government, all of whom express much desire for the speedy establishment of schools *throughout* Chile. We have the largest apartment in the University for a school-room. The joiners are busy fitting it up, and we only wait their finishing to begin operations.

He also quotes the following letter from the government to Don Manuel Salas, one of the leading citizens, as showing the zeal with which the supreme dictator, O'Higgins, proposed to aid the plan for the education of the children of Chile:

Mr. Thomson, who has been engaged to establish in this city the new system of mutual instruction, has already arrived in Valparaiso. His Excellency, the director, has a decided wish that public education may be general and is very anxious to give all possible aid to this establishment for elementary instruction, as preparatory to the higher branches. He has, for this reason, appointed you with full powers to forward this object, in conjunction with Mr. Thomson and the president of the Board of Public Education. You will, therefore, do all in your power to establish it as soon and as perfectly as possible. A copy of this order is to be sent to the president of Public Instruction and to Mr. Thomson.

Three Lancasterian schools were established in Santiago— the principal of which was for the training of teachers who were to be sent to other parts of the country—one in Valparaiso, and another in Coquimbo. Thomson's contract, however, called for but one year of service and he was anxious to go north where he hoped to continue his work. General José de San Martín was then at the height of his power and had invited Thomson to go to Lima for the purpose of establishing schools. Consequently, it was necessary to obtain another teacher, and this was done through the Chilean legation in London. The choice fell on Mr. Anthony Eaton, who, it appears, knew both French and Spanish, as well as English. Due to political changes, and, especially, to the fact that he soon fell ill, the stay of Eaton in Chile was brief and it was not long until the suspicions of the clergy were aroused against the whole Lancasterian movement. This opposition of the Church was the deathknell of the movement.

The decision rendered by one Guzmán, a friar, relative to a proposition made by Thomson to bring artisans and agriculturists to Chile is an interesting document. This proposition was referred to the ecclesiastical commission, in conformity with the law of that time, and the above mentioned friar, in the name of the commission made the following report:

A memorial presented by Mr. James Thomson, in which he proposes to the supreme government to bring to Chile excellent foreign artisans and farmers, is that which gives rise to the present discussion.

Since it is not incumbent on our commission to discuss the utility of said proposition, I will limit myself to an examination from the religious standpoint for the purpose of determining whether or not such a procedure would be consonant with the interests of the religion of the state, which is the chief concern of this commission.

It is a terrible thing for one who is a patriot by nature and a Christian by profession to give a decision in which the interests of the country and religion seem to be in conflict! And, who would not say, at first thought, that this offer ought to be accepted and that a thousand thanks ought to be given to the author for his kindness and philanthropy? To bring people to a country which is almost desert, and which is in need of population, of arms to cultivate its fertile fields, of skilled labor to utilize its raw materials, and of men who are fitted to establish commerce, both foreign and domestic, is all that our young republic could desire and that is what the proposition seems to represent.

But, if we analyze it, in a religious sense, as is fitting in a Catholic state, as is ours, we find not a few difficulties to be overcome before we admit the proposition.

These foreigners, whom it is proposed to bring to our republic, may be Catholic Christians. In that case, there is not the slightest objection to receiving them and to allow as many to come, with their families, as the government wishes, and to establish themselves in the country.

But, they may be Protestants and of diverse religions and sects, as appears to be indicated in the proposition. It is equally true that they may be married or single, transient or permanent, and may bring with them their religion or worship and have their meetings and congregations to hold worship according to their own rites and liturgy. These are the great difficulties which are concealed or involved in the proposition and which must be cleared up and overcome before the plan can be considered.

As was to be expected, in view of this stand of the chief of the ecclesiastical commission, Thomson's plan was condemned as contrary to religious unity in the country and was rejected by the government. Continuing, the report states:

It would not be prudent to receive these devouring vipers (the foreigners who are not Roman Catholics) into the bosom of a state which desires to conserve pure, clean, and inviolable the religion which it professes. The coming to Chile of foreign families would ruin the Catholic religion.

One such who pretends to live here should content himself with the tolerance or civil permission which the government has granted to all foreigners to carry on business, free from molestation in regard to their morals and dogmas, provided they do not preach them nor otherwise interfere in religious matters; for, in such case, they should be expelled from the republic as disturbers of the peace, public order, and tranquillity.

Quite different was the attitude of Director General O'Higgins toward the establishing of the Lancasterian school system. His decree, which has a special historic interest, was as follows:

The Lancasterian system of mutual instruction, now introduced in most parts of the civilized world, and to which many places already owe an improvement in their habits, has been established among us and in such a manner as gives promise of beneficial results. The propagation of this system holds out the surest means of extirpating those principles formed among us in times of darkness. The government has resolved to protect this establishment zealously and, as the best way of fulfilling its intentions, has resolved to unite with it in this object those persons who have the same sentiments on the subject and who, at the same time, possess that activity, zeal, and energy which this important matter demands.

In all places this system of instruction prospers and extends itself under the fostering care of societies. This circumstance at once determines me to follow the example thus set before us and immediately to organize a society for this object. Of this society I will be the protector and a member. My first minister of state will be the president. The solicitor general of the city, the protector of the city schools, and the rector of the national institute will be members *ex officio* of the committee of management.

The object of this society shall be to extend throughout Chile the benefits of education, to promote the instruction of all classes but especially the poor, and to point out those means by which it may be best adapted to the circumstances and necessities of the country. . . . (Signed) O'HIGGINS.

In one of the volumes of his monumental work, *La Historia de Chile*, which has served as the basis of all modern writers on the subject, the author, Claudio Gay, refers to the work of Thomson and the value of the Lancasterian schools as a means of moralizing the people. As to the schools, he declares that they were costly, in the extreme, and, besides, "gave no result whatever". In regard to Thomson, he mistakenly declares that it became necessary to dismiss him. The real facts, as indicating the high esteem in which Thomson was held, may be deduced from the following decree of Director General O'Higgins:

In view of the wellknown patriotism of James Thomson, a native of Scotland, and the unusual merit with which he has labored in Chile, as principal of the schools of mutual instruction according to the system of Lancaster which are established in this capital, of the normal schools and others, which have been opened by persons who have received his instruction—which instructions, divulged, as they are being divulged, throughout the country, will open a wide field for the education of the youth and will end to the bettering of the customs of the inhabitants in general; and desirious of remunerating him in the way which is within the reach of the government: I have decided to declare him, and do hereby declare him, a citizen of Chile, and, consequently he is and must be considered as a Chilean, with rights equal to all natives of the country and of enjoying all favors and privileges which are due them.

Therefore, all inhabitants of the state of Chile will receive him and regard him as such. Let the courts take due notice, as also all others who may be concerned, in order that my decree may be properly obeyed. Given in the Palace at Santiago, Chile, May 31, 1822.

(Signed) BERNARDO O'HIGGINS.

The deathblow to the work of the system in Chile seems to have been given by the commission in charge of public instruction more than eleven years after Thomson had left the country. Proper teachers had not been secured and the results of the work of the monitors were not satisfactory in the opinion of the commission. Already, the school had been divided into two sections and only that in which free tuition was given remained under the rule of the mutual system of instruction. The pronouncement of the commission was as follows:

The commission of studies, in recent session, has had under consideration the faulty organization and scanty progress which are to be observed in' the Free School, due to the method of mutual instruction adopted in it. The commission has seen the practical result of this system of education which, far from corresponding to our hopes, not only has retarded the students in their studies but has also proved to be defective.

This is the natural consequence of a method according to which the instruction of a child is given over to an older one whose knowledge is scarcely greater. He thus acquires defects which are not corrected and in reading, especially, his progress is hindered by the scant capacity of his monitor.

As a result, we find today with sorrow that there are but one or two in each class who know how to read correctly. In view of this, the commission has deemed it prudent to abolish the method of mutual instruction, limiting to sixty the number of students, which is the maximum that can come under the immediate inspection of the master.

This report was sent to the president of the Republic, the government at once adopted it, and the Lancasterian system was abolished from the "Instituto Nacional" of Chile and, as it was supposed, from the schools of the country. But it was to be heard from again, in connection with the so-called Sunday schools which were established, through the initiative of Don Andrés Bello, the great Venezuelan who gave to Spanish America the first complete treatises on Spanish grammar and, in Chile, was influential in the production of the civil code of laws.

Bello had been one of the chief opponents of the Lancasterian system in the public schools, yet, when, at his suggestion, the Sunday schools were established for the instruction of the soldiers of the Chilean army and other adults, the system employed was that of Lancaster. In 1840, four schools of this class were established in Santiago and the government gave orders to print a new edition of the texts that had been used in the former schools of mutual instruction. No attempt, however, had been made to provide suitable monitors or assistant teachers, and the failure of the system was once more assured. A new adversary had also come, who attacked the method of mutual instruction. This was no other than the great Sarmiento of Argentina, then in Chile, and the Sunday schools were suppressed in 1843.

The reasons for the failure, says Sarmiento, were easily found. They were, in brief, as follows:

1. The difficulty of teaching a man who does not want to learn, and who studies simply because ordered to do so by his superior officer.

2. The complexity and absurdity of the system called "mutual instruction," which was the one employed. This method was enough to ʇtire out and discourage any man, however anxious he may have been to learn.

3. The incomplete application of the system, since there were not enough monitors well prepared for their work.

It is probable that in the last point we have the real explanation of the failure of the Sunday schools. Inasmuch as its whole genius lay in its having a large number of monitors, well prepared for their work, it could hardly be expected to prove a success if these elements were lacking.

In his work on Popular Education, Sarmiento makes a final reference to the work of the Lancasterian system in Chile. He says:

In Aconcagua I made a trial of this system, with the scarcity of material which I could get together. For the effects of the system the government of Chile had ordered published a number of texts— one for reading, another for arithmetic, and a third for writing and dictation. These establishments have now entirely disappeared, without leaving any trace of their influence, and with them has disappeared, also, any doubt we may have had in regard to their efficiency.

This paragraph, which may be considered the epitaph of the system in Chile, forms a part of the book of the great Argentine educator which was published in 1849, twenty-seven years after Thomson had left Chile for Perú and other northern countries.

Peru

In June, 1822, Thomson sailed from Valparaiso for Peru and, after ten days of navigation, reached Callao, the port of Lima. On the same day that he reached Lima, which was then held by the liberating army under General José de San Martín, he called on the commander in chief and received a warm welcome. San Martín expressed his great pleasure in welcoming him to Peru and pledged his support in furthering plans for the establishing of the Lancasterian schools throughout the country. On the following day, with true Hispanic American politeness and punctiliousness, San Martín returned the call and together they planned for the opening of the schools at an early date. The members of the constituted government gave every encouragement and one of the convents of the city was cleared of its occupants and given over to the uses of the first school to be organized. In this connection, Thomson naïvely remarks:

I believe that the number of convents will decrease as the schools multiply in number!

He also remarks on the unusual celerity with which the orders of the government were carried out in the matter of dis-occupying the convent, and cites this as a proof of the entire submission of the ecclesiastical authorities to the civil power. He says:

This order for the friars to remove was given on Saturday. On Monday they began to remove, and on Tuesday the keys were delivered up.

He at once proceeded to draw up a plan for the inauguration of his work. This was presented to San Martín, who suggested certain changes, although he declared that, as a whole, the plan was "excellent". One phrase, in particular, met the approbation of the Chilean minister, who was aiding Thomson, as also that of San Martín. This phrase read:

The men who will be most useful to South America are men truly religious and of sound morality.

"That is very true", was the comment of San Martín.

In view of the facilities given him, and in the light of his experience, gained through years of travel in South America in association with its principal men, Thomson had a deep sense of responsibility for the evangelization of the continent. It was while still at the beginning of his work in Peru that he gave expression to his thoughts in words which have often been quoted and which, although uttered almost a century ago, are still true today. He exclaimed:

What an immeasurable field is South America! And how white it is to the harvest! I have told you this repeatedly, but I have pleasure in telling it to you again. I do not think that, since the world began, has there been so fine a field for the exercise of benevolence in all its parts. The man of science, the moralist, the Christian, have all fine scope here for their talents. God, who has opened such a door, will surely provide laborers!

The promises of San Martín were not empty words. He at once published a decree relative to the Lancasterian schools, of which the following is a translation:

Preamble: Without education there is not, properly speaking, such a thing as society. Men may indeed live together without it, but they can not know the extent of the duties and the rights that bind them one to another, and it is in the right knowledge of these duties and rights that the wellbeing of society consists. The bringing of education to any degree of perfection is, from the very nature of things, a slow work. To accomplish it, time is required and some degree of stability in the government, as well as other circumstances, both natural and moral. All these must combine in order that the education of the people may become general and that a foundation may thus be laid for the continuance of those institutions which may be established among them.

Of the various improvements which the government has been desirous of making, none has been more earnestly and constantly kept in view since the moment of its assumption of power than the reformation of public education. In those intervals of public tranquillity which have been enjoyed, when the clamor of arms has ceased, this object has occupied the attention of the government, and, although the sun has not stood still, it has found in activity the secret of doubling the length of the day.

It has already been announced in various decrees of the government that the introduction of the Lancasterian system in the public schools was one of the plans under study. It is not yet possible to calculate the revolution which will be produced in the world by this system of mutual instruction when its use has become generalized throughout the civilized nations. When this shall take place, ignorance will come to an end, or, at least, shall be reduced to certain limits beyond which it shall never be allowed to pass.

The time is now arrived to set this system a-going in this country and the commencing of it is worthy of the month of July—a month in which posterity will record many events of importance—and we trust that the justice will be done us to declare that we have desired to make this time memorable by deeds which philosophy applauds and which spring from the noblest principles of all human society, namely, the love of glory, founded on the promotion of the prosperity and happiness of mankind.

The above are the reasons on which the following decree is based.

The Supreme Deputy, with the advice of the privy council, decrees:

1. There shall be established a central or principal school, according to the system of Lancaster, under the direction of Mr. Thomson.

2. The College of Santo Tomás shall be appropriated for this purpose. The friars at present residing in it shall remove to the large

convent of Santo Domingo, leaving only so many as may be necessary for the service of the church which is attached to it.

3. In this establishment the elementary parts of education shall be taught, together with the modern languages. The necessary teachers for this purpose shall be appointed agreeably to the arrangements which shall be pointed out in the plan for the National Institute of Peru.

4. At the expiration of six months all public schools shall be closed, which are not then being conducted according to the system of mutual instruction.

5. All the masters of the public schools shall attend the central schools with two of their most advanced pupils, in order to be instructed in the new system, and, in studying it, they shall attend to the method prescribed by the director of the establishment.

6. As soon as the director of the central school shall have instructed a sufficient number of teachers, these shall be employed, with competent salaries, in establishing public schools on the same principles in the capital city of each province.

7. At the first public examination which shall take place in the central school, those masters who have been most attentive in learning the system and shall have made such progress as to be able to conduct schools according to it, shall receive the award of a gold medal to be offered for that purpose by the minister of state.

8. For the preservation and extension of the system, the Patriotic Society of Lima is particularly requested and commissioned to take such measures as may be considered necessary for these purposes, and they are desired to make known to the government those things in which its cooperation may be required in order to carry forward effectually the important object.

9. In order that the advantages of this system may be extended to the female sex, which the Spanish government has always treated with culpable neglect, it is especially recommended to the Patriotic Society to take into consideration the most likely means for establishing a central school for the instruction of girls.

10. The salary of the director and other necessary expenses for this establishment shall be defrayed by the government. The minister of state is authorized to issue all the orders necessary for the punctual fulfillment of this decree.

Given in the Government Palace in Lima, July 6, 1822.

In his letters written from Lima at this time Thomson enters into considerable detail in his description of this stirring period of American history. He particularly defends San Martín against the imputation that he wished to make himself king or dictator of the conquered provinces, and declares his belief that the commander in chief stood only for a republican form of government. Other and better known—though, it is probable, less well prepared—historians have fully endorsed this belief of Thomson. A committee had drawn up the outlines of a political constitution for the country and congress was engaged in its discussion, article by article. The article on religion had excited great interest and Thomson's description of the scene in congress while it was under discussion merits reproduction as a whole. Referring to this historic discussion of the form of religion that should prevail in the newly constituted republic, he says:

The form of Government has been unanimously declared to be republican, agreeably to what I hinted to you in one of my late letters. In the "Outlines" the Article on Religion runs thus,—"*The religion of the State is the Catholic Apostolic Church of Rome.*"

One of the members wished to add the word *only* or *exclusive*, but, since the rest did not agree with him, he entered his protest. On this account, as well as for the general interest in the subject, the matter was keenly discussed. I went, as you may well suppose, to hear what should be said on both sides and to see the result.

The first who ascended the tribune to speak was a clergyman, carrying in his hand a book about the size of a New Testament. He began by stating that it was his sincere desire that all men might be of the Roman Catholic Church. He then stated that the only proper way, in his opinion, of bringing men into the Church, was not by force nor by persecution, in any shape, but solely by persuasion, by the force of reason. After speaking a few minutes to this effect, he went on to treat of the Article as stated in the "Outlines." He regretted the divisions among Christians and the distinctive names one body and another had taken.

He then opened the book which he held in his hand, which I now found to be one of the Bible Society's New Testaments in Spanish. He read the 12th and 13th verses of the first chapter of the first Epistle to the Corinthians and proceeded to make some remarks on the passage and to apply it to the Article in question. It appeared to him, he said, very like the divisions censured by Paul to see the Article stated in the words *Roman, Catholic, Apostolic*. Having done this he proposed that the Article should be stated in this manner,—

"*The Religion of Jesus Christ is the Religion of the State.*"

He then made some observations on the propriety of stating it in this way, in preference to the way it stands in the "Outlines," and thus concluded his speech.

As might have been expected, this alteration or amendment was opposed. . . . After being fully discussed the vote was taken,—First, whether the Article should stand as stated in the "Outlines," or be altered. It was carried that it should stand as stated. The next question was, if the word "exclusive" should be added, and it was, unfortunately, carried in the affirmative. The Article now reads thus,—

"*The Roman Catholic Apostolic Religion is the Religion of the State and the exercise of every other is excluded.*"

A congress had been elected in Peru, as well as a president of the Republic and other national officers, and Thomson seems to have gained the respect and favor of all these men of influence.[6]

His plans now reached beyond the mere establishment of schools and the circulation of the Bible in Spanish.

[6] San Martín had already gone north, where he held the now historic interview with Simón Bolívar. This was more than an interview between two individuals; it was a *pour parler* between two radically distinct theories of government. Although there is no authoritative account of what passed between these two sphinx-like men in their few hours of conversation in the little town under the equator, when they met for the first and only time, there is good reason to conclude that San Martín saw the futility of opposing the ambitions of his younger colleague. Dedicated to the proposition that each of the states of South America ought to be free and independent, a complete entity in itself, self-governing and with self-perpetuating institutions, he could not acquiesce in the plan of Bolívar to establish a Federation of States, something after the plan of the Delian League, in Greece, with Bolívar himself, as was evidently his ambition, as its permanent head. Consequently, this great-hearted patriot, the Washington of South America, turned his face again toward the south and, resigning all his posts in the army and in the government, went into voluntary exile, leaving Bolívar supreme in the newly established republics of the West coast. He returned to Buenos Aires and thence crossed to France. He died in Paris in 1850, and, thirty years afterward, his body was brought back by his grateful countrymen, who had now learned the debt due his memory, and now rests in the beautiful cathedral of Buenos Aires.

In a letter to the Bible Society, he says:

Your are aware, I suppose, that the inhabitants of Peru do not all speak the Spanish language. The descendants of the ancient Peruvians are very numerous and most of them speak only the language of their ancestors. In some parts of the country, they have assumed the manners and the language of their conquerors, but in other parts,—and these by far the most populous,—their ancient tongue is the only medium of communication.

I have long had my eye on this interesting part of the population of the country and have, at length, obtained a fair prospect of being able to plant schools among them and also to hand them the Word of God in their native tongue. An officer belonging to a native regiment, called the "Peruvian Legion," and who thoroughly understands the Quechua, or Peruvian, language, has taken a great liking to our system and is extremely desirous of benefitting his countrymen by communicating instruction to them. He is at present attending our school for this purpose and I entertain a pleasing hope regarding the results of his operations.

It was a time, however, of great political unrest and the plans of Thomson were to miscarry in many important particulars. The Spaniards again secured possession of the city, driving out the republican armies, and, although Thomson gained the friendship of the Spanish commander, he could do little in his work while the city was under martial influence. Bolívar finally arrived from the north and the Spaniards were driven out and Lima definitely passed into the power of the liberators. In a letter written near the close of the year 1823 he describes his impressions of the new commander in chief as follows:

I mentioned to you in my last that Bolívar had arrived in the city. Some days after his arrival I was introduced to him and was very favorably received. He is, in appearance, a very modest unassuming man. . . . He appears very active and intelligent, but I could not read anything of an extraordinary nature in his countenance. He has not the eye of San Martín, whose glance would pierce you through in a moment. Bolívar's weather-stained face tells you that he has not been idle. No man, I believe, has borne so much of the burden, or has toiled so much in the heat of the day, in the cause of the independence of South America, as Bolívar. His labors in his own country are already crowned with success. Colombia may be considered free and independent. According to all accounts that reach us, the Congress of that country is going on with great steadfastness. The following, I believe, is a very pleasing trait in the character of Bolívar. When invited to come here, he replied that he would gladly come, without a moment's delay, but that he could not allow himself to obey his feelings in the matter, as an Article in the Constitution of Colombia prohibits the President from going out of the State without the leave of the Congress. From this circumstance, he said, and from a desire to give an example of subjection to laws, he could not come until he could obtain leave. He accordingly wrote to the Congress for permission and although, from the distance from the Capital, he was long in receiving an answer, and in the interval was strongly urged from this quarter, yet he remained in Guayaquil until the permission from the Congress arrived and then he immediately sailed for this place.

Thomson had succeeded in establishing a good work in Lima, in spite of the political difficulties of the times. The central school had two hundred and thirty students. Another school had been initiated and already had eighty children in attendance, and he was planning to open a school for girls. Three masters were also giving all their time to the study of the system with the purpose of introducing it into other cities of Peru. But, in view of the continued war and the unsettled conditions of the time, he decided to leave Peru and start for Colombia. In reviewing his work in the principal viceroyalty of Spanish America, it is remarkable that he had been able to enlist the sympathy and active help of not only San Martín and Bolívar, in his plans for the education of the children of Peru, but also of the general of the Spanish forces in control of the city and the very Catholic governor.

His reasons for leaving Peru are very freely and frankly set forth in one of his last letters from Lima. After referring to the progress made by the children, in spite of so many difficulties, he adds that he had already packed his goods, preparatory to leaving the country. He continues:

I had indeed resolved to sail for Guayaquil with the first ship, and was inquiring for a passage. My reasons for doing so were quite solid.

My salary, as you know, is paid by the government. Under present circumstances, the payment of the troops is the first thing attended to, and to procure sufficient funds for this purpose requires great exertions in the present exhausted condition of the place. To obtain this supply, all the ordinary sources of revenue are laid hold of and other heavy contributions are laid on the inhabitants to make up the deficiencies. This being the case, there was no prospect of my obtaining supplies, more especially as persons in the immediate employ of the Government and who have salaries assigned them could obtain nothing . . . . As you know, I have no supplies but what my own hands provide me with, and it became an imperative duty to remove when my usual resources were dried up.

However, he found that he could not leave his school at once. The parents of the children, all of them poor and already burdened with the contributions that were forced on all the inhabitants of the city for the support of the troops, and in spite of the high prices that prevailed and made their very existence difficult, came to him and begged him to remain, promising to pay a small fee for the education of their children. In view of their insistence, and because of his great devotion to the work, he postponed his going for three months.

Colombia

In his journey to the north, with the capital of Colombia as his destination, Thomson was importuned to stop in both Trujillo and Guayaquil and establish schools on the Lancasterian basis. But he felt that he could not interrupt his journey to the more important centers of Quito and Bogotá, and his interest was now largely centered in the work of the British and Foreign Bible Society. In fact, his school work may be said to have ended when he left Lima, except that he sought out the school authorities in all points which he visited and endeavored to encourage education in every way possible. But he himself was unable to give his time to the organization of new schools and resolutely set his face toward the northern coast of the continent, from which he hoped to embark for London in order that he might give an account of his work during a period of seven years in the principal countries of South America.

The journey from Callao to Guayaquil could then be made in comparative ease and comfort by any one of the numerous sailing vessels that were engaged in commerce along the coast. But, from Guayaquil to Quito and, thence, to Bogotá, the conditions were completely changed. The route now lay along the aligator-infested river, as far as Babahoyo, a distance of about forty miles. This was a journey of three days in a small canoe, and the crowded condition of the small boat, the heat, and the swarms of stinging insects combined to make it an experience that was far from pleasant. He also notes that in addition to the alligators, of which he counted as many as forty lying together on the sand, the shores of the river were frequented by cougars, jaguars, and, in particular, by serpents peculiar to the tropics.

From the small port that marked the end of the river journey, he proceeded on mule back along the Indian trails and under the shadow of giant Chimborazo until, after having safely passed through many dangers, of which he makes but scant mention, he reached the city of Quito, situated on the equator and at that time one of the principal cities of Colombia.

During this journey up the mountain slope from Guayaquil he had been hospitably entertained by the governors of the various provinces which he had crossed, and by other influential men of the communities visited, and, in many cases, he lodged with the friars in their convents and was greatly aided by them in the sale of the copies of the Scriptures which he carried with him. Writing from Quito, and in review of his long journey, he says:

I have been much pleased with my journey, in the prosperity I have had in the distribution of the sacred volume. I have observed a very general desire to possess this book, and I have had the pleasure of seeing great numbers flock together, not to receive it as a present, but to buy it.

Of upwards of fifteen hundred New Testaments which I had at the outset, not many remain. I had no Bibles, and was sorry for it, as, from its being generally asked for, I am sure that I could have sold many copies.

The condition of education in Quito at that time, as well as Thomson's plans for the establishing of his own work, can best be understood by the following quotation from one of his letters, written from that city in November, 1824:

Before I speak of the state and progress of education in Quito, I shall mention two circumstances which have occurred to me since I left Lima. I notice these because they are encouraging, as it respects the progress of education, and because they tend to prove what I have so often stated to you,—that there is a very general desire throughout this country for extending the benefits of education to all, and with all possible speed.

The circumstances referred to occurred in Trujillo and Guayaquil. In both these places I received proposals from the magistrates to remain among them, in order to establish schools on our plan, and to promote the objects of education in general. In both cases I had a struggle with my feelings, though not with my judgment, in declining the honor offered me. Though my duty bade me pursue my journey, yet, in consequence of these proposals, I can not help taking an additional interest in the progress of education in the places mentioned; and through the intercourse that took place upon this subject during my short stay in these towns I expect some good will result, of which I shall afterward inform you.

I come now to speak of the state and prospects of education in this city. The state of elementary education here is very low, but its prospects are more encouraging. Perhaps you are aware that the Colombian government is taking steps to extend education all over its share of South America. Some time ago a school on the Lancasterian plan was established in Bogotá, the Capital, by a friar who had been banished from his native country on account of his then so-called revolutionary principles, and who had learned the system during his exile. Upon his return to America he established this school which has now existed for two or three years. It is the wish of the Government to put a model school in the capital of each department, and from these schools to send out masters to all the towns and villages the department contains. For this purpose, the friar whom I have mentioned, has lately arrived here and is getting his school-room prepared. I have had several conversations with him, and have been much pleased in observing the lively interest he takes in the education of the youth, as well as in the general progress of knowledge throughout his native country. . . .

The next thing I have to notice is of some interest and respects female- education. You are aware that the education of this sex is very much limited in South America. It is so in Quito, as might be expected. From the consideration that this is a large place and the chief city of a large and populous district of country, I was very desirous of doing something toward establishing a Female Seminary or school here. . . . I am lodged in the home of the Marquis de San José, where I am very kindly treated, and I wished the Marchioness to take the lead in the affair, as a matter of courtesy on my part, and principally because she is the person of most influence in the place. I stated to her the plan proposed and was happy to find that she entered heartily into it. . . . And such is the interest taken by the Government in these matters that I have no doubt of its complete success.

Thomson remained three weeks in Quito and was cordially entertained by influential persons, among them the principal and the professors of the leading school of the city. Before leaving Lima he had bought two copies of a book entitled "The Evidences of Christianity", written by the Bishop of London and translated into Spanish. One copy was sold to one of the leading men of the city, who not only read it with the greatest profit and interest, but passed it around among his friends who also studied it with great satisfaction. So great was the interest aroused in this subject that the ladies of the city took a subscription for the purpose of having an edition published in Quito. Thomson's remarks on the need of just this class of literature are interesting. He says:

I suppose that I need not tell you that a work on the evidences of Christianity is not a little wanted in many parts of this country, as there are many who are verging towards, or have already gone into, deism. On this account, as well as on others, it behooves the friends of Christianity to bestir themselves on behalf of South America. The present is a very interesting and a very critical period for this country. Much, very much, may be done at present, through prudent and zealous means, to instruct and confirm the wavering, and even, perhaps, bring back those who have apostatised from the faith. These measures were connected with means of instruction, as far as can be done. Regarding the true principles and practices of Christianity, as taught in the Holy Scriptures, a very plentiful harvest, through the blessing of God, might be reaped. If it should please the Lord to spare me and to enable me to reach my native land, I trust that I shall find many ready to lend their aid towards such a sacred object.

From Quito to Bogotá the route to be followed by Thomson lay through tropical valleys and over high mountain ranges, a total distance of over eight hundred miles. A recent traveler who was "vagabonding down the Andes"[7] reports that he took fifty-seven days for the trip from Bogotá to Quito, and that his pedometer marked eight hundred and forty-four miles as the distance walked. Thomson, with his usual disregard for the spectacular in the account of his travels, simply remarks in his first letter written from Bogotá that he had had a "long and by no means an agreeable journey. The distance from Quito to this place is considerable, the roads are very bad, and, in passing through one district there is considerable danger". On this journey, however, three schools were discovered which had been established on the Lancasterian plan. One of these was in the town Yahnará and the other two in Popayan. One of these last was for girls.

The establishing of these schools in the provincial districts of Colombia, says Thomson,

is the result of a general plan of education upon this system in connection with a central school established some time ago in Bogotá, the Capital. On arriving at that city, I visited this model school and hoped to meet there the Director of the establishment, to converse with him in regard to the number and efficiency of the various provincial schools. I was, however, disappointed in seeing him, as he was actually engaged on a tour through some of the provinces to promote the formation of schools. I can not, therefore, state how many schools were in operation, but I have good reason to think the existing number is calculated to encourage the friends of education, and that it goes on increasing.

I received from the Minister of the Interior a set of the lessons used in the schools. One regrets to find that the Scriptures are not there, nor any extracts from a volume so much calculated to benefit us, in youth and age, in time and eternity. With this important exception,

[7] H. A. Franck.

the lessons are good and in every way superior to the trash formerly used in the schools of South America.

One part of the lessons is worthy of notice. The Constitution of the country is divided into portions and sections and is read in the schools. By this means the children get acquainted in early life with the real nature and circumstances of their native land, and thus become better citizens and more useful to each other. This plan is worthy of imitation in other quarters. It is to be hoped that ere long this judicious plan, which has been adopted for the purpose of imbuing the early mind with a knowledge of the statutes of the country will be adopted also with regard to the Statutes of God unfolded in the Holy Scriptures.

One further reference must be made to the work of Thomson as the agent of the British and Foreign Bible Society, namely, the formation of a Bible society in Bogotá with the title "The Colombian Bible Society". The president of the University of Chile, to whose book reference has been made, has the following paragraph in regard to this society and its founder:

In Bogotá Thomson had the unspeakable satisfaction of founding a "Colombian Bible Society," whose only aim was the publication and distribution of the Holy Scriptures, in Spanish.

There was some resistance on the part of the clergy, but, on the other hand, the society counted on the help of the Government, of distinguished members of the clergy, and of many highly respectable citizens.

The first meetings for the organization were held in the chapel of the University, in the building which had been the principal convent of the Dominicans. The gifts toward the society, in a short time, reached the sum of one thousand three hundred and eighty pesos.

The minister of foreign relations was named president of the society, and the minister of finance and the vice-president of the republic supported the plan of founding the society and generously supported it.

Ten of the twenty members of the executive committee of this society were clergymen of the Roman Catholic Church.

Mexico and the Antilles[8]

From Colombia, in 1825, Thomson returned to England. But his heart was in the work which he had begun in Hispanic America and, in January, 1827, he accepted an appointment from the British and Foreign Bible Society to undertake the introduction of the Scriptures in Mexico. He reached that country at the end of April, of the same year, and proceeded at once to the capital, probably going up over the route that is now followed by the railway from Veracruz.

From this center different parts of the republic were visited and a large number of books were sold. In the mining regions, in particular, he met with an unusually warm welcome from the miners and their families, of which he has the following to record:

The rich and well populated mining districts through which I have passed were supplied, by means of this visit, with a treasure more precious than that which they were digging from the mines. And it was a pleasure to see the people recognize, at least once, the superiority of the treasure which I offered to that which they had taken from the ground. They showed their preference by giving me, at one time,— not to mention others,—some seventy pounds of the precious metal which they had taken out, in exchange for copies of the Sacred Volume which I put into their hands.

However, orders prohibiting the further sale of the Bible, caused Thomson to withdraw from Mexico, although he cherished hopes of returning later to that country. He had been well received by many of the leading citizens, some of them ecclesiastics, and he was defended in the papers by some of these men who regretted his departure from the country and the consequent cessation of his work. However, he considered that his time might be better occupied elsewhere and he returned to England to make his report on conditions as he had found them in the ancient land of Moctezuma.

[8] For much of the material of this section the author is indebted to a recent book, *Diego Thomson, Apóstol de la Instrucción Pública, e Iniciador de la Obra Evangélica en la América Latina*, por Juan C. Varetto, Imprenta Evangélica, Buenos Aires, 1918.

He had maintained but an indirect connection with the work of education in Mexico, inasmuch as a former *chargé d' Affaires* of Mexico in London had learned the principles of the Lancasterian system and, on his return to his own country, had been active in securing the establishment of schools on that basis. In a report which this gentleman, Sr. Rocafuerte, made to the "British and Foreign School Society", and which was afterward published, occurs the following relative to the work of the Lancasterian system in Mexico:

In Mexico, the first Lancasterian school was opened on the twenty-second of August, 1822, and, by one of those strange occurrences in revolutions, the halls of the Inquisition, so inimical to this institution, were converted into a public school, into a nursery of free men, into a true temple of reason. Three hundred children are taught to read in this school according to the new system of education, a system that will lead to the moral perfection of the world, as the mariner's compass led to the geographical perfection of the globe. This first school was called "*La Escuela del Sol*" [*i.e.,* "*The School of the Sun*"].

Some time afterward, the government granted to the Lancasterian Association of Mexico the large and beautiful convent of Bethlehem, and a second school was formed there. This establishment is divided into three parts. . . . The first part is calculated for six hundred and sixty children; they learn to read, write, and cipher; they are also instructed in the political and religious catechism, orthography, arithmetic, and Spanish grammar. The parents of the children who can pay give a dollar a month. The children of the poor pay nothing.

The second department will contain four hundred scholars, who pay two dollars a month, or nearly five pounds a year. It is a model or central school for forming teachers and good professors who are afterward to be sent into the different provinces in order to fulfill the desire of the government which is to place in every village throughout Mexico a Lancasterian school, a printing press, and a chapel.

The third department will contain three hundred scholars, and these pay three dollars a month, or seven pounds a year. The object intended in this department is to teach Latin, French, geography, and drawing, on the principles of the Lancasterian system.

In 1823 there were introduced into the Lancasterian schools of Mexico the lessons used in your schools of London, taken from the Bible, without note or comment. Some old priests opposed the introduction of these, stating that it was prohibited to read extracts from the Bible without notes. The secretary of the Lancasterian Association . . . . supported the opposite opinion and succeeded in establishing in the schools the use of these extracts. The consequence is that our children are acquiring a taste for the perusal of the Scriptures, and they are, hence, learning to be virtuous, charitable, tolerant and free. . . .

. . . . This vast plan of human improvement is the great object of your noble institution, an institution which truly deserves the gratitude of the world and the most cordial support of all who are influenced by the *love of their country and the principles of Christianity.*

Although the remaining years of the life of Thomson were given up to the work of the British and Foreign Bible Society rather than to that of education, it will be well to follow him in his travels until his work is finished. Having been obliged to leave Mexico, he offered his services to the society for work in the West Indies. He was gladly accepted and in carrying out his commission visited practically every island of the Lesser Antilles, as also the larger islands of the groups to the north. From Cuba he wrote the society in 1837, as follows:

I am writing you from the Island of Cuba, a place which has been long in my thoughts with mingled desire, hopes and fears,—the first and third of these sentiments prevailing over the other. But your work and mine is to offer and introduce the Sacred Scriptures in all places and to all men of all continents, and even to those in the far-off islands of the sea. This is the last island of the West Indies, both as regards its position and the visit of your Agent,—and it is also the last in many respects which I do not now care to mention. But, although last, it is not the least, since, in size, it is the largest of all the islands of the Antilles, and it is also the largest as regards the need of help from your Society. It is the twentieth island which I have visited on my trips through the archipelago . . . . and in all these places the Word has free entrance and complete acceptation, except in Porto Rico.

Returning to England, Thomson made a trip to Canada, and was then appointed agent of the Bible Society in Spain and Portugal. He also visited France and even crossed over into Morocco. He died in London, in 1854.

In the report of the Bible Society for the same year are to be found the following words:

The Society can not receive the news of the death of its lamented friend, Dr. James Thomson, who, from 1823 to 1844 acted as one of its Agents abroad, without recording its acknowledgment of the faithful and valuable services given by him during that long period, in South America, the Antilles, in British America, in Mexico, and other places, and, lately, when, at the request of the Society, he took. charge of a provisional mission to Spain.

The Society remembers with special appreciation the personal piety of Dr. Thomson, his freedom from sectarian spirit, his devotion to the work, his zeal and tact, and his untiring perseverance in carrying out the same. Also, it can not fail to record that since he ceased to have an official connection with the Society, he has been constantly solicitous for its welfare and ready to serve the countries which had been the scene of his former labors. And many will bear witness of the voluntary aid which he gave, so far as he was able, and always with the greatest satisfaction, to the various institutions and projects whose object was that of the evangelization of all the world,—an object always dear to his heart.

WEBSTER E. BROWNING.

BOOK REVIEWS

Lecciones de Historia Argentina. By RICARDO LEVENE. 2 vols.
(Buenos Aires: J. Lajoune y Cia, 1920. Pp. xxxi, 436, 516.)

These volumes compose the revised fifth edition of a textbook of the history of Argentina written by a member of the new school of Argentine historians. The present edition is scarcely as attractive typographically as the fourth edition: it is printed in a somewhat more compact format; and the paper is scarcely of such a good quality. A small amount of illustrative material is omitted from this edition. Although it has no formal bibliography, yet it is equipped with footnotes.

The first volume is devoted to the colonial epoch. Its introductory chapter deals with the sciences auxiliary to history with some attention to Argentina's libraries, museums, and archives. The second chapter is concerned with the age of Columbus. Then the early discoverers and explorers of the Río de la Plata are described. The aborigenes of the Platean basin are characterized and mention is made of the activities of the Incas in that region. Considerable space is given to the temporal and spiritual conquest of southern South America by the Spaniards. The spread of settlement into the interior of that continent, the reduction of the Indians, and early indications of discontent with Spanish rule are successively considered. Economic conditions in the viceroyalty of la Plata receive special attention; for a chapter is allotted to each of the following topics: colonial commerce, economic life, the administration of the royal treasury, and economic institutions. A similar amount of space is assigned to judicial institutions, church organization, colonial journals, and colonial society. Four chapters are concerned with the English invasions of the Platean viceroyalty, other antecedents of the Argentine struggle for independence, and the revolution of May, 1810, in Buenos Aires. All in all, this volume furnishes a suggestive epitome of the colonial history of Argentina which utilizes the most recent scientific contributions of Argentine scholars.

The second volume is occupied with the revolutionary period of Argentina's history and with national organization. Only a few more

99

pages are allotted to the years from 1810 to 1916 than to the colonial period. Of the thirty-five chapters which compose this volume fifteen are concerned with the troublous although interesting history of Buenos Aires and the United Provinces of la Plata which ended by the adoption of the Argentine constitution of 1826. Chapter twenty-six carries the story through the battle of Monte Caseros and discusses the resulting downfall of Dictator Juan Manuel de Rosas. The four following chapters mainly deal with the national reorganization which took place during the years from 1852 to 1861. A chapter accorded to the war of certain South-American nations with Paraguay in which Argentina played an important rôle is naturally written from the Argentine viewpoint. The epoch from 1868 to 1916 is summarily disposed of in some fifty pages. In consequence many topics of interest and significance in the recent history of Argentina, such as electoral reform under President Roque Sáenz Peña, the relations between the national government and the provinces, and the attitude of Argentina toward the World War, receive little or no attention. There may, of course, be reasons why the author of a history of Argentina that is intended for use in the schools of his country may wish to avoid describing in detail the portion of his nation's history about which the passions of some of his compatriots still run high. To the reviewer, however, the neglect to allot more space to the half century of Argentine development under the existing constitution is a cause for regret.

In spite of this shortcoming—which the reviewer hopes may be somewhat remedied in the next edition—Levene's history is among the best works that deal with the history of a nation of Hispanic America. May its tribe increase.

WILLIAM SPENCE ROBERTSON.

Isabel of Castile and the Making of the Spanish Nation, 1451-1504. By IERNE L. PLUNKETT. [Heroes of the Nations series.] (New York and London: G. P. Putnam's Sons. 1919. Pp. xi, 432. Illustrated.)

The full title of this work indicates, it is to be presumed, a purpose to write a biography not only, but a history of "the making of the Spanish nation". With a writer of such talent in the portrayal of character and the narration of events as the author, the biographical element, however, receives an unequal share of attention to the detriment of the story of the evolution of the Spanish nation. Notwithstanding this disproportion, emphasis was placed upon the contributions to Spanish nationhood which were consequent effects of the marriage of Isabella and Ferdinand, the formation of that peculiar union of Castile and Aragon, and the institutional and administrative reforms of those rulers. On the other hand, such fundamental factors as sectionalism in Spain and the racial make-up of the people receives little notice.

The book is divided into thirteen chapters, the whole being adorned with some forty-five well chosen illustrations taken in the main from the works of Valentín Carderera y Solano, Lafuente, and Amador de los Rios. One map is provided. The first three chapters are devoted to a description of the political conditions in Castile of the fifteenth century with special reference to the misgovernment, feudal disorders, and civil wars of the reign of Henry IV., and to an analysis of the intrigues and involved politics which related to the marriage of "Isabel" and Ferdinand and their accession to power. There follows, in the fourth, the story of the Portuguese War, fought about the succession in Castile, and that of the final elimination of Isabella's rival, La Beltraneja. With respect to the first 120 pages, it is safe to say that nothing new is presented. In the chapter on "Organization and Reform", the problems and achievements in administrative, judicial, and financial reform are discussed with consummate brevity; and the history of the incorporation into the crown of the masterships of the military orders, the service of the *Santa Hermandad*, and the enforced restitution by the nobles of wrongly appropriated royal properties is written with a due sense of its significance to the process of suppressing seigniorial anarchy. However excellent this chapter may be in clearness and as an achievement in compression, it leaves much to be desired as a study of institutions. The author is happier in the narration of events in the final wars against the Mohammedans and the fall of Granada. The study of the Inquisition (ch. X) and the story of the expulsion of the Jews and the Mudéjares (ch. XI) are particularly vivid in the characterizations of such men as Cardinal Mendoza, Ximénez de Cisneros, Talavera, and Torquemada. The chapter (pp. 285–318) on Columbus—based entirely on Irving, Filson Young, and Thacher—is of little value. In addition there are chapters on "Isabel and her children", which is one of the best; "The Italian Wars", which is of doubtful pertinence; and "Castilian Literature", in which Isabella is shown to have been a deeply interested patroness of educational and cultural activities and institutions.

The author is conscious of the extremes between extravagance of praise and severity of condemnation in the interpretations of Isabella, but this book is neither extravagant nor severe. Isabella is presented as having an "independent and clear-sighted mind"; as an able politician capable of taking care of herself in the midst of court intrigues; as a ruler of firm justice tempered on occasion not so much by mercy as by expediency; as a wife and mother deserving of "unstinted admiration". Her "bigotry" in religion is explained as an "inheritance" shared in common with "the greater part of her race", yet the "relentless cruelty" of her persecutions is viewed with "sick disgust". Isabella rendered great service in restoring the crown as a "symbol of national justice" and in securing domestic peace.

In view of the works of Prescott and Irving, to attempt a book of a semi-popular character was a bold undertaking. The result is a clearly and interestingly written volume which justifies a worthy position in the series in which it appears. Yet it may be questioned if it "will take the place" of Prescott's *History of the Reign of Ferdinand and Isabella*. This work adds little if anything in the way of information; and, although Altamira and Lafuente are included in the brief bibliographical list, little use was made in the main body of the book of any authority which had not been employed by Prescott. The present work most frequently quotes from the writings of Hernando del Pulgar, Jerónimo Zurita, Andrés Bernaldez, Marineo Siculo, and Sabatini, with scattered excerpts from Peter Martyr. Excepting Sabatini, of course, these are writers constantly referred to by Prescott in his heavily documented history.

WILLIAM WHATLEY PIERSON, JR.

A Syllabus of Hispanic-American History. By WILLIAM WHATLEY PIERSON, JR., PH.D., Professor of History in the University of North Carolina. Third edition. Revised and reprinted. (University of North Carolina: 1920. Pp. 44. $0.50.)

This *Syllabus*, the preface states, "is designed primarily for the use of students of the University of North Carolina as a guide to the introductory study of Hispanic-American history". The aim of the author is to stress economic and institutional history, rather than political, which can best be sacrificed when the limitations of time must receive consideration. The outline consists of an introduction bearing upon the European background and thirteen detailed chapters, the first entitled "The Period of Discovery," and the last, "Contemporary History, Problems, and Achievements of Hispanic America". A goodly number of bibliographical references, including works in Spanish and French, as well as in English, accompany the various topics. Careful scholarship and regard for sound pedagogical principles characterize the work. Without doubt, Professor Pierson has performed a service of more than local character; for men and women who have had no formal training are constantly being called upon to teach courses in the Hispanic American field. To them the *Syllabus* should prove a special boon, but it will not be without interest to high school teachers who are anxious to introduce our neighbors to the south in connection with the course in United States history.

In view of such large opportunity for usefulness, it seems legitimate to call attention to a few respects in which, in the opinion of the reviewer, the *Syllabus* might be improved. Judging from the briefest possible mention given to the Aztecs and Incas (p. 14), the author feels that they deserve but slight attention in an introductory course. This is a mistake, for a study of these peoples not only throws valuable light upon the cultural possibilities of their descendents, but appears absolutely essential to an understanding of political, economic, religious, and moral conditions in present-day Hispanic America. Chapter four, dealing with geography and resources, seems out of place in its position immediately preceding the chapter on "The Struggle for Independence". Surely the logical position for this is the first part of chapter one, where it would furnish the needed setting for the historical narrative which follows. Some of the details listed for economic history might be omitted in order to secure time for more attention to the political history of the leading nations, such as the A. B. C. republics; for a year's course in Hispanic American history should give sufficient stress to the leading political figures to make these stand out in the minds of the students as real personalities; and unless more attention is given to the biographical thread than is indicated in the *Syllabus*, this end will not be accomplished.

To make the *Syllabus* of more general value, it would also be desirable to add more of the standard works in Spanish, such as Pelliza's *Historia Argentina* and Galdames's *Historia de Chile*, or to substitute them for some of the more inferior volumes of the South American series. Dr. Oliviera Lima's very helpful analysis of *The Evolution of Brazil compared with that of Spanish and Anglo-Saxon America* (Stanford University Press) should be given a place. And *Inter-America*, the *Pan-American Magazine*, the *Mexican Review*, *Cuba Contempo-ránea*, and other periodicals of similar standing, which contain much valuable matter, should be included.

Goucher College.

MARY WILHELMINE WILLIAMS.

Paraguay. A Commercial Handbook. By WILLIAM LYTLE SCHURZ. Department of Commerce, Bureau of Foreign and Domestic Commerce, Special Agents Series, No. 199. (Washington: Government Printing Office, 1920. Pp. 195. Folding map. Paper. 40 cents.)

No other book equally enlightening and accurate concerning present-day Paraguay has yet appeared. Its author is a trained historical worker who was given absence from his post in the historical faculty of the University of Michigan where he taught Hispanic American history, in order that he might visit Paraguay as trade commissioner for the Bureau of Foreign and Domestic Commerce. As the title of Dr. Schurz's work indicates, the volume is intended primarily for the use of North Americans from the United States who are interested in foreign trade. It contains, however, a wealth of information that is of importance in the classroom to those not only interested in the trade of South America but as well to students of the history of the southern continent, for it presents the necessary background that can be obtained nowhere else in such convenient form.

The introduction gives brief data relative to geography, climate, history, government, religion, education, and population. Other main topics discussed are the following: cities and towns; agriculture; stockraising; meatpacking; forest industries; mineral resources; manufactures; transportation and communication; labor; immigration, colonization, and land; foreign trade; investments; banks and banking; money and exchange; and public finances. The result is an excellent social and economic study that should give the volume a place on the shelves of every student of Hispanic American history. The author personally visited all parts of the country except those parts of the Chaco district that have not yet been visited by any white man so far as known. The large folding map is credited to Cleto Romero, former director of the National Department of Engineers in Paraguay, but it contains various emendations and additions by Dr. Schurz. This map shows the extreme claims of Paraguay to the mysterious and largely unknown Chaco district.

While Paraguay is as yet mainly an undeveloped country, potentially it is of considerable wealth, and the future will undoubtedly see this republic—the old domain of the Jesuit order—advance rapidly because of its agricultural and cattle possibilities. The country is a vast storehouse only awaiting the world's necessity to make its importance fully realised. In this connection the section on Transportation and communications will be of interest. A handbook by the same author, who has recently returned to South America as commercial attaché for the Bureau of Foreign and Domestic Commerce at Rio de Janeiro, is now in press.

JAMES ALEXANDER ROBERTSON.

New Mexico the Land of the Delight Makers. ["See America First" Series.] By GEORGE WHARTON JAMES. (Boston: The Page Company, [•1920]. Map, Illustrated. Index. $5.00.)

The sub-title of this volume well describes its contents: "The History of its Ancient Cliff Dwellings and Pueblos, Conquest by the Spaniards, Franciscan Missions; Personal Accounts of the Ceremonies, Games, Social Life and Industries of its Indians; A Description of its Climate, Geology, Flora and Birds, its Rivers and Forests; A Review of its rapid Development and Reclamation Projects and Educational System; with full and accurate accounts of its Progressive Counties, Cities and Towns". This is not a scientific treatment of New Mexico, but a tribute to its historic past, its interesting present, and its developing future, written by one who went thither in search of health and for over thirty years lived in the out-of-doors of this state, learning its natural characteristics and its people at first hand instead of from books. The volume is an intimate narration, written *con amore*, and rightly has a place in the "See America First" Series.

In addition to its introduction, there are thirty-one chapters in the book, as follows: Why "The land of the delight makers"; The exploration and subjugation of New Mexico; The Homeric epic of New Mexico; The great Pueblo rebellion of 1680; The world's greatest autograph album, Inscription Rock; My adventures at Zuni; Among the witches; Hunting with Indians in New Mexico; Acoma, the city of the cliffs; Katzimo—the enchanted mesa; The arts and industries of the Indians; The religion of the Indians; Indian songs and music; The native architecture of New Mexico; The pueblo of Taos; The antiquities of New Mexico, Its ancient dwellings, its mission churches; The American

passion play; The mountains of New Mexico; The national forests of
New Mexico; The bird life of New Mexico; The flora of New Mexico;
The influence of New Mexico upon literature; The influence of New
Mexico upon art; The Taos society of artists; Ancient and modern
methods of seeing New Mexico; New Mexico as the nation's play-
ground; Education in New Mexico; The university and special schools
of New Mexico; The art museum of Santa Fe; Irrigation in New
Mexico; Albuquerque, the commercial metropolis of New Mexico;
The population of New Mexico.

The title of the book comes of course from Bandelier's *The Delight
Makers*, as the author explains in his first chapter—a name chosen by
Bandelier for his novel "from the clowns who performed their antics
and bufoonery for the delectation of the prehistoric dwellers in the
cliffs"; and James adopts it because New Mexico with its wealth of
archaeological and ethnological material, its past history, and its
natural wonders is a land of delight to all who visit it. He describes
New Mexico as "a land of rich fertility and of hopeless barrenness;
where irrigation has been practiced for centuries, even long before
Columbus sailed from Spain on his voyage of discovery". He expresses
a wish that the book may "lead a few people of intelligence each year
to break loose from the traditional and conventional routes of travel
and give themselves the joy of roughing it in New Mexico". In his
statement that without New Mexico "there would be no accepted
science of American archaeology to the outside world", he forgets that
the United States is not all of America, and that the richest fields of
American archaeology do not lie in this country but in the lands to the
south.

The historical chapters dealing with the history of the Spaniards in
New Mexico are written mainly from secondary material. Most
interesting, perhaps, of these chapters is that treating of *El Morro* or
Inscription Rock, on which many autographs have been cut, some of
which are reproduced. The most interesting of all is that of Juan de
Oñate, but in transcribing this, James has made several blunders,
which are rather inexcusable as the inscription is perfectly legible.
Instead of reading "Paso por aqui el adelantado de don Jan de Oñate
el descubrimiento de la mar del sur a 16 de Abril ao 1606", this inscription should read "Paso por aq̃i el adelantado don J°n de oñate Del
descubrimyento de la mar del sur a 16 de abril del 606". His descriptions of the people are good, considerable use being made of Cushing's
work as well as that of other writers. His remarks on the passion

play are interesting although too wordy at times, and with too great a preponderance of the pronoun "I". In this connection, it must be remembered that under the United States flag is still to be seen another set of *penitentes*, namely, those of a small town in the Philippine Islands, of whom what James says of the class and character of many of *penitentes* in New Mexico is equally true.

The mechanical appearance of the book which is dedicated to Jesse Walter Fewkes, chief of the Bureau of American Ethnology, is excellent. The binding is attractive and the illustrations, eight of which are colored, are good. The map is serviceable but would be better if it were larger. As a whole the work conveys much information of many different kinds. In its execution, it is uneven in its style and too frequently accuses the easterner of ignorance of the west. Its first hand history is valuable, even although this is rather a popular book than one for the student; but its history taken from books adds nothing new to what is known already, although the author could scarcely have omitted these portions of his narrative in a work of this nature. It is very probable that a large edition of the volume will be sold.

JAMES ALEXANDER ROBERTSON.

Colección de Documentos relativos a las Islas Filipinas existentes en el Archivo de Indias de Sevilla. Publicada por la Compañía General de Tabacos de Filipinas. Tomo III (1519–1522). (Barcelona: Imprenta de la Viuda de Luis Tasso, 1920. Pp. vi, 383, 1 leaf. 15 pesetas. Bound in stiff paper.)

The third volume of the remarkable *Colección General de Documentos relativos a las Islas Filipinas* contains documents nos. 86–126 inclusive. The printing of this volume, as stated in the colophon, was completed on June 18, 1920. A slip tipped on to the page containing the half title of the series is as follows: "The untoward circumstances which have affected work in general since the middle of the year 1919 furnish a prime cause for the delay in publishing this volume, for although normal conditions are now reigning, production remained liable to great delays, due to the accompanying press of work. These are difficulties which could not be overcome earlier notwithstanding all our good intentions. We believe firmly that the next volume will be published this same year [1920], unless causes beyond our control frustrate our intentions".

The documents of this volume are as follows: Doc. 86, The cost of the five vessels intended for the discovery of the Spicery under Ferdinand Magellan, Seville, 1519. Doc. 87, Cost of the vessels, supplies, ammunition, etc., of Magellan's fleet, Seville, 1519. Doc. 88, Pay of sailors, common seamen, and boys of Magellan's fleet, Seville, 1519. Doc. 89, News relative to a fleet despatched to the Indies by the king of Portugal, [Lisboa?, 1519]. Doc. 90, Judicial inquiry made by order of Ferdinand Magellan with the object of ascertaining events aboard the ship *San Antonio*, Port San Julian, April 26, 1520. Doc. 91, Royal cédula addressed to the officials of the House of Trade relative to the salary of Nicolás de Artieta, Coruña, May 16, 1520. Doc. 92, Patent as treasurer of the Trade of the Spicery granted to Bernardino Mélendez, and his oath, Coruña, May 17, 1520. Doc. 93, Letter of Ruy Falero to the Cardinal Governor of Castile informing him that he had been arrested, and requesting him to have the goodness to have the king of Spain write in his behalf to the king of Portugal, Cubillan, July, 1520. Doc. 94, Letter from the officials of the House of Trade to the Cardinal Governor informing him of the imprisonment of Ruy Falero in Portugal, and about other matters, Seville, July 31, 1520. Doc. 95, Royal cédula directing that 15,000 maravedís be paid annually to Martín de Mezquita until the return of Magellan's fleet, although by his Majesty's order he did not accompany the fleet, Valladolid, August 26, 1520. Doc. 96, Royal cédula directing that no pilot make the voyage to the Indies without being examined by the chief pilot Sebastian Cabot, Valladolid, September 26, 1520. Doc. 97, Pay directed by his Majesty to be given to the captains and officers of Magellan's fleet, Seville, 1520. Doc. 98, Geographical description from the Cape of Good Hope to China, 1520–1528. Doc. 99, Letter from the accountant, Juan López de Recalde to Archbishop Fonseca, informing him of the arrival at the port of Seville of the ship *San Antonio*, one of Magellen's five ships, etc., Seville, May 12, 1521. Doc. 100, Continuation of Recalde's letter. Doc. 101, Letter from the Bishop of Burgos to the officials of Seville in answer to a communication in which the officials informed him of the arrival of the ship *San Antonio*, Burgos, May 26, 1521. Doc. 102, Letter from Licentiate Matienzo to his Majesty informing him of the arrival at Seville of the ship *San Antonio*, and as to what its crew say about the reason for returning, Seville, May, 1521. Doc. 103, Letter from Bishop Fonseca to the House of Trade, directing that the ship *San Antonio* be delivered over to Don Juan de Velasco, June 30, 1521. Doc. 104, Inventory of the rigging, arms, artillery, and other appurtenances of the ship *San Antonio*, and resolution taken by the officials of the House of Trade on delivering over the ship over to Don Juan de Velasco, Seville, July 12, 1521. Doc. 105, Book of the treaties of peace and friendship made with the kings of the Moluccas, [Moluccas], September-December, 1521. Doc. 106, Royal cédula directing that Esteban Gómez's pay as pilot be given him, and that his effects be placed in deposit until the rendering of a decision as to what shall be done with those who returned in the ship *San Antonio*, Burgos, October 4, 1521. Doc. 107, Royal cédula directing that the cargo brought by the ship *San Antonio* be delivered to Cristóbal de Haro and their value be spent in the preparation for the despatching of the new fleet which is being fitted up to continue the discovery of the Spicery, Burgos, October 4, 1521. Doc. 108, Power of attorney given by Cristóbal de Haro in favor of Diego Díaz, authorizing him to take charge of the cargo of the ship *San Antonio*, Burgos, October 4, 1521. Doc. 109, Instructions to Captain Juan Nicolás de Artieta directing him to build three ships, which are to be sent to the Moluccas fleet, Burgos, December 7, 1521. Doc. 110, Note of the goods taken by the Portuguese from the ship *Trinidad* in the Moluccas, Tidore, December 16, 1521. Doc. 111, Expenses incurred by Cristóbal de Haro, factor of the House of Trade, from the moneys received by him for the despatch of the fleets, September 20, 1521–January 10, 1528. Doc. 112, Royal cédula addressed to Nicolás de Grimaldo relative to the delivery of a certain sum to the Bishop of Burgos to spend on the fleet, which is now being prepared for the continuation of the discovery of the Spicery, Vitoria, May 6, 1522. Doc. 113, Inventory of the cargo of the ship *San Antonio*, of which Diego Díaz took charge in the name of Cristóbal de Haro, Seville, May 8, 1522. Doc. 114, Letter from Cortés to his Majesty discussing the importance of the discovery of the South Sea, Cuyuacan, May 15, 1522. Doc. 115, Log of Magellan's voyage from the Cape of San Augustín in Brazil until the return of the ship *Victoria* to Spain, written by Francisco Albo, September, 1522. Doc. 116, Several papers containing information relative to the goods on the ship *Victoria*, its arms, ammunition, etc., September 1522. Doc. 117, Relation of all who died on the Magellan expedition, September 1522. Doc. 118, Pay given to the members of Magellan's fleet until the return of the ship *Victoria* to Seville, [Seville], September, 1522. Doc. 119, Rigging, arms, and artillery of the ship *Victoria*, which were taken charge of by the accountant Domingo de Ochandiano, Seville, September 12–October 14, 1522. Doc. 120, Royal cédula directing the officials of the House of Trade to send all the books and documents made at the time of the despatch of Magellan's fleet, Valladolid, October 10, 1522. Doc. 121, Royal cédula to the same directing that they deliver to Cristóbal de Haro all the cloves brought from the Moluccas in the ship *Victoria* and keep samples of the spices, Valladolid, October 10, 1522. Doc. 122, Royal cédula to the same directing that the amount of pay still due Pedro de Alva, a Portuguese pilot, be given him, October 10, 1522. Doc. 123, Royal cédula directing that the samples of drugs and spices brought by the ship *Victoria* be delivered to Cristóbal de Haro, in order that he might send them to certain persons, Valladolid, October 17, 1522. Doc. 124, Power of attorney from Haro in favor of Diego Díaz, authorizing the latter to get the cloves on the ship *Victoria*, and receipt given in Seville for them, Valladolid, October 17-Seville, November 14, 1522. Doc. 125, Judicial inquiry before the alcalde of Valladolid, Díaz de Leguizamo, relative to several occurrences during the voyage of Magellan's fleet, Valladolid, October 18, 1522. Doc. 126, Weight of the sacks of cloves brought by the ship *Victoria* and delivered to Diego Díaz, factor for Cristóbal de Haro, Seville, November 6, 1522.

Of these interesting documents, thirteen had been previously published, several in part only or in abstract, while the remainder had existed only in manuscript form, although it is more than likely that they have been used by authors of the period. The documents published heretofore are as follows: nos. 87, 90, 99, 100, 115, and 125, by Navarrete and Medina; nos. 93, 117, and 118, by Medina; no. 94, by Llorens Asensio; no. 101, by Pastells in his edition of Colin and by Llorens Asensio; no. 102, by Pastells (fragment); no. 105, by Navarrete (abstract), and Pastells (fragments). The published documents have been drawn upon frequently in Blair and Robertson's *The Philippine Islands*. There is a paucity of annotation, as in the other volumes, notes being limited to five and being bibliographical in character rather than historical. In the first note the editor confesses that he had some doubt as to whether doc. 89 properly belonged to this collection, but finally admitted it in accordance with the opinion of a student of the period who thought that it had been sent to the king or his council as showing that Portugal was trying to anticipate the Spaniards in their discoveries. The second note explains that docs. 99 and 100 really form one document, and were so published by both Navarrete and Medina, but in order to preserve the originals as far as possible, they

were published as two documents. It is explained that the two parts
of the document in the Archivo de Indias were evidently copied from
an older original by two distinct persons, as shown by the difference in
orthography. The editor of this series, by the way, who signs himself
simply J. S. G. in the first volume, it has been ascertained is Sr. Don
Jose Sánchez Garrigos, the librarian of the Compañía General de
Tabacos de Filipinas. It might not be amiss to mention also that one
of the members of the company who had been especially interested
through his love of history and letters in the publication of this series,
namely, the Conde de Churruca, has recently died.

The chief interest of the student will naturally center around the
documents now published for the first time, and from which a more
complete knowledge of the expedition of Magellan and its immediate
aftermath can be obtained. The several documents treating of the
expenses of the expedition are especially interesting and invite comparison with modern expeditions. In doc. no. 96, warning is given
that "muchos pilotos hazen el dho viaje de q los tratantes e pasageros
e otras personas rresciben daño e los pasajes son mas largos e mas
peligrosos por no saber levar los dhos navios", to obviate which examination before Cabot is necessary. In general, the documents are technical in character and furnish considerable information relative to the
machinery of the expedition, and as such they are not without value
for the economic history of the period.

JAMES ALEXANDER ROBERTSON.

NOTES AND COMMENT

A NEW FORM OF PAN-AMERICANISM: THE EXCHANGE OF STUDENTS

A great deal has been said within the last few years about a so-called exchange of students between the universities of the United States and Hispanic America. So far as I have been able to observe, these plans have been concerned only with the bringing of students from Hispanic America to the United States. They have not contemplated reciprocity: they have not included the sending of American students to the universities of Hispanic America. A reciprocal arrangement has recently been made by a few schools and the results of this experiment will be watched with great interest.

I am informed by Dr. Lord, Dean of the Boston University School of Business Administration, that the school he represents has opened a branch in Havana which will give an opportunity to Americans to study in Cuba. It is stated that this same institution will open other foreign branches. Georgetown University has recently announced a group of affiliated colleges in all parts of the world at which credit towards graduation will be given by the Georgetown Foreign Service School. Both of these plans contemplate undergraduate work along lines running parallel with the work done in the home institution.

The University of Notre Dame has recently inaugurated a system of exchange that contemplates the sending of graduates of the Department of Foreign Commerce to do advanced work in the Universities of Hispanic America, and the bringing of students from Hispanic America for either graduate or undergraduate work at Notre Dame. The first students to go to South America under this plan are Mr. John T. Balfe of Beacon, New York, who graduated from the University of Notre Dame in June, 1920, and entered the University of Buenos Aires in September, and Mr. John C. Powers of Urbana, Ohio, who will enter the Catholic University of Santiago, Chile, in March, 1921, in time for the opening of the fall term. Four students have come to Notre Dame under the plan: Mr. Manuel Vial, of the Catholic University of Santiago, who is working for the Doctorate in Civil Law; Mr. Ivan Pra Balmaceda of the same university, who is a sophomore in Agriculture; Mr. Juan Pedro Scaron Pallares of the University of Montevideo, who is a sophomore in the Department of Electrical Engineering; and Mr. Edward W. Sullivan, from an English high school in Buenos Aires, who is a freshman in Foreign Commerce. Applications for further exchange next year are now receiving consideration.

While opinion as to the ultimate success of this plan is divided, it seems to be the belief of the majority of persons consulted that this exchange will have a very decided influence in the development of a new Pan Americanism. The objections to the plan fall under two main heads: First, it is feared by some that the young Americans who go to study in Hispanic America will fail on moral grounds;- second, it is stated by others that it is impossible to superimpose the culture of one race upon the basic elements of another race.

The first objection might seem at first sight to have a sound basis. There is not a single commercial center of any importance in Hispanic America that has not traditions and often actual examples of young Americans who have gone into moral and intellectual decay, but I think that the causes for these shipwrecks can be found very readily and can be absolutely eliminated in the case of graduate students. These causes and their remedies may be summarized as follows:

1. Lonesomeness. The young American away from home for the first time finds himself in what he feels to be a hostile social atmosphere, and he finds consolation in drink and its attendant vices. An American college man with a knowledge of Spanish and armed with good letters of introduction, will be admitted quite freely into the best native society, and will be just as safe, if not safer, from a dangerous moral environment than he would be in a metropolitan center at home.

2. Idleness. Idle hours are most dangerous, and are often a pitfall for the young American business man in South America. The student can have his full time occupied whether through business employment during the hours he is free from class or through research work in history or some other line for which there are excellent facilities available. Perhaps a combination of business employment and research work is the ideal one.

3. Bad example and bad counsel. Certainly the American college man should be able to use sound judgment in picking his friends among the English-speaking colony and avoid those whose failure seeks companionship among new arrivals. The student will be especially

independent of this sort of influence if he concentrates his attention upon good native society, and he will be a much more successful business man later for having cultivated this social contact.

The college that pays no attention to character training is certainly false to its trust and is receiving tuition under false pretenses. I like to feel that most American educators have a keen sense of their responsibility in this matter, have a realization of the fact that the discipline of the will is a more important function of education than the discipline of the intellect. And any college that fulfills its duty towards its students in the matter of character training will send out men who are above the temptations that have wrecked the career of other Americans abroad.

The college also has a special duty, I believe, to select for study such subjects as will best prepare the student for an appreciation of the culture of the country in which he expects to reside. In South America especially one finds a tendency to a broad cultural education more common among the better class of business men than is the case in the United States. The merchant there wants to be able to think of something besides business outside of business hours. Literature, music, art, historical study, economics, and world politics, claim their devotees among the business men of South America, who feel that their business minds lose nothing of their clearness through these elevating distractions. The same sort of appreciation, and some sort of international viewpoint may be instilled into the American student while he is still in college, and if he is wise he will be very glad to have two or three points of contact with his future customer instead of one, and that the very material one of business.

The second objection has practically been answered in considering the remedies for the first, but it deserves a word of special comment. It may be a difficult and tedious process to superimpose the culture of one race upon the basic stock of another, but we know from history that it has been accomplished time and again. However, the plan of the University of Notre Dame does not contemplate any such a radical change. It proposes to give to the college graduate an enthusiastic appreciation of Hispanic American culture and thus form a nucleus of enlightened Americans who will counteract decisively the influence of thoughtless persons who have done so much harm to our interests in South America by inflicting unkind, unjust, and very often malignant, criticism. It is hoped that the formation of a group of this sort will have a strong influence towards overcoming the provincialism which has been so much of an obstacle to our development of friendly relations abroad.

On the positive side, I believe that many advantages will result from the exchange of students. The American boys who go to South America will perfect themselves in Spanish, will gain more thorough knowledge of South American industrial and commercial opportunities than they could gain by a hundred years of study at home, will learn the point of view and the business psychology of the South American merchant, will be better Americans for their broader knowledge of Americans foreign relations, and will be towers of strength for American business. If such an exchange of American students had been made a working corollary of the beginning of diplomatic relations with Hispanic America a hundred years ago, the Monroe Doctrine and Pan Americanism would now be so solidly established that no non-American power could hope for any advantages on American soil without the consent of the United States of America.

The presence of these young men in South America will have a wonderful effect upon the regard of the South Americans for us. Speaking frankly, the South Americans regard us as barbarians so far as culture and the finer things of life are concerned. They know us only as wonderful inventors, geniuses for manufacturing and industrial organization, and colossi of business. It is our fault that they have this unfavorable impression of us. We have shown them only the more material and less favorable side of our character. The only news from the United States that we used to receive in South American countries referred to such items as powder explosions, murders, divorce statistics, tall buildings, attempts to ride Niagara Falls, lynchings, anti-trust activities of the Supreme Court, and speeches on the Monroe Doctrine. They knew that we paid large sums of money to Caruso and other operatic stars, but they felt that this was shallow mimicry of the *nouveau riche* and they laughed at what they considered our clumsy essays in culture.

The South American social fabric is more closely woven than our own, and the presence of a cultured group of college men from the United States in university centers will have a profoundly pleasing effect. The students will be gossiped about at every tea and reception of the university set, and since the professors of the universities are generally men holding high positions in law or politics, the university set has a more influential position in high society than is usually the case in our large cities. The people will be prepared for favorable impressions because the idea of sending young men to learn from them is a gracious compliment. The students will have it in their power to correct many, if not all, the misunderstandings into which our relations have blundered during the past hundred years.

Students who come to the United States from South America will always absorb a satisfactory amount of Americanism and will confirm the good work done by our own students. A high official of the Argentine Government told me recently that the average Argentine who spends some time in the United States becomes a most enthusiastic lover of our institutions and admirer of our culture, even when his previous training has been antagonistic to such impressions. He said that in the case of the United States and Germany, a residence of considerable time was necessary to gain this effect. He himself was educated in Germany and is now an enthusiastic admirer of most things German. He said further that the opposite holds true in the case of France, where the first pleasant impression is more superficial, and is likely to be spoiled by too prolonged a residence.

Four years spent in an American college should be sufficient to fix an appreciation of American ideals in the mind of the South American, and it might not be wise to prolong the residence of the student more than this time, because to prolong an absence from home gives rise to another objection which has been formulated by several members of the governments of Peru, Chile and Argentine. Their fear is that the student will lose contact with his friends if he remains too long away from home, and will find himself isolated when he begins his business or political career at home.

All in all, I believe that the plan inaugurated this summer has everything to commend it and will result in the formation of a generation of Americanists who will assure the future of Pan Americanism.

JOHN F. O'HARA, C.S.C.

ECONOMIC CONDITIONS IN ARGENTINA

It has been stated so many times of late that the interest and welfare of one country is the concern of all that one hesitates in making so prosaic a statement. However, it is so clearly shown in some specific cases today, that it well merits a rating as a classical expression. Argentina is an example of a country that has recorded world-trade conditions almost as sensitively as a barometer records pressure. In fact that country has almost at times seemed a barometer of world-trade conditions. This is true for two reasons. First, Argentina depends upon foreign capital for the production of raw materials within its boundaries, and also to move these commodities from its farms and industrial centers to foreign markets. Second, Argentina's prosperity depends upon the sale of its products abroad and any dull periods in the foreign demand is certain to record a depression in home industries.

During the war the increased demands made upon Argentina for such products as wool, wheat, hides and skins, and foodstuffs, created an enlarged export balance and prosperity was the natural result. This continued after the war, but as is usually true with all postwar prosperity its strength was certain to be spent within a short time. The latter part of May, 1919, a world trade depression began and almost simultaneously a depression in the trade of Argentina was recorded. Gold deposits abroad were drawn down, exports decreased, and exchange which had previously been favorable began to decline rapidly. In the short space of five months Argentina's exchange on the American market dropped from a two per cent premium to a twenty-five per cent discount. The stringency in the money markets of foreign countries curtailed the flow of capital to Buenos Aires and the result was shown both by a decrease in production and a sluggish flow of commodities. Argentina's recovery depends upon improved money conditions abroad and increased demands for its products.

EDWIN BATES.

South America is overstocked with goods it cannot pay for but not with goods it does not need, according to my view of the matter. Exchange started going against South America just as soon as we rectified our unfavorable trade balance by shipping gold. The bottom fell out of their market for raw materials in this country and they were forced to pay a premium of from thirty to fifty per cent on the dollar. It seems to me that there are two ways of rectifying this. The first is to wait for the natural laws of economics to work out and settle the trade balance, and the second is to make permanent investments in South America that will absorb the surplus of the trade balance.—JOHN F. O'HARA, C. S. C.

At the annual meeting of the American Historical Association, held at Washington, December 27–30, 1920, the afternoon session of the last day was devoted to "Pan American Political and Diplomatic Relations". This was a joint session of the above mentioned association and the American Political Science Association, and was held at the Pan American building. Under the chairmanship of Dr. Leo S. Rowe, director of the Pan American Union, papers were read as follows:

"Recent Constitutional Changes in Latin America", Herman G. James, University of Texas.

"The Monroe Doctrine as a Regional Understanding", Julius Klein, Harvard University.

"Pan-Americanism and the League of Nations", Manoel de Oliveira Lima, Catholic University of America.

The last two papers will appear in a future issue of this REVIEW. The papers were discussed by a number of those present.

During the meeting one of the group luncheons was for those interested in Hispanic American history. This was presided over by Dr. William R. Shepherd, of Columbia University, who spoke eloquently on Hispanic America and the League of Nations, and there was an attendance of over 60. Among speakers were Dr. Víctor Andrés Belaúnde, of Peru, Dr. Manoel de Oliveira Lima, formerly of Brazil, now of Washington, Dr. Bolton, Dr. Samuel Guy Inman, Dr. Chapman, Dr. Mary W. Williams, and others.

A Congress of Geography and History will meet at Seville in the spring. It is understood that various of the Hispanic American countries will be represented, especially Argentina and Colombia. It is hoped that the United States will send many delegates. This is an important occasion and should be taken advantage of by all American nations. It would have been very fitting had the opening date been set for La Fiesta de la Raza. It is suggested that institutions of the United States which wish to be represented, but can not send a delegate, consider the appointment of Miss I. A. Wright to act as such. She has the advantage of being on the field.

Peru has issued a call for the third Pan American Scientific Congress to be held at Lima, during the month of July, 1921.

A group of Stanford Alumni who have had business experience in Mexico, have, in coöperation with Stanford University and the National University of Mexico, established an annual inter-collegiate debate in Mexico for the "Medal of Stanford University". The debate, which is open to students of the schools of Jurisprudence of the Mexican Republic, will be held each year in the City of Mexico during the

month of July. It is to be an extempore discussion modeled on the
annual Joffre debate between Stanford and the University of California.
The subject debated each year must relate to Hispanic American countries and to the relation between these countries and the United States,
the purpose of the debates being "to encourage the study of problems
of Hispanic American countries and of the relation of those countries
to each other and to the United States, and to bring about a better
understanding between them". The leader in the enterprise is V. R.
Garfias, who graduated from Stanford in 1907, and who was afterward
a professor in the Geology and Mining Department. He has also
been actively connected with mining engineering projects in Mexico.
A group of other Stanford men, geologists, and mining engineers, who
have also carried on engineering enterprises in Mexico, have established
a fund, the interest of which will furnish the annual gold "Medal of
Stanford University", and provide for printing and distributing the
speech of the winner of the debate. The design for this medal is now
being completed. The specific topic for discussion each year will
be announced only two hours before the debate and the contestants
will be assigned their side of the debate at the same time. These contestants will be selected through a series of preliminary debates to be
held three days before the final contest. The speech of the winner
each year, and of such others as may be considered worthy of it, will
be published in English and in Spanish by Stanford University and
distributed to the Universities and centers of culture of Mexico, North
America, and other countries.—PERCY ALVIN MARTIN.

Six scholarships, each for $600, have been founded by the regents of
the University of Texas for Mexicans students who will study in the
above named University. Five students have already been appointed,
namely: Ruperto de León of Piedras Negras; Ramón Beteta, Roberto
Córdova, and Elan Escobar, of Mexico City; and Sabas Ricardez, of
Tabasco. All these young men have entered the freshman class.
Ruperto de León is a graduate of San Antonio High School. The
second and third above named have studied in the College of Laws
which forms part of the University of Mexico. The other two have
been students at the Normal School at Coyoacan. It is thought that
scholarships will also be established by the Mexican government so
that students from the United States may have the same advantage.
This exchange of students between the two countries should be developed in other institutions.

A recent number of *Hispania* contains an interesting article by Dr. Guillermo A. Sherwell, describing the trip of a party of students of Georgetown University under his direction to the West Indies and Venezuela. It seems to the present writer that the plan conceived and executed by Georgetown University might well be extended by coöperation of the universities of this country in the organization of yearly excursion trips for such students of Spanish as could afford the expense or whose expense might be borne by special funds, scholarships, etc. The development of such a yearly pilgrimage—a sort of *peregrinatio ad loca sancta*—could become a most valuable factor, not only in practical instruction, linguistic and commercial, but also in promoting by actual contact a real acquaintance with our southern neighbors that should produce positive results in improving and establishing American relations. The development of the plan initiated by the Foreign Service School of Georgetown University and successfully directed by Dr. Sherwell seems thoroughly worthy of consideration by the Association of University Presidents, the American Association of Teachers of Spanish, and all other organizations and agencies interested in this field.—C. K. JONES.

Don Antonio Gómez Izquierdo, representative of the Centro Mercantil of Buenos Aires, has published a patriotic article setting forth the fact that during the war, Spanish commerce was a very important source of supply for South America along certain lines and that in spite of the short time which has elapsed since the war, Spain has already lost a great many of those markets, especially the Argentine markets, because Spanish commerce has not known how to conserve the advantages thrown in its way. It is the opinion of Sr. Gómez Izquierdo that now is the opportune time for Spain to regain those markets and that in any effort made, it will be able to count upon the sincere coöperation of the Hispanic-American countries. He points out that the first step necessary for this economic reconquest should be the inauguration of fairs and expositions of Spanish products. These should be coincident in time with the projected visit of His Majesty Alfonso XIII to South America, and would thereby contribute to the regeneration of Spain's commercial; as well as political and social, influence in Hispanic America, which is indispensable for the aggrandizement of those countries and of Spain.—CHARLES H. CUNNINGHAM.

The press of Spain is enthusiastic over the news that five Spanish speaking Republics of Central America have formed a single State which is to be known internationally as the United States of Central America. The *A. B. C.* states that Spain had often feared for the independence and liberty of these small republics on account of their dangerous proximity to the United States. After the triumph of Mr. Harding, who, this paper states, is an advocate of the Monroe Doctrine in its most egoistic interpretation, the fears of Spain for these republics had more foundation than ever. These five Republics, conscious of this danger, form a blockade to stop the encroachment of the new conquering nation. The United States of Central America form a solid opposition to the economic, diplomatic, or territorial annexation projected by the Anglo-Saxons. "These Republics will be the guardians of the heritage given by Spain to the peoples of the New Continent, to whom she gave life and civilization. The language, traditions, and the moral virtues of Spanish America which have resisted all the influences of migration of these centuries, are made more than ever secure by the barrier formed by Guatemala, Honduras, San Salvador, Nicaragua, and Costa Rica against the invasion from the North. This Confederation safeguards each of these Republics and guarantees its future. United, they will be strong enough to defend themselves and in international relations where nothing counts but numbers, they will acquire a personality which they did not have in their isolation." The enthusiasm is somewhat dampened, says this paper, by the fact that all of the Central American republics have not joined this Confederation, for instance Venezuela, Colombia, and Panama. However, the confederation of these five republics proves to skeptics that the dream of a united Spanish America is not entirely a Utopian dream, for this is only the beginning. The rest may soon come into the Confederation, which shall extend from the Mexican Frontier to Tierra de Fuego, in which each Republic shall preserve its autonomy and yet be united to the others by common origin, language, and by the necessity of defending themselves against Anglo-Saxon imperialism, now more formidable than ever since the European War has left the nations of Europe too weak to oppose Monroism.

Dr. Herbert E. Bolton, of the University of California, gave a series of lectures in the Lowell Institute, Boston, during the last of last year and the first part of the present year. Dr. Bolton's subject was concerned with the Spanish colonization in America.

A new college of commerce and business training has been authorized by the Peruvian government in accordance with a recent law for complete reorganization of Peru's educational system. It will be located in Lima and is expected to begin work during the coming year. This new college will be organized along typically American lines, and will be affiliated with some of the leading institutions of higher business education in the United States. The aim of the Peruvian Ministry of Public Instruction is to have the work developed along practical lines which will aid in the growth of Peru's business and industries. Dr. W. E. Dunn, recently manager of the New York export office of Simmons Hardware Company will be director of the new school. He has had excellent training for the post, combining academic scholarship with practical business. After six years of university teaching experience he became assistant chief of the Latin American Division of the Bureau of Foreign and Domestic Commerce, in Washington, and was later in charge of the Latin American Section of the *New York Sun and Herald*. During the last Pan American Commercial and Financial Congress he acted as secretary of the Colombian group committee. Dr. Dunn has written several books and monographs on Hispanic American subjects as well as a number of articles on foreign-trade topics.

Dr. Charles W. Hackett, of the University of Texas, accompanied Governor Hobby's party, as the delegate of the University, to the inauguration of President Obregón. The expenses of the whole party from San Antonio to Mexico City and return were borne by the Mexican Government, and the delegates were treated sumptuously during the entire time. Opportunity was given the party to see something of the economic conditions of Mexico. The *Galveston Daily News* of December 18 states that the only outside invitation accepted by President Obregón during the inauguration period was that to the luncheon given by the Texans at Chapultepec Café. President Obregón sent a delegation under General Treviño to attend the inauguration ceremonies of Governor Neff, the Governor of Texas, which were held in January of this year. General Treviño made a brief address upon the occasion of the inauguration, which was reproduced in full in the *Austin American* of January 19.

One of the two essays to gain honorable mention from the Military History Prize Commission was that by Professor W. P. Webb, of the

University of Texas, entitled "The Texas Rangers in the Mexican War". The prize was awarded to Mr. Thomas Robson Hay, of Pittsburgh for his essay, entitled "Hood's Tennessee campaign". The other essay to gain honorable mention was "What happens in battle", by Captain J. N. Greeley, General Staff, U. S. A.—MILLEDGE L. BONHAM, JR.

Mr. Henry P. Dart, of the New Orleans law firm of Dart, Kernan and Dart, who is interested in the preservation of the old Louisiana French and Spanish documents, notes in a recent letter that the work of sorting out the material which has lain unmolested in boxes for some fifty or sixty years has been begun with the aid of two assistants. These documents consist almost entirely of the records of litigation during the French and Spanish régimes, being practically all law documents. They are very valuable from the legal, as well as from the historical, standpoint. Mr. Dart published a number of these documents, both in the original language and in English translation, together with some comment by himself in a recent number of the *Louisiana Historical Journal.*

Professor Percy Alvin Martin, of Leland Stanford Jr. University, will give the Albert Shaw lectures on Diplomacy at Johns Hopkins University during the first two weeks in May, 1921. The lectures will deal with the general topic of Hispanic America and the war.

Mr. Philip Ainsworth Means was installed as the Director del Museo Nacional de Arqueología of Peru on November 22, 1920. In his new office, Mr. Means contemplates plenty of work. Among the many tasks which he is finding to do, are the rearrangement of the valuable collection in such a manner that it will clearly show the chronological development of the ancient Peruvian cultures; the making of a good technical catalogue of the collection; and the publication of a number of monographs by competent Peruvian investigators and others on the various aspects of Peruvian archaeology. The Museum has the apparatus for printing its own publications.

Arthur S. Aiton and J. Lloyd Mecham, who have been doing research work in the Archivo de Indias at Seville, as holders of the fellowships founded by the Native Sons of the Golden West, are finishing their work and are making preparations to leave Seville. The first has been working on "New Spain, 1535–1550", and the second on "The Northern Frontier of New Spain in the later Sixteenth Century".—I. A. WRIGHT.

Dr. Rómulo S. Naón, former ambassador for Argentina to the United States, is now a member of the law firm of Naón, Iriondo & Beccar Varela. This firm and the firm of Curtis, Mallet-Prevost & Colt have lately become consolidated for the practice of law in Argentina, Uruguay, and Paraguay. Dr. Manuel M. de Iriondo was former Minister of Finance of Argentina, and Dr. Horacio Beccar Varela was former Director General of Justice in Argentina. The office of this unique law firm will be located in Buenos Aires. The firm will still maintain a New York office and a Brazilian office. The latter office will be in charge of Frederick A. Whitney, Dr. J. M. Macdowell da Costa, Dr. Paulino J. Soares de Souza Neto, and Dr. Cumplido de Sant'Anna.

Professor Henry Pittier, formerly with the Department of Agriculture of the United States, has been for the last three years in Venezuela, where he has made an ecological map of great value. Accompanying the map is an excellent pamphlet descriptive of various economic factors of Venezuela. Both map and pamphlet are in Spanish, and are published by the Venezuelan government.

James A. Robertson will conduct a seminar on the history of the Philippine Islands at the University of North Carolina, during the week of March 6–12. He will also give several public addresses and talks.

It may not be amiss to mention that Miss Irene A. Wright, well known for her writings on Cuban history, is in Seville making investigations in the Archivo General de Indias. Scholars who require research and copying in Spanish archives, but who can not do the actual work themselves because of other more pressing duties, will probably be able to make arrangements with Miss Wright to lend her good offices to them. Miss Wright has recently been engaged by the Netherlands government to make researches among the documents in Seville relative to Dutch activity in Hispanic America beginning with the late sixteenth century.

Dr. Estanislao S. Zeballos, former Argentine minister to the United States, three times minister of foreign affairs in Argentina, professor of private international law at the University of Buenos Aires, and editor of the greatest South American paper, *La Prensa*, has recently published the third and fourth volumes of his important work, *La Nationalité*, the publication of which had been interrupted by the war. With these two volumes this excellent work is brought to a close. In this work, originally written in French, Dr. Zeballos, who is not only one of the most remarkable statesmen but also one of the most successful lawyers of South America, deals exhaustively with the problems of nationality in the New World. Besides this he is the author of over one hundred volumes and pamphlets, which treat especially of law, history, sociology, and diplomacy—a remarkable and excellent output. In addition to this, his wellknown *Revista de Derecho, Historia y Letras*, which has been published for thirty-two years with the greatest of punctuality, contains essays of importance written by him, political notes on domestic and foreign policy, excellent bibliographical material, and reviews of all books received by the *Revista.*—MANOEL DE OLIVEIRA LIMA.

BIBLIOGRAPHICAL SECTION

HISPANIC AMERICAN BIBLIOGRAPHIES

(*Continuation*)

CENTRAL AMERICA

See also:
Costa Rica,
Guatemala,
Honduras,
Nicaragua,
Panama,
Salvador.

465. Bancroft, Hubert Howe. History of Central America. San Francisco, A. L. Bancroft & company, 1882–87.

3 v. illus. (maps) fold. map. 24 cm.
"Authorities quoted": v. 1, p. xxv–lxxii.
The bibliographic notes are of great value.

466. Bandelier, Adolph Francis Alphonse. Notes on the bibliography of Yucatan and Central America; comprising Yucatan, Chiapas, Guatemala (the ruins of Palenque, Ocosingo, and Copan), and Oaxaca (ruins of Mitla). A list of some of the writers on this subject from the sixteenth century to the present time. Worcester [Mass.] Press of C. Hamilton, 1881.

39 p. 24½ cm.
"From Proceedings of the American antiquarian society, October 21, 1880."

467. Barrios, Roberto. La literatura de Centro-América; su pasado y su presente.

(*In* Centro-América. Guatemala, 1915. 24½ cm. p. 42–44.)

468. Bibliografía y cartografía centro-americanas.

(*In* Centro-América, Guatemala, 1913. 24½ cm. Vol. 5, p. 182–196.)

469. Brigham, William Tufts. Guatemala: the land of the quetzal. New York, C. Scribner's sons, 1887.

xv, 453 p. front., illus., pl., port., maps. 22½ cm.
A list of works relating to Central America: p. 430–442.

469a. Cundall, Frank. Bibliography of the West Indies (excluding Jamaica). Kingston, The Institute of Jamaica, 1909.

3 p. l., 179 p. 21½ cm.
Includes sections on Central America, etc.

126

470. International bureau of the American republics. A list of books, magazine articles, and maps relating to Central America, including the republics of Costa Rica, Guatemala, Honduras, Nicaragua, and Salvador. 1800–1900. Prepared by P. Lee Phillips. Comp. for the Bureau of the American republics. Washington, Govt. print. off., 1902.

109 p. 23½ cm.

471. Joyce, Thomas Athol. Central American and West Indian archæology. London, P. L. Warner, 1916

xvi, 270 p., 1 l. incl. front , illus. plates, fold. map. 22½ cm.
Bibliographical appendix: p. 258–263.

472. Munro, Dana Gardner. The five republics of Central America, their political and economic development and their relations with the United States. Ed. by David Kinley ... New York, Oxford University press, 1918.

xvi p., 1 l., 332 p. front. (map). 25 cm. (Carnegie endowment for international peace.)
Bibliography: p. 321–326.

473. Slade, William Franklin. The federation of Central America. Worcester, Mass. [1917].

1 p. l., p. 79–150, 204–275. 23 cm.
"Reprinted from the Journal of race development, vol. 8."
"Selected bibliography": p. 270–275.

474. Spain, Archivo general de Indias. Relación descriptiva de los mapas, planos, etc. de la Audiencia y Capitanía general de Guatemala (Guatemala, San Salvador, Honduras, Nicaragua y Costa Rica) existentes en el Archivo general de Indias. Madrid, Tip. de la Revista de archivos, 1903.

214 p.
By Pedro Torres Lanzas.
From Revista de archivos, bibliotecas y museos, 3. época, 2 (1898), 8 (1903), 14 (1906).

475. Squier, Ephraim George. Monograph of authors who have written on the languages of Central America, and collected vocabularies or composed works in the native dialects of that country. New York, C. B. Richardson & co., 1861.

xv, [17]–70 p. 22½ x 18½ cm.

476. —— —— London Tribune & Co., 1861.

xv, [17]–70 p. 22½ x 18½ cm.

477. Uriarte, Ramón. Galería poética centro-americana. Colección de poesías de los mejores poetas de la América del Centro; precedidas de ligeros apuntes biográficos y breves juicios críticos ... Guatemala, 1883.

3 v. 8°.
+. 1.

478. —— —— [2. ed.] Guatemala, Tip. "La Unión", 1888.

2 v. 25 cm.

479. Abel Rosales, Justo. Bibliografía del literato D. Miguel Luis Amunátegui, ministro de estado, diputado al Congreso, secretario jeneral de la Universidad, profesor de literatura e historia del Instituto nacional, miembro correspondiente de la Real academia española i del Instituto histórico i jeográfico del Brasil, etc. Santiago de Chile, Impr. de la Libertad electoral, 1888.

30 p. 18½ cm.

480. Ahumada Maturana, Rómulo. Revista de revistas. (In Revista de artes y letras. Santiago de Chile, 1886, t. v–vi.)

A bibliographical study of 26 literary and scientific reviews published in Chile before 1882.

481. Amunátegui, Miguel Luis. Ensayos biográficos. Santiago de Chile, Imprenta nacional, 1893–96.

4 v. 26½ cm.

482. Amunátegui Solar, Domingo. Bosquejo histórico de la literatura Chilena. Período colonial. Santiago de Chile, Impr. universitaria, 1918. 106 p.

Cited in Revista de filología española t. 6, 1919, cuaderno 4.

482a. ———— Bosquejo histórico de la literatura Chilena. Santiago de Chile, Imprenta universitaria, 1920. 669, [1] p.

An important study of the literature since the revolution. Edition limited to 100 copies.

483. ———— La sociedad Chilena del siglo xviii, mayorazgos i títulos de Castilla; memoria histórica presentada a la Universidad de Chile. Santiago de Chile, Impr. Barcelona, 1901–04.

3 v. 26 cm.

"Se compone de una serie de monografías de familias Chilenas, de todas aquellas que en nuestra sociedad del siglo XVIII podían ostentar un título de Castilla o enorgullecerse con la posesión de un mayorazgo fundado en Chile."

484. Anales de la Universidad de Chile. Indice alfabético y analítico de los trabajos publicados, 1843–1887. Por Eduardo Valenzuela y Gusmán. Santiago, Imprenta nacional, 1890.

164 p.
René Moreno. Bib. bol. 2. sup., no. 6069.

485. ———— Índice general de los Anales de la Universidad de Chile, dispuesto por rigoroso orden alfabético de materias y apellidos, y comprensivo de trece años, esto es, desde 1843 inclusive hasta 1855 también inclusive. compuesto ... por Don Ramón Briseño ... Santiago, 1856.

111, xx p.

486. ———— Índice de los trabajos contenidos desde 1888 hasta 1899. Santiago, Imprenta Cervantes, 1900.

50. p.
René Moreno. Bib. bol., 2. sup., no. 6090.

487. Anrique Reyes, Nicolás. Bibliografía de las principales revistas i periódicas de Chile.

(In Anales de la Universidad de Chile. Santiago de Chile, 1904. 26 cm. t. 115, p. 121–162.)

488. ——— Bibliografía marítima chilena (1840–1894). Santiago de Chile, Impr. Cervantes, 1894.

205 p., 1 l. 19½ cm.

489. ——— Ensayo de una bibliografía dramática chilena. Santiago de Chile, Imprenta Cervantes, 1899.

2 p. l., [3]–184 p. 26½ cm.
Publicado en los "Anales de la Universidad."
Bibliografía: I. Teatro estranjero relativo a Chile (1612–1886). II. Teatro nacional (1602–1899).

490. ——— Ensayo de una bibliografía histórica i jeográfica de Chile; obra premiada con medalla de oro en el certamen de la Universidad para presentarla al Congreso internacional deciencias históricas i jeográficas de Roma; por Nicolás Anrique R. i L. Ignacio Silva A. Santiago de Chile, Imprenta Barcelona, 1902.

xix, 679 p. 23 cm.
2,561 titles, classified. Author index.

491. Arellano y Yecorat, Juan. Los periodistas de la democracia ante la historia [1891–1894]. Santiago, Impr. B. Vicuña Mackenna, 1894.

xxiii, [24]–277 p., 1 l. ports. 19 cm.
73 biographies, dates given in some cases.

492. ——— Semblanzas parlamentarias (1897–1900). Santiago, Impr. de "El Imparcial" [1900?].

313 p., 1 l. illus. (ports.) 19½ cm.

493. Barrett, Robert South. Chilean market for paper, paper products, and printing machinery. Washington, Gov't. print. off., 1917.

72 p. front., pl. 25 cm. (Dept. of Commerce, Bureau of foreign and domestic commerce. Special agents series, no. 153.)
Contains a useful list of Chilean newspapers and magazines, with subscription price and other data.

494. Barros Arana, Diego. El doctor Don Rodolfo Amando Philippi, su vida i sus obras; obra escrita por encargo del Consejo de instruccion pública. Seguida de una bibliografía de las obras del doctor Philippi por Don Carlos Reiche. Santiago de Chile, Impr. Cervantes, 1904.

vii, 248 p. port., facsim. 26½ cm.

495. Briseño, Ramón. Catálogo por el orden alfabético de sus títulos de las publicaciones que por la prensa hizo Don Benjamín Vicuña Mackenna. Santiago de Chile, Imprenta nacional, 1886.

29 p.
Also in Anales de la Universidad de Chile. 2. seccion, v. 70 (1886).

496. ——— Catalogo razonado de la biblioteca chileno-americana de Don Ramón Briseño. Santiago de Chile, Impr. de "La Estrella de Chile", 1874.

105, [1] p. 28 x 20½ cm.

497. ——— Catálogo de la biblioteca chileno-americana de Don Ramón Briseño. Santiago de Chile, Impr. Gutenberg, 1889.

XVI, [2], 376 p. port.
Comp. by Luis Montt.

498. ——— Estadística bibliográfica de la literatura chilena. Santiago de Chile, Imprenta chilena, 1862–79.

2 v. 32 cm.

CONTENTS.—t. 1. 1812–1859. Impresos chilenos. Obras sobre Chile. Escritores chilenos.— t. 2. 1860–1876. Prólogo. Prensa chilena por órden alfabético. Prensa chilena por órden cronolójico. Prensa periodística chilena. Bibliografía chilena en el país, desde 1812 hasta 1859 inclusive. Bibliografía chilena en el extranjero, desde 1860 hasta 1876 inclusive. Curiosidades bibliográfico-chilenas.

499. Cabezón, Carlos. Neógrafos kontemporáneos; tentatiba bibliográfika (Kongreso zientífiko chileno de 1894). Santiago de Chile, Impr. Zerbántes, 1896.

21 p. 27 cm.

500. Catálogo de los libros y folletos impresos en Chile desde que se introdujo la imprenta.

(In Revista de ciencias y letras. Santiago de Chile, 1858. t. 1. p. 739–768.)

501. Chacón del Campo, Julio. Reseña histórica de la prensa de Parral y relacion de sus fiestas cincuentenarias. Parral, Chile, Imp. la Democracia, 1915.

84 p. illus. (port.) 18½ cm.
At head of title: Julio i Nazario Chacón del C.
"Periódicos publicados en Parral": p. [47]–52.

502. Chamberlain, Alexander Francis. On the Puelchean and Tsonekan (Tehuelchean), the Atacameñan (Atacaman) and Chouoan, and the Charruan linguist c stocks of South America (In American anthropologist, Lancaster, Pa., 1911, 24½ cm. p. 458–471).

Contains bibliographies.

503. ——— The present state of our knowledge concerning the three linguistic stocks of the region of Tierra del Fuego, South America. (In American anthropologist. Lancaster, Pa., 1911. 24½ cm. p. 89–98.)

"This important paper, largely based on Mitre, contains a critical discussion of most of the sources for the study of the Fuegian languages".—Cooper. Bibl. of the tribes of Tierra del Fuego.

504. Chiappa, Victor M. Bibliografía de Don Diego Barros Arana (ensayo). Temuco, Imprenta alemana, 1907.

3 p. l., [3]–112 p. 26½ cm.

505. ——— Biblioteca Medina. Noticias acerca de la vida y obras de Don José Toribio Medina. Santiago de Chile, Impr. Barcelona, 1907.

lxix p., 2 l., 276 p., 1 l. front. (port.) 24 cm.

506. ——— Noticias bibliográficas sobre la Colección de historiadores de Chile y documentos relativos a la historia nacional. Santiago de Chile, Impr. de E. Blanchard-Chessi, 1905.

XIII, 44 p.

507. Chile. Dirección de contabilidad. Résumen de la hacienda pública de Chile. Summary of the finances of Chile. Desde la independencia hasta 1900. Editado en castellano e ingles por la Direccion jeneral de contabilidad, 1901. From the independence to 1900; pub. in Spanish and English by the Accountant general's department. [Santiago] 1901.

[757] p. incl. tables. 23 col. pl. facsims. 26½ cm. x 38 cm.

Prepared for the Pan-American exposition, 1901.

List of "Political leaders who have governed in Chile from 1536 to 1901."—Introd., p. [16]-20.

"A Chilian bibliography of the national finances": [chap.] VIII (64 p. at end).

508. Chile. Ministerio de colonización. Recopilacion de leyes i decretos supremos sobre colonizacion. 1810-1896. 2. ed. Santiago de Chile, Imprenta nacional, 1896.

lxx, 1464 p. 24½ cm.

At head of title: Julio Zenteno Barros.

"Bibliografía de las obras i publicaciones sobre colonización e inmigración nacional": p. [1443]-1464.

509. Chile. Ministerio de marina. Catálogo de los planos i cartas hidrográficas i topográficas que existen en el Ministerio de marina de la república de Chile. Santiago, Imprenta nacional, 1863.

11 p. 30 cm.

510. Chile. Ministerio de relaciones exteriores. Servicio consular de Chile y consules extranjeros constituidos en Chile hasta el 1.° de abril de 1915. Santiago de Chile, Impr. "Bellavista" [1915].

45 p.. 26½ cm.

511. Cooper, John Montgomery. Analytical and critical bibliography of the tribes of Tierra del Fuego and adjacent territory. Washington, Govt. print. off., 1917.

ix, 233 p. maps. 23½ cm.

Smithsonian institution. Bureau of American ethnology, Bulletin 63.

512. Cruchaga, Alberto. Los primeros años del Ministerio de relaciones exteriores. Santiago de Chile, Imprenta universitaria, 1919.

3 p. l., [11]-142 p., 2 l. pl., ports. 18½ cm.

513. Cuadra Gormaz, Guillermo de la. Los de Larraín en Chile; trabajo publicado en la Revista chilena de historia y geografía. Santiago de Chile, Imprenta universitaria, 1917.

19 p. 26 cm.

514. ——— Origen de doscientas familias coloniales de Santiago. Santiago de Chile, Imprenta universitaria, 1914.

196 p. 22½ cm.

"Publicado en el número 15 de la Revista chilena de historia y geografía."

515. Dabbene, Roberto. Los indígenas de la Tierra del Fuego. (In Boletín del Instituto geográfico argentino. Buenos Aires, 1911. 26½ cm. t. 25, p. 163-226, 247-300, illus.)

Bibliografía: p. 288-300.

516. Delfín, Federico T. Catálogo de los peces de Chile. (In Revista chilena de historia natural. Valparaíso, 1899-1900. 23 cm. t. 3-4.)

Contains a bibliography.

517. Desmadryl, Narciso. Galería nacional, o Colección de biografías y retratos de hombres célebres de Chile, escrita por los principales literatos del país, dirigida y publicada por Narciso Desmadryl. Santiago, Imprenta chilena, 1854–61.

2 v.

518. Echeverría y Reyes, Aníbal. Bibliografía de los codigos chilenos. Santiago de Chile, Imprenta Cervantes, 1890.

31 p.

519. ———— Disquisiciones: La lengua araucana. El puente de cal y canto. La batalla de Rancagua. Primeros almanaques publicados en Chile. El cólera. Santiago de Chile, Imprenta nacional, 1889.

100. [1] p.
The first, fourth and fifth papers are bibliographical studies.
Laval no. 103.

520. ———— Ensayo bibliográfico sobre la revolucion de 1891. Santiago de Chile, G. E. Miranda, 1894.

28 p. 23 cm.

521. ———— Ensayo de una biblioteca chilena de legislación y jurisprudencia. Santiago de Chile, Imprenta nacional, 1891.

viii, 155. [2] p.

522. ———— Voces usadas en Chile. Santiago [de Chile] Imprenta elzeviriana, 1900.

xxii, 246 p. 19½ cm.
"Bibliografía: p. [1]-21.

523. Enrich, Francisco. Historia de la Compañía de Jesús en Chile. Barcelona, Rosal, 1891.

2 v.

524. Ferrada, U. J. Eclesiásticos que se distinguieron en el descubrimiento y Conquista de Chile. (In Revista católica de Santiago de Chile, 1919, t. 37, p. 16–27, 95–102.)

Cited in Revista de filología española, t. 7 (1920) cuaderno 1., p. 83.

525. Ferrer, Pedro Lautaro. Historia general de la medicina en Chile (documentos inéditos, biografías y bibliografía) desde el descubrimiento y conquista de Chile, en 1535, hasta nuestros dias. Talca, Imp. Talca, de J. Martin Garrido C., 1904.

v. 1. 24 cm.
t. I. Desde 1535, hasta la inauguración de la Universidad de Chile en 1843.

526. Figueroa, Pedro Pablo. Álbum militar de Chile, 1810–1879: obra histórica ilustrada con documentos i retratos de militares i marinos notables de la República. Santiago de Chile, Impr. Barcelona, 1898–1906.

4 v. ports. 28 cm.
No more published.

527. ———— Diccionario biográfico de Chile. 4. ed. ilus. con retratos. Santiago de Chile, Impr. y encuadernacion Barcelona, 1897–1902.

3 v. ports. 26 cm.
An important work on Chilean biography and bibliography.

528. ——— Diccionario biográfico de estranjeros en Chile. Santiago de Chile, Imprenta moderna, 1900.

258 p., 2 l. front. (port.) 27 cm.

529. ——— La librería en Chile; estudio histórico y bibliográfico del canje de obras nacionales establecido y propagado en Europa y América, por el editor y librero Don Roberto Miranda 1884–1894. 2. ed. Paris, Garnier hermanos, 1896.

186 p., 1 l. fold. map. 18½ cm.

530. ——— Pensadores americanos. Santiago de Chile, Impr. de "El Correo," 1890.

137 p., 2 l. 24 cm.
CONTENTS.—Bartolomé Mitre—Alberto Palomeque.—Lázaro María Pérez.—Ignacio Ramírez.
—Juan Carlos Gómez—Familias de escritores americanos.—José Antonio Soffia—Novelistas contemporáneos de América.—Francisco Sosa.—Dardo Rocha.—Héctor F. Varela.—Francisco Octaviano.—Poetas de Venezuela.—Periodistas del Brasil.—Ramón J. Cárcano.—Sarmiento artista.

531. Fuensalida, Enrique Amador. Galería contemporánea de hombres notables de Chile (1850–1901), Tomo 1. Valparaíso, Universo, 1901.

358 p. ports. 27 cm.
No more published.

532. Fuensalida Grandón, Alejandro. Lastarria i su tiempo (1817–1888) su vida, obras e influencia en el desarrollo político e intelectual del Chile. Santiago de Chile, Impr. Barcelona, 1911.

2 v. ports., fold. facsim. 26 cm.
1st edition pub. in 1893.
"Bibliografía i notas bibliográficas": v. 2, p. 273–315.

533. Gasulla, Policarpo. Los primeros Mercedarios en Chile, 1535–1600. [Santiago de Chile] [Impr. la Ilustración, 1918?]

xvi, 491 p., 1 l. fold. map. 27 cm.
At head of title: Séptimo centenario, 1218–1918.

534. Huneeus y Gana, Jorge. Cuadro histórico de la producción intelectual de Chile. [Santiago de Chile, 1910?]

xvi, 890 p. 22 cm. (Biblioteca de escritores de Chile. 1.)

535. Ignacio de Pamplona. Historia de las misiones de los PP. Capuchinos en Chile y Argentina (1849–1911). Santiago de Chile, Imprenta "Chile", 1911.

3 p. l., [ix]–xv, 567 p. illus. (incl. ports.) 25½ cm.

536. Introducción de la imprenta en Chile. (In Anuario estadístico de la República de Chile. Santiago de Chile, 1861. 32½ cm., entrega 2, p. 143–156.)

Includes a Catálogo de obras publicadas en Chile, 1812–1858.
Short titles arranged by years, without imprints or collations.

537. Latcham, Ricardo E. Bibliografía chilena de las ciencias antropológicas, 1–2. serie. (In Revista de bibliografía chilena y extranjera. Santiago de Chile, 1915. 23 cm. año III, p. 148–185; 229–261.)

Also published separately.

538. Laval, Ramón A. Bibliografía de bibliografías chilenas. Santiago de Chile, Imprenta universitaria, 1915.

71 p. 23 cm.
From Revista de bibliografía chilena y extranjera, año III, 1915.

539. ———— Un incunable chileno, Modo de ganar el jubileo santo, año de 1776; noticia bibliográfica. [Santiago de Chile] Imprenta universitaria, 1910.

16 p., facsim.: 1 p. l., [7] p. 19½ cm.
Includes facsimile reproduction of the oldest Chilean printed book thus far known.

540. Lillo, Samuel A. Literatura chilena. Santiago de Chile, Casa editorial "Minerva", 1918.

171 p.
Cited in Revista de filología española, t. 6, 1919, cuaderno 2.

541. Lira, Pedro. Diccionario biográfico de pintores. Santiago de Chile, Impr., encuadernación y litogr. Esmeralda, 1902.

viii, 551, [1] p. 23½ cm.

542. Lista alfabética de los abogados recibidos en Chile desde el 13 de diciembre de 1788 hasta el 22 de noviembre de 1899. Santiago de Chile, Imprenta nacional, 1899.

158 p. 24½ cm.

543. Maturana, Víctor. Historia de los Agustinos in Chile. Santiago de Chile, Imprenta Valparaíso, de F. T. Lathrop, 1904.

2 v.
Laval, no. 165.

544. Medina, José Toribio. Bibliografía de la Araucana. (In Ercilla y Zúñiga, Alonso de. La Araucana ... Ed. del centenario ... la publica J. T. Medina, Santiago de Chile, 1910–18. 39 cm. Ilustraciones, p. 1-60).

48 editions described.

545. ———— Bibliografía de la imprenta en Santiago de Chile desde sus orígenes hasta febrero de 1817. Santiago de Chile, Impreso en casa del autor, 1891.

xli, 179, [2] p. port., facsims. 27½ cm.

546. ———— Bibliografía de santo Toribio Mogrovejo, arzobispo de Lima (capítulo incompleto de un libro inédito). [Lima, Impr. S. Pedro, 1907.]

lxxxii p. 19 cm.
"Publicado en: Estudios históricos sobre santo Toribio, por Monseñor Manuel Tovar, arzobispo de Lima. Tomo III.—Impreso en 1907".—Laval, no. 171.

547. ———— Biblioteca hispano-chilena (1523–1817). Santiago de Chile, Impreso y grabado en casa del autor, 1897–99.

3 v. facsim. 29 cm.
"No tratamos de ningún libro impreso en este país, pues de ellos nos hemos ocupado ya en nuestra Bibliografía de la imprenta en Santiago [1891]; ni de manuscritos, ni de obras publicadas en idiomas extranjeros ... ni de las reales cédulas impresas."
876 titles, arranged chronologically; transcribed line for line, with references to authorities and to libraries where copies are to be found. Copious quotations and critical and bibliographical notes.

548. ———— Diccionario biográfico colonial de Chile. Santiago de Chile, Impr. elzeviriana, 1906.

viii, [9]-1004 p. illus. (incl. ports.) 31 cm.

549. ———— Prieto del Río, Luis Francisco. Muestras de errores y defectos del "Diccionario biográfico colonial de Chile por José Toribio Medina." Santiago [de Chile] Impr. y encuadernacion Chile, 1907.

124 p. 18½ cm.

550. ———— Ensayo acerca de una mapoteca chilena ó sea de una colección de los títulos de los mapas, planos y vistas relativos a Chile arreglados cronológicamente, con una introducción histórica acerca de la geografía y cartografía del pais. Santiago de Chile, Impr. Ercilla, 1889.

cxxviii, 254 p., 1 l. 30 cm.

551. ———— Ensayo de una bibliografía de las obras de Don José Miguel Carrera. [La Plata] Talleres del Museo de La Plata, 1892.

ix, 36 p. port. 28 cm.
Del tomo IV de la Revista del Museo de La Plata, pág. 53 y siguientes.

552. ———— História de la literatura colonial de Chile. Santiago de Chile, Impr. de la Librería del Mercurio, 1878.

3 v. 25 cm.

553. ———— Índice de los documentos existentes en el archivo del Ministerio de lo interior. Santiago de Chile, Impr. de la República, de J. Nuñez, 1884.

viii, 809 p.
Chiappa, no. 16.

554. Mission scientifique du cap Horn: t. vii. Anthropologie, ethnographie, par P. Hyades et J. Deniker. Paris, Gauthier-Villars, 1891.

Bibliography: p. 393-402.

555. Molina A., Evaristo. Ensayo bibliográfico chileno sobre la hacienda pública. Santiago de Chile, Imprenta nacional, 1901.

64 p.
A list of the works on public finance found in Briseño's Estadística bibliografica, Toro y Melo's Catálogo and the Anuario de la prensa chilena. Cf. Laval.

556. Montessus de Ballore. Bibliografía general de temblores y terremotos ... Santiago de Chile, Imprenta universitaria, 1915-17.

pts. 1-7. 27 cm.
5. pte. América, tierras antárticas y océanos.

557. Montt, Luis. Bibliografía chilena, precedida de un bosquejo histórico sobre los primeros años de la prensa en el pais. Tomo II. 1812-1817. Santiago, Imprenta Barcelona, 1904.

xx, 499 p., 2 l. 5 facsim. (incl. front.) 26 cm.
"Los pliegos impresos (264 p.) del tomo 1, que debían rehacerse según las intenciones del Señor Montt fueron vendidos por la imprenta como papel inútil, y los del 3. (160 p.) se quemaron en el incendio que destruyó la Imp. universitaria en 1909". Laval, no. 230.

558. Muñoz Olave, Reinaldo. Las monjas trinitarias de Concepción, 1570-1822; relato historico, Santiago de Chile, Impr. de San José, 1918.

ix, [11]-272 p. 19 cm.

550. ———— Rasgos biográficos de eclesiásticos de Concepción, 1552-1818. Santiago de Chile, Impr. "San José", 1916.

2 p. l., [3]-548 p., 1 l. 20 cm.

560. Nieto del Río, Félix. La alta prensa diaria en Chile. (*In* Cuba contemporánea, Habana, 1918. 26 cm. v. xvi, p. [303]-309.)

561. Núñez Olaechea, Samuel. Los ferrocarriles del estado. 1. Reseña histórica. 2. Esplotación. 3. Diccionario biográfico. Santiago de Chile, Impr. i. encuadernación, Chile, 1910.

328 p., 1 l. front. (port.) 26 cm.

562. Phillips, Philip Lee. A list of books, magazine articles, and maps relating to Chile. Comp. for the International bureau of the American republics. Washington, Govt. print. off., 1903.

110 p. 23 cm.

563. Ponce, Manuel Antonio. Bibliografía pedagójica chilena (anotaciones). Santiago de Chile, Imprenta elzeviriana, 1902.

xii, 307, [1] p. 27 cm.

665 titles, classified "en seis secciones cronolójicas ... pedagojía jeneral, sistemática (organización escolar jeneral e interna), metodolojía, lejislación, historia de la enseñansa i periódicos profesionales."

564. ———— Reseña histórica de la enseñanza de lectura en Chile (siglos xvi-xix). Santiago de Chile, Imprenta Barcelona, 1905.

135 p. pl.

A complete inventory of readers and spellers without indication of size and number of pages. Cf. Laval, no. 257.

565. Porter, Carlos E. Bibliografía chilena de antropología y etnología. Trabajo presentado al 4° Congreso científico (1° Pan-Americano). Con un prólogo de Ricardo E. Latcham. Ed. del autor. Buenos Aires, Impr. "Juan A. Alsina", 1910. 44 p.

Anales del Museo nacional de Buenos Aires, t. xx, ser. 3, t. xiii.

Continued by Latcham in Revista de bibliografía chilena y extranjera, t. II, p. 49-52. Cf. Laval (nos. 258-274) for a list of Porter's bibliographical contributions.

566. ———— Bibliografía chilena de ciencias antropológicas. Santiago, Imprenta "Santiago", 1912.

62 p.

567. ———— Catálogo razonado de los trabajos histórico-naturales hechos desde enero de 1894 hasta junio de 1905. Valparaiso, Impr. Gillet, 1905.

32 p. illus., port. 23½ cm.

568. ———— Ensayo de una bibliografía chilena de historia natural. Valparaíso, Impr. Gillet, 1900.

68 p.

From Revista Chilena de historia natural.

569. ———— Literatura antropológica y etnológica de Chile. Santiago, 1906.

36 p.

570. Real y Prado, Julio. Boletín bibliográfico de la Librería de Julio Real y Prado, Valparaíso, 1875–79.

23 nos.

"Sin embargo de ser catálogo de librería, contiene datos interesantes sobre publicaciones chilenas, que difícilmente se hallarán en otra parte". Laval, no. 280.

571. Reiche, Karl Friedrich. Grundzüge der pflanzenverbreitung in Chile. Leipzig, W. Engelmann, 1907.

xiv, 374 p. plates, maps. 26 cm. (Die vegetation der erde, hrsg. von A. Engler und O. Drude, VIII.)

"Literarische hilfsquellen": p. 1–47.

Lists 627 publications.

572. Revista de bibliografía chilena y extranjera. Publicada mensualmente por la Sección de informaciones de la Biblioteca nacional. año 1– enero 1913– Santiago de Chile, Imprenta universitaria, 1913–.

v. l—. 22 cm.

Valuable not only for current bibliography but for the special bibliographies it contains.

573. Santiago de Chile. R. Audiencia. Catálogo del Archivo de la Real audiencia de Santiago. Santiago de Chile, Impr. Barcelona, 1898–11.

v. 1–3. 25½ cm.

574. Santiago de Chile. Biblioteca nacional. Anuario de la prensa chilena, pub. por la Biblioteca nacional. 1886–1913. Santiago de Chile, 1887–1914.

28 v. 24–28 cm.

Catalog of books deposited in the library under law of 1872; and, from 1891–1913 books by Chilean authors, or relating to Chile, published in other countries.

From 1892–1913 each volume, except 1895, contained an appendix of "publicaciones omitidas" from previous volumes. Musical compositions are entered in vols. for 1896–1900.

575. ———— Bibliografía general de Chile. Por Emilio Vaïsse, jefe de sección en la Biblioteca nacional de Chile. t. 1. Santiago de Chile, Imprenta universitaria, 1915.

v. 1. 23 cm.

Reprinted from Revista de bibliografía chilena y extranjera.

CONTENTS.—1. pte. Diccionario de autores y obras (biobibliografía y bibliografía). t. 1. Bibliografía de bibliografías chilenas, por R. A. Laval. Diccionario: A-Barros Arana.

576. ———— Bibliografía musical. Composiciones impresas en Chile y composiciones de autores chilenos publicadas en el extranjero. 2. parte. 1886–1896. Santiago de Chile, Estab. poligráfico Roma, 1848.

89 p.

Prepared by Ramón A. Laval, and reprinted from Anuario de la prensa chilena, 1896.

The first part has not been published.

577. ———— Boletín. no. 1–92; oct. 31, 1901– julio a dic. de 1913. Santiago de Chile, 1901–[13?].

92 nos. plates, ports., fold. facsims., diagrs. 25 cm.

Monthly, Oct. 1901–Dec. 1902; irregular, 1903–13.

Publication suspended during 1907.

578. ———— Catálogo alfabético i por materias de las obras que contiene la Biblioteca nacional Egaña de Santiago de Chile. Santiago, Impr. de la Sociedad Egaña, 1860.

149 p. tab. 32 cm.

The collection of Mariano Egaña, containing some 9000 volumes, was acquired by the Biblioteca nacional in 1846.

579. ———— Catálogo de la exposición retrospectiva de la prensa chilena, abierta el 13 de febrero de 1912 en conmemoración del centenario de la "Aurora de Chile". 2. ed., corr. y aum. [Santiago de Chile] Imprenta universitaria, 1912.

75 p. 25½ cm.

CONTENTS.—Incunables chilenos, o sea primeros trabajos tipográficos hechos en el país.—La "Aurora de Chile".—Periódicos publicados en Santiago hasta el año 1826.—Primeros periódicos fundados en cada una de las demás ciudades, pueblos y comunas.—Revistas y anuarios principales (1821-1912).—Publicaciones periódicas en idioma extranjero —Periódicos de caricatura.—Diarios y periódicos con más de 25 años de duración—Epocas de las guerras de 1879 y 1891.—Periódicos chilenos impresos en el extranjero.—Bibliografía concerniente a la introducción de la imprenta en Chile, etc.

Prepared by Enrique Blanchard-Chessi.

580. ———— Catálogo de la sección americana. América en general. Santiago de Chile, Imprenta universitaria, 1902.

1 p. l., 153, [2] p. 25 cm.

581. ———— Catalogo de los manuscritos relativos a los antiguos Jesuítas de Chile que se custodian en la Biblioteca nacional. Santiago de Chile, Imprenta Ercilla, 1891.

4 p. l., 543 p. 24 cm.

Compiled by José Manuel Frontaura y Arana. 2753 items.

582. ———— Catalogo por órden alfabético de los libros que contiene la Biblioteca nacional de Santiago de Chile. Santiago, Impr. de la Sociedad, 1854.

216 p. 26 cm.

583. Santiago de Chile. Instituto pedagógico. Catálogo de la biblioteca del Instituto pedagógico. (*In* Memoria del Ministerio de justicia e instrucción pública. 1896. p. 72-196.)

584. Santiago de Chile. Universidad católica. Biblioteca de la Universidad católica de Santiago. Santiago de Chile, Impr. de E. Perez L., 1902.

227 p., 1 l. 25½ cm.

585. ———— Bodas de plata de la Universidad católica de Santiago y proclamación de los premios a sus alumnos, 1888-1913. Santiago de Chile, Imprenta Chile, 1913.

3 p. l., [3]-102 p. ports., diagr. 26 cm.

"Personal directivo y docente desde su fundación en 1888 hasta 1913": p. 47-55.

"Nómina de los alumnos que han recibido el título profesional": p. 57-69.

586. Santiváñez, José María. Rasgos biograficos de Adolfo Ballivián. Santiago [de Chile] Impr. de "La República" de J. Núñez, 1878.

1 p. l., iii, [3]-145, 19 p. 24½ cm.

"Escritos de don Adolfo Ballivián": Apéndice, p. [3]-19.

587. Schuller, Rodolfo R. El vocabulario araucano de 1642-1643, con notas críticas i algunas adiciones a las bibliografías de la lengua mapuche. Santiago de Chile, Impr. Cervantes, 1907.

2 p. l., [3]-286 p. pl., fold. map, facsims. 27 cm.

508. Silva Arriagada, Luis Ignacio. La novela en Chile. Santiago de Chile, Impr. y encuadernación "Barcelona", 1910.

4 p. l., [3]-523 p., 1 l. illus. (ports.) 19 cm. (Ensayos bibliográficos sobre la literatura chilena.)

CONTENTS.—1. pte. Novelas.—2. pte. Cuentos y artículos de costumbres.—3. pte. Miscelánea literaria, leyendas, tradiciones, histórico-literarias, etc. Addenda. Indice alfabético de autores y nombres citados en la obra.

530. Silva Catapos, Carlos. Lista de canónigos de la Iglesia catedral de Santiago, con breves datos biográficos desde el año 1563. [Santiago, Impr. de San José] 1916.

17 p. 24 cm.

560. Silva y Molina, Abraham de. Oidores de la Real audiencia de Santiago de Chile durante el siglo XVII. Santiago de Chile, Impr., Barcelona, 1903.

75 p. 26 cm.
Publicado en los Anales de la Universidad, t. CXIII, julio i agosto de 1903.

531. Suárez, José Bernardo. Rasgos biográficos de hombres notables de Chile. Santiago de Chile, Imprenta nacional, 1863.

290 p., 1 l. 16 cm.
60 biographies.

532. Sundt, Roberto. Bibliografía araucana. (In Revista de bibliografía chilena y extranjera. Santiago de Chile, 1917–18. 22 cm. t. 5, p. 300–315; t. 6, p. 3–21, 87–101, 182–213, 269–286.)

533. ———— Bibliografía dental chilena. Santiago, Imprenta universitaria, 1918.

66, [1] p.
Cited in Revista de bibl. chilena y extranjera, Sep.-Oct. 1918.

534. Thayer Ojeda, Luis. Apuntes genealógicos relativos a familias chilenas. Santiago de Chile, Imprenta universitaria, 1911.

v. 1, 19 cm.

535. Thayer Ojeda, Tomás. Memoria histórica sobre la familia Álvares de Toledo en Chile (Publicado en los Anales de la Universidad, t. cxiii). Santiago de Chile, Imprenta Barcelona, 1903.

168 p., 1 l. 26½ cm.

536. ———— Santiago durante el siglo xvi. Constitución de la propiedad urbana i noticias biográficas de sus primeros pobladores. Santiago de Chile, Imprenta Cervantes, 1905.

249 p. plates. 24 cm.
Published in the Anales de la Universidad, 1905.

537. Toro Melo, David. Catálogo de los impresos que vieron la lus pública en Chile desde 1877 hasta 1885 inclusives. Santiago, Impr. "Gutenberg", 1893.

504 p.
"Comprende sólo la 1.ª parte: Libros y folletos, y cataloga 2453 piezas. No existen de esta publicación más de 5 ejs. formados con los pliegos que se reti raban de la imprenta a medida que se imprimían. El resto de la edición desapareció enel incendio que consumió el establecimiento que lo daba a lus en 1894".—Laval, no. 330.

598. Torres, José Antonio. Oradores chilenos; retratos parlamentarios. Santiago de Chile, Impr. de la Opinión, 1860.

vi, 189 p., 1 l. 21½ cm.

599. Valdivia, Luis de. Nueve sermones en lengua de Chile reimpresos á plana y renglón del único ejemplar conocido y precedidos de una bibliografía de la misma lengua por José Toribio Medina. Santiago de Chile, Imprenta elseviriana [1897].

xvi, [17]–73, [2], 76 p., 1 l. 31½ cm.
The "Bibliografía" (p. 17–73) comprehends 101 titles.

600. Valenzuela, Pedro Armengol. Los regulares en la iglesia y en Chile Roma. Impr. tiberina de F. Setth, 1900.

512 p.
Contains bibliographical data regarding both printed works and manuscripts. Laval, no. 334.

601. Vega E., M. Album de la colonie française au Chili. Cette œuvre a pour but de faciliter le rapprochement des membres de la colonie; la faire connaître au dedans et au dehors du pays et démontrer par une scrupuleuse statistique le rôle important qu'elle remplit au Chili. Éditeur & propriétaire M. Vega E. Santiago de Chile, Impr. et lithogr. franco-chilienne, 1904.

4 p. l., 3–263, xxix p., 1 l. illus. (incl. ports.) 26½ cm.
2. ptie. Profils et biographies.—6. ptie. Guide général de la colonie française.

602. Venturino, Agustín. Grandes familias chilenas descendientes de ingleses, franceses e italianos. Santiago de Chile, Imprenta frano-chilena, G. Gregoire, 1918.

Cover-title. 12 p. 26 cm.

603. Vicuña Cifuentes, J. Contribución a la historia de la imprenta en Chile. Santiago, Impr. Cervantes, 1903.

50 p. pl.
"Tirada aparte de la Introducción que encabeza la reproducción paleográfica de la Aurora de Chile publicada en 1903".

604. Vicuña Mackenna, Benjamin. Bibliografía completa de las obras de don B. Vicuña Mackenna. (Única nómina completa, revisada i autorizada por el autor) Santiago de Chile, Imprenta del Centro editorial, 1879.

1 p. l., 15 p.

605. ——— Bibliografía del general O'Higgins. (In La corona del héroe. Recopilación de datos i documentos para perpetuar la memoria del general Don Bernardo O'Higgins. Santiago de Chile, 1872. 26 cm. p. 561–572.)

Laval, no. 341.

603. ——— Catálogo de la biblioteca y manuscritos de D. Benjamín Vicuña Mackenna. Santiago de Chile, Imprenta Cervantes, 1886.

281 p.
Prepared by Carlos Castro Ruiz.
The collection was acquired by the Biblioteca nacional in 1887.

607. Wagemann, Ernst. Die wirtschaftsverfassung der Republik Chile; zur entwicklungsgeschichte der geldwirtschaft und der papierwährung. München und Leipzig, Duncker & Humbolt, 1913.

vii, 253 p., 1 l. 24½ cm.
"Quellen und literatur": p. 238-246.

608. Zanelli López, Luisa. Mujeres chilenas de letras. Santiago, Imprenta universitaria, 1917.

4 p. l., [7]-203 p., 2 l. port. 18 cm.

COLOMBIA

608a. Acosta, Joaquín. Compendio del descubrimiento y colonización de la Nueva Granada en el siglo decimo ¡sexto. 2. ed. Bogotá. Camacho Roldáu & Tamayo, 1901.

xvi, 296 p. 24½ cm.
"Catálogo de libros y manuscritos que se han tenido presentes al escribir este Compendio", p. 271-291.

609. Acosta de Samper, Soledad. Biografías de hombres ilustres o notables de la época del descubrimiento o colonización de Colombia. Bogotá, Impr. de "La Luz", 1883.

xvi, 447 p. 21 cm.
"Lista de las obras": p. [445]-447. 287 biographies.

610. Añez, Julio. Parnaso colombiano; colección de poesías escogidas, por Julio Añez. Estudio preliminar de D. José Rivas Groot: Bogotá, Camacho Roldán & Tamayo, 1886-87.

2 v. 20 cm.
With bio-bibliographical sketches.

611. Arango Mejía, Gabriel. Genealogías de las familias de Antioquia. [Medellen, Imprenta Editorial, 1911.]

Cover title, 5 l., 774, [1] p. 22 cm.
Half-title: Genealogías de Antioquia. Libro 1. Cabezas de familia. Contiene la lista de los fundadores de casi todas las familias antioqueñas de origen español que vinieron desde el año 1540 a-1810 a-establecerse a 'nuestras montañas.
Dates of birth and death not given.

612. Arboleda, Gustavo. Diccionario biográfico general del antiguo departamento del Cauca, colonia, independencia, república. Quito, Ecuador, J. I. Gálvez [1910].

cover-title, viii, 151 p. 24 cm.

613. ———— Historia contemporánea de Colombia (desde la disolución de la antigua república de ese nombre hasta la época presente). Bogota, Camacho Roldán y Tamayo [etc.] 1918.

v. 1. 25 cm.
Vol. 1, Fines de 1829—principios de 1841.
Contains much biographical information.

614. Arrieta, Diógenes A. Colombianos Contemporaneos, t. 1. Caracas, 1883.

615. Baraya, José María. Biografías militares, o Historia militar del país en medio siglo. Bogotá, Impr. de Gaitán [1874].

xvi, 288, 133 p. 24½ cm.
72 biographies.

616. Bogotá. Biblioteca nacional. Catálogo de las obras existentes en la Biblioteca nacional. Bogotá, Impr. de "El Neo-granadino, 1855-56.

4 v. 27 cm.

617. ——— ——— Catálogo de las obras hispano-americanas existentes en la Biblioteca nacional de Bogota. Bogota, Imprenta de Zalamea hermanos, 1897.

2 p. l., 360 p. 24 cm.

618. ——— ——— Catálogo de los mapas, planos, cartas, hidrográficas &c, existentes en la Biblioteca nacional, formado por Saturnino Vergara. 1881. (In Anales de la instrucción pública en los Estados Unidos de Colombia. Bogotá 1882. No. 16, enero de 1882, p. 456-466.)

619. ——— ——— Catálogos de periódicos y libros de la Biblioteca nacional de Bogota. Edición oficial. Bogota, Imprenta nacional, 1914.

315 p. 24½ cm.
"Suplementos" classified, short titles, place and date, without indexes.

620. Bogotá, Colegio mayor de Nuestra Señora del Rosario. Constituciones del Colegio mayor de Nuestra Señora del Rosario, pub. por D. Rafael María Carrasquilla. Bogota, Medardo Rivas & cª-, 1893.

viii, 86 p. 24½ cm.
"Catálogo de los señores rectores del Colegio": (p. 67-80) gives full names and in most cases, dates.

621. Bogotá. Facultad de derecho y ciencias políticas. Catálogo de la Biblioteca. Bogotá, 1904.

622. Boletín de la Librería Colombiana. Bogotá, Camacho Roldán y Tamayo.

A useful trade list.

623. Borda, José Joaquín. Historia de la Compañía de Jesús en la Nueva Granada. Poissy, S. Lejay et cª, 1872.

2 v. front. (port.) 22 cm.

624. Colombia. Archivos nacionales. Indice analítico, metódico y descriptivo por F. J. Vergara y Velasco. Bogota, Imprenta nacional, 1913.

v. 1, 24 cm.
1. serie: La colonia, 1544-1819; t. 1. Gobierno en general; 1. v. Cedulario, Gobierno, Real audiencia, Virreyes.

625. Colombia. Ministerio de instrucción pública. Revista de la instrucción pública de Colombia. Bogotá.

"Lista de los libros y folletos recibidos en la Biblioteca nacional": v. 2, in no. 8-10, Aug.-Oct., 1893.
"Catálogo de las obras americanas existentes en la Biblioteca nacional": v. 3-5, in no. 16-22, 24, April-Oct., Dec., 1894; no. 25-27/28, Feb.-March and April, 1896.
"Catálogo de las obras hispano-americanas existentes en la Biblioteca nacional adicional al publicado e 1897": v. 10, in no. 59-60, 62-64, June-July, Sept.-Nov., 1899.

626. Colombianos contemporáneos. Los poetas. La lira nueva. Bogotá, 1886.
24, 417 p.
Blake's Bulletin, Apr. 1917.

627. Eder, P. J. Select bibliography [of Colombia]. (In Colombia, London, 1913, p. 289–301.)
Cited by Quelle, Verzeichnis wissenschaft. einrichtungen, zeitschriften und bibliographien der ibero-amerikan. kulturwelt.

628. Franco V., Constancio. Rasgos biográficos de los próceres y mártires de la independencia. Bogotá, Rivas, 1880.
[5], 288 P.
René-Moreno. Bib. boliviana, 1. sup., p. 257.

629. Gómez Restrepo, Antonio. La literatura colombiana. (In Revue hispanique. New York [etc.] 1918. 25 cm. t. xliii, p. 79–204.)

630. Los héroes y los mártires de la independencia. Bogotá, 1919. vi, 115 p. 22½ cm.

631. Ibánez, Pedro M. La imprenta en Bogotá, desde su introducción hasta 1810. (In Revista literaria de Bogotá, nos. 7–8, Nov.–Dec., 1890; reprinted in La Gaceta municipal de Guayaquil, Aug. 13, and Oct. 1, 1898.)

632. ———— Memorias para la historia de la medicina en Santafe de Bogota. Bogotá, Impr. de Zalamea hermanos, 1884.
3 p. l., [5]-202, p. 23½ cm.

633. Isaza, Emiliano. Antología colombiana. París, México, Vda de Ch. Bouret, 1895–96.
2 v. 18 cm.

634. Laverde Amaya, Isidoro. Apuntes sobre bibliografía colombiana, con muestras escogidas en prosa y en verso. Con un apéndice que contiene la lista de las escritoras colombianas, las piezas dramáticas, novelas, libros de historia y de viajes escritos por colomrianos [!] Bogotá, Impr. de Zalamea hermanos, 1882.
3 p. l., ii, viii, 240 p., 1 l., [3]-252, iii, [1] p. 21 cm.
"Seudónimos de colombianos": p. 237-240.

635. ———— Bibliografia colombiana. Tomo i. Bogotá, M. Rivas, 1895.
iv, 296 p. 24 cm.
No more published.
Contents.—t. 1. Abadía Méndez-Ovalle.

636. ———— Fisonomías literarias de colombianos. Curazao, A. Bethencourt e hijos, 1890.
341 p., 1 l. 17½ cm.

637. León Gómez, Adolfo. Directorio general de los abogados de Colombia. Bogotá, 1899.
Cited in Catálogos de periódicos y libros de la Bib. nac. de Bogotá, 1914, p. 200.

638. Libro azul de Colombia. Blue book of Colombia. Bosquejos biográficos de los personajes más eminentes. Historia condensada de la república. [New York, The J. J. Little & Ives Co.] 1918. 4 p. l., 725 p. col. front., illus., ports., map. 31½ cm.
Spanish and English.

639. Llona, Numa Pompilio.   Bosquejos de literatos colombianos.   Bogotá, 1886.

640. Matute, Santiago.   Los padres candelarios en Colombia, o Apuntes para la historia.   Bogotá, Tip. de E. Pardo, 1897–1903.

6 v. plates, ports. 23½ cm.

641. Medina, José Toribio.   La imprenta en Bogotá (1739–1821).   Notas bibliográficas.   Santiago de Chile, Imprenta elzeviriana, 1904.

101 p., 1 l. 24 cm.

642. ———— La imprenta en Cartagena de las Indias (1809–1820).   Notas bibliográficas.   Santiago de Chile, Imprenta elzeviriana, 1904.

70 p., 1 l. 24 cm.

643. Mesa Ortiz, Rafael M.   Colombianos ilustres (estudios y biografías) con juicio de la Academia nacional de historia y prólogo de D. Antonio Gómez Restrepo.   Bogotá, Impr. de "La República, 1916–19?

v. 1–3. ports. 26 cm.

644. París, Gonzalo.   The young writers of Colombia.   (In Inter-America. New York, 1919.   25½ cm.   English, v. 2, p. [241]–248.)

Translated from Cuba Contemporánea, v. 19 (1919) p. 395–402.

645. Patiño, Alberto.   Bibliografía dental colombiana.   Bogotá, 1910.

Cited in Bib. nac., Catálogos, 1914, p. 293.

646. Pereira, Ricardo S.   Documentos sobre limites de los Estados-Unidos de Colombia, copiados de los originales que se encuentran en el Archivo de Indias de Sevilla, y acompañados de breves consideraciones sobre el verdadero *Uti possidetis juris* de 1810.   1. serie: Limites entre el antiguo vireinato de la Nueva-Granada y las capitanias generales de Venezuela y Guatemala.   Bogotá, C. Roldan y Tamayo, 1883.

3 p. l., xvi, 167, [1] p. fold. map, 22½ cm.
"Apéndice bibliografico": p. [157]–161.

647. Pérez, Rafael.   La Compañía de Jesús en Colombia y Centro-América después de su restauración.   Valladolid, L. N. de Gaviría, 1896–98.

3 v. plates, ports. 23½ cm.

648. Pineda, Anselmo.   Biblioteca del ex-coronel Pineda, ó colección de publicaciones hechas en el Vireinato de Santa Fé y en las repúblicas de Colombia y Nueva Granada, desde 1774 á 1850, y de varios manuscritos nacionales, é impresos extranjeros, relacionados con los negocios de la república anteriores, contemporáneos y posteriores a la revolución de 1810.   Bogotá, Imp. de El Tradicionista, 1872–73.

2 v.
Cited by Babcock, Reference list of bibliographies in Books and magazine articles received in the Columbus memorial library of the Pan American Union, Supp. 2, 1914, p. 124.

649. Posada, Eduardo.   Bibliografía bogotána.   Bogotá, Imp. Arboleda y Valencia, 1917.

v. 1. (Biblioteca de historia nacional, v. xvi.)
Vol. 1 contains all books, pamphlets, broadsides, etc. printed in Bogotá, from 1738 to 1820.

650 ———— La imprenta en Santa Fé de Bogotá en el siglo xviii. Madrid, V. Suárez, 1917.

2 pl. l., [vii]-xii, 153 p. facsims. 27½ cm.
88 publications are described, 1739-1800.

651. Samper, José María. Galería nacional de hombres ilustres ó notables; ó sea Colección de bocetos biográficos, t. 1. Bogotá, 1879.

652. Schumacher, Hermann A. Südamerikanische studien; drei lebens—und cultur—bilder: Mutis, Caldas, Codazzi, 1760-1860. Berlin, E. S. Mittler & sohn, 1884.

xiii, 559, [1] p. 23½ cm.
The "Anmerkungen" (p. 421-559) are of bio-bibliographical interest.

653. Soto Borda, Clímaco. Siluetas parlamentarias; Congreso nacional de 1896. Corr. y aum.

Cited in Boletín de la Librería colombiana, May, 1920.

654. Uribe Villegas, Gonzalo. Los arzobispos y obispos colombianos desde el tiempo de la colonia hasta nuestros días. Bogotá, Impr. de "La Sociedad", 1918.

3 p. l., [iii]-v, [5]-792, 1p. 24 cm.

655. Vergara y Vergara, José María. Historia de la literatura en Nueva Granada desde la conquista hasta la independencia (1538-1820) 2. ed., con prólogo y anotaciones de Antonio Gómez Restrepo. Bogota, Libreria americana, 1905.

xxvii, 515, [1] p. port. 22½ cm.

656. Vesga y Ávila, J. M. Perfiles colombianos. 1. ser. Diputados y ministros. Bogotá, 1908.

Cited in Bogota, Bib. nac. Catál., 1914, p. 209.

657. Zamora, Alonso de. Historia de la provincia de San Antonio del Nuevo Reyno de Granada del Orden de predicadores. Barcelona, Impr. de J. Leopis, 1701.

10 p. l., 537, [1] p. 10 l.
Medina. Bib. hisp. americana, 2053.

COSTA RICA

658. Biolley, Pablo. Bibliografía; obras publicadas en el extranjero acerca de la República de Costa Rica durante el siglo xix. (In Revista de Costa Rica en el siglo xix. Tomo 1. San José, 1902. 29½ cm. p. [363]-404.)

656. Costa Rica. Facultad de farmacia. Memoria general presentada a la Asamblea general anual, reunida en esta ciudad el 14 de enero de 1917, por el secretario de la Facultad, Lic. Alonso Pérez Calvo. San José, "Alsina", 1917.

748, [4] p. plates, ports. 25½ cm.
"Apuntes biográficos": p. 198-211, 232-236, [603]-605, [618]-619.

630. Costa Rica. Inspección general de enseñanza. Bibliografía pedagógica y medios materiales de enseñanza, por B. Corrales, secretario de la Inspección general. San José, Tipografía nacional, 1896.

45, [1] p. 20 cm.

661. Revista de Costa Rica en el siglo xix. Tomo primero. San José, Tipografía nacional, 1902.

x p., 1 l., 404, a-c p. incl. illus., tables. plates, ports. 29½ cm.

Pub. by "Comisión conmemorativa de Costa Rica en el siglo xix", ed. by Francisco M. Iglesias and Juan F. Ferraz.

No more published.

CONTENTS.—Iglesias, F. M., y Ferraz, J. F. Prólogo.—Thiel, B. A. Monografía de la población de Costa Rica en el siglo xix.—Iglesias, F. M. Memoria histórica ... los veinte primeros años del siglo (reproducción)—Soto Hall, M. Capítulos de un libro inédito.—Jiménez, M. J. Cuadros de costumbres.—Soto Hall, M. Episodios nacionales, 1856-1857. Día de la independencia.—Ferraz, J. F. Tres fiestas del 15 de setiembre.—Lächner Sandoval, V. Apuntes de higiene publica.—Soto Hall, M. Rasgos biográficos ... de un libro inédito.—Thiel, B. A. La Iglesia católica en Costa Rica durante el siglo xix.—Valenciano, R. J. Breve reseña de la jerarquía eclesiástia, 1851-1900.—Biolley, P. Bibliografía: obras publicadas en el extranjero acerca de la Republica de Costa Rica durante el siglo xix [1826-1900].

662. San José, Costa Rica. Biblioteca nacional. Boletin, año 1- agosto 1898- San José, 1898-.

Two numbers published.

The Biblioteca nacional is publishing its catalogue which is expected to be completed by the end of 1920.

663. San José, Costa Rica. Biblioteca nacional. Informe de la Biblioteca nacional oficina de depósito y cange de publicaciones San José. Tip. nacional.

663a. Sotela, Rogelio. Valores literarios de Costa Rica. San Jose, Impr. Alsina, 1920.

293, [2] p. 22 cm.

CUBA

664. Acevedo, Luciano de. La Habana en el siglo xix descrita por viajeros extranjeros (ensayo de bibliografía crítica) La·Habana. Cuba contemporánea, 1919.

52 p. 24 cm.

665. Alcover y Beltrán, Antonio Miguel. El periodismo en Sagua; sus manifestaciones. (Apuntes para la historia del periodismo cubano.) Habana [Tip. "La Australia"] 1901.

2 p. l., v, 227, [1] p., 1 l. illus. 17½ cm.

666. Asociación de la prensa médica de Cuba. Homenaje al Señor Carlos M. Trelles y Govín, socio de honor. Matanzas, Impr. de J. F. Oliver, 1919.

1 p. l., 90 p. 25½ cm.

"Bibliografía del Señor Carlos Manuel Trelles y Govín por el dr. Jorge Le-Roy y Cassá:" p. 24-35.

667. Bachiller y Morales, Antonio. Apuntes para la historia de las letras, y de la instrucción pública de la isla de Cuba. Habana, Impr. de P. Massano [etc.] 1859-61.

3 v. 24 cm.

CONTENTS.—t. 1. pte. 1. De la educación primaria. pte. 2. Educación secundaria y facultativa profesional. De la instrucción facultativa literaria. Enseñanzas universitarias.—t. ii. pte. 3. Imprenta en la isla. Periódico. Canciones. Poema lírico y dramático. Historiadores. Renacimiento. Publicaciones periódicas: catálogo rasonado y cronológico hasta 1840 inclusive. [Miscelánea].—t. iii. pte. 4. Galería de hombres útiles. Adiciones. Catálogo de libros y folletos publicados en Cuba desde la introducción de la imprenta hasta 1840. Adiciones.

."Suplementos y adiciones á los catálogos de la bibliografía cubana [312 titles]" in Revista de Cuba, v. 7. p. 354-364, 491-498; v. 8. p. 71-78, 124-135, 250-254, 363-372.

662. British museum. Cartografía cubana del British museum; catálogo cronológico de cartas, planos y mapas de los siglos XVI al XIX. Por Domingo Figarola-Caneda. 2. ed., corr. Habana, Impr. de la Biblioteca nacional, 1910.

21 p. 27 cm.

669. Calcagno, Francisco. Diccionario biográfico cubano. <Comprende hasta 1878.> New-York, N. Ponce de Leon, 1878[-86].

3 p. l., viii, [7]-727 p. 26 cm.

670. Cotarelo y Mori, Emilio. Doña Gertrudis Gómez de Avellaneda; indicaciones bibliográficas con motivo de un libro reciente. Madrid, Tip. de la "Revista de arch., bibl. y museos", 1915.

24 p. 24½ cm.
"Del 'Boletín de la Real academia española'"; also in Cuba intelectual, no. 40-42.

671. El Criollo. Album de el Criollo; semblanzas. Habana, Est. tip. O'Reilly número 9, 1888.

350 p. incl. ports. 25 cm.
"Ofrecemos al público coleccionados en el presente volumen, los retratos de los famosos insurrectos y revolucionarios cubanos que han galardonado las páginas de el Criollo."

672. Cruz, Manuel de la. Cromitos cubanos (Bocetos de autores hispano-americanos). Habana, Est. tip. la Lucha, 1892.

xv, 436 p., 2 l. illus. (ports.) 20 cm.
"Bibliografía de los cromitos cubanos": p. 423-436.

673. Cuba. Congreso. Cámara de representantes. Catálogo de las obras existentés en la biblioteca. Habana, Impr. y. papeleria de Rambla y Bousa, 1905.

30 p. 22 cm.
Signed: Manuel González Iglesias, bibliotecario.

674. ———— Catalogo de las obras que forman su biblioteca: secciones de hacienda pública y de comercio y transporte. Habana, Imp. de Suárez, Carasa y ca, 1913.

[272] p. 27½ cm.
Prepared by Luis Marino Pérez.

674a. Cuba. Congreso. Senado. Biblioteca. Catálogo de las obras existentes en la referida biblioteca, año de 1916. Habana, Impr. de Rambla, Bousa y ca., 1917.

xliii p., 2 l., [3]-350 p. 27 cm.
Signed: Valentín Villar, jefe de la sección.

675. Escoto, José Augusto. Ensayo de una biblioteca herediana. (In Cuba y América, Habana, 1904. 24 cm. v. 14, p. 148-149, 261-269.)

676. Figarola Caneda, Domingo. Bibliografía de Enrique Piñeyro, con una introducción, notas y complemento. (In Anales de la Academia de la historia. Habana, 1919- 28½ cm. t. 1, no. 1-, p. 64-91- ports.)

In progress.

677. —— Bibliografía de Luz y Caballero. 2. ed., corr. y. aum. Habana, Impr. "El Siglo xx" de A. Miranda, 1915.

xix, 272 p., 2 l. plates, ports., facsims. 26 cm.

"Las cinco primeras partes de esta obra se dieron a la estampa en la Revista de la Facultad de letras y ciencias de nuestra Universidad (1914-1915). Ahora se reproducen corregidas, aumentadas, completas con las abreviaturas y una tabla metódica.

678. —— Bibliografía de Rafael M. Merchán. 2. ed., corr. y aum. Habana, Imp. y pap. La Universal, 1905.

xxvii p., 1 l., 48 p., 1 l. 22½ cm.

679. —— El doctor Ramón Meza y Suárez Inclán; noticia biobibliográfica. 2. ed., corr. Habana, Impr. de la Biblioteca nacional, 1909.

21 p. port. 27½ cm.

From "Revista de la Biblioteca nacional," v. 1. p. 31-51.

679a. Figarola-Caneda, Domingo. Donativo Bustamante: Catálogo de derecho internacional. (In Revista de la Biblioteca nacional. Habana, 1911-12. t. 5, p. 46-55; t. 7, p. 124-133.)

En 1917 se ha publicado el primer tomo completo del Catálogo, Habana, Imp. de la Biblioteca nacional, vii, [1], 47, [1] p. 173 números.

Nos 679a-b- c, 686a and 69?a are cited in a list of Cuban bibliographies (mss.) compiled by Mrs. E. Figarola-Caneda. This list, examined with the permission of the compiler, was received too late to permit of the insertion in the present list of all the titles. Mrs Figarola-Caneda is preparing also a dictionary of Cuban pseudonyms with biographical data

679b. —— Indice de los títulos contenidos en las diversas colecciones facticias de la biblioteca adquirida por compra hecha al Sr. Dr. Vidal Morales y Morales. Habana, Impr. de la Biblioteca nacional, 1905.

64 p.

679c. —— Para la biografía de José Martí. (In Revista de la Biblioteca nacional. Habana, 1909. t. 1, p. 138-160).

680. González Alcorta, Leandro. Datos para la historia de Vuelta-Abajo. Pinar del Rio, Impr. "La Constancia", 1902.

v. 1. 22 cm.

1. pte. Exploraciones bibliográficas.

681. Guía-directorio de la República de Cuba (Bailly-Bailliere-Riera); comercio, industria, agricultura, ganadería, minería, propiedad, profesiones y elemento oficial. Barcelona, Pub. por "Anuarios Bailly-Bailliere y Riera reunidos", s. a., 1920.

888 p. map. 28 cm.

682. Havana. Biblioteca nacional. Revista de la Biblioteca nacional; publicación mensual. año 1- t. 1- enero 1909- Habana, Impr. de la Biblioteca nacional, 1909-.

Editor: Jan. 1909-. D. Figarola-Caneda.

683. Havana. Censor principal de teatros. Indice de las piezas dramáticas permitidas sin atajos ni correcciones, de las permitidas con ellos y de las absolutamente prohibidas, presentado al gobierno superior civil de la isla por el censor principal de teatros de esta capital. Habana, Impr. del Gobierno y capitanía general por S. M., 1852.

58, 6 p. 30 cm.

684. Havana. Colegio de Belén. Album conmemorativo del quincuagesimo aniversario de la fundacion en la Habana del Colegio de Belen de la Compañía de Jesús. Habana, Impr. Avisador comercial, 1904.

[iii]-viii, 435 p., 1 l. plates, ports. 25 cm.

685. Lagomasino A., Luis. Patricios y heroinas. Bocetos históricos. Habana, Tip. del Boletín nacional de historia y geografía, 1912.

v. 1. illus. pl., ports, facsim. 20 x 10 cm.

CONTENTS.—v. 1. J. de Agüero, I. Armenteros, F. Hernández, F. Estrampes, F. V. Aguilera D. del Marmol, P. Figueredo, I. Moray Pera, F. Sánches Betancourt, M. G. Gutiérres, A. Lordo.

686. Le Roy y Cassá, Jorge. Bibliografía de la estadística en Cuba durante el siglo xx. (In La Reforma social, Habana, 1917. 24 cm. t. ix, p. [134]-150.)

686a. ——— Bibliografía del Dr. Juan Santos Fernándes. Habana, Imp. de Lloredo y ca.

97 p. Contains 928 numbers.

686b. Libro azul de Cuba: The Blue Book of Cuba, 1917. Habana, Solana y cía., 1917.

xi, 352 p. illus., ports. 32 cm.

687. El libro social de la Habana. New York, Impr. de W. Green [°1906-

v. 1. 19½ cm.

"Originado y compilado por Louise Wintzer de vom. Dorp, propietaria, revisado por Enrique Fontanilla".

688. Llaverías, Joaquín. Historia de los archivos de Cuba. Prólogo de F. de P. Coronado. Habana, Imp. de Ruiz y comp. (s. en c.) 1912.

xxiv, 382 p., 1 l. illus., fold. plan. 27 cm.

689. Lópes Prieto, Antonio. Parnaso cubano. Colección de poesías selectas de autores cubanos desde Zequeira a nuestros días, precedida de una introducción histórico-crítica sobre el desarrollo de la poesía en Cuba, con biografías. Habana, M. de Villa [1881].

lxxxi, 370 p. 23 cm.

690. Medina, José Toribio. La imprenta en La Habana (1707–1810). Notas bibliográficas. Santiago de Chile, Imprenta elseviriana, 1904.

xxxii, 199 p., 1 l. 24 cm.

691. Mitjáns, Aurelio. Estudio sobre el movimiento científico y literario de Cuba. Habana, Imp. de A. Alvares y ca., 1890.

xxxi, [5]-395 p. 20 cm.

Contains many data in the field indicated by the title, but the want of index and table of contents greatly impair its value as a reference book.

692. ——— Historia de la literatura cubana. Del Monte. Heredia. Milanés. Saco. Gertrudis Gómes de Avellaneda. Zenea, etc., etc. La vida y la obra de Mitjans, por Manuel de la Cruz. Madrid, Editorial-America [1918?]

389 p. 19½ cm. (Biblioteca Andrés Bello, t. 1.)

692a. Monte, Domingo, del.   Lista cronológica de los libros inéditos e impresos que se han escrito sobre la isla de Cuba y de los que hablan de la misma desde su descubrimiento y conquista hasta nuestros días, formado en París en 1846.   Habana, Est. tip. de la Vda. de Soler, 1882.

50 p.

693. Morales y Morales, Vidal.   Iniciadores y primeros mártires de la revolución cubana.   Prólogo del dr. Nicolás Heredia.   Habana, Impr. Avisador comercial, 1901.

xv, 680 p., 1 l. front. (port.) col. pl. 28 cm.

· 694. Muñoz Sañudo, Lisardo.   Periodistas y periódicos masónicos de Cuba.   Habana, 1917?

695. Parker, William Belmont.   Cubans of to-day.   New York and London, G. P. Putnam's sons, 1919.

xvii, 684 p. front., ports. 17 cm. (Hispanic notes and monographs ... issued by the Hispanic Society of America.)

696. Péres, Luis Marino.   Apuntes de libros y folletos impresos en España y el extranjero que tratan expresamente de Cuba desde principios del siglo xvii hasta 1812 y de las disposiciones de gobierno impresas en la Habana desde 1753 hasta 1800.   Con varios apéndices é índice.   Habana, C. Martines y compañía, 1907.

xv, 62, 16, [7] p. 23½ cm.
Apéndices: Impresos de la Real sociedad patriótica y del Real consulado de la Habana. Adiciones á la Imprenta en la Habana de José Toribio Medina. Imp. de "Cuba y América". 1907.

697. ———— Bibliografía de la revolución de Yara; folletos y libros impresos de 1868 a 1908.   Historia y política.   Biografías.   Masonería.   Asuntos eclesiástico-políticos.   Esclavitud.   Asuntos económicos.   Asuntos administrativos.   Literatura patriótica.   Habana, Impr. Avisador comercial, 1908.

x, 73 p. 23½ cm.

698. Péres Beato, Manuel.   La imprenta en la Habana.   (In El Curioso americano, Habana.   1908.   25½ cm.   p. 109–112, 152–155.)

699. ———— La imprenta en Santiago de Cuba.   (In El Curioso americano. Habana, 1908.   25½ cm.   p. 19–24, 33–38, 107–109.)

700. Pesuela y Lobo, Jacobo de la.   Diccionario geográfico, estadístico, histórico, de la isla de Cuba.   Madrid, Impr. del estab. de Mellado, 1863–66.

4 v. tables (partly fold.) 27½ cm.

701. Quesada, Gonzalo de.   Cuba.   Washington, Govt. print. off., 1905.

541 p. front. (fold. map) pl. 23 cm.
At head of title: International bureau of the American republic, Washington, D. C., U. S. A.
"Books relating to Cuba.   Compil d by Mr. A. P. C. Griffin": p. 315–446.
"Maps relating to Cuba.   Compiled by P. Lee Phillips": p. 447–512.   .

702. Ramíres, Serafín.   La Habana artística.   Apuntes históricos.   Habana, Imp. del E. M. de la Capitanía general, 1891.

iii-xv, 684, [7] p. 22 cm.

703. Risquet, Juan F. Rectificaciones: la cuestión político-social en la isla de Cuba. Habana, Tipografía "América", 1900.

xiii, [15]-205, ii, p., 1 l. 21½ cm.
Contains biographical matter.

704. Rosain, Domingo. Necrópolis de la Habana. Historia de los cementerios de esta ciudad. Con multitud de noticias interesantes, Habana, Impr. "El Trabajo", 1875.

vii, [9]-543, xiii p., 1 l. 23 x 18 cm.

705. Torralbas, Federico. Bibliografía del Dr. José I. Torralbas. Habana, Impr. Avisador comercial, 1910.

ix p., 1 l., 53 p. port. 24 cm.

706. Trelles y Govín, Carlos Manuel. Bibliografía cubana del siglo XIX. Matanzas, Impr. de Quirós y Estrada, 1911-15.

3 v. 26 cm.
A continuación of the author's "Ensayo de bibliografía cubana de los siglos XVII y XVIII" pub. 1907, with supplement 1908.
CONTENTS.—t. 1. 1800-1835.—t. 2. 1836-1840. Seguida de una Relación de periódicos publicados en Cuba en el siglo XX, por F. Llaca, y unas Noticias curiosas referentes á escritores de los siglos XVII y XVIII, por M. Pérez Beato.—t. 3. 1841-1855.—t. 4. 1856-1868.—t. 5. 1869-1878.— t. 6. 1879-1885.—t. 7. 1886-1893.—t. 8. 1894-1899. Apéndices: I. Adiciones; II. Notas biográficas; III. Juicios críticos; IV. Alfabetos, Ultimas adiciones; V. Ensayo de biblioteca cubana del siglo XIX.

707. —— Bibliografía cubana del siglo XX. (1900-1916) Matanzas, Impr. de la vda. de Quiros y Estrada, 1916-17.

2 v. 26 cm.

708. —— Bibliografía de la segunda guerra de independencia cubana y de la hispano-yankee. Publicada en la revista ilustrada "Cuba y América". Habana, 1902.

cover-title, 69 p. 24 cm.
Arranged chronologically, 1895-1900; includes references to articles in periodicals.

709. —— Bibliografía geográfica cubana. Matanzas, Impr. de J. F. Oliver, 1920.

3 p. l., iv, 340 p. ports., maps. 25 cm.

710. —— Bibliografía médico-farmacéutica cubana. (In Revista de medicina y cirugía. Habana, 1906-07. 25 cm. t. xi-xii.)

Describes 2000 books, pamphlets and articles.

—— —— Indices. Habana, Impr. Avisador Comercial, 1907.

31, [1] p. 25½ cm.

711. —— Biblioteca científica cubana. Matanzas, Impr. de J. F. Oliver, 1918-19.

2 v. illus., pl., ports., facsims. 25 cm.
CONTENTS.—t. 1. Matemáticas, astronomía, Ciencias militares, físicas y naturales, Biología, Antropología, Agricultura.—t. 2. Ciencias médicas, Ingeniería.

712. —— Los ciento cincuenta libros mas notables que los cubanos han escrito. Habana, Impr. "El Siglo XX," de A. Miranda, 1914.

61 p. 18 cm.
From Cuba y América, v. 17, no. 1, October 1913.

713. ———— Ensayo de bibliografía cubana de los siglos XVII y XVIII. Seguido de unos apuntes para la bibliografía dominicana y portorriqueña. Matanzas, Impr. "El Escritorio", 1907.

xi, 228 p., 1 l., xxviii p., 1 l. 26 cm.

"Notas y adiciones". (In El Curioso americano, Habana, 1907, p. 27, 30, 43, 46, 62, 64, 94, 96.)

———— ———— Suplemento. Matanzas, Impr. "El Escritorio," 1908.

2 p. l., ii, 76 p. 26½ cm.

714. Trujillo, y Cárdenas, Enrique. Album de "El Porvenir". New York, Impr. de "El Porvenir", 1890-95.

5 v.

A rich source of biographical information: cf. Pérez, de Biol. la revolución de Yara, no. 350-354.

715. U. S. Library of Congress. List of books relating to Cuba, including references to collected works and periodicals; by A. P. C. Griffin; with a bibliography of maps by P. Lee Phillips. Washington, Govt. print. off., 1898.

61 p. 23½ cm. (U. S. 55th Cong., 2d sess., 1897-98. Senate. Doc. no. 161.)
"Appendix: A synoptical catalogue of manuscripts in the Library of Congress relating to Cuba. Comp. by Herbert Friedenwald": p. 58-61.

716. Valdés Domínguez, Eusebio. Bibliografía cubana. (In Revista cubana. Habana, 1879. 26 cm. t. 5, p. [368]-379, [581]-592; t. 6, p. [85]-89.)

Unfinished.

717. Valle, Rafael Heliodoro. Cuban authors and thinkers. (In The Hispanic American historical review. Baltimore, 1920. 27 cm. vol. III, p. 634-638.)

718. Velasco, Carlos de. La Academia de la historia de Cuba, los académicos de número. (Pub. en la Revista de la Biblioteca nacional) Habana, Impr. de la Biblioteca nacional, 1910.

68 p. incl. ports. 26½ cm.

ECUADOR

719. Andrade, Manuel de Jesús. Ecuador. Próceres de la independencia; índice alfabético de sus nombres con algunos bocetos biográficos. Quito, Tip. de la Escuela de artes y oficios, 1909.

3 p. l., 417 p. 20½ cm.

719a. Andrade Coello, Alejandro. Intellectual development in Ecuador. (In Bulletin of the Pan American Union, Washington, 1920. 24½ cm. v. 50, p. 265-275.)

"English version of an article in Revista de la Universidad de Córdoba".

720. Anrique Reyes, Nicolás. Noticia de algunas publicaciones ecuatorianas anteriores a 1792. Santiago de Chile. 1891.

23 p.

721. Anuario de la prensa ecuatoriana, publ. por la Biblioteca municipal de Guayaquil. [año I]–III; 1892–1894. Guayaquil, 1893–95.

3 v. 21½ cm.
"Publicaciones de autores ecuatorianos o relativas al Ecuador, impresas en el extranjero durante los años [de] 1892[–1894]": 1893, p. [81]–83; 1894, p. [106]–109.
Diarios, periódicos y revistas": 1894, p. [90]–105.
No more published?

722. Campos, Francisco. Galería biográfica de hombres célebres ecuatorianos. Guayaquil, 1885.

723. Ceballos, Pedro Fermín. Ecuatorianos ilustres. Reproducción hecha por Ernesto C. Monge para el centenario del autor. Quito, Impr. "La Juventud", 1912.

2 p. l., [3]–58 p. 20 cm.
Ed. by Celiano Monge.
Reprinted from El Iris, 1861.

724. Ceriola, Juan B. El periodismo en el Ecuador. Quito? 1909.

725. Compte, Francisco María. Varones ilustres de la Orden seráfica en el Ecuador, desde la fundación de Quito hasta nuestros días. 2. ed., corr. y aum. por el mismo autor. Quito, Impr. del clero, 1885.

2 v. 22½ cm.

725. Destruge, Camilo. Album biográfico ecuatoriano. Guayaquil, Ecuador, Tip. "El Vigilante", 1903–05.

v. 1–5. ports. 24½ cm.
CONTENTS.—t. 1. Hombres notables del reino de Quito. Hombres notables de la época colonial.—t. 2. Hombres notables de la independencia.—t. 3. Presidentes de la república.—t. 4. Hombres notables de varias épocas (fallecidos).—t. 5. Hombres notables contemporáneous (fallecidos).

726a. Endara, Julio. La cultura filosófica en el Ecuador durante la colonia. (In Revista de filosofía. Buenos Aires, 1920. 26 cm. año 6, no. 6 (noviembre) p. 400–429.)

727. Gonsáles Suárez, Federico. Bibliografía ecuatoriana. La imprenta en el Ecuador en tiempo de la colonia, 1750–1792. Quito, Impr. de la Universidad, 1892.

36 p.

728. Guayaquil. Biblioteca municipal. Boletin. t. 1– marzo 1910– Guayaquil, 1910–.

23 cm.
"Sección histórica" included in each no.

729. Medina, José Toribio. La imprenta en Quito (1760–1818). Notas bibliográficas. Santiago de Chile, Imprenta elseviriana, 1904.

36 p., 1 l. 24 cm.

730. Mera, Juan Léon. Antología ecuatoriana. Cantares del pueblo ecuatoriano, precedida de un estudio sobre ellos, ilustrada con notas acerca el lenguaje del pueblo y seguida de varias antiguallas curiosas. Ed. hecha por orden y bajo el auspicio de la Academia ecuatoriana. Quito, Impr. de la Universidad central del Ecuador, 1892.

2 p. l., xxvi p., 1 l., 504 p. 26 cm.

731. ——— Ojeada histórico-crítica sobre la poesía ecuatoriana, desde su época más remota hasta nuestros días. Quito, Impr. de J. P. Sanz, 1868.

1 p. l., vii, 503, [5] p. 17½ cm.

732. Muñoz, Bonifacio. Biblioteca de alquiler; catálogo especial de 30,000 obras dedicado al pueblo ecuatoriano; Librería "Sucre" de Bonifacio Muñoz. Quito, Impreso por N. Romero D., 1918.

1 p. l., 424 p. pl. 24½ cm.
A dealer's catalogue: "Sección nacional:" p. 335-365.

733. ——— Obras de autores ecuatorianos; catálogo especial de las librerías "Sucre" ... Quito, Tip. y encuadernación salisianas [1919].

144 p. 25 cm.

734. Orellana, Gonzalo. Patria intelectual. Album biográfico ecuatoriano.

Cf. Catalogue of Bonifacio Muñoz.

735. Pérez, Juan. Rasgos biográficos de personas notables de Ambato. Quito y del Ecuador.

3 v.

736. ——— Rasgos biográficos de personas notables de Guayaquil. Guayaquil? 1906.

737. Pino Roco. Establecimiento de la imprenta en Guayaquil, 1821. Guayaquil, Impr. Gutenberg, 1906.

738. Rolando, Carlos A. Catálogo de la bibliografía nacional del Dr. Carlos A. Rolando. Guayaquil, Imp. mercantil [1913].

2 p. l., 135 p. 25½ cm.
"El catálogo está arreglado hasta el 31 de diciembre de 1912."

739. ——— Pseudónimos de escritores nacionales y extranjeros en la prensa guayaquileña. (In Boletín de la Sociedad ecuatoriana de estudios históricos americanos. Quito, 1919, t. 3, p. 273-275.)

739a. Váscones, Francisco. Historia de la literatura ecuatoriana. Quito, Tip. de la Prensa católica, 1919.

v. 1—

GUATEMALA

740. Academia guatemalteca. Biografías de literatos nacionales, publicación de la Academia guatemalteca. t. 1. [Guatemala] Estab. tip. "La Unión," 1889.

v. 1. 24½ cm.
CONTENTS.—R. García Goyena, I. Gómez, M. Diéguez Olaverri, J. Batres, J. Diéguez Olaverri, A. Marure.

741. Guatemala. Facultad de derecho. Catálogo de la biblioteca de la Facultad de derecho y notariado del Centro. Sección latino-americana. Guatemala, Siguere y cía, 1898.

p. 217-300.

742. Guatemala. Instituto nacional. Biblioteca Catálogo. Guatemala, 1887.

Cited in Catálogos de periódicos y libros de la Biblioteca nacional de Bogotá, 1914, p. 189.

742a. Guatemala. Secretaría de relaciones exteriores. Lista diplomática y Consular. Guatemala, Tip. nacional, 1920.

21 p.

743. Medina, José Toribio. La imprenta en Guatemala (1660–1821). Santiago de Chile, Impreso en casa del autor, 1910.

lxxxv p., 1 l., 696, [2] p. illus., facsims. 33 cm.

744. O'Ryan, Juan Enrique. Bibliografía de la imprenta en Guatemala enlos siglos XVII y XVIII. Santiago de Chile, Imprenta elzeviriana, 1897.

xvi, [17]-120 p., 1 l. facsims. (1 fold.) 19 cm.
"Bibliografía": p. [17]-20.

744a. Rodríguez Beteta, Virgilio. La imprenta y los impresores en Centro América durante la colonia. (In El arte tipográfico. Nueva York, 1920—, t. xviii—).

Introducción a la historia del periodismo en el antiguo reino de Guatemala.

745. Salazar, Ramón A. Historia del desenvolvimiento intelectual de Guatemala. Tomo 1. La colonia. Guatemala, 1867.

403 p.
With bibliography. Cited in Blake's bull. Dec. 1917, no. 716.

746. Spain. Archivo general de Indias. Relación descriptiva de los mapas, planos, etc. de la audiencia y capitanía general de Guatemala (Guatemala, San Salvador, Honduras, Nicaragua y Costa-Rica) existentes en el Archivo general de Indias; por Pedro Torres Lanzas ... Madrid, Tip. de la Revista de arch., bibl. y museos, 1903.

214 p. fold. maps, plans. 17 cm.
"De la Revista de arch., bibl. y. museos."

HONDURAS

747. Albir, Francisco José. Writers of Honduras. (In Bulletin of the Pan American Union, Washington, 1919. 24½ cm. v. 49, p. 187–190.)

Published also in the Spanish edition of the Bulletin, June, 1919.

748. Directorio nacional de Honduras, América Central. New York, Spanish-American directories Co., 1899.

502 p. front. (port.) illus. 24 cm. Compiled by G. R. Perry.

749. Durón y Gamero, Rómulo Enrique. Honduras literaria; colección de escritos en prosa y verso, precedidos de apuntes biográficos por Rómulo E. Durón ... Tegucigalpa, Tipografía nacional, 1896–99.

2 v. 27 cm.

750. Honduras. Biblioteca nacional. Catálogo metodico de la Biblioteca nacional, seguido de un índice alfabético de autores y otro de materias. 1906 [i. e. 1915] Tegucigalpa, Tipografía nacional [1915]

293 p., 1 l. 28 cm.
The author and subject indices are wanting in the copy I have collated.

751. Revista del Archivo y Biblioteca nacional de Honduras ... **Tegucigalpa,**
1904–

752. Valle, Rafael Heliodoro. Índice bibliográfico hondureño. (In Centro-
América, vol. 5 (1913) p. 583–587.)

———— Bibliografía que interesa a Honduras. (In Centro-América, vol.
7 (1915). 24½ cm. p. [530]–534.)

C. K. JONES.

(*To be continued.*)

———————

LA SECCIÓN DE MANUSCRITOS DE LA BIBLIOTECA NACIONAL DE CHILE

I. SU ORIGEN Y DESARROLLO

En cumplimiento de una ley especial, adquirió el Gobierno de Chile
en 1846 la biblioteca del eminente patriota don Mariano Egaña, de la
que formaba parte una colección de manuscritos de las más variadas
materias, que sirvió de base para crear mas tarde la Sección de Manuscritos de la Biblioteca Nacional, y que era la 6.ª de las que contaba
este establecimiento cuando se dictó su Reglamento en 8 de agosto de
1861.

Años mas tarde, en 1867, la colección constaba de seiscientas piezas,
distribuidas en 113 volúmenes en esta forma: 48 volúmenes en folio,
60 en 4° y 5 en 8°.

En mayo de 1876 ingresó a la Biblioteca Nacional la biblioteca particular de Monseñor don José, Ignacio Víctor Eyzaguirre, que además
de 4,000 libros contaba con una colección de documentos que el erudito
y progresista sacerdote legó al mencionado establecimiento.

Añadiéronse sucesivamente a estas colecciones otra serie de papeles
utilizados por don Claudio Gay para escribir su *Historia General de
Chile*, los libros y expedientes tramitados en el tribunal del Consulado,
y el archivo del Estado Mayor del Ejército Peruano, referente a la
primera etapa de la guerra del Pacífico, caído en poder del ejército
chileno en 1879.

En julio de 1885 un conocido periodista y activo investigador de la
historia patria don Justo Abel Rosales, publicó un extenso y nutrido
artículo en el que abogaba por la creación de una verdadera Sección de
Manuscritos, donde se guardasen los diversos archivos históricos diseminados en varias oficinas públicas. Hasta entonces la Biblioteca
Nacional sólo contaba con 116 volúmenes de manuscritos del Fondo

Antiguo; 12 de Reales Cédulas, muchas de ellas impresas, y 223 legajos de documentos sin empastar ni catalogar, correspondientes a los archivos de Eyzaguirre, Consulado, Guerra del Pacífico, Inquisición y Jesuitas, los que representan a lo sumo unos 1250 volúmenes mas, valiosos sin duda, pero de consulta casi imposible por entonces.

A pesar de su crecimiento, la Sección de Manuscritos llevó por esto una vida lánguida hasta que un nuevo Director de la Biblioteca, don Luis Montt, le dió vigoroso impulso en 1886. Gracias a sus esfuerzos pasaron a formar parte de ella el archivo de la antigua Capitanía General, cuya traslación se ordenó por decreto supremo de 25 le septiembre de ese año; los Registros de los Escribanos de Santiago, los archivos de la Real Andiencia, de la Contaduría Mayor, de las Intendencias de Biobío y parte del Judicial de Concepción. Adquirióse también por entonces la colección de manuscritos del reputado escritor y político chileno don Benjamín Vicuña Mackenna; el archivo de don Carlos Morla Vicuña, obsequiado por su señora viuda y otra serie de documentos diseminados en poder de particulares.

El señor Montt, que a su vasta erudición de bibliógrafo, unía su interés por el estudio de la historia patria, dió así forma práctica a lo que a manera de aforismo repetía él con frecuencia: "no hay papel inútil", consiguiendo que prevaleciera su elevado criterio sobre el de los que opinaban que algunos de esos ricos archivos debían destruirse por carecer ya de todo valor.

El señor Montt debe, por tanto, ser reputado como el verdadero creador de la Sección, en la que trabajó no sólo como investigador, sino también en la revisión de los catálogos y aun en la ordenación misma de los papeles.

Cuando ocurrió la muerte del señor Montt en 1910, la Sección de Manuscritos contaba ya con más de 12,500 volúmenes, distribuidos en la forma siguiente:

Archivos	Volúmenes
Antiguo de la Biblioteca	198
Capitanía General	1,045
Cédulario	104
Consulado	50
Tribunal de Minería	14
Contaduría Mayor	5,000
Copias de Indias	63
Eyzaguirre	60
Inquisición	600
Jesuitas	467

Archivos	Volúmenes
Escribanos (1559–1800)	976
Real Audiencia	3,098
Vicuña Mackenna	336
Morla Vicuña	125
Guerra del Pacífico (1879)	33
Judicial de Concepción (1820–1854)	90
Intendencia de Concepción	136
Intendencia de Bío-Bío	105
Copias de la Oficina Hidrográfica	19
Total	12,519

Por desgracia las salas de la Biblioteca Nacional destinadas para la Sección de Manuscritos llegaron a ser estrechas y más aun cuando fue menester demoler una de ellas para facilitar la construcción del Palacio de los Tribunales y las restantes quedaron dañadas a consecuencia del terremoto de Agosto de 1906. Con todo, en el último decenio han ingresado a la Sección 328 volúmenes distribuidos como sigue:

Archivo del Cabildo de la Serena	36
" de la Gobernación de Angol	59
" particular de don Benjamín Vicuña M.	52
" del Fondo Antiguo	23
Agregados a diversos archivos	158

Dentro de muy poco tiempo se dará comienzo a la construcción de la parte que en el nuevo edificio de la Biblioteca Nacional se ha destinado a la Sección de Manuscritos. Con capacidad para guardar más de 200,000 volúmenes y con todas las comodidades necesarias para su seguridad y fácil consulta la Sección está llamada a experimentar un rápido incremento, pudiéndose calcular desde luego que duplicará su existencia actual de 13,000 volúmenes, cuando reciba los antiguos archivos notariales, los de las Intendencias y Gobernaciones y judiciales de los corregimientos coloniales y muchos otros que se hallan repartidos por las provincias de un extremo al otro de la república.

II. DESCRIPCIÓN PARTICULAR DE LOS DIFERENTES ARCHIVOS

La composición heterogénea de algunos archivos dificulta la tarea de dar una somera idea de cada uno de ellos, inconveniente tanto mayor cuanto que el valor de los documentos varía según se les aprecie por su valor intrínseco, por su rareza, por los antecedentes de las personas de quienes proceden, o por los detalles curiosos que contengan o se relacionen con el origen de ellos, o por otra serie de causas que aun es difícil recordarlas en un momento. La reseña resultará por consiguiente incompleta por la omisión de noticias de interés, y deficiente por la concisión con que es menester apuntar las demás para no dar a este artículo un desarrollo mayor del que su naturaleza le corresponde.

Archivo del Fondo Antiguo.—Consta hoy de 223 volúmenes de tan diferentes materias que en conjunto semejan una enciclopedia. Hay en ellos obras de jurisprudencia, informes en derecho, memorias jurídicas, reales cédulas; textos didácticos y teológicos, de literatura, poesía e historia; apuntes sobre medicina, mineralogía, meteorología chilenas, obras públicas, educación, materia de gobierno, diarios de navegación, comercio, industria, artes, estadística, etc., y una colección de documentos relativos al Tribunal de la Inquisición o a la historia de Chile, copiados en el Archivo de Indias de Simancas.

Como curiosidades se pueden enumerar los manuscritos originales de la *Crónica del Reyno de Chile*, de Mariño de Lobera, 1595; del Cautiverio Feliz, de Pineda y Bascuñan, 1673; el Empadronamiento de españoles e indios de la Provincia de Chiloé, 1785; el Cronicón sacro-imperial de Chile, por Ramírez, 1805; los antecedentes sobre la fundación del Colegio de Naturales, erección de la Academia de San Luis en 1796, plan de estudios y creación del Instituto Nacional en 1813; las cartas y papeles de Vera y Pintado, don Manuel de Salas, el padre Camilo Henriquez y otros patriotas sobre la Independencia americana.

Archivo de la Capitanía General.—Comprende los papeles relativos al gobierno político y militar durante la Colonia. Son muy escasas las piezas pertenecientes al siglo XVI, pero aumentan gradualmente y ya desde mediados del siguiente y hasta los primeros años del siglo XIX la documentación es variada y abundante, estimándose en mas de 20,000 el número total de piezas existentes.

El archivo está subdividido en diversas secciones, en cada una de las cuales predominan ciertas materias, pero sin que exista en realidad una rigurosa clasificación. Siguiendo el orden numérico de los volúmenes las materias a que se refieren son las siguientes:

Causas particulares . . . . Vols. 1 a 227
Causas relativos a minas . . . . " 228 a 279
Causas criminales . . . . " 280 a 339
Expedientes sobre el derecho de alcabala . . . . . " 340 a 357
Expedientes relativos a la navegación . . . . . . " 358 a 381
Libros de Procuradores . . . . " 382 y 383
Asuntos administrativos . . . . " 384 a 422
Expedientes relativos a Temporalidades de Jesuitas . " 423 a 472

Sobre mercedes de tierras y encomiendas de indios	Vols.	473 a 566
Solicitudes particulares, memoriales sobre servicios, denuncio de tierras valdías, etc	"	567 a 575
Expedientes de la jurisdicción de Aconcagua	"	576 y 577
Tierras sobrantes	"	578 y 579
Memoriales antiguos	"	580
Expedientes relativos a extranjeros	"	581
Recibos diversos	"	582 a 584
Asuntos mercantiles	"	586 a 589
Sobre las bodegas de Valparaíso	"	590 a 596
Sobre funcionarios públicos	"	597 a 609
Sobre escribanías públicas	"	610 a 621
Sobre obras públicas, correspondencia oficial, asuntos administrativos particulares de Real Hacienda	"	622 a 714
Colección de Reales cédulas 1576–1816	"	715 a 798
Correspondencia oficial, copiadores de decretos, bandos, acuerdos y otras materias de gobierno	"	799 a 814
Sobre milicias, ejército, montepíos, fortificaciones, juicios de residencia, situados, plazas de armas, guerra con Inglaterra, gobierno de Juan Fernández, plazas y presidios y refacción de cuarteles	"	815 a 876
Sobre deudas y caudales públicas, media annata, capitales consolidados, impuestos, balanza, donativos, aduanas, resguardos, comisos, real hacienda, rentas y diezmos	"	877 a 927
Policia urbana, obras públicas, fundaciones de pueblos y ciudades, Casa de Moneda, Correos, caminos, puentes, tajamares y canal de Maipo	"	928 a 954
Sobre fomento de la agricultura, el Colegio Carolino, el de Naturales, la Universidad	"	955 a 959
Sobre cárceles, obras pías, hospitales y epidemias	"	960 a 967
Elecciones y remates de cargos concejiles y otros expedientes análogos de los cabildos de Cuyo y Concepcion	"	968 a 998
Asuntos eclesiásticos, jesuitas, etc	"	999 a 1036

Los volúmenes que siguen corresponden al período de la Independencia o de la República y son de carácter netamente administrativo.

Estimado en conjunto el archivo de la Capitanía General es el que mejor sirve para estudiar las instituciones del gobierno colonial, muy poco conocido todavía pero bastante mal juzgado por la generalidad de los historiadores.

Difícil es dar una idea clara de la verdadera importancia de este archivo para investigaciones históricas sobre el tema indicado. Con todo trataremos de apuntar siquiera algunos detalles.

La correspondencia del Presidente con las autoridades subalternas, en los años de 1781 a 1804, encerrada en 11 volúmenes consta de 17,970 piezas y muchas de ellas son circulares enviadas simultáneamente a muchos funcionarios.

La correspondencia con el Rey, por la vía reservada está copiada en 5 volúmenes, y alcanza a cerca de 3,000 cartas escritas en el mismo lapso de tiempo. Tan eólo estos cinco volúmenes han suministrado material suficiente para un interesante y útil trabajo que realiza y concluirá en el presente año el profesor Mr. Charles E. Chapman con un grupo de alumnos del Instituto Pedagógico.

Los libros copiadores de las mercedes de tierras y encomiendas de indios concedidas entre los años de 1670 y 1708, son catorce y contienen 420 títulos de tierras y cerca de 900 de encomiendas. Los primeros son provechosos para conocer el origen de la propiedad rural y para reconstituir la toponimia indígena y los segundos encierran numerosas matrículas de indios, con millares de nombres indígenas, rico e inexplotado material para estudios de filología americana, como también memoriales y certificaciones de méritos y servicios y de filiaciones de los miembros más prestigiosos de la sociedad colonial.

Entre los expedientes administrativos son de interés particular los que se refieren a las fundaciones de ciudades, pueblos y fuertes; los que tratan de los parlamentos celebrados con los indios, de la guerra araucana y de las tentativas para convertir a la fe cristiana o civilizar al indígena; y, finalmente, los juicios de residencia y otros procesos instruidos con el objeto de esclarecer la conducta de las autoridades subalternas y demás funcionarios en el desempeño de sus cargos.

Archivo de Cédulas y Reales Órdenes.—Contiene más de 8,000 piezas correspondientes a todo el período de la Colonia, de las cuales talvez la décima parte sean impresas. Existen además otros 10 volúmenes de *Índices* y copias de documentos de esta clase guardados en los archivos de la Real Andiencia, Contaduría Mayor, Arzobispado y Municipalidad de Santiago y en el antiguo del Cabildo de la Serena. Aunque sea talvez innecesario decirlo, todos esos documentos contienen resoluciones y órdenes reales tanto de carácter general como particular sobre el gobierno de Chile. Entre estos últimos hay multitud de nombramientos de funcionarios civiles y militares, concesiones de mercedes y pensiones, permisos para contraer matrimonio, indultos de penas, expulsión o naturalización de extranjeros y sobre muchas otras materias. Por cierto que los de interés general, leyes, ordenanzas, reglamentos y aclaración o interpretación de sus disposiciones son los de major importancia.

Archivo del Tribunal de Minería.—Este tribunal fue creado en Chile en cumplimiento de lo dispuesto por Real Orden, dada en Aranjuez en 12 de Febrero de 1797. Contiene gran parte de los expedientes que formó el Administrador General del Ramo de Minería don Antonio Martínez de Mata, en la visita general a todos les asientos mineros del pais, verificada en los años de 1788 a 1790, con el objeto de crear y fijar los límites de las Diputaciones, examinar el estado de las labores mineras, trapiches, fundiciones y conocer las necesidades premiosas para fomentar el desarrollo de la Minería en Chile. Hay expedientes análogos pero de menor importancia correspondientes a los últimos años del período colonial como asimismo litigios entre partes.

Complemento de este archivo por la materia que contienen son los volúmenes 228 a 279 de la Capitanía General, formados por pedimentos y juicios de minas, tramitados antes de la creación del tribunal especial.

Aparte de su utilidad para conocer el desarrollo de la Minería en Chile, este archivo ofrece un campo inexplotado y lucrativo, como base para organizar exploraciones mineras en antiguos y tal vez ricos asientos que permanecen abandonados o desconocidos al presente.

Archivo del Tribunal del Consulado.—Contiene documentos y expedientes tramitados en este Tribunal, creado en cumplimiento de una Real Orden, fechada en 28 de marzo de 1795, para propender al desenvolvimiento del comercio y conocer los asuntos netamente comerciales.

Archivo de la Contaduría Mayor.—En este voluminoso archivo se guarda cuanto se relaciona con el cobro o inversión de las rentas de la Real Hacienda. Contiene algunos documentos del siglo XVI, y es muy abundante en los de los siglos siguientes hasta 1840, año en que concluye la parte guardada en la Biblioteca Nacional.

En realidad está formado por no menos de una veintena de archivos diversos, de otras tantas oficinas o repartimientos administrativos entre los cuales son los principales los de las Tesorerías de Santiago y Concepción; de las Aduanas de Valparaíso, Copiapó, Huasco, Coquimbo, Constitución, Talcahuano, Valdivia y Chiloé; el de la Casa de Moneda, el de la Renta de Tabacos y construcciones de obras públicas, puentes, tajamares, etc.

Históricamente considerada, la documentación más valiosa es la que se refiere a los ejércitos, tanto realista como patriota, que pelearon en la guerra de la Independencia. Las listas de revista permitirán reconstituir ambos ejércitos, conocer las efectivos que combatieron en las batallas, las bajas que tuvieron, y hasta las nombres de los muertes o heridos. Otros documentos dan noticias del armamentos, revelan detalles, permiten rehacer las hojas de servicios, y hasta descubrir a veces los planes militares.

Como la rendición de las cuentas era muy prolija, se hallan como comprobantes de las partidas de ingreso o egreso copias íntegras de memoriales o títulos de mercedes o nombramientos en los cuales constan los servicios de los agraciados; de los documentos que acreditaban la calidad de extranjeros de los que debían pagar el derecho de extranjería, los pormenores de la pruducción de los obrajes de jarcías, paños, frazadas, etc., para el aprovisionamiento del ejército y muchos otros comprobantes de índole muy diversa pero susceptibles de ser utilizados en investigaciones especiales, sobre la inmigración extranjera y desarrollo de las industrias en el período colonial; desenvolvimiento del comercio de importación y exportación después de la Independencia y en general de los temas que se relacionan con la economía política.

Archivo de Copias de Indias.—Formado por copias de documentos referentes a Chile guardados en el Archivo de Indias de Sevilla, descubiertos en las búsquedas de los señores Vicuña Mackenna, Medina y Morlá Vicuña y otros investigadores nacionales. Algunos han sido publicados en la Colección de Documentos Inéditos del señor Medina, en el Estudio Histórico del señor Morla Vicuña, y en diversas obras del señor Vicuña Mackenna, pero la mayor parte no ha sido aprovechada todavía para ahondar el estudio de la historia patria.

Archivo de Eyzaguirre.—Encierra papeles de muy diversas materias, aunque predominan los de carácter religioso. Entre éstos se cuentan los expedientes sobre las visitas episcopales del obispo Alday a la diócesis de Santiago y del obispo Marán a la de Concepción; el recurso interpuesto por Rodríguez Zorrilla contra el Cabildo eclesiástico de Santiago en 1808, y papeles tocantes al obispo de Epifania.

Entre las obras más interesantes se pueden citar las relaciones de los viajes del Padre Mascardi a las regiones de Nahuelhuapi, 1667–1672, y de don Luis de la Cruz desde Concepción a Buenos Aires, 1806; los originales de las historias de Córdoba y Figueroa y de Rodríguez Ballesteros y un "Diario" de los sucesos ocurridos en Santiago en los años de 1765–1773, escrito por don Fernando Antonio de los Ríos, Vice-Rector de la Universidad de San Felipe.

Pero los papeles más importantes de este archivo son los pertinentes al período de la guerra de la Independencia y entre éstos sobresale un tomo de decretos originales de las Juntas Gubernativas, correspondientes a los años 1810–1816, y, por último, dentro del período republicano, el proceso instruido al Almirante Blanco Encalada, en 1821.

Archivo de la Inquisición.—Comprende casi exclusivamente los papeles tocantes a la parte económica del tribunal del Santo Oficio, como ser remates de los bienes de los condenados, ejecuciones y cobranzas de las deudas que otras personas reconocían por censos u otros motivos a favor del mismo tribunal; existen, sin embargo, copias de cartas o comunicaciones con otros tribunales españoles.

La sede del Tribunal de la Inquisición era Lima, pero su jurisdicción abarcaba toda la costa del Pacífico, desde Panamá de manera que la Capitanía General de Chile estaba dentro de los límites asignados a este tribunal.

El estudio de la documentación arrojaría mucha luz sobre el comercio colonial, y los procedimientos inquisitoriales en asuntos financieros que la competían. También serán provechosos para abordar el problema de la inmigración hebrea a la América latina, y las persecuciones de que fueron objeto sus miembros, sobre todo los judíos portugueses con quienes fue implacable la pesquisa y castigo inquisitoriales.

Archivo de los Jesuítas.—Esta valiosa colección perteneció a don Antonio de Paz, oficial de la Biblioteca Nacional de Madrid, a quien se la compró el Gobierno de Chile, por intermedio de don Carlos Morla Vicuña, a la sazón Secretario de la legación de Chile en Francia, quien en informe fechado en Sevilla el 24 de agosto de 1876 escribía lo siguiente:

La collección de manuscritos que existe en poder del Señor Paz, consiste en su mayor parte de originales pertenecientes a los Jesuitas de Hispano-América desde Méjico hasta Chile. Estos documentos que fueron trasladados a la Península en 1767, inmediatamente después de la expulsión de la Compañía de Jesús de aquel continente, estuvieron archivados en un departamento del Ministerio de Gracia y Justicia, llamado de las Temporalidades, que fue desbaratado durante la última revolución. Los papeles fueron vendidos al peso a bodegones y pulperías, y se hallaban ya en vía de completa destrucción, cuando en Señor Don M. Javier Bravo, español residente en Buenos Ayres, que se encontraba accidentalmente en Madrid, tuvo noticia de su existencia y los adquirió. El Señor Bravo devolvió parte de la colección al Gobierno español y emprendió la publicación de lo restante. No hallándose preparado por estudios anteriores para este género de trabajos, el Señor Bravo no tuvo éxito en su empresa, y hubo de dejar la colección de manuscritos referida de la que quedaba debiendo a sus colaboradores literarios y al editor de los dos primeros volúmenes de la publicación.

Esta colección es la que fue ofrecida en venta al Supremo Gobierno por mi intermedio hace dos años, y la que el Señor Ministro de Relaciones Exteriores autorizó a V. S. [el Ministro de Chile en Francia] para adquirir, si lo juzgaba conveniente. Hasta hoy no se había tomado resolución en este particular, porque no habiendo habido ocasión de examinar personalmente los manuscritos, se ignoraba su calidad y si valían o no el gasto que iba a demandar su adquisición.

Como he dicho a V. S. antes, esta vez he tenido oportunidad para examinar la mencionada colección por mí mismo. Está contenida en diez enormes baúles, y separada en cajas de cartón figurando volúmenes, siguiendo la distribución el órden de las diversas secciones en que estuvo dividida la América Colonial. Esta clasificación permitiría formar un catálogo completo, papel por papel y legajo por legajo, de todo el contenido, sin gran dificultad ni empleo de tiempo y facilitaría la entrega de la colección para el uso público.

La sección correspondiente a Chile, aun cuando de las menos abundantes, se compone de muy interesantes documentos que a cualquiera costa debiera de adquirirse para la Biblioteca Nacional de Santiago. Hay entre ellos, cartas originales de los Padres Luis de Valdivia, Gaspar Sobrino, Luis del Castillo, Antonio y Gonzalo de Covarrubias, Diego Rosales, Alonso de Ovalle, &c, todos varones famosos en nuestros anales históricos, los unos como misioneros y pacificadores y los otros como cronistas chilenos. La parte de esta sección que se refiere a la guerra defensiva, con que, a proposición del Padre Valdivia se emprendió en 1610 la reducción de los Araucanos, es completísima bajo el punto de vista de los Padres misioneros, y aún hay entre sus papeles muchas de las informaciones adversas y críticas que hacían al nuevo plan los jefes militares que deseaban la continuación de la guerra activa. En esta misma sección se encuentran todos los documentos referentes a las propiedades rurales y urbanas que tuvo en Chile la Compañía de Jesús, con sus escrituras y planos, muchos de ellos coloreados, anexos. La falta de estos documentos ha producido en Chile, según ha llegado a mi noticia, mas de un litigio sobre deslindes de haciendas, y su existencia en la Biblioteca Nacional, aún cuando no hubiera de servir para dirimir cuestiones semejantes, sería siempre muy útil en un sentido meramente literario e histórico. No es menos considerable el número de cartas y expedientes relativos a los colegios, iglesias y misiones que los Jesuitas tenían a su cargo en todo la extensión del pais.

Las secciones de la colección correspondientes al Perú y al Paraguay que incluía las Provincias de Tucumán y Río de la Plata, según la distribución de Provincias de los Jesuitas, tienen indudablemente muchísimos documentos que interesan igualmente a Chile y que serían de cierto valor en la presente cuestión de límites de cuyo estudio me hallo encargado.

Las partes que corresponden al Brasil, al Vireinato de Santa Fé y a Méjico son ya mas ajenas a Chile y no le interesan sino por una que otra incidencia directa, pues muchos de los religiosos que se distinguían en Chile solían ir a continuar sus trabajos en esas regiones y vice-versa; pero estas como las otras tienen intrínsecamente su valor para la historia de los paises referidos y a caso sea la de Méjico la mas rica.

La colección entera se compone de trece mil piezas mas o menos, entendiéndose por pieza documentos y expedientes muchos de los cuales son voluminosos.

Todavía agrega en nota el señor Morla Vicuña estas otras noticias:

Esta colección fue adquirida por el Estado, y ha sido remitida a Chile. Yo emprendí su organización documento por documento, y aún hice el catálogo detallado de una parte considerable de ellos, pero en esta tarea, como en la del estudio de la cuestion de límites, fuí interrumpido por las exigencias de la última guerra [del Pacífico].   Conviene, sin embargo, que se imprima lo que hay hecho del catálogo, y será cosa sencilla el continuar en Santiago el arreglo y clasificación.   La colección que se hallaba en poder del Señor Pas ha sido completado con varias otras partidas de papeles pertenecientes al mismo archivo, que se hallaban en manos de libreros revendedores de Madrid.   Los manuscritos procedentes de las casas que tenían los Jesuitas en España, y que no se refieren a América se hallan desde hace años en poder de los eruditos Señores Zabalburu, y estos con nuestra colección y los documentos escogidos regalados por el Señor Bravo a le Academia de la Historia de Madrid, constituyen todo lo que queda de los archivos secuestrados a la Compañía de Jesús cuando fué suprimida.[1]

A lo expuesto por el señor Morla Vicuña conviene agregar que la mayor parte de los papeles de esta colección son posteriores a la expulsión de los Jesuítas de los dominios españoles, y consisten en los autos formados para dar cumplimiento a la órden de extrañamiento, en los inventarios y remates o administración de los bienes secuestrados y constancia de los pagos de las pensiones a los religiosos expulsos, algunos de los cuales vivían todavía cuando sobrevino la emancipación americana; encierra por tanto documentación correspondiente a todo el período colonial, y no solo de las colonias hispano-americanas sino también de Filipinas, Canarias y aún de algunas casas de la misma España.

Cuando el archivo llegó a la Biblioteca Nacional este establecimiento carecía todavía de un taller de encuadernación, de manera que era menester enviar a talleres particulares los libros y manuscritos para hacerlos empastar.   Esto motivó una pérdida casi irreparable de unos cuarenta volúmenes que resultaron semi-destruidos en un incendio que ocurrió en la encuadernación donde se realizaba ese trabajo.

El número total de volúmenes inclusos los deteriorados era de 498; pero a fin de facilitar la consulta se reuniéron dos o mas libros de cuentas en un solo volúmen, disminuyendo en 18 la suma total, que se distribuye de la siguiente manera:

Chile	Volúmenes numerados de 1 a 136A
España	137 a 150
España, Canarias y Filipinas	151
Italia (sobre las pensiones)	152 y 153
Bolivia	154–170 y 436 y 437
Perú	171 a 232
República Argentina	233 a 298

[1] C. Morla Vicuña, *Estudio Histórico sobre el Descubrimiento y Conquista de la Patagonia y de la Tierra del Fuego*, pags. 34 y 35.

Méjico . . . . Volúmenes numerados de 299 a 380
Paraguay . . . . 381 y 382
Quito . . . . 383 a 396
Bogotá . . . . 397 a 419
Panamá 420
Antillas . . . . 421 a 425
Filipinas . . . . 426 a 428
Varios . . . . 429 a 435
Semi-quemados en el incendio . . 42 volúmenes guardados en ca-
torce cajas.

Aparte de la nomenclatura anacrónica, esta clasificación adolece indudablemente de un grave yerro cometido al no conservar la antigua separación de los documentos pertenecientes a cada Virreinato y Capitanías Generales de ellos dependientes, de manera que el investigador debe tener presente tal división geográfica de la América, para no exponerse a un posible fracaso, como le ocurría sin duda a quien se limitase a revisar los volúmenes 381 y 382 para recoger noticias del Paraguay y prescindiese de los sesenta y cinco referentes a la República Argentina.

El archivo de los Jesuítas ha sido utilizado por diversas repúblicas en las defensas de sus derechos en los litigios que han sostenido con los paises vecinos sobre cuestiones de límites.

. Está también llamado a servir de provechosa fuente de información para la etnografía americana, tanto para fijar las regiones donde vivía cada pueblo, como también por la abundancia de nombres indígenas geográficos o personales que se conservan en esos papeles.

Los inventarios de las bibliotecas, de los enseres y semovientes de las estancias, el número de los esclavos y de los bienes muebles en general, todo ofrece un vasto campo para la investigación histórica, que permitirá conocer mejor no solo la actuación tan discutida de la Compañía de Jesús sino también el grado de desarrollo de la sociedad colonial.

Archivo de los Escribanos.—Comienza con un fragmento del registro del escribano Pedro de Salcedo del año 1559; le sigue un volumen de Juan de la Peña, 1564-1566; otros fragmentos de los protocolos de Alonso del Castillo 1578, 1579, 1580, 1593 y 1594 y desde 1585 hasta 1800 siguen ya los registros sin solución de continuidad, aún cuando faltan uno que otro protocolo de algunos de los varios escribanos que desempeñaban al mismo tiempo sus funciones.

Aparte de los protocolos de Santiago, existe un volumen con fragmentos de registros de diversos notarios de Concepción que actuaron entre los años de 1769 y 1843.

El número total de las escrituras excede tal vez de 200,000 y su contenido suministra el más vivo y fiel cuadro de lo que fué Chile y de lo que fueron nuestros mayores en pasados siglos. La variación de las costumbres sobre todo es fácil de comprobar y aún de seguir su evolución examinando esos documentos.

Los testamentos eran más comunes que hoy y en ellos nadie dejaba de encomendar su alma a Dios y a los santos, de hacer protestas de fe; algunos añadían datos minuciosos sobre su vida o su progenie y muchas declaraciones por demás curiosas. El testamento más extenso es el del Maestre de Campo General Jerónimo de Quiroga, otorgado en 1716 y consta de 141 páginas.

Las cartas de dotes, o sea la constancia del caudal que de ordinario entregaban los padres o deudos de la novia al marido al tiempo de celebrarse el matrimonio, son asimismo muy numerosas y recuerdan una costumbre que ha caido ya en total desuso.

Entre las escrituras curiosas conviene recordar las promesas de no jugar, de no hacer préstamos u otras semejantes, en que el otorgante se imponía no solo multa a beneficio del denunciante, de la Real Hacienda o de alguna institución religiosa, sino que también se condenaba a sí mismo a sufrir una prisión por un tiempo señalado; las escrituras de perdón de algun delito, extendidas por lo común previo arreglo pecuniario entre los interesados; los testimonios de acontecimientos reputados como milagrosos; las "exclamaciones", instrumentos en que los firmantes declaraban haber suscrito otras escrituras contra su voluntad y a los que por consiguiente les negaban todo valor o efecto; los "asientos" o contratos de servicios domésticos y sobre otra variedad de asuntos.

En el Archivo de los Escribanos se puede observar el desenvolvimiento de la sociedad, la evolución de las costumbres, el progreso de la industria y del comercio y en general, de la Colonia misma.

Archivo de la Real Audiencia.—Este tribunal se estableció primativamente en Concepción en 1568; suprimido en 1575; fué restablecido en Santiago en 1609, donde funcionó hasta 1817, exceptuando un corto período de la Patria Vieja, 1811–1814.

Existen, sin embargo, en este archivo expedientes antiguos desde 1552, otros varios iniciados asimismo en el siglo XVI, documentos en copia desde 1544 y originales desde 1550; pero la gran mayoría de las piezas son posteriores a la creación de la Audiencia de Santiago.

Como la esfera de acción de la Real Audiencia era mucho mayor que la de los actuales tribunales de Justicia, ejerciendo además funciones fiscalizadoras sobre las demás autoridades del país, se han en este archivo muchos expedientes, sobre competencias de jurisdicción, aplicación de leyes o reglamentos, cuestiones de etiquetas, recursos de fuerza, etc. Pero entre todos los de mayor interés para la historia son los juicios de residencia, que como se sabe, se instruían a los Presidentes y Capitanes Generales, Corregidores y demás autoridades subalternas al cesar en sus funciones, y en los que después de oir los cargos que le hacián los agraviados, y los descargos del funcionario cesante se le condenaba o absolvía según el mérito que arrojasen los autos.

La materia de los procesos y juicios entre partes no difieren, como es fácil presumirlo, de los que se promueven ahora. Hay, sin embargo, muchos expedientes seguidos entre esclavos o indios y sus amos o encomenderos, por malos tratamientos y otros agravios que les inferían, los que son provechosos para conocer las relaciones de las diversas castas entre sí y las leyes que protegían a las inferiores contra los abusos del peninsular.

El número aproximado y de las piezas que contiene es de 14,000 clasificadas como sigue:

Pleitos civiles ordinarios	10,200
Expedientes de valor histórico	2,200
Expedientes sobre encomiendas de indios, esclavos, etc. . .	700
Expedientes en materia criminal	600
Expedientes sobre minas	300

Completan este archivo una colección de reales provisiones, sentencias de vista o revista expedidas por la Real Audiencia durante todo el tiempo que funcionó. Esta serie de papeles que forman hasta el presente mas de 60 volúmenes y quedan todavía muchos otros por ordenar es particularmente interesante por cuanto se hallan noticias de muchos expedientes pérdidos y a veces la síntesis completa, con inserción de los documentos principales en las sentencias pronunciadas por el Tribunal.

Archivo Vicuña Mackenna.—Como acontece con frecuencia en colecciones particulares la composición de esta es heterogénea, componiéndola principalmente apuntes y borradores originales del señor Vicuña Mackenna; su archivo y correspondencia particular; una serie de copias tomadas en el Archivo de Indias; documentos y cartas sobre los principales acontecimientos políticos ocurridos en Chile y de las personajes que actuaron en ellos; nultitud de recortes de diarios o revistas; expedientes coloniales, etc.

Sobresalen por su valor los archivos que pertenecieron a los Padres de la Patria Generales don Bernardo O'Higgins y don José Miguel

Carrera y el manuscrito original de la Historia de Chile del Padre Diego Rosales.

Archivo Morla Vicuña.—Consta principalmente de dos grandes grupos de papeles, a saber: los borradores autográficos de don Claudio Gay, los documentos originales y las copias de otros coleccionadas por el mismo señor Gay para escribir su *Historia de Chile;* y las copias tomadas en España por don Carlos Morla Vicuña para su *Estudio Histórico sobre el descubrimiento y conquista de la Patagonia y de la Tierra del Fuego* y sobre todo para la defensa de los derechos de Chile en la cuestión de límites con la República Argentina.

El archivo está distribuido en la forma siguiente:

Manuscrito de la Historia de Chile, de Gay	Vols. 1 a 7
Manuscritos antiguos originales	" 8 a 40
Manuscritos antiguos y apuntes tomados por Gay	" 41 y 42
Copias de documentos, reunidas por Gay	" 43 a 53
Copia de la Relación Geográfica e Hidrográfica del Reino de Chile enviada al Rey por el Presidente don Manual de Amat en 1761	54
Documentos Geográficos sobre Chile	55
Copias y extractos de papeles antiguos sobre Chile	" 56
Copias de antiguos cronistas e historiadores de Chile, Pineda Bascuñan, Córdoba y Figueroa, Olivares, Péres García, Martines, etc.	" 57 a 65
Copias de "Diarios de Navegación"	66
Copia de la Historia del Reino de Chile por Fray Antonio Lors, 1780	67
Copia del Diario político de don José Miguel Carrera	68
Copia de la Historia de lu revolución de Chile, por fray Melchor Martínes	69
Atlas con cartas geográficas de Chile	70
Papeles originales sobre el gobierno de la isla de Juan Fernández, 1832–1834	" 71
Copias de documentos del Archivo de Indias	" 72 a 123
Relación original sobre la navegación del Río Bermejo, 1790	" 124
Memoria del Virrey de Buenos Aires Marqués de Loreto, 1790	125

Archivo de la Guerra del Pacífico.—Formado casi en su totalidad por la documentación del Estado Mayor del ejército peruano; que cayó en poder de los chilenos a fines de 1879. Es el complemento de la documentación y de mucha utilidad para juzgar con mayor acierto e imparcialidad sobre la primera etapa del conflicto internacional.

Se distribuye como sigue:

Notas oficiales, abril a noviembre 1879 . . . . . . Vols. 1 a 7
Asuntos reservados . . . . " 8
Ordenes generales a la Reserva . . . . " 9
Estados diarios de las fuerzas, altas, bajas, etc. . . . " 10 a 13
Cuentas sobre aprovisionamiento, gastos de hospitales
    militares, etc . . . . " 14 a 17
Copiador de instrucciones, decretos y pasaportes . . . " 18
General en Jefe y Comandantes Generales de división . " 19
Comunicaciones con diversas autoridades . . . . . " 20
Correspondencia General . . . . " 21 y 22
Mesa de partes (Indice alfabético de individuos del ejér-
    cito y de noticias a ellos pertinentes) . . . . . . " 23
Copias de Comunicaciones telegráficas 24
Parque General y su delegación 25
Provisión General y sus dependenciás 26
Comisaría General y su delegación 27
Correspondencia de la Comandancia General Naval . . " 28
Altas y bajas de armamento 29
Diario de Bitácora del monitor Huascar, desde abril de
    1879 hasta su captura en el combate de Angamos, 8 de
    octubre del mismo año 30
Diario de la campaña comenzada el día 16 de mayo de
    1879, contra Chile, a bordo del monitor Huascar, escrito
    por el teniente 2° don Jorge F. Velarde. Este marino
    pereció en el combate de Iquique (21 de mayo de 1879)
    y siguió el Diario hasta el 29 del mismo mes el teniente
    2° graduado don Pedro Gárezon 31
Diario del capitan de fragata de la marina chilena don
    Manuel Thompson, de marzo a junio de 1879 . . . 32
Diario de navegación del aspirante don Ernesto Riquelme, a
    bordo de la *Esmeralda* y *Covadonga* 1874–1875. Riquelme
    fue uno de los heroes de la epopeya de Iquique y la
    Esmeralda y la *Covadonga* las naves chilenas que en
    ella tomaron parte 33

Archivo Judicial de Concepción.—Compuesto por juicios criminales y civiles, contiene algunos procesos por conspiraciones subversivas que peuden interesar para la historia política; comienza en 1810 y alcanza hasta 1854.

Archivos de las Intendencias de Concepción y Biobío.—El primero corresponde a los años de 1819 a 1840 y el segundo a los de 1829 a 1875, y ambos son netamente administrativos. En el de Concepción se hallan sin embargo algunos documentos tocantes a la campaña de Chiloé que concluyó allí con la dominación española en 1826.

Copias de la Oficina Hidrográfica.—Son copias de documentos tocantes a la historia náutica, que en gran parte corren impresos en el Anuario Hidrográfico de la Marina de Chile.

Archivo de la Gobernación De Angol.—También es archivo moderno, de carácter administrativo, que puede servir para estudiar cuestiones relacionadas con los indios y su pacificación definitiva.

Archivo del Cabildo de la Serena.—Comienza en el año 1680 y concluye en 1818, pero existen además algunos documentos anteriores y posteriores a los años indicados. La clasificación de las materias de los papeles es la que sigue:

Volúmenes 1 a 3—Actas del Cabildo	. . . .	1778–1800
" 4 a 9—Cédulas, bandos, etc	. . . .	1698–1823
" 10 y 11—Reales provisiones	. . . .	1680–1813
" 12 y 13—Visitas de indios	. . . .	1692–1792
" 14 y 16—Causas civiles	. . . .	1682–1818
" 17—Causas criminales	. . . .	1720–1813
" 18 a 21—Expedientes sobre minas	. . . . .	1714–1812
" 22 a 25—Oficios y comunicaciones diversas	. .	1780–1814
" 26—Hospital	. . . .	1740–1816
" 27—Sobre milicias	. . . .	1775–1814
" 28—Asuntos tocantes a los indios	. . .	1690–1811
" 29 a 31—Materias de Gobierno	. . . . . .	1600–1808
" 32—Rentas de Balanza y Propios	. . . .	1810–1817
" 33—Rentas del Estanco	. . . .	1755–1813
" 34 Expedientes sobre tierras	. . . . .	1790–1817
" 35—Copias de diferentes escrituras	. . .	1716–1892
" 36—Libro de recibos de San Agustín		

Este archivo contiene sin duda algunos papeles útiles para completar la historia de varios incidentes de la guerra de la Independencia; pero los más importantes son los que se refieren a los indígenas, por relacionarse con la etnología chilena muy poco estudiada y que en Coquimbo reviste mayor interés por haber estado sometido sus habitantes a la influencia de culturas americanas diversas por el norte y este y probablemente también por el sur.

Manuscritos Diversos.—Son dignos de mención entre estos documentos un mapa o croquis de Chile, dibujado en España en 1768, por don Ambrosio O'Higgins, después Presidente de Chile y Virrey del Perú, con el objeto de dar una idea del número y ubicación de las propiedades de los Jesuítas expulsos; un "Antiguo Testamento" al que don J. Sylvester, profesor de idiomas y de hebreo en el colegio rabínico de Varsovia, calculó una antigüedad de mil años, basándose en la alteración del color del pergamino, desgaste de los hilos, o cuerdas de violín,

de las costuras y en los carácteres muy imperfectos de la escritura,
según lo expresó en un informe de fecha 30 de agosto de 1875; y dos
planos, levantados en 1760 por órden del Virrey del Perú don Manuel
de Amat, y que contienen un proyecto de irrigación de los valles de
Arica y Tarapacá.

Estos últimos podrán quizás servir de base para un estudio sobre
una posible modificación de las condiciones meteorológicas y climatéricas
de esas provincias, porque hay marcadas regiones "que eran cultivadas
antes cuando llovia" y otras que lo eran todavía en 1760 y que sin
embargo son ahora estériles. Los datos consignados en esos planos
concuerdan con los que existen en la parroquía de Iquique en expedientes encaminados a refrenar los desórdenes e inmoralidades de que
eran teatro esas regiones en tiempo de las cosechas. Existen además
otros indicios y aún fundamentos para creer que las condiciones inhos-
pitalarias de los desiertos del norte de Chile han empeorado en los
cuatro últimos siglos, pero esa materia no puede dilucidarse en este
artículo.

Entre los otros manuscritos se peuden recordar "El Vasauro", poema
inédito del licenciado Pedro de Oña, el más antiguo de los poetas chilenos, nacido en Angol en 1570; y la Historia de la provincia dd Chiloé
bajo la dominación española, escrita en cuatro volúmenes, y que dejó
inconclusa don Abraham de Silva, muerto prematuramente en diciembre
de 1908.

III. DISPOSICIONES, FACILIDADES, Y CATÁLOGOS PARA LA CONSULTA DE LA SECCIÓN

El título VIII del Reglamento de le Biblioteca Nacional decretado
el 12 de Junio de 1890, se refiere a la Sección de Manuscritos y tocante
a la consulta de los documentos contiene estas disposiciones:

Art. 17.—Son obligaciones del Jefe de esta sección:

1ª. Facilitar a los lectores los manuscritos que soliciten, prévia entrega de un
recibo firmado en que se exprese la fecha de la solicitud, el número del volúmen,
el archivo a que pertenece y el domicilio del solicitante;

2ª. Cuidar que las personas que sacan copias o apuntes no deterioren o man-
chen los manuscritos escribiendo sobre ellos o haciéndoles cualquiera clase de
señales.

. . . .

Art. 18.—No se podrán sacar de los manuscritos especialmente reservados sin
permiso del Director.

Art. 19.—La serie de manuscritos reservados constará de un índice formado
por el Director y aprobado por el Ministro de Instrución Pública.

Art. 20.—Los jóvenes menores de 20 años no podrán ser admitidos en esta
sección en calidad de lectores.

Dentro de estas disposiciones se procura dar al público todas las facilidades para que pueda trabajar con mayor provecho y comodidad. La catalogación de los manuscritos es deficiente todavía; pero la subdivisión de los archivos y el ordenamiento cronológico de algunos de ellos simplifica y acelera de ordinario la investigación.

El mejor de los catálogos existentes y que servirá de modelo para los futuros es el del archivo de la Real Audiencia. Adolece tal vez del defecto de ser demasiado voluminoso por el tipo de letra muy grande usado en la impresión, pero en cambio es fácil de manejar. Consta de tres tomos, que comprenden 6210 piezas, contenidas en los volúmenes numerados de 1 a 2100 inclusive.

Como la mayor parte de las piezas son juicios entre partes se han colocado las descripciones de ellas por el órden alfabético de los apellidos de los demandantes, o de la persona, funcionario, o corporación a quien interese principalmente o se refiera la pieza catalogada. Se añaden además citas, o llamadas, con los nombres de los demandados y notas debajo de la descripción principal en que se mencionan los documentos principales, reales cédulas, mercedes y planos de mensuras de tierras, cartas dotales, testamentos o poderes para testar, y en general de aquellos de valor histórico y que sin ese procedimiento sería difícil descubrir, y de todos se hacen asimismo llamadas en el órden alfabético indicado. La trascripción que sigue dará a comprender mejor el procedimiento seguido:

ALHUÉ (Tierras de).—Véase *Merced* (Convento de la), No. 1000.

GUZMÁN (Beatriz de).—Véase *Merced* (Convento de la), No. 1000.

1000   MERCED (Convento de la).—Juicio seguido con Guzmán (Beatriz de), sobre mejor derecho a las tierras del valle de *Alhué*. 1634–1643.

Vol. 310.—309 hojas.—La primera parte de este juicio se encuentra en la . pieza 2ª del volumen 599.

Contiene el testamento de don Rodrigo de Quiroga (24 de febrero de 1580); y una merced, en copia, hecha por don Pedro de Valdivia a favor de doña Inés Suárez de las tierras del valle de Alhué (11 de julio de 1546).

QUIROGA (Rodrigo de).—Véase *Merced* (Convento de la), No. 1000.

SUÁREZ (Inés).—Véase *Merced* (Convento de la), No. 1000.

VALDIVIA (Pedro de).—Véase Merced (Convento de la), No. 1000.

Como se ve, esta pieza tiene cinco referencias, y quien busque noticias de las personas mencionadas, o de las tierras en litigio, o en general de la historia de esa época tiene a su alcance los datos que necesita para orientar la investigación.

El catálogo del archivo de los Jesuitas referente a Chile, está confeccionado de una manera análoga, pero contiene una doble referencia a los páginas del volúmen y hojas de que consta la pieza, lo que suele entorpecer el manejo, para quien no está habituado a consultar ese índice. Las referencias se hallan escritas en la forma que sigue: 1797. Vol. 86, p. 10, pág. 263 hojas 19; o sea; ano 1797; volúmen 86, pieza 10ᵃ, página 263, del volumen y en la que comienza la pieza; 19 hojas, son las que forman el manuscrito.

El catálogo de la Capitanía General es más bien un inventario, y no completo, de las piezas que contiene cada volumen. Con todo, aunque su consulta sea más lenta e insegura que la de los catálogos de la Real Audiencia y de los Jesuítas, su revisión facilita mucho la investigación. Se ha comenzado además la catalogación minuciosa de este archivo, con muy buen resultado, pues los primeros setenta volúmenes han dado más de 2,000 piezas, o sea un 40 por ciento mas de las 1245 que constan en el índice actual, sin las referencias que de seguro excederán de 3,000. Diferencia tan grande se debe a que el primer trabajo hubo de realizarse en un corto plazo, dentro del cual era imposible catalogar multitud de solicitudes y pequeños expedientes de una, dos o tres fojas de extensión, pero que exigía cada uno tanto tiempo como un voluminoso legajo, los que por este motivo quedaron englobados bajo el rubro de primera, segunda, o tercera serie de papeles diversos.

El catálogo del archivo Vicuña Mackenna es también un mero inventario, con algunos comentarios sobre el valor de ciertos documentos. Consta de 229 páginas en 4° a dos columnas y puede revisarse con rapidez porque está subdividido en series de papeles de muy diversa naturaleza y que nadie ha de revisar al mismo tiempo, como puede comprobarse comparando algunas de las principales que se indican a continuación.

Vols. 33 a 35—La revolución del 20 de abril de 1851.
" 42 a 44—La Guerra a muerte. 1819–1820.
" 47 a 50—La revolución de 1859.
" 85 á 112—Archivo del General O'Higgins.
" 113 a 122—Archivo del General Carrera.
" 195 a 221—Campaña contra el Perú y Bolivia. 1837–1839.
" 222 a 255—Campaña contra el Perú y Bolivia, 1879–1883; y otros sucesos
 referentes a ese período.
" 265 a 304—Copias de documentos del Archivo de Indias de Simancas,
 1532–1700.

Para facilitar la consulta del archivo de los Escribanos se ha impreso una "Guía" en la que se enumeran los testamentos y poderes para testar, las cartas de dotes y algunos otros documentos de especial interés. La parte publicada ya comprende hasta el volumen 591, pero se continua la impresión de lo restante. Además muchos de los volúmenes tienen índice de las escrituras que contienen, de manera que la revisión o búsqueda de documentos no ofrece gran dificultad.

De los demás archivos sólo existen inventarios manuscritos y aun algunos carecen de ellos por no ser posible su confección sin ordenar previamente los papeles que contienen y que ingresaron a la Sección completamente revueltos.

Próxima a ser trasladada provisionalmente al nuevo edificio de la Biblioteca Nacional, mientras se construye el extenso y cómodo local que con tal objeto se levantará al costado poniente del mencionado palacio de la Biblioteca, la Sección de Manuscritos quedará organizada definitivamente en poco tiempo más, en condiciones que le permitan eliminar los defectos de que adolece ahora y experimentar sin tropiezos el ensanche de sus servicios, consiguiente a su violento desarrollo a causa de los nuevos archivos que recibirá entonces, y que la convertirán en uno de los más ricos, sino en el más valioso, de los archivos históricos de la América hispánica.

Tomás Thayer Ojeda,
Jefe de la Sección de Manuscritos
de la Biblioteca Nacional de Santiago de Chile.

[TRANSLATION]

THE MANUSCRIPTS SECTION OF THE BIBLIOTECA NACIONAL OF CHILE

I. ITS ORIGIN AND DEVELOPMENT

By virtue of a special law, the government of Chile, in 1846, acquired the library of the illustrious patriot, Don Mariano Egaña. A portion of this library consisted of a collection of manuscripts treating of the most varied matters, which served later as a base for the creation of the Manuscripts Section of the Biblioteca Nacional. This was the sixth section of the above institution at the time of the enactment of the Ordinance of August 8, 1861.

A few years later, in 1867, the collection consisted of six hundred pieces distributed in 113 volumes, to wit: 48 folio volumes, 60 quarto, and 5 octavo.

In May, 1876, there was added to the Biblioteca Nacional the private library of Monseñor Don José Ignacio Victor Eyzaguirre, which contained, in addition to 4,000 books, a collection of documents which the erudite and progressive priest bequeathed to the above mentioned institution.

In succession there were added to these collections another series of papers used by Don Claudio Gay in writing his *Historia General de Chile;* the books and expedientes of cases in the tribunal of the *Consulado;* and the archives of the general staff of the Peruvian army relative to the first stage of the war of the Pacific, which had come into the possession of the Chilean army in 1879.

In July, 1885, a wellknown journalist and an active investigator of the national history, Don Justo Abel Rosales, published an extensive article, bristling with facts, in which he pleaded for the creation of a real Manuscripts Section, in which should be housed the several historical archives scattered about in various public offices. Until that time the Biblioteca Nacional had only 116 volumes of manuscripts of the Fondo Antiguo, 12 volumes of Royal cédulas, many of which were printed, and 223 legajos of unbound and uncatalogued documents from the archives of Eyzaguirre, the *Consulado,* the War of the Pacific, the Inquisition, and the Jesuits, which represent, at the most some 1250 volumes more, valuable beyond any doubt, but at that time almost impossible of consultation.

In spite of its creation, the Manuscripts Section led a languid existence until a new director of the library, in 1886, namely, Don Luis Montt, gave it a vigorous impulse. Thanks to his efforts, the following collections were joined to it: the Archives of the old Capitanía General, the transfer of which was ordered by a supreme decree of September 25 of that year; the Registers of the Notaries of Santiago; the Archives of the Royal Audiencia, of the Contaduría Mayor, of the Intendencies of Bíobío and part of the Judicial district of Concepción. At that time the manuscript collection of the famous Chilean author and politician, Don Benjamin Vicuña Mackenna was also acquired, as well as the archives of Don Carlos Morla Vicuña, which were presented by his widow, and another series of documents scattered about here and there in the possession of private persons.

Señor Montt, who united with his vast bibliographical erudition, his interest in the study of our national history, thus gave practical form to what he was wont to repeat frequently as an aphorism, namely, "There is no such a thing as a useless paper", and his elevated judgment successfully prevailed over the judgment of those persons who were of the opinion that some of those rich archives ought to be destroyed as now totally lacking in value.

Señor Montt must, therefore, be considered to be the real creator of the Section, in that he worked not only as an investigator but also in the revision of the catalogues and even in the arrangement itself of the papers.

Upon the death of Señor Montt in 1910, the Manuscripts Section already had 12,500 volumes, distributed in the following form:

Archives	Volumes
Old archives of the Library	198
Capitanía General	1,045
Collection of cédulas	104
Consulado	50
Mining tribunal	14
Contaduría Mayor	5,000
Copies of manuscripts from Archivo de Indias	63
Eyzaguirre	60
Inquisition	600
Jesuits	467
Notaries (1559–1800)	976
Royal Audiencia	3,098
Vicuña Mackenna	336
Morla Vicuña	125
War of the Pacific (1879)	33
Judicial district of Concepción (1820–1854)	90
Intendency of Concepción	136
Intendency of Bíobío	105
Copies from the Hydrographic Office	19
Total	12,519

Unfortunately the rooms of the Biblioteca Nacional set aside for the Manuscripts Section proved to be small. Moreover, it was even necessary to demolish one of them in order to facilitate the construction of the palace of the Tribunals, and the other rooms were damaged in consequence of the earthquake of August, 1906. Nevertheless, in the last decade, 328 volumes have been received in the Section, as follows:

Archives of the Cabildo de la Serena	36
Archives of the Government of Angol	59
Private archives of Don Benjamin Vicuña M.	52
Archives of the Fondo Antiguo	23
Added to various archives	158

Within a very short time will be begun the construction of that part of the new building of the Biblioteca Nacional which has been set aside for the Manuscripts Section. With a shelving capacity of more than 200,000 volumes, and provided with all the conveniences necessary for keeping them safe and making them easy of consultation, the Section is called upon to experience a rapid increase. It can be estimated that the Section will immediately duplicate its present collection of 13,000 volumes when it receives the old notarial archives, those of the Intendencies and Governments and the judicial records of the colonial corregidor districts, besides many others which are now scattered about the provinces from one end of the Republic to the other.

II. PARTICULAR DESCRIPTION OF THE SEVERAL ARCHIVES

The heterogeneous make-up of some of the archives renders it a difficult task to give a slight idea of each of them—a disadvantage rendered much greater since the value of the documents varies according to whether they are estimated at their intrinsic value, according to their rarity, according to the rank of the persons from whom they proceed, or according to the interesting details set forth in them or having a bearing on their origin, or according to another series of causes which it is even difficult to remember in a moment. The review will consequently be incomplete because of the omission of matters of interest concerning them, and faulty because of the brevity with which it is necessary to discuss the rest in order not to spin out this article to a greater length than belongs to it from its character.

Archives of the Fondo Antiguo.—This consists of 223 volumes composed of matters so different that taken as a whole they resemble an encyclopedia. Among them are found works of jurisprudence, law reports, judicial memoirs, royal cédulas; didactic and theological texts and works of literature, poetry, and history; notes on Chilean medicine, mineralogy, and meteorology, public works, education, government matters, logs of voyages, commerce, industry, arts, statistics, etc., and a collection of documents relative to the tribunal of the Inquisition or to the history of Chile, copied from the Archives of the Indies of Simancas.

As curiosities may be enumerated the original manuscripts of the *Crónica del Reyno de Chile,* by Mariño de Lobera, 1595; of the *Cautiverio Feliz,* by Pineda y Bascuñan, 1673; the Register of Spaniards and Indians of the Province of Chiloe, 1785; the *Cronicón Sacro-Impe-*

rial de Chile, by Ramírez, 1895; the preliminaries in regard to the founding of the College of the Natives, the erection of the Academy of San Luis in 1796, the plan of studies and creation of the Instituto Nacional in 1813; the letters and papers of Vera y Pintado, Don Manuel de Salas, Father Camilo Henriquez, and other patriots of American independence.

Archivo de la Capitanía General.—This contains the papers relating to the political and military government during the colony. There are very few pieces belonging to the sixteenth century, but they increase gradually, and indeed from the middle of the following and up to the first years of the nineteenth century the documentation is varied and abundant. The total number of pieces is estimated at more than 20,000.

The archives are subdivided into various sections, in each of which certain matters predominate, although there is really no hard and fast classification. Following the numerical order of the volumes, the matters to which these refer are as follows:

Private causes	Vols. 1–227
Causes relating to mines	" 228–279
Criminal causes	" 280–339
Expedientes relative to the alcabala	" 340–357
Expedientes relative to navigation	" 358–381
Books of attorneys	" 382–383
Administrative matters	" 384–422
Expedientes relative to Temporalities of the Jesuits	" 423–472
In regard to grants of land and encomiendas of Indians	" 473–566
Private petitions, memorials regarding services, denouncements of waste lands, etc	" 567–575
Expedientes relative to the jurisdiction of Aconcagua	" 576–577
Surplus lands	" 578–579
Ancient memorials	" 580
Expedientes relative to foreigners	" 581
Various receipts	" 582–584
Mercantile matters	" 586–589
Relative to the warehouses of Valparaiso	" 590–596
Relative to public functionaries	" 597–609
Relative to notaries public	" 610–621
Relative to public works, official correspondence, private administrative matters of the royal treasury	" 622–714
Collection of royal cédulas, 1576–1816	" 715–798
Official correspondence, copy books of decrees, edicts, resolutions, and other governmental matters	" 799–814
Relative to the militia, army, pensions, fortifications, residencia judgments, subsidies, garrisons, war with England, government of Juan Fernández, fortified towns, and presidios and repairs of barracks.	" 815–876

Relative to debts and public wealth, the half annats,
consolidated capitals, imposts, balance, gifts, customs, guards, confiscations, royal treasury, incomes,
and tithes . . . . Vols. 877–927
Urban police, public works, foundations of towns and
cities, mints, mails, roads, bridges, cutwaters and
canal of Maipo . . . . " · 928–954
Relative to the encouragement of agriculture, the Caro-
lino College, the college for the natives, and the University . . . . " 955–959
Relative to prisons, *obras pias*, hospitals, and epidemics " 960–967
Elections and auctions of public offices, and other similar expedientes of the cabildos of Cuyo and Concepción " 968–998
Ecclesiastical matters, Jesuits, etc . . . . " 999–1036

The volumes following belong to the period of independence or to
that of the Republic, and are of a purely administrative character.

Estimated as a whole, the archives of the Capitanía General are the
best for a study of the institutions of colonial government, which are
very little known as yet, but very poorly estimated by the generality
of historians.

It is difficult to give a clear idea of the real importance of these
archives for historical investigations relative to the above mentioned
title.   However, we shall endeavor to set forth a few details.

The correspondence of the president with subordinate officials during
the years 1781–1804 consists of 17,970 pieces bound in 11 volumes.
Many of them are circulars sent simultaneously to many functionaries.

The confidential correspondence with the king is copied into five
volumes and contains about 3,000 letters written during the same
period of time.   These five volumes alone have supplied enough material for an interesting and useful piece of work which was planned and
will be concluded during the present year by Professor Charles E.
Chapman with a group of students of the Instituto Pédagógico.

The copybooks of grants of lands and encomiendas of Indians made
between the years 1670 and 1708 number fourteen and contain 420
land titles and about 900 encomienda titles.   The first are useful for
ascertaining the origin of rural property and for the reconstruction of
the native place names, while the second contain many lists of Indians
with thousands of native names, a rich and unexploited material for
the study of American philology, as well as memorials and certificates
of rewards and services and of lists of the most prominent members of
colonial society.

Among the administrative expedientes those are of special interest which relate to the foundations of cities, towns, and forts; those concerning conferences with the Indians, of the Araucanian war, and of the attempts to convert the natives to the Christian faith or to civilize them; and lastly, sentences of residencias and other processes drawn up for the purpose of setting forth the conduct of subordinate officials and other functionaries in the discharge of their duties.

Archives of Cedulas and Royal Orders.—These archives contain over 8,000 pieces all belonging to the colonial period, one-tenth perhaps of which are printed. In addition there are ten other volumes containing indices and copies of documents of this class which are kept in the Archives of the Royal Audiencia, Contaduría Mayor, Archbishopric, Municipality of Santiago, and in the ancient Archives of the Cabildo de la Serena. Although it may not be necessary to state as much, all those documents contain resolutions and royal orders both of a general and particular nature in regard to the government of Chile. Among these last named there are a multitude of appointments of civil and military functionaries, concessions of rewards and pensions, permissions to contract matrimony, pardons from fines, expulsion or naturalization of foreigners, and many other matters. Of course those of general interest, such as laws, ordinances, regulations, and explanation or interpretation of their provisions are of chief importance.

Archives of Mining Tribunal.—This tribunal was created in Chile in fulfilment of a royal order given in Aranjuez, February 12, 1797. It contains a large portion of the expedientes drawn up by the administrator general of the department of mining, Don Antonio Martínez de Mata, in his general inspection of all the mining settlements of the country which was made during the years 1788–1790, for the purpose of creating and defining the boundaries of the deputations, examining into the condition of mine labor, sugar mills, and foundries, and ascertaining the urgent needs in order to encourage the development of mining in Chile. There are similar expedientes, but of less importance belonging to the latter years of the colonial period, as well as lawsuits between parties.

Supplemental to these archives because of the material which they contain are volumes 228–279 of the Archives of the Capitanía General, comprehending petitions and mine sentences which were made before the creation of the special tribunal.

Aside from their usefulness in ascertaining the development of mining in Chile, these archives offer an unexploited and lucrative field as a base for the organization of mining explorations in old and perhaps rich mine districts which are abandoned or unknown at present.

Archives of the Tribunal of the Consulado.—These contain documents and expedientes which passed before this tribunal which was created in obedience to a royal order dated March 28, 1795, for encouraging the development of commerce and trying matters purely commercial.

Archives of the Contaduría Mayor.—In these rich archives are kept whatever bears on the collection or expenditure of the revenue of the royal treasury. They contain some documents of the sixteenth century, and very many documents of the following centuries down to 1840, the year to which those conserved in the Biblioteca Nacional go.

In reality these archives are made up from no less than a score of different archives, from as many other offices or administrative divisions. Chief of these latter are those of the treasuries of Santiago and Concepción; the custom houses of Valparaiso, Copiapo, Huasco, Coquimbo, Constitución, Talcahuano, Valdivia, and Chiloé; those of the mint; those of the tobacco revenue; and those of the construction of public works, bridges, cutwaters, etc.

Historically considered, the richest documentation is that relating to the armies, both royalist and patriotic, which fought in the war for independence. The muster lists will allow the reconstruction of both armies, to learn the effectives who fought in the battles, the list of casualties suffered, and even the names of those killed or wounded. Other documents give news of the armaments, reveal details, permit the remaking of service sheets, and at times even show military plans.

As the rendition of accounts was very tedious, there are found as proofs of the items of receipts and expenses, entire copies of memorials or patents of rewards or appointments in which appear the services of those favored; of documents proving the foreign status of those who were to pay the tax to which foreigners were liable; details of the production of the manufactures of rigging, cloth, blankets, etc., for supplying the army; and many other vouchers of very different kinds, but which may be of use in special investigations relative to foreign immigration and the development of industries during the colonial period; to the development of commercial importing and exporting after the gaining of independence, and, in general, to matters connected with political economy.

Archives of Copies from Archivo de Indias.—These consist of copies of documents relative to Chile conserved in the Archivo de Indias of Seville. These documents were discovered during the investigations of Señores Vicuña Mackenna, Medina, and Morla Vicuña, and other investigators of Chile. Some have been published in the *Colección de Documentos Inéditos* of Señor Medina, in the *Estudio Histórico* of Señor Morla Vicuña, and in various works of Señor Vicuña Mackenna, but the greater part of them have not yet been used for investigating the study of the history of the country.

Archives of Eyzaguirre.—These contain papers on very diverse matters, although those of a religious nature predominate. Among them are found expedientes relative to the episcopal visits of Bishop Alday to the diocesis of Santiago and of Bishop Marán to that of Concepción; the appeal sanctioned by Rodríguez Zorrilla against the ecclesiastical cabildo of Santiago in 1808; and papers relative to the bishop of Epifania.

Among the most interesting works may be cited the narratives of the voyages of Father Mascardi to the regions of the Nahuelhuapi, 1667–1672 and of Don Luis de la Cruz from Concepción to Buenos Aires, 1806; the originals of the histories of Córdoba y Figueroa and of Rodríguez Ballesteros; and a journal of the events occurring in Santiago during the years 1765–1773, written by Don Fernando Antonio de los Ríos, vice rector of the University of San Felipe.

But the most important papers of these archives are those pertaining to the period of the war of independence and among these especially one volume of original decrees of the government *juntas* corresponding to the years 1810–1816, and lastly, during the republican period, the process drawn up against Admiral Blanco Encalada in 1821.

Archives of the Inquisition.—These contain almost exclusively papers relative to the economic side of the tribunal of the Holy Office; for instance, auctions of the goods of condemned persons, executions, and collections of debts which other persons allotted as pensions or for other reasons in favor of the same tribunal. There exist, however, copies of letters or communications with other Spanish tribunals.

The seat of the tribunal of the Inquisition was at Lima, but its jurisdiction embraced all the Pacific coast from Panama down, so that the captaincy general of Chile lay within the boundaries assigned to this tribunal.

The study of the documents would throw much light on colonial trade and the inquisitorial proceedings in financial matters which competed with it. They will also be useful for investigating the problem of the immigration of Jews to Latin America, and the persecutions of which their members were the object, especially the Portuguese Jews against whom the inquisitorial investigation and punishment were implacable.

Archives of the Jesuits.—This rich collection belonged to Don Antonio de Paz, an official of the Biblioteca Nacional of Madrid, from whom the government of Chile bought it, through the intermediary of Don Carlos Morla Vicuña, then secretary of the Chilean legation in France. The latter in a report dated Seville, August 24, 1876, wrote as follows:

The manuscript collection in possession of Señor Paz consists for the most part of originals belonging to the Jesuits of Hispano-America from Mexico to Chile. These documents which were transferred to the Peninsula in 1767, immediately after the expulsion of the Society of Jesus from that continent, were housed in a department of the Ministry of Grace and Justice, called the Temporalities, which was broken up during the last revolution. The papers were sold by the pound to butcher shops and groceries, and were fast on the way to complete destruction when a gentleman named Don M. Javier Bravo, a Spaniard living in Buenos Aires, who was then by chance in Madrid, heard of their existence and acquired them. Señor Bravo returned part of the collection to the Spanish government and undertook the publication of the rest. As he did not have any preparation by special studies for this kind of work, Señor Bravo was not successful in his undertaking and had to give up the manuscript collection above mentioned for the amount he was owing to his literary collaborators and to the editor of the first two volumes of the publication.

This collection is the one offered for sale to the Supreme Government two years ago through my mediation, and which the Minister of Foreign Relations authorized your Excellency [the Chilean minister in France] to buy if I judged it advisable. As yet no determination has been made relative to this matter, since as I had no opportunity to examine the manuscripts personally, I was ignorant of their value and whether or not they were worth the expense that their acquisition would require.

As I have told your Excellency before, this time I have had the opportunity to examine the above mentioned collection personally. It is kept in ten enormous trunks. It is divided into cardboard sections forming volumes, the distribution following the order of the various regions into which colonial America was divided. This classification would permit of the formation of a complete catalogue, paper by paper, and legajo by legajo, of all the material, without any great difficulty or space of time, and would facilitate the preparation of the collection for the use of the public.

The section corresponding to Chile, although one of the least abundant, is composed of very interesting documents which ought to be acquired for the Biblioteca Nacional of Santiago at any cost. Among them are original letters from Fathers Luis de Valdivia, Gaspar Sobrino, Luis del Castillo, Antonio and Gonzalo de Covarrubias, Diego Rosales, Alonso de Ovalle, etc.—all of them famous in our historical annals, some as missionaries and pacifiers and the rest as Chilean chroniclers. That part of this section which refers to the defensive war, by which at the advice of Father Valdivia the reduction of the Araucanians was undertaken in 1610, is very complete from the point of view of the father missionaries. There are also among their papers many adverse reports and criticisms made against the new plan by the military chiefs who desired to continue active warfare. In this same section are found all the documents referring to the rural and urban properties owned by the Society of Jesus in Chile, with their deeds and plans annexed, many of which were in colors. The want of these documents has provoked in Chile, as I have noted, more ,than one lawsuit in regard to the boundaries of estates. If they were in the Biblioteca Nacional, even should they not serve to solve such questions, they would always be very useful in a purely literary and historical sense. The number of letters relative to the colleges, churches, and missions, of which the Jesuits had charge throughout the whole extent of the country is not less considerable.

The sections of the collection corresponding to Peru and to Paraguay, which included the provinces of Tucumán and Río de la Plata, as the provinces were divided by the Jesuits, undoubtedly have very many documents which are of equal interest to Chile and which would be of certain value in the present boundary questions, with the study of which I am charged. The portions corresponding to Brasil, the Viceroyalty of Sante Fé, and Mexico are quite far distant from Chile and do not interest it except for one or more direct incidents, for many of the religious who distinguished themselves in Chile usually went to continue their labors into these regions and vice versa. However, these documents like the others are of intrinsic value for the history of the countries above mentioned, and in the case of Mexico, the richest.

The entire collection is composed of thirteen thousand pieces more or less, understanding by "piece" documents and expedientes, many of which are voluminous.

Señor Morla Vicuña also adds these words in a note:

This collection was acquired by the state and has been sent to Chile. I undertook its organisation, document by document, and I even made the detailed catalogue of a considerable part of them; but in this task as well as in that of the study of the boundaries question, I was interrupted by the exigencies of the late war [of the Pacific]. It is advisable, however, that as much of the catalogue as has been completed be printed, and it will be a simple matter to continue the arrangement and classification in Santiago. The collection which had been owned by Señor Paz has been completed with various other items of papers pertaining to the same archives which were found in possession of old book dealers in Madrid. The manuscripts proceeding from the houses owned by the Jesuits in Spain and which do not refer to America, were found some years ago in possession of the erudite Señores Zabalburu. These with our collection and the choice documents presented by Señor Bravo to the Academy of History in Madrid, constitute all that is left of the archives secuestrated from the Society of Jesus when it was suppressed.[1]

To the words of Señor Morla Vicuña, it is fitting to add that the greater part of the papers of this collection are posterior to the expulsion of the Jesuits from the Spanish dominions, and consist of ordinances

[1] C. Morla Vicuña, *Estudio Histórico sobre el Descubrimiento y Conquista de la Patagonia y de la Tierra del Fuego*, pp. 34, 35.

issued in order to obey the order of expulsion, of inventories and auctions, or administration of the secuestrated goods and proofs of the payment of pensions to the expelled religious, some of whom were still living when American emancipation took place. This collection contains, therefore, documentation covering the entire colonial period, and not only of the Hispano-American colonies, but also of the Philippines, Canaries, and even of some houses of Spain itself.

When the archives reached the Biblioteca Nacional, this institution still was without a bindery, so that it was necessary to send the books and manuscripts to private binderies for binding. This caused an almost irreparable loss of some forty volumes which were half destroyed in a fire that broke out in the bindery where this work was being done.

The total number of volumes, including the impaired ones, was 498, but in order to facilitate consultation, two or more account books were bound into a single volume, thus decreasing the total number of volumes by 18, which are distributed as follows:

Chile	Volumes numbered from 1–136A
Spain	137–150
Spain, Canaries, and Philippines	151
Italy (relative to pensions)	152–153
Bolivia	154–170 and 436–437
Peru	171–232
Argentine Republic	233–298
Mexico	299–380
Paraguay	381–382
Quito	383–396
Bogotá	397–419
Panama	420
Antilles	421–425
Philippines	426–428
Various others	429–435

Half burned in the fire
42 volumes kept in fourteen boxes.

Aside from the anacronic nomenclature, this classification undoubtedly suffers from the commission of a serious error, namely, that of not preserving the old separation of the documents belonging to each viceroyalty and the captaincies general dependent on them, so that the investigator must keep in mind the geographical division of America in order not to lay himself open to some possible downfall such as would happen without doubt to the person who limited himself to examining volumes 381 and 382 to find information about Paraguay and should pass by the sixty-five volumes referring to the Argentine Republic.

The archives of the Jesuits have been utilized by various republics in the defense of their rights in the lawsuits concerning boundary questions sustained with neighboring countries.

They are also called upon to serve as a useful source of information for American ethnography, both for the fixing of the regions where each people lived, and also because of the abundance of native geographical or personal names which are conserved in those papers.

The inventories of the libraries, of the tools and animals of the estates, the number of the slaves and of the household goods in general, all offer a vast field for historical investigation which will permit not only of a better knowledge of the so greatly discussed activities of the Society of Jesus, but also the degree of development of colonial society.

Archives of the Notaries.—These begin with a fragment of the register of the notary Pedro de Salcedo in the year 1559. This is followed by a volume of Juan de la Peña, 1564–1566; other fragments of the registries of Alonso del Castillo, 1578, 1579, 1580, 1593, and 1594, and from 1585 to 1800 follow the registers without any attempt at continuity even when one or the other of the registries of any of the notaries who discharged their duties at the same time are missing.

Aside from the registries of Santiago, there is a volume containing fragments of registers of various notaries of Concepción who held office between the years 1769 and 1843.

The total number of instruments is perhaps in excess of 200,000 and their contents furnish the most vivid and faithful picture of Chile and our ancestors in past centuries. The change in customs especially can be shown easily and its evolution even followed by examining those documents.

Wills were more common than they are today, and in them no one neglected to commend his soul to God and to the saints, or to make his confession of faith. Some added minute data relative to their life or to their progeny and many highly interesting statements. The most extensive will is that of the maestre de Campo General Jerónimo de Quiroga, which was signed in 1716 and consists of 141 pages.

Dotal letters or the evidence of the money which the parents or relatives of the bride usually gave to the husband at the time of the celebration of marriage are also very numerous and recall a custom which has now fallen into complete disuse.

Among the interesting instruments it is of interest to note the promises not to gamble, not to make loans, and other similar promises, in which the signer imposed on himself not only a fine for the benefit of the denouncer, of the royal treasury, or of some religious institution, but also condemned himself to go to jail for a certain time; instruments of pardon for some crime usually extended after a money settlement between the interested parties; testimonies of happenings accounted miraculous; "exclamations", or instruments in which those signing them declared that they had signed other instruments against their will, and to which consequently they denied all value or effect; the "agreements" or contracts for domestic services, and documents relative to a variety of other matters.

In the Archives of the Notaries, one may observe the development of society, the evolution of customs, the progress of industry and commerce, and in general of the colony itself.

Archives of the Royal Audiencia.—This tribunal was established in Concepción first in 1568, suppressed in 1575, and reestablished in Santiago in 1609 where it functioned until 1817 except for a short period of the Old Country, 1811–1814.

However, old expedientes dating from 1552 are conserved in these archives, as well as various others initiated in the sixteenth century, documents,—copies dating from 1544 and originals dating from 1550. But the great majority are posterior to the creation of the Audiencia of Santiago.

Inasmuch as the sphere of action of the Royal Audiencia was much greater than that of present-day tribunals of justice, and it exercised in addition functions of criminal jurisdiction over the other authorities of the country, these archives contain many expedientes relative to competency of jurisdiction. The application of laws or regulations, questions of etiquette, appeals to force, etc. But among them all, those of greatest historical interest are the residencia sentences, which as one knows were drawn up against the presidents and captains general, the corregidors, and other subordinate authorities upon leaving office, and in which after the charges made against the departing official by aggrieved parties and the rebuttal made by the departing official had been heard the latter was condemned or absolved in accordance with the merits shown by the records.

The matter of processes and sentences between parties does not differ, as one may easily imagine, from those nowadays. There are, however, many expedientes of cases between slaves or Indians and their masters or encomenderos because of bad treatment and other injuries which were inflicted on them which are useful for ascertaining the relations of the various classes among themselves and the laws protecting inferiors from abuses by the peninsular.

The approximate number of pieces contained in these archives is 14,000, classified as follows:

Ordinary civil suits 10,200
Expedientes of historical value 2,200
Expedientes relative to encomiendas of Indians, slaves, etc. . 700
Expedientes of criminal matter 600
Expedientes relative to mines 300

These archives are completed by a collection of royal provisions, sentences of examination or review expedited by the royal audiencia during the entire time that it functioned. This series of papers which so far forms more than 60 volumes, although many others are still to be formed, is particularly interesting because there are found here notices of many expedientes that have been lost and sometimes the complete synthesis of them with the main documents inserted in the sentences pronounced by the tribunal.

Archives of Vicuña Mackenna.—As happens frequently in private collections the make up of these archives is heterogeneous, and it is composed principally of notes and original drafts of Señor Vicuña Mackenna, his archives and private correspondence, a series of copies made in the Archivo de Indias; documents and letters relative to the chief political events of Chile and of the persons concerned therein; a multitude of newspaper or magazine clippings; colonial expedientes, etc.

The archives that belonged to the Fathers of the Country, Generals Don Bernardo O'Higgins and Don José Miguel Carrera and the original manuscript of the *Historia de Chile* by Father Diego Rosales are the most valuable of all.

Archives of Morla Vicuña.—These consist principally of two large groups of papers, namely: the autographic drafts of Don Claudio Gay, the original documents and copies of other documents collected by the aforesaid for the writing of his *Historia de Chile;* and the copies made in Spain by Don Carlos Morla Vicuña for his *Estudio Histórico sobre el Descubrimiento y Conquista de la Patagonia y de la Tierra del Fuego*, and especially, for the defense of the rights of Chile in the boundaries question with the Argentine Republic.

The archives are distributed in the following manner:

Manuscript of the *Historia de Chile*, by Gay	Vols.	1- 7
Old original manuscripts	"	8–40
Old manuscripts and notes made by Gay	"	41–42
Copies of documents collected by Gay	"	43–53
Copy of the *Relación Geográfica e Hidrográfica del Reino de Chile*, sent to the king by the president Don Manuel de Amat in 1761		54
Geographical documents relative to Chile		55
Copies and extracts of old papers relative to Chile . .		56
Copies of old chroniclers and historians of Chile, namely, Pineda Bascuñan, Córdoba y Figueroa, Olivares, Pérez García, Martínez, etc.		57–65
Copies of Logs		66
Copy of the *Historia del Reino de Chile* by Fray Antonio Lors, 1780		67
Copy of the *Diario Político* by Don José Miguel Carrera	"	68
Copy of the *Historia de la Revolución de Chile*, by Fray Melchor Martínes		69
Original papers relative to the government of the island of Juan Fernández, 1832–1834	"	71
Copies of documents from the Archivo de Indias . . .	"	72–123
Original relation relative to the navigation of the Rio Bermejo, 1790		124
Memoirs of the viceroy of Buenos Aires, Marqués de Loreto, 1790		125

Archives of the War of the Pacific.—These consist almost entirely of documents from the general staff of the Peruvian army, which fell into the hands of the Chileans at the end of 1879. It complements the Chilean documentation and is of considerable use for passing a more accurate and imparial judgment on the first part of the international conflict. They are distributed as follows:

Official notes, April to November, 1879	Vols.	1–7
Confidential matters	"	8
General orders to the reserves	"	9
State diaries of the forces, returns, casualties, etc. . .	"	10–13
Accounts relative to provisions, expenses of military hospitals, etc	"	14–17
Copybook of instructions, decrees, and passports . . .	"	18
General in chief and commandants general of division. .	"	19
Communications with various authorities	"	20
General correspondence	"	21–22
Table of persons (alphabetical index of individuals of the army and of information pertaining to them)	"	23

Judicial Archives of Concepción.—These are composed of criminal and civil sentences, and contain some processes because of subversive conspiracies that may have an interest for political history. They begin in 1810 and end about 1854.

Archives of the Intendencies of Concepción and Biobío.—The first corresponds to the years 1819–1840 and the second to those of 1829–1875, and both are purely administrative. However, in that of Concepción are found a few documents relative to the campaign of Chiloé which put an end to the Spanish domination there in 1826.

Copies from the Hydrographic Office.—These are copies of documents relative to nautical history. They were printed in great part in the *Anuario Hidrográfico de la Marina de Chile.*

Archives of the Government of Angol.—These are also modern archives of an administrative character. They may be useful for the study of questions having to do with the Indians and their definitive pacification.

Archives of the Cabildo de la Serena.—These commence in the year 1680 and end in 1818, but they contain also a few documents anterior and posterior to the years indicated. The classification of the matters treated in the papers is as follows:

Volumes	1– 3	Acts of the cabildo	1778–1800
"	4– 9	Cedulas, edicts, etc	1698–1823
"	10–11	Royal provisions	1680–1813
"	12–13	Visitas of the Indians	1692–1792
"	14–16	Civil causes	1682–1818
"	17	Criminal causes	1720–1813
"	18–21	Expedientes relative to mines	1714–1812
"	22–25	Dispatches and various communications . .	1780–1814
"	26	Hospital	1740–1816
"	27	Relative to militia	1775–1814
"	28	Matters relative to the Indians	1690–1811
"	29–31	Matters of government	1600–1808
"	32	Revenues of balance and estates	1810–1817
"	33	Revenues from the monopoly	1755–1813
"	34	Expedientes relative to lands	1790–1817
"	35	Copies of various legal writs	1716–1829
"	36	Book of receipts of San Agustin	

Beyond doubt these archives contain some papers that will prove useful for completing the history of various incidents of the war of independence. The most important, however, are those referring to the indigenes, and these have a bearing on Chilean ethnology which has been very little studied, and which is clothed with greater interest in Coquimbo whose inhabitants have been submitted to the influences of several American cultures from the north and east, and probably as well from the south.

Miscellaneous manuscripts.—Among these documents are worthy of mention a map or sketch of Chile designed in Spain in 1768 by Don Ambrosio O'Higgins, later president of Chile and viceroy of Peru, for the purpose of conveying an idea of the number and location of the properties of the expelled Jesuits; an "Old Testament" to which Don J. Sylvester, professor of languages and of Hebrew in the rabbinical college of Varsovia, ascribed an age of a thousand years, basing his opinion on the change of color in the parchment, the wear of the catgut with which it was sewed, and the very imperfect characters of the writing, according to his statement in a report of August 30, 1875; and two plans executed in 1760 by order of the viceroy of Peru, Don Manuel de Amat, which contain a project for the irrigation of the valleys of Arica and Tarapacá.

The last might perhaps serve as a base for a study relative to a possible modification in the meteorological and climatic condition of those provinces, for they contain marked regions "which were cultivated formerly when it rained" and others which were still cultivated in 1760, but which are nevertheless sterile at the present time. The data noted on those plans accord with those existing in the parish of Iquique in expedientes drawn up for the purpose of checking the disorders or immoralities of which those regions were the scene during the time of the harvests. There are also other indications and even foundations for believing that the inhospitable conditions of the deserts of northern Chile have grown worse during the last four centuries, but that matter can not be elucidated on in this article.

Among the other manuscripts may be mentioned "El Vasauro", an unpublished poem by Licentiate Pedro de Oña, the oldest of Chilean poets, who was born in Angol in 1570, and the "Historia de la Provincia de Chiloé bajo la Dominación Espanola", written in four volumes, and left unfinished by Don Abraham de Silva, who died prematurely in December, 1908.

III. REGULATIONS, FACILITIES, AND CATALOGUES FOR CONSULTING THE
SECTION

Título VIII. of the Regulations of the Biblioteca Nacional, enacted June 12, 1890, refers to the Manuscript Section and contains the following rules relative to the consultation of documents:

Art 17. The duties of the Chief of this Section are as follows:
1. To furnish to readers the manuscripts for which they ask after having received a signed receipt on which are noted the date of the petition, the number of the volume, the archives to which it belongs, and the residence of the petitioner.
2. To see that the persons who make copies or notes do not damage or spoil the manuscripts by writing on them or by making any kind of mark.
. . . .
Art. 18. Manuscripts especially reserved can not be examined without permission from the director.
Art. 19. The series of reserved manuscripts shall consist of an index made by the Director and approved by the Minister of Public Instruction.
Art. 20. Persons below the age of 20 years can not be admitted to this section as readers.

Within these rules it is aimed to give the public all the facilities by which they can work to the greatest advantage and comfort.

The cataloguing of the manuscripts is still deficient, but the subdivision of the archives and the chronological arrangement of some of them simplifies and usually accelerates investigation.

The best of the existing catalogues and the one which will be used as a model for future catalogues is that of the Archives of the Royal

Audiencia. It suffers, perhaps, from the defect of being too voluminous, because of the very large type used in printing it, but on the other hand it is easy to manage. It consists of three volumes, which comprehend 6,210 pieces contained in the volumes numbered from 1–2100 inclusive.

Inasmuch as most of the pieces are judgments between parties, the descriptions of these pieces have been set down according to the alphabetical order of the surnames of the complainants, or of the person, functionary, or corporation of whom the catalogued piece especially treats or refers. In addition are added the citations or summonses, with the names of the defendants and notes under the main description in which are mentioned the principal documents, royal cédulas, grants and plans of surveys of lands, total letters, wills or powers for bequeathing; and in general of those of historical value and which without that method it would be difficult to find. Of all these citations are made in alphabetical order as above said. The following transcription will give a better understanding of the procedure followed:

ALHUÉ (Tierras de).—See *Merced* (Convento de la), No. 1000.

GUZMÁN (Beatriz de).—See *Merced* (Convento de la), No. 1000.

1000 MERCED (Convento de la).—Judgment followed with Gusmán (Beatriz de), relative to a better right to the lands of the valley of *Alhué*. 1634–1643.

Vol. 310. Pp. 309.—The first part of this judgment is found in the second piece of volume 599.

It contains the will of Don Rodrigo de Quiroga (February 24, 1580); and the copy of a concession granted by Don Pedro de Valdivia in favor of Doña Inés Suárez of the lands of the valley of Alhué (July 11, 1546).

QUIROGA (Rodrigo de).—See *Merced* (Convento de la), No. 1000.

SUÁREZ (Inés).—See *Merced* (Convento de la), No. 1000.

VALDIVIA (Pedro de).—See *Merced* (Convento de la), No. 1000.

As above seen, this piece has five cross references, so that the person looking for information relative to the above mentioned persons or of the lands in litigation, or in general of the history of that epoch has within reach the data necessary for the locating of the material.

The catalogue of the Archives of the Jesuits relating to Chile is made up in like manner, but contains a double reference to the pages of the volume and the sheets contained in the piece, but this generally makes it confusing to one not accustomed to consult that index. References are written in the following form: 1797; Vol. 86, p. 10, page 263, sheets 19; or Year 1797; volume 86, piece 10th, page 263 of the volume in which the piece commences; the manuscript is made up of 19 sheets.

The catalogue of the Capitanía General is rather an inventory, and incomplete, of the pieces contained in each volume. Nevertheless, although it is much slower and less accurate to consult than the catalogues of the Royal Audiencia and of the Jesuits, investigation is considerably facilitated by examining it. Moreover, the minute cataloguing of these archives has been begun with excellent results, for the first seventy volumes have yielded more than 2,000 pieces or 40 per cent more than the 1,245 that appear in the present index, not counting cross references which must exceed 3,000. This so striking difference is due to the fact that the first work had to be done in a space of time, so that it was impossible to catalogue a multitude of petitions and small expedientes one, two, or three sheets long, yet each of which required as long a time as a voluminous legajo. For this reason such papers were massed together under the symbol of first, second, or third series of miscellaneous papers.

The catalogue of the Archives Vicuña Mackenna also consists of a mere inventory, with a few commentaries as to the value of certain documents. It consists of 229 pages in double column quarto and can be examined rapidly, inasmuch as it is subdivided into series of papers of very diverse character which no one need examine at the same time, as can be proved by comparing some of the chief ones which are indicated below.

Vols. 33–35.—The Revolution of April 20, 1851.
"   42–44.—War to the death, 1819–1820.
"   47–50.—The revolution of 1859.
"   85–112.—Archives of General O'Higgins.
"   113–122.—Archives of General Carrera.
"   195–221.—Campaign against Peru and Bolivia, 1837–1839.
"   222–255.—Campaign against Peru and Bolivia, 1879–1883; and other events
                relative to that period.
"   265–304.—Copies of documents from the Archivo de Indias from Simancas, 1532–1700.

In order to facilitate the consultation of the Archives of the Notaries, a *Guía* has been printed, in which are enumerated the wills and powers for making wills, dotal letters, and some other documents of special interest. The part already published takes up to volume 591, but the printing of the balance is being continued. In addition, many of the volumes are provided with an index of the documents contained therein, so that the examination or search for documents entails no great difficulty.

Manuscript inventories only are found for the other archives, and are even lacking to some of them, as it is impossible to make them without first arranging their papers which came into the Section in complete disorder.

Soon to be transferred provisionally to the new edifice of the Biblioteca Nacional, while the extensive and commodious building which is being constructed west of the above mentioned palace of the library, the Manuscripts Section will be definitively organized within a short time under conditions which will permit the elimination of the defects from which it is suffering at present and to experience without obstruction the extension of its services in consequence of its violent development because of the new archives which it will then receive and which will convert it into one of the richest, if not one of the most valuable of the historical archives of Hispanic America.

TOMÁS THAYER OJEDA

Chief of the Manuscripts Section
of the Biblioteca Nacional of Santiago,
Chile.

THE PUBLICATIONS OF THE HISTORY SECTION, FACULTY OF PHILOSOPHY AND LETTERS, UNIVERSITY OF BUENOS AIRES, ARGENTINA

Because of the augmenting importance of the volumes of documents which the National University of Buenos Aires is publishing through the History Section of its Faculty of Philosophy and Letters, it is desired, in this article, to give an idea of their value, and of the scope of the vast and admirable undertaking of which each of these volumes is a carefully prepared, harmonious part. As source material for history, the documents presented in the series under consideration usually relate solely to the territory now constituting the Argentine Republic, although occasionally, with respect to matters which cannot be so definitely segregated, there is furnished the whole related process of laws and procedure, which, in affecting the Spanish colonies of America, concerned Argentina among the rest. The value of the volumes which the University of Buenos Aires is issuing, is, however, more than solely the historical value of the documents they so accurately present. As models and encouragement they are invested with another, and possibly as great an interest, for all students of history, especially those most appreciative of undiluted, unadulterated, limpid sources.

Editorially these books meet the requirements of the most exacting criticism. From a good beginning the series has improved in each successive volume, as the work done in various archives has trained those in charge of investigations to recognize and master difficulties, and their experience has taught the editors how more nearly to achieve their own advancing ideal with respect to presentation. The latest volume is close indeed upon the history student's conception of perfection in this particular field of work.

It was Sr. D. José Nicolás Matienzo who, when dean of the University of Buenos Aires, conceived the plan of publishing in serial groups, documents covering determined epochs in Argentine history. Under his auspices appeared volumes entitled *Documentos para la historia del Virreinato del Rio de la Plata, Documentos relativos a los antecedentes de la Independencia de la República Argentina*, and *Documentos relativos a la Organización Constitucional de la República Argentina*, to which must be added *Gobierno del Perú* (sixteenth century) by Licentiate Juan de Matienzo. These form ten volumes of selected documents.

Under Sr. D. Norberto Piñero, dean, certain editorial reforms were effected, and there emerged the University's Section of History, placed under the special direction of Sr. D. Luis M. Torres, with Sr. D. Emilio Ravignani in charge of investigations.[1] They were assisted by Drs. Romulo D. Carbia, Diego Luis Molinari and Carlos Correa Luna, all specialists in these matters, with reputations established among Argentine students of history. Then began the new series of publications, which still continues, under the general title of *Documents for Argentine History*.

Under succeeding deans (Sr. D. Rodolfo Rivarola, and the present incumbent, Sr. D. Alejandro Korn) the volumes of this series have steadily improved, each upon the preceding, until, as has been said, the latest, Volume IX., *Administración Edilicia de la Ciudad de Buenos Aires*, is a model of its kind. It is the flower of a well surveyed, well cultivated field.

Sr. Torres classifies the requirements which must be met in prepara-

---

[1] Since this article was written Sr. Torres has resigned the direction of the History Section, to become director of the Museo de la Plata, but he will continue to collaborate in its work, which is now in the hands of the former chief of investigations, Sr. Ravignani.

tion of each volume of the series, under four different heads, which he considers fundamental:[2]

1. Investigation and determination of sources. *I.e.*, Exploration of public and private archives, both national and foreign, and provincial and municipal. Preparation of catalogues and special bibliographies.
2. Extrinsic criticism of sources. *I.e.*, Determination of origin (date, place, person) and certification of authenticity.
3. Classification: General character—Classification of materials a) Antecedents; b) Form; c) Function. Chronological and geographical order—The concordant indices (by subject, person, place, date).
4. Publication: General Series; Partial Series; Preliminary interpretation of the value of the documents; Bibliography by subjects; Partial indices (authors, patronymics, topics); Concordant indices of each partial series.

The History Section has carried forward its investigations in the principal archives of Argentina, and in certain archives of Europe, among them the Archivo General de Indias, at Seville. In each instance a thorough survey has been made of the archives in general, of its content relative to Argentina in particular, with careful preparation of notes sufficiently detailed to enable the History Section to identify, compare, and select intelligently from the wealth of material so made available.

The general plan for publications, which Sr. Torres presents in a recent volume of the series, classifies the volumes yet to appear into large serial groups which cover only the epoch embraced between the erection of the viceroyalty of Rio de la Plata and the year 1810, when Argentina became independent. In view of the excellence of the work which the History Section is doing, students will certainly desire that its labors shall extend to preceding periods of Argentine history, including as far as possible matters of general interest to all Hispanic America, as was done, for instance, in *Antecedentes legales del comercio libre de Indias*.

The plan according to which the History Section is working is the following:

Territory and Population:
Geographical explorations and cartography of the viceroyalty
Extent and population of the city and vicinity of Buenos Aires (1726–1809)
Extent and population of the cities, towns, military districts, and *corregimientos* (civil and religious census reports and similar rosters)

[2] "La Seccion de Historia de la Facultad de Filosofia y Letras en el Congreso Americano de Ciencias Sociales reunido en Tucumán, el 5 de Julio de 1916," in *Revista Argentina de Ciencias Políticas*, Buenos Aires, 1916, Year VI., Vol. XII., No. 70.

Native and black elements of population in the cities, towns, and country estates of the viceroyalty; life and customs
Boundaries.
Trade and Commerce in America:
  Legal antecedents (1713–1778)
  Free trade (1778–1791)
  Commercial organizations (*consulado*), slave and foreign trade (1791–1809)
  Commercial memorials and representations (1771–1810)
  Customs administration (1778–1810)
  Administration of commercial organizations (*consulado*) (1785–1810)
Economics and Royal Treasury:
  Industries and technology
  Exploitation of miner
  Currency and credit
  Guilds
  Property
  Imposts
  Ways and means of communication.
Political:
  Foreign—
    Differences with Portugal
    Differences with England
    Differences with France
  Domestic—
    Tupac-Amaru uprising
    Precursory subversive movements
    The revolutions of 1809 and 1810.
Administration:
  Viceroyalty—
    Antecedents of its erection (1771–1776)
    Establishment (1776–1778)
    Duration (1778–1805)
  Audiencia
  Royal Treasury
  Intendencies
  Councils
  Municipal administration
  Organization of military institutions
  Government of indigenous peoples
  Consequences of the expulsion of the Jesuits.
Culture:
  Public instruction
  Literature and bibliography
  Habits and customs
  Artistic manifestations
  Folklore
  Iconography
  Biography.

Church:
  Diocesan organisation
  Parishes
  Ecclesiastical justice
  Tithes[2].

Further, the History Section purposes to translate into Spanish the accounts written by certain English travelers and chroniclers of the 18th and early 19th centuries, who visited or described the Plate countries, and recorded their experiences and opinions in curious books, full of singular and astute observations. These will be published in critical editions, supplemented by extensive studies by specialists.

Those persons who interest themselves in matters of this sort will recognize the immensity of the task which the History Section of the Faculty of Philosophy and Letters of the University of Buenos Aires is undertaking; but an inspection of the later volumes which have been issued furnishes full assurance that the work is in preeminently competent hands. In the volumes already issued appear names of illustrious Argentine historians who have furnished prologues to certain of the selections presented. Omitting the names of members of the Section itself, who have already been cited, there may be mentioned Juan Agustín García, Ricardo Levene, and Enrique del Valle Iberlucea.

Parallel with this work, there is being published a collection of monographs, intended to throw light upon, or to revise, certain historical questions still of true interest, which, thanks to documents heretofore unknown, now being discovered in the rich archives which the History Section is exploring, can today be treated with greater certainty and wider knowledge. Collaborators in this new collection, up to the present, are Luis M. Torres, Emilio Ravignani, Juan Álvarez, Roberto Lehmann-Nitsche, and Rómulo D. Carbia.

It is not too much to say that among the current publications which deal with American history, none are issued on so carefully premeditated a plan as this one, so especially correlated to deal with all the factors in the life of the past centuries of Hispanic American colonization and development, nor do any so satisfactorily fulfil the highest modern concept of what critical presentation of sources should be. The History Section of the Faculty of Philosophy and Letters of the National University of Buenos Aires honors Argentina, in honoring itself with these excellent publications, which are a magnificent exponent of the

[2] Plan for Historical Investigation and Publication of the History Section, foreword to Volume V., *Documentos para la Historia Argentina*, Buenos Aires, 1915.

degree of perfection in research which is being attained in Argentina, the nicety of historical discipline there maintained, to the end of dissipating legends and setting forth the far more valuable truths of American history—so long unknown, distorted or ignored.

Furthermore, to students whose interests lie outside Argentina, this series is of vital interest, for it rises like a goal ahead which can, and will, certainly be attained by analogous institutions of other countries, when intermittent and desultory investigations shall have been consolidated and correlated on some such plan as the one here described. Only such forethought, determination, persistance, and exacting care as the University of Buenos Aires is now exercising through its History Section of the Faculty of Philosophy and Letters can accomplish permanent and creditable work in this field of endeavour.[4]

I. A. WRIGHT.

Seville, Spain, May, 1920.

NOTES

ITEMS IN COMMERCE REPORTS FOR THE PERIOD OCTOBER-DECEMBER, 1920

Additional steamship service for Mexico. No. 287, December 7.

American commercial aeroplanes in Mexico. No. 273, November 19.

American paper and office supplies in Mazatlan, Mexico, No. 269, November 15.

American tractors and agricultural machinery in southern Brazil. No. 288, December 8.

American trolley cars in Buenos Aires. No. 282, December 1.

Anomalies of exchange in Trinidad. No. 237, October 8.

Argentina's exports for first nine months of 1920. No. 271, November 17.

Argentine export duties for December. No. 285, December 4.

The Argentine market for calcium carbide, glycerine, and other chemical products. No. 279, November 27.

Argentine market for drugs and veterinary remedies. No. 283, December 2.

[4] The only North American university which has undertaken any serious, continuous work in Hispanic American research, is the University of California, which, while proceeding upon quite another course, is, nevertheless, accomplishing much, thanks to possession of a central plan.

Argentine sugar prospects. No. 238, October 9.

Argentine state railways show improvement. No. 274, November 20.

Argentine trade notes. No. 275, November 22.

Argentine-United States exchange. No. 273, November 19.

The Artificial flower industry in Argentina. No. 274, November 20.

Automobile show to be held in Mexico in March. No. 304, December 28.

Bahia port improvements. No. 249, October 22.

Bandages, gauze and absorbent cotton manufactured in Argentina. No. 263, November 8.

Banking situation in Colombia. No. 289, December 9.

Beet-sugar industry in Uruguay. No. 259, November 3.

Bids desired for port works at Rio de Janeiro, Brazil. No. 281, November 30.

Bids for electrification of Chilean railway. No. 241, October 13.

Bolivia repeals law relative to selling foreign drafts. No. 260, November 4.

Brazilian imports of textiles show increase in 1918. No. 257, November 1.

Brazilian market for portable houses. No. 288, December 8.

Brazilian sugar crop for 1920. No. 304, December 28.

Brazilian supreme court decision affecting registration of trademarks. No. 267, November 12.

Brazil's crude rubber exports in October. No. 289, December 9.

Cacao growers form syndicate in Bahia, Brazil. No. 294, December 15.

Cancellation for orders of merchandise by Mexican importers. No. 271, November 17.

Changes in the Bureau's offices in Latin America. No. 232, October 2.

Chihuahua city streets to be repaved. No. 294, December 15.

Chilean budget for 1921. No. 251, October 25.

Chilean customhouse receipts in July. No. 238, October 9.

Chilean import trade. No. 262, November 6.

Chilean products available for export. No. 280, November 29.

Coal strike developments in Mexico. No. 278, November 26.

Cocoa dryers for Trinidad. No. 240, October 12.

Coffee shipments from Maracaibo, Venezuela, during October. No. 304, December 28. *Id.* during November, No. 307, December 31.

The coffee situation in Venezuela. No. 252, October 26.

Commercial and financial readjustment in Chile. No. 263, November 8.

Commercial and private failures in Argentina. No. 280, November 29.

The Commercial district of Bogotá, Colombia. No. 253, October 27.

Conditions in Habana harbor.   Nos. 282, 284, and 304, December 1, 3, and 28.
Condition of cotton crop in Lower California.   No. 246, October 19.
Construction work in the city of Buenos Aires.   No. 276, November 23.
Continued business depression in Chile.   No. 285, December 4.
Continued improvement in congested conditions in Habana.   No. 242, October 14.
Copper deposits in Chile.   No. 241, October 13.
Cotton cultivation in Tucumán, Argentina.   No. 251, October 25.
Cotton textile industry of Mexico.   No. 255, October 29.
Crude rubber exports from Brazil in November.   No. 306, December 30.
Cuban purchasers of railroad rolling stock.   No. 281, November 30.
Cuban regulations governing shipments during moratorium.   No. 265, November 10.
The Cuban situation.   No. 246, October 19.
Cuban terminal port closed to entry.   No. 306, December 30.
Declared exports during August from Panama.   No. 282, December 1.
Demonstration of American agricultural machinery in Salvador.   No. 267, November 12.
Development of sugar industry in Nicaragua.   No. 306, December 30.
Development of trade with Mexico.   No. 305, December 29.
Dispatch of merchandise continues in Habana.   No. 251, October 25.
Dominican rules governing sales of patent and proprietary medicines.   No. 287, December 7.
Economic conditions in Brazil.   No. 288, December 8.
Economic conditions in Entre Rios, Argentina.   No. 250, October 23.
Economic conditions in Mexico.   No. 233, October 4.
Economic notes from Uruguay.   Id.
Establishment of American consulate at Arica, Chile.   No. 306, December 30.
Establishment of free ports in Mexico.   No. 246, October 19.
Establishment of publicity bureau in Guatemala.   No. 251, October 25.
Establishment of school aviation in Ecuador.   No. 305, December 29.
Exports for September quarter from Isle of Pines to United States.   No. 260, November 4.
Exports for the third quarter of 1920 from Santa Marta.   Id.
Exports to the United States from Paraguay.   No. 281, November 30.
Extension of Cuban prohibition on import of rice.   No. 277, November 24.

Extension of moratorium in Cuba. No. 285, December 4.

Final figures for 1919–1920 Cuban sugar crop. No. 256, October 30.

Financial conditions in Para, Brazil. No. 269, November 15.

Financial situation in Salvador. No. 263, November 8.

Financial situation in Nicaragua. No. 276, November 23.

Fluctuation of Peruvian exchange. No. 263, November 8.

Foreign tariffs. Nos. 233, 242, and 248, October 4, 14, and 21; 260, November 4; and 284, December 3.

Formation of syndicate of banana growers in Tabasco, Mexico. No. 305, December 29.

Government irrigation project in Sonora. No. 257, November 1.

Guatemala paper currency. No. 258, November 2.

Gum arabic available from Argentina. No. 246, October 19.

High prices demanded by grain haulers in Argentina. No. 294, December 15.

Higher prices for livestock in Honduras. No. 307, December 31.

How exchange affects business in Chile. No. 243, October 15.

Ice factory for Matamoros. No. 276, November 23.

Import prohibitions in Salvador. No. 282, December 1.

Importation of leather and shoes into Cuba. No. 294, December 15.

Importers of rubber goods and clothing in Canada, Europe, and Latin America. No. 250, October 23.

Improvement in congested conditions in Habana. No. 237, October 8.

Inauguration of direct cable from Cartagena to Colon. No. 286, December 6.

Inauguration of through Pullman service from San Antonio to Mexico City. No. 244, October 16.

Incorporation and corporation taxes in Latin America. No. 286, December 6.

Increased activity in Argentine butter market. No. 269, November 15.

Increased duties in Guatemala. No. 286, December 6.

Increased interest in Argentine cotton cultivation. No. 301, December 23.

Indications of oil in Uruguay. No. 305, December 29.

Interest charges under Cuban moratorium. No. 263, November 8.

Integral loan issued by Argentine Republic. No. 244, October 16.

Investments in agricultural and mining properties in Mexico. No 248, October 21.

Laws regulating exploitation of petroleum mines in Salvador. No. 264, November 9.

Limited shipments of hides from Chihuahua, Mexico. No. 251, October 25.

Lists of importers in Bolivia. *Id.*

Lists of tile manufacturers in Argentina. No. 261, November 5.

Manufacture of acids in Argentina. No. 272, November 18.

The Manufacture of brooms and brushes in Argentina. *Id.*

Manufacture of flax straw waste in Argentina. No. 258, November 2.

Manufacture of floor tiles in Argentina. No. 259, November 3.

Manufacture of straw hats in Argentina. No. 271, November 17.

Market conditions in Venezuela. No. 234, October 5.

Market for American agricultural machinery in southern Brazil. No. 268, November 13.

Market for building materials in Lima, Peru. No. 276, November 23.

Market for fruit preserves in Argentina and Uruguay. No. ·257, November 1.

Market for industrial drums and chemicals in Argentina. No. 263, November 8.

Market for jute bags at Mazatlan, Mexico. No. 252, October 26.

Market for mining supplies in Mexico. No. 281, November 30.

The Market for oils in Argentina. No. 286, December 6.

The Market for paraffin wax, stearic acid, and rosin in Argentina. No. 280, November 29.

The Market for sodium and potassium in Argentina. No. 270, November 16.

Mining and petroleum laws of Venezuela available. No. 263, November 8.

Moratorium diminishing discharge in Habana. No. 257, November 1.

Moratorium established in Paraguay. No. 270, November 16.

Moratorium interfering with discharge of merchandise in Habana. No. 262, November 6.

National wool-scouring plant at Montevideo. No. 260, November 4.

New bibliography in lumber trade in Latin America. No. 286, December 6.

New branch of the Banco Frances de Mexico opened. No. 262, November 6.

New Chilean magazine devoted to American interests. No. 257, November 1.

New consular fees in Chile. No. 264, November 9.

New import duties in Peru. No. 280, November 29.

New insurance company in Paraguay. No. 262, November 6.

New line of steamers between the United States and Brazil. No. 261, November 5.

New paper pulp industry in Argentina. No. 273, November 19.

New Peruvian customs tariff. No. 265, November 10.

New Portuguese steamship line to Brazil. No. 283, December 2.

New road projected in Ecuador. No. 303, December 27.

New service to Brazil and River Plate. No. 268, November 13.

New steamship line to Brazil. No. 293, December 14.

New steamship line to Mexico. No. 288, December 8.

New steamship lines from Colon-Cristobal. No. 275, November 22.

New sulphuric acid laboratory for Montevideo. No. 234, October 5.

New theater for Pointe-a-Pitre, Guadeloupe. No. 243, October 15.

No moratoriums in Colombia. No. 259, November 3.

October exports from Nogales to United States. No. 288, December 8.

Official study of Argentine coal fields. No. 261, November 5.

Opportunity for sale in Paraguay of cotton piece goods. No. 287, December 7.

Organization formed in Argentina to protect trade in grain bags. No. 250, October 23.

Output of the government oil reserves at Comodoro Rivadavia, Argentina. No. 277, November 24.

Panama canal traffic for August, No. 244, October 16. *Id.*, for September. No. 269, November 15.

Panama's trade for October. No. 306, December 30.

Paraguay government to issue currency in aid of banks. No. 257, November 1.

Parcel post to Venezuela. No. 292, December 13.

Peruvian centennial to be held in 1921. No. 249, October 22.

Peruvian statistics for 1919. No. 259, November 3.

The Petroleum industry and laws of Colombia. No. 243, October 15.

Petroleum production by American companies in Trinidad. No. 274, November 20.

Plan for increased railway communications in Colombia. No. 279, November 27.

Present conditions in Habana harbor. No. 274, November 20.

Production and exportation of Chilean nitrate of soda during August. 1920. No. 243, October 15.

Production of Cacao in Tabasco. No. 289, December 9.

Production of minerals in Mexico. No. 234, October 5.

Prohibition on import of rice into the Dominican Republic. No. 231, October 1.

Projected development of the merchant marine of Mexico. No. 259, November 3.

Projected port improvements at Manzanillo, Mexico. No. 267, November 12.

Proposed bill for an association of nitrate products of Chile. No. 268, November 13.

Proposed fuel-oil station at Cuba. No. 273, November 19.

Proposed petroleum law in Peru. No. 274, November 20.

Proposed sanitation of Salvador. No. 307, December 31.

Proposition for establishment of beet-sugar industry in Argentina. No. 250, October 23.

Prospects of wood-pulp production in Chile. No. 249, October 22.

Publication of Venezuelan railroads available for reference. No. 258, November 2.

Purchase of aviation materials by Brazil. No. 288, December 8.

Railways acquire Argentine oil fields. No. 247, October 20.

Peat fields near La Paz, Bolivia. No. 253, October 27.

Recent shipments of wood from Ecuador. No. 306, December 30.

Reclamation project in northeastern Brazil. No. 303, December 27.

Relaxation of Brazilian embargo on sugar. No. 237, October 8.

Remission of duty on cattle and sheep and certain food products in Bolivia. No. 258, November 2.

Removal of Brazilian embargo on food products and articles of prime necessity. No. 275, November 22.

Removal of Argentine embargo on flour. No. 294, December 15.

Removal of import duty on certain iron piping in Mexico. No. 258, November 2.

Resources and trade of the Amazonian region of Bolivia. No. 246, October 19.

Results of sugar season in Dominican Republic. No. 236, October 7.

Rich tungsten ore in Argentina. No. 304, December 28.

River dredges desired in Ecuador. No. 266, November 11.

River navigation renewed in Argentina. No. 236, October 7.

Rubber industry of Bolivia. No. 251, October 25.

Rubber stamps and enameled signs in Argentina. No. 292, December 13.

Samples of flax-straw fiber and waste from Argentina available. No. 261, November 5.

School of wireless telegraphy established in Venezuela. No. 252, October 26.

September rubber exports from Brazil. No. 276, November 23.

Serious coal shortage in Mexico. No. 257, November 1.

Sisal cultivation in Jamaica. No. 239, October 11.

Situation in Habana remains unchanged. No. 291, December 11.

Six months' exports from Paraguay to United States. No. 261, November 5.

Specifications for Mexican wireless stations available. No. 262, November 6.

Specifications for water cocks and pipe fittings in Venezuela. No. 254, October 28.

Sugar industry in Brazil. No. 237, October 8.

Sulphur ores available in Mexico. No. 272, November 18.

Summary of recent news from Vera Cruz. No. 278, November 26.

Terms of Cuban moratorium. No. 245, October 18.

Timber contract let by Honduras government. No. 252, October 26.

Tobacco crop in the Dominican Republic. No. 258, November 2.

Trade lists in Europe and South America. No. 263, November 8.

Trade notes from Argentina. No. 241, October 13; no. 259, November 3; and No. 293, December 14.

Trade notes from Central America. No. 304, December 28.

Trade notes from Colombia. No. 257, November 1.

Trade notes from Mexico. No. 251, October 25, nos. 260, 262, 264, and 276, November 4, 6, 9, and 23; and no. 288, December 8.

Trade notes from Peru. No. 270, November 16.

Trade notes from Venezuela. No. 238, October 9.

Trade of United States with Ecuador during first quarter of 1920. No. 287, December 7.

Trade publications wanted for Cuban agricultural schools. No. 256, October 30.

Typewriter market in Brazil. No. 281, November 30.

Uruguayan company to purchase Mihanovich fleet. No. 282, December 1.

Uruguayan trade for first eight months of 1920. No. 307, December 31.

Uruguay's foreign trade for first seven months of 1920. No. 271, November 17.

Vanilla production in Mexico. No. 274, November 20.

Wool shipments from Argentina. No. 236, October 7.

Yucatan offers subvention for new henequen industry. No. 293, December 14.

Annual publications have appeared as follows:

Brazil. No. 43b. November 14, 1920: Bahia. By Consul Thomas Bevan, pp. 1–10. Pernambuco. By Vice Consul Edward Power, pp. 10–16.

Costa Rica. No. 27b. November 29, 1920. By Consul Benjamin F. Chase, San José. Pp. 7.

Dominican Republic. No. 29b.· December 9, 1920: Dominican Republic. By Vice Consul George A. Makinson, pp. 1–5. Puerto Plata. By Consul W. A. Bickers, pp. 6–10. The Sanchez Agency. By Consular Agent J. E. Lerousa, p. 10.

Panama. No. 38a. November 22, 1920. By Consul Julius D. Dreher. Pp. 4.

Among pamphlets issued by the Bureau are the following:

Garry, L. S.: Textile markets of Brazil. Special Agents Series, no. 203. Pp. 47. Price 10 cents.

Schurz, William Lytle: Paraguay. A commercial handbook. Special Agents Series, no. 199. Pp. 195. Price 40 cents.

NOTES ON MEXICO AND CENTRAL AMERICA

México Moderno is one of the leading literary magazines of Mexico. It is published in Mexico, D. F., by the "Compañía Editorial" directed by Professor Agustín Loera y Chávez, and the president of the Board of Directors is Dr. Enrique González Martínez, one of the foremost poets of modern Spanish. The "Editorial México Moderno" also publishes "Cultura", a library of world authors; "La Novela Quincenal" and "Revista de Libros", under the surveillance of Manuel Toussaint; and "Revista Musical" in the last named of which Manuel M. Ponce displays his qualities as musical critic and composer. To "México Moderno" contribute María Enriqueta, the authoress of the exquisite poems *Rumores de mi Huerto;* the Colombians Leopoldo de la Rosa and Ricardo Arenales, the second residing in San Antonio, Texas, where he has in charge in *El Imparcial* a section entitled "Indice de las Ideas"; Ramón López Velarde, whose volume of poems *La Sangre Devota* has deserved recently a second edition; and Jaime Torres Bodet, who is showing a very strong personality in his review of reviews for the magazine. Other contributors are Genaro Estrada, author of *Poetas Modernos de México,* who concerns himself chiefly with the bibliographical section; José Vasconcelos, the Rector of the University, whose recent address of welcome to Manuel Márquez Sterling, from Cuba, as Doctor "honoris causa" of the University, is a master-piece of diction and thought; José Juan Tablada, who has established the best Romance bookstore in New York City; Ezequiel A. Cháves, former Assistant Secretary of Public Education and Fine Arts, and Director of the National Preparatory School; Carlos Pereyra, diplomat and man of letters, whose critical·works (on the Monroe Doctrine, *Bolívar y Washington, Historia del Pueblo Mexicano, Hernán Cortés y la Epopeya del Anahuac*", and *Humboldt en América*) have been widely commented on; Alejandro Quijano, Dean of the Faculty of Law, author of *En Casa de Nuestros Primos*, and translator of Eca de Queiros's *Analectas*, who gives his views on a letter of the Conqueror of Colombia, Don Gonzalo Jiménez de Quezada; and Federico Mariscal, architect, who explains "The Beauty of our Walls." Through Luis González Obregón, the most attractive and erudite chronicler of old Mexico, and ex-Director of the National Archives, we know the history of an *Encomienda* of the sixteenth century. Antonio Caso, Director of the High School, and a philosopher of no mean caliber, argues on "The hierarchies of Thought as the Foundation of Belief". Alfonso Reyes, Secretary of the Mexican Legation in Madrid, who quite recently published *El Plano Oblícuo*, is also a contributor. The Director of the National Museum, Luis Castillo Ledón (his historical monography *El Chocolate* ought to be mentioned) presents some pages of his biography of Padre Hidalgo; and El Marqués de San Francisco, Librarian of the National Archives, proves with his prose of "El Papagayo de Huichilobos" that he is the witty writer of "Los Jardines de Nueva España".

Don Victoriano Salado Alvarez, now residing at San Francisco, Cal., is, no doubt, the most reliable authority on the Mexican War and the Intervention and the Empire. In his article "Un Filósofo Histo-riador", in *La Prensa*, San Antonio, Tex., speaking on "Factors in the Historical Evolution of Mexico" by Lic. Toribio Esquivel Obregón, which was published in THE HISPANIC AMERICAN HISTORICAL REVIEW, he says that this is a substantial monography, and he examines many of its viewpoints in its excellent discussion of the fundamental national problems of his country. Lic. Esquivel Obregón with Manuel Calero, Francisco Carvajal, Juan B. Castelazo, Jesús Flores Magón, Tomás McManus, Miguel Ruelas, and Jorge Vera Estañol, all of them well-known men of Mexican past administrations, have published in New York *Ensayo sobre la Reconstruccion de México*, in which they treat of matters ranging from the public suffrage to the agrarian problem. One of the contributors to this important essay, Lic. Vera Estañol, former Secretary of the Interior and of Public Education, has reprinted his articles on *Carranza and his Bolshevik Régime*, advocating the rehabilitation of the Constitution of 1857. "Is a new political party to be formed and is Work its program, its platform?" asks Salado Álvarez.

Below follow mention of the successful books published by Mexicans last year: *El Verdadero Díaz y la Revolución*, by Dr. Francisco Bulnes, the author also of *El Verdadero Juárez*—a sensation in the political world, as no author before Bulnes has displayed so boldly the different aspects of the great revolutionist; *Li-Po y Otros Poemas*, by José Juan Tablada, Imprenta Bolívar, Caracas, a collection of very original poems written according to the "Ultraism" rules; *Una Victoria Financiera. Capítulos para la Historia*, by Carlos Díaz Dufoo (published by Librería Bouret), the distinguished journalist of *El Imparcial* and *Excelsior*, who ably and frankly reviews the financial situation in Mexico since the Independence and especially during the new era started by Limantour, the famous Minister of the Treasury; *Divagaciones Literarias*, by José Vasconcelos, Lectura Selecta, a representative of the present philosophical movement in Spanish America and whose *Pitágoras*, with preface by Henríquez Ureña, placed him among the educators of youth; *La Vida Intacta*, by Eduardo Colín, Secretary of the Mexican Legation in Venezuela, in which he explains the mental influence and personalities of thinkers and authors like the Belgian Verhaeren, the Portuguese De Queiros, the Colombian Guillermo Valencia (of *Ritos*), and the Mexican Luis G. Urbina (of *Ingenuas, Puestas de Sol*, and *Antología del Centenario*); *Rosario la de Acuña*, by José López Portillo y Rojas, Librería Española,—a leaf of the literary history of Mexico not only as a biography of the unhappy Manuel Acuña and of the picturesque creature of one of his poems, but as first hand information of men like Ignacio Manuel Altamirano, Ignacio Ramírez, and Juan de Dios Peza; "El Rebozo", a remarkable historical article by José de J. Núñez y Domínguez, editor of the weekly *Revista de Revistas*, Secretary of the Society of Geography and Statistics, and who is worthy of mention for his opusculos *Holocaustos, La Hora del Ticiano*, and *Los Poetas Jóvenes de México; Retratos Reales e Imaginarios*, Lectura Selecta, a selection of the articles on many literary topics of today, by Alfonso Reyes, the young master; and *La Vida en México*, by Marquesa Calderón de la Barca, edited by Bouret, but unpublished as it was only known fragmentarily, until Enrique Martínez Sobral translated it. Other books are: *Sátiros y Amores*, by Ricardo Gómez Robelo, Los Angeles, Cal. (illustrations by Roubaix de L'Abrie-Richey); *Bajo el Haya de Títiro*, by Juan B. Delgado; *El Pan Nuestro de Cada Día*, by José Gómez Ugarte (El Abate Benigno); *Caro Victrix*, sonnets by Efrén Rebolledo; *Jardines de Provincia*, by José Zavala; *Las Alamedas del Silencio*, by Gilberto Ruvalcaba, published by El Ateneo Reissig, México; and *Se Apoderará Estados Unidos de América de Baja California?* (*La invasión filibustera de 1911*), by R. Velasco Ceballos.

In the memorial of Pedro Requena Legarreta held in Mexico City, under the suggestion of the University, Carlos Pellicer Cámara, made touching remarks about the young poet who died recently in New York, and whose translations of Tagore and other English and French poets deserve high praise among scholars. We have also to mention with regret the deaths of Jesús Urueta, the wellknown polished orator and champion of Greek cúlture; and of Genaro García, the historian, who accomplished a great task as investigator of early Mexican history and who was Director of the National Museum of Ethnology and History of Mexico. García owned the richest collection on Mexico, and his own written works reach many volumes, among the latter being the priceless *Documentos para la Historia de México, Leona Vicario, heroína insurgente; Historia Verdadera de la Conquista de Nueva España, por Bernal Diaz del Castillo; and Don Juan de Palafox y Mendoza*.

Mexican past history is tempting Enrique Gómez Carrillo, the delightful chronicler, and he is busily collecting all material useful for writing the history of the pre-Cortesian epoch of Mexico. He believes that colonial Mexico is monotonous and gray, and that Chocano's poems about that epoch are not in full accord with reality.

Following are some of the latest books published in the United States and dealing with Mexico: *The Near Side of the Mexican Question*, by Jay S. Stowell, New York, George H. Doran Co.; *Mexico and the Caribbean*, a series of addresses during the conference upon those countries at Clark University, May, 1920, and edited now by George H. Blakeslee, New York, G. E. Steckert & Co.; *Through the Grand Canyon from Wyoming to Mexico*, by Ellsworth L. Kolb, New York, Macmillan, on the author's trip, 1911, for securing photographs and moving pictures of the Colorado River; and *The People of Mexico*, by Wallace Thompson, edited by Harper & Brothers.   Mr. Thompson gives first-hand information, as he has been in Mexico more than fifteen years closely connected with the American Consular Service and as a newspaper man. Badger has published *The Land Beyond Mexico*, by Rhys Carpenter.

Lectura Selecta, Mexico, has printed a new edition of *El Hombre que Parecía un Caballo y el Trovador Colombiano* by the Central American poet Rafael Arévalo Martínez, with a foreword by Alfonso Reyes, who highly commends this attractive novel, the first effort in Central America to write a psychological novel; as well as *El Alma de la Escuela*, by Luis Zulueta, Biblioteca Renovación, Costa Rica, against the Catholic teaching of that country; *Fuentes Iluminadas*, by R. Álvarez Berrocal, San José; *Valores Literarios de Costa Rica*, by Rogelio Sotela, editor of the magazine *Athenea*; and *Filosofía de la Crítica* and *Voces Lejanas*, by M. Vicenzi.

"La deuda Ethelburga, negocio de los banqueros" by Juan Ramón Áviles, *La Noticia*, Managua, December 5 and 7, 1920; and "Los Enemigos del Córdova" (the Nicaraguan money), by Frutos Ruiz, *El Comercio*, Managua, November 17th are very interesting contributions to the study of the Central American financial situation.   One should also read the article "Foreign Debts Factor in Move to Effect Central American Union", by Mr. Edward Perry, published in the *Newark Evening News*, January 10, 1921.

Salado Alvarez proves in a substantial article, "El Prohibicionismo en México", *La Prensa*, San Antonio, Texas, December 25, 1920, that the Prohibition campaign in that country is a serious problem for statesmen, for during the eighteenth century the Mexicans indulged in more than thirty alcoholic beverages.   One of the prohibitionist pioneers was the viceroy Marques de Mancera, in 1671.

Emilio Rabasa, in *La Evolución Histórica de México*, a historical essay, shows that he is still the same distinguished scholar who wrote years ago *La Constitución y la Dictadura*. In his latest book Sr. Rabasa makes a deep study of the Indian problem in Mexico, although it is said he does not treat the subject from the ethnological point of view.   The life and work of Father Antonio Remesal (author of the famous *Historia de la Provincia de San Vicente de Chiapa y Guatemala*) was the topic of Don Francisco Fernández del Castillo before the Mexican Academy of History. He explained how Father Remesal was prosecuted on account of his book, a fact which had remained unknown hitherto.

To honor the poet's influence on the mental activities of the new generation, Professor Joaquín García Monge, has published "Rubén Darío en Costa Rica" in two volumes. Sr. García Monge is the public librarian and editor of "El Convivio", popular library, "Ediciones Sarmiento" and *Repertorio Americano*, a fortnightly magazine devoted to continental interests. At the same time, Regino E. Boti, of Cuba, has collected in *Hipsipilas* the less known poems of Darío. García Monge is the author of *Mala Sombra y Otros Sucesos* and his superb literary taste is always shown in his publications. Under his auspices there are published the following books: *La Miniatura*, sketches of the colonial period and short-stories, by Ricardo Fernández Guardia; *Las Coccinelas del Rosal*, by Octavio Jiménez; *Los Cuentos de mi Tía Panchita*, folklore pages by Carmen Lira; *En el Taller del Platero*, *De Variado Sentir*, and *De Atenas y la Filosofía*, by Rómulo Tovar; *Poesías*, by José Olivares, of Nicaragua; *El Hombre que Parecía un Caballo*, by Rafael Arévalo Martínez, of Guatemala; and *El Rosal del Ermitaño*, by Rafael Heliodoro Valle, of Honduras. Luis Dobles Segreda, with his *Rosa Mística* (Heredia); Napoleón Pacheco with *Las Guarias del Crepúsculo* (Falco y Borrase, publishers); and Luis Andrés Zúñiga of Tegucigalpa, with *El Banquete*, prose and verse, are also contributions to literary bibliography. Zúñiga is a poet laureate, has an excellent record as a journalist, and wrote *Los Conspiradores*, a sort of historical drama based upon that passage of General Francisco Morazán, the Central American hero, when his enemies tendered to him the dictatorship which he indignantly refused. In accordance with this patriotic tendency among students of history of the Isthmus to exalt the virtues of the pioneers of their nation, Dr. Sixto Barrios delivered in the University of Salvador, a lecture on the life of Dr. Isidro Menéndez, as legislator and orator; and there is a magazine, *Próceres*, edited by Dr. Rafael V. Castro, with contributions of Víctor Jerez, Alberto Luna, Rómulo Durón, Manuel Valladares, M. Castro Ramírez and Francisco Gavidia. In the last issue, no. 5, volume IV, appear articles on the Captain General of Guatemala, José de Bustamante y Guerra (1814), and the first President of Central America, General Arce, beside an eulogy of José Matías Delgado, by Dr. Victor Jerez, Rector of the University. Central America is on the eve of the first centenary of its political independence.

. In his anthology of Hispanic American prose writers, recently printed in Buenos Aires, Leonardo Bazzano presents pages from Gavidia, Mayorga Rivas, Arturo Ambrogi, and Alberto Masferrer, the last named an excellent teacher and writer, who has in press *Ideas y Formas*. At the same time, Virgilio Rodríguez Beteta, former editor of *Diario de Centro-América*, in Guatemala, has lectured in the Atheneum of Madrid, on the literature of his country; and "El Arte Tipográfico", New York City, is publishing the most interesting chapters of *La Imprenta en Centro-América* (preface to his history of journalism in the old kingdom of Guatemala). His old friend, Víctor Miguel Díaz, with his "Crónicas Viejas" in the *Diario*, gives reliable information relative to Antigua Guatemala, as does Eduardo Martínez López, librarian of Honduras, with "Colonial Time" in *Los Sucesos*, a weekly of Tegucigalpa; and Ricardo Fernández Guardia with the origin of a poem written in Costa Rica by one of the Conquerors, a paper read in December last in a festival to honor José Santos Chocano as guest of that country.

Managua has *Nicaragua Informativa* and *Los Domingos* two weekly periodicals edited, respectively, by Hernán Robleto and Salvador Ruiz Morales. In the issue of the last one, November 28, 1920, appears the magnificent "Salutación a Chocano" by Azarías H. Pallais, Doctor of Belles-Lettres and Theology and the author of the poems *A la Sombra del Agua* and *Espumas y Estrellas*. *La Revista de Costa Rica*, edited by Dr. J. F. Trejos Quiñós, has the support of the best scholars of the country, among them Anastasio Alfaro, the biologist, and Cleto González Víquez, former President of the republic and one of the most able investigators of the past. In this review have recently appeared the following interesting articles: "A visit to the volcano of Irazú", by R. Fernández Peralta; "Final Geological and Geographical Report about Costa Rica", by Donald F. MacDonald and other geologists; "Cartago and Cariay", by Carlos Gagini; "Climatology and Forestry", by Elías Leiva; "The South-western Coasts of Costa Rica", by M. Obregón L.; and "San José and its Beginnings", by Cleto González Víquez.   RAFAEL HELIODORO VALLE.

Twenty-three Clark University Addresses, edited by Professor George H. Blakeslee, of Clark University, have been published by G. E. Stechert & Co., under the title *Mexico and the Caribbean*. These addresses were all given at Clark University during the Conference 'upon Mexico and the Caribbean, May 20–22, 1920. This volume, which will be reviewed later in the columns of this periodical, is full of interest and value. Among contributors are Toribio Esquivel Obregón, Frederick Starr, James Carson, Ellsworth Huntington and others. The addresses deal with matters on which people desire information.

Dr. Webster E. Browning, a paper by whom is published in this number, has published through the Committee on Co-operation in Latin America, a small pamphlet on *The Republic of Ecuador. Social, Intellectual and Religious Conditions Today.* Interesting data concerning this country will be found in this work.

The distinguished Argentine scholar Alberto Ghiraldo has undertaken the preparation and publication (March, 1920) of an *Antología americana* which is intended to present a comprehensive picture of the intellectual and artistic life of the Hispanic American countries. The work will be divided into twenty volumes under the following titles: 1 and 2, *Precursores;* 3, *Lira Clásica;* 4, *Lira Romántica;* 5, *Historiadores y Filósofos;* 6, *Los Ensayistas;* 7, *La Musa del Pueblo;* 8, *Tradicionalistas y Costumbristas;* 9, *Los Tribunos;* 10, *Leyendas y Anécdotas;* 12, *El Verbo nuevo;* 11, *Poesía Festiva;* 13, *Crítica contemporánea;* 14, *El Libro de los Cuentos;* 15, *El Libro de las Ciencias;* 16, *El Libro de los Niños;* 17, *Biografía Americana;* 18, *Teatro;* 19, *Hoy* (prosa); and 20, *Hoy* (verso).—C. K. JONES.

The Mesta: A Study in Spanish Economic History, 1273–1836, by Julius Klein, has recently appeared from the Harvard University Press at Cambridge. The volume is published under the direction of the Department of Economics. The subject is treated by Dr. Klein in seventeen chapters and forms an important work in the economic history of Spain. A copious and useful bibliography is a welcome part of the volume. This work will be reviewed in a later issue of the Review. Dr. Klein has lately severed his connection with the Bureau of Foreign and Domestic Commerce and is now Assistant Professor of Latin American History and Economics in Harvard University. His volume fulfills part of the requirements necessary for his doctor's degree at Harvard.

Dr. Fernando Ortiz, Professor in the University of Habana, in his *Los Negros Esclavos; Estudio sociológico y de Derecho Público,* has written a chapter in the history of Cuba that must be consulted by the historian who wishes to write the history of this important island. The volume shows a great deal of original research, and is well documented. Dr. Ortiz expects to reissue the work in several parts as monographs.

Foreign Tariff Notes, No. 36, recently issued by the Bureau of Foreign and Domestic Commerce, contains notes on the tariff of several Hispanic American countries.

The Americas for December, 1920, publishes the following: "Canada gaining in Caribbean trade"; "Cuban situation should greatly improve within six months"; and "Plan new railroad across the Andes mountains".

The Catholic Historical Review publishes in its number for October, 1920, an excellent communication relative to "Father Kino's name"; and "The martyrdom of Father Juan de Santa María", by Lloyd Mecham.

Cultura Venezolana (Caracas), for August 1920, contains Los Aborígines del estado Falcón", by Pedro M. Arcaya; "El Vértice victorioso", by Gabriel Espinosa; "Las Ensenadas de la historia", by Eloy G. González; "Aldea de Aquelarre", by Ramón Hurtado; "Campañas y cruceros", by W. G. Mahoney; "Miranda como filósofo y erudito", by Manuel Segundo Sánchez; and "Como podría obtenerse la unión espiritual y material de la América Hispana y la Anglo Sajona", by Guillermo A. Sherwell.

"Del Potomac al Guaire" is the title of an article in the November *Hispania*, and its author is Guillermo A. Sherwell, a Mexican scholar resident in Washington, D. C. The issue of this paper for December publishes: "El Alma de Toledo", by M. Romera-Navarro; "Impresiones de España", by Carolina Marcial Dorada; "Six weeks in Madrid", by Medora Loomis Ray; "Spanish American poets of today and yesterday: II. José Santos Chocano, el poeta de América", by George W. Umphrey.

In *Inter-America* for October, 1920 are found : "Antecedents of Argentine history", transl. from *La Unión* (Buenos Aires), May 24, 1920; "The Bolivian doctrine", by J. L. Andara, transl. from *Cultura*

Venezolana (Caracas), June, 1918; "General Leonard Wood and public instruction in Cuba", by Aurelio Hevia, transl. from *Cuba Contemporánea*, July, 1920; "A Great Bolivian writer", by Juan José de Soiza Reilly, transl. from *Nuestra América* (Buenos Aires), March, 1920; "A knightly pirate", by Ricardo Fernández Guardia, transl. from *Revista de Costa Rica* (San José, Costa Rica), March, 1920; "A wedding in the Quechuan great world", by Alfredo Palacio Mendoza, transl. from *El Hogar* (Buenos Aires), June, 1920. In the number for December are the following; "American policy", by Armando Solano, transl. from *El Espectador* (Bogotá), August 13, 1920; "An Argentine artist", by R. Ramis Togores, transl. from *Nosotros*, July, 1920; "Baja California", transl. from *Revista de Revistas* (Méjico), August 8, 1920; "Independence Day and the Central American union", by Ramón Rosa, transl. from *Revista de la Universidad* (Tegucigalpa), April 15, 1920, and reprinted from *La Paz*, no. 278, 1882; "José Asunción Silva", by Rafael A. Estenger, transl. from *Cuba Contemporánea*, May, 1920; "Rafael Obligado", by Calixto Uyuela, transl. from *Nosotros*, April, 1920; "Rubén Darío in Heredia", by Luis Dobles Segreda, transl. from *Athenea* (Costa Rica), July, 1920; "In search of a new volcano", by Ricardo Fernández Peralta, transl. from *Revista de Costa Rica* (San José, Costa Rica), July, 1920; "Theoretical and practical politics", by Leopoldo Lugones, transl. from *Centro-América* (Guatemala) April–June, 1920.

In recent numbers of *Mercurio Peruano* (Lima), occur the following articles: July 1920—"El Cuzco: Meca del turismo de la América del Sur", by Alberto A. Giesecke; "Europa después de la gran guerra", by Juan Bautista de Lavalle; "La Revolución de Bolívar". August—"Classificationes estéticas", by A. O. Deustua; "Augusto Madueño" (eulogy); "El Romanticismo contemporánea". September—"El Americanismo en los nuevos poetas anglo e hispano-americanos", by George W. Umphrey; "El Artista y el hombre", by José Leonidas Madueño;" "El Ayllo", by Carlos Valdez de la Torre. October—"D. Toribio Rodríguez de Mendoza", by Jorge Guillermo Leguia; "Don Ricardo V. García (eulogy); "Grados estéticos", by A. O. Deustua; "La Labor arqueológica de Sylvanus Griswold Morley", by Philip Ainsworth Means; "El Perú y España", by Manuel G. Abastos; "La Poesía contemporánea en los Estados Unidos", by George W. Umphrey; "Un Vaso esculpido de San Agustín Acasaguastlan, Guatemala", by Philip Ainsworth Means. November—"El Alma americana", by Webster E. Browning; "Dr. Don Luis Felipe Villarán" (editorial); "Régimen de la propiedad durante los incas", by Carlos Valdez de la Torre; "Un Sacerdote de la cultura", by Edwin Elmore; "La Universidad de Yale. Los métodos de enseñañza y la vida del estudiante en una gran universidad de norteamericana", by César Antonio Ugarte. In each number is also a part of the "Crónicas de Norteamérica," by the Peruvian scholar, Sr. Víctor Andrés Belaúnde, who is now in the United States.

The issue of *La Nueva Democracia* (New York) for November, 1920, contains: "La Guerra y la América", by E. Rodríguez Mendoza; "Herencia material del continente americano" (III.), by Webster E. Browning; and "El Pro y el contra de los Estados Unidos", by R. de Zayas Enríquez.

The Pan-American Magazine, for January, 1921, contains: "Argentina's butter trade"; "The coming sugar crop"; "Hydro-electric developments and prospects in South America"; "Mexican vanilla"; "Nicaragua's coffee"; "Peru protects the vicuña"; "Santo Domingo, old and new", by Samuel Guy Inman; "The South of South America", by W. W. Rasor; "United States foreign trade and its correlative factors"; "The Y. M. C. A. in Mexico, Brazil, Cuba, Uruguay".

The following items are published in various recent numbers of *The Pan American Review;* September, 1920—"The Christ of the Andes"; "Concerning Latin American center in New York" (editorial); "Intellectual intercourse with Hispanic America" (editorial); "Luncheon to President of Panama"; "Mexican possibilities", by R. De F. Boomer; "A Pan American college of commerce" (editorial); "Report of the Conference Committee for Chile". October—"Argentina", by Leonard Mathers; "Guatemala's citizen president", by Thomas R. Dawley; "Michael P. Grace"; "The new director general of the Pan American Union" (editorial); "New Latin American courses" (editorial); "Report of the Conference Committee for Colombia". November—"Biological expedition to explore the Amazon valley" (editorial); "How Latin America views Harding's election" (editorial); "Pan American propaganda" (editorial); "Report of the Conference Committee for Cuba"; "Striving for women's rights in South America" by Carlos Puyo D.; "Twelve years of progress"; "Women's activities in Latin American educational circles". The last section of each number of this Review is devoted to "Telegraphic Briefs", which are short, snappy items of interest from all parts of Hispanic America.

In *The River Plate American* (Buenos Aires) for January 9, 1921, appear the following: "The League of Nations"; "North American money"; "Our Latin American trade"; and "The Pioneer" [in Argentina], by Harry A. Kirwin.

The following titles are to items published in various numbers of the new Chilean review *Revista América;* October 5, 1920—"Construcción de caminos en Panama"; "Un Ferrocarril que unirá a Nicaragua y Honduras"; "Forman compañía para el subterráneo en la Habana"; "La Maestranza de San Bernardo"; "Penetración ferroviaria de la América del Sur"; "Se proyecta fundar en Panamá un instituto en homenaje a W. G. Gorgas"; "Una Tierra romantíca" (California), by Charles E. Chapman. October 19, 1920—"La Asociación Cristiana de Jovenes en Sud-América", by Ralph C. Scott; "Costa Rica da libre entrada a los ganados"; "Ecuador como productor de petróleo"; "Méjico avalua el petróleo y cobra el impuesto fijo"; "Nuevo partido político en Costa Rica"; $75,000,000 pide Méjico para su rehabilitación"; "Se dará maquinaría a los pequeños agricultores"; "Servicio postal aereo entre Estados Unidos y Cuba"; "La Poesía contemporánea en los Estados Unidos", by George Wallace Umphrey. November 7, 1920—"A. Mitchell Palmer", by Carlos Castro Ruiz; "Condición general de los negocios en Estados Unidos"; "El Despertar de Hispano-América"; "Exproprian tierras para un acqueducto" [Venezuela]; "La Habana es el primer puerto de Hispano-América"; "Méjico será el futuro centro mundial de petróleo"; "Los Estados Unidos no intervendrán jamás en Méjico"; "Gran proyecto sobre marina para Méjico"; "Por que los anunciantes dicen la verdad", by Carl Hunt; "Se forma en la zona del Canal una liga cívica. Los norteamericanos allá residentes quieren que se les otorgue el voto"; "Warren G. Harding: Presidente electo de los Estados Unidos. Declaraciones con respecto a Sud América".

Revista Argentina de Ciencias Políticas for August, 1920, contains: "Acefalía en la presidencia", by R. Wilmart; "Delitos contra la vida", by Rodolfo Rivarola and E. Gómez; "En el Brasil", by Rodolfo Rivarola; "Hojas de mi diario", by Luis B. Tomini; and Telasco Castellanos", by Angel F. Avalos.

Revista Bimestre Cubana in its number for January-June, 1920 has the following: "La Antonomía de los primitivos municipios cubanos", by Marío Alonso; "Los Estados Unidos y la independencia americana", by Camilo Destruge; and "Los Judíos en Cuba", by Max J. Kohler.

Revista de Derecho, Historia y Letras (Buenos Aires) for December, 1920, contains "El Gobierno de Martín Rodríguez", by J. C. Garay; "Homenaje escolar a Belgrano"; "La Jurisdicción sobre los ferrocarriles en el derecho constitucional argentino", by J. N. Matienzo. "Política unitaria", by J. Mendoza Zells; and "El Problem chileno-argentino", by J. Vial Solar; Dr. Estanislao S. Zeballos, the editor, contributes "Analecta", "Bibliografía", and "Oro y cambios".

Revista de Filosofía for September, 1920 contains "Aspectos sociales de la religión búdhica", by C. S. Saenz Peña;"De Drago a Tchitcherin", by A. Orzabal Quintana; "Democracia política y democracia económica" by A. Bunge; "La Personalidad de Alberdi", by A. S. Mújica; "La Reforma universitaria en Córdoba" by A. Orgaz and A. Capdevila; and other articles of more technical character.

The South American for January, 1921, appears under a new format, which greatly improves its appearance. In this number the following articles and items are worthy of mention: "Advertising in Latin America", by James C. Carson; "The agricultural college at Santiago" [Chile]; "Argentina quits league assembly" (editorial); "Bad financial situation in Nicaragua"; "Colombia faces her troubles"; "Conspiracy thwarted in Peru"; "The Country of Bolívar and Miranda", by Guillermo A. Sherwell; "Direct steamers to Guayaquil"; "German goods reappear in Chile"; "Indians of the Paraguayan Chaco"; "Made in Argentina" by Sir Woodman Burbridge; "Mexican outlook most promising"; "Mexico's amazing oil potentialities"; "The mission of Secretary Colby (editorial); "Obstacles to American trade with the South American republics", by John F. O'Hara, C. S. C.; "Plant life in Jujuy"; "Sketches of northern Argentina"; and "The Y. W. C. A. in Argentina".

The Southwestern Historical Quarterly, January, 1921, continues the "Minutes of the Ayuntamiento of San Felipe de Austin, 1828–1832", by Eugene C. Barker, and "Mirabeau Buonaparte Lamar", by A. K. Christian. William Ray Lewis presents in addition "The Hayes administration and Mexico".

"José de la Luz y Caballero", and "La Visita Española a Chile", are the titles of two articles appearing in *La Unión Hispano-Americana* (Madrid), for December, 1920.

RECENT PUBLICATIONS

BOOKS

Acevedo Díaz, Eduardo: Geografía de América, física, política y económica. 3d ed. Buenos Aires, P. García, 1920. Pp. 390.

Affairs in Mexico. Partial report of foreign relations committee (Senate. 66:2). Senate Réport no. 645. Washington, Government Printing Office, [1920?]. Pp. 93. N. t.

Antología americana; selección y prólogo de Alberto Ghiraldo. Vol. I. Madrid, G. Hernández y G. Sáez, 1920. Pp. 222.

Arquedas, Alcides: Historia de Bolivia: la fundación de la república. La Paz, Escuela tip. del Colegio Don Bosco, 1920. Pp. xviii, 442.

    Raza de bronce. La Paz, Gonzáles y Medina, 1919. Pp. 373.

Ascarruns, Moises: El Partido liberal en el poder. A traves de los mensajes presidenciales. 2 vols. La Paz, Arno Hermanos, 1918.

Avalos, Angel F.: Problemas del federalismo argentino, Córdoba, 1920.

Ayarragaray, Lucas: La iglesia en América. Buenos Aires, 1920.

Bacardí Moreau, Emilio: Florencio Villanova y Pío Rosado, 1854–1880. Habana, 1920. Pp. 164.

Baldivia, G.: Páginas históricas; Tacna y Arica. 2d ed. La Paz, 1919. Pp. VIII, 146, II.

Ballivián, Adolfo: Bolivia; recuerdos y futuro. Londres, Estab. Tip. de Sandford, 1920. Pp. 66.

Barreto, José María: Un año en Bolivia. La Paz, 1919. Pp. 310.

Bilbao, Francisco: El evangelio americano y páginas selectas. Selección, prólogo y notas de Armando Donoso. Barcelona, 1920. Pp. 254.

Blakeslee, George H. (ed.): Mexico and the Caribbean. Clark University Addresses. New York, G. E. Stechert & Co., 1920. Pp. x, 363.

Blas Uvua, ——: La historia de Carranza. México, 1920. Pp. 131.

Blasco Ibáñes, Vicente: El militarismo mejicano. Valencia, 1920. Pp. 250.

    Mexico in revolution. Transl. by Arthur Livingston and José Padín. New York, E. P. Dutton Co., 1920. Pp. 245.

Bolivia. Su estructura y sus derechos en el Pacífico. La Paz, Librería Editora Arno Hermanos, 1919. Pp. 377, VI.

Bott, Ernesto J. J.: El comercio entre los Estados Unidos y la América latina durante la gran guerra. Buenos Aires, Talleres Tip. "Oceana", 1919. Pp. 359.

Breceda, Alfredo: México revolucionario (1913–1917). Vol. I. Madrid, Tip. Artística, 1920. Pp. 506.

Brown, Everett Somerville, Ph.D.: The Constitutional history of the Louisiana purchase, 1803–1812. Berkeley, University of California Press, 1920. Pp. xi, 248.

Browning, Webster A.: The republic of Ecuador. Social, intellectual, and religious conditions today. New York, Committee on Cooperation in Latin America, 1920. Pp. 31.

Bulnes, Gonzalo: Las causas de la guerra entre Chile y Perú. Santiago de Chile, Soc. Imprenta-Litografía "Barcelona", 1918. Pp. 139.
Chile and Peru; causes of the war of 1879. Santiago de Chile. Impr. Universitaria, 1920. Pp. VIII, 160.

Bunau-Varilla, Philippe: The great adventure of Panama. Wherein are exposed its relations to the great war and also the luminous traces of the German conspiracies against France and the United States. Garden City, Doubleday, Page & Company, 1920. Pp. xv, 267.

Bunge, Augusto: La inferioridad económica de los argentinos nativos: sus causas y remedio. Buenos Aires, Imprenta Mercatali, 1919. Pp. 95.

Bunge, Carlos Octavio: Nuestra América. (Ensayo de Psicología Social.) Buenos Aires, Administración General Casa Vaccaro, 1918. Pp. 317.

Bustamante y Ballivián, Enrique: Auctóctonas. La Paz, 1920. Pp. 165.

Capo-Rodríguez, Pedro: Aspectos jurídicos de las relaciones entre los Estados Unidos y Puerto Rico. Washington, D. C., 1920. Pp. 73.

Carbia, Rómulo D.: Manuel de historia de la civilización argentina. Vol. I, Buenos Aires, Franzetti y Cía., 1917. Pp. 509.

Carrio, V. M.: Crónicas americanas. La Paz, 1919. Pp. 218.

Castro y Oyanguren, Enrique: Boletines del exterior. Lima, Peru. Edición 'Cervantes', 1920. Pp. viii, [9]–328.
Entre el Perú y Chile. La cuestión de Tacna y Arica. Páginas de divulgación histórica. Lima, Imprenta del Estado, 1919. Pp. 93.

Centeno, Francisco: Precursores de la diplomacia argentina. Buenos Aires, 1920.

Cobos Daract, Julio: Historia argentina. 2 vols. Buenos Aires, Edición "Virtus", [1919?].

Código electoral de Cuba. Ley de 8 de agosto de 1919. Habana, Imp. de Rambla, 1919. Pp. 312.

Collins, James H.: Straight business in South America. New York, London, D. Appleton and Company, 1920. Pp. xi, 305.

Cortijo A., L.: La música popular y los músicos célebres de la América Latina. Madrid, [1919?]. Pp. 443.

Constitución de la República Oriental del Uruguay. Montevideo, Librería la Facultad, 1919. Pp. 51.

Contreras, Francisco: Les écrivains contemporaines de l'Amérique Espagnole. Paris, 1920.

El Convenio de la Liga de las Naciones. Ministerio de Relaciones Exteriores, Santiago, Imp. Universitaria, 1920. Pp. 134.

Criado, Eduardo: La ciudad de los rascacielos (Nueva York). Sevilla, Tip. Leopio y Jiménez, 1919. Pp. 178.

Crus, Ernesto de la: Epistolario de O'Higgins, Santiago de Chile, 1916.

Cuervo Márques, Carlos: Prehistoria y viajes americanos. Estudios arqueológicos y etnográficos. 2d. ed. revised and enlarged. 2 vols. Madrid, Imp. de J. Pueyo, 1920.

La Cuestión chileno-peruana. No. 2. Santiago de Chile, Imprenta Universitaria, 1919. Pp. 46.

La Cuestión chileno-peruana: El Debate diplomático de 1918. Santiago de Chile, Imprenta Universitaria, 1919. Pp. 62.

La Cuestión chileno-peruana. La política de la República Argentina. Santiago de Chile, Emp. Zig-Zag, 1919. Pp. 117.

Cuestión de Límites con Bolivia. 1915-1917. Vol. I. Asunción, Paraguay, 1917. Pp. 396. (Ministerio de Relaciones Exteriores.) ·

Cuestiones internacionales. Bolivia Paraguay. [La Paz], Imprenta Nacional, 1918. Pp. 82.

Currencies after the war; a survey of conditions in various countries. Comp. under the auspices of the International Secretariat of the League of Nations. London, Harrison & Sons, [1920]. Pp. XVI, 254.

Denis, Pierre: L'Argentine moderne. Buenos Aires, Coni Freres, 1916. Pp. 122. La République Argentine; la mise en valeur du pays. Paris, A. Colin, 1920. Pp. 299. Maps; bibliographie, pp. 283-299.

Deustua, Ricardo A.: Petróleos peruanos. Lima, 1919. Pp. 48.

Días, José Virginio: Historia de Saravia; contribución al estudio del caudillaje en América. Montevideo, Barreiro y Cía., 1920. Pp. 256.

Días Romero, Belisario: Ensayo de prehistoria americana: Tiahuanaca y la América primitiva. 2d ed. La Paz, Arno Hermanos, 1920. Pp. II., 198.

Dies de Medina, Eduardo: Apuntes sobre tópicos internacionales. La Paz, Arno Hermanos, 1919. Pp. 170. (Preface by Carlos Calvo.)
Bolivia—Chile. La Paz, 1919. Pp. 153.
Derecho público. La Paz, 1919. Pp. 383.
De la Faena patriótica. La Paz, 1919. Pp. 210.
Paisajes criollos. La Paz, 1919. Pp. 68.

Domíngues, Manuel: El Alma de la rasa. Asunción, Casa Editora de Cándido Zamphiropolos, 1918. Pp. 265.
Paraguay—Bolivia, Cuestión de límites. Asunción, Talleres Gráficos, 1917. Pp. 43.
The same. Asunción Talleres Gráficos del Estado, 1918. Pp. 30.

Domville-Fife, Charles: The states of South America. New York, The Macmillan Co., [1920?].

Duque-Estrada, Osorio: A aboliçao (esboço historico)1831-1888. Com um prefacio do conseheiro Ruy Barbosa. Rio de Janeiro, Leite Ribeiro & Maurillo, 1918. Pp. XII. 6-328.

Emiliani, Rafael P.: Reorganisación económica política y social . Buenos Aires, J. Lajouane y Cía., 1920.

Enoch, C. R.: Spanish America, its romance, reality and future. New York, Charles Scribner's Sons, 1920. 2 vols.

Estrado, Dardo: Páginas de historia. Montevideo, 1920. Pp. 141.

Ferreccio, Horacio: El problema del Pacífico. La Paz, Gonsáles y Medina Editores, 1919. Pp. 103.

Ferreres, Joanne B., S. J.: Institutiones canonicae juxta novissimum codicem Pii X a Benedicto XV promulgatum juxtaque praescripta Hispaniae disciplinae et Americae Latinae. 2 vols. New and revised ed. by Eugenio Subirana, Barcelona, 1920.

Ferrés, Carlos: Compañía de Jesús en Montevideo. Barcelona, 1920.
Época colonial; la Compañía de Jesús en Montevideo. Montevideo, 1919. Pp. 237.

Fregeiro, Clemente L.: Estudios históricos. La batalla de Ituzaingó. Buenos Aires, 1919. Pp. xxxv, 331.

Gálvez, Juan Ignacio: Conflictos internacionales. El Perú contra Colombia, Ecuador y Chile. Santiago de Chile, Soc. Imprenta y Litografía Universo, 1919. Pp. 246. Map.

Gamarra, Abélardo M.: Los norteamericanos en el Perú. (Lima, 1919?]. Pp. 16.

Gancedo, Alejandro: Justicia social hacia la paz. Buenos Aires, Imp. Rinaldi hnos., 1920. Pp. v, (7)–79.

García, Jacinto S.: San Martín, Bolívar, Gamarra, Santa Cruz, Castilla y las constituciones del Perú. Lima, 1920.

García Calderón, Francisco: Ideas e impresiones. Precede un estudio sobre F. García Calderón por G. París. Madrid, Editorial América, 1919. Pp. 256.

Garry, L. S.: Textile markets of Brasil. Washington, Government Printing Office, 1920. Pp. 47. (Department of Commerce, Bureau of Foreign and Domestic Commerce, Special Agents Series, no. 203.)

Gásperi, Luis de: Geografía del Paraguay. Buenos Aires, Talleres "Casa Jacobo Peuser", 1920. Pp. 305.

Groussac, Paul: Estudios de historia argentina. Buenos Aires, 1919. Pp. 350.
El Viaje intellectual; impresiones de naturalesa y arte. 2. serie, Buenos, Aires, 1920. Pp. 381.

Harrison, Benjamin: Vida constitucional de los Estados Unidos. Traducción de Toribio Esquivel Obregón. New York, Doubleday, Page & Co., 1920. (Biblioteca Interamericana.)

Helbing, Robert: Beiträge sur topographischen Erschliessung der Cordilleras de los Andes swischen Aconcagua und Tupungato. Vol. 23, Jahresbericht Akad. Alpenclub Zürich, 1918. Pp. 77.

Herrero, Luis Alberto de: Buenos Aires, Urquisa y el Uruguay. Montevideo, Barreiro y Cía, 1919. Pp. 141.
La Encuesta rural; estudio sobre la condición económica y moral de las clases trabajadoras de la campaña. Montevideo, 1920. Pp. 76.

Huarte y Echenique, Amalio: Apuntamientos sobre el adelantamiento de Yucatán. Salamanca, Est. Tip. de Calatrava, 1919. Pp. 30.

Inman, Samuel Guy: The present situation in the Caribbean. Reprinted from The Journal of International Relations, II, No. 2, October, 1920.

Investigation of Mexican affairs. Foreign Relations Committee (Senate, 66:1–2). 23 parts. Washington, Government Printing Office, 1919–1920.

Irala, Antolín: La causa aliada en el Paraguay. Asunción, Talleres Zamphirópolos, 1919. Pp. 26.

Ispizua, Segundo de: Los Vascos en América. Historia de América. Vol. 6, Venesuela, tomo III., La ascendencia vasca de Simón Bolívar, libertador de América. Madrid, Mateu, 1919. Pp. xvi, 244.

Itier D., Luis: La chilenización de Tacna. Opiniones del General Armstrong. Santiago de Chile, Imprenta Chile, 1916. Pp. 36.

Jiménez, G.: Amado Nervo y la crítica literaria. México, Imp. Franco-Mexicana, [1919]. Pp. 190.

Klein, Julius: The Mesta. A study in Spanish economic history, 1273–1836. Cambridge, Harvard University Press, 1920. Pp. xviii, 444.

Latorre, Germán: Relaciones geográficas de Indias contenidas en el Archivo General de Indias de Sevilla. La Hispano-América del siglo XVI: Colombia, Venezuela, Puerto Rico, República Argentina. Sevilla, Tip. Zarzuela, 1919. Pp. xi, 153.

Lavalle, Juan Bautista de: Páginas de historia diplomática contemporánea. El Perú y la gran guerra. Lima, Imp. Americana, 1919. Pp. xv, 439.

Lemos R., Gustavo: Semántica o ensayo de lexicografía ecuatoriana Guayaquil, J. F. Molestina, 1920. Pp. 222.

Lequia, Jorge Guillermo: Lima en el siglo XVIII. Lima, [1919?]. Pp. 11.

Levillier, Roberto: Santo Toribio Alfonso Mogrovejo, arzobispo de los Reyes (1581–1606). Madrid, Sucesores de Rivadeneyra, 1920. Pp. 34.

Lira Mexicana. Madrid, Jiménez y Molina, 1920. Pp. 327.

Loayza, Hiram: La riqueza petrolífera de Caupotecan y norte de Bolivia. La Paz, Gonzáles y Medina, 1920. Pp. 70.

López, Manuel Antonio: Recuerdos históricos de la guerra de independencia. Colombia y el Perú (1819–1826). Madrid, J. Pueyo, 1919. Pp. 328.

López Valencia, Federico: Cuadros americanos. Escenas de la vida en los Estados Unidos. Madrid, M. Albero, 1920. Pp. 211.

Lugones, L.: Rubén Darío. Buenos Aires, Ediciones Selectas América, 1919.

Luttrell, Estelle: Mexican writers. University of Arizona, Tucson, Ariz., (1920?). Pp. 83.

Macedonio Urquidi, José: Bolivianos ilustres. 2 vols. La Paz, 1919.

Maitrot, Général ———: La France et les Républiques sud-américaines. Paris, Berger-Levrault, [1920?]. Pp. xvi, 392.

Martí, José: Cartas inéditas de Martí; anotadas por Joaquín Llaverías. Habana, Impr. "El Siglo XX", 1920. Pp. 39.

Martínez, Martín C.: Ante la nueva constitución. Montevideo, 1919. Pp. 193.

Martínez Paz, Enrique: Dalmacio Vélez Sarsfield y el código civil argentino. Córdoba, 1920.

Maúrtua, V. M.: La cuestión del Pacífico. Lima, Imp. Americana, 1919. Pp. xxxv, 651. Map.

Meissner, Walther: Argentiniens Handelsbeziehungen zu den Vereinigten Staaten von Amerika. Cöthen (Anhalt) O. Schulze, 1919. Pp. xiii, 363. (Bibliothek der "Cultura Latino-Americana".)

Memoire sur Tacna et Arica présenté au secretariat de la Société des Nations par le delegué de la Bolivie à la Conference de la Paix. (Memorandum regarding Tacna and Arica presented to the Secretariat of the League of Nations by the delegate from Bolivia to the Peace Conference.) London, Edward Stanford, Ltd., 1920. Pp. 21 + 21. In both French and English. Map of South America.

Mercado M., Miguel: El Chaco boreal. La Paz, 1920. Pp. xvii, 230.
Charcas y el Río de la Plata. La Paz, Gonzáles y Medina, 1919. Pp. 295. Map.

Molins, W. Jaime: Paraguay. Crónicas americanas. Buenos Aires, Est°. `Gr°.
    "Oceana", 1916. Pp. 307, [10].
Morales, José Agustín: Legislación municipal. La Paz, 1919. Pp. 138.
More, Federico: La próxima conflagración suramericana. La Paz, La Editorial
    "Los Andes", 1918. Pp. 250, [3].
Muñoz, Luis J., S.J.: Notas históricas sobre la Compañía de Jesús restablecida
    en Colombia y Centro-América. Oña, Imprenta privada del Colegio, 1920.
Muriel, Domingo: Historia del Paraguay desde 1747 hasta 1767. Obra latina tra-
    ducida al castellano, por el P. Pablo Hernández. Madrid, Impr. Clásica
    Española, 1919. Pp. 659. (Colección de Libros y Documentos referentes
    a la Historia de América, vol. 19.)
Navarro, Gustavo A.: Los cívicos. La Paz, 1919. Pp. 254.
Nervo, Amado: Mis filosofías. Madrid, J. Pueyo, 1920. Pp. 226.
    Serenidad. Madrid, J. Pueyo, 1920. Pp. 222.
Olascoaga, Laurentino: Instituciones políticas de Mendoza. 2 vols. La Paz,
    Escuela Tipográfica Salesiana, 1919.
Olazábal, Alejandro de: Hacia la emancipación económica. Buenos Aires, 1920.
O'Leary, Juan E.: Nuestra epopeya (Guerra del Paraguay, 1864–70). Asunción
    del Paraguay, Imprenta y Librería La Mundial, 1919. Pp. 649. (Biblio-
    teca Paraguaya del Centro e de Derecho.)
Oliveira Lima, Manuel de: La evolución histórica de la América Latina. Bosquejo
    comparativo. Transl. into Spanish by A. C. Rivas. Madrid, Editorial-
    América, [1917].
Ortega, Afredo: Ferrocarriles colombianos. Bogotá, Impr. Nacional, 1920. Pp.
    XII, 232.
Ortiz, Fernando: Los negros esclavos. Estudio sociológico y de derecho público.
    Habana, Revista Bimestre Cubana, 1916. Pp. viii, 536.
Ortiz Rubio, Pascual: Historia de Michoacán. Morelia, Tip. Comercial, 1920.
    Pp. 43. Plates.
O'Shaughnessy, Edith: Intimate pages of Mexican history. New York, Doran
    & Co., 1920.
Otero, José Pacífico: Nuestro nacionalismo. Buenos Aires, J. Roldán, 1920. Pp.
    186.
Palma y V., José: Principios de derecho civil. La Paz, 1919. Pp. 405.
Park, Julian: A journal of the expedition against Cuba. University of Buffalo
    Studies. Monographs in history No. 1. Reprint of Vol. 1, No. 4, pp. 231–
    244. 1920.
Pastells, Pablo, S.J., and Constantino Bayle: El descubrimiento del estrecho de
    Magallanes. Madrid, Sucesores de Rivadeneyra, 1920.
Peñuela, Cayo Leonidas: Album de Boyaca. Vol. 1. La Campaña de 1819.
    Bogotá, Arboleda y Valencia, 1919. Pp. 407+263.
Pérez Petit, V.: Rodó, su vida, su obra. Montevideo, 1919.
Pinochet, Tancredo: The gulf of misunderstanding; or, North and South America
    as seen by each other. New York, Boni & Liveright, [1920]. Pp. vii, 275.
Pinilla, Sabino: La creación de Bolivia. Madrid, Editorial América, [1917].
    Pp. 371.
Pittier, Henry: Esbozo de las formaciones vegetales de Venezuela con una breve
    reseña de los productos naturales y agrícolas. Caracas, Litografía del

Comercio, 1920. Pp. 44. (Accompanied by a "mapa ecológico" entitled "Mapa ecológico de Venezuela que demuestra las zonas naturales, los cultivos, las vías de comunicación y los principales centros mineros, etc.")

Planas Suáres, Simón: Condición legal de los extranjeros en Guatemala. Madrid, Hijos de Reus, 1919. Pp. 62.

Prack, Enrique B.: Lo que debemos hacer por el obrero. Mar del Plata, 1920.

Priestley, Herbert Ingram: The Carranza débâcle. Reprint from *The University of California Chronicle*. July, 1920. Pp. 17.

El Problema del Pacífico. Santiago de Chile, Imprenta Universitaria, 1919. Pp. 96.

Progreso norteamericano en Chile, 1920. Santiago, J. Beaya A., 1920. Pp. 142.

Ramallo, General ——: Guerrilleros de la independencia; los esposos Padiera. La Paz, Gonsáles y Medina, 1919. Pp. 310.

Restrepo Tirado, Ernesto: Descubrimiento y conquista de Colombia. 2 vols. Bogotá, Imp. Nacional, 1917–1919.

Reyes, César: Los superhombres argentinos. La Rioja, 1920.

Reyes, José Luis: Diccionario general de legislación policiaria. La Paz, Gonsáles y Medina, [1920?]. Pp. 268.

Rodó y sus críticos. París, 1920. P. 352. (Biblioteca Latino-Americana.)

Rodríques del Busto, N.: ¿Adonde va la democracia? Tucumán, 1920.

Rodríguez Villa, Antonio: El teniente general D. Pablo Morillo, primer conde de Cartagena, marqués de la Puerta (1778–1873). Vol. 1. Madrid, J. Pueyo, 1920. Pp. 334. (Biblioteca Ayacucho.)

Rohde, Jorge M.: Estudios literarios. Buenos Aires, Coni Hermanos, 1920.

Romero, Carlos: Las taras de nuestra democracia. La Paz, 1920. Pp. 278.

Romero, Genero: Los problemas nacionales. Asunción, Talleres Gráficos del Estado, 1915. Pp. 92.

Salas, Julio C.: Civilisación y barbarie. Estudios sociológicos americanos. Barcelona, Talleres Gráficos "Lux", 1919. Pp. 175.

Etnografía americana. Los indios caribes. Estudios sobre el origen del mito de la antropofagia. Barcelona, Talleres Gráf. "Lux", 1920. Pp. 233.

Lecciones de sociología aplicada a la América. Barcelona, Soc. General de Publicaciones. Pp. 86.

Sánches Bustamante, Daniel: Bolivia y sus derechos en el Pacífico. La Paz, 1919. Pp. 380.

Las taras de nuestra democracia. La Paz, Arno Hermanos, 1920. Pp. v, 277.

Santibañez del Río, Conde de: Portugal y el hispanismo. Madrid, 1920. Pp. 69.

Sarmiento, Domingo F.: Conflicto y armonías de las razas en América. Buenos Aires, "La Cultura Argentina", 1915. Pp. 458.

Schurs, William Lytle: Paraguay. A commercial handbook. Washington, Government Printing Office, 1921. Pp. 195. Paper. Map. (Department of Commerce, Bureau of Foreign and Domestic Commerce, Special Agents series, no. 199.)

Sherwood, Guillermo A.: Glimpses of South America. New York, The Century Co., 1920.

Sotela, Rogelio: Valores literarios de Costa Rica. San José, Impr. Alsina, 1920. Pp. 293, [2].

Statistical abstract of the republic of Chile. Santiago de Chile, Sociedad Imprenta y Litografía Universo, 1918. Pp. IX, 146.

Suárez, Constantino: La desunión hispano-americana y otras cosas. Barcelona, Imp. de B. Bausá, 1919. Pp. 312.

Tejadas, S., J. L.: Bolivia. Plea of a sister nation for an outlet to the sea. [New York?, 1920:] Pp. 8.

Torres Lanzas, Pedro: Catálogo de legajos del Archivo General de Indias, Secciones 1 y 2. Patronato y Contaduría de Indias. Sevilla, Tip. Zarzuela, 1919. Pp. 203.

Travieso, Carlos: Memorias militares del General Don Ventura Rodrigues; guerra grande: sitio de Montevideo. Montevideo, Barreiro y Cía., 1919. Pp. 230.

Trelles, Carlos M.: Biblioteca Geográfica Cubana. Matanzas, Imprenta de Juan F. Olivier, 1920. Pp. 340.

United States. Bureau of Navigation (Navy Department): Ports of the world. Buenos Aires. Washington?, 1920? Pp. 5–28.

Urrea, Beas: La herencia de Carranza. México, Imp. Nacional, 1920. Pp. 131.

Urrutía, Francisco José: La evolución del principio de arbitraje en América. La Sociedad de Naciones. Madrid, J. Pueyo, 1920. Pp. 298.

Urtasún, V.: Historia diplomática de América. Pamplona, 1920.

Vallenilla Lanz, Laureano: Cesarismo democrático. Caracas, 1919. Pp. 310.

Varela, Alfredo: Duas grandes intrigas. Mysterios internacionaes attinentes a Portugal, Brasil, Argentina, Uruguay e Paraguay. 2 vols. Porto, [1919?].

Vargas Vila, ———: Ante los barbaros. (Los Estados Unidos y la guerra). Barcelona, Imprenta de José Anglada, 1918. Pp. 247.

Vera Estañol, Jorge: Carranza and his bolshevik régime. Los Angeles, Cal. Wayside Press, 1920. Pp. viii, (3)–247.

Vignaud, Henry: The Columbian tradition on the discovery of America and of the part played therein by the astronomer Toscanelli. A memoir addressed to the professors Hermann Wagner of the University of Göttingen and Carlo Errera of Bologna. Oxford, at the Clarendon Press, 1920. Pp. 62.

Villalobos, Rosendo: Pedazos de papel. La Paz, 1–20. Pp. 179.

Walker, Martínez, Joaquín: Clamores de intervención diplomáticas. (La cuestión del Pacífico). Santiago de Chile, Imprenta Chile, 1919. Pp. 96.
Una revancha con sangre ajena. (La cuestión del Pacífico.) Santiago de Chile, Imprenta Chile, 1919. Pp. 112.

Walther, Karl: Líneas fundamentales de la estructura geológica de la República Oriental del Uruguay. Montevideo, 1919. Pp. 220.

Williams, John H.: Argentine international trade under inconvertible paper money, 1880–1890. Cambridge, Harvard University Press, 1920. Pp. xiv, 282. Bibliography, pp. 263–271.

Wilmart de Glymes, R.: El senado romano. El senado de Estados Unidos. Buenos Aires, 1920.

Zeuny, H.: Historia de los gobernadores de las provincias argentinas. Vol. 3. Buenos Aires, 1920.

IN PERIODICALS

Abastos, Manuel G.: El Perú y España. In *Mercurio Peruano* (Lima), October, 1920.

Adams, Charles C.: The zoogeography of northwesternmost South America. In *The Geographical Review*, August, 1920. Maps.

The Agricultural college at Santiago [Chile]. In *The South American*, January, 1921.

Alonso, Mario: La autonomía de los primitivos municipios cubanos. In *Revista Bimestre Cubana*, January–June, 1920.

Altamira, Rafael: La personalidad hispánica. In *Revista del Centro de Información Española* (reproduced in *La Lectura*, Madrid).

Andara, J. L.: The Bolívar doctrine. In *Inter-America*, October, 1920 (transl. from *Cultura Venezolana*, June, 1918.)

Antecedents of Argentine history. In *id.* (transl. from *La Unión*, Buenos Aires, May 24, 1920).

Argentina quits league assembly. Editorial in *The South American*, January, 1921.

Argentina's butter trade. In *The Pan-American Magazine*, January, 1921.

Askin, E. H.: Cotton growing in the department of Piura, Peru. In *The Compass*, October, 1920.

Augusto Madueño. Eulogy in *Mercurio Peruano*, August, 1920.

Avalos, Angel F.: Telasco Castellanos. In *Revista Argentina de Ciencias Políticas*, August, 1920.

Bad financial situation in Nicaragua. In *The South American*, January, 1921.

Baja California. In *Inter-America*, December, 1920 (transl. from *Revista de Revistas*, México, August 8, 1920).

Balance of payments of the Argentine Republic for the economic year 1918/1919. In *The Review of the River Plate*, December 3, 1920.

The Banco Mercantil y Agricola de Buenos Aires is formally opened. In *The Compass*, December, 1920.

Barker, Eugene C.: Minutes of the Ayuntamiento of San Felipe de Austin, 1828–1832. In *The Southwestern Quarterly Review*, October, 1920 (continuation).

Beals, Carleton: Mexico changes its president. In *North American Review*, August, 1920.

Belaúnde, Víctor Andrés: Crónicas de Norteamérica. In *Mercurio Peruano*, July–November, 1920.

Berry, Edward W.: The Andes from the Isthmus to Magellan's Strait. In *The New York Times Book Review and Magazine*, November 14, 1920.

Biological expedition to explore the Amazon Valley. Editorial in *The Pan American Review*, November, 1920.

Bloom, J.: Gold shipments abroad. In *The Compass*, October, 1920.

Boomer, R. DeF.: Mexican possibilities. In *The Pan American Review*, September, 1920.

Bayle, C.: El centenario de Magallanes. In *Razón y Fe* (Madrid), November, 1920.

El próximo congreso de las juventudes hispanoamericanas. In *id.*, October, 1920.

Browning, Webster E.: El alma americana. In *Mercurio Peruano*, November, 1920.
Herencia material del continente americano. In *La Nueva Democracia* (New York), November, 1920 (continued).
Bunge, A.: Democracia política y democracia económica. In *Revista de Filosofía* (Buenos Aires), September, 1920.
Burbridge, Sir Woodman: "Made in Argentina." In *The South American*, January, 1921.
Canada gaining in Caribbean trade. In *The Americas*, December, 1920.
Carson, James C.: Advertising in Latin America. In *The South American*, January, 1921.
Castro Ruiz, Carlos: A. Mitchell Palmer. In *Revista América* (Santiago), November 7, 1920.
Chapman, Charles E.: Una tierra romántica (California). In *Revista América*, October 5, 1920.
Chessher, H. B.: U. S. foreign trade and its correlative factors. In *The Pan-American Magazine*, January, 1921.
The Christ of the Andes. In *The Pan American Review*, September, 1920.
Christian, A. K.: Mirabeau Buonaparte Lamar. In *The Southwestern Historical Quarterly*, October, 1920 (continued).
Colombia faces her troubles. In *The South American*, January, 1921.
The coming sugar crop. In *The Pan-American Magazine*, January, 1921.
Concerning a Latin American center in New York. Editorial in *The Pan American Review*, September, 1920.
Condición general de los negocios en Estados Unidos. In *Revista América*, November 7, 1920.
Conspiracy thwarted in Peru. In *The South American*, January, 1921.
Construcción de caminos en Panamá. In *Revista América*, October 5, 1920.
Costa Rica da libre entrada a los ganados. In *id.*, October 19, 1920.
Cox, Isaac J.: The Mexican problem: a possible peaceful solution. In *The Mississippi Valley Historical Review*, July, 1920 (extra no.).
Crowder's mission to Cuba. Editorial in *The Journal of Commerce*, January 5, 1921.
Cuban situation should greatly improve within six months. In *The Americas*, December, 1920.
Dawley, Thomas R.: Guatemala's citizen president. In *The Pan American Review*, October, 1920.
El Despertar de Hispano-América. In *Revista América*, November 7, 1920.
Destruge, Camilo: Los Estados Unidos y la independencia americana. In *Revista Bimestre Cubana*, January–June, 1920.
Deustua, A. O.: Clasificaciones estéticas. In *Mercurio Peruano*, August, 1920. Grados estéticos. In *id.*, October, 1920.
Diaz, Carlos: El Carbón de leña en polvo como combustible. In Universidad de Tucumán: *Informes del Departamento de Investigaciones Industriales*, No. 11, 1920.
Esterilización del agua potable de la ciudad de Tucumán por el método de cloruración. In *id.*
Vacimientos mineros de la provincia de Tucumán. In *id.*

Direct steamers to Guayaquil. In *The South American*, January, 1921.

Dobles Segreda, Luis: Rubén Darío in Heredia. In *Inter-America*, December, 1920 (transl. from *Athenea*, Costa Rica, July, 1920).

Dr. Don Luis Felipe Villarán. Editorial in *Mercurio Peruano*, November, 1920.

Don Ricardo V. García. Eulogy in *id.*, October, 1920.

Dorado, Carolina Marcial: Impresiones de España. In *Hispania*, December, 1920.

Drafts on South America. In *The Compass*, November, 1920.

Dulanto, Ricardo E.: El Romanticismo contemporáneo. In *Mercurio Peruano*, August, 1920.

Ecuador como productor de petróleo. In *Revista América*, October 19, 1920.

Eder, Phanor James: Pan-Americanism and the bar. In *The Compass*, October, 1920.

Elisalde, Rafael H.: Address. In *International Conciliation*. Interamerican Division. Bulletin no. 23. November, 1920. (Reproduced in *La Lectura*, Madrid).

Elmore, Edwin: Un Sacerdote de la cultura. In *Mercurio Peruano*, November, 1920.

Espinosa, Gabriel: El Vértice victorioso. In *Cultura Venezolana* (Caracas), August, 1920.

Los Estados Unidos no intervendrán jamás en Méjico. In *Revista América*, November 7, 1920.

Esténger, Rafael A.: José Asunción Silva. In *Inter-America*, December, 1920 (transl. from *Cuba Contemporánea*, May, 1920).

Exchange position in Argentina. In *The Times Trade Supplement* (London), October 23, 1920.

Exproprian tierras para un acqueducto [en Venezuela]. In *Revista América*, November 7, 1920.

Fairchild, Fred Rogers: The problem of Santo Domingo. In *The Geographical Review*, September, 1920.

Father Kino's name. In *The Catholic Historical Review*, October, 1920.

Fernándes Guardia, Ricardo: A knightly pirate. In *Inter-America*, October 1920 (transl. from *Revista de Costa Rica* (San José, Costa Rica), March, 1920).

Fernándes Peralta, Ricardo: In search of a new volcano. In *id.*, July, 1920.

Un Ferrocarril que unirá a Nicaragua y Honduras. In *Revista América*, October 5, 1920.

La Fiesta de la raza. In *Plus Ultra*, August, 1920.

Forman compañía para el subterráneo en la Habana. In *Revista América*, October 5, 1920.

Franck, Harry A.: The South American metropolis. In *The Century*, January, 1921.

Garay, J. C.: El gobierno de Martínez Rodrígues. In *Revista de Derecho, Historia y Letras*, December, 1920.

German goods reappear in Chile. In *The South American*, January, 1921.

Giesecke, Alberto A.: El Cusco: Meca del turismo de la América del Sur. In *Mercurio Peruano*, July, 1920.

Gonsáles, Eloy G.: Las ensenadas de la historia. In *Cultura Venezolana*, August, 1920.

Gran proyecto sobre marina para Méjico. In *Revista América*, November 7, 1920.

La Habana es el primer puerto de Hispano-América. In *id*.

Hardy, O.: Current developments in Peru. In *The Compass*, December, 1920.

Hevia, Aurelio: General Leonard Wood and public instruction in Cuba. In *Inter-America*, October, 1920 (transl. from *Cuba Contemporánea*, July, 1920).

Homenaje escolar a Belgrano. In *Revista de Derecho, Historia y Letras*, December, 1920.

Hurtado, Ramón: Aldea de Aquelarre. In *Cultura Venezolana*, August, 1920.

How Latin America views Harding's election. Editorial in *The Pan American Review*, November, 1920.

Hunt, Carl: Por que los anunciantes dicen la verdad. In *Revista América*, November 7, 1920.

Hydro-electric developments and prospects in South America. In *The Pan-American Magazine*, January, 1921.

Indians of the Paraguayan Chaco. In *The South American*, January, 1921.

Inman, Samuel Guy: Santo Domingo, old and new. In *The Pan-American Magazine*, January, 1921.

Intellectual intercourse with Hispanic America. Editorial in *The Pan American Review*, September, 1920.

Johnson, James Weldon: Self-determining Haiti. In *Nation*, August 28, September 4, 11, and 25, 1920.

José de la Luz y Caballero. In *La Unión Hispano Americana* (Madrid), December, 1920.

Kirwin, Harry A.: The pioneer [in Argentina]. In *The River Plate American* (Buenos Aires), December 2, 1920 (in both English and Spanish).

Kohler, Max J.: Los judios in Cuba. In *Revista Bimestre Cubana*, July–August, 1920.

Lara Pardo, Luis: La actualidad mejicana. In *Philippine Free Press* (Manila), October 23, 1920.

Laut, Agnes C.: Mexico at the crossroads. In *Current Opinion*, January, 1921.

Lavalle, Juan Bautista de: Europa después de la gran guerra. In *Mercurio Peruano*, July, 1920.

The league of nations. In *The River Plate American*, January 9, 1920 (in both English and Spanish).

Leguia, Jorge Guillermo: D. Toribio Rodríguez de Mendoza. In *Mercurio Peruano*, October, 1920.

Lewis, William Ray: The Hayes administration and Mexico. In *The Southwestern Historical Quarterly*, October, 1920.

Lindberg, A. F.: Nicaraguan finances. In *The Compass*, October, 1920.

Lugones, Leopoldo: Theoretical and practical politics. In *Inter-America*, December, 1920 (transl. from *Centro-América*, Guatemala, April–June, 1920).

Lull in Peruvian trade. In *The Times Trade Supplement* (London), October 23, 1920.

Luncheon to president of Panama. In *The Pan American Review*, September, 1920.

MacDermot, T. H. How Britain got her West Indies. In *Canadian Magazine*, September, 1920.

Madueño, José Leonidas: El artista y el hombre. In *Mercurio Peruano*, September, 1920.

La Maestranza de San Bernardo: In *Revista América*, October 5, 1920.

Mahoney, W. G.: Campañas y cruceros. In *Cultura Venezolana*, August, 1920.

Mathieu, Beltran: The neutrality of Chile during the European war. In *The American Journal of International Law*, July, 1920.

Matienzo, J. N.: La jurisdicción sobre los ferrocarriles en el derecho constitucional argentino. In *Revista de Derecho, Historia y Letras*, December, 1920.

Matters, Leonard: Argentina. In *The Pan American Review*, October, 1920.

Meader, W. G.: Trade with Costa Rica. In *The Compass*, December, 1920.

Means, Philip Ainsworth: La labor arqueológica de Sylvanus Griswold Morley. In *Mercurio Peruano*, October, 1920.

Un vaso esculpido de San Agustín Acasagaastlan, Guatemala. In *id*.

Mecham, J. Lloyd: The martyrdom of Father Juan de Santa María. In *The Catholic Historical Review*, October, 1920.

Méjico evalua el petróleo y cobra el impuesto fijo. In *Revista América*, October 19, 1920.

Méjico será el futuro centro mundial de petróleo. In *id*., November 7, 1920.

Mendoza Zells, J.: Política unitaria. In *Revista de Derecho, Historia y Letras*, December, 1920.

Mexican outlook most promising. In *The South American*, January, 1921.

Mexican vanilla. In *The Pan-American Magazine*, January, 1921.

Mexico's amazing oil potentialities. In *The South American*, January, 1921.

Michael P. Grace. In *The Pan American Review*, October, 1920.

The mission of Secretary Colby. Editorial in *The South American*, January, 1921.

Moore, John Bassett: Address in honor of Dr. Belisario Porras. In *International Conciliation*. Interamerican Division bulletin, no. 23. November, 1920.

The Pan-American financial conferences and the inter-American High Commission. In *The American Journal of International Law*, July, 1920.

Mújica, A. S.: La personalidad de Alberdi. In *Revista de Filosofía*, September, 1920.

The new director general of the Pan American Union. Editorial in *The Pan American Review*, October, 1920.

New Latin American courses. In *id*.

Nicaragua coffee. In *The Pan-American Magazine*, January, 1921.

North American money. In *The River Plate American*, December 2, 1920 (in both English and Spanish).

Nuevo partido político en Costa Rica. In *Revista América*, October 19, 1920.

Obregon, the one-armed Mexican president. In *Current Opinion*, January, 1921.

O'Hara, John F., C.S.C.: Obstacles to American trade with the South American Republics. In *The South American*, January, 1921.

Orgas, A., and A. Capdevila: La reforma universitaria en Córdoba. In *Revista de Filosofía*, September, 1920.

Orsábal Quintana, A.: De Drago a Tchitcherin. In *id*.

Our Latin American Trade. In *The River Plate American*, December 2, 1920 (in both English and Spanish).

Oyuela, Calixto: Rafael Obligado. In *Inter-America*, December, 1920 (transl. from *Nosotros*, Buenos Aires, April, 1920).

Palacios Mendoza, Alfredo: A wedding in the Quechua great world. In *id.* (transl. from *El Hogar*, Buenos Aires, June, 1920).

A Pan American college of commerce. Editorial in *The Pan American Review*, September, 1920.

Pan American propaganda. In *id.*, November, 1920.

Penetración ferroviaria de la América del Sur. In *Revista América*, October 5, 1920.

Peru protects the Vicuña. In *The Pan-American Magazine*. January, 1921.

Physiography and life forms of Panama. In *The Geographical Review*, October, 1920.

Plans new railroad across the Andes Mountains. In *The Americas*, December, 1920.

Plant life in Jujuy. In *The South American*, January, 1921.

Porras, Belisario: Address. In *International Conciliation*. Interamerican Division Bulletin, no. 23, November, 1920.

Prendergast, William A.: Our Central American Neighbors. In *Review of Reviews*, August, 1920.

Present conditions in Cuba. In *The Compass*, November, 1920.

Puyo D., Carlos: Striving for women's rights in South America. In *The Pan American Review*, November, 1920.

Ramis Togores, R.: An Argentine artist. In *Inter-America*, December, 1920 (transl. from *Nosotros*, Buenos Aires, July, 1920).

Rasor, W. W.: The south of South America. In *The Pan-American Magazine*, January, 1921.

Ray, Medora Loomis: Six weeks in Madrid. In *Hispania*, December, 1920.

Report of the Conference Committee for Chile. In *The Pan American Review*, September, 1920.

Id. for Colombia. In *id.*, October, 1920.

Id. for Cuba. In *id.*, November, 1920.

Resúmenes crónico-mundiales. In *La Nueva Democracia* (New York). November, 1920.

La Revolución de Bolivia. In *Mercurio Peruano*, July, 1920.

Ribeiro da Silva, Raul: Sugar industry in Brasil. In *The Compass*, November, 1920.

Rippy, J. Fred: Diplomacy of the United States and Mexico regarding the Isthmus of Tehuantepec, 1848–1860. In *The Mississippi Valley Historical Review*, March, 1920.

Rivarola, Rodolfo, El Brasil. In *Revista Argentina de Ciencias Políticas*, August, 1920.

Rivarola, Rodolfo, and E. Gómez: Delitos contra la vida. In *id.*

Rodríguez Mendoza, E.: La guerra y la América. In *La Nueva Democracia* (New York), November, 1920.

Romera-Navarro, M.: El alma de Toledo. In *Hispania*, December, 1920.

Rosa, Ramón: Independence day and the Central American union. In *Inter-America*, December, 1920 (transl. from *Revista de la Universidad* (Tegucigalpa), April 15, 1920; a reprint here from the newspaper *La Paz*, no. 278, 1882).

Rovillain, Eugene E.: The latest Mexican revolution. In *Atlantic Monthly*, October, 1920.

Saenz Peña, C. S.: Aspectos sociales de la religión búdhica. In *Revista de Filosofía*, September, 1920.

Sánches, Manuel Segundo: Miranda como filosófo y erudito. In *Cultura Venezolana* (Caracas), August, 1920.

Santos Cristóbal, Epifanio de los: Marcelo H. del Pilar. In *The Philippine Review*, August and September, 1920 (continued).

Scott, Ralph C.: La Asociación Cristiana de Jóvenes en Sud-América. In *Revista América*, October 19, 1920.

Se dará maquinaria a los pequeños agricultores. In *id*.

Se proyecta fundar en Panamá un instituto en homenaje a W. G. Gorgas. In *id*., October 5, 1920.

Se forma en la sona del Canal una liga cívica. Los norteamericanos allá residentes quieren que se les otorgue el voto. In *id*., November 7, 1920.

Servicio postal aereo entre Estados Unidos y Cuba. In *id*., October 19, 1920.

$75,000,000 pide Méjico para su rehabilitación. In *id*.

Sherwell, Guilermo A.: Como podría obtenerse la unión espiritual y material de la América Hispana y la Anglo Sajona. In *Cultura Venezolana*, August, 1920.

The Country of Miranda and Bolívar. In *The South American*, January, 1921.

Del Potomac al Guaire. In *Hispania*, November, 1920.

Sketches of northern Argentina. In *The South American*, January, 1921.

Soisa Reilly, Juan José de: A great Bolivian writer. In *Inter-America*, October, 1920 (transl. from *Nuestra América*, Buenos Aires, March, 1920).

Solano, Armando: American policy. In *id*., December, 1920 (transl. from *El Espectador*, Bogotá, August 13, 1920).

Tomini, Luis B.: Hojas de mi diario. In *Revista de Ciencias Políticas*, August, 1920.

Trade of British Guiana and British Honduras. In *The Economist* (London), October 30, 1920.

Twelve years of progress. In *The Pan American Review*, November, 1920.

Ugarte, César Antonio: La Universidad de Yale. Los métodos de enseñanza y la vida del estudiante en una gran universidad norteamericana. In *Mercurio Peruano*, November, 1920.

Ugarte de Ercilla, E.: Tercer centenario del P. Diego Álvares de Pas. In *Rasón y Fe* (Madrid), December, 1920.

Umphrey, George W.· El americanismo en los nuevos poetas anglo e hispano-americanos. In *Mercurio Peruano*, September, 1920.

La poesía contemporánea en los Estados Unidos. In *id*., October, 1920.

Id., in *Revista América*, October 19, 1920.

Spanish American poets of today and yesterday. II. José Santos Chocano, el poeta de América. In *Hispania*, December, 1920.

Valdes de la Torre, Carlos: El Ayllo. In *Mercurio Peruano*, September, 1920.

Régimen de la propiedad durante los incas. In *id*., November, 1920.

Vial Solar, J. El problema chileno-argentino. In *Revista de Derecho, Historia y Letras*, December, 1920.

Victoria, Federico P. The need for juvenile courts in the Philippines. In *The Philippine Review*, October, 1920.

La Visita española a Chile. In *La Unión Hispano Americana* (Madrid), December, 1920.

Warren G. Harding, presidente electo de los Estados Unidos. Declaraciones con respecto a Sud América. In *Revista América*, November 9, 1920.

Wilmart, A.: Acefalía en la presidencia. In *Revista Argentina de Ciencias Políticas*, August, 1920.

Women's activities in Latin American educational circles. Editorial in *The Pan American Review*, November, 1920.

The Y. M. C. A. in Mexico, Brasil, Cuba, Uruguay. In *The Pan-American Magazine*, January, 1921.

The Y. W. C. A. in Buenos Aires. In *The South American*, January, 1921.

Zayas Enríques, R. de: El pro y el contra de los Estados Unidos. In *La Nueva Democracia* (New York), November, 1920.

Zeballos, Estanislao S.. Analecta. In *Revista de Derecho, Historia y Letras*, December, 1920.

Bibliografía. In *id*.

Oro y cambios. In *id*.

The Hispanic American Historical Review

Vol. IV   MAY, 1921   No. 2

PAN AMERICANISM AND THE LEAGUE OF NATIONS[1]

This hall of Americas, where we meet today in such a cordial gathering, speaks for itself. It proves that at least one league of nations exists on earth and that it has been successful since it is a reality. Why? Because it was founded on the theory of equality; it has tried to act according to justice and it has for its aims peace and prosperity for all the countries of the New World. We must only bear in mind that practice does not always correspond to theory and that human justice is far from perfection. Our Pan American league may, however, stand as a model.

The great trouble with the larger and more recent league of nations—may I say the late league of nations—which was said to be universal but in fact was restricted to a managing and patronizing board, was that it resembled too much an old fashioned school, with a severe set of masters, frightened pupils, and even a whip lying on the table for the correction deemed indispensable. Politically it was a council, it was never a league. Yet precedence pointed to a different way.

In 1914–15, France was beaten and invaded, Napoleon had been for fifteen years at least the ogre of Europe—a new scourge of God;—the vanquished sat, however, at the same table with

[1] Read at the joint conference of the American Historical Association and the American Political Science Association, December 30, 1920, at the Pan American Union, Washington, D. C.

the victors and Talleyrand, who always found the proper words for the occasion, certainly because he changed his words according to the occasion, could boldly say to the Czar of Russia that right ought to precede national conveniences. It is true that the Czar replied that right was nothing more than the conveniences of Europe. He was a wise man and he acted according to his wise saying; but the Holy Alliance did not try to deceive the world, as it proclaimed itself a trust organized by kings against peoples. On the contrary now, or rather lately, it has not been said that democracy and oligarchy have practically the same meaning. Democracy has been exalted as the basis and the *raison d'être* of a league which recently established military success as the best qualification for admission to its body.

In 1855, Russia had been detained on its way to Constantinople—this same Byzantium which is described as a den of vice worse than in its worst times of corruption, now that the Turks have ceased effectively to rule on the Bosphorus. The Congress of Paris met under Louis Napoleon's sleepy eyes and enigmatic smile; Russia was not absent from the meeting where Turkey obtained a new lease of life and Cavour laid the foundations of the kingdom of Italy.

In 1878, Turkey had another collapse which was, as always, considered to be the last; but Bismarck acted as a physician, more perhaps as a surgeon, and once more the Ottoman Empire recovered. Both Turkey and Russia were side by side playing the game of politics on the green cloth of the German Chancery.

At Versailles the recollections of the Roi Soleil tended so much towards absolutism that under this powerful suggestion there was a bench of judges with certain criminals at the bar. That was the thing that spoiled a plan which had been the offspring of generous intentions. The world resulted more divided than ever and instead of civilization being restored by a concourse of good will, it had to face disintegration and a decay fostered by so much hatred.

On this side of the Atlantic we never thought of establishing leagues so exclusive that they barred out some nations in favor, not even of the majority, but of a few initiated. Bolívar dreamt of a league of nations—we call it a dream because the hour had not yet struck for the realization of such a lofty ideal;— but when he attempted it, he did not relegate even Haiti to a black place.

We have had since the Congress of Panama other Pan American meetings, and we started thirty years ago, under the auspices of James G. Blaine, who had the faculty of seeing far ahead, a Bureau of American Republics, which has been irreverently called your Department of Colonies, but which became this Pan American Union, precisely because you did not endeavor to create dependencies. A union cannot imply exceptions or it would be necessary to look for another word for it.

It is true that a certain big stick made its appearance, but a big stick is not exactly the negation of family feelings. It may be fraternal; it is not necessarily tyrannical. Blows do not hurt less for that, but we must always look to intentions, as they may prove good and in spite of the saying, Humanity is guided by intentions more than by anything else.

Our common tradition is a tradition of law, although the particular traditions of each nationality may have been altered by human violence. America was conquered from its native races and the European invaders disputed parts of it among themselves; but generally right prevailed over might and the settlers obeyed when fixing their boundaries the distribution of lands delineated by European diplomacy. Even before the discoveries, carried to their utmost limit, had disclosed what an immense world this unknown world was, America had been apportioned according to a famous papal bull. So public conventions ruled its evolution and when the time for independence came, the principle of *uti possidetis*, fixing for the new countries the same boundaries of the old colonies, avoided many a bloody struggle between these Spanish possessions which, unlike Brazil, had disrupted their former union and did not keep the imperial unity.

This is a case of equality before the public law which is more difficult to ascertain than equality before the private law. The

Monroe Doctrine did not contradict such a tradition and change it into oppression because the Monroe Doctrine was originated in this way. The United States understood that the new countries of America were under the pressure and menace of European intervention and as the strongest power of the continent, they took the leadership and, at England's advice— as England also had matter of complaint and desired to curtail the power of the Holy Alliance—formulated the famous doctrine of defense for all and national safety for every one of the newly emancipated nations.

The United States acted towards them as a kind of guardian. At the end of a century of responsible life, some of those countries showed that they did not need tutorship any more, one or two even plainly stating so, although cherishing grateful remembrance for past services. A few, however; had to become regular wards under the circumstances, which may change as the condition of the world is not perpetually stagnant. We may consequently infer that the Monroe Doctrine was in its beginnings a policy of protection and that it may nowadays have been sometimes a policy of control; but the truth is that it pretends and endeavors to be a policy of cooperation.

For the United States the best policy to follow is surely a policy of solidarity. Its place will always be the first but it is better to acquire by persuasion what might be denied to imposition. The Monroe Doctrine is to be a common continental doctrine; if not, Hispanic America will remain beyond the pale of a responsible destiny within any league of nations. More than a regional understanding, it must be an American doctrine in the broad sense of the word.

The war—I mean the great war—strengthened Pan Americanism, in spite of the neutrality preserved by some of the nations, not so much because the freedom of the New World or the liberties in the New World were endangered through the extension of European hegemonies, but simply because it helped to fortify the conception of right and America always had for right in its concrete, and also in its abstract, meaning, an almost superstitious respect which we would in vain look for in Europe in the same degree. I do not know whether the term "superstitious" can be justly applied to such a noble feeling: my only desire is to emphasize the nature of a respect which has rather the elements of worship.

Pan Americanism ceased entirely to be a catchword or a diplomatic trick to become much more than before the point of convergence of a number of aspirations, the framework of a regular association, the backbone of a solid organization. Above Pan Americanism there is only Pan Humanism to which the former may lead some day, bestowing upon all mankind the principles of law which are now the privilege of a part only of humanity and which we Americans theoretically and usually practically substitute for conquest and force.

Force is even thought incompatible with Pan Americanism and the United States will have to abstain from force if it is to govern the world morally. Material interests act as a bad counsellor: good advice comes from intelligence, from the centers of education, especially the universities, where Pan Americanism has received its scholarly form and which we may say has inspired its soul. Even the apostles of idealism may sometimes err, despite conventionalities and have spells of disrespect for forms, just as the followers of what was called *real politik* contributed so much to disparage an aspect of German thought before public opinion.

The world shifts decidedly to a period of greater cosmopolitism notwithstanding the revival of nationalism, but such a cosmopolitism must rest upon mutual duties and rights. If the leadership of a world so new is to be the lot of the United States, it is owing to the identification of the United States with freedom and peace, not to any device of annexation of land and suppression of liberties.

Rome cannot live twice with its spirit at once juridical and military. A new Rome will have to choose between the two forms, as the people is no longer content with being fed and amused: *panem et circenses*. People begin everywhere to be conscious of what is due to labor, and huge immoral profits are henceforth to be abolished in industry as well as in politics.

Proconsuls like Verres are no more to be tolerated than nabobs sprung from the war at the cost of their brother's blood. I once wrote that war would cease to be courted if it became a poor heiress.

If it was not so, it would be to despair of the justice of history, which although it may be fallible, is one of the beliefs that support mankind in its hours of agony. American people as a whole are too honest to think otherwise and the last league of nations that was attempted was only a victim of the egoism grafted in it through the statecraft of international politicians causing the loss of its original altruism.

The form of a league of nations may be political, but its substance must be juridical. This is why its most important and efficient feature ought to be the organization of the Supreme Court to deal with interpretations, differences, and controversies which can all be reduced to judicial terms. I myself would like to see within the Pan American Union a court of that kind to which American disputes could be submitted. Of course it would have to lie, like the Union itself, on the basis of equality, a basis which permitted this result of the first Pan American conference, created especially for commercial and economical purposes, to become a moral power and to stride with giant's steps to the goal of an inalterable concord.

The world has heard of other leagues of nations before this last attempt and Sully describes in his *Memoirs* the one planned by his soverign Henri IV. It was also to be exclusive, confined to christian nations, but the end of wars was really to be attained by the action of an international court of justice. *Le bon roi Henry* belonged, however, to the kind of pacifists who want first to take every advantage of the old system and to have their own way by means of war before ceasing to fight; he wished to begin by crushing Austria.

Shortly before the great war in May, 1914, a French pacifist—he called himself so —expressed to me in Paris quite similar views. We must, he told me to my great dismay, have a general scramble and then work for peace. The adepts of the balance of power do not speak a different language. In America, fortunately, things are not the same and we have a better conception of that so called balance of power. It must not be a see-saw; it has to be a *carousel*.

In fact we never built up systems of alliances, or at least those which have occurred in the course of events have been so occasional and ephemeral that they cannot be called a system. The United States since its very beginning as a continental power refused to enter into alliances, even with the other nations of this hemisphere. Such American alliances were equally considered entangling.

Brazil, when menaced by Portugal in 1823, immediately after its independence was proclaimed, proposed in Washington a pact which was politely declined. The only part to which they would subscribe, the only pacts which all of us have subscribed to, are pacts to improve interamerican relations and they had consequently to rest upon equity.

Our continent is, however, acquainted with more than one initiative of a league of nations. Bolívar was not the only American to express this ideal in 1815, in his famous letter-program of Kingston, and to promote its realization in 1826 at the Congress of Panama. Portugal, which was the first European power to acknowledge the new Spanish American nationalities, showed in 1822, shortly before the separation of Brazil, a more acute vision of the balance between the Old and the New World than Canning seemed to have.

That happened when one of its statesmen proposed to build up what he called the "Confederation of the independent nations". It was but a league and Silvestre Pinheiro Ferreira, who suggested it, was a remarkable political thinker, whom the constitutional uprising of 1821 in Brazil brought to the front as a member of the royal cabinet as well as one of the philosophers and writers on public law quoted in his time as authorities in Europe.

His confederation, which he thought of starting with the United Kingdom of Portugal and Brazil, Spain, Greece, and the American countries, was destined in his conception to work as the *contre partie* of the Holy Alliance. The latter tended to protect legitimacy and autocracy, the first to protect democracy or at least constitutional government. They were in truth antagonistic. At the head of the second, Silvestre Pinheiro Ferreira wanted to place the United States of North America— as he called them—declaring himself afraid, in the diplomatic instructions he wrote for his agents and for foreign governments, of the Holy Alliance's aim. In his words this blessed league would seek to destroy liberty throughout all the civilized world and especially in the New World, using for that purpose Russia's ambition and England's sea power.

The *casus foederis* in every case of foreign aggression was to be decided by a majority vote, as well as the form of help to be extended to the victim, in order to offer a common resistance. The project comprised equal treatment for citizens of each of the confederate countries in the other countries of the league, equality of taxes on navigation, freedom of commerce, banking facilities, reciprocal validity of the awards of prize courts, etc.

Countries of Iberian descent in the New World had then a standing which their political unrest greatly impaired afterwards. Hispanic America has recovered it and has gained much prestige in late years, not through feats of arms but through the action of its culture. So it was that Pan Americanism has deserved to be called "a dynamic force" in the world of today. Twenty years ago, when I was secretary of the Brazilian Legation in Washington, not a few of the European diplomats used to look upon their South American colleagues as creatures of a different kind, although there were among these, men of refined education and high learning like Salvador de Mendonça, Don Matías Romero, Garcia Merou, Morla Vicuña and others, who were positively superior to most of the Old World representatives.

Through the efficiency of such men—I am proud to have had Salvador de Mendonça as my chief and professor of diplomacy, the fault being all mine if I was a bad pupil—a Pan American conscience has been growing and teaching that the permanent development of the New World requires absolute union among its countries. They may differ in race, in language, in religion, in traditions, even in form of government, as when Brazil was an empire, a peaceful and well meaning empire: there is always a community of purposes since there is an identity of ground and the tie binding them together is public law.   It is the unity of juridical principles which has risen above that diversity of conditions, political or social; which has gathered us; which has called and kept us attentive to the attainment of a common moral law and which will bind us forever.   If there is a destiny which cannot be denied or avoided, this is the one: it is as manifest as it will be glorious.

M. DE OLIVEIRA LIMA.

THE MONROE DOCTRINE AS A REGIONAL
UNDERSTANDING[1]

The purpose of the present paper is not to venture upon one more discussion of that much discussed question as to the relationship between the Monroe Doctrine and the League of Nations. It is proposed rather to examine briefly certain new developments, largely economic, which have taken place in Hispanic America since 1914 and especially since 1918, which have a direct bearing upon the diplomatic and political relations between that region and the United States. If we assume that the interests of all of the American nations still demand the maintenance of the Monrovian principle—the exclusion of political aggrandizement by non-American nations—a question arises, namely: Has not the world-wide political and economic upheaval of the past few years exerted some influence upon the general situation in Hispanic America, affecting thereby the effective enforcement of the Doctrine? Among the amazing transformations wrought by the war upon the southern republics, have there been any which bear upon what might be called the inter-regional problems, the political and economic relations of the American nations, both north and south? Can a unilateral, defensive declaration, such as the Monroe Doctrine—not even a policy, but rather a changing point of view or position varying from passive disinterestedness or even negligence and non-enforcement on some occasions to outspoken threats of war on others—can such a concept be made the basis of an international engagement or a regional understanding?

One of the most significant effects of the war upon the southern republics was the change which it wrought in their relations

[1] Read at the joint conference of the American Historical Association and American Political Science Association, December 30, 1920, at the Pan American Union, Washington, D. C.

248

with one another. I do not refer to the formation of such political or diplomatic associations as the so-called A. B. C. arbitration league of May, 1915, which has not yet been fully ratified. More significant and fundamental, though far less spectacular than this, are the prosaic commercial, economic, and social bonds which have grown up among them during the enforced cessation of many of their contacts with the outside world from 1914 to 1919. For the first time in their history they were compelled to become acquainted with one another and the effects of this are strikingly apparent to any observer who has been in a position to compare pre-war impressions with those of today. The colonial history of this area was marked by the most carefully devised administrative dependence directly upon the Castillian crown. The nineteenth century was a period of turbulent political and economic internal readjustment with considerable assistance on the economic side from Europe but with practically no inter-Hispanic American contacts save at the points of bayonets.

Then came 1914, and just as the preoccupations of Europe in its previous great cataclysm, the Napoleonic War, enabled Hispanic America to achieve her political independence, so has the recent upheaval in the old world given the southern republics their first real appreciation of their own capacity for self-development and inter-regional cooperation along economic and social lines.

It would be absurd of course to suggest that the years 1914–1918 had delivered Hispanic America from any further economic dependence upon Europe; but in view of certain significant facts to be reviewed in a moment, it would be equally ridiculous to assume that Hispanic America will continue to look to Europe, or even to the United States, for the fulfillment of all of her needs for manufactured commodities, and even for capital and fuel. The amount of evidence on this point is ample and instead of falling off after 1918, it has steadily increased. Let us take, for example, a few isolated instances in the financial field. Argentine citizens recently loaned one and a half billion lire to the Italian government; the Argentine government has advanced

£40,000,000 to the allies and is now said to be contemplating negotiations of a similar nature with Austria and Germany. Chilean financiers have, within the past two years, assumed a prominent position in the Bolivian tin industry and have lately been active in planning the exploitation of petroleum and other mineral products in Argentina. Since 1918 detailed plans or arrangements have been made for the construction in Hispanic America of at least five international railways and six or more international cable and telegraph lines. It is unnecessary to comment upon these very material and effective expressions of the new desire for more inter-regional bonds, nor need we be reminded of the profound effect, both economic and political, that such ties will have. The noteworthy point is the fact that the majority of these enterprises are being undertaken with local capital.

Commercial changes of the same sort are noticeable on every hand, due especially to the extraordinary diversification of industries and production in the past six years. Since 1914 the trade between Argentina and Brazil has grown 500 per cent and all the latest statistics point to even further expansion. Mexican commerce with the more important South American countries, including such items as food stuffs, oil, fibers and even newsprint paper, has been more than quadrupled during the war, and the most rapid growth has come in the past two years. During 1919 and 1920 at least five inter-Hispanic American congresses were held, not with the object of exchanging those beautiful expressions of fraternal affection which too frequently befog the atmosphere of such assemblages. Quite the contrary; their subject matter in each case was prosaic and unpicturesque, but at the same time definite and constructive: dairying and pastoral agriculture, police regulations, immigration, architecture, and physical education.

These are but a few random items, but they could be duplicated many times over, even in the case of the smaller republics of the tropics. They point unmistakably to the beginnings of a new adjustment of the Hispanic American international situation. The bearing of such significant economic developments upon political and diplomatic affairs is too obvious to require explanation. Hispanic America may still be dependent upon Europe for immigrants, capital, ingenuity and manufactures, but that dependence—especially with reference to the last three items—is decreasing relatively. The opportunities and necessities for European incursions and exploitations in Hispanic America are on the wane and the native means available within the southern republics for their individual or cooperative defense against any such intrusions which might be unwelcome are slowly but surely growing.

The effect of this rapprochement upon the Monroe Doctrine must therefore be inevitable. In fact, the prophecy made in June, 1918, by Professor G. G. Wilson seems to be nearing fulfillment: The Doctrine is evidently passing to a wider field of influence. Whereas the economic readjustment in the south is altering profoundly the relations between Hispanic America and Europe, the change has been far less dangerous to our economic interests primarily because those interests had only come to the fore during the years just before the war and their relative youth made them far more plastic, more adjustable to the new situation than were their older and now seriously embarrassed European competitors. The results of this situation are well known; for the purposes of the present discussion, the great increase in trade values is less significant than the appearance of real, permanent bonds between the two regions— material ties which make for better understanding and a lasting community of interests. It is well, in this connection, to recall that before 1914 there was not one American branch bank in Hispanic America while today there are over a hundred; that there are nearly a dozen American Chambers of Commerce in the southern republics, the oldest of them having been founded about two years ago; that important new American cable connections and the valuable services of the two great American news-gathering associations have been greatly extended in that field; and that American ships are now sufficiently numerous in southern waters to carry nearly fifty per cent of our trade there, which is five times the proportion carried in 1914.

The Inter-American High Commission has since 1915 been unostentatiously but surely working out a definite and effective series of bonds in the shape of uniform commercial law and practice—a constructive program of the highest value.

This marked increase in inter-American contacts suggests at once the possibility, and even the probability of a restatement of the Monroe Doctrine along more friendly lines. President Wilson's efforts along this line are well known; we may recall especially the proposal to the visiting Mexican journalists on June 7, 1918, that "all American republics, including the United States, should give guarantees for the political independence and territorial integrity of all"—a phrase which, according to the President's subsequent explanation, was the origin of the idea later expressed in Article X of the League of Nations covenant. In view, however, of the disputed boundaries in many parts of Hispanic America, it is difficult to see how such a firm, unconditional territorial guarantee can be established. But the desirability of such an inter-American guarantee as applied to the sovereign independence of the various republican governments cannot be questioned; our recent experiences in Central America and the West Indies show plainly the necessity of reiterated, formal assurances on our part that we feel bound by such a guarantee.

President Brum of Uruguay outlined in April, 1920, a plan of an American League which "would consider jointly all American problems, would place all American republics on an equal footing and would defend each one of them against menaces from Europe or from any American government". This proposal for "American solidarity" has been greeted with skeptical criticism in various Hispanic American capitals as a Utopian dream which has already been dispelled by the aggressions of the United States in the Caribbean area. The suggestion of the distinguished Uruguayan probably is ahead of the times, but so far as it concerns our submission of the Monroe Doctrine to other American governments for judgment, we may recall that for several years we have already been bound by treaties with no less than fifteen of the twenty Hispanic American republics to "submit all disputes of every nature whatsoever", including presumably those involving the Monroe Doctrine, to joint commissions for investigation (though not for a final and a binding arbitration) during a period of one year. Former President Taft's memorandum to President Wilson dated March 21, 1919, regarding Article X of the Covenant of the League, indicated a readiness to accept the above principle and to carry it even further in the form of a definite acquiescence in the protection of the sovereignty of any American state or states by any other such state or states, a position which he believes to be "the Monroe Doctrine pure and simple".

One further evidence of the new trend of events may be noted. "The war has reduced to dust the ancient legend of the calibanism of North America", as Semprum, the distinguished Venezuelan man of letters has expressed it; we are no longer "rude and obtuse monsters whose newspapers and feet are large" as we were described by the great poet, Darío; no longer a towering menace, "swift, overwhelming, fierce and clownish" (even though our own widely circulated motion picture films seem to confirm some at least of those impressions). More than one Hispanic American publicist has observed in the words of one of them, that "the part the United States has played in this war is the noblest that has ever fallen to any people". Saenz Peña, the late president of Argentina, may have been partially right when he wrote in 1914 that "we South Americans have only unwelcome memories of our friends in the North"; he was certainly correct in stating that at that time there were more points of material contact between South America and Europe than there were between the two Americas. But as has been noted above, much, very much has happened to alter that situation during the past six years. For one thing, we have become a great creditor nation and some of the larger Hispanic American republics have also appeared as lenders of capital. In consequence of that fact a prediction made some eleven years ago by Professor A. C. Coolidge of Harvard has been fulfilled: irresponsible borrowers in the new world are finding themselves answerable to creditors nearer home and the

Drago Doctrine defense of debtors is being examined by the American nations from a new angle, with a new understanding of the interests and point of view of the creditor.

It is certainly encouraging to have a well-known Hispanic American from one of the smaller republics declare that "absolute stability of credit is the only positive basis of national and individual prestige". Then he goes on to note that the Monroe Doctrine has become a precept of the American family whose closer economic and commercial ties help the autonomy and defensive powers of each one. And it is interesting to note that one of the recent stimuli to this new regional rapprochement is the threatening danger of incursions of radical agitators from eastern Europe which is even now presenting a very grave problem to the southern republics as well as to ourselves. The Monroe Doctrine of 1823 was aimed in part at Russian political aggressions in the new world. One of the factors which will stimulate a united American stand upon a new and broader principle as we approach the centennial of the Doctrine, may very well be the defense of America against the menace of Russian bolshevism and its attendant evils.

Nevertheless, we hear from certain sensitive and suspicious critics the condemnation that "the United States is giving the Monroe Doctrine an economic imprint . . . the Doctrine has come to express the ambitions of the United States to keep business Europe rather than political Europe out of Latin America"; that every effort on our part toward economic cooperation with the southern republics means just one more attempt to clinch our economic hegenomy over that area. And yet, when in May, 1920, American bankers refused to renew a loan of $50,000,000 to the Argentine Republic, we were denounced as insincere and unfaithful to the principles of Pan Americanism, and our prestige in Hispanic America suffered the worst blow which it has had in many years.

Our intentions should not and do not by any means contemplate any exclusive or monopolistic arrangement for economic cooperation with Hispanic America. If, for example, the Pan Spanish movement should take an economic turn—and there are already signs of such a tendency—our purpose should be to meet it in a spirit of frank and friendly rivalry and to let our Hispanic American friends choose between the two.

This much seems, then, to be clear: the marked strengthening of economic relations and bonds among the Hispanic American republics on the one hand and between them and the United States on the other points very definitely toward a new epoch in the history of the Monroe Doctrine in which regional understandings, primarily perhaps along economic lines but nevertheless affecting inevitably the diplomatic and political relationship, will play an important part.

JULIUS KLEIN.

"YANKEE IMPERIALISM" AND SPANISH AMERICAN SOLIDARITY: A COLOMBIAN INTERPRETATION

On August 16 last, the anniversary of Santo Domingo's independence, the Congress of Colombia offered the customary congratulations to the neighboring island republic with which the country has always maintained very close relations. As originally presented these resolutions embodied phrases that involved a third power—the United States. For this reason they deserve our careful attention.

In the Chamber of Deputies, the original resolution expressed the wish that Santo Domingo might speedily recover its sovereignty, "ground under the heel of a foreign military occupation." This expression and the prayer of the Senate that "circumstances that deprived our Sister Republic of its sovereignty should cease to operate" were struck out of the final resolutions. A like fate overtook the Senate provision that the Minister of Foreign Relations should address the message to the President of Santo Domingo, Doctor Henríquez y Carvajal, now living in self-imposed exile.

"A Shameful Silence", proclaimed Eduardo Santos next day, on the front page of *El Tiempo*. "Timidity or rather inexplicable cowardice," continued this frank-spoken, liberal editor, "marked the failure of Congress to protest against the further occupation of Santo Domingo." This was the blackest crime yet committed by "Yankee Imperialism" in Hispanic America. An iniquitous domination, he averred, which "simply appealed to violence, rough, implacable, cruel. Suppressing all liberties, impeding every manifestation of free thought, [it] employed machine guns to dominate a people who refused to sacrifice their independence". Under such conditions the colorless greetings from the Colombian Congress savored of sarcasm.

The bitterness of Santos was inspired by resentment against that imperialistic aggression which once despoiled his own

256

country. But Colombia's suffering had not surpassed the woe of Santo Domingo. The latter's president was driven from power and its officials were without their salaries, because they would not accept a treaty that subjected them to an American protectorate. In solemn procession their women folk had offered their jewels to maintain their hospitals and other public charities without the aid of the usurpers. Their touching protest, eloquently voiced by their archbishop, had finally awakened an echo even in the American House of Representatives. Argentina had sent a warship to salute the Dominican flag, pointedly ignoring that of the usurper. Even the Parliament of Spain requested Washington to release its former colony from servitude. Only Colombia, "mutilated and grieving"—Colombia that had once "felt the pains of solitude and of abandonment"—Colombia, unwilling to acknowledge that another people had suffered more than itself—did not "dare express sympathy for a people among whom all rights have been violated and all liberties refused recognition."

Santos is obviously too rhetorical to carry full conviction, but he bears a reputation in Bogotá for saying what he thinks. "Not thus", he stated, "does a people preserve its right to live. Infamous is the pathway of aggression and suicidal. A hesitating course is not only suicidal but humiliating, and by pursuing it, we lose everything, even honor. Precisely because danger threatens us are we prohibited from keeping silence when neighboring peoples fall victims of the evil we fear".

To the same effect, but with more caution, writes Armando Solano in *El Espectador*. Counseling neither submission nor hostility, he pointed out that the greatest cohesive force in America was the United States, with which Colombia needed closer relations. From that power alone could their country obtain the capital necessary for speedy progress. Tacitly or through timidity European nations forebore to dispute with the United States for economic hegemony in Hispanic America. The United States could greatly aid in their economic development, but more to the point it could teach them important lessons in moral orientation. "On its intimate side the North American people are loyal, sincere, pure, and generous.   Its fireside life is patriarchal; its sentiments are pious and just".

The editor pointed out the antithesis, all too familiar to Colombians, between popular ideals and official life.   To officials in the United States, Colombia owed her grievous past injuries, but this should not prevent a "noble and spontaneous" friendship with the North American people.   Such a friendship required no shameful manifestations of servility.   "He who renounces his personality, and denies his history, his name, his antecedents, his ideals, loses voluntarily and necessarily the right to call himself another's friend. . . .   Servitude, vassalage, protectorates, have their rules", but they are not the precepts of friendship.   The United States wishes friends, not slavish admirers.   Public opinion there promptly responds to the call of justice and of urgent need.   Business men and college professors alike protested against the "crime of Panama", and if the people at large knew more of its details they would long since have forced suitable reparation.

It is a false interpretation of patriotism that requires Colombians to prostrate themselves before "Yankee Imperialism".   The people of the United States wish their Hispanic American neighbors to be friends.   "Its public men are trying to elevate South America through education, wealth, and public hygiene, because they need our cooperation, not our shameful and sterile hesitancy".   Above all they will not rejoice to find under a slightly brunette complexion the spirit of African subserviency.

The editor of *El Nuevo Tiempo*, the leading conservative organ, evidently felt called upon to defend the course of Congress. The resolutions as at first presented, he stated, would have been acceptable in a political club or a newspaper, or even when expressed by individual senators and representatives.   But the Minister of Foreign Relations could not address the exiled president of Santo Domingo, unjustly though the latter had been treated, as long as the Colombian government maintained official relations with the United States.   On Bolivia's natal day the minister did not feel impelled to send the resolutions then adopted to her recently exiled president.   Very properly, therefore, the Senate modified the Santo Domingan resolution to conform to diplomatic usage.

This defense provoked from Santos a prompt reply. Under the caption "Worse than it Was", he pointed out that international usage certainly would not require the Colombian minister to send resolutions to an American naval officer who, "contrary to all right, law, and justice, persecutes the Dominicans and with violence and the barbarity of brute force suppresses every manifestation of free thought. . . . Miserable will be the lot of us weaker peoples when Latin American countries recognize this military usurper as chief executive of Santo Domingo".

Such recognition, he continued, would be "simply criminal and make us accomplices in the offense committed against that people". Bolivia did not represent a parallel case. Its own people had expelled their executive and replaced him with the man of their choice. The Navy Department of the United States dominated Santo Domingo and the original protests of the Colombian Congress against that control differed little in wording from the resolution of the North American House of Representatives. In attempting to excuse the shameful silence of the final resolutions, *El Nuevo Tiempo* assumes a worse attitude than the members themselves. Words fail to describe the condition of Colombia, if its people are unable to express their sympathy with neighbors whose sovereignty is violated. But they do sympathize with the Dominicans and therefore, he concluded, "let us fold up this page inspired by the unjustifiable fear of certain parliamentarians—this page around which the editor of *El Nuevo Tiempo* has written so strange a border."

That same afternoon Augustín Nieto Caballero continued the discussion in *El Espectador*. "In an idealistic people like our own," he stated, "one will always encounter an echo of protest against force or a fraternal word for the fallen, although neither one or the other answers any practical end, and both because of obvious conditions are simply platonic. Such a habit may seem inconvenient and may arouse prejudice against us, but it is a beautiful habit worthy of sympathy and respect".

After this characteristic and truthful introduction, he adds that Colombia can do nothing for Santo Domingo. The latter is "a sheep fallen into the jaws of the wolf", whose fate the great Powers seem tacitly to accept just as they sanctioned the plundering of Colombia. While it will not materially aid the tortured island to know that Colombians mourn its lot, the news that "a noble people of America accompanies its people in their *via crucis*" will create a salutary moral impression. For this a fraternal greeting by those members of the Colombian Congress who most "feel the fate of the captive isle" would have been sufficient.

Nieto Caballero acknowledges that Doctor Henríquez y Carvajal—"today an austere wandering Jew"—is a great American personality, before whom even the citizens of the United States uncover. He flatters the discernment of the North American people, but they should at least try to merit the courteous exaggeration. As for the resolution, he felt that it should not officially emanate from Congress nor pass through the ministry of foreign relations. In the United States Congress had expressed itself vigorously over Ireland, but the Secretary of State had made no untoward representations to the British Foreign Office nor had the administration recognized De Valera. As little could the Colombian government officially approach a president who was without office. This course was harsh but necessary if the country was to avoid continual bickerings with other powers or maintain with them any relations whatever.

In his answer Santos informed Nieto Caballero that Ireland had never been free, so her case afforded no parallel to that of Santo Domingo. Moreover, he published a protest issued in 1856 by the Minister of Foreign Relations of New Granada, Lino de Pombo. The country that later called itself Colombia did not then hesitate to express its opposition when the United States recognized in Nicaragua a government supported by the filibuster, William Walker. That, in Santos's concept, was "a marvelous note which condensed with insuperable grace the sentiments and well-being of the weak American nations. It is all there, and all its phrases apply to the present incident.

It is a page of gold which may be read with pride, when thinking of what we were, and with sadness, when noting what has occurred yesterday and today. It is a lesson from the past that we ought to receive with respect and it should teach us the only way a free people can proceed to a realization of its destiny".

"As *El Tiempo* recognizes we are in accord with that paper in acknowledging the outrages committed by Yankee forces in the island of Santo Domingo", calmly wrote the editor of *El Espectador* that same day. "*El Nuevo Tiempo* is likewise in accord with our colleague and ourselves, and so are all newspapers and probably all citizens. The unmerited woes of a sister people undoubtedly arouse in the innermost being of each the noble sympathy that affords consolation and the noble indignation against the oppressor which serves to stimulate the oppressed".

Nieto Caballero believes in a popular expression of this sympathy; Santos in an official one. Such official action, the former thinks, would render international relations impossible. The plight of Ireland shows how international law limits the champion of public faith. If Colombia must always hold herself ready to break a lance in the name of mere justice, then it makes no difference whether a people finds itself oppressed by internal factions or by alien hands; whether it belongs to the same race and inhabits the same continent as its would-be defender; whether it seeks autonomy or simply freedom from economic tutelage. He enumerates a list of quarrels that await Colombia in both hemispheres, if it essays the doubtful role of world justiciar.

Their country, as his editorial caption suggests, must preserve a "Sense of Proportion". A newcomer in the concert of nations, it must not pattern after Tunja's municipal assembly. That body once declared war against Napoleon III. because he invaded Mexico. The purpose was idealistic; the outcome laughable. Such would be the result of a quixotic declaration by Colombia alone concerning Santo Domingo. If the country really wished to do something worth while, let her ministers exert themselves to bring about a collective note signed by all the chanceries of the continent.

In his "Final Words" Santos resents the irony of his fellow editor, but he is not less bitter against the invader of Santo Domingo. No other independent country in Hispanic America, within the last half century, had been invaded by Yankee military forces, deprived of its sovereign authorities, and subjected to alien courts-martial. "This is the supreme outrage committed by Yankee Imperialism in Latin America. The loyal sons of the Dominican Republic struggle unceasingly to end that outrage, to terminate that scandalous occupation. We have asked that the Congress of Colombia might lift up its voice in behalf of their sacred cause and by so doing bring into relief the solidarity that should exist among sister nations, menaced by the same danger. We have believed that such a course was rigidly in accord with the principles of American international law and conducive to the well-being of all countries bordering on the Caribbean."

Such being the case, Santos continued, Colombia should not hold its peace, but should follow the worthy precedent set by Lino de Pombo, seventy-five years before, in protesting against acts that deprive free people of their sovereignty. This action, whatever the importance of the protesting nation, was the privilege of every continental state. But when Santos had reiterated this idea, he provoked only an ironical comparison with the humble municipality of Tunja. "Let the tiger eat us one by one", he bitterly concluded. "When the lot falls to a neighbor, we will maintain serene composure, so as to afford no occasion for laughing at our manifestations of indignation or surprise. If the fatal day arrives for us, let us take care not to ask aid or sympathy from people of our race, nor from any one, and certainly not from the God of Nations, who, it seems, is a decided partisan of the law of majorities."

Nieto Caballero regretted the other's resentment. After all, he observed the following day, they did not greatly differ in sentiment. The words of Santos do credit to his heart and character, but he should not employ them uselessly. A simple note from the Colombian minister would not in the least help Santo Domingo, but it might once more arouse against Colombia the resentment that seemed to be disappearing, even in the Senate of the United States. A protest would have been in order when the occupation began. Made today, after the people of the United States have promised to restore the sovereignty of Santo Domingo and when, in the midst of a presidential campaign, they are condemning the policy that violated it, its only effect would be to arouse the hostility of the entire nation and defeat the pending treaty that means so much to Colombia.

The editor of *El Espectador* prides himself on his patriotism as truly as does his colleague. "We feel," he avers, "what he feels and if we were in a position to challenge the Colossus, we should favor the organization of an expedition to liberate Santo Domingo with the same romantic and beautiful ideals that inspired the Crusades. But as we are weak and for that reason unequal to such a task, we prefer to show our deep sympathy for our captive brothers by means of the press, without exposing our country in a most noble but imprudent manner to reprisals that we could not measure until it was altogether too late".

Nieto Caballero spoke wisely, but even his moderate phrases contain few words of approval for the United States. Most of his contemporaries, especially those of the comic press, were far less charitable. A popular cartoon represented Uncle Sam astride the Colombian Congress, appropriately in the posture of the ever-present mule, before whose nose, at a safe distance, dangled a tempting morsel labelled "Twenty-five Millions". The familiar *motif* in its immediate application seemed to hit the popular fancy, but the response shows no growing fondness for the United States.

Nor should this tendency surprise us. For more than six years, Colombia has patiently awaited the ratification of a treaty that promised partial recompense for the purloined Panama Railroad—not for the revolted department itself. On various pretexts the chief despoiler—who openly boasted that he "took" Panama—and his friends, have put off this simple act of justice. The petroleum interests, it is charged, have used the deferred instrument as a club, wherewith to fight unacceptable decrees. Possibly they have acted with some justification, but the sinister connection between their protests and the failure of the Senate to consider the treaty has been noted by Colombian leaders—noted and deeply resented. Not by such methods will the great Northern Republic improve its reputation in Hispanic America.

We must realize that this newspaper controversy is not a mere sporting exhibit of journalism in Colombia. Few important questions arise there, in Congress or in the press, that may not be turned to the disadvantage of the United States. Legislators debate the possible forfeiture of a contract with the Santo Marta Railroad. Immediately the discussion turns to the United Fruit Company and its methods, projected as they believe by the American government. The unsettled boundary with Panama arouses fears for the mining district of Chocó, where Colombian gold and American currency circulate together with distressful ease. A great banking corporation with ramifications throughout the Republic is, they charge, only the precursor of political as well as economic subjection. The wave of prosperity coincident with its operations appears but a temporary measure to lull them into fancied security. The recent 'fall in the price of coffee, hides, and other staples, with the consequent slump in exports, unfavorable exchange, and general commercial demoralization, seems to confirm their fears. Even men of saner views and of innate courtesy do not wholly escape these forebodings.

It is high time that our people awoke to the significance of this propaganda. Its psychological effect on a potential market of five million people is not to be despised. But the mischief spreads through all Spanish America. We remember that during the late war Colombia was one of the few American powers that neither declared war nor broke relations with Germany. Now its statesmen are unceasingly agitating closer commercial relations with Chile and Japan—an obvious slap at ourselves. We can only blame our past folly, and above all the indirect intervention of 1903, for this unfortunate situation. That event caused other dirt to fly than its protagonist intended. Therefore the sooner we clear up the dispute the better for both countries. At least, favorable action on the treaty will remove pretexts for further journalistic discussion such as we have summarized above.

ISAAC JOSLIN COX.

Northwestern University,
Evanston, Illinois.

MINISTERIAL ORDER OF JOSÉ DE GÁLVEZ ESTAB-
LISHING A UNIFORM DUTY ON THE IMPORTATION
OF NEGRO SLAVES INTO THE INDIES; AND CON-
VENTION BETWEEN SPAIN AND THE UNITED
PROVINCES REGULATING THE RETURN OF DE-
SERTERS AND FUGITIVES IN THEIR AMERICAN
COLONIES

The two documents here given are to be found in the collection
of East Florida papers in the Division of Manuscripts in the
Library of Congress.   The first is found in 39 M 3, the second
in 46 G 4.   The Spanish is from photostat prints of the originals.

The Ministerial Order of José de Gálvez is evidence of the
knowledge that the Minister of the Indies possessed of the conditions in the Spanish Americas.   Those who have read the
scholarly work of Doctor Priestley[1] are familiar with the means
by which he had acquired this knowledge.   The training and
experience gained by José de Gálvez as Visitor-General of New
Spain from 1765 to 1771 had eminently well fitted him for the
arduous duties of Minister of the Indies in the reign of the
enlightened ruler, Charles III.   The document is evidence also
of views held at that time of the economic conditions of Spain
and its colonies.   Agriculture and mining are held to be basic
industries upon which depend commerce and the happiness of
the king's subjects.   The labor problem in the Indies is acute and
can be improved by facilitating the importation of negro slaves
into those dominions.   For Gálvez finds that negro slaves are
the only laborers who can be used most widely in the colonies.
For this reason import duties on negro slaves are to be made
uniform; and facilities for their importation into the Indies are
to be improved and enlarged.   Hence this order of 1784.

[1] Herbert Ingram Priestly: *José de Gálvez, Visitor-General of New Spain, 1765–
1771.* University of California Publications in History, Volume V. University
of California Press, Berkeley, 1916.

The document is of importance further as an evidence of the enlightened colonial policy of Charles III. and his ministers. By the commercial code of 1778,[2] Charles III. had declared free the principal ports of Spain and its possessions. The monopoly which Sevilla and Cadiz, Vera Cruz and Porto Bello had enjoyed for so many years had by this act been abolished. The principal ports of the Indies could therefore freely trade with Sevilla, Cadiz, Barcelona, Malaga, Santander, San Sebastian, Bilbao, Vigo, Gijon, and San Lúcar; and among themselves. The Count of Floridablanca (Jose Moñino), the First Minister of State of Charles III. from 1777 to the death of the king in 1788, and of Charles IV. to the time of his dismissal in 1792, was, in the opinion of the writer, the man primarily responsible for the enlightened colonial policy of those last, eleven years of the reign of Charles III. True, José de Gálvez had been made Minister of the Indies in 1776, a year before Floridablanca became First Minister of State and President of the Council of Ministers. The great influence which Floridablanca exerted over Charles III. from the very beginning of the ministry[3] leads the writer to conclude that the colonial policy was the policy of Floridablanca and not of José de Gálvez. The larger knowledge of national and international affairs possessed by Floridablanca enabled him to make this colonial policy a part of his general policy. The imperative need of conciliating the vassals of those kingdoms—to use the language of Gálvez's order—was fully realized by Charles III. and Floridablanca. The recent rôle that Spain had been compelled to play in the international struggle against Great Britain had placed it in a most trying position in its relations with the colonists. Floridablanca had

[2] This was the famous *Reglamento para el comercio libre de España á Indias* of 12th October, 1778. See Moses, *Spain's Declining Power in South America*, p. 166.

[3] There are interesting passages in the correspondence of the minister of Catherine II. of Russia, M. Etienne de Zinowief; and of the Austrian Ambassadors at the court of Spain, two sons of the great Austrian Chancellor, Prince Kaunitz-Rietberg, in the Royal and Imperial Archives of Austria at Vienna. Excerpts from these bearing on the great influence of Floridablanca with Charles III. are given in the writer's doctor's thesis on *Floridablancas Handelspolitik gegen Oesterreich, 1777–1792*, 1913. Munich.

really been forced to take up arms in behalf of a group of rebellious English colonists in a war with the mother country. And Spain had played no mean part in the war for its threat to invade England prevented the British from using a larger naval force against the United States.[4] Floridablanca realized fully too the importance of the suggestion of Count Aranda in 1783 to Charles III. for a division of the Indies into three kingdoms with a Bourbon prince over each and all under the rule of Charles III. as Emperor. The colonists in the Americas were therefore conscious of change bound to come sooner or later in the form of their government. The spirit of revolution thrives upon notions of inevitable change. The movements too of the newly created nation in North America must be closely watched. Boundary questions were becoming very acute especially as regards the Mississippi. Louisiana and the Floridas were to be set in order—no mean problems in themselves. So great caution, foresight, and sagacity were needed on the part of Spain if it were to prevent a war of even greater proportions than that between Great Britain and the thirteen American colonies. The order of José de Gálvez here given was only part of the general scheme of conciliating the Spanish American colonies. For the order is larger than that which would facilitate the importation of negro slaves into the Indies. The order should therefore be considered as only another bit of evidence of the general policy of Floridablanca in national as well as international affairs.

The other document, the convention between Spain and the United Provinces, very naturally calls to mind our Fugitive Slave Law of 1793. There need not necessarily be any connection between the two documents. The fact that they appear so closely together is itself of interest.

There are certain humane features about the Dutch-Spanish methods of procedure that should arrest our attention. Article five, for example, specifically stipulates that the punishment for desertion alone shall be humane. The death penalty, mutila-

---

[4] See Charles E. Chapman, *A History of Spain*, p. 397.

tion, perpetual imprisonment, etc., may not be inflicted upon a fugitive slave who is guilty of no crime other than desertion. The fugitive slave alleged to have committed a crime punishable by death shall have charges of criminal offense made and proved against him at the time of his capture and before the judge of the territory into which he had escaped. Article six, too, is important and rather novel. But if religious freedom were to obtain in the dominions of their High Mightinesses, why not effective in the case of returned fugitive negro slaves?

N. ANDREW N. CLEVEN.

The University of Arkansas,
    Fayetteville, Arkansas.
        January 22, 1921.

CONVENCION ENTRE EL REY NUESTRO SEÑOR Y LOS ESTADOS GENERALES DE LAS PROVINCIAS UNIDAS, PARA LA RECÍPROCA RESTITUCION DE DESERTORES Y FUGITIVOS ENTRE SUS COLONIAS DE AMÉRICA. FIRMADA EN ARANJUEZ Á 23 DE JUNIO DE 1791. RATIFICADA POR S. M. EN SAN LORENZO EL REAL Á 19 DE AGOSTO, Y POR SS. AA. PP. EN EL HAYA Á 22 DEL MISMO MES Y AÑO. [Cut] DE ORDEN DEL REY. EN MADRID, EN LA IMPRENTA REAL.

El Rey de España y los Estados Generales de las Provincias Unidas, movidos de las quejas reiteradas de sus respectivas Colonias en América, y deseosos de cortarlas de raiz, han tenido por oportuno para conseguirlo concluir una Convencion por la qual se establece la restitucion recíproca de sus Desertores y Fugitivos entre sus Colonias respectivas; cuya disposicion al paso que impedirá en adelante la desercion y sus conseqüencias perniciosas, estrechará los lazos de amistad y union entre los Colonos de ambas partes, y no dexará que desear á S. M. y SS. AA. PP.

A este fin, y para arreglar las condiciones de esta Convencion tan deseada, han conferido las Altas Partes Contratantes sus Plenos Poderes, por parte de S. M. Católica á D. Josef Moñino, Conde de Floridablanca, Caballero de la insigne Orden del Toyson, Gran Cruz de la de Cárlos III, primer Secretario de Estado y del Despacho; y por los

Estados Generales á D. Jacobo Godefroi, Conde de Rechteren, su Embaxador cerca de S. M. Católica; los quales despues de varias conferencias relativas á los mutuos intereses de sus Soberanos, han convenido en los Artículos siguientes.

ARTÍCULO PRIMERO.

Se establece la restitucion recíproca de los Fugitivos Blancos ó Negros entre todas las Posesiones Españolas en América, y las Colonias Holandesas, particularmente entre aquellas en que las quejas de desercion han sido mas freqüentes, á saber, entre Puerto Rico y S. Eustaquio, Coro y Curazao, los Establecimientos Españoles en el Orinoco, y Esequebo, Demerary, Berbices y Surinam.

ARTÍCULO II.

Se verificará la mencionada restitucion con toda legalidad al precio establecido en el Artículo siguiente, y á la primera reclamacion que hagan los Colonos sus Dueños, los quales tendrán que executarla en el término de un año, contado desde el dia de su desercion; pues pasado este tiempo no habrá ya lugar á reclamar los Esclavos, los quales pertenecerán desde entonces al Soberano del parage á que se hayan refugiado.

ARTÍCULO III.

Luego que se reclamen algunos Negros ó Negras, el Xefe ó Gobernador, que es á quien debe hacerse la reclamacion, tomará las medidas mas eficaces para su arresto, y para que despues de presos se entreguen á sus Dueños, los quales han de pagar á razon de un real de plata al dia por la manutencion de cada uno, desde aquel en que se les asegure, y además una gratificacion de veinte y cinco pesos fuertes por cada Esclavo para atender á los gastos de su prision, y recompensar á los que hayan contribuido á su arresto.

ARTÍCULO IV.

Animados los Plenipotenciarios de los mismos sentimientos de humanidad estipulan, que en adelante los Negros ó Negras Fugitivos no podrán ser castigados á su vuelta por causa de su desercion con pena capital, mutilacion, prision perpetua &c. á menos que además de la fuga fuesen reos de otros delitos, que por su naturaleza y calidad merezcan la pena de muerte; en cuyo caso deberán hacerlo presente al tiempo de reclamarlos.

ARTÍCULO V.

Si en los parages donde se hubiesen refugiado los Negros ó Negras Fugitivos, hubiesen cometido algun delito digno de castigo, los Jueces de aquellos lugares entenderán en la causa, y no restituirán los Esclavos sino despues de dexar la Justicia satisfecha. Si hubiesen cometido algun robo, no se entregarán hasta que sus Amos hayan satisfecho el valor de él; y para que no haya que hablar de las deudas que los Fugitivos hayan podido contraer, se remediará este abuso publicando por una y otra parte, quedan incapaces de contraerlas durante su fuga ó su prision.

ARTÍCULO VI.

Como la Religion no debe servir de pretexto ni motivo para reusar la restitucion, los Fugitivos Holandeses, que durante su residencia en las Colonias Españolas hubiesen abrazado la Religion Católica, podrán perseverar en ella á su vuelta á las Colonias Holandesas, donde gozarán, sin ser molestados, de la libertad de culto establecida por el gobierno de SS. AA. PP. en todos sus Dominios.

ARTÍCULO VII.

Habiéndose comprehendido á los Soldados Desertores baxo la denominacion de Desertores Blancos en el Artículo primero, se establece igualmente la restitucion recíproca de los que abandonando el servicio en las Colonias Españolas ú Holandesas, se refugiaren á las de los Españoles ú Holandeses; pero con la restriccion expresa de no pagarse por estos gratificacion alguna, satisfaciendo puramente los Dueños que los reclamen los gastos de su prision, y los que se juzguen indispensables hasta su restitucion, que deberá hacerse con los vestidos, armas, y quanto llevasen encima.

ARTÍCULO VIII.

Se dará noticia á los Xefes, Gobernadores y Comandantes de las Colonias vecinas respectivas de la presente Convencion, encargándoles su exâcta execucion, y que á este efecto la den toda la publicidad posible en sus Gobiernos y distritos respectivos.

ARTÍCULO IX.

La presente Convencion será ratificada y confirmada en el término de dos meses contados desde el dia de su firma.

En fe de lo qual Nosotros los infrascritos Plenipotenciarios de S. M. Católica y SS. AA. PP. hemos firmado en sus nombres y en virtud de sus Plenos Poderes la presente Convencion, y la hemos puesto los sellos de nuestras Armas.

En Aranjuez á 23 de Junio de 1791.

EL CONDE DE FLORIDABLANCA.   COMTE DE RECHTEREN.

[Seal]   [Seal]

[TRANSLATION]

Convention between the King our Lord and the States-General of the United Provinces for the Mutual Return of Deserters and Fugitives in their Colonies of America.
Confirmed at *Aranjuez* on the twenty-third of June, 1791.
Ratified by his Majesty at *San Lorenzo el Real* on the nineteenth of August, and by their High Mightinesses at the Hague on the twenty-second of the same month and year.

By order of the King.

The King of Spain and the States-General of the United Provinces, moved by the reiterated complaints of desertion in their colonies of America and desiring to remove (uproot, *cortarlas de raiz*) the causes for desertion, and to make impossible further complaints of desertion, consider the moment opportune for the adoption of a plan for the mutual return of deserters and fugitives. The plan should prevent desertion and its vicious consequences in the future, and should also aid in establishing a closer bond of union and amity among their colonists in America which cannot fail to be satisfactory to His Majesty and to their High Mightinesses.

With this end in view and in order to determine the nature of the provisions of this highly desired convention, the high contracting parties have conferred full and plenary powers on, for His Catholic Majesty, Don Josef Moñino, the Count of Floridablanca, Knight of the Order of the Golden Fleece, Knight of the Order of the Grand Cross of Charles the Third, First Minister of State and Dispatch; and on, for the States-General of the United Provinces, Don Jacobo Godfroi, the Count of Rechteren, their Ambassador near to His Catholic Majesty. These Plenipotentiaries, after having held various conferences touching the mutual interests of their respective sovereigns, have agreed upon the following articles.

Article One.—It is hereby ordered that there shall be a mutual return of fugitives (white and negroid) between all the Spanish possessions in America and the Dutch Colonies, particularly between those districts in which complaints of desertion have been most frequent, namely, between Puerto Rico and S. Eustaquio, Coro and Curazao, the Spanish Establishments on the Orinoco and Esequebo, Demerary, Berbices and Surinam.

Article Two.—The mutual return ordered in the article above shall be made in conformity with due process of law; and at the price stipulated in the articles following. Claims upon deserters and fugitives shall be made within the period of a year, counting from the date of desertion. After the expiration of one year claims cannot legally be made for the return of the fugitive. The slaves shall, after the expiration of one year from the time of desertion, belong to the ruler of the territory to which the slaves have escaped.

Article Three.—When fugitive slaves (negro men and women) have been identified, the governor, who is the proper person to whom claims for the return of the fugitives shall be made, shall take the most effective means for the arrest of the fugitives. After capture the slave shall be returned to the owner who shall pay a fee of a silver *real* per day for the maintenance of each slave from the date of capture; and, in addition, a fee of twenty-five *pesos* for each slave in order to pay for the cost of the slave in prison, and to reward those who were instrumental in the slave's capture.

Article Four.—Fugitive slaves (negro men and women) shall not henceforth be punished with capital punishment, mutilation, perpetual imprisonment, etc., for desertion unless guilty of crimes other than desertion which by their nature and degree deserve the penalty of death. In every case such crime shall be preferred and proved against the slave at the time that claims for his return are made.

Article Five.—Fugitive slaves (negro men and women) who have committed crimes in the districts to which they have escaped shall be tried by the judge in that district. The judge shall not permit the return of the slave until justice has been satisfied. The fugitive slave who has committed a theft or other robbery shall not be returned to the owner until the amount of the loss has been paid. Fugitive slaves can contract no debt during the period of their desertion or while in prison for which the owner shall be held responsible.

Article Six.—Religion shall not be considered as a cause or pretext for refusal to return fugitive slaves. Dutch fugitive slaves who may have become converts to Roman Catholicism while fugitives in Spanish territory shall not be compelled to renounce this faith upon their return to Dutch territory but shall have full freedom of worship which has been established by Their High Mightinesses in their dominions.

Article Seven.—Dutch or Spanish military deserters who shall have escaped to Holland or Spain, or into Dutch and Spanish colonies shall upon demand of the proper authorities be returned to their respective governments. It shall be expressly understood that when deserters are identified no fee shall be paid by those who claim them except such as shall be necessary to pay for their imprisonment and for their clothing, arms, and such other equipment as shall be deemed absolutely necessary.

Article Eight.—Notice shall be given to the chiefs, governors, and commanders of colonies adjoining those concerned in this convention, charging them with the definite execution of the provisions of this convention and with giving the provisions of this convention all possible publicity in their respective governments or districts.

Article Nine.—The present convention shall be ratified and confirmed within the period of two months from the date of the signing of the same.

In witness whereof the respective Plenipotentiaries have signed their names and affixed the seals of their arms.

THE COUNT OF FLORIDABLANCA   THE COUNT OF RECHTEREN
[Seal]   [Seal]

ÓRDEN DEL MINISTRO JOSÉ GÁLVEZ DEL 4 DE NOVIEMBRE DE 1784

Desvelado siempre el paternal amor del Rey nuestro Señor en proporcionar á sus amados Vasallos de América todos los medios que conduzcan á su mayor prosperidad, y riqueza, regula que uno de los mas útiles, y necesarios á este efecto, es el de facilitarles la introduccion de Negros Esclavos en aquellos dominios, como únicos brazos en la mayor parte de ellos para la agricultura, y trabajo de las Minas, que son los ramos de que depende el Comercio, y la felicidad de estos, y aquellos Reynos. Con este objeto se ha servido S. M. reducir en varias partes de Indias los derechos de entrada de los Negros, establecidos por Leyes, y Reales disposiciones, y concedido en otras, por motivos particulares, libertad absoluta de contribucion. Y siendo su Real ánimo, que todos sus Vasallos en general logren de la rebaxa de derechos, ha resuelto, que en donde no estuviere concedida la entera exêncion de ellos, se cobre solo un seis por ciento de introduccion de cada Negro, regulado su valor en ciento y cincuenta pesos, aunque tenga mayor precio, y sin diferencia de edad, sexô, ni clase, de modo que por cada cabeza se satisfagan únicamente por ahora nueve pesos en ambas Américas Españolas, llevándose á ellas en Naves'que lo sean, ó en virtud de permisos particulares que se hayan despachado, ó se dieren en adelante para que se puedan conducir en Embarcaciones extrangeras. Comunícolo á V. S. ya V. mas. de órden de S. M. para que disponga su cumplimiento en el distrito de su mando.

Dios guarde á VS. y Vmd. muchos años. San Lorenzo 4 de Noviembre de 1784.

JPH DE GALVEZ (rubric).

On the printed document is written:

S.ª Agustin de la Florida 16 de M.ᵐᵒ de 1785.

Tomese la razon de esta R.¹ Orden en la Contaduria Prãl de Real Hazda de esta Plaza, para su devido cumplim.ᵗᵒ siempre que ocurra lo que se previene en el asumpto.

Viz.ᵗᵉ Man.¹ de Zespedes (Rubric).

Tomese la razon en la Contad.ª prãl de Extõ de esta Plaza. S.ª Agustin de la Florida, 16 de Marzo de 1785.

Gonzalo Zamorano (rubric).

Addressed: "S.ʳᵐ Gov.ᵒʳ y Oficiales R.ˢ de S.ª Agustin de la Florida."

Docket:

S.ª Lorenzo 4 de Nov.ʳᵉ de 1784

R.¹ orñ Comunicada por el Ex.ᵐᵒ s.ᵒʳ D.ⁿ Jph de Galvez, al Gov.ʳ y ofiz.ˢ R.ˢ de S.ⁿ Ag.ⁿ de la Florida.

Para que en donde no estubiere conzedida la entera libertad de derechos p.ˢ la introducion de Negros esclavos, en ambas Americas, se cobre solo un Seis por Ciento, por Cada uno, regulado su valor en 150 p.ˢ aunq.ᵉ tenga mayor precio, sin distincion de edad ni sexo.

[TRANSLATION]

Ministerial Order of José de Gálvez of November 4, 1784

The paternal love of the King our Lord ever zealous in providing his beloved vassals of America with all those means which will contribute to their greatest prosperity and wealth, recognizes that one of the most useful and necessary means to this end, is that of facilitating the introduction of negro slaves into those dominions, as the only laborers (*brazos*) in the greater part of those dominions for agriculture and mining which are the bases upon which depend the commerce and happiness of these and those kingdoms. With this end in mind His Majesty has been pleased to reduce in different parts of the Indies the duties on the importation of negro slaves established by laws and royal orders; and has permitted in others, for particular reasons, absolute freedom from taxation. And since it is his royal will that all his vassals in general should enjoy the reduction in duties has ordered that where the duties have not been abolished there shall be collected a duty of only six per cent on the introduction of each negro slave, placing the value of each slave at one hundred and fifty *pesos*, although the slave be worth more, and without distinction as to age, sex, and class; so as to make the duty per head at the present time only nine *pesos* in both of the Spanish Americas on negro slaves transported thence in ships of the regular line, or in ships having special permits for such service, or in foreign ships which may have received special permission to transport negro slaves. I communicate this to your Excellencies and Lordships by order of His Majesty in order that you may arrange for the execution of it in the districts under your jurisdiction.

God protect your Excellencies and Lordships many years.

San Lorenzo the fourth of November, 1784.

JPH DE GALVEZ (rubric).

The printed document is indorsed as follows:

San Agustin de la Florida, March 16, 1785.

Let account of this Royal Order be taken in the chief accountancy of the Royal Treasury of this Fort, so that it may be duly observed whenever what is provided in this regard happens.

Vicente Manuel de Zespedes (rubric).

Let account be taken in the chief accountancy of the Army of this fort. San Agustin de la Florida, March 16, 1785.

Gonzalo Zamorano (rubric).

Addressed: The Governor and Royal Officials of San Agustin de la Florida.

Docket:

San Lorenzo, November 4, 1784.

Royal order communicated by his Excellency Don Joseph de Galves to the Governor and Royal Officials of San Agustin de la Florida.

Ordering that in all cases in which complete exemption of duties has not been granted for the introduction of negro slaves into both Americas, a duty of six per cent only be collected on each one, assessed at a value of 150 pesos, although his price may be in excess of that amount, without any distinction being made for age or sex.

BOOK REVIEWS

Bosquejo de la Literatura Chilena. By Domingo Amunátegui Solar. (Santiago de Chile: Imprenta Universitaria, 1920. Pp. 669, [1]. Paper.)

In this work, the edition of which was limited to one hundred copies —a reprint from the *Revista Chilena de Historia y Geografía*— Dr. Amunátegui Solar, the rector of the University of Chile, whose scholarly competency has been demonstrated in other works in this or related fields, notably in his *Encomiendas de Indíjenas en Chile* and *Sociedad Chilena del Siglo XVIII*, has made an important contribution to the history of the intellectual life and literary movements of Hispanic America. It is an important field to students of the southern republics in this country as ancillary to political history and as a means of social interpretation and its importance has been recognized in valuable studies by Coester, Goldberg, and others. In the general field of literary history several important critical works have been published by Hispanic American scholars of which may be noted: Roxlo, *Historia de la Literatura Uruguaya*, in eight volumes; Picón Febres, *Historia de la Literatura Venezolana;* Romero, *Historia da Literatura Brazileira;* and Rojas, *Historia de la Literatura Argentina.* The third volume of the last work, *Los Proscriptos*, is of special interest to the student of Chilean literature owing to the intimate relations that existed between the two countries in the period following the revolution.

Considering the literary history of Chile, the present work fills a lacuna, forming as it does a complete and critical review of the subject. There are, to be sure, other works treating directly or indirectly of the intellectual life and activities of the country, such as Lastarria's *Recuerdos Literarios*, Fuenzalida Grandón's *Lastarria y su Tiempo*, Huneeus Gana's *Producción Intelectual de Chile*, the works of Barros Arana, and others. In the present work, however, Dr. Amunátegui has had the benefit of the labors of his predecessors, and has produced a book that is a real addition to our knowledge of Chilean literary productions and history.

National character is clearly shown in Chilean literature. Menéndez y Pelayo has said—and his statement is quoted and confirmed by Dr. Amunátegui—that the Chileans are positive, practical, and prudent, little inclined toward ideals. Colonial conditions in large measure determined this character. Remote from Lima, the seat of the vice-regal court, and from the Atlantic seaboard, with its greater accessibility to European influences, colonized largely by settlers of Basque origin, conducting largely upon its own resources and throughout almost the whole colonial period a sanguinary war against the Araucanos, it was inevitable that such factors should exercise a strong formative influence upon intellectual life and national character. The Araucanian war itself was a most important feature of the colonial life, and was the theme of Ercilla y Zúñiga's Araucania, affording a basis for Bello's assertion that Chile is the only country in modern times whose establishment has been immortalized by an epic.

Chilean literature, then, is relatively weak in works of the imagination, poetry and fiction. It has, to refer again to the great Spanish critic, a certain habitual dryness. There are no "orgies of the imagination." It is solid but rarely graceful. On the other hand it is astonishingly rich in historical works. There is hardly a period, aspect, or personality that has not been thoroughly studied. The published results of such intellectual activities form a most impressive collection of critical and thoroughly documented historical studies.

In the present work—to note some of the general features—the author is neither discursive nor eulogistic. He is succinct, analytical, critical, conforming to the best methods of the Chilean historical school. Historical, political, ethnic, and social factors and influences are everywhere noted. The significance of periodicals as prime elements of literary activity is carefully set forth. The establishment of educational institutions, and the organization of literary societies are noted, their spirit, tendencies, and influence weighed, and the general relation of the state to education, a matter of major importance in the nascent republic, carefully stressed. Characteristic quotations are freely introduced, but never in such a degree as to obscure the historical and expositive method of the author. Free use is made of footnotes for biographical and bibliographical data. The lack of an index is measurably compensated by an analytical table of contents that greatly facilitates reference use.

The author has included in this study the period from the revolution to the present. He has also published a history of the literature of the colonial period which the present reviewer has not yet been able to examine.

The early period which we may consider as extending to the year 1842 is an interesting one. It is a period of stress, of national organization and orientation, of the adaptation of social and political life to largely different conditions. Important among the early events in the new republic were the initiation of national journalism with the foundation in 1812 of the Aurora de Chile under the editorship of Camilo Henríquez, and the establishment in 1813 of the Instituto Nacional, its abolishment by the royalist restoration, and its reorganization under the government of O'Higgins in 1819.

A feature of interest in this period of national parturiency is the influence exercised upon the intellectual and educational development by expatriates from other countries who, in acceptance of offers from the government or induced by the more orderly and stable conditions, became domiciled in Chile. Among these were Mora, former agent of Ferdinand VII., who was an important factor in the educational activities, and Andrés Bello, the great Venezuelan, who, arriving in Chile in 1829 after a sojourn of many years in England, exerted a profound and beneficial influence upon the intellectual growth of the younger generation. From Argentina also came many who had been driven out by the conditions under the Rosas regime—Sarmiento, Mitre, Fidel López, and others—who took an active and influential place in educational activities and journalism. The polemic which developed between the latter and the followers of Mora and Bello is an interesting and important episode of the period. Dr. Amunátegui has summarized this as follows:

With the design of forwarding the romantic movement which had for some years prevailed in Europe and with the frank object of discouraging Spanish literature, the Argentine writers opposed by Vallejo and San Fuentes . . . feel themselves justified in expressing their views on the causes of Chilean literary sterility, thus giving offense to former students of Mora and followers of Bello. Sarmiento, especially, sustained the opinion that the methods of the distinguished Venezuelan instead of stimulating his students, deterred them by the fear of incorrectness of language, and by an exaggerated regard for the models proposed by Bello as standards. . . .

Happily, in Chile the lessons of Bello and Mora triumphed. . . . Thus it has resulted that in our country Spanish is better spoken than in the other republics of America.

An interesting account of this discussion which became quite acrimonious will be found in Lastarria's *Recuerdos Literarios*, somewhat

more critical of Bello and written by one who was an important partici-
pator in the events of that period.   Rojas also, in the chapter on "La
Escuela Cuyana", in the third volume of his *Historia de la Literatura
Argentina* has discussed it from the Argentine point of view.

The establishment of the University of Chile in 1843, under the wise
direction of Bello was a notable event in the cultural history of the
country especially in its influence upon the development of scientific
and historical studies.   The act creating the university provided that
there should be prepared every year by some member of the faculty
to be designated by the rector a monograph on some important question of national history.   From this provision have sprung a notable
series of historical monographs which Dr. Amunátegui has noted with
critical appreciations.

During the period from 1842 to the present, Chilean literature has
shown the general character expressed previously in this review.   The
author has given a luminous outline of the historical work of Barros
Arana, Vicuña Mackenna, Miguel Luis Amunátegui, and others who
have distinguished themselves in this field.   He has devoted special
chapters to poetry, the drama, and fiction, analyzing the work of Guillermo Matta, the greatest Chilean poet and of Alberto Blest Gana
whom he considers the real founder of the Chilean novel.

Of the latter, Dr. Amunátegui says:

Without doubt, Alberto Blest Gana is an exceptional case in Chilean letters of
the past century.   In all the forms of literary activity cultivated in our country,
the initiators or founders were soon equaled by others who succeeded them.
This is seen in history, lyric poetry, and journalism.   Nothing like this took
place in the case of the novel.   Blest Gaña from the first notably surpassed all
of his compatriots who devoted their pens to the novel. . . .   We must come
to the present century to find authors of novels or stories who, if they do not contest the palm with Blest Gana, can at least be placed in the same class with
him without exaggeration.

A special chapter is given to the literary school of the ecclesiastical
colleges, to the activities of the Jesuits, and to a review of their organ,
La Estrella de Chile.

The final chapter of this valuable work contains "general observations on Chilean letters in the 19th century, new tendencies, evolution
of journalism and parliamentary oratory, influence of Pedro Antonio
González and Rubén Darío on lyric poetry, and the future of the novel
and drama".   The concluding paragraph is as follows:

It can be affirmed that social questions will dominate in the period that is beginning. For the successful solution of these it will be necessary that history continue presenting its fruitful lessons in order that present problems be thoroughly studied. With the same object, statesmen should lend attentive ear to the voice of the novelists, dramatists and poets.

C. K. JONES.

List of Works for the Study of Hispanic-American History. By HAYWARD KENISTON. (New York: The Hispanic Society of America, 1920. Pp. XVIII, (2), 451.) [Hispanic notes and monographs . . . issued by the Hispanic Society of America, V.]

An important element in the judgment of a book should be a consideration of the author's objective.

In the present case the author's purpose has been clearly and succinctly expressed in the preface and the reviewer feels that he cannot do better than quote the author's words:

> No one has undertaken work in the field of Hispanic-American history without feeling the handicap which the lack of a . . . [bibliographical] guide imposes upon him. . . . It is to meet this need, to provide, if not a complete bibliography, at least a list which may serve as a basis for an eventual definitive work, that the present work has been compiled.
>
> It has been my purpose to include the essential works, both primary sources and secondary studies. . . . Biography has naturally been given a place of equal importance with the narration of events, and the story of the missions has everywhere been included. . . . For the fields ancillary to history (antiquities, anthropology and ethnology; cartography and geography; constitutional law, government, and political economy; linguistics and literature), I have included only bibliographical and general works. And I have made a similar limitation in the list of works on the non-Hispanic Colonies of Guiana and the Antilles. In every case I have tried to record any bibliographical work on a period or subject. . . .
>
> Certain types of work have been omitted altogether: (1) Government publications of the individual Hispanic-American Republics since the declaration of independence . . . (2) calendars of state papers or catalogues of archives of European governments other than Spain or Portugal; (3) state documents of the United States. . . .

The compiler has grouped the works under Hispanic America in general and individual countries or states. Under each main heading are: (1) Works concerning the whole history and (2) Works on special periods: 1. Aborigines (to 1492), 2. Discovery and conquest (1492–1550), 3. Colonies (1550–1810), 4. Revolution (1810–1830). Sections under the first or general division are: A. Bibliography, B. Periodical publications (including publication of learned societies and civic institutions), C. Collections either of documents or of standard works, D. Individual works. Under special periods are grouped: A. Bibliography, B. Collections, C. Sources, D. Secondary works.

Under the modern name are placed works treating specifically of that district, e. g., works on Alto-Perú and Potosí under Bolivia. Works on the principal "liberators", Bolívar, Miranda, San Martín, and Sucre are placed under Hispanic America in general, Revolution.

Since my purpose was not to describe but to identify the works, I have given brief titles only and have not included the name of the publisher or printer . . ."
The number of volumes, when more than one, is given, but collections of single volumes and all bibliographical and critical annotations are omitted. This omission the compiler recognises as a defect, unavoidable because "the task . . . must obviously be the work of a considerable group of specialists in the field." To compensate for this lack and to give the work a certain usefulness to the casual student or to the librarian . . . I have ventured to star the works which are generally recognised as authoritative or fundamental.

In the preceding words the compiler has clearly indicated the object and plan of this bibliography. It is fitting, perhaps, that the reviewer should venture an opinion as to how fully this object has been realized, and as to the general and special value of the work.

The arrangement is good; the separate grouping of bibliography, periodical publications, collections, and sources is especially useful. The absence of collations and all bibliographical and critical notes is for obvious reasons regrettable, particularly in relation to the rare and expensive works and collections.

The present reviewer cannot express an authoritative opinion as to the adequacy of the selection. From an examination of those sections with which he feels familiar it seems that the compiler has shown scholarly discrimination and comprehensive knowledge in including the valuable material, and that he has prepared a list that represents the historical literature relating to Hispanic America of much greater value to students than any preceding compilation.

Dr. Keniston's work will be of great value, not only to students, but to reference librarians and to librarians who are building up collections of Hispanic Americana. Even those in charge of extensive collections in this field should find it worth while to check up this list. It would, moreover, form an excellent basis for the preparation of a critical manual of this literature.

In conclusion, some titles may be noted the reason for the exclusion of which is not patent to the reviewer: *A catalogue of books relating to the discovery and early history of North and South America forming part of the library of E. D. Church*, compiled by George Watson Cole, with its magnificent equipment of bibliographical data; Picón Febres, *Literatura Venezolana;* Rojas, *Literatura Argentina;* Laverde Amaya, *Bibliografía Colombiana;* Rocha Pombo, *Historia do Brazil,* 10 v.; Cejador, *Lengua y Literatura Castellana,* including Spanish American authors; Laval, *Bibliografías Chilenas;* Binayán, *Bibliografías Argentinas;* Amunátegui Solar, *Literatura Chilena; Mercurio Peruano; Inventario dos Documentos Relativos ao Brasil, existentes no Archivo de Marinha e Ultramar, organisado . . . por Eduardo de Castro e Almeida.* The *Annaes da Bibliotheca Nacional,* in which the last work is contained, are mentioned.

C. K. JONES.

La Personalidad de Manuel Belgrano. Commemorative Historical Essay by EMILIO RAVIGNANI. (Buenos Aires: 1920. Pp. 32. Paper.)

As part of the ceremonies held in Buenos Aires in June, 1920, in commemoration of the centenary of Belgrano's death, Dr. Ravignani read an address which has just been published by the History Section of the Faculty of Philosophy and Letters of the National University of Buenos Aires, in the form of a pamphlet, which is No. 6 in that faculty's series of monographs. There is included in this pamphlet an appendix presenting six letters written by Belgrano, 1810–1819, the originals of which are preserved in the Academy of Philosophy and Letters of the University. These letters are reproduced in the very satisfactory form now followed by the History Section of the Faculty, of which Section Dr. Ravignani has recently become director—a form which, in itself, imparts confidence in that it gives evidence of careful and intelligent editorial work.

Dr. Ravignani briefly reviews Belgrano's life, from his birth in Buenos Aires in 1770, to his death, in that same city, on June 20, 1820; and, dividing its activities into two large aspects—civil and military—in few pages indeed presents a striking "profile" of the man: "Bachelor in law of the University, and advocate in chancery of Valladolid, general commanding his country's armies—Don Manuel Belgrano y González".

Son of an Italian who chose to render his name Pérez, by a creole mother, although he was educated in Spain, Belgrano was "one of the best of Argentinians". Offspring of the merchant class, he was an intellectual—an optimistic, altruistic advocate of popular culture, and a constructive force which advanced his country toward his ideals. From a responsible government position, to which the king of Spain appointed him, youth of twenty-three that he was, in 1793, he sought to disseminate new ideas on economics in a bureaucratic atmosphere which smothered him. To improve the social conditions amid which he found himself, he established the third newspaper issued in Argentina. To the same end he advocated schools, and founded them. To alter political conditions, he labored for Argentine independence. Drawn into military life by his country's fight for freedom, he ran up for the first time the flag which still symbolizes Argentine nationality, and out of an undisciplined rebel horde, the conduct of which had antagonized the inhabitants of regions where it fought, he created an army with ideals of honor, lived up to by its officers and its men. In a revolutionary period Belgrano was serene, modest, and generously free from envy.

Considered from a certain point of view, he was a precursor. . . . Without the creative energy of those who are all originality and minus the stubborn persistence of those who succeed in perfecting their undertakings, he nevertheless cleared the path along which others were to pass to success.

Dr. Ravignani remarks that a centenary celebration is an occasion for eulogy rather than for the emission of a historian's cold judgment. "Every biographical study," he adds, "makes its principal object the determination of the man's influence upon his epoch, and of the extent to which it absorbed him. . . ." If a great influence and a thorough absorption are the hall-mark of a "hero" truly worthy "an essay *a lo Macaulay*", to quote Dr. Ravignani, then it would seem that Argentina is justified in hanging Belgrano's picture (as is done) in the schools, for this essay displays him as an efficacious advocate of popular education, in both the English and the Spanish sense of that word.

I. A. WRIGHT.

Justo Arosemena (Obra Premiada en el Concurso del Centenario). By OCTAVIO MÉNDEZ PEREIRA. (Panamá: *Imprenta Nacional,* 1919. Pp. 568. Paper.)

Don Justo Arosemena (1817–1896) was a native of Panama and throughout his long and useful life, strongly attached to the interests of his section. At the same time as a citizen of Colombia, he played an active part for nearly fifty years, in the various changes that marked the political development of that country. He was elected to membership in the Cabildo of Panama in 1839 and retired from his post as government representative in connection with the work of the Interoceanic Canal Company, in 1885. In the interim he had held almost every post of importance in Panama, including the governorship, had served as representative and senator from the province, department or state (according to Panama's varying status in the republic), and had taken a prominent part (although not an actively hostile one) in asserting the interests of that section against possible injustice at the hands of the Bogotá authorities. In the capital itself he not only represented Panama but during his younger years served the central government as a subordinate in the ministries of finance and foreign relations, and later in life held important diplomatic posts in Europe, United States, Peru, Chile, and Venezuela. During this same period he maintained active business connections with many of the chief enterprises of the Isthmus. Through these connections he kept in touch with New York, London, and other financial centers. His personal activities as well as political efforts were extensive, reasonably successful, and highly honorable in character.

As a journalist, Don Justo stood high in Peru and Chile, as well as in his native Panama. He was an orator of distinction, a prolific writer, an effective pamphleteer, an author of enduring reputation. His *Estudios Constitucionales* passed through several editions, each one enriched by the results of his own political experience. During his residence abroad it was his good fortune to take an active part in the Congress at Lima, in 1864, and to work in favor of the Wyse-Lessups Canal Contract in the United States. He thus participated in two measures of importance for Colombia, but without achieving the permanent results his efforts merited. He took part in framing the liberal Constitution formed at Río Negro in 1863, and while he recognized later that this document must be seriously modified, regretted that the conservative reaction of 1886 thrust it wholly aside. This overturn practically ended his political career, but not his business and literary labors.

A mere enumeration of Arosemena's activities is impressive. A catalogue of his publications, ephemeral though many of them are, shows his manifold intellectual power. Criminal and political problems, measures of social reform, philosophical and religious topics, juridical measures, general literature—all alike inspire his ready pen.

It is as political writer that he will best be remembered and few have done so much to reveal the spirit of moderate liberalism that ruled in Colombia during the mid years of the last century.

Dr. Méndez Pereira has performed his task well. The thirty-six chapters show the productive work as well as the political activity of his hero. His biography is extremely favorable but not too partisan. He quotes extensively from Arosemena's writings, so that the reader may gain an idea of their character and recognize the importance of the present work for an understanding of the various issues that formerly divided Colombians. He thinks that Arosemena would have favored the cause of Panama, had he survived to 1903, but we may well believe he would have exerted his influence against precipitate separation. The work, as the sub-title indicates, gained the prize in the competition authorized by the Panamanian government in commemoration of the centenary of Arosemena's birth.

                                                        ISAAC JOSLIN COX.

Cuba y los Cubanos. By E. K. MAPES, Professor of Modern Languages, Westminster College, Fulton, Missouri, and M. F. DE VELASCO, Professor of Languages, Havana, Cuba. (New York, Chicago, Boston, etc.: The Gregg Publishing Company. [c 1920] Pp. viii, 213. $1.00.)

This little textbook, which is designed for the use of students studying the Spanish language, was compiled in the belief "that the ideal foreign language reader is produced by the collaboration of a native of the country treated in the text, who furnishes first-hand information as to facts and authentic knowledge of the language as actually spoken there, and an American teacher of the language, who is familiar with the pedagogical features necessary to adapt the material to the needs of the American classroom". The result has been a very interesting book and one that can be used to advantage because of its practical bearing.

In fact, this is more than a language reader. It could be read to advantage by persons about to visit Cuba for the first time, for it gives in small compass considerable useful information. The book is divided into twenty-eight chapters. The first five of these are formed into a section entitled "La llegada" (The arrival) and give a few salient and interesting facts regarding the approach to the island and life thereon. This section is followed by sections on "La Isla" (The island), of four chapters; "Las provincias del oeste" (The western provinces), of four chapters, in one of which the city of Habana is described; "Productos e industrias" (Products and industries), of seven chapters; "Las provincias centrales y del este" (The central provinces and those of the east), of six chapters; one chapter on history; and one consisting of brief comments on Cuban literature. These are followed by a section of questions and exercises, various explanatory notes, and a full vocabulary.

The work admirably conserves its purpose. The text is simple, although proceeding continually to more complex expressions and descriptions, while the notes give many interesting data regarding Cuba. This is not intended primarily as a history but many historical data, all necessarily of a secondary character, are presented.

J. A. R.

NOTES AND COMMENT

GOVERNMENT COMMERCIAL ACTIVITIES IN HISPANIC AMERICA

In 1913 the total foreign commerce of Hispanic America amounted to $2,874,612,151, of which $1,321,861,199 was imports and $1,552,750,952 was exports. By 1919 the total foreign commerce of Hispanic America had increased to $5,064,588,740, of which $1,934,747,794 represented imports and $3,129,840,946 exports, that is an increase of 46 per cent in imports and 102 per cent in exports and an increase in the total trade of 74 per cent. Hispanic America's total imports from the United States for the three years 1915–18 increased 99 per cent over the total imports for the three years 1910–13, while its imports from the United Kingdom increased but 49 per cent and from France 30 per cent during the same period. The value of our trade with the five leading Hispanic American countries show the following increases from 1913 to 1920 (each in per cent): Cuba, 523; Brazil, 172; Mexico, 198; Argentina, 421; Chile, 274.

Although the increase in our trade with Hispanic America is partially due to the higher values of commodities, this expansion has been gradual. The important position which the United States has come to occupy in Hispanic American trade is attributable to some extent to the World War. The United Kingdom during that period had diverted its attention largely from the promotion of its foreign trade to the business of winning the war, while Germany had been compelled to withdraw from the Hispanic American field. The question is, can we maintain our new position, which was virtually forced upon us?

Since the United States has engaged in large financial undertakings in Europe, it has neglected to strengthen its position in Hispanic American investments. It is estimated that Great Britain has above five and a half billion dollars invested in Hispanic American countries, which will enable that country to secure a large amount of business that might otherwise go elsewhere. This is a serious handicap under which the United States must labor and one which will become more powerful as conditions return to normal. Our competitors will exert every effort to regain their former hold upon this lucrative trade and the United States will only be able to maintain its position in this field through the exercise of superior ability.

Since 1914, the United States government has assiduously applied itself to the problem of promoting its Hispanic American commerce. Through the commercial attaché and trade commissioner services of the Department of Commerce it has investigated markets for American products and reported upon economic developments. The first commercial attachés were sent abroad in 1914, an appropriation of $100,000 having been granted by Congress for the establishment of such a service.

The commercial attaché is appointed and assigned to his post by the Secretary of Commerce after proper examination, and he is given his official designation as an officer of the embassy or legation by the Secretary of State. Although his work is directed by the Bureau of Foreign and Domestic Commerce of the Department of Commerce he is required to follow a policy while abroad in accord with that of the chief of the diplomatic mission.

The duties of the commercial attaché are threefold. As this position had been created to fill the long-felt need for a permanent government official abroad who was wholly concerned with trade problems, it is his first duty to report upon business conditions and markets for American goods. Usually the commercial attaché has lived or traveled extensively in the country to which he is assigned, and he is always thoroughly familiar with the language, both written and spoken. He reports regularly to the Bureau of Foreign and Domestic Commerce upon tariff changes, banking regulations, commercial statistics, etc. Investment opportunities and specifications for new construction projects are submitted by him. Important and pressing matters are cabled to the Bureau and recently a monthly cabled report upon economic conditions has been required of all foreign representatives. In his capacity as commercial attaché he is the commercial adviser and assistant to the chief of the diplomatic mission. An official of the Department of Overseas Trade, which is the department of the British Government which supervises the British commercial attaché service, estimated that 95 per cent of the work of the British embassies and legations in Hispanic-America was handled by the British commercial attachés. Although the proportion is not nearly so large in the American service, the duties placed upon the commercial attachés by the embassies are not light. A large number of American business firms call upon the commercial attaché, both personally and through correspondence, for assistance of various kinds. As the representative of the Department of Commerce the commercial attaché is required to assist in every legitimate manner the business firms which call upon him. Frequently the representative of an American firm is put directly in touch with government or private purchasers by the commercial attaché. American business men have learned that when abroad they can call upon the commercial attaché and secure the latest information concerning business conditions in the country, tariff changes, and trade opportunities. Several Hispanic American countries have not reached the high plane of efficiency in the preparation of trade statistics which the United States occupies and it is consequently a great advantage to American business men traveling abroad to have the latest trade statistics available in the office of the commercial attaché. The office of the commercial attaché has gradually developed into a clearing house for economic information bearing upon the country in which it is located.

In 1914, commercial attachés were assigned to the embassies in Río de Janeiro, Buenos Aires, Santiago (Chile), and Lima, and in 1919 a commercial attaché was assigned to Mexico City. Insufficient funds have prevented the assignment of a commercial attaché to Cuba.

These offices quickly justified their establishment and within a short time the volume of work had increased to such an extent that it became necessary to assign assistants to the various commercial attachés. These assistants were called trade commissioners, but they should not be confused with the trade commissioners of the Department on special assignment, which will be described below. At the present time (March 1921) there is a trade commissioner assisting the commercial attaché at Buenos Aires and two assistant trade commissioners in the office of the commercial attaché at Río de Janeiro. The trade commissioners and assistant trade commissioners are unfortunately without diplomatic privileges and have no formal relation with the embassy. This feature becomes a matter of importance and embarrassment when the trade commissioner or assistant trade commissioner is required to assume charge of the office in the absence of the commercial attaché.

It is the practice of the Bureau to have the members of its foreign service return to the United States every few years. These visits have a double purpose. It is essential that the commercial attachés and trade commissioners renew their contact with American business conditions regularly in order to appreciate the needs of the domestic manufacturers and exporters. Continuous residence abroad tends to alienate one and is especially detrimental to a commercial representative who is endeavoring to interpret conditions abroad to his home office. The second reason for these periodic visits is to stimulate among American business men an interest in conditions abroad and in foreign trade generally. These officials visit many sections of the United States studying conditions and conferring with business men and trade associations. In their addresses and conferences with American business men they are able to present the latest and most reliable information relating to business conditions in the country to which they are assigned and to give sound and practical advice regarding the development of foreign commerce.

For seven years prior to the inauguration of the commercial attaché service the Bureau of Foreign and Domestic Commerce had sent special representatives abroad to investigate foreign markets for American products and to prepare surveys of economic conditions in various countries. Among the markets investigated in Hispanic America are included the following: Boots and shoes; construction materials and machinery; electrical goods; furniture; investment opportunities; jewelry and silverware; textiles. Economic surveys have been made of Bolivia, Colombia, Danish West Indies, Mexico, Paraguay, Venezuela.

These investigations were made by trade commissioners on special assignment who traveled extensively and had no direct relation to the embassies or legations of the United States. Such trade commissioners are chosen because of their particular fitness to conduct a special investigation, frequently being recognized experts in their field. Their investigations ordinarily consume from six to eighteen months, and when their reports are completed they are published by the Bureau and are available to anyone at a nominal price. At the present time the Bureau has a trade commissioner investigating markets for industrial supplies in South America.

In addition to its large Latin American Division the Bureau of Foreign and Domestic Commerce has various specialized divisions in Washington which are continuously studying Hispanic American trade statistics, investment opportunities, tariffs, export trade methods, etc. These studies are given to the American business community through Commerce Reports, the bulletin of the Bureau which is issued every week day, exclusive of holidays. Special circular letters are also issued from time to time and a very large number of inquiries are answered by mail every day.

Although the trade promotional activities of the Bureau can never be more than a supplement to the activities of private firms and American business men, this service is capable of tremendous expansion. The United States increased its productive capacity immensely during the War and it is imperative that we maintain a large proportion of the world's foreign commerce if our factories are to be kept in operation and our labor employed. During the next few years when the United States will be handicapped by the foreign exchange factor in its trade with Hispanic America and when our competitors will be doing their utmost to regain their lost position the foreign service of the Bureau will be put to the test. But the value of this service will always be dependent upon the extent to which the American business community utilizes it.

WALTER LOWRY MILLER.

REGULATIONS OF THE UNIVERSITY OF RIO DE JANEIRO

The *Jornal de Commercio,* of Rio de Janeiro, in its issue of December 28, 1920, published the following regulations governing the University of Rio de Janeiro:

The Minister of Justice has approved by decree the following:

CHAPTER I

The University

Article 1. The University of Rio de Janeiro instituted by virtue of decree N° 11,530 of March 18, 1916, and N° 14,343 of Sept. 7, 1920, for the purpose of stimulating the study of science, strengthening the ties of intellectual solidarity among the professors and improving the methods of teaching, shall be located in the city of Rio de Janeiro and shall comprise the Polytechnic School of Rio de Janeiro, the Faculty of Medicine of Rio de Janeiro and the Faculty of Law of Rio de Janeiro.

Article 2. The University of Rio de Janeiro shall be conducted and managed by a Director and by a Council of the University.

Article 3. The estates of the different institutions constituting the University shall continue to be independent and shall be administered as heretofore.

Article 4. All expenses arising out of the erection of the University, independently of expenses proper to each section of it, shall be met by the sums set apart for this purpose in the general budget of the Republic, until the time when the University shall possess such income as shall make it independent of any official subsidy.

Only paragraph. The Faculty of Law shall continue to meet all its own expenses from the income of its estates, without other official aid or advantages to its professors beyond those already provided for in the respective statutes.

Article 5. The University shall have its office under the direction of a Secretary and Staff to be appointed by the Council after approval by the Minister of Justice.

Sec. 1. The secretary who shall have graduated from one of the Government high schools, shall be appointed by ministerial act.

Sec. 2. The other members of the Secretary's office shall be chosen by the Director of the University.

Sec. 3. The Council shall control the service of the office of the University.

CHAPTER II

The Director of the University

Article 6. The Director shall be the President of the Superior Council of Teaching.

Article 7. The duties of the Director shall be:

1) To superintend the functions of the institutes of Superior Teaching which constitute the University.

2) To preside at the meetings of the Council, calling the meetings with notice of 48 hours (at least) and designating the matter to be discussed except in cases of secret deliberations.

3) To see that the regulations, laws and decisions of the Government and Council of the University are properly carried out by the directors of the Faculties.

4) To exchange correspondence in the name of the University with public authorities and with national and foreign scientific institutions.

5) To obtain from the component institutions of the University all information which shall be deemed necessary.

6) To promote by all means within reach the good relations with other colleges, universities, etc., and to establish an interchange of publications and works of the authorship of their respective professors.

7) To supervise the cash books of the University and to order the payment of all expenses authorised by the Director of Council.

8) To appoint and dismiss all employees of the Secretary's office whose appointments shall not come under the Government control.

9) To exercise disciplinary jurisdiction over the Council and Director's office.

10) To bring to the Council's notice all communications received from superior institutions of learning—components of the University—relative to all extraordinary occurrences whatsoever encountered in the service and work of the same and to promote the adoption of all measures for the perfect course of teaching and administration.

11) To sign, together with the respective directors of the Faculties, all diplomas or titles conferred by the University, the same to bear the great seal of the said University, which shall be used by the Director only.

12) To publish the publications of the University—authorised by the Council —which shall be printed by the Government's printing office.

13) To present to the Minister of Justice and Interior, up to the 28th of February of each year, a full report of the work of economic situation of the Uni-

versity, and then to propose all necessary measures and improvements which the Council shall have approved.

Article 8. Until such time as there shall be appointed a president of Higher Teaching—in accordance with Art. 31, of law 3,454 of January 6, 1918—the Director of the University shall be replaced by a Sub-Director to be appointed by the Government from the University Council.

CHAPTER III

The Council of the University

Article 9. The Council shall consist of the Director, the directors of the Faculties which compose the University and two active professors from each Faculty who shall be elected bi-annually by the respective congregations.

Only Paragraph. The professors, who shall represent at the Council the congregation of the respective Faculties may be reëlected after an interval of not less than two years.

Article 10. Should a professor who shall have been elected, not be present at two consecutive meetings of the Council, the Director of the University shall communicate this fact to the respective Faculty in order that a substitute be named.

Article 11. The Council shall meet from March 15, to December 31, of each year—once every month—and the sessions shall last as many days as necessary; extraordinary meetings shall be called in urgent cases or when five of the Council's members shall demand it—declaring the motive of such meeting.

1. The quorum necessary at the Council's meetings shall be the absolute majority of the Council's members.

2. No subject outside of that which provoked the call for an extraordinary meeting shall be discussed by the Council at such extraordinary meetings.

Article 12. The duties of the University Council shall be:

1. To exercise together with the Director, the high jurisdiction over the University.

2. To draw up its internal regulations.

3. To approve or modify the regulations of the institutions that constitute the University, harmonizing them as far as possible.

4. To create and grant, whenever possible, cash prizes as well as scholarships in order to stimulate the cultivation of science in Brazil.

5. To confer on Brazilians and eminent professors the degree of 'Doctor' or 'honoris causa' (honorary degrees) of the University of Rio de Janeiro—such degrees to be proposed by three members of the Council and accepted by a majority of votes at a secret ballot.

6. To attend to and settle all claims from functionaries and students of the University—as well as to report on those addressed to the Government coming from professors and candidates to office.

7. To organize, at the proposal of the Director, the annual budget, of the University, which shall be submitted to the Government for approval.

8. To examine all annual accounts presented by the Director, reporting thereon.

9. To accept and to take charge of donations, endowments, etc., to the University, and to authorize the purchase of estate.

10. To submit to the Government any necessary reforms to the present set of regulations.

Article 13. At the sessions of the University Council, the Secretary of the University shall act as secretary to the meeting.

Article 14. The Secretary of the Council shall:

1) prepare and draw up all documents, papers, etc., which are to be submitted to the Council;

2) draw up the minutes of the meetings;

3) edit all correspondence relative to the meetings;

4) supply all information, upon request, which shall be required in discussing Univesity matters at the meetings of the Council.

Article 15. In the absence of the Secretary of the University, he shall be substituted by the first officer of the Secretary's bureau.

CHAPTER IV

The Congregations of Directors of the Institutes or Faculties

Article 16. The powers of the Congregations and Directors of the Institutes which compose the University of Rio de Janeiro are described in decree N° 11,530 of March 18, 1915, and in the internal regulations of the University.

General and Temporary Provisions

Article 17. All provisions established by the present regulations shall be subservient to the articles of decree N° 11,520 of March 18, 1915, adapted to the University "régime," in accordance with paragraph 2 of Art. 6 of said decree.

Article 18. The University of Rio de Janeiro shall enjoy didactic and administrative autonomy in accordance with the present regulations and shall be represented at the Superior Council of Teaching.

Article 19. The Director's office, Council's office, University and office of the University shall be located in the building of the Superior Council of Teaching until special buildings shall have been erected or chosen for them.

Article 20. The congregations of the component Institutions of the University shall put into effect the provisions of Art. 9, of the present regulations within 30 days of their publication.

Article 21. The present regulations shall come into force on January 1st, 1921—all former provisions to be hereby revoked.

On the 17th of December, there was celebrated a session of the Central Committee of the Spanish American League, which adopted the following resolutions:

First. To call the attention of His Majesty to the harm done by the imposing of the income tax on Spanish steamship companies trading with England, in the form in which the Government of the United Kingdom intends to execute it.

Second. To petition the Government to prorogue the law now in force, of June 14, 1909, with respect to naval construction under the temporary conditions authorized by the law of budgets and now that world conditions are normal, that the Government consider the principles laid down by the Maritime League as the basis of a new law, as a complement to the Tariff dealing with navigation and commerce and to the general laws protecting industry.

Third. To petition the Minister of Fomento to make good the premiums for naval construction due from 1917 up to the present budget, for which premiums the Minister of Hacienda, on last October, put the necessary credits at the disposal of the Ministerio de Fomento.

This Association made various other recommendations for the protection of maritime interests.

———————

Dr. Sturgis E. Leavitt, professor of Romance languages in the University of North Carolina, is putting the finishing touches on a study of Chilean literature which will take the form of a bibliography of literary criticism, biography, and literary controversy. Magazine articles as well as books will be included in the references. In the case of books, in addition to the usual bibliographical data, notes will be included indicating the content or the scope of the work. There will also figure in this bibliography four of the leading newspaper critics—Rómulo Mandiola, Pedro Nolasco Cruz, Ricardo Dávila Silva and Emilio Vaisse (Omer Emeth), with a list of their contributions to the newspapers of Chile. This will be the fourth of a series of studies resulting from researches made in South American libraries by Dr. Leavitt who was the holder of a Sheldon Traveling Fellowship from Harvard University during the year 1919-1920. A bibliography of Ricardo Palma appeared in the Mercurio Peruano (Lima), October–November, 1919; a biography of the same author was published in THE HISPANIC AMERICAN HISTORICAL REVIEW in February, 1920; and bibliographies of Peruvian and Bolivian literature will shortly be brought out in the *Romanic Review*. The bibliography of Chilean literature will be followed by a similar study of Argentine literature.

BIBLIOGRAPHICAL SECTION

HISPANIC AMERICAN BIBLIOGRAPHIES

(Continuation)

MEXICO. NUEVA ESPAÑA

753. Abadiano, Eufemio. Catalogue of a portion of the remarkable library of Senor Eufemio Abadiano ... consisting more particularly of Mexicana, and works relating to Central and South America ... Mexican history, biography and discovery ... Mexican hieroglyphics and dialects ... also:—general literature and other Americana. [New York, D. Taylor, printer, 1888]

42 p. 25 cm.

754. Acosta, Francis J. The Acosta directory of the English speaking residents of the republic of Mexico for 1910 ... including a directory of the ... mining companies, plantations, government departments and officials, diplomatic corps. Mexico City, F. J. Acosta [1910].

iv, 330 p. 23 cm.

755. Agüeros, Victoriano. Escritores mexicanos contemporáneos. Mexico, I. Escalante, 1880.

756. Aguilar y Santillán, Rafael. Bibliografía geológica y minera de la República Mexicana, completada hasta el año de 1904. México, Impr. de la Secretaría de fomento, 1908.

xiii, 330 p., 1 l. 33 cm. (Instituto geológico de México. Boletín núm. 17)
First edition, listing publications up to the end of 1896, appeared 1898 as "Boletín del Instituto geológico de México, num. 10."

757. ——— Bibliography of Mexican geology and mining. (In Transactions of the American institute of mining engineers. New York, 1903. 24 cm. v. 32, p. 605-680.)

758. ——— Bibliografía meteorológica mexicana que comprende las publicaciones de meteorología, física del globo y climatología hechas hasta fines de 1889. México, Edición de la Sociedad "Antonio Alsate," 1890.

44 p., 2 l. 24½ cm.

759. ———— Indice general del Boletín de la Sociedad mexicana de geografía y estadística. Comprende desde el tomo 1 de la primera época hasta el tomo VII de la quinta época, 32 tomos, 1839–1918. México, Departamento de aprovisionamientos generales, 1919.

96 p. 22 cm.

760. Alegre Francisco Javier. Historia de la Compañía de Jesús en Nueva España que estaba escribiendo el P. Francisco Javier Alegre al tiempo de su espulsión Publicala ... Carlos María Bustamante. Mexico, Impresa por J. M. Lara, 1841–42.

3 v. 21 cm.
For continuation see Dávila y Arillaga.

761. Altamirano, Ignacio Manuel. Revistas literarias de Mexico. Mexico, T. F. Neve, impresor, 1868.

203 p. 18 cm.

762. ———— ———— Edicion de "La Iberia." México, F. Dias de León y S. White, impresores, 1868.

202 p., 1 l. 20½ cm.

763. Anderson, Alexander Dwight. Mexico from the material stand-point. A review of its mineral, agricultural, forest, and marine wealth, its manufactures, commerce, railways, isthmian routes, and finances. Washington, D. C., A. Brentano & co.; New York, Brentano bros., 1884.

1 p. l., [5]-156 p. pl., 3 maps (2 fold.) 24 cm.
"American and English authorities": p. 143-156.

764. ———— The silver country or the great southwest, a review of the mineral and other wealth, the attractions and material development of the former kingdom of New Spain. New York, G. P. Putnam's sons, 1877.

221 p. 21 cm.
The authorities: p. 130-187.

765. Andrade, José María. Catalogue de la riche bibliothèque de D. José María Andrade. Livres manuscrits et imprimés. Littérature française et espagnole. Histoire de l'Afrique, de l'Asia et de l'Amerique. 7000 pièces et volumes ayant rapport au Mexique ou imprimés dans ce pays. Leipzig, List & Francke; Paris, Librairie Tross, 1869.

ix p., 1 l., 368 p. 23 cm.
Preface by P. Deschamps.

766. ———— Prix d'adjudication des articles de la bibliothèque de D. J. M. Andrade; vente faite à Leipzig le 18 janvier 1869 et jours suivants ... Leipzig, List & Francke; Paris, Librairie Tross, 1869.

11 p. 23 cm.

767. Andrade, Vicente de Paula. Los capitulares de la insigne Nacional colegiata parroquial Santa María de Guadalupe. Datos biográficos. México. 1893.

230, [36] p.
50 copies printed.
Blake's bulletin, Feb., 1918, no. 1046.

768. —— Datos biográficos de los señores capitulares de la Santa iglesia catedral de Mexico. Mexico, 1908.

vi, [5]-279, [4] p. 16½ cm.

769. —— Ensayo bibliográfico mexicano del siglo XVII. 2. ed. México, Impr. del Museo nacional, 1899 [1900].

vii, 803, [1] p. port., facsim. 23 cm.
Reprinted, in part, from the Boletín de la Sociedad Alzate, 1894.
Forms, with García Icazbalceta's Bibliografía mexicana del siglo XVI (1886) and Nicolás León's Bibliografía mexicana del siglo XVIII (1902-) a continuous bibliography of Mexican literature, 1539-1800.
1228 titles, transcribed line for line. Arranged chronologically and followed by alphabetical indexes of authors and anonymous works.

770. —— Noticia de los periódicos que se publican dentro y fuera la Capital. Mexico, 1901.

771. —— Noticias biográficas de los Ilmos. Sres. obispos de Chiapas. 2. ed. Mexico, Imprenta guadalupana, de Reyes Velasco, 1907.

198, [2] p. 21½ cm.

772. —— Noticias biográficas sobre los ilustrísimos prelados de Sonora, de Sinaloa y de Durango. 3. ed. México. Impr. del Museo nacional, 1899.

IV, 342 p. 24 cm.

773. Anuario bibliográfico nacional. (1888) Por Luis González Obregón; año I. México, Officina tip. de la Secretaría de fomento, 1889.

155 p. 17 cm.
No more published.

774. Anuario coahuilense para 1886, por Esteban L. Portillo. Año I. Saltillo, A. Prado, 1886.

v. 1. 16 cm.
"Galería de Coahuilenses ilustres": p. 5-76.

775. Arróniz, Marcos. Manual de biografía mejicana o Galería de hombres célebres de Méjico. Paris, Rosa, Bouret y cía; New-York, G. R. Lockwood, 1857.

viii, [9]-317 p. 16 cm. (Enciclopedia popular peruana)

776. Bancroft, Hubert Howe. Mexico ... San Francisco, A. L. Bancroft & company, 1883-88.

6 v. illus., maps. 24 cm. (History of the Pacific states of North America. vol. IV-IX)
"Authorities quoted": v. 1, p. XXI-CXIII.
The bibliographical notes are of great value.

777. Basalenque, Diego. Historia de la provincia de San Nicolás de Tolentino, de Michoacán, del orden de N. P. S. Augustín. Edición de la "Voz de México." Mexico, Tip. Barbedillo y comp., 1886.

3 v. 19 cm.
1st edition, Mexico, 1673.

778. Bazán, Hernando. Memorial del número de religiosos y de sus cualidades, que hay en esta provincia de Santiago de Méjico y pertenecen a ella, de la Orden de predicadores, y de sus conventos, colegios y doctrinas de indios. (In Colección de documentos inéditos para la historia de España. Madrid, 1891. 22 cm. t. 100, p. 480–491.)

779. Beauvois, Eugène. Les publications relatives à l'ancien Mexique depuis une trentaine d'années. Paris, Au siège de la Société, 1899.

23 p.
Congrès bibliographique international tenu à Paris du 13 au 16 avril 1898, sous les auspices de la Société bibliographique. Extrait du Compte rendus des travaux, t. 1, p. 475–497.

780. Beristáin de Sousa, José Mariano. Biblioteca hispano-americana septentrional; o, Catálogo y noticia de los literatos, que o nacidos, o educados, o florecientes en la America Septentrional española, han dado a luz algún escrito, o lo han dexado preparado para la prensa. México [A. Valdés] 1816–21.

3 v. 29½–33 cm.

781. ———— Biblioteca hispano americana setentrional. 2. ed. Publícala el presbítero Br. Fortino Hipolito Vera ... Amecameca, Tip. del Colegio católico, 1883.

3 v. 20 x 15 cm.

782. ———— ———— Tomo iv comprende los anónimos que dejó escritos el autor, las adiciones del Dr. Osores y otras añadidas posteriormente por las personas que se expresan. José Toribio Medina publícalo ahora con una introducción bio-bibliográfica. Santiago de Chile, Impr. elzeviriana, 1897.

liii, 196, [1] p. 20 cm.

783. ———— ———— Adiciones y correcciones que a su fallecimiento dejó manuscritas el Sr. Lic. D. José Fernando Ramírez, y son las que cita con el nombre de "Suplemento"; o, "Adición" en las apostillas que pasó a su ejemplar de la Biblioteca hispano-americana del Dr. D. J. Mariano de Beristain y Sousa. Publícanlas por vez primera el Lic. Victoriano Agüeros y el Dr. N. Leon. México, Impr. de el Tiempo, 1898.

xlvii, [4], 662 p., 1 l. front. (port.) 18 cm.
An indispensable work for the American bibliographer despite its defects, notable among which is his practice of altering titles of works cited.

784. Bermúdez de Castro, Diego Antonio. Theatro angelopolitano, o Historia de la ciudad de la Puebla. Lo publica por vez primera el Dr. N. León. (In León, Nicolás. Bibliografía Mexicana del siglo XVIII. México, 1908. 30 cm. Sección 1., 5. pte. p. 121–354.)

785. Bibliotheca mejicana, a catalogue of an extraordinary collection of books relating to Mexico and North and South America, from the first introductiom of printing in the new world, A. D. 1544 to A. D. 1868. Collected during 20 years' official residence in Mexico. [n. p., n. d.]

312 p. 21½ cm.

786. Bibliotheca mexicana; catalogue d'une collection de livres rares (principalement sur l'histoire et la linguistique) réunie au Méxique par M. ... attaché a la cour de l'émpereur Maximilien. Paris, Librairie Tross, 1868.

2 p. l., 47 p. 23 cm.

787. Bibliotheca mexicana; sammlung des barons Kaska: I. Mexikanische u. spanische handschriften; II. Bücher über geschichte, sprachwissenschaft, naturgeschichte usw. Mexikos; III. Varia. Berlin, J. A. Stargardt, 1911.

54 p. facsim. 24½ cm.
Section 2 contains 632 titles.

788. Blake, Willson Wilberforce. Catalogue of second hand books. México, 1892?—

A very useful catalogue with many notes. The business is continued by A. M. Blake, and a monthly list, Blake's bulletin, is being published.

789. Bliss, Porter Cornelius. Catalogue of the library of the late Porter C. Bliss, including his very rare collection of Spanish Americana and Mexicana ... sold ... July 27th and 28th, 1885 ... Geo. A. Leavitt & co., auctioneers ... New York, 1885.

100 p. 24 cm.

790. Boban, Eugène. Documents pour servir à l'histoire du Mexique; catalogue raisonné de la collection de M. E.-Eugène Goupil (ancienne collection J.-M.-A. Aubin); manuscrits figuratifs, et autres sur papier indigène d'agave mexicana et sus papier européen antérieurs et postérieurs à la conquête du Mexique (XVIe siècle), avec une introduction de M. E.-Eugène Goupil et une lettre-préface de M. Auguste Génin. Paris, E. Leroux, 1891.

2 v. 2 port. 36 cm. and atlas of 80 pl. 37 x 46 cm.
Collection formed originally by L. Boturini Benaduci and acquired by the Bibliothèque nationale, Paris.
"Notes biographiques sur M. J.-M.-A. Aubin": v. 1, p. [31]-30.
"Biographie du chevalier Lorenzo Boturini Benaduci, (d'après M. A. Chavero)": v. 1, p. [31]-51.

791. ——— Table analytique générale des matières contenues dans les deux volumes des Documents pour servir à l'histoire du Mexique. Paris, E. Leroux, 1891.

cover-title, 16 p. 36½ cm.

792. Boletín bibliográfico y escolar. Organo de la Biblioteca pública "Romero Rubio" y de las escuelas. Revista quincenal destinada a coadyuvar a los progresos del municipio de Tacubaya, y en particular a los de la enseñanza ... t. 1- enero 16, 1891-. México, Impr. del gobierno federal en el ex-arzobispado, 1891-

   26 cm.
   Edited by Ramón Manterola.

793. Boturini Benaduci, Lorenzo. Idea de una nueva historia general de la América Septentrioal. Madrid, Impr. de J. deZuñiga, 1746.

   2 v. 21 cm.
   "Catálogo del Museo histórico indiano del cavallero Lorenzo Boturini Benaduci": 96 p. at end of v. 2.

794. Brasseur de Bourbourg, Charles Étienne. Bibliothèque mexico-guaté-malienne, précédée d'un coup d'œil sur les études américaines dans leurs rapports avec les études classiques et suivie du tableau par ordre alpha-bétique des ouvrages de linguistique américaine contenus dans le même volume; rédigée et mise en ordre d'après les documents de sa collection américaine par M. Brasseur de Bourbourg. Paris, Maisonneuve & cᵗᵉ, 1871.

   2 p. l., xlvii, 183, [1] p. 26 cm.
   Acquired by A. L. Pinart, of whose collection a sale catalogue was issued in 1883.
   This collection is rich in rare manuscripts of real importance and in works on the Indian languages, especially on those of Mexico and Central America.

795. Brinton, Daniel Garrison. The missing authorities on Mayan antiquities. Washington, Judd & Detweiler, 1897.

   p. 183-191.
   Reprinted from American Anthropologist, June, 1897.

796. Bustamante, Luis F. Perfiles y bocetos revolucionarios. Mexico, 1917.

   183 p.

797. Carrillo y Ancona, Crèscencio. Disertación sobre la historia de la lengua maya o yucateca. México, Impr. del gobierno, 1872.

   2 p. l., 63, 257-271 p. pl. 26 cm.
   Disertación sobre la literatura antigua de Yucatán: p. 257-271.
   Also in Boletín de la Sociedad de geografía y estadística de la República Mexicana, v. 4 (1872), p. 134-195.

798. ——— El obispado de Yucatán; historia de su fundación y de sus obispos desde el siglo XVI hasta el XIX. Tomo 1. Mérida de Yucatán, R. B. Caballero, 1892.

   274 p. 27½ cm.

799. Casasús, Joaquín Demetrio. En honor de los muertos. Mexico, Impr. de I. Escalante, 1910.

   2 p. l., [7]-254, [4] p. 23 cm.

800. Castillo, Gerónimo. Diccionario histórico, biográfico y monumental de Yucatán. Desde la conquista hasta el último año de la dominación española en el país. Tomo I, A-E. Mérida, Impr. de Castillo y compañía, 1866.

vii, [9]-315 p. 22 cm.
No more published.

801. Castillo Negrete, Emilio del. Galería de oradores de México en el siglo XIX. Mexico, Tip. de S. Sierra, 1877-80.

3 v. front. (port.) 22 cm.
Contains biographical sketches.

802. Catalogus personarum et officiorum provinciae Mexicanae Societatis Jesu. In Indiÿs 1764. Mexici, typis reg. & Ant. D. Ildefonsi (Reprinted in León, Nicolás. Bibliografía mexicana del siglo XVIII. México, 1906. 30 cm. Sección 1, 3. pte., p. 76-118)

Index alphabeticus cognominum sociorum in provincia Mexicana (with date of birth): p· 101-113.

803. Chapman, Charles Edward. Catalogue of materials in the Archivo de Indias for the history of the Pacific Coast and the American Southwest. Berkeley, University of California press, 1919.

2 p. l. III-v, 755 p. 26 cm. (University of California publications in history. v. VIII)

804. Chavero, Alfredo. Apuntes viejos de bibliografía mexicana. México, Tip. J. I. Guerrero y cia, 1903.

2 p. L, [5]-89 p., 2 l. 24½ cm.
CONTENTS—Códice Telleriano remense.—Pinturas de los soles.—Peregrinación azteca.—Cronistas Tenochcas: Códice Ramírez. Durán. Acosta. Tesozomoc.—Motolinía.—Mendieta.—Sahagún.—Vétancurt.

805. ——— Sahagún; estudio. México, Impr. de J. M. Sandoval, 1877.

100 p., 1 l.

806. Cowan, Robert Ernest. A bibliography of the history of California and the Pacific west 1510-1906, together with the text of John W. Dwinelle's address on the acquisition of California by the United States of America. San Francisco, The Book club of California, 1914

xxxi, p., 1 l., 318 p., 2 l. 27 cm.

807. Cruzado, Manuel. Bibliografía jurídica mexicana. México, Tip. de la Oficina impresora de estampillas, 1905.

2 p. l., 385 p. 23½ cm.
830 titles.

808. Dávila Padilla, Agustín. Historia de la fundación y discurso de la provincia de Santiago de México de la Orden de predicadores, por las vidas de sus varones insignes, y casos notables de Nueva España. Madrid, En casa de P. Madrigal. 1596.

7 p. l., 815, [26] p. pl. 30½ cm.
For continuations, see Franco y Ortega and Ojea.

809. Dávila y Arrillaga, José Mariano.   Continuación de la historia de la Compañía de Jesús en Nueva España del P. Francisco Javier Alegre.   Puebla, Imp. del Colegio pío de artes y oficios, 1888–89.

2 v. 23½ cm.

810. Denison, Thomas Stewart.   Mexican linguistics: including Nauatl or Mexican in Aryan phonology; The primitive Aryans of America; A Mexican-Aryan comparative vocabulary; Morphology and the Mexican verb; and The Mexican-Aryan sibilants; with an appendix on comparative syntax, by T. S. Denison, together with an introduction by H. W. Magoun.   Chicago, T. S. Denison & company [1913]

[449] p. front. (port.) 24½ cm.
Contains bibliographies.

811. Diccionario universal de historia y de geografía obra dada a lus en España y refundida y aum. considerablemente para su publicación en México con noticias históricas, geográficas, estadísticas y biográficas sobre las Américas en general, y especialmente sobre la República Mexicana.   México, Tip. de Rafael, 1853–56.

10 v. 28 cm.
Vols. 8–10: Apéndice—Colección de artículos relativos a la República Mexicana recogidos por M. Orosco y Berra.

812. Domínguez, Ricardo.   Galería de escritores y periodistas de la "Prensa asociada."   México, Impr. de "El Partido liberal," 1890.

123 p. 16 cm.

813. Eguiara y Eguren, Juan José de.   Bibliotheca mexicana; sive, Eruditorum historia virorum, qui in America Boreali nati, vel alibi geniti, in ipsam domicilis aut studijs asciti, quavis linguâ scripto aliquid tradiderunt; eorum præsertim qui pro fide catholicâ & pietate ampliandâ fovendâque, egregiè factis & quibusvis scriptis floruere editis aut ineditis.   Tomus primus, exhibens litteras A B C.   Mexici, ex nova typographia in ædibus authoris editioni ejusdem Bibliothecæ destinata, 1755.

80 p. l., 543, [1] p. 30 x 21 cm.
No more published.

814. Escalafón del cuerpo diplomatico mexicano.   1. julio de 1913– México, Müller hnos, 1913–

815. Escandón, Luis A.   Poetas y escritores mexicanos.   1. ed.   México, Impr. de. I. Paz. 1889.

126, [1] p. 19 cm.

816. Espinosa, Isidro Félix de.   Chronica apostolica, y seraphica de todos los colegios de propaganda fide de esta Nueva-España, de missioneros franciscanos observantes: erigidos con autoridad pontificia, y regia, para la reformacion de los fieles, y conversion de los gentiles.   Consagrada a la milagrosa cruz de piedra, que como titular se venera en su primer Colegio de propaganda fide de la muy ilustre ciudad de San-Tiago de Queretaro, sita en el arzobispado de Mexico. [Mexico] Por la viuda de J. B. de Hogal, impressora, 1746-92.

2 v. 30 cm.

Vol. 2 has title: Crónica seráfica y apostólica del Colegio de propaganda fide de la Santa Cruz de Querétaro en la Nueva España. Escrita por el P. Fr. Juan Domingo Arricivita. 2. parte. México, Por F. de Zúñiga y Ontiveros, 1792.

817. ———— Crónica de la provincia franciscana de los apóstoles San Pedro y San Pablo de Michoacán; la publica por vez primera el Dr. Nicolas León. México, Imp. de "El Tiempo," 1899.

1 p. l., [5]-574 p. 27 cm.

818. Fernández del Castillo, Francisco. Libros y libreros en el siglo XVI. Mexico, Tip. Guerrero hnos., 1914.

2 p. l., iv, 608 p. 24 cm. (Estados Unidos Mexicanos. Secretaría de relaciones exteriores. Publicaciones del Archivo general de la nación, VI)

Interesting documents on the book trade in Mexico and on the control exercised by the Inquisition.

819. Fewkes, Jesse Walter. Catálogo de los objetos etnológicos y arqueológicos exhibidos por la expedición Hemenway. Madrid, Jaramillo, impresor, 1892.

115 p. 22½ cm.

820. ———— Commemoration of the fourth centenary of the discovery of America. Columbian historical exposition, Madrid. Catalogue of the Hemenway collection in the Historico-American exposition of Madrid. By Dr. J. Walter Fewkes. From the report of the Madrid commission, 1892. Washington, Gov't print. off., 1895.

1 p. l., 279-327 p. 24½ cm.

CONTENTS: Catalogue of the Hemenway collection in the Historico-American exposition of Madrid.—The Bandelier collection of copies of documents relative to the history of New Mexico and Arizona. <From the Archives of the Hemenway expedition>—Exhibit of the Peabody museum.

821. Francisco de Burgoa. Palestra historial de virtudes y exemplares apostólicos. Fundada del zelo de insignes héroes de la sagrada Orden de predicadores en este Nuevo Mundo. Mexico, I. Ruyz, 1670.

12 p. l., 209 numb. l., 5 l.

Medina, Impr. en México, no. 1019.

822. Franco y Ortega, Alonso. Segunda parte de la Historia de la provincia de Santiago de México, Orden de predicadores en la Nueva España, año de 1645 en Mexico. Mexico, Impr. del Museo nacional, 1900.

1 p. l., 573 p.

A continuation of Dávila Padilla's Historia ... de la provincia de Santiago de México; edited by José María de Agreda y Sánchez.

823. Fusco, Federico M. Los hombres que rodean al señor general Porfirio
Díaz. Semblanzas políticas, por Federico M. Fusco y Félix M. Iglesias.
México, 1896.

120 p.
Cited in Blake's Bulletin, Aug.-Sept., 1920.

824. Galindo y Villa, Jesús. El Panteón de San Fernando y el futuro panteón
nacional. Notas históricas, biográficas y descriptivas. México, Impr.
del Museo nacional, 1908.

cover-title, 216 p. illus., plates. 29½ cm.
From Anales del Museo nacional de México, 2. época, t. 4 (1907), p. 337-552.

825. ——— Las pinturas y los manuscritos jeroglíficos mexicanos. Nota
bibliográfica sobre los más conocidos e importantes. (In Anales del Museo
nacional de México. México, 1905. 29½ cm. 2. época. t. 2., p. 25-56.)

No more published?
Contains 1, Colección de Boturini; 2, Publicaciones del barón Humboldt; 3, Colección de lord
Kingsborough; 4, Antigua colección Aubin.

826. Gallo, Eduardo L. Hombres ilustres mexicanos; biografías de los personages notables desde antes de la conquista hasta nuestros días, por
I. M. Altamirano, M. Acuña ... y varios escritores de los estados. Mexico, Impr. de I. Cumplido, 1873-74.

4 v. plates ports. 23½ cm.

827. García, Esteban. Crónica de la provincia agustiniana del Santísimo Nom-
bre de Jesús de México. Libro 5. Pub. por la Provincia del Santísimo
Nombre de Jesús de Filipinas en su Archivo histórico hispano-agustiniano.
Madrid, G. Lópes del Horno, 1918.

xxxi, 404 p.

828. García, Genaro. Bernal Díaz del Castillo; noticias bio-bibliográficas.
México, Impr. del Museo nacional, 1904.

75 p. front. (port.) facsim., 29½ cm.
From Anales del Museo nacional de México. 2. época, v. 1, p. 306-375.

829. ——— Don Juan de Palafox y Mendoza, obispo de Puebla y Osma,
visitador y virrey de la Nueva España. México, Bouret, 1918.

426 p. incl. front. (port.) 24½ cm.
Bibliografía: p. 319-423.

830. ——— Índice alfabético de la "Colección de documentos para la historia
de la guerra de independencia de México, de 1808 a 1821," formada por
J. E. Hernández Dávalos. (In Anales del Museo nacional de México.
México, 1907. 29½ cm. 2. época, t. 4, p. 225-306.)

831. ——— Indice alfabético de los "Documentos para la historia de México"
publicados en cuatro series por D. Manuel Orozco y Berra. (In Anales
del Museo nacional de México. México, 1906. 29½ cm. 2. época, t. 3,
p. 523-540.)

832. ———— Juárez; refutación a Don Francisco Bulnes. México, Vda de C. Bouret, 1904.

viii, 276, [2] p. front. (port.) 22½ cm.
Bibliografía, p. 195–276.

833. García Cubas, Antonio. Diccionario geográfico, histórico y biográfico de los Estados Unidos Mexicanos. México, Antigua impr. de Murguia, 1888–91.

5 v. illus. 31 cm.

834. García Icazbalceta, Joaquín. Apuntes para un catálogo de escritores en lenguas indígenas de América. México, 1866.

1 p. l., [v]–xiii, 157 p. 15½ cm.
Se han impreso 60 ejemplares en la imprenta particular del autor.
A second ed. appeared in Obras de D. J. García Icazbalceta, México, 1898, t. viii, p. [5]–181. 175 titles.

835. ———— Bibliografía mexicana del siglo xvi. Primera parte. Catálogo razonado de libros impresos en México de 1539 á 1600. Con biografías de autores y otras ilustraciones. Precedido de una noticia acerca de la introducción de la imprenta en México. Obra adornada con facsímiles fotolitográficos y fototipográficos. México, Andrade y Morales, 1886.

xxix, 419, [3] p. illus., facsim. 29 cm.
The second part (intended to cover 16th century writers whose works were either published after 1600, or remained in ms.) was never published.
116 titles, transcribed line for line. Copious quotations, bibliographical and historical notes, references to authorities and libraries, owning copies, etc.

836. ———— León, Nicolás. Adiciones a la Bibliografía mexicana del siglo xvi del señor don Joaquín García Icazbalceta. (In Boletín del Instituto bibliográfico mexicano. México, 1903. 30 cm. núm. 2, p. 41–64, facsims.)

837. ———— Don fray Juan de Zumárraga, primer obispo y arzobispo de México; estudio biográfico y bibliográfico. Con un apéndice de documentos inéditos o raros. México, Andrade y Morales. 1881.

3 p. l., 371, 270, vii, [1] p. facsim. 22½ cm.

838. ———— Obras. México, Imp. de V. Agüeros, editor, 1896–99.

10 v. front. (port.) 16½ cm. (Biblioteca de autores mexicanos. Historiadores. [1–3, 6, 9, 12, 14, 18, 20, 23])
CONTENTS:Opúsculos varios.—Biografías.—Biografía de D. Fr. Juan de Zumárraga.

839. ———— Galindo y Villa, Jesús. D. Joaquín García Icazbalceta; biografía y bibliografía. (In Boletín del Instituto bibliográfico mexicano. México, 1903. 30 cm. núm. 2, p. 1–39, port.)

840. Gestoso y Pérez, José. Documentos para la historia de la primitiva tipografía mexicana. Carta dirigida al Sr. D. José Toribio Medina. [Sevilla] Tip. de la Andalucía moderna, 1908.

14 p., 1 l. 26 cm.

341. Gloner, Prosper. Les finances des États-Unis Mexicains d'après les documents officiels. Berlin, Puttkammer & Mühlbrecht, 1896.

> viii, 703 p., 1 l., incl. tables. 29½ cm.
> Bibliographie: p. 683-691.
> Contains a useful list of Memorias de la Secretaría de hacienda y crédito público.

342. González, Pedro. La bibliografía histórica nacional. (In Boletín de la Sociedad mexicana de geografía y estadística. México, 1912. 23½ cm. 5. época, t. 5, p. 295-298.)

343. Gonzáles de la Puente, Juan. Primera parte de la Choronica avgvstiniana de Mechoacan, en qve se tratan, y escriuen las vidas de nueue varones apostolicos, Augustinianos. [Cuernavaca, Tip. de R. C. Miranda, 1907?]

> 2 p. l., 509, ix p. 23½ cm. (Colección de documentos inéditos y raros para la historia eclesiástica mexicana. t. 1)
> Preface signed: Dr. N. León. No more published.

344. Gonzáles Obregón, Luis. La Biblioteca nacional de México, 1833-1910, reseña histórica. México, 1910.

> 110, [2] p. incl. illus., 2 pl. facsim. fold. plan. 19 cm.

345. ———— El capitán Bernal Díaz del Castillo, conquistador y cronista de Nueva España. Noticias biográficas y bibliográficas. México, Oficina tip. de la Secretaría de fomento, 1894.

> 88, ii p., 1 l. 23½ cm.

346. ———— Don José Joaquín Fernández de Lizardi (el Pensador mexicano) apuntes biográficos y bibliográficos. México, Oficina tip. de la Secretaría de fomento, 1888.

> xii, 91 p. front. (port.) 23 cm.

347. Grijalva, Juan de. Crónica de la Orden de N. S. P. Augustin en las provincias de la Nueva España. En cuatro edades desde el año de 1533 hasta el de 1592. *Colophon:* Mexico, En el convento de S. Augustin, y impr. de I. Ruyz, 1624].

> 4 p. l., 218 l.
> Medina, Impr. en México, no. 368.

348. ———— García, Esteban. Crónica de la provincia agustiniana del Santísimo Nombre de Jesús de México libro quinto compuesto por el P. M. Fr. Esteban García y pub. por la provincia del Santísimo Nombre de Jesús de Filipinas en su Archivo histórico hispano-agustiniano ... Madrid, Impr. de G. López del Horno, 1918.

> xxi, 404, [2] p. 23½ cm.
> A continuation of Juan de Grijalva's Cronica de la Orden de N. P. S. Augustin en las provincias de la Nueva España.

349. Guadalajara. Biblioteca pública del estado. Catálogo de los libros que existen en la Biblioteca pública del estado. Guadalajara, Tip. de S. Banda, 1874, '73·

> 2 v. 24½ cm.
> By José María Vigil.

860. Guadalupe Romero, José. Noticia de las personas que han escrito o publicado algunas obras sobre idiomas que se hablan en la República. In Boletín de la Sociedad mexicana de geografía y estadística. Mexico, 1860. 25 cm. t. VIII, p. 374–386.)

861. ———— Noticias para formar la historia y la estadística del obispado de Michoacán; presentadas a la Sociedad mexicana de geografía y estadística en 1860. México, Impr. de V. Garcia Torres, 1862.

251 [1] p. port., fold. maps. 27 cm.

862. Haebler, Konrad. Die maya-litteratur und der mayaapparat su Dresden. (In Centralblatt für bibliothekswesen, v. XII (1895) 24 cm., p. 537–575.)

863. Haferkorn, Henry Ernest. The war with Mexico, 1846–1848; a select bibliography on the causes, conduct, and the political aspect of the war, together with a select list of books and other printed material on the resources, economic conditions, politics and government of the republic of Mexico and the characteristics of the Mexican people. With annotations and an index. Washington barracks, D. C., 1914.

4 p. l., 93, xxviii p. 23 cm. (Supplement no. 1, Professional memoirs, March–April, 1914, vol. VI, no. 26. Bibliographical contributions. Bulletin no. 1)

864. Henríquez Ureña, Pedro. Bibliografía de Sor Juana Inés de la Cruz. (In Revue hispanique, New York [etc.] 1917. 25½ cm. v. 40, no. 97, p. 161–214.)

865. ———— La literatura mexicana de la época de la independencia (1800–1821). (In Anales del Museo nacional de arqueología, historia y etnología. México, 1913, t. V, 14 p.)

866. Heredia, Carlos M. Los jesuítas de la Nueva España, catequistas. (In Razón y fé, Madrid, 1914, t. 38, p. 462–474.)

867. Hernández, Carlos. Mujeres célebres de México. San Antonio, Texas, Casa editorial Lozano, 1918.

188, [3] p. incl. pl., ports. 23½ cm.

868. Herrera y Ogazón, Alba. El arte musical en México; antecedentes,—El Conservatorio, compositores e intérpretes. México, Dirección general de las bellas artes, 1917.

227 p., 1 l. 19½ cm.

869. Horta, Aurelio. Mexicanos ilustres. Lión, J. Villapando, 1891.

870. Hrdlička, Aleš. Physiological and medical observations among the Indians of southwestern United States and northern Mexico. Washington, Gov't print. office, 1908.

ix, 460 p. plates, tables, diagrs. 34 cm.
Smithsonian Institution. Bureau of American Ethnology, Bulletin 34. Bibliography: p. 407–425.

861. Iguíniz, Juan B. La imprenta en la Nueva Galicia 1793–1821. Apuntes bibliográficos. México, Imp. del Museo n. de arqueología, historia y etnología, 1911.

2 p. l., p. [253]-326. plates. 29 cm.
Sobretiro del tomo III de los "Anales del Museo nacional de arqueología, historia y etnología."

862. ———— Las publicaciones del Museo nacional de arqueología, historia y etnología. Apuntes histórico-bibliográficos. México, Imp. del Museo n. de arqueología, historia y etnología, 1912.

2 p. l., [5]-99, [1] p. plates, ports., facsims. 23½ cm.
Bibliografía: p. 51-95.

863. Jefes del ejército mexicano en 1847; biografías de generales de división y de brigada y de coroneles del ejército mexicano por fines del año de 1847. Manuscrito anónimo, adicionado en gran parte y precedido de un estudio acerca de la participación del ejército en la vida política de Mexico durante la primera mitad del siglo XIX, con numerosos documentos inéditos, por Alberto M. Carreno. Mexico, Impr. de la Secretaría de fomento, 1914.

cccxxxiv, 258 p., 1 l. ports., facsims. 24 cm.
At head of title: Sociedad mexicana de geografía y estadística.
"Hay una serie de circunstancias que me hacen creer que el manuscrito ... es obra del general D. Gabriel Valencia."—Prólogo.

864. Jiménez de la Espada, Marcos. La imprenta en México. (In Boletín del Instituto bibliográfico mexicano. México, 1905. 30 cm. núm. 6, p. 7-16.)

A letter to Don F. de T. dated Aug. 11, 1878.

865. Jones, Cecil Knight. Bibliography of the Mexican revolution. [Baltimore, 1919]

cover-title, p. [311]-314. 27 cm.
Reprinted from the Hispanic American historical review, vol. II, no. 2, May 1919.

866. Larrainzar, Manuel. Algunas ideas sobre la historia y manera de escribir la de México, especialmente la contemporánea desde la declaración de independencia en 1821, hasta nuestros días. Memoria escrita y presentada a la Sociedad mexicana de geografía y estadística. México, Impr. de I. Cumplido, 1865.

v, 105 p. 27½ cm.
Catálogo de los principales historiadores de México, y otros autores que han escrito sobre las cosas de América: p. 92-105.

867. Leduc, Alberto. Diccionario de geografía, historia y biografía mexicanas, por Alberto Leduc y Dr. Luis Lara y Pardo para los artículos históricos y biográficos, y Carlos Roumagnac para los artículos geográficos. México [etc.] V^{da} de C. Bouret, 1910.

viii, 1109 p., 1 l. 18 cm.

868. Lehmann, Walter. Methods and results in Mexican research. Tr. by Seymour de Ricci. Paris, 1909.

2 p. l., 127 p. 21 cm.
From Archiv für anthropologie v. 6 (1907), p. 113-168.
A valuable handbook with an excellent bibliographical equipment.

869. Lejeal, Léon. Les antiquités mexicaines (Mexique, Yucatan, Amérique-Centrale). Paris, A. Picard et fils, 1902.

cover-title, 78, [1] p. 25 cm. (Bibliothèque de bibliographies critiques, publiée par la Société des études historiques. 19)
A classified list of 388 titles.

870. León, Nicolás. Apuntamientos bibliográficos sobre el Concilio IV mexicano. (In Boletín del Instituto bibliográfico mexicano. México, 1902. 30 cm. núm. 3, p. 71–78.)

871. ———— Apuntes para una bibliografía antropológica de México. (Somatología.) México, Impr. del Museo nacional, 1901.

1 p. l., 18 p. 24½ cm.

872. ———— La bibliografía en México en el siglo XIX. (In Boletín del Instituto bibliográfico mexicano. México, 1902. 30 cm. núm. 3, p. 53–66.)

873. ———— Bibliografía mexicana del siglo XVIII. México, 1902–

v. 1–. facsims. 30 cm. (Boletín del Instituto bibliográfico mexicano)
Publication first begun in Anales del Museo michoacano, 1890.
"Constará de dos secciones, una puramente bibliográfica y otra biográfica, histórica y crítica.
Sección 1: 1. pte., A–Z (1000 titles) 1902; 2. pte., A–Z (999 titles including reprint of the Gaceta de México and Mercurio de México) 1903–05; 3. pte., A–Z (400 titles) 1906; 4. pte., A–Z (400 titles) 1907; 5. pte., A–Z (500 titles)

874. ———— Biblioteca botánico-mexicana. Catálogo bibliográfico, biográfico y crítico de autores y escritos referentes a vegetales de México y sus aplicaciones, desde la conquista hasta el presente. Suplemento a la materia médica mexicana publicada por el Instituto médico nacional. México, Oficina tip. de la Secretaría de fomento, 1895.

372 p. 23 cm.

875. ———— Ex libris de bibliófilos mexicanos. (In Anales del Museo nacional de arqueología, historia y etnología. México, 1913. t. v. p. 65–124.)

876. ———— Los ex libris simbólicos de los bibliófilos mexicanos. (In Boletín del Instituto bibliográfico mexicano. México, 1903–05. 30 cm. núm. 2. p. 65–68; núm. 6, p. 3–6, plates.)

877. ———— Hombres ilustres y escritores michoacanos; galería fotográfica y apuntamientos biográficos. Morelia, Impr. del gobierno, a cargo de J. R. Bravo, 1874.

vii, 104 p. ports.

878. ———— La imprenta en México; ensayo histórico y bibliográfico. México, Tipog. de "El Tiempo," 1900.

38 p. 18 cm.
A list of presses in Mexico about 1827 not included in Dr. Osores' Adiciones à la Biblioteca de Beristain. cf. p. 6.
———— (In Boletín del Instituto bibliográfico mexicano. México, 1902. 30 cm. núm. 3, p. 27–51)

879. ———— Las lenguas indígenas de México en el siglo XIX. Nota bibliográfica y crítica. (In Anales del Museo nacional de México. México, 1905. 29½ cm. 2 época, t. 2, p. 180–191.)

880. ———— Profr. dr. N. León: noticia de sus obras, originales impresas e inéditas, las de varios autores por él editadas, sociedades científicas a que pertenece, comisiones y empleos públicos por él desempeñados hasta el año 1908, 25° de su graduación médica. Mexico, Typ. vda. de F. Días de Léon, sucs., 1908.

34 p., 1 l. illus., pl. 19½ cm.

881. ———— Tres obras de Sigüenza y Góngora, nota bibliográfica. Morelia, Impr. del gobierno, 1886.

22 p.
From Gaceta oficial del gobierno del estado de Michoacán, 1886.

882. McCaleb, Walter Flavius. The press of Mexico. (In The Hispanic American historical review, Baltimore, 1920. 27 cm. vol. III, p. 443–450.)

883. Maneiro, Juan Luis. Joannis Aloysii Maneiri Veracrucensis De vitis aliquot Mexicanorum aliorumque qui sive virtute, sive litteris Mexici inprimis floruerant. Bononiæ, ex typ. Laelii a Vulpe, 1791–92.

3 v. 19½ cm.

884. Martínez Alomía, Gustavo. Historiadores de Yucatán. Apuntes biográficos y bibliográficos de los historiadores de esta península desde su descubrimiento hasta fines del siglo XIX. Campeche, Tip. "El Fénix," 1906.

2 p. l., xii, 360 p. 23½ cm.

885. ———— Introducción de la imprenta en Campeche y cien portadas de impresos mexicanos, estudio bibliográfico. (In Boletín del Instituto bibliográfico mexicano. México, 1902. 30 cm. núm. 3, p. 1–25.)

886. The Massey-Gilbert blue book of Mexico; a directory in English of the city of Mexico. Mexico, The Massey-Gilbert company, °1901·

372 p. incl. plan. 20 cm.

887. Maudslay, Alfred Percival. Bibliography of Mexico. (In Días del Castillo, Bernal. True history of the conquest of New Spain. London, 1908. 22½ cm. p. 309–368.)

888. Means, Philip Ainsworth. History of the Spanish conquest of Yucatan and of the Itzas. Cambridge, Mass., The Museum, 1917.

xv p., 1 l., 206 p. 7 pl. 25 cm. (Papers of the Peabody museum of American archaeology and ethnology, Harvard university. vol. VII)

"The maps of Yucatan, 1501–1800": p. [192]–199.
Bibliography: p. [202]–206.

889. Medina, Baltasar de. Chronica de la santa provincia de San Diego de Mexico, de religiosos descalços de N. S. P. S. Francisco en la Nueva-España. Vidas de ilvstres, y venerables varones, que la han edificado con excelentes virtudes. Mexico, J. de Ribera, 1682.

23 p. l., 259 numb. l., [20] p. map. 29½ cm.

Descriptive, historical and biographical. The Province of San Diego included approximately the modern states of Oaxaca, Puebla, Guerrero, Morelos, Mexico, Michoacán, Hidalgo, Querétaro, Jalisco, Guanajuato and Aguascalientes.

890. Medina, José Toribio. D. José Mariano Beristain de Souza; estudio biobibliográfico. Santiago de Chile, Imprenta elseviriana, 1897.

xlix, 52 p. 20 cm.

891. ———— La imprenta en Guadalajara de México (1793-1821), notas bibliográficas. Santiago de Chile, Imprenta Elzeviriana, 1904.

104 p. 24 cm.

892. ———— La imprenta en Guadalajara, Mérida de Yucatán, Oaxaca y Veracruz. (In Boletín del Instituto bibliográfico mexicano. México, 1905. 30 cm. núm. 6. p. 17-32.)

893. ———— La imprenta en Mérida de Yucatán (1813-1821), notas bibliográficas. Santiago de Chile, Imprenta elzeviriana, 1904.

23 p. 24 cm.

894. ———— La imprenta en México (1539-1821). Santiago de Chile, Impreso en casa del autor, 1907-12.

8 v. illus., facsims. 31½ cm.
12,412 entries.
"Introducción" (v. 1) contains: (I. Preliminares; II. Los impresores; III. Los grabadores; IV. Los libreros; V. Los bibliógrafos; VI. Leyes y privilegios)

895. ———— La imprenta en México. Epítome (1539-1810). Sevilla, Impr. de E. Rasco, 1893.

291, [1] p. 26 cm.
2599 titles.

896. ———— La imprenta en Oaxaca (1720-1820), notas bibliográficas. Santiago de Chile, Imprenta elzeviriana, 1904.

29 p., 1 l. 24 cm.

897. ———— La imprenta en la Puebla de los Angeles (1640-1821). Santiago de Chile, Imprenta Cervantes, 1908.

L p., 2 l., [3]-822 p. illus., facsims. 26½ cm.

898. ———— La imprenta en Veracruz (1794-1821), notas bibliográficas. Santiago de Chile, Imprenta elzeviriana, 1904.

24 p., 1 l. 24 cm.

899. ——— Introducción de la imprenta en América; carta que al Sr. D. José Gestoso y Pérez dirige J. T. Medina. Santiago de Chile, Impr. Cervantes, 1910.

viii, [9]-104 p. 26½ cm.
"Tirada de cincuenta ejemplares numerados y sólo para la circulación privada."
From the introductory matter to vol. 1 of the author's Imprenta en México.

900. Memorial de los conventos, doctrinas y religiosos desta provincia del Santísimo nombre de Jesús de Guatemala, Honduras y Chiapa de los frailes menores. (In Colección de documentos inéditos para la historia de España. Madrid, 1891. 22 cm. t. 100, p. 492-502.)·

901. Mexico. Biblioteca nacional. La Biblioteca nacional en 1909- 22½ cm.

902. ——— Boletin ... año 1- (núm. 1- julio 1904- México, 1904- 33cm.

903. ——— Catálogos de la Biblioteca nacional de México, formados por el director José M. Vigil. México, Oficina tip. de la Secretaría de fomento, 1889-

v. 1-9. 30 cm.

——— ——— Primeros suplementos de las divisiones 3ª., 5ª., 6ª., y 8ª. México, Oficina tip. de la Secretaría de fomento, 1895.

1 p. l., 9, 26, 31, 23, 33 p. 32½ cm.

904. ——— Catálogos de la Biblioteca nacional de México, formados por el director José M. Vigil. Biblioteca nocturna. México, Oficina tip. de la Secretaría de fomento, 1897.   .

2 p. l., 251, xxxii p. 32 cm.

905. ——— Concurso de bibliografía y biblioteconomía convocado por la Biblioteca nacional; estudios premiados dados a luz bajo la dirección de Juan B. Iguíniz. México, Departamento de aprovisionamientos generales, 1918.

x p., 4 l., [7]-92, 43, 114. 28 p. ports. 26 cm.
CONTENTS: Bibliografía de la revolución mexicana de 1910-1916, por Ignacio B. del Castillo.—Bibliografía de la imprenta de la Cámara de diputados, por Ignacio B. del Castillo.—Los historiadores de Jalisco, por Juan B. Iguíniz.—Los grabadores en México durante la época colonial, por Manuel Romero de Terreros.

906. Mexico, Escuela nacional preparatoria. Catálogo de abras de la biblioteca. México, Tip. de "La Voz de oriente, 1889."

276, 2 p.

907. Mexico. Instituto bibliográfico mexicano. Boletín. México, 1902-08.

v. 1-10. 30 cm.
Includes León's Bibliografía mexicana del siglo xviii, etc.

908. Mexico. Instituto científico de San Francisco de Borja. Catálogo de los alumnos, año escolar de 1907. México, 1907.

2 p. l., 7-70 p., 1 l. plates. 22 cm.

909. Mexico. Ministerio de fomento, colonización e industria. Catálogo de las principales obras impresas en la Oficina tipográfica de dicha secretaría y que se remiten a la exposición internacional de Chicago. México, Oficina tip. de la Secretaría de fomento, 1893.

30 P. 22½ cm.

910. Mexico. Ministerio de hacienda. Memoria de hacienda y crédito público, correspondiente al cuadragésimoquinto año económico. Presentada por el Secretario de hacienda al Congreso de la Unión el 16 de setiembre de 1870. Mexico, Impr. del gobierno, 1870.

4 p. l., 1075, [129] p. 33 cm.
"Catálogo de los volumenes que se han examinado," p. 1061-1075.
Useful for: official publications.

911. Mexico. Secretaría de industria, comercio y trabajo. Catálogo de publicaciones. México, Poder ejecutivo federal, 1919.

No. 1 (16 p.) 22½ cm.

912. Mexico. Secretaría de relaciones exteriores. Escalafón del Cuerpo consular mexicano. Enero 1914. México, Impr. de F. S. Soria, 1914.

50 p. 22½ cm.
Full names and dates of birth.

913. —————— Guía diplomática y consular. 2. ed. oficial, 1902. México, Impr. de F. Días de León, 1902.

220 p. 23½ cm.
Full names and dates of birth.

914. New York. Public library. List of works in the New York public library relating to Mexico. New York, 1909.

cover-title, 186 p. 26 cm.
"Reprinted from the Bulletin, October-December, 1909."

915. Oaxaca. Biblioteca del estado. Catálogo alfabético. Oaxaca, Imprenta del estado, 1887.

2 p. l., 270 p. 21½ cm.

916. Ojea, Hernando. Libro tercero de la historia religiosa de la provincia de México de la Orden de Sto. Domingo. México, Impreso por el Museo nacional, 1897.

xvi, 73, [1] p., 1 l., 41, [1] p. 33½ cm.
Written as a continuation of Dávila Padilla's Historia de la fundación y discurso de la provincia de Santiago de México de la Orden de los predicadores. Edited by J. M. de Ágreda y Sánchez.

917. Olaguíbel, Manuel de. Impresiones célebres y libros raros. México, Impr. del "Socialista" de M. López y comp., 1878.

143 p. 22 cm.

918. ——— ——— México, Impr. de F. Días de León, 1884.

153 p.   23 cm.

919. ——— Memoria para una bibliografía científica de México en el siglo XIX. México, Oficina tip. de la Secretaría de fomento, 1889.

99 p.   24 cm.
"Sección primera: Botánica."   No more published.

920. Olavarría y Ferrari, Enrique de. Reseña histórica del teatro en México. 2. ed. México, Impr. "La Europea," 1895.

4 v. in 2.   25½ cm.

921. Orosco y Berra, Manuel. Materiales para una cartografía mexicana. Edición de la Sociedad de geografía y estadística. México, Imprenta del gobierno, 1871.

xii, 337, [2] p.   29½ cm.

922. Ortega y Pérez Gallardo, Ricardo. Estudios genealógicos. México, Impr. de E. Dublán, 1902.

365 p.   17 cm.

923. ——— Historia genealógica de las familias más antiguas de México. 3. ed. corr. y aum. con profusión de datos y documentos históricos e ilustrada con hermosas eromolitografías. México, Impr. de A. Carranza y comp., 1908-10.

3 v.   front. (port.) plates, ports.   33 cm.

923a. Ortiz de Ayala, Tadeo. México considerado como nación independiente y libre, o sean Algunas indicaciones sobre los deberes más esenciales de los mexicanos. Burdeos, Impr. de C. Lawalle sobrino, 1832.

506, [1] p.   20 cm.
Chapter 5, De los beneficios del cultivo de las ciencias y las artes (p. 173-256) contains a review of authors, artists, etc., from the 15th to the 19th centuries.

924. Osores y Sotomayor, Félix. Noticias bio-bibliográficas de alumnos distinguidos del Colegio de San Pedro, San Pablo y San Ildefonso de México (hoy Escuela n. preparatoria). México, Vda. de C. Bouret, 1908.

2 v.   plates.   20½ cm.   (Documentos inéditos ó muy raros para la historia de México, pub. por Genaro García.   t. xix-xxi)

925. Pareja, Francisco de. Crónica de la provincia de la visitación de Ntra. Sra. de la Merced redención de cautivos de la Nueva España. Escrita en 1688. 1. ed. México, Impr. de J. R. Barbedillo y cª, 1882-83.

2 v.   20½ cm.

926. Paris. Bibliothèque nationale. Catalogue des manuscrits mexicains. Paris, E. Bouillon, 1899.

2 p. l., 64 p., 2 l.   25½ cm.

"Extrait de la Revue des bibliothèques, 1898 et 1899."   Preface by Henri Omont.
385 of the manuscripts described formed the Goupil-Aubin collection acquired by the Bibliothèque nationale in 1898. A complete catalogue of this collection will be found in Eugène Boban's Documents pour servir à l'histoire du Mexique.

927. Pavía, Lázaro. Apuntes biográficos de los miembros más distinguidos del poder judicial de la República Mexicana. t. 1. México, Tip. y lit. de F. Barroso, hermano y cª., 1893.

510, ii p. front., ports. 22 cm.
No more published.

928. ———— Breves apuntes biográficos de los miembros más notables del ramo de hacienda de la República Mexicana, tomo 1. México, 1895.

640 p.
64 biographies. No more published.

929. ———— Los estados y sus gobernantes; ligeros apuntes históricos, biográficos y estadísticos. México, Tip. de las Escalerillas núm. 20, 1890.

xi, 431, ii p. front., ports. 22 cm.

930. ———— Ligeros apuntes biográficos de los jefes políticos de los partidos en los estados de la República Mexicana. México, Tip. de J. Guerra y Valle, 1891-[92]

2 v. ports. 22½ cm.

931. Paz, Ireneo. Los hombres prominentes de México. Les hommes éminents du Mexique. The prominent men of Mexico. México, Impr. y litografía de "La Patria," 1888.

1 p. l., 488, ii p. ports. 29½ cm.
Spanish, French and English in parallel columns. Introduction to the Spanish signed Ireneo Paz; to the French, J. L. Regagnon, and to the English, José F. Godoy.
Contains 211 biographies.

932. Peña y Reyes, Antonio de la. Vidas y tiempos. Diccionario biográfico mexicano. t. 1. A-D. Habana, Impr. "El Renacimiento," 1915.

v. 1. 23 cm.
Vol. 1 contains 349 biographies.

933. Peñafiel, Antonio. Bibliothek des dr. Antonio Peñafiel, herausgeber der "Monumentos del arte mexicano antiguo." Berlin, J. A. Stargardt, 1912.

cover-title, 80 p. 24 cm.

934. Pérez de Ribas, Andrés. Corónica y historia religiosa de la Provincia de la Compañia de Jesús de México en Nueva España. México, Impr. del Sagrado corazón de Jesús, 1896.

2 v. in 1. 25 cm.

935. Pérez Hernández, José María. Diccionario geográfico, estadístico, histórico, biográfico, de industria y comercio de la República Mexicana, escrito en parte y arreglado en otra por el general José María Pérez Hernández, consultando sus tareas con los distinguidos escritores Lics. D. Manuel Orosco y Berra y D. Alfredo Chavero. México, Impr. de Cinco de mayo [etc.] 1874–75.

4 v. front. (port.) 29 cm.
A–C only; no more published.

936. Pesa, Juan de Dios. La vida intelectual mexicana; poetas y escritores modernos en México, revista crítico-biográfica del estado intelectual de la República Mexicana. (In Nueva revista de Buenos Aires. Buenos Aires, 1883. 24½ cm. t. VIII, p. 550–579; t. IX, p. 124–144, 448–471, 596–618.)

937. Pilling, James Constantine. Proof-sheets of a bibliography of the languages of the North American Indians. Washington, Gov't print. off., 1885.

xl, 1135 p. 29½ cm.
"List of authorities": p. xi–xxxvi.

938. ——— The writings of Padre Andrés de Olmos in the languages of Mexico. Washington, Judd & Detweiler, 1895.

cover-title, 18 p. 24 cm.
From American anthropologist, v. 8, no. 1.

939. Pimentel, Francisco. Historia crítica de la literatura y de las ciencias en México desde la conquista hasta nuestros días. Poetas. México, Librería de la enseñanza, 1885.

736 p. 12 port. 23½ cm.
Includes the poets only; no more published.

940. ——— Historia crítica de la poesía en México. Nueva ed. corr. y muy aum. México, Oficina tip. de la Secretaría de fomento, 1892.

976. ii, p. 23 cm.

941. Pinart, Alphonse Louis. Catalogue de livres rares et précieux, manuscrits et imprimés, principalement sur l'Amérique et sur les langues du monde entier, composant la bibliothèque de M. Alph.-L. Pinart et comprenant en totalité la bibliothèque Mexico-Guatémalienne de M. l'abbé Brasseur de Bourbourg. Paris, Vve A. Labitte, 1883.

2 p. l., [v]–viii, 248 p. 25 cm.
1440 entries.

942. Prantl, Adolfo. La ciudad de México; novísima guía universal de la capital de la República Mexicana, directorio clasificado de vecinos, y prontuario de la organización y funciones del gobierno federal y oficinas de su dependencia. México, J. Buxó y compañía, 1901.

xxiv p., 1 l., 1005, [2] p. pl., port., map, plan. 20 x 15½ cm.
At head of title: Adolfo Prantl y José L. Groso.

942. Priestley, Herbert Ingram. José de Gálves, visitor-general of New Spain (1765-1771). Berkeley, University of Califorina press, 1916.

xiv, 449 p. front., pl., maps. 25 cm. (University of California publications in history, vol. 5).
Bibliography: p. 391-408.

944. ———— Mexican literature on the recent revolution. (In Hispanic American historical review. Baltimore, 1919. 27 cm., v. 2, p. 286-311.)

943. ———— Modern Mexican history. New York, 1920.

36 p. 23 cm. (Institute of international education. International relations clubs. Syllabus 6)
A valuable guide to the study of Mexican history, with bibliographies. Sections: 1. The territory of Mexico and the people; 2. The Spanish colonial régime; 3. The war of independence; 4. The war of the reform and the French intervention, 1857-67; 5. The presidency of Porfirio Díaz, 1876-1910; 6. The revolution under Madero, 1910-13; 7. Huerta and the United States, Feb. 19, 1913-July 15, 1914; 8. The government of Carranza, July 15, 1914-May 5, 1920; 9. The petroleum controversy; 10. The problem of the land.

945. Puttick & Simpson. Bibliotheca mejicana. A catalogue of an extraordinary collection of books & manuscripts, almost wholly relating to the history of North and South America, praticularly Mexico. To be sold by auction, by Messrs. Puttick & Simpson. [London, 1869].

2 p. l., 312 p. 23 cm.
2,962 entries.

———— Bibliotheca mejicana. Sold by auction, June 1st to June 10th, 1869. Prices and purchasers' names. [London, G. Norman and son, printers, 1869].

41 p. 23 cm.

947. Ramíres, José Fernando. Bibliotheca mexicana; or, A catalogue of the library of rare books and important manuscripts relating to Mexico and other parts of Spanish America, formed by the late Señor Don José Fernando Ramírez. Sold by Puttick and Simpson. London [G. Norman and son, printers] 1880.

iv, 165 p. 25½ cm.

947a. Ramíres de Arellano, Angel. Apuntes para un catálogo de libros notables impresos en México de 1539 a 1599. México, 1895.

45 p. facsims.

948. Rea, Alonso de la. Crónica de la Orden de N. seráfico de P. S. Francisco, provincia de San Pedro y San Pablo de Michoacán en la Nueva España. Mexico, 1882.

15,488 p.
Reprint of the rare edition of 1643.

949. Ríos Arce, Francisco R. de los.   Puebla de los Angeles y la Orden dominicana.   Estudio histórico para ilustrar la historia civil, eclesiástica, científica, literaria y artística de esta ciudad de Los Angeles.   Puebla, "El
Escritorio," 1910–11.

   v. 1-2.   fold. plan.   23½ cm.

950. Rivera, Agustín.   Los hijos de Jalisco o sea El catálogo de los catedráticos
de filosofía en el Seminario conciliar de Guadalajara desde 1791 hasta 1867.
Guadalajara, 1897.

951. Rivera Cambas, Manuel.   Los gobernantes de México.   Galería de biog·
rafías y retratos de los vireyes, emperadores, presidentes y otros gobernantes que ha tenido México, desde Don Hernando Cortes hasta el C.
Benito Juárez.   Mexico, Imp. de J. M. Aguilar Ortiz [1872]–73.

   2 v.   ports.   30 cm.

952. Rodríguez Escandón, Aristeo.   Breve reseña de la vida pública i hechos
notables de los miembros del clero mejicano, en pro del sostenimiento i
progreso de la religión católica.   2. ed.   Méjico, Impr. de E. Dublán,
1900.

   3 p. l., [5]-382, ii p.   ports.   22½ cm.

953. Romero, José.   Guía de la ciudad de México y demás municipalidades del
Distrito Federal.   México, Porrúa hermanos, 1910.

   2 p. l., 431, xxxii p.   illus., ports., fold. plan.   17 cm.

954. Romero, José Guadalupe.   Noticia de las personas que han escrito o publicado algunas obras sobre idiomas que se hablan en la República.   (In
Boletín de la Sociedad mexicana de geografía y estadística.   México,
1860.   v. 8, p. 874–886.)

955. Salado Álvarez, Victoriano.   Breve noticia de algunos manuscritos de
interés histórico para México, que se encuentran en los archivos y bibliotecas de Washington, D. C.   México, Impr. del Museo nacional, 1908.

   xi, 24 p.   29 cm.
   Extractado del t. 1 de la tercera época de los Anales del Museo nacional.

956. Sánchez Mármol, Manuel.   National letters.   (In Sierra, Justo.   Mexico,
its social evolution, Mexico, 1900.   t. 1, v. 2, p. 603–663.)

   Published also in Spanish.

957. Sociedad científica "Antonio Alzate."   Revista científica y bibliográfica,
1888–89– México, Impr. del gobierno federal, 1888– illus., plates, ports.,
maps.   23 cm.

958. Sociedad mexicana de geografía y estadística.   Memoria, presentada a la
Sociedad mexicana de geografía y estadística por el primer secretario Lic.
Ignacio M. Altamirano, en enero de 1880.   México, Impr. de F. Díaz de
León, 1887.

   1 p. l., 348 p.   24½ cm.
   Includes lists of the honorary and corresponding members of the society, 1868-1881.
   Catálogo de libros de la sociedad: p. 71-207.
   Catálogo de cartas.—Cuadros sinópticos, geográficos, estadísticos e históricos.—Vistas.—
Retratos: p. 208-334.

959. Soriano, Manuel S. Bibliografía médica nacional. (In Boletín de la Sociedad mexicana de geografía y estadística. México, 1902–07. 23½ cm. 5. época, t. 1, p. 722–724; t. 2, p. 22–28.)

960. Sosa, Francisco. Biografías de mexicanos distinguidos. México, Oficina tipográfica de la Secretaría de fomento, 1884.

xii, 1115, 8 p. 23 cm.

961. ———— Efemérides históricas y biográficas. México, Tip. de G. A. Esteva, 1883.

2 v. 15 cm.

962. ———— El episcopado mexicano; galería biográfica ilustrada de los illmos. señores arzobispos de México desde la época colonial hasta nuestros días. México, H. Iriarte y S. Hernández, 1877–79.

xvi, 232, [235]–252 p. pl., ports. 32 cm.
"Autores consultados para escribir esta obra": p. 241–245.

963. ———— Manual de biografía yucateca. Mérida, Impr. de J. B. Espinosa e hijos, 1866.

228, [3] p.

964. Sotomayer, José Francisco. Historia del Apostólico colegio de Nuestra Señora de Guadalupe de Zacatecas, desde su fundación hasta nuestros días, formada con excelentes datos, por el presbítero José Francisco Sotomayor. Editor, Lic. Rafael Ceniceros y Villareal. 2. ed. corr. y aum. por el autor Zacatecas, Imp. de "La Rosa" á cargo de M. Ceniceros, 1889.

2 v. 18½ cm.
Vol. 2 contains "biografías ... de los religiosos que se han distinguido en el Colegio."

965. Starr, Frederick. Recent Mexican study of the native languages of Mexico. Chicago, The University of Chicago press, 1900.

19 p. illus. (ports.) 24 cm. (The University of Chicago. Department of anthropology Bulletin IV)
Annotated list of 75 titles.

966. Tello, Antonio. Libro segundo de la Crónica miscelanea, en que se trata de la conquista espiritual y temporal de la Santa provincia de Xalisco en el Nuevo Reino de la Galicia y Nueva Viscaya y descubrimiento del Nuevo México. Guadalajara, Impr. de "La República literaria," de C. L. de Guevara y ca., 1891.

2 p. l., xxiv, 886, xxvii p. 23½ cm.
Introducción bibliografica by José López Portillo y Rojas.

967. Thomas, Cyrus.   Indian languages of Mexico and Central America and their geographical distribution, by Cyrus Thomas, assisted by John R. Swanton. Accompanied with a linguistic map.   Washington, Govt. print. off., 1911.

vii, 108 p. fold. map. 24½ cm. (Smithsonian institution. Bureau of American ethnology. Bulletin 44)
Issued also as House doc. 416, 61st Cong., 2d sess.
Bibliography: p. 97-100.

968. ————— Notes on certain Maya and Mexican manuscripts.

(U. S. Bureau of American ethnology. Third annual report, 1881-82. Washington, 1884. 29½ cm. p. 3-65. illus., pl. I-IV)
CONTENTS: Tableau des Bacab.—Plate 43 of the Borgian codex.—Plate 44 of the Fejervary codex.—Symbols of the cardinal points.

969. Torre, Juan de la.   Guía para el estudio del derecho constitucional mexicano.   La constitución federal de 1857, sus adiciones, reformas y leyes orgánicas con notas que indican las fuentes adonde debe ocurrirse para su estudio.   México, Tip. de J. V. Villada, 1886.

xxiv, 392 p. 19½ cm.
Bibliografía: p. xiii-xxiv.

970. U. S. War dept.   Index of publications, articles and maps relating to Mexico, in the War department library.   Washington. Govt. print. off., 1896.

v, 120 p. 29½ cm.
CONTENTS: pt. 1. General literature.—pt. 2. Interoceanic canals and railroads.—pt. 3. Mexican war, 1846-48, and Texan-Mexican war.—pt. 4. French intervention and Maximilian period.

971. Urbina, Luis G.   Antología del centenario, estudio documentado de la literatura mexicana durante el primer siglo de independencia; obra comp. bajo la dirección del Señor licenciado Don Justo Sierra por los Señores Don Luis G. Urbina, Don Pedro Henríquez Ureña y Don Nicolás Rangel. México, Imp. de M. León Sánchez, 1910-

2 v. 23½ cm.
"Bibliografía general": v. 1, p. ccxlvi-cclvi.
1. pt. 1800-1821. 2 v.

972. Valverde Téllez, Emeterio.   Bibliografía filosófica mexicana.   México, Tip. de la viuda de F. Díaz de León, 1907.

4 p. l., 218 p. 29 cm. (Obras de Don Emeterio Valverde Téllez. III)

973. Varones ilustres de la Compañía de Jesús.   2. ed., tomo 3.   Misiones de Filipinas, Méjico, Canadá, Brasil.   Bilbao, Administración del Mensajero del Corazón de Jesús, 1889.

650 p. 24 cm.

974. Velásquez, Primo Feliciano.   Obras.   México, Imp. de V. Agüeros, editor, 1901.

viii, 454 p. front. (port.) 18 cm. (Biblioteca de autores mexicanos. 34)
Bibliografía científica potosina: p. 273-454.

975. Vera, Fortino Hipólito. Tesoro guadalupano. Noticia de los libros, documentos, inscripciones, &c. que tratan, mencionan o aluden a la aparición y devoción de Nuestra Señora de Guadalupe. Amecameca, Impr. del "Colegio católico," 1887-89.

2 v. pl. 20½ cm.
Includes publications from 1531 to 1731.

976. Vera, Pedro de. Relación fidedigna, hecha en la provincia de Mechoacán de la Nueva España, por mandado del ilustrísimo señor conde de Lemos y de Andrade, en que se refiere el número de conventos que hasta el día de la fecha hay en esta provincia de San Nicolás de Tolentino, de la Orden de Santo Agustino, y los religiosos della, fecha por noviembre del año de mil y seiscientos y tres. (In Colección de documentos inéditos para la historia de España. Madrid, 1891. 22 cm. t. 100, p. 459-476.)

977. Vetancurt, Agustín de. Teatro mexicano. Descripción breve de los sucesos ejemplares, históricos, políticos, militares y religiosos del Nuevo mundo occidental de las Indias. México, Impr. de I. Escalante y ca., 1870-71.

4 v. 20 cm. (Biblioteca histórica de la Iberia. t. 7-10)
Vol. 4: Menologio franciscano de los varones mas señalados que con sus vidas ejemplares, perfección religiosa, ciencia, predicación evangélica, en su vida y muerte ilustraron la provincia del Santo Evangelio de México.
1st edition, Mexico, 1698.

978. Villaseñor y Villaseñor Alejandro. Biografías de los héroes y caudillos de la independencia. México, Imp. de "El Tiempo," de V. Agüeros, 1910.

2 v. plates, ports. 21 cm.

979. Wagner, Henry R. Bibliography of printed works relating to those portions of the United States which formerly belonged to Mexico. Santiago de Chile, Imp. Diener, 1917.

43, [1] p. 23 cm.

980. Winship, George Parker. Early Mexican printers. Cambridge [Mass.] 1899.

10 p. 24½ cm.
"Reprinted from the Proceedings of the Massachusetts historical society, Jan. 12, 1899."

981. Winsor, Justin. Cortés and his companions, [with a critical essay on the documentary sources of Mexican history, and notes]

(In his Narrative and critical history of America. Boston and New York, 1884-89. 32 cm.
v. 2, p. 349-430.

982. ——— Mexico and Central America, [with a critical essay on the sources of information, and notes]

(In his Narrative and critical history of America. Boston and New York, 1884-89. 32 cm.
v. 1, p. 133-207.

963. Wright de Kleinhaus, Laureana. Mujeres notables mexicanas. México, Tipografía económica, 1910.

2 p. l., 246 p. front., ports. 23 cm.

964. Zelis, Rafael de. Catálogo de los sugetos de la Compañía de Jesús que formaban la provincia de México el día del arresto, 25 de junio de 1767. Contiene: los sugetos por orden alfabético, por orden de edad, por orden de grado: los colegios, las misiones y los difuntos. México, Impr. de J. Escalante y ca., 1871.

202, [3] p. 24 cm.
"Après la mort du P. de Zelis, le P. Pierre Marques compléta la liste des défunts. Ce volume a été publié par le P. André Artola. cf. Backer-Sommervogel.

965. Zerecero, Anastasio. Memorias para la historia de las revoluciones en México. México, Impr. del gobierno, 1869.

1 p. l., ii, 608 p. 20 cm.
Indice célebres de la República Mexicana, o biografías de los más notables que han florecido desde 1521 hasta nuestros días: p. 436-531.

C. K. JONES.

(*To be continued.*)

BIBLIOGRAFÍA ANTILLANA

Voy a disertar ligeramente sobre un tema que interesa de modo peculiar a los que vivimos en esta región del Nuevo Mundo, y que hasta ahora ha ocupado poco la atención de los hombres estudiosos.

Me refiero a la Bibliografía Antillana, que ha tenido escasos cultivadores como se verá a continuación.

El primer autor que debe haber fijado su atención en los escritores de las Antillas supongo sea el peruano Antonio de León Pinelo, que publicó en Madrid en 1629 el *Epítome de la Biblioteca Oriental y Occidental, Náutica y Geográfica*. Esta es la primera bibliografía americana que se ha impreso y la cual no he tenido la suerte de consultar.

Es probable que en ella se mencionen algunos escritores de Santo Domingo, del siglo diez y seis. Puerto Rico tuvo uno en dicha centuria, Juan Ponce Troche de León (1582), que dudo mucho llegara a ser conocido de Pinelo; y de Cuba, muy atrasada entonces, no se tiene noticia de un solo escritor en el referido siglo. Los primeros, Pedro de la Torre Sifuentes, Juan Rodríguez Sifuentes y José Hidalgo, florecieron en 1606 y 1637.

En la segunda edición de la obra de Pinelo, dada a luz en Madrid en 1737 por Andrés González Barcía, en tres tomos en folio, se citan únicamente tres escritores cubanos, a saber: Francisco Diaz Pimienta, Ambrosio Zayas Bazán y el Presbítero Juan Ferro Machado.   No tengo en estos momentos a la vista ese libro; pero es seguro que consignará los nombres de algunos dominicanos, y tal vez, el de uno o dos portorriqueños.

Casi un siglo mas tarde, el famoso bibliógrafo mexicano José M. Beristaín de Sousa en su *Biblioteca Hispano-Americana Septentrional* (México, 1816–1819) suministra numerosas noticias sobre los escritores de las tres Antillas, a que me estoy refiriendo.   Dicho bibliógrafo estuvo en la Habana en 1789 y probablamente en 1794, recogiendo antecedentes para su monumental bibliografía.

El eminente polígrafo D. Marcelino Menéndez y Pelayo, el más grande de los escritores españoles del siglo XIX, en su magnífica obra *Antología de Poetas Hispano-americanos* (Madrid, 1893) se fija con detenimiento y estudia de modo magistral (en el tomo 2°) a los poetas de las Antillas hermanas por el idioma; estudio que amplió en la segunda edición de dicha obra, publicada con el título de *Historia de la Poesía Hispano-Americana* (Madrid, 1911, 1913, dos volúmenes).

El autor que traza estos humildes renglones tuvo la satisfacción de poner su grano de arena en el edificio de la Bibliografía Antillana; pues al publicar en 1907 su *Ensayo de Bibliografía Cubana de los siglos XVII y XVIII* lo adicionó con unos ligeros "Apuntes para la Bibliografía Dominicana y Portorriqueña", dando a conocer algunos autores y libros ignorados u olvidados, y tuvo la suerte de poder descubrir uno de los primeros folletos impresos en Santo Domingo, a saber, los *Estatutos de la Regia y Pontificia Universidad de Santo Thomas de Aquino; en el convento imperial de predicadores de la ciudad de Santo Domingo en la Isla Española.*   En Santo Domingo, en la Imprenta de Andrés Josef Blocquerst, impresor de la comisión del Gobierno Frances.   Año 1801.   En 8° M, 53 Ps.

Este precioso folleto lo encontré en la rica biblioteca de mi apreciado amigo el Licenciado D. Elias de Zúñiga (de la Habana), y constituye una joya bibliográfica; pues es, en realidad, el más antiguo folleto que se conserva en estos tiempos de las prensas dominicanas.   En efecto, se cita una *Novena a Nuestra Señora de Netagracia* (Santo Domingo, 1800), que se ha perdido y nadie ha descrito con precisión; y aunque el escritor Moreau de Saint Méry en su *Description topographique de la partie Espagnole de l'isle Saint Domingue* (Philadelphia, 1796) afirma que la imprenta existía en la capital de Santo Domingo en el año acabado de citar, no describe con amplitud ningun impreso de esa época.

No deja de ser curioso el hecho de que los introductores de la imprenta en Cuba y Santo Domingo, Carlos Habré (1720) y Andrés J. Blocquerst (1801) fueron franceses.

Poco después de publicados los "Apuntes" mios apareció la primera y genuina Bibliografía Antillana que hasta ahora ha visto la luz, debida a la pluma de un prolífico autor inglés, Mr. Frank Cundall, y cuyo título es: *Bibliography of the West Indies (excluding Jamaica)*. Kingston Institute of Jamaica, 1909. En 4°, 179 ps.

Este es el primer ensayo que se ha llevado a cabo de una Bibliografía de todas las Antillas, y es sensible que su autor no lo haya ampliado por medio de una segunda edición. Cundall acaba de publicar en colaboración con Mr. Pietersz la interesante obra *Jamaica under the Spaniards* (Kingston, 1919) en la que se encuentran multitus de noticias del todo nuevas.

In 1912 la New York Public Library imprimió una relación de las numerosas obras que contiene esa formidable Biblioteca, con el título de *List of Works relating to the West Indies* (New York, 1912. En 4° M,, 392 ps.); y aunque su propósito no fuera dar a luz una Bibliografía Antillana, de hecho resulta la más nutrida de las hasta ahora publicadas.

Por último, se está imprimiendo en la actualidad una obra importantísmia, escrita por el Catedrático de la Universidad Central de Madrid, el famoso lingüista Dr. Julio Cejador, en cuya obra intitulada *Historia de la Lengua y Literatura Castellana* (Madrid, 1915–1920. Doce vols. en 4°) se incluyen por primera vez en una literatura española los escritores hispano-americanos, y en ella se pueden encontrar referencias a los libros publicados por todos los autores antillanos. Esta obra verdaderamente monumental ha prestado un servicio inestimable a la literatura hispano americana, alcanza hoy a 1907 y se terminará el año próximo con la publicación de dos nuevos volúmenes. El autor ha dedicado el tomo XI "A los ilustres escritores, críticos y poetas (dominicanos) Pedro y Max Henríquez Ureña". Se propone reunir después, en uno o dos tomos, todo lo relativo a los autores de la América Española.

Tales son los trabajos que tratan en conjunto de la Bibliografía Antillana; pero existen otros muchos que se ocupan de cada Antilla en particular, y han aparecido además, numerosas monografías sobre determinados asuntos de cada uno de estos paises. Mencionarlos todos sería hacer este trabajo interminable; pues solo de Cuba podría enumerar mas de cien.

Por este motive me limitaré a señalar algunos de los trabajos más importantes de los publicados en cada Isla.

De Cuba pueden citarse los siguientes:

Domingo Delmonte. Biblioteca Cubana. Habana, 1882. En 4°, 48 ps.

Antonio Bachiller. Catálogo de Libros y Folletos publicados en Cuba de (1720 a 1840). Habana, 1860.

José T. Medina. La Imprenta en la Habana (1707–1810). Santiago de Chile, 1904. En 4°, 200 ps.

A. P. C. Griffin. Books relating to Cuba. Washington, 1905.

Carlos M. Trelles. Bibliografía Cubana (de 1600 a 1916). Matanzas, 1907–1917. Doce volúmenes en 4°.

———— Biblioteca Científica y Geográfica Cubana. Matanzas, 1918–1920. Tres volúmenes en 4°.

José A. Rodríguez García. Bibliografía Gramática y Lexicografía castellanas. Habana, 1903–1913. Dos volúmenes en folio.

Andrés G. Weber. Bibliographia y Biblioiconographia estomatológica. Diez y seis volúmenes.

De Santo Domingo

L. G. Tippenhauer. Die Insel Haiti. Leipzig, 1893. En 4°, M. 693 ps. Menciona al final de la obra numerosos libros de Santo Domingo.

Henry L. Roth. Bibliography and Cartography of Hispaniola. (En Royal Geographical Society, London, 1899.)

Pedro Henríquez Ureña. Cultura antigua de Santo Domingo. ("El Ateneo," Santo Domingo, Nobre, 1910.)

———— Literatura Dominicana. New York, Paris, 1917: En 4° M., 26 ps.

José N. Escoto. Estado intelectual de los cubanos en el siglo XVI. (*Revista Histórica de la Literatura Cubana* 1916.) Con interesantes datos sobre Santo Domingo.

De Puerto Rico

Manuel M. Sama. Bibliografía Puerto-Riqueña. Mayagüez, 1887. En 4°, 156 ps.

Abelardo Morales Ferrer. Bibliografía Puerto-Riqueña (por 1892).

A. P. C. Griffin. A List of Books on Porto Rico. Washington, 1901. En 4° M., 55 ps.

De otras Antillas

Se pueden recordar estos impresos:

Bibligrafía de Haiti (V. Tippenhauer (1893) y en el *Bulletin of the New York Public Library* (1912).

Frank Cundall. Bibliotheca Jamaicensis. Kingston, 1895. En 8° M., 38 ps.

———— Bibliographia Jamaicensis. Kingston, 1902. En 8°, 83 ps.

———— Suplemento a esta obra. Kingston, 1908. En 8° M., 38 ps.

G. Watson Cole. Bermuda in periodical literature. Boston, 1907. 275 ps.

A. P. C. Griffin. A List of Books on the Danish West Indies. Washington, 1901. En 4°, 18 ps.

De esta enumeración se puede deducir que Cuba tiene ya casi completa su bibliografía; la de Puerto Rico se encuentra a medias, y en Santo Domingo sería conveniente que alguno de sus hijos se dedicase a dárnosla a conocer íntegra.

CARLOS M. TRELLES.

[TRANSLATION]

BIBLIOGRAPHY OF THE ANTILLES

I am going to touch lightly upon a theme which has a peculiar interest for those of us who live in this region of the New World, and which has hitherto held the attention of studious men but little.

I refer to the Bibliography of the Antilles, which has had a scarcity of wooers as will be seen immediately.

The first author who must have bestowed any attention on the writers of the Antilles, was, I suppose, the Peruvian, Antonio de León Pinelo, who published his *Epítome de la Biblioteca Oriental, y Occidental, Naútica y Geográfica*, in Madrid, in 1629. This is the first American bibliography to be printed, but I have not had the good fortune to consult it.

It is probable that it mentions several writers of Santo Domingo of the sixteenth century. Puerto Rico had an author in the above mentioned century, namely, Juan Ponce Troche de León (1582), but I doubt very much that he could have come to the attention of Pinelo. Of Cuba, very backward at that epoch, there is no notice of a single writer in the abovesaid century. The first ones, Pedro de la Torres Sifuentes, Juan Rodríguez Sifuentes, and José Hidalgo flourished in 1606 and 1637.

In the second edition of Pinelo's work, published in three folio volumes at Madrid in 1737, by Andrés Gonzáles Barcía, only three Cuban writers are cited, namely, Francisco Dias Pimienta, Ambrosio Zayas Bazán, and the Presbyter Juan Ferro Machado. I do not have that book before me just now, but it will certainly give the names of some Santo Domingans, and perhaps the name of one or two Porto Ricans.

Almost a century later, the famous Mexican bibliographer, José M. Beristaín de Sousa, in his *Biblioteca Hispano-Americana Septentrional* (Mexico, 1816–1819) supplied numerous bits of information relative to the writers of the three Antilles to which I am referring. The aforesaid bibliographer was in Havana in 1789 and probably in 1794, gathering data for his monumental bibliography.

The eminent polygraphist, Don Marcelino Menéndez y Pelayo, the greatest of all Spanish writers of the nineteenth century, in his magnificent work, *Antología de Poetas Hispano-Americanos* (Madrid, 1893) gives close attention to and studies in a masterly way (in volume 2) the poets of the Antilles (those that are sisters by language)—a study which he amplified in the second edition of the aforesaid work which was published under the title *Historia de la Poesía Hispano-Americana* (Madrid, 1911–1913, in two volumes).

The author who writes these humble lines had the satisfaction of placing his grain of sand in the edifice of the Bibliography of the Antilles; for when he publisbed his *Ensayo de Bibliografía Cubana de los Siglos XVII y XVIII*, he added to it a few light "Apuntes para la Bibliografía Dominicana y Portorriqueña" (*i.e.*, "Notes on Santo Domingan and Porto Rican Bibliograpny") in which he pointed out several authors and books not known or forgotten, and had the good fortune to discover one of the earliest pamphlets printed in Santo Domingo, namely, *Estatutos de la Regia y Pontificia Universidad de Santo Thomas de Aquino; en el convento imperial de predicadores de la ciudad de Santo Domingo en la Isla Española.* Santo Domingo in the Printing House of Andrés Josef Blocquerst, printer of the commission of the French Government, 1801. Large 8vo. Pp. 53.

I found this precious pamphlet in the rich library of my estimable friend, Licentiate Don Elias de Zúñiga (of Havana) and it constitutes a bibliographical jewel, for it is, in fact, the oldest pamphlet of the Santo Domingan press to be conserved at the present time. In fact, that pamphlet cites a *Novena a Nuestra Señora de Netegracia* (Santo Domingo, 1800), which has been lost and which no one has exactly described; and although the writer, Moreau de Saint Méry, in his *Description topographique de la partie Espagnole de l'isle Saint Domingue* (Philadelphia, 1796) asserts that the printing press existed in the capital of Santo Domingo in the year just cited, he does not give a full description of any book of that period.

The fact that the introducers of printing into Cuba and Santo Domingo, Carlos Habré (1720) and Andrés J. Blocquerst (1801) were French, can not fail to be considered strange.

A little while after the publication of my "Apuntes", there appeared the first genuine bibliography of the Antilles which has so far been published. It was due to the pen of a prolific English author, Mr. Frank Cundall, and it is entitled *Bibliography of the West Indies (excluding Jamaica)*. Kingston, Institute of Jamaica, 1909. 4to. Pp. 179.

This is the first attempt to be realised of a bibliography of all the Antilles, and it is to be regretted that its author has not amplified it by means of a second edition. Cundall, in collaboration with Mr. Pieterss, has just published the interesting work entitled *Jamaica under the Spaniards* (Kingston, 1919) in which are found many altogether new notices.

In 1912, the New York Public Library printed a list of the numerous works contained in that rich library, under the title *List of Works relating to the West Indies* (New York, 1912, large 4to. Pp. 392). Although its purpose was not to publish a bibliography of the Antilles, it is, in fact, the richest of all those yet published.

Finally, there is now being printed a very important work written by the Catedrático of the Central University of Madrid, the famous linguist, Dr. Julio Cejador. In his work, entitled *Historia de la Lengua y Literatura Castellana* (Madrid, 1915–1920, twelve volumes in 4to) Hispanic American writers are included for the first time in a work on Spanish literature. In this work reference can be found to the books published by all the writers of the Antilles. This truly monumental work has lent an inestimable service to Hispanic American literature. It has now reached down to 1907, and will be finished next year with the publication of two new volumes. The author has dedicated volume XI "To the illustrious writers, critics, and poets (Santo Domingan) Pedro and Max Henríquez Ureña." It is later proposed to collect into one or two volumes everything relating to the authors of Spanish America.

330 THE HISPANIC AMERICAN HISTORICAL REVIEW

Such are the works which treat of the bibliography of the Antilles as a whole. There are many others which treat of each one of the Antilles especially. In addition, a considerable number of monographs have appeared which treat of certain matters of each one of these countries. To mention all of these would make this work interminable, for more than one hundred could be enumerated of Cuba alone.

Consequently I shall limit myself to noting a few of the most important of those works published in each island.

[For this list, see *ante*, p. 327.]

From the above list, one may deduce that Cuba has already almost completed its bibliography. That of Puerto Rico is only about half complete As for Santo Domingo it would be fitting if one of its sons would devote himself to giving us full information of its bibliography.

CARLOS M. TRELLES.

COLOMBIAN LITERATURE[1]

An important New York paper in its review of Mr. Isaac Goldberg's recently published book entitled *Studies in Spanish American Literature*,[2] declares that the lack of knowledge in the United States concerning South American literature is deplorable. Ask any reader, it continues, what he knows of the literature of our southern neighbors, and the reply will be that he hardly supposes they have a literature of their own. On the other hand, what do we South Americans know of the literature of the North? To be sure, we honor the names of Poe, Whitman, Longfellow, but if questioned as to a knowledge of present-day authors, the reply would hardly be more complimentary. In fact, our impression from actual observation of North American life is that every one is too much pre-occupied with business to think of literature. Hence, arises the prevailing conception of South America as a land whose only source of interest is its mine fields. Neither of these replies is entirely true, and therefore a serious effort should be made on both sides, while opportunity is knocking at our doors, to spread a mutual knowledge of what each continent has done and is doing in the world of letters, and thus accomplish an intellectual work of importance.

[1] Lecture delivered in Spanish at Columbia University, New York, March 6, 1920, before the American Association of Teachers of Spanish. The translation into English was made by Señorita Dora Gomes Casseres, a Colombian living in New York.

[2] New York, Brentano's, [°1920]. See a review of this work in this REVIEW, May, 1920, p. 199.

On reviewing the situation, it is encouraging to find that there are certain intellectual groups in the United States seriously occupied in making Hispanic-American literature known, and in teaching our language, actual proof of which we have in the work of the widely known Association of Teachers of Spanish, whom I now have the honor of addressing.

In Colombia little is known as yet of this enterprise, owing to the difference in language and the difficulty of geographical position, as well as to the comparatively recent publication of certain works on the subject. Mr. A. Coester is the author of *The Literary History of Spanish America*,[3] a work which covers the literature of the periods of the Conquest, Colonial occupation, and Independence, as well as that of each separate republic of South America. Prof. J. D. M. Ford of Harvard University published a work last year entitled *Main Currents of Spanish Literature*,[4] which describes the high achievements of literary efforts in the South. Mr. Goldberg's work appears last, a study of our present-day literature, unknown as yet in the United States if we except a few English translations of such representative works of a past period as the Colombian novel, *María*,[5] which has won great popularity.

The Hispanic Society of America has just published a small *Spanish Anthology*[6] which contains English translations of some of the greatest gems of Spanish and South American poetry, revealing at the same time the names of those who have thus interpreted Colombian classics and the "leaders" of the Colombian modernist movement. There we shall find the verses of Rafael Pombo, "Our Madonna at Home", originally written in English, and "At Niagara", translated by Mr. Thomas Walsh; "On the Lips of the Last of the Incas", by Mr. Coester, who styles its author, J. E. Caro, "the Puritan of South American literature"; "Spain and America" by R. Carrasquilla, translated by Roderick Gill; "Eyes" and "The Generalife" by Gómez Restrepo, translated by Mr. Walsh. Here too we shall enjoy in the language of Byron the poems of Silva, "Nocturne", a fine example of the modernist, "A Poem", and "the Serenade"; as well as "Turris Eburnea" and other works by Guillermo Valencia, also translated by Mr. Walsh. The poems of Julio Flórez and Luis C. López are also represented in this anthology.

If through this medium our verse is to become known abroad, we have reason to cherish the same hopes for our prose, seeing that a

---

[3] New York, The Macmillan Co., 1916.
[4] New York, Henry Holt & Co., 1919.
[5] By Jorge Isaacs.
[6] Edited by Thomas Walsh.

recent translation has appeared of the Colombian novel, *Paz*, by Lorenzo Marroquin, a work truly representative of our literature and our local life, this being the first of a contemplated series of English translations of works of this type. This movement will undoubtedly so develop as to enable us, on the other hand, to study, through Spanish translations, the poets and authors of North America and the work done by the Universities and the Hispanic Society, all of which will be an immense contribution to the cause of culture and to the objects of the Pan American Union.

The traditional intellectual culture of Colombia has been synthesised in the name given to Bogotá— "the Athens of South America"—for its culture, according to Menéndez y Pelayo, is "as ancient as the Conquest itself"; and in spite of the various influences of French, English, and German literature, that of Colombia has preserved a peculiarly national form and sentiment, born of its atmosphere, its natural resources, and its history, no less than from the deep roots planted as a rich inheritance by the mother country, Spain, it being an admitted fact that intellectual independence in Colombia was never accomplished. Not Silva himself, who produced some of the most advanced examples of modern thought, has been able to depart from Spanish tradition, nor have Pérez Triana and other representatives of European culture in Colombia, though they have indeed strengthened our position in the modern trend of literature.

The appearance of distinguished authors in New Granada dating as far back as the Conquest, started the work of gradually molding the civic character of the nation, which continued to grow under the influence of the universities and through the study of natural science and jurisdiction during the seventeenth and eighteenth centuries. Don Juan Valera who in his famous *Cartas Americanas* wrote about Colombian literature so as to give an idea, as he expressed it, "of what that nation is and of the importance and significance of its intellectual life", says: "Ever since the New Kingdom of Granada fell under Christian and Spanish influence, poets and historians have abounded. . . . Colombian literature is a part of Spanish literature and will continue so to be as long as Colombia remains what it is".

Not less than the above factors have the beauty and exuberance of its tropical vegetation contributed to this aspect of Colombian letters. The Conquest, involving as it did an immense struggle, produced no literary effort worthy of mention. The conquerors, as Jules Superveille says, stood amazed at the country's native wealth, and remained equally spellbound at the spectacle of a sunset on the banks of the Magdalena. But while the conditions of life gradually grew easier, not only in Nature did Colombian poets find inspiration for beautiful song, but in the haunting sadness of those early colonial cities, their customs and their patriarchal mode of existence. This superiority of Colombian literature, recognized as early as the eighteenth century by Humboldt and other European authorities, has continued undiminished throughout the nineteenth and twentieth centuries. Menéndez y Pelayo has said: "No one can be offended by the statement of a truth so wellknown, namely, that Colombian literature at the present day excels in quality, if not in quantity, that of every other country of the New World." Sr. Valera, after reading the work of the distinguished Argentine, Cané, manifested a desire to know Bogotá which, he said, was "a democratic Republic possessed of an extraordinary facility for verse, . . its poetry is aristocratic, cultured and ornate"; and again, referring to the location of that city, he thus compares it to another in Greek mythology: "Similarly, on learning of the tremendous obstacles to be overcome before reaching Bogotá, and of the subsequent pleasure and delight afforded by the life of Bogotá, I recalled the ancient Greek fable about the country of the Hyperboreans which was only accessible by traversing distant snow-clad mountains, exceedingly perilous and quite beyond the reach of human abodes of any kind. Once past the barbarity and horror of these mountains, however, the traveler found himself amid an excellent community, a privileged people favored of the god Apollo, where hardly a native but sang and played delightfully on the lyre, where beautiful women danced and sang with equal ease and elegance, and all hearts were captivated by their genius and grace."

Ruben Darío too, to quote an impartial observer, has sung our country's praises in a masterly sonnet:

> Colombia es una tierra de leones:
> El esplendor del cielo es su oriflama;
> Tiene un grito perenne, el Tequendama,
> Y un Olimpo divino, sus canciones.[7]

Referring to Bogotá in another study which best displays the original, florid style of this master of modernism, he says, "it is a city long famous for its pursuit of intellectual culture; a city, as it were, both Greek and Latin, which, in spite of its constant touch with the world's progress, has always gloried in a gallant show of past deeds of chivalry and ancient manners; worldly-wise yet ingenuous, sparkling with the cordial graces of a colonial age; versed in the grammar of its language, and endowed

[7] Colombia is a land of lions; the splendor of the sky is its banner; the Tequendama holds a roar eternal, and its songs an Olympus divine.

with the lyric gift, abounding in parchments of the illustrious sons of India, and in learned lawyers and scholars sheltered in their distant midland nook whence never a glimpse of the ocean's blue is to be had . . . . " The marvellous tide of civilization approaches Bogotá nearer each day from Atlantic and Pacific shores, but its fundamental features remain such as Darío in his masterly lines has pictured that city, and may they never be effaced.

Other impartial criticisms from distinguished English writers such as Cunningham Grahame, etc., might now be quoted, but lest your attention be wearied, I shall only recall that of one of the most discussed of South American writers among North American critics, viz. Sr. Blanco Fombona, the Venezuelan, who in one of his most recent works declares that "no country of the South American continent can justly dispute the intellectual supremacy of Colombia". The most learned among recent American writers and critics—Mr. Coester, Mr. Ford, and Mr. Goldberg—are agreed in this opinion, that Mexico, Colombia and Peru are in the vanguard of South American intellectuality.

You will realize from what I have said, ladies and gentlemen of the American Association of Teachers of Spanish, that the study of a literature such as Colombia's is no easy task and it has already been done so admirably by various erudite Spaniards and learned Colombians and other Americans, that all I need to do on this occasion is to review the general outlines of our subject, without invading the field of other scientific investigations which have been and still are being carried on in our country by experts specially appointed in each department.

The renaissance period of the Spanish Peninsula was just beginning toward the end of the sixteenth century, the names of Calderón, Lope, Cervantes, and Quevedo being still unknown, when the firstfruits of our literature began to appear in the then recently discovered New Kingdom of Granada. It would seem that the conquering cavaliers were only waiting to throw off the helmets and swords of their military trappings to pick up the pen and lay the foundations of an enterprise which was destined to a long and glorious career. Unusually striking and interesting is the figure of the founder of Santa Fé de Bogotá, Don Gonzalo Jiménez de Quesada, a soldier and scholar, true type of the Castilian nobility, author of "*Compendio historial de la conquista del Nuevo Reino*" and "*Colección de sermones*", works which unfortunately have been lost and which he wrote during moments of ease from his expeditions. The heroic deeds of that time found their Homer in another discoverer who at the end of the sixteenth century wrote "with the rustic majesty of the primitive poets", the longest poem of the Spanish language, namely Don Juan de Castellanos, a priest of that noble and loyal city called Santiago de Tunja. His works include "Elegias de los varones ilustres de Indias" and "Historia del Nuevo Reino de Granada", which won him a place among Spanish classic writers. This "garrulous old man", as Menéndez y Pelayo calls him, used to gather around him in Tunja a small group of contemporary poets, a practice then common throughout the Viceroyalty among the poet-loving sons of New Granada.

Towards 1554 the government at Madrid established in its new dominions a system of public instruction, founded seats of learning in the convents and village schools for the Indians, as well as colleges and universities in various important cities. At Santa Fé, the capital, the college of El Rosario, holding privileges equal to those at Salamanca, and that of San Bartolomé have always remained the center and cradle of patriotism and Colombian learning.

With this advantage the seventeenth century, though presenting little poetry that was not affected by the Gongorism of the period, produced various notable writers and historians whose works are of recognized importance:—Piedrahita, Padre Simón, Oviedo, Rodríguez Fresle, Zamora; and grammarians such as Lugo, Dadey, Veraix, besides several religious chroniclers. Later came Álvarez de Velasco and the poet, Vélez Ladrón de Guevara, both of high standing.

Towards 1690 appeared by order of her confessors, and written from her convent cell, "in the dignified prose of the sixteenth century" the "Vida" and "Sentimentos espirituales" of Madre Castillo, a rival of the Doctora of Avila, who without the literary defects of her time, has left us an immortal treasure in her beautiful writings. Her prose was limpid and eloquent, and her poetry, though less remarkable, was full of inspiration. Behold a sample of her verse:

> El habla delicada
> Del amante que estimo
> Miel y leche destila
> Entre rosas y lirios.
>
> Su meliflua palabra
> Corta como rocio
> Y en ella florece
> El corazon marchito.[8]

[8] The tender speech of the lover I esteem as honey and milk distilled amid roses and lilies;
Its mellifluous word falls like the dew, and in it blossoms the withered heart.

At the beginning of the eighteenth century appeared D. Francisco Álvarez de Velasco y Zorrilla, a Bogotá poet, who was perhaps the only representative of poetic culture at that period when, as in Europe, a scientific rather than a literary movement was sweeping all over New Granada, "which seemed to place it at a single bound at the head of all the other American countries, not excluding Mexico". This period during the second half of the eighteenth century was known in Colombia as that of the *Botanical Expedition*, an Institution founded in 1782 by the Archbishop Viceroy, Caballero y Gongora, by order of the government at Madrid. It was this movement which marked the true beginning of that intellectual life which produced a brilliant array of naturalists and writers, geographers and botanical researchers headed by D. José Celestino Mutis, the director of the Expedition, "a giant in science and virtue", to quote Caldas, whose name shines forth brilliantly in the annals of Colombian science, liberty, and martyrdom.

Inseparable from the record of that period is the figure of Baron Humboldt at Sante Fé in the year 1802, whose interest in the scientific movement in the New Kingdom led him to seek permission of the Royal Crown to go to visit its vast dominions. Great was the surprise of the German sage to find in that corner of the Andes an intellectual center of such perfection, and greater still his appreciation of Caldas, who was then revealing his creative genius in Popayan. At the same period D. Jorge Tadeo Lozano, marquis of San Jorge, wrote among other things *La fauna cundinamarqueza;* and various other writers published scientific memoirs in the *Semanario* of Caldas, whose scientific fame was closely seconded by such men as D. Francisco A. Zea, subsequently Vice-President of Colombia; D. Camilo Torres, the Demosthenes of New Granada; and D. Antonio Nariño, the forerunner, as it were, of the whole scientific movement.

These men of genius in their sublime endeavor brought forth scientific questions which prove the intellectual temper of the colony to have been not, as many have supposed, clouded over by ignorance, but decidedly scientific, a characteristic which was stimulated by the universities as far as the resources of the times permitted. By far the most illustrious of these men was Caldas, "the ever regrettable victim of the ignorant ferocity of a soldier to whom in an evil hour Spain entrusted the pacification of its overseas colonies", to quote the author of *Heterodoxos Españoles,*[9] who also opined that "that country owes

[9] M. Menéndez Pelayo.

to Caldas a monument in expiation". In him we have combined the geographer, botanist, astronomer, and physicist; explorer also he was, and director of the observatory of Santa Fé, dean and director of the *Semanario*, a publication including pages "worthy of Buffon, Chavanis or Humboldt". As a republican he gave distinguished service to the cause of independence, and was shot on October 29th, 1816, a day on which, as the historian, Acosta, has fitly expressed it, "tropical nature veiled herself with a funeral robe".

Similar to the fashion then prevailing in France and Spain, towards 1800 literary circles called "Tertulias" became popular at Santa Fé, the most notable being that of Doña Manuela Santamaría de Manríque, called "Buen Gusto", whither flocked during the evening the literary youth of Santa Fé. A number of distinguished writers appeared at that time, among whom might be mentioned D. Manuel del Socorro Rodríguez, librarian and dean of Colombian journalism, editor of *Papel Periódico de la Ciudad de Santa Fé*, an author of various works; and D. Francisco Javier Caro, the satirist, father of D. José Eusebio, and grandfather of D. Miguel Antonio. He wrote stanzas of scathing irony against persons of note, and that curious *Diario de la Secretaría del Virreinato*".

This period also witnessed the rise of the theatre in Bogotá, beginning with the production of *El Zagal*, by D. José Miguel Montalvo, who later became a martyr to the Republic.

With the approach of the nineteenth century, the colleges and the Botanical Expedition began to pour forth numbers of brilliant young men destined before long to take their part in the tragic scene of the Revolution for Independence which came to interrupt the tranquillity of colonial life, and to usher in a period of strife and bloodshed which culminated in the final triumph of Boyacá in 1819. During the first period of republican life, beginning on July 20th, 1810, known by the name of "Patria Boba" (slow country), literary production was almost at a standstill; barely a few patriotic hymns were written in honor of the conquerors. During the reconquest of 1816, D. José de Torres y Peña, the realistic writer, wrote a long poem entitled "Santa Fé cautiva", which was destined to blacken the republican cause even then practically defeated. It seems more interesting from the historical than from the literary viewpoint, and contains much interesting data. With the victory of Boyacá, August 7, 1819, the republican system of government became established. Since then Colombia has led an uninterrupted life of political intensity which, nevertheless, has not interfered with its intellectual development, seeing that many of the leaders of its political conflicts, who have also held the presidential chair, have been poets and writers.

The intellectual movement during a century of independent life may be thus divided: the first period, which produced only three notable poets, for the true songsters of those glorious days were the Venezuelan, Bello, and the Ecuadorian, Olmedo; then with the rise of the Grand Republic of 1831, came the beginning of the Romantic period, lasting through two generations and destined to a long career; and lastly, the reaction, bringing in the realistic school with its two aspects of festive verse and sketches of national customs. Between the years 1870 to 1890 a group of notable poets appeared, and the Academy of Language associated with that of Spain, launched forth its glorious work over the continent, the fruits of which were shown in those two brilliant representatives of·the Spanish tongue, Caro and Cuervo. About 1886 arose another generation of poets educated in the ruling tastes of the Peninsula, already tending toward that modernism which was to appear with the twentieth century. The remaining part of the present century calls attention to two important phases of literature: the poetic, already so deeply rooted; and the historic, with its modern methods of research and impartial criticism, the old prejudices against Spain, for the most part ill-founded, having now worn away, giving place in the new light of experience to a new estimate of the glories of the fatherland without, however, forgetting those points that a distributive justice would still retain.

Three names which New Granada contributed to the poetic literature of Greater Colombia were José María Salazar, Fernández Madrid, and Vargas Tejada. Salazar's earliest efforts appeared towards the decline of the colonial period, and in 1804 he wrote the romance entitled, *El placer público de la Nueva Granada*, in honor of Viceroy Amar. He also rendered distinguished service as a diplomat, and sang in poems of epic style the "Victoria de Boyacá" and "La Colombiada". In Venezuela he wrote biographies of the martyrs of 1816, giving valuable historical data. His work is influenced by the pseudo-classic school of the eighteenth century, as seen in his youthful composition, "El soliloquio de Aeneas" and "El sacrificio de Idomeneo".

It fell to the lot of Fernández Madrid to chant the funeral hymns of our country in 1816. His personality has been much discussed, though there is no question as to the literary value of his work. He sang with exquisite feeling the sentiments of the home, and he proclaimed the glories of Bolívar in a manner which aroused much severe criticism. His ode to the Nations of Europe and his poem "La Hamaca" are well known, also his two tragedies *Atala* and *Guatimoc*.

Vargas Tejada was among the most celebrated writers of the new republic, both for his vast culture and for the passionate devotion of a short life to politics, which drew him among the number of conspirators of 1828. He wrote verses in French and poems of exquisite beauty such as "El anochecer". Of his dramatic productions, *Las Convulsiones* was played in Bogotá as recently as 1916. Vargas was called the Colombian Chenier, and his life ended unhappily by the unknown shores of a distant river. "The death of this genius", says Sr. Menéndez, "marks a pause in the literary history of Colombia". However two other names of mark should in justice be mentioned namely, D. Andres Marroquín, the festive poet, and García del Río. The latter, according to Sr. Gómez Restrepo, was the "trade d'union" between Greater Colombia and New Granada, a man of international renown who left an historic record in the impassioned pages of his *Meditaciones colombianas*.

French influence brought the wave of romanticism to our shores. It is difficult to describe in words the significance of José Eusebio Caro, one of the greatest lyric poets of Spanish America, "whose life and works give the most vivid impression of genius." He threw himself eagerly into the struggle against materialistic philosophy. His verses, though unpolished as to form, are a sublime expression of the brilliant inspiration he drew from the universal themes of poetry. His stormy but exemplary life gave evidence of civic virtues which made him "a greater man than poet". To his lot fell the leadership of the opposition against the tyranny of French radicalism introduced into Colombia in 1849, in which year he was banished from the country and came to the United States whose institutions he admired and eulogized in his poem entitled, "La libertad y el socialismo":

> Eso es la libertad: la que he previsto
> Entre los raptos de mi ardiente edad;
> La que en la tierra de Franklyn he visto,
> La que ofrece en sus promesas Cristo;
> Eso es la libertad![10]

[10] That is Liberty: that which I have foreseen in the visions of my ardent youth, which I have seen in the land of Franklin, which Christ in his promises offers—that is Liberty!

Next in order was Julio Arboleda, poet and soldier, a typical cavalier of the golden age of Spain, whose turbulent, romantic life found expression in poems which, to quote the illustrious critic above named, "bear the odor of dust", and "appear rather like the roaring of lions than as works of art". Such is the impression given by the poems "Estoy en la Carcel", "Escenas democráticas", "El congreso granadino", and others. His fragmentary work, "Gonzalo de Oyon" is the finest example of South American poetry in epic narrative sytle.

Master of the classic ode, lyricist and catholic controversialist, a delicate singer of the sentiments of village churchyards and colonial cities, was D. José Joaquín Ortiz. In verses worthy of Quintana and Querol he sang the glories of Bolívar and Colombia:

> Oh, la bandera de la patria es santa
> Flote en las manos que flotare![11]

These three greatest figures at the beginning of the romantic period were closely followed by D. José María Samper, one of the most prolific writers in South America; D. J. M. Torres Caicedo, of high literary standing in Europe; D. Manuel M. Madiedo, author of the poem translated and published in English by Agnes Blake Poor, under the title of "The Guaili" in a book of *Pan-American Poems*.[12] Dr. Madiedo also wrote various interesting studies in politics and philosophy.

The middle of the century brought other distinguished representatives of the same school of literature: Rafael Pombo, Rafael Nuñez, and Jorge Isaacs, all influenced largely by the English school. Pombo was the most complete of the poets of Colombia; his lyric utterances were sublime and humorous, mystic and erotic, satirical and descriptive. The falls of Niagara inspired him no less than his native falls of Tequendama, the waters of the Hudson no less than those of the Magdalena river, and the artisocratic blondes of Broadway no less than the "ñapangas" of Popayan:

> Ñapangas que por modelo
> Las quisiera un escultor . . . .

His fables in verse for children are an immortal gift to the mothers of Colombia. Other fables he wrote and translations from the ancient Latin classics which, in a beautiful and masterly manner, preserve the

---

[11] O! the flag of my country is sacred, let it float in whose hands it may!
[12] Boston, the Gorham Press, 1918.
[13] Rustic beauties whom for models a sculptor well might wish . . . .

tones of his own magic lyricism. I take particular pleasure in here noting that it was in New York towards the year 1859 that Pombo spent the most brilliant period of his life, and reached the highest flights of his inspiration. It was then he wrote the poem, "A las norteamericanas en Broadway", a passionate and at the same time humorous tribute to the belles of Broadway:

> Oh! cada hermosa es una amable autócrata;
> Ley sus sonrisas, sus palabras ley,
> Y una marcha triunfal entre sus súbditos
> Cada excursión por la imperial Broadway.
>
> . . . .
>
> Lindas como esos iris, risa falas del Niagara;
> Vagas como ellos y caprichosas;
> Efímeras como ellos,
> Crueles cual ese abismo de aguas y cadáveres
> Que erisa los cabellos . . . .
> Y asi atrayentes, vertiginosas.[14]

Unexcelled in philosophic and erotic verse, energetic and sententious in style, was Rafael Nuñez, a distinguished name associated with the most important political and administrative reorganization of Colombia, despite the fact that his life was continually tormented by doubt, which vented itself in such outbursts as, "Que sais-je?", according to Mr. Coester "one of the most skeptical poems that has ever been written":

> Oh confusión, Oh caos! Quién pudiera
> Del sol de la verdad la lumbre austera
> Y pura en este limbo hacer brillar!
> De lo cierto y lo incierto, quién un día,
> Y del bien y del mal, conseguiría
> Los límites fijar![15]

Jorge Isaacs achieved immortal literary fame with his novel *Maria*, the most popular and charming of South American novels, which has been translated into several languages. Not only in prose did his

[14] O! each Beauty is a lovable autocrat: her smiles are the law, her words are the law: a triumphal march among her subjects is each excursion through imperial Broadway. . . . .
Beautiful as those rainbows, laughter false of Niagara; vague and capricious like them; like them ephemeral, as cruel as that abyss of waters and dead bodies which raise the hair . . . . fascinating, vertiginous.

[15] O confusion, O chaos! Who shall be able to make the stern, pure light of the Sun of Truth shine in this limbo! Of certainty and uncertainty, of good and evil, who shall ever fix the limits!

romanticism find expression, but also in beautiful poems of deep sentiment.   Worthy of mention among the so-called minor romantic poets
were German Gutiérrez de Piñeros, and Lázaro M. Pérez, and of novelists of the already decadent school of fiction, Angél M. Galan, whose
work, *El Doctor Temis* appeared in 1850.   False imitators of Zorilla
urged on the advance of the realistic school expressed in poems of festive verse and sketches of national customs.   The earliest representative was Gregorio Gutiérrez González, a poet of ineffable charm, who
sang of his loves, his griefs, and his patriotic ardor in simple, popular
verses which recall one's infancy:

> Hoy tambien de ese techo se levanta
> Blanco-azulado el humo del hogar;
> Ya ese fuego lo enciende mano extraña,
> Ya es agena la casa paternal.
>
> . . . .
>
> Infancia, juventud, tiempos tranquilos,
> Visiones de placer, sueños de amor,
> Heredad de mis padres, hondo rio,
> Casita blanca . . . . . y esperanza, adios![16]

The Spanish taste for sketches of national customs found fruitful
ground in Colombia, where a literary center was soon established called,
"El Mosaico", which published a review of the same name in Bogotá
in 1865.   The following are among those who cultivated this delightful species of literature: José María Vergara y Vergara, who also wrote
La Historia de la Literatura de la Nueva Granada; José Caicedo Rojas,
the *"Mesonero Romanos"*, of Colombia; and the reincarnation, as it were,
of the patriarchal period of Santa Fé; Juan de Dios Restrepo, pupil
of Larra, who under the pseudonym of Emiro Kastos wrote one
of our most prized volumes, *Recuerdos y Apuntamientos;* Ricardo Silva,
father of José Asunción Silva, similar in some respects to Restrepo;
José David Guarín, prominent as a social critic; Eugenio Díaz, author
of *Manuela*, an admirable picture of rural life in Colombia; and Manuel
Pombo, distinguished author of poems, travels, and social anecdotes.
More renowned even were José Manuel Marroquín, and Ricardo Carrasquilla.   The work of the former, according to one of hiscritics, "gives

---

[16] Today too from that roof rises the bluish-white smoke of the hearth-fire; now
the stranger's hand kindles that fire, now strangers occupy the paternal home,

. . . .

Infancy, youth, tranquil days, visions of pleasure, dreams of love, heritage of
my fathers, deep river, little white house. . . . . . and hope, adieu!

the impression of a winter landscape". The latter's contributions to festive verse, to the novel, and to valuable works on classic education, are enduring; while his conservatism, his gift for oratory, and his famous "Sofismos anticatólicos vistos con microscopio," bespeak high merit. To this group of writers also belong Joaquín Pablo Posada and César Conto, poets both satiric and graceful, the former an improviser, and the latter a translator of Byron, and author of *Apuntes sobre la lengua inglesa.*[17]

Previous to the establishment of the Academy of Language mentioned above, which marked an event of great significance, many interesting works on politics, history, geography, international affairs, legislation, and other subjects, had been written by various authors of determined and often opposite ideas, whose political and intellectual personality appeared to be almost inseparable. Poets too were not lacking at that period, but these we must pass over in order to speak of the more recent history of the Academy. I have already mentioned it as one of the most reputable and scholarly institutions of the Spanish language in Colombia. The date of its foundation is one of the greatest in our annals, for it has always held, and even today holds highest the banner of science and patriotism in Colombia. My study would be incomplete without it, and without the names of those who have honored its chairs even in the past: Rufino José Cuervo, "the most distinguished philologist of the Spanish race in the nineteenth century"; Miguel Antonio Caro; Rafael Nuñez; Sergio Arboleda; Venancio G. Manríque; Liborio Zerda; Rafael Uribe Uribe; Carlos Calderón; Martínez Silva; Ruperto S. Gómez; and others. Its present director, Rafael M. Carrasquilla, "la primera ilustración y la primera virtud de Colombia", as Sr. Caro describes him; and Marco Fidel Suárez, the distinguished grammarian, humanitarian, and scholar who now presides over the destinies of the nation; Antonio Gómez Restrepo, renowned critic and poet; Hernando Holguín y Caro; Miguel Abadia Méndez; José Joaquín Casas; Guillermo Camacho; Ismael E. Arcimegas; Martín Restrepo Mejía; Diego R. de Gúzman; Emiliano Isaza; and a few others;—these constitute our "forty immortals", as they say in France.

Together with the founding of the Academy arose another center of art and poetry, and history and music, directed by Alberto Urdaneta, founder of the School of Fine Arts, director in 1887 of the *Papel Periódico Ilustrado* which contains literary masterpieces from the pen of notable men whose names are to be found in the *Romancero colombiano*, then published in honor of the great Liberator.

[17] That is, *Notes on the English Language.*

The appearance of *La Lira Nueva* introduced another generation of poets whose work was noticeably influenced by Núñez de Arce and Becquer. Two names stand out among its large number of inspired contributors, to the latter of whom Mr. Goldberg devotes several pages in his *Studies in Spanish-American Literature*, namely Julio Florez, the romantic disciple of Espronceda and Zorrilla, whose verses display "all the fire and reflected images of a tropical sun"; and José Ascunción Silva, who "would have disputed with Ruben Darío the leadership of the modernist school of poetry in Spain and South America", if he had not at so early an age taken his own life.

With these illustrious names we now arrive at the height of the modernist movement. Toward the close of the past century, French literature began to present an aspect of intense and astonishing renovation, which soon spread its influence through the writings of the "sad old father", Verlaine, and Baudelaire, into the domain of the Castilian tongue, where the movement was heralded by Ruben Darío, and to which, as Mr. Coester says, "Colombia had the honor of contributing in the person of José Ascunción Silva". Of a refined spirit molded both by France and by his own native Bogotá, with touches of English and North American inspiration, a strong admirer of Poe and Whitman, this original and unique singer, simple yet profound, was one of those poets whose work continues from day to day to emphasize those particular features which have given it a high place in the world of letters and art. Silva was born, as Victor M. Londoño says,

> Para llevar sobre la frente rosas,
> Para besar las frentes de las diosas
> Bajo los sacros pórticos de Atenas.[18]

The name of Londoño figures among the list of our present-day poets. With a particular taste for Greek art and literature, the perfection of his few but striking productions has won him a distinguished place among contemporary writers, while he has also unquestionably the gifts of a critic and a diplomat. Other names are Guillermo Valencia, the superb master of verse and lover of Greek tradition; Max Grillo, famous for his poems, "En Espiral," "Al Magdalena," etc., his dramas and critical and historical studies; Angél M. Céspedes, whose genius and style are of the French order, an "enfant prodigue" recognized by Rostand; Alfredo Gómez Jaime, whose "Rimas del Trópico" and other

---

[18] To wear roses on his brow, to kiss the brows of goddesses beneath the sacred porches of Athens.

verses exhibit a quick imagination and fine poetic gifts; Cornelio Hispano, historian and critic who wrote "Elegias caucanas"; Ricardo Nieto, a singer of the Valle section; Eduardo Castillo, profound connoisseur of foreign literature; Martínez Mutis, winner of two prize contests at Paris and Madrid; Victor E. Caro, who recalls the glories of his ancestors in masterly sonnets; Daniel Arias Argaez, representing the culture of Bogotá; Rivas Frade, immortalised by his composition, "Como se aléja el tren . . . ."; Carlos Villafañe, a chronicler of fine equipment; G. Manríque Terán; Samuel Velásquez, poet and novelist; and a group of younger men whose faith and enthusiasm are already pointing towards a future of glorious days. Critical opinion which is closely watching their progress, observes that they show certain distinct tendencies without, however, marking a definite path; but this apparent contradiction is explained both by the disuse into which the so-called "decadent" modernists have fallen, and by our present state of civilization which seems, in a diversity of forms, to be going through a painful crisis leading towards surprising issues which a not too distant future will reveal. Whatever these results may be, as Dr. Gómez Restrepo observes, the peculiar features of our Colombian poetry are not to be lost in reaching toward the morrow's needs.

Aside from poetic writers, other forms of literature are represented by contemporary authors such as Emilio Cuervo Márquez and Alfredo Ramas Urdaneta, novelists and intellectual co-workers; Gustavo and Hernando Santos, whose literary reviews and contributions to the daily press show a knowledge of foreign literature and art criticism; Tomás Rueda Vargas, whose book, *Sabana de Bogota*, has recently appeared; and a group of essayists, journalists and other novelists. In the theatrical field much fruitful work has been accomplished by the "Sociedad de Autores," chief among whom are: Antonio Álvarez Lleras, Ricardo Rivas, Miguel S. Valencia, Pedro Gómez Corena, and Carlos Castello.

A few months ago in Bogotá occurred the death of a prominent person whose name symbolises a significant movement in the field of national history. I refer to Dr. Pedro M. Ibáñez, permanent secretary of the Academy of History, author of *Crónicas de Bogota*, and one of the last representatives of the period of Urdaneta's *Papel Periódico Ilustrado*, a gentle master, with a deep respect for historical truth. I take this opportunity to express once more the profound grief his death has caused us.

History was recorded by the few chroniclers of the Conquest during the early colonial period; at the beginning of the Republic, by José Manuel Restrepo, J. M. Groot, Plaza; "Memoirs" were written by distinguished persons such as Santander, Posada Gutiérrez, López, Obando, and Espinosa, followed by chronicles of lesser importance. At that time there prevailed a strong feeling against Spain, since documentary evidences were not sought among the archives, and its rule in the South was of recent date. Almost all the work of that time, though patriotic in spirit, was written with a passion for politics which dominated the entire imagination and activities of the time. In 1902, the Academy of History was formed, and a few years later debates on the same subject took place at the Colegio del Rosario. The directors of the Academy are Restrepo Tirado, Diego Mendoza, Eduardo Zuleta, Tulio Ospina, Cuervo Márquez, Eduardo Posada, Francisco José Urrutia, José Joaquín Guerra, Gerardo Arrubla, J. D. Monsalve, Adolfo León Gómez and others who, in encouraging research liberally, continue to arouse and win the enthusiastic support of the youthful prize-winners of the Rosario contests. Thus throughout the Republic, the Academy, far from being considered narrow-minded, is acknowledged as an active, progressive center whose doors are open wide to all lovers of history irrespective of difference of creed. It will suffice to name from its exhaustive list of publications only the most important among them, namely: *La Biblioteca de Historia nacional,* numbering more than twenty volumes; the *Archivo del General Santander,* volumes equalling in proportions the *Memorias de O'Leary; La Conquista y Colonización de Colombia,* by E. Restrepo Tirado; *La Vida de Márquez,* by Carlos Cuervo Márquez; volumes on bibliography by Eduardo Posada; *Páginas de Historia diplomática,* by Dr. Urrutia; *La Vida de Miranda,* written in English by Professor Robertson of the University of Illinois, and translated by Dr. Diego Mendoza, author of *La Expedición Botánica* and *Memorias de Aquileo Parra,* only the first volume of which has thus far been published. *El Album de Boyacá* by Dr. C. L. Peñuela, was published last year, and a very vigorous work, *Historia Contemporánea de Colombia,* by Gustavo Arboleda, has recently appeared. Raimundo Rivas, now president of the Academy, wrote *Historia de las Relaciones de los Estados Unidos con Colombia,* and some brilliant character sketches of such persons as Mosquera and Fernández Madrid, and of such romantic figures as Viceroy Solís. His interest in genealogical research is also shared by José María Restrepo Saenz who inherited from the historian, Restrepo, the gift of accuracy and minuteness of detail in giving personal data; Luis Augusto Cuervo, who published the *Archivo de D. Rufino Cuervo*, and in the style of Lenotre and Mason, has written brilliant pages on Bolívar; Fabio Lozano y Lozano, who in original, graceful style wrote his valuable work, *El Maestro del Libertador* and various other biographical studies; Roberto Cortazar; Álvaro Uricoechea; Gabriel Porras Troconis; B. Matos Hurtado; Arturo Quijano; E. Otero D'Acosta; and others—all engrossed in unearthing relics of the past and renewing the glories of our country, with the motto of the Academy ever before them: *Veritas ante omnia*.

Ruben Darío in his charming, flowery language bequeathed us this phrase: "Colombia is the land of verses and of emeralds." We pray the muses that the serene fountains of Colombia's inspiration and learning may be as exhaustless as are the precious mines which reach far down beneath the soil of our country!

NICOLAS GARCÍA SAMUDIO,
Of the Colombian Academy of History.

NOTES

ITEMS ON HISPANIC AMERICA PUBLISHED IN COMMERCE REPORTS JANUARY–MARCH, 1921

Advice to Cuban shippers. No. 24, January 29.

American company awarded wireless contract in Honduras. No. 60, March 15.

American company in Paraguay to extend its activities. No. 44, February 23.

American consulate at Bahia Blanca to be closed. No. 3, January 5.

American mining concern in French and Dutch Guiana. No. 44, February 23.

American trade with Colon. No. 38, February 15.

Annual trade and economic review of Honduras. No. 50, March 2.

Id. of Jamaica. No. 51, March 3.

Id. of Mexico. No. 67, March 23.

Areas sown to leading crops in Argentina. No. 4, January 6.

Argentine crop estimates. No. 12, January 15.

Argentina's exports during 1920. No. 54, March 8.

Authorization of additional paper money issue in Brazil. No. 13, January 17.

Authorization of Brazilian preferential tariff on United States goods.
No. 3, January 5.

Authorization of loan signed by president of Chile.   No. 18, January 22.

Automobile show in Mexico City.   No. 48, February 28.

Bahia cacao shipments.   No. 38, February 15.

Bakeries and baking machinery in Buenos Aires.   No. 33, February 9.

Bank notes to be circulated in Paraguay.   No. 24, January 29.

Bids asked for construction of customhouse and wharf at Guayaquil.
No. 11, January 14.

Bids requested for electrification of Chilean railway.   No. 59, March 14.

Bolivian commerce in recent years.   No. 57, March 11.

Brazilian budget law for 1921.   No. 70, March 26.

Brazilian exports for the year 1920.   No. 43, February 21.

Brazilian government to aid in railway improvements.   No. 9, January
12.

Brazilian protection of trade-marks registered through the Habana
bureau.   No. 19, January 24.

Canadian steamship service with Jamaica.   No. 67, March 23.

Cassava farine available in Trinidad.   No. 71, March 28.

Cessation of work on public improvements in Dominican Republic.
No. 46, February 25.

Chicle industry in Campeche, Mexico.   No. 61, March 16.

Chilean company places order for German trucks.   No. 7, January 10.

Chilean nitrate statistics for November, 1920.   *Id.*

Closing of bank in Mexico City.   No. 3, January 5.

Closing of banks in Mexico.   No. 6, January 8.

Coffee shipments from Maracaibo.   No. 34, February 10, and No. 61,
March 16.

Commercial handbook on Paraguay.   No. 13, January 17.

Concession for construction of port works at Progreso.   No. 31, February 7.

Conditional exemption of cereals from Argentine export surtax.   No.
67, March 23.

Conditions in Habana harbor.   No. 8, January 11, and No. 70, March
26.

Congestion in Habana harbor almost eliminated.   No. 63, March 18.

Construction of new pier and sewerage system at Arica, Chile.   No.
50, March 2.

Continued depression of the nitrate market in Chile.   No. 11, January
14.

Continued improvement in Habana harbor conditions. No. 29, February 4, and No. 42, February 19.

Contract awarded for completion of Bolivian railway. No. 55, March 9.

Cotton production in Venezuela. No. 58, March 12.

The crisis of the association of agriculturists in Ecuador. No. 52, March 5.

Crude rubber exports from Brazil in January. No. 66, March 22.

Cuba-Jamaica passenger service. No. 34, February 10.

Customs receipts at Puerto Plata, Dominican Republic. Id.

Declared exports from Arica, Chile, to United States. No. 21, January 26.

Declared exports from Bahia to United States, for 1920. No. 34, February 10.

Declared exports from the Guianas. No. 69, March 25.

Decongestion of Habana harbor practically accomplished. No. 59, March 14.

Economic and financial situation in the Dominican Republic. No. 17, January 21.

Economic conditions in Colombia. No. 47, February 26.

Economic and trade notes from Chile. No. 46, February 25.

Economic program of new Chilean administration. No. 47, February 26.

Ecuadorian trade review. No. 13, January 17.

Ecuador's declared exports to the United States. No. 70, March 26.

Electrification of Brazilian railways. No. 3, January 5.

Establishment of postal money order system in Dominican Republic. No. 29, February 4.

Exchange rate on Brazilian money. No. 61, March 16.

Explosives imported by Uruguay. No. 68, March 24.

Export of crude rubber from Brazil and Peru in December. No. 57, March 11.

Exportation of lumber and timber from Brazil. No. 36, February 12.

Exports from Montevideo in 1920. No. 61, March 16.

Exports from Port Limon, Costa Rica, to United States. No. 70, March 26.

Extension of moratorium in Cuba. No. 2, January 4.

Favorable conditions for outlook in Habana harbor. No. 23, January 28.

Fire insurance carried by merchants in Central and South American countries. No. 27, February 2.

Fish supplies in Tabasco, Mexico. No. 17, January 21.

Foreign tariffs. No. 21. January 26 (Cuba, Mexico and Uruguay); No. 27, February 2 (Uruguay); No. 31, February 7 (Panama and Uruguay); No. 33, February 9 (Chile, Cuba, Mexico, Paraguay); No. 45, February 24 (Chile, Colombia, Ecuador, Guatemala, Peru, and Salvador); No. 53, March 7 (Mexico and Panama); No. 61, March 16 (Chile, Dominican Republic, Mexico, and Paraguay); No. 73, March 30 (Venezuela).

Foreign trade of Peru. No. 9, January 12.

German competition in Latin American markets. No. 28, February 3.

Grinding of sugar crop in Dominican Republic delayed. No. 52, March 5.

Guadeloupe's coffee, cocoa, and vanilla crops. No. 7, January 10.

Guadeloupe's vanilla crop. No. 42, February 19.

The henequen situation in Mexico. No. 59, March 14.

Hygienic houses for Paraguayan workers. No. 29, February 4.

Immediate outlook for American trade in Chile. No. 71, March 28.

Imports of automobiles into Uruguay. No. 22, January 27.

Improved health conditions in Vera Cruz, Mexico. No. 36, February 12.

Imports into Paraguay since 1916. No. 66, March 22.

Improvements in port facilities at Santiago de Cuba. No. 42, February 19.

Income of the Rio de Janeiro customhouse in 1920. No. 32, February 8.

Increased import duties in Chile. No. 50, March 2.

Industrial yarns, threads, and twine in Argentine. *Id.*

Influence of gold exportations upon Colombian exchange. No. 25, January 31.

Installation of electric light plant in Dominican Republic. No. 37, February 14.

Installation of wireless stations in Venezuela. No. 21, January 26.

Internal dairy exhibits to be held in Argentina. No. 74, March 31.

Investment of Argentine capital since 1914. No. 7, January 10.

Investments on Venezuelan resources. No. 71, March 28.

Jamaica's export trade in January. No. 62, March 17.

Latin American markets for optical goods. No. 1, January 3.

Laws of Cuba with respect to personal property. No. 17, January 21.

Liquidation of French loan by Bolivia. No. 10, January 13.

Lists of Chilean firms available. No. 16, January 20.

Lists of importers in Dominican Republic. No. 26, February 1.

Id. in Nicaragua. No. 74, March 31.

Id. in Paraguay. No. 7, January 10.

Lumber markets and timber resources of Mexico. No. 51, March 3.

Lumber markets in Latin America. No. 9, January 12.

Manufacture of lamp wicks and elastic webbing in Argentina. No. 11, January 14.

Manufacture of soap in Argentina. No. 41, February 18.

Manufacture of soft hats in Argentina. No. 58, March 12.

Manufacture of toilet preparations in Argentina. No. 43, February 21.

Market for American hardware in Paraguay. No. 47, February 26.

Market for internal combustion engines in Argentina. No. 29, February 4.

Market for playing cards in Mexico. No. 25, January 31.

Market for silk and cotton thread in Argentina. No. 1, January 3.

Market for spark plugs in Argentina and Brazil. No. 18, January 22.

Market for tractors and agricultural machinery in Chile. No. 50, March 2.

Market in Guatemala for bathroom and kitchen equipment. No. 10, January 13.

Markets to certain Latin-American countries. No. 31, February 7.

Mexican export duty on chicle. No. 57, March 11.

Id. on copper. No. 12, January 15.

Mexico to purchase railroad equipment. No. 23, January 28.

Motor-bus service for Curacao. No. 27, February 2.

Monthly cable service (cables on financial and general conditions from Argentina, Brazil, Chile, Mexico, and Peru). No. 7, January 10; No. 32, February 8; and No. 55, March 9.

Moratorium extended in Paraguay. No. 1, January 3.

More encouraging outlook in situation at Habana. No. 18, January 22.

Movement for a uniform currency for British Guiana and the West Indies. No. 71, March 28.

Municipal purchase of local water-works in Puerto Plata. No. 33 February 9.

Name of American company awarded Bolivian contract incorrect. No. 57, March 11.

Necessity for immediate sale in Habana. No. 47, February 26.

New building for cable company in Cristobal. No. 27, February 2.
New customs regulations in Honduras. No. 65, March 21.
New records for Panama Canal traffic. No. 7, January 10.
New Scandinavian-Argentine bank. No. 1, January 3.
New steamship service between Marseille and South America. No. 21,
    · January 26.
Id., between New York and the Dominican Republic. No. 8, January
    11.
Id., to South America. No. 23, January 28.
New telegraph lines in Venezuela. No. 31, February 7.
New wharves at Santa Marta, Colombia. *Id.*
Norwegian paving blocks for Cuba. No. 9, January 12.
Notes from Brazil. No. 73, March 30.
Official estimates of livestock in Argentina. No. 32, February 8.
Opportunity for development of Guatemalan pineapple industry.
    No. 41, February 18.
Paraguay as a market for American flour. No. 65, March 21.
Paraguayan government obtains Argentine wheat. No. 30, February
    5.
Payment of obligations incurred during Cuban moratorium. No. 55,
    March 9.
Peruvian banking statistics. No. 4, January 6.
Peruvian copper production for four years. No. 67, March 23.
The petroleum industry in Venezuela. No. 37, February 14.
Port tonnage for Cienfuegos for 1920. No. 12, January 15.
Postponement of Argentine exposition. No. 42, February 19.
Postponement of conversion of paper money in Chile. No. 1, January
    3.
Practice of handling bills of exchange in Peru. No. 14, January 18.
Present conditions in Habana harbor. *Id.*
Present economic situation in Mexico. No. 22, January 27.
The present unfavorable for immigration to Mexico. No. 18, January
    22.
Production of blackstrap molasses in Cuba. No. 52, March 5.
Progress of the air service in Ecuador. No. 69, March 25.
Projected dredging of Magdalena River by German firm. No. 16,
    January 20.
Projected oil concessions in Argentina. No. 40, February 17.
Proposals for stimulation of Brazilian coffee exports to the United
    States. No. 71, March 28.

Removal of Argentine export duty on wool and skins. No. 29, February 4.

Renewal of Brazilian preference to certain American goods. No. 58, March 12.

Renewed activity in manganese mines in Argentina. No. 19, January 24.

Reopening of bank of London and Mexico. No. 46, February 25.

Reopening of bank in Mexico. No. 16, January 20.

Reopening of the port of Encontrados, Venezuela. No. 46, February 25.

Reorganization of the Brazilian Lloyd steamship lines. No. 71, March 28.

Reorganization of the Comisión Reguladora de Mercado de Henequen. No. 11, January 14.

Reorganization of Lloyd Brazileiro Steamship Co. No. 29, February 4.

Report of Argentine National Mortgage Bank. No. 2, January 4.

Report on economic conditions in Mexico available. No. 73, March 30.

Resources and trade of Santa Cruz district, Bolivia. No. 3, January 5.

Restoration of Bolivian duty on foodstuffs. No. 11, January 14.

Return of Mexican bank to owners. No. 60, March 15.

Resumption of Brazilian tariff discussion. No. 57, March 11.

Revival of German competition in Chile. No. 62, March 17.

Rio de Janeiro's leading exports to the United States. No. 67, March 23.

Salvador permits circulation of American bills. No. 27, February 2.

Sample contract for Peruvian industrial exhibition available. No. 15, January 19.

Sao Paulo authorizes internal loan. No. 71, March 28.

Serious economic situation in Nicaragua. No. 16, January 20.

Settlement of strike among employees of Mihanovich steamship Co. (Buenos Aires). No. 49, March 1.

Shipments of vegetables and grapefruit from the Isle of Pines. No. 67, March 23.

Slight improvement in congested conditions in Havana. No. 2, January 4.

Small market for leather belting in British Guiana. No. 73, March 30.

Storage charge on parcel post package sent to Mexico. No. 23, January 28.

Substitution of alcohol for gasoline in Pernambuco, Brazil. No. 60, March 15.

Sugar exports from Cuba to United States. No. 29, February 4.

Suspension of export duty on rubber in Peru. No. 63, March 18.

Tenders for supplies to Jamaica government invited. *Id.*

Textile industry in Argentina. No. 51, March 3.

Third bonded warehouse in Colon. No. 2, January 4.

Trade between the United States and Porto Rico in 1920. No. 63, March 7.

Trade notes from Argentina. No. 17, January 21; No. 36, February 12; No. 63, March 18.

Id., from Brazil. No. 7, January 10; No. 43, February 21.

Id., from British Guiana. No. 35, February 11.

Id., from Central America. No. 27, February 2, No. 47, February 26.

Id., from Chile. No. 22, January 27.

Id., from Dominican Republic. No. 52, March 5.

Id., from Mexico. No. 13, January 17; No. 30, February 5; No. 40, February 17; No. 45, February 24; No. 65, March 21; No. 71, March 28.

Id., from Nicaragua. No. 51, March 3 No. 73, March 30.

Id., from Paraguay. No. 44, February 23; No. 64, March 19.

Id., from Peru. No. 24, January 29.

Id., from Uruguay. No. 70, March 26.

Trade of foreign countries in 1920 and 1921. No. 64, March 19.

Trade review of Sao Paulo, Brazil. No. 58, March 12.

Transfer of the Bahia-Blanca-Patagones Railway. No. 24, January 29.

Transportation conditions in Mexico. No. 41, February 18.

Unfavorable economic conditions in Guadaloupe. No. 16, January 20.

Uruguayan animal-quarantine regulations. No. 6, January 8.

Uruguayan loans under consideration to alleviate the critical wool situation. No. 68, March 24.

Uruguay's foreign trade in 1919. No. 17, January 21.

Use of woven-wire cloth in Argentine. No. 53, March 7.

Vegetable seed oil extraction in Argentine. No. 65, March 21.

CENTRAL AMERICAN AND MEXICAN NOTES

COSTA RICA

A second edition of *Geografía Ilustrada de Costa Rica*, edited by Trejos Hermanos of San José, bears the date of 1919. The publication is well illustrated and contains material of value for those who plan to visit the country or describe its politics and history.

Two publications of the Escuela Normal de Costa Rica, bearing the stamp of the Imprenta Nacional have some historical interest. In the first, Don Cleto González Víquez, an ex-president of the republic, puts forward the claim that President Jesús Jiménez, in 1869, established the system of primary education and normal schools in Costa Rica at the cost of the state, and was also instrumental in introducing a better type of secondary education. This system was afterwards re-established and amplified by Don Mauro Fernández. Among the other public services of Jiménez, the writer stresses the construction of highways. For these two measures of enlightened policy, the writer ranks Jiménez high among his country's benefactors.

In the same number Don Pedro Pérez Zeledón pays just tribute to the cultural activity of Doctor José María Castro, the founder of the Republic of Costa Rica. Castro was instrumental in establishing the University of Santo Tomás, where six presidents were afterwards trained, and also in providing normal instruction for women. It was fitting that the first number of the publication should be devoted to these two pioneers in education.

The second number of this publication, bearing the date 1919, is devoted to a study of Luís Felipe González entitled, *La Obra Cultural de don Miguel Obregón*. The monograph is a fitting tribute to a worthy educator, who at present holds the post of minister of public instruction. Don Miguel's work has been primarily that of organizer, and his influence has been felt in the field of primary and secondary instruction, in the training of teachers, and in public libraries. In addition, his writings upon the technical phases of education have obtained wide recognition. The two publications may be obtained at a moderate fee from the Secretaría de la Escuela Normal de Costa Rica, Heredia, C. R. The proceeds of the sales are destined to serve as a publishing fund for the school.

On December 8, 1918, the city of Punta Arenas dedicated a monument to the memory of Juan Rafael Mora, thrice elected president of Costa Rica, and his faithful companion, General José María Cañas. The former was especially revered for his services as executive during the formative period of Costa Rica's history, and both men did excellent service in the campaigns against the filibuster, William Walker. Like many of their contemporaries they found themselves in 1860 at the head of a revolt against the constituted authorities, were defeated near Punta Arenas, captured, and shot. The celebration mentioned above represents a tardy recognition of their services. Under the title "*Apuntes y Documentos*", an illustrated booklet describes the measures initiated and carried through on that occasion by the Comité

Central-Ejecutivo pro Mora-Cañas of Punta Arenas and gives some facts of historical interest regarding these famous caudillos.

Five small booklets, under the general caption, *Para la Historia de Costa Rica* (*Coleccion de Folletos*) are devoted to *La Revolución de 22 de Febrero de 1918*. The movement therein described was initiated by Rogelio Fernández Güell and his companions against the government of Tinoco and the work, dedicated to their memory, has value for the historian of contemporary events.

The *Colegio de Señoritas* of San José, Costa Rica, through its director Señor J. Fidel Tristán, is publishing a series of scientific leaflets of considerable local interest.

Señor Eladio Prado has recently published a local study of unusual merit: *Nuestra Señora de Ujarrás*. The brochure is well illustrated with photographs showing the valley in which the church devoted to the former patroness of the colony was situated, the ruins of the ancient edifice, images, representations of miracles, etc. While a work of devotion and local pride rather than of critical character, it is an important contribution to the cultural history of Costa Rica.

In the December number of *Inter-America*, Señor Luís Dobles Segreda contributes an interesting sketch of the poet, Rubén Darío, and his brief visit to Heredia. Señor Dobles is one of the progressive educators of Costa Rica, as well as a writer of note. At present he is the director of the Instituto at Alajuela.

Under the title, *Mi Tierra Nativa*, Francisco María Núñez-Monge describes the canton of Desamparados, Costa Rica. The work is a pretentious monograph of some 170 pages, well illustrated, and contains a variety of useful information of historical and general character. It is a pleasure to note that as a token of appreciation the local council of the canton paid for the publication of the work.

Under the present administration in Costa Rica, Doctór Joaquín García Monge is serving as director of the National Library. He recently acted as minister of public instruction.

Señor Anastasio Alfaro González, author of *Arqueología Criminal Americana* (San José, 1906), is now in charge of the Museo Nacional de Costa Rica, at San José.

Señor Ricardo Fernández Guardia, of Costa Rica, easily holds first place among contemporary Central American historians. To the documentary series begun by his father, Lic. Don León Fernández, under the title *Colección de Documentos para la Historia de Costa Rica* (5 vols. Paris, 1886), he added five volumes more (Barcelona, 1907). He also published, after the untimely death of his father, the latter's *Historia de Costa Rica durante la Dominación Española*, 1502–1821 (Madrid, 1889). His own *Historia de Costa Rica, El Descubrumiento y la Conquista*, appeared in San José (1905) and has since been translated into English. *Cuartilla Histórica de Costa Rica* (San José, 1909) is a brief text for school use, but it will also serve as a useful guide for advanced students. A new edition of *Cartas de Juan Vázquez de Coronado* appeared in Barcelona in 1908.

A recent work, *Reseña Historia de Talamanca* (San José, 1918), describes in 198 pages the development of that province, comprising the south eastern extremity of Costa Rica, from its discovery by Columbus to the advent of the railroad. Its Indian population has afforded material for the missionary and the scientist and its frontier position has given it prominence in the territorial and commercial disputes with Colombia and the United States. It is a most commendable study in local history. Señor Fernández Guardia is also the author of a number of literary works of which the best known is his *Cuentos Ticos*. At present he is actively engaged in editing other manuscript material of the colonial period.

PANAMA

Doctor Octavio Méndez Pereira is director of the Instituto Nacional of Panama, where the Pan American College of Commerce will be established for the time being. The *Instituto* is magnificently housed in a series of large buildings constructed with just such a purpose in view. Dr. Méndez has written a brief *Historia de la Instrucción Pública en Panamá* and is also the author of an elaborate study of the life, literary labors, and political and diplomatic activities of Justo Arosemena (1817–1896). The latter was one of the leading characters in the history of Colombia during the nineteenth century. The work received the premium offered by the National Assembly for the best study of Arosemena's life and its appearance formed part of the celebration of his centenary. It bears the imprint of the Imprenta Nacional and elsewhere we shall give it more extended notice.

NICARAGUA

The name of Roscoe R. Hill appears as *Comisionado*, in an extensive two-volume, fiscal report bearing the title: *Republicá de Nicaragua. Informe de la Comisión de Credito Público*, 1917–1919. The report was presented to the president of the Republic as part of the work of the High Commission of which Mr. Hill is a member.

MEXICO

Under the title *La Instrucción Rudimentaria en la República*, Señor Gregorio Torres Quintero reviewed for the First Mexican Scientific Congress, the action taken by the various states of Mexico upon the law of May 30, 1911, providing for national aid in founding rudimentary schools (*escuelas rudimentarias*). These were essentially rural in character, designed primarily to instruct the Indian population and were to be supported by the federal government. With few exceptions the various states welcomed this supplemental aid but subsequent political disturbances prevented the plans from being carried out. Professor Torres Quintero has recently devoted several months to a study of the primary and secondary schools of the United States with a view to improve the corresponding schools of Mexico. A third edition of his *La Patria Mexicana*, a history text for elementary schools, has just come from the press.

Doctor Manuel Barranco, author of a valuable monograph describing the educational problems of Mexico and recently connected with the General Directory for Public Instruction of the Federal District, is now engaged in special research at Columbia University. Señor Moíses Sáenz, recently director of the *Escuela Preparatoria*, and prominent in the work of the Committee on Cooperation in Latin America, is also at the same institution.

Señor Ezéquiel Chávez, Sub-Secretary of Public Instruction during the time of Díaz, is now director of the *Escuela Preparatoria*. He is

·an alumnus of that institution and had much to do with its development while serving in the ministry of Don Justo Sierra. He was recently associated with Señores Paulino Machorro Narváez and Alfonso Pruneda in preparing *Una Eucuesta sobre Educación Popular*, which appeared under the auspices of Señor Alberto J. Pani.

I. J. C.

Students interested in Hispanic American commercial law will find extensive bibliographical lists in *Latin-American Commercial Law*, by T. Esquivel Obregón, with collaboration by Edwin M. Borchard. This work is published by The Banks Law Publishing Company (New York, 1921).

Dr. Herbert I. Priestley, of the University of California, has performed a useful service for students and teachers in preparing his syllabus, *Modern Mexican History* (New York, 1920, Institute of International Education, International Relations Clubs, Syllabus, No. VI). It is divided into ten sections, as follows: (1) The territory of Mexico and the people; (2) The Spanish colonial régime, 1519–1810; (3) The war of independence, 1820–21; (4) The war of reform and the French intervention, 1857–67; (5) The presidency of Porfirio Diaz, 1876–1910; (6) The revolution under Madero, 1910–13; (7) Huerta and the United States, February 19, 1913–July 15, 1914; (8) The government of Carranza, July 15, 1914–May 5, 1920; (9) The petroleum controversy; (10) The problem of land. Each section is preceded by a luminous study outline and followed by an excellent bibliography, including periodical literature.—C. K. JONES.

Señor Luis Alberto Sánchez has just published (Lima, 1921) the first volume of his *Historia de la Literatura Peruana*. This is entitled *Los Poetas de la Colonia*. The second volume, *Los prosadores de la Colonia*, is announced to be in course of preparation. The first volume is an important work, valuable not only for its historical and critical features, but also for the bibliographical data it contains.—C. K. JONES.

Señor Manuel Segundo Sánchez, director of the National Library at Caracas, has added to his notable bibliographical contributions the following work: *El Publicista de Venezuela; Capítulos del Libro en Preparación; Los Incunables Venezolanos*, (Caracas, 1920, pp. 25). This paper contains a detailed historical and bibliographical account of the periodical founded by virtue of a resolution of the First Congreso Constituyente of Venezuela, in 1811.—C. K. JONES.

Volume 13 of Dr. Julio Cejador y Franca's *Historia de la Lengua y Literatura Castellana* (Madrid, 1920), forms the first part of the Época Contemporánea: 1908–1920. This work is invaluable for reference regarding Hispanic American authors.—C. K. JONES.

Professor Clemens Brandenburger, in his *Neuere brasilische wissenschaftliche Litteratur*, which is reprinted from *Mitteilungen des Deutsch-Sudamerikanischen und Iberischen Instituts* (Köln), VIII. 1920, pp. 49–61, has made an excellent contribution to Brazilian bibliography, especially along historical and sociological lines during recent years. Dr. Brandenburger is at the head of the Board of Brazilian scholars who are preparing the great geographical, biographical, bibliographical, etc., Dictionary which the Instituto Historico de Rio de Janeiro is to publish in celebration of the centenary of the independence of Brazil. He is himself writing the Introduction which will form the first volume of this publication. The part relating to Pernambuco was compiled by Dr. Mario Melo, secretary of the Historical Association of Pernambuco (Instituto Archeologico-Geographico Pernambucano).—MANOEL DE LIMA OLIVEIRA.

Noronha Santos, chief of the section of the Municipal Archives, has compiled a very useful work, namely, *Indice da Revista Archivo do Districto Federal com Extracto Alphabetico de Assumptos* (Rio de Janeiro, 1919). This contains an alphabetical index of all documents since the sixteenth century relating to the Brazilian capital and published in the records of the municipality.—MANOEL DE LIMA OLIVEIRA.

Limites interestaduaes (Rio de Janeiro, 1920), is the name of a recent work by Thiers Fleming. This was a lecture given by its distinguished author at the Public Library of Rio de Janeiro, November 11, 1920, relative to the boundary question between the states of the Brazilian union. Most of these questions have been settled, either by direct negotiation between the governments of the states, or by arbitration. Some were very important, as, for instance, that between Parana and Santa Catharina regarding the Misiones territory granted to Brazil by the award of President Cleveland in 1895. A few are to be decided shortly as a result of the meeting at Rio de Janeiro of all the delegates who had been especially appointed to deal with this matter. Only those concerning Bahia remain unsettled.—MANOEL DE LIMA OLIVEIRA.

A recent book of considerable interest is *S. Paulo nos primeiros Annos* (1554–1601); *Ensaio de Reconstituição Social* (Tours, 1920). Its author is Affonso d'Escragnolle Taunay, who is the son of one of the most brilliant of Brazilian writers, and the author of the famous *Retraite de la Laguna* an episode of the Paraguayan war, in which he took part as an officer. He is now the director of the Museu Paulista and is himself an historical writer. His new book, which is based on the admirably preserved records of the municipality of San Paulo, constitutes a curious and reliable reconstruction of Brazilian life in the sixteenth century.—MANOEL DE LIMA OLIVEIRA.

La Revue de Geneve, No. 5, November, 1920, published an article by Dr. Manoel de Lima Oliveira, entitled "Brésil (La Guerre, la Paix, et la Neutralité). Two other articles by the same author will also appear in the same review, namely, "Le Retour des Cendres", and "Le République Militaire et la République Civile".

Revista do Brasil (published at San Paulo) in its issue for November, 1920, contains an article by Dr. Percy Alvin Martin, entitled "O Brasil no segunda Conferencia Pan Americana".

Professor W. W. Pierson, Jr., of the University of North Carolina will give two courses in Hispanic American history at the University of Texas during the coming summer school session. Professor Pierson is working on a syllabus on Hispanic American history for the Institute of International Education.

Professor Isaac Joslin Cox will give two historical courses in the summer school at Northwestern University next summer.

Sr. D. Pedro Aguirre y Cerda, formerly head of the Chilean commission that arranged for the exchange of professorships between Chile and the United States, and former minister of public instruction and justice, has recently been appointed premier of the new Chilean cabinet, taking the portfolio of minister of the interior. Sr. Aguirre is the president of the radical or progressive party, which numbers in its ranks many of the young voters of the country, whose interests are broad and progressive. Sr. Aguirre is especially interested in educational reform, and he has extensively studied forms of education in the United States.

Sr. D. Carlos Cruz, the head of the Biblioteca Nacional of Chile, is the minister of war of the new cabinet. Sr. Cruz, who is a radical in politics, is the author of a number of works on folklore and history.

As exchange professor to Chile, Professor Gilmore, of the College of Agriculture of the University of California has been chosen for the current year. In return Chile has sent Professor Gálvez, who enjoys a high reputation in South American educational circles, both for his grasp of pedagogical principles and his ability to put them into practice. Sr. Gálvez will be in the United States between the months of April and November. The University of California, which has the management of the exchange professorships from the United States side, endeavored to have a professor from one of the eastern institutions chosen for Chile this year, but it was impossible to arrange dates for that purpose. The University of California is really not entitled to this exchange this year, for Dr. Chapman was sent to Chile by that institution last year, and the basic principle of the exchange is to have it shared in by all the best institutions of the United States.

Sr. D. Víctor Andrés Belaunde, the Peruvian scholar, who has been delivering addresses in a number of Universities of the United States, is the owner and editor of *Mercurio Peruano*, one of the foremost reviews of South America. Among the notable addresses that have been given are one on "Inca Communism", and one on "Hispanic American Culture and Ideals".

STATEMENT OF THE OWNERSHIP, MANAGEMENT, CIRCULATION, ETC., REQUIRED BY THE ACT OF CONGRESS OF AUGUST 24, 1912,

Of THE HISPANIC AMERICAN HISTORICAL REVIEW, published, Quarterly at Baltimore, Md. for April 1, 1921.

State of Washington, D. C.

Before me, a Notary Public in and for the state and county aforesaid, personally appeared James A. Robertson, who, having been duly sworn according to law, deposes and says that he is the Managing Editor of THE HISPANIC AMERICAN HISTORICAL REVIEW and that the following is, to the best of his knowledge and belief, a true statement of the ownership, management (and if a daily paper, the circulation), etc., of the aforesaid publication for the date shown in the above caption, required by the Act of August 24, 1912, embodied in section 443, Postal Laws and Regulations, printed on the reverse of this form, to wit:

1. That the names and addresses of the publisher, editor, managing editor, and business managers are:

Publisher:

Board of Editors of THE HISPANIC AMERICAN HISTORICAL REVIEW, care Williams & Wilkins Company, Mount Royal and Guilford Avenues, Baltimore, Maryland.

Editors:

Isaac J. Cox, Northwestern University, Evanston, Illinois.

William R. Manning, 4701 Fessenden St. N.W., Washington.

Percy Alvin Martin, Leland Stanford Jr. University, Leland Stanford, California.

W. W. Pierson, Jr. University of North Carolina, Chapel Hill, North Carolina.

Herbert I. Priestley, University of California, Berkeley, California.

James A. Robertson, 1422 Irving St. N.E., Washington D. C.

Advisory Editors:

Herbert E. Bolton, University of California, Berkeley, California.

William R. Shepherd, Columbia University, New York, N. Y.

Managing Editor:

James A. Robertson, 1422 Irving St. N.E., Washington, D. C.

Business Managers:

None.

2. That the owners are: (Give names and addresses of individual owners, or, if a corporation, give its name and the names and addresses of stockholders owning or holding 1 per cent or more of the total amount of stock.)

Board of Editors of THE HISPANIC AMERICAN HISTORICAL REVIEW:

Isaac J. Cox, Northwestern University, Evanston, Illinois.

William R. Manning, 4701 Fessenden St. N.W., Washington, D. C.

Percy Alvin Martin, Leland Stanford Jr. University. Leland Stanford, California.

W. W. Pierson, Jr. University of North Carolina, Chapel Hill, North Carolina.

Herbert I Priestley, University of California, Berkeley, California.

James A. Robertson, 1422 Irving St. N.E., Washington, D. C.

3. That the known bondholders, mortgages, and other security holders owning or holding 1 per cent or more of total amount of bonds, mortgages, or other securities are: (If there are none, so state.) None.

4. That the two paragraphs next above, giving the names of the owners, stockholders, and security holders, if any, contain not only the list of stockholders and security holders as they appear upon the books of the company but also, in cases where the stockholder or security holder appears upon the books of the company as trustee or in any other fiduciary relation, the name of the person or corporation for whom such trustee is acting, is given; also that the said two paragraphs contain statements embracing affiant's full knowledge and belief as to the circumstances and conditions under which stockholders and security holders who do not appear upon the books of the company as trustees, hold stock and securities in a capacity other than that of a bona fide owner; and this affiant has no reason to believe that any other person, association, or corporation has any interest direct or indirect in the said stock, bonds, or other securities than as so stated by him.

5. That the average number of copies of each issue of this publication sold or distributed, through the mails or otherwise, to paid subscribers during the six months preceding the date shown above is   (This information is required from daily publications only.)

JAMES A. ROBERTSON.

Sworn to and subscribed before me this 23d day of March, 1921.

[Seal.]   WILLIAM R. NAGEL,
                                                Notary Public, D. C.
                        (My commission expires October 21, 1925.)

The Hispanic American Historical Review

Vol. IV   AUGUST, 1921   No. 3

LA PRIMERA NEGOCIACIÓN DIPLOMÁTICA ENTA-
BLADA CON LA JUNTA REVOLUCIONARIA DE
BUENOS AIRES

Ha venido siendo creencia generalmente admitida hasta hoy, que las primeras negociaciones diplomáticas que sostuvo la Junta revolucionaria de Buenos Aires, a raíz de su constitución, se verificaron con el Gobierno de Su Magestad Británica; y para fundamentar este aserto, se alegaba que a los cuatro días de haberse producido la revolución, o sea, el 29 de Mayo de 1810, se dieron por la Junta cartas credenciales a D. Matías Irigoyen, para presentar al Gobierno de Londres y negociar con él, el reconocimiento de la Junta formada en la capital del Plata.

Y en efecto, si sólo se atiende a esta circunstancia, no será extraño que se asevere que la primera potencia que estuvo en relación con los revolucionarios porteños, fué la Gran Bretaña. Pero, si examinamos, aunque sea ligeramente, esta cuestión, nos evidenciaremos de que no fué al gobierno inglés a quien corresponde la primacía, sino al gobierno portugués establecido en Rio de Janeiro, que acreditó cerca de la Junta revolucionaria a D. Cárlos José Guezzi, con el carácter de enviado secreto, el cual se presentó a la Junta el día 17 de Julio de 1810; siendo así, que el enviado argentino Irigoyen llegó a Inglaterra el 5 de Agosto del mismo año, presentándose en el Foreing Office al día siguiente.

Si lo dicho no fuera definitivo, otras circunstancias podrían demostrar el hecho; pues aun prescindiendo de esta misión diplomática, siempre correspondería la prioridad al gobierno portugués, ya que desde la constitución de la Junta se mantuvieron relaciones entre Río de Janeiro y Buenos Aires, de gobierno a gobierno.

En este breve estudio nos proponemos tratar de la negociación diplomática que realizó en Buenos Aires el enviado portugués Carlos José Guezzi, así como también de los resultados y consecuencias que produjo. Esta misión secreta se desarrolla en el lapso de tiempo comprendido entre 17 de Julio de 1810, fecha de la llegada a Buenos Aires de Guezzi, y el 20 de Diciembre del mismo año, en que salió de Buenos Aires el citado emisario.

Para la exposición, desarrollo y resultados que produjo, tenemos como base y aprovechamos por tanto, una colección de documentos rigurosamente inéditos, que comprende tres partes: 1ª Correspondencia de Guezzi con la Junta revolucionaria de Buenos Aires. 2ª Correspondencia de Guezzi con el Conde de Linhares. 3ª Esposiçao de quanto me accorreo durante a demora que fiz em Buenos Ayres desde 17 de Julho ate 26 Decembro 1810;—la primera, integrada por 5 documentos; la segunda por 7; y la tercera por uno muy extenso.

I

Al producirse la revolución de Buenos Aires, y llegar a conocimiento del gobierno portugués en Río de Janeiro la noticia de la constitución de una Junta de Gobierno en la vecina capital del Plata; pasado el primer momento de estupor producido por el inesperado acontecimiento, comenzó el Conde de Linhares, primer ministro a la sazón del Príncipe Regente del Brasil, a dar cabida en su inquieta imaginación a la idea de entrar en inmediatas relaciones con el incipiente gobierno revolucionario, siquiera haciéndolo con cierto carácter secreto, por la evidente razón de que por el momento no ofrecía condiciones de estabilidad el citado gobierno. Esto aparte de que como aliado que era el gobierno portugués del de España, no podía, sin faltar a esta alianza, entrar, no ya en negociaciones, sino simplemente en relaciones diplomáticas.

Pero a ello le impulsaban motivos de diversa índole, y que brevemente vamos a exponer. En primer término, no se le ocultaban al perspicaz ministro portugués las consecuencias que para el Brasil pudieran sobrevenir, al producirse en los estados vecinos una convulsión revolucionaria con marcado carácter de rebeldía y tendencias inequívocas hacia la independencia de su metrópoli; y que como es natural, los directores de este movimiento procurarían hacerlo extensivo a cuantos territorios sud-americanos se encontrasen en la misma situación del Río de la Plata, esto es, en el estado de colonia dependiente de una metrópoli; y esa era la situación en que se hallaba el Brasil, siquiera en él variasen las circunstancias por el hecho de hallarse, aunque transitoriamente, la corte portuguesa residiendo en esta su principal colonia; lo cual no era óbice para que el peligro citado surgiese amenazador.

En otro orden de cosas, el gobierno portugués tenía diversos proyectos sobre anexión de ciertos territorios pertenecientes al virreinato sublevado; proyectos que no eran desconocidos en Buenos Aires, y que por lo tanto podían ser la causa que determinara la animosidad del nuevo gobierno e impidiese su realización. Y en este sentido se explica perfectamente que el Conde de Linhares pretendiera entablar estas relaciones diplomáticas, pues consciente de que el Brasil era el único estado que de una manera positiva y eficaz podía ayudar a la naciente República del Plata, procuraba de esta manera atraerse las simpatías de su gobierno, para poder en su día exigir, con cierto derecho, compensaciones que muy ardientemente perseguía, y este era el único medio para conseguirlas.

Sabido es tambien que la infanta Dª Carlota Joaquina de Borbón esposa del Príncipe Regente del Brasil, venía realizando desde 1808 determinadas gestiones para erigirse con una regencia en el virreinato de Buenos Aires, gestiones que se hallaban paralizadas hacía algún tiempo, y de las cuales quería ahora aprovecharse el gobierno portugués con determinados fines, que no eran ciertamente los que impulsaban a la hija de Carlos IV a emprenderlas.

Las apuntadas, entre otras muchas razones, podrían alegarse para determinar con toda claridad los motivos que indujeron al citado ministro portugués para enviar cerca de la Junta de Buenos Aires a D. Carlos José Guezzi, con el carácter de emisario secreto del gobierno de Rio de Janeiro.

Decidido pues, el conde de Linhares, a acreditar un enviado en Buenos Aires, eligió para desempeñar esta misión, y para evitar sospechas, al citado Guezzi, que era un aventurero italiano expulsado de Buenos Aires cuando ocurrieron los ataques ingleses el año 1806, y que refugiado en Rio de Janeiro, se puso allí en relación con otros expulsados como él, entre los que se encontraban D. Saturnino Rodríguez Peña, Felipe Contucci, M. de Parosin, los hermanos Perichón. . . .; individuos todos ellos muy conocidos por sus ideas, y que en un sentido o en otro hicieron destacar su personalidad con motivo de los sucesos de Buenos Aires, y algunos antes de dichos sucesos; ya que primeramente se habían dedicado a colaborar con Rodríguez Peña, cuando este anduvo en relaciones con la Infanta Dª Carlota Joaquina para coronarla en Buenos Aires, y que después se habían mezclado en intrigas políticas de todo género y condición que pudieran proporcionarles algún medio de subsistencia.

El tener una inteligencia despierta y viva y acentuado talento social, el conocer suficientemente los negocios de la América meridional, y poseer una regular cultura, como se demuestra por sus escritos, hicieron que el conde de Linhares fijara su atención en Guezzi, como persona apta para desempeñar la misión de que se trataba cerca de la Junta revolucionaria de Buenos Aires; ya que a las condiciones anteriormente expuestas reunía la de conocer personalmente a alguno de los individuos que ejercían visible influencia en la vecina capital.

Las instrucciones que el Conde de Linhares dió a Guezzi, no fueron, ni podían serlo, concretas y determinadas, ya que lo que deseaba el gobierno portugués era conocer con algún detalle los propósitos que abrigaba la Junta de Buenos Aires, para obrar en consecuencia de ellos.

Claramente se advierte que para conseguir esto, se necesitaba de un motivo o causa que justificase de alguna manera la presencia de un enviado portugués en Buenos Aires; y en este sentido si pueden suponerse las instrucciones que fueron dadas a Guezzi por el Conde de Linhares, y que facilmente se deducen de los escritos de ambos.

Así pues, el primer punto que Guezzi debía tratar con la Junta se refería a desvanecer los recelos que con justa causa debían tener los prohombres argentinos respecto a la política y manera de conducirse del gobierno portugués en los últimos tiempos, y en todo aquello que tenía relación con el virreinato; y a este efecto, se le encargó que hiciera constar a la Junta, que el gobierno portugués había obrado con justicia negándole al Marqués de Casa Irujo, embajador de España en Rio de Janeiro, el permiso necesario para detener a los argentinos refugiados allí, y que simpatizaban y trabajaban de común acuerdo con sus compatriotas de Buenos Aires para producir el movimiento que se llevó a cabo el 25 de Mayo de 1810. Lo cual estimaba el Conde de Linhares que había de causar excelente efecto entre los individuos de la Junta revolucionaria.

En segundo término, debía Guezzi atraerse la simpatía de la Junta, haciendo ante ella formal declaración, de que S.A.R. el Príncipe Regente de Portugal y Brasil, no quería mezclarse, ni tomar parte en asuntos que pudieran ser causa de desagrado entre los habitantes españoles del virreinato del Plata; esperando como justa compensación a esta benevolencia, que liberalmente se ofrecía, que a su vez los patricios argentinos supiesen guardar el respeto y consideración que merecían la Augusta persona del Regente y la de su esposa la infanta Dª Carlota Joaquina, la cual, como no podía ocultarseles, poseía auténticos derechos sobre la sucesión de la monarquía española; no debiendo olvidar además que esta infanta no deseaba usar de estos derechos sino en beneficio y provecho de los pueblos hispano-americanos. Como complemento a todo ello, debía manifestar que los sentimientos del Príncipe eran en todo pacíficos y favorables respecto de los últimos acontecimientos ocurridos en el virreinato.

Estas manifestaciones, que Guezzi debía hacer a la Junta, llevaban envuelta otra indicación de mayor transcendencia, como era, el reconocimiento, por parte de la Junta, de los derechos de Dª Carlota, a que hemos aludido; lo que fué motivo de gran discusión.

Por lo demás, segun se desprende de los documentos que vamos a examinar, Guezzi fué investido de facultades suficientemente amplias para tratar otros puntos que no podían precisarse desde Rio de Janeiro.

Los motivos expuestos, no tenían mas virtualidad que la de justificar la presencia en Buenos Aires del enviado protugués, el cual tenía como misión principal la de inquirir los diversos planes y proyectos que pretendiera realizar la Junta, ya que estos no podían saberse, ni aún sospecharse, desde Rio de Janeiro.

II.

En los primeros días de Julio de 1810, partió Carlos José Guezzi de Rio de Janeiro con dirección a la Capital del Plata, a donde arribó el día 17 del mismo mes. En ese mismo día 17 trató de ser recibido por la Junta, lo que no consiguió por las muchas ocupaciones que aquella tenía, pero se le ofreció que sería recibido al día siguiente.

En la misma fecha visitó con carácter particular a D. Manuel Belgrano y a Castelli, que formaban parte de la Junta y que eran, sobre todo el primero, personas muy influyentes en ella, y por lo tanto podrían indicarl la opinión que se había formado del gobierno portugués, y si sería bien recibido como representante de tal gobierno.   Así pues, y juzgándolo conveniente, les expuso las instruciones que le habían sido dadas por el Conde de Linhares, y a las cuales ya hemos hecho referencia; inquiriendo a la vez, si entraba en los propósitos de la Junta reconocer los derechos que Dª Carlota Joaquina tenía a la corona de España, derechos que habían sido reconocidos por la Junta Central de este país.

Conocidas que fueron por Belgrano y Castelli tales pretensiones, respondieron con cierta ambigüedad, que desde luego la Junta no tenía el menor motivo de queja respecto del gobierno portugués; y en lo relativo a los derechos de la Infanta, creían ellos que entraba en las miras de la Junta, no sólo el reconocerlos, sino también que, a su debido tiempo, sería llamada a regir los destinos del virreinato; siendo de la misma opinión el resto de los Vocales de la Junta. Ahora bien, el realizar esto llevaba consigo muchas dificultades que vencer, no solamente por parte de los patricios argentinos, ya que estos deseaban que así ocurriese, sino de los europeos, que habían de ser los que más dificultades opusieran; y en consecuencia, lo más oportuno era esperar a que se reuniera el Congreso General, y que este decidiese la cuestión.

A primera vista parece extraño que los revolucionarios argentinos, por boca de uno de sus directores, dieran tal contestación a un asunto en el que ni siquiera se pensaba; pero no hay que olvidar que Belgrano y Castelli fueron de los que aún no hacía dos años, habían pretendido coronar a la infanta D* Carlota en Buenos Aires: proyecto en el que puso gran interés Belgrano, y que fracasó por falta de ambiente en el virreinato del Río de la Plata, por la tenaz oposición que hizo el embajador inglés en Rio de Janeiro, Lord Strangford, y por diferencias surgidas entre los patricios argentinos y D* Carlota Joaquina.

La entrevista que el día 18 de Julio tuvo Guezzi con la Junta, resultó interesante por los extremos que en ella se trataron. Después de agradecer la Junta los sentimientos que manifestaba el Príncipe Regente por medio de su enviado, relativos a mantener la amistad y buena armonía necesarias a los dos Gobiernos, trataron los vocales de justificar ante Guezzi la necesidad tan urgente en que se había visto la ciudad de Buenos Aires para destituir al virrey y establecer una Junta de Gobierno, para evitar, según ellos, que llegasen a efecto las maquinaciones francesas, que ponían en peligro la seguridad del virreinato; lo cual era totalmente falso. Después le fué preguntado sobre el efecto que habían causado en el Brasil los últimos sucesos de Buenos Aires y, a la vez, si consideraba de conveniencia que la Infanta hiciera uso de sus derechos.

Dada la importancia que encerraban las preguntas, y la no menor transcendencia que arrastraban las respuestas, Guezzi contestó soslayando el hacer una manifestación categórica, diciendo que la corte portuguesa no había formado juicio definitivo sobre los sucesos de Buenos Aires, desde el momento en que estos se conocían muy imperfectamente y no sabían por tanto cuales eran las intenciones y los fines que abrigaban los argentinos al cambiar de Gobierno; y respecto a los derechos de D* Carlota Joaquina, él creía que puesto que habían sido formalmente reconocidos por la Junta Central de España, era de esperar que todos los pueblos sud-americanos estarían conformes con tal decisión. A lo cual respondió D. Cornelio Saavedra, presidente de la Junta revolucionaria, que "nisto não podia caber duvida, e que ainda quando toda a nação fosse de opinião contraria, o Povo de Buenos Ayres, e a Junta que tinha a honra de o mandar, serião os primeiros a impunhar a espada para a conservação dos seus direitos".

Al dar esta contestación Saavedra, puede asegurarse que faltaba en absoluto a la verdad, y a sabiendas; pues nunca había sido propósito de los revolucionarios tal reconocimiento de derechos. En realidad, lo que pretendió fué, que el gobierno portugués considerase esta respuesta como una halagadora promesa, que no era tal desde el momento en que se hacía uso de ella, en el mismo sentido y para causar los mismos efectos que pretendían conseguir los argentinos, presentando siempre como justificación de sus actos el nombre de Fernando VII y desde este punto de vista ningún compromiso encerraba tal declaración.

Puede decirse, pues, que la Junta recibió de buen grado al emisario del gobierno portugués, aunque muy pronto hubo de entibiarse tal cordialidad, que no era más que aparente; ya que las pretensiones de cada una de las partes eran contrapuestas y con distintos fines: las del enviado portugués, ya las conocemos; y las del gobierno de Buenos Aires también se referían a conocer los propósitos y proyectos de la corte de Rio de Janeiro, a quien desde el primer momento consideraron como un futuro próximo enemigo, ya que necesariamente tenían que ser opuestas las políticas de ambos gobiernos.

Como por el momento convenía, al menos oficialmente, hacer constar la satisfacción que habían producido a la Junta las manifestaciones de Guezzi, redactóse un Oficio para que fuera enviado al Conde de Linhares, en el que se manifestaba agradecimiento a la Corte portuguesa, y se hacían falsas protestas de amor y fidelidad a España.[1]

El enviado portugués no era hombre que se dejara llevar de palabras vanas y promesas verbales, aunque ellas proviniesen de labios tan autorizados como eran los del Presidente de la Junta de

---

[1] Oficio de la Junta a D. Carlos José Guezzi. Buenos Aires 20 de Julio de 1810.

Gobierno, y por esta razón decidió dar cierto carácter oficial a sus negociaciones, esto es, presentando escritos con las peticiones que formulaba, y exigiendo las contestaciones en la misma forma.

En tal sentido, el día 20 de Julio pasó un oficio a la Junta, manifestando que el Gobierno portugués trataría de conservar buenas relaciones con el de Buenos Aires, siempre que de esta parte no se atentase contra la integridad de la monarquía española bajo el dominio de Fernando VII; indicando a la vez la conveniencia de que los pueblos sud-americanos ayudasen y auxiliasen en la medida de sus fuerzas a la metrópoli.

Apesar del lenguage mesurado en que Guezzi hizo la manifestación, causó muy mal efecto en la Junta semejante pretensión, adoptándose la cómoda postura de no tomar en consideración tales indicaciones de Guezzi, dejándolas por tanto sin contestación; sirviendo únicamente ellas para ganarse la animosidad de la Junta y la de los enemigos de esta, que lo censuraron empleando satíricas burlas, como él mismo hace constar en su Exposición.[1]

III.

En el virreinato del Río de la Plata hubo continuamente, y sobre todo en el primer período de la revolución, grandes discordias políticas que ocasionaron la demora por cierto tiempo del fin que se propusieron los revolucionarios. Las más notables de estas divergencias fueron las existentes entre la capital y las provincias del virreinato. En la Argentina ocurrió como en casi todos los países coloniales al pretender independizarse, el mismo hecho sucedido en los Estados Unidos en sus primeros tiempos de independencia, esto es: que en casi todos ellos se dió el caso, de discordias intestinas entre los dos partidos que se formaron al producirse las sublevaciones: estos partidos fueron el republicano unitario y el federalista.

[1] "Este officio teve a desgraca de desagradar aos dos partidos extremos. Por terme explicado com alguma cortezía de tarifa en louvor dos Individuos da Junta, os oppositores de Esta, me tratarao com demasiada superficialidade, como *Manolo* ou Revolucionario, E por ter dito que a Junta debía auxiliar, e manterse em unidad com a Metrópoli, os *Manolos*, com mais razao me Chamarao *Saraceno*."

Claramente se entiende que en cada uno de los países presentó caracteres y peculiaridades diferentes, que en el fondo eran lo mismo. Así se observa que la lucha entablada en Estados Unidos entre republicanos y federalistas, se reproduce para la América del Sur, en general, con la formación de grandes partidos a los que pudiéramos llamar moderados y separatistas: los primeros deseaban únicamente reformas liberales que los redimiesen de la opresión a que se hallaban sometidos; los segundos trataban de romper todo lazo de unión con la Metrópoli.

Estos partidos se transformaron más tarde y al producirse ya las primeras convulsiones revolucionarias, del fuerte tronco de los separatistas, se desgajaron dos ramas que vinieron a debilitarlo: los republicanos y los federalistas.

Particularizando, apúntase que en Nueva Granada, a raíz de las primeras insurecciones, se distinguen ya los dos partidos últimamente mencionados, con la singularidad de que los primeros toman el nombre de unitarios; no limitándose a una lucha meramente política, sino que llegan a la guerra civil, con grave detrimento del fin común que ambos partidos perseguían.

En las provincias chilenas, este fenómeno político presenta caracteres diferentes. Aquí la discordia surge porque las provincias del Sur, deseando los procedimientos radicales como medio de acción más eficaz, eran hostiles a la superioridad que pretendía ejercer la ciudad de Santiago, donde predominaba el elemento moderado. Esta lucha llegó a agudizarse hasta el punto de que en el año 1812 se separaron las provincias del Sur de las del Norte formando cada una su Junta de Gobierno.

Por último, en la ciudad de Buenos Aires y en todo el virreinato se complicó más esta situación, pues aquí no solamente existían los dos grandes partidos de republicanos radicales y moderados, sino que las principales discusiones partieron de la manifiesta oposición existente entre la capital y las provincias, desde el momento en que la primera pretendía constituir un gobierno perfectamente centralizador, que pudiéramos llamar republicano unitario; y las provincias, por el contrario, odiando la supremacía de la capital, deseaban ardientemente el establecimiento de un régimen federal.

La causa de este hecho la encontramos perfectamente explicada en las diferencias existentes entre la población de la capital y la de las provincias; en la primera predominaba considerablemente el elemento burgués comerciante, industrial, y hasta cierto punto culto; en una frase, la capital representaba el espíritu *criollo*. Por el contrario en las provincias predominaba el elemento indígena compuesto de agricultores y pastores, reducidos a un ínfimo grado de civilización, y cuyo tipo se dibuja con firmes trazos en el *gaucho*. En esta lucha tenaz y partidista triunfó Buenos Aires, por ser más civilizada que las provincias.

La situación de Buenos Aires no llevaba ciertamente camino de consolidarse y cada día surgían nuevos obstáculos que a ello se oponían: fuera de la ciudad, el virreinato se hallaba, no sólo dividido en tendencias y banderías, sino que estaba sumido en la anarquía, muy difícil de contener, apesar de que la Junta encaminaba sus trabajos a ello. Tampoco dentro de la capital andaban muy conformes las opiniones, pues se habían formado distintos partidos, y continuamente se oye hablar de *europeos*, como individuos opuestos a los *criollos*, y dentro de estos últimos los había representando las tendencias mas diversas: quienes eran partidarios de los procedimientos pacíficos y conciliadores, quienes por el contrario preferían y consideraban la violencia como el mejor medio; y en el seno mismo de la Junta de Gobierno había gran disparidad de criterios dificilmente conciliables, ya que el interés general lo posponían al particular, y todos deseaban ponerse a la cabeza del gobierno.

Aunque ajeno por completo a estas intrigas, el emisario portugués dióse perfecta cuenta de la situación; y como según todos los caracteres que esta presentaba, era de esperar que en lugar de caminar hacia la estabilidad se llegase en breve tiempo al estado de anarquía revolucionaria, cosa que el gobierno portugués no estaba dispuesto a tolerar, decidió tomar medidas preventivas, y al efecto dirigió con fecha 1 de Agosto de 1810 un oficio a la Junta de Gobierno, en el cual hace constar que si el Príncipe Regente ha manifestado ciertos sentimientos de benevolencia hacia los habitantes y autoridades del Río de la Plata, lo ha hecho únicamente con el objeto de proveer a la seguridad del virreinato por primario objeto, coadyubar con mayor eficacia a la Causa General, que es el objeto principal para la Metrópoli y sus aliados. Pero la división de opiniones en las Provincias, y aun en la misma Capital, hacen recelar que uno y otro objeto sean igualmente inasequibles, y si por desgracia a las medidas ruidosas que se adoptan para reunir las voluntades, vienen a suceder una guerra civil, es muy dudoso que las intenciones de Vd. consiguiesen establecer una forma de Gobierno provisional, capaz de cumplir con las obligaciones que la Metrópoli y sus aliados tienen derecho a exigir de todos los miembros de la Monarquía Española.

A continuación Guezzi sintetizó en cuatro puntos la situación del virreinato, y los propósitos del gobierno portugués como conse-. cuencia, y eran los siguientes: 1° Que la división de opiniones que se había manifestado en la capital y en las provincias, inquietaba seriamente a la Corte del Brasil. 2° Que no pudiendo el Gobierno provisional establecido ofrecer ninguna garantía en sus relaciones tanto interiores como exteriores, en virtud de su propia organización no podía calmar las alarmas de la misma Corte. 3° Que esta, ya había declarado en 3 y 24 de Abril, que tenía todas sus fuerzas preparada para extinguir o contener, cualquier movimiento revolucionario que pudiese manifestarse en el Río de la Plata. 4° Que para evitar torcidas interpretaciones que podrían darse sobre los sucesos de Buenos Aires, sería conveniente mandar un Diputado al Brasil, para que solicitase de este gobierno sus buenos oficios para la convocación del Congreso General y para el establecimiento de un orden fijo e invariable de la administración; y que, a no dudar, la Corte sería la garantía del nuevo sistema provisional de Gobierno.[3]

Indicaba a la vez, la conveniencia de que a este diputado que se pedía se le invistiera de las facultades necesarias para establecer un arreglo comercial con el Brasil.

En la carta que Carlos José Guezzi dirigió al Conde de Linhares con motivo de lo que se deja expuesto, es mas explícito en sus

[3] Oficio de Carlos José Guezzi al Presidente y Vocales de la Junta Provisional Gubernativa de las Provincias del Rio de la Plata. 1 Agosto.

Exposicao de quanto me accorreo durante a demora que fiz em Buenos Ayres desde 17 de Julho ate 20 Decembro de 1810.

manifestaciones, y como persona bien enterada y percatada de la situación de las provincias platenses, apunta algunas ideas que podían ser una solución para acabar con las actuales discordias, y entre ellas merece consignarse la siguiente: decía Guezzi que el peligro revolucionario desaparecería en el momento que el poder ejecutivo, antes en manos de los virreyes, y usurpado después por la Junta que se constituyó en 25 de Mayo, se entregase en manos de los diputados de cada una de las provincias, pues éstas seguramente elegirían para ejercer la diputación personas de probidad reconocida y de talento bastante para obrar con rectitud y justicia; siendo este momento el adecuado para que la Metrópoli interviniese fomentando iniciativas, satisfaciendo aspiraciones y deseos, y en suma, atrayéndose al buen camino por la persuasión y las concesiones oportunas, a las provincias que, no queriendo soportar por más tiempo la rapiña y el mal gobierno de las autoridades españolas, habían sacudido en un momento de dignidad el yugo que de largos años venían pacientemente sobrellevando, pero que al hacerlo, habían querido volar libres e independientes cuando no tenían alas ni fuerzas para ello.

Indica también Guezzi al Conde de Linhares, la necesidad de hacer una demostración militar en la frontera del virreinato, con objeto de intimidar en lo posible a los revolucionarios que, temiendo el castigo, no cometieran excesos y atropellos.[4]

Según testimonio de Guezzi, el oficio que dirigió a la Junta con fecha 1 de Agosto, y del cual ya hemos hecho mención, causó impresión muy buena, pues comprendieron los individuos que formaban parte de la Junta, que la intervención de la corte del Brasil en sentido favorable o contrario, sería decisiva para el porvenir del Río de la Plata; pero a la vez que los argentinos advertían esta importancia, temían por otra parte la ingerencia de una potencia para ellos tan poderosa como era el Gobierno portugués, pues aunque contaban con el apoyo inglés, este apoyo era puramente moral. Durante todo el mes de Agosto y parte del de Septiembre negoció la Junta con el enviado Guezzi sobre la con-

[4] Carta de Carlos José Guezzi al Conde de Linhares. Buenos Aires 5 Agosto 1810.

veniencia y ventajas, y a la vez sobre los inconvenientes que podían resultar de la mediación portuguesa.

Como la Junta tenía que resolver asuntos de mayor importancia que el que se expone, evitó dar una contestación definitiva sobre el asunto, esperando que el curso de los acontecimientos y las circuntancias determinarían si convenía o no aceptar tal mediación.

Ya se ha indicado como la Junta revolucionaria tuvo decidido interés en justificar ante el gobierno portugués las causas que habían motivado los sucesos del 25 de Mayo. Pues bien, este mismo sistema siguió para cuantos actos de violencia se realizaron durante el primer período de la revolución, con el fin de no atraerse la animosidad del gobierno portugués, único enemigo de consideración y el más temible de cuantos contaba. Esta manera de obrar se patentizó bien claramente cuando, con motivo de los fusilamientos que Castelli realizó en las personas de Liniers, Concha, Allende y otros, Belgrano preguntó a Guezzi (y este calificó de imprudente tal pregunta) sobre la impresión que habría causado en Rio de Janeiro tal suceso; a lo que contestó Guezzi, que seguramente la impresión habría sido malísima, ya que el proceder de los fusilados no podía nunca justificar tal hecho; no sirviendo de nada el argumento que le hizo Belgrano diciendo que ya se convencería de la justicia de este acto, cuando conociese la correspondencia de estos rebeldes con José Bonaparte; lo cual ciertamente nunca pudo demostrar.

Honda preocupación ocasionó a la Junta el conocimiento de un oficio del Conde de Linhares anunciando la concentración de tropas portuguesas en la frontera del virreinato; y como no se conocían las causas de tal determinación, Belgrano interrogó a Guezzi sobre ellas, pues este hecho era una contradicción respecto de las manifestaciones de amistad, poco tiempo antes comunicadas por el gobierno portugués. Guezzi respondió que desconocía los motivos que habían impulsado al ministro portugués a tomar tal determinación, pero que indudablemente lo habría hecho por el estado de inseguridad que ofrecía el virreinato; insistiendo con este motivo sobre la necesidad y conveniencia que resultaría de tener la Junta un diputado en Rio de Janeiro, pues de esta manera tendríanse informes seguros sobre los acontecimientos.

Como la situación no era en verdad muy halagüeña en el virreinato, cuenta Guezzi cómo una gran masa de opinión era partidaria de que el Brasil con su mediación procurase la reconciliación de las provincias del Río de la Plata; y que de esta manera de pensar no participaba solamente el pueblo, que era quien principalmente sufría las consecuencias de la revolución, sino que también prestaban su asentimiento a tal idea personas tan importantes como lo era, y lo fué más todavía posteriormente, el Dean de La Catedral de Córdoba del Tucumán, Dr. Gregorio Funes, quien apuntó a Guezzi la idea de que en el momento en que se arreglasen las provincias y se reuniera el Congreso General, sería de necesidad absoluta que éste fuera protegido por una fuerza portuguesa "sin cuya circunstancia, dice, jamais gozaria da libertade suficiente para manifestar as suas opinioes".

Y en verdad que esta pudo haber sido la solución más rápida y satisfactoria, pues según Guezzi, el único modo de arrebatar a la Junta el poder que tan tiránicamente ejercía, era la reunión del Congreso General o la guerra; e indica al Conde de Linhares la necesidad de tomar uno u otro camino.[6]

De todo lo expuesto se desprende que Guezzi se mostraba de opinión de que el gobierno portugués interviniera directamente en los negocios del Río de la Plata, pues su inacción sería interpretada por la Junta como temor o debilidad, cosa que no convenía a los fines portugueses; por lo tanto, pedía el inmediato envío de fuerzas navales·a Buenos Aires, y dice al Conde de Linhares que "Se V. E. trata o que passa nestas Provincias por huma bagatela, está muy equivocado. São 200 mil furiosos sem principios a quen não faltão se não armas para desafiar todo o poder da España e do Brazil. Deixeme organizar, unir, extender, e veremos as consequencias". ¡Con cuánta clarividencia conoció Carlos José Guezzi la fuerza que llevaba la revolución argentina, sino se ponía inmediato coto a sus demasías! El tiempo se encargó de darle la razón cumplidamente.

[6] Oficio de Carlos José Guezzi al Conde de Linhares. Buenos Aires 16 de Septiembre de 1810.

El Dean, Dr. Gregorio Funes, era muy considerado por la Junta de Buenos Aires, y según referencias de Guezzi se precuraba siempre conocer la opinión que formaba de los acontecimientos, y casi siempre se respetaban las soluciones que él proponía; por él supo Guezzi que, habiendo hablado con Belgrano, éste se mostró opuesto a la mediación portuguesa. Entonces el Dean le preguntó al enviado portugués si no sería mejor solución que, en lugar de la mediación portuguesa, se admitiese la inglesa. Comprendiendo el alcance de la pregunta, Guezzi respondió airado "Que a Inglaterra podía ser mediatriz se quizessen; porem que a Corte do Brazil, devía selo, *quizessen ou não quizessen*; que esta a mais de amiga, y aliada tinha o titulo de vizinha, e interesada nos negocios do paiz. Que não se imaginasse que os direitos da Señora Princeza ficavão esguecidos por se ter demorado e execucao da justa reclamacao, e que devia estar na inteligencia, que a recusacao dos officios amigaveis, e paternaes em materia tao grave era huma manifiesta provocaçao, e legitimaba e emprego de forca". ¡Lastima que el espiritu y carácter enérgico de este enviado no fuera secundado en Rio de Janeiro por el Conde de Linhares!

Siéndole indicado a Guezzi por la Junta de Buenos Aires, la conveniencia de que manifestase por escrito las proposiciones que podrían ser agradables a la corte de Rio de Janeiro, lo hizo así, y estas proposiciones fueron las siguientes: 1ª El reconocimiento de los derechos eventuales de la Serenísima Sra. Princesa del Brasil. Al hacer Guezzi esta proposición la acompañó de los argumentos necesarios para demostrar el fundamento de tales derechos y el uso que la Infanta pensaba hacer de ellos. 2ª Aceptación por parte de la Junta de la mediación del gobierno portugués, el cual únicamente exigiría como base de aquella, el reconocimiento del Gobierno Supremo establecido en España y el compromiso de ayudar a la defensa de la Metrópoli.[6] Las anteriores dos proposiciones fueron ampliamente discutidas por el Secretario de la Junta, D. Mariano Moreno, y por Guezzi: el primero opuso muchas dificultades a ambos puntos, quedando

[6] Oficio de Guezzi a Mariano Moreno. Buenos Aires 17 Novbre. 1810.

convenidos en que serían sometidas a la consideración y deliberación de la Junta y ella daría una respuesta definitiva.

En efecto, pocos dias después de presentadas las proposiciones, fué Guezzi a recoger la respuesta que se le había prometido. Mejor que glosarlo, para darlo a conocer preferimos reproducir, traducido integramente del original, el diálogo que con este y otros motivos sostuvo el Dr. Moreno con Guezzi, y que éste tuvo la felicísima idea de reproducir en la Exposición que escribió, de cuanto le aconteció en Buenos Aires durante su estancia.

DIÁLOGO

Moreno.—La Junta no estima conveniente mandar un Diputado a la Corte del Brasil. Esta debe estar satisfecha con la prueba de confianza que se la ha dado, comunicándole las cartas que el Marqués de Casa Irujo dirigió al Virrey Cisneros.

Guezzi.—No creo que baste esta comunicación. Desde Julio hasta aquí han ocurrido tales novedades que necesariamente deben precisar nuevas explicaciones.

Moreno.—No ha habido otras novedades que las precisas para organizar el Gobierno interior, bajo el plan que se ha elegido.

Guezzi.—Pero el plan que se ha elegido y el modo de organizarlo, puede ser tal, que sea incompatible con los intereses del Brasil.

Moreno.—La Junta no se ocupa de los intereses del Brasil, sino de los intereses del virreinato del Río de la Plata.

Guezzi.—El Sr. Moreno no puede disimular que la Corte del Brasil tiene legítimos intereses a deslindar con este país; pero prescindiendo de ellos, diré en general, que de no querer separarse de todo el Mundo, es preciso que el Gobierno de Buenos Aires combine sus intereses con los de las Potencias vecinas. En este sentido por lo menos, me será concedido hablar de los intereses del Brasil.

Moreno.—El comercio del Brasil fué favorecido y los vasallos de S.A.R. protegidos y respetados.

Guezzi.—S.ᵃA.R. no dejará de agradecer estas atenciones, pero ellas son de segundo orden; el principal interés del Brasil, es que se conserve la paz y la unión en el Virreinato; que una Provincia no quiera esclavizar a otra; y que por ahora todas concurran en cuanto puedan a la defensa de la causa general.

Moreno.—Esto es justamente de lo que se ocupa el Gobierno. Y culpa es de los sublevados, si hasta ahora no se ha podido conseguir.   .

Guezzi.—Si la Junta hubiese adoptado, o adoptase el arbitrio de la mediación que propongo, no habría resistencia ni oposición, ni se necesitaría de los medios violentos que se han empleado. Aún estamos a tiempo de remediar muchos males, si la Junta quiere avenirse a esta proposición.

Moreno.—¿Y bajo que términos aceptaría la Corte del Brasil el oficio de Medianera?

Guezzi.—Yo lo ignoro, pero me parece que no se reusaría en ningún término que fuese justo y razonable.

Moreno.—¿Y quién nos asegura que de Mediadora, no quiera pasar la Corte del Brasil a ser Señora de estas Provincias?

Guezzi.—Esta sospecha no tiene fundamento. Lo que se halla impreso en la justa reclamación[7], y las alianzas actuales con la Península, excluyen toda idea de conquista.

Moreno.—Pero la Corte del Brasil ha de querer emplear la fuerza, y de este modo la mediación es inadmisible.

Guezzi.—Es cierto que una fuerza es indispensable; con ella puede garantizar una Protección igual a Españoles y Patricios, reprimiendo a aquellos que fomenten divisiones. Sin la presencia de una fuerza se perpetuarían las desconfianzas, y pronto se pasaría a violencias, en precaución de violencias más temidas.

Moreno.—De modo que en opinión de V. M., un Ejército Portugués debe venir a consolidar la paz en las Provincias del Río de la Plata?

Guezzi.—No digo tal cosa. El Ejército no pasaría de sus fronteras, escepto si lo promovedores de disturbios rompiesen los pactos que fuesen sancionados bajo la garantía del Brasil.

Las consecuencias del anterior e interesante diálogo no pudieron ser más inesperadas.   Creyendo el Dr. Moreno que el gobierno

---

[7] Se refiere al Manifiesto que publicaron la infanta Dª Carlota y el infante D. Pedro Carlos, el 19 Agosto de 1808.

portugués estaba decidido, según acababa de oir de labios de su enviado a intervenir directamente en la política bonaerense y que esta intervención iba a ser apoyada por un numeroso ejército, dió cuenta inmediata a la Junta de la conversación que acababa de tener con Guezzi, y con no menos rapidez la Junta tomó el siguiente acuerdo, que fué transmitido a Guezzi:

La Excma. Junta Provisional Gubernativa de las Provincias del Río de la Plata, ha resuelto decididamente que Vd., en el primer buque que salga para el Rio Janeiro, se restituya a aquel destino, a cuyo efecto con esta misma fecha, da orden al Capitan del Puerto, para que esté a la mira del cumplimiento de esta providencia, y lo aviso a Vd. para su intelgencia. Dios guarde a Vd. muchos años. Buenos Aires 20 de Noviembre de 1810.

CORNELIO SAAVEDRA,

[Addressed:] Sr. D. Carlos José Guezzi.

Aunque no lo manifiesta, grande debió ser la sorpresa del enviado portugués al recibir una tan conminatoria orden de partida, que tenía todos los caracteres de expulsión, tanto más inesperada cuanto que había convenido con el Dr. Moreno que formularía por escrito la propuesta que ya conocemos, propuesta que sería contestada por la Junta en igual forma.

Como le unían lazos de amistad al Dr. Funes, a éste acudió para darle cuenta del oficio que acababa de recibir, informándole a la vez de la conversación que le había precedido con el Dr. Moreno, yendo también con la idea de que le explicase, si podía, la causa que había motivado su expulsión. Y en efecto, no salió Guezzi defraudado de su entrevista con el Dr. Funes, pues este le explicó la causa de la actitud adoptada por la Junta; y no sólo esto, sino que le dió a conocer claramente los propósitos que abrigaba la Junta revolucionaria.

La expulsión tuvo por causa, según el Dr. Funes, el considerar la Junta como un grave delito cualquier proposición que se le hiciera sobre mediaciones o arreglos, y mucho más si estos eran apoyados, como en la portuguesa, por un ejército. De donde claramente se deduce que el objeto de la Junta, desde el primer momento, fue entretener al enviado portugués con dilaciones y vanas palabras, para dar tiempo a que la situación del virreinato se consolidase al adquirir fuerza, y como resultado, hacer inútil por tardía la intervención portuguesa.

En cuanto a los propósitos que abrigaban los próceres argentinos, el Dr. Funes hizo saber a Guezzi, que lo que se pretendía a toda costa era que el virreinato del Plata se gobernase por un régimen democrático propio e independiente, y como esto no se podía conseguir ni se podía esperar ayuda para ello más que de la Gran Bretaña, tenían que procurar separarse totalmente de la Metrópoli y de Portugal, procurando el virreinato por sí solo la consecución de sus propósitos.

Guezzi, aún comprendiendo que su presencia no podía ser del agrado de la Junta, se decidió a partir, si, pero no sin antes sacar todo el partido posible de la Junta, en el sentido de conocer en toda la amplitud posible sus proyectos, que, después de lo dicho por el Dr. Funes, eran todavía de más interés para el gobierno portugués que lo habían sido antes.

Así pues, y con excusa de tener que recoger ciertos papeles que obraban en poder de la Junta, demoró su partida, y entre tanto buscó ocasión propicia de hablar con el Dr. Moreno, consiguiéndo conversar con él tres veces, siendo el último diálogo el que resumió todos los anteriores, y el cual se verificó a petición de Moreno y en su propia casa, el día 13 de Diciembre a las 10 y media de la noche, con ocasión en que se hallaba en la casa el vocal de la Junta, Larrea, que también terció en la conversación.   He aquí el diálogo, literalmente traducido.

Moreno.—Por noticias particulares me consta que la Corte del Brasil reune fuerzas en la frontera.

Guezzi.—Ignoro lo que pasa en la frontera del Brasil, pero he de presumir, en efecto, que la Corte toma algunas precauciones en vista de las agitaciones de estas Provincias.

Moreno.—Quien produce estas agitaciones son los sublevados y rebeldes, engañados por los marinos.   Los Pueblos de Montevideo y Paraguay ya estarían reunidos a la Capital, si estos fuesen expulsados.

Guezzi.—La Corte del Brasil no entra en estas averiguaciones. Ve un incendio y desea apagarlo, sin preguntar quien ha sido el autor de él.

Moreno.—Si la Corte del Brasil adopta el arbitrio de la Guerra, ella se arrepentirá, pues excitará en su propio país el fuego que pretende apagar en el ajeno.

Guezzi.—La Corte del Brasil no provoca la guerra. Esto lo tiene probado con las contemplaciones tal vez excesivas, que guardó con esta Capital. Pero el Sr. Moreno estará persuadido como yo, que la forma de Gobierno adoptada por la Junta, y los principios inculcados en los Pueblos del Virreinato, obligan a la Corte del Brasil, a sofocar en su origen un incendio que, como dice el Sr. Moreno, puede extenderse al Brasil.

Moreno.—Esta Capital no se ocupa sino de su Régimen interior, el cual nada tiene que ver en el Brasil.

Guezzi.—La Corte del Brasil debe mirar por el estado de estas Provincias, como Vecina, como Aliada de España, y como interesada en los sucesos de estos Dominios, en los Casos determinados por la Constitución. Es por tanto locura pensar que ha de prescindir de estas razones de estado, y que debe ser indiferente sobre lo que pasa en estas Provincias.

Moreno.—La Junta tiene dado prueba de espiritu de paz y de confianza que tiene en la Corte del Brasil, mandando retirar las guarniciones de la Frontera.

Guezzi.—Eso, así será, pero es probable que en Brasil se de a esta retirada una interpretación nada favorable.

Moreno.—Y qué fuerzas tiene el Brasil en la Frontera?

Guezzi.—¿Yo lo ignoro; pero creo que hallándose prevenido de Oficio, que era intención del Virrey Cisneros armar 12 mil hombres el Brasil por precaución reuniría una igual fuerza.

Moreno.—¿Cree Vd. que las fuerzas del Brasil se juntarán con los Españoles de la Banda Oriental?

Guezzi.—Nada sé; pero si estas provincias fieles al gobierno de la nación, que la Corte del Brasil reconoce, imploran su patrocinio, ninguna duda tengo de que las protegerá.

Moreno.—Pues nosotros también tenemos jurado a Fernando VII y sus legítimos sucesores.

Guezzi.—Si este juramento comprende la debida fidelidad y obediencia al mismo soberano, es preciso entonces que las desavenencias hayan nacido de falta de entenderse; y renuevo por tanto la instancia tantas veces hecha, de mandar una persona a Rio de Janeiro para dar y pedir las explicaciones necesarias ya, que los Españoles entre sí no se pueden entender.

Moreno.—La Junta también desearía mandar un Diputado, pero no conoce una persona capaz de una comisión tan delicada.

Guezzi.—Sobran en esta ciudad Personas de talento, y yo podría nombrar muchas que gozan de completa confianza de la Junta.

Larrea.—Yendo V.M. excusamos mandar un Diputado; V.M. puede dar al Ministro Portugués una idea verídica de las intenciones y procedimientos de la Junta.

Guezzi.—Creo que el Sr. Larrea se burla de mi. Trátase de mandar una Persona que lleve la palabra de la Junta, y que diga lo que ésta piensa y quiere. Yo nunca podría ser intérprete fiel ni acreditado, porque nunca diría sino lo que pienso yo mismo de la Junta.

Larrea.—No debemos mandar un Diputado para ser desairado. El Ministro Portugués nunca quiso escribir a esta Junta, lo que indica que no quiere entenderse con Ella.

Guezzi.—El Gabinete Británico no desairó al Diputado que se le mandó, apesar de que nunca escribió ni respondió a las proposiciones de la Junta. La etiqueta de los Gabinetes no permite que los Secretarios de Estado tengan correspondencia directa con Gobiernos iguales, y mucho menos con Gobiernos subalternos.

Larrea.—Podía responder por vía del Ministro Español.

Guezzi.—(Contesté con una carcajada.)

Larrea.—O por lo menos entenderse con el Gobierno de España.

Guezzi.—No dudo que el Ministerio Portugués está en inteligencia con el Gobierno de España. Pero ¿desde cuándo reconoce la Junta este gobierno?

No es necesario proclamar la importancia y transcendencia política del diálogo que se acaba de transcribir. Por su sola lectura, y sin hacer el menor comentario, pueden apreciarse ambas circunstancias. Este diálogo representa el momento culminante de la misión secreta de Guezzi en Buenos Aires, y sintetiza toda su actuación en dicha ciudad.

Tanto en esta como en la anterior conversación, pueden así mismo observarse las condiciones diplomáticas de los interlocutores. Del Dr. Mariano Moreno, es fama universal que poseía un talento preclaro, y estaba dotado de inmejorables condiciones diplomáticas, siendo sin duda un enemigo temible para cualquier negociación, como claramente lo demuestra en los diálogos antecedentes, sobresaliendo sus cualidades en el último de ellos; y así se le ve descargando en otros culpas que únicamente a los revolucionarios correspondían. Para persuadir, emplea simultáneamente la amenaza y el deseo de contemporizar; con gran rapidez de pensamiento procura desvirtuar los sólidos y bien fundamentados argumentos de su interlocutor; no duda en emplear sofismas y en falsear a conciencia la verdad, para tratar de persuadir; tiene la facilidad de desviar habilmente la conversación, cuando no le conviene contestar a ciertas preguntas, y a la vez muy sutilmente procura averiguar los proyectos de sus contrarios, no concediendo importancia a ciertas interrogaciones que en el fondo la tienen. Todo esto demuestra que el Dr. Moreno fué un diplomático de excelentes condiciones.

Pero en la ocasión presente el Dr. Moreno, aún poniendo a contribución sus cualidades diplomáticas, bien pocas consecuencias de importancia pudo aprovechar de sus conferencias con el enviado portugués; pues si inteligente y persuasivo era Moreno, Guezzi no era menos sagaz y astuto; y aunque de inferior inteligencia este último, con las cualidades dichas suplía las diferencias que entre ambos existían. No se olvide que Guezzi era italiano, y estaba dotado de gran perspicacia y habilidad para ver y tratar las cuestiones políticas; por eso puede apreciarse a través del diálogo, que en cuantas contestaciones da a las cuestiones que propone y pregunta Moreno, responde siempre con gran habilidad, acogiéndose a la ignorancia cuando así lo estima conveniente, y dando importancia y aún exagerando las cosas, cuando le conviene causar determinados efectos; así no es de extrañar que atribuya al gobierno portugués gran alteza de miras en su política, y en sus proposiciones; lo cual en realidad estaba bien alejado de ser cierto. Observese también que cuando Moreno con gran conocimiento de causa le hace ver que el Brasil desea introducirse en asuntos que no le competen, responde excusándose en los perjuicios que muy verosímilmente pueden ocasionarse al gobierno que representa, por lo cual éste no es extraño que concentre sus ejércitos en la frontera y tome toda clase de precauciones, esforzándose en demostrar que no le animan en la actualidad instintos bélicos, sino que le impulsan a intervenir deseos de paz y tranquilidad que debe procurar en todas las colonias vecinas; por último, Guezzi sostiene con gran habilidad la polémica empleando argumentos y dando contestaciones que le colocan a la altura de su interlocutor.

La intervención que en diálogo tuvo el Vocal de la Junta, Larrea, no pudo ser mas desafortunada, pues pretendiendo afianzar los razonamientos de Moreno, aduce tan torpes razones que provocan la hilaridad de Guezzi.

Como resúmen a estas consideraciones puede decirse que el Dr. Moreno representa la inteligencia y la alta diplomacia; y que el enviado portugués es el prototipo de la astucia y sagacidad políticas.

Después de las conversaciones referidas aún tuvo ocasión Guezzi de hablar con el Dr. Moreno, pero lo tratado en los últimos coloquios no debía encerrar gran importancia cuando el enviado portugués no los consideró dignos de mención detallada, limitándose a consignar que los tuvo.

Pasó luego Guezzi a despedirse del Dean Funes, quien le indicó la conveniencia de que demorase se salida, porque se esperaba de un momento a otro la sustitución del actual gobierno por otro que seguramente atendería mejor sus proposiciones. Pero viendo que transcurrían días sin que esto sucediera, y ante el temor de un apercibimiento, el día 20 de Diciembre de 1810 embarcó Guezzi en el navío *Belisario*, a cuyo capitán entregó un oficio que el Dr. Moreno dirigía al Conde de Linhares, y pasó luego a la nave inglesa *Quem* que como había de permanecer cierto tiempo en la rada de Buenos Aires le permitía esperar allí, con objeto de ver si ocurría el cambio de gobierno que se esperaba; pero sin que nada sucediera permaneció a bordo hasta finales del mes de Enero del año 1811.

Desde la indicada fecha se pierde el rastro de este personaje, no sólo en su actuación política, sino fuera de esta, en su condición social, habiendo resultado inútiles cuantas investigaciones he realizado para saber de Guezzi con posterioridad al citado año de 1811.

Considero interesante dar a conocer ciertos brevísimos juicios que formó Guezzi de la revolución argentina y de alguna de los personajes principales actores en ella.   La importancia de estos juicios se origina de que el enviado portugués conoció bastante profundamente tanto la revolución como sus hombres, ya que vivió la primera, y trato a los segundos; y como tuvo la buena idea de consignar estas sus apreciaciones al final de la Exposición a que hemos hecho referencia varias veces, vamos a glosarlas siquiera sea ligeramente.

Hablando de la personalidad del Dean de la Catedral de Cordoba del Tucumán, Dr. Funes, le considera como hombre dedicado preferentemente a las letras, aunque apasionado por las cuestiones políticas; adornado de las excelentes cualidades personales sencillez y modestia, lo que según Guezzi predisponía a cobrarle pronto efecto; de maneras insinuantes y muy tenaz para sus propósitos, era un verdadero patriota que encaminaba todo su valer al servicio del país, y que como hijo que era de una provincia, no fué nunca partidario de la supremacía que Buenos Aires quiso ejercer sobre el resto del virreinato del Río de la Plata.

Por sus merecimientos, el Dr. Funes, se había hecho acreedora verse favorecido y ensalzado por los poderosos, especialmente por el virrey Liniers y por la infanta Dᵃ Carlota, que, considerándole como persona de gran influencia, mantuvo con él una extensa correspondencia.

Sin buscar popularidad, procuró encauzar la opinión de los argentinos, y convencido del desgobierno que reinaba desde la formación de la Junta en 25 de Mayo de 1810, fué opuesto a cuantos actos de violencia verificó ésta.   Su actitud de moderación y templanza causó muy mal efecto en los avanzados espíritus de los caudillos argentinos.   Apesar de estas cualidades, era ferviente partidario de la independencia de su patria, predominando en él las ideas democráticas, según Guezzi atestigua; y consideraba como más favorable para su país la intervención, o mediación, de Inglaterra que la de Portugal.

Son por demas curiosos los comentarios que a Guezzi le sugirieron la Junta Provisional y los individuos que de ella formaban parte; así por ejemplo, considera al Dr. D. Mariano Moreno como "el Robespierre del día"; y estima a cuantos le rodean como individuos sin ningun valer personal, pero que juntos y unidos son "oportunos y ardientes instrumentos de la Tiranía"; y que como finalidad de su actuación se proponían fundar una República sobre la base del terrorismo.

Acremente censura a los criollos, especialmente a los incultos provincianos a quienes llama "asta vil del campo"; y tiene para los principales la siguiente frase: "En Cordova, una manada de Patricios se presentó al Gobierno, pidiendo licencia para matar *sarracenos.*"[8] Sin embargo, distingue entre los patricios cultos, que no simpatizan con los medios violentos puestos en práctica por la Junta, y los partidarios de Saavedra, presidente de la misma "porque dice, son la clase militar y forman una especie de *sansculottes*, porque efectivamente son todos pobres y hambrientos; los partidarios de Moreno son como la *Montaña* entre los Jacobinos".

En lo apuntado se sintetiza el juicio que Guezzi formó de la revolución y de los revolucionarios del Río de la Plata. Es indudable que las frases envuelven un apasionamiento muy pronunciado; pero no por esto dejan de ser notas tomadas de la realidad vivida. Y está fuera de duda que la revolución argentina tuvo momentos y. personas que sólo alabanzas merecen de la posteridad; pero no es menos cierto que, como todas las revoluciones, tuvo también tiranos y momentos de crueldad.

Así esbozada, esta fué la primera negociación diplomática que se realizó cerca del primer gobierno independiente del Virreinato del Río de la Plata. Si en justicia no se la puede considerar como de una importancia suprema y decisiva, tampoco se la debe menospreciar hasta el punto de no hacer siquiera mención de ella, como hasta hoy ha venido ocurriendo.

JULIAN MARIA RUBIO Y ESTEBAN

[8] Así denominaban a los españoles.

[TRANSLATION]

THE FIRST DIPLOMATIC NEGOTIATIONS WITH THE REVOLUTIONARY JUNTA OF BUENOS AIRES

There has been a belief generally admitted up to the present that the first diplomatic negotiations celebrated by the revolutionary junta of Buenos Aires, soon after its creation, were those with the government of his Britahnic Majesty. As foundation for this assertion, it was alleged that within four days after the outbreak of the revolution, that is, on May 29, 1810, credentials were given by the junta to Don Matías Irigoyen, for presentation to the London government in order to negotiate therewith for the recognition of the junta created in the capital of the Plata.

And in fact, if this circumstance alone be considered, it will not be surprising to affirm that Great Britain was the first to enter into relations with the revolutionists of Buenos Aires. However, if we examine this question, even very lightly, we shall prove that the priority does not belong to the English government, but to the Portuguese government established at Rio de Janeiro. The latter government accredited Don Carlos José Guezzi to the revolutionary junta with the character of secret envoy, and he presented himself to the junta on July 17, 1810, while the Argentine envoy, Irigoyen, reached England on August 5 of the same year, and presented himself at the Foreign Office on the day following.

If the above were not definitive, other circumstances could demonstrate the fact, for even if this diplomatic mission be left out of account, the priority would always belong to the Portuguese government, since that from the time of the creation of the junta, relations were maintained between Rio de Janeiro and Buenos Aires, from government to government.

In this brief study, we propose to discuss the diplomatic negotiations carried on in Buenos Aires by the Portuguese envoy, Carlos José Guezzi, together with the results and consequences produced. This sècret mission took place in the interim between July 17, 1810, the date of Guezzi's arrival at Buenos Aires, and December 20 of the same year, when the abovesaid emissary left Buenos Aires.

For the exposition, development, and results produced, we have as a source and use especially a collection of documents unpublished in their entirety consisting of three parts; 1. Correspondence of Guezzi

with the revolutionary junta of Buenos Aires; 2. Correspondence of
Guezzi with the Count of Linhares; 3. Relations of all events during
my stay in Buenos Aires, from July 17 to December 20, 1810. The
first consists of five documents, the second of seven, and the third is
very extensive.

I.

Upon the outbreak of the revolution of Buenos Aires, and as soon
as news of the creation of a government junta in the neighboring
capital of the Plata reached the Portuguese government at Rio de
Janeiro, and after the first moment of surprise produced by this unexpected occurrence, the Count of Linhares, then prime minister of the
prince regent of Brazil, began to revolve in his restless imagination the
idea of entering into immediate relations with the incipient revolutionary government, although under a certain character of secrecy,
for the simple reason that the abovesaid government for the time being
offered no conditions of stability—this aside from the fact the Portuguese government, since it was allied with that of Spain, could not,
without committing a breach of that alliance, enter either into negotiations or even into diplomatic relations.

However, he was urged thereto by motives of a diverse nature,
which we shall demonstrate briefly. In the first place, the keen Portuguese minister was not ignorant of the consequences that might happen
to Brazil from the outbreak in the neighboring states of a revolutionary
convulsion which had a marked character of rebellion and unmistakable
tendencies for independence from their mother country; and that, as
is natural, the leaders of this movement would try to have it spread
to all the South American territories that were in the same situation
as the Río de la Plata, that is, in the condition of a colony dependent
on a mother country. That was the situation of Brazil, although
circumstances there were different, because the Portuguese court was
then residing although only temporarily in this its chief colony. But
this was no obstacle to the fact that the abovesaid danger might become
a threatening one.

On the other hand, the Portuguese government had several projects
in regard to the annexation of certain territories belonging to the
revolted viceroyalty—projects not known in Buenos Aires—and which
consequently, might be the cause of incurring the hostility of the new
government and so preventing their realization. This explains perfectly why the Count of Linhares should try to establish these diplo-

matic relations, for aware that Brazil was the only state which could aid the nascent republic of the Plata in a positive and effective way, he tried to extend the sympathies of his government in this manner, so that he might demand with a certain right when the time was ripe, those compensations which he was very ardently asking, and which this was the only means of getting.

It is also well known that the Infanta Doña Carlota Joaquina de Borbón, the wife of the prince regent of Brazil, had been making certain efforts since 1808 to establish herself at the head of a regency of the viceroyalty of Buenos Aires—efforts which had been paralyzed for some time, but of which the Count of Linhares now desired the Portuguese government to take advantage, for certain ends which assuredly were not the same which urged on the daughter of Carlos IV. to seize them.

The above, among many other reasons, might be alleged in order to determine quite clearly the motives that induced the above mentioned Portuguese minister to send Don Carlos José Guezzi to the junta of Buenos Aires as a secret emissary of the government of Rio de Janeiro.

The Count of Linhares, then, having resolved to accredit an envoy to Buenos Aires, he chose the said Guezzi as the one to undertake this mission, and to avoid suspicion. The latter was an Italian adventurer who had been expelled from Buenos Aires at the time of the English attacks in 1806, and who having sought asylum in Rio de Janeiro allied himself with other refugees like himself. Among these were Don Saturnino Rodríguez Peña, Felipe Contucci, M. de Parosin, and the Perichón brothers, all men whose ideas were very well known, and who, in one way or another, caused their personalities to stand out because of the events of Buenos Aires, and some even before the said events. For, in the first place they had devoted themselves to aiding Rodríguez Peña when the latter had entered into relations with the infanta Doña Carlota Joaquina in order to crown her in Buenos Aires, and had afterward been mixed up in political intrigues of all kinds and conditions that might furnish them means of subsistence.

The fact that he was of a wideawake and keen intellect and of accentuated social talent, that he had a good understanding of the affairs of South America, and that he possessed the correct status of culture, as is shown by his writings, caused the Count of Linhares to select Guezzi as a person suitable to undertake the mission that he had in mind at the revolutionary junta of Buenos Aires, and since, in addition to the qualities above mentioned, he had the good fortune to know personally some of the men who exercised visible influence in the neighboring capital.

The instructions given to Guezzi by the Count of Linhares, were not, nor could they be, concrete and definite, since what the Portuguese government desired to know in some detail was the purpose that the junta of Buenos Aires had in mind, in order that it might act in consequence thereof.

He was clearly aware that in order to accomplish this, a reason or cause was needed which would justify in some way the presence in Buenos Aires of a Portuguese envoy. In this way the instructions given to Guezzi by the Count of Linhares which can easily be deduced from the writings of both men, can be explained.

Consequently, the first point which Guezzi had to treat with the junta had reference to putting to flight the fears which the Argentinian leaders must have had with respect to the policy and methods of the Portuguese government in recent times, and with everything connected with the viceroyalty. For this purpose, he was charged to state to the junta that the Portuguese government had acted justly in refusing to allow the Marquis of Casa Irujo, the ambassador for Spain at Rio de Janeiro, to arrest the Argentinian refugees there, and that the latter sympathized and were working in common accord with their compatriots of Buenos Aires to bring about the movement which had been brought to a head on May 25, 1910. The Count of Linhares thought that this would have an excellent effect on the members of the revolutionary junta.

In the second place, Guezzi was to get the sympathy of the junta by making a formal declaration before it to the effect that his Royal Highness, the prince regent of Portugal and Brazil had no wish to mix in nor take part in matters that might be the cause of displeasure to the Spanish inhabitants of the viceroyalty of the Plata. He hoped that, as a just compensation for this benevolence, which was freely offered, the Argentinian patriots in their turn would keep the consideration and respect which they owed to the august person of the regent and of his spouse, the infanta Doña Carlota Joaquina, who, as they could not lose sight of, possessed authentic rights to the succession of the Spanish monarchy. They should not forget, moreover, that the said infanta had no wish to make use of those rights except for the advantage and wellbeing of the Hispanic American peoples. As a complement to all this, he was to make clear that the sentiments of the prince were entirely pacific and favorable with respect to the late happenings in the viceroyalty.

These manifestations which Guezzi was to make to the junta, involved another indication of greater importance, namely, the acknowledgment on the part of the junta of the rights of Doña Carlota, to which we have alluded. This was a motive for serious dissension.

For the rest, according to the documents which we are about to examine, Guezzi was invested with powers sufficiently ample to discuss other matters which could not be precisely stated from Rio de Janeiro.

The reasons above set forth had no other purpose than that of justifying the presence of the Portuguese envoy in Buenos Aires. That envoy had as his chief mission that of investigating the various plans and projects which the junta was trying to realize, since these could not be known or even suspected from Rio de Janeiro.

II.

During the first part of July, 1810, Carlos José Guezzi left Rio de Janeiro for the capital of the Plata, which he reached on the 17th of the same month. On that day, the 17th, he tried to be received by the junta, but did not succeed because that body was so busy with other things. However, he was promised that he would be received the next day.

On the same day, and in his private capacity, he visited Don Manuel Belgrano and Castelli, who were members of the junta, and who were, especially the first, men of great influence on it. In consequence of this, they would be able to tell him what opinion had been formed relative to the Portuguese government, and whether he would be well received as the representative of that government. Therefore, in as much as he deemed this advisable, he showed them the instructions that had been given him by the Count of Linhares, to which we have already referred. At the same time he asked them whether the junta was prepared to recognize the rights of Doña Carlota to the Spanish crown, rights which had been recognized by the central junta of that country.

When such claims were learned by Belgrano and Castelli, they replied somewhat ambiguously that the junta had not the slightest reason for complaint against the Portuguese government and that so far as the rights of the infanta were concerned, they believed that the junta was considering, not only recognizing them, but also calling her in due time to rule the destinies of the viceroyalty, and that the other members of the junta were of the same opinion. But the realization of this carried with it many difficulties that would have to be overcome, not only on the part of the native Argentinians since these already desired it, but of the Europeans who would be those to oppose most difficulties. For this reason, it would be best to await the assembly of the general congress, which would decide the question.

At first sight it seems strange that the Argentinian revolutionists should make such a reply through the mouth of one of their directors, with respect to a matter which had not even been considered, but it must not be forgotten that Belgrano and Castelli were among those who less than two years before had tried to crown the infanta Doña Carlota in Buenos Aires—a project in which Belgrano had been intensely interested. The plan fell through for lack of ventilation in the viceroyalty of Rio de la Plata, through the tenacious opposition of the English ambassador in Rio de Janeiro, Lord Strangford, and because of differences that arose between the native Argentinians and Doña Carlota Joaquina.

The interview held by Guezzi with the junta on July 18, proved of interest because of the widely separate things which were discussed. After the junta had expressed gratification over the sentiments expressed by the prince regent through the medium of his envoy relative to a maintenance of the friendship and good relations necessary to the two governments, the members tried to justify before Guezzi the very urgent need of the city of Buenos Aires in exiling the viceroy and establishing a government junta, which was done, in order to prevent, as they said, the success of the French machinations, which were endangering the security of the viceroyalty. This was completely false. After that the envoy was questioned as to the effect produced in Brazil by the late occurrences in Buenos Aires, and at the same time, as to whether he considered it advisable for the infanta to make use of her rights.

Considering the importance of these questions and the no less consequence involved in the answers, Guezzi, shying off from making a categorical declaration, answered by saying that the Portuguese court had not formed any definitive judgment on the occurrences, in Buenos Aires, since they knew these very imperfectly and consequently did not know what were the intentions of the Argentinians in changing their government. So far as concerned the rights of Doña Carlota Joaquina, he believed that since she had been recognized formally by the central junta of Spain, it was to be hoped that all the South American peoples would be in accord with such decision.   Don Cornelio Saavedra, president of the revolutionary junta, replied to this that "there could be no doubt of this, and that although all the nation was of a contrary mind, the people of Buenos Aires and the junta which he had the honor to govern, would be the first to seize the sword for the preservation of her rights".

When he gave this reply, it can be assumed that Saavedra departed entirely from the truth and knowingly so, for such recognition of rights had never been the purpose of the revolutionists.   In fact, it was intended that the Portuguese government should consider this reply as a flattering promise, but it did not have that meaning from the moment of utterance and was meant to cause the same effect which the Argentinians were trying to obtain, always presenting as a justification of their actions the name of Ferdinand VII.; and from this point of view, such a declaration involved no promise.

One may say, then, that the junta received the emissary of the government with a good grace, although very soon their cordiality, which was only assumed, was to grow lukewarm, since the claims of each of the two parties were opposed and of distinct ends.   We already know the ends of the Portuguese envoy, and the ends of the government of Buenos Aires were directed to ascertaining the purposes and projects of the court of Rio de Janeiro which they considered from the first moment as a nearby future enemy, since they would necessarily be opposed to the policies of both governmants.

As it was considered advisable for the present, at least officially, to show the gratification of the junta at the declarations made by Guezzi, a despatch was drawn up for transmission to the count of Linhares, in which gratitude was expressed to the Portuguese court, and false protestations were made of love and fidelity to Spain.[1]

The Portuguese envoy was not a man to be carried away by vain words and empty promises, although they proceeded from such authoritative lips as those of the president of the government junta.   For that reason, he decided to give a certain official character to his negotiations, namely, by presenting documents with petitions which he formulated, and by requesting answers in the same form.

For that reason, on July 20, he delivered an official paper to the junta, in which he stated that the Portuguese government would strive to preserve good relations with the government of Buenos Aires, so

[1] Despatch from the junta to Don Carlos José Guessi.   Buenos Aires, July 20, 1810.

long as the latter should not make any attempt against the integrity
of the Spanish monarchy under the rule of Ferdinand VII. At the
same time he expressed the advisability of the South American peoples
aiding and helping the mother country to the best of their ability.

In spite of the measured language of Guezzi's statement, that pretension had a very bad effect on the junta, which adopted the easy
position of not considering such declarations of Guezzi, which they
accordingly failed to answer. They only had the effect of gaining
the animosity of the junta as well as that of the enemies of the latter,
who censured it with satirical jests, as he himself has set forth in his
relation.[1]

III.

In the viceroyalty of Río de la Plata, especially during the first
period of the revolution, there were continual and serious political
disagreements which delayed the purposed end of the revolutionists for
a certain time. The most noteworthy of these differences were those
existing between the capital and the provinces of the viceroyalty. In
Argentina the same thing happened as in almost all colonial countries
that try to obtain independence, and which happened in the United
States during the first period of its independence, namely, internal
quarrels between the two parties which arose at the outbreak of the
rebellions. These parties were the centralized republicans and the
federalists.

Obviously, it is understood that distinct characters and peculiarities
were produced in each one of the countries, but at the bottom they
were all the same. Accordingly, it is to be observed that the struggle
which arose between republicans and federalists in the United States,
was reproduced so far as South America is concerned by the formation
of large parties, which we might call moderates and separatists. The
first desired only liberal reforms which might redeem them from the
oppression from which they were suffering; the second tried to break
every bond of union with the mother country.

These parties later suffered a change, and at the very first outbreak
of the revolution, two branches were lopped off the strong trunk of

[1] "This despatch had the ill fortune to disappoint the two extreme parties.
Because I expressed myself with some courtesy in praise of the individual members of the junta, the opponents of that body treated me with too great super-
ficiality as *Manolo* or revolutionist; and because I said that the junta ought to
aid and maintain unity with the mother country, the *Manolos* with greater reason
called me *Saracen*."

the separatists, which weakened it, namely, the republicans and the federalists.

To particularize, it is noted that at the beginning of the first outbreaks in. New Granada, the two parties last mentioned are already distinguished, with the singularity that the first take the name of unitarians and do not limit themselves to a purely political struggle, but engage in civil war, to the serious harm of the common end that both parties desired.

In the Chilean provinces, this political phenomenon presents different characteristics. There discord arose because the southern provinces which desired to take radical measures as the most effective course of action, were hostile to the superiority which the city of Santiago, the stronghold of the moderate element, claimed to exercise. That struggle even reached such a point that in 1812 the southern provinces separated from those of the north, and each formed its own government junta.

Lastly, in the city of Buenos Aires, and throughout the viceroyalty, this situation was even more complicated, for there existed not only the two great parties of the radical and moderate republicans but the main discussions arose from the manifest opposition existing between the capital and the provinces from the moment when the first tried to constitute a perfectly centralized government which we might style unitarian. republican; while the provinces, on the contrary, in their hatred of the supremacy of the capital eagerly desired the establishment of a federal regime.

We find the cause of this fact perfectly explained in the differences existing between the population of the capital and that of the provinces. In the first the commercial and industrial bourgeois element predominated, and up to a certain degree, the cultured class. In a word, the capital represented the *creole* spirit. On the other hand, the native element composed of farmers and shepherds predominated in the provinces. These were reduced to a low degree of civilization, a type drawn with bold lines in the *gaucho*. Buenos Aires was the victor in this tenacious and partisan struggle, because it represented a higher type of civilization than the provinces.

The situation of Buenos Aires carried no certain path of consolidation, and new obstacles arose daily to oppose it. Outside the city, not only was the city divided into tendencies and bands, but was also steeped in anarchy which was very difficult to restrain, in spite of the junta directing its work to that end. Inside the capital, opinions were not in any harmony either, for distinct parties had formed, and there was heard continual talk of *Europeans* as individuals opposed to the *creoles*, and among these last there were those of the most diverse tendencies. Some were partisans of pacific and conciliating means of procedure. Others on the contrary, preferred and considered violence as the best means to employ. In the very midst of the government junta, there was a great disparity of standards that could with difficulty be harmonized, since the general interest was placed after the particular, and all desired to be at the head of the government.

Although he was quite outside these intrigues, the Portuguese emissary kept himself thoroughly informed of the situation; and since, according to all the possibilities, it was to be expected that instead of affairs becoming stable, they would shortly reach a status of revolutionary anarchy—a condition which the Portuguese government was not disposed to tolerate—he resolved to take preventive measures. In fact, on August 1, 1810, he sent an official communication to the government junta. In this, he stated that although the prince regent had manifested certain sentiments of benevolence toward the inhabitants and authorities of Río de la Plata, he had done so only for the purpose of

providing for the security of the viceroyalty as the primary object and aiding the general cause more efficiently, which is the chief cause for the mother country and its allies. But the division of opinion in the provinces and even in the capital itself makes him fear lest both objects are equally impossible of attainment, and if unfortunately in consequence of the clamorous measures which are being adopted in order to unite the consent of all, a civil war breaks out, it is very doubtful whether your designs to form a provisional government capable of meeting the obligations which the mother country and its allies have a right to demand from all the members of the Spanish monarchy will succeed.

In continuation, Guezzi analyzed the situation of the viceroyalty under four heads, and then the resulting proposals of the Portuguese government, as follows: 1. That the division of opinion in the capital and in the provinces was seriously disturbing the Brazilian court. 2. That since the provisional government that had been established could offer no guaranty either in regard to its domestic or foreign relations, by virtue of its own organization, he was unable to restrain the alarm of the above mentioned court. 3. That the latter had already stated on the 3d and 24th of April that it had all its forces ready to kill or restrain any revolutionary movement that might show itself in Rio de la Plata. 4. That in order that twisted interpretations which might be published concerning events at Buenos Aires, might be avoided, it would be a good idea to send a deputy to Brazil in order to solicit from that government its good offices for the convocation of the general congress, and for the establishment of a fixed and invariable order of the administration, and no doubt the court would be the guarantee of the new provisional system of government.[3]

At the same time, he stated that it would be a good thing for the deputy for whom he asked to be invested with the powers necessary for the establishment of a commercial arrangement with Brazil.

In the letter which was written to the count of Linhares by Carlos José Guezzi telling of the above action, the latter was more explicit in his statements, and as one who was fully conversant and fully aware of the situation in the provinces of La Plata, he pointed out some ideas that might serve as a solution in relieving the present lack of harmony. Among these, the following deserve mention: Guezzi said that the revolutionary danger would disappear as soon as the executive power, formerly in the hands of the viceroys, and later usurped by the junta which was constituted on May 25, would be delivered, as was soon to be done, into the hands of the deputies of each one of the provinces. For the latter would surely choose as deputies persons of known probity and of ability sufficient to work with rectitude and justice. This moment would be the proper time for the mother country to intervene by encouraging the initiation of new laws, by satisfying aspirations and desires, and in short, by attracting the provinces along the right road by persuasion and opportune concessions, for these not wishing to endure longer the rapine and poor government of the Spanish authorities, had withdrawn in a moment of dignity from the yoke which they had been patiently enduring for many years, but upon doing this they had tried to become free and independent when they had neither wings nor strength for it.

Guezzi also told the count of Linhares of the necessity of making a military demonstration on the frontiers of the viceroyalty for the purpose of intimidating as much as possible the revolutionists who, fearful of punishment, would not commit excesses and depredations.[4]

According to the testimony of Guezzi, the official communication which he sent to the junta under date of August 1, and of which we

[3] Despatch of Carlos José Guezzi to the president and members of the provisional government junta of the provinces of Río de la Plata. August 1.

Relation of what happened to me during my sojourn in Buenos Aires, from July 17 to December 20, 1810.

[4] Letter from Carlos José Guezzi to the count of Linhares. Buenos Aires, August 5, 1810.

have already spoken, caused an excellent impression, for the individuals who composed the junta understood that according as the intervention of the court of Brazil was favorable or unfavorable, it would be decisive for the future of the Río de la Plata. However, at the same time that the Argentinians took notice of this important fact, on the other hand they feared the interference of a power so powerful to them as was that of the Portuguese government. For, although they counted on English support, that said support was purely moral. During the whole month of August and a part of that of September, the junta negotiated with the envoy, Guezzi, in regard to the advisability and advantages, and at the same time, of the disadvantages that might result from Portuguese intermediation.

Since the junta had to decide matters of greater import than that mentioned above, it avoided giving a definitive reply in regard to the matter, hoping that the course of events and circumstances would determine whether or not it was best to accept that mediation.

It has already been stated that the revolutionary junta had a decided interest in justifying before the Portuguese government the causes that had produced the events of May 25. Then as a matter of fact, it followed the same procedure for all the acts of violence which took place during the first period of the revolution, in order not to draw down upon itself the animosity of the Portuguese government, the single considerable enemy and the most fearful of all that it counted on. This manner of acting was quite plainly seen, when Belgrano, in regard to the shooting of Liniers, Concha, Allende, and others, asked Guezzi (and the latter qualified such a question as imprudent) what impression had been created in Rio de Janeiro by that event. To this Guezzi replied that the impression must surely have been a very bad one since the actions of those who had been shot could never justify such an act. Belgrano's argument that he would be convinced of the justice of the act when he should learn of the correspondence of these rebels with Joseph Bonaparte had no weight with him. This assuredly could never be proven.

Knowledge of a despatch of the count of Linhares, announcing the concentration of Portuguese troops on the frontier of the viceroyalty caused considerable disturbance to the junta. Since the reasons for such a determination were unknown, Belgrano interrogated Guezzi in regard to them, inasmuch as this act was in contradiction to the expressions of friendship which had been shortly before communicated by the Portuguese government. Guezzi replied that he was unaware of the reasons which had impelled the Portuguese minister to make such a decision, but undoubtedly he must have taken it because of the unsafe condition of the viceroyalty, and he insisted for this reason on the necessity for the junta to maintain an agent in Rio de Janeiro, and the resulting advantage therefrom for in this way they would have accurate information in regard to events.

Since the situation in very truth was not very flattering in the viceroyalty, says Guezzi, as a widespread opinion existed that Brazil, by means of its mediation, should obtain the reconciliation of the provinces of the Rio de la Plata; and that in this way of thinking not only did the people share, who would be the first to suffer the consequences of the revolution, but also persons of importance lent their consent to such an idea. Still later the dean of the catheral of Cordoba del Tucumán, Dr. Gregorio Funes, communicated to Guezzi the idea that as soon as the provinces should come to an agreement, and the General Congress should assemble, it would be an absolute necessity for that body to be protected by a Portuguese force, "for if not", he says, "never would it enjoy sufficient liberty to declare its opinion".

And in truth this might have been the quickest and most satisfactory solution, for according to Guezzi, the only way of depriving the junta of the power which it was exercising in so tyrannical a manner, was the assembly of the general congress or war; and he communicated to the count of Linhares the necessity for taking one way or the other.[5]

From all the above, it appears that Guezzi expressed the opinion that the Portuguese government should intervene directly in the affairs of the Rio de la Plata, for its inaction would be interpreted by the junta as fear or weakness—a thing that was not advisable for the Portuguese ends. Therefore, he asked that naval forces be sent to Buenos Aires immediately, and he says to the count of Linhares "If your excellency regards what is taking place in these provinces as a mere trifle, you are much mistaken. There are 200,000 madmen without principles, to whom only arms are lacking to defy the whole power of Spain and Brazil. Allow me to organize, unite, and extend, and we shall see the consequences." In such a clearsighted manner did Carlos José Guezzi recognize the force which the Argentinian revolution would have, unless an immediate end were put to its excesses. Time showed that he was entirely right.

[5] Despatch of Carlos José Guezzi to the count of Linhares. Buenos Aires, September 16, 1810.

The dean, Dr. Gregorio Funes, was very well considered by the
junta of Buenos Aires, and according to the references of Guezzi, he
was always trying to obtain his opinion on events, and almost always
the solutions which he proposed were respected. From him, Guezzi
found that having spoken to Belgrano, the latter was opposed to Portuguese mediation. Then the dean asked the Portuguese envoy whether
it would not be a better solution for them to admit the English rather
than to have Portuguese mediation. Comprehending the object of
the question, Guezzi answered angrily "England might be a mediator
if they wished. Nevertheless, the court of Brazil would mediate
whether they wished or not, for more than friend and ally, Brazil has the
title of neighbor, and has an interest in the affairs of the country. It
should not be imagined that the rights of the princess would be forgotten by being postponed and would be executed by just demand,
and it ought to be understood that the refusal of friendly and paternal
offices in so serious a matter was a manifest provocative and legalized
the display of force." It was a pity that the energetic spirit and character
acter of this envoy were not seconded in Rio de Janeiro by the count
of Linhares.

Guezzi having been notified by the junta of Buenos Aires that it
would be advisable for him to express in writing these propositions
that might be agreeable to the court of Rio de Janerio, he did so. Those
propositions were as follows; 1. The recognition of the eventual rights
of her highness the princess of Brazil. When Guezzi made this point,
he accompanied it by the necessary arguments to prove the foundation
of such rights, and the use that the infanta expected to make of them.
2. Acceptance on the part of the junta of the mediation of the Portuguese government, which would only demand as the base thereof the
recognition of the supreme government established in Spain and the
promise to aid in the defense of the mother country.[*] The two above
propositions were discussed at length by the secretary of the junta,
Don Mariano Moreno, and by Guezzi. The former opposed many
difficulties to both points, but they came to an agreement that they
would be submitted to the consideration and deliberation of the junta
and that it would give a definitive answer.

In fact, a few days after the presentation of the propositions, Guezzi
went to get the reply that had been promised him. Rather than to
summarize it, in order that it might be known, we prefer to reproduce,

[*] Despatch from Guezzi to Mariano Moreno. Buenos Aires, November 17,
1810.

translated literally from the original, the dialogue which Dr. Moreno had with Guezzi for this reason as well as for other reasons, and which Guezzi had the very happy idea of reproducing in the account which he wrote of all events in Buenos Aires during his sojourn there.

DIALOGUE

Moreno.—The junta does not consider it advisable to send a deputy to the court of Brazil. That court must be satisfied with the proof of confidence which has been given it to, by communicating to it the letters which the Marquis of Casa Irujo sent to Viceroy Cisneros.

Guezzi.—I do not believe that this communication is sufficient. From July to this date such innovations have occurred that new explanations should necessarily be made.

Moreno.—There have been no other innovations than those necessitated for the organization of the internal government under the plan that has been adopted.

Guezzi.—But the plan which has been chosen and the method of organization may be such that they may be incompatible with the interests of Brazil.

Moreno.—The junta is not concerned with the interests of Brazil, but with the interests of the viceroyalty of Rio de la Plata.

Guezzi.—Señor Moreno can not hide from himself that the court of Brazil has legitimate interests to thresh out with this country. But leaving them aside, I shall say in general that unless the government of Buenos Aires wish to separate itself from the whole world, it must combine its interests with those of the neighboring powers. In this consideration, at least, it will be conceded to me to speak of the interests of Brazil.

Moreno.—The commerce of Brazil was favored and the vassals of his royal highness protected and respected.

Guezzi.—His royal highness will not fail to render thanks for these attentions, but they are of a secondary class. The chief interest of Brazil is that peace and union be preserved in the viceroyalty; that one province should not try to enslave another; and that for the present all concur as much as possible in the defense of the general cause.

Moreno.—This is exactly what is before the government. The blame lies at the door of the insurgents if it has not been able to obtain this up to the present.

Guezzi.—If the junta had adopted or should adopt the expedient of mediation which I propose, there will be no resistance nor opposition, nor would it be necessary to use the violent means which have been employed. We have still time to remedy many evils if the junta desire to agree to this proposition.

Moreno.—And under what terms would the court of Brazil accept the office of mediator?

Guezzi.—I do not know, but I believe that it would make use of no expedient unless it were just and reasonable.

Moreno.—And who can assure us that the court of Brazil from being mediator may not desire to become mistress of these provinces?

Guezzi.—This suspicion has no foundation. What is printed in the just claim[7] and the present alliance with the Peninsula exclude all idea of conquest.

Moreno.—But the court of Brazil desires to employ force, and by this method mediation is not admissible.

Guezzi.—A force is surely indispensable. By means of it, equal protection can be guaranteed both Spaniards and natives by restraining those who incite division. Without the presence of a force suspicions would be perpetuated. A force would soon take violent measures in order to prevent more fearful acts of violence.

Moreno.—Consequently, in your Grace's opinion, a Portuguese army should come to consolidate peace in the provinces of the Rio de la Plata?

Guezzi.—I say no such thing. The army would not pass its frontiers unless agitators should break the pacts which had been sanctioned under the guarantee of Brazil.

The consequences of the preceding interesting dialogue could not be more unexpected. Dr. Moreno believing that the Portuguese government had resolved, as he had just heard from the lips of its envoy, to intervene directly in the politics of Buenos Aires, and that this intervention was to be supported by a numerous army, reported the conversation that he had just had with Guezzi to the junta. No less promptly, the junta adopted the following resolution, which was transmitted to Guezzi:

The very excellent provisional government junta of the provinces of Rio de la Plata, has resolved unalterably that by the first vessel sailing for Rio de Janeiro, you shall return to that place. For this purpose, the captain of the port is ordered on this same date, to carry out this provision. You are advised thereof for your information. May God preserve you many years. Buenos Aires, November 20, 1810.

CORNELIO SAAVEDRA.

[*Addressed:*] Don Carlos José Guessi.

---

[7] Reference is made to the manifesto published by Infanta Doña Carlota and Infante Don Pedro Carlos, on August 18, 1808.

Although he does not express it, the surprise of the Portuguese envoy on receiving so threatening an order to leave, must have been great. It had all the character of expulsion and was so much the more unexpected because he had agreed with Dr. Moreno to formulate in writing the proposition which we have already seen—a proposition which would receive an answer from the junta in like manner.

Since Guezzi was united in bonds of friendship with Dr. Funes, he called on him in order to tell him of the despatch which he had just received, informing him at the same time of the conversation with Dr. Moreno which had preceded it. He went to Dr. Funes also so that the latter might tell him if he could the reason for his expulsion. In fact, Guezzi came from his interview with Dr. Funes under no delusions, for the latter told the reasons for the action adopted by the junta. Not only that, but he informed him thoroughly of the plans of the revolutionary junta.

The reason for his expulsion, according to Dr. Funes, was that the junta considered as a heinous crime any proposition which might be made it relative to mediation or regulation, and especially if these were supported, as was the Portuguese proposition, by an army. Whence it is clearly deduced that the object of the junta was from the very first to entertain the Portuguese envoy with delays and empty words in order to allow time for the viceroyalty to become consolidated by the acquisition of an armed force, and as a result thereof to render Portuguese intervention of no avail through delay.

In regard to the proposition of the Argentine leaders, Dr. Funes informed Guezzi that what was desired at all cost was that the viceroyalty of the Plata should be governed by a self democratic and independent system. Since this could not be obtained nor could other aid than that of Great Britain be hoped for, they were about to separate entirely from the mother country and from Portugal, the viceroyalty trying by itself to obtain its purposes.

Guezzi understanding that his presence could not be agreeable to the junta, decided to leave, but not before getting as much information as possible from the junta, in respect to discovering so far as possible its projects which, after what had been told him by Dr. Funes, were of still more interest to the Portuguese government than they had been before.

Consequently, and under the excuse of having to recover certain papers, which were in the possession of the junta he delayed his departure. Meanwhile, he sought a propitious occasion to talk with Dr.

Moreno. He succeeded in holding three conversations with him, the last dialogue summarizing all the others. This took place on request of Moreno and in his own house, on December 13, at half after ten at night, at a time when the member of the junta, Larrea, was present, who also took part in the conversation. The dialogue, literally translated, follows:

Moreno.—Through private information, it has come to me that the court of Brazil is massing forces on the frontier.

Guezzi.—I do not know what is taking place on the frontiers of Brazil, but I must assume, in fact, that the court is taking certain precautions because of the disturbed conditions of these provinces.

Moreno.—Those producing these disturbances are the insurgents and rebels, who have been deceived by the marines. The towns of Montevideo and Paraguay would already be united to the capital if those people were expelled.

Guezzi.—The court of Brazil is taking no part in these investigations. It sees a fire and wishes to quench it without asking who has set it.

Moreno.—If the court of Brazil adopts the gage of war, it will repent it, for it will excite in its own country the fire that it is trying to put out in another.

Guezzi.—The court of Brazil is not provoking war. This it has proven by the complaisance, perhaps excessive, which it has had toward this capital. But Señor Moreno must be as certain as I am that the form of government adopted by the junta and the principles inculcated among the peoples of the viceroyalty oblige the court of Brazil to suffocate in its beginning a fire, which as Señor Moreno says, may extend to Brazil.

Moreno.—The capital is occupied only with its internal government, which has nothing to do with Brazil.

Guezzi.—The court of Brazil must consider the condition of these provinces, as a neighbor, as an ally of Spain, and as one interested in what happens in these domains, in the cases determined by the constitution. It is consequently madness to think that it must leave out of consideration these questions of state and that it ought to be indifferent to what is taking place in these provinces.

Moreno.—The junta has given proof of the spirit of peace and confidence which it has in the court of Brazil, by ordering the withdrawal of the frontier garrisons.

Guezzi.—Yes, that will be so, but it is probable that an interpretation will be given in Brazil relative to this retirement that will be not at all favorable.

Moreno.—And what forces has Brazil on the frontier?

Guezzi.—That I do not know. But I believe that, being warned by a despatch, it was the intention of Viceroy Cisneros to arm twelve thousand men. Brazil for precaution's sake will assemble an equal number.

Moreno.—Do you believe that the Brazilian forces will join with the Spaniards of the Banda Oriental?

Guezzi.—I know nothing. But if these provinces which are faithful to the nation which the court of Brazil recognizes implore its protection, I have no doubt that it will protect them.

Moreno.—But we ourselves have sworn fealty to Ferdinand VII. and his legitimate successors.

Guezzi.—If such an oath comprehends the fidelity and obedience due to the said sovereign, it must be then that misunderstandings have arisen from lack of getting together. Consequently, I renew the petition made so many times, namely, that a person be sent to Rio de Janeiro in order to make and request the necessary explanations since the Spaniards can not come to any understanding among themselves.

Moreno.—The junta would also like to send a deputy, but it does not know a capable man to entrust with so delicate a mission.

Guezzi.—There are more than enough persons of talent in this city, and I could name many who enjoy the complete confidence of the junta.

Larrea.—Since your Grace is going, we shall not need to send a deputy. Your Grace can give the Portuguese minister a true idea of the intentions and actions of the junta.

Guezzi.—I believe that Señor Larrea is jesting with me. We are discussing the sending of a person who may carry a message from the junta, and who may tell what the junta thinks and wishes. I could never be a faithful or accredited interpreter, for I would never say anything except what I myself think of the junta.

Larrea.—We ought not to send a deputy to be slighted. The Portuguese minister never cared to write to this junta, which indicates that he does not care to come to an understanding with it.

Guezzi.—The British cabinet did not slight the deputy who was sent to it, in spite of the fact that it never wrote to or answered the propositions of the junta. The etiquette of cabinets does not permit secretaries of state to have direct correspondence with equal governments, and much less with subordinate governments.

Larrea.—He could have answered through the Spanish minister.

Guezzi.—(I answered this with a burst of laughter.)

Larrea.—Or at least he could have come to an understanding with the Spanish government.

Guezzi.—I have no doubt that the Portuguese minister has come to an understanding with the Spanish government. But since when has the junta recognized that government?

It is not necessary to state the importance and political significance of the dialogue which has just been transcribed. By a mere reading of it, and without making the least comment regarding it, both circumstances can be appreciated. That dialogue represents the culminating moment of Guezzi's secret mission to Buenos Aires, and explains his whole activity in said city.

Both in this and in the preceding conversation, the diplomatic conditions of those taking part in it can be observed. It is well known that Dr. Mariano Moreno was possessed of distinguished qualities, and that he was endowed with the highest diplomatic gifts, doubtless being as was clearly demonstrated in the foregoing dialogues a formidable enemy in any negotiation, and his qualities showing forth especially in the last of them. Thus he is seen to unload on others faults that belonged only to the revolutionists. In order to persuade he employs simultaneously threats and a desire to temporize. With extreme nimbleness of thought, he endeavors to destroy the solid and well founded arguments of his interlocutor. He does not hesitate to employ sophisms and to falsify the truth consciously in order to try to persuade. He has the faculty of cleverly turning the conversation, when it is not convenient for him to reply to certain questions, while at the same time he very subtly tries to get at the plans of his opponents by not conceding any importance to certain questions that in the last analysis are important. All this shows that Dr. Moreno was a diplomat of excellent caliber.

But in the present occasion, Dr. Moreno, although he exhibited his diplomatic qualities, could gain but few important results from his conference with the Portuguese envoy. For although Moreno was intelligent and persuasive, Guezzi was no less sagacious and astute; and although the latter was of less intelligence he made up the difference between the two of them by the qualities above mentioned. It is not forgotten that Guezzi was an Italian and was endowed with remarkable keenness and ability to see and discuss political questions. Consequently, one can appreciate that, throughout the course of the dialogue he always answered with great cleverness to all the questions proposed and asked by Moreno, taking refuge in ignorance when he thought that advisable, and giving importance and even exaggerating things when it was advisable for him to cause certain effects. Consequently, it is not to be wondered at that he attributes to the Portuguese government a great nobleness of view in its policy and in its plans, which in fact, was very far from being the truth. It should be observed also that when Moreno, with full understanding of the reason, shows that Brazil desires to mix in matters that do not belong to it, he answers by excusing the harm which may very easily be occasioned to the government which he represents, by which it is not surprising that that government should concentrate its forces on the frontier and take every manner of precaution, exerting himself to show that in reality Brazil is not animated by hostile feelings, but that the desire of peace and tranquility which must be procured in all neighboring colonies impel it to intervene. Finally, Guezzi sustains the controversy very cleverly by employing arguments and by giving answers which place him at the height of his interlocutor.

The part taken in the dialogue by the member of the junta, Larrea, could not have been more unfortunate, for while he attempted to give credit to the reasoning of Moreno, he adduces such stupid reasons that they provoke Guezzi's laughter.

As a summary to these considerations, it might be said that Dr. Moreno represents intelligence and high diplomacy, and that the Portuguese envoy is the prototype of political astuteness and sagacity.

After the conversation above mentioned, Guezzi had another occasion to talk with Dr. Moreno, but what was said in the last conversations could not have been of great importance, for the Portuguese envoy did not consider them worthy of detailed mention, saying only that they occurred.

Thereupon Guezzi went to bid farewell to Dean Funes, who told him that it would be advisable for him to delay his departure, for at any moment he was expecting the substitution of the present government by another government which would certainly pay better heed to his propositions. But after the lapse of some days without that happening, and urged by his fear of a summons, Guezzi took ship on December 20, 1810, on the *Belisario,* to whose captain he gave a despatch which Dr. Moreno had written to Count de Linhares. Then he went immediately to the English ship *Quem,* which since it was to stay for some time in the roadstead of Buenos Aires, would allow him to wait there, for the purpose of seeing whether the change of government which was expected would occur. But he stayed on board that ship until the end of the month of January, 1811, without anything happening.

After the abovenamed date, all trace of that personage are lost, not only as concerns his political activity, but outside of that as concerns his social status, for all my investigations to learn anything of Guezzi after the above mentioned year 1811 have been in vain.

IV.

I consider it of interest to report certain very brief opinions formed by Guezzi concerning the Argentine revolution and of a few of the chief personages who were actors in it. The importance of these opinions arises from the fact that the Portuguese envoy knew quite thoroughly both the revolution and its men, since he lived through the first and treated with the second; and since he had the excellent idea of noting his estimates at the end of the relation to which we have several times made reference, we shall summarize them although very briefly.

In speaking of the personality of the dean of the cathedral of Córdoba del Tucumán, Dr. Funes, he considers him as a man devoted preferably to letters although very much interested in political questions; adorned with excellent personal qualities, simplicity, and modesty, which according to Guezzi, predisposed him to give him his ready affection; of insinuating manners and very tenacious in his purposes, he was a true patriot who directed all his valor to the services of his country, and who being a native of one of the provinces, was never partial to the supremacy which Buenos Aires desired to exercise over the rest of the viceroyalty of the Rio de la Plata.

By his deserts Dr. Funes had become accredited and favored and exalted by those in power, especially by Viceroy Liniers and by the infanta Doña Carlota, who considering him to be a person of great influence, maintained an extensive correspondence with him.

Without seeking popularity he endeavored to lead the opinion of the Argentinians, and convinced of the misgovernment which ruled from the formation of the junta on May 25, 1810, he was opposed to all the acts of violence committed by that body. His moderate and mild attitude caused a very bad effect on the radical spirits of the Argentinian leaders. In spite of these qualities, he was a fervent partisan of the independence of his country, and democratic ideas predominated in him as Guezzi testifies. He considered the intervention or mediation of England as better for his country than that of Portugal.

Moreover, the commentaries which the provisional junta and the individual persons forming a part of it suggested to Guezzi are interesting. Thus, for instance, he considered Dr. D. Mariano Moreno as "the Robespierre of the day;" and he considered all who surrounded him as persons without any personal value, but who joined and united together are "fit and ardent instruments of tyranny", and who as the finality of their activities proposed to found a republic on the base of terrorism.

He bitterly censures the creoles, especially the rustic provincials whom he calls "a vile breed of the fields," and for the chief men he has the following expressions: "In Córdoba, a crowd of natives came before the government, requesting permission to kill *saracens.*"[8] However, he distinguishes between cultured natives, who do not sympathize with the violent means employed by the junta and the partisans of Saavedra, the president of the junta, "for" as he says, "they are the military class and form a sort of *sansculottes*, for they are all really poor and starving; the partisans of Moreno are like Montaigne among the Jacobins."

In the above is set forth the opinion which Guezzi formed concerning the revolution and the revolutionists of Rio de la Plata. Beyond all doubt, his sentences involve a very pronounced bias; but for all that they do not cease to be notes taken from real life; and it is not to be doubted that the Argentine revolution had moments and persons which deserve only praise from posterity, but it is no less certain that as in all revolutions it also had tyrants and moments of savage cruelty.

Thus lightly summarized was the first diplomatic negotiations which were realized in regard to the first independent government of the viceroyalty of Rio de la Plata. If it can not in justice be considered as having supreme and decisive importance, yet it ought not to be disregarded to the point of making no mention of it at all, as has been done heretofore.

JULIAN MARIA RUBIO Y ESTÉBAN.

[8] This was a name applied to the Spaniards.

PIEZAS JUSTIFICATIVAS[1]

CORRESPONDENCIA DE GUEZZI CON EL CONDE DE LINHARES

Oficio del Conde de Linhares a Guezzi

Havendo constado a S. A. R. o Principe Regente, Nosso Senhor, que V. M. se propunha retirarse a Bueños Aires, ordenoume o mesmo Augusto Senhor que fizesse entregarlhe copias dos officios que por ordem de S. A. R. dirigí ao Enviado Extraordinario e Ministro Plenipotenciario de S. M. Catolica negandole a entrega que pedía dos Hespanhoes que se achavaõ aqui refugiados, e que V. M. poderá comunicar com a debida descriçaõ aos membros do actual Governo, para que conheçaõ que S. A. R. se naõ quir tomar parte alguna que pudesse ser nociva e desagradavel aõs Habitantes Hespanhoes da América Hespanhola; e que o mesmo Augusto Senhor espera que elles conheçaõ quanto les convem mostrar todo o respeito é consideraçaõ para un taõ Augusto Soberano, e cuya Augusta Esposa ten todo o dereito a futura successaõ da Monarchía Espanhola, e he por consecuencia merecedora de que os membros do actual Governo lhe trebuten toda a veneraçaõ e respeito que por todos os titulos merece; tanto mais que S. A. R. naõ deseja usar desta prerrogativa, se naõ a beneficío dos povos Hespanhoes da América.

Lisongeime que V.M. me de noticias mas depois que chegar a Buenos Aires, que muito estimarei recebir.

Deos guarde a V.M. Palacio do Rio de Janeiro em 19 de Junho de 1810.

CONDE DE LINHARES.

[Addressed:] Senhor Carlos José Guezzi.

Oficio del Conde de Linhares a Guezzi

Havendo constado a S. A. R. o Principe Regente Nosso Senhor que V.M. se dispunha a partir para Buenos Ayres o mesmo Augusto Senhor, aprovando a sua viagen, o encarriga de facer ahí constar os sentimentos pacificos e de benevolencia con que S. A. R. considera os habitantes da América Espanhola, e que esperando sempre que se naõ separen da obediencia que deben aõ seu legitimo Soberano o Senhor D^r. Fernando 7° naõ deseja se naõ establecimiento de tudo o que pode concorrer para

---

[1] Todos los documentos que siguen se encuentran en el Archivo Histórico Nacional de Madrid en el legajo 5871. TRANSLATION: All the following documents are found in the National Historical Archives of Madrid, in legajo 5871.

a sua felicidade, e que estes sao os mais puros inalteraveis sentimentos que sempre o animarão a respeito dos mesmos; e que S.A.R. espera que V.M. lhe partecipe o que achar a respeito da disposiçaõ dos animos dos mesmos habitantes.

Deos guarde a V.M. Palacio do Rio de Janeiro em 20 de Junho de 1810.

CONDE DE LINHARES.

[*Addressed:*] Senhor Carlos José Guezzi

Oficio de Guezzi al Conde de Linhares

Exmo. Sr: Inclusa receberá V.E. a copia da carta que dirigi a Junta. A expatriaçaõ do Vice-rey e da Audiencia, a resistencia manifiesta de Montevideo e Cordova a aposiçaõ tacita dos principaes habitantes desta Capital, a falta de reconhecimento da Regencia, e sobre todo os meyos violentos de que me consta sem usado os individuos da Junta e seus partidarios para formar a segunda Junta eraõ causas bastantes graves para que naõ devera manifestar a estes povos os pacificos e benevolos sentimentos de S:A.R. ate nova ordem de S.E.

Por outra parte alguns individuos da Junta em particular me asegurarāõ que os direitos do seu legitimo soberano serían defendidos, os da Senhora Princeza atendidos quando as circunstancias o permitierem. A Junta fei as mesmas promesas e ayuntou que hia a metter na presença de S.A.R. os documentos originaes por onde se comprobaría a necesidade en que se tinha visto o Povo de renover as autoridades principaes para segurança destas Provincias. Esta ultima circunstancia foi a que me determinou a dirigilhe o oficio do dia 20 de Julho no qual para evitar mas interpretaçoes Julguei dever agregar algumas explicaçoes referentes as abrigaçoes que tenhaõ com a metropoli; como V.E. conhecera pelo contesto do mesmo oficio.

Para mayor preeauçaó o dia da conferença com a Junta lhe pedi licencia para dicerlhe no successivo por escrito o que julgasse conveniente e entendi diverme valer a permisaõ conceda logo em 1° de Agosto en cuyo dia lhe dirigi o officio B. que por copia remetto tamben a V.E. Ainda que nele tinha procurado desfauçar do millor modo posivel o motivo que me determinaba a escrivelo. A Junta naõ pode deixar de conhecer que e huma amenaza semi-oficial para o caso en que pretenda separarse dos seus deveres, e da fidelidade devida ao seu soberano.

Os opositores da junta acusaõ aos Criollos de aspirar a democracia: e estes acusaõ aos Europeos de querer a sujeitar estas Provincias a José Bonaparte. Algum fundamento ha habido para estas sospeitas em outros tempos: por agora creio hum e outro suceso imposivel.   O que mais probablemente pode originarse, e huma anarquía completa, da qual renacerá o ordem quando . . .   e outros tinhaõ aprendido por experiencia que a situacaõ da Monarquía naõ consente partidos extremos.

Remito a V. E. a colecçaõ do gacetas: sirvase V. E. tomar em consideraçaõ a do dia 3 de Julho, o que diz o don Cañhete me parecen verdades evangélicas: porem os arbitrios que sugger para obviar aos mais previstos se destruyen pelos seus mesmos principios.   Suporto que naõ existe na América nem a força Real, nem a força de opiniaõ; como defenderaõ os Virreys, o edificio provisional que levantem?   No meo conceito as juntas particulares saõ preferiveis.   As extraordinarias e sinceras demostraçoes de allegria que den o povo de Buenos Aires quando se formou a primeira Junta, prova quanto se julgaba util e necesaria nas circonstancias a mesma necesidade ou mayor se acha no Perú.   Se cada Provincia tivesse a sua Junta, resultaria a grande ventagem de disolver a terribel massa de Virreinados, aislar por asin dicer as Provincias, debilitar a força que podesse nacer de sua uniaõ, concentrar cada huma a mirar pelos seus propios intereses e dar tempo aos restos da Peninsula.   A procurar auxilios para conservar e mantener na devida uniaõ e obediencia o total das Provincias ultramarinas.   He taõ verdade que se debilitaria a força de resistença pelas Juntas provinciales que a de Buenos Aires se guardaria ben de a consenter.

Outro papel digno de attençaõ de V. E. he o inscrito na gaceta de 16 de Julho.   Ele he do D^r. Funes Deaõ da Sede Cordova.   A zizanía entre Europeos e Criolhos he antigua e naõ dubido que sara o resorte principal de todos os movimientos populares: na imposibilidade de a poder desvanecer con sillogismos creyo que o milhor partido saría defenderse completamente que existe, e nunca dicer ou facer cousa que pudese interpretarse dirigida a facer triumphar hum partido sobre outro.

Na minha opiniaõ a revoluçaõ de Buenos Aires deixaría de ser perigrosa se o poder executivo antecedentemente confiado aõ Virrey pasase por agora aos diputados das provincias.   He probavel que estes forem persoas instruidas e de facultades: e naõ haviaõ de comprometer o seu ben estar para ir atras de teorias e quimeras.   Aten de que naõ ha Provincia que naõ tinha as suas pretençoes particulares: fomentadas estas aproposito, a metropolí adquiriría Patronos a sua causa, ya que se supoe que naõ pode mandar defensores: Se agregaría tamben que os Deputados obligados a seguir as instrucçoes que lhes dessen as Provincias, estas ficaraõ en todo tempo habilitadas a resistir a qualquer arbitrariedade ou exceso que sahiese do Congreso como contrario as ordens dos seus instituientes.

Sobre estes principios me determinei de propor a mediaçaõ de S. A. R. sin ter instrucçoes para o efeito: e estou tan convencido da ma utilidade que a naõ admitirla ou solicitala a Junta, me parece que se le debería propor de oficio pela mesma Corte. Esto evitaría grandes calamidades que naõ podem deixar de suscitarse saõ abandonados a si mesmos estes Povos no grado de effervescencia e exaltacaõ en que se achaõ todas as mas passoes.

Contemplo huma felicidade para o Vice-rey e Oidores que tinhaõ sido embiado a Hespanha tinha quando se mantivesen mais tranquilos que Cordeiros, era imposivel que naõ servissem de pretexto a disturbios e inquietudes grandes tanto em hum como en outro partido ha cabezas quentes capaces de cometter qualquer desatino.

Hum grande apparato de força na fronteira me parece de primeira necesidade. O medo guarda a vinha. Saria util tambem que houvesse aquí hum par de Bergantines, tanto para alcanzar mais frecuentes noticias como para dar a entender que a Corte do Brazil esta a mira do que se pasa. Pode ser que fosse conveniente que estivese a bordo de hum deles huma pessoa autorizada a fallar quando a necesidade fosse urgente. O grande objecto deve ser o de evitar as primeiras desordens. Se a Junta comette algunas o medo do castigo a precipitará em huma rebeliaõ aberta, e naõ ametterá meyos para arrastrar no seu principio a parte do povo ignorante a preocupado que forma o mayor numero, especialmente nas Provincias interiores.

Vejo que he imposivel offrecer huma opiniaõ que seja inteiramente exempta de escolhos. A proposta que fiz penso que por ninhum principio pode comprometter a Corte do Brazil nen ser perjudicial aos intereses generaes. A moderacaõ conseguirá facilmente o que a força acaso naõ podera conseguir, e que no meu conceito debe reservarse para o caso em que naõ hayaõ sortido effeito os bons e amigaveis officios.

Estas saõ as consideraçoes que me tomo a libertade de por na presença de V. E. suplicandao queira aceptalas como opinioes individuaes formadas en poucos dias de observaçaõ e que podem ser enteiramente erradas. V. E. com a sua acostumada prudenca e penetraçaõ poderá juzgar milhor que Eu, do que convenha obrarse.

A pessoa de V. E. E. D. M. A. Buenos Ayres 5 de Agosto de 1810.

Oficio de Guezzi al conde de Linhares

Exmo. Sr.: O dia 26 de Agosto os Presos de Cordova foraõ assasinados no meyo de hum caminho por Castelli Vogal da Junta, Penha, hirmaõ do que esta no Rio, nomiado Segretario Militar, e French

Comandante de hum destacamento que se mandou de proposito. Se prohibio nas Igresas de Buenos Ayres que se lhes ficessem sufragios. Desta acçaõ V. E. formará o juicio que eu naõ posso detalhar em papel: porem naõ posso deixar de dizer que sendo imperdoavel, precipitará a Junta em huma rebeliaõ aberta, e fará o posivel para inducir o populacho a cometer novos attentados para interessalo na ma defesa.

Belgrano tive a imprudencia de perguntarme que impresaõ tinha feito esta noticia; respondi que de horrorizar a todo o mondo e indispor contra a Junta os espiritos os mais parciaes. Eles se desenganharaõ, repetio ele, quando apareça a correspondencia destes rebeldes com o Rey José. Estos expressoes me fazen sospeitar que probavelmente estaõ forjando alguma correspondencia suporta para a publicar na gazetta. Disto sei que saõ capaces, porque me consta que quizeraõ practicar o mesmo com o Vice-Rey Cisneros. O mesmo Belgrano em 11 Septembro me fiz ler huma carta que chegou a Junta, dirigida aberta por V. E. aõ governador e Capitan General do Rio Grande. O seu contexto parece que a atemorizou, e Belgrano me preguntou como se combinaba o seu contenido com as manifestaçoens de amizade e paz, feitas pouco antes: Respondi: Que em nada o Oficio me parecia opposto a estes sentimentos, e que o que se pedía era menos do que a Junta me tinha prometido. Me repetió as difficultades que debiaõ encontrarse. Propuz em taõ que a Junta para evitar responsabilidades com a Corte do Brazil fizesse a proposta por via dos Curas das Parroquias convidando aõ Povo a manifestar individualmente a ma vontade por hum respeito aõ reconhecimento dos direitos eventuaes da Sra. Princeza, si, ou hum naõ posto debaxo da pregunta sencilhamente feita. Me respondeo que naõ podía ser. Insisti em taõ para que mandasen hum Diputado aõ Brazil para explicarse. Conveyo nisso, e me disse que se comissionaría a Don Saturnino Peña: lhe indiquei que este sujeto naõ convinha porque naõ podía merecer a confiança de ninguen, nem podia ter a representacaõ conveniente.

O dia despois Belgrano me disse que se tinha nomiado hum sujeito de fora da Terra, e que se mandariá vir com toda a prontidato. Veremos si cumpre a Junta con esta promessa; o que se verificará se dura o medo e prevee resistencias insuperaveis da banda do Peru.

O bloqueyo desta Capital fornece a V. E. hum novo motivo para conservar algumas embarcaçoes destacadas neste Rio, sendo urgentisima a necesidade de ter promptas e frequentes noticias do que se pasa na Capital. Alem de que a ma presencia servirá, a manifestar que a Corte do Brazil se ocupa do allivio de hums e castigo de outros.

He preciso que a esperança se naõ perda enteiramente. O bloqueyo naõ faz prejuicio aõ comercio portuguez; pelo contrario faz enganhar aõs primeiros introductores de frutos e impide que venhaõ outros novos a arruinarse.

Inclusas achava V. E. as gacetas. A carta de Dᵣ. Ambrosio Funes, hirmaõ do deaõ Funes, que ven na gaceta de 30 agosto, se tem interpretado como a expresaõ dos sentimentos de ambos, e lhes faz muy pouca honra. Se ajunta que ambos, contribuiraõ aõ arresto dos Officiaes de Cordova tentacido a felicidade dos que os seguiaõ, e cubrindo por esta indigna acçaõ a milicia de Cordova de hum obbrobrio eterno. Do Deao em particular se falla muito mal. Todas as passoes achandose desenfreyadas he posivel que se levanten muitas calumnias e imposturas: o tempo descubrirá a verdade das cousas, e nao se deben precipitar juicios.

Pelos Diputados de algumas Provincias que ja se tem elegido parece que os povos naõ faltaõ de juizo o discernimento. Os que foraõ por Cordova Juan . . e Santiago, goçao de boã reputacaõ, ou pelo menos a goçavaõ antes dos successos actuaes: e isto prova quanto seria ventajoso o Congreso, para sacar da maõ da Junta o poder que exerce com tanta tirannía. As cousas ja ten chegado a tomar huma tal extencaõ que naõ veyo modo de a acabar se naõ pela guerra ou pelo Congreso. V. E. sabrá qual caminho he preferivel, porem como a guerra he de todos os maes o peyor, me parece que se devería reservar para o caso extremo e quando se tivessem apurado todos os meyos de conciliaçaõ.

Contemplo o Perú perdido naõ por o que dicen as gaçettas, porem por o que dicen algumas cartas particulares: ninhum daquelles Governadores ten ainda dado hum paso proporcionado a gravidade do perigo, e permanecen na confianza de que as tropas mandadas desde Buenos Aires naõ hao de chegar lá.

Incluyo a V. E. la proclama do Vice-Rey de Lima, naõ vale nada, nem pelo estilo, nem pelos argumentos. Ja se tem visto como algumas expresoes dirigidas individualmente contra os Vogaes da Junta esta, os applica a todos os criolhos. E huma reflexaõ que aquel Vice-Rey devia fazer, e naõ se deben usar palabras que possao aplicarse ainda que malignamente a classe mais numerosa dos habitantes da America. Os insultos e os improperios por isto que saõ taõ familhares nos revoltosos nunca deven acharse baxo da firma dos Gefes de hum Governo regular. Este sistema determina a rebelliaõ, e as circunstancias actuaes me parece que exigen imperiosamente que se contemporize, e como diz con muito juizo o D^r. Funes que se capitule com os vicios, ainda que seja murmurando, e se elija dos maes o menor.

A noticia da insurreiçaõ de Caracas, deu hum alento formidavel aòs amigos da independencia de este paiz, e se arrepenten de naõ ter feito tanto como os Caraguenhos.

Havería muito que dizer e muy digno de attençaõ de V. E. porem he perigoso fallar dicendo a verdade, e se podem causar equivocaçoes disminuindo a naturaleza dos succesos.   Esta en maõ de V. E. procurarse instrucçoes exactas mandando aquí alguma embarcaçaõ de guerra:

A pessoã de V. E. G. D. m^a a^s Buenos Aires 16 Septembro 1810.

Oficio de Guezzi al conde de Linhares.

Exmõ Sr: A Junta se ten dado por muy offendida de que o Capitan Elliot consentisse no bloqueyo, e os Ingleses negociantes estaõ divididos entre si.   Naõ ha especie de humilhaçoes, a que naõ se assujeita a Junta para manter o favor de alguns negociantes.   Belgrano e Passo me falharaõ para que escrevisse a V. E. que mandase aqui algumas forças para proteger o commercio Portuguez contra a violencia dos de Montevideo.   Ja escrevi em data de 16 o que pensava sobre isto: com tudo renovarei a instancia de mandar as tropas pedidas, naõ para impedir o bloqueyo, porem para valerse das occasioes pedir explicaçoes e facerse respeitar a temer.   Que ben pode resultar a Corte do Brazil porem huma absoluta indifferencia?   Ninhum absolutamente ninhum. Se V. E. trata o que se passa nestas Provincias por huma bagatela, está muy equivocado.   Saõ 200 mil furiosos sem principios e quem naõ faltaõ se naõ armas para desafiar todo o poder da Espanha e do Brazil. Deixeme organizar, unir, extender, e veremos as consequencias.

Naõ sei em que possa commetterse a Corte intromettendose nas . . . destes Paizes pelo menos como medianeira.   He posivel que a penetraçaõ de V. E. naõ lhe suggera ninhum caminho de reconciliaçaõ?   Porem ainda quando naõ houvesse ninhuma esperanza as calamidades de huma guerra civil saõ taõ horrorosas que naõ se devería deixar para mover a fin de conseguir algum ajuste e acudir inmediatamente as armas, se se descubrise huma resistencia obstinada e cega. Em que veyo o perigo he, na demora e naõ na actividade, qualquer que seja o arbitrio que se adopte.

Aqui tem aparecido manuscritas duas cartas dirigidas pela Serenisima Señora Princeza do Brazil aõ Cabildo de Montevideo.   Em a Junta seja facciosa ninquem ha duvida, que tiraniza, e oprime o povo de Buenos Aires, este mesmo povo o experimenta a hum punto de o naõ poder duvidar. Porem hay verdades que naõ devem acharse bajo a firma de hum Principe, e se tivesse que propor hum exemplar a seguir saría o de Enrique IV no sitio de Paris. De aqui a pouco veremos que la Junta fará crer a os seus partidarios que a Señora Princeza os trata de facciosos que ja naõ ha perdaõ para eles; que vale mais precer com as armas na maõ que deixarse inforçar e assim teremos huma rebeliaõ universal e decidida por meya duzia de palabras que se podiaõ excusar sem que em nada padesesse a opiniaõ da boa causa.

Remito as gazettas nas quaes achará V. E. algumas cousas interesantes.

A pessoa de V. E. - G. D. mª aª Buenos Aires 5 Octubre 1810.

Oficio de Guezzi al Conde de Linhares.

Exmõ Sr: Segundo o muito que se tinha voziado se esperava con grande expectaçaõ a exposçiaõ dos motivos verdadeiros ou forjados que determinaraõ o assesinato de Liniers e seus companheiros. O manifesto de Santa que finalmente sahió e a mais completa justificaçaõ daquelles innocentes. O autor deste escrito he o Segretario Sano.

A Junta que se installou em Chile naõ he propiamente da misma natureza como a de Buenos Aires segun de V. E. verá pela acta que remetto. Houvo poucos alborotos e deve esperarse que naõ se alterar o sossego pelo succesivo porque os verdadeiros agitadoes naõ prevaleceraõ. Para precaverse destes he que foi sustituida a Junta e per evitar maes majores, o que me na opiniaõ de que estas Juntas seriaõ a salvaçaõ de America se se erigiesem em tempo como se debe. Se o Presidente e Intendentes de Charcas, Potosi e Paz tivesem instituido Juntas Provinciaes independientes humas de outras, em lugar de agregarse aõ Vice-Reinato de Lima, e fizesen o que con tanto juicio e discernimento fei o . . . do Paraguay, se tivesen aberto inmediatamente os portos intermedios aõ comercio ingles: os intereses do Peru se seriaõ achado em oposiçaõ com os desta Capital e o Perú ficava salvo. Esta forma de gouverno parecerá monstruosa: por em agora naõ se trata de conservar o regimen antiguo ou establecer regas perpetuas. A única cousa que se debe pretender he que a Metropoli conserve a sua superioridade sobre as Colonias, e ja que naõ pode manter con a força, debe provisionalmente dividir para vencer. Se suscitaraõ sem duvida muitos mais e muitos inconvenientes: Por em . . hum deles aõ equivalente da per . . . da America.

Vera V. E. o que diz o redactor da Gaceta sobre huma carta da S. Princeza, ele naõ publicou a carta que os trata de facciosos: porem em particular naŏ deixará de fazer creser que a S. Princeza trata de facciosos a todos os Criolhos o que he certamente hum mal, e mal grande para a causa da S. Princeza muito mayor que o que lhe pode nacer das reflexoes impressas.

Em raçaŏ da inclinaçaŏ que o Deaŏ Funes manifestou em outro tempo a causa da S. Princeza julguir develo visitar. Alguns amigos me dijerao que desconfiese dele; porem como nada tenho a diser em privado que ja naŏ tenha dito a mesma Junta, e a qualquer que me queira ouvir, aprecio o aviso sem julgar deber estar em cautela. Ele figurará certamente muito por que tem muita eloquencia e parece moderado. A Junta procura captivarse huma deferencia absoluta a todas as mas opinioes e previniendolhe as vontades.

Os enterminios ordinarios tendose feitos comunes ja naŏ se reparava neles: porem o do Cabildo despertou a gente. He excusado dizer tudo quanto se faz circular para justificar esta acçaŏ. Ele estaba determinada desde o principio, segundo ouvi falhar logo na minha chegada. Soto fara pasos de gigante si naŏ se atalha.

Vi huma carta de Chile que dizia que o Agente da Junta de Buenos Ayres tinha solicitado de aquella Junta que não se consentisse a arribada de navios ingleses a os portos de aquel Reyno. Buenos Ayres pertende ser o árvitro de estes payses, e esta pretençaŏ manifesta a facilidade que havería havido en metter todas as demais provincias em oposição com a Capital cada huma pelos seus particolares intereses.

Em proporção que vaŏ prosperando os negocios de Buenos Ayres no interior, e em quanto ese o seu sistema geralmente propagado em América os principios democraticos se vão desenvolvendo e ja se falla nelles e se escreve com mais libertade.

Todos travallan em ler o estudiar constituiçoes e a dos Estados Unidos se acha na boca de todos. Funes me diju que sobre todas prefería a de Suecia, me esqueri a preguntarlhe a de que ano.

Em 3 novᵉ a Junta me mandou chamar para saber se tinha remetido os oficios que me entregou o 30 julho: Respondi, que si. Me preguntou porque naŏ restituiria os papeis originaes hiaŏ neles: respondi que naŏ sabía, porem que savía por esquecimento, e que se o desejavaŏ os pediría. Disie entaŏ hum dos Voguaes que era conveninte fosse eu mesmo. Supliqué ser dispensado de este viagem pela pouca importancia do objeto, manifestando que somente apreciaría emprenderla quando a Junta tivesse alguma proposiçaŏ agradavel para facer a Corte do Brazil. Disie em taŏ Saavedra que o objeto anterior se agregaría outra comisaŏ importante, e que o Segretario ficara encarregado de formar as instrucçoes.

No dia . . . foi ao Segretario e qual me preguntou quaes sariaõ as proposiçoes que podessem agradar a Corte do Brazil, respondi que a de reconhecer os direitos eventuaes da S. Princeza, ou admitir a mediaçaõ do Brazil; ou pelo menos embiar la huma pessoa para explicarse sobre os puntos que podem causar inquietaçaõ aquella Corte. Me fei mil dificultades sobre cada hum destes puntos, humas reaes outras imaginarias. Por ultimo ficamos em que faría a proposig a Junta e me comunicaría a explicaçaõ final.

Incluyo as Gacetas algumas das quaes saõ importantes. A Pessoa de V. E.—E. D. a. M.—Buenos Ayres 9 novº 1810.

Oficio de Guezzi al Conde de Linhares.

Ilmõ. Exmõ. Sr: Desde a minha última que tive a honra de dirigir V. E. em data de 9 novº, naõ se me offreció mais occasiaõ excepto a do Belisario, da qual naõ podí aprofitar pelo muito que tinha que dizer, e pelo perigo de consignar em papel estando en Buenos Aires algumas verdades que precisamente debía escrivir. Como o que me accorreo desde principios de novº ate agora, he consequencia dos passos dados e proposiçoes feitas desde a minha chegada a Buenos Ayres julgueí que V. E. me perdonaria a molestía que lhe ocasiono recopilando em huma especie de memoria todas as minhas operaçoes, ditos e escritos, para que a vista do succeso que tiveraõ, possa V. E. tomar as resoluçoes que a sua penetraçaõ julgue mais convenientes.

Anda muy valido en Buenos Ayres o rumor que a Corte do Brazil fornece a Montevideo algunas forças para obrar hostilmente contra Buenos Ayres. Continuando a valerme da bondade com que V. E. se digna oirme, permittame que manifeste a minha opiniaõ sobre este particolar.

Que o Brazil debe manter forças na fronteira para renderse respeitavel he fora de toda duvida: que debe esmerarse em suffocar a semente de huma revoluçaõ toda democratica que prepara a América siglos de desgraças he tambem evidente: que isto que no se pode conseguir com a forza, e que a de Montevideo e Paraguay auxiliada pelo Brazil he suficiente para asujeitar Buenos Ayres tampoco padece duvida; porem ignoro se estas forças saõ bastante grandes para evitar a contingencia de hum combate, e sem embargo este he o fin principal a que se debe aspirar. No meu conceito as forças deveriaõ ser taes e tantas que Bª Ayª se viese obligado a̱ assujeitarse sem hum so tiro de espingarda para naõ dar lugar a que se principie huma guerra civil e se una o espírito de venganza aõ amor das cousas novas que se acha geralmente propagado.

Porem antes de tudo me parece que o Brazil deberia em qualidade de medianeira fazer alguma proposiçaõ directa de conciliaçaõ, a qual me lisongeio que saria aceptada quando Buenos Ayres vise a firme resoluçaõ e os meios preparados para o obligar com a força a reconciliarse com as Provincias de Paraguay e Montevideo. Quando a Corte do Brazil naõ saccasse outra vintagem com este passo, conseguiria o muy importante fin de dar a conhecer que naõ obra con vistas de facer conquistas para si, nen de aproveitarse das dissensoes intestinas do Paiz.

Huma circunstancia que V. E. naõ deve perder de vista he que os Autores dos motins en Buenos Ayres naõ tem propriamente nemhum projecto fixo de governo que os una, e que o unico principio de uniaõ que os faz obrar, he a determinaçaõ de naõ assujeitarse a superiores de origen Europeõ, ou mandados de Europa. Se este modo de pensar existiese somente en Buenos Ayres saria de pouca consequencia porque os Europeos saõ em numero iguaes aos criolhos; porem como nas Provincias interiores aquelles saõ a estes como hum a cen, V. E. comprendera que a pretençaõ de Buenos Ayres por desatinada e injusta que seja, merece alguma attençao, e que podendose salvar o esencial que he a uniaõ e dependencia da Metrópoli, nao se deve insistir nos accesorios com tanta pertinacia, que a nao conformidade a todos os caprichos e pertençoes de hum partido seja precisamente hum motivo de hostilidade.

O Brazil devería facer as funçoes de huma Potencia absolutamente neutra, imparcial, inculcar muita moderaçaõ, dolçura, e esguecimento do passado a Europeos e Criolhos, porem aõ mesmo tempo mostrarse firme e decidida a queirer ver reducida a Capital a antigua obediencia ou pelo menos a buena forma de gouverno compativel com os intereses geraes da monarquía Hespanhola e dos seus alliados. O bon succésso da mediaçaõ do Brazil depende sem embargo da prontidaõ.

Se as boas noticias que temos de Espanha succeden noticias tristes, duvido que Montevideo, Paraguay e o mesmo Brazil possaõ prevalecer contra a massa de forças que pode reunir Buenos Ayres e sobre todo se consegue manter a opiniaõ do vulgo en su favor em consequencia de nova forma que tomou o Governo.

A pessoa de V. E. G. D. mª aˢ—Em Rada 19 Janeiro 1811.

CORRESPONDENCIA DE GUEZZI CON LA JUNTA REVOLUCIONARIA DE BUENOS AYRES.

Oficio de la Junta a Guezzi.

Ha sido muy satisfactorio para esta Junta el oficio en que Vm. manifiesta los pacíficos y amistosos sentimientos de la Corte del Brasil con estas Provincias. El interés general de todos los pueblos de este vasto Continente exige una entera conformidad en las medidas contra la ambición del Usurpador de la Europa; pues todos correran igual riesgo si la dominación de este fuese reconocida en un solo punto; y si las relaciones de recíproca conveniencia se han colocado diestramente por los antiguos gefes, influiran con toda su fuerza baxo un gobierno que ha jurado no reconocer otros derechros que los de su Augusto Monarca el Sr. D. Fernando 7°. La Junta aprovecha el ofrecimiento de Vm. para dirigir por su conducto el adjunto pliego en que ratifica estos sentimientos, esperando al mismo tiempo se servirá Vm. manifestar al gabinete del Brasil la buena fé, sinceridad y constante adhesión de esta Junta a quantos medios conduzcan a la conservación de los derechos del Sr. D. Fernando 7° en estas Provincias, y recíproca seguridad de todas las que forman este vasto Continente.

Dios guarde a Vm. m⁸ a⁸ Buenos Ayres 20 de julio de 1810.

CORNELIO DE SAAVEDRA   Dr. JUAN JOSÉ CASTELLI
MANUEL BELGRANO   MANUEL DE AZCUENAGA
Dr. MANUEL ALBERTI   DOMINGO MATEU
JUAN LARREA   Dr. MARIANO MORENO,
                                     secretario.

[Addressed:] Sr. D. Carlos Guesei

Oficio de Guezzi a la Junta

Exmõ Sr: Acuso la recepción del oficio fecha 2o del pasado con que Vd. se ha dignado favorecerme, y la del pliego que le acompaña para el Exmõ Señor Conde de Linhares, a quien será dirigido en primera ocasión.

Al mismo tiempo aprovechando de la libertad que Vd. se ha dignado facultarme de poner en su presencia las reflexiones que se dirigiesen al bien de este pais, y a la conservacion de la buena armonía con sus vecinos, espero que Vd. me permitirá añadir a mi oficio del 20 algunas observaciones que nacen de las circunstancias del dia, y tienen una inmediata relación con la comisión de que tube el honor de ser encargado . por el Ministerio Portugués.

Vd. acreditaría facilmente que uno de los principales motivos que han podido inducir a Su Alteza a anticipar la manifestación de sus amistosos y pacíficos sentimientos acia los Havitantes de estas Provincias, ha sido la esperanza de ver de una vez disipada la injusta y demasiado repetida imputación de las asechanzas de la corte del Brasil, y quando esta declaración, y la importancia de los intereses que se agitan en la Peninsula pudiesen dejar alguna duda, espero que será suficiente para desvanecerla la formal declaración que Vd. observará en el documento oficial fecha 29 de Mayo de 1810 que tengo el honor de ofrecer a su superior consideración.

Creo igualmente que la manifestación de los sentimientos de S. A. A. serán para Vd. un testimonio no equívoco de que han cesado en la Corte del Brasil los recelos que se le habián echo concebir sobre la posibilidad de que tubiesen buen exito las tentativas que pudiesen practicar los franceses contra estas Provincias. Cometida su guardia y defensa a un Pueblo tan leal y generoso, aquella Corte no podía dudar un instante que serián inútiles todas las fuerzas, y baldadas todas las maquinaciones al común enemigo.

Nada faltaría pues para el sólido establecimiento de una recíproca y cordial amistad y confianza, si la actual organización del govierno de Buenos Ayres pudiese llenar las miras que sin duda se ha propuesto en su instalación; esto es proveer a la seguridad del Virreynato por primario objeto, y coadyubar con mayor eficacia a la defensa de la Causa general que es el objeto principal para la Metrópoli y sus aliados. Pero la división de opiniones en las Provincias, y aun en la misma Capital, hacen recelar que uno y otro objeto serán igualmente inasequibles, y si por desgracia a las medidas ruidosas que se adoptan para reunir las voluntades, viniese a suceder una guerra civil, es muy dudoso que las mejores intenciones de Vd., consiguieren establecer una forma de gobierno provisional, capaz de cumplir con las obligaciones que la Metropoli y sus aliados tienen derecho de exigir de todos los miembros de la monarquía Española.

Vd. comprende quanto sería dificil en este caso que la Corte del Brasil pudiese vivir enteramente libre de alarmas, en medio de la incertidumbre que acompaña a las conmociones populares, y quanto sería justificado el recelo de que a la suspensión temporaria del reconocimiento, unión y cooperación viniese a suceder una separación absoluta de la metrópoli, no ciertamente por la voluntad y concurso de Vd. pero por el inevitable encadenamiento de los sucesos, que acaso no estará al alcance de Vd. poder prevenir.

Quanto me ha servido de complacencia el honor de haver sido encargado de manifestar a Vd. los pacificos sentimientos de S. A. A.: tanto me juzgo ahora obligado a ofrecer sin dilación a la superior consideración de Vd., los inclusos documentos oficiales fecha 3 y 24 de Abril. La llenaza y sinceridad con que el Ministro Portugués se expresa sobre el caso posible, y no esperado, de algun movimiento revolucionario en estas Provincias, me lisongeo que Vd. la tomaría como la prueba mas convincente del anhelo de la Corte del Brasil para la conservación de la paz interior di este Virreynato, y de ver removida qualquiera causa que pueda reproducir nuevas simientes de desconfianzas e inquietudes.

En tal estado de cosas, ¿ no sería por acaso conveniente que la Corte del Brasil, la qual tiene un interés tan inmediato a la quietud y orden de estas Provincias interpusiese sus buenos oficios para el establecimiento de la buena armonia y paz interior, y para la organización de un sistema regular que provisionalmente exerciese el anterior poder egecutivo? Si es indispensable a la felicidad del Virreynato la Convocación de los Diputados de las Provincias, no dudo que la Corte del Brasil se prestaría gustosa a remover amigablemente los obstaculos que se oponen a su pronta reunión, y garantida una vez la libertad de opinar en el Congreso, Vd. tendría la satisfacción de ver al instante renacida la subordinación y el orden, respetada su propia autoridad, y renovados los vinculos con la Metrópoli, sin cuyas circunstancias Vd. mismo ha previsto y anunciado males imponderables que deben afligir al Virreynato.

Si Vd. no juzga indiscreta mi propuesta y prevee que puede venir un caso en que sea admisible, y puesta en ejecución, permitame añadir que en los citados documentos anexos a esta, hallará Vd. indicados algunos motivos de queja particulares, cuyo allanamiento contribuiría a consolidar la buena inteligencia y amistad entre los dos Pueblos. Desde el 26 de Marzo de 1808 se han hecho en nombre de S. A. A. algunas propuestas relativas al comercio, las quales quedaran sin respuesta, al paso que se han rendido mas pesadas condiciones bajo las quales antecedentemente se egercia, Vd que conoce quanto influyen los enlaces y conveniencias mercantiles en la conservación de la paz entre naciones vecinas y de mutua natural dependencia, podría aprovechar la ocasión del envio de un comisionado a aquella Corte para arregar de un modo equitativo aunque provisional, el sistema bajo del qual hayan de girarse las relaciones comerciales entre el Brasil y la Capital del Rio de la Plata.

Los tres documentos que Vd. hallará inclusos, se servirá Vd. devolvérmelos despues de haverse impuesto de su contenido. Por su inspeccion se hallará Vd. en situación de distinguir lo que deve considerar como declaración del Govierno Portugues, y lo que no es mas que opinión mia particular, en cuyo último número con especialidad deve Vd. contar la propuesta que hago, de la mediación de aquella Corte, para hacer lo qual declaro no tener la menor autorizacion ni insinuación; pero me he animado a hacerla en la suposición, que pudiese contribuir al bien y felicidad de estas Provincias, y con la seguridad de que por ningun modo se ofenderian las relaciones de amistad y alianza que tan estrechamente ligan al Gobierno Portugués con el Gobierno supremo de la Nación Española.

Aprovecho esta ocasión para renovar a Vd. los sentimientos de la mas alta estima y consideración con la qual tengo el honor de declararme. Buenos Ayres 1° de Agosto de 1810.   De Vd.

[Addressed.]   Exmo. Sr. Presidente y Vocales de la Junta Provisional Gubernativa de las Provincias del Rio de la Plata.

Oficio de Guezzi a D. Mariano Moreno

En la conferencia que V. M. se sirvió concederme ayer ofrecí mis propuestas por escrito para ponerlas en presencia de la Exma Junta, si las juzga merecedoras de su atención, y convenientes a las circunstancias del dia, lo que voy a cumplir con la mayor concesión posible, refiriendome en lo demás a lo que tube el honor de decir a V. M. de palabra.

La Corte del Brasíl ha pedido el reconocimiento de los derechos eventuales de la Serenisima Sra. Princesa del Brasil. Estos derechos fundados en la antigua constitución, reconocidos individualmente por las cortes de 1789, y reconfirmados en 1809 por una declaración expresa de la Suprema Junta Central, son títulos sobrantes para no necesitar el reconocimiento parcial de una única Ciudad. Parece pues que la voluntad de la Corte del Brasil no deve considerarse como un arbitrio para adquirir títulos, sino como un acto amistoso dirigido a desvanecer las sospechas que hayan podido nacer respecto de las intenciones futuras de la Exma. Junta, y como un nuevo testimonio para creer que es sincera la declaración anteriormente echa de fidelidad y obediencia al Sr. D. Fernando 7° y sus legitimos sucesores.   No veo que del solicitado reconocimiento pueda originarse el menor comprometimiento, y las utilidades son tan palpables que (puede) ofender la penetración de Vm. en detallarlas.   Solo una circunstancia añadiré por que me hallo autorizado a declararla de oficio, como ya lo verifiqué verbalmente con la Exma. Junta, y es, que la intención de S. A. A. la Sra Princesa Carlota es de no hacer valer sus derechos sino en el uso y del modo preciso determinado por las leyes y constitución de la Monarquía. Esta declaración excluye por consiguiente la idea de una Regencia actual, o de una gestión qualquiera contraria al voto y al interés nacional.

La segunda propuesta que hice desde el 1° de Agosto y que he renovado ayer es, la de aceptar la mediación de la Corte del Brasil, en la inteligencia que esta propuesta era puramente mia y que de ningun modo ni de palabra ni por escrito estaba autorizado a hacerla.

La unica condición preliminar que a mi ver exigiría la Corte del Brasil, aceptando el cargo de medianera, sería el reconocimiento del Gobierno Supremo establecido en España, y el concurso sincero y eficaz del Virreynado a la defensa de la Metrópoli. Estos dos objetos son de tanta primaria importancia que todos los demas intereses desaparecen enteramente al frente de estos.

Respecto a las pretensiones del govierno actual de Buenos Ayres, como ignoro quales sean, no puedo anticipar mi opinión sobre si serán o no apoyadas, pero en general juzgo que se garantirían todas aquellas que no reduciesen la dependencia del Govierno Supremo a un puro acto nominal, y que no ocasionasen una real separación del resto de la monarquía baxo las apariencias de unión, como viene a ser el caso de Caracas.

La reunion del Congreso, ni creo que pueda hallar oposición en la Corte del Brasil, por que esta organización provisional pertenece al arreglo interior del Virreynato, respecto al qual ya ha declarado de oficio la misma Corte no querer embarazarse por ningun medio directo ni indirecto: Pero la libertad de los Diputados es una materia de tanta importancia y trascendencia que a no circunscribirse con exactitud sus privilegios y funciones, jamás podría hallar apoyo en la Corte del Brasil. Es claro que el Congreso no podrá ser considerado como la representación de un estado soberano e independiente que forma una constitución, pero como una comisión destinada a exercer interinamente el poder ejecutivo baxo el auspicio de las leyes existentes, o que de nuevo exámen de la legítima representación nacional.

Estos son las dos propuestas que por el momento creo puedan merecer la atención de la Corte del Brasil. Si Vm. juzga que pueden contribuir al restablecimiento del sosiego, y a la union de las provincias del Virreynato: ofrezcolas a la consideración de la Junta Suprema que dispondrá en este caso de mi voluntad y obediencia como mejor la convenga.

Aprovecho esta ocasión para renovar los sentimientos de la estima
y consideración con que tengo el honor de declararme. De Vd. Buenos
Ayres 17 de Noviembre de 1810.

[Addressed:]   Sr. D. Mariano Moreno.

ESPOSICIÓN

*Exposiçao de quanto me accorreo durante a demora que fiz em Buenos
Ayres desde 17 Julho ate 20 Decembro 1810.*

Cheguei o 17 julho em Buenos Ayres: me presentei a Junta inmediatamente; porem as suas ocupações naõ lhe permitiraõ darme audiencia
ate o día sucessivo.   Ocupei este intervalo em visitar aos Vogaes
Belgrano, e Castelli: Ambos me asegurarão que permaneciaõ invaria-
veis nos antiguos sentimentos: Que os direitos da Serenísima Sra.
Princesa sarião reconhecidos e chamada logo que as circunstancias da
Peninsula, e do Virreinado o permittissen: Que o restante de os Vogaes
da Junta pensavaõ do mesmo modo; porem que eu mesmo sabía as
muitas dificultades que deviaõ superarse tanto por parte dos Europeos,
como dos Patricios; as precaucões que deviaõ tomarse, e o tempo que
se necessitava: Que a reuniaõ do Congresso podia abbreviar a caminho
e dissipar os embaraços, e que somente pelo mesmo Congresso se podía
dar aõ reconhecimento da Senhora, ó grado de dignidade correspon-
dente a taõ relevante materia.

No dia 18 tive audiencia da Junta: se manifestou somamente agra-
decida aos sentimentos de paz, e benevolencia que S. A. R. se dignava
manifestar; me pedio que lhe os comunicase por escrito, e que em senhal
do seu reconhecimento poría na presença de S. A. R. os documentos
originaes por onde ficasse convencido da urgente necessidade em que
se tinha visto o Povo de mudar o Gouverno para assegurarse contra as
maquinaçoes francesas, e de expulsar o Vicerey e Audiencia cujo progecto era asujeitar o Vicereynado a Metrópoli qualquier que fosse a
sorte desta.   Me preguntaraõ se tinha alguna recomendaçaõ de parte
da Senhora Princeza; se sabía como se tinha recibido a noticia dos
sucessos de V. E. e se julgaria que esta era a ocasiaõ opportuna para
fazer valer os seus direitos: Respondi que naõ tinha recommendaçaõ
alguma, nem sabia como S. A. R. tivesse recevido noticias dos aconte-
cimentos de Buenos Ayres: Que pelo demais tendo ja a suprema Junta
central reconhecido os seus Direitos, era natural que S. A. R. confiasse
na lealtade Hespanhola para o seu cumprimento e contasse especialmente
com o voto dos Povos destas Provincias.   Disse entaõ Saavedra que

nisto naõ podia caber a menor duvida, e que ainda quando toda a nacaõ fosse de opiniaõ contraria, o Povo de Buenos Ayres, e a Junta que tinhí. a honra de o mandar, seriaõ os primeiros a impunhar a espada para a conservacaõ dos seus direitos. Antes de concluir a conferencia supliquei a Junta quisesse facultarme a libertade de comunicarlhe por escrito as opinioes, duvidas, ou propostas que as circunstancias rendessem necessarias, e mirassem aõ bem geral, ou a conservaçaõ da boa harmonia establecida com a Corte do Brazil; que foi liberalmente concedido.

No dia 20 passei a Junta o officio que foi impresso na Gazeta. Para elle me serviraõ de guia em quanto ao essencial as instruccoes que tinha, e respeito as formalidades, e cerimonias a Carta de Lord Strangford; Porem observando que a mançan da discordia era o naõ reconhecimento da Regencia, julguei deber o circunscrivir do milhor modo possivel a interpretaçaõ que se debía dar a expressaõ dos sentimentos pacificos e amigaveis de S. A. R. dando a entender no mesmo officio que em tanto approvaria S. A. R. as reformas do Gouverno, em quanto estos se dirigissem a manter intacta a Monarquía Hespanhola debaxo do Domínio do seu Legitimo Soberano, a conservar a paz e concordia entre os Povos, a concorrer a comun defenza, a estreitar a uniaõ com a Metrópoli socorrela, auxiliala, etc.

Este officio teve a desgraça de desagradar aos dous partidos extremos. Por terme explicado com alguma cortezia de tarifa em louor dos Individuos da Junta, os oppositores de Esta me trataraõ com demasiada superficialidade, como *Manolo* ou Revolucionario. E por ter dito que a Junta devia auxiliar, e manterse em unidad com a Metrópoli, os Manolos com mais razaõ me chamaraõ *saraceno*.

Em 30 Julho recebi a resposta da Junta aõ meu officio de 20, e com ella hum prego para o Exmo Sr. Conde de Linhares, no qual se me asseguraba que hiaõ fecha dos os documentos originaes por onde ficaria a Corte do Brazil convencida das maquinações que se estaraõ forjando para entregar estes dominios a o Rey que fosse de Hespanha.

A pesar da lisongeira e somamente satisfactoria comunicaçaõ do dia 18, julguei que saría conveniente usar da libertade de fallar, e escrever que me tinha sido concedido pela junta, e em 1° de Agosto lhe dirigi hum officio ou carta que por copia remetti ao Exmo. Sr. Conde de Linhares, cujo objecto era facer entender a Junta:

1° Que a divisaõ de opiniões que se tinha manifestado na capital, e nas Provincias, inquietaria a Corte do Brazil.

2° Que o gouverno provisional estabelecido naõ podendo ofrecer ninhuma garantia nas suas relaçoes exteriores, e interiores em virtude da propia organisaçaõ, nao podería calmar as alarmas da mesma Corte.

3° Que esta ja tinha formalmente declarado em 3 ó 24 de Abril que se achava com todas as forças promptas para extinguir e conter qualquier movimento revolucionario que podesse manifestarse no Rio da Plata.

4° Que para evitar qualquer sinistra interpretacaõ que se quizesse dar aõs sucessos de Buenos Ayres, saria conveniente mandar hum Diputado a Corte do Brazil, suplicala a interpor os seus bons officios para a convocaçaõ do Congresso, e para estabelecimento de huma ordem fixa e invariavel de administraçaõ, e que a mesma Corte sahisse garante do novo sisthema provisional de gouverno.

Esta proposita fo toleravelmente bem recebida pela Junta, e por muítos individuos a quem a comuniquei conceptuando os ter alguma influencia sobre a opinion do Povo, e hum resto de sentimento das suas obrigações e conveniencias.   Porem era visivel que a sua adopçaõ dependia princeiramente do bon ou maõ sucesso que tivesse a expediçaõ do Perú, e em segundo lugar da parte activa e vigorosa que a Corte do Brazil se mostrase decidida a tomar nas desavenzas do Paiz.   Por isso a Junta por via de algums Vogaes com quem tinha relaçaõ, nunca cessou de lisonjarme que abraçaria o proposto ainda que procurasse sempre novos e especiosos pretextos para dudar as minhas sollicitaçoes.

As ventagens que deviaõ resultar da mediaçaõ sao patentes.   Ganhavaose os dous partidos opostos dispensando a debida proteiçaõ a Europeos, e Empregados, e fazendo conceder alguns favores aõs Patricios.   Por outro qualquier meyo deve necessariamente resultar hum partido enemigo, e talvez com o tempo os dous.   A permaçaõ destas ventagens me fez insistir con pertinacia desde Agosto ate Decembro no mesmo plano, ainda despois que a Junta descubrió os seus designios, e quando era extremamente perigoso o contradizela, ou querer imbaracqalhe a sua marcha.

Carta del 16 de Setembro. id 5 Octubro — De quanta importancia era para o resultado dos negocios do Paiz o tono que tomasse a Corte do Brazil o conheci clarmente quando o Vogal Belgrano me fez ter o officio que o Exmo. Sr. Conde de Linhares dirigió aõ governador e Capitan General do Rio Grande.   Me prevaleú do temor momentaneo que me parecía haver inspirado a Junta o contendo do citado officio para renovar as instancias de que se mandase hum Deputado a Corte do Brazil, e por esta vez me foi respondido que ja estava elegido, porem que se tinha escolhido hum sujeito de fora da capital para que fosse izento de espíritu de partido e naõ excitasse emulações; que se tinha mandado sir, e que em breve chegaria. Se este saudavel temor tivesse podido ser permanente naõ duvido que as diferencias do Vicerreynado estariaõ compostas, ou pelo menos em disposiçaõ de receber a direcçaõ que a Corte do Brazil julgase suficiente para aredar o incendio de lha Caza. O Terror, a consternaçaõ e o disconcerto tendose feito generaes o progecto da mediaçaõ do Brazil para a reconciliaçaõ das Provincias orientaes do Rio da Prata se fez popular e teve apoyo em persoas de primeira importancia, e de grande influencia. Entre estas corresponde o primeiro lugar aõ Dr. Don Gregorio Funes, Deputado de Cordova, aõ qual desde muito tempo tinha comunicado de palabra, e por escrito as minhas ideas sobre os negocios do dia. Naõ somente se mostrou satisfeito delas porem apuntou que ainda quando as Provincias se composessem, e chegasse a realiçarse o Congresso, era necessario que este fosse protegido por huma força portugueza sem cuya circunstancia jamais gozaría da libertade suficiente para manifestar as suas opinioes.

Em principio de Novembro o mesmo Doctor Funes me disse que tinha fallado aõ Segretario Moreno, neste tempo o Corifeo da Junta, sobre a proposta mediaçaõ porem que perceberá que naõ estaba disposto a admitirla, ainda que lhe naõ tivesse dito nada de positivo em contrario, e logo despois me preguntou, se naõ me parecia que incontraria menos dificultade a mediaçaõ de Inglaterra? Estranhei infinitamente esta proposta feita por huma persoa que de dous años a esta parte affectou tanto fervor para a causa da Senhora Princeza, e lhe respondi: Que a Inglaterra podia ser mediatriz se quizessem; porem que a Corte do Brazil devia selo quizessem ou naõ quizessem; que esta a mais de amiga e alliada tinha o titulo de vizinha, e interessada nos negocios do paiz: Que naõ se immaginasse que os direitos da Senhora Princeza ficavaõ esguecidos por se ter demorado a execuçaõ da justa reclamaçaõ, e que devía estar na intelligencia que a recusaçaõ de officios amigaveis, e paternaes em materia tao grave era huma manifesta provocaçaõ, e legitimaba o emprego da força.

9 Novembro : Poucos dias despois foi chamado pela Junta; informei logo aõ Exmo. Sr. Conde de Linhares da proposiçaõ que nela se me fez de hir aõ Rio de Janeiro a reclamar as cartas originaes escritas pelo Marques de Casa Irujo aõ Vicerey Cisneros; como me recusei a esta comissaõ offecerendome com tudo a passar aõ Rio de Janeiro se a Junta tivesse alguma proposiçaõ agradavel a fazer a aquella Corte, e que perguntandoume o Segretario quaes podriaõ ser as proposições agradaveis respondi: a de reconhecer os direitos eventuaes da Sra.

Princeza: ou admittir a mediaçaõ da Corte do Brazil para compor as differencias do Vicerreynado. Sobre o que ficou o Segretario em receber e darme a resposta da Junta.

Em 16 de Novembro foi pela resposta. O que sigue he o resumo do dialogo que tive com Moreno.

Moreno.—A Junta naõ acha conveniente mandar hum Deputado a Corte do Brazil. Esta debe acharse satisfeita com a prova de confianza que se lhe tem dado comunicandolhe as cartas que o Marqués de Casa Irujo dirigia aõ Virrey Cisneros.

Guezzi.—Naõ creyo que baste esta comunicaçao. Desde Julho ate aqui houverao taes novidades que necesariamente deven precisar de novas explicaçoes.

Moreno.—Naõ houveraõ outras novidades que as precisas para organizar o Gouverno interior baxo o plano que se tem elegido.

Guezzi.—Porem o plano elegido, e o modo de organizalo pode ser tal que seja incompativel com os intereses do Brazil.

Moreno.—A Junta naõ se ocupa dos intereses do Brazil porem dos intereses do Vicerreynado do Rio da Prata.

Guezzi.—O Senhor Moreno naõ pode dissimular que a Corte do Brazil tem legítimos intereses a deslindar com este Paiz; porem prescindindo deles, direi em geral, que a naõ quererse separar de todo o Mondo he preciso que o Gouverno de Buenos Ayres combine os seus intereses com os das Potencias vizinhas. Neste sentido pelo menos me sera concedido fallar nos intereses do Brazil.

Moreno.—O comercio do Brazil foi favorecido, e os vassados de S.A.R. protegidos e respeitados.

Guezzi.—S. A. R. naõ deixará de agradecer estas attençoes; porem ellas saõ de segunda ordem; o principal interesse do Brazil he que se conserve a paz e a uniaõ no Vice-rreynado; que huma Provincia naõ queira esclavizar a outra, e que por agora todas concorraõ em quanto podem a defeza da causa geral.

Moreno.—Isto he justamente em que se ocupa o Gouverno. He culpa dos sublevados se ate agora o naõ tem podido conseguir.

Guezzi.—Se a Junta tivesse adoptado, ou adoptasse o arbitrio da mediaçaõ que propuz naõ haveria resistencias nem opposiçoes, nem se necessitariao os meyos violentos que se tem empregado. Ainda estamos em tempo de remediar a muitos maes se a Junta quer uniformarse a esta proposta.

Moreno.—E baxo que termos aceptaria a Corte do Brazil o officio de Medianeira.

Guezzi.—Eu o ignoro; porem me lisongeo que naõ se recusaría a ninhum termo que fosse justo e racionavel.

Moreno.—E quem nos assegura que de Medianeira naõ queira passar a Corte do Brazil a ser Senhora destas Provincias?

Guezzi.—Esta sospeita he sem fundamento. O que se acha impresso na justa reclamaçaõ, e os empenhos actuaes com a Peninsula excluen toda idea de conquista.

Moreno.—Porem a Corte do Brazil ha de querer empregar a força e de este modo a mediaçaõ e inadmisivel.

Guezzi.—He certo que huma força he indispensavel; so Ella pode garantir huma Proteiçaõ igual a Hespanholes e Patricios, reprimindo aquelles que fomentem divisoes. Sem a presença de huma força se perpetuaraõ as desconfianças e prompto se passaria a violencias em precauçaõ de violencias temidas.

Moreno.—De modo que na opiniaõ de V. M. hum Exercito Portuguez deve vir a consolidar a paz nas Provincias do Rio de Prata.

Guezzi.—Naõ digo tal cousa. O Exercito naõ passaria as suas fronteiras, excepto se os promovedores de novedades rompessem os pactos que ficassem sancionados baxo a garantia do Brazil.

Ajoutei mil cousas para comprovar a utilidade e urgencia desta medida e me offerece a darlhe a minha proposta por escrito para que a comunicasse a Junta, o que verifiquei no dia seguinte. O dia 20 pela tarde recebi o officio seguinte:

"La Exma Junta Provisional Gubernativa de las Provincias del Rio de la Plata ha resuelto decididamente que Vd. en el primer buque que salga para Rio de Janeiro se restituya a aquel destino, a cuyo efecto con esta misma fecha da orden al Capitan del Puerto para que esté a la mira del cumplimiento de esta Providencia, y lo aviso a Vd. para su inteligencia. Dios guarde a Vd. m⁸ a⁸. Buenos Ayres 20 de noviembre de 1810. "CORNELIO SAAVEDRA."

Informei aõ Dr. Funes da ordem recebida, e da conversaçaõ que a tinha precedido. Me instruio entaõ em detalhe das causas que a tinhao motivado: Me disse que era hum delitto para a Junta fallar em mediaçoes ou composiçoes. Que o que a Junta queria era hum Gouverno Democratico, e que para conseguilo devia principiar por separarse enteiramente da Hespanha e do Portugal, e conservarse ella mesma no posto en que se tinha collocado. Conhecido pois que tendo taes intençoes a Junta, debía verme de mal olho, me preparei a partir, bem decidido com tudo a explicarme mais claro logo que se me proporcionasse huma ocasiaõ favoravel, a qual naõ me podia faltar com motivo de haver de reclamar alguns papeis que estavaõ em poder do segretario.   Com efeito tres veces tive proporçaõ de fallar: Excuso referir os dialogos como se succederaõ, porque o argumento sendo sempre o mesmo se reducem a ultimo que tive em 13 Decembro, dia em que foi convidado pelo mesmo Moreno a passar a sua caza, adonde disse que tinha muito que fallar consigo.   Foi as' dez e meya da noute, e o encontrei com o Vogal Larrea.   O resumo do dialogo que tivemos he seguinte:

Moreno.—Por noticias particulares me consta que a Corte do Brazil reune forzas sobre a fronteira.

Guezzi.—Ignoro o que se passa na Fronteira do Brazil, porem he de presumir que com efeito a Corte tome algumas precauçoes a vista das agitaçoes destas Provincias.

Moreno.—Quem produz as agitaçoes saõ os sublevados e rebeldes enganhados pelos marinhos.   Os Povos de Montevideo e Paraguay ja estariaõ reunidos a Capital se estes fossem expulsados.

Guezzi.—A Corte do Brazil naõ entra nestas averiguaçoes.   Ve hum incendio, e descja apagalo sem perguntar quem he Autor dele.

Moreno.—Se a Corte do Brazil adopta o arbitrio da guerra ella se arrepentará; pois excitará no propio Paiz, o fogo que pretende apagar no alheio.

Guezzi.—A Corte do Brazil naõ provoca a guerra.   Isto o tem provado com as contemplaçoes tal vez excesivas que guardou com esta Capital.   Porem o senhor Moreno estará persuadido como Eu, que a forma de gouverno adoptada pela Junta, e os principios inculcados nos povos do Vicerreynado obrigaõ a Corte do Brazil a suffocar na sua origen hum incendio que como diz o Sr. Moreno pode extenderse' ate aõ Brazil.

Moreno.—Esta Capital naõ se ocupa se naõ do seu Regimen interior, com o cual nada tem que ver o Brazil.

Guezzi.—A Corte do Brazil debe mirar pelo estado destas Provincias, como Vizinha, como Alhada de Hespanha, e como intersada na successaõ destes Dominios, nos casos determinados pela Constituiçaõ.   He portanto loucura pensar que ha de prescindir destas raçoes de estado, e que dive ser indifferente sobre o que se passa nestas Provincias.

Moreno.—A Junta tem dado prova do seu espírito de paz, e da confianza que tem na corte do Brazil, mandando retirar as guarniçoes da Fronteira.

Guezzi.—Isso assim sera; porem he probavel que no Brazil se de a esta retirada huma interpretaçaõ nada favoravel.

Moreno.—E que forzas tem o Brazil na fronteira?

Guezzi.—Eu o ignoro; porem creyo que achandose prevenido de Officio que era intençaõ do Vice-rey Cisneros armar 12 mil homens, o Brazil por precauçaõ reuniría pelo menos huma igual força.

Moreno.—Cre Vm. que as forças do Brazil se juntaraõ com os Hespanholes da Banda Oriental?

Guezzi.—Nada sei, porem se estas provincias fieis aõ Gouverno da Naçaõ, que a Corte do Brazil reconhece, imploraõ o seu patrocinio nim huma duvida tenho que as protegerá.

Moreno.—Porem nos tambem temos jurado a Fernando 7mo e os seus legítimos sucessores.

Guezzi.—Se este juramento comprehende a debida fidelidade e obbediencia aõ mesmo Soberano, he preciso entaõ que as desavenças tenhaõ nacido de falta de entenderse, e renovarei portanto a instancia tantas vezes feita de mandar huma pessoa aõ Rio de Janeiro para dar e pedir as explicaçoes necessarias, ja que os Hespanhoes entresi naõ se podem entender.

Moreno.—A Junta tambem desejaria mandar hum Deputado, porem naõ conhece huma pessoa capaz de huma commissaõ taõ delicada.

Guezzi.—Subejaõ nesta Cidade Pessoas de talento, e Eu poderia nomiar muitas que gozaõ da completa confianza da Junta.

Larrea.—Hindo Vm. excusamos mandar hum Deputado, Vm. pode dar aõ Ministro Portuguez huma idea veridica das intençoes e procedimentos da Junta.

Guezzi.—Creyo que o Sr. Larrea se burla de min. Tratase de mandar huma Pessoa que leve a palabra da Junta, e diga o que esta pensa e quere. Eu nunca poderia ser interprete fiel nem acreditado, porem nunca diria se naõ o que penso eu mesmo da Junta.

Larrea.—Naõ devemos mandar hum Deputado para ser desairado. O Ministerio Portuguez nunca quiz escrever a esta Junta, indicio que se naõ quer entender com Ella.

Guezzi.—O Gabinete Britannico naõ desairou o Deputado que se lhe mandou a pesar que nunca escreveo nem respondeo as propostas da Junta. A etiquetta dos Gabinetes naõ permitte que os Segretarios de Estado tenhao correspondencia com Gouvernos iguaes, e muito menos con Gouvernos subalternos.

Larrea.—Podiá responder por via do Ministro Hespanhol.

Guezzi.—(Contestei com huma risada.)

Larrea.—Ou pelo menos intenderse directamente com o gouverno de Hespanha.

Guezzi.—Naõ duvido que o Ministerio Portuguez esteja de intelligencia com o gouverno de Hespanha?   Porem desde quando reconhece a Junta este gouverno?

————

Esta conferencia durou mais de hora e meya; porem como me apercebi que nada se concluiría, me despedí, e figuei em hir buscar os meus papeis o dia 17.

Ao tempo de os entregar, Moreno me fez ler o Officio que dirigia em nome da Junta aõ Exmo Sr. Conde de Linhares.   No primeiro parrafo se queixa de que naõ lhe fosseiu restituidas as Cartas originaeis dirigidas pelo Marqués de Casa Irujo a o Vicerrey Cisneros; no segundo falla dos movimentos hostis que supoe na fronteira do Brazil, e se refere a min por o que pertenece a informes sobre a conducta e opinioes da Junta. Despois de o ser lido dissi a Moreno: Que me parecía irregular que se chamassem sublevados os officioes de Montevideo escrevendose a huma Corte Extrangeira, e em quanto a min, me queixe de que me tivesse nomiado como legítimo interprete das intencoes da Junta quando elle mesmo sabía o muito que diferenciabamos, tanto no modo como nos fines.   Porem como Moreno se achava muito alterado por algumas ocurrencias desagradaveis da noute anterior imbrolhou o officio em huma especie de papel pardo, o lacrou sem sello, e m'o entregou sem pronunciar nem huma palabra.

Passei a dispedirme do Canónigo Funes: me informou das tentativas feitas nos dias anteriores para que se admittissen desde ja os Diputados das Provincias na Junta: Dos debates violentos que houveraõ nela; da resistencia que opposeraõ quatro dos seus Vogaes; porem que a pluralidade sendo en favor dos Deputados, naõ duvidaba que se vencesse a pertencaõ.   Me pidió que me detivesse hum par de semanas na Rada por que o sistema de Gouverno debendo necessariamente mudar podía ser que se abrisse hum camino a projectada mediacaõ; a cujo effecto necessitava de min.

Com effeito o dia 18 de Dezembro ficou resolvida a quistaõ em favor dos 9 Deputados, e se estava organizando o modo e forma de recepcaõ. Os 4 Vogaes dissidentes deviaõ ter assento na Junta sem voto, entre estes se alhao os dous segretarios.   O plano final parece que se dirige a conseguir que Buenos Ayres nomeye hum ou dous Deputados para o Congresso, e acabe a jurisdicçaõ da Junta.

O dia 20 me embarquei no Bregantin Belesario a cuyo Capitan Joaõ de Souza de Carvalho entreguei baxo recibo a carta que Moreno me confiou para o Exmo. Sr. Conde de Linhares a quem naõ me foi possivel pela brevidade do tempo, e porque o que devía dizén naõ se podia lançar em papel sem risco, estando em terra; e passei logo a bordo do navio Yngléz Quem que estava na Rada.

Em 21 foi a visitar o Comandante da Corveta Mercurio aõ momento em que despedia hum Parlamentario para a Capital com officios de Hespanha. O informei do que me ocorria, da mudança que tinha havido em razaõ da qual naõ duvidaba que o Parlamentario fosse recebido com decencia; porem duvidei que reconhecesem as Cortes. A total e perpetuo separaçaõ da uniao e dependencia da Metrópoli e creyo hum artigo decidido tanto para a Junta como para os Deputidos se naõ me deya eforça que faça variar este propósito.

Como tenho fallado tanto do Dr Gregorio Funes e como probabelmente representará o primeiro papel nesta nova transformaçaõ de Gouverno creyo que sería conveniente facelo conhecer milhor para calcular o que dele se debe esperar ou temer.

Ele he Dean da Se de Cordoba, unicamente dedicado as Letras, reservado no fallar e com hum ar de simplicidade e modestia que preven en seu favor. Manifesta desejar a felicidade do seu Paiz aquella que se nace da coltura de Espirito, e da propagaçaõ das luzes. He tenaz nos propósitos que emprende, e sabe todas as artes para conseguir. Recebeo muitos beneficios da Corte de Hespanha; obsequios e favores dos Vicerreys, especialmente de Liniers.

S.A.R. a Sra. Princeza Carlotta o honrou com huma correspondencia distinguida, e que manifesta o aprecio que lhe merecia. He autor de hum Escrito com data de 5 de Julho dirigido aõ Exmo Sr. Conde de Linhares firmado se naõ me enganho pelo Dr. Carvalho seu Primo: Se tem manifestado opportissimo as operaçoes da Junta, tanto em publico como em privado, e sempre pareceo inclinado a moderaçaõ, a ordem, e a boa harmonia das Provincias. Porem este mismo Dr. Funes he acusado pela voz publica de ter dirigido o Povo de Cordova, e ser contribuido a desgraça de Liniers o seus compañeros. He autor dos tres escritos da Gazetta firmados "Un Ciudadano". Nunca pronunciou huma unica sobre os direitos da Sra. Princeza; nem dem a conhecer qui podía vir hum caso em que Ele os apoyasse. Manifestou preferir a mediacaõ de Inglaterra a do Brazil, mais sejura, mais inmediata e mais legal. Me fez dicer pelo Dr. Carvalho que escrevesse aõ Exmo. Sr. Conde de Linhares: que por agora naõ fizesse uso do papel de 5 de Julho. Parece infatuado de principios democraticos, a fixo na resoluçaõ de que naõ se deven admittir novos Empregados Europeos, nem dependencia da Metrópoli.

Se esta ultima conducta he a conselhada pela inmoralidade e barbarie do Gouverno passado, merecerá o Dr. Funes o título de prudente e circonspecto: do contrario será o mais iniquo hipocrita e impostor que ha naturaleza tenha produzido.

He superfluo fallar da Junta e dos seus principios. Moreno e o Robespierre do dia. Os outo companheiros saõ nullos para o ben, porem opportunos e ardentes instrumentos da Tirannia. Todos juntos pretenderaõ fundar huma Republica sobre o terrorismo; e pelo menos ten conseguido propagar este. Entre os seus progectos favoritos se conta o de levar a revoluçaõ no Brazil. Ja a deraõ por feita em principio de Decembro, naõ sei sobre que noticias, e o seu recosijo foi extremo.

A divisaõ entre Europeos e Patricios he conhecida e certa e me parece irreconciliavel se a Metropoli naõ triunfa. He increivel como se tem propagado esta anticipatia especialmente na casta vil do Campo. Em Cordova huma manada de Patricios se presentou aõ gouvernador pedindo licencia de matar saracenos, e em Buenos Ayres a cada novidade meyo desagradavel, e a tecla que logo se tocca.

Os Patricios saõ divididos entre si: A mayor parte dos que pertenecem a familhas decentes detestaõ os procederes violentos, arbitrarios e crucis da Junta. Os partidarios de Saavedra que saõ a classe militar formaõ huma especie de sansculottes, porque efectivamente saõ todos pobres e famicutos; os partidarios de Moreno saõ como a Montanha entre os Jacobinos.

A pesar destas dissençoes naõ devo deixar ignorar que em hum punto parece concordaõ os Patricios de todas classes e condiçoes, e he de querer formar huma Republica, e naõ reconhecer superioridade no Gouverno Hespanhol.

A divisaõ entre os partidarios de Saavedra e Moreno a causou hum oficial levado que em hum convite fez hum brindis Saavedra, primeiro imperador de America. O caso parece despreciavel; porem se naõ foz osote de Saavedra pode ser que naça outro a quem se possa applicar a passagem de Tacito: "Capere duo manipulares transferre Imperium Populi Romani, et transtulerunt."

Os Patricios estao persuadidos que tarde ou sedo a Metropoli mandará forças para os assujeitar; e se lisongeaõ de ter tambem forças para resistirlhe. Porem em caso de apuro ouir dizer a muitos que prefeririaõ trattar com o Brazil, antes que com os Hespanhoes, porque aquelle naõ tem venganzas a tomar nem justiças a exercitar como estes. Era esta a principal razaõ que me animava a insistir na mediacaõ por que me parecía ser o unico arbitrio que podia acabar as disenções sem samgue sem guerras e sem deixar sementes de animosidades que possaõ occasionar catastrofes no sucessivo.

As armas de fogo sendo a unica falta que a Junta experimenta no seu plano de resistencia emprega todos os esforços em estabelecer huma fábrica delas nas visinhanças de San Miguel de Tucuman. Para estc fim ja dirigió a aquel destino huma porçaõ consideravel de ferro, adonde se diz que pensa retirarse ella mesma con todas as tropas e munições se por acaso as forças que atacassem Buenos Ayres fossem demasiado superiores. Este plano me parece inverificavel, porque os que naõ estaõ complicados nos crimes da Junta naõ se querao seguir: porem he muito possivel que Ella tente fugir para o interior com os que voluntariamente queiraõ correr a ma fortuna.

Estas eraõ as disposiçoes da Junta e dos Patricios em geral antes que se agregassem aõ Gouverno os 9 Deputados. As mudanças que deste accidente resulten deficilmente se poden pronosticar. Haverá mais moderaçaõ, porem os principios seraõ os mesmos. Sobre todo o tono que tome a Corte do Brazil decidirá da sorte futura desta Capital. Os povos em geral tomaõ a prudencia por debilidade, e desprezaõ o poder que naõ se lhes faz temivel. Para elles ha a fabula das Rans.

A bordo do Navío Mercante Inglez "Quem," na rada de Buenos Ayres a 26 de Decembro 1810

D. CARLOS JOSÉ GUEZZI.

THE OLD SPANISH TRAIL

A STUDY OF SPANISH AND MEXICAN TRADE AND EXPLORATION
NORTHWEST FROM NEW MEXICO TO THE GREAT BASIN
AND CALIFORNIA[1]

SUMMARY

The present study is but a chapter in the larger theme, "The
Opening Of The Southern Trails To California". This
entire subject has generally been minimized or entirely overlooked in the study of the opening and development of the West.
There is usually but one trail from New Mexico to California
marked on the maps dealing with the subject. This is the so-
called "Old SpanishTrail to California", which is indicated as
passing through Abiquiú and northwest down the Dolores and
across Grand and Green rivers, thence west to the Sevier, and
southwest to the Virgin and Mohave rivers and through Cajon
Pass to Los Angeles. As a matter of fact, this trail was not
opened until the region had ceased to be Spanish territory. The
Old Spanish Trail, properly so-called led to the Great Basin only,
and was developed as a result of the Spanish trade with the Yutas.
This trade began with the first exploration of the region and continued until after the country was settled by whites.

During the decade between the time of the Rivera expedition to
the Gunnison River (1765) and that of the Domínguez-Escalante
exploration (1776) Spanish traders made frequent visits to the
Yutas, remaining with them, in some cases, months at a time.
These activities were possibly confined to the region east of the
Colorado and south of the Gunnison. After Domínguez and
Escalante had explored a route to the Great Basin, however, and

[1] The writer wishes to acknowledge gratefully in the preparation of the following paper the suggestive help of Dr. H. E. Bolton under whose direction it has
been written.

444

had established friendly relations with the Timpanogos Indians in the vicinity of Utah Lake and the Bearded Yutas along the Sevier River, traders pushed into that region, also, and although no other *official* expeditions are known to have been made from New Mexico into the Great Basin during Spanish or Mexican dominion there, still Spanish *traders* continued to frequent that region for the purpose of obtaining pelts and Indian slaves until after the middle of the nineteenth century.

Recent research has considerably increased our knowledge of this subject. Anza's campaign against the Comanches through the San Luís Valley (1779) has been missed hitherto by students of that section because Bancroft had erroneously referred to it as having gone northeast instead of northwest from Santa Fé. Documents relating to the activities of the Yuta interpreter, Mestas, who made a trip to the Timpanogos after stolen animals in 1805, indicate intercourse with those Indians not previously recognized. Another hitherto unknown expedition is the one which was led by Mauricio Arze and Lagos García in 1813 to the Timpanogos and as far as the Bearded Yutas on what they called Rio Sebero (Sevier River). Even the Armijo expedition to California, 1829-30, seems to have been entirely overlooked by writers on the subject. Still another expedition which is not generally known is the one that was directed by Pedro León in 1851 through Salt Lake, Utah, and Sanpete valleys for the purpose of obtaining Indian slaves The Spaniards even operated as far north as Spokane River, in the northeastern part of the present State of Washington, as late as 1853.

The trail to California which has become known as the Old Spanish Trail apparently was not opened until 1829. The misnomer arose from the fact that parties going from New Mexico to California by the northern route naturally traveled as far as the Colorado River along the Old Spanish Trail, and were, therefore, said to have gone to California by way of that trail. The name thus became applied to the entire trail to California instead of just to the first portion of it.

The purpose of the present paper is to clarify this entire subject. An account of the various expeditions, their purposes and results and the routes traveled, will be given in some detail, showing the gradual extension of Spanish and Mexican activity northwest from New Mexico to the Great Basin and California.

THE RIVERA EXPEDITION TO THE GUNNISON RIVER, 1765.

Possibly the first expedition of white men northwest from New Mexico as far as the La Plata Mountains of today was the one led by Juan María de Rivera by order of Tomás Vélez Cachupín, Governor of New Mexico, in the year 1765.[2] Although Rivera's journal of the expedition has been lost, its content is partly known to us by its having been known and used by Domínguez and Escalante, who seem to have followed it more or less closely as a guide on their expedition in 1776, referring here and there in their diary to places described by Rivera.

By this means we are able to trace the general course of Rivera's route from Santa Fé northwest to the San Juan River (possibly named in honor of Rivera) and across the southern spur of the La Plata Mountains, which seem to have been prospected to some

[2] The date of the Rivera expedition, according to the printed copy of the *Diario y derrotero* of Domínguez and Escalante is 1761 (*Documentos para la historia de Mexico*, sér. 2, tomo 1, Mexico, 1854, p. 409). Domínguez and Escalante also speak of the region's having been explored under the orders of Tomás Véles Cachupín, governor of New Mexico, but without giving any date of the expedition (id., p. 389.) If these statements are both correct it would mean that there were two official expeditions over this territory within at least a few years of each other, since the date, 1761, falls between the dates of the two administrations of Véles (1749–1754 and 1762–1767). This of course is not impossible, but it suggests the question of error in the date of the Rivera expedition. As a further indication of the possibility of such an error, Cesáreo Fernández Duro, on the authority of a manuscript copy of the Domínguez-Escalante diary in the Real Academia de la Historia, dates the Rivera expedition in the year 1765 (Fernández Duro, Cesáreo, *Don Diego de Penalosa y su descubrimiento del reino de Quivira*, Madrid, 1882, pp. 139, 142). Philip Harry also gives 1765 as the date of the expedition in his summary of the Domínguez-Escalante narrative based upon a manuscript copy then in the possession of Peter Force, now in the Library of Congress, and which apparently had been copied from what was regarded as the original in the archives of the City of Mexico (J. H. Simpson, *Report of explorations across the Great Basin, 1859*, Washington, 1876, p. 490). I have adopted this date because it seems to fit the general situation better than the other one does. Since writing the above note, a copy of the Domínguez-Escalante journal, made from a copy in the Seville archives, has been received in the Bancroft Library. In this copy the date of the Rivera expedition is given as 1765.

extent and given their present name because of the finding in them of what appeared to be silver ore.[3] Continuing northwest the party descended either the Dolores or San Miguel River[4] (probably the Dolores) and, turning to the northeast, crossed the Uncompahgre Plateau and descended the Uncompahgre River to the Gunnison.[5] Here, after sending a couple of men across the river in search of Yutas, Rivera began his return journey, presumably retracing his previous route.

PRIVATE TRADING EXPEDITIONS AMONG THE YUTAS, 1765–1776.

Although no other official expeditions are known to have been made into that section for more than a decade, private individuals, among whom were members of Rivera's party, began to look with interest upon the region just explored. Thus began a movement which was to last more than three-quarters of a century. It is a movement, however, that is most difficult to follow in detail because, unlike official expeditions, there were no records kept of these private ventures. In fact, owing to government restric-

[3] *Doc. para la hist. de Mex.*, *ut supra*, p 389. *See also* Juan Bautista Anza *Diario* in *Doc. para la hist. de Nuevo Mexico*, II. 874—Ms. in Bancroft Library.

[4] While on the San Miguel, Dominguez and Escalante noted going down the same precipitous trail described by Rivera in his journal (*Doc. para la hist. de Mex., ut supra*, p. 401. *Cf.* W. R. Harris, *The Catholic Church in Utah* (1909), 140.

[5] It was while in about this location eleven years later that Dominguez and Escalante recorded: "There came to these two rivers in the year 1765 Don Juan María de Rivera, crossing the same *sierra de los Tabehuachis*, on the summit of which is the place that he named *El Purgatorio*, according to the description that he gives in his journal. The plain on which he camped for the purpose of fording the river and on which he says he cut a cross in a young poplar together with the initials of his name and the year of the expedition, are still found at the junction of these rivers on the southern bank, as we were informed by our interpreter Andrés Muñiz, who came with the said Don Juan María the year referred to, as far as the Tabehuachis Mountains, saying that although he had remained behind three day's journey before reaching the river, he had come the past year, 1775, along the bank of the river with Pedro Mora and Gregorio Sandoval who had accompanied Don Juan María through the whole of his expedition. They said that they had come as far as the river at that time, and from that point they had begun their return journey; only two persons having crossed the river, being sent by Don Juan María to look for Yutas on the bank opposite the plain on which they were camping, and from which they returned." (*Doc. para la hist. de Mex., (ut supra,)* pp. 409–410. *Cf.* Harris, *The Catholic Church in Utah*, p. 146.)

tions on Indian trading, it was frequently to the advantage of the persons concerned to cover up all trace of their activities. It is only by occasional, incidental references, therefore, that one is able to get a glimpse of what seems to have been happening more or less continuously during this entire period.

The first definite reference that we have to any of these private enterprises is the statement made by Domínguez and Escalante concerning the expedition of Pedro Mora, Gregorio Sandoval, and Andrés Muñiz who went as far as the Gunnison in the year 1775 where at the mouth of the Uncompahgre they examined the young cottonwood on which Rivera had cut a cross, together with the initials of his name and the year in which he was there.[6] All three had accompanied Rivera in 1765 and may have been on other expeditions into that region in the intervening decade, but of such activities we have as yet no specific record.

That there were other expeditions such as this, however, is evidenced by statements in the diary of Domínguez and Escalante. That document states that while among the Sabuaganas (who lived on the headwaters of the North Fork of the Gunnison) the interpreter had misinterpreted a certain portion of the padre's speech either for the purpose of not offending the Indians, or in order that he might not lose their goodwill, which he had gained by traffic in pelts, which, the document adds, the Spaniards frequently carried on with those Indians even in violation of the prohibitions of the governors of the kingdom.[7] It further refers to the apparently rather common custom which the Spaniards had of going to the Yutas and remaining there a great while — two, three, and four months at a time for the purpose of obtaining pelts.[8]

By the time of the Domínguez-Escalante expedition (1776) the region east of the Colorado and as far north as the Gunnison seems to have been fairly well known to the Spaniards of New Mexico. This is clear from the fact that most of the more important physical features of the country were referred to in the diary

[6] *Doc. para la hist. de Mex., ut supra*, p. 410. *See ante* note 5.

[7] *Ibid.*, p. 518.

[8] *Ibid.*, p. 519.

of Domínguez and Escalante by names that are still on the map, and in a way that would lead one to think that those names were in more or less common use at that time. It was also definitely stated by Nicolás de la Fora who accompanied the Marqués de Rubí on his tour of inspection through the northern provinces in 1766-1767 that the country to the north along the *Cordillera de las Grullas*[9] was at that time known to the Spaniards for a hundred leagues above New Mexico.[10]

DEMAND FOR OVERLAND COMMUNICATION BETWEEN NEW MEXICO AND CALIFORNIA.

So far the movement might be considered purely local in character. But at this point it takes on a broader aspect. Urged on by the Russian advance down the Pacific coast, Spain had colonized Alta California. The first expeditions had been by water. But the need of an overland route was keenly felt both as a means of protection and as an economic saving in transportation. From Sonora, Anza had led a party to California in 1774 and another in 1775–76. But the route was far from satisfactory. Even if the Colorado desert had proved less formidable there would still have been the desire of opening a direct road between New Mexico and California if that should prove possible.

---

[9] La Sierra de Las Grullas (sometimes written La Grulla) was the name applied to that spur of the Rocky Mountains beginning in the vicinity of Marshall Pass at the northern end of San Luís Valley and running towards the southwest for about one hundred and twenty-five miles to the La Plata Mountains of today thus forming the western boundary of San Luís Valley and serving as the divide between the waters of that valley and those of the Colorado River. For a description of these mountains by Domínguez and Escalante see *Doc. para la hist. de Mex.*, *ut supra.* p. 407, and *passim.*

[10] *Relacion del viaje que de orden del Excelentíssimo Señor Virrey Marquez de Cruillas hizo El Capitán de Ingenièros Dn Nicolás de la Fora, en compañia del Mariscal de Campo Marqu^s de Rubí, Comissionado por Su Magesstad, a la revista de los presidios internos, situados en la frontera de la parte de la America septentrional perteneciente al Rey.* Ms. transcript in Bolton Collection (original in Biblioteca Nacional, Mexico).

THE DOMÍNGUEZ–ESCALANTE EXPEDITION TO THE GREAT BASIN,
1775.

For this purpose, coupled with the desire of becoming acquainted
with the Indians to the north and northwest and of exploring their
country with the view to establishing missions, a company was
organized under the leadership of two Franciscan friars — Francisco Athanasio Domínguez and Silvestre Vélez de Escalante.[11]

In addition to the two fathers the party consisted of the
following members: Juan Pedro Cisneros, *alcalde mayor* of the
pueblo of Zuñi; Bernardo Miera y Pecheco, a retired captain and
citizen of Santa Fé;[12] Joaquín Lain, a citizen of Santa Fé;
Lorenzo de Olivares of the pueblo El Paso del Norte; the interpreter and guide Andrés Muñiz of Bernalillo, who had been a member of the Rivera expedition of 1765; his brother Antonio Lucrecio
Muñiz of Embudo; Juan de Aguilar of Bernalillo; and Simón
Luzero, a servant of Cisneros.[13]

[11] The official title given Domínguez was "Comisario visitador de esta custodia
de la conversion de San Pablo del Nuevo Mexico". Very little is known of his
previous or later life. Escalante, whose name really should be written Véles de
Escalante except for the fact that he is so much better known simply as Escalante,
was "ministro doctrinero de la mision de Nuestra Señora de Guadalupe de Zuñi."
This position he occupied from 1774 to 1778. His various letters and reports
during this period indicate that he was actively interested in opening a road
between New Mexico and Alta California. In April, 1778, at the request of Father
Morfi, he wrote an historical account of New Mexico. Very little is known of
his later activities.

[12] There is some suggestion that the expedition was actually under the command of Miera y Pacheco. Escalante, writing on the day that the party set out,
says that he had recommended Miera as a useful member of the party "no para
comandar la expedicion sino para construir un mapa del Terreno que se andubiesse" (letter to Fr. Ysidro Murillo, in P. Otto, Maas, *Viages de misioneros
franciscanos á la conquista del Nuevo Mexico*, Sevilla, 1915, p. 89.)

[13] The chief source of information concerning the expedition is the diary kept
by Domínguez and Escalante. Manuscript copies of this dairy can be found
in the Archivo General, Mexico (Bolton, *Guide to materials for the history of the
United States in the principal archives of Mexico*, pp. 28, 39), the Archivo General
de Indias, Seville (Chapman, *Catalogue of materials in the Archivo General de
Indias for the history of the Pacific coast and the American Southwest*, p 425), and
in the British Museum (Pascual de Gayangos y Arce, *Catalogue of the manuscripts
in the Spanish language in the British Museum*, p. 412). The first printed edition
is that published as a part of *Documentos para la historia de Mexico* (sér. 2, tomo
1, pp. 375-558) Mexico, 1854. Recently P. Otto Maas published a portion of the

Leaving Santa Fé July 29, 1776, the company, ten in number, directed its course northwest through the little town of Santa Clara on the Río del Norte and Abiquiú on the Chama, across Río Cebolla and Río Nutrias to the Chama at about the point of the present El Vado.[14] On August 5, they arrived at the Navajó River where it turns from the southwest to the northwest about three leagues before it enters the San Juan. Passing on the company camped three leagues below the junction of the two rivers near the present town of Caracas, naming the place Nuestra Señora de las Nieves. Continuing to the northwest they crossed Río Piedra, Río Los Pinos, Río Florida, Río Las Ánimas, Río La Plata (also mentioned by the name of San Joaquín), and Río Mancos (which they also called San Lázaro).

On August 12, they arrived at Río Dolores at the place where it turns from the southwest to the northwest near the present city of Hogg. From here they followed the general downward course of the river but usually at some distance to the west of it. Upon touching it on the 17th, somewhere in the vicinity of Disappointment Creek, they discovered recent signs of Yuta Indians whom, however, they were unable to locate.

journal from a manuscript copy in the Archivo General de Indias, in his *Viages de misioneros franciscanos á la conquista del Nuevo Mexico* (Sevilla, 1915), but unfortunately there is only a portion of the return trip included in this publication. Rev. W. R. Harris, in *The Catholic Church in Utah* (Salt Lake City, 1909), prints a translation of the diary. It is so poorly done, however, that the work is practically worthless. Such mistakes as the following occur frequently: *Septentrional* is rendered "southern;" *ochenta*, "eight;" *de*, "to;" *o*, "and." Also entire phrases which are essential to the meaning of the context are frequently omitted altogether, and there is a complete confusion as regards directions.

[14] Harris concludes that they crossed the Chama river at about the present site of Chama on the Denver and Rio Grande railroad and from there followed the present route of the railroad west. This however, seems improbable from the fact that they reached the Chama after traveling only three leagues from the Nutrias and at a point where the river was said to run to the south and from which point it turned to the east (*de oeste*). To the west they were told there were two lakes. Stinking Lake is directly west of El Vado and Boulder Lake is about six miles to the north. In going about four leagues to the northwest and north from their crossing they passed an opening in the mountains "in which is another lake." Boulder Lake satisfies this condition if the party crossed the Chama in the vicinity of El Vado (The Ford).

An effort was now made to find a road leading to the west but after searching a day and a half nothing was discovered but a trail to the southwest which was seen to be soon obstructed by table-lands and cañons. A council was then held in which each member of the party disagreed with each of the others as to the direction that should be taken. With this feeling of uncertainty prevailing, they finally decided to follow the trail to the Yutas and there endeavor to obtain a guide. Leaving the Dolores they pursued a northeasterly course crossing the San Miguel River, which they called Río San Pedro,[15] and the Uncompahgre Plateau, which they referred to as the Sierra de los Tabehuachis, and finally on the 26th of August, "entered the pleasant valley and river of San Francisco, called by the Yutas the Ancapagari". From about thirty miles from the junction of the Uncompahgre with the Gunnison they descended to within about ten miles of its mouth when they turned north to the Gunnison, which they named San Xavier and which they said the Indians called the Tomichi. Going up the Gunnison and the North Fork of the Gunnison they came to some villages of the Sabuaganas Yutas. Here they met Indians belonging to the Timpanogos, or Lagunas,[16] tribe, "to whose country", the journal significantly states, "we were already intending to go."[17]

Thus far their course had led over territory fairly well known. The interpreter, Andrés Muñiz, had been over most of it at least twice before, and probably other members of the party had also been over part of it. But from now on their route was to lead them into territory apparently never before explored by white men.

Having secured the services of two Lagunas as guides, the party set out on September 2, intent upon finding the home of the Lagunas. Going generally to the northwest they crossed the Grand and White rivers and, on September 13, arrived at

[15] The San Miguel is the first river to be referred to by a different name than that by which it is known today.

[16] Also called Timpangotsis, Timpaiavats, etc.

[17] "Á cuya tierra intentábamos ya pasar". *Doc. para la hist. de Mex.*, sér. 2, tomo I, p. 411.

the banks of Green River (called by thém *San Buenaventura*) near the mouth of Brush Creek a little above the present site of Jensen, Utah. Crossing the river they directed their course to the southwest until they arrived at the junction of the Uinta and Du Chesne rivers. Going up the Du Chesne and Strawberry rivers and crossing the summit they seem to have descended along Diamond Creek and Spanish Fork River to the settlements of the Timpanogos on the eastern shores of Utah Lake, where they arrived September 23, 1776.[18]

Of this region—its geography, inhabitants, and possibilities of development—the padres speak in considerable detail. They mention four rivers which flow into the lake, the first of which, beginning at the south, was named Aguascalientes on account of the hot springs that had been observed while descending it. This was Spanish Fork River, down which the party had just come. The second, three leagues to the north, was named San Nicolás, and corresponds fairly well to Hobble Creek except for the statement in the diary that it contains more water than the first one, which is hardly the case. However, they seem to have left the Aguascalientes shortly after it entered the open plain and to have struck the San Nicolás farther down in the valley which would make it appear relatively larger than if compared with the Aguascalientes at the same distance from the mountains. Three and a half leagues farther to the northwest was the third river, containing more water than the other two. This they named San Antonio de Padua. It is clearly the present Provo River.

[18] There seems to be considerable disagreement as to the route followed by the party after leaving the summit. Bancroft has them coming down the Provo River which he imagines they called the Purísima. As a matter of fact the river they called the Purísima was on the east of the summit and, according to the diary, runs to the southeast (*sueste*). The company crossed it on September 21 and then climbed to the summit and, on the 23d, descended a stream running to the southwest which turned to the west as it joined another small stream. Just below the junction of the two were a number of hot springs which suggested the name of Aguascalientes for the river. They continued down the Aguascalientes to the open plain and then northwest six and a half leagues to the Indian villages. These various details and the daily routes traveled and the directions of the rivers seem to indicate that they came down Diamond Creek to its junction with Spanish Fork River and then on down that stream. The Castella Hot Springs just below the mouth of Diamond Creek seem to make this conclusion imperative.

To the northwest they could see a fourth river which they were told carried as much water as the others. They named this the Río de Santa Ana, but did not visit it. It was, evidently, the American Fork River of today.[19]

The valleys of these rivers, it was said, contained wide-spreading meadows of rich irrigable land with plenty of water for irrigation so that there might be established in the region as many pueblos of Indians as there were in New Mexico.

The Indians were said to be good featured. They spoke the Yuta language but with a noticeable variation of accent. They were docile, living principally upon fish, rabbits, wild fowls, seeds, and herbs. They were but poorly clothed; their most decent dress being a shirt or jacket of buckskin with moccasins and leggings of the same material. For cold weather they had blankets made of rabbit skins. Their dwellings were huts made of willow brush.

The Spaniards were told of a larger lake of salt water to the north with which this one connected, but they did not visit it. Obviously, this was Great Salt Lake.

After spending three days visiting the tribes on the eastern shore of the lake as far north as Provo River, the party resumed its journey towards Monterey. Taking a course south-southwest

[19] Bancroft identifies the four rivers flowing into the lake as follows: "Their Aguascalientes", he says, "is Currant Creek; the second, their San Nicolás though more than three leagues from the first, and not corresponding in every other particular, is the Spanish Fork River; the San Antonio de Pudua is the Provo; and the Santa Ana, the River Jordan" (*History of Utah*, p. 14). But the diary distinctly states that the party entered the valley along the Aguascalientes. How they could have done this if Currant Creek were the Aguascalientes Bancroft does not explain. Furthermore Spanish Fork River is at too great a distance from Currant Creek to be the San Nicolás if Currant Creek be the Aguascalientes and Provo River is too far from the Spanish Fork to be the third if the Spanish Fork be the second. Also looking to the northwest from Provo River the company certainly would have seen the American Fork instead of the Jordan. Moreover, they regarded all four as flowing into the lake whereas the Jordan flows out of it. Harris identifies the four rivers as follows: The Aguascalientes, he concludes, was the Spanish Fork; the San Nicolás, the Provo; the San Antonio de Padua, the American Fork; and the Santa Ana, the Jordan (*The Catholic Church in Utah*, p. 248). The objections to this arrangement is the fact that the Provo is at too great a distance from the Spanish Fork, Hobble Creek is ignored, and the Jordan flows in the wrong direction.

they arrived on the 29th, unexpectedly, on the banks of the
Sevier River, named by them the Santa Isabel. Here they made
special note of meeting Indians having extra thick beards—
"much thicker", they said, "than those of the Lagunas",—by
which circumstance these Indians were said to be differentiated
from all others hitherto known.[20] From the statement that the
territory of these bearded Indians began at this Santa Isabel
(Sevier) River it is possible to trace more definitely the routes of
later expeditions which refer to these Indians as the Bearded
Yutas.

Crossing the Santa Isabel (Sevier) River near the site of the
present town of Mills they traveled south about five leagues and
then west until they again reached the Sevier in the vicinity of
the present Oasis and Desert. Here they turned to the southwest, taking the course at present followed by the Los Angeles
and Salt Lake Railroad through the valley of Beaver River.

On October 5, when in the vicinity of the present town of
Blackrock, their Laguna guide, whom they had secured before
leaving Utah Lake, left them after a quarrel with members of
the party. To add to their difficulties, a heavy snow storm set
in, which brought very forcibly to their minds the nearness of
the approaching winter. Being snowbound and out of provisions, on October 8 they recorded: "The winter had now set in
with great rigor, and all the mountain ranges that we could see
were covered with snow." They began to realize that long before
they could reach Monterey the mountain passes would be closed,
and they feared that they would be obliged to remain some two or
three months on some mountain where they would be unable to
provide themselves with the necessary food to sustain life. Under
these conditions it was finally decided to give up the project and
return to Santa Fé by way of the Cosnina, Moqui, and Zuñi
Indians. It was hoped that in this way a better road might be
discovered by a more southern route.

But without a guide the return trip was no simple matter.
Directing their course to the south through Cedar Valley, down
Ash Creek, and across the Virgin River they soon reached the

[20] *Doc. para la hist. de Mex.*, sér. 2, tomo 1, pp. 473, 476.

high tablelands of the cañon of the Colorado. For a month they wandered over extremely difficult trails seeking a crossing of the great river. Finally after much tribulation, the river was crossed, November 7, at a point about thirty miles below the mouth of the San Juan just north of the Utah-Arizona line. Concerning the crossing, which has subsequently been known as the Crossing of the Fathers, the record says:

The ford of this river is very good; it is a little more than a mile wide at this point and here the Navajo and Dolores come incorporated with all the others that we have mentioned in this diary as flowing into either of them.[21]

The effort was now made to find the Cosnina Indian villages, which, however, were discovered to be empty when they were finally reached on November 14—the Indians apparently being away in search of pine-nuts in the adjacent mountains. On the 16th the party arrived at the town of Oraybi, one of the Moqui villages. The Moquis both here and at the towns of Xongopabi, Mossanganabi, and Gualpi were willing to supply the Spaniards with provisions and help them on their way but were not willing to treat with them on other matters, saying that they wished to be friends of the Spaniards but not Christians.

Leaving the Moqui towns on November 20, the priests with three companions hurried on to the Zuñi settlements leaving the rest of the company to follow more leisurely with the weaker animals.[22] After two or three weeks stay at Zuñi they continued their journey, passing through San Estéban de Ácoma, San José de la Laguna, Álamo, San Agustín de la Isleta, San Francisco Xavier de Albuquerque, Nuestra Señora de los Dolores de Sandía, Santo Domingo,[23] and, finally, on January 2, 1777, arrived at the city of Santa Fé.

So far as opening a road to California was concerned the Domínguez-Escalante expedition was a failure. But by means

[21] *Id.*, p. 535.
[22] At Zuñi the priests forwarded a report of their travels to governor Pedro Fermín de Mendinueta. See Bolton, *Guide*, p. 37, and Chapman, *Catalogue*, p. 434.
[23] All the stops between Zuñi and Santa Fé were referred to as missions except Álamo.

of it a large portion of the interior of North America was explored for the first time by white men, the Great Basin was visited and, the Indian tribes about Utah Lake and the Sevier River were made friends of the Spaniards.

When at the Timpanogos settlements, Domínguez and Escalante had promised to return the following year and establish a mission. Indeed this was given as one of the reasons for not going on to Monterey, as that would delay the establishment of the mission too long.[24] But it seems that the priests were unable to convince the authorities of the necessity of such a move, and so the promise was not fulfilled. No mission was established in the Great Basin, but, as we shall see later, Spaniards from New Mexico continued to visit that region for the purpose of trading with the Indians.

ANZA'S EXPEDITION THROUGH THE SAN LUÍS VALLEY, 1779.

Up to this time travel north from New Mexico and west of the continental divide seems to have taken a northwesterly route around the southern spur of the La Plata Mountains and then northeasterly along the western slope of those mountains to the Gunnison River.[25] So far as is known no white man had passed through the San Luís Valley until Juan Bautista de Anza led an expedition there in 1779.[26]

The occasion for this expedition was Indian disturbances. The Comanches had been especially troublesome for some time. One of their chiefs, Cuerno Verde, (Green Horn) whose father had been killed in an encounter with the Spaniard, had taken it

[24] *Doc. para la hist. de Mex.*, sér. 2, tomo 1, p. 484.

[25] East of the continental divide there had been a number of expeditions north from New Mexico previous to this time. In 1706, Juan de Uribarri led a company over the mountains from Taos, and north along the eastern foothills through Jicarilla, thence north and east to El Cuartelejo in what is now southeastern Colorado. In 1719 Valverde, governor of New Mexico, led an expedition over very much the same ground except that he did not go as far east as El Cuartelejo. And in 1720 the fateful Villasur expedition made its way along the eastern foothills to about the vicinity of Fort Morgan on the South Platte.

[26] Our authority for this expedition is Anza's dairy *Ms.* in the Archivo General de Mexico, Sección de Historia, Tomo XXV, no. 36, a copy of which is in the Bancroft Library (*Doc. para la historia de Nuevo Mexico*. II. 861-922).

upon himself to avenge his father's death. He had led numerous attacks against the Spaniards, "killing hundreds and taking many prisoners who m he afterwards sacrificed in cold blood". In an effort to quell these disturbances Anza, who had recently been made governor of New Mexico, organized an expedition against the Comanches. In making his attack he says that he selected a different route from that by which all previous expeditions against the Comanches had been made in order that he might not be discovered long before reaching the country inhabited by the enemy as had been the case with all former operations against them.

With an army of 645 men he set out from Santa Fé on the 15th of August, 1779. Following the Camino Real to the northwest and north, they passed through San Juan, crossed the Río del Norte, and continued to Ojo Caliente, some seven leagues from their crossing, where the Camino Real ended. Between Ojo Caliente and their next crossing of the Río del Norte, the diary mentions passing to following six streams: Las Nutrias (Nutritas), San Antonio, Conejos, Las Jaras (La Jara), Los Timbres (Río Alamosa), and San Lorenzo (Piedra Pintada Creek).

While on the Río del Norte, Anza took occasion to record a few items that throw light on the geographic information of the time. He says:

This river, as is known, empties into the North Sea and the Bay of Espíritu Santo. It has its own source fifteen leagues or a little more from this place in the Sierra de la Grulla which is the same one on the skirts of which we have traveled since the 17th . . . .[27] The Yuta nation accompanying me,[28] who reside at the said source, and three civilians who have explored it, tell me that it proceeds from the interior of a great swamp, which is formed, . . . by the constant melting of the snow on some mountain peaks that are very near it.

The same persons tell me that after crossing fifteen leagues breadth of the land seven rivers come for very short distances, and after uniting

[27] For a description of La Sierra de la Grulla (sometimes called La Sierra de las Grullas) see above, note 8.

[28] On August 20, while on the Conejos, two hundred Yutas and Apaches had joined the expedition.

they form one of considerable size which flows to the west. This river . . . I judge to be the river called Colorado, which, after uniting with the Gila, empties into the Gulf of California, where, among the nations which live on it and with whom I have communicated in my journeys there, I have received information quite circumstantial of the Yuta nation from which I infer that the two are not far distant from each other.[29]

Anza further said that the three civilians mentioned above explored the said seven rivers by order of Governor Don Tomás Vélez. They were, therefore, probably members of the Rivera party.

From the Río del Norte the company proceeded north through the San Luís Valley,[30] and then crossed the mountains to the head waters of the Arkansas River, where, by coming upon the Comanches from the north Anza was able to surprise and defeat them. The location is still recorded in the name of the Greenhorn (Cuerno Verde) Mountains. He then recrossed the divide[31] and continued south along the foothills to Taos and Santa Fé.

[29] *Doc. para la Historia de Nuevo Mexico*, II. 872.

[30] It is difficult to trace the exact route of the expedition through the San Luís Valley. Judging from the course pursued from the time the company crossed the Río del Norte near San Juan until they reached it again at the point they named El Paso de San Bartolomé, the latter place must have been in the vicinity of the present Del Norte. From San Bartolomé the journal states that they traveled four leagues to the north and then four to the north-northwest when they arrived at a beautiful lake (*ciénega*) which they named San Luís. If the present San Luís lake is meant the direction traveled must be inaccurate. Furthermore, there is no place on the Del Norte from which they could have reached the San Luís Lake after traveling the given distance and directions. There seems to be a mistake in the direction given. San Luís Lake is about due east from where they must have crossed the river. But notwithstanding the confusion at this point, it is perfectly clear that they proceeded north until the mountains on the west (La Grulla) and the ones on the east (Sierra Almagre) approach each other so closely that there is nothing but a cañon between them. It was here that the crossing was made to the waters of the Napeste (Arkansas).

[31] There is confusion again at this point. The diary states that they reached the arroyo of La Sangre de Cristo on September 3, and that they crossed the divide the following day and at the foot of the mountains arrived at the place of the lake (al sitio de la ciénega). It seems that they must have called one of the tributaries of Huérfano River the arroyo of La Sangre de Cristo and that they must have crossed the mountains by either the Sand Hill or Mosca Pass and not by the Sangre de Cristo Pass as would naturally be supposed from reading the diary.

This was the last official expedition north or northwest of New Mexico during the period in which Spain held control of which we have any record. The reason for this apparent lack of interest in the region may not be difficult to understand when one looks at the activities of Spain as a whole. The strained European conditions, the war with England which directed attention to the Mississippi valley and the Atlantic coast, and the increasing demand for protection of California and the Pacific northwest gave little time for further exploration of the Rocky Mountain region. The fact, also, that no important pueblos had been found tended to cool the ardor for governmental activity.

CONTINUED ACTIVITY OF INDIAN TRADERS IN THE GREAT BASIN

But the Indian trader usually knew or cared little about international affairs. Nor was he dismayed by not finding Indian pueblos. He was frequently of that type of individual who cared little for settled life and was just as much at home with a tribe of roving Indians as in the more highly civilized pueblos. To him the Yutas along the tributaries of the Colorado and in the Great Basin offered opportunities for both a life and living which were highly suitable to his inclinations. As we have already seen, at least as early as the time of Domínguez and Escalante traders were in the habit of visiting the Yutas and staying with them for months at a time for the purpose of gathering peltries. That these activities continued there can be but little doubt, although, for the next twenty-five years or so we have slender data on which to make any very definite statements At the end of that time, however, there are a few documents which enable us to pick up the thread again.

On September 1, 1805, Joaquín de Real Alencaster who had but recently become governor of New Mexico, in writing to the commandant-general on the merits of a Yuta interpreter says: "Manuel Mestas, a Genizaro, seventy years old who, for approximately fifty years has served as Yuta interpreter, was the one who reduced them to peace," and further in recounting Mestas's virtues Alencaster says:

In the short time that I have governed this province, he has recovered from the aforesaid heathen eight horses which he himself searched for and brought back. In the month of July he went back to the country of the aforesaid people and not only succeeded in bringing back eleven mules and horses, but, according to the report of other Yutas, called Jimpipas, shortly started out on a trip of about a month's duration for the purpose of retaking, not only the aforesaid eleven animals, but also twenty mules and eight horses, which among other things, had been stolen from men of this province last year in the country of the said Jimpipas, by Cumanches, and were retaken by the Yutas Timpanagos during a war with the aforesaid Cumanches.

It seems from this that Mestas had set out for the land of the Timpanogos for the purpose of recovering the animal stolen from the Spaniards by the Comanches and retaken by the Timpanogos.[32]

On November 20, 1805, Alencaster again wrote to the commandant-general informing him that Mestas had returned

without recovering more than nine animals, since the pack mules of which he went in search, as a result of the cruel war which the Caiguas (Kiowas) were waging against the Yutas Timpanagos, in an attack, had been captured by the Caiguas.[33]

These communications suggest more or less continual intercourse between the Spaniards of New Mexico and the Yutas, some of which seems to have been carried as far as the Timpanogos, that is, to the Utah Lake region of today.

THE ARZE EXPEDITION TO RIO SEBERO (SEVIER RIVER), 1813

Recently I have discovered a document in the Spanish Archives of New Mexico, now located in the Library of Congress, which throws new light upon the activities of the period. It gives an account of a trading expedition to the Timpanogos and the

[32] Alencaster to Commandant-General Salcedo, September 1, 1805 (Ms. Spanish Archives of New Mex., Library of Congress; photographic copy in Bancroft Library; cf., Twitchell, Spanish Archives of New Mexico, II. 478—no. 1881).

[33] Alencaster to Commandant-general Salcedo, November 20, 1805. (Ms. Spanish Archives of New Mex., Lib. of Congress; photographic copy in Bancroft Library; cf., Twitchell, Spanish Archives of New Mexico, II. 487—(no. 1925).

Bearded Yutas west of the Sevier River in the year 1813.   The company consisted of seven men under the command of Mauricio Arze and Lagos García.   They left Abiquiú on the sixteenth of March, 1813, and returned to that place after a trip of some four months, on the twelfth of July.   On the first of September, the governor of New Mexico, having received information regarding the affair ordered the members of the party to appear before Manuel García as alcalde of the "Villa de Santa Cruz de la Cañada" and report what had taken place on the trip.   Between the sixth and tenth of the month affidavits were sworn to by the following five members of the party: Miguel Tenorio, Felipe Gómez, Josef Santiago Vejil, (Vigil), Gabriel Quintana, and Josef Velásquez.[34]

In the main these affidavits duplicate each other, with only here and there a unique detail.   None of the accounts give any particulars as to the route followed between Abiquiú and the lake of the Timpanogos, possibly because that route was so well known that nothing needed to be said.   The company remained at the lake of the Timpanogos three days carrying on a little trade while waiting for the Indians of two rancherías to come together.   When all were assembled a council was held, but, if we may rely upon the statements of the Spaniards in their affidavits, the Indians would trade nothing but Indian slaves, "as they had done on other occasions",[35] the documents add. This the Spaniards refused to do.   Whereupon some of the Indians fell upon the horses of the Spaniards and began killing them.   Before they could be stopped eight horses and a mule had been killed, when one of the chiefs succeeded in quieting his people and stopping the slaughter.   Warned by this injury the Spaniards collected their remaining horses and, after standing guard over them all night, set out on the following day for Río Sebero (Sevier River).

Here they met a Yuta of the Sanpuchi (Sanpete) nation who promised to take them to a place where they could trade with a

[34] The document has no title, but is listed by Twitchell as number 2511 in his *Spanish Archives of New Mexico*, II. 577.   A photographic copy is in the Bancroft Library.

[35] "Como lo abian verificado en otras ocasiones."

tribe of Yutas as yet unknown to them. Two of the company, Felipe Gómez and Gabriel Quintana, were left in charge of the pack train while the other five, guided by the Sanpuchi, set out to the west. After traveling three days they came upon a tribe of Indians who were characterized as having heavy beards, clearly the bearded Indians of the Domínguez-Escalante journal, whose territory we are there told began at the Río Santa Isabel (the Sevier of today).[36]

Domínguez and Escalante had found these Indians very gentle and affable, but now they met the Spaniards with "their arms in their hands, saying their trade would be arrows". They were finally quieted, however, and arrangements were made to trade on the following day. But in the evening the Spaniards overheard the Indians discussing a plan by which they proposed to kill their visitors. Taking advantage of this information the Spaniard stole away

travelling stealthily all night and day until they reached the place where their companions and pack train were. Thence they took the road to the Rio Grande, (Colorado)[37] on which they found the little ranchería of Guasache, who was waiting on the road to trade with them *as was his custom.*

At the ranchería of Guasache the party met with the same sort of treatment that they had received on the other portions of their trip. At first they were treated kindly but when they refused to trade for the Indian slaves offered them, the Indians took offense. This time, however, the commandant, having been informed of the extremity of the resentment of the Indians, called his men together and gave them permission to purchase the slaves, "in order," as the affidavits state "not to receive another injury like the past one." As a result of this decision, twelve slaves were bought, after which the Spaniards continued their journey with no other incident worthy of note except the loss of a mule and a horse by drowning in crossing the Río Grande (Colorado).

[36] *Doc. para la hist. de Mex.,* 2 sér. I. 473, 476.
[37] The Río Grande here, and usually during this period, refers to the Colorado, not the Río Grande del Norte.

Besides the slaves mentioned above, the Spaniards collected on their trip a total of one hundred and nine skins. This, however, was stated to be "but a few". None of the statements tell what kind they were.

That the country over which the company had traveled was fairly well known seems to be implied from the fact that nothing to the contrary is stated and that no difficulties regarding the route are mentioned. The only place where they speak of having had a guide was from the Río Sebero to the Bearded Indians.

These, it was stated, were unknown to the traders which seems to imply that the traders were at least somewhat acquainted with the others whom they visited.

AMERICAN TRADERS WITH THE SPANIARDS ON THE COLORADO[18]

By 1824, Americans from Missouri were trapping and trading with the Indians in the mountains along the tributaries of the Colorado and Green rivers, and it is frequently supposed that the Spaniards had given way to the more aggressive traders from the United States. This is hardly a correct statement of the case, however. While it is true that American traders built up an extensive industry on the waters of the Colorado with Santa Fé as a supply base and that they continued active in that region and from there to California for the next twenty years or more, it is also true that Spaniards from New Mexico carried on an important trade with the Indians of the same region all during that period.

THE ARMIJO EXPEDITION TO CALIFORNIA, 1829

One of the factors of prime importance in the opening of the trails to the far west at this time was the Missouri-Santa Fé trade and its demand for mules. California had great numbers of mules which were noted for their size and quality. This led to the organization of numerous expeditions to that country in

---

[18] A suggestive article on the activities of the Americans in this region was published by Dr. T. M. Marshall in the *Southwestern Historical Quarterly* for January, 1916 (XIX, 251–260.)

the effort to supply the demand of the Missouri traders. Perhaps the first of these expeditions was the one led by Antonio Armijo.

In the fall and winter of 1829–'30, a company of some sixty Mexican traders under the command of Antonio Armijo succeeded, in opening a road from New Mexico to California by a route north of the Grand Cañon of the Colorado. The expedition set out from Abiquiú on November 7, 1829, and arrived at the mission of San Gabriel on January 31, 1830. After a month spent in California the return journey was begun March 1st and completed April 25 when the party reached Jémez, New Mexico.[19]

Armijo, instead of following the Rivera and Domínguez-Escalante trail (the "Old Spanish Trail") northwest to the Navajó, Dolores and Gunnison rivers took a more southerly route west from Abiquiú to Cañon Largo and down that stream to its junction with the San Juan. Crossing the San Juan he proceeded down the valley (a few miles to the north of the river) across Las Ánimas and La Plata rivers and as far as the Mancos, which he descended to its junction with the San Juan. Here he recrossed the San Juan and directed his course to the west across Río de Chelly to the Colorado which he crossed on the eighth of December at the "Ford of the Fathers", apparently the one used by Domínguez and Escalante on their return from the Great Basin in 1776. Here the party turned to the north and on the twentieth reached "Rio Severo". For the next ten days they seem to have directed their course, in a general way, down the Sevier River to its outlet in Sevier Lake which their itinerary mentions on December 29. On the first of January they reached what they supposed to be the Río Grande (Colorado) but which probably was the Virgin River.

Here an item of more than ordinary interest occurred. Upon the return of the scouting party which had been out reconnoitering it was learned that one, Rafael Rivera, was missing. Several days were spent in search for him as the party moved down the

---

[19] Antonio Armijo, *Itinéraire du Nord-Mexico a la Haute-California, parcouru en 1829 et 1830 par soixante Mexicains.* (*Bulletin de la société de geographie*, Paris, 1835, ser. 2, III. 316–323). This was first published in Spanish in the *Registro oficial del gobierno de los Estados-Unidos mexicanos* (Mexico, 1830).

river, but without success. On January 7 he came into camp with the report that "*he had examined the ford where he had crossed the Río Grande the preceeding year in going to Sonora*". It would seem, therefore, that he had just made the trip from California to New Mexico by way of Sonora, but of his expedition we have no other information. Nor is it stated what influence he had in directing the course of the present expedition. The fact, however, that he was acting as one of the scouting party suggests that possibly he was more than just an ordinary member.

The day following Rivera's return was spent in reconnoitering after which the party set out to the west across the Mohave Desert and along the Mohave River to the San Bernardino Mountains which they crossed through the "San Bernardino Cañon" (Cajon Pass) on the twenty-eighth of January. Three days later they arrived at the San Gabriel Mission.

Of their return journey, which was made in a month less time than the outgoing trip, nothing is known except that it began on the first of March and ended at Jémez, New Mexico, on the twenty-fifth of April.

The expedition, as has been intimated, had been made for the purpose of trading New Mexican products for California mules. What the outcome was, is not stated but the inference is that it was fairly successful. It at least made clear the possibility of direct overland communication between the two provinces, each of which contained commodities such as to stimulate trade.

AMERICANS OPEN ROAD TO CALIFORNIA ALONG SO-CALLED OLD SPANISH TRAIL, 1829

American traders soon followed the example of Armijo. In fact one company, led by Ewing Young of Tennessee, seems to have made the trip at about the same time that Armijo did. But we have no contemporary account of this expedition. J. J. Warner, writing some forty or fifty years later, says:

In 1829 Ewing Young of Tennessee, who had traded in New Mexico, and had also trapped beaver in the northern part of that territory, fitted out a trapping party at Taos, traveled westerly to the tributaries of Grande River, and down that river and across Green River, entering California upon the Jedediah S. Smith trail. In the valley he found Ogden with his large party of trappers from Fort Vancouver. After spending some little time on the streams emptying into Tulare Valley lakes and upon the San Joaquin River and its affluents, he came into the settlements of California with his party.[40]

After remaining a few days at Los Angeles he returned to New Mexico reaching Taos in the summer of 1830.

From this account of the expedition it appears that Young led his party over the trail which later became known as the "Old Spanish trail to California". As already stated, this is evidently a misnomer. There was no old *Spanish* trail to California, through this region. Apparently the first expeditions to make their way from New Mexico to California by routes north of the Grand Cañon of the Colorado were made, as we have seen, in the fall and winter of 1829–1830, when the region was Mexican rather than Spanish territory. Even then, of the two expeditions making the trip at that time only one could be said to be really Mexican. The other was led by an American from Tennessee and, while it contained a number of native New Mexicans, it was perhaps more American than Mexican. Of these two companies it was the American company that made its way over the so-called "Old Spanish Trail". The Mexican party went somewhat to the south of that trail.

The confusion of names seems to have arisen from the fact that expeditions from New Mexico to California in the second quarter of the nineteenth century usually traveled to the vicinity

[40] *Reminiscence of Early California,* in Hist. Soc. of Southern Cal., *Annual publications,* 1907–1908 (Los Angeles 1909), p. 184. See also *An historical sketch of Los Angeles county, California* (1876), by J. J. Warner, Benj. Hayes, and J. P. Widney. Here (p. 18) Warner says: "In 1828–1829 Ewing Young, of Tennessee, who had for some seasons been engaged in trapping beaver in the north of New Mexico, made a hunt in the Tulare Valley and on the waters of the San Joaquin." . . . If his statement, however, in his *Reminiscences,* namely, that he met Ogden in the San Joaquín Valley, be correct, his expedition must have been made in the fall and winter of 1829–1830 instead of 1828–1829, since the published journal of Ogden for 1828–1829 shows clearly that Ogden was not in the San Joaquín Valley that season. *Cf.* Oregon Historical Society, *Quarterly,* XI. 381–396 (1909).

of the Colorado along the trail that had been used by the Spaniards since the time of Rivera (1765) in their trade with the Yutas in the Great Basin, and which had thus become known as the Old Spanish Trail. But the Old Spanish Trail, properly so-called, extended only to the Indians of the Great Basin and not to California.

Upon the return of Ewing Young to New Mexico in 1830, he and William Wolfskill, a native of Kentucky but coming to New Mexico from Missouri, fitted out another party at Taos for the purpose of trapping on the San Joaquin and Sacramento rivers from which Young had but recently returned. According to Warner,[41] they followed a westerly course from Taos to the headwaters of the San Juan River, which they descended a short distance and then, turning more northerly, they fell upon the tributaries of Grand River, which they followed until it turned nearly south. Here they left it and traveled westerly to Green River which they crossed and followed down to its junction with the Grand, where it takes the name of Colorado. Continuing down the Colorado fifty miles or more and finding that it ran into a cañon and was so walled in as to be unapproachable, they left the neighborhood of the river and took a westerly course to the Sevier, from which their route led southwest toward California. But becoming entangled in the irregular mountains, enveloped in snow, and suffering from cold and scarcity of food, the company composed of various discordant elements—New Mexicans, Americans, St. Louis Frenchmen, and Canadians—became demoralized and disorganized and was forced to abandon its route for one farther to the south. They finally crossed the mountains through the Cajon Pass and reached the Pueblo of Los Angeles in February, 1831.

Some of the New Mexicans had taken a number of woolen blankets with them for the purpose of trading with the Indians, but which they now found they could dispose of to a very good advantage to the Californians in exchange for mules. "The appearance of these mules in New Mexico", says Warner, "owing to their large size, compared with those at that time used in the

[41] *Reminiscences of Early California*, p. 185.

Missouri and Santa Fé trade, and their very fine form, as well as the price at which they had been bought in barter for blankets, caused quite a sensation in New Mexico, out of which sprang up a trade, carried on by means of caravans of pack animals, between the two sections of the same country, which flourished for some ten or twelve years. These caravans reached California yearly during the before mentioned time. They brought the woolen fabrics of New Mexico, and carried back mules, and silk and other Chinese goods."

Los Angeles was the central point in California of the New Mexican trade. Coming by the northern or Green and Virgin River routes, the caravans came through Cajon Pass and reached Los Angeles. From thence they scattered themselves over the county from San Diego to San Jose, and across the bay to Sonoma and San Rafael. Having bartered and disposed of the goods brought, and procured such as they wished to carry back, and what mules they could drive, they concentrated at Los Angeles for their yearly return.[42]

Warner seems not to have known of the Armijo expedition of 1829–30 but gives Young and Wolfskill the entire credit for inaugurating the growing trade between California and New Mexico. This may have been because Warner, at the time, was at Taos, and the expeditions to which he refers left that section, whereas Armijo left Abiquiú. The movement, however, was more or less general and was the outgrowth of the Missouri trade with New Mexico.

The task undertaken by Domínguez and Escalante some fifty years before had at last been accomplished. Direct communication between New Mexico and California had been established by way of the Great Basin.

CONTINUED ACTIVITY OF THE MEXICANS AMONG THE YUTAS OF THE
GREAT BASIN.

For the next twenty years Santa Fé was a recognized supply base for the Rocky Mountain fur trade. Enterprising Americans like Robidoux carried on an extensive commerce along the trib-

---

[42] *An historical sketch of Los Angeles County*, p. 18.

utaries of the Colorado and Green Rivers, transporting a large portion of their furs to Santa Fé where they procured their outfits and supplies. Miles M. Goodyear, in 1841, is supposed to have obtained a Mexican grant for the region now known as Ogden and to have stocked it as a rancho with sheep, goats, cattle, and horses from Mexico. But not all of the trade fell into the hands of Americans. Even after the Mormons established themselves in the Great Salt Lake Valley companies of Mexican traders continued to frequent that region. Friction between these parties and the Mormon authorities is responsible for a number of documents throwing light on the activities of the Mexican traders of the period. Some of these may be here noted. In the preamble of a law "for the further relief of Indian slaves and prisoners", passed by the Utah legislature January 31, 1852,[43] it was stated that

From time immemorial, the practice of purchasing Indian women and children, of the Utah tribe of Indians by Mexican traders, has been indulged in, and carried on by those respective people, until the Indians consider it an allowable traffic, and frequently offer their prisoners or children for sale; . . . .

A little over a year later, under date of April 23, 1853, Brigham Young, as governor of Utah, saw fit to issue the following proclamation:[44]

Whereas it is made known to me by reliable information, from affidavits, and various other sources, that there is in this Territory a horde of Mexicans, or outlandish men, who are infesting the settlements, stirring up the Indians to make aggressions upon the inhabitants, and who are also furnishing the Indians with guns, ammunition, etc., contrary to the laws of this Territory and the laws of the United States:

[43] Utah, Laws ,statutes, etc., *Acts, resolutions and memorials* (Great Salt Lake City, 1855), p. 171.

[44] This proclamation appeared in the *Deseret News* of April 30, 1853, (see Bancroft, *History of Utah*, p. 476) and from that was translated and published in an extended editorial, by *La Crónica de Nueva-York* from which it was copied by *El Siglo Diez y Nueve* (Mexico), in its issue of July 16, 1853. It is reproduced in O. F. Whitney, *Hist. of Utah* (Salt Lake City, 1892), I. 512. On July 20, 1853, *El Siglo Diez y Nueve* devoted its entire front page to the subject in opposition to the action taken by the Governor of Utah.

And whereas it is evident that it is the intention of these Mexicans or foreigners to break the laws of this Territory and the United States, utterly regardless of every restriction, furnishing Indians with guns and powder, whenever and wherever it suits their designs, convenience, or purposes:

Therefore, I, Brigham Young, Governor and Superintendent of Indian affairs for the Territory of Utah, in order to preserve peace, quell the Indians and secure the lives and property of the citizens of the Territory, hereby order and direct as follows:

1st. That a small detachment consisting of thirty men, under the charge of Captain Wall, proceed south through the entire extent of the settlements reconnoitering the country and directing the inhabitants to be on their guard against any sudden surprise.

. . . .

3rd. The officer and party hereby sent upon this service are hereby authorized and directed to arrest and keep in close custody every strolling Mexican party, and those associating with them . . . and leave them safely guarded at the different points of settlement to await further orders . . .

. . . .

5th. All Mexicans now in the Territory are required to remain quiet in the settlements and not attempt to leave under any consideration, until further advised; and the officers of the Territory are hereby directed to keep them in safe custody, treating them with kindness and supplying their necessary wants. . . . .

SLAVE BUYING EXPEDITION TO THE GREAT BASIN LED BY PEDRO LEÓN, 1851

A single specific case will serve to illustrate the practice which seems, from the documents quoted, to have been a rather common custom. On November 15, 1851, the *Deseret News* called attention to the fact that one Pedro León and a party of about twenty Mexicans were at Manti in Sanpete valley for the purpose of trading horses for Indian children and that he had a license dated Santa Fé August 14, 1851, and signed by Governor James S. Calhoun.[44] León and seven of his companions were arrested and tried before the Justice of the Peace at Manti during the

[44] Bancroft, *Hist of Utah*, p. 475. Whitney, *Hist of Utah*, I. 508–510.

winter of 1851–52.´ The case later came before Zerubbabel
Snow as judge of the First District court.   In summing up the
case, Snow made the following statement:

In September last, twenty-eight Spaniards left New Mexico on a
trading expedition with the Utah Indians, in their various localities
in New Mexico and Utah.   Twenty-one of the twenty-eight were sever-
ally interested in the expedition.   The residue were servants.   Among this
company were the Spaniards against whom these suits were brought.
Before they left, Pedro León obtained a license from the governor of
New Mexico to trade on his own account with the Utah Indians, in
all their various localities.   Another member of the company also had
a license given to blank persons by the Governor of New Mexico.   The
residue were without license.   They proceeded on their route until
they arrived near the Rio Grande, where they exchanged with the
Indians some goods for horses and mules.   With these horses and
mules, being something more than one hundred, they proceeded to
Green River, in this Territory, where they sent some five or six of their
leading men to see Governor Young, and exhibit to him their license;
and as the Spanish witness said if that was not good here, then to get
from him another license.   Governor Young not being at home, but gone
south, they proceeded after and found him November 3rd at Sanpete
Valley.   Here they exhibited to the Governor their license, and informed him they wished to sell their horses and mules to the Utah Indians, and buy Indian children to be taken to New Mexico.   Governor
Young then informed them that their licence did not authorize them
to trade with the Indians in Utah.   They then sought one from him,
but he refused to give it, for the reason that they wanted to buy Indian children for slaves.   The Spaniards then promised him they would
not trade with the Indians but go immediately home.   Twenty of the
number, with about three-fourths of the horses and mules, left pursuant
to this promise and have not been heard from since.   The eight who were
left behind are the men who are parties to these proceedings.[44]

Snow decided against the eight defendants, and the Indian
slaves in their possession were liberated and the Mexicans sent
away.

[44] Whitney, *Hist. of Utah*, I. 510–511.

SPANIARDS ON SPOKANE RIVER

New Mexicans, of course, were, at this time, United States citizens, but that they were regarded still as Mexicans in language and sentiment not only by the Mormons but by themselves and United States government agents is indicated by an incident narrated by Lieutenant R. Saxton in his "Report of the Route from the Columbia Valley to Fort Owen and thence to Fort Benton", in 1853. When in the vicinity of Spokane River in the northeastern part of the present state of Washington, Saxton found the Indians suspicious and almost inclined to be hostile. As an explanation he recorded in his journal under date of August 2, 1853:

The Indians told me that a Spaniard had been along a few days before, and told them that a large body of American soldiers were coming to cut them off and take possession of their homes.[47]

It is not stated that this Spaniard was from New Mexico, but it may, perhaps, be safely presumed that such was the case. Incidentally, this indicates the extent to which activity of Mexican traders was carried as late as the middle of the nineteenth century.

JOSEPH J. HILL.

Bancroft Library,
University of California.

[47] U. S. Engineer dept., *Reports of explorations and surveys to ascertain the most practical and economical route for a railroad from the Mississippi River to the Pacific Ocean.* I. 256. (U. S. 33d cong., 2d sess., Senate, Ex. doc. 78).

SOME SOCIAL ASPECTS OF THE MEXICAN CONSTITUTION OF 1917[1]

The constituent convention met at Querétaro, it will be remembered, from December 1, 1916, to January 31, 1917, for the purpose of amending the constitution of 1857.[2] On February 5, 1917, about two months from the first date, the amended constitution was promulgated. The fact that this was possible within a comparatively short space of time is all the more remarkable when we consider the unsettled political, social, and economic condition of the people during the recent revolutionary period. More than that, in view of the disadvantages under which Mexico has labored for practically centuries, the breadth of mind and deep insight into present-day problems, as revealed by the various provisions of this document, are especially worthy of note. It embodies reforms which many students of modern social progress deem essential in any comprehensive scheme for social welfare. Various phases of social activity, usually left to the police powers of the nation, state, and municipality, are here deemed worthy of insertion into a national constitution. At least three national constitutions, framed and adopted since 1917, incorporate reforms of very similar nature: namely those of Germany (1919), of Peru (1919), and of Czechoslovakia (1920). A comparison of these four documents will reveal the fact that the constitution of Mexico is neither unduly radical nor unduly proletarian in character.

It is not the purpose of this paper to present a comprehensive study of the social aspects of this constitution. The subject is far too large and the necessary materials far too difficult of

[1] Read before Annual Meeting Southwestern Political Science Association. Austin, Texas, March 25, 1921.
[2] Sources: *Constitución de los Estados Unidos Mexicanos* (official edition); and H. N. Branch, The Mexican Constitution of 1917 compared with the Constitution of 1857. Annals of the American Academy of Political and Social Science. May, 1917.

access to warrant such a complete study at this time. That which is important after all is the instrument itself. The paper will, therefore, deal in condensed form only with those sections of the constitution which emphasize more particularly problems of social welfare.

The reasons for incorporating social reforms in the document itself are often found in legislation proposed after the adoption of a constitution. An act of this nature is the famous agrarian measure presented by President Obregón to the Congress, December 1, 1920.[1] The preamble recites that it is time to put into effect the plan of the revolutionists to improve more effectively the land, abolish the political and economic slavery of the proletariat, and establish peace and harmony in the state. The native soil, it continues, is capable of supplying the necessities of life for a large population and should furnish the foundation for a strong and progressive country. The nation is not strong and progressive, however,

because of the monopoly of land which impedes its cultivation and discourages the utilization of its fertility . . . . The monopoly of land is responsible for the enormous extent of uncultivated land, about ninety per cent of the territory in the Republic suitable for agricultural purposes. Such a state of affairs was the cause of the amortization of church property during the reform period, and would at present amply justify a similar measure in favor of the rural and city proletariat, which lack property of any kind, and which is eager to use and reap the benefits even of a small part of the land which legally belong to it. . . . . Whatever may be the ideas expressed concerning social justice and the rights of man, his inherent and inalienable right to the land for its cultivation and for the enjoyment of the whole product of his labor must be recognized, since the soil which sustains him constitutes the natural field for his productive activity and the sole origin of all wealth, both for the elements most essential to his subsistence and for the raw materials of industry. Such being the case, the privilege which the law grants to the monopolies of national territory can reach such a point, in accordance with these same laws, as to bring about absolute privation to those who

[1] "Mexican Land Reform," in *The Nation*, February 9, 1921, CXII, No. 2901, pp. 218–221.

lack such privileges; and even though such an extreme situation has not arisen yet, there is no doubt that as long as the present state of rural proprietorship remains unchanged the workers will be faced by the imperative necessity of accepting the conditions imposed upon them in exchange for permission to use the land which is absolutely necessary for their existence.

Article One of the measure contains the revolutionary principle that

The Government recognizes the inalienable and inherent right of every man to possess and cultivate for himself a piece of land, which, with reasonable care, shall be sufficient for his personal needs and those of his family.

To carry out this principle, lands will be expropriated from rural estates, from real property undeveloped for the past five years, and from lands cultivated by crude and antiquated methods. Rural properties, however, which have established modern ways of cultivation will not be expropriated. The holdings granted to each individual must not be less than five nor more than twelve hectares. The grantee must in every case be a Mexican citizen, either by birth or naturalization, and in the full enjoyment of civil rights. The measure excludes citizens owning more than twenty hectares and those who do not possess habits of industry and the ability to cultivate the land properly. The grantee has, however, no rights to forests and waters on the property so granted; these resources are governed by special laws. Moreover, the grantee must continue to cultivate the soil regularly. If the land remains uncultivated for only one year, the grantee loses right to the land but has the right to the improvements which he has made on it. The price paid by the grantee will be the same that the nation must pay the expropriated plus five per cent for organization and distribution. The grantee has a time allowance of twenty years, but he must make annual payments. The title to the land, however, rests in the nation until the whole amount is paid. The size of the plots granted should be inversely proportional to the value of the land, computing this value as much by the intrinsic quality of the soil as by the location with respect to the highways of traffic and the consuming centers. The size of the plots must in all cases be sufficient to maintain a farmer and his family and in addition must permit the accumulation of small savings to encourage thrift. "Elderly Mexican women and widows will also have the right to acquire pieces of land for their own benefit and not for the benefit of other persons." Agrarian commissions will be created having control of the granting of these holdings in each community.

The constitution gives to the people themselves very large powers in the control of the natural resources. Through the federal government the people regulate the development of these resources, and likewise prevent their deterioration, in order to conserve them and to distribute equitably the public wealth. The government may, therefore, impose limitations upon private property whenever the public weal may demand, just as it protects property from damage detrimental to human society in general. It may aid settlements or hamlets situated on private property by providing them with additional land and water from adjoining estates in sufficient amount to satisfy the needs of their inhabitants. In order, however, to respect carefully the rights of small land holdings, the famous land grants of January 6, 1915, are confirmed (Art. 27).

The nation, moreover, has sovereign and inalienable rights of ownership in all minerals and mineral substances from which metals and commercial metaloids are made. It also possesses the right of ownership in the case of precious stones, rock salt, salt lakes, products derived from the decomposition of rocks, fertilizing phosphates, solid fuels, petroleum, and all solid, liquid, and gaseous hydro-carbons (Art. 27).

In accordance with this doctrine, Mexico maintains the position that the ownership of surface soil does not confer ownership of subsurface resources, unless such additional rights have been granted. Such a stand is of international importance, at least in the question of petroleum. May we not say that Mexico is definitely within her rights, since she is proceeding according to the interpretation of sound public law? The United States

Supreme Court, for example, in the celebrated case *The Ohio Oil Company versus Indiana* (177 U. S. 209), held that ownership in oil and gas beneath the soil does not vest in the owner of the surface soil, or in the ultimate product, until such oil and gas have been brought to the surface and reduced to possession; and that by the very nature of petroleum, it

is a public thing, subject to the absolute control of the State, which, although it allows it to be reduced to possession, may at its will, not only regulate it, but wholly forbid its future taking.

If a commonwealth of the United States of North America possesses this right, the sovereign, independent nation of Mexico assuredly possesses a similar or even greater one. Such right does not, of course, excuse Mexico from failure to comply with its treaty obligations nor with laws Mexico has itself enacted in this regard, unless there are valid reasons for the abrogation of such treaties and for the repeal of such laws.[4]

The nation possesses full control and ownership of all territorial seas, lakes, inlets of bays, interior lakes, and natural formations connecting flowing waters, principal rivers and their tributaries; rivers, streams, and ravines, bounding national territory or that of a state; waters extracted from mines; waters in beds, banks of lakes and streams already mentioned; and the development of waters passing from one landed property to another (Art. 27).

The constitution is no less explicit in prescribing the method of acquiring ownership in the national lands and water rights. Ownership in these properties can be acquired only by native born or naturalized citizens, and by Mexican civil and commercial companies. Foreigners may acquire ownership in such properties only by agreeing, through the Department of Foreign Affairs, to be considered Mexicans in respect to such ownership, and by renouncing absolutely the right to invoke the protection of their governments in respect to such ownership. Any attempt to evade this regulation, will entail complete forfeiture of such

[4] "Sub-Surface Petroleum is not Private Property" in *The Mexican Review*, December, 1920, pp. 6–8.

rights. Under no circumstances, however, will the Mexican Government confer such rights within one hundred kilometers of the frontier, or within fifty kilometers of the seacoast. "Concessions to develop mines, waters, or mineral fuels in the Republic of Mexico" are subject to the same rules and regulations (Art. 27).

A large place is, in addition, given to labor and social welfare. The national and state legislative bodies are clothed with large powers regulating social betterment. Certain specific reformative measures are to be passed governing every specie of contract labor. Legislation shall establish a maximum eight hour day and a seven hour night of labor for all male employees; and a maximum six hour day for children between the ages of twelve and sixteen. "Children under the age of twelve may not be made the subject of a contract" at all. Women of whatever age, and children under the age of sixteen, may not engage in occupations in factories at night nor in commercial establishments after ten o'clock. They may not work in dangerous and unhealthful occupations. Women may not perform any considerable physical work during the three months immediately preceding and one month following childbirth; but they are to receive full pay and to enjoy the rights acquired as employees, despite the interruptions incident to childbirth. In addition, mothers are to have two extra half hours each day for rest and in order to nurse their children. Every employee is allowed one day in seven for rest. Overtime work may not exceed three hours nor extend over more than three consecutive days. In no case may women of whatever age and children under the age of sixteen engage in overtime work. A citizen contracting to do work in a foreign country must have his contract legalized before a competent municipal authority and viséed by the consul of the country to which he is going. There must be the distinct understanding that in addition to the usual clauses there shall be special stipulations whereby the employer assumes the cost of repatriation. Definite provisions are made for safeguarding the interest of the employees in contractual relations. Labor contracts become null and void when their terms demand notoriously excessive work; when the wage is insufficiently remunerative; when the terms provide for more than one week before payment of wages; when it provides for the assigning of amusement places, hostelries, saloons, and shops for the payment of wages when the employees thereof are not included; when there is a direct or indirect obligation to purchase articles of consumption in specified places; when the terms permit the retention of wages for fines; when the terms constitute a waiver on the part of the employees for the indemnities to which they are entitled; and when the terms imply the waiver of any right belonging by law to the employees. Moreover, employees may not be discharged without due notice and without cause for such discharge having been given to the Board of Conciliation and Arbitration. The employees who decline to abide by the decision of the board may terminate their contract at will; but the employers who decline to abide by the decision of the board may not terminate the contract without paying employees a sum of money equal to three months' wages and such damages as the employees may have incurred as a result of the termination of the contract by the employers (Art. 123).

The provisions for wage legislation are equally definite and precise. The minimum wage for the employee, head of a family, must be sufficient, according to the standards in the different sections of the state, to satisfy the normal needs of the employee, and for his education and lawful pleasures. In addition to the normal wage, the employees are entitled to a share in the profits of the establishment in which they are engaged as determined by special commissions in the different communities. The minimum wage is exempt from attachment, set off, or discount. This is likewise true in the case of bankruptcy or in composition. The claims, too, of the employees for wages must be preferred over that of any other claims. Wages must be paid in legal currency and not in merchandise, orders, counters, or in any other substitutes. Debts incurred by employees in favor of their employers, or the employers' associates, subordinates, or agents, may be charged against the employees themselves only and in no case and for no reason against the members of their families. Debts due the employers from the employees can be deducted only from the wages for one month.   Neither sex nor nationality may in any way affect the wages paid.   Property legally constituting the family patrimony is inalienable and cannot be mortgaged or in any way attached, and may be bequeathed in due succession proceedings (Art. 123).

There are, moreover, many provisions governing the duties of the employers toward their employees and the community in addition to those already described.   The employers are to furnish housing facilities for their employees in every place where one hundred or more employees are engaged.   Rents not to exceed one half of one per cent of the assessed valuation of the properties may be charged by the employers for the upkeep of such dwellings.   Employers must also furnish schools, dispensaries, and other services necessary.   In labor centers with a population of at least two hundred there is to be set aside a space of land not to exceed five thousand square meters for the establishment of public markets, the construction of buildings for municipal services, and places of amusement.   Saloons and gambling houses may not, however, operate in such centers. All places of work are, of course, to comply with all the regulations tending to insure hygienic and sanitary working conditions.   Due care is to be taken to prevent accidents in the use of machinery, tools, and all working materials.   Employers are to be at all times responsible for the accidents to the employees and for occupational diseases arising from such work.   Indemnification is to be made by the employers in accordance with the nature of the accident and death from diseases or disabilities (Art. 123).

There are also provisions permitting employees and employers the legal right to unite for purposes of protection and of improving their conditions.   Syndicates and unions are recognized as legal institutions with permission to function as long as they comply with the law.   The right to strike and to lockout is also recognized as legal weapons to be used in case of necessity.   This right is, however, denied the employees of the federal government and those in all military establishments in times of peace as well as war, and to those engaged in industries which may be necessary for the successful prosecution of war.   Ten days' notice must be given the Board of Conciliation and Arbitration before a strike or a lockout may be called. Differences between labor and capital are to be referred to this board for final settlement. The board is to be made up of an equal number of representatives from labor and capital with one representative from the federal government. Finally, employment bureaus, municipal offices, and other private or public agencies, finding work for employees, may charge no fees whatsoever for their services (Art. 123).

The federal and state governments are also to encourage the organization of social insurance (*Cajas de Seguros Populares*) for old age, sickness, life, unemployment, accidents, and other misfortunes. This is done "in order to instil and inculcate popular habits of thrift" (Art. 123). There are provisions, furthermore, safeguarding the individual's right to choose whatever occupation he may desire and to receive compensation on his own part for services rendered (Art. 5). The document is equally definite in matters dealing with unfair competition and monopolies. Any attempt to stifle competition, to corner the market, or to create unfair and exclusive advantages in favor of any one person or persons to the detriment of the public in general, or of any special class of society, are to be severely dealt with. But associations of labor, cooperative associations, or unions of producers, are not to be deemed monopolies providing they operate in defense of their own interests or those of the general public. Exemption from taxation, any restriction of personal liberty, even under cover of protection to industry, and all private and governmental monopolies are to be forbidden. Those monopolies regulating the coinage of money, the postal, telegraphic, and radio-telegraphic services, the issuance of bills by a single banking institution, all are to be controlled by the federal government. The law is also to concede to authors, artists, and inventors the privilege for a definite period of time of reproduction of their work (Art. 28).

Religious reform, in addition, is given a very important place. The student of clericalism as a political factor readily comprehends the genuine repugnance of the Mexicans to the political activities of the Church, and understands fully the reasons for the thorough and complete subordination of the Church to the

State. The very grave wrongs and the injury done the Mexican
people by clericalism will be accepted by the student as ample
justification for this complete elimination of ecclesiastical interests
from the civil affairs of the State. A very large majority of the
people have long desired to rid themselves, root and branch, of
clerical domination admittedly the cause of a large share of the
national ills. The historian will not fail to realize that these
reforms are directed against clericalism, of whatever nature, and
not against religion as such. He understands full well that the
Mexicans are a very devout people and that the great majority
of them—fully ninty-eight per cent—worship according to the
rites of the Roman Catholic Apostolic Church. The damage
done to church property by the soldiery during the recent revolution was not committed because of hatred of Roman Catholicism,
but rather as a protest against the abuses of many of the conservative clergy in spreading propaganda inimical to the best interests
of the people. The reforms, therefore, are directed against those
forms of religious activity, irrespective of creeds, considered a
menace to republican institutions and a grave danger to the
State. Very many of the reforms inserted in the constitution
of 1917 will be found in the constitution of 1857, in the famous
Laws of Reform (*Leyes de Reformas*) of 1874, as well as in the
philosophical writings of *Gómez Farías.*

The complete control over all religious worship and all outward ecclesiastical forms is placed in the federal authorities. The
privilege to embrace the religion of one's choice, and to practice
all ceremonies, devotions, or observances of any particular creed,
either in places of public worship or at home, is fully guaranteed,
provided always that these do not constitute an offense punishable
by law. Every act of public worship is to be performed within
assigned places; these places must at all times be under direct
governmental supervision (Art. 24). The congress has no right
to enact any law establishing or prohibiting any particular form
of religion in Mexico. Moreover, "the law recognizes no juridical
personality (*personalidad alguna*) in the religious institutions
known as churches". All establishments of monastic and religious orders are absolutely forbidden. The ministers of whatever creed are considered merely as persons exercising a profes-

sion, and are accordingly subject to the laws governing professions. "Only a Mexican by birth may be a minister of any religious creed in Mexico." In addition, and with evident purpose of controlling clerical activities of a political nature, it is provided that religious institutions of whatever description, and all ministers of whatever creed, shall have no legal capacity to acquire ownership in real properties or in water rights. Moreover, no religious institution and no ecclesiastic shall have a legal right to hold or administer properties or to make loans on real estate. All property in possession of religious institutions, and of all individuals exercising the profession of religion, at the time of the adoption of this constitution, are confiscated and the ownership of such property is vested in the nation. The state and territorial governments are to determine which of the religious buildings shall be used for temples of public worship, the number of such temples, as well as the number of ministers of each community, New structures may be erected only with the permission of the Department of the Interior (*Gobernación*). The temples so constructed belong to the nation and may be used for public worship only. Such temples are always subject to the careful supervision and inspection of the governmental authorities. The caretaker, together with ten citizens is to be directly responsible under the government for the proper management of the houses of public worship. Moreover, it is provided that episcopal residences, rectories, seminaries, orphan asylums, collegiate establishments of religious institutions, convents, and other buildings constructed or designed for the administration, propaganda, or teaching of the tenets of any religious creed, shall belong to the nation. All such buildings are to be used exclusively for religious services. In addition, all charitable institutions, private and public; all institutions for scientific research, or for the diffusion of knowledge; all buildings of mutual aid societies, or organizations formed for any lawful purpose, may in no case whatsoever be under the patronage, direction, administration, or supervision of religious corporations, institutions, or ministers of any creed, or of any of their dependents. It is furthermore provided that these institutions and persons may not acquire ownership in lands or make loans on real property where the terms of the contract exceed five years. No ecclesiastic may inherit either in his own name, or through any agent, real property of any kind; he is also legally incapable of inheriting by will any real property or money from a fellow ecclesiastic, or from any person to whom he is not related by blood to within the fourth degree. To prevent the resumption of clerical influence in politics, it is expressly provided that no minister has a right to vote, to hold a public office, to be a candidate, or to take part in any way in political affairs. Meetings of a political nature may not be held in the temples of public worship. Religious periodicals of every kind are strictly forbidden to criticize the fundamental laws of the land, the public authorities, or in any way to interfere with the policies of the different governmental bodies (Art. 130).

In the field of education, there are likewise to be very definite restrictions upon the privileges of religious institutions and all ministers. Religious organizations may not engage in primary instruction, either in private or in public institutions: all such education must be secular and gratuitous (Art. 3). As if to put a finality to it all, trial by jury for the infraction of any of the laws dealing with religious matters is strictly forbidden (Art.130).

Such are the more important social aspects of the new Mexican Constitution of 1917. The question that naturally arises is whether or not these reforms will be put into practical use. To be sure the Mexicans may not be able to solve their problems under the present régime. There may even be need of other constitutions. Yet, with forceful convictions, resolute minds, and determined ambitions, the people themselves are bound ultimately to triumph. It is, after all, the men at the helm in Mexico in whom the world at large is more especially interested. The men now at the helm are "new" men, the sons of revolutions. In them there appears an earnest desire to carry out the wishes of the mass of the people. When this is done, Mexico will be one of the most enlightened and genuinely democratic of modern nations. It is in the furtherance of this end, through altruistic motives, that the people of the United States of North America can render Mexico and humanity the greatest service.

N. ANDREW N. CLEVEN.

BOOK REVIEWS

The Colonization of North America, 1492–1783. By HERBERT E.
BOLTON, PH.D., Professor of American History in the University
of California, and THOMAS M. MARSHALL, PH.D., Professor of History
in Washington University. (New York: Macmillan Company,
1920. Pp. xiv, 609. $4.25.)

In no particular does the reviewer dissent from what seems to be
the consensus of opinion among all who have thus far appraised the
value of this book: first, that such a treatment of the subject was much
needed; secondly, that Professors Bolton and Marshall have done their
work well. The authors in their preface state that this volume is an
attempt to treat the subject of colonization in North America entirely
and completely, neither confining it to the story of the one nation whose
colonies happened to be the nucleus of the United States, nor limiting
it to the history of the thirteen colonies which revolted. This
plan of presentation is so obviously the natural and correct one that
it is now to be wondered why it had not before been attempted. Professor C. M. Andrews has in many places pointed out as incomplete and
illogical the common custom of segregating individual efforts at colonization, and of studying these as independent phenomena, without
regard to the unity of the whole movement. If this treatment of the
subject has been thus lacking in dealing with the English nation, one
can appreciate the completeness and excellence of a work, like the one
under review, which grasps the full significance of the whole colonial
enterprise and the accomplishment of every nation concerned.

So the establishment of the colonies of Bermuda, Guiana, the Lesser
Antilles, and Providence Island is given proper place in the colonial
system. The colonizing efforts of Spain and of the other countries
which played a part in the settlement of North America are presented
not as unconnected, spasmodic events, but as results of a definite
movement, with more than ordinary emphasis placed on the interre-
lations of the different nations, and with the European background so
clearly pictured that the reader easily understands the reaction in
America. An adequate index, carefully selected and recent references
for further reading, and forty-nine well-adapted line maps make the
volume more helpful.

Of 424 pages in which the story is brought down to the Revolutionary period, approximately 185 pages are devoted to the development of English colonization; 129 to the study of Spanish expansion; 92 to the French colonies; and 15 to those of the Dutch and Swedes. As one would expect from Professor Bolton's connection with the volume, the part played by Spain in our era of beginnings is at last shown in its proper form and proportion. The teacher of United States history may complain that some of the Spanish explorations beyond the present confines of the country, especially the conquest by Cortés of Mexico, are given in too much detail. But this was probably considered necessary in order to visualize to the student the empire as a whole. Spain discovered the New World (the discussion of this event breaks away from the old theory of the Turks' blocking the trade-routes, thereby sending Columbus on a western route in an endeavor to reach the Indies); she opened up new paths of commerce; she established an empire which in time extended from the straits of Magellan to Nova Scotia. All of this is described by one who is saturated with the subject. Spain's colonial policy and administration are outlined clearly and fully. It will probably shock those of the old prejudices to learn that in the sixteenth century "there never was a time when the right of petition was not freely exercised, and with great effect on actual administration"; and that emigration also was encouraged. By 1574, there were two hundred towns and cities in North and South America, and a Spanish population in North America of 100,000 to 125,000. "Half a century before Jamestown was founded by the English, the University of Mexico was conferring degrees upon graduates in law and theology." It was not in her colleges and seminaries, though these were creditable, that Spain left her strongest impress on the New World: it was in her endeavor to lift millions of Indians to a higher plane of morality and civilization. The work of the friars and of the early missions is sympathetically told. Spain broke down in her colonial program, but she must have consoled herself by the reflection that before surrendering her American dependencies she had implanted in them the elements of civilization.

If that portion of the book devoted to Spanish exploration and settlement is here given more attention than other divisions, it is because this is the "new matter" not heretofore found in books of this scope, and not because the rest of the volume is less excellent in its presentation. The French settlements in Louisiana and in the Northwest are given fuller treatment than usual; the accounts of colonial administration, whether of France or of England, show familiarity with recent studies; the enumeration of parliamentary acts relating to the colonies is not confined to the few one generally finds in a text-book; and the later emigrations of Germans and Scotch-Irish are followed not merely into the states but into the very counties in which they finally settled.

Altogether, this volume, of interest to teacher, student, and general reader, merits the popularity it is destined to enjoy. Revisions of text-books now in use will not likely be made without reference to it. There is a cry in some quarters to make American history "safe for Americans". There is no propaganda in this study of the period of colonization. Every race whose early efforts helped in any reasonable degree to make America what it is will find here a fair and unbiased record.

LEO F. STOCK.

Encyclopedia e Diccionario Internacional. Edited by W. M. Jackson. (Lisboa, Rio de Janeiro, São Paulo, Londres, Pariz, Nova York, 1921. 20 vols.)

Under the above title a Portuguese-Brazilian encyclopedia has just been published, which answers most adequately its purpose. Encyclopedias must naturally have a general character, and some, indeed, try to be really and thoroughly international, but they can not be completely so, and a larger place is always allowed to the subjects touching the original country of their publication. The *Encyclopedia Britannica*, for instance, is first of all "Britannica" and secondly cosmopolitan. The title does not deceive in this case.

Such a remark as the above is most effectively applied regarding countries of less comprehensive influence in the world, and yet, to gain entire information, one can not work with a single encyclopedia. French subjects are to be studied in Levasseur's *Grande Encyclopédie*, German subjects in Meyer's *Lexikon*, Spanish and especially Spanish-American subjects in the work in course of publication by Espasa (Barcelona).

To the encyclopedia, which forms the subject of this review, many of the best Portuguese and Brazilian writers have contributed, which explains the accuracy of most of the articles on Portugal and Brazil. It is much to be regretted that the initials or names of the respective authors do not appear at the foot of the articles, as this procedure would give those articles greater authority—especially so when contributions are written by men like Theophilo Braga, Sylvio Romero,

Ricardo Jorge, Oswaldo Cruz, Carolina Michaelis de Vasconcellos, and José Verissimo.

The work seems indispensable to every student of things Portuguese and Brazilian. The biographical, bibliographical, historical, geographical, and artistic parts are very well developed—we may say, nearly complete in their special aspects: however, it is not to be implied that general scientific and literary matters are not treated in a very clear, comprehensive, and scholarly manner. The illustrations are numerous, though not too many, and excellent, and furnish efficient help to the reader. The work is not too extensive—20 volumes in royal octavo, thus forming a very convenient size. The pages have two columns each and the type faces are properly chosen.

MANOEL DE OLIVEIRA LIMA.

NOTE: Dr. Oliveira Lima has contributed various important and authoritative articles to this work.—J. A. R.

Argentine International Trade under Inconvertible Paper Money, 1880–1900. By JOHN H. WILLIAMS. (Cambridge: Harvard University Press, 1920.)

It would indeed have been unfortunate had the results of this experiment in inconvertible paper money gone by unnoticed and Dr. Williams is to be complimented for acting upon the suggestion of Professor Taussig in preparing this study of Argentina's financial history from 1880 to 1900.

In 1881 Argentina nationalized its currency system, and the developments in the years following this present many interesting problems for any student of Hispanic American finance. By the end of 1883 its monetary system had been established on a convertible basis. A panic in the year following forced a return to the inconvertible basis, and increased issues of paper money just previous to 1890, together with the Baring panic, prevented resumption of specie payments until 1899. Thus for a period of about fifteen years we are able to observe the results of this system.

The period, however, is different from that of the present day in Europe, as regards the buying of exchange, in that exchange remained on a gold basis. Gold was bought with the inconvertible paper money through private agencies and with this gold the exchange was purchased. Thus there were really two distinct monetary systems, the inconvertible paper which circulated in domestic trade and the gold with which exchange operations were conducted. Needless to say there was a great opportunity for speculation in exchange in that the ratio of paper to gold fluctuated violently.

In part I of this volume a study is made of the balance of international payments under the inconvertible régime by carefully analyzing the borrowings of the country and the interrelation of borrowing with the paper money system. The effect of borrowing upon the foreign exchange rate is also analyzed. Here might be found a reason for the present condition in Argentine exchange, namely, that of a curtailed flow of capital from abroad. The effects of the Baring panic give evidence of the sensitive manner in which Argentina responds to conditions prevailing in the monetary centers of the world. The indications of recovery from the crisis during the period of the Baring panic appeared when foreign borrowings were renewed. The relation between the value of paper money and the balance of international payments concludes the first part of the study and it is here brought out "that the balance of international payments did in fact exercise a powerful influence upon the value of Argentine inconvertible paper money".

Part II takes up the study of the effects of inconvertible paper money upon the balance of merchandise trade. The period of Dr. Williams's investigation, it should be borne in mind, is peculiar in that the first five years was a period of prosperity and expansion and the following half-decade one of financial stringency. These conditions must be taken into account as complicating the problem.

The fluctuation of internal prices occasioned by the movements of gold was a factor of considerable importance during this period. Owing to the fact that export prices varied as the ratio of paper to gold, and internal prices in which production costs were figured were not so sensitive to this change, exports tended to increase as the ratio of paper to gold became greater. Import prices, conversely, rose as the ratio of paper to gold became greater and imports were curtailed as the premium on gold increased.

A consideration of the relation of paper money, prices, and wages to export trade is one of the interesting features of the later half of this study. This is followed by a detailed analysis of the chief exports of the country. Here is brought out a very important characteristic of Argentina's trade which will undoubtedly continue to affect the situation—the fact that its exports are almost entirely agricultural products subject to the influence of climatic conditions. Added to this is the fact that the demand for its products even in favorable years depends upon conditions prevailing in foreign commodity markets. A chapter is also devoted to paper money and prices in import trade.

This is an excellent study and is a clear analysis of the financial history of the country during this period. An extensive bibliography is included.

EDWIN BATES.

Kino's Historical Memoir of Pimería Alta. A contemporary account of the Beginnings of California, Sonora, and Arizona, by Father Eusebio Francisco Kino, S. J., Pioneer Missionary, Explorer, Cartographer, and Ranchman, 1683–1711. Published for the first time from the original manuscript in the Archives of Mexico; translated into English, edited and annotated, by HERBERT EUGENE BOLTON, PH.D., Professor of American History and Curator of the Bancroft Library, University of California. 2 vols. (Cleveland: The Arthur H. Clark Company, 1919. Map. Illustrations. Index. $10.00.)

What was accomplished for the history of early northern exploration in territory now a part of the United States by the publication of the Lewis and Clark manuscripts by Dr. Thwaites has been accomplished for the history of the exploration and settlement of part of our own southwest by Dr. Bolton in his publication of Kino's lost manuscript. The putting into type of the latter is in a way even more striking than was the former, for, as its editor aptly says, "the publication of this long lost manuscript puts on a new basis the early history of a large part of our Southwest". It is only now that the world is able to perceive what it owes to Kino, Jesuit, missionary, church builder, explorer, cartographer, and ranchman.

These two volumes, while appearing as an entity in themselves, form volumes III and IV of a series entitled "Spain in the West". The first two volumes, namely *Athanase de Mezières and the Louisiana-Texas Frontier, 1768–1780*, were also translated, annotated, and edited by Dr. Bolton, and published by the Arthur H. Clark Company, in 1914. Like those two volumes, the Kino is given a dignified and attractive format and exterior quite in keeping with its character, which the historical public has learned to expect from the publications of the house abovementioned.

Dr. Bolton had the good fortune to discover Kino's manuscript in the Archivo General y Público of Mexico after it had lain untouched for a century and a half. By its discovery, he has been able to prove beyond all question that Venegas, Ortega, and Alegre all know of this work and used it in their own volumes. The complete title of the work is "Favores Celestiales de Iesus y de Maria Ssma. y del gloriosissimo

Apostol de las Yndias S. Francisco Xavier experimentados en las nuevas Conversiones del nuevo Reino de la Nuevo Navarra desta America Septentrional yncognita, y Passo por Tierra a la California en 35 grados de Altura con su nuevo Mapa cosmografico de estas nuevas y dilitadas Tierras que hasta Aora havian sido yncognitas, dedicados a la Rl. Magd. de Felipo. V. mui Catolico y gran Monarca de las Españas, y de las Yndias". The translation of the manuscript was made by Miss Elizabeth Howard West and the editor. In publishing the translation, the form of the original was adhered to as strictly as possible, and any changes made were those indispensable editorial changes that the best critical historical usage has sanctioned.

In his introduction to the text, Dr. Bolton has produced an excellent historical essay which the reader wishes were longer. Here he discusses the name and family of Kino, his early training, his mission work in Lower California, his explorations and other labors in Pimería Alta, and his death. He reveals Kino as a very human individual, an indefatigable worker, unsparing of himself, tender toward others, enthusiastic in his work, whether in the saving of souls, in the administration of the mission, in the business of ranching, which he undertook so that his converts and others might have food, or in his explorations, as untiring in the saddle as any cowboy ever was, a good friend—in short one of those men whom it is the good fortune of the world to breed up every now and then, so that he may become an inspiration to later generations. He was able to do a great many things and to do them all well, for he had in great measure an original mind that did not balk at obstacles. The Jesuit order has a right to be proud of him.

Kino, whose name was properly Chino and not Kühn, was of Italian, and not German origin as many have conjectured, but his early education and training were German. In connection with his name, an interesting communication was published not long ago in a number of the *Catholic Historical Review*, which should be read by all interested in Kino and his work.

Kino was assigned to Pimería Alta in 1687, of which what is now northern Arizona formed a part. There he founded many missions and made those explorations that must forever establish him as one of the pioneer makers of America (the word is used in its broadest sense). He first of all, as Dr. Bolton notes, mapped Pimería Alta on the basis of actual exploration. He first of white men saw the Gila River since the men of the Oñate expedition in 1605. One of the most striking accomplishments of this man was the adducing of proof of the peninsularity of California. That California was a peninsula was known to the Spaniards two centuries before Kino, but the belief had arisen that it was no peninsula but an island—and this has been one of the great hoaxes of geographers which was copied from generation to generation in the maps, the error persisting in many maps even long after Kino's time. Kino has left this evidence in his map of 1701, which so far as known was first published in 1705. Of his discovery of the peninsularity of California Dr. Bolton says:

After 1699, aside from his search for souls in the Pimería, Kino's most absorbing quest was made in search of a land route to California. Since the days of Cortes and Cabrillo many views had been held regarding the geography of California, some regarding it as a peninsula and others as an island. Kino had been taught by Father Aygentler, in the University of Ingolstadt, that it was a peninsula, and had come to America firm in this belief; but in deference to current opinion, and as a result of certain observations of his own, he had given up the notion, and as late as 1698 he wrote of California as "the largest island of the world". But during the journey of 1699 to the Gila occurred an incident that caused him to turn again to the peninsular theory. It was the gift, when near the Yuma junction, of certain blue shells, such as he had seen in 1685 on the Pacific coast of the Peninsula of California, and there only. If the shells had come to the Yumas from the South Sea, he reasoned, must there not be land connection with California and the Ocean, by way of the Yuma country? Kino now ceased his work on the boat he was building at Caborca and Dolores for the navigation on the Gulf, and directed his efforts to learning more about the source of the blue shells. For this purpose he made a journey in 1700 to San Xavier del Bac. Thither he called the Indians from all the villages for hundreds of miles around, and in "long talks" at night he learned that only from the South Sea could the blue shells be had.

This assurance was the inspiration of his remaining journeys. In the same year, 1700, he for the first time reached the Yuma junction, and learned that he was above the head of the Gulf, which greatly strengthened his belief in the peninsular theory. In the next year he returned to the same point by way of the Camino del Diablo, passed some distance down the Colorado, and crossed over to the California side, towed on a raft by Indians and sitting in a basket. Finally, in 1702, his triumph came, for he again returned to the Yuma junction, descended the Colorado to the Gulf, and saw the sun rise over its head. He was now satisfied that he had demonstrated the feasibility of a land passage to California and had disproved the idea that California was an island.

The map was first published in *Lettres Edifiantes*, edition of Paris, 1705, vol. V., and in the same year also in the *Mémoire de Trévoux*.

The editor includes in his essay a list of Kino's writings in which to the titles already known he has been able to add an even longer list of titles of writings which were incorporated in Kino's manuscript, as well as other titles of writings which he found in the Mexican archives. To the ten titles that had been known, Dr. Bolton adds 24 new titles—a notable achievement.

Kino's work itself is full of interest and of valuable information in many directions, not the least being his remarks on the Indians of the regions through which he passed. Kino was always observant and let slip no detail that would be useful to him in his work. His descriptions and geographical notes are of the highest order; and for the historian of the missions his chapters giving details of his spiritual work are of the utmost value. Finally, for the beginning of the civilized history of a portion of our own southwest, the narrative has a peculiar value, and students must have recourse to Kino for the complete understanding and interpretation of the history of the southwest.

In his essay, the editor speaks (p. 61) of the "untamed savages", which is a looseness of speech common among historians in connection with American aborigines. No Indians of this continent can be accurately described as "savages", but they were "barbarians", a very different thing from savages, and belonged to a higher culture than do savages. Outside of this common error, the reviewer has found no slips. The editorial notes are excellent and add to the information of the narrative.

The first volume contains a good reproduction of Kino's map of Pimería Alta, which is reproduced from the *Mémoire de Trévoux*, a later version of the same map reproduced from a manuscript in the Archivo de Indias, Seville; a map by Kino of the part of Lower California where Kino and Atondo labored, 1683–1685; and a plan of the settlement at San Bruno, 1683. The second volume contains a present-day view of the mission of San Zavier del Bac, which was founded by Kino in 1700; a facsimile of the title page of Picolo's Informe (1702); and a map of Pimería Alta, 1687–1711, compiled by the editor from Kino's Memoir and other contemporary sources. As a whole the work has been well done, and Dr. Bolton deserves the thanks of students for making available another prime source of American history.

JAMES ALEXANDER ROBERTSON.

Cartas Históricas del Perú. Primera Serie y Segunda Serie. Recopilada y anotada por JUAN PEDRO PAZ-SOLDÁN. (Lima: Librería e Imprenta Gil, 1920 and 1921. 2 vols. pp. 426 and 452.)

These two volumes constitute one of the most important bibliographical achievements relating to the struggles of Peru for independence. The editor of these letters is a well-known historical investigator, author of a number of interesting and scholarly historical monographs and a member of a family which has for generations been of great importance in the intellectual life of Peru.

Paz-Soldán, in his preface, aptly calls the decade from 1819 to 1829 a "trágico decenio". It was tragic, but it was stirring and noble, too. It was a time of many currents and cross-currents, a time of struggles to accomplish worthy aims and a time of struggles to realize evil projects. It was a period wherein social institutions were severely tested and wherein some of them succumbed under the burden placed upon them. It was a decade in which it was determined whether the social and political orgnization of the unhappy past of Peru should survive or whether the invigorating breath of more liberal-minded men should be allowed to prevail and to make the newly born states robust. Unhappily an insensate conservatism not at all incompatible with a paradoxically perverted trend toward "democracy" was prevalent in the end; unhappily, also, arrogance, selfishness, materialism and stupidity were able to triumph over high-minded idealism, self-devotion, and generous far-sightedness.

Being as it was, it is not astonishing that the decade of 1819 to 1829 was full of fascinating events. The compilation of Señor Paz-Soldán offers to students the necessary basis for all who wish to understand and to interpret the revolutionary movement in Peru and neighboring countries.

The documents in the two volumes relate to Generals San Martín, Bolívar, Sucre, La Mar, Torre-Tagle, Guido, Heres, Necochea, La Fuente, Admiral Guise, Riva-Agüero, Monteagudo, Sánchez-Carrión and other chief figures of the period. No inedited material is here published, but the documents thus gathered together and supplied with good notes are found scattered in the Venezuelan collections of O'Leary and Blanco and in the Argentine collection called "Archivo de San Martín."

To many people the most interesting pages in the two volumes are pages 51 to 54 of the First Series, where will be found an interesting letter from General San Martín to General Miller, written from Brussels, April 19, 1827, in which is described the famous "interview of Guayaquil" between San Martín and Bolívar. In this letter San Martín states that his only object in the interview of Guayaquil was to obtain from Bolívar military aid with which to terminate the war in Peru. He says that after the Battle of Pichincha the Colombian army had about 9,600 bayonets, but that of this number Bolívar would send to the succor of Peru only 1,070, a number which rightly seemed to San

Martín ungenerous. His conversation with Bolívar had as its purpose that of persuading the Colombian liberator to cooperate more unreservedly with the Peruvians. This Bolívar never did, and for his failure to do so he was well castigated by the vitriolic pen of the brilliant Manuel Lorenzo Vidaurre.

The Second Series is especially rich in material referring to the unseemly manner in which Bolívar and his followers conducted themselves while in Peru.

In a word, this is a piece of work of great importance to specialists in this particular field. The two volumes are beautifully printed on good paper, and the proofreading has been most scrupulous. One wishes that there were some inedited letters among the rest, but otherwise he is well satisfied.

PHILIP AINSWORTH MEANS.

Los Poetas de la Colonia. By LUIS ALBERTO SÁNCHEZ. (Lima: Editorial "Euforión." 1921. Pp. 301.)

Heretofore those of us who have sought to write about Peruvian literature have had to turn first of all to Menéndez y Pelayo, then to Prado y Ugarteche, and finally to Ventura Garcia-Calderón. Now a fourth is added to these three indispensable writers. It is a rare and real pleasure to greet so young, so diligent, so skilful and so conscientiously complete a writer as Luis Alberto Sánchez. He is barely 21 years old, and his youth would demand gentle handling were it not for the fact that his book is so mature as to make it possible to judge it upon its merits only.

The first chapter treats of the poets of the conquest. In it appears Sánchez's peculiar power of portraying in a few lines the qualities of an entire epoch and of contrasting them with those of some other period. His style is magnificent; his erudition is profound but never soporific. The book is so well written that it is no effort to read it in a train or on a crowded steamer. It has quaint flashes of humor now and then, or rapier thrusts of piercing satire, or dashes of perhaps indecent, but not vulgar, wit. These light places relieve the whole without in any way lessening its importance as a work of historical reference and literary criticism.

The function of the first chapter is to prepare the bases of the history of Peruvian letters in colonial times. Every page is rich in bibliographical notes and in sagacious comments on various matters of importance. There are innumerable remarks tending to correct the errors of previous writers; there are notes of interest on writers but little known or entirely unknown before. At the end of the first chapter, Sánchez speaks of one Pedro Vaca de la Cadena, who, though he lived as late as 1659, is considered a "poet of the conquest" because his chief, 'Los actos y hazañas valerosas del Capitán Diego Fernández de Serpa", is of belicose and virile nature, similar to those other martial compositions written earlier in the stormy days of the conquest and of the civil wars of Peru. It is a question whether the mere possession of such characteristics is sufficient grounds for including the poem in question among those of the conquest. Rather, it seems, that poem should be regarded as a late survival of the warrior spirit in times when courtier-like softness was beginning to prevail.

Chapters II. and III. discuss the courtier poets of the period between about 1550 and about 1610. In that period the viceroyalty of Peru was passing through a transition stage, and from it emerged the final social and governmental forms of the colony, forms destined to remain almost unchanged down to 1821. Enrique Garcés, native of Portugal, Diego Mexía de Fernangil, native of Seville, "Clarinda", an anonymous writer whose sex is not surely known, Diego de Aguilar y Córdoba, and others of the period are all treated more or less extensively.

In reviewing a book which treats of so vast a subject, one must perforce skip much. Chapters IV. and V. discuss the work of Ercilla, Oña, and Barco Centenera. Chapter VI. does the same for the great religio-epic poet Diego de Hojeda, author of the "Cristiada" so generally praised in spite of its many wearisome stretches. Chapter VII. is of special importance for the reason that it presents a new identification of the baffling poetess "Amarilis". Her great work was her "Silva a Lope", in which she deluges with chaste love Lope de Vega, himself a poet of first rank and worthy to receive verses so wonderful as those of his distant Peruvian admirer. Don Ricardo Palma was the chief foe of Amarilis's claim to womanhood, and it is pleasant to be able to assert that Sánchez joins with Menéndez y Pelayo, Medina, Riva-Agüero y Osma and V. García-Calderón in supporting it. The name fixed upon by Sánchez as being that of "Amarilis" is the sonorous one of Doña María Tello de Lara y de Arévalo y Espinoza, her parents being, according to him, Juan Tello de Lara and María de Arévalo y Espinoza. His proofs, of the genealogical variety, seem valid.

A long leap to chapter XV. is necessary. The intervening pages are thoroughly excellent, but their material is not so supremely new as that in chapter XV., wherein an unknown poet, Toribio Bravo de

Lagunas Castilla y Zavala, member of a great family and a creditable bard of the last half of the eighteenth century, is discussed.

The book is excellent and indeed indispensable. Its chief lack is that of an alphabetical index. It is well printed on good paper.

PHILIP AINSWORTH MEANS.

The Goldsmith's Art in Ancient Mexico. By MARSHALL H. SAVILLE. Published by the Museum of the American Indian, Heye Foundation. (New York: 1920. Pp. 264.)

To most people the search for gold seems to have been the chief, if not the sole, motive of the Spanish conquerors in America. Nearly everyone has notions, however incorrect and nebulous, of the vast wealth of the native empires vanquished by Castile and by her tumbled in the dust. This small book by Professor Saville gives a vast amount of information about what the goldsmith's art of one of those empires really was.

Pages 8 to 107 inclusive are taken up with textual transcripts of inventories, notes and explanatory text revealing in great detail what was the nature of the gold found by the Spaniards in Mexico and to what persons it was assigned. The material here given is based on the accounts of Bernal Díaz del Castillo, Cervantes de Salazar, Cortés, and various inedited lists of loot existing in the archives of the Indies. Lists given by López de Gómara, Peter Martyr and other writers also appear. The impression created by reading these accounts of plunder is one of surprise at the great variation in the workmanship reported upon and admiration for the manner in which gold was combined with fine woods, cotton, feathers, deerskins, precious stones, and other objects either to make things of great beauty or to form a treasure of great value.

Pages 108 to 189 are taken up with excerpts from many ancient accounts of Mexican goldsmith's work. Especially important is Sahagún's account, in Nahuatl, published here on pages 125–142 with a translation into English of Seler's French version of the original. The entire goldworking technology of the Aztecs is here made very clearly understood by one of the most important writers. This particular part of Sahagún's work is relatively little known, as it was omitted by Sahagún himself in his abridged Spanish version. The remainder of the work is taken up with notes and an excellent index.

This will remain a first-rank work of reference for an important subdivision of the artistic life of the ancient Mexicans. The illustrations, both those which are colored and those in black-and-white, are admirable.

The proofreading has been carefully attended to. It is to be regretted that so excellent a monograph should have been given a format which does not harmonize with its character, and which must act as a deterrent to the intrinsic value of the work itself.

PHILIP AINSWORTH MEANS.

Mexican writers: a Catalogue of Books in the University of Arizona Library with Synopses and Biographical Notes. By ESTELLE LUTRELL, Librarian of the University of Arizona. (Tucson: 1920. Pp 83. Portraits.)

This useful reference work on Mexican bibliography is published as University of Arizona record, vol. XIII, no. 5, Library bibliography, no. 5. Full names and dates are given with important bio-bibliographical data of the more prominent Mexican authors of the modern period. The bibliography is arranged in five sections: Mexican writers; Literature in Spanish upon Mexican themes by authors native to other countries; Collections, literary criticism, biography; Bibliographies; and Mexican language. Miss Lutrell's contribution will be very helpful to students, and especially to librarians and cataloguers, since it contains much necessary information by no means easily accessible.

C. K. JONES.

Santo Domingo and Haiti. A Cruise with the Marines. By SAMUEL GUY INMAN, Executive Secretary of the Committee on Co-operation in Latin America. Report of a visit to these island republics in the summer of 1919. (New York: Committee on Co-operation in Latin America, 1920. Pp. 96. Sketch map. Paper.)

Dr. Inman's small volume is a "brief digest of religious, social, and educational conditions in the Dominican Republic and Haiti". Beyond his own observations, the writer claims no original investigation, and has made considerable use of the few sources available, including Schoenrich's *Santo Domingo, a Country with a Future*. He reproduces in whole or in part a report of United States Consul Clement S. Edwards relative to Santo Domingo, and a portion of a memorandum prepared for his use by an American resident of Haiti, besides making quotations from various religious writers. The work is timely and is an addition to our rather meager knowledge of these two republics that lie right at our own doorway. Santo Domingo is treated in six short chapters, namely:

General observations and travel notes; history, government, American occupation; commerce, transportation, resources; the people and their social problems; and eduction and religion.   Haiti is treated in seven chapters, namely: History; crossing the island; problems of American occupation; commerce and natural resources; education and sanitation; the people; and missions in Haiti.   The volume is concluded by a bibliographical list of six pages which will be found useful.

The impression left on the reader is the need for more concrete, complete, and universal knowledge concerning these two republics.   Dr. Inman is never wearisome in his descriptions, and writes throughout in a broad, tolerant spirit quite free from religious cant.   He has gone though this island, one of the richest in the world, with an eye open to all about him, and if the conditions which he has found are at times awful he has told them simply, while on the other hand he has not failed to praise what there is to praise.   In so small a compass as this pamphlet, it was impossible to give much of the history of the island; in fact only as much being given as will lead to an understanding of the work.   Considerable useful economic information is brought out, as well as social and educational.   Dr. Inman's discussion of the United States marines, the problems affecting them, and the effort to bring peace and prosperity to the island is sane.   Taking the work as a whole, one feels that there is the beginning of a book which Dr. Inman should write and in which better proportions might be shown than were possible in a volume of this small size.

JAMES ALEXANDER ROBERTSON.

Cuba Past and Present.   By A. Hyatt Verrill.   Revised edition with 1919 facts and figures.   (New York: Dodd, Mead & Company, 1920. Pp. (13), 240.   Illustrations.   Maps.)

The first edition of this volume, which was written as a popular handbook, was copyrighted in 1914.   In the eighteen chapters presented, the last, "Cuba's Share in the Great War," is new.   Other revisions are apparently slight, and consist in general of commercial and other data.   The aim of the writer in compiling the book is "to tell what the visitor to Cuba may expect, just how to see the various points of interest, how to travel from place to place, what to do and what *not* to do, . . . to paint Cuba as it really is—not as the steamship folders or the hotel advertisements would have us believe; and not to exaggerate its attractions nor to disparage it."   The first chapter dealing with the past history of Cuba is a mere summary; the second is also a cursory summary of various geographical factors; and the third is a slight discussion of Cuba's health and sanitation, past and present, education, agriculture, and immigration.

With chapter IV., the real purpose of the volume begins to be manifest, and the writer takes the traveler through Habana and its suburbs and the six provinces of the island, with a short excursion (chapter XI) to the Isle of Pines. These chapters are readable and give the traveler who is not too particular an excellent perspective of Cuba. Chapters XIII. to XVII. describe the highroads of Cuba; commercial and financial customs; Cuba's model clubs, hotels and restaurants and other items; and a few facts and figures, some of which are for 1918 and 1919.

The chapter on Cuba's model club, the Asociación de Dependientes del Comercio de la Habana", or Commercial Clerks' Club, which has a membership of at least 30,000, is of interest. The Gallegos Club has a membership of 37,000 Galician workmen, and there are other important clubs in Habana, including an American Club. Altogether, the book contains considerable information, and would make a handy companion to the traveler. The old saying that "It takes three Jews to beat a Greek, and three Greeks to beat an Armenian", appears as "It takes two Jews to beat a Greek, and two Greeks to beat a Gallego". The cost of living in Habana has risen considerably, partly due to reconstruction problems and partly to the prohibition amendment to the Constitution of the United States, which sends many people from this country to Cuba, inasmuch as Cuba is still a "wet" region. There is an occasional slip in the types and the illustrations are only fair.

                                        JAMES ALEXANDER ROBERTSON.

Cuba y las Costumbres Cubanas. By FRANK C. EWART, Professor of Romance Languages in Colgate University. (Boston, New York, etc.: Ginn and Company [°1919]. Pp. xxx, xiv, 157.)

Cuba y las Costumbres Cubanas was prepared "in harmony with the action of the Modern Language Association of America", which recommended that "the textbooks (of Spanish) embrace works dealing with the geography, history, and customs of Spanish-America as well as of Spain". The work "is the result of several months spent in Cuba", one purpose in its making being "to furnish . . . information with reference to the Spanish-American republic whose relations to the United States are the closest, and concerning which, above all others, we should be informed". The text is intended for high school and college use, and with the exception of certain selections from the

Boletín de la Unión Panamericana, was written in Cuba under the criticism of a Spanish teacher, probably Sr. José Fortuna y Salvado, of Habana, to whom the work is dedicated. This was in turn reviewed and in some places recast by Sr. T. Esquivel Obregón of New York.

The volume is one of the newer type of readers which of late have been helping to make the study of the modern languages in this country more sane than was formerly the case, for it appeals to the sense of the practical; and, after all, this is a criterion which cannot be neglected in the judgment of a work. The majority of people in the United States who study Spanish do so with a practical object in view rather than the merely cultural, and this volume, while its main object is to aid in the teaching of Spanish, gives useful information about one of our Hispanic American nieghbors. In its fourteen chapters, the author treats of the climate of Cuba, the port of Habana, first impressions of Habana, El Morro y La Cabana, the Plaza de Armas; Parks and streets; the Columbus cemetery; public education; notes on the future; Habana, the city with the most clubs of the world; a national fiesta; Christmas holidays; trip to Matanzas; and gives the words and music of the national hymn. A map of Cuba, questions, exercises, notes, and a vocabulary complete the reader. The volume is well illustrated by the author's own pictures. It should stimulate its readers to read the history of Cuba.

J. A. R.

Argentina: Legend and History. Readings selected and edited by GARIBALDI G. B. LAGUARDIA, A. M., and CINCINATO G. B. LAGUARDIA, A. B., of the United States Naval Academy. (Chicago, etc.: Benjamin H. Sanborn & Co. [°1919]. Pp. lviii, 411. Maps. Vocabulary.)

As one of the Hispanic Series which is being prepared under the editorship of Professor John D. Fitz-Gerald, of the University of Illinois, this volume will undoubtedly find considerable use. Like the volume mentioned above, it is one of the new type of reader that is revolutionizing the study of Spanish in the United States. The preface states that "the editors offer reading material which will give the student some idea of the history of Argentina, of her great men, of her development since the dawn of independence, and of her wonderful possibilities". The work is intended both for high school and for college use.

Selections are given from the writings of fourteen authors, of each of whom short biographical sketches are presented in English. These authors are Vicente López. Planes, the poet; Vicente Fidel López, the jurisconsult; Domingo F. Sarmiento, the educator and statesman; Carlos Octavio Bunge, a modern author; Manuela Gorriti, authoress and educator; Marcos Sastres, educator; Juan María Gutiérrez, lawyer, journalist, and educator; Pedro Lacassa, agriculturist and patriot; Bartolomé Mitre, historian, poet, soldier, and stateman; Ernesto Nelson, educator; Lucio V. López, political writer and critic; Vicente Blasco Ibánez, the Spanish novelist (the only author in the collection not an Argentinian); Luis María Drago, jurist, and author of the Drago Doctrine.

The text is preceded by an introduction in English of considerable length, in which the editors give a few of the main facts of Argentinian history. The selections are interesting and on the whole well chosen, and a number of illustrations of historical character add value to the volume.

J. A. R.

NOTES AND COMMENT

THE SECOND CONGRESS OF HISPANO-AMERICAN HISTORY AND GEOGRAPHY, SEVILLE, MAY, 1921

The Second Congress[1] of Hispano-American History and Geography, held at Seville, Spain, May 2-9, 1921, had two distinct aspects: one political and the other scientific. The Spanish policy was announced at the very beginning by the president of the congress, the Marqués de Laurencín. Its import is "the rehabilitation" of Spain, and Spain's investiture with the direction of world affairs through a "league of

[1] The writer is not aware that any society or organisation other than the committee in charge stands behind these congresses, the first of which was held at Seville in 1914. That they have the approval of the Spanish government is obvious; that government appropriated 60,000 *pesetas* to this second congress and doubtless was generous to the first. At the head of the organising committee stands the Marqués de Laurencín. He is actively assisted by Sres. Jerónimo Bécker and Joaquín Ciria. The first congress, held, as above said, at Seville in 1914—just before the war—attracted other than Hispanic-American delegates; for instance, Dutch and French, Netherlands and France having been invited to be represented because, as the Marqués de Laurencín explained to the writer, "of the part they took in the discovery and colonisation of America". The second congress seemed to have a somewhat different orientation. Asked if the United States had been invited to be represented at this second congress, its president, the Marqués de Laurencín, and its secretary, Sr. D. Jerónimo Bécker, explained to the writer that it had not, because the congress was "a family affair" (words of the Marqués de Laurencín) to which only Spanish-speaking independent nations were asked. The marquis said that this restriction was drawn in accordance with the unanimous opinion of the organisers of the congress. Inasmuch as the fourth section into which the congress was divided was devoted to the history and geography of the Philippines, the writer especially lamented the omission of these islands, but was informed that they had been invited to attend. Asked whether they had been invited as "an independent nation", or how, the Marqués de Laurencín replied that the organisers had not gone into that matter ("en eso no nos metimos"). The invitation was extended to "the superior authorities" of the Philippine Islands. [On the other hand, a prominent Spanish archivist is credited with the statement that invitations had been issued to historians of all countries, including the United States, but that no response had been received from the latter country.—J. A. R.]

nations" comprising "the race", *i.e.*, Spain and Hispanic America (including Portugal and Brazil).[2]

On the other hand, it appeared that, face to face with this policy, America has a policy of its own, for Argentina, throughout the proceedings of the congress, in the activities of the Argentine government delegate, Pascual Guaglianone, presented "Americanism, as we in America understand it"—a Pan-Americanism which was aptly worded by the Cuban delegate, Salvador Massip, when, in the course of debate, he defined: "America! From Alaska to Patagonia, without distinction of race, language, creed, or nationality!" In the closing address, given by Dr. Guaglianone, Argentina foretold for America, so defined, a leadership in world affairs which America will exercise in all fraternity, for liberty, justice, and advancement.

During the sessions of the congress the gradual defining of the issue noted above was marked by numerous incidents, never unpleasant, the most notable of which arose over the Argentine resolution to establish in the Archives of the Indies "an American public library" to consist of as many sections as there are republics in the New World. When this resolution came up for discussion a member of the congress (Father Linares, S. J.) asked what finality lay behind the use of the inclusive word "American", rather than the term "Hispano-American", and argued that the latter should be preferred, in order that the library so established might constitute a "monument to the race". The Argentine government delegate (Guaglianone), supported by the Cuban delegate (Massip), by the representative of the Ateneo Hispano-

---

[2] ". . . nuestra total rehabilitación ante el mundo. . . " (*Discurso leído en la Sesión inaugural del II. Congreso de Historia y Geografía Hispano-Americanas, celebrada en Sevilla en 2° de Mayo de 1921 por el Excmo. Sr. Marqués de Laurencín*, Madrid, 1921, p. 14). ". . . la unidad espiritual, la identidad del pensamiento, la comunidad en los ideales infinitamente superior a la unidad territorial y única capaz de volver a nuestra raza la influencia, el poderío, la grandeza que merece por sus gloriosas tradiciones en todas las esferas de la actividad humana. . . ." (*ibid.*, pp. 14–15). ". . . excelso ideal una Hispania que comprende a España y Portugal y a toda esa América* (Spanish-speaking) . . . *Hispania, sociedad de naciones*. . ." (Ramon Manjarres, in "La Denominación de América Latina", a paper presented to the congress which ended in a resolution, according to which the congress declared "the term Latin America improper; the term Ibero-América unnecessary", advocating instead "Hispanic" to mean that which is common to Spain and Portugal and to apply "to the America which proceeds from both". Sr. Manjarres's resolution was adopted; but the secretary, Sr. Bécker, did not read it at the closing session.

Americano of Buenos Aires (Carranza), and by the representative of the Centro Oficial de Estudios Americanistas of Seville (Gérman Latorre), favored the resolution as formulated, frankly defending the intentional use of the word "American" in its full, inclusive meaning. The further suggestion that ecclesiastical censorship should be established over the library, if founded, met with opposition from all quarters, Spanish and American alike, but finally, when the question was brought to a vote, the Guaglianone resolution passed with only one voice against it, that of Rev. Pablo Pastells, S. J.

In its scientific aspect, the congress was somewhat of a disappointment, especially to delegates who had come from a great distance on the supposition that they had been summoned to attend an important gathering of historians and geographers assembled for end solely scientific. Colombia was especially well represented, by eminent intellectuals: three government delegates—Raimundo Rivas, Eduardo Posada, president and secretary of the Academy of History at Bogotá, Ernesto Restrepo Tirado, for the Academy at Cartagena;—Luciano Herrera, chargé d'affaires of the Colombian legation at Madrid, invited by the organizers to attend and by the congress made chairman of the history section; and J. M. Pérez Sarmiento, Colombian consul at Cádiz. Cuba was represented by Salvador Massip and José María Chacón, both government delegates. Mexico was represented by the poet, Francisco A. de Icaza; Costa Rica and Guatemala, by their ministers accredited to France, the Marqués de Peralta and Manuel Valladares; Brazil, by its minister at Madrid, Alcibiades Peçanha; Honduras, by Pelayo Quintero, for the Academia Hispano-Americana of Cádiz, who presided over the first section; Argentina, by its government delegate, Pascual Guaglianone; Adolfo S. Carranza, for the Ateneo Hispano-Americano of Buenos Aires; Marcos H. Ayala, for the Academia Americana de Historia of Buenos Aires; José R. del Franco, for the Junta de Estudios Históricos of Cordoba.

For Spain were present Señores the Marqués de Laurencín, Bécker, Beltran y Rospide, and Blázquez from the Academy of History, but without special commission. Sr. Blázquez presided over the fourth section. The Sociedad Geográfica Comercial of Barcelona was represented by Roberto Beltran y Rospide, who presided over the third section; the Royal Geographic society by Sres. Beltran y Rospide and Ciria; the Centro Cultura Hispano-Americana, by Manuel Rodríguez Navas; the Union Ibero-Americano, by its president, the Marqués de Figueroa; the Royal Academy of Exact, Physical, and Natural Sciences,

at Madrid, by Gustavo Fernández de Bastos.[3] The presence of other
individual members of the congress helped to maintain the average
attendance at its sessions at about thirty persons.

The inaugural session was held in the Classic Arts buildings on the
Hispano-American fair grounds; the others were held in the assembly
room of the Chamber of Commerce in the Lonja building. The congress was divided into four sections: 1st, Pre-Spanish history, America
and the Philippines; 2nd, History of America; 3rd, Geography of
America; 4th, History and Geography of the Philippines.

To all intents and purposes no special requirements nor standards
were specified for the papers presented to the congress. No degree of
excellence or originality was demanded. In consequence, together
with certain papers of unquestioned excellence, books and pamphlets
previously published, a special edition of a propagandist periodical,
and some papers of little or no merit were presented and received with
indiscriminate courtesy.[4] As noted above, however, the grist was not
without kernels of real worth.[5]

Among these were notable[6] the papers proffered by the Colombian
delegates, Sres. Rivas and Posada—"A Biography of Gonzalo

---

[3] Inasmuch as no official list of delegates seems to have been prepared, complete accuracy of the foregoing cannot be guaranteed.

[4] The papers fell easily into two classes: propaganda, and contributions to
knowledge of history and geography. Among the former may be mentioned:
"Criollos empleados", by Manuel de Castro y López: a defense of Spain against
charges of discrimination in government employment; "Textos escolares", by
the same: a protest against exaggerated ("false and anti-Spanish") text books;
"La Denominación 'América Latina'" by Ramón Manjarres; "España en
América", by Adolfo S. Carranza; "Carácter de la Colonización Española en
América" by Rev. Angel Clavero Navarro, Córdoba (R. A.): a protest against
"hate" and "indignation" in opinions concerning Spain's policies; "La Enseñanza de la Historia y la Solidaridad Hispano-Americana", by José R. del
Franco.

[5] Official but incomplete lists of the papers presented in the first, third and
fourth sections were available. No official list covering the second section could
be had.

[6] In the very few days during which most of the papers presented to this congress
lay upon the table for examination, the writer had not the time to formulate a
fair judgment of them. Those mentioned seemed, however, to constitute fresh
contributions to general knowledge, and, by their outward form and in their
substance, to show respect for sources and for accepted standards of presentation. As is stated, there was absolutely no discussion of the work laid before
the congress, which might have brought out a fairer estimate of real values than
any one person in a hasty inspection could possibly hope to make for himself.

Jiménez de Quesada", and "A Biographical Dictionary of the Discoverers and Conquerors of the Kingdom of New Granada", by
Sr. Rivas; "Bibliographical Data concerning the Native Languages of
Colombia"; "A Vocabulary, Indigenous Languages of Colombia",
and "Cartography of Colombia", by Sr. Posada. Sr. Rivas's "Biographical Dictionary of the Discoverers and Conquerors of the Kingdom of New Granada" will consist when complete of 160 biographical
sketches of the men who served under Gonzalo Jiménez de Quesada,
of which Sr. Rivas was able to present twenty-five to the congress.
Needless to say, these works are all based upon original research and
are properly annotated.

The Rev. Constantino Bayle, S. J., presented a good work on the
accomplishments (geographical and colonization) of the Jesuits in
California, with an appendix of documents, a list of still others consulted, and a collection of maps (photographs) from the Archives of the
Indies. Rev. Atanasio López, O. S. F., editor of *La Revista Archivo
Ibero-Americano*, a magazine published in Madrid, devoted to setting
forth the record of the Franciscans in America, gave an account of
that review which showed valuable contribution made to the available
supply of material for history, in the shape of rare and inaccessible
documents it has printed. The same gentleman laid before the congress an account of "The first twelve Apostles in Mexico", constituting
that mission which reached Vera Cruz on May 13, 1524.

Jesús Pabón and Luis Jiménez-Placer y Ciaurrez presented "Some
Documents from the Archives of the Indies concerning Chilean Cities"
(articles of foundation, titles of "loyal", etc.), with an appendix of
six good photographs of related maps.

Among contributions sent from Argentina was one entitled "Formalidades Forenses en la Época Colonial", presented on behalf of
Rev. Pedro Grenón, S. J., of Córdoba. This consisted of documents
which set forth the curious old forms used in taking possession, for
instance, of an estate, in founding a city, a church, in transferring a
house, etc. The presbyter, D. Pablo Cabrera, of Córdoba also, sent
in a study of "El Famatina", a "lost" poem by Rosas de Oquendo.

Of a similar character was the paper on "El Espejo de Paciencia"
by Silvestre de Balboa, written concerning the sequestration of Bishop
Cabezas of Cuba, in 1604, and preserved in Bishop Morel's history of
that island, long supposed to be lost. This paper, with an appendix of

unedited documents (including the bishop's account of the incident) was presented by the Cuban delegate, José María Chacón y Calvo.[7]

Among good papers laid before the congress in the third section (geography) was "A Pre–Colombian Voyage of the Chinese to North America", by Salvador Massip, and in the fourth section attention was drawn to three unedited, valuable manuscripts. One, "Un Nuevo relato de la expedicion de Garcia Loaisa", presented by Antonio Blázquez, is to be found in the National Library at Madrid and is attributed to Jeronimo de Santiesteban. Another, "Retrato Geografico-historico-apologetico de las Islas Filipinas con un apendice de las Islas de Palaos o Carolinas y de las Marianas", 139 folios, quarto, 1789, attributed to Juan Antonio Tornos, is preserved in the Academy of History, Madrid; the paper concerning it was presented to this congress by Angel Blázquez Jiménez. The third, presented by Francisco V. Silva, is an "Itinerario Maritimo de California al Rio de la Plata" (National Library, Madrid, MSS. Division, No. 2957), folio, parchment, 151 pages, anonymous.

The congress passed various resolutions, among which should be mentioned those (generally originating with Argentina) which sought to initiate, encourage, or direct methods and opportunities for scientific work.[8] In adjourning, the congress resolved to meet in Seville in 1924, when, it is hoped, the Hispanic American exposition will be held; it was further resolved to meet in Buenos Aires in 1926.[9]

IRENE A. WRIGHT.

[7] Miss Wright should also have mentioned her own work, which was presented to the congress in English on "Don Pedro de Valdes, Governor of Cuba, 1600–1608," with an appendix of sixty-one documents from the Archives of the Indies, and consisting of letters and memorials of Valdes. The introductory study is a history of Cuba in the first decade of the seventeenth century and carries Miss Wright's work on Cuba forward in the chronological order she has followed in her several works.—J. A. R.

[8] The writer has been unable to obtain a copy of the resolutions passed by the c···ress in its sections, and approved at the closing session, as read by the ϝ···· ⁻v, but doubtless a request addressed to Sr. D. Jerónimo Bécker, Lista 22, M   · ·ould bring any inquirer the official record of the congress, which is t(· ·   ʾ·ᴅ.

[9] · ·   ʌent of the third congress was left in the hands of the same cᴜᴍᴀ·'·   ᴄh organized the second, of which committee Sr. D. Jerónimo Bécker, :   22, Madrid, is secretary, to whom all correspondence should be addresseʋ

Apropos of the Hispano-American Congress, report of which appears above, *El Sol*, of Madrid, in its issue of April 26, 1921, says:

The Congress of Hispanic American history and geography which will be inaugurated at Seville on May 1, . . . promises to be a real event. The majority of the states of Spanish America have already sent their delegates, and the arrival of others is expected before the end of the month.

Argentina will be represented by the subinspector general of teaching, D. Pascual Guglianone; Chile, by the illustrious historian, Don José Toribio Medina; Colombia, by the minister at Madrid, Don Francisco José de Urrutia, ex-president of the senate and ex-minister of foreign relations, by Sres. Rivas and Posada, president and secretary of the Academia de la Historia de Bogotá, by General Restrepo Tirado, and by its consul general in Cádiz, Sr. Pérez Sarmiento; Guatemala, by its minister at Paris, Don Manuel Valladares; Ecuador, by Don Jacinto Jijón y Caamaño; Peru, by Don Luis Ulloa; Brazil, by its plenipotentiary at Madrid, D. Alcibiades Peçanha; Costa Rica, by its minister to Spain, Don Manuel María Peralta; and Cuba, by the university professor, Salvador Massip.

Delegates from various cultural centers of America and Spain will also be present. The Academia de Estudios Diplomáticos de Bogotá, will be represented by Dr. González Brun; the Academia de la Historia de Cartagena de Indias, by Sr. Restrepo; the Academia Americana de la Historia de Buenos Aires, by Don Marcos H. Ayala; the Ateneo Hispanoamericano of the same capital, by Don Adolfo S. Carranza; the Unión Iberoamericana de Madrid, by its president, the Marquis of Figueroa; the Academia Hispanoamericano de Ciencias y Artes de Cádiz, by Sres. Quintero, Pérez Sarmiento, Cebrián, Solier y Ayala (Don Sebastián); the Real Academia de Ciencias Exactas, Físicas y Naturales, by Sr Fernández Bastos; the Junta de Estudios Históricas de Córdoba (Argentina), by Don José R. del Franco. The Instituto Histórico y Geográfica de Rio de Janeiro, the Universidad Central, the Real Academia de la Historia, and the Real Sociedad Geográfica will also be represented. In addition to those mentioned above, several others of the American representatives accredited to Madrid propose to be present, for instance, Sr. Levillier, of Argentina; Don Ismael G. Fuentes, of Salvador; Sr. Ortega, of Guatamala; and Don Luciano Herrera, of Colombia. The president of the Comisión Mexicana de Estudios e Investigaciones Históricas en los Archivos Nacionales de Europa, Sr. Icaza, will also be present.

At the inaugural session, the president and secretary of the congress, the Marquis of Laurencin and Sr. Bécker, one of the authorities of Seville, the minister of Brazil, Sr. Peçanha, the minister of public instruction, Sr. Aparicio, and probably the president of the Academia de la Historia de Bogotá, Sr. Rivas, will make addresses.

The organizers of the congress propose that the resolutions adopted shall be eminently practical and signalize the beginning of a vigorous and effective campaign for the intellectual drawing together of all the countries of Spanish origin.

Independently of the sessions of the congress, and during the period of its celebration, the marquis of Figueroa and Sr. Bécker will hold meetings in Seville in regard to the problem of Hispanic America.

PERU'S PROGRESSIVE EDUCATIONAL PROGRAM

The twentieth century has witnessed two notable examples of the ability of American educators to evolve satisfactory systems of public education for countries in which fundamental conditions are radically different from those prevailing in the United States. The remarkable degree of success whch has been achieved in implanting new school systems in the Philippine Islands and in Porto Rico within a short span of years is now usually admitted by those who are familiar with the work that has been in progress in those countries. It is doubtless on account of the adaptability and efficiency manifested in the work done in these former colonies of Spain that American educational experts have again been called upon to undertake a third great experiment in modern education. This latest task is the complete reorganization and initial administration of the entire system of public instruction in one of the most traditionally conservative of the South American republics—that of Peru.

During the past Hispanic America usually looked to Europe rather than to the United States for inspiration in educational matters. British and German schools were founded in many of the southern republics, while French ideas have been so influential that it is a common saying that Paris has been the intellectual capital of the countries of Hispanic origin in America. Of late years, however, the influence of the United States has been growing. South American students in increasing numbers are now seeking their education in the northern continent. Various of the Hispanic American governments have sent groups of teachers to study our methods of teaching. An interchange of professors between certain of the institutions of higher learning in the United States and Hispanic America has been recently inaugurated. Peru is the first of the southern republics, however, to take the radical step of turning over its entire system of public education to an American mission on the ground. It is for this reason that special interest is attached to the Peruvian educational program now under way, affording as it will another severe test of the ability of Americans to adapt their pedagogical methods to a foreign environment.

The ground has been cleared for the present movement in Peru by a new law of public instruction promulgated during the past year. This legislation, which is the result of ten years of investigation and study by Peruvian and American experts, has merely erected the framework of the new system, leaving the final details to be worked out by the American administrators in view of local conditions encountered and of the experience acquired in the actual operation of the law.

The first step taken in the execution of this law was the selection of experienced men to administer it. The Peruvian government entrusted this important task to Dr. Harry Erwin Bard, well known in American educational circles, who has been associated with educational reform in Peru since the inception of the present movement. He was a member of the original commission appointed in 1910 during the first administration of President Leguía. The labors of this body were continued under successive administrations, and when President Leguía was reelected in 1919 he again called upon Dr. Bard to supervise the final revision of the plan that had been formulated, in consequence of which the recent legislation was enacted by the Peruvian congress.

Returning to the United States in the summer of 1920, Dr. Bard engaged twenty-four American educators, each a specialist in his respective field, to aid in the administration of the new law. Several of the men formerly held important posts in the Philippine school system, where Dr. Bard also had extensive experience. All are now in Peru, and have entered upon the active discharge of their duties, under the supervision of Dr. Bard, who has been appointed Director General of Education for the entire republic.

The assignments to the more important administrative posts are as follows: Frank A. Crone, director of schoolhouse construction; William W. Andrew, regional director for the Center; Glenn L. Caulkins, regional director for the South; Forrest B. Spaulding, director of school libraries and museums; Lester M. Wilson, director of examinations and studies; Frank L. Andrews, director of athletics and students' activities; Herbert G. Lull, dean of the Superior School of Pedagogical Sciences; Ernest C. Phillips, dean of the Superior School of Industrial Arts; and William E. Dunn, dean of the Superior School of Commerce. Fourteen other Americans have been assigned to various positions in colleges of secondary instruction throughout the republic.

The new Peruvian law provides for a well coordinated system of public intruction from the primary schools to the universities. Particular emphasis has been placed on the training of teachers. In Peru, as in many other Hispanic American countries, teaching has been done largely by men who devote most of their time to some other profession or business. Especially is this true of the higher branches of instruction. The law endeavors to remedy this fundamental evil by establishing modern normal schools, by insisting upon full-time service, and by granting adequate compensation, with pensions for long service, thus making it possible to build up a permanent corps of competent professional teachers. Facilities are also provided for the training of Peruvians in the science and technique of administration so that they may be qualified to take over the direction of the school system as soon as practicable.

Another important innovation is the introduction of vocational studies into the secondary schools and higher institutions of learning. This feature should be of especial value for Peru in view of the heritage of technical skill which has come down from the days of the old Inca empire. Ancient Peru was the seat of the most highly developed industries found in the western hemisphere, some of the work done in weaving and the decorative arts not being surpassed by modern artisans, and it is hoped that these ancient traditions will be speedily revived.

Important additions have been made to Peru's facilities for higher education. The University of San Marcos, the oldest in the New World, remains under the law the crowning glory of the system. This venerable institution, founded in 1551—more than three-quarters of a century before the United States could boast of its first university— enjoys a well deserved prestige as the guardian of the best cultural traditions of the southern continent, and its influence is still more potent perhaps than any other university in Hispanic America.

To meet the trend of modern educational thought along the lines of vocational training, however, a new University of Technical Schools has been created. It is composed of the National Schools of Engineering and of Agriculture, already well established and of new Schools of Pedagogical Sciences, of Industrial Arts, and of Commerce. Provision is made in the law for the incorporation of these schools as integral parts of the University of San Marcos if such a step later seems desirable. There is some opposition in Peru, as is to be expected in a country which for three centuries was a stronghold of Spanish conservatism, to any departure from the traditional lines of university instruction, but such opposition will doubtless gradually disappear, as has been the case in other countries where practical vocational training is now given in the oldest and most conservative universities.

In certain respects the problems of the American educational mission to Peru will be more difficult than those encountered in the Philippine Islands or in Porto Rico. Public education in Hispanic America is inseparably connected with politics. The independence enjoyed by

the schools and colleges of the United States is inconceivable in the
southern republics. The American educators in Peru will undoubtedly
have to face a certain amount of opposition arising from political motives.
They will have the advantage, on the other hand, of working among a
people whose influential classes are famed for their national patriotism,
their enlightened culture, and their sympathetic attitude toward the
United States.

Financial handicaps must also be overcome. While Peru is potentially perhaps the richest country in South America, it is still in the
early stages of development. The standard of living of the bulk of
the population, at least half of which is of pure Indian stock, does not
yet demand the creation of great wealth. It speaks well for the
courage and vision of the present administration in Peru that it is
persevering in its educational program in spite of the present world-
wide financial depression which has seriously affected the national
revenues. The present stringency, however, is not expected to interfere with the work of the educational mission, although the necessity
for economy may make progress at the outset slower than had been
anticipated. The success of the experiment will depend chiefly on
the extent to which all elements in Peruvian society lend it their
support. Peru's good record in matters affecting its national prestige
and progress affords every reason for believing that the nation as
a whole will do its part.

WILLIAM E. DUNN.

At a scientific international congress celebrated at Buenos Aires in
1910, it was decided to draw up a project for an international Hispanic
American Union of Bibliography and Technology. This plan was
drawn up by the Argentine engineer, Sr. Santiago E. Barabino and by
the Spanish delegate, Sr. Leonardo Torres Quevedo. The primary
purposes of such a Union was to prepare a catalogue of the best
scientific works, to be published in Spanish; the elaboration and publication of a dictionary on technology in Spanish; and the establishment
of a scientific and technical library of Spanish works, which would
publish original works as well as translate works from other languages,
works which are considered fundamental in the different branches of
human knowledge. For the past ten years this plan seems to have
been forgotten but has been recently revived in Spain with a great
deal of enthusiasm by the Spanish Academy, which was inspired to
some extent by the recent Postal Congress which met in Madrid during

November and December. It was decided that Spain take the initiative in this important scientific project which will mean so much to the science of all Spanish-speaking peoples. A commission has been created to have charge of Spain's part in this great undertaking.

The general regulations of the International Congress of the History of America to be held in Brazil in 1922 in celebration of the centenary of the independence of Brazil have been issued under the following title: Congresso Internacional de Historia de America. Promovido pelo Instituto Historico e Geographico Brasileiro para commemorar o centenario da Independencia do Brazil, a 7 de Setembro de 1922. Regulamento Geral. Theses da 15ª secção Historia do Brasil. This bears imprint Rio de Janeiro, Imprensa Nacional, 1921, and is a pamphlet of 38 pages. The sections of the congress will be as follows: General history of America; history of the United States of North America; history of Mexico; history of Guatemala; history of Honduras; history of San Salvador; history of Nicaragua; history of Costa Rica; history of Panama; history of Colombia; history of Venezuela; history of Ecuador; history of Peru; history of Bolivia; history of Brazil; history of Paraguay; history of Chile; history of the Argentine Republic history of Uruguay; history of Cuba; history of the Dominican Republic; history of Haiti; history of the Dominion of Canada; history of English Guiana; history of Dutch Guiana; history of French Guiana; history of the English insular colonies of America and of British Honduras; history of the French insular colonies in America; history of the Dutch insular colonies in America; history of the Danish insular colonies in America—30 sections in all. Each section is subdivided into the following subsections: general history; history of geographical explorations; history of archeological and ethnographical explorations; constitutional and administrative history; parliamentary history; economic history; military history; diplomatic history; literary history and history of the arts. The 15th section is the History of Brazil. The pamphlet gives for each subsection of this section the subjects that have been approved by the Central Executive Committee of the Congress. If the program is carried out as planned this promises to be one of the most notable and important historical gatherings ever celebrated on the American continent. It is hoped that many historical scholars from the United States of North America will attend these meetings. The congress has been planned in an excellent and far reaching manner.

The *Boletín del Centro de Informacion Comercial* of February 28 publishes an article from the Spanish Consul at San José, Costa Rica, which urges that Spain take advantage of the present propitious conditions in Hispanic America to introduce more Spanish literature into Hispanic America, not only as a means of cultural propaganda but commercial propaganda as well. He states that since the war Spain has gained added prestige in the Hispanic American countries and that the other European countries have lost in this respect, which has given rise to a keener interest in all things Spanish, especially in Spanish literature. French literature, which was so popular in Hispanic America before the war, is losing its hold and the way is clear for Spanish editors to supply the market left open by the French. This writer believes that the Spanish book can be the means of close intellectual and political, as well as commercial, relations between Spain and the Hispanic American countries. He urges the Spanish editors especially to take an active interest in the Exposición Feria-Muestrario Española which is to be held in San José from the 15th to the 30th of September, 1921, and at which one section will be dedicated to Spanish literature.

Professor Milledge L. Bonham, Jr., in a letter to the editor of the *Utica Daily Press*, of May 26, 1921, apropos of an editorial note in that paper relative to propaganda against the United States in Hispanic America, calls attention to the fact that the widespread feeling of suspicion against the United States in Hispanic America is perhaps in some degree justified and that much of it is based on a misunderstanding of the purposes and principles of our foreign policy. Professor Bonham says that as there is a very large illiterate element in Hispanic America, it is quite easy for unscrupulous native demagogues and agents of our trade rivals to foment distrust of the United States for their own purposes. Continuing, Professor Bonham says:

Many of the leaders of thought in Hispanic America fully understand our reasons for intervention in Cuba, Haiti, Santo Domingo, Nicaragua and Honduras, and more recently, in the dispute between Panama and Costa Rica. These leaders trust the purity of our intentions. Others, however, believe these incidents, and such incidents as the recognition of Panama, the Mexican war, the Chilean incident of 1891-92, even the actions of Presidents Cleveland and Roosevelt in protecting Venezuela from foreign aggregation, show that the United States is using the Monroe Doctrine as a "big stick" to keep Europe off, while Uncle Sam establishes his own hegemony in Hispanic America. Prof. Dunning has pointed out that the historical importance of a theory is not its truth, but the degree to which the people of a given area and epoch believe it to be true.

So though you and I are perfectly certain that we have no such aim, it cannot be doubted that many Hispanic Americans do so believe.

In the course in Hispanic American history at Hamilton College, the effort is made to impress upon the students the necessity of comprehending the Hispanic American viewpoint in order to help remove just such misunderstandings. I feel sure that this is true of every college and university giving a course in Hispanic American history.

But only a small percentage of our citizens ever have an opportunity to take such a course. Yet it is quite feasible for any citizen interested in promoting the country's best interests to get abundant information from the public libraries. So it is the intention of this letter to bring to the attention of your readers some of the most accessible sources of information.

THE HISPANIC AMERICAN HISTORICAL REVIEW is a quarterly that publishes much valuable information, both past and current, about Hispanic America. I wish to call especial attention to the following articles:

Obregon, "Factors in the Historical Evolution of Mexico," May, 1919.

Baum, "German Political Designs with Reference to Brazil," November, 1919.

Perry, "Anti-American Propaganda in Hispanic America," February, 1920.

Dunn, "Post-war Attitude of Hispanic America Toward the United States," May, 1920.

Dr. Percy A. Martin of Stanford University, in his excellent pamphlet, *Latin America and the War* (Published by the World Peace Foundation), points out that German teachers and German officers in South American armies have long kept up a pro-German and anti-United States agitation. Its effects were particularly noteworthy in Chile and Argentina in 1917.

I sincerely wish that every citizen of the United States would read carefully Dr. Dana G. Munro's masterly monograph *The Five Republics of Central America*. In this he shows clearly some of the reasons why Uncle Sam is disgusted in Hispanic America and suggests means of counteracting this.

Prof. E. A. Ross in his *South of Panama* points out that to the Hispanic American, with his courtly, if somewhat florid manners, the brusquer manners of the North American do not indicate a greater frankness or sincerity, but a cold, selfish avariciousness. Again, both in Canada and Hispanic America we find a resentment of our arrogation of the term "American" to describe a citizen of the United States. The Chileno, the Brazilian, the Manitoban or the Mexican feels that he is just as much an American as the native of the United States.

Prof. W. R. Shepherd's little monograph, in the Home University Library, *Latin America*, presents an excellent though brief survey of Hispanic American civilization, from a sympathetic viewpoint.

Of course the bulletins of the Pan-American Union are invaluable for a knowledge of social, political, and economic progress in the countries of Hispanic America. From these publications, as from countless other sources, the manufacturers and exporters of the United States can learn, if they will, that to succeed in capturing and holding Hispanic American trade, they must study closely and sympathetically the needs of these customers, and supply their wants. British, French, and German business men had been doing this for many years, so that it is not surprising that in 1913 these countries handled 54 per cent of

Hispanic American foreign commerce, while the United States controlled only about 17 per cent.

Two articles in the *Journal of International Relations* also deserve careful perusal:

Volume X, page 135: "The Pan-American Union and the Monroe Doctrine." Same, page 392: "The Future of the Monroe Doctrine."

In the annals of the American Academy of Social and Political Science, volume 54 can be found a series of fine articles on Pan-American relations, including a study of the Hispanic American view of the Monroe Doctrine.

In conclusion, I wish to urge the reading of two illuminating volumes by distinguished Hispanic American scholars.

F. Garcia-Calderon, *Latin America*, and Rafael Reyes, the *Two Americas*. Nor should Lord Bryce's brilliant book, *South America*, be overlooked.

Yours very truly,

MILLEDGE L. BONHAM, JR.

It is gratifying to note the organization of a "subcommittee on library coöperation with Latin America" of the American Library Association. There is obviously a field for such an organization in developing intellectual and cultural relations between the American republics, while serving the more immediate and practical purpose of improved trade relations. The Report of the subcommittee prepared for the recent meeting of the Libarary Association by Frederick C. Hicks and Peter H. Goldsmith is in four sections: (1) Work accomplished by existing institutions; (2) Library conditions in the Hispanic American countries; (3) work accomplished by the subcommittee: a list of Hispanic American book publishers and dealers; (4) Proposals as to future work. To quote from the last section the objectives set up by the subcommittee:

Such a committee would serve: (1) As a medium for exchange of thought between the libraries and library organizations of the respective countries; (2) To inform libraries of the United States and of the Hispanic countries of the development of publications in the other countries; (3) To communicate the names of new publishers and booksellers; (4) To give advice to librarians of the United States and Canada regarding books and periodicals published in the Hispanic countries, and to those of the Hispanic countries regarding books or magazines published in the United States and Canada; (5) To assist libraries to acquire by subscription reviews and magazines published in the American countries; (6) As a link between the Association and other organizations with which it might coöperate in the same field.

The appendix gives a description of the material illustrative of Hispanic-American periodicals exhibited at the Swampscott conference.—C. K. JONES.

Senator Francos Rodríguez of the Spanish senate is greatly interested in the development of closer relations between Spain and the countries of Hispanic America. He has made a number of speeches in the Spanish senate with that object in view.

Professor Halford L. Hoskins, of Tufts College, has prepared an extensive syllabus on Hispanic American history, which it is expected will soon be published. Professor Hoskins is scheduled to teach in the summer session of the Cleveland School of Education and Western Reserve University, at Cleveland this year. His course, which is "History Si6S," is entitled "History of Latin America" and is described as follows:

A general course, intended particularly for those interested in the expansion of the Hispanic languages and institutions, and, from a more practical viewpoint, those desiring to promote better political and commercial relations with Latin America. The course aims to present the salient facts in the development of the Latin American republics from a sympathetic point of view as a means of removing prejudice and providing the basis for better understanding with our southern neighbors. Beginning with the expansion of Spain and Portugal the central theme will follow rapidly the stages of colonial development, the wars of independence, and the evolution of types of Hispanic American nations, reserving for more detailed and careful consideration recent and contemporary cultural advancement, domestic problems, foreign political and commercial contact, and the idea of Pan-Americanism. Primarily a lecture course, requiring broad, general reading, and reports on special topics. 1 hour daily. 2 semester hours credit.

This class has a large enrolment of enthusiastic students, some of whom are expecting to enter business in Hispanic America. Mr. Hoskins will also give courses in "The Rise and Expansion of the British Empire" and "Europe since 1815".

Mr. Gilberto de Mello Freyre, of Pernambuco, Brazil, is attending the graduate school of Columbia University. He will present a thesis on "Social Conditions of Brazil from 1855 to 1860, including the organization of the family, the social life, the means of traveling, business customs, and the industrial and economic organization. Mr. Freyre, who holds a scholarship in American history at Columbia for the coming year, has recently been elected a member of the Academy of Letters of Pernambuco, He recently revised Dr. J. C. Branner's Portuguese edition of the Geology of Brazil. After obtaining his Ph. D. at Columbia, Mr. Freyre plans to spend at least one year at Oxford.

Professor Percy Alvin Martin selected for the title to his course of Lectures, given as the Albert Shaw Foundation lectures in Johns Hopkins University in spring of this year, "Hispanic America and the War". The course embraced the following matters: Lecture I. Introduction. Scope and character of the series. Discussion of the material used. Brief survey of Hispanic America on the eve of the war. II. Cuba and the war. III. Brazil and the war. IV., V. and VI. Argentina and the war. VII. and VIII. Chile and the war. IX. The remaining Hispanic American Republics and the war. X. The remaining Hispanic American Republics and the war. The results of the war as affecting the national and international status of the Hispanic American Republics and their relations with the United States. The lectures will shortly be published and the appearance of Dr. Martin's book will be awaited with interest.

Dr. William W. Pierson, Jr., of the University of North Carolina is teaching in Summer School at Texas University this year. He will give courses in Hispanic American history.

Professor William R. Shepherd, of Columbia University, attended as delegate for Columbia University the Anglo-American conference of Professors of History at London, in July. Beginning with September of this year, he will be professor of American History in the Centro de Estudios Históricos at Madrid, under the auspices of the Junta para Ampliación de Estudios. During this period, he will probably also lecture on historical subjects before Spanish universities. Next spring, Professor Shepherd will lecture before British universities under the auspices of the Institute of International Education.

Mr. Philip Ainsworth Means, who was recently appointed curator of the National Museum of Lima, Peru, has resigned his position and has returned to the United States. This review has published two papers by Mr. Means, besides a number of book reviews written by him.

Sr. D. Rafael Heliodoro Valle, who was connected with the Honduran mission in Washington, D. C., for some time, has been appointed Chief of the Division of Publications of the Museo Nacional de Arqueología, Historia y Ethnología of Mexico City. Sr. Valle contributes bibliographical notes relative to Mexico and Central America in this number of the REVIEW.

Professors Charles E. Chapman and Herbert Ingram Priestley, of the Unversity of California, spent part of the summer in Mexico.

The death on October 7, 1920, of Dr. Homer J. Webster, acting head of the history department of the University of Pittsburg, threw the department into some disorder and it became necessary to reorganize the department immediately. Dr. Webster had planned for the academic year, 1921, a two-hour semester course in Hispanic American history. This work was taken up after his sudden demise by Assistant Professor James. The course was accordingly introduced, and was made open only to juniors, seniors, and graduate students. Enrollment for the first semester was thirty and for the second twenty-five. During the first semester, Latané's *The United States and Latin America* was used for an outline text and considerable collateral reading required. During the second semester, something of the history of Spain, Portugal, and early discoveries, explorations, and colonizations was studied, use being made of Pierson's *Syllabus of Hispanic American History*. It was fully realized that the first semester's work should have been given during the second semester, but in the disorganization caused by Dr. Webster's death it was impossible to obtain material for a study of the discovery and subsequent exploration and colonization. "Strange to say," says Dr. James, "things worked out well. This was the path of association, the psychological approach to the subject for upper classmen who were already familiar with the history of the United States. While unsound chronologically and wrong from the standpoint of logical evolution, no regret for this necessary procedure was seen by any one concerned." Great interest was displayed in the course by the students and the situation for the future of the study of Hispanic American history in the University of Pittsburgh is excellent.

BIBLIOGRAPHICAL SECTION

HISPANIC AMERICAN BIBLIOGRAPHIES

Continuation

966. Bibliografía y cartografía de Nicaragua.   (*In* Centro-América, Guatemala, 1914.   24½ cm.   v. 6, p. 548–561.)

A short reading list, with notices of 78 maps, 1822–1900.

967. Kalb, Courtenay de.   A bibliography of the Mosquito Coast of Nicaragua. (*In* Journal of the American geographical society.   New York, 1894. 24½ cm.   v. xxvi, p. 241–248.)

968. Lévy, Pablo.   Notas geográficas y económicas sobre la república de Nicaragua, y una exposición completa de la cuestión del canal interoceánico y de la de inmigración con una lista bibliográfica, la mas completa hasta el día, de todos los libros y mapas relativos á la América central y general y á Nicaragua en particular.   Paris, E. Denné Schmitz, 1873.

xvi, 627, [1] p.   fold. map.   26½ cm.
Bibliografía y cartografía: p. [603]–613.

969. Nicaragua.   Biblioteca nacional.   Catálogo general de los libros de que consta la Biblioteca nacional de la República de Nicaragua.   Managua, Tip. de Managua, 1882.

1 p. l., 90 p.   30½ cm.

——— ——— Managua, 1906.

990. Nicaragua.   Ministerio de relaciones exteriores.   Cuerpo diplomático y consular.   Managua, Compañía tip. internacional, 1907.

16 p.   24 cm.

991. Pector, Désiré.   Exposé sommaire des voyages et travaux géographiques au Nicaragua dans le cours du XIX siècle.   Paris, Bibliothèque des Annales économiques, 1891.

8p. 24 cm.

992. Aguilera, Rodolfo.   Galería de hombres públicos del Istmo.   Panama, Tip. Casis y cia, 1906.

3 p. l., 103 p.   port.   22 cm.

993. ——— Istmeños ilustres de la emancipación.   Panamá, 1887.

994. Bridgeport, Conn. Public library. Panama and the Pacific; a reading list on the Panama canal, South and Central America, Mexico, California and the west and Alaska. Bridgeport, Conn., 1915.

12 p. 19 cm.

995. Guía-directorio de la ciudad de Panamá; guía del extranjero, consultor y auxiliar del comerciante, cicerone del tourista. año 1- Panama, Tip. Chevalier, Andreve & cía., 1906-. plates, ports. 21½ cm.

996. Méndes Pereira, Octavio. Parnaso panameño, con prólogo y biografías. Panama, Tip. el Istmo, 1916.

3 p. l., ix, 392, [7] p. 18 cm.

997. New York. Public library. American interoceanic canals; a list of references in the New York public library. Comp. by John C. Frank. New York, Public library, 1916.

iii, 90 p. 25½ cm.
"Reprinted ... from the Bulletin of the New York public library of January 1916."

998. Riverside, Cal. Public library. Panama canal; an old way to California made new. Riverside, 1912.

16 p. 17 cm. (Its Bulletin 75)

999. Scott, John. A bibliography of printed documents and books relating to the Darien company. By John Scott, rev. by George P. Johnston. Edinburgh, Priv. print., 1903.

54 p. 30 cm.

————— ————— With additions and corrections by George P. Johnston, Edinburgh, Priv. print., 1906.

1 p. l., [55]-75 p. 30 cm.

1000. U. S. Library of Congress. List of books and of articles in periodicals relating to interoceanic canal and railway routes. By Hugh A. Morrison. Washington, Govt. print. off., 1900.

174 p. 23 cm. (56th Congress, 1st session. Senate doc. 59).

1001. ————— List of references on the Panama Canal and the Panama Canal Zone. Prepared under direction of H. H. B. Meyer, chief bibliographer. Washington, Govt. print. off., 1919.

cover-title, 21 p. 31 cm.

1002. U. S. Superintendent of documents. Bibliography of United States public documents relating to interoceanic communication across Nicaragua, Isthmus of Panama, Isthmus of Tehuantepec, etc. Washington, Govt. print. off., 1899.

29 p. 23 cm.

1003. ————— Panama canal and the Canal Zone. Public documents for sale by the superintendent of documents, Washington, D. C. [Washington, Govt. print off.] 1914.

18 p. 24½ cm.

1004. ——— Panama canal, Canal Zone, Republic of Panama, Colombia treaty, Suez canal, Nicaragua route; publications relating to the above subjects for sale by the superintendent of documents. 4th ed. Washington, Govt. print. off., 1917.

14 p. 25 cm.

1005. Williams, Mary Wilhelmine. Anglo-American Isthmian diplomacy, 1815-1915. [Baltimore, The Lord Baltimore press, 1916]

xii, 356 p. map. 18½ cm. (Prize essays of the American historical association. 1914) Bibliography: p. 331-345.

PARAGUAY

1006. Azara, Félix de.   Geografía física y esférica de las provincias del Paraguay y misiones guaraníes.   Bibliografía, prólogo y anotaciones por Rodolfo R. Schuller.   Montevideo, 1904.

cxxxii, 478 p.   plates, ports., tables, maps.   25½ cm.   (Análes del Museo nacional de Montevideo.   Sección histórico-filosófica, t. 1.)

1007. Báez, Cecilio.   Cuadros históricos y descriptivos.   Asunción, Talleres nacionales de H. Kraus, 1906.

344 p. port. 26½ cm.
Contains biographical sketches.

1008. Catálogo de la Biblioteca paraguaya "Solano López".   Asunción, Talleres nacionales de H. Kraus, 1906.

984 p.

1009. Decoud, José Segundo.   A list of books, magazine articles, and maps relating to Paraguay.   Books, 1638-1903.   Maps, 1599-1903.   A supplement to the Handbook of Paraguay, pub. in Sept., 1902, by the International bureau of the American republics.   Washington, Gov't print off., 1904.

53 p. 23 cm.

1010. Guía general del Paraguay.   Asunción 1916.

1 v. illus. 26½ cm.
A state register and directory.

1011. Hernández, Pablo.   Reseña histórica de la misión de Chile-Paraguay de la Compañía de Jesús desde su origen en 1836 haste el centenario de la restauración de la compañía en 1914.   Barcelona, J. Pugés (s. en c.) 1914.

7 p. l., [5]-319 p. illus. (incl. ports.) fold. map. 26 cm.
"Principales libros que se han publicado": p. 258-266.

1012. Mosqueira, Silvano.   Semblanzas paraguayas.   Asunción, Talleres nacionales de H. Kraus, 1908.

v. 1. 24 cm.

1013. Peramas, José Manuel.   De vita et moribus sex sacerdotum paraguaycorum.   Faventiæ, ex typ. Archii, 1791.

xxxix, [1], 299 p. 21½ cm.
Contains biographical sketches of Emmanuel de Vergara, Emmanuel Querini, Petrus Joannes Andreu, Joannes Escandon, Vincentius Sans and Sigismundus Griera.

1014. ——— De vita et moribus tredecim virorum paraguaycorum. Faventiæ, ex typ. Archii, 1793.

xxvii, 462, [2] p. plan, 2 tab. 21 cm.

Includes biographical sketches of Ignatius Morro, Joannes Mesner, Joannes Suares, Ignatius Chome, Franciscus Ruis de Villegas, Joannes Angelus Amilaga, Antonius del Castillo, Stephanus Pallosius, Clemens Baigorri, Franciscus Urrejola, Joachimus Iribarren, Cosmas Agullo and Martinus Schmid.

1015. Techo, Nicolás del. Historia provinciæ Paraquariæ Societatis Jesv. Leodii, ex officina typog. J. M. Hovii, 1673.

20 p. l., 390, [20] p. 34 cm.

1016. Xarque, Francisco. Insignes missioneros de la Compañía de Jesús en la provincia de Paraguay. Estado presente de sus missiones en Tucumán, Paraguay, y Rio de la Plata, que comprehende su distrito. Pamplona, J. Micón, impressor, 1687.

12 p. l., 432 p. 21 cm.

1017. Zinny, Antonio. Historia de los gobernantes del Paraguay, 1535–1887. Buenos Aires, Impr. y librería de Mayo, 1887.

1 p. l., xvi, 515, 5 p. 23 cm.

PERÚ

1018. Angulo, Domingo. La orden de Santo Domingo en el Perú; estudio bibliográfico. Lima [1910]

Cited in Courtney's Register of national bibliography, v. 3, p. 79.

1019. ——— Santa Rosa de Santa María. Estudio bibliográfico. Prólogo de Carlos Alberto Romero. Lima, Sanmarti y cía., 1917.

1 p. l., ix, 249, [1] p. ports. 22 cm.

1020. Barreda y Laos, Felipe. Vida intelectual de la colonia (educación, filosofía y ciencias; ensayo histórico crítico. Lima, Impr. "La Industria." 1909.

422 p. 22 cm.

1021. Barrett, Robert South. Paper, paper products, and printing machinery in Peru, Bolivia, and Ecuador. Washington, Gov't print off., 1917.

77 p. front. 23 cm. (Dept. of Commerce. Bureau of foreign and domestic commerce. Special agents series, no. 143.)

Contains a useful list of newspapers, and magazines published in these countries.

1022. Bermúdes, José Manuel. Anales de la catedral de Lima. 1534 á 1824. Lima, Imprenta del estado, 1903.

419 p. 24½ cm.

Contain biographical data but is without index.

1023. Biblioteca peruana. Apuntes para un catálogo de impresos. Santiago de Chile, Biblioteca del Instituto nacional, 1896.

2 v. 25½ cm.

Ed. by Gabriel René-Moreno.

CONTENTS.—I. Libros y folletos peruanos de la Biblioteca del Instituto nacional.—II. Libros y folletos peruanos de la Biblioteca nacional; y Notas bibliográficas.

1024. Bibliotheca peruviana; a catalogue of books, tracts and manuscripts chiefly relating to North and South America, comprising works printed at Lima. London, 1873.

1025. Boletín bibliográfico, publicación mensual (1. de enero de 1888 hasta el 15 de julio de 1901). Lima, 1888–1901.

> Edited by Carlos Prince; no. 81 forms "un erudito y rasonado catálogo de obras sobre los idiomas quichua y aimará":—cf. René-Moreno, Ensayo de una bibliografía general de los periódicos de Bolivia, no. 1350.

1026. Cabello, Pedro M. Guía política, eclesiástica y militar del Perú para el año de 1861. Lima, Impr. de J. M. Masias, 1861.

> 392, xxxiv, [8] p.

———— ———— 1873. Lima. Impr. del estado, 1873.

> Cf. Bib. peruana, v. 1, nos. 774–775.

1027. Calancha, Antonio de la. Corónica moralisada del Orden de San Avgvstin en el Perv, con svcesos egenplaers vistos en esta monarqvia. Dividese este primer tomo en qvatro libros; lleva tablas de capítulos, i lugares de la Sagrada Escritura. Barcelona, P. Lacavalleria, 1639.

> 15 p. l., 922, [37] p. illus., pl. 34 cm.
> "A second ... volume of this work was printed at Lima in 1653 [or 1654] but was never published, owing probably to certain obnoxious passages contained in it. It is a smaller volume than the first, and is of very rare occurrence."—Stevens, Hist. nuggets, v. 1, 1862, p. 108. This second volume was written in part by Bernardo de Torres, whose "Cronica de la provincia pervana del Orden de los ermitaños de S. Avgvstin," Lima, 1657, was also published as a supplementary volume to the first volume of Calancha's work and included an epitome of it. cf. Rene-Moreno, Bolivia y Perú; notas hist. y bibl., 1905, p. [1]–9; Bibl. peruana, t. 1, 1896, nos. 404, 412; Medina, Bibl. hisp.-amer., t. 2, 1900, no. 977.

1028. Chaumette des Fossés, A. Catalogue des livres imprimés et manuscrits composant la bibliothèque de M. A. Chaumette des Fossés ... Paris, 1842.

> 2079 titles, chiefly Peruvian.

1029. Coronel Cegarra, Félix Cipriano. Santa Rosa de Lima (Isabel Flores y Oliva) Estudio bibliográfico. (In Concurso literario en honor de Santa Rosa de Lima celebrado ... en el tercer centenario de su nacimiento, 30 de abril de 1886. Lima, Impr. de Torres Aguirre, 1886. p. 61–128).

1030. Córdova y Salinas, Diego de. Corónica de la religiosissima provincia de los doze apóstoles del Perú, de la Orden de N. P. S. Francisco. Lima, I. Lópes de Herrera, 1651.

> 18 p. l., 214, 690, 679–695, [2] p.
> Cf. Medina, Impr. en Lima, no. 339.

1031. Cueva Ponce de León, Alonso de la. Apuntes para la historia eclesiástica del Perú hasta el gobierno del VII arsobispo. Lima, Tip. de "La Sociedad", 1873.

> vii, 9–516, [7] p.
> "La genealogía y otras partes biográficas pueden verse en el Diccionario de Mendiburn ... otra historia eclesiástica publicada en Lima, el año 1876 por ... Pedro García Sans, viene a servir de complemento." Bib. peruana, v. 1, no. 114.

1032. Dorsey, George Amos. A bibliography of the anthropology of Peru. Chicago, U. S. A., 1898.

2 p. l., p. 55-206. 24½ cm. (Field Columbian museum. Publication 23. Anthropological series. vol. II, no. 2)

1033. García Calderón, Ventura. La literatura peruana (1535-1914). (*In* Revue hispanique. New York, 1914. 25½ cm. v. xxxi, p. 305-391.)

1034. García Salazar, Arturo. Guía práctica para los diplomáticos y cónsules peruanos, por Arturo García Salazar y Jorge Linch. [Lima, Tip. americana] 1918.

2 v 3 pl. 21½ cm.
Contains chronological lists of the presidents, ministers of foreign affairs and diplomatic representatives.

1035. Larrabure y Unanue, Eugenio. Monografías histórico-americanas. Lima, Impr. de Torres Aguirre, 1893.

xii, 426 p. illus., map. 21 cm.

1036. Lavalle, José Antonio. Galería de retratos de los arzobispos de Lima (1541-1891). Lima, 1892.

ix, 48, [1] p. 34 ports.

1037. ———— Galería de retratos de los gobernadores y virreyes del Perú (1532-1824), pub. por Domingo de Vivero, texto por Don J. A. de Lavalle, láminas por Don Evaristo San Cristóbal. Barcelona, Tip. de la Casa editorial Maucci, 1909.

184 p., 1 l. ports. 24 cm.

1038. ———— Galería de retratos de los gobernantes del Perú independiente (1821-1871), pub. por Domingo de Vivero, texto por Don J. A. de Lavalle, láminas por David Lozano. Barcelona, Tip. de la Casa editorial Maucci, 1909.

112 p., 1 l. ports. 24 cm.

1039. Leubel, Alfredo G. El Perú en 1860 o sea Anuario nacional. Política, comercio, estadística, literatura, industria, agricultura. Lima, Impr. de Comercio, 1861.

viii, 306, [1] p.
Cf. Bib. peruana, v. 1, no. 1271.

1040. Lima, Biblioteca nacional. Boletín de la Biblioteca nacional, tomo 1-núm. 1- enero de 1919-. Lima. Imprenta del estado, 1919-.

1041. ———— Catálogo de los libros que existen en el salon América, por Ricardo Palma. (Director de la Biblioteca nacional) Lima, Imp. de T. Aguirre, 1891.

iv, 217 p. 34 cm.

1042. Lima. Universidad mayor de San Marcos. Catálogo de la Biblioteca de la Universidad mayor de San Marcos. Lima, Impr. San Pedro, 1907.

113 p.

———— ———— 1. suplemento. Lima, Impr. San Pedro, 1908.

132 p.

———— ———— 2. suplemento. Lima. Impr. San Pedro, 1909.

127 p.

1043. Maldonado, Juan Martín. Breve svmma de la provincia del Perv del Orden de los ermitaños de San Avgvstín nuestro padre y de los insignes, y memorables conventos, hijos, y sugetos que tiene en el estado y siglo presente de este año de 1651. Roma, F. Moneta, 1651.

51 p.

1044. Markham, Clements Robert. The Inca civilization in Peru [with a critical essay on the sources of information, and notes].

(In Winsor, Justin, ed. Narrative and critical history of America. Boston and New York 1884-89. 32 cm. v. 1. (1889) p. [209]-283. illus.)

1045. Means, Philip Ainsworth. A survey of ancient Peruvian art. New Haven. Conn., Yale university press, 1917.

p. [315]-[422] incl. xvii pl. map. 24½ cm. (Transactions of the Connecticut academy of arts and sciences, v. 21.

Bibliography: p. 394-401.

1046. Medina, José Toribio. Bibliografía de Santo Toribio Mogrovejo, arzobispo de Lima. Lima, Imp. S. Pedro, 1907.

lxxxii p. 19 cm.

"Publicado en Estudios históricos sobre Santo Toribio, por Monseñor Manuel Tovar, arzobispo de Lima, tomo III, impreso en 1907."—Laval. Bibl. chilenaa, no. 171.

1047. ———— La imprenta en Arequipa, el Cusco, Trujillo y otros pueblos del Perú durante las campañas de la independencia (1820-1825); notas bibliográficas. Santiago de Chile, Imprenta elzeviriana, 1904.

71, [1] p. 24 cm.

1048. ———— La imprenta en Lima (1584-1824). Santiago de Chile, Impreso y grabado en casa del autor, 1904-07.

4 v. facsims. 28 cm.

1049. Meléndez, Juan. Tesoros verdaderos de las Indias en la historia de la gran provincia de San Juan Bautista del Perú, de el Orden de predicadores. Roma, N. A. Tinassio, 1681-82.

3 v.

1050. Mendiburu, Manuel de. Diccionario histórico-biográfico del Perú. Parte primera que corresponde a la época de la dominación española. Lima, Impr. de J. F. Solís, 1874-90.

8 v. 21 cm.

"Catálogo de las obras y manuscritos que deben consultarse.": v. 1, 25 p.

1051. ———— ———— Polo, José Toribio. Historia nacional. Crítica del Diccionario histórico-biográfico del Perú del señor general Mendiburu. Lima, Impr. de "El Comercio" por J. R. Sánchez, 1891.

33, [2] p.
Cf. Bib. peruana, v. 1, no. 808.

1052. Mortimer, William Golden. Péru. History of coca, "the divine plant" of the Incas; with an introductory account of the Incas, and of the Andean Indians of to-day. New York, J. H. Vail & company, 1901.

xxxi, 576 p. incl. front., illus. 24 cm.
Bibliography: p. [517]-544.

1053. Paz Soldán, Mariano Felipe. Biblioteca peruana. Lima, Imprenta liberal, 1879.

xi, 544 p.
Cf. Bib. peruana, v. 1, no. 176.

1054. ———— Historia del Perú independiente. 1835-1839. Buenos Aires. Imp. del Courrier de la Plata, 1888.

3 p. l., xxviii, 408, xliv p. 26 cm.
Catálogo de documentos manuscritos e impresos que han servido para escribir esta obra": xliv p.

1055. Paz Soldán, Mateo. Geografía del Perú. Obra póstuma cor. y aum. por Mariano Felipe Paz Soldán. París, Didot hermanos, 1862-63.

2 v. front. (port.) 27 cm.
Noticia bibliográfica: v. 1, p. 715-723.

1056. ———— Géographie du Pérou. Traduction française par P. Arsène Mouqueron. Paris, A. Durand, 1863.

2 p. l., xxxi, 533 p. front. (port.) 27 cm.
Catalogue bibliographique: p. 475-484.

1057. Peru. Congreso. Cámara de senadores. Catálogo de las obras de la biblioteca de la h. Cámara de senadores. Octubre 22 de 1906. Lima, Impr. la Industria, 1906.

67 p. 25½ cm.

1058. ———— Catálogo de la biblioteca, formado por el oficial primero Don Rafael Belaúnde. 31 de julio de 1913. Lima, Emp. tip. "Unión," 1913.

75 p. 25 cm.

1059. Peru. Ministerio de relaciones exteriores. Lista del cuerpo consular extranjero y peruano, marzo de 1905. Lima, Impr. de la Industria, 1905.

53 p. 20 cm.

1060. Peru. Ministerio de fomento. Guía bibliográfica consultiva de obras, folletos, revistas y publicaciones, sobre temas relacionados con la agricultura y la ganadería nacionales, por José G. Otero. Lima, Impr. de "La Académica," 1906.

99 P. 23 cm.
"Indice de las principales leyes, decretos, y resoluciones pertinentes a la agricultura y ganaderías nacionales, 1821-1905": p. 51-99.

1061. Peru. Oficina de reparto, depósito y canje internacional de publicaciones. Catálogo de las publicaciones que la "Oficina de reparto, depósito y canje internacional" tiene disponibles para distribuir. [Lima, 1905]

10 p. 23 cm.

1062. Prado y Ugarteche, Javier. El genio de la lengua y la literatura castellana y sus caracteres en la historia intelectual del Perú. Lima, 1918.

1063. Pret, C. A. Bibliographie pérouvienne. Paris, 1903.

1064. Prince, Carlos. Bibliografía nacional. Los peruanófilos anticuarios del siglo XIX. Lima, Imp. de la Escuela de ingenieros. 1908.

2 p. l., [3]-283, [1] p. 23½ cm.
First published in Revista de ciencias.

1065. ———— I. Bosquejo de la literatura peruana colonial, causas favorables y adversas a sv desarrollo. II. Biblioteca peruana de la colonia. Lima, Impreso en casa del autor, 1910-11.

3 p. l., [5]-311 p. 21 cm.
Periódicos de la época colonial impresos en Lima: p. 229-242. Obras inéditas: p. 277-278.

1066. ———— Libros doctrinarios en idiomas y dialectos índicos peruanos. (*In* Congreso científico latino americano. Primera reunión. Buenos Aires, 1900. 23½ cm. v. 5, p. 299-360)

1067. Revista de archivos y bibliotecas nacionales; época colonial, guerra de independencia. Lima, 1899-1900.

5 v. 28 cm.
"Noticia bibliográfica" por C. A. Romero, v. 1, p. vii-xvii.

1068. Revista peruana, fundada por Mariano Felipe Paz Soldán. Carlos Paz Soldán, editor. v. 1-4. enero 1879-Junio 1880. Lima, M. Fernández, 1879-80.

4 v. pl. 26½ cm.
Ceased publication with the first number of vol. 5, June 1880.
Contains much of bibliographical value, especially M. F. Paz Soldán's Biblioteca peruana, arranged as follows: 1. Publicaciones periódicos, giving number of issues, character of contents and an Indice cronológico; 2. Bibliografía americana; 3. Viajes, geografía, estadística, límites; 4. Historia. Among the contributions of value for biographical data may be noted: Los obispos de Cuzco; Los obispos de Trujillo; Apuntes históricos sobre las encomiendas del Perú by E. Torres Saldamando; Las fuentes de la historia eclesiástica, by M. Gonsáles de la Rosa.

1069. Riva Agüero, José de la. Carácter de la literatura del Perú independiente. Lima, 1905.

1070. ———— La historia en el Perú. Lima, Imp. nacional de F. Barrionuevo, 1910.

2 p. l., [7]-558, [2] p. 21½ cm.
CONTENTS: Introducción.—Blas Valera. Garcilaso de la Vega.—Cronistas de convento.—Don Pedro Peralta.—El general Don Manuel de Mendiburu. Don Mariano Felipe Paz Soldán.—Epílogo.

1071. Salas, Carlos I.   Bibliografía del coronel Don Federico Brandsen.   Buenos Aires, Compañía sud-americana de billetes de banco, 1909.

5 p. l., 10–311 p., 1 l.   2 pl.   2 port.   8 facsim.   22½ cm.
CONTENTS: Bibliografía.—José de la Riva Agüero.—Antonio José de Sucre.—José Bernardo de Torre Tagle.—Andrés de Santa Cruz.

——— ——— 2. ed., considerablemente aum.   Buenos Aires, Compañía sud-americana de billetes de banco, 1910.

418 p., 1 l. incl. front.   ports.   21 cm.

1072. Sánchez, Luis Alberto.   Historia de la literatura peruana.   1. Los poetas de la colonia.   Lima, 1921.

3 p. l., 301 p.   17 cm.

1073. Sancho, Pedro.   An account of the conquest of Peru, written by Pedro Sancho, secretary to Pizarro and scrivener to his army; tr. into English and annotated by Philip Ainsworth Means.   New York, The Cortes society, 1917.

203 p.   21 cm.   (Documents and narratives concerning the discovery and conquest of Latin America, no 2)
Bibliography: p. 199–203.

1074. Sarmiento de Gamboa, Pedro.   History of the Incas by Pedro Sarmiento de Gamboa, and the execution of the Inca Tupac Amaru, by Captain Baltasar de Ocampo; tr. and ed., with notes and an introduction, by Sir Clements Markham.   Cambridge, Printed for the Hakluyt society, 1907.

3 p. l., [v]–viiia, [ix]–xxii p., 1 l., 395 p.   pl., port., 2 fold. maps, 8 facsim.   23 cm.   (Works issued by the Hakluyt society ...2 d ser., no. XXII)
"Bibliography of Peru. 1526–1907": p. 267–358.

1075. Schütz zu Holzhausen, Damian, freiherr von.   Der Amazonas.   Wanderbilder aus Peru, Bolivia und Nordbrasilien.   2., durchgesehene und erweiterte aufl., unter besonderer berücksichtigung der vom verfasser gegründeten tirolisch-rheinischen kolonie Pozuzo, hrsg. von Adam Klassert.   Freiburg im Breisgau, St. Louis, Mo. [etc.] Herder, 1895.

xviii, [1], 443, [1] p.   illus., plates, 2 port., 2 maps.   24 cm.   (Illustrierte bibliothek der länder-u. völkerkunde)
Litteratur: p. 427–433.

1076. Sociedad geográfica de Lima.   Primera sección.   Catálogo de la biblioteca.   Lima, L. H. Jiménez [1898].   1 pt.   26½ cm.

1077. Spain.   Archivo general de Indias.   Relación descriptiva de los mapas, planos, etc. del Virreinato del Perú (Perú y Chile) existentes en el Archivo general de Indias (Sevilla), por Pedro Torres Lanzas.   Barcelona, Imp. Henrich y cᵃ, 1906.

135 p.   18 cm.

1078. Torres, Bernardo de.   Crónica de la provincia Peruana del Orden de los ermitaños de S. Agustín.   Lima, Impr. de J. Santos de Saldaña, 1657.

The second part is an epitome of Calancha's Crónica (1551–1563); the first part continues this chronicle from 1594 to 1657.   Cf. Medina, Impr. en Lima, no. 381.

1079. Torres, J. Leopoldo. Guía bibliográfica consultiva; descripción de minas y oficinas metalúrgicas en el Perú, clasificadas por departamentos; compilación de estudios generales y locales, informes de mineralogía, geología, explotación de minas y metalurgia insertos en las obras y publicaciones de la biblioteca de la Escuela de ingenieros de Lima.   Lima, E. Morenó, 1904.

27p. 21½ cm.

1080. —————— ——————   3. ed., corr. y. aum.   Lima, Tip. de "El Lucero," 1914.

97 p.   26 cm.

1081. Torres Saldamando, Enrique.   Los antiguos Jesuitas del Perú; biografías y apuntes para su historia.   Lima, Impr. liberal, 1882.

xv, 400 p.   24 cm.
Contains extensive bio-bibliographical notices of 157 16-17th century authors.

1082. Unanue, José Hipólito.   Guía política, eclesiástica y militar del virreynato del Perú, para el año 1793-[1797].   Lima, Impr. real de los huérfanos, 1793-97.

5 v.
"Catálogo de los títulos de Castilla de este virreynato, según la antigüedad de su creación ... y de los señores que actualmente lo poseen," in Guía para 1793.

1083. Varones ilustres de la Compañía de Jesús. 2. ed., tomo 4. Misiones del Perú, Nueva Granada, Quito, Paraguay, Chile. Bilbao, Administración de "El Mensajero del Corazón de Jesús, 1889.

642 p.   24 cm.
By Juan Eusebio Nieremberg.

1084. Vidaurre, Pedro N.   Relación cronológica de los alcaldes que han presidido el ayuntamiento de Lima desde su fundación hasta nuestros días.   Formada de orden de la Alcaldía, y en vista de documentos auténticos, que originales se conservan en el archivo de la ciudad.   Lima, Impr. de J. F. Solís, 1889.

V, [3]-109, VIII p. 21 cm.

1085. Winship, George Parker.   Early South American newspapers, by George Parker Winship.   Worcester, 1908.

14 p., ll. illus. 20 cm.
Reprinted from the Proceedings of the American antiquarian society for October, 1908.
"List of news sheets printed at Lima in Peru, 1621-1767, recorded in J. T. Medina's La imprenta en Lima, Santiago de Chile, 1904": p. 10-[15]

PORTO RICO

1086. Ateneo puertorriqueño.   Catálogo por orden alfabético de autores y de materias, de las obras existentes en la biblioteca del Ateneo puertorriqueño.   Puerto-Rico, Tip. de "El Pais," 1897.

63 p   21 cm.

1087. Berniér, Félix Matos.   Muertos y vivos.   San Juan, Puerto Rico, Tip. "El pais." 1905.

248 p., 1 l.   22 cm.

1088. Fernández Juncos, Manuel. Antología portorriqueña, prosa y verso, para lectura escolar ... New York, Filadelfia, Hinds Noble & Edredge, 1913.

v, [3], 267, [1] p. 19½ cm.
Biographical notices of 28 authors.

1089. Figueroa, Sotero. Ensayo biográfico de los que más han contribuido al progreso de Puerto.-Rico, con un prólogo del lcdo. en ciencias Don José Julián Acosta y Calvo. Ponce, Est. tip. "El Vapor," 1888.

xvii p.. 2 l., [3]-356 p., 1 l., [2] p. 23½ cm.
30 biographies.

1090. González Contreras, José María. Guía general de Puerto Rico. Puerto-Rico, Impr. de la Gaceta, 1897.

636 p. 2 port. (incl. front.) 22 cm.

1091. Lloréns Torres, Luís. América (estudios históricos y filológicos). Colección de artículos escritos y ordenados por D. Luís Lloréns Torres, con una carta-prólogo de D. Antonio Cortón. Madrid, V. Suárez [1898].

204 p. 21 cm.
Reseña bibliografica. p. 190-196.

1092. Neumann Gandía, Eduardo. Benefactores y hombres notables de Puerto-Rico; bocetos biográficos-críticos, con un estudio sobre nuestros gobernadores generales. Ponce, Est. tip. "La Libertad," 1896-99.

2 v. plates, ports., map, facsim. 22½ cm.

1093. Paniagua Oller, Angel. Episcopology of Porto Rico; a catalogue of the bishops who have occupied this see, including bishops-elect who did not take possession. Tr. by Henry Grattan Doyle. (*In* Catholic historical review. Washington, D. C., 1918. 25½ cm. v. iv, p. [348]-364.)

1094. Porto Rico. Colegio. Lista de abogados del ilustre Colegio de Puerto-Rico. Puerto Rico, 1876.

1 v. 20 cm.

1095. Porto Rico. Secretary's office. Register. San Juan [1901]-23½ cm.

1096. Porto Rico. Tribunal supremo. Listas cronológicas y alfabéticas de los abogados y notarios inscritos en este tribunal. Lista cronológica de los abogados inscritos en la Corte de distrito de los Estados Unidos para Puerto Rico. San Juan, Bureau of supplies, printing and transportation, 1914.

44 p. 22 cm.

1097. Sama, Manuel María. Bibliografía puerto-riqueña. Trabajo premiado en el certamen del Ateneo puerto-riqueño, celebrado el 29 de enero de 1887, de conformidad con el laudo del jurado calificador de la Asociación de escritores y artistas de Madrid. Mayaguez, P. R., Tipografía comercial—marina, 1887.

3 p. l., 159 p. 22 cm.

1098. U. S. Library of Congress. A list of books (with references to periodicals) on Porto Rico. By A. P. C. Griffin. Washington, Govt. print off., 1901.

56 p. 26 cm.

SALVADOR

1099. Album patriótico. [San Salvador, Imprenta nacional] 1915.

266, 5, [1] p. incl. illus., ports. ports. 24 cm.

A collection of political and patriotic articles, with biographical notices of President Meléndez, and other citizens of Salvador.

1100. Guía del Salvador, del comercio, industrias, profesiones, empresas de ferrocarriles, etc., etc. San Salvador, J. M. Lacayo [1907]

1 v. tables. 23½ x 12 cm.

1101. Labor del gobierno del general Fernando Figueroa, presidente constitucional de la República, 1907–1909. San Salvador, Impr. Meléndez [1909]

209 p. ports. 26 cm.

1. pte.: Biografías cortas.

1102. Mayorga Rivas, Román. Guirnalda slavadoreña. Colección de poesías de los bardos de la república del Salvador, precedidas de apuntes biográficos y juicios críticos sobre cada uno de sus autores. Con un prólogo del Dr. Don Tomás Ayón. San Salvador, Impr. del doctor F. Sagrini, 1884–86.

3 v. 21½ cm.

1103. San Salvador. Biblioteca nacional. Catálogo alfabético y por materias de todos los libros que contiene la Biblioteca nacional de El Salvador formado por Rafael U. Palacios. San Salvador, Tip. el Cometa, 1887.

1 v.

———— ———— 1. Apendice ... por Eduardo Martinez Lopez, San Salvador, 1890.

1104. ———— Catálogo general alfabético. San Salvador, 1896–97.

3 v.

1105. ———— ———— San Salvador, 1905.

URUGUAY

1106. Almanaque-guía de "El Siglo" para el año 1918, año LVI. Montevideo, 1918.

1 v. 25 cm.

1107. Araújo, Orestes. Diccionario popular de historia de la República O. del Uruguay. Montevideo, Dornaleche y Reyes, 1901–03.

3 v. 24 cm.

Contains much biographical information.

1108. ———— Gobernantes del Uruguay. Montevideo, Impr. de Dornaleche y Reyes, 1903.

2v. ports. 17½ cm.

CONTENTS: t. 1. Advertencia. Los treinta y tres. Rivera y Lavalleja. El primer gobierno local. Independencia y anexión. Triunfos y derrotas. Sarandi Incorporacion á la Argentina. Primeros conflictos. Ituzaingó. Dictadura de Lavalleja. Conquista de Misiones. La independencia. Gobierno de Rondeau.—t. 2. Presidencias y dictaduras. Gobierno de Rivera. Presidencia de Oribe. Segunda presidencia de Rivera. Gobierno de Suárez. Después de la guerra grande.

1109. Arechavaleta, J. Naturalistas en el Uruguay. (*In* Revista histórica de la Universidad. Montevideo, 1907. 25½ cm. v. 1, p. [478]–506, [828]–842. ports.)

Bio-bibliographical data concerning naturalists who have studied the flora and fauna of Uruguay.

1110. Ateneo del Uruguay. Reglamento y catálogo general de la Biblioteca pública del Ateneo del Uruguay. Montevideo, Impr. de la Idea, de Flores hermanos, 1880.

38 p. 21 x 27 cm.

1111. Bauzá, Francisco. Historia de la dominación española en el Uruguay. 2. ed. Montevideo, A. Barreiro y Ramos, 1895–97.

3 v. fronts. 25 cm.

Reseña preliminar (v. 1, p. vii–lviii) contains: Bibliografía y archivos coloniales.—Primeros cronistas e historiadores de Indias-Escritores y viajeros subsiguientes.—Bibliografía jesuítica.—Complementación de los trabajos historiales y jurídicos.—Azara.—Movimiento bibliográfico de principios del siglo 19.—Bibliografía argentina.—Bibliografía brasileira.—Bibliografía uruguaya.

1112. Boletín bibliográfico "Barreiro" Montevideo, A. Barreiro y Ramos.

A useful publisher's list.

1113. Carve, Luis. Apuntaciones biográficas. (*In* Revista histórica de la Universidad. Montevideo, 1907–09.)

25½ cm. v. 1, p. [30]–57, 355–371, 651–670, v. 2, p. 99–108, 430–434, 459–465, 724–734. ports.
Contents: S. Vásques, J. B. Blanco, M. Herrera y Obes, L. J. de la Peña, J. B. Lamas, C. Juanicó, E. Echeverría, F. Castellanos, L. A. Fernández, F. Ferreira, A. Lamas, J. G. Palomeque, F. A. Antuña, F. Acuña de Figueroa, F. Ferreira y Artigas, J. A. Varela, G. Pérez Gomar, F Araucho, J. M. Besnes Irigoyen, C. M. Ramírez, T. Narvaja, A. de Villegas, J. L. Terra, J J. de Herrera, M. Herrero y Espinos a, J. C. Blanco.

1114. De- Maria, Isidoro. Rasgos biográficos de hombres notables de la República Oriental del Uruguay. Montevideo, 1879–80.

3 v.

1115. Estrada, Dardo. Historia y bibliografía de la imprenta en Montevideo 1810–1865. Montevideo, Librería Cervantes, 1912.

318, [2] p. 26 cm.

1115a. ———— Fuentes documentales para la historia colonial; conferencia leída el día 28 de julio de 1917, con un discurso preliminar del doctor Gustavo Gallinal. Montevideo, Impr. y casa editorial "Renacimiento," 1918.

39 p. 20 cm.

1116. Fernández Sáldaña, J. M. Pintores y escultores uruguayos. (*In* Revista histórica de la Universidad Montevideo, 1913. 24 cm. t. 6. p. 428–450, 710–731.)

1117. ——— ——— Montevideo, Imp. "El Siglo ilustrado" de G. U. Mariño, 1916.

108 p. front., plates, ports. 23 cm.

1118. Fernández y Medina, Benjamín. La imprenta y la prensa en el Uruguay desde 1807 a 1900. Montevideo, Impr. de Dornaleche y Reyes, 1900.

87 p. 18½ cm.

Reprinted with additions from Orestes Araújo's Diccionario geográfico del Uruguay, 1900.

1119. Fors, Luis Ricardo. Las bibliotecas de Montevideo; examen y reseña de las mismas. La Plata, Impr. y enc. "La Popular," 1903.

43 p., 1 l. 21½ cm.

Appendix: 1. Clasificaciones del catálogo metódico decretado por el Gobierno oriental para la Biblioteca de Montevideo.—2. Secciones del primitivo catálogo formado por el D. Mascaró para la Biblioteca de Montevideo.—3. Clasificación del catálogo para la Biblioteca pública de La Plata, adoptada por su director Don Clodomiro Quiroga hasta 1898.—4. Catálogo sistemático de la Biblioteca pública de La Plata.

1120. García Calderón, Ventura. La literatura uruguaya (1757–1917) por Ventura García Calderón y Hugo D. Barbagelata. (In Revue hispanique. New York [etc.] 1917. v. 40, p. 415–542.)

A useful review with dates of prominent contemporary authors.

1121. "Guia nacional" de la República Oriental del Uruguay, año 8. Montevideo, 1908.

1 v. 23½ cm.

Edited by O. J. Arias.

1122. Henríquez Ureña, Max. Rodo y Rubén Dario. La Habana, Sociedad editorial Cuba contemporánea, 1918.

153 p., 1 l. 23 cm.

Bibliografía: p. 63–69, 141–149.

1123. Jalabert, Ricardo M. Album biográfico ilustrado y descripción histórico geográfica de la República Oriental del Uruguay, año 1904; directores propietarios: Ricardo M. Jalabert y Rodolfo Cabal. Buenos Aires, Ortega y Radaelli, 1903.

254, [2] p. incl. illus., ports. 35½ cm.

1124. Larrañaga, Dámaso Antonio. Centenario de la Biblioteca pública de Montevideo. 1816–26 de mayo—1916. Discurso que en el acto de la inauguración pronunció el presbítero Dámaso Antonio Larrañaga. Con varias anotaciones históricas sobre la ceremonia por Arturo Scarone. Montevideo, Talleres gráficos del estado, 1916.

24 p. 23½ cm.

1125. Maeso, Carlos M. El Oriental; descripción general de la República Oriental del Uruguay, su comercio, industrias, rentas y riquezas, narraciones históricas, rasgos biográficos de Uruguayos célebres, etc. Montevideo, Impr. de Ríus y Becchi, 1884.

206 p.

1126. ——— Tierra de promisión: descripción general de la República O. del Uruguay: su comercio, industrias, rentas, riquezas, educación y progresos. Situación de los extranjeros en ella. Narraciones históricas. Rasgos biográficos de próceres de la independencia, etc. Montevideo, Impr. á vapor de la Nación, 1900.

1 p. l., [5]–211 p. 24½ cm.

1127. Montevideo. Biblioteca nacional. Anales de la bibliografía uruguaya. Año 1895. Tomo 1. Montevideo, 1896.

127 p.
Pages 95–113 give list of periodicals.
No more published?

1128. ———— Biblioteca nacional; recopilación de leyes, reglamento, plan de catálogo metódico y otras disposiciones y antecedentes relativos a dicha institución, por el director doctor Felipe Villegas Zúñiga. Años 1815 á 1906. Montevideo, Talleres gráficos A Barreiro y Ramos, 1914.

152 p. 21½ cm.

1129. ———— Memoria. Montevideo, 1881–85.

3 v. fold, tables. 27½ cm.
Includes catalogs of accessions to the library.
"Relación de todos los periódicos que aparecen en la república": 1880, fold, tab. following p. 197: "Relación de los grabados, mapas, planos y fotografías, que posée la Biblioteca nacional": 1880, p. 211–237.
Others issued?

1130. Núñez Regueiro, Manuel. Contemporary Uruguayan literature. (*In* Inter-America. New York, 1920. 24 cm. v. 3, p. 306–315.)

From Nuestra América, Buenos Aires, June, 1919.

1131. Los oradores de la Cámara; retratos, bocetos y caricaturas de algunos diputados de 1873. Montevideo, Impr. el Obrero español, 1876–. 18½ cm.

1132. Roxlo, Carlos. Historia crítica de la literatura uruguaya. Montevideo, A. Barreiro y Ramos, 1912–16.

7 v. 23 cm.
CONTENTS: t. 1–2. 1810–1885. El romanticismo.—t. 3–5. 1885–1898. (t. 3. El arte de la forma. t. 4–5. La influencia realista.)—t. 6. 1885–1898. El cuento nativo y el teatro nacional.—t. 7. 1900–1916. La edad ecléctica.

1133. Scarone, Arturo. La Biblioteca nacional de Montevideo; reseña histórica con motivo del primer centenario de su fundación, 1816—26 mayo—1916. Montevideo, Talleres gráficos del estado, 1916.

157 p. illus., ports. 24 cm.

1134. ———— Uruguayos contemporáneos; obra de consulta biográfica. Diccionario de datos referentes a compatriotas ... y de algunos extranjeros desde largo tiempo incorporados y descollantes en nuestra vida pública. 1 ed., con un apéndice. Montevideo, "Renacimiento," 1918.

2 p. l., [vii]–xv, 676 p. illus., ports. 18½ cm.

1135. Uruguay. Archivo y Museo histórico nacional. Revista histórica. Montevideo, 1907–. 25½ cm.

Bibliographies interspersed.

1136. Uruguay. Ministerio de relaciones exteriores. Anuario diplomático y consular de la República Oriental del Uruguay. Año 1917. Montevideo, Imprenta nacional, 1917.

343 p., 2 l. 25 cm.
"Estado de servicios de los miembros del Cuerpo diplo mático y consular" (with full names and dates): p. 205–213.

1137. Uruguay. Oficina de depósito, reparto y canje internacional de publicaciones. Lista de las publicaciones existentes en la Oficina de depósito, reparto y canje internacional. Montevideo, 1890. 21½ cm.

1138. Zinny, Antonio. Historia de la prensa periódica de la República Oriental del Uruguay 1807-1852. Bienos Aires, C. Casavalle, 1883.

xxix p., 1 l., 504 p. 23½ cm.

VENEZUELA

1139. Album bibliográfico de Venezuela; año 1-, 1916-. Caracas, Litografía del comercio, 1917-. 23½ cm.

By Manuel Segundo Sánchez.
Cf. also no. 1160.

1140. Anzola, Juvenal. Abogados venezolanos. Caracas, Imp. Colón, 1904.

222 p.

1141. Asociación venezolana de literatura, ciencias y bellas artes. Primer libro venezolano de literatura, ciencias y bellas artes, ofrenda al gran mariscal de Ayacucho. Contiene retratos e ilustraciones. Caracas, Tip. El Cojo, i parte; Tip. Moderna, ii parte, 1895.

2 p. l., A-ABC, cocxxxvi, 216, ii p. illus. (incl. ports.) plates. 37 x 29½ cm.
By the Asociación venezolana de literatura, ciencias y bellas artes, under the special direction of R. F. Seijas.
CONTENTS: 1. pte. Las buenas letras. Las ciencias. Las bellas artes. La bibliografía.—
2. pte. La antología general. Las notas biográficas. Las últimas páginas. El índice.

1142. Briceño, Luis F. La imprenta en el Táchira. [Caracas, Impr. Bolívar, 1883].

1 p. l., 16 p. 31 cm. (Ofrenda al Liberator en su primer centenario. Impresa por disposicion del presidente de los Estados Unidos de Venezuela, general Gusmán Blanco.)
Noticia cronologica de los periódicos que desde el año de 1845 hasta el de 1883 se hanpublicado en la sección Táchira: p. 8-16.

1143. Calcaño, Julio. Parnaso venezolano; colección de poesías de autores venezolanos desde mediados del siglo XVIII hasta nuestros días precedida de una introducción acerca del origen y progreso de la poesía en Venezuela. Caracas, Tip. de "El Cojo" 1892-

v. 1-. 24½ cm.

1144. ———— Reseña histórica de la literatura venezolana. Caracas, Tip. de El Cojo, 1888.

29 p.

1145. Castro, Enrique María. Historia de los obispos de Mérida de Maracaibo Valencia. Tip. de F. Rodríguez, 1888.

iv, 5-234 p.

1146. ———— Rasgos biográficos de algunos curas ejemplares de la antigua provincia de Barinas. Caracas, Imp. de "La Religión," 1890.

269 p.

1147. Dalton, Leonard Victor. Venezuela, London, T. F., Unwin, 1912. 320 p. front., plates, map. 23 cm. (The South American series, v. 8.)
Bibliography: p. 287-313.

1148. Dávila, Vicente. Próceres merideños. Caracas, Imp. Bolívar, 1918.
vi p., 1 l., 278 p., 1 l. ports. 24½ cm.
Sketches of Ribas Dávila, Campo de Elías, Antonio Rangel, Uscátequi Dávila, Juan Antonio Paredes, Rodríguez Picón, Gabriel Picón, Ruiz Valero, Justo Briceño, Fernández Peña, Félix Uscátegui, Manuel Nucete, García de Hevia.

1149. Ernst, A. Ensayo de una bibliografía de la Guajira y de los guajiros. (In Revista científica de la Universidad central de Venezuela. Caracas, 1890, no. 20, p. 341-357)

1150. Indicador de Caracas y de la República, 1919-1920. Caracas, Empresa del Indicador de Caracas y de la República [1919]
2 p. l., cclxxxviii, 964 p. 24 cm.
Includes the administrative personnel, a directory of the diplomatic and consular representatives, and of the church, a general and classified directory of Caracas and the states of the union, periodicals, etc.

1151. Landaeta Rosales, Manuel. Indice de los trabajos históricos y estadísticos de Manuel Landaeta Rosales. Caracas, Tipografía americana, 1909.
30 p., 1 l. 23 cm.

1152. Macpherson, Telasco A. Diccionario histórico, geográfico, estadístico y biográfico del estado Lara. Puerto Cavello, J. A. Segrestaa, 1883.
xi, 516 p.

1153. ———— Diccionario histórico, geográfico, estadístico y biográfico del estado Miranda. Caracas, Imp. de "El Correo de Caracas, 1891."
556 p.

1154. Medina, José Toribio. La imprenta en Caracas (1808-1821); notas bibliográficas. Santiago de Chile, Imprenta elzeviriana, 1904.
29, [1] p. 24 cm.

1155. Méndez y Mendoza, J. de D. Historia de la Universidad Central de Venezuela. t. 1. Caracas. Tip. Americana.
ix p., 2 l., 414 p. 1 l. 24 cm.
Contains lists of rectors, faculty and graduates up to 1837.

1156. Montenegro, M. V. Esbozos de venezolanos notables. Cartagena, Tip. de García e hijos, 1902.
154 p.

1157. Phillips, Philip Lee. Guiana and Venezuelan cartography. Washington, Gov't. print. off., 1898.
1 p. l., 681-776 p. 24½ cm.
From the Annual report of the American historical association for 1897.

1158. Picón-Febres, Gonzalo. La literatura venezolana en el siglo diez y nueve (ensayo de historia crítica). Caracas, "Empresa el Cojo," 1906.
5 p. l., 429, ii p. illus. (incl. ports.) 30 cm.

1159. Rojas, José María.   Biblioteca de escritores venezolanos contemporáneos, ordenada con noticias biográficas.   Carácas, Rojas hermanos, 1875.

xix, 808 p. 28 cm.

1160. Sánchez, Manuel Segundo. Bibliografía venejolana. Nómina de los principales libros y folletos venezolanos publicados en los primeros meses de 1918.

(In Revista de bibliografía Chilena y extranjera. Santiago, 1918. 23½ cm. Año VI, nos. 7-8-, julio-agosto-.)
Cf. also no. 1139.

1161. ———— Bibliografía venezolanista; contribución al conocimiento de los libros extranjeros relativos a Venezuela y sus grandes hombres, pub. o reimpresos desde el siglo XIX.   Caracas, Empresa el Cojo, 1914.

x p., 1 l., 494, [2] p. front. (port.) 25½ cm.

1162. ———— La imprenta de la expedición libertadora; capítulo de la obra en preparación: Historia y bibliografía de la imprenta en Venezuela. (Ed. de 50 ejemplares) Caracas, Litografía del Comercio, 1916.

[12] p. facsims. 24 cm.

1163. ———— El Publicista de Venezuela; capítulo del libro en preparación "Los incunables venezolanos." Caracas, Talleres de "El Universal," 1920.

25 p. facsim. 18 cm.

1164. Spence, James Mudie. The land of Bolivar, or War, peace and adventure in the Republic of Venezuela.   London, S. Low, Marston, Searle & Rivington, 1878.

2 v. 23 cm.
Bibliography: v. 2, p. 271-293.

1165. Tejera, Felipe. Perfiles venezolanos; o, Galería de hombres célebres de Venezuela en las letras, ciencias y artes.   Caracas, Imprenta Sans, 1881.

xviii, 478 p. front., ports. 20½ cm.

1166. Vaïsse, Emilio. Bibliografía de Don Andrés Bello. y de sus descendientes, 1781-1916. Santiago de Chile, Imprenta Universitaria, 1917.

125 p.

1167. Venezuela. Ministerio de relaciones interiores. Directorios médico y farmacéutico de Venezuela. Caracas, Tip. moderna, 1916.

Cover-title, 35, [2] p. 31 cm.
An alphabetical list, by states, of physicians, dentists and pharmacists. Full names are not always given.

1168. Venezuela. Universidad central. Catálogo de la biblioteca de la Universidad de Caracas, formado de orden del ilustre americano general Guzmán Blanco. Caracas, F. T. de Aldrey, 1875.

viii, 279 p. 28 cm.
Prepared by Adolfo Ernst.

See also: Cuba and Porto Rico.

1169. Advielle, Victor. L'Odyssée d'un Normand à St. Domingue au dix-
huitième siècle. Paris, Challamel, 1901.
292 p. 20 cm.
Notes bibliographiques: p. 285-290.

1170. Boissonnade, Prosper Marie. Saint-Domingue à la veille de la révolution.
Paris, P. Geuth, 1906.
1 p. l., 299, [1] p. 25½ cm.
Sources et bibliographie: p. 290-294.

1171. Bonneau, Alexandre. Haiti, ses progrès, son avenir; avec un précis historique sur ses constitutions, le texte de la constitution actuellement en
vigueur, et une bibliographie d' Haïti. Paris, E. Dentu, 1862.
176 p.

1172. Brooklyn. Public library. A list of books on the West Indies and the
Bermuda islands in the Brooklyn Public library. Brooklyn, 1904.
12 p.

1173. Cundall, Frank. Bibliography of the West Indies (excluding Jamaica).
Kingston, The Institute of Jamaica, 1909.
3 p. l., 179 p. 21½ cm.
Contains also sections on Florida. Honduras, Nicaragua, Costa Rica, Panama, Colombia,
Venezuela, the Guianas, etc.

1174. ———— Political and social disturbances in the West Indies. A brief
account and bibliography. Kingston, Pub. for the Institute of Jamaica
by the Educational supply company, printers; London, H. Sotheran &
co., 1906.
35 p. 20½ cm.

1175. Dampierre, Jacques de. Essai sur les sources de l'histoire des Antilles
Françaises (1492-1664) Paris, A. Picard et fils, 1904.
2 p. l., xl, 238 p., 1 l. 25½ cm. (Mémoires et documents publiés par la Société de l'École des
chartes, vi.)
Principales bibliographies américaines: p. xix-xl.

1176. Deschamps, Enrique. La República Dominicana; directorio y guía general, Santiago de los Caballeros, República Dominicana [Barcelona, Impr.
de la vda. de J. Cunill, 1906?]
3 p. l., 13-383, 336 p. illus., col. pl., ports., fold. map. 26 cm.

1177. García, José Gabriel. Rasgos biográficos de dominicanos célebres. 1. ser.
Santo Domingo, García hermanos, 1875.
191, [1] p.
René-Moreno. Bib. bol., 2. sup., no. 6323.

1178. García Godoy, Federico. Dominican intellectual life. (In Inter-America.
New York, 1920. 24 cm. v. 3, p. 298-303)
First published in Spanish in Nuestra América, Buenos Aires, July, 1919.

1179. ———— La literatura dominicana. (In Revue hispanique; New York, 1916. 24½ cm. v. 37, p. 61–104)

1180. Garrett, Mitchell Bennett. ` The French colonial question 1789–1791; dealings of the Constituent assembly with problems arising from the revolution in the West Indies. Ann Arbor, Mich., G. Wahr [1918]

iv p., 1 l., 167 p. 23½ cm.
Bibliography: p. 135–160.

1181. Hazard, Samuel. Santo Domingo, past and present, with a glance at Hayti. New York, Harper & brothers, 1873.

xxix p., 1 l., 511 p. incl. front., illus. plates, 2 maps (1 fold.) 21 cm.
Bibliography of Santo Domingo and Hayti: p. xxi–xxix.

1182. Henríquez Ureña, Pedro. Literatura dominciana. (*In* Revue hispanique New York, 1917. 24½ cm. v. 40, p. 273–294])

Intended to supplement Garcia Godoy's paper (Revue histanique, v. 37, p. 61–104).

1183. Hovey, Edmund Otis. Bibliography of literature of the West Indian eruptions published in the United States. (In Bulletin of the Geological Society of America. Rochester, 1904, v. 15, p. 562–566)   .

1184. Inman, Samuel Guy. Through Santo Domingo and Haiti, a cruise with the marines. Report of a visit to these island republics in the summer of 1919. New York city, Committee on co-operation in Latin America [1919]

96 p. illus. (maps). 21 cm.
Bibliography: p. 91–96.

1185. New York. Public library. List of works relating to the West Indies. New York, 1912.

2 p. l., 392 p. 26½ cm.
Reprinted at the New York public library, from the Bulletin, January-August, 1912.

1186. Peytraud, Lucien. L'esclavage aux Antilles Françaises avant 1789. Paris, Hachette et cie., 1897.

xxii, 472 p. 25½ cm.
Notice bibliographique: p. xiii–xxii.

1187. Roth, Henry Ling. Bibliography and cartography of Hispaniola.

(*In* Royal geographical society. Supplementary papers. London, 1887. 24½ cm. v. 2, pt. 1, p. 41–97)

1188. Stoddard, Theodore Lothrop. The French revolution in San Domingo. Boston and New York, Houghton Mifflin company, 1914.

xviii p., 1 l., 410 p., 1 l. front. (port.) 2 maps. 20½ cm.
Select annotated bibliography: p. 395–410.

1189. Tippenhauer, Louis Gentil. Die insel Haiti. Leipzig, F. A. Brockhaus. 1893.

xviii, 693, [1] p. illus., plates. 32½ cm.
Bibliographie: p. 672–693.

1190. Trelles y Govín, Carlos Manuel. Ensayo de bibliografía cubana de los siglos XVII y XVIII. Seguido de unos apuntes para la bibliografía dominicana y portorriqueña. Matanzas, Impr. "El Escritorio," 1907.

xi, 228 p., 1 l., xxviii p., 1 l. 26 cm.

———— ———— Supplemento. Matanzas, Impr. "El Escritorio," 1908.

2 p. l., ii, 76 p. 26½ cm.

1191. Treudley, Mary. The United States and Santo Domingo, 1789–1866. Worcester, Mass. [1916]

1 p. l., p. 83–145, 220–274. 23 cm.
Reprinted from the Journal of race development, v. 7, no. 1, July 1916, no. 2, October 1916.
Bibliography: p. 269–274.

ADDITIONS

1192. Andrade Coello, Alejandro. Intellectual Ecuador, an index to the recent literary movement. (In Inter-America. New York, 1920. 24 cm. v. 3, p. 144–156)

1193. Annuaire général des médecins de la langue française des trois Amériques ... Les noms et adresses des professeurs, médecins et chirurgiens du Canada, des États-Unis et dépendances, du Mexique, des Antilles, des républiques de l'Amérique Centrale et de l'Amérique du Sud. 3. éd. Montréal, C. Deom et Granger frères, 1918.

428 p. 25 cm.

1194. Bandelier, Adolph Francis Alphonse. On the sources for aboriginal history of Spanish America. (In Proceedings of the American society for the advancement of science, Salem, 1879. 27th meeting, 1848, p. 315–337)

1195. Blanco y Sánchez, Rufino. El año pedagógico hispanoamericano. Monografías pedagógicas, crónica mundial de la enseñanza, 2,000 notas bibliográficas. Madrid, Perlado, Páez y Cia., 1920.

330 p.

1196. Borsari, Ferdinando. La letturatura degl' indigeni americani. Napoli, L. Pierro, 1888.

76 p. 21 cm.

1197. Bravo, Francisco Javier. Atlas de cartas geográficas de los países de la América Meridional, en que estuvieron situadas las más importantes misiones de los Jesuitas; como también de los territorios sobre cuya posesión versaron allí las principales cuestiones entre España y Portugal; acompañado de varios documentos sobre estas últimas, y precedido de una introducción histórica Madrid, Impr. y estereotipia de M. Rivadeneyra, 1872.

xxiii, 51 p. 6 fold. maps. 31 cm.
"Catálogo de los documentos relativos a las cuestiones entre españoles y portugueses en el Río de la Plata y Amazonas, y que forman parte de mi colección": p. 33–40.
"Catálogo de los documentos relativos a los tratados ajustados entre España y Portugal sobre límites de los territorios que poseian en América ambas naciones (De mi colección):" p. 41–51.

1198. Denis, Pierre. La République Argentine; la mise en valeur du pays. Paris, A. Colin, 1920.

2 p. l., 299 p., 2 l. maps. 22½ cm.
Bibliographie: p. 283-299.

1199. Desdevises du Dezert, Georges Nicolas. Les sources manuscrites de l'histoire de l'Amérique latine á la fin du xviii e siècle (1760-1807). (In Nouvelles archives des missiones scientifiques et littéraires. Paris, 1914. Nouv. sér., xii.)

1200. Directorio social de Cuba, Habana, conteniendo los nombres de familias y personalidades de la sociedad habanera, año 1919. [Habana] L. Angulo y M. A. Mendoza, 1919.

8 p. l., 312 p. 26 cm.

1201. Ecuador. Biblioteca nacional. Boletín de la Biblioteca nacional del Ecuador. Nueva serie. Num. 1- Quito, Talleres tip. nacionales, 1920-. 31 cm.

1202. Esquivel Obregón, Toribio. Latin-American commercial law. With the collaboration of Edwin M. Borchard. New York, Banks law publishing co., 1921.

xxiii, 972 p. 24 cm.
Contains extensive bibliographies.

1203. Field, Thomas Warren. An essay towards an Indian bibliography. Being a catalogue of books, relating to the history, antiquities, languages, customs, religion, wars, literature, and origin of the American Indians in the library of Thomas W. Field. New York, Scribner, Armstrong and co., 1873.

iv, 430 p. 23 cm.

1204. Filsinger, Ernst B. Commercial travelers' guide to Latin-America. Washington, Govt. print. off., 1920.

592 p. and portfolio of 30 maps. 20½ cm. (Bureau of foreign and domestic commerce. Miscellaneous series, no. 89)
Bibliography: p. 580-592.

1205. Flórez de Ocariz, Juan. Las genealogías del Nuebo Reyno de Granada. Madrid, 1674.

2 v.

1206. Foulché-Delbosc, R. Manuel de l'hispanisant. New York, G. P. Putnam's Sons, 1920.

v. 1. 22½ cm.
By Foulché-Delbosc and L. Barrau-Dihigo.
Published by the Hispanic Society of America.
A most valuable repertoire of Spanish and Portuguese biographies, bibliographies and related works.

1207. Garcia Acevedo, Daniel. Documentos inéditos de Lozano. (In Revista histórica de la Universidad. Montevideo, 1907-09. 24 cm. año 1, p. 862-894; año 2, p. 147-170)

1208. García Calderón, Ventura. Semblanzas de América. Rodó, Silva, Herrera y Reissig, Palma, Chocano, Gómez Carrillo, Almafuerte, Zorrilla de San Martín, Reyles, Prada y Montalvo. Madrid. Imp. de G. Hernández y G. Sáez [1920]

206 p.

1209. Gayangos, Pascual de. Catalogue of the manuscripts in the Spanish language in the British museum. London, The Trustees, 1875-93.

4 v.

Class 5 (v. 2 and 4): Spanish settlements in America.

1210. Gómez de Rodeles. Cecilio. La Compañía de Jesús catequista. Madrid, Impr. G. L. Horno, 1913.

415 p.

1211. ———— Imprentas de los antiguos jesuitas en Europa, América y Filipinas. (In Razón y Fé, 1909-)

1212. Grosvenor library, Buffalo, N. Y. Catalogue of books on Latin-America. Buffalo, The Library, 1901.

30 p. 26½ cm. (Bulletin, no. 1, 1901)

1213. Hernández, Pablo. Reseña histórica de la misión de Chile-Paraguay de la Compañía de Jesús desde su origen en 1836 hasta el centenario de la restauración de la Compañía en 1914. Barcelona, Editorial ibérica, 1914.

7 p. l., [5]-319 p. front. (fold. map) illus., ports. 25½ cm.
"Principales libros que se han publicado." p. 258-261.

1214. Hodge, Frederick Webb. Bibliography of fray Alonso de Benavides. New York, Museum of the American Indian, Heye foundation, 1919.

39 p. 17 cm (Indian notes and monographs, vol. III, no. 1)

1215. Jones, Cecil Knight. Hispano-Americana in the Library of Congress. [Baltimore, 1919]

p. 96-104. 27 cm.
Reprinted from the Hispanic American historical review, vol. 2, no. 1, February, 1919.
Published in Spanish in inter-América, July 1919.

1216. ———— Suggested readings in Spanish-American prose. (In Hispania. Stanford University, California, 1920. 24 cm. v. 3, p. 207-212)

1217. Keniston, Hayward. List of works for the study of Hispanic-American history. New York, The Hispanic society of America, 1920.

xviii p., 1 l., 451 p. 17 cm. (Hispanic notes and monographs, 5)
A valuable guide for students of Hispanic American history and bibliography.

1218. Latorre, Germán. Relaciones geográficas de Indias contenidas en el Archivo general de Indias de Sevilla. La Hispano-América del siglo XVI: Colombia, Venezuela, Puerto Rico, República Argentina. Sevilla, Tip. Zarzuela, 1919.

xi, 153 p.

1219. Latin American libraries: Argentine library conditions; The National library of Mexico; Library experiences in Mexico; Latin Americana collections in the United States. (In Library journal. New York, 1919. 24½ cm. v. 44, no. 4.)

1220. Macedonio Urquidi, José. Bolivianas ilustres. Prólogo de Ismael Vásquez. La Paz, 1919.·
　2 v.

1221. Méndez Bejarano, Mario. Bio-bibliografía, o Papeletas bio-bibliográficas de escritores nacidos en la provincia de Sevilla que han tratado de las tierras y misiones de ultramar. Madrid, Impr. del Patronato de huérfanos de intendencia e intervención militares, 1915.
　218 p.　21 cm.

1222. Mitre, Bartolomé. Ulrich Schmidel, primer historiador del Río de la Plata, con notas bibliográficas y biográficas. La Plata, 1890. (In Anales del Museo de La Plata. Sección de historia americana)

1223. Montero Pérez, Francisco. Noticias acerca de algunos naturales de la provincia de Alicante que se distinguieron en América. Alicante, Talleres tipográficos de "El Día", 1919.
　46 p.

1224. Morel-Fatio, Alfred. Bibliothèque nationale. Département des manuscrits. Catalogue des manuscrits espagnols et des manuscrits portugais. Paris, Imprimerie nationale, 1892.
　xxvii, 422 p.

1225. Murray, John Lovell. A selected bibliography of missionary literature. New York, Student volunteer movement 1920.
　58 p.　23 cm.
　Latin America: p. 33–35.

1226. Museum of the American Indian. List of publications of the Museum of the American Indian, Heye foundation. New York, Museum of the American Indian, 1921.
　38 p.　16½ cm.　(Indian notes and monographs.)

1227. Mussio, Julio A. Diccionario histórico y biográfico de la República Argentina. Buenos Aires, J. Roldán [1920?]
　2 v. ports., plates.

1228. New York. Public library. Latin-American periodicals current in the reference department. New York, 1920.
　7 p.　25½ cm.
　From Bulletin of the New York Public Library, Sept., 1920.

1229. Ochoa, Eugenio de. Catálogo razonado de los manuscritos españoles existentes en la Biblioteca real de Paris, seguido de un suplemento que contiene los de las otras tres bibliotecas (del Arsenal, de Sta. Genoveva y Mazarina) Paris, Imprenta real, 1844.
　x, 708 p.

1230. Pan American union. Section of education. Latin American secondary schools; courses of study. Washington, D. C., 1920.

32 p. 23½ cm. (Monograph, no 1.)
Prepared by Arturo Torres.
Contains references to sources.

1231. Parker, William Belmont. Argentines of today. New York. The Hispanic society of America, 1920.

2 v. (Hispanic notes and monographs, v. 5.)
The author is also preparing Bolivians of to-day, Chileans of to-day, Paraguayans of to-day, Peruvians of to-day and Uruguayans of to-day.

1232. Paz, Julián. Catálogo de los mapas que se conservan en el Archivo general de Simancas, sección de "Límites de América." (In Revista de archivos, bibliotecas y museos. Madrid, 1899. 24½ cm. 3. época, t. 3, p. 524–548)

1233. Pierson, William Whatley. A syllabus of Hispanic-American history. 3d ed. University of North Carolina. 44 p.

1234. Quaritch, Bernard. A catalogue of geography, voyages, travels, Americana. London, 1895.

2 p. l., 200 p. 18½ cm.

1235. Rich, Obadiah. Catalogue of a collection of manuscripts principally in Spanish, relating to America, in the possession of O. Rich. London, Printed by W. Bowden [1845?]

44, [4] p. 19 cm.
Original autograph letters: [4] p.

1236. Rolando, Carlos A. Cronología del periodismo ecuatoriano. Pseudónimos de la prensa nacional. Guayaquil, Imp. Monteverde y Velarde, 1920.

166 p.

1237. Schuller, Rodolfo R. Sobre el orijen de los Charrúa; réplica al doctor Jorje Friederici. Publicado en los Anales de la Universidad de Chile, t. cxviii. Santiago de Chile, Imprenta Cervantes, 1906.

158 p. map. 25½ cm.
Contains bibliographies.

1238. Sociedad cubana de ingenieros. Catálogo abreviado de la biblioteca. Habana, Imp. de P. Fernández y cía., 1915.

42 p.

1239. Thayer Ojeda, Tomás. La sección de manuscritos de la Biblioteca nacional de Chile. (In Hispanic American historical review. Baltimore, 1921. 27 cm. v. 4, no. 1, p. 156–197)

With English translation.

1240. Torres, Lanzas, Pedro. Catálogo de legajos del Archivo general de Indias, secciones 1 y 2. Patronato y contaduría de Indias. Sevilla. Tip. Zarzuela, 1919.

203 p.

1241. Trillo, José Alejandro. Bibliografía del alienista argentino Lucio Melén-
des. Buenos Aires, 1920.

1242. Warden, David Baillie. Bibliotheca americana, being a choice collection
of books relating to North and South America and the West Indies, including voyages to the southern hemisphere. Paris, 1831.

   2 p. l., 138 p., 1 l.
   Reprinted, Paris, 1840.

   This collection "was purchased ... by the state of New York ... It
   numbers 1118 works, beginning with the Translation of Munster by Belle-
   forest (ed. of 1570) and, with the exception of some rare charts, does not
   contain anything of special interest to bibliographers.—Harrisse, B.A.
   V., p. xxvi.

1243. Winship, George Parker. Index of titles relating to America in the "Colección de documentos inéditos para la historia de España." (In Bulletin
of the Public Library of the city of Boston. Boston, 1894. 27 cm. v. 13,
p. 250-263)

1244. Anglo-South American handbook for 1921 (incorporating Mexico and
Central America). Edited by W. H. Koebel. London. Federation of
British industries, 1921.

   cxiv, 929 p. map. 19 cm.
   Bibliography of works on South America from 1870: p. 891-907.

1245. Bolton, Herbert Eugene. The colonization of North America, 1492-1783,
by Herbert Eugene Bolton ... and Thomas Maitland Marshall ... New
York, The Macmillan company, 1920.

   xvi p., 1 l., 609 p. illus. (maps) 22½ cm.
   "Readings" at end of each chapter form a valuable guide for the student.

1246. ―――― Guide to materials for the history of the United States in the
principal archives of Mexico. Washington, D. C., Carnegie institution
of Washington, 1913.

   xv, 553 p. 25½ cm. Carnegie institution of Washington. Publication no. 163.

1247. ―――― Kino's Historical memoir of Pimería Alta; a contemporary account
of the beginnings of California, Sonora, and Arizona, 1683-1711, pub. for
the first time from the original manuscript in the Archives of Mexico;
translated into English, edited and annotated by Herbert Eugene Bolton,
Cleveland, The A. H. Clark company, 1919.

   2 v. fronts. 26 cm.
   Bibliography (printed works and manuscripts): v. 2, p. 277-296.

1248. ―――― Spanish exploration in the Southwest, 1542-1706. New York,
C. Scribner's sons, 1916.

   xii p., 2 l., 3-487 p. 3 maps. 22½ cm. (Original narratives of early American history.)
   CONTENTS: Exploration and plans for the settlement of California: The Cabrillo-Ferrelo expedition; the Viscaino expedition.—Exploration and settlement in New Mexico and in adjacent regions:

The Rodríguez expedition; the Espejo expedition; the Oñate expeditions and the founding of the province of New Mexico.—Exploration and settlement in Texas: the Bosque-Larios expedition; The Mendoza-López expedition to the Jumanos; The De León-Massanet expeditions.—Arizona; the Jesuits in Pimería Alta.
The introductions contain reviews of bibliographical sources.

1249. ———— Texas in the middle eighteenth century; studies in Spanish colonial history and administration. Berkeley, University of California press, 1915.

x p., 1 l., 501 p. front., maps (part fold.) facsim. 24½ cm. (University of California publications in history. vol. III.)
Bibliography: p. 447-470.

1250. Boston Public Library. A selected list of books on the commercial relations of South America, principally with the United States. Boston, The Trustees, 1918.

2 p. l., 19 p. 17 cm. (Brief reading lists, no. 4).

1251. Brandenburger, Clemens. Neuerebrasilische wissenschaftliche literatur. (in Mitteilungen des Deutsch-Südamerikanischen und Iberischen Instituts in Köln. Stuttgart und Berlin, 1920. 24½ cm. heft 1-2, p. 49-61).

1252. Candioti, Marcial R. Bibliografía doctoral de la Universidad de Buenos Aires y catálogo cronológico de las tesis en su primer centenario 1821-1920. Buenos Aires, 1920, 804 p.

"Las tesis de jurisprudencia, incluyendo las de derecho canónico, son 3450, las de teología 22, las de medicina son 3860, los proyectos.de la Facultad de ciencias exactas 1014, las tesis de la Facultad de filosofía y letras 46, agronomía y veterinaria 215 y ciencias económicas 79; lo que hace el total de 8686 de la colección. Los diez y nueve capítulos que sirven de introducción a la obra, son un verdadero tratado de crítica literaria sobre las tesis"—cf. Dr. E. S. Zeballos' review in Rev. de derecho. hist. y letras, April, 1921.

1253. Cortijo Alahija, L. Musicología latino-americana La música popular y los músicos celebres de la América-latina. Barcelona, Maucci, 1920.

443 p.

1254. Cuba Congreso. Cámara de representantes. Bibliografía sobre bancos y crédito, obras que se hallan en la biblioteca. Edición preliminar. Habana, Impr. "El Siglo xx," 1921.

59 p.
Prepared by Luis Marino Pérez.

1255. Espejo, Juan Luis. Indice de documentos relativos a Chile existentes en el Public record office de Londres, Archivo de las órdenes militares de Madrid y Archivo general de Indias de Sevilla. Santiago de Chile, 1915.

1256. ———— Nobiliario de la antigua Capitanía general de Chile. Santiago de Chile, Imprenta universitaria, 1917.

309, [1] p. coats of arms. 26 cm. Ensayo bibliográfico: p. 291-296.

1257. Francia, Felipe. Genealogía de la familia del Libertador Simón Bolívar. [Caracas] Tip. Emp. el Cojo, 1911.

30 p. plate. 21½ cm.

1258. García Samudio, Nicolás. Colombian literature. (In the Hispanic American historical review. Baltimore, 1921. 27 cm. v. 4, p. 330–347).

1259. Griffin, Grace Gardner. Writings on American history, 1906.—A bibliography of books and articles on United States and Canadian history, with some memoranda on other portions of America. New York, The Macmillan company, 1908—. 24½ cm.

"With respect to the regions lying south of the continental United States. . . the intention has been to include all writings on the history of these regions published in the United States or Europe; but the products (not relating to the United States) of South America and other southward regions has been left to their own bibliographers."—Preface, 1917.

1260. Hasse, Adelaide Rosalie. Index to United States documents relating to foreign affairs, 1828–1861. Washington, D. C., Carnegie institution of Washington, 1914–21.

4 v. 29½ cm. (Carnegie institution of Washington. Publication no. 185.)

1261. Instituto do Ceará. Revista trimensal do Instituto do Ceará, sob a direcção do barão de Studart. Ceará-Fortaleza, 1887?—. 22½ cm.

Contains much of biographical and bibliographical value, such as bio-bibliographical notices of deceased members, lists of journals published in Ceara, Estrangeiros e Ceará, etc.

1262. Lehmann, Walter. Zentral-Amerika. 1. teil. Die sprachen Zentral-Amerikas. Berlin, D. Reimer, 1920.

xii, 596 p. map. 32 cm. With extensive bibliographical references.

1263. Lutrell, Estelle. Mexican writers, a catalogue of books in the University of Arizona Library, with synopsis and biographical notes. Tucson, 1920.

83 p. parts. 23½ cm. (University of Arizona record, v 13, no. 5, Library bibliography no. 5.)

A very useful contribution to the bibliography of modern Mexican literature. Authors names are given in full with dates, followed by bio-bibliographical notes. It is arranged in five sections: 1. Mexican writers; 2. Literature in Spanish upon Mexican themes by authors native to other countries; 3. Collections, Literary criticism. Biography; 4. Bibliographies; 5. Mexican language.

1264. Navas V., José Buenaventura. Evolución social del obrero en Guayaquil; obra histórica. Guayaquil, Imp. Guayaquil, 1920.

63, [1] p. illus., ports. 19 cm.
Contains many biographical notices.

1265. Noronha Santos, Francisco Agenor de. Indice da Revista Archivo do Districto Federal com extracto alphabetico de assumptos. Rio de Janeiro, 1919.

"Contains an alphabetical index of all documents since the 16th century relating to the Brasil-capital and published in the records of the municipality." cf. Dr. Oliviera Lima's note in Hisp. Am. hist. rev., May 1921. p. 361.

1265a. Pérez, Luis Marino. Guide to the materials for American history in Cuban archives. Washington, D. C., Carnegie institution, 1907.

ix, [1] 142 p. 26 cm. (Carnegie institution of Washington. Publication no. 83.)

1266. Revista de filología española, t. 1- . Madrid, 1914—. 25½ cm. Quarterly.

Edited by Ramón Menéndes Pidal.

In addition to the critical articles and reviews the Revista contains a classified bibliography of books and articles dealing with Spain and Latin America in all languages. For convenience in filing a special edition of this indispensable bibliography is printed on one side only.

1267. Rivet, P. Bibliographie américaniste 1914–1919. (Journal de la Société des Américanistes de Paris. Paris, 1919. 28 cm. Nouv. sér., t. xi, p. 677–739).

1268. Rodríguez Lendián, Evelio. Elogio del doctor Ramón Meza y Suárez Inclán. (In Anales de la Academia de la historia. Habana, 1919—. 28½ cm. t. 1—, núm. 1—).

Includes bibliography.

1269. Salas, Carlos I. Estudio biografico-bibliográfico de la vida y obras del doctor Pedro Mártir de Angleria. Buenos Aires?, 1921.?

Only 50 copies printed.
Reviewed in La Prensa, New York, May 25, 1921.

1270. Salvador Ministerio de relaciones exteriores. Lista diplomática y consular. San Salvador, Imprenta nacional, 1920.

32 p.

1271. Serrano, Pedro. Hispanistas mexicanos. Vol. 1. Mexico, 1920.

1272. Sociedad económica de los amigos del país de la Habana. Catálogo de la biblioteca (In Revista cubana bimestre. Habana, 1920—. 24 cm.)

1273. Sparn, Enrique. Bibligraía de la geología, mineralogía y paleontología de la República Argentina. Córdoba, 1920.

56 p.

1274. Studart, Guilherme, barão de. Estrangeiros e Ceará. (In Revista trimensal do Instituto do Ceará, Ceará-Fortaleza, 1918. 22 cm. t. 32, p. 191–274.)

Lista dos auctores e de suas obras tendo referencia ao Ceará: p. 269–274.

1275. Thayer Ojeda, Luis. Navarros y vascongados en Chile. Santiago de Chile, 1904.

1276. Thayer Ojeda, Tomás. Los conquistadores de Chile. Santiago de Chile, Impr. Cervantes, 1908–13.

3 v. 26 cm.

1277. Torres Saldamando, Enrique. Los títulos de Castilla en las familias de Chile. Santiago de Chile, 1894.

2 v.

1278. Trelles y Govín, Carlos Manuel. Bibliografía antillana. (In the Hispanic American historical review. Baltimore, 1921. 27 cm. v. 4, p. 324–330).

1279. Urquidi, José Macedonio.   Bolivianas ilustres.   La Paz, Arnó hermanos, 1919.

   2 v. ports. 19 cm.

1280. Vicuña Mackenna, Benjamín.   Los orígenes de las familias chilenas Santiago de Chile, G. E. Miranda, 1903.

   3 v.

1281. Zeballos, Estanislao Severo.   Bibliographie argentine de droit international privé, par ordre chronologique.   (In Bulletin argentin de droit international privé, fondé et publié par Estánislao S. Zeballos.   Buenos Aires, 1903-10.   23 cm.   v. 1-2).

   An important contribution to the bibliography of the subject, the value of which is greatly enhanced by the authorative critical comments of the compiler a distinguished statesman, jurist, author and editor, former professor of private international law in the University of Buenos Aires, and three times minister of foreign affairs of Argentina.   The Bulletin contains also other sections, Bibliographie étrangère, Bibliographie générale, etc., reviewing the current literature of the subject with critical appreciations.

   The Revista de derecho, historia y letras, also founded and directed by Dr. Zeballos and now in its 68th volume (1921) is a valuable source of information concerning current Hispanic American bibliography, giving titles of recent publications, not only in Argentina but also in other countries.   A special section "Bibliografía (catálogo rasonado de mi biblioteca) gives full titles and collations, with critical reviews by the editor.

(*To be concluded*)

C. K. JONES.

THE ARCHIVO GENERAL DE INDIAS

The ever-increasing present-day interest in Hispanic America offers ready acceptance to anything which aims at a wider dissemination of information regarding it—whether it be commercial opportunity or historical background.[1]   The study of the history of the territory lying to the south of the United States has a most brilliant future, and, in the succeeding years the sources of its history, particularly those located in the archives of Spain, will be mined more and more extensively.   No collection in Spain, indeed, no collection throughout the world, is so rich in materials concerning that region, as is the Archivo General de Indias, located in Seville.   It is to be expected, therefore, that those archives are destined to be the goal of a great majority of those who elect research in Spanish American History.   There are numerous guides in print to the Archivo General, but they are primarily catalogues to materials—what is needed is a practical aid to direct one through the intricacies of archive routine.   It is the aim of this article to present such a guide in brief scope, one that the authors of this article would have welcomed when they began their work in Seville.

Investigation in foreign archives necessarily presents to American students the problems of travel and residence aboard.   In Spain these difficulties are accentuated.   Hence, next to aids in actual archive complexities, it is expedient to point out how inconveniences in travel and residence can be reduced to a minimum.   The prospective investigator should plan to arrive in Seville no earlier than September

[1] The best-known guide of this character is William R. Shepherd, *Guide to materials for the history of the United States in Spanish archives* (Washington, 1907), which also gives a general description of the Archives and the organisation of their contents.   Roscoe R. Hill's *Descriptive catalogue of the documents relating to the history of the United States in the Papeles procedentes de Cuba deposited in the Archives General de Indias at Seville* (Washington, 1916) is a guide to materials of a more particular nature.   It also supplements Shepherd's *Guide* as regards arrangement and archival rules.   A bibliography of works treating of the Archivo General de Indias is to be found on p. vii of this catalogue.   Another guide to particular material in the Archivo General is, Charles E. Chapman's *Catalogue of Materials in the Archivo General de Indias for the History of the Pacific Coast and the American Southwest*, Berkeley, 1919.   Its introduction contains a brief, but useful, description of the Archives.

as the terrific summer heat makes work wellnigh impossible. This
will enable him to spend the other three seasons quite comfortably
in research.

The routes to Seville from America are as varied as are their relative merits. In reality, however, these can be classified under two
heads: sea and land approaches. There are Spanish transatlantic
steamship lines running direct to Cadiz, British lines to Gibraltar,
and French lines to Lisbon. These constitute the sea approaches.
They involve a long, slow passage across the Atlantic, several train
changes to Seville, and little opportunity for sight-seeing. On the
other hand, one can make a rapid, direct passage to France on any one
of a dozen steamship lines, and travel overland to Seville by way of
Paris and Madrid at no greater expense, and with the added induce-
ment of better service and instructive sightseeing. In regard to route
therefore, the most preferable one is that by way of France.

The selection of living accomodations in Seville is obviously a relative matter, determined by the sex, age, and position in life of the
student. In general, however, there are certain criteria which must
be adhered to in choosing quarters; the first and most important of
which is good food and warmth during the winter. The winters in
Seville, though comparatively mild, can nevertheless be most uncom-
fortable due to the lack of heating facilities. One should aim, therefore, in order to escape the damp cold, to secure quarters as high above
the ground as is possible, and which receive sunlight sometime during
the day. Of equal importance to health and unimpaired efficiency is
wholesome food and pure drinking water. Spanish food, though plentiful, is invaribly prepared in olive-oil which, beneficial in its natural
state, is highly indigestible as cooked grease. Nor can too much care
be exercised in drinking nothing but boiled or distilled water, as the
local supplies are typhoid-laden. The impression is current that
syphon-water is safe, but even its use should be dispensed with, as it
is made from undistilled water. The proximity of living quarters to
the archives is an obvious advantage which needs but to be mentioned.

The most accessible stopping-places in Seville are the hotels and
fondas, which are, as a rule, quite comfortable, and are to be recommended to people who contemplate only a short stay. Prices range
from seven pesetas a day, to eighteen pesetas at the Hotel Inglaterra,
Seville's most pretentious hostelry. For parties of people who intend
to make a more prolonged stay the renting of an apartment is recommended. These, well furnished, can be easily secured at a moderate

price. Extreme Andalusian conservatism renders it well-nigh impossible to live with a Spanish family with the idea of coming in contact with Spanish life and improving one's knowledge of the Spanish language. Moreover the Spanish dialect spoken in Andalusia, makes it a most unsatisfactory place to acquire correct Spanish.

People accustomed to. keep in trim by a certain amount of active, outdoor exercise, will find that all Seville affords are long walks. Even tennis is out of the question, due to the absence of tennis courts. Physical recreation being thus summarily disposed of there remains mental diversion. There are no public libraries, nor institutions resembling the Y. M. C. A. Hence, one is compelled to fall back on clubs, cafes, and théaters for amusement.

The building in which the Archivo General de Indias is housed can be located with little difficulty. It is a two-storied, square, unimposing structure, adjoining the Cathedral in the heart of the city, and is known to the Sevillanos as the Casa Lonja. It was built in 1598 as the seat of the Casa de Contratación, which purpose it served for over a hundred years. With the removal of the merchant's exchange to Cadiz, the building was left unoccupied until 1785, when, by royal decree, it became the repository for the Archivo de Indias. That purpose it has served to the present time—the collection being increased constantly by accessions from Simancas and similar sources. Despite the simple severity of the Casa Lonja's exterior, it's interior still retains some vestiges of former splendor. On the lower floor, surrounding a patio, adorned only by a statue of Columbus are galleries for exhibiting documents, and the summer research-room. The second floor, more ornate. than the first, is given over to document stacks, exhibition halls, and the winter workrooms of the Archives.

The provision of workrooms to fit the seasons may seem curious. This is made necessary because of the marked change from suffocating summer-heat to penetrating winter-dampness. The Sevillian custom is to vacate the lower floor during the winter months to escape the invading moisture, and in this the Archives are no exception. Even these measures are futile, for, in the absence of heating appliances, one is forced to work heavily wrapped in overcoats and blankets. For these reasons it is advisable to be provided with clothes suitable for both extreme heat and cold.

Admission to the Archives for the purpose of investigation can be readily obtained. There are practically no formalities, and, once admittance has been gained, there is little restriction. Letters of introduction, and similar credentials, attesting the good character and serious intent of the bearer, will be found valuable. No fees are required; however, it is customary to give a small *"propina"* to the *"ordenanzas,"* or attendants, who deliver the documents. Students are assigned permanent study-tables where they may carry on their investigations unmolested, and, though paper is not furnished, pens and good ink are supplied.

The necessity of adequate preparation and thorough training before attempting archive research cannot be too strongly urged. Above all, a thorough acquaintance with all secondary material on a given subject, as well as of printed sources and transcripts of manuscripts that are available, should be acquired. In particular there should be at hand, at all times, a complete index of known material on the subject. This will not only give direction to work in the Archives, but will prevent useless duplication. One should not expect to find library facilities at his disposal in Seville. There is a small reference library in the Archivo General, but the very meager collection is kept behind lock and key. The University Library has little value for modern research, and the Columbine Library is limited in its scope.

The training in auxillary sciences necessary to historical analysis will be determined by the nature of the subject under investigation. Obviously, every researcher in the Archivo General de Indias must be equipped with a knowledge of the Spanish language. This knowledge must be more and more specialized as one works back toward the Middle Ages. The study of subjects belonging to the earlier centuries, or the religious field, demand a thorough training in Latin in addition. Modern Spanish orthography presents no difficulties, but any work prior to the seventeenth century necessitates a mastery of palaeography.[1] The Archives' very rich collection in old maps makes, at least, an elementary acquaintance with cartography highly desirable. It is for the particular investigator to determine whether his subject requires training in diplomatics, heraldry, genealogy, sphragistics, or any other of the sciences auxiliary to history.

The great mass of manuscripts in the Archivo General has never been satisfactorily calendared. There are inventories which vary as greatly in physical makeup as they do in utility. They are of various sizes,

[1] The most practical work on Spanish palaeography is, D. Jesus Muños y Rivero, *Manual de Palaeografía Diplomática Española de los Siglos XII al XVII*, Segunda edición corregida y aumentada, Madrid, 1917. It can be procured from the editor, Daniel Jorro, at 23 Calle de la Paz, Madrid.

ranging from small, octavo volumes to huge unwieldy folios—all hand-written. Some of the catalogues, still in use, were prepared over a century ago. Naturally, they are somewhat worn, and, in many cases, are almost illegible; but, most serious of all, they are quite out of date, as archive science has made tremendous strides since they were prepared. Their .ack of uniformity is also marked by different systems of entry, presence or absence of indices, and variability in accuracy and complete-ness. The result is that, while one is dependent upon these catalogues for general direction, these materials are of little assistance beyond providing the necessary shelf-numbers for *legajos*.[3]

The summary entries of these inventories have been recently pub-lished in a small volume by the officials of the Centro at the Archivo de Indias in Seville.[4] It indicates the main divisions into which the *legajos* have been grouped, their numbers and inclusive dates, and some indi-cation of the nature of the material contained. The lack of shelf-numbers makes this publication of little value. Realizing this, the Archives officials have undertaken the publication, *in extenso*, of all the inventories to the Archives collection. The only one of these published to date is, *Catálogo de Legajos del Archivo General de Indias, Secciones Primera y Segunda, Patronato y Contaduría General del Consejo de Indias*.[5]

Inasmuch as one can have recourse to no more satisfactory catalogues, a detailed description of those existing may prove useful. The some sixty million documents, assembled in the forty-five thousand *legajos*, which comprise the manuscript collection of the Archives, are divided into twelve great sets, each with its individual catalogue. These sets are: Patronato Real, Contaduría General del Consejo de Indias, Casa de Contratación de las Indias, Papeles de Justicia de Indias, Consejo de Indias y Distintos Ministerios Procedentes de Simancas, Escribanía de Camara del Consejo de Indias, Secretaría del Juzgado de Arribadas de Cádiz y Comisión Inteventora de la Hacienda Pública de Cádiz,

---

[3] *Legajos* are bundles of manuscripts ranging in size from a few documents, or bound volumes, to as many as two thousand manuscrips each. They are located by *estante* (stack), *cajón* (shelf), and *legajo* numbers, and a combination of the three forms the *legajo* call-number. For example, *Estante 2, Cajón 2, Legajo 3*, is commonly written 2-2-3.

[4] *Catálogo, Cuadro General de la Documentación del Archivo General de Indias*, Bibliotepa Colonial Americana, Tomo I, edited by the officials of the Centro at the Archivo de Indias, Seville, 1918.

[5] Biblioteca Colonial Americana, Tomo II, edited by the director of the Centro at the Archivo de Indias, Seville, 1919.

Papeles de Correos, Papeles de Estado, Papeles de Ministerio de Ultramar, Papeles de la Isla de Cuba, and Papeles de Cádiz. They vary in size from the 105 *legajos* of the Estado Group to the 18,860 *legajos* of the Simancas Consejo Papers.

The first and best known set is the Patronato Real. It represents selections from the consignments from Simancas made by Don Diego Juárez, head of the Archivo de Indias, in 1814, of what he considered the most interesting.⁶ The collection of 294 *legajos*, occupies two *estantes* in the "Salón del Patronato", thus named, probably, from the fact that some of the first documents to be stored there referred to Patronato Real.⁷ These documents, relating almost exclusively to the sixteenth and seventeenth centuries, are particularly rich in materials for the "era of the conquistadores". Their inventories, completed by Juárez in 1819, by virtue of royal authorization, comprise two volumes.

Volume I catalogues, first, seven *legajos* of Pontifical Bulls and Briefs concerning Real Patronato, erection of cathedrals and churches, and the appointments of archbishops and bishops during the years 1493 to 1703; second, forty-three *legajos* on discoveries, new lands and descriptions of them, for the period 1486–1640; third, 120 *legajos* relating to the merits and services of the first discoverers and conquistadores, 1514–1646. Volume II, also divided into three parts, catalogues papers concerning government, navigation, commerce, fortification, history, geography, Real Armada, astronomy, and other specific subjects. These papers, collected into 126 *legajos*, cover the period 1480–1790. There are items of extreme interest to be found in these catalogues to the Patronato Real, to which particular reference should be made. For example, there are eight *legajos* devoted to Christopher Columbus and his descendants; three to Magellan's expedition, and four to Hernando Cortés and his descendants. Under the heading

⁶ *Catálogo, Cuadro General*, p 47. Chapman (in his *Catalogue of Materials*, p. 7, n. 18) says "They represent the selections of Juan Bautista Muñoz of the materials which he considered the most valuable of the Archives, as such they have been used by investigators more than any other equally valuable sets, and they constitute the principal source for the much cited *Colección de documentos inéditos relativos al descubrimiento, conquista, y organización de las antiguas possesiones españolas de America y Oceanía*, 42 vols., Madrid, 1864–1884.

⁷ Chapman (*Catalogue*, p. 7, n. 18) and Shepherd (*Guide*, p. 79) agree regarding the title of these papers saying that they derive their name from the fact that the papers were stored in a room which was formerly the office of that branch of royal administration.

THE ARCHIVO GENERAL DE INDIAS

"History", in Volume II., is a *legajo* of papers pertaining to Fray Bartolomé de Las Casas, and a similar *legajo* for Miguel de Cervantes Saavedra. Under "Real Armada" are a number of *legajos* concerning corsairs of various nations, the most important of whom was Sir Francis Drake.

The inventory to the second great set of papers, the Contaduría General del Consejo de Indias, which, as its name indicates, proceeds from the Council of the Indies, is to be found in four volumes. This work was concluded by Don Juan Agustín Cean Bermúdez in January, 1792. In all 1,956 *legajos*, embracing the years 1514 to 1778, were catalogued under various subheadings. The first, Papers pertaining to the Consejo de Indias and its Dependencies, contains accounts of receivers, treasurers, and porters of the Council, and copies of royal *cédulas* granting individuals permission to go to the Indies. Negro slavery in the New World constitutes the second subheading. The third subdivision of the inventory, is a calendar of papers referring to the Casa de Contratación de Sevilla, dealing solely with commerce and its protection. Following this is a section pertaining to the papers of the Consulados de Sevilla y Cádiz. The balance of the inventories to the Contaduría General concerns accounts of the Royal Treasury in Nueva España, Guatemala, Santo Domingo, Puerto Rico, Cuba, Filipinas, Nuevo Reino de Granada, Venezuela, Perú, Buenos Aires, and the Orinoco.

There are four inventory volumes to the Papers of the Contratación de Sevilla. These, the work of Don Agustín Cean Bermúdez (1793), list the materials proceeding from the Casa de la Contratación de las Indias, for the years 1492 to 1795.· They are collected into 5,876 *legajos*, and constitute the third main grouping of *legajos* in the Archives. The greater part of the first volume of the inventory is given over to an enumeration of wills filed in the Contratación. In this volume are also to be found items referring to the examination of pilots and legal cases concerning commerce. Volume II. is concerned primarily with legal disputes arising out of commerce. The registers for the entrance and clearance of ships are catalogued in volume III. The most interesting papers of the Contratación are. listed in the last volume of the inventory. They deal with trade companies both in Spain and in the New World, passengers, appointments of admirals and generals of the fleet, salaries, and other matters concerning the Armada. At the end of each of the four volumes is to be found a resumen, which furnishes the student with a short cut to its contents. The four inventories are supplemented by parallel index volumes.

The catalogue of the Justicia Papers consists of two volumes, one an inventory and the other an alphabetical index. They were prepared by Isidoro de Antillón and date from 1809. The papers listed constitute 1,187 *legajos* collected in six *estantes*, and comprise the years 1515 to 1664. The Papeles de Justicia de Indias, likewise transferred from Simancas, is one of the most important collections of the Archives. It is especially valuable for the earlier period, for in it are grouped *residencias* and *visitas*. The importance of this type of material will be given consideration later in this article. In the inventory volume the *legajos* are arranged according to *audiencias*, in each of which the papers are subdivided into cases between individuals, cases in which the government is a party, *residencias*, *visitas*, and commissions. Deviations from these set subdivisions constitute mainly, appeals to the Council of the Indies, with the *informaciones* and *probanzas* that accompany them. The index volume of the catalogue is merely a cross reference to the inventory and furnishes no additional information. Documents of more than ordinary interest to be found in the Justicia Papers are the Viceroy Mendoza visita taken by Tello de Sandóval, the Coronado residencia, and the residencia of Hernando Cortés. The extreme value of these papers is paralleled by their great bulk, for the first mentioned *visita* constitutes no less than twenty *legajos*.

Three very meager guides are provided for what is perhaps the richest set of all—Papeles del Consejo de Indias y Distintos Ministerios procedentes de Simancas. This set, familiarly known as the Simancas Papers, is collected in 103 *estantes*, totaling 18,860 *legajos;* it being therefore, the greatest in point of numbers in the Archives. In the first two volumes of the above-mentioned guides are the papers of the *distritos* divided into as many groups as there were *audiencias* in the Indies. The distribution of the documents corresponding to each *audiencia* conforms to the following classification: first, under the secular branch (*ramo secular*) are royal orders, civil government, correspondence, *expedientes*, treasury, war, marine, and commerce; second, under the ecclesiastical branch (*ramo· eclesiástico*) are royal orders, nominations, correspondence, *espedientes*, special subjects, and religious orders. Of the *legajos* listed those that lend themselves most readily to profitable research are those which contain the correspondence of the viceroys, royal officials, and ecclesiastical dignitaries. For particular information concerning persons, the *hojas de servicios* (certificates of services) and *informaciones de oficio y partes* yield the best results.

In the third volume is a list of the papers called Indiferente which deal with America in general, not being referable to any particular district. There are also collected in this set material, not necessarily from Simancas, which arrived too late for classification in other inventories. It is, therefore, a growing set.[8] The inventory to the Indiferente can be most conveniently considered under three heads, the Indiferente of New Spain, the Indiferente of Peru and the Indiferente General. The same system of subdivision employed in the catalogues of the Simancas Papers proper is used for the Indiferente of New Spain and Peru. Under the title, Indiferente General, as widely varying subjects as royal orders for the formation of the Archivo General de Indias, Asientos concerning Negroes, Flotas and Armadas, and Diplomatic relations with Rome concerning Patronato Real, are to be found.

This classification of the Simancas Papers was made in accordance with Article 29 of the *Ordenanzas of the Archivo General de Indias*, January 10, 1790. Since that date the papers have retained their original classification, no improvements or alterations having been attempted. Nor have the provisional inventories, made long ago, been replaced by more permanent and serviceable guides.

The Escribanía de Cámara del Consejo de Indias has an inventory of seven volumes bound in sheepskin. None of them has an index, nor are the cover-titles legible, so one is compelled to go through the volumes page by page to find the desired reference. The catalogues itemize minutely the records of the Royal Secretariat for the years 1525 to 1761. They are a continuation in chronological order of section four of the Justicia Papers. They comprise in all 1,194 voluminous *legajos*, and are installed provisionally on the lower floor of the Archives. The original classification in which they were transferred to the Archivo General, i.e. by *audiencias*, has been retained. Under these heads legal cases, *residencias*, *visitas*, and commissions are treated.

To the *legajos* of the next set—the Secretaría del Juzgado de Arribadas de Cádiz y Comisión interventora de la Hacienda Pública de Cádiz, there are two inventories. The maritime and financial documents, with which they deal, were sent to Seville from their respective centers in 1822. The Secretariat of the Tribunal Papers comprise 369 *legajos*, to which have been added the 224 *legajos* of the Supervisory Commission. The first named includes the years 1674 to 1822, and the latter

[8] Shepherd, *Guide*, p. 67.

1560 to 1821. Although thus combined they constitute one of the twelve major sections of the Archives Collection, as the title indicates their value and usefulness is restricted, due to their particular nature.

Espedientes concerning the mails to and from the Indies, for the years 1764 to 1825, were brought to the Archivo General de Indias in 1864, and constitute the eighth general division of the Archives. They are classified geographically and chronologically, with a group on America in general. The general contents of the 484 *legojos* which comprise the set, are described in the *Indice e Inventarios de los Papeles de Correos*. The principal matters contained, with reference to each *audiencia*, are the following: correspondence and *espedientes*, maritime mails, accounts, and ship-logs.

The collection known as the Papeles de Estado is composed of 105 *legajos* dating from 1686 to 1860. In 1871 they were consigned to the Archivo General by the Ministry of State (*Estado*). They are organized similarly to the Simancas Papers and are classified in the same manner, that is, into thirteen subdivisions by colonial districts, with an additional section called America in general. There is a valuable topical guide, *i.e.*, by *espedientes*, to the set. In addition *papeletas* are provided for each *legajo*, as the index failed to cover the last ten *legajos* of America in general. In this set are assembled part of the papers exchanged between the Consejo de Indias and the Departmento de Estado concerning state affairs. In addition to the Indies in general, the Papeles de Estado group is particularly rich in items bearing on the history of the Pacific Ocean and the American southwest.[9]

Matter concerning the Ministry of Ultramar was turned over to the Archivo in Seville in 1887. It consists of 880 *legajos* and refers to Cuba, Puerto Rico, Luisiana, Florida, Filipinas, and America in general for the years 1605 to 1868, thus supplementing and continuing the Papers of the Audiencias. For the classification of each one of these groups the same plan was followed as was employed for the Simancas Papers. In the *Inventario de los papeles remitidos por el Ministerio de Ultramar al Archivo General de Indias* the *legajos* are numbered consecutively. These *legajos* are provisionally installed in the new cases on the lower floor of the Archivo.

The Papeles Procedentes de la Isla de Cuba are comparatively wellknown to American students due to Roscoe R. Hill's admirable *Descriptive Catalogue*. The Cuban Papers derive their name from the

---

[9] *Ibid.*, p. 33.

fact that they were formerly in Havana in the Archivo General de la Isla de Cuba, from which place they were sent to Seville in thirteen shipments, during the years 1888–1889. They reach a total of 2350 *legajos*, and embrace the period 1669 to 1866. The various shipments to the Archivo de Indias were accompanied by checklists, made by taking the first entries from earlier inventories existing in the Archivo General de Cuba, or by copying the titles from the tags on the *legajos*. These checklists were placed together in the order of receipt, and are the only official index of the papers existing in the Archivo de Indias.[10]

It is interesting to note that this great collection of manuscript material was almost lost to the world of scholarship at the time of its removal to Spain. On arrival in Seville, due to lack of shelf-space, it was placed in the principal rooms of the Archives on wooden platforms prepared for this purpose. It was soon noted, however, that paper-moths had made appreciable inroads on the collection, making it necessary to transfer it to the lower floor, to prevent the spread of the pest. Before being permanently located they were carefully cleaned, ventilated, and inspected. Thanks to the very great care exercised, the destruction was stopped, and the moths have never reappeared.[11]

The Papeles de Cuba are classified in thirteen divisions which correspond to the thirteen shipments from Cuba. In the first three divisions are documents concerning the government of West Florida. In them are contained the correspondence of the governors of New Orleans, Pensacola, and Louisiana, as well as that of the intendents and others. The fourth, fifth, and sixth are made up of treasury accounts and official correspondence in East and West Florida and Louisiana. The seventh group of documents concerns the official correspondence of New Orleans, Cartagena de Indias, Nuevo Reino de Granada, Costa Firme, Sante Fé de Bogotá, Vera Cruz, Puerto Cabello, Castillo del Morro, and Santo Domingo. In the eighth, ninth, and tenth sets, are collected *documentos de Cuba y Santo Domingo*. These are largely the military correspondence of the Captaincies General. The last three divisions, America in general, cover a variety of subjects. As pointed out in Hill's *Descriptive Catalogue* (p. xi), the Cuban Papers offer the finest opportunity for research in United States History of all the sets in the Archivo General de Indias.

[10] Hill, *Descriptive Catalogue*, p. xi.
[11] *Catálogo, Cuadro General*, p. 147.

The twelfth and final major group, the Papeles de Cadiz, is an accession made in 1903. It came from the Biblioteca Provincial de Cádiz, where it had been known as the Archivo de Indias de Cádiz. From the slight index (*Libro de Actas*) one learns that it is made up of 1260 *legajos*, and approximately 750 account books. The *lagajos* do not have guidecards indicating place, subject, and date, nor are their size uniform. Their utility, for these Archives, is doubtful, since the majority of them do not refer to the Indies but rather to the House of Trade in Cadiz. They are assembled in a separate room to protect the rich collection of the Archives from the moth-pest with which they are infected.

Next to unsatisfactory inventories and indices, one of the greatest difficulties that confronts the investigator in the Archivó General is the matter of limited working hours. At present, the Casa Lonja is officially open for work from 9.00 a.m. to 3.00 p.m. on week days. In actual practice, however, this time is shortened to about five hours a day. Holidays, however, do not come with the frequency that one might expect in a European Catholic country, so, in this respect, there is no reason for complaint.

The securing of *legajos* for examination presents little in the way of difficulties. One has but to fill out a call-slip, known as a *papeleta de pedido*, and present it to the official in charge. An *ordenanza* secures the desired *legajo* and brings it to the student's table. When a new *legajo* is delivered the old one must be returned to the shelves; beyond this restriction, one is free to call as many as he desires.

There are other rules, however, regarding the handling of material. The most rigid of these is that documents are not to be carried about except by attendants, who should be called for that purpose. Since most of the manuscripts have been arranged separately in chronological and topical order, the research-worker is urged not to disturb this sequence. The marking of manuscripts and tracing over them is likewise prohibited. This rule, notwithstanding, is not strictly obeyed; nor is the prohibition against smoking in the archives building rigidly enforced. It is permitted in the corridors, and is even winked at in the workroom. Not infrequently an archives official can be seen smoking over a precious manuscript which, were it to be destroyed, can never be replaced.

Another archives regulation, more recently adopted, requires that a record be kept of all documents copied by investigators. To carry this out a blank form (*cedula de resultado de investagacion*) with spaces for date, name, and nationality of investigator, subject of investigation, number and title of *legajo*, destination of copies and extract of subject matter, has been provided. It was believed that this system would remove one of the greatest difficulties that confronted students in the Archives, *i.e.*, the lack of any record of previous investigation, which led to useless duplication of work.[12] Though this effort was most laudable, its resultant utility is almost negligible; for, it was begun too late to secure a complete record, it lists only transcripts and not student's notes, and lastly, its files are not accessible. Nor are the back files of the callslips obtainable should one desire to consult *legajos* examined by previous investigators.

Having thus outlined the character of the collection in the Archivo General de Indias which awaits the investigator in Hispanic American History, there now remains for consideration the best methods of meeting the problems presented. Although research methods are largely relative in character, there are certain rules for procedure in these Archives which are applicable to all persons. Obviously, one should direct his attention to materials which will yield the best results. The most valuable kinds of documents for the majority of research subjects are *hojas de servicios*, *residencias*, and *visitas*. In the *hojas de servicios* are to be found records, not only of official services, but complete biographies as well. *Residencias* sum up entire incumbencies of royal officials by means of testimonies and replies to charges. They include also, all official papers to which reference is made in the investigation. In them are to be found the most complete and compact accounts of viceregal reigns, governorships, or any other tenure of office. *Visitas* are valuable for similar reasons, although they do not cover entire terms of office. Informing letters, such as the correspondence of the viceroys and other royal and ecclesiastical officials, furnish a broad background that cannot be secured from such personal sources as *informaciones* and *hojas de servicios*.

[12] James A. Robertson (in his *List of documents in Spanish archives relating to the history of the United States which have been printed or of which transcripts are preserved in American libraries*, Washington, 1910,) made the first attempt to assemble results of investigations in Spanish archives, but it has lost a considerable part of its value due to the fact that many manuscripts have been copied and published since 1910—more, perhaps, than existed at that time. There is no task so vital to the successful promotion of American research in Spanish archives as is the bringing of Robertson up-to-date. Of equal importance is a similar work applicable to all the Americas.

When, therefore, the investigator goes to the catalogues, he should mark as much of this type of material as is possible. These annotations should be made on uniform slips of paper arranged in the desired order of investigation. This system will obviate the necessity of constant reference to the catalogues. Moreover, one will always have, ready at hand, a record of what remains to be done. New leads are constantly appearing as one investigates, and can be immediately fitted into their proper place in the file.

Being thus equipped, the student can consult the *legajos* to better advantage. On the discovery of useful information, some uniform system of marking it should be employed. The use of colored slips of paper is perhaps the most satisfactory method. At the same time, careful record of what is marked should be kept in a file similar to that made for "*legajos* to be consulted". It is advisable to delay the copying of manuscripts until everything has been examined, for until then, their relative value cannot be properly determined.

Once the list of "*legajos* to be consulted" has been exhausted, the investigator can decide what is to be rejected, what is to be copied, and what is useful only for scattered notes. In some cases the making of *regestas* rather than complete copies, is recommended. Competent typists can be hired in the Archives at a nominal price for the making of transcripts. Those who plan to have transcripts made should bring a supply of typewriting paper and carbons with them, as the local shops provide inferior paper at exorbitant rates. This is also true as regards note-paper. In order to insure the safe arrival in the United States of one's work, it is a wise precaution to have all transcripts made in duplicate—sending one by registered mail, and bringing the other in person.[13]

Under archival routine there remains the consideration of the photographing of maps. The excellent collection has been catalogued in great part by Sr. D. Pedro Torres Lanzas, head of the Archives.[14] Ready access, therefore, can be had to many of the maps, and should one desire to procure photographic copies, this can be easily arranged through the official photographer.

[13] It is very necessary to point out the unreliability of the Spanish mail system. Nothing of value should be sent unregistered, and even then, safe delivery is not assured. In having money remitted to Seville, it is advisable to act through the agency of the Anglo-South American Bank, which has branches in both New York and Seville.

[14] See Hill, *Descriptive Catalogue*, p. vii, for titles.

Finally, the friendly reception accorded foreigners by the Archivo General needs but to be mentioned. The comparatively recent realization of the New World that its early history can best be studied in Spanish archives, has been heartily endorsed by Spain which is meeting American students with unalloyed sympathy and approval. This is evidenced by the attempt to create a great center about the Archivo General de Indias in Seville for the study of colonial history. The idea was conceived at the Congreso Hispano-Americano held in Barcelona in 1911, and, by royal order of 1914, "El Centro de Estudios Americanistas de Sevilla" was founded. The aims were, as expressed in the order of foundation: "a más de ser un lugar de investigación histórica un vivero donde perfeccionen ·sus estudios los archiveros españoles y americanos y donde sobre los materiales acumulados de histórica colonial, prácticamente se preparen para el inventario, la catalogación y explotación de los documentos históricos que queden a su cuidado, siendo finalmente un lazo de unión entre los hispano-americanos, con los vínculos de la documentación histórica común y donde tantas lagunas hay que llenar y tantos errores que desvanecer".[18] Invitations were sent to American students to work in the Archives under expert direction, but, due to the outbreak of the war, students were prevented from coming, and so, the project failed. Its official publication, *El Boletín del Centro*, continues to exist, and is now in its seventh year. Quite recently this movement was revived, and it is hoped, now that the war is over, that transatlantic students will be attracted in increasing numbers to Seville. It is to these students, coming from the United States, that this article is directed in the hope that it may be some assistance in guiding them through the archive labyrinth.

ARTHUR S. AITON,
J. LLOYD MECHAM,
Native Sons' Fellows in Pacific Coast
History, University of California

Seville, Spain, January 7, 1921.

[18] *Catálogo, Cuadro General*, p. 156.

NOTES ON MEXICO AND CENTRAL AMERICA

Titles of some interesting books and pamphlets recently published in Central America are the following: *Con el Eslabón*, by the Cuban philosopher, Enrique José Varona, *Pensamientos y Formas. Notas de Viaje*, by Alberto Masferrer, *La Propia* (second edition), by Manuel González Zeledón, and *La Ventana y Otros Poemas*, by the Colombian writer Dmitri Ivanovitch, all published by García Monge; *Cuentos Germánicos*, translations by Carlos Durán; *El Sacerdocio Católico y la Ciencia*, by a Salesian Father; *El Cambio*, by Manuel F. Jiménez; *Algo de Matemáticas*, by Vital Murillo; *Novia*, by Professor Luis Dobles Segreda; *Pacto de Unión de Centro-America celebrado en San José de Costa Rica, el 19 de enero de 1921*, special edition by Alsina's; and *Cuentos de Amor y de Tragedia*, by Vicente Sáenz. In Honduras were published *Aventuras de un Cónsul*, by Enrique Sturitza, who is the Argentine representative in Tegucigalpa; *Maximo Hermenegildo Zepeda*, by the journalist Alemán Bolaños, Tipografía Pro-Patria, La Ceiba; and *Proyecto de Reforma Monetaria presentado al Soberano Congreso Nacional Legislativo*, by the Minister of the Treasury, Señor Eduado Guillén, and comments by Dr. Arthur Young, who is the American financial expert for the Honduras Government. In Salvador, appeared *Leer y Escribir*, by Alberto Masferrer; *Historia del Salvador* (third edition), by Dr. Rafael Reyes; *Principios Elementales de Música*, by Raúl Santamaría; and *Recuerdos Salvadoreños*, volumen II., by José Antonio Cevallos. In Guatemala were published *La Señora es Así*, by Carlos Gustavo Martínez, the editor of the *Studium* magazine; and *Las Rosas de Engaddi*, poems by Rafael Arévalo Martínez. In the last country the publishing company "El Sol", of Ayestas, will devote some special editions in honor of the first centenary of the Central American emancipation.

Books to appear soon in Central America are as follows: Adrian Vidaurre, a keen observer, has in print what he has written on the political events of Guatemala during the last thirty years; *Apuntes sobre Bibliografía de Costa Rica*, by Adolfo Blen; *Costa Rica Precolombina*, by Professor Carlos Gagini; *Crónicas Coloniales*, by Ricardo Fernández

568

Guardia, Trejos Hermanos, San José; and a botanical dictionary of the three Americas, by Dr. Sixto Alberto Padilla, from Salvador.

Two new books on Central America are on sale in the United States: "*Sailing South*", by Philip S. Marden (Houghton, Mifflin), who gives his impressions and experiences about Cuba, Costa Rica and the Canal Zone; and "*The Land Beyond Mexico*", by Rhys Carpenter (Badger), a tribute to the old cities of Copan and Quiriguá, both.of which had been visited by the author.

Among the literary activities of the Central American men of letters abroad, I have to mention the work of José Rodríguez Cerna, from Guatemala, who is in San Francisco publishing *Centro-America*, a weekly paper, with the assistance of Dr. Timoteo Miralda, from Honduras, and Gabry Rivas, from Nicaragua. Adolfo Vivas is the new editor of *Mercurio*, the Spanish magazine of New Orleans. Roberto Barrios is on the editorial staff of *Universal Ilustrado*, of Mexico City, with Francisco Zamora, both of them Nicaraguans. Barrios writes on the new Cuban poets (Agustín Acosta, Federico de Ibarzábal and Felipe Pichardo Moya) in the issue for March 27th; and Zamora pleases his readers with the humorous pages "*Mundo, Demonio y Carne*". Other distinguished sons of Nicaragua are Dr. Dámaso Rivas, from the University of Pennsylvania, who has recently disclosed his scientific investigations in *Human Parasitology, with notes on Bacteriology, Mycology, Laboratory diagnosis, Hematology and Serology*, edited last year by Saunders Company, Philadelphia; and Dr. Juan B. Sacasa, former Dean of the Faculty of Medicine in León, in the January number of the *Bulletin of the Pan-American Union*, offers his views on the work done by the Rockefeller Foundation in the Isthmus. *Las Ventajas de los Mercados Industriales del Valle del Mississippi y del Puerto de New Orleans para el Comercio de la Republica de Honduras*, by Dr. Eusebio Toledo López, Crescent Printing Company, New Orleans, 1921, comes to help the commercial propaganda of his country.

Some articles dealing with Central American topics are as follows: "El Pacto Centro-Americano de San José de Costa Rica" by A. M. Herradora, in *El Fígaro* (Habana), March 6; "In Search of a Volcano Investigations among the Mountains of Costa Rica", in *The South American*, March (New York); "El Neoyorkino más Popular en Centro-

America" (Minor Keith), in *La Tribuna* (New York) February 5; "Á Glance at Guatemala", by Aaron Hardy Ulm, in *The Dearborn Independent* (Michigan), Febuary 12; "La Union de Centro-America", by Dr. Policarpo Bonilla, in the March number of *La Reforma Social*, the remarks of his lecture given at the Instituto de las Españas of Columbia University; "El General Rafael Antonio Gutiérrez" (a former President of Salvador, who died this year), by Modesto Barrios, in *La Prensa* (San Salvador), March 14; "Clarín Patriótico" (a selection of the war songs against Walker in 1857, first issued by Imprenta de la Paz, Costa Rica, of that time and now reprinted by *Diario de Costa Rica;* "Latin American Republics Shy at Being Refuge for Northern Wets", in *Newark Evening News*, April 5, a comment upon the last annual message to the Honduras National Congress by the Minister of the Treasury; "El Pueblo de Nicaragua y los Estados Unidos", by Gustavo Aleman Bolaños, in *Atlántida*, a weekly paper from La Ceiba, Honduras; and "The Economic Conditions of Guatemala", by Dr. Julio Bianchi, in *The South American* for February.

From the Central American magazines we may select some material. In the March issue of *Repertorio Americano*, the fortnightly paper edited by García Monge in San José de Costa Rica, appear "Walter Pater", an essay by Salomón de la Selva, with a translation of "La Gioconda" of the above mentioned master, by Pedro Henríquez Ureña; "Del Folk-Lore Costarricense", by Salvador Umaña, who is collecting these songs for the children of his country; and some notes about textbooks for the study of Spanish, by Professor Brenes Mesén, now teaching at Syracuse University. In *Los Sucesos*, a weekly paper of Tegucigalpa, appear "La Misión de las Universidades de Centro-America" and "El Delito Político en Centro-America" by Dr. Céleo Dávila; "La Bótica de su Magestad en San Jorge de Olancho", by Eduardo Martínez López, the National Librarian; and "El Maestro Delgadillo" (the author of *Consideraciones sobre Arte Musical en Nicaragua* and *Comentarios a los Consejos de Schumann*), by Manuel Adalid y Gamero, a writer and musical composer. In *Orientaciones*, edited by Salvador Merlos, San Salvador, is published "La Función Electoral" by Dr. Alonso Reyes Guerra. In *Los Domingos*, Managua, published by Salvador Ruiz Morales, appears "Ultimos Días de Darío," by Octavio Rivas Ortiz. *Centro America*, the official organ of the Oficina Internacional Centro-Americana, Guatemala, is reprinting "El Popol-Vuh", a true translation of the sacred book of the Indians, which also is widely commented on in *The Mythology of Latin American Races*, by Hartley Burr Alexander, not long ago reviewed by J. Warshaw in *The South American*, of New York. In the *Gaceta Oficial* of Costa Rica, Professor Carlos Gagini will conduct the publication of those important documents which are in danger of being destroyed. *Revista de Costa Rica* of J. F. Trejos Quirós, San José, in the February and March issues brings these good contributions: "Apuntes sobre el Volcan Rincón de la Vieja", by J. Fidel Tristán; "Fray Rodrigo Pérez", by Pedro Pérez Zeledón; and a monograph on the Costa Rican fruits by Señorita María Jiménez Luthmer.

Following are some of the new Mexican books edited in Mexico; *La Evolución Histórica de México*, by Emilio Rabasa, Librería de la Vda. de Bouret (already reviewed by Victoriano Salado Alvarez in his article "El Problema de México juzgado por un Mejicano Eminente", in *La Prensa*, San Antonio, Tex., March 13); *Saturnino Herrán y su Obra*, by Manuel Tousssaint, Ediciones "México Moderno" (which are appreciations on Herran's work as a painter and portrait artist); *El Mundo de las Sombras*, on the moving pictures, by Carlos Noriega Hope (Botas e Hijo); *Los Lidiadores*, on the art of the bull-fighters, by Armando de María y Campos, Talleres Tipográficos de "Don Quijote"; *Fray Andrés de Castro*, with data for the history of Toluca, by Miguel Salinas, Imprenta de J. I. Muñoz; *México Viejo*, an orthographical essay, by Salvador Villalpando, Imprenta "Hesperia", *Tipos Populares*, by E. de Oria y Sentíes, Imprenta de Botas y Cía.; *Las Carreteras Nacionales*, by Adolfo A. López, Talleres Gráficos Nacionales; *Conveniencia de las Asociaciones Agrícolas*, by Gonzalo Cámara, Imprenta de la "Revista de Yucatán", Mérida; and *El Trabajo en Mexico durante la Época Colonial* (Ordenanzas de Gremios de la Nueva España), a digest made by Genaro Estrada of the three volumes of *Compilción Nueva de Ordenanzas de la Muy Noble, Insigne y Muy Leal e Imperial Ciudad de México*, by Francisco del Barrio y Lorenzot, who was a member of the Royal Audiencia. Estrada is the well known author of *Poetas Modernos de México*, who writes the bibliographical notes for the magazine *Mexico Moderno*, and has recently published *Visionario de la Nueva España*, a selection of short-stories. In the forty-three chapters of his very useful work *Latin American Commercial Law*, published by The Banks Law Publishing Comany, New York, Toribio Esquivel Obregón offers material for business men and lawyers, from mercantile registry and contract of transportation overland to conflict of laws in

Hispanic American countries. In *La Vida Tumultuosa*, Carlos González Peña describes his trip to the United States during the summer of 1918. Ricardo García Granados, with *Historia de México desde la restauración de la República en 1867 hasta la Caída de Porfirio Díaz;* Luis Cabrera, with his *Obras Políticas del Licenciado Blas Urrea;* Jorge Rueda, with *Pluma Falsa*, an answer to the unjust attacks made by Blasco Ibáñez in *El Militarismo en México;* and Artemio Valle-Arizpe, with his masterful prose-book *Vidas Milagrosas*, Tipografía Artística Cervantes, Madrid, are other contributors to the literary and political history of the southern republic. Valle-Arizpe, now residing in Madrid, is the author of *La Gran Ciudad de México Tenustitlán, Perla de la Nueva España*, and has announced that other works, namely, *En el Solar de mis Abuelos, La Dama del Soplillo* (novel), and *La Ruta de Santa Teresa*, are being printed. *La Cuestión del Petróleo*, by Carlos Díaz Dufoo, is a remarkable work wherein is found first-hand information about the history, economics and legal side of the oil riches of Mexico. *Pitágoras. Una Teoría del Ritmo*, by Jose Vasconcelos, has been printed by "Cultura".

Under the direction of Manuel Gamio, the prominent anthropologist of "Ethnos", there has been written a book about the people of the Teotihuacán Valley, where the student may find valuable information in regard to the customs and the economic and artistic history of that Valley. Engineer Ezequiel Ordóñez gives the geological notes; Professors Moisés Herrera and Alberto N. Chávez study the fauna and flora of the region; José Reygadas y Vértiz contributes with his paper on stratigraphical excavations made in the above mentioned zone (the first essay of this kind in México); Professor Roque J. Cevallos Novelo explains certain intellectual tendencies of the Teotihuacans in the two best periods of their existence; Professor Ignacio B. del Castillo describes the valley during its colonial period; and there are in the book many other papers on archeology written by Gamio, Ramón Mena, Carlos I. Betancourt, José M. Arreola, Ignacio Marquina and Antonio Cortés, and Professor Hermann Beyer. From the last named, who is a member at the faculty of superior studies in the University of Mexico, we have read these noteworthy articles in *Revista de Revistas:* "Las Ruinas de Mitla", "Un Instrumento Musical de los Antiguos Mexicanos, la Sonaja de Hueso", "El Huehuetli, el Tambor de los Antiguos Mexicanos", "Las Ruinas de Palenque" and "El Tesoro del Cacique de Huejotzingo".

Professor William Gates, President of the "Maya Society," announced at the last meeting of the society, which was held at The Johns Hopkins University, that American archeologists will soon commence exhaustive investigations in Central America and Yucatan for the purpose of studying medical knowledge of the aborigines and the economic resources of those regions. Victoriano Salado Álvarez has written for *La Prensa*, (San Antonio, Texas, March 18) an article entitled "Sabiduría Popular". This is a most important guide for the collection of the data of Folk-Lore in Mexico. Licenciado Carlos Pereyra gives valuable suggestions in "Las Noticias Secretas de America. El Libro y su Influencia" (published in 1822), in *El Heraldo de Mexico* (Los Angeles, California, March 23).

To encourage the spiritual brotherhood with Spain there has been reorganized the Commission of Mexican Culture which is presided over by Francisco A. de Icaza. The secretary of this body is Miguel Toussaint, formerly of the staff of the National University. In the Alzate Society Mrs. Zelia Nuttall lectured upon some published documents, almost unknown, relative to Mexican History; Professor Hermann Beyer on "Notas bibliográfica y crítica acerca del tomo V de la Colección de Memorias del Dr. Seler", and Professor Elpidio López on "Climatología de la República Mexicana". The poet Ricardo Arenales has been active in Monterrey in the initial work of founding an Academy of Fine Arts. This is being done by a series of lectures. Among lecturers already have been Santiago R. de la Vega, who spoke on the Mexican cartoonists, and Professor Fortunato Lozano and Licenciado Ramón Treviño, who spoke on the literature of Nuevo León during the seventeenth century. The rector of the National University, Licenciado José Vasconcelos, is touring the country, accompanied by his secretary, the poet Jaime Torres Bodet, and Professor Agustín Loera y Chávez, as the first steps for the reorganization of a Federal Department of Public Education and Fine Arts. Dr. Juan B. Iguíniz, Assistant to the National Librarian, is preparing a bibliographical essay on the short-stories and novel writers of Mexico.

In *Revista de Revistas*, the leading magazine edited by José de Jesús Núñez y Domínguez, appear the following items: "Dina Rosa-Rosolimo, Poetisa Fatalista y Viril" by H. Tejera, with the poems "Mis Puñalitos", "La Lluvia", and "La Doncella"—all exceedingly interesting; Alfonso Toro criticises *Doña Catalina Xuárez Marcayda, primera esposa de Hernán Cortés y su Familia*, by Francisco Fernández del Castillo, and he also writes on "La Verdadera Historia de San Felipe de Jesús", as written by Salado Álvarez in the daily *La Prensa* of Texas; "El Abánico de Mlle. Mallarmé", translation and notes by Alfonso Reyes; and "Decadencia del Cultivo del Cacao", by Julio Riquelme Inda.

Núñez y Domínguez is the leader of the national movement to restore this year, on the first centenary of the independence, the name of Agustín de Iturbide, as one of the true liberators of the country. There will be in the capital a numismatic exposition, where amateurs will find not only the money coined during Iturbide's days but also those copper pieces, so scarce now, which were used during the term of the first Viceroy of Nueva España, for whom they were minted, and a few copies of the money issued by Morelos. The Academy of History, assisted by the National Museum, is making arrangements for an exposition of historical papers. In accordance with the suggestions made by Alfonso Toro the press of the present time will have another exposition, and there has been established a prize for the best printed paper of the year, under the patronage of Rafael Alducín, the editor of *Excelsior*. Under the auspices of the National Museum, there will be edited some papers especially prepared for the occasion: the bibliography of Iturbide from 1821 to 1824 by Engineer Jesús Galindo y Villa; "Iturbide and O'Donojú", by Ramón Mena; "La Corte de Agustín I", by Manuel Romero de Terreros; "El Mobiliario y los estilos artísticos de la época de Iturbide", by Antonio Cortés; and "La Antropología Física de los Restos de Iturbide", by Dr. Nicolás de León. In connection with the festival, at the suggestion of Enrique Santibáñez, the Sociedad de Geografía y Estadística has called a National Congress of Geography to meet from September 27 to October 2, 1921.

At the funeral of Jesús Urueta, and in regard to the work and national deeds of the greatest orator of Mexico, Alfonso Teja Zabre made some very impressive remarks, his eulogy appearing in the *Excelsior* of March 30. Guatemala has lost one of its best students of the past, Licenciado Francisco Quinteros Andrino, whose writings on the colonial epoch are well appreciated by the readers of the magazine *Centro-América*. El Salvador regrets the death of Juan Antonio

Solórzano, who sketched many of the Indian traditions of Central America. Dr. Simeón Pereira y Castellón, the beloved bishop of León de Nicaragua, leaves fine remembrances as a man of letters and as spiritual leader. A splendid tribute has been paid him by Dr. Gustavo A. Prado in "Anecdotario de Monseñor". Dr. Alberto Membreño, from Honduras, is dead. He had been appointed minister in Madrid to settle the boundary dispute with Nicaragua, and had won the royal award of Alfonso XIII. in favor of the rights of Honduras. As minister in Washington he suggested to the governing board of the Pan American Union a peace plan for the western hemisphere (see the *New York Times*, April 23, 1915). Membreño was assistant secretary to the minister of public works (1886), president of the Honduran delegation to the First Central American Congress of Education which met in Guatemala (1893), and president of the Republic of Honduras (1915). He was the author of *Elementos de Práctica Forense en materia civil según la Legislación Hondureña"* (1893), *Repertorio Alfabético de Jurisprudencia* (1894), *Hondureñismos*, a study of the provincialisms of the country with some hints on the Indian vocabularies (three editions, the third one in Mexico (1912); the *Agrarian Law of Honduras* (1898), *Alegato presentado a Su Magestad Católica el Rey de España*, and *Réplica al Alegato de Nicaragua* (both in Madrid, 1905), at the time of the boundary dispute with the latter Republic; *Astequismos de Honduras* (Mexico, 1907); *Nombres Geográficos de la República del Salvador* (México, 1908), and a plan to make a comparative study of tropical flora, which was published in the *Proceedings of the Alzate Society*, Mexico, D. F. Dr. Karl Sapper in *Globus*, 1898, gave a review of *Hondureñismos*, and Dr. Antonio Peñafiel, in *Ciudades Coloniales y Capitales de la República Mexicana. Estado de Tlaxcalla* (Mexico, 1909), praises Membreño's scholarship as a philologist. Membreño was also highly commended by Benot and Cejador y Frauca from Spain and Cuervo from Venezuela.

RAFAEL HELIODORO VALLE.

NOTES

· Brazilian exports of oil-producing nuts and fruits. No. 88, April 16.

Brazilian exports to Germany. No. 108, May 10.

Brazilian government aid to importation of livestock. No. 88, April 16.

Brazilian income tax law. No. 146, June 24.

Brazilian industrial notes. No. 142, June 20.

Brazilian railway notes. No. 131, June 7.

Brazilian revenues for 1920. No. 130, June 6.

Brazilian shipping notes. Nos. 80 and 141, April 7, and June 18.

Brazilian trade for the first four months of 1921. No. 145, June 23.

British bank established in Colombia. No. 146, June 24.

British railways in Argentina, Uruguay, and Paraguay show gain. No. 103, May 4.

Business depression in Cuba. No. 121, May 25.

Business opportunities in Brazil. No. 109, May 11.

Cement manufacturing machinery needed in Ecuador. No. 130, June 6.

Census of the provinces of Lima and Callao, Peru. No. 123, May 27.

Change in date for increased Mexican duties on textiles. No. 86, April 14.

Change in date of Mexican trade conference. No. 84, April 12.

Change in Mexican export duty on chicle. No. 97, April 27.

Chile seeking new foreign loan. No. 143, June 21.

Chilean duty on rubber tires unchanged. No. 89, April 18.

Closing of branch banks in the Dominican Republic. No. 109. May 11.

Coal production in Peru. No. 99, April 29.

Coastwise transportation facilities at Mexican ports. No. 137, June 14.

Coffee production in Salina Cruz consular district. No. 113, May 16. *Id.*, during March, No. 114, May 17.

Coffee shipments from Maracaibo during February. No. 75, April 1. *Id.*, during April. No. 137, June 14. *Id.*, during May. No. 150, June 29.

Commerical failures in Argentina during the first four months of 1921. No. 139, June 16.

Competition for railway supplies for Argentina. No. 150, June 29.

Completion of wireless station at Baranquilla, Colombia. No. 129, June 4.

Condition of Chilean finances. No. 122, May 26.

Conditions in Habana harbor. No. 76, April 2.

Confirmation of Peruvian government decree in regard to banks. No. 121, May 25.

Congestion at the port of Vera Cruz. Nos. 110 and 116, May 12 and 19.

Construction of new port at Pernambuco, Brazil. No. 148, June 27.

Construction work in Colombia. No. 110, May 12.

Consular agency established in Haiti. No. 123, May 27.

Continued unfavorable economic conditions in Dominican Republic. No. 144, June 22.

Contract for construction of slaughter house in Brazil. No. 105, May 6.

Contract for financing and construction of the La Quiaca-Atocha Railroad. No. 94, April 23.

Correction for statement on Cuban rice embargo. No. 85, April 13.

Cotton crop in Lower California. No. 113, May 16.

Cotton in the Argentine Chaco. No. 149, June 28.

Cotton in Vera Cruz. No. 94, April 23.

Crop prospects in Mexico. No. 142, June 20.

Crop reports of the Yaqui Valley, Sonora, Mexico. No. 134, June 10.

Cuban commerce with Germany, No. 136, June 13.

Cuban imports and exports of chemicals. No. 75, April 1.

Cuban imports of chemicals, gums, etc. No. 144, June 22.

Cuban imports and exports of iron and steel products. No. 75, April 1.

Cuban labor conditions. No. 150, June 29.

The currency system in Chile. No. 88, April 16.

Date growing in Lower California, Mexico. No. 134, June 10.

Declared exports from Jamaica to U.S. for April. No. 128, June 3.

  Id. from Paraguay to U.S. in 1920. No. 76, April 2.

  Id., from Puerto Plata to U.S. No. 127, June 2.

Decrease for demand for Jamaica dyes. No. 119, May 23.

Decree regulating the Brazilian livestock industry bureau. No. 123, May 27.

Development of Peruvian cattle and grazing industry. No. 93, April 22.

Direct all-American cable from Brazil to Europe. No. 151, June 30.

Dominican automobile law available. No. 119, May 23.

Drought damage to Bermuda. No. 91, April 20.

Dutch trade promotion in South America. No. 121, May 25.

Economic condition in Argentina during 1920. No. 85, April 13.

  Id., in Bahia, Brazil. No. 103, May 4.

  Id., in Mexico. No. 100, April 30.

  Id., on the east coast of Nicaragua. No. 122, May 26.

Economic notes from Colombia. No. 119, May 23.

  Id., from Ecuador. No. 96, April 26.

  Id., from Mexico. Nos. 110 and 136, May 12 and June 13.

Economic situation in Cuba. No. 116, June 19.

Electrification of Jamaica railroads. No. 121, May 25.

Emergency loan arranged for Nicaragua. No. 129, June 4.

Equipment for Mexican sugar mills. No. 142, June 20.

Establishment of clearing house in Cuba. No. 110, May 12.

Estimate Brazilian cacao crop. No. 130, June 6.

Estimate of 1921 trade balance for Ecuador. No. 135, June 11.

European bids on steel rails in Chile. No. 100, April 30.

Exhibiting British goods suitable for South America. No. 103, May 4.

Experiments in British Guiana to utilize alcohol as fuel. No. 101, May 2.

Export duty on bananas in Colombia. No. 103, May 4.

Exportable surplus of cereals in Argentina. No. 78, April 5.

Exporters of crossties in Santo Domingo . No. 75, April 1.

Exports from Argentina during the first quarter of 1921. No. 121, May 25.

Id., from Bahia, Brazil, to U.S. No. 124, May 28.

Id., from Callao, Peru, to U.S. No. 123, May 27.

Id., from Paraguay to U.S. No. 122, May 26.

Exports of naval stores from U.S. in 1920. No. 125, May 31.

Exports of rubber from Brazil and Peru during May. No. 148, June 27.

Extension of import embargo on rice in Cuba. No. 79, April 6.

Favorable crop reports from Salvador. No. 113, May 16.

Financial and banking situation in Ecuador. No. 133, June 9.

Financial condition in Salvador. No. 123, May 27.

Financial depression in Jamaica. No. 117, May 20.

Financial measures in Cuba. No. 139, June 16.

Flour mills for Argentina. No. 117, May 20.

Foreign commerce of Cuba during 1919–20. No. 127, June 2.

Foreign competition in Mexico. No. 125, May 31.

Foreign debts of states of Brazil. No. 91, April 4.

Foreign tariffs: Mexico, Nos. 92, 113, 132, 137, 141, 147, April 21, May 16, and June 8, 14, 18, and 25. Uruguay, Nos. 92 and 113. British Honduras, No. 113. Guatemala, Nos. 113 and 141. Peru, Nos. 132 and 151, June 8 and 30. Bolivia, No. 137. Salvador, Nos. 147 and 151. Paraguay, No. 151.

Foreign trade of Brazil for 1920. No. 88, April 16.

Id., of Mexico for first half of 1919 and 1920. No. 91, April 20.

Id., of U.S. in toilet preparations. No. 116, May 19.

Freight congestion at Piedras Negras, Mexico. No. 143, June 21.

Id., at Vera Cruz. Nos. 122 and 129, May 26 and June 4.

Freight on hand at Vera Cruz, Mexico.   No. 140, June 17.
French bank for Brazil suspends payments.   No. 98, April 28.
German development in south of Chile.   No. 138, June 15.
German trade with Santiago de Cuba.   No. 128, June 3.
Germany's trade with Argentina.   No. 77, April 4.
Growing market for farm tractors in Ecuador.   No. 76, April 2.
Guatemala encourages manufactures of industrial alcohol.   No. 144, June 22.
Guatemalan market for American flour.   No. 135, June 11.
Guatemalan ochre for American paints.   No. 117, May 20.
Hand-made clothing available in Porto Rico.   No. 82, April 9.
Harness and saddle makers' wares in Argentina.   No. 96, April 26.
Highway development in Brazil.   No. 103, May 4.
Immigration into Paraguay during 1920.   No. 121, May 25.
Importation of cement into Cuba,   No. 121, May 25.
   Id., into Santiago, Cuba,   No. 117, May 20.
   Id., into the Maracaibo district,   No. 114, May 17.
Importation of automobiles into Peru.   No. 77, April 4.
Imports and exports for May by countries.   No. 146, June 24.
Improvements for Chiapas and Tabasco, Mexico.   No. 128, June 3.
Importation of coal into Puerto Cabello, Venezuela.   No. 128, June 3.
Income tax bill pending in Chilean congress.   No. 80, April 7.
Incorporation and corporation taxes in Latin America.   No. 101, May 2.
Increase in certain Mexican import duties.   No. 140, June 17.
Increase in freight rates from Europe to Vera Cruz.   No. 101, May 2.
Increase of price of henequen in Mexico.   No. 117, May 20.
Increase of Mexican duty on rubber tires.   No. 102, May 3.
Increased Mexican duties on cotton goods.   Nos. 130 and 146, June 6 and 24.
Increased immigration into Argentina.   No. 99, April 29.
Increasing the oil storage capacity at Cristóbal.   No. 113, May 16.
Information on automobile market in Latin America available.   No. 100, April 30.
Inspection of banks and corporations in Paraguay.   *Id.*
Jamaica proposes sugar loan.   No. 150, June 29.
Japanese capitalists investigating copper mines in Chile.   No. 110, May 12.
Jerked beef industry in Brazil.   No. 120, May 24.
Kingston, Jamaica, harbor improvements.   No. 128, June 3.

Kingston proposed as free port. No. 119, May 23.

Lack of demand for Paraguayan petit grain. No. 124, May 28.

Legislation toward economic reconstruction in Chile. No. 93, April 22.

Lignum-vitae available in Haiti. No. 87, April 15.

Limited market for trunks in Guatemala. No. 144, June 22.

List of agents and representatives in Mexico. No. 137; June 14.

List of banks in Brazil. No. 128, June 3.

Lists of importers in Chile available. No. 118, May 21.

Lists of importers in Colombia. No. 150, June 29.

Lloyd Brazileiro using national coal. No. 76, April 2.

Looting in Amazonas and Acre. No. 103, May 4.

Lower prices predicted in Dominican Republic. No. 123, May 27.

Lumber markets in Central America. No. 121, May 25.

Manufacture of cigars and cigarettes in Argentina. No. 101, May 2.

    Id., of handbags and pocketbooks. No. 108, May 10.

    Id., of iron and brass beds. No. 113, May 16.

    Id., of paints and varnishes. No. 77, April 4.

    Id., of trunks and suit cases. No. 112, May 14.

Manufacturing industries in Argentina. Nos. 108 and 139, May 10 and June 16.

Maracaibo wireless station completed. No. 150, June 29.

Market for American soap in Nicaragua. No. 103, May 4.

Market for building materials in Costa Rica. No. 147, June 25.

Market for paints and varnishes in Mexico. No. 89, April 18.

Market for railroad equipment in Monterey. No. 82, April 9.

Market for toilet soap in Mexico. No. 114, May 17 .

Market for toys in Argentina. No. 142, June 20.

Market for typewriters in Peru. No. 144, June 22.

Material required for a Brazilian college. No. 124, May 28.

Members of liquidating board for the Banco Nacional of Cuba. No. 90, April 19.

Merchandise to enter free for the Peruvian centennial exhibition. No. 80, April 7.

Merchant vessels for west coast of Mexico. No. 117, May 20.

Metallurgical industry in Argentina. No. 95, April 25.

Mexican census to be taken. No. 129, June 4.

Mexican central bank of issue. No. 136, June 13.

Mexican debt. No. 137, June 14.

Mexican duty on imported livestock. No. 148, June 27.

Mexican garbanzo crop damaged. No. 113, May 16.

Mexican shipments for March. No. 110, May 12.

Mexican trade in 1920. No. 146, June 24.

Monthly cable service. Including reports on Argentina, Brazil, Chile, Mexico, and Peru. Nos. 82, 107, and 133, April 9, May 9, and June 9.

Motor pictures in Brazil. No. 94, April 27.

Motor lorries proving successful in Jamaica. No. 121, May 25.

Motor transportation in Brazil. No. 115, May 18.

Motor vehicles in Ecuador. No. 126, June 1.

Movement in Brazilian ports in 1920. No. 109, May 11.

Negotiations for purchase of oil in Chile. No. 115, May 18.

New Argentine loan. No. 148, June 27.

New banking regulation in Brazil. No. 133, June 9.

New Brazilian freight transportation tax. No. 77, April 4.

New Brazilian mining law. No. 102, May 3.

New customs regulations and charges at Callao, Peru. No. 130, June 6.

New fire insurance law in Salvador. No. 123, May 27.

New flour mill in Chile. No. 143, June 21.

New fuel oil company in Cienfuegos, Cuba. No. 94, April 23.

New law proposed on Bolivian mineral taxation. No. 77, April 4.

New oil field in Northern Mexico. No. 115, May 18.

New steamship line to Para. No. 89, April 18.

New steel mill for Brazil. No. 91, April 20.

New train service for Mexico. No. 151, June 30.

New wireless service for Peru. No. 78, April 5.

Id., for Ecuador. No. 126, June 1.

Nonacceptance of merchandise in Peruvian ports. Id.

Notes from Brazil. No. 135, June 11.

Opening of bids for railway equipment in Chile. No. 82, April 9.

Opening of branch bank in Dominican Republic. No. 122, May 26.

Operations of the Canadian merchant marine with British Guiana. No. 151, June 30.

Operations of the Curacao Petroleum Co. No. 111, May 13.

Opportunity for a construction company in Brazil. No. 114, May 17.

Packing of milk and butter in Colombia. No. 113, May 16.

Packing of prepared flours for shipment to Argentina. No. 125, May 31.

Panama canal traffic for February. No. 80, April 7. Id., for March. No. 99, April. Id., for April. No. 127, June 2.

Paper-mill supplies in Argentina. No. 119, May 23.

Paraguay's foreign commerce for 1920. No. 77, April 4.

Paraguay's foreign debt. No. 117, May 20.

Partial moratorium in Peru. No. 116, May 18.

Peruvian banking decree. No. 104, May 5.

Peruvian exchange situation. No. 113, May 16.

Peruvian financial legislation. Nos. 120 and 125, May 24 and 31.

Peruvian government limits the interest charged on loans. No. 112, May 14.

Peruvian protection of merchandise in custom house. No. 126, June 1.

Petroleum exports from Tampico during March. No. 94, April 23.

Port conditions at Vera Cruz. No. 97, April 27.

Possible purchase of railway and construction of new line by Chilean government. No. 77, April 4.

Price and grade of mahogany in Guatemala. No. 110, May 12.

Probable effects of the new Chilean tariff. No. 90, April 19.

Production of coconuts in Guatemala. No. 136, June 13.

Prohibition of importation of firearms in Peru. No. 87, April 15.

Promotion of cotton industry in northeastern Brazil. No. 151, June 30.

Promotion of French trade in Salvador. No. 123, May 27.

Proposed airplane mail service between Bahamas and Florida. No. 129, June 4.

Proposed harbor improvements of Caibanen, Cuba. No. 112, May 14.

Proposed increase in Cuban consular fees. No. 138, June 15.

Proposed railway in the Amazonian region. No. 108, May 10.

Proposed repeal of the 4 per cent profit tax in Cuba. No. 110, May 12.

Public finance of the state of Rio Grande do Sul, Brazil. No. 120, May 24.

Public improvement for Ciudad Juarez, Mexico. No. 114, May 17.

Purchase of electric light plant by Dominican municipalities. No. 116, May 19.

Quarantine in Uruguay. No. 84, April 12.

Receipts and expenditures of the Brazilian states during 1919. No. 144, June 22.

Reclamation work around the bay of Rio de Janeiro. No. 138, June 15.

Registration of trade mark "Superior" in Argentina. No. 131, June 7. *Id.*, "Victor" in *id.* No. 132, June 8.

Relaxation of Peruvian embargo on exportation of rice. No. 79, April 6.

Removal of Mexican export duty on sugar. No. 87, April 15.

Reopening of bank of Nuevo Leon, Mexico. No. 122, May 26.

Reported loan to Uruguay by British bank. No. 144, June 22.

Result of trade promotion by American consulate of Acapulco. No. 90, April 19.

Resumption of sugar trade with Colombia. No. 113, May 16.

Revised list of dealers in motor cars in Curacao. No. 134, June 10.

Revision of Commercial Traveler's Guide to Latin America. No. 120, May 24.

Ratification of Canada-West Indies agreement by Barbados. No. 122, May 26.

Railway construction and improvements in Mexico. No. 75, April 1.

Railway situation in Mexico. No. 143, June 21.

Railway extension in Jamaica. No. 128, June 3.

Railway construction in Brazil in 1921. No. 126, June 1.

Rise of land values in the Argentine province of Entre Rios. No. 134, June 10.

River transportation difficult in Colombia. No. 117, May 20.

Rubber exports from Brazil in February, 1921. No. 86, April 14.
    Id., In March, 1921, No. 108, May 10.

Sale of meat products allowed in Paraguay. No. 100, April 30.

Salt industry in Mexico. No. 125, May 31.

Shipping at the port of Rio de Janeiro for 1920. No. 78, April 5.

Shipping between Tampico and the U.S. No. 143, June 21.

Shipments of oil from Tampico for January, 1921. No. 79, April 6.
    Id., for February. No. 104, May 5.

Soft drinks in Argentina. No. 145, June 23.

Sonora irrigation project. No. 124, May 28.

Statistics of Brazilian foreign trade. No. 129, June 4.

Steamship lines calling at Ecuadorian ports. No. 125, May 31.

Steamship service for Caribbean and western ports of Central America. No. 133, June 9.

Study of cotton culture in Brazil. No. 113, May 16.

Suspenson of payments by Chilean bank. No. 82, April 9.

Three new ships for Houston line. No. 89, April 18.

Trade at the port of Santos, Brazil, for three months. No. 140, June 17.

Trade of Argentina in vegetable oils and vegetable-oil material. No. 91, April 20.
    Id., of Brazil. No. 92, April 21.
    Id., of Chile. No. 139, June 16.
    Id., of Cuba. No. 113, May 16.
    Id., of Peru. No. 96, April 16.

Trade in yerba mate in Argentina. No. 132, June 8.

Trade notes from Argentina. Nos. 91, 115, 128, and 138, April 20, May 18, and June 3 and 15.

  Id., from Brazil. Nos. 75, 83, 85, 102, 105, 118, 124, 132, 144, and 147, April 1, 11, and 13, May 3, 6, 21, and 28, June 8, 22, and 25.

  Id., from Chile. Nos. 94 and 116, April 23 and May 19.

  Id., from Costa Rica. Nos. 79 and 104, April 6 and May 5.

  Id., from the Guianas. No. 130, June 6.

  Id., from Mexico. Nos. 91, 126, 133, 149, and 151, April 20, June 1, 6, 28 and 30.

  Id., from Paraguay. Nos. 111 and 122, May 13 and 26.

  Id., from Venezuela. No. 82, April 9.

Trade of foreign countries in 1920 and 1921. No. 83, April 11.

Trade of Paraguay for 1920. No. 143, June 21.

Text of recent Peruvian banking decree. No. 138, June 16.

Trade of U.S. with Latin America, 1920. No. 79, April 6.

Trade review of Maracaibo, Venezuela. No. 105, May 6.

  Id., of Para. No. 83, April 11.

  Id., of Puerto Cortes, Honduras. No. 87, April 15.

Trade statistics for British Guiana. No. 110, May 12.

Traffic movement on the Paraguayan Central Railroad. No. 122, May 26.

Transportation difficulties in Mexico. No. 115, May 18.

Two new sugar factories in Jamaica. No. 129, June 4.

Unemployment in Uruguay. No. 99, April 29.

Unfavorable economic situation in Paraguay. No. 110, May 12.

Uruguayan foreign trade by countries for 1920. No. 103, May 4.

Uruguayan foreign trade for 1920. No. 82, April 9.

Venezuelan trade statistics. No. 97, April 27.

Vera Cruz custom house receipts. No. 113, May 16.

Wireless installation for Chihuahua, Mexico. No. 134, June 10.

Withdrawal of Brazilian moratorium proposal. No. 118, May 21.

Wool shipments from Montevideo during March. No. 137, June 14.

Two valuable books have recently been published, one in Brazil and the other in Portugal. *Populações Meridionaes do Brazil*, by Oliveira Vianna, vol. I. (Monteiro Lobato e Cia., *Revista do Brazil*, São (Paulo); and *Historia de Antonio Vieira*, by J. Lucio d'Azevedo, vol. II. (Livraria Classica, Editora, Lisboa). The first is one of the few contributions to a sociological study of Brazil. It points out especially the rural character of the populations of its southern central regions—the *paulistas, fluminenses*, and *mineiros*— and explains in a clear and comprehensive manner the genesis of the clans, the colonial anarchy under the great territorial *caudillos*, and the conflict between these disintegrating political elements and the unifying, orderly action of the crown, which embodies the function of the state.

Senhor J. Lucio d'Azevedo is a Portuguese scholar who lived in northern Brazil (Pará) for many years and became well known as a publicist. He is the author of two excellent books, namely, *Os Jesuitas no Grão Para*, and *O Marquez de Pombal*. The latter is by far the best essay on the great Portuguese statesman of the eighteenth century.

Father Antonio Vieira is a most attractive subject for a writer. Senhor Azevedo describes the diplomat, the preacher, and the missionary, the three chief aspects of the activity of the famous Jesuit, who was one of the literary glories of Portugal—certainly its most eloquent religious orator—and was intimately associated with court intrigues and the international policy of the time, so much so that several secret missions were intrusted to him. In this second volume the aspects considered are the visionary—who attracted the attention and the persecution of the Inquisition; the rebel—against his enemy and against fate; and the vanquished Vieira, who died after he had reached the age of ninety in Bahia (Brazil), where his genius first revealed itself in the pulpit. The whole work is based on personal and original research in the Portuguese and foreign archives. This makes it a first-class historical monograph concerning Portugal and Brazil of the seventeenth century.—MANOEL DE OLIVEIRA LIMA.

Manuel Segundo Sánchez, Delegate from Venezuela to the recent inauguration of the Bolívar statue in New York, has presented us his pamphlet *Miranda como Filósofo y Erudito*, and *El Publicista de Venezuela*, a chapter from *Los Incunables Venezolanos*, both published in Caracas, 1920. Sánchez is the Librarian of the Venezuelan capital, and one of the distinguished Hispanic American bibliographers, who counts among his works *Apuntes para la Iconografía del Libertador* (Litografía del Comercio, Caracas, 1916); *Los Restos de Sucre* (1918); *La Imprenta de la Exposición Pacificadora* (1916); and *Anuario Bibliográfico de Venezuela* (first year, 1916). He also was the editor of the *Biblioteca de Venezuela*, a select literary library. His distinguished countryman, Dr. Luis Churión, secretary of the Venezuelan legation in the United States, lectured on Venezuela in the Hispanic American Athenaeum of Washington, his remarkable speech being published in *La Prensa*, New York, April 12. As a token of devotion to Simón Bolívar, Dr. Guillermo A. Sherwell has sketched the life and work of the hero, in a volume printed by Byron S. Adams, Washington. He consulted all the documents, articles and papers suggested by Dr. Manuel Segundo Sánchez, above mentioned, and the notes taken by Dr. Julius Goebel of the University of Virginia about certain papers existing in the files of the State Department. Dr. Sherwell gives in the twenty-one chapters of his book a concise and important notice of the deeds of the father of five nations, and his volume will give substantial information to American students.

RAFAEL HELICDORO VALLE.

The Government Bureau of Statistics in Lima has published a statistical abstract of Peru covering the year 1919. An English edition has also been issued for the first time. The bulletin (of 149 pages) contains much interesting and valuable information concerning Peru. Some of the more important features included are the following: Statistics of area and population, administrative subdivision, activities of the postal and telegraph services, ecclesiastical matters, foreign and coastwise tonnage, exchange fluctuations, coinage and production of precious metals, banking, agriculture, mining, public charities, education, national revenues and budgets, railway traffic, and foreign trade. The statistics relating to the foreign commerce of Peru are given under a number of subdivisions, such as total values and volumes annually from 1877 to 1919; exports and imports by years, and by countries of destination and of origin, value by customs districts; and values according to commercial nomenclature. The official figures indicate that the total foreign commerce of Peru for 1919 reached the value of $190,296,214. Imports increased by 25.75 per cent over those of 1918, amounting to $59,389,985. Exports increased by 34.68 per cent over the preceding year, their total value being $130,906,229. The United States enjoyed by far the largest share of Peruvian foreign commerce. Peru bought American goods to the value of $36,740,398, and sent exports to the United States to the value of $60,827,398. Great Britain was second in this trade, with Chile third, and British India fourth. Japan had only a comparatively small share, importations from that country being valued at $1,542,233 and exports at $444,464.

The Bureau of Statistics was organized in 1918, and is now under the direction of Dr. Oscar F. Arrúz. The staff is engaged on a number of interesting scientific studies. It is the only agency in the republic that keeps a series of index numbers. A recently issued bulletin showed in statistical form the successive increases in the cost of living in the capital since 1913. The Bureau has also been entrusted with the supervision of the national census that has been ordered by the executive. —W. E. DUNN.

The Literary Review of the New York *Post*, for March 19, 1921, contains an interesting communication from Mr. Charles M. Pepper, Director of the Chile-American Association, relative to the gift to Chile of representatve books in English dealing mainly with the United States. Both the letter and the list of books are reproduced here:

SIR: The study of Spanish in the schools and colleges of the United States has now broadened to include something of the literature, the history, and the institutions of Spanish-American countries by authors in that language. It may therefore interest your readers to learn something of a reciprocal movement to spread the knowledge of the United States through books in English.

Señor Santiago Severin, a philanthropic business man of Chile, after visiting the United States, presented to the city of Valparaiso a fine library building. His death, a few months ago, left incomplete the plans for filling its shelves with books. The Chile-American Association, in its general work of promoting better knowledge of the two countries, each by the other, found the field an inviting one. The members of the association comprise leading companies and business firms interested in Chilean industry, and trade. Many of them know the country and its people somewhat intimately. They therefore make provision for the gift of a collection of 100 books which it is expected will serve as a unit for addition from time to time.

In establishing the Chile-American Association collection the members had in mind such books as would illuminate the historical development of the United States from the romantic days of Spanish colonization and they were aware that in a Spanish-speaking country more than Plymouth and Jamestown were desirable. A background of political and social institutions and the diverse elements which have entered into the blood stream of our national life was essential, however limited it might be. Both history and national character as reflected and interpreted in biography, with no prejudice against anecdotal biographers, and equally biographies which deal with not only statesmen and soldiers but with leaders in industry and commerce who represent achievement, formed part of the plan. Something of the spirit which adventures abroad was likewise to be exhibited, especially where it has a savor of the sea, which appeals especially to a maritime people such as Chileans. Fiction, both the novel and the short story, naturally would be drawn on and for that reason it was given full recognition, even to excursions into historical fiction and sectional or geographical aspects of American life and manners. The United States as seen by observers from other countries was not to be overlooked and some of their observations therefore found place. Moreover, it was steadily kept in view that the purpose was not to provide a reference library, but a readable collection of books. Uniform literary merit was not aimed at.

With these motives understood the director prepared a tentative list of seventy or seventy-five books based on his knowledge of Chilean psychology. This list was submitted with an explanation of the purpose to librarians in half a dozen cities and to some professional students of Latin America as far away as Stanford University. Those busy men offered pertinent and practical suggestions. Following their suggestions, elisions and additions were made until the list was completed.

Omissions doubtless will be noted and the usual query made as to why this or that book was left out. The answer is to repeat that the initial gifts are simply a beginning and that the intention is to make additions to the collections from time to time.

CHARLES M. PEPPER,
Director, Chile-American Association.

NEW YORK, February 1, 1921.

List of books presented by the Chile-American Association:

Our Chief Magistrate. W. H. Taft.

Congressional Government. Woodrow Wilson.

The American Commonwealth. James Bryce.

American Government and Politics. Beard.

The Critical Period of American History. John Fiske.

History of the United States (in one volume). Elson.

Principles of American Diplomacy. John Bassett Moore.

Address on International Subjects. Elihu Root.

Speeches in South America. Elihu Root.

The Making of an American. Jacob A. Riis.

The Promised Land. Mary Antin.

From Alien to Citizen. Edward A. Steiner.

The Americanization of Edward Bok. Bok.

Life of Washington. Woodrow Wilson.

The Many Sided Franklin. Paul L. Ford.

The True Thomas Jefferson. W. E. Curtis.

Alexander Hamilton. Henry J. Ford.

The Conqueror (Hamilton in Fiction). Gertrude Atherton.

The True Andrew Jackson. Cyrus Townsend Brady.

James Monroe. Daniel Coit Gilman.

Henry Clay. Carl Schurz.

Abraham Lincoln. Lord Charnwood.

Lincoln, Master of Men. Alonzo Rothschild.

Life of Ulysses S. Grant. Hamlin Garland.

Robert E. Lee. Bruce.

Up From Slavery. Booker T. Washington.

Autobiography of Andrew Carnegie.

Theodore Roosevelt and His Time. Bishop.

American Contemporary Biography. (two volumes).

Who's Who in America.

Edison, His Life and Inventions. Dyer and Martin.

Life of Westinghouse. Leupp.

Memories of Buffalo Bill. Louisa F. Cody.

Herbert Hoover—The Man and His Work. Vernon Kellogg.

The Men Who Are Making America. Forbes.

Letters to His Children. Roosevelt.

Spain in America. E. G. Bourne.

The Colonization of North America. Bolton and Marshall.

The Founding of Spanish California. Chapman.

Our Hispanic Southwest. Ernest Peixotto.

The Old Sante Fé Trail. Inman.

The French in the Heart of America. John H. Finley.

The Louisiana Purchase. James K. Hosmer.

The Winning of the West. Theodore Roosevelt.

Conquest of the Old Southwest. Henderson.

The Oregon Trail. Parkman.

Pathfinders of the West. Agnes C. Laut.

Old Cape Cod. Mary R. Bangs.

The Panama Gateway. Joseph B. Bishop.

Indians of the Painted Desert. George Wharton James.

The Mississippi River. Chambers.

Our Inland Seas. Mills.

The Land of the Strenuous Life. Abbe Klein.

America of To-morrow. Abbe Klein.

The Future in America. H. G. Wells.

The Land of Contrasts. Muirhead.

With Americans of Past and Present Days. Jusserand.

America Through the Spectacles of an Oriental Diplomat. Wu Ting Fang.

Letters from America. Rupert Brooke.

Character and Opinion in the United States. George Santayana.

People of Destiny. Philip Gibbs.

The Gulf of Misunderstanding. Tancredo Pinochet.

The United States and Latin America. Latané.

Two Years Before the Mast. R. H. Dana.

Ships and Sailors of Old Salem. Ralph D. Paine.

White Shadows in the South Seas. Frederick O'Brien.

The Rise of Silas Lapham. W. D. Howells.

The Turmoil. Booth Tarkington.

Life on the Mississippi. Mark Twain.

The Virginian. Owen Wister.

The Grandissimes. George W. Cable.

The Rainbow Trail. Zane Grey.

The Trail of the Lonesome Pine. John Fox.

The Call of the Wild. Jack London.

The Age of Innocence. Edith Wharton.

A Poor Wise Man. Mary Roberts Rinehart.

Java Head. Joseph Hergesheimer.

To Have and to Hold. Mary Johnston.

The Great Desire. Alexander Black.

The Voice of the People. Ellen Glasgow.

The Riders of the King Log. Holman Day.

The Freedom of the Seas. Cyrus Townsend Brady.

The Pit, a Story of Chicago. Frank Norris.

Alice of Old Vincennes. Maurice Thompson.

The House of the Seven Gables. Hawthorne.

Hugh Wynne. S. Weir Mitchell.

Ramona. Helen Hunt Jackson.

The Crossing. Winston Churchill.

Nathan Burke. Mary S. Watts.

The Man Without a Country. Edward Everett Hale.

The Hon. Peter Sterling. Paul L. Ford.

The Portygee. Joseph Lincoln.

The Great Modern American Stories. W. D. Howells.

The Luck of Roaring Camp. Bret Harte.

Marjorie Daw. T. B. Aldrich.
In Ole Virginia; or Marse Chan.
  Thomas Nelson Page.
The Four Million. O. Henry.
Old Chester Tales. Mrs. Deland.
The Splendid Idle Forties. Gertrude
  Atherton.

The Little Book of American Poets.
  Jessie B. Rittenhouse.
The Little Book of Modern Verse.
  Jessie B. Rittenhouse.
The Second Book of Modern Verse.
  Jessie B. Rittenhouse.

Doubleday, Page & Co. has recently opened a department of Spanish
books to be conducted under the management of Miss Harriet V.
Wishnieff. The above company has been appointed the representative in the United States of a number of the leading publishers of
Spain, and of some in Hispanic America. Volumes carried in stock
by this company number well into the thousands, and any desired
number of publications will be imported on request. Arrangements
have been made to have library orders bound in Spain. Miss Wishnieff is preparing a doctor's thesis on Spanish literature, and is in an
unusual position to supply all kinds of bibliographical information,
special book lists, and to assist librarians in forming their Spanish
collections. This service is available to libraries quite independently of
the purchase of books. Under her direction a catalogue is being compiled which will contain over 3,000 titles of the most important books in
Spanish, both classical and modern. The company announces that a
copy of this work will be sent to those who desire it if request be sent
to the Spanish Book Department.

Sr. Benjamin Monroy, a well-known professor and grammarian of
Spain, who has wrtten a number of textbooks, has recently compiled a
Spanish grammar for elementary and introductory uses. The work is
described as graphic and as taking up the instruction step by step,
leaving no vacant places for the imagination of the pupil to fill in as
so many of these books do when hastily prepared. The book contains
100 lessons, and is intended primarily for the use of children who can
not attend school, for adult illiterate workmen, and for the elementary
schools of all countries where Spanish is taught. It is claimed for the
work that, by its use, one can learn to read and write without the
aid of a teacher. It is understood that the author would consider a
proposition to publish this volume in the United States.

Señor Carlos I. Salas has issued recently *Estudio biográfico bibliográfico de la vida y obras del doctor Pedro Mártir de Angleria*, which is

said to be the most important study of the first historian of the Indias, and to contain a full bibliography. Only fifty copies were printed. Señor Salas, who has previously published several valuable bibliographies, notably his *Bibliográfia del general San Martín y de la emancipación sudamericana* in 5 volumes, has been elected a corresponding member of the Real Academía de la Historia of Spain.—C. K. JONES.

A pamphlet of 34 pages entitled *A Brief Description of Actual Conditions in Mexico*, written by Samuel G. Vazquez, colonization agent for Mexico in Los Angeles, California, has recently been issued by The Mexican Products Exhibit, of Los Angeles. "A plain statement of the policy of the Mexican Government" by President Obregón precedes the "Description" by Vazquez. This is dated April 3, 1921, and is both in English and in Spanish, and first appeared in Spanish in the Mexican newspapers. This statement is to the effect that complete pacification has been accomplished; that all national debts are to be paid; that foreigners are to be protected; that guarantees are given to all of fair treatment. Relative to the foreign debt of Mexico, the statement says:

An invitation has been issued to all holders of our exterior debt asking them to appoint their representatives and enter into arrangements with the Government concerning all its debts, upon the basis that the Government will not use any subterfuge or evasions, but on the contrary found its settlement upon an ample spirit of equity such as has served heretofore as a standard for all its acts, until they be completely satisfied.

In his Description, Vazquez discusses briefly the following matters: Wrong conception of Mexico; Mexico's past; reasons for revolution; Mexico today: serious problems; excursions to Mexico; American spirit in Mexico; economic conditions in Mexico; Mexico's indebtedness; inducements for capital; Mexico (area, etc.); industrial Mexico; the Mexican cotton industry; industrial possibilities; industrial facilities in Mexico; timber; vegetable products; mining; oil; where Mexico could lead the world; what the Mexican government is doing to encourage immigration and agricultural development; lands; water and irrigation; petroleum imports from Mexico nearly doubled in year, and exports gained rapidly; and petroleum biggest factor.

Sr. D. Domingo Figarola-Caneda, founder and former director of the National Library of Habana, member of the Academy of History of Cuba, and director of the *Anales de la Academia de la Historia*, has quite recently compiled a work entitled *José Antonio Saco.—Documentos para su Vida*. Sr. Figarola-Caneda has annotated the volume and written an introduction for it. The volume has been issued in two editions, one a *de luxe* edition of 200 numbered copies, which sells at five dollars, and the other of 800 copies, which sells at two dollars. It is understood that the work is on sale in all the bookstores in Habana. The proceeds from the sale of this interesting work are to be employed in publishing the second volume which is now in course of preparation and to restore Saco's monument in the cemetery of Colón.

Luis Araquistaín, the author of a book entitled *El Peligro Yanqui* (printed in Madrid, and now being sold in Argentina) was in the United States some two months. The principal tenet of his work is the materialism of the people of the United States who strive only for power and money. The United States view relative to woman suffrage and rule of woman over the home are proofs of that tenet. The book characterizes the people of the United States as cherishing a hatred toward races of color. The Federation of Labor is held up as a most powerful organization which opposes recognition of equality to the Japanese. The United States is said to be the center of an intense rivalry for power as between England, Japan, and themselves. In the United States, the Gulf of Mexico is considered as a modern Mediterranean, and Panama and the Antilles, as well as Central America and Mexico, are considered to be but economic colonies. Capitalists of this country are said to be the most powerful in the world, and to be ready to extend their influence into any country that gives an opening, as can be seen in the case of the oil resources of Mexico. Even the present study of the Spanish language in this country is taken as an indication of our desire for the economic conquest of Hispanic America. Later, when the time is ripe the Spanish language in these countries will be suppressed and English imposed in its stead as has been done in Porto Rico, Panama, and the Philippines.

STATEMENT OF THE OWNERSHIP, MANAGEMENT, CIRCULATION, ETC., REQUIRED BY THE ACT OF CONGRESS OF AUGUST 24, 1912,

Of The Hispanic American Historical Review, published quarterly at Baltimore, Maryland, for October 1, 1921.

City of Washington, ⎫
District of Columbia⎭ ss.

Before me, a Notary Public in and for the city and District aforesaid, personally appeared James A. Robertson, who, having been duly sworn according to law, deposes and says that he is the Managing Editor of The Hispanic American Historical Review and that the following is, to the best of his knowledge and belief, a true statement of the ownership, management (and if a daily paper, the circulation), etc., of the aforesaid publication for the date shown in the above caption, required by the Act of August 24, 1912, embodied in section 443, Postal Laws and Regulations, printed on the reverse of this form, to wit:

1. That the names and addresses of the publisher, editor, managing editor, and business managers are:

Publisher:

   Board of Editors of The Hispanic American Historical Review, care Williams & Wilkins Company, Mount Royal and Guilford Aves., Baltimore, Maryland.

Editors:

   Isaac J. Cox, Northwestern University, Evanston, Illinois.

   William R. Manning, 4701 Fessenden St., N.W., Washington, D. C.

   Percy Alvin Martin, Leland Stanford Jr. University, Leland Stanford, California.

   W. W. Pierson, Jr., University of North Carolina, Chapel Hill, North Carolina.

   Herbert I. Priestley, University of California, Berkeley, California.

   James A. Robertson, 1422 Irving St., N.E., Washington, D. C.

Advisory Editors:

   Herbert E. Bolton, University of California, Berkeley, California.

   William R. Shepherd, Columbia University, New York, N. Y.

Managing Editor:

   James A. Robertson, 1422 Irving St., N.E., Washington, D. C.

Business Managers:

   None.

2. That the owners are: (Give names and addresses of individual owners, or, if a corporation, give its name and the names and addresses of stockholders owning or holding 1 per cent or more of the total amount of stock.)

Board of Editors of The Hispanic American Historical Review:

   Isaac J. Cox, Northwestern University, Evanston, Illinois.

   William R. Manning, 4701 Fessenden St., N.W., Washington, D. C.

594

Percy Alvin Martin, Leland Stanford Jr. University, Leland Stanford, California.

W. W. Pierson, Jr., University of North Carolina, Chapel Hill, North Carolina.

Herbert I. Priestley, University of California, Berkeley, California.

James A. Robertson, 1422 Irving St., N.E., Washington, D. C.

3. That the known bondholders, mortgagees, and other security holders owning or holding 1 per cent or more of total amount of bonds, mortgages, or other securities are: (If there are none, so state.)   None.

4. That the two paragraphs next above, giving the names of the owners, stockholders, and security holders, if any, contain not only the list of stockholders and security holders as they appear upon the books of the company but also, in cases where the stockholder or security holder appears upon the books of the company as trustee or in any other fiduciary relation, the name of the person or corporation for whom such trustee is acting, is given; also that the said two paragraphs contain statements embracing affiant's full knowledge and belief as to the circumstances and conditions under which stockholders and security holders who do not appear upon the books of the company as trustees, hold stock and securities in a capacity other than that of a bona fide owner; and this affiant has no reason to believe that any other person, association, or corporation has any interest direct or indirect in the said stock, bonds, or other securities than as so stated by him.

5. That the average number of copies of each issue of this publication sold or distributed, through the mails or otherwise, to paid subscribers during the six months preceding the date shown above is.................................(This information is required from daily publications only.)

JAMES A. ROBERTSON,
Managing Editor.

Sworn to and subscribed before me this 22nd day of September, 1921.

[SEAL.]   C. C. WEIDEMANN.

(My commission expires September 23, 1923.)

The Hispanic American Historical Review

Vol. IV NOVEMBER, 1921 No. 4

THE DUTCH AND CUBA, 1609-1643[1]

I

THE WEST INDIA COMPANY

(To 1628)

The Netherlands had been fighting Spain for liberty since 1568, with England and France for allies. In 1579 the southern Catholic provinces yielded to Alexander Farnese, but the seven northern provinces in 1581 proclaimed their complete independence, and, with varying fortunes, fought on, toward the twelve years' truce agreed upon in 1609.

During this long war the Netherlands, through various East India companies, acquired profits and possessions in the orient. Encouraged by amazing success there, they turned inquiring eyes north, to Greenland, south to Brazil, and they by no means overlooked the Caribbean, in the west.

Henry IV. of France became interested in the possibilities of conquest and of revenues which he saw were open in distant quarters of the world. Together, experienced Dutchmen and the French king considered establishing a French East India Company. To protect the Dutch East India Company in which the government as government was concerned, from the rivalry thus threatened, the Netherlands' states-general in 1606

[1] Based on documents preserved in the General Archives of the Indies, Seville, Spain.

conceived a plan of diverting Henry's attention from the east, by suggesting, through their French ambassador, François Aerssens, and François Francken, the establishment of a West India Company. Francken had repeatedly discussed this with the able navigator and merchant, William Usselincx, with Linschoten, and the learned Plancius. Oldenbarnevelt (universally acknowledged political leader of the United Netherlands) was ready to adopt a plan of a West India Company with Holland capital and French support, as he saw an opportunity of inflicting injury in Spanish America.[2]

That such a project existed was known to the archduke, Albert, who represented Spain in the loyal southern provinces. Prior to November of 1606 he informed[3] Philip that "among Hollanders and merchants" there existed a scheme to raise an armada of seventy or eighty ships and six thousand men, the king of France contributing along with them, "up to a total of eighty thousand ducats and a thousand francs a day". This armada was to attack Puerto Bello and Cartagena, and especially the island of Cuba. The principal objective was Havana, in seizing which port it was intended to cripple Spanish colonial commerce irremediably. The expedition was to clear for Indies in the spring of 1607.

"But in 1607 practical difficulties", presenting themselves to the Dutch,

seemed too great to warrant the execution of this plan. Merchants were afraid to risk their capital; the increasing hope of peace (with Spain) decided Oldenbarnevelt and other statesmen not to add to their (already serious) difficulties in East India (any further complications in the Spanish West Indies). The matter was dropped, to the great annoyance of the zealous Usselincx, who thought that this company promised "the greatest traffic in the world".[4]

Philip, however, was not immediately convinced that the danger of a West Indian Company was not imminent.

[2] Petrus Johannes Blok, *History of the People of the Netherlands* (New York, G. P. Putnam's Sons, 1900), III., *The War with Spain*, pp. 296–7.
[3] A. de I., 147–5–16, *Junta de guerra* to crown.
[4] *See above*, Note 2.

He referred the archduke's warning to the council for war in Indies.[5] *Cedulas* were despatched[6] to Governor Valdes, at Havana warning him of Dutch designs on that part. His attention was called to the harbor of Matanzas where, the crown was informed, this enemy got supplies (as the French had very long been doing), from an estate which Valdes was asked to consider removing farther inland. Don Pedro seems to have felt livelier alarm lest invaders come into his capital by a nearer route, via Chorrera, where, he said[7], Maldonado's saw mill and sugar estate exposed the road to the town. Conclusion of the truce of 1609 quieted this alarm: the West India Company was not to materialize until twelve years later.

Article V. of that truce contained a general stipulation

that there should be mutual freedom of trade (between Spaniards and Netherlanders). In the Spanish dominions within Europe, the inhabitants of those provinces could not trade without the king's express permission, but outside of them should be allowed full freedom of entry. In a secret article, this permission herein mentioned was expressly given by the deputies from the enemy (Spain) in the name of the king and the archdukes, "on condition that the trade be free and assured".[8]

These agreements can have affected Dutch traders in Indies very little: both before and after conclusion of the truce, they

[5] *See above*, note 2. As "by all means the most important and efficacious opposition which may be offered to everything which the enemy can attempt and the most certain means to frustrate his designs", the council recommended the creation of a Caribbean squadron (*armada de barlovento*), the history of which the author has given in another article so entitled, published in *La Reforma Social*, New York, in 1919. Also, while turning to Alonso de Sotomayor for accurate information as to the condition of things in Havana, the council recommended that the crown appoint to the governership of Cuba, to succeed don Pedro de Valdes, at this juncture (October–November 1606) "suspended", as a consequence of Nuñes de Toledo's *visita*, some person who should be "very much of a soldier, made to defend places, entirely satisfactory in his administration of both military and civil affairs", who, with a hundred and fifty men to reinforce the garrison at Havana, should depart for Cuba at once, in fast vessels. Eventually, Ruis de Pereda was chosen to succeed Valdes.

[6] A. de I., 78-2-2, V. 5, p. 70 r., *cedula*, November 20, 1606; 54-2-8, memorandum for a *cedula*, February 18, 1607.

[7] A. de I., 54-1-16, Valdes to the crown, Havana, July 13, 1607.

[8] Blok, *History of the People of the Netherlands*, III., *The War with Spain*, p. 311.

sailed westward out of Netherland ports to carry spoons, forks, knives, wines, cheese, butter, and negroes to Indies, and returned thither with hides, sugar, tobacco, and dyewood—or did not return, as their luck may have run. No matter what rights they may have acquired under the truce of 1609, to Spaniards in Cuba they, like all other foreigners, remained pirates (heretics and enemies), that is, persons with whom business must, unfortunately, be done more or less surreptitiously.[9]

[9] When Manso de Contreras finished his campaign against illicit trade between the colonists of Cuba and foreigners, the king had been assured (1607–8) that the *vecinos* of the island said they would kill, or at least stone out of the *res publica*, any person who indulged in *rescates*, ever again. "It seems incredible," Manso de Contreras himself admitted, that the evil of illicit traffic should have been so completely eradicated. On April 14, 1612, Governor Pereda reported it as "most certain" that this nefarious business was reviving. On December 18, 1612, in writing of the prize money which proceeded from Valdes's campaigns against pirates, Governor Pereda said that through all these years Cuba's coasts were infested with "small pirate craft". They did damage to the king's subjects who lived by the coasting trade, for they were prone to pillage by sea; they also did damage to the king's revenues, for they captured the market when they came ashore, to barter. The English were abroad: of ten pirates captured on the Isle of Pines in the spring of 1612, seven were of that nationality. "For worthy reasons" the life of one was spared; the rest were executed. In Spain it was at this time (1611) considered best policy to placate the English, and orders were issued to spare the vessels of the king of Great Britain all cause for complaint, but if these orders were ever addressed to Cuba they at least arrived too late to save the men in question. These pirates informed Pereda of the English colony of Virginia; that Jamestown existed was news to him. The Spaniards understood that the French were out with some sort of authority from their government: some said that they were cleared by the French authorities, but at their own risk. It would seem that French courts (1615) held that vessels taken west of the Terceras were lawful prizes. The crown could think of no remedies for the situation: no removal of causes was attempted—only the old superficial treatments of effects. In 1614, the president of the council was peremptorily ordered to put a stop to all communication between Spaniards in Indies and foreigners along the coasts: without awaiting further provocation, past infractions of the laws against such intercourse were to be punished, and those officials who might have prevented it, but had failed to do so, were to be deposed from office. Penalties against communication with enemies were to be increased, "in order to inspire terror in those concerned". Governor Pereda was most interested to learn who in Cuba were most concerned, in favoring these enemy traders: he knew that without encouragement it would not have been possible for them to linger off shore so long, so comfortably. Certainly they had friends on land. These friends, however, were not the merchants and traders of the island, with whose interests the illicit business which the colonists transacted with pirates constituted a ruinous competition.

Their activities gave the king of Spain no rest at all. When he bought ship-building materials of them and admitted their vessels to Havana to deliver same, the materials not only turned out to be unsatisfactory, but a clerk aboard, who was said to be an old pirate, made the most of the opportunity offered him by the freighter's stay there, to sound and chart that harbor![10] Behind every such incident his majesty descried great governmental designs to seize and hold ports or islands of the Caribbean, especially Havana. Nor were his fears unjustified: Dutch commerce had built the Netherlands an empire in the orient.

Usselincx, whose dream it was that it should do as much in the occident, revived the project for a West India Company,

and carried it so far by 1614 that the estate of Holland finally gave ear to his representations. But the opposition of Oldenbarnevelt and the East India Company again caused the failure of his plans, and Usselincx went back to the Beemster. . . And not alone Usselincx had turned his attention to the west. . . The East India Company itself was continually seeking a shorter route to India by way of the western hemisphere.

Now it was that Hudson, in the service of that company sought the northwest passage; and found instead his river and his bay.

The publication of a placard of the states-general in 1614, wherein a forty years' commercial monopoly in the localities was offered to those who should discover "any new passages, ports, lands or localities," aroused a still greater zeal for discovery in the west. A Company of New Netherland was founded. This established Fort Nassau and another fort on the island of Manhattan at the mouth of the Hudson, while the American coast was further explored and the voyages thither continually increased."[11]

The king of Spain, however, was less disturbed by these humble beginnings of mighty matters in the north, than he was by events on the southern continent and around the smaller,

---

[10] A. de I., 147-5-17, *Junta de guerra* to the crown, April 30, 1612, etc. (*see* 143-5-5).

[11] Blok, *ut supra*, III., *The War with Spain*, pp. 329-330.

neglected islands of the Caribbean, which lie in a curving line from Florida to the Orinoco. Holland and Zealand owners, banded into companies, even before the truce had sent out "more than two hundred ships"[12] on business cruises; a damaging proportion of them frequented the shores of Brazil, Guayana, Araya—the coasts of the Caribbean and all its islets; whereon, along with their friends, the French and English, the Dutch were becoming permanently at home.

As the twelve years' truce between Spain and the Netherlands wore on, both parties to it came to realize that it would not be renewed, nor converted into a peace. So, too, war with England threatened Philip: it was in 1617 that Sir Walter Raleigh was permitted to undertake his expedition to the Orinoco. Informed of this, and fearing further aggression, the crown in 1618[13] reinforced the garrisons of Porto Rico and Santo Domingo; Havana was to get any surplus men, and it was at this time, too, that Santiago de Cuba received a garrison of twelve and certain arms and munitions.[14]

Because it was believed[15] (in January, 1619) that the Dutch contemplated aggression against Havana, Alonso de Sotomayor was sent[16] there with arms, munitions and biscuit. The governor[17] was instructed[18] to lay in still more supplies, and to arm the townspeople—at their expense—adding as many of them as he might see fit to the forts' garrisons. He was warned not to rely upon Havana's strength, nor upon the difficulties an enemy must overcome to attack the place, nor on the existing truce, because the preparations which were being made in the Netherlands indicated that to capture so important a place, the Dutch were ready to undertake and to risk, anything. All the Indies were advised that a project against Havana was afoot, and of the

[12] *Ibid.*
[13] A. de I., 78-2-2, VII., p. 46 r., *cedula*, September 18, 1618.
[14] A. de I., 78-2-2, VII., pp. 46 r., *cedulas*, September 18, 1618.
[15] A. de I., *Junta de guerra* to the crown, January 22 and January 26, 1619.
[16] A. de I., 78-3-9, VII. pp. 143, 144, *cedulas* concerning Alonso de Sotomayor.
[17] The governor was now Sancho de Alquisa, who had succeeded Pereda.
[18] A. de I., 78-2-2, VII., p. 63, *cedula*, February 12, 1619.

possibility that, failing there, the Dutch would endeavor to console themselves elsewhere.[19]

In 1620 the council for war in Indies expressed the opinion[20] that

given the state of affairs in Germany, England and Holland . . a small occasion will suffice for the Hollanders to disregard what is left of the truce, and for the English to break the peace,

which small occasion the council thought they were likely to discover in the despatch of Spanish auxiliary armies to Germany.

Whether a definite plan to attack Havana was formulated in the Netherlands, at this time, or not, certainly the West India Company was shaping up. Oldenbarnevelt had fallen from power and the indefatigable Usselincx believed that his removal opened opportunity to his designs on Spanish possession of the west. Usselincx therefore returned in the autumn of 1618 from Zealand, whither he had fled to escape his creditors, and came to Holland to act as adviser to the states of that province and to the states-general, in the matter of the new company and its charter. He could not even now carry out all of his plans, nor impose what he considered essential ideas,[21] wherefore he with-

[19] The *cedula* addressed to Alquiza, and the arms, munitions, and supplies which Sotomayor brought, arrived in Havana after that governor's death. Quero was in command. He reported that he had put Havana into good shape and meant "to try to punish the enemy as advantageously as possible". He bade the governor of eastern Cuba mobilize men and supplies, to send to Havana if they were needed, and he informed Mexico of the situation, preparatory to calling upon the viceroy for help, if necessary. Quero stated that to enable him to provide for Havana's forts as ordered, 30,000 ducats would be required, whereas there was not "one single *real*" in the treasury. He purposed calling on passing armada generals for money.

[20] A. de I., 147-5-18, *Junta de guerra* to the crown.

[21] "Usselincx was a stern Calvinist and enemy of all heretics and erring spirits, and he now desired not only a limitation of the power of the directors over the shareholders, better and completer accounts, the planting of colonies of freemen closely bound to the mother country, but also the promotion of civilisation and Christianity among the natives, and especially a regular supervision by the state of the doings of the merchants "who have gain for their north star and greed for a compass, and who would believe the ship was keeping to its right course, if it were almost wrecked by profits." Little heed was paid his ideals. He disapproved of the scheme as finally agreed upon and entered the service of the king of Sweden, still in hopes from that northern court to realise his great plans.

drew from the business, to which he had given all his years and all his means.

The truce with Spain expired in 1621. The West India Company was chartered on June 3 of that year. It was not[22] simply a commercial corporation; it was also a political association formed to injure an enemy, to stanch the source of his power, and perhaps to develop its own and the Netherlands' revenues and empire in that enemy's territory, at his expense. In the orient the Dutch had already demonstrated not only the defects, but also the ruthless efficiency of such an institution. The king of Spain was not unaware of them.

Neither was he unadvised as to what were supposed to be this West India Company's piratical intentions, at the very commencement of its career. Via England, where its organization was resented because it might interfere with English designs on Guiana, he was informed some months before its chartering that the company's purpose was to capture that year's galleons.

In September, 1621, from Brussels, the *infanta* Isabel sent[23] Philip IV. a map, and details, said to come from a reliable source, of what she was assured were the company's designs on Havana via Matanzas. Havana was the objective, for the Dutch reckoned it to be the vital center of the Indies trade. Because they believed the place to be strongly held, they considered that it would be unwise to attack it directly, even with all their might; instead, they planned to seize Matanzas bay, fortify it, establish a permanent colony there, whence, the intervening woodlands having been destroyed by fire, the Dutch would attack Havana from land, on which side they understood that it was weak. Whoever presented this scheme to the company, displayed accurate and appreciative acquaintance with Matanzas bay, the lay of its fertile lands and its fresh waters, its climate and the fact that Spaniards had not improved any of these natural advantages. It was held that from Matanzas as a strongly fortified base, the company would be able to play havoc with Spanish shipping frequenting Havana, *i.e.*,

[22] Blok, *ut supra*, IV., pp. 3–5.
[23] A. de I., 147–5–8, September 24, 1621.

with all of it, from the southern continental shore of the Caribbean, from the Isthmus, from Mexico. They would be aided,
it was said, by the Spaniards' erroneous supposition that navigation was not feasible from Matanzas through the Bahama
channel; the Dutch claimed to have learned better, by experience.

This plan against Matanzas, and Havana, having been laid[24]
before the council for war in Indies—in the words, it was said,
of the Dutch themselves—the council recommended that the
governor[25] be ordered to inspect Matanzas, in company with
engineers and other intelligent persons, and send a map of the
port and plans for fortifications there, these fortifications to be
provided with guns and garrison from Havana at small expense;
but, the council added, in recommending that the governor send
a map of all the island as well, and report on other ports, it was
no lack of fine harbors which had deterred, or would deter, the
Dutch from such a project as this described. The council
believed that they might make their choice of even better loca-
tions than Matanzas. The real difficulty—indeed, the impossi-
bility—of such a scheme, lay in cost of maintenance, once a
base were established. The Spaniards believed that English
experience in Virginia and Bermuda had demonstrated as much:
Philip was assured that these outposts had through many years
cost England dear without returning any profit whatsoever.[26]
The *cedula* to Venegas was duly issued, ordering him to inspect,
map, and report on Matanzas.[27]

No sooner had the council so comfortably disposed of this
alarm than the ambassador, Cardinal de la Cueva, sounded it
again, from Brussels, in reporting[28] that Count Maurice was

[24] A. de I., 147-5-18, *Junta de guerra* to the crown, October 23, 1621.

[25] Venegas had succeeded Alquiza, deceased. In 147-5-18, there is an undated memorandum of what appears to be an order in council to indite a *cedula*
to Venegas.

[26] This view with respect to Virginia is especially clear in a set of documents
bearing on the subject, which Dr. Jameson has recently secured from the archives
of Simancas and Seville. See "Spanish Policy toward Virginia, 1606-1612," in
the American Historical Review, vol. XXV, No. 3, by I. A. Wright.

[27] A. de I., 78-2-2, VII., p. 143, October 28, 1621.

[28] A. de I., 147-5-8, March 5, 1622.

secretly and rapidly arming three vessels in Zealand, intended for some enterprize in Indies; he, too, mentioned Matanzas.

Former Governor Pereda, then in Brussels, on being consulted in the matter, and shown a Dutch map of Cuba, called[29] attention to the fact that he had previously expressed fears for Matanzas. Nevertheless, he believed that the enemy would not find it easy to attack Havana overland from as far away as that harbor; he knew the intervening country to be rough, wooded, threaded only by narrow trails. He thought that the saddles the Dutch were said to be carrying along, would be of little service on the ponies which were all the mounts they would find. Heat and mosquitoes would trouble them. One great advantage the Spaniards possessed: they were acclimatized, whereas the Dutch were not. Pereda foresaw that sickness would fight on the Spaniards' side. Without depleting the ordinary garrisons, Havana could muster six hundred men armed with arquebuses, pikes, and very few muskets. Thirty-five or forty horsemen would be available, mounted on "reasonably" good animals, and armed with lances and targets. The east could send up not more than two hundred men, who would be badly armed, but valuable in their acquaintance with the country. He believed that a great danger lay in the negroes of the island, slaves, and *cimarrones* "who all desire liberty". If they joined the enemy they would be useful as guides and in building fortifications, at no cost to his supplies, since they would continue to live on bananas, *cazabe*, and wild cattle. Pereda thought it unnecessary to describe "the inquietude and notable damage" which would result if the Dutch fortified themselves at Matanzas, forming a base there for naval operations. Fleets and armadas en route to Spain must pass that harbor. He called attention to the facility with which it could be reached from both Virginia and Bermuda, and they from it.

Some persons believed[30] that it was Count Maurice's intention to attack Morro Castle, at Havana, or the promontory of the same name at Santiago de Cuba. Venegas was warned.[31]   He

[29] A. de I., 147-5-8, March 4, 1622.
[30] A. de I., 54-2-20, Juan de Cirica to the president of Indies, March 16, 1622.
[31] A. de I., 78-2-2, VII., p. 152 r., March 27, 1622.

replied[32] that Morro castle at Havana was by reason of its position almost impregnable; moreover, it now possessed fifty bronze guns, eighteen to ninety-seven hundred weight, and a garrison of two hundred soldiers. It commanded the country for two leagues around. There were at Havana two other forts, and still other soldiers, to a total fighting force of eight hundred well trained men; thirty of them, cavalry. He was not inclined to fancy that Count Maurice would attack with three ships out of Zealand. Surely it must be Morro at Santiago which was threatened.

Again, in August of 1622, the crown referred to the council for war in Indies further advice from Flanders[33] that the Dutch purposed establishing a strong naval base in Indies. In November following, Venegas was warned[34] again: Count Maurice's three vessels had become six 600-ton ships, three 300-ton ships, three caravels and four supply ships. The governor was told to be on guard, but not to alarm the country or to occasion unnecessary expense. Venegas replied[35] that neither was this expedition enough to reduce his majesty's forts at Havana, and since the land in itself offered little bait (in gold, silver, or jewels), he still felt sure that the Dutch would waste no time, men, or powder on Cuba.

In Spain, in the spring of 1623, the idea nevertheless persisted[36] that the enemy's objective in Indies was Matanzas. The Dutch expedition was now described as twenty vessels, approximately two thousand men, with building tools among their baggage. It was reported to have sailed on April 29th—for Havana, for Matanzas, for Cape San Antonio, or for San Miguel (ten or twelve leagues from Panama), or for the salt beds of Araya. In fact, this first fleet of the West India Company, under Lhermite and Willekens, held its course straight for

[32] A. de I., 54-1-17, Venegas to the crown, August 12, 1622.
[33] A. de I., 54-2-10, August 12-13, 1622.
[34] A. de I., 78-2-2, VII., p. 194, November 24, 1622.
[35] A. de I., 54-1-17, Venegas to the crown, April 15, 1623.
[36] A. de I., 147-5-8, Secretary Cirica to the *Junta de guerra*, March 30, 1623; memorandum, dated April 11, 1623; royal order, May 2, 1623.

South America.[27]   On May 26, 1623, Venegas was warned[38] again: to expect at San Anton, or Havana, or Matanzas, the Prince of Orange's fleet (it was so designated), consisting of twenty large vessels, forty guns, and one hundred and fifty men each, outside the crew.   The crown expected Venegas[39] to have inspected Matanzas ere this.   He was ordered to keep Havana well protected, but at the same time to defend that neighboring port.

Through 1624, fear of the Dutch did not abate.   It considerably disturbed the usual course of Spanish traffic from Indies.   Normally, there were still the two fleets a year from Spain, one to Mexico, and one to Tierra Firme.   The galleons of the guard accompanied the latter.   The former, being less protected, was especially liable to be forbidden to sail at all, in times of danger.[40]   It had been the rule for these two fleets to meet in Havana harbor and recross the Atlantic together, for mutual protection.   A couple of galleons from Honduras carrying very valuable cargoes also made Havana their rendezvous. This arrangement occasioned delay, especially to the merchants of Mexico, whose fleet was usually the first to arrive at Havana. It therefore became usual for them to leave their more precious cargo and specie in Havana's forts, to be picked up, at one

[27] A month after it had gone the council for war in Indies was still arguing to the crown that it would be impossible for the Dutch to take Havana, with its eight hundred or a thousand fighting men and three castles—impossible, if the governor in charge were a soldier.   Venegas, now, the council described as an honorable gentleman—but a sailor.   The council was assured and so assured the crown, that the enemy could not sustain a force of fifteen or twenty thousand men, for fifteen days, in Cuba: the climate would spoil their food, and the eating of it would breed sickness, which alone would suffice to destroy the invaders.   It had been suggested that the Dutch might fortify themselves on Cape San Antonio. This notion the council dismissed, relying upon an informant who was certain that as good statesmen as the Dutch were would direct their attentions to more profitable regions.

[38] A. de I., 78-2-2, VII., p. 203 r., May 26, 1623.

[39] A. de I., 147-5-8, Venegas to the crown, September 5, 1622.

[40] For instance, in 1606-7, when its omission incommoded Havana, and gave excuse for petitions to clear "loose vessels", i.e., which sailed independently of the fleets, with foodstuffs for that port.

period by Texeda's frigates[41] and later by the galleons of the guard, when they came by, escorting the Tierra Firme fleet, the Mexican fleet meanwhile proceeding on its way home alone: twenty, thirty or more merchantment convoyed by a *capitana* and an *almiranta* and each pretty well able to defend itself.

When the *armada de averia* to guard the Indian trade routes was established, at Seville's expense, in return for Seville's monopoly of Spain's colonial trade[42], it consisted of eight galleons and three shallops. In 1611 scarcity of money eliminated two galleons. To cover this weakness in numbers it was ordered in 1612 that the Mexican fleet should again await the galleons in Havana and cross with them, but, presently, the risk of danger from enemies seeming less expensive than the certain delay to the merchant fleet, it again became usual for the vessels from Mexico to come on without waiting for the galleons, for which, however, they left their more valuable cargo in Havana.

These galleons of the guard, which loaded Peruvian silver and gold at the Isthmus, and at Havana picked up still more gold and silver from Mexico and Honduras, had succeeded Texeda's frigates to the romantic title of "plate fleet". Though they continued to convoy merchantmen to and from the mainland, it was a matter of discussion whether they should be so handicapped or not, in their chief duty, which was to fetch themselves with the plate safe home. The king in Spain was always well pleased to learn that his Mexican merchant fleet had cleared, or arrived, safely; but it was for the armada of these galleons of the guard, and for the cargo they carried, that he appropriated six or eight hundred ducats a year, or more, to buy candles and prayers. "God bring them safe home", was his annual petition. When the Almighty was pleased to permit storm or enemies to

[41] The author has dealt with the interesting matter of these admirable frigates in a paper which was presented before the Congress of the Spanish Society for the Progress of Sciences at Seville in 1917, and printed in *La Reforma Social* (New York).

[42] The author has shown the effect of this monopoly on Cuba in a paper entitled *Rescates* which was presented before the Congress for the Progress of Science at Bilbao in 1919, and published in THE HISPANIC AMERICAN HISTORICAL REVIEW (Washington), August, 1920.

interfere with the granting of this prayer, his most Catholic majesty was divided between surprise and resentment; when his desires were granted he accepted that indication of divine favor with relief and complacency.⁴³ To capture this armada was supposed to be the grand desideratum of the Dutch.

Early in 1625, because of rumor that this enemy purposed attacking the Mexican fleet in the vincinity of La Tortuga, the governor at Havana was ordered⁴⁴ to patrol the sea from San Anton to Tortuga, and to advise that fleet, and the armada, if hostile sails were seen. No plate was sent from Peru that year, for the viceroy there believed that the enemy was out in force upon the Pacific. Havana rejoiced when the Honduras galleons came in, safe.⁴⁵

On November 7, 1625, the acting governors⁴⁶ of Havana first heard that the Dutch had landed on Porto Rico (September 25) and were besieging Governor Juan de Haro in his castle there. The West India Company achieved a great success in the conquest of Bahia, or San Salvador, in Brazil, seat of the Portuguese

⁴³ On September 5, 1622, the armada and the mainland fleet it convoyed, twenty-seven or twenty-eight sail, under the Marqués de Cadereyta, were struck by a hurricane one day out from Havana. It is recorded that eight vessels, three of them treasure galleons, and five hundred persons, were lost. The *almiranta*, which was the galleon *Margarita*, was among these; she went down on Matacumbe keys off the Florida coast and her sunken hulk was for years thereafter a goal for pirates and for Spanish salvaging expeditions, seeking to recover the bullion and specie she took down. The Mexican fleet was also damaged by this storm. This bad luck was made the occasion, if it was not the cause, of a moratorium in Spain. In 1623 Oquendo's armada and the mainland merchantmen got into Havana on September 12, and after two attempts to leave which were defeated by bad weather, decided in early October to winter in that harbor. Eight frigates which came up from Honduras that year in company with the two regular galleons, arrived twelve days after the Mexican fleet had cleared, and were, therefore, held up with the mainland galleons for the winter. This armada left for Spain on April 9, 1624, and en route home two galleons were lost. On his arrival Oquendo and his subordinates were subjected to investigation because of this delay in Havana, and the loss of the two galleons in transit. All this occasioned hard times in Sevelle.

⁴⁴ A. de I., 147-5-18; 87-5-2, VII., p. 202 r., *cedula*, March 16, 1625.

⁴⁵ A. de I., 54-1-17, Dr. Velasquez de Contreras to the crown, Havana, July 30, 1625.

⁴⁶ Venegas had died. Aranda was *gobernador de la guerra;* Velasquez, *gobernador de la paz.* A. de I., 54-2-10, November 7, 1625.

government, where the vice-admiral, Pieter Pieterzoon Heyn, distinguished himself uncommonly[45]; but Bahia had been recovered in this year of 1625 by a Spanish-Portuguese armada, under don Fadrique de Toledo, and so ousted from there, the Dutch had descended upon Porto Rico. On November 16 two vessels with men, munitions and supplies left Havana[47] to relieve Haro. Havana at once appealed to Mexico for more powder and biscuit.[48]

On November 16—the very day Havana's reinforcements were despatched—the enemy left Porto Rico. It was understood[49] that his plan was to careen his ships, come on to Cuba, and attack the fleet off Cuban coasts. Up to late March, 1626,[50] Havana had no news of him; in April it was said[51] that he had sacked La Margarita. In May or very early June, fourteen or more sail were reported[52] from Saint Philip's keys, near the Isle of Pines. There the Dutch captured a frigate whose escaping crew they insulted with a Spanish epithet ("*Bellacos españoles!*") called after them, with a foreign accent. This enemy squadron sailed under a tricolor flag, striped red, white, and blue. On June 14 the Dutch were at Cabañas.

A slave named Matheo Congo brought the news to Havana, telling how, at eight o'clock on the morning of that day, enemy frigates and launches had entered that harbor[53]. Spaniards and negroes who were building a ship there for Juan Perez Oporto, and the owners and workmen of nearby cattle ranches, all fled toward the town. The Dutch burned the unfinished vessel and killed hogs and hens. They then sailed on, and lay to off Havana, a menacing aggregation of about twenty-three sail.

[47] Blok, *ut supra*, IV., p. 36. A. de I., 54-2-10, Cristobal de Aranda to the crown, Havana, January 5, 1626, 54-1-17, *id.* to *id.*, January 28, 1626.

[48] A. de I., 54-1-17, Dr. Velasquez to the crown, February 28, 1626. Florida later complained that the "relief" Havana furnished Porto Rico was afforded at her expense, in that the things sent had been intended for that northern colony. Mexico responded properly (as usual).

[49] A. de I., 54-1-17, Cristobal de Aranda to the crown, March 28, 1626; 54-2-10. Dr. Velasquez to the crown, March 30, 1626.

[50] A. de I., 54-1-17, Cristobal de Aranda to the crown, March 28, 1626.

[51] A. de I., 147-5-19, Cristobal de Aranda to the crown, April 3, 1626.

[52] A. de I., 54-1-17, an *informacion*.

[53] *Ibid.*

Here their commander died, on July 2.[44] His admiral, a Fleming, succeeded. But the crews and soldiers of the squadron were already in a stage of dissatisfaction bordering upon mutiny even before their superior officer's death; though arms, munitions, and artillery were still plentiful aboardship, food was scarce and the time for which the men had signed on, was up. They had been held in check only by prospect of capturing the Mexican fleet: their commander had been determined not to return with as little as had been accomplished prior to his arrival off Havana—for Porto Rico and La Margarita taken, Cumana, Araya, Jamaica, Caracas, and Grand Cayman visited, had yielded no considerable profit, nor had the six frigates captured off Cuba.

The Flemish general who succeeded to command studied Havana through his glasses, and showed a Spanish prisoner his maps of that place, and others, upon which the very streets were named. He admitted that it looked strong ("*mucho fuerte*") as against attack from sea; but he quarreled with the Spaniard for denying that he could take it by land. He did not, however, attempt the feat at this juncture. Instead, he moved on, to Matanzas.

On receipt of news that the enemy had appeared at Cabañas, the *alcaide* of Morro castle (Aranda), started soldiers in that direction, under Lucas Maldonado; hearing that the Dutch had not remained in that western port, Maldonado and thirty men hurried to Matanzas, to defend that watering place. In a skirmish with the enemy the Spaniards captured a few prisoners, and may have prevented the Dutch from taking on water enough.

On July 11, 1626, the enemy set ashore fifty-two prisoners, whom they evidently did not desire to carry across the Atlantic and burned certain vessels they had, which presumably they did not consider fit for the crossing. They thereupon took their departure. Even from their own point of view, they had accom-

---

[44] The Spanish versions of his name, in the documents at Seville, are "Bodoyn", "Boydoyno Enrico", "Vaude Vin Enrique", "Pedro Petre Enriques". He died of a fever which followed a cold caught in the rain at Cabañas, where he was first ashore.

plished nothing. Prisoners said that they had lost heavily—perhaps fifty per cent of their men—and they were sailing home poor, and on short rations of bread and soup. But they had harassed Havana by a "siege" of thirty-two days.[55]

Within a month after the Dutch had gone, the treasure galleons of the guard came into Havana with the Tierra Firme fleet. It would seem that the enemy had purposely avoided any encounter with these warships. Indeed, neither the Dutch the English, nor the French had any real desire to meet any Spanish armada. Their avoidance of any such engagement was attributed to cowardice; whereas, in fact, it was based on good business sense. Profit, not glory, was what the Dutch sought in Indies. It is the object of most offensive warfare, such as they were waging against the Spaniards in the New World. The galleons of the guard were too expensive to attack, unless scattered or in distress. The fleets, especially the comparatively unprotected Mexican fleet, were a different matter.[56]

In the spring of 1627, at the entrance to the channel, General Thomas Larraspuru sighted thirteen Dutch sail, which fled from his Armada; only by what the Spaniards considered a Godsent miscalculation did they fail to fall upon either or both of the two Mexican fleets, one sailing for Vera Cruz and the other leaving that port, at about this time.[57] The governor at Havana[58] feared lest the Dutch squadron which had shown Larraspuru its heels wait in some capacious comfortable port until he should depart, to commence, in the summer "some undertaking with which to offset the many misfortunes which had befallen the enemy and the thin picking he had found".[59]

Instead, in July, 1627, the divine protection, to which the escape of the Mexican fleets was ascribed, being for the moment

[55] The source for this account of the matter is the *informacion* cited, A. de I., 54-1-17. *See also* 54-1-17, Aranda to the crown, Sept. 6, 1626.
[56] It is to be observed that Spanish galleons when engaged in transporting treasure, or convoying fleets, had just as little appetite for fight. Not cowardice, but policy, was at the bottom of the conduct of both parties.
[57] A. de I., 54-1-17, Cabrera to the crown, April 19, 1627.
[58] The governor was now don Lorenzo de Cabrera y Corbera.
[59] A. de I., 54-1-17, Cabrera to the crown, April 19, 1627.

somewhat withdrawn, the Dutch attacked the two galleons which were, as usual, escorting a few merchantmen up from Honduras. This little fleet had long feared some such catastrophe. In response for an appeal for help to strengthen it, the governor at Havana had just reinforced it with a hundred musketeers from the garrison there, with munitions and ten pieces of ordnance (one piece bearing the august name of Charles V.) despite all which the Dutch on July 8, 1627, took the *almiranta* and the treasure it carried. It cost a fight, which occurred off Coximar. The Spaniards came near to losing the *capitana* as well: certainly that galleon too was hard-pressed and went aground.[60]

Now, the year 1627 had been profitable for the Dutch: fifty-five vessels, large and small, had been captured, "and in the next year three great squadrons steered for the west."[61]

Havana was warned[62] that the enemy had designs, perhaps on Pernambuco, perhaps on Bahia, but, failing these objects, might attack Santo Domingo or Porto Rico. In August of 1628[63] a Dutch fleet, of twenty-three ships, was off the Havana coast.

[60] A. de I., 54-2-11; 141-1-12; 147-5-19; 54-2-10, Aranda to the crown, August 12, 1627. Picturesque details of this fight have been preserved. Governor Cabrera had sent infantry overland to relief of the Honduras ships. One of these infantrymen, named Francisco Isidro, saved the *capitana's* flag: he stabbed a Dutchman, who had just killed the Spanish color-bearer, wrapped the flag about his body, leaped overboard and swam ashore. Alvaro de la Cerda, *cabo* (in command) of the Honduras vessels, must have deserted his post, for Isidro pushed him to land on a piece of wreckage. He afterwards swam back to the *capitana* and brought ashore three sailor friends of his who could not swim. Governor Cabrera, who, with other officials and soldiers, watched the struggle from the land, praised Isidro for his bravery, and he was given the flag he had saved as a trophy. The Dutch did not succeed in capturing the *capitana*; on July 12, battered and blood-stained, it limped into port. The enemy were six days off Coximar. The authorities in Havana quarreled hotly over the question whether or not to despatch a punitive expedition against them. The noes had it.

[61] Blok, *ut supra*, IV., p. 36.

[62] A. de I., 141-1-12, council to the crown, January 9, 1628; 54-1-17, Fonseca Betancur to Cabrera, Puerto Principe, January 26, 1628; 78-2-3, VIII., p. 121 r. *cedula*, June 20, 1628.

[63] A. de I., 147-5-19.

It was commanded by Piet Heyn himself. Many of the fifteen warnings sent from Havana to the fleet, then due from Mexico, must have been intercepted by the enemy, since none of them reached their destination, and, therefore, in the dawn of September 8 this fleet sailed tranquilly into the midst of the enemy squadron, as it lay off Matanzas.[64]

The Dutch easily took nine vessels. The *capitana* and the *almiranta* made the shelter of Matanzas bay that night, followed by two fat merchantmen, preparing, they later said, to fight. When Benavides, commanding this Mexican fleet, presently took evidence to defend his judgment in so entering Matanzas harbor, one witness declared that Spanish prisoners watching events from aboard the enemy flagship, felt that his course was inspired by the Holy Ghost! Nevertheless, some of these fleeing vessels went on the shoals in that harbor and their passengers being ordered ashore, obeyed with alacrity. The intention was to burn the ships and what part of their cargo could not be landed, but, in the clear light of an unkind moon, the enemy followed fast into the bay, firing as he came. The Dutch swarmed aboard the Spanish ships from small boats. Their appearance seems to have created a panic, for certainly the Spaniards hastily deserted the king's treasure[65] and all the merchandise—departing in great disorder—and Piet Heyn found himself in possession of the four best vessels (and two shallops) which had constituted the strength and the wealth of the Mexican fleet. The thousand ducats which the king of Spain next month ordered[66] spent in masses and charity, for the safety of the fleets and armadas, were spent in vain.

In capturing that fleet Piet Heyn had done what no seaman before him—not the boldest of them—had ever succeeded in doing.

Fabulous indeed were the captured treasures of silver, gold, pearls, indigo, sugar, Campeachy wood, and costly furs, which sold in the

[64] A. de I., 147-5-19; 54-1-17.
[65] The fleet had not yet reached Havana, to discharge any cargo.
[66] A. de I., 141-1-12, council to crown, October 25, 1528.

Netherlands for no less than fifteen million guilders. The rejoicing over the news (there) was boundless, and Heyn himself showed some vexation at the excessive praises bestowed upon him for this easy victory, after his previous and more important exploits had been greeted with much less enthusiasm.[67]

The capture of the Mexican fleet is, indeed, what keeps his name alive to posterity.[68]

On September 18 or 19, Heyn disembogued.[69] Nothing in all its history had so angered Cuba as his capture of the Mexican fleet. "Who," later cried[70] one especially wrathful gentleman named Pedro Gutierrez Ortiz, voicing as great and lasting indignation in Spain,

who can hear of this and not seize high heaven itself in angry hands? Who, at the risk of a thousand lives, if he had them, would not avenge so grievous an affront? . . The Hollander has so degraded us that commonly, in adjacent kingdoms, where formerly they called the Spaniards unchained lions, they now call us embroidered Marias with braided hair and padded legs!

[67] Blok, ut supra, IV., p. 37.

[68] The school children of Holland, to a gay melody, still sing: "Piet Hein's name his small, but his deeds are great—he has captured the silver-fleet!" No song records his capture of Bahia, although on his statue in Delft harbor it is written: "Gold before silver but honor before all", which was his motto. Two despatch boats conveyed to Holland news of his adventures at Matanzas and even before he arrived home the story of his great haul was in circulation in print and picture. While the writer was engaged upon this paper there was at Seville, occupied in investigation among papers referring to the Dutch, F. E. Baron Mulert, a special admirer of Piet Hein, who possesses an engraving of the time, depicting the capture of the Mexican ships in Matanzas bay. It is stated on the picture that the Dutch got thirty-six tons of silver.

[69] A. de I., 54-1-17, an incomplete letter from Cabrera to the crown, Havana, September 30, 1628.

[70] A. de I., 141-1-7, Pedro Gutierrez Ortiz to the crown, June 23, 1637. To enable Spaniards to recover lost repute, Pedro Gutierrez advocated an armada— an immense armada. He advised that all enemies captured be executed forthwith, in order "so to terrorize the world that, where it once stood, the name of Spain may stand again!"

II

INCIDENTAL EFFECTS OF DUTCH COLONIZATION IN BRAZIL

(To 1640)

As a matter of fact, Piet Heyn's capture of the Mexican fleet was a happy accident. Fortune never again so beamed upon Dutch adventures against Spanish West Indian traffic. Since success prefers to crown determined efforts specially directed to single definite objectives, it may be that the enemy's failure to repeat Piet Heyn's exploit was due to the fact that Dutch attacks on Spanish commerce became merely incidental, minor features of larger affairs in South America, on which the ambition of the Netherlands settled. Dutch squadrons which troubled Cuba in the decade ending with 1640, cleared from home for Brazil, for possession of which the Dutch were contending with the Portuguese; having done their business there, they returned via the Caribbean, in hopes to happen by the way upon Spanish ships under circumstances which would enable them to make the expenses of their expeditions, which were primarily directed, however, to Brazil. When, as part of the truce entered into between the Netherlands and Portugal in 1641, hostilities abated in Brazil, and such expeditions were no longer necessary there, it was not found good business to despatch them especially against Spanish traffic in the Caribbean, particularly since peace with Spain again appeared possible and desirable upon the horizon of the United Netherlands. The period of Dutch influence upon Cuba's affairs dwindled away, but not before fear of the Dutch had erected fortifications at Havana,[71] just as, previously, fear of the French and fear of the English had done.

Their adventures in Indies, around about 1628, heartened the Dutch, and, in corresponding degree, disheartened the Spanish, who found themselves paralyzed by lack of money. Try as he

[71] And at Santiago de Cuba. The effect of Cornelis Cornelissoon Jol's visitation to Santiago on March 15, 1635, has been indicated in the author's *Santiago de Cuba and its District* (Madrid, 1918), and the matter is therefore omitted from this paper.

would, his most Catholic majesty simply could not "raise the wind", which Piet Heyn had taken out of his sails at Matanzas!

The governor at Havana was demanding reinforcement "for the love of God": he wanted two hundred men, and firearms, powder, fuse and lead in proportion.[72] He declared that more than seventy of his garrison of four hundred were useless. Remarking that as long as the Dutch found war profitable to them and costly to Spain, the king must reckon the Indies as his frontier, don Antonio Oquendo estimated Havana's effective force at about two hundred and fifty men, whereas it should be a thousand, and recommended the despatch thither of two or three hundred infantry, well equipped.[73] Governor Cabrera asked an appropriation for the pay of additional men, and urged that Havana's *situado* for that year, which the Dutch had taken with the Mexican fleet that conveyed it, be made good from crown revenues passing in the armada, "for otherwise it will not be possible to maintain the garrison".[74] His letter found the authorities in Spain in receipt of news from the north which inclined them to believe the governor's apprehensions justified.

The king was informed that the West India Company's projects were four in number, three of them concerning ports wherein the Spanish were established, and the fourth contemplating the seizure of some comparatively unoccupied place, perhaps Jamaica.[75] Certainly it was their intention to obtain a permanent foothold in the Caribbean from which to make continuous warfare upon Spain's colonial traffic.[76] The company was said to be equipping great armadas, one of which, described as the finest that had been raised in the United Provinces, was to attack the treasure galleons as they left Havana. That port itself[77] was to be taken—its castles were to

---

[72] A. de I., 54-1-17, Cabrera to the crown, Sept. 30, 1628.

[73] A. de I., 147-5-8, Oquendo to the crown, Lisbon, Oct. 11, 1630.

[74] A. de I., 147-5-19, *Junta de guerra* to the crown, January, 1629; 78-2-3, VIII., pp. 133, 134 r., *cedulas*, January 22, 1629.

[75] A. de I., 147-5-8, *Junta de guerra* to the crown, December 26, 1629. Such were the company's plans, according to the Infanta Isabel's informant.

[76] A. de I., 147-5-8, March 20, 1629: according to warnings received from Cardinal de Cueva.

[77] A. de I., 147-5-8, the king to the grand chancellor for Indies, March 31, 1629.

be "besieged by hunger"—or now the Dutch would indeed occupy the harbor of Matanzas. Dutch ships were said to be clearing from their ports one by one as though to meet at a rendezvous: Tenerife counted more than fifty sail as they went by.[78] And the French, encouraged by all this, were reported to be arming eight ships for Indies![79]

The council for war in Indies would have sent don Antonio Oquendo out with an armada.[80] The council for Indies approved of the idea but declared that it must not be looked to for the money: it was bankrupt. It was the king who cried his council courage: "Now is no time to yield", he wrote late in 1630. "If the Indies are well cared for this coming year, it will compensate for all the damage done and bring our enemies to sue for peace."[81]

On January 11, 1629, Cabrera was ordered[82] to lay in supplies of food and water, to call on Mexico for provisions if necessary, and, because it was understood that the Dutch might attack from the Chorrera, to permit no timber whatsoever to be cut in that vicinity. The council for war recommended[83] that General Larraspuru be instructed to leave in Havana, from crown revenues aboard the galleons, the equivalent of the lost *situado*, and the crown so decreed. The council further recommended that men, and the arms and munitions which the governor wanted, be sent to him at once. The crown, agreeing, ordered[84] the Marques de Leganes, captain general of artillery, to furnish two hundred muskets, two hundred arquebuses, two hundred hundred-weight of powder and one of fuse, for Havana. The Duke de Medina Sidonia was ordered to recruit two hundred men.

It was here (1629) that difficulties of a financial order arose, irritatingly. It was usual to bring over a good sum of money

[78] A. de I., 147-5-8, *id.* to *id.*, May 9, 1629.
[79] A. de I., 147-5-8, royal order, June 10, 1630; February 7, 1631.
[80] A. de I., 147-5-8, April 24, 1630.
[81] A. de I., 141-1-13, November 30, 1630.
[82] A. de I., 78-2-3, VIII., p. 132 r., *cedula*, January 11, 1629.
[83] A. de I., 147-5-19, *Junta de guerra* to the crown, January 12, 1629.
[84] *Ibid* and A. de I., 147-5-19, *Junta de guerra* to the crown, January 26, 1629.

annually from Mexico to pay for arms and munitions for Indies: Piet Heyn had carried that year's money off to Holland with other spoils of the Mexican fleet. Therefore the captain general of artillery asked[85] the council for war to furnish seven thousand two hundred ducats to cover the cost of the muskets, arquebuses, powder, and lead for Havana. The council recommended[86] that the shipment be sent forward on credit, since the need was imperative and delay dangerous. The captain general of artillery, who had not a musket on hand to deliver, insisted[87] that since he had to deal with northern factories who transacted business on spot cash basis, he must have cash, or nothing could be done. In March, 1629, the council threw up its hands.[88] Governor Cabrera, who, in January, had been assured[89] that the armada was bringing him arms and munitions, was told in April[90] to send eight thousand six hundred ducats in "double silver" to pay for these means for Havana's defense—otherwise, they could not be provided.

The House of Trade, which was making ready a vessel to convey these supplies, and soldiers, to Havana, sent in an itemized bill showing nineteen thousand seven hundred and eighty seven ducats needed for the purpose.[91]

And the Duke de Medina Sidonia met with mutiny and desertion when he attempted to raise men for Cuba: they did not believe that they were being recruited for Indies.[92]

The council for war in Indies urged[93] that the duke be advised that the two hundred men must be found—perhaps among those recruited for service aboard galleons of the guard, and that the House find money to clear the ship for Cuba regardless of previous warrants against artillery funds, because

[85] A. de I., 147-5-19, *Junta de guerra* to the crown, January 26, 1629.
[86] *Ibid.*
[87] A. de I., 147-5-19, *Junta de guerra* to the crown, March 5, 1629.
[88] *Ibid.*
[89] A. de I., 54-1-35, Castañeda and Armeñiteros to the crown, Oct. 7, 1629.
[90] A. de I., 78-2-3, VIII., pp. 137 r., 144, *cedulas*, April 27, 1629.
[91] A. de I., 147-5-19, *Junta de guerra* to the crown, April 26, 1629.
[92] *Ibid.*
[93] *Ibid.*

according to advices concerning the enemies' designs on the Indies, confirmed every day from various quarters, the relief of Havana is to-day one of your majesty's most imperative obligations, inasmuch as in holding this place we may remedy other damage if, because of our sins, God permit it to occur—damage which without Havana would be almost beyond your majesty's power to repair; and although Havana is strong and well defended even by its very situation, precisely for that reason if the enemy attempts to invade, it will be with great force by land and by sea, and cutting off all means of relief,

wherefore the council urged the king to take every possible measure to prevent a loss which would be so very difficult to retrieve.

Despite all this alarm, lack of funds continued to check action. The special vessel direct to Cuba could not be cleared, nor the two hundred men recruited. What arms and munitions were sent went with an armada under don Fadrique de Toledo. Since January (1629) the crown had been trying to get this armada off—"to punish the enemy and protect the mainland galleons and the Mexican fleets"—and it cleared, finally, in the following summer.[94]

As stated, Cabrera had been warned in January; at the end of May still another despatch was sent to him,[95] advising that late news from Flanders confirmed previous reports: that the Dutch meant to besiege Havana, that vessels enough to constitute a powerful armada were slipping out of enemy harbors one by one, wherefore he would do well to prepare for attack from Matanzas, or from the Chorrera where, the king understood, the way had been opened by the clearing of the land for sugarcane fields.

Meanwhile, from June until mid-September of that year of 1629, enemy vessels patroled the Cuban north coast; the port of Havana was as good as closed. On August 22 "Perin Pettre" (Pater) stood off the city, with an armada said to consist of thirty sail, though only fourteen were seen.[96]

[94] A. de I., 141-1-12.
[95] A. de I., 78-2-3, VIII., p. 149, cedula, May 28, 1629.
[96] A. de I., 54-1-35, Castañeda and Armenteros to the crown, October 7, 1629; 54-2-11, Matheo Varona to the crown, Havana, November 3, 1629; 54-1-17, Fonseca Betancur, Bayamo, November 15, 1629.

Cabrera had summoned the militia from the interior: men arrived the first week in June. On one occasion a hundred were rushed in great haste to the Chorrera; they arrived there hot, a giant of a sergeant among them waded into the sea to cool off, and died very soon after the bath, but there were no further casualities.[97]

It was at this time that Cabrera threw up a trench from Punta to the old gun foundry (the *Maestranza*) despite objections, voiced by Pedro de Armenteros y Guzman, for instance, who thought that no enemy would attempt to land there, under the batteries of three forts, and that to man this trench left the inlet, Punta Brava and the Chorrera weakened. The work was done, however, and a redoubt built in which ordnance was placed. It was paid for out of the tax levied to raise funds for the *armada de barlovento*. To erect certain houses considered necessary, the citizens contributed.[98]

Meanwhile, the Mexican fleet for 1629 and the ships from Honduras came safe into Havana, and decided to lie there. That they were safe was glad news to Seville. The king ordered thanks given to "Our Lord for extending favor to us, and also for protecting us from harm".[99] Don Fadrique de Toledo with his armada and the mainland fleet arrived in Havana on March 15, 1630. He had encountered only rumors of enemies about: after he had left that vicinity he heard that they had burned Santa Marta. He sent three galleons and a shallop out to strengthen still another Mexican fleet which he expected to find in Havana, waiting for him. It came in on April 3 and Don Fadrique presently got off to Spain with a very large and correspondingly valuable lot of shipping in his convoy.[100] Cabrera expressed[101] "a million thanks" for the arms and munitions

[97] A. de I., 54-1-35, Castañeda and Armenteros to the crown, October 7, 1629; 54-1-35, Pedro de Armenteros y Guzman to the crown, Oct. 7, 1629; and documents in 54-2-11.

[98] A. de I., 54-1-35, Pedro de Armenteros y Guzman to the crown, Oct. 7, 1629.

[99] A. de I., 147-5-19, council to crown, Dec. 3, 1629; 141-1-12, January 24, 1630, council to crown; 139-6-23, III., p. 112, *cedula*, February 3, 1630.

[100] A. de I., 141-1-12, don Fadrique de Toledo to the crown, Havana, April 3, 1630.

[101] A. de I., 54-1-17, Cabrera to the crown, Havana, April 26, 1630.

Don Fadrique had brought him: he hoped to persuade him to leave also some men and artillery. The governor believed that now he could put Havana into shape to defend itself, "with the help of God".

Apparently considerable such assistance was going to be necessary, for the Dutch had not departed from the neighborhood. In mid-May of 1630, when Don Fadrique and his fighting ships must have been still in Havana harbor, a despatch boat from Mexico was intercepted by enemies so close to Havana that what papers it carried were brought overland from Cabañas. Its news was that an enemy squadron of eighty sail was to be expected.[102] In the following August General Larraspuru[103] at Cartagena with the treasure galleons of that year, heard that these eighty sail were lying in wait for him: twenty-two were said to be off Havana then. He commended his voyage to "the Blessed Souls", and in the king's name promised them a thousand ducats for safety. He had 6,887,800 *pesos* worth of cargo in his keeping, of which 5,851,850 were specie and bullion.[104] If the enemy continued to hang off Cuba he purposed abandoning the regular route home, avoiding San Anton by sailing east between Cuba and La Española, and although it would appear that the at least two dozen enemy sail which had been off Havana, disembogued in September of 1630, Larraspuru appears to have considered it safer so to alter his course.[105] His doing so, and the failure of the Mexican fleet to pass through on schedule, left Havana without the usual means of exporting its products that year.

On March 10, 1631, the governor[106] at Havana was informed[107] that eight enemy hulks had been seen off Cape Corrientes. He sent forth warnings, and urged Mexico to hurry along the six hundred hundred-weight of biscuit he had already sent for,

---

[102] A. de I., 147-5-20.
[103] A. de I., 141-1-12, Thomas Larraspuru to the crown, Cartagena, August, 1630.
[104] Cheap insurance, as rates have been running.
[105] A. de I., 54-1-17, Bitrian to the crown, January 21, 1631.
[106] The governor was now Admiral Don Juan Bitrian de Biamonte y Navarra.
[107] A. de I., 54-1-17, Bitrian to the crown, June 29, 1631.

as the crown had bidden him do, if he fell short, and, for good measure, he now asked for an additional thousand hundred-weight. On April 17 (it was Holy Thursday) the eight vessels of which he had heard appeared off Havana. They hung about for a month, and then shifted to Matanzas. The governor sent a hundred soldiers to that port under Captain Don Gonzalo Chacon de Narvaez. The enemy set thirty-seven prisoners ashore and departed. These persons said that the enemy squadron was twenty-six sail, though Havana had seen only eight, carrying eight hundred men of whose courage the Spaniards who had been among them thought very little indeed. They had plenty of ammunition but were short of food. On May 20, they reappeared off Havana and lingered until June 4. Depite their presence, twenty-six ships made the port safely, including those bringing one thousand six hundred hundred-weight of biscuit from Mexico. Nevertheless, the governor felt real alarm when still other Spaniards who had been prisoners of the enemy arrived at the end of that month, to repeat assurance that eighty enemy sail were to be expected![108]

Happily for his peace of mind, General Thomas Larraspuru with an armada came into port on August 24, 1631. He had not seen or heard of any but insignificant enemies. Having taken on water this armada went out again, to San Anton, to await the Mexican fleet, which had orders not to leave Vera Cruz until advised that the enemy had disembogued and a Spanish squadron stood ready to meet it at San Anton. Larraspuru was obliged to return to port to pass the equinox but again fared forth on October 2. The Mexican fleet did not come up until early December, and a storm knocked it to pieces. The Tierra Firme fleet arrived on December 12, and on February 24, 1632, Larraspuru left for Spain convoying fifty-eight sail (ten of which were to drop away to Indies ports on emerging from the channel). He was escorting over 8,211,683 *pesos* in cargo, of which 1,395,303 were the king's, in bullion and coin.[109]

[108] A. de I., 54-1-17, Bitrian to the crown, June 30, 1631.
[109] A. de I., 141-1-13, August-December, 1631.

An armada under the Marques de Cadereyta made Havana on September 30, 1633. He had just cleaned the enemy out of San Martin. Vessels of a small squadron coming to reinforce him met Dutchmen off San Anton in Augest, and Miguel Redin, admiral commanding them died in the fight (or soon after, of wounds) "in a manner becoming a gentlemen and his blood". This squadron, minus the admiral's ship, made Havana between September 7 and 9. It was reported that the enemy had sackek Campeche, and perhaps Truxillo. Governor Bitrian plumed himself that they kept away from Cuba because it was known that he was ready to receive them there becomingly.[110]

Early in 1638 the council for Indies was informed that "Peg-Leg the Pirate" had cleared for the West Indies—he was "Corniel Cornieles de Jol", according to the Spaniards' reading of his signature (Cornelis Corneliszoon Jol). Don Carlos de Ybarra was warned[111] that he had left for Indies with ten ships, to join fourteen others pirating there; it was understood that Peg-Leg's intention was to convey certain relief to Pernambuco, where the Dutch were in sharp contest with the Portuguese for possession of Brazil, and then to come up to the Caribbean to encounter Ybarra's armada. The Spaniard was ordered to avoid the encounter, if possible; but if this were not possible, then to "punish" Jol. Timely receipt of a warning held the Mexican fleet at Vera Cruz, with 2,519,401 pesos aboard, of which 1,822,772 were the crown's, but the armada—the priceless galleons—in August, off the west end of Cuba, fell in with Peg-Leg who was lying in wait, for them or for the fleet, with eleven ships of his own, reinforced by half a dozen hangers-on—little birds of prey who scented possibilities of spoil. The armada, in obedience to Ybarra's orders, beat hasty retreat toward Mexico. The galleon *Carmen*, commanded by Sanchez de Urdanivia, fought a rear-guard action which, described by Urdanivia himself, stands forth among the more prosaic documents of the Archives of the Indies like a highly colored painting of a vigorous sea

[110] A. de I., 54-1-17, Bitrian to the crown, October 13, 1633; 147-5-20.
[111] A. de I., 141-4-8.

fight, touched by a ray of sunlight falling into a darkened picture gallery![112]

The enemy's *capitana* bore down upon Ybarra's, while the enemy's *almiranta* picked up the Spanish *almiranta* as her antagonist, and they interchanged broadsides and sweeping musketry fire. In advancing to this attack, the enemy *almiranta* passed close enough to the *Carmen* to enable Urdanivia to "offend" it with all his artillery and musketry. The enemy answered in kind. The *Carmen* then swung in, and prevented three supporting vessels which followed from joining in the attack upon the Spanish *almiranta*. Two hours Urdanivia fought these three vessels, at close quarters—so close that his rigging became entangled with theirs.

The enemy now withdrew but only to choose an admiral to replace one they had lost in the combat (so prisoners taken said later), and to replace certain captains whose valor was not equal to the test of existing circumstances. The Dutch were lost to view for two days, but on the third resumed the attack with thirteen ships.

The enemy *capitana* renewed its duel with the Spanish, but soon dropped away, bested in the encounter. The *Regla*, the *Sanctiago* and the *Carmen* were the rear of the Spanish squadron and on them now fell the brunt of the Dutchmen's determination to get some profit out of this meeting, so that presently, according to its commander, the *Carmen* found itself engaging twelve enemy ships, alone, unaided by any other Spanish vessel, despite the fact that it was broad daylight and the roar of its guns and the rattle of its musketry were waking the echoes through the Organo mountains on the shore. Only when the *Carmen*, with masts broken and rigging down, seemed about to yield to the force of superior numbers, did the rest of the armada turn back, with evident intention to bring relief. Thereupon the Dutch withdrew.

[112] A. de I., 147-5-22; 141-1-16, two letters written by Sancho de Urdanivia, November 15 and 16, 1638, and the council's communication, dated January 14, 1639, referring these letters to the crown.

Inspection showed the *Carmen* to be beyond hope of saving. What plate it carried was transferred to another vessel, and with twenty dead and twenty-eight wounded aboard, it limped into Bahia Honda bay (three leagues away), where its artillery, munitions, copper and indigo were landed, and the wreck that was left of the ship itself, burned.

Its commander was blamed for the concentrated attack upon the *Carmen*. He resented this criticism bitterly; he said that he was the rear guard—a rear guard was necessary, given the plan of battle determined upon previous to the event—and no galleon disputed the place with his vessel nor sought to share its dangers. If to break out standards and pennants without orders to do so were an error, it was news to him that a commander needed specific instructions to permit him to make his ship "as ferocious and bizarre as his equipment allowed".

And if, as my general seems to think, the adornments of war and a disposition to fight were an invitation to the enemy to seek me out and attack me with especial earnestness—if in so dressing my galleon I erred against your majesty's best interests, a greater display and a greater fault would it have been to garland it with hencoops and litter its bridge and decks with corrals for live stock, as does sometimes happen upon this Indian route!

Ask Holland, he exclaimed, how the armada conducted itself that day, and how the galleon with the standards spread, bore it itself among the rest! The enemy had eyed that beflagged galleon close and long enough to report upon it accurately!

Peg-Leg set his prisoners ashore at Bahia Honda and left for home. He, or his hangers-on, may have taken some of the smaller craft which were travelling in the armada's company, but he captured no galleons, nor any treasure of any account; and the fight had cost him dear. Nevertheless, he was back in two years, but fortune had indeed deserted the Dutch.

On September 4, 1640, thirty-six sails appeared off the Havana coast. The city had been warned and was in good shape to resist any attack, for the governor [113] had drilled the citizens, reinforced Coximar and the Chorrera, hurried provisions into Morro and anchored fire-boats at the entrance to the bay.[114]

On September 11 a violent storm scattered the enemy right and left.[115] The first news Havana had of this disaster arrived on the 14th to the effect that a hundred-ton shallop was ashore three leagues from town. It was not a valuable prize, for its cargo was pitch and thatch. Next day came news of a four hundred ton hulk ashore still farther west; its thirty-two guns (a dozen bronze) and a hundred prisoners, fell into the hands of the party which Governor de Luna sent out after them. Farther on was wrecked still another hulk, which to the Spaniards' spoils added nineteen guns (six bronze), but only twenty-two men of the hundred and thirty who had been abroad. The crew of still another, ashore at Herradura, was reported to be marching toward Havana, in a company numbering about a hundred and eleven men, a dozen or so having remained behind with what was left of their ship, said to have carried twenty-two guns (six bronze).

The governor sent out infantry to gather in these prisoners, and the artillery; and to burn the wrecks. The Spaniards regretted to have to burn the ship ashore at Herradura, for it was new and undamaged, but they were compelled to do so lest the enemy recover it, as they had already recovered two of its guns.

When the reckoning was taken, the Spaniards found themselves the richer by a windfall of seventy-two pieces of artillery a good proportion of which were bronze, to say nothing of cables, masts, sails, fifteen pounds of powder, a hundred muskets, and

[113] The governor was now Don Alvaro de Luna Sarmiento, who took possession of his office on September 15, 1639. He considered that the greatest menace to the colony's welfare was the enemy who infested the coasts: the lessee of the customs dues had collected only 5,000 *pesos* during immediately preceding years, whereas these collections had formerly been 18,000 per annum. Coastwise trade traveled in canoes, not even these vessels being safe. The pirates actually troubled business done ashore, for they had penetrated two and three leagues inland to plunder and burn.

[114] A. de I., 54-1-17, Luna Sarmiento to the crown, September 15, 1639.

[115] *Ibid.*, and 54-2-11, Riaño to the crown, September 17, 1639.

over two hundred prisoners, whom the governor purposed sending at once to Spain along with certain other objectionable foreigners whom he had rounded up from all over the island.

Peg-Leg, for it was indeed he, coming up from Brazil as Cuba had been warned that he would, on September 20 or 21 sent a small boat under a white flag toward the port of Havana, to which the Spaniards sent out another like it, which brought in a letter in which Peg-Leg proposed an exchange of prisoners. He admitted that Governor de Luna had a larger number of his men than he of Spaniards, but still he had forty or fifty on hand—Franciscan priests, soldiers, civilians—and could, moreover, catch as many more as he chose, along those coasts. He promised to extend to the Spanish prisoners the same treatment the Spaniards meted out to the Dutch.

Governor de Luna replied courteously, condoling with Jol on the catastrophe which had befallen him, saying that his sympathy had moved him to hasten food to the wrecks, and men to bring the prisoners into Havana where, he said, they were comfortable and well treated. The governor said that he knew what in humanity was due to an enemy who has surrendered, and therefore he expected similar good treatment to be extended to the Spaniards in Jol's hands. He said that he would like to make the exchange suggested, but lacking orders to that effect he must now send his prisoners to Spain. This quaint letter ends with expression of Governor de Luna's hope that Jol may meet the Spanish armada well supplied with everything necessary that its victory over him may be the more brilliant, and terminates with the stereotyped form of conclusion: "May God guard you as I desire"![116]

Peg-Leg moved on to Matanzas, where he did what damage he could. There he released certain of his prisoners (among them the Franciscan priests, from Florida). They reported that Jol's loss was six good men-o'-war and a shallop. Although he was said to have intended to go on to Santiago, where he was assured he could seize twenty thousand *arrobas* of sugar, Peg-

[116] A. de I., 54-1-17, Luna Sarmiento to the crown, September 17, 1639.

Leg disembogued with twenty-four sail on October 17th, 1640. and with him vanished all real danger to Cuba from the Dutch.

The governor sent Don Pedro Salgado de Barros to Spain with news of the destruction of Peg-leg's squadron on the Cuban coast. This messenger inadvertently put into a Portuguese port—and to his chagrin learned that the Duke of Braganza as John IV. was in revolt against the king of Spain. The curtain had gone up upon another phase of Cuba's checkered history.[117]

The period which had passed left permanent monuments behind, for Havana and her governor had had (1633) an active procurator at court, named Simon Fernandez Leyton,[118] who brought before the crown many matters in which Cuba was interested. As his principal mission he represented that it was necessary to open loopholes in Morro's landward walls, to repair the barracks, build drawbridges, etc., there; that it was necessary to repair La Fuerza; and that it was necessary to build a tower at the Chorrera and another at Coximar, each to accomodate four guns.[119] His representations, together with former Governor Cabrera's opinion thereon, were seen in the council for war in Indies, in February, 1633, and the council recommended[120] that the captain general of the next armada to sail that way be instructed to make an inspection along with the governor and royal officials of Havana, and report upon the work Havana wanted done. The council thought that pending the crown's action on this report what repairs those so inspecting considered "most necessary and inexcusable", might be made, Mexico to provide the money. The crown agreed to most of these recommendations, for under date of April 11, 1633, the Marqués

[117] A. de I., 147-5-23, January 25, 1641. Further references to the Dutch around about Cuba exist, for instance: A. de I., 55-1-38, 54-2-11, Riaño to the crown, September 17, 1639; 147-5-23, January 1641; 141-4-9, February 7 (?), 1641; 78-2-3, XI., pp. 65, 68; 141-1-18, September 7, 1641 (?), etc., etc.

[118] Fernandez Leyton was Portuguese by birth, a *vecino* of Havana, married to the daughter of a Spaniard; it had cost him 300 ducats "double silver" to get out naturalization papers which (November 2, 1627) entitled him to do business in Indies and in Spain.

[119] A. de I., 55-5-24, *memorial*, Captain Simon Fernandez Leyton, February 3, 1633.

[120] A. de I., 55-5-24, May 30, 1634, a *relacion*.

de Cadereyta and Don Carlos de Ybarra, admiral of the armada, were ordered to make the inspection, along with Bitrian, the treasurer and accountant of Cuba, "and other experienced and intelligent persons". The governor was instructed accordingly, under the same date.[121] He was told to "dispose the minds of the *vecinos* toward aiding with their slaves and materials", in any work it might be deemed necessary to do at once; if these local resources were not sufficient, the crown would order the balance supplied from Mexico.

On October 6, 1633, the inspection was made.[122] Governor Bitrian, the Marqués de Cadereyta, Don Carlos de Ybarra, Captain Damian de Vega, *alcayde* of Morro, Diego Diaz Pimienta accountant (the treasurer was too ill to be present), and various other persons, including three engineers (Joseph Ydalgo, Juan Bautista Vandazo, Don Francisco de Tessa), looked Morro over and listed desirable repairs and alterations, to an estimated cost of 52,000 ducats. They inspected Fuerza and found 1750 ducats worth of work to be done. They recommended the building of towers at the Chorrera and Coximar, 20,000 ducats. Total, 73,750 ducats. Their report was duly forwarded to court. Some details in connection with it, which it was considered not desirable to entrust to writing, were to be reported verbally by the procurator. On May 30, 1634, the council for war in Indies approved this report and the matter came before his majesty. On October 19, 1634, the crown ordered[123] the council's recommendations carried out. This order took the shape of a *cedula*[124] dated January 30, 1635, bidding the governor[125] do "what was urgent, and build the towers" (at the Chorrera and Coximar), which, if he considered them vitally necessary to Havana's safety, were to be erected simultaneously with other work. Mexico was ordered[126] to deliver twenty thousand ducats and to furnish ten thousand yearly, to the total of 73,750 ducats which it had been estimated were required.

[121] A. de I., 78-2-3, IX., pp. 39, 41 r.; 147-5-20, *cedula*, April 11, 1633.
[122] A. de I., 147-5-20; 55-5-24, Bitrian to the crown, October 12, 1633.
[123] A. de I., 147-5-20, *Junta de guerra* to the crown, October 19, 1634.
[124] A. de I., 78-2-3, IX., p. 121 r., *cedula*.
[125] The governor was now Don Francisco de Riaño y Gamboa.
[126] A. de I., 78-2-3, IX., p. 126 r.; 127 r.

The governor was to use the money carefully and do only necessary work.

When the Dutch and the rebel Portuguese entered into a truce, the governor[127] feared lest, united, they fall upon Havana. He felt a revived[128] interest in the towers planned for the Chorrera and Coximar.

He inspected both sites.[129] He found himself handicapped in executing the work, ordered in 1635, because Mexico had not sent the appropriation made for it. The governor despatched an emissary[130] to Mexico for this money, who returned without it, or the munitions for which, also, he had asked. The crown repeatedly ordered[131] the viceroy to remit.[132]

In view of his delay in complying with these orders, and alarmed by news from Brazil[133] the governor was constrained to

[127] The governor was Don Alvaro de Luna Sarmiento.

[128] A. de I., 54-1-17, November 6, 1640, Luna Sarmiento to the crown.

[129] Riaño had reported on May 25, 1635, that, recognizing the necessity of placing the Chorrera in a position not only to defend itself, but also to offend any enemy fleet seeking to anchor there, he and General Antonio de Oquendo, accompanied by veteran soldiers and engineers, made various inspections of the vicinity, and of Coximar, and drew up plans, which Captain Juan Alferes presented at court. These resuscitated interest in the projected work, but it was the fear which Luna Sarmiento expressed, lest the Dutch and Portuguese together attack, which finally built the forts—after all danger from the enemy (the Dutch) to whom they are a monument, had disappeared. *"El socorro del español . . ."*

[130] A. de I., 54-1-17, Luna Sarmiento to the crown, September 15, 1639, and November 6, 1640; 54-1-18, *id.* to *id.*, December 28, 1641. Juan de Esquivel was the emissary.

[131] A. de I., 78-2-3, XI., pp. 62½, 69 r., 81 r., 82 r., *cedulas*, December 25, 1640, August 28, 1641, June 20, 1642.

[132] Irregularities in the Mexican fleet service, the wintering of the fleets and armada in Vera Cruz in 1639 and their failure to call at Havana in passing, had created a serious situation for Cuba. Don Alvaro found the king's strongboxes about empty. The crown reminded armada generals of previous orders to leave from whatever treasure they had aboard whatever accounts showed to be due Cuba when they called. From Don Geronimo de Sandoval, presumably in 1639, the governor got 50,000 ducats on account, and in 1641 Dias Pimienta left 105,000 ducats (239,000 *pesos* were then due, it appears). But it must be borne in mind that Havana had local revenues at disposal.

[133] A. de I., 54-1-18, Luna Sarmiente to the crown, December 28, 1641; 55-5-24, August 26, 1642, *id.* to *id.* The crown's announcement of Portugal's rebellion did not reach Luna Sarmiento as it should; he got his first news of that event via Brazil, accompanied by alarming rumors that from Brazil the Dutch and Portuguese would attack Havana.

call the citizens into consultation, and to tax them, each according to his ability to pay, thus raising money, ostensibly to wall the city. To take charge of the work he summoned Juan Bautista de Antoneli[134] from Santiago de Cuba, the fortifications here being in such condition that they could well be finished in the engineer's absence. When Antoneli arrived he decided that the work to be done in Havana should begin by the erection of the two towers which the crown had approved, so long before, one at the Chorrera and one at Coximar.

The fort at the Chorrera, on a rocky islet, where the river (now called the Almendares) comes into the sea, was built eighty feet square by forty high, five guns to play from a height of twenty feet, and six more from the top. It would seem that Antoneli was guided by plans which in July, 1641, General Luis Fernandez de Cordoba laid before the crown[135] as embodying his ideas of what was wanted. The model was the style of tower which Spain had found useful against the Moors:

Two thirds solid and the other third hollow, for the lodging of some six or eight soldiers, and on top one or two small pieces, to prevent launches from entering the said inlet; and the entrance . . as high up as the solid part goes, access by a rope ladder, for the greater safety of the whole.

For the rope ladder, at the Chorrera Antoneli substituted a draw bridge, and he built in a reservoir, storehouses, and barracks in such manner that the structure was reported to accommodate fifty men.

The fort at Coximar was similar—eighty feet square, but inasmuch as the rock upon which it stood was high, the walls were but fifteen feet to the guns on the seaward side; on the landward, they were thirty-five and there was a five foot moat.[136]

[134] There were two brothers named Juan Bautista Antoneli, one of whom, commonly called Bautista Antoneli, came to Havana with Don Juan de Texeda, to build Morro and Punta castles, commencing in 1589. The Juan Bautista Antoneli here mentioned is this man's son, born out of wedlock in Cartagena but later legitimized; he was heir to his father's name, talents, bad bills against the government, and also to his title of king's military engineer. He had a son, also of the same name, who was born in Porto Rico *circa* 1634.

[135] A. de I., 54-2-12.

[136] Good descriptions of the towers are contained in the governor's and Antoneli's letters to the crown: A. de I., 55-5-24, August 26, 1642; June 1, 1643.

The crown had appropriated 20,000 ducats for these towers.[137] They cost 20,000 *pesos* each, and, Don Alvaro de Luna wrote on August 26, 1642, "they will be finished within four months without the expenditure of a *real* of your majesty's revenues . . . ." Before the end of May, 1643, the governor reported fort Santa Dorothea de Luna at the Chorrera done,[138] and eleven guns in place. The fort at Coximar seems to have been finished well toward the end of the year 1643.

Four years before royal approval[139] of this work extended in 1647, had arrived in Havana, came a *cedula* to the governor dated May 4, 1643, ordering[140] that, for the good of his majesty's service, any Hollanders taken prisoners be neither molested nor maltreated, but rather exchanged to avoid irritation. These were black hours for Spain: this *cedula* was issued within a few days of the defeat at Rocroy. The immediate future held the Peace of Munster. The Dutch had won their fight. Havana's new forts, like her old ones, were monuments erected to dangers that had passed.

I. A. WRIGHT.
Archival Commissioner of the
Dutch Government.

[137] *See above*, page 633.

[138] In fact, he reported one fort done before the end of 1642. A. de I., 54-1-18, Luna Sarmiento to the crown, January 5, 1643; *id.* to *id.*, March 10, 1643; 55-5-24, *id.* to *id.*, May 29, 1643.

[139] A. de I., 55-5-24, *Junta de guerra* to crown, January 12, 1645; Geronimo de Sandoval's report, February 14, 1645; *Fray* Antonio Camaso's opinions, February 15, 1645, etc. Don Alvaro asked for powder, munitions, firearms, and a garrison of fifty for each of the new forts, including for each a captain, sergeant, drummer, fifer, chaplain, barber and four artillerymen. He reported that he had appointed Captain Pedro Henriquez de Noboa, former warden of Punta, to be warden at Coximar temporarily, and, similarly, he had selected Don Pedro Salgado for the fort at Chorrera. Salgado was assistant to Sergeant Major Lucas de Carvajal, whom the governor praised for the help he had given to the work of building the forts. The governor asked that his appointments be approved, and meanwhile from the other forts' garrisons he assigned men temporarily to both Coximar and the Chorrera. In 1647, Antonio Hurtado del Clavo went to court with a memorial showing why, and how, these forts were built. He had succeeded Pedro Salgado as Alvaro de Luna's choice for warden at Chorrera.

[140] *See also* A. de I., 147-5-24, a document dated June 25, 1647; *Junta de guerra* to the crown, September 9, 1647; 78-2-4, XII., pp. 38 r., 42, 45 r., *cedulas* of September 17, 1647.

THE MONROE DOCTRINE AND HISPANIC AMERICA[1]

The Monroe Doctrine has been for the American continent at once the most powerful unifying force and the greatest cause of division and misunderstanding. From the standpoint of the United States it might be called "the American fetish". Along with the Washington Doctrine of no entangling alliances it has been the cardinal principle of our foreign policy. As Jefferson said, "It is the offspring of the American Revolution and the most momentous question offered to my contemplation since the Independence". Like many an important principle, it has through the passage of time come to be more of a sentiment than a principle or a policy. And like every sentiment it has as many interpretations as there are kinds of persons who deal with it. To the average North American it means the divine right—as sacred and clear as was ever such right to any monarch—to act as the big brother of all the other American nations. This means first to protect them from all outside interference and, second, to help them in their own difficulties when they seem to have lost their way politically, financially or economically. It makes no difference what question concerning Hispanic America may arise in this country or what difficulty may arise in the south which affects the life of the United States, many immediately call out the Monroe Doctrine as arbiter.

"Why has General Crowder gone to Cuba?" was the question recently appearing from a reader of one of our prominent dailies. "It is due to the Monroe Doctrine, which makes us responsible for fair elections in Cuba," answered the all-wise editor. And no doubt the questioner was entirely satisfied with this simple answer. Because we North Americans are so sure of our generous desire to help all who are in need and so sure of our superiority to all the rest of America, many of us suppose that all Hispanic

[1] This paper is chapter V. of a forthcoming volume entitled *Problems in Pan Americanism*.

American government must be highly appreciative of the help which the Monroe Doctrine makes us in honor bound to give. Of course if the young sinner proves recalcitrant, we, as the unselfish and more experienced brother, desirous only of the other's improvement, must compel him to be good. If anyone questions at all whether this is the right procedure he is met with "We do not discuss the Monroe Doctrine, we enforce it".

It is this attitude of the North American toward the Doctrine, rather than the Doctrine itself, that explains why it has been such a cause of division and misunderstanding. In other words it is a certain interpretation of the Doctrine (a false interpretation, I believe) and not the Doctrine itself, that is so much opposed in Hispanic America. Indeed the original Monroe Doctrine was well received in the south, and from that time until today the declaration in its original sense has been approved by the best minds of Hispanic America.

In these days when all international relations are in flux and when every principle of life is being stripped of its accretions and thoroughly examined, we need a fresh study of the original purposes of the Doctrine which has been the basis of more discussion and more varied interpretation than any other document ever issued by the president of a republic.

ORIGIN OF THE DOCTRINE

The substance of this doctrine, which calls for the exclusion of European colonization and interference in American affairs, had often been stated before the Monroe pronouncement both by North American and South American statesmen. But in 1822, it seemed probable that the efforts of the Holy Alliance to strangle all democratic development in Europe might be extended to the western hemisphere. So Monroe and his advisors felt it necessary to take steps to forestall any such movement. Great Britain was also opposed to the extension of the influence of the Holy Alliance to America, for with the reconquest of Spanish America a large part of the conquered territory might be turned over to France and the large commerce which had been diverted to Great Britain on account of the revolt of the colonies would be seriously affected.

At this time the British Foreign Secretary was the celebrated Canning, one of the most astute men that ever held that office, a man who exercised almost a charmed influence over Hispanic American statesmen of those days, as well as an exaggerated place in the judgments of later Hispanic American historians. His proposal to the United States of an agreement that would checkmate the influence of the Alliance (and incidentally that of the United States) in Hispanic America, has led many historians to erroneously credit him with originating the Monroe Doctrine. At least two strong proofs of the falsity of the "Canning myth", as it has rightly been called, are these: First, the doctrine that Europe must not meddle in American affairs had been stated many times both in North and South America, before it was formally announced by Monroe. Second, the Doctrine had no more strenous opponent than Canning himself. He later said:

It is not easy to say how much the previous British propositions influenced the message, but the doctrine, if such it can be called, of the presidential message prohibiting all future colonization on the American continent, is absolutely unacceptable to my government and to France. This extraordinary principle will be combated by my government with all its force.

The private correspondence of Canning with some of his friends shows that he did everything possible to combat the Doctrine. In fact, Great Britain has generally been a strong opponent, Lord Salisbury writing to Secretary Olney during the Venezuela controversy that the Monroe Doctrine was not entitled to anyone's respect.

When Canning was asked why he had not sought to prevent the French invasion of Spain, he said:

I sought for compensation in another hemisphere. . . . . I resolved that if France had Spain it should not be Spain with the Indies; I called the new world into existence to redress the balance of the old.

This, of course, was nonsense, as the Spanish American colonies had won their independence by their own efforts and had been recognized by the United States as independent governments two years before Great Britain took any action in the matter. Canning was so irritated by the Monroe Doctrine that he did not permit the United States to participate with Great Britain and Russia in the settlement of the Alaska boundary question. As long as he remained in public life he opposed the Monroe Doctrine in every possible way, and continually impressed upon the Hispanic American republics the advantage to them of an alliance with Great Britain over an alliance with the United States.

And yet, with all this evidence to the contrary, great students like Alberdi have believed this Canning myth and attribute the success of the colonies' struggle for independence to the friendship of Great Britain. Many Hispanic Americans erroneously hold this to be a very important point in showing what they claim was the indifference of the United States to Hispanic America's struggle for independence.

Canning did send to Minister Rush of the United States, who was in London at the time, five proposals concerning the recognition of the independence of the Spanish colonies and their protection from the schemes of the Holy Alliance, which he suggested the two governments might jointly announce. But Monroe, advised by his Secretary, Adams, chose rather to announce a purely American doctrine that would be sustained by American authority. This is a most important matter for Hispanic Americans to understand. And for North America it is imperative to realize that the circumstances surrounding the announcement of the Doctrine all point to the fact that our statesmen did not have the least idea that we were providing for ourselves any special privileges in America. As John Quincy Adams, the man who historians believed worded the Doctrine itself, wrote in his diary:

Considering the South Americans as independent nations, they themselves, and no other nation had the right to dispose of their condition. *We* have no right to dispose of them, either alone or in conjunction with other nations. Neither have any other nations the right to dispose of them without their consent.

The most salient features of the famous Doctrine, which was contained in President Monroe's annual message to Congress on December 2, 1823, are the following:

The occasion has been judged proper for asserting as a principle in which the rights and interests of the United States are involved, that the American continents, by the free and independent condition which they have assumed and maintain are henceforth not to be considered as subjects for future colonization by any European power.

The citizens of the United States cherish sentiments the most friendly in favor of the liberty and happiness of their fellow-men on that side of the Atlantic.   In the wars of the European powers in matters relating to themselves we have never taken any part, nor does it comport with our policy to do so.   It is only when our rights are invaded or seriously menaced that we resent injuries or make preparation for our defense. With the movements in this hemisphere we are, of necessity, more immediately connected, and by causes which must be obvious to all enlightened and impartial observers.   The political system of the allied powers is essentially different in this respect from that of America. This difference proceeds from that which exists in their respective Governments.   And to the defense of our own, which has been achieved by the loss of so much blood and treasure, and matured by the wisdom of their most enlightened citizens, and under which we have enjoyed unexampled felicity, this whole nation is devoted.   We owe it, therefore, to candor, and to the amicable relations existing between the United States and those powers, to declare that we should consider any attempt on their part to extend their system to any portion of this hemisphere as dangerous to our peace and safety.   With the existing colonies or dependencies of any European power we have not interfered and shall not interfere.   But with the Governments who have declared their independence, and maintained it, and whose independence we have, on great consideration and on just principles, acknowledged, we could not view any interposition for the purpose of oppressing them, or controlling in any other manner their destiny, by any European power, in any other light than as the manifestation of an unfriendly disposition toward the United States.

The late events in Spain and Portugal show that Europe is still unsettled.   Of this important fact no stronger proof can be adduced than that the allied powers should have thought it proper, on any principle satisfactory to themselves, to have interposed, by force, in the internal concerns of Spain. To what extent such interposition may be carried, on the same principle, is a question in which all independent powers whose Governments differ from theirs are interested, even those most remote, and surely none more so than the United States.[2]

HOW THE DOCTRINE WAS RECEIVED IN HISPANIC AMERICA

What was Hispanic America's attitude to this new doctrine? Bolivar seems not to have heard of it for quite a while. He never really made any long pronouncement upon it. He did, however, applaud the declaration, and in a letter to the Spanish general whom he was endeavoring to persuade to join the liberal cause, said:

England and the United States protect us. These two nations, which form today the only two powers in the world, will not permit that help be given to Spain.

The Brazilian government, through its minister, Rebello, proposed an alliance between the United States and Brazil which the other Hispanic American republics were invited to join. That government invoked the message of Monroe and the necessity of making impossible any tendency of the mother countries to reconquer their old colonies, observing that

the United States is obliged to place in practice the principle announced in the message (Monroe) giving proof of the generosity and the consistency which animates that government, without counting the eventual sacrifice of men and money.[3]

On April 6, 1824, Vice-President Santander sent a message to the Colombian Congress in which he referred to the Monroe Doctrine as follows:

The President of the United States has lately signalized his administration by an act eminently just and worthy of the classic land of liberty; and in his last message to the Congress he has declared that he will regard every interference of any European power directed to op-

[2] James Daniel Richardson, *A Compilation of the Messages and Papers of the Presidents*, pp. 778, 786–788.
[3] Helio Lobo, *Causas Diplomaticas*.

press or violate the destinies of the independent governments of America as a manifestation of hostile disposition toward the United States. That Government considers every attempt on the part of the Allied Powers to extend their system to any portion of the American hemisphere as perilous to the peace and safety of the United States. This policy, consolatory to human nature, would secure to Colombia a powerful ally should its independence and liberty be menaced by the Allied Powers. As the Executive cannot regard with indifference the march which the policy of the United States has taken, it is sedulously occupied in reducing the question to decisive and conclusive points.

About the same time Santander addressed a note to Secretary Adams in which he said:

My Government has received with the greatest pleasure the message, worthy of its author, which expresses the sentiment of the country over which he presides.

He even went so far as to propose an alliance between the United States and Colombia to sustain the principles of the Monroe Doctrine.

From Buenos Aires United States Minister Rodney wrote on February 10, 1824, to President Monroe that his message had been received two days before, that it had inspired the Argentine people, and that it would have the "happiest effect throughout the whole Spanish provinces". On May 22nd he wrote Secretary Adams that the frank and firm message of the President had been productive of happy effects; but that he looked not so much to its temporary influence as to its permanent operation. "We had it immediately translated", he wrote, "into the Spanish language, printed and generally circulated in this quarter, Peru and Chile."

On December 16, 1824, the congress of the United Provinces of Río de la Plata opened its sessions at Buenos Aires. In a message of the government of Buenos Aires, laid before that body on the same date, the American policy of the United States was referred to in the following terms:

We have fulfilled a great national duty toward the republic of the United States of North America. That republic, which, from its origin, presides over the civilization of the New World, has solemnly acknowledged our independence. It has at the same time made an appeal to our national honor by supposing us capable of contending single-handed with Spain; but it has constituted itself the guardian of the field of battle in order to prevent any foreign assistance from being introduced to the aid of our rival.

Governor Las Heras, of Buenos Aires, on receiving United States Minister Forbes a little later, said:

The Governor of the United Provinces recognizes the importance of the two principles which the president of the United States has announced in his message to Congress and, convinced of the usefulness of their adoption by each of the states of this continent, will consider it his duty to back them, and for this purpose will accept any opportunity that is presented.

Chile gave a most genuine response to President Monroe's message. The papers of Santiago seemed to discover in the Monroe Doctrine a frank and explicit promise of effective protection for the Spanish American republics against the political combinations and military projects of European monarchs. A delegate of the chief executive, upon the occasion of receiving Mr. Allen, the newly-appointed Minister of the United States to Chile, expressed the gratitude of his government for the recognition of the independence of the new states and for the recent declaration of President Monroe which placed them beyond the reach of the coalitions of European monarchs.

The cordial declarations of the Foreign Office of the Central American Government in 1825, also heartily approved the Doctrine.[4]

It would be easy to present other indorsements of the Monroe Doctrine by the Hispanic American countries in those early days, but these are sufficient to show that at that time they had no idea of anything being involved in the doctrine which made it dangerous to Hispanic America. It will be remembered that in the call for the Panama Congress it was proposed to make the

---

[4] Cited in another chapter of the volume from which this chapter is taken (see note 1).

Monroe declaration a common principle of all the American governments. This is one of the strongest indications that the correct interpretation of the Doctrine rejects the inference that the United States reserves to itself the privilege of doing the things it will not suffer Europe to do. If this earlier interpretation had been retained in practice the present bitterness against the Doctrine would never have developed in Hispanic America.

The Monroe message states very clearly the three following propositions: first, that there shall be no future colonization in America by European powers; second, that there shall be no extension of the monarchical system to republican America; third, that the United States will defend the independence of these American countries against European aggression. During the years that followed we seem to have added two corollaries to these three propositions: that European governments must not acquire any of the American governments' territory, even with the consent of the nation involved or by the adjustment of boundaries; and that non-American governments cannot occupy any portion of the American republics even temporarily for the satisfaction of any kind of claims against these republics. The first three of these proposals are the original Doctrine. The latter two are interpretations allowed by the Doctrine and which have developed out of recent experience in dealing with the Caribbean countries.

INTERPRETATIONS OF THE DOCTRINE

One of the greatest questions most often debated concerning the Doctrine is whether or not it is a purely selfish one, announced merely to protect the United States or designed as one of those altruistic services which we North Americans like to think we are doing to help smaller nations. Let us listen to what some present North Americans say about that phase of the subject: Mr. Root says:

The Doctrine is not international law, but it rests upon the right of self-protection and that right is recognized by international law. The right is a necessary corollary of independent sovereignty. It is well understood that the exercise of the right of self-protection may and frequently does extend in its effect beyond the limits of territorial jurisdiction of the state exercising it. . . . The most common exercise of the right of self-protection outside of a state's own territory, and in time of peace, is the interposition of objection to the occupation of territory, of points of strategic military or maritime advantage, or to indirect accomplishment of this effect by dynastic arrangement. . . . Of course each state must judge for itself when a threatened act will create such a situation. If any state objects to a threatened act and the reasonableness of its objection is not assented to, the efficacy of the objection will depend upon the power behind it.

It is doubtless true that in the adherence of the American people to the original declaration there was a great element of sentiment and sympathy for the people of South America who were struggling for freedom and it has been a source of great satisfaction to the United States that the course which it took in 1823 concurrently with the action of Great Britain played so great a part in assuring the right of self-government to the countries of South America. Yet is it to be observed that in reference to the South American Governments, as in all other respects, the international right upon which the declaration expressly rests is not sentiment or sympathy or a claim to dictate what kind of government any other country shall have, but the safety of the United States.

Mr. John Bassett Moore says:

The Monroe Doctrine was in its origin a defiance to those who would suppress independent governments and restore the system of commercial monopoly and political absolutism on the American continents. It was in this sense that it found an enthusiastic response in popular opinion.

Ex-president Taft has seen this point very clearly and says:

The Monroe Doctrine was proclaimed for the purpose of upholding the territorial dignity and political independence of the nations of South and Central America. It binds the United States to the exact course which the League of Nations demands of all nations.

Mr. Henry W. Taft says:

The Monroe Doctrine is not a principle of international law. It is a national policy based on the right of every nation to protect itself against acts tending to embarass it in preserving its own national interests or political institutions. It is founded upon the same right as the familiar concert of European powers, except that it affects a greater number of nations more widely separated geographically, and is asserted by a single powerful nation, able, without the sanction of treaty stipulations, to maintain it. It does not become effective so much by the acquiesence of the American nations subject to its operation as from its recognition by nations of other parts of the world as a political policy which cannot be disregarded by them except at the risk of war with the United States.

Mr. John Bigelow says:

In order properly to appreciate the significance of the Monroe Doctrine it must be clearly recognized that it was designed primarily for the protection of the United States, the safeguarding of its territory and political institutions, the effect of which would be, indirectly, to work to the advantage of the Latin American countries by affording them the opportunity to work out their problems without interference from European powers.

Secretary of State Lansing gave the Senate the following account of the conversations which led to the Lansing-Ishii agreement:

Then it was during the same interview that we mentioned "paramount interests," and he (Ishii) made a reference to the Monroe Doctrine of the Far East; and I told him that there seemed to be a misconception as to the underlying principle of the Monroe Doctrine; that it was not an assertion of primacy or paramount interest by the United States in its relation to other American republics; that its purpose was to prevent foreign powers from interfering with the separate rights of any nation in this hemisphere and that the whole aim was to preserve to each republic the power of self-development. I said further that so far as aiding in this development the United States claimed no special privileges over other countries. . . .[5]

Rear-Admiral Chester says:

The first principle of the Monroe Doctrine—self-preservation—is axiomatic and immutable, and all other considerations must give way

[5] For a luminous discussion of the Monroe Doctrine in all its aspects political and economic, see *Proceedings of the American Society of International Law*, 1914.

to it. The second principle, like the constitution of a country, is amenable to changes and amendments that will bring it into accord with new conditions that may arise in the country. The question now, therefore, is, do the same conditions prevail on the western continent today as in 1823?   .   .   .   Many of the twenty other American Republics are no longer the weaklings they were when the policy was formulated, but are now strong enough to share the common defense of the continent. We cannot, however, with propriety form an alliance, for that word has been tabooed by an unwritten law of the land, but we can engage in an "entente," as foreigners call it, with the republics of South America that will give them a share in the responsibility of maintaining a policy which looks to the good of all parties concerned.

As Admiral Chester says, the doctrine is partly selfish and partly altruistic, as every natural principle should be.   It seems very natural to suppose that the United States, being a weak nation in the early days, was particularly interested in protecting itself and also in advancing the great idea of democracy of which it was the pathfinder.   Democratic government it selfishly and unselfishly desired to see grow—selfishly in that the development of such government on the American continent would tend to strengthen its own life, unselfishly in that it wished to encourage and assist other small nations to realize the same ideal.

A more practical question concerning the application of the Monroe Doctrine is the extent to which the United States assumes responsibility before the world for the shortcomings of the other American nations.   If we say to Europe, "You are to keep completely out of this continent", how far do we expect to see to the just settlement of European complaints against those countries?   Consider, for example, the matter of the collection of debts.   If we will not let France enter Santo Domingo and take a couple of ports in payment of a ten million dollar debt, how far shall we interfere to make Santo Domingo pay?   If an English subject is killed in Mexico and we do not allow England to obtain satisfaction by seizing Mexican territory, how far are we to assume the authority to punish Mexico and force her to deal fairly with England?

We have stated (Roosevelt said it, and it has been intimated many times by our government) that we will not keep European

governments from collecting their debts in the American republics. In fact we have permitted them to take measures to enforce payment of such debts as long as this did not mean territorial acquisition by them. At the time when interventon in
Mexico was begun, with the announced purpose of collecting
debts which that country owed Great Britain, France, and Spain
the United States was invited to join with them. The situation
was tried out to ascertain our attitude, and Secretary Seward
wrote that the United States had no objection to these countries
collecting their debts from Mexico. When it came to the
establishment of a monarchy in Mexico, however, our attitude
was very different.

We have never agreed with the claims of certain Hispanic
American statesmen that debts should never be collected forcibly.
We have adopted the Hague agreement that the question of
debts of this kind shall be arbitrated, but we have undertaken
to use moral suasion and more recently have actually assumed
responsibility for managing the finances of certain republics in
order to save them from a foreign foreclosure. We have thus
assumed a protectorate over both Santo Domingo and Haiti
because it was claimed that these countries were likely to be
seized by European countries for non-payment of debt. But
we have still to determine how far we will go in straightening out
the financial difficulties of Hispanic American countries that
seem to be in danger from European creditors.

The precedent of Santo Domingo, Haiti, and Nicaragua seems
to indicate pretty clearly that, at least in the Caribbean, or
what Admiral Chester calls the "larger Panama Canal Zone",
we will take action before risking that of any foreign country.
Indeed diplomatic aid in resuscitating the finances of Honduras,
Cuba, Costa Rica, and possibly Mexico is now being extended by
the United States, although in the case of Mexico the proceedings
are still in the formative stage. It is interesting to note that the
shift in world credit due to the war makes it altogether probable
that the United States will itself more and more assume the
rôle of creditor to these republics and that problems in connection with payment of debts will be given an entirely new turn.

European nations are not in position to finance foreign governments to any great extent, however profitable it might be.

It has been suggested by some thoughtful students that the Monroe Doctrine should be limited to Caribbean countries or at least those north of the Amazon, for the reason that the zone of defense of the Canal and of the continental United States extends no farther than that, and also for the reason that the countries farther south have grown strong in their own power and neither need nor appreciate our proffered protection. While a formal pronouncement of any such limitation of the Doctrine will probably never be made, it is almost certain that its application will be limited to this northern zone, as has been the case in the past. It may well be recalled in this connection that even when England and France intervened in Argentina, and Spain in Chile and Peru, the United States did no more than express sympathy to these countries. In this connection Dr. Estanislao Zaballos, of Buenos Aires, has said:

What other countries of America have the same world problems as Panama or Mexico, the latter on the frontier of the United States and the former at the throat of the continent itself. They have nothing in common with the problems of the River Plate or the shores of Brazil or the coasts of Chile. The Monroe Doctrine is necessary today to the United States. The Caribbean washes the shores of the richest part of the United States and it is necessary that it be dominated by them in order to guarantee the independence and security of the United States.

The most important question concerning the Doctrine is whether it means that Europe must stay out of Hispanic American affairs and that the United States may go in, or simply that Europe shall stay out. It is difficult to see anything in the Monroe Doctrine to justify the assumption of an aggressive policy on the part of the United States toward Hispanic America. The original doctrine claims nothing for the United States that it does not concede to every other American nation. If in the Monroe Doctrine the United States arrogates to itself supremacy in the western hemisphere, it is only with respect to non-American powers, and with respect to them it wishes every American nation to be supreme. There is nothing in it that makes its provisions a monopoly by the United States. The proclamation of a similar doctrine by each of the other American nations would strengthen rather than impair the force of the Monroe declaration.

In his address at the unveiling of the Bolivar statue in New York, President Harding clearly emphasized that the United States reserves no special privileges to itself under the Monroe Doctrine. Speaking to the entire Hispanic American diplomatic corps, he said:

There have been times when the meaning of Monroeism was misunderstood by some, perverted by others and made the subject of distorting propaganda by those who saw in it an obstacle to the realization of their own ambitions. . . . They have falsely charged that we sought to hold the nations of the Old World at arm's length in order that we might monopolize the privilege of exploitation for ourselves. Others have protested that the doctrine would never be enforced if to enforce it should involve us in actual hostilities.

The history of the generations since that Doctrine was proclaimed has proved that we never intended it selfishly; that we had no dream of exploitation. On the other side, the history of the last decade certainly must have convinced all the world that we stand willing to fight, if necessary, to protect these continents, these sturdy young democracies, from oppression and tyranny.

Nevertheless the Monroe Doctrine has been a continual source of irritation to the Hispanic American nations. At first they accepted it gladly, as we have seen, as protecting them from Europe, but later we see it becoming in their eyes an instrument through which the United States presumed to dictate to them. "America for the Americans", they say, means "America for the North Americans".

In the early days no such talk was heard as this of Señor José de Astorga, writing recently in *La Revista de America*:

. . . The importance of securing concerted movement and unanimity of action among the countries of Latin America in order to offset the imperialistic ambitions of the United States is urgent and of extreme importance. The protests of con-fraternity, of disinterestedness and of respect for the political sovereignty and the commercial independence of Latin America which the Government of the United States sets forth so freely on every occasion, are not able to counteract or to lessen the eloquence of deeds, and these are the deeds: Tutelage over Cuba; the abduction of Panama; the embargo on the custom houses of Santo Domingo; economic and military intervention in Central America; the "big stick," "dollar diplomacy", and the Lodge declaration.

The Hispanic Americans, however, are not alone in interpreting the Monroe Doctrine as meaning that the United States retains the right to control the western hemisphere. There are not a few North Americans who hold this view. These extracts from *America Among the Nations*, by Professor H. H. Powers, are certainly disquieting:

It is difficult to follow the expansion of America in the Caribbean without feeling that it will go farther. Whether it should go farther is not the question. This is neither an indictment nor a propaganda, but a study. No more is assumed than that national character shows a certain continuity, and that incentives which have been potent in the past are likely to be potent in the future. If so much be conceded, then the further development of Caribbean domination seems assured. If the considerations which have impelled us to restrict the liberty of Cuba, to take over the financial problems of Santo Domingo and to assume the management of Hayti, are legitimate then there is more work of this kind for us to do. Conditions were no worse in Hayti than in other Caribbean countries. Utter recklessness and incompetency have characterized the management of every one of these pseudo-states which the preoccupations of the real nations have temporarily abandoned to independence. It was a matter of chance which one of the dancers should first pay the piper, but all have danced and all must pay. As each faces in turn the inevitable crisis, the same problem presents itself. What reason is there to believe that we shall not meet it in the same way? (P. 140)

To the independence party Central America is its own little world. To the imperialistic party it is but a pawn on the mighty chessboard of world empire. We may sympathize with the one or the other but we must not judge the one by the standards of the other. The United States plays the vaster game, must play it and play it well, for the stake is its existence. (P. 140.)

We have learned subtler ways of winning, more varied ways of ruling. We have found new reasons for old impulses, and old impulses have renewed their youth.

Finally, we are still confronted with opportunity. More than any other people we have prizes within our grasp. And we are grasping them. Never was our frontier more alive than it is today. Acquisition of new territory has become a commonplace and passes unnoticed. Not one American in a hundred realizes that we have a protectorate over Hayti and that our control is creeping out through all these southern seas. If he knew, his only reaction would probably be a slightly increased complacency. The door is thus opened wide for a government, embarrassed by the mischievous irresponsibility of these petty make-believe states, to take refuge in an ever broadening imperialism. Unless the leopard changes his spots this must carry our frontier to the limits we have mentioned. (P. 159.)

Nor is the call of the tropics the only one. The war upon which we have now embarked has incalculable possibilities. We are committed not merely to the redressing of our grievances to date, but to the vastly larger program of settling such difficulties as the war itself may create. Without taking too seriously the fascinating program of "making the world safe for democracy," it is well to remember that the war is to be fought on European soil and in conjunction with nations having possessions in every part of the world. When the peace conference meets we shall hear very little of the sonorous slogans which heralded the war's beginning and much of the concrete problems for which these phrases suggest no very tangible solution. (P. 160.)

Such arguments as these certainly do not represent the best North American thought yet they are common enough to spread wide alarm in Hispanic America.

Probably the most illuminating discussion of the present Hispanic American attitude toward the Monroe Doctrine was the debate in 1914 in the columns of the *Atlantic Monthly* between Professor Hiram Bingham and Señor F. Garcia Calderón. Professor Bingham's article was entitled "The Monroe Doctrine, an Obselete Shibboleth." He argues for the abandonment of the Monroe Doctrine on the following grounds:

1. The Doctrine was proclaimed under a false conception of (a) geographical proximity, for the great centers of South American life

are nearer to Europe than to the United States, and (b) the existence of natural sympathy, which is difficult to encounter in Latin Amerca.

2. Latin America resents our attitude of being "practically sovereign on the continent" and opposed our war with Spain, our interference in Panama, Santo Domingo, etc.

3. It places the United States in the false position of being the collector of Europe's debts, bringing our intervention in these states on many false grounds and thus multiplying the prejudice of Latin America against us.

4. The great growth of some of the South American states in recent years is ignored in the application of the Doctrine. Viscount Bryce represents them as saying, "Since there are no longer rain clouds coming up from the East, why should our friend, however well-intentioned, insist on holding an umbrella over us?"

Professor Bingham concludes:

Let us face clearly the fact that the maintenance of the Monroe Doctrine is going to cost the United States an immense amount of trouble, men and money. Carried out to its logical conclusion it means a policy of suzerainty and interference which will earn us the increased hatred of our neighbors, the dissatisfaction of Europe, the loss of commercial opportunity and the forfeit of time and attention which would better be given to settling our own difficult internal problems. The continuance of adherence to the Monroe Doctrine offers opportunity to scheming statesmen to distract public opinion from the necessity of concentrated attention at home by arousing mingled feelings of jingoism and self-importance in attempting to correct the errors of our neighbors.

Señor Calderón, whom readers of his *Latin America, Its Rise and Progress* would certainly not accuse of being partial to the United States, strongly maintained the usefulness of the Doctrine and its acceptability to Hispanic America if properly interpreted. He said:

If the United States would affirm that it also is in accord with the sovereign republics of the south, that it respects the territorial *status quo* in this American continent which its own triumphant expansion seems to threaten, an American system of law would be established, and the union of the two races which govern this huge continent would become a political fact of most far-reaching consequence. We should be face to face, then, with a new Monroeism as the doctrine of American autonomy, accepted and proclaimed by all the people oversea, who would agree to protect one another against all future attempts at conquest, and then, in place of this vexing and harassing tutelage, we should have a sturdy declaration of American solidarity.

Even by 1911 these generous plans showed signs of development. The United States, Brazil, and Argentina, through friendly intervention, averted an imminent war between Peru and Ecuador. When they pacified Central America, Mexico came to their aid, and thenceforward their action no longer bore any resemblance to the intrusion of foreigners. It was in the name of a doctrine not only North American but Pan American that the peoples of the New World addressed the powerful nations which stood ready to tear them in pieces. No one then criticised this intervention of the great countries of the New World, of North Saxon and South Latin. The United States played its part also—which made its moral influence acceptable to the Spanish American nations.

In principle the Monroe Doctrine is an essential article in the public code of the New World. Two newspapers of Buenos Aires, *La Argentina* and *La Razón*, have come to recognize it as such. In them we read that the United States is the "safeguard of American interests", and they praise the North American republic for the paternal protection which it offers. It is only the brutal expression of the doctrine, the cynical imperialism which is deduced from it, which becomes dangerous to the moral unity of the continent.

The wisest statesmen have no thought of divorcing this doctrine from the future history of America, even when they criticise its excesses most severely.

The men of the North have a civilizing function to fulfil in a continent wherein they exercise supreme power. If their behavior is disinterested, if they prevent war, if they fertilize these new countries abundantly with the gold of their banks, if they become apostles of peace and international justice, no one will ever forget the grandeur of their political rôle in the world's politics.

In considering the behavior of the United States toward its neighbors, we must distinguish quite clearly between its attitude regarding Panama and its policy toward countries south of the Isthmus. Toward South America its intervention deserves only respect. The purely selfish interest of the United States evidently lay in the acceptance of war and anarchy, in accordance with the classical formula "divide and rule"; yet the United States has kept the peace. From Panama to the La Plata it is working for the union of the peoples and for civilization.

Here, then, is an aspect of the Monroe Doctrine of perpetual usefulness: the struggle against the wars which threaten to ruin the New World, still poor and thinly populated—intervention with the olive branch. In stimulating the union of South American republics the United States is at the same time protecting its own commercial interests, menaced by this perpetual turmoil. If its action were to halt there, if it renounced all territorial acquisition and set its face against all interference with the internal affairs of every state, the doctrine so often condemned would seem born anew and no one would dare to criticise its efficacy. Most of all, it is on the score of irregular political practices, of fomenting revolution, that the excessive tutelage of the United States comes in for most widespread condemnation. An Argentine writer, Manuel Ugarte, has summarized this sentiment in the phrase, "We wish to be brothers of the North Americans, not their slaves". Even if this tutelage were designed to prepare democracies without democratic tradition for self-government after the Saxon method; even if, as in the case of Cuba, it is granted partial liberty and provisional privileges, the passionate feeling for independence which is so widespread throughout America would be exceedingly irritated by this rather contemptuous method of education. Great Britain pays more repect to the autonomy of her colonies than the new Saxon democracy is willing to bestow upon the still fragile independence of some American republics. What would be thought of the attitude of a Conservative minister of Great Britain who put a veto on the action of the Socialist government of Australia by dissolving the colonial Parliament and criticising the laws of the free "Commonwealth"? One cannot comprehend the policy which American peoples are often obliged to endure in their relations with Washington.

In Latin America people do not understand the United States. A few offhand judgments often control the decision which leads Latin Americans to antagonism or to unreflecting infatuation. The Americans of the North are thought to be "practical people". Men say that they are intensely covetous of riches. They have no morality. The business man, always hard and arrogant in mind and brutal in method, is the symbol of the nation. Ideals, dreams, noble ambitions, never stir their breasts. These characteristics of the North American the men of the South, according to their individual ideas, admire or despise.

They forget how austere is the grandeur that Americans of the North acquire from their superb idealism, from their strong Puritan tradition, from the lust of gold made subservient to ambition for power and for influence over men. They are ignorant of the mysticism which forever flourishes in the United States, continually creating new sects, the perpetual Christian Renaissance whose energy was so greatly admired by William James. We must admit that in South American countries, with their narrow and superficial religiosity, we do not find this great concern regarding the line which divides the ideal from the fact. The example of the United States, the reading of its poets, the study of Emerson, the influence of its universities, an examination of the part which wealth has played in this democracy, would, I conceive, go far toward reforming the bad manners of the South and make it appreciate the true fundamentals of the grandeur of North America.

In my book on the Latin democracies I have set forth the contrasts which may easily be established between the Catholicism of the Spanish Americans, the state religion, uniform and formal, and the restless and active Protestantism of the United States; between the mixture of races in the South and that racial pride, "the white man's burden" which controls northern opinion. It would be very easy to push this analysis further and to set forth the strength of aristocratic prejudices among the Spaniards and the very democratic spirit which exists among the Saxons; to contrast the idealism of the North with the less vast, less generous ambition of the South; or the stanch, puritanical domestic life among the South Americans with a certain license of morals which exists in North America. But, in spite of this sharp contrast, there are resemblances not less evident than the divergent traits, an Americanism which gives a certain unity to the entire New World. All evidence points to the conclusion that if the United States acts in accord with Latin America, if the Monroe Doctrine loses its aggressive character, the influence of these twenty nations will be a force in the world's progress which cannot be despised.

That is the serious judgment of one of the great Hispanic American writers and diplomats, a man who becomes most indignant when he discusses North American imperialism.

CONFUSION OF THE MONROE DOCTRINE WITH OTHER POLICIES

With the passing of the years the Monroe Doctrine has been confused with at least three new ideas that have grown up during the period of our relations with the rest of the American continent. In the first place, we have confused it with the headship of the United States in America.

The United States has developed a hundred times more rapidly than any other country in America, and as a natural outgrowth of that development it has necessarily assumed the headship of the American nations. It is more or less the story of all history. The process is similar to that by which the Bishop of Rome became the Pope—the smaller bishoprics sent their problems to the great man in the city and thus his influence developed until he became supreme. In the same way the United States has grown very naturally into a position of leadership on the American continent. Whether we like it or whether Hispanic America likes it, there is no way of preventing the most advanced and most powerful nation in the group from exercising the greatest influence.

This headship signified, among other things, that we must lead in the building of the Panama Canal, though of course it did not prescribe the method. It likewise meant that we must acquire naval stations and zones of influence for the protection of the Canal and all that that implies. But the Monroe Doctrine has nothing whatever to do with this. These things came about from the position we necessarily assumed as the greatest nation on the continent. Perhaps we did not have to do it in quite the way we did; better ways could have been found. Nevertheless the burden was laid upon us and we could not get away from it, so we took the lead just as other great nations have done in other parts of the world where their influence was dominant. Thus the various "Pan American Congresses" met with little success until the greatest American nation entered and lent its overpowering influence to their promotion.

The second principle with which the Monroe Doctrine is confused is that of imperialism. Imperialism has nothing to do with the Monroe Docrtine, but is merely one of those tendencies of modern nations to take over smaller and more poorly organized countries. We have been following other peoples in doing that, for the tendency is not only world wide but is a factor in the economic as well as the political field today. Most of our territory has really been gained at the expense of other nations. Let it be said to our credit, however, that in contrast with most modern imperialistic nations, we bought most of the territory acquired. This is our imperialistic policy, a thing apart from the Monroe Doctrine. Let us remind our Hispanic American friends that Chile, Brazil, and Argentina have done like things. The big nations in South America have done as the big nation in North America. Of course it is easy to think the United States is the only sinner in the world, but every big nation is imperialistic. It is not the Monroe Doctrine that prompts us to do these things, it is the great and prepossessing idea of empire building. We are not nearly as guilty on this score as Great Britain.

The third point of confusion is with the idea of Pan Americanism. By Pan Americanism we understand the recognition of a community of interests among all American countries and a determination to work these out coöperatively to the best advantage of all concerned. The present tendency is to create a concert of American powers to act together for mutual protection and help, the maintenance of peace and the promotion of better commercial, political and intellectual relations. And this is not the Monroe Doctrine.

These three matters of headship, imperialism, and Pan Americanism have all exerted an appreciable influence in our relations with Hispanic America, but they should not be confounded with Monroeism. We will clarify our action and our understanding of all inter-American relations as soon as we cease lumping everything related to Hispanic America under the one conception of Monroeism, which, after all, is to the average citizen of the United States largely a sentiment.

The address of President Wilson to the Mexican editors probably delighted Hispanic America more than any other official utterance with the exception of Mr. Root's famous speech at Rio de Janeiro. Mr. Wilson said:

The famous Monroe Doctrine was adopted without your consent, without the consent of any of the Central or South American states.

If I may express it in the terms that we so often use in this country, we said, "We are going to be your big brother whether you want us to be or not". We did not ask whether it was agreeable to you that we should be your big brother. We said we were going to be. Now that was all very well so far as protecting you from agression from the other side of the water was concerned, but there was nothing in it that protected you from aggression from us, and I have repeatedly seen the uneasy feeling on the part of representatives of the states of Central and South America that our self-appointed protection might be for our own benefit and our own interests and not for the interests of our neighbors. So I said, "Very well, let us make some arrangement by which we will give bond. Let us have a common guarantee, that all of us will sign, of political independence and territorial integrity. Let us agree that if any one of us, the United States included, violates the political independence or the territorial integrity of any of the others, all the others will jump on her."

THE MONROE DOCTRINE AND THE LEAGUE OF NATIONS

What effect has the World War, which has affected all international relations, had on the Monroe Doctrine? In answering this question one is again confronted with the basic question of the meaning of the Doctrine. President Wilson said, in addressing the Senate on June 22, 1917, that "The nations should with one accord adopt the doctrine of President Monroe as the doctrine of the world." He explained that under this world doctrine no nation should seek to extend its policy over any other nation or people, but that every people should be left free to determine its own policy, its own way of development, unhindered, unthreatened, unafraid, the weak along with the great and powerful.

President Wilson's understanding of the Monroe Doctrine is here clearly revealed. It is certainly not the same as Professor Bingham had when he advocated its abandonment because it kept us from being well regarded in Hispanic America. The simple Monroe and Wilson insistence that each nation shall have the right to develop along its own lines, without interference from the outside, that, "good faith and justice toward all nations" shall prevail, represents an entirely different conception. While Monroe's proposal was that no European nation should seek to extend its authority over an American nation, Wilson proposed that no nation in any part of the world should seek to extend its policy over any other nation or people.

This interpretation of the Doctrine was the one given it by President Cleveland in dealing with the Venezuelan boundary dispute, when he said that the Doctrine found its basis "in the theory that every nation shall have its rights protected and its just claims enforced". At the same time Secretary Olney pointed out to Great Britain that "the people of the United States had a vital interest in the cause of self-government" and that the British attitude toward Venezuela so threatened the American policy that if the power of the United States was adequate to prevent the carrying out of British purposes it would be done.

It is natural that this doctrine, maintained for a century and resulting in giving weaker nations in America a chance to develop without outside interference, should be of value in developing a world policy that would protect small nations. That the efficacy of the Monroe Doctrine has depended on the force the United States could bring to its support, suggests of course the need of force to support any world application of the same principle—the principle which has been recognized in the formation of the League of Nations.

Just as the Hispanic American peoples had favored the original Monroe Doctrine and appreciated its protection from Europe, so they immediately welcomed the extension of the doctrine to the whole world as embodied in the League of Nations. For strangely enough our southern neighbors, believing that the United States has shifted from the original purpose of the Doctrine and is now using it merely for its own selfish purposes, saw in the proposal to bring the world into the agreement a guarantee that Hispanic America would not only be protected from Europe but from the United States itself.

The League of Nations was received with the greatest enthusiasm by all the southern countries. Here was the movement that would get the American nations beyond the *impassé* which had been reached in the much talked-of Pan Americanism.   For though on one hand the United States could not give up the historic Monroe Doctrine, on the other the Hispanic Americas could never come into free relations with their northern neighbor within that Doctrine if it meant, as it seemed to have come to mean, the hegemony of the United States in the Pan American family.

But here was the way out of the dilemma—make the doctrine world wide.   The United States would surrender nothing of its historic insistence that European nations must not project themselves into American life, and Hispanic America would have its fears and its implied inferiority removed, since the United States would thus assume the same obligation to respect the independence of the small American states as did all other nations.   Thus the greatest difficulty in the way of continental solidarity would disappear without embarrassment to any of the parties.

This feeling was well expressed by the Cuban, Orestes Ferrara, in his review, *La Reforma Social*, as follows:

When Mr. Wilson and Mr. Taft refer to the declarations of President Monroe and insist that the detachment of American nations will not receive a blow but on the contrary will be more absolute because the doctrine is universally accepted by the establishment of the League, they say something that reveals very clearly how their minds turn to the past when the principle of the independence of American nations was threatened by the transference of the consequences of another great European conflict to American soil.   Evidently Wilson and Taft regard the Monroe Doctrine in its original sense, the most just to other rights. It is not so with Senators Knox and Lodge.   They think of the Doctrine as it has been practised for the last twenty-five years, which seems to have justified the relations with Panama, Nicaragua, Santo Domingo, Haiti, etc., and which has established the absolute dominion of the United States over the Americas.   The difference is therefore paramount, being on the one hand a principle and on the other a selfish interest.

The truth is that there has never been a declaration in the international life of the world with purer ideas and more noble purposes than the Monroe Doctrine.   The North American statesmen of that time had the most unselfish ideas about it. Jefferson, from his retirement, gave to it the whole endorsement of his serene mind and tranquil soul. But in the course of time the formula "The United States standing before Europe in defense of the Americas" naturally brought the predominance of the United States in America. And if the United States had not practised in her international relations the Anglo-Saxon principle that the rights of others shall not be interfered with unless one's own interests are clearly threatened, a situation of this kind would have been fatal to the rest of America.

To be more specific, we may affirm that if any other nation than the United States had had her hands free in America as she has, with power to make or unmake the map south of the Rio Grande and even to do so with the blessings of Europe, the rights of Latin America would have suffered profoundly.

But this relative prudence has not vitiated the change of form of the Monroe Doctrine which makes it not the old powerful and unilateral declaration of the early days, but a real program of action which permitted the presidents of the United States to dictate rules for American international politics and even national political rules to apply to other countries. Thus the Caribbean has come to be considered as a *mare nostrum*. The United States has come to regard the Monroe Doctrine, thus transformed, as backing those other policies—trade follows the flag, and dollar diplomacy.

Thus Wilson and Taft on the one hand and Lodge and Knox on the other, since they speak of different periods of the Monroe Doctrine, are both right when one maintains that the League of Nations will maintain the Doctrine intact and the others contend that the opposite is true.

Discussing the question of the League, if the United States, having helped to break the balance of power in Europe by defeating Germany, should remain outside the alliance of the victorious nations, her isolation will not mean her strength but her weakness. The obligations of the Monroe Doctrine would not then be carried against a divided Europe, but before an alliance of states victorious on sea and land. It is not easy to prophesy the difficulties of the future, but it can be seen that the mission assumed by the United States will be full of difficulties, as it has in the past. To share jointly these responsibilities should mean the obviating of conflicts or diminishing the possibility of conflicts which may take place not in Europe but in the tranquil Americas.

On abandoning the rights of exclusive protection, she would be free of multiplied responsibilities and know that, if a conflict occurred, it would be concerning matters that affected her directly and not remotely. The principles of Washington and Monroe would have passed through a complete evolution and become the admitted principles of all humanity, not simply the canons of American law.

The Monroe Doctrine could thus become the doctrine of the world. Only the aspirations of conquest which make of the doctrine of defense of the small nations of this continent an excuse for continual aggression approaching an American Prussianism, will have died forever.

But this wise and just solution of the Pan American *impassé* was not to be. A group of North Americans who appreciated the necessity of protecting their own prerogatives but not those of any other nations, insisted on the Covenant of the League making specific acknowledgment that, while all the nations of the world would surrender all special privileges and rights of interference with their neighbors, the United States must still have the special privilege of determining the course of national development in the western hemisphere. So the following was inserted as Article XXI, of the Covenant:

Nothing in this covenant shall be deemed to affect the validity of international engagements such as treaties of arbitration or regional understandings like the Monroe Doctrine, for securing the maintenance of peace.

If this article had gone further and defined the Monroe Doctrine as not giving the United States any special privileges on the American continent, but meaning, as President Wilson had intimated, that every people should be left free to determine its own policy, there could have been no objection. But this was not done. And so at one stroke the old situation was continued and made worse. For it looked as if this was a move to have the whole world agree to leave with the United States the determination of all American questions. And, of course, if the Hispanic American nations signed the covenant, they themselves became guarantors of an arrangement which those who insisted on the inclusion of this reservation stated to mean that the

United States would have the right to interfere in the national life of the other American nations whenever it deemed such a course expedient.

Here was Hispanic America's dilemma: If it stayed out of the League it lost the opportunity of being linked up with the only organization that offered to help the small nation. If it went in it signed a document which might mean its agreement to complete domination by its great northern neighbor. Hispanic America was much in the position of a man who is forced to borrow a certain sum of money to escape ruin, but who is asked to sign a note for an unknown amount in order to get the money. It leaves him in doubt as to whether he is to be ruined now or later.

This was what led little Salvador to direct a note to our Department of State asking for a definition of the Monroe Doctrine. This note, in the first place, recites that despite its neutrality in the war, Salvador manifested "its sympathy on every occasion for the ideals which animated the Government of the United States in entering the war", praises President Wilson for "having crystallized the legitimate hopes of a fruitful peace by submitting the draft of a League of Nations covenant", says Salvador, "manifests the desire to adhere to this treaty which sanctions arbitration as the only method of settling disputes between nations", and continues:

The whole text of the treaty is both suggestive and attractive. In it there is a return to those principles of life long awaited by sociologists and publicists. And indeed it seems as if from the ruins of war there have arisen with greater strength and potency the beautiful gospels which in a moment of folly were relegated to the discard by those who through the immutable laws of international interdependence were especially charged with sustaining and upholding them.

The text of the treaty contains however, one article which has awakened warm discussions throughout the whole American continent including the United States, due no doubt to its brevity and lack of clearness. I refer to Article XXI, drafted in the following terms: Nothing in this covenant shall be deemed to affect the validity of international engagements, such as treaties of arbitration or regional understandings like the Monroe Doctrine, for securing the maintenance of peace.

The legal scope of this provision from an international viewpoint is open to differing interpretations, since in the vast scheme of the League of Nations treaties of arbitration and regional understandings, such as the Monroe Doctrine, are recognized and sanctioned, despite the fact that as to the highly peaceful purpose of the latter doctrine there does not exist harmonious meeting of minds nor an absolute criterion.

From the year 1823, in which the distinguished James Monroe rejected all intervention by European nations in the affairs of the American continent to the present day, this doctrine has undergone different applications depending upon the diverse political tendencies prevailing at that particular time in the United States.

It would be unnecessary, Mr. Secretary, to undertake any detailed exposition of the various views of prominent thinkers and public men of the United States as to the genuine and correct interpretation of the Monroe Doctrine, which former Secretary of State Elihu Root regarded as "a declaration based on the right of the people of the United States to protect itself as a nation, and which could not be transformed into a declaration, joint or common, to all the nations of America or even to a limited number of them".

My Government recognizes that the Monroe Doctrine consolidated the independence of the Continental States of Latin America, and saved them from the great danger of a European intervention. It realises that it is a powerful factor in the existence of the democratic form of government on this continent and that it raises a barrier to European colonization.

Since, however, the covenant of the League of Nations does not set forth nor determine the purposes nor fix a definite criterion of international relationship in America, and since, on the other hand, the doctrine will be forthwith transformed—in view of the full sanction of the nations of the world—into a principle of universal public law, *juris et de jure*, I request that your Excellency will be good enough to give the authentic interpretation of the Monroe Doctrine as it is understood in the present historical moment and in its future application by the Government of the United States, which must realize that my Government is keenly desirous of securing a statement which shall put an end to the divergence of views now prevailing on the subject, which it is recognized by all is not the most propitious in stimulating the ideals of true Pan Americanism.

Contrary to the authorized and respected view of former Secretary of State Root, the Monroe Doctrine through its inclusion in the covenant of the League of Nations will be converted without doubt into a genesis of American international law.

Since any amendment to the text of the treaty and even the rejection of all of its provisions by the American Senate would still leave intact the various points which this international agreement covers as to the other signatory nations, by virtue of their general and expressed acceptance, the principle embraced in the League of Nations, and therefore the Monroe Doctrine, would be virtually accepted as a fundamental principle of public American law by all those countries that signed or manifested their adherence to the Peace Treaty.

The necessity of an interpretation of the genesis and scope of the Monroe Doctrine not only in the development of the lofty purpose of Pan Americanism, but in order that that Doctrine may maintain its original purity and prestige, is rendered all the more urgent.

Even before El Salvador had written its now famous note to the Department of State, Ex-president Bonilla of Honduras, who represented his country at the Peace Conference, presented to that body the following communication:

In this covenant all peoples represented in this Conference are directly interested; the smaller nations, like that which I represent, more if possible than the greater ones. Its bases, as expressed by the Commission, are not known; but the public press has asserted that amendments have been proposed: among these a proposal by the delegation of North America, to declare that "the pact shall not affect the validity of other international conventions such as the arbitration treaties or regional understandings, like the Monroe Doctrine, to assure the maintenance of peace".

The Monroe Doctrine affects the Latin American republics directly. As it has never been written into an international document, nor been expressly accepted by the nations of the Old Continent, nor of the New World; and as it has been defined and applied in different manners by presidents and other statesmen of the United States of America, I believe that it is necessary that in the pact about to be subscribed it should be defined with entire clearness, in such way that it may be incorporated in the written international law.

The North American delegation is presided over by the Honorable Woodrow Wilson, and it is certain that if the Monroe Doctrine was not defined the delegation had in mind the definition of interpretation that Mr. Wilson, as President of the United States, has given to it in his various addresses from that which he voiced at Mobile 'in 1913 to the last in the current year. In these he declared that the Doctrine is not a menace, but is a guaranty for the feeblest of the nations of America; and he repudiated expressly the interpretations that had been made to signify that the United States had a right to exercise a kind of tutelage over the other republics of America.

Especially in his discourse with the Mexican journalists on June 7th, 1919, he declared that the guaranty that this Doctrine implied in favor of the feeble countries is not with relation to the powers of the Old World only, but relates to the United States also; and that he spoke of the celebration of a Pan American pact that might be realized and might include this point. Such declarations have made President Wilson the best of the exponents of the ideals of the peoples of Latin America.

All these facts induce me to present the accompanying proposition, which I hope will merit a favorable reception by the delegation of the United States, and will be supported by the Latin American republics, which with it will pay their tribute of admiration and respect to the First Magistrate of the North American republic, that has given such proofs of its love of justice.

If the American amendment to which I referred is phrased in the terms published, or in others like them, the pact of the League of Nations will be no obstacle to a union or confederation of other form, by the peoples of Latin America, that will tend to a realization of the dream of the immortal Bolívar.

The clause which Dr. Bonilla offered as an addition to the proposed compact of the League of Nations may be translated as follows:

This Doctrine, that the United States of America has maintained since the year 1823, when it was proclaimed by President Monroe, signifies that: All the republics of America have a right to independent existence; that no nation may acquire by conquest any part of the territory of any of these nations, nor interfere with its internal government or administration, nor do any other act to impair its autonomy or to wound its national dignity. It is not to hinder the "Latin" American countries from confederating or in other forms uniting themselves, seeking the best way to realize their destiny.

The view taken generally in Hispanic America of the Salvadorean note is well illustrated by the following editorial utterance of *El Universal*, of Mexico City:

We published yesterday the Note addressed by the republic of El Salvador to the Secretary of State of the North American Union asking for an exact interpretation of the 21st article of the protocol of the League of Nations, referring to the recognition of the Monroe Doctrine by the Latin American nations. It is a document of far-reaching importance.

On the appearance in 1823 of the Monroe Doctrine, it had the character, as has been expressed by the eminent Chilean statesman, Don Alejandro Alvarez, of a sort of gospel of the New World. President Monroe, according to Alvarez, though taking his stand exclusively on the interests of his own country, in his famous message to Congress summarized and expressed admirably and clearly the political situation and aspirations of the whole New World. Circumstances then obtaining in Europe made some such declaration urgent. There was a controversy on between Russia and England over the boundaries of their possessions in America; and besides—and graver still—the countries signatory to the Holy Alliance were suspected of the purpose of coming to the help of Spain for reconquering her lost American colonies. When, therefore, the United States proclaimed its affirmation that the New World ought to be governed by republican organizations, and that all the countries on this side are free and equal, as relates to Europe, the independence of the bourgeoning republics was assured—an attitude on the part of the Northern Republic which cannot fail to meet with the goodwill of the other countries.

Up to that point, and for the reasons set forth, the Monroe Doctrine could not be considered a particular expression of the sentiments of the United States; it was rather the crystallization in international relations of the aspirations of all America. But since then, as the various countries of the continent have gone forward in their evolution, the Latin republics have not always moved harmoniously with the United States —nor even with one another. Thus it has come about that while some publicists consider the Monroe Doctrine as a sort of tacit agreement among all the American nations for warding off the occupation of territory by Europe, or its active intervention in American affairs, there are others who have come to believe that the only thing the United States had in view in promulgating the Doctrine was to substitute their own intervention for that of Europe in the affairs of the other nations of this continent, and, in that connection, it has not yet been settled whether acts of imperialism, deliberately engaged in by the United States against the sovereignty of Latin American republics, are or are not subject to regulation by the Monroe Doctrine.

It is a state of things which has resulted in many misunderstandings. We do not know, really, what to think; as, in view of diverse and even contrary interpretations by different statesmen, the Monroe Doctrine or "Monroeism" has become something extremely foggy and obscure. It is to this fact that is due the lack of confidence in it on the part of the Latin republics; to this, and to nothing else, was due the statement on the part of our Government recently that it did not recognize that Doctrine.

President Wilson himself seemed to justify that want of confidence when he suggested in his address to the Mexican editors in June, 1919, that all the Latin American countries should undertake a revision of that Doctrine and should come to an agreement that would put the question of their independence outside the danger of any imperialistic encroachment. If thus the very author of the League of Nations admitted less than a year before that it was only natural that the Monroe Doctrine should inspire some want of confidence in Latin America, as not being a real community pact, how can those nations, which have not yet been called into the consultation, adhere to the League of Nations in which the Monroe Doctrine is explicitly recognized?

As we see the matter, El Salvador has put a finger on the sore spot, as the saying goes, in this most complicated matter of American politics. Will its note bring about a general revision, a Pan American revision such as Wilson intimated, of the Monroe Doctrine? Unless some such thing happens, we do not see how the Latin American nations can sign a compact, such as that of the League of Nations, unless some light can be thrown on a matter that so profoundly concerns their interests.

The framing of a reply to Salvador taxed the ingenuity of our Department of State. But a way out was happily found by a simple citation of the address of President Wilson before the Second Pan American Scientific Congress, where the President had discussed the Monroe Doctrine as follows:

The Monroe Doctrine was proclaimed by the United States on her own authority. It has always been maintained, and always will be maintained, upon her own responsibility.   But the Monroe Doctrine demanded merely that European governments should not attempt to extend their political systems to this side of the Atlantic.   It did not disclose the use which the United States intended to make of her power on this side of the Atlantic.   It was a hand held up in warning, but there was no promise in it of what America was going to do with the implied and partial protectorate which she apparently was trying to set up on this side of the water, and I believe you will sustain me in the statement that it has been fears and suspicions on this score which have hitherto prevented the greater intimacy and confidence and trust between the Americas.   The states of America have not been certain what the United States would do with her power.   That doubt must be removed.   And latterly there has been a very frank interchange of views between the authorities in Washington and those who represented the other states of this hemisphere, an interchange of views charming and hopeful, because based upon an increasingly sure appreciation of the spirit in which they were undertaken.   These gentlemen have seen that, if America is to come into her own, into her legitimate own, in a world of peace and order, she must establish the foundations of amity, so that no one will hereafter doubt them.

I hope and believe that this can be accomplished.   These conferences have enabled me to foresee how it will be accomplished.   It will be accomplished, in the first place, by the states of America uniting in guaranteeing to each other absolute political independence and territorial integrity.   In the second place, and as a necessary corollary to that, guaranteeing the agreement to settle all pending boundary disputes as soon as possible and by amicable process; by agreeing that all disputes among themselves, should they unhappily arise, will be handled by patient, impartial investigation and settled by arbitration; and the agreement necessary to the peace of the Americas, that no state of either continent will permit revolutionary expeditions against another state to be fitted out on its territory, and that they will prohibit the exportations of munitions of war for the purpose of supplying revolutionists against neighboring governments.

This reply was received by Salvador with diplomatic expressions of appreciation, but that country's leaders, as well as those of other Hispanic American countries, recognize that the sentiments expressed by one of our presidents before a scientific gathering cannot be considered as an authoritative and binding definition of any fundamental policy like the Monroe Doctrine. They want rather a declaration in which the executive and legislative branches of the government, after a discussion which allowed public opinion to express itself, would officially state the position of the nation.

The following words of Señor A. de Manos-Albas, written a few years ago in the English *Review of Reviews*, still remain true:

The means to accomplish unity of sentiment and to dispel the misgivings between the United States and Latin America is not far to seek. It is only required to amplify the Monroe Doctrine to the full extent of its logical development. . . . . If the United States should declare that the era of conquest on the American continent has been closed to all and forever, beginning with themselves, the brooding storm of distrust will disappear from the Latin American mind, and an international cordiality of incalculable possibilities will ensue, not only for the welfare of the American nations, but universally for the cause of freedom and democracy.

At this writing the United States is in a most peculiar position. Having insisted upon inserting the Monroe Doctrine clause into the Covenant, a clause in which no other nation in the world was interested and to which many were opposed, the United States finds itself the only nation of consequence out of the League. The Hispanic American countries were so enthusiastic for the League idea that fourteen out of twenty of them signed, with the Monroe Doctrine clause and all, almost without debate. The United States was expected to join as well. Most of these countries followed the United States into the war and they all thought they were going with that country into the League. Now they are awakening to the fact that their supposed leader is not with them, and the situation is a bit disconcerting to some of them.

The situation reminds one of an incident in the French Revolution when a group of politicians sat discussing matters of state. A great mob rushed by the building. One of the group jumped to his feet, ran to the door and exclaimed, "There go my people. I must hurry and follow them, for I am their leader!"

The complaisant North American may smile at the mention

of the possibility of our losing our position of dominance on this continent, but the present situation at least suggests the development of a condition which will unite the rest of America with Europe rather than with us.   It is easy to note that among Hispanic Americans there is great confusion over the situation, and some frankly say that the present division may mean a final separation of the Hispanic American countries from North America. Commenting on the presidential election in the United States, *La Nación*, of Buenos Aires, a paper which all during the war ardently supported the United States, said:

Confronted with the dilemma of abandoning either the League of Nations or the Monroe Doctrine, the Latin American countries probably would choose to abandon the latter.   Many people in the United States have believed that the various South American countries, members of the League, would withdraw in order to follow the policy inspired by the United States, and contrary, naturally, to the League. . . .

The declaration on the Monroe Doctrine Senator Harding made to the correspondent of *La Nación* hardly seems an adequate cause for the South American members of the League to abandon it.   In effect Senator Harding told our correspondent that the Monroe Doctrine was not an international pact or agreement but a declaration of policy by the United States which promised protection against abuses or aggressions by European nations, precisely an interpretation which causes the greatest resistance from most, if not all, of these countries, and which is contrary to the interpretation President Wilson has given, according to which the Doctrine established among the American nations a most perfect equality—an equality that cannot exist if the question of protection that is not asked is the product entirely of the one-sided resolution of a power declaring itself the protector against dangers in which no one believes.

If the United States does not form part of the League, these southern countries will find themselves in a different camp from the United States, having acquired a special status in relation to other members of the League, and will be forced to consider the United States as a factor to some extent foreign to the development of their peaceful policy. This surely will not be satisfactory either to them or to us, in view of the sincere desire of both parties that an accord shall exist between the two sections of the continent.

This reported interview with President Harding raises an important question concerning the Monroe Doctrine about which there is absolute difference of opinion. The President is reported as intimating that the Doctrine is not to be considered as an international agreement, but solely as a declaration of the United States, maintained by the power of the United States. Secretary Root, already quoted, also said that it would under no circumstances become a joint agreement.

But President Roosevelt said, in an address at Rio de Janeiro:

All the nations which are sufficiently advanced, such as Brazil and the United States, should participate on an absolute equality in the responsibilities and development of this doctrine so far as the interests of the western hemisphere as a whole are concerned. It must be made a continental and not a unilateral doctrine. . . . If ever, as regards any country, intervention does unfortunately become necessary, I hope that wherever possible it will be a joint intervention by such powers as Brazil and the United States, without the thought of self-aggrandizement by any of them, and for the common good of the western world.

As has already been shown, President Wilson accepted the same idea of the Monroe Doctrine being extendable not only to all America but to the whole world. In this same spirit were his words in addressing Congress December 7, 1915, when he said:

There was a time in the early days of our great nation and of the republics fighting their way to independence in Central and South America, when the government of the United States looked upon itself as in some sort the guardian of the republics to the south of her as against any encroachments or efforts at political control from the other side of the water; felt it its duty to play the part even without invitation from them; and I think that we can claim that the task was undertaken with a true and disinterested enthusiasm for the freedom of the Americas and the unmolested self-government of her independent peoples. But it was always difficult to maintain such a rôle without offense to the pride of the peoples whose freedom of action we sought to protect, and without provoking serious misconceptions of our motives, and every thoughtful man of affairs must welcome the altered circumstances of the new day in whose light we now stand, when there is no claim of guardianship or thought of wards, but, instead, a full and honorable association as of partners between ourselves and our neighbors, in the interest of all America, north and south.

It is this spirit faithfully carried out that will make all Hispanic America join with us in the support of the Monroe Doctrine and be at one with us in building a continental solidarity. The following comment by *La Prensa*, of Buenos Aires, on this message is expressive of the way all Hispanic America responds to such sentiment:

There has been a gradual and continuous change in the American policy toward the republics of this continent. These changes have been coincident with the visits of prominent Americans to South America, with the result that a better knowledge of the state of civilization which has been reached by South Americans has become more general. This has been the principal cause of the gradual transformation. The Monroe Doctrine is now essentially modified. It is necessary that it should no longer have the character of tutelage that it had at the time of its origin, but it must undergo an evolution toward Pan Americanism.

No higher, more fundamental, more authoritative utterance has been made on the subject that that embodied in President Wilson's message. President Wilson made his statement without reserve and with sincerity, showing that it was the result of serene reflection. According to President Wilson, Monroeism will be a means of defense of this continent, but all the American states will be members of the international community, the United States having the same sovereign rank as the others.

President Wilson's message will be as transcendent as was President Monroe's, both being in accord with regard to solidarity, but differing in regard to the conception of circumstances. President Wilson's program does not lack anything necessary to the high development of ideals.

Let all America then unite in supporting the Monroe Doctrine, and when all have gone into a World League of Nations, let a sub-division of that league act as the American League, suggested by Bolivar in 1826 and by Wilson in 1917, to promote peace and mutual prosperity among all American nations.

Dr. Baltasar Brum, President of Uruguay, in an address before the University students of the capital of his country, has suggested this League of American Nations in the following important declarations:

Owing to the state in which European countries remain after the struggle, it may be said that fear of invasion by them in America has been removed for many years. But is that sufficient reason for us to take no interest in the future and turn away from the Monroe Doctrine with the pretext that it is now unnecessary? I believe that today, more than ever, we should use foresight in searching for formulas that may assure forever the peace and full independence of American countries.

The principles of American solidarity, based on the constitution of a continental league, is more ample than the Monroe Doctrine, because it will not only defend the countries of America against foreign invaders but also against imperialistic tendencies which might arise among themselves.

The formation of this league, in my opinion, would be a logical consequence of the Treaty of Versailles, which, in recognizing and expressly accepting the Monroe Doctrine, seems to be desirous of limiting its field of action, so far as American affairs are concerned. On the other hand, the Supreme Council of the League of Nations is composed principally of the delegates of the great powers, nearly all the American countries having been excluded. These countries need, therefore, to create a powerful organization to look after their interests in the decisions arrived at by the League of Nations. Harmonious and joint action by the "American League" would avoid European intervention in our affairs.

Some have objected to this League of American Nations because they fear it would become a rival to the World League. But there seems to be no reason why such a league would not really strengthen the world league by assuring its unanimous support by all American nations. These nations would naturally discuss beforehand the questions to come before the League and decide upon the attitude of all the American nations. Indeed it could easily and profitably develop into a kind of sub-committee of the committee of the whole, to consider purely American matters. By such a relationship the American nations could settle their own questions, but with the double advantage that these smaller nations would have some final appeal in case of absolute injustice by the one American power that is easily able to impose its will on all the rest of the continent; also the cis-Atlantic nations would be enabled to have direct touch with the American nations in working toward the peace and prosperity of the world at large.

We are today in the midst of one of those great world epochs when all relations with and inheritances from the past are in flux. The best of the past must be readjusted, reformed, redefined to contribute to the future—the new day, which, whether, we like it or not, is different from the old.

The Monroe Doctrine has been the greatest influence on the American continent for preserving the republican form of government. It is today neither an "obsolete shibboleth" nor an "international impertinence", if understood in the original and true sense. There is no question that the Doctrine has been made to cover a multitude of sins, political and commercial, and is abused by North American jingoes. The wrong appeal to and interpretation of the Doctrine has developed among the Hispanic American peoples a prejudice against it, and among the statesmen of the south an insistent demand for a definition of its present application. If we can be big enough to put ourselves in the place of our southern neighbors we must acknowledge that they have a right to a clear understanding of how far the Doctrine means "America for the Americans" and how far it means "America for the North Americans". If we are to retain our leadership in America and in the world in this new age when the rights of the small nation and the common man are the concern of all and when a righteous peace in the world is the pearl of great price for which all else may be sacrificed, we will turn toward world friendship rather than shrivel into a Prussian nationalism.

And if we are honest, as we believe we are, in our contention that, as Secretary Root said, "We wish for no victories but those of peace, for no territory except our own", and as Roosevelt said, "This Doctrine has nothing to do with the commercial relations of any American powers save that it in truth allows each of them to form such as it desires", and, as President Wilson said, "Let us have a common guarantee that all of us will sign, an agreement of political independence and territorial integrity"—if we really mean these things, let us make them so clear and so authoritative that our worst enemies cannot but admit that our relations with Hispanic America are guided, as John Hay said they were with China, by the open door and the golden rule, and that the Monroe Doctrine is the simple expression of our commitment to the principles of American democracy, developed without outside interference, and of our willingness to give the last drop of our blood for its defense.

SAMUEL GUY INMAN.

FRENCH VIEWS OF THE MONROE DOCTRINE AND THE MEXICAN EXPEDITION

From the beginning of its history, the United States has followed more or less consciously a policy of isolation. This tendency, noticeable as early as 1780 in the statements of Thomas Pownall, John Adams, and others, was continued by Washington, Jefferson, Adams, and Madison, until it found more definite expression in the famous statement of Monroe in 1823. This state of affairs was early recognized in Europe, as well; but however much the separation of the American continent in policy and in fact may have been appreciated by European statesmen, they have ever been careful to give it as little formal recognition as possible.

It was only in the United States, then, that the converse of our isolation policy—that of European aloofness—took shape. One phase of the doctrine, however, was as natural and inevitable as the other; and in order to impress on Europe our convictions as to the separation of the two hemispheres, it became necessary to formulate and state the further idea that it was the natural province of the United States, as the leading American power, to keep Europe from altering conditions in America. So it came about that the United States asserted its self-assumed authority as the natural guardian of the western hemisphere on a number of occasions. And it has been this phase of the policy which has given rise to a uniformly hostile attitude of European states, no less hostile because it has been for the most part latent or potential.

European unwillingness to accept our protective authority in the New World, or even in North America, has been displayed on practically every occasion when such an attitude could be shown to the possible advantage of European interests. Any indulgence or respect which has been displayed toward our traditional policy has been due to European rivalries and preoccupation elsewhere, or to the vigorous and easily-displayed strength of the United States, or, more particularly, to the Atlantic Ocean—the factor which first prompted our isolation policy and which has more than any other single thing made its continuation possible.

Now and then some particular issue has focused the attention of one power or another on the status in the New World and elicited a storm of criticism and disapproval in the foreign press. It is, of course, impossible to cite here the particular attitude of European states toward this characteristic policy of the United States in each specific instance where definite issues have been raised. The armed invasion of Mexico by the French, however, is a striking case in point, which offers a good opportunity for the study of European attitude toward the jealous American doctrine, not only because this was the only thorough violation of the Monroe Doctrine, but also because it was instituted by a combination of the three European colonizing Powers; England, France, and Spain. Moreover, it was no accident that the year 1861, when the United States was in the midst of a terrible civil struggle, was chosen for the only successful attempt ever made by a foreign state to plant a colony in America against the will of an Hispanic American state.

In this instance, the causes of intervention were many and confused, beginning with the Mexican revolt from Spain in 1821. From that time there had been internal war and anarchy in Mexico. For a number of years a contest raged between two parties, styled Liberals and Clericals. In that civil war, considerable damage was suffered by subjects of foreign nations, and notably by French, English, and Spanish nationals. Claims for damage in each case mounted high. England complained because of the long mistreatment of its subjects and the denial of the usual privileges to its diplomatic representatives. Besides the British Legation at Vera Cruz had been seized and rifled of a sum of £150,000 on November 16, 1860. Spain was wroth because the government of the Juárez faction, having the upper hand in 1861, refused to recognize a Spanish treaty of 1859 made with the then *de facto* government, whereby the validity of certain long-standing Spanish claims had been recognized. To that had been added the expulsion of the Spanish minister later.[1]

The claim of France for reparation rested on supposed injuries to French subjects, culminating in the refusal of the Juárez government to honor the so-called Jecker bonds, which one of the many factional leaders, Miramon, had issued before his defeat and deposition somewhat earlier. Juárez agreed to repay the 5 per cent ($750,000), which had been advanced by France in cash, but refused to pay the face value of the bonds, which amounted to $15,000,000. The determination to press this unjust claim (Jecker was, moreover, a Swiss banker, naturalized in France under unusual conditions) led to the only instance where France offered a greater threat to the Monroe Doctrine than any other European power.[2] And France appears to have had the weakest case against Mexico of any of the injured powers in 1861.[3]

The first phase of the intervention was not wholly unreasonable. Having failed to receive satisfaction from separate presentation of their claims, the three powers formed a triple alliance at London, October 31, 1861, wherein they vowed that,

> The high contracting parties engage not to seek for themselves, in the employment of the coercive measures contemplated by the present Convention, any acquisition of territory, nor any special advantage, and not to exercise in the internal affairs of Mexico any influence of a nature to prejudice the right of the Mexican nation to choose and to constitute freely the form of its Government.[4]

This pledge was kept by Spain and England, which at first coöperated with France in preparing a punitive expedition. A triple fleet, loaded with troops and commanded by a Spanish General (Prim), sailed for Mexico and prepared to bombard

[1] Daniel Antokolets, *La Doctrine de Monroe et l'Amérique Latine*, p. 38; Hector Petin, *Les États-Unis et la Doctrine de Monroe*, p. 167.

[2] M. de Barral-Montferrat, *De Monroë à Roosevelt*, p. 95.

[3] Petin, *op. cit.*, p. 167; a quite different view.

[4] *British and Foreign State Papers*, LI, 947. *Cf.* also Petin, *op. cit.*, p. 175; and Maurice D. Beaumarchais, *La Doctrine de Monroe, l' Évolution de la Politique des États-Unis au XIXe Siecle*, p. 80.

Vera Cruz. In view of the fleet, the *de facto* government asked to treat, offering to pay all the indemnities which had been asked and to give security for the execution of the agreement. England and Spain declared themselves satisfied, and signed a Convention at Soledad February 19, 1862, which brought their action to an end.[5]

However, the French plenipotentiary, Admiral Gravière, refused to sign, maintaining that the indemnities offered were insufficient, and demanding the entire redemption of the Jecker bonds. This furnished a pretext, at least, for further French action.[6] Hostilities were commenced shortly after by the French forces, while the government complained bitterly of the "violation" of the treaty of 1861 by its allies.[7]

France had from the first intended to seize Mexico, if possible, regardless of the attitude of Europe, the United States, or Hispanic America. Shortly after the expedition had begun, Napoleon III informed his military commander that he would need to remain in Mexico in order to assist those Mexicans who might desire a strong government, and added that it would be prudent if the two governments (England and Spain) did not discourage those efforts which might be attempted by the country to extricate itself from the anarchy into which it was plunged.[8]

The French lawyer and historian Petin states that it was obviously to the interests of both England and France to see a strong government set up in Mexico which would be favorably disposed toward them; the more so if the Confederate States won, for then there would be a desire on the part of both North and South to compensate themselves in Mexico. Also he states an European policy for America, by saying:

Such an event could not be looked upon with indifference by England and by France, and the principal obstacle which could prevent its ac-

[5] Antokoletz, *op. cit.*, p. 39.
[6] *Ibid.*, p. 39 f.
[7] Barral-Montferrat, *op. cit.*, p. 95.
[8] Beaumarchais, *La Doctrine de Monroe*, p. 80.

complishment would be the reconstitution of Mexico by a government strong enough to stop internal dissolution; but the elements of a strong government do not exist in Mexico.[9]

Petin reiterates that the sole French motive in this intervention was to see anarchy succeeded by a stable government, at the same time recognizing the infringement of such an attempt on the Monroe Doctrine.

Other motives are, however, confessed by some French authorities, though all have constantly held that the Mexican enterprise was something of an errand of kindness. For instance:

Napoleon wished to oppose to the supremacy of the Anglo-Saxon race in America, as in Europe, a formidable union of Latin peoples; he began to see the need of an expedition from abroad to assist the realization of these policies. . . .

Also the French Government was brought to conceive the grandiose idea, that if she should succeed, she would be in conformity with the voices of the Mexican people—to make of Mexico otherwise a French colony, or at least, a kind of French protectorate.[10]

The Emperor had discerned all that the Monroe Doctrine contained of anti-Europeanism. He had seen that the declaration of the fifth President of the United States was nothing else than a declaration of war on the Old World, and he wished to show America that Europe had taken up the challenge. . . .

Napoleon was a dreamer. . . . . He had adopted the principle of nationalities in his European policy. . . . He wished a federation of Latin races opposed to the federation of Anglo-Saxon peoples.[11]

Napoleon himself stated his motives in continuing his aggression in Mexico in a letter, dated July 3, 1863, to General Forey, commanding the French troops in Mexico. Among other things, he said:

Thus, France has extended her beneficent influence into the center of America. . . . It is, in fine, military honor, political exigencies,

[9] Petin, *op. cit.*, pp. 166, 175.
[10] Beaumarchais, *op. cit.*, p. 80.
[11] Petin, *op. cit.*, p. 186.

industrial and commercial interests, which have imposed the obligation of marching on the capital of Mexico.[12]

According to French writers, Napoleon III was originally not alone in his intentions to flout the Monroe Doctrine and set up a new régime in Mexico. To quote:

That which they did not write into the treaty (the London Convention) they mutually said, however, in their despatches and exchanges of views, which was that they hoped that the presence of the allied forces would inspire the sane part of the (Mexican) nation to set up those institutions most conducive to the reëstablishment in the country of the order and security needed. . . . They believed that the . . . country would never be pacified in a definite fashion except by an authority more firm and stable than that of divers presidents, who deposed each other time after time every two or three years. In consequence, they would see with pleasure the adoption by Mexico of a monarchical constitution and would give her for a sovereign any prince belonging to the ruling families of Europe.[13]

This desire for intervention, however, is partly justified by the statement that,

This desire for intervention was in a certain measure warranted by the anarchical condition in Mexico, which in 40 years had had 73 presidents and had modified its form of government 36 times.[14]

Article 4 of the Convention of 1861 provided for inviting the United States to join in the Mexican affair. Secretary of State Seward refused the joint invitation on the ground of United States traditional policy and sympathy for Mexico. In this connection, Petin remarks:

That reflection of the Secretary of State was clearly useless; every one knows, since the war that they have waged against Mexico, that they eagerly desire its annexation.[15]

[12] Cepedes, *La Doctrina de Monroe*, p. 278 f.; cf. also, Antokolets, *op. cit.*, pp. 42-3.

[13] Barral-Montferrat, *op. cit.*, p. 92.

[14] Beaumarchais, *op. cit.*, p. 80, note.

[15] *Op. cit.*, p. 180.

The French thought the United States would have bitterly opposed any project of reparation whatever, had not its hands been tied by war, pointing out that this country had strongly protested to Spain in 1858 when that country was meditating single action against Mexico. The statement of the United States government to the contrary apparently was not convincing.[16]

As a final answer to the invitation of the powers, Seward said on December 4, 1861:

It is true that the United States have on their part claims against Mexico. Meanwhile, after mature reflection, the President is convinced that it would be inopportune at the moment to actually seek to obtain satisfaction by adhering to the Convention. Among the reasons which have led to this decision are these: In the first place, the United States prefer, as far as is practicable, to hold to the traditional policy which has been their legacy from the father of their country; a policy of which experience has shown the happy effects, and which keeps them from forming alliances with foreign nations. In the second place, Mexico is a neighbor of the United States; her system of government resembles ours in many respects. The United States, then, have naturally benevolent sentiments for that Republic, and are interested in her security, her prosperity and her welfare".[17]

In addition to a refusal to sign, the United States attempted to relieve the pressure by backing Mexico financially, proposing to guarantee the interest on the Mexican debt. This was rejected by the European alliance. "The claims of European countries were too strong to be satisfied by guarantees."[18]

But before the occupation of Mexico had begun, the government of France had decided to overturn that of Mexico. A future Mexican prince, Archduke Maximilian of Austria, had even been chosen, who was deemed acceptable to England and Spain as he was to France.[19] The French persuaded themselves that they were acting in as unselfish a manner as when in 1829,

[16] *Ibid.*, p. 178.
[17] Henry Wheaton, *Elements of International Law*, p. 349.
[18] Beaumarchais, *op. cit.*, p. 82; Petin, *op. cit.*, p. 182.
[19] Barral-Montferrat, *op. cit.*, pp. 93–4; Petin, *op. cit.*, p. 175.

France, England, and Russia had helped to liberate Greece
and had placed on the new throne a prince from a country not
participating. The only concession to be made to American
traditions was indicated by an intimate friend of Napoleon's,
Michel Chevalier, who remarked in 1862:

> For a republic which is nominal and derisive, there will be substituted
> a monarchical system, but a monarchy perfectly independent, and as
> liberal as possible.[20]

Following the withdrawal of England and Spain from the
Mexican project, the work of the French went merrily on. The
French government alternately complained of the "desertion"
of its allies and asked for their moral support. This desertion
was not prompted entirely by the satisfaction of their claims
in Mexico, and certainly not by sympathy with the views of the
United States. England had commercial interests which it
conceived would be advanced by withdrawing from the affair.
Spain turned its attention to the reconquest of Santo Domingo,
which was as much a violation of the Monroe Doctrine as the
Mexican venture itself. Ignoring an emphatic protest from
the United States, the Spanish officially proclaimed Santo
Domingo "reannexed", though the attempt to hold the island
in subjection proved too much and the project was entirely
abandoned in 1865 with the partial recovery of the American
Union.[21]

Meanwhile, the French under General Forey had entered
Mexico City on June 10, 1863. By decree a provisional government was established, consisting of 35 notables. These named a
triumvirate of Mexican citizens, charged with the exercise of
executive powers, to convoke an assembly of 205 notables, who
should decide the future of the Mexican government.[22]

The Assembly which had these powers represented only a
small part of the entire nation. However, it drew up a constitu-

[20] M. Chevalier. L'Expedition europenne au Mexique", in *Revue des Deux
Mondes*, Apr. 1, 1862, p. 514. *Cf.* also the article by Mazade, "La Guerre de Mexique et les puissances europennes", in the same journal for August 1, 1862.

[21] *Cf.* A. B. Hart, *The Monroe Doctrine, An Interpretation*, p. 151.

[22] Petin, *op. cit.*, p. 188.

tion providing for a limited monarchy, and designated Maximilian of Austria as Emperor. This arrangement was validated by a plebiscite, held under the auspices of the French army.[23]

Maximilian, believing himself regularly chosen, reluctantly accepted the position. He arrived in Mexico City, June 12, 1864, and was immediately recognized by most of the European powers. At the same time, a convention was signed whereby the expenses of the French expedition were to be paid by the new monarchy; and arrangements were made for the temporary establishment in Mexico of 25,000 French troops, 8,000 of whom were to remain permanently.[24] Thus was inaugurated the new government which was to have been "perfectly independent, and as liberal as possible".

At no time was there any doubt in French minds as to the violation of the Monroe Doctrine.

The Treaty of London had violated the Monroe Doctrine. If a monarchy were set up under a European prince, it would be still more menacing. To remove that danger, the United States should have subscribed to the Treaty of London, and abandoned, as in 1850 (in the Clayton-Bulwer Treaty), the principles of their foreign policy and practice with the Powers. They would then have the right to intervene and collect their own damages.[25]

That the French may have been acting under some serious misconceptions in undertaking the Mexican project in the belief that they might secure the consent, if not the aid, of the Confederate States, appears from historical comment later.

The North was of the Anglo-Saxon race, which was accustomed through its origin to liberty. It was Protestant in religion, largely Puritan. For the development of industries, it had adopted a protective tariff. The population of the South, on the contrary, had the traditions of autocracy. They were partly Catholic, and belonged to the Latin race. Moreover, the South was a country of great culture, and

[23] Barral-Montferrat, op. cit., p. 97; Beaumarchais, op. cit., p. 179; Petin, op. cit., 188; Wheaton, op. cit., II, 362.

[24] Petin, op. cit., pp. 189–90.

[25] Ibid., p. 180. Cf. Antokolets, p. 40.

was anxious to exchange cotton for European goods. It was, in consequence, wedded to free trade.[26]

The delusion that the people of the south were Latin in sympathy, at least, was rudely terminated when the Confederate government was approached on the subject of a Franco-Confederate alliance against the North. This suggestion was summarily dismissed. A little later the United States government intercepted a letter which Benjamin, Secretary of State for the Confederacy, had addressed to Mr. Slidell, Confederate agent at Paris. In this letter, Benjamin showed the intrigues of the French government in Texas for keeping it from the Confederacy. The proofs for it were sufficient to have the French consul expelled from Galveston. Not only did the Emperor Napoleon have the design of retaining Mexico as a colony, but he desired to see a buffer state of little strength separate his new colony from the Confederate States.[27]

In the mean time, the government at Washington was unable to cope effectually with these events. Diplomatic protests were made on several occasions, but care was taken not to offend France seriously. It was necessarily assumed that the French were acting in good faith. The United States did not deny that France was justified in recovering satisfaction for losses. Secretary Cass is quoted as saying in September, 1860:

We do not deny to any European Power the right to take measures against Mexico for the reparation of damage caused. The Monroe Doctrine, altogether opposing the taking possession of any part of that country, is not opposed to the waging of hostile operations against that Republic for the satisfaction of certain substantial losses of which she has been the occasion.[28]

And Secretary Seward wrote in June, 1863:

France has the right to make war against Mexico and to arrange such affairs herself. We have the right and the interest to insist that France

[26] Barral-Montferrat, *op. cit.*, p. 86.
[27] Thomas J. Lawrence, *Principles of International Law*, II. 359 f. *Cf.* also, Beaumarchais, *op. cit.*, p. 84.
[28] Quoted in Antokolets, *op. cit.*, p. 40.

shall not profit by the war which she makes to establish in Mexico a government anti-Republican and anti-American, or for maintaining there any such government. . . .[29]

The United States consequently refused to recognize the Mexican Empire, and declared,

that the people of the United States have the firm conviction that progress is not possible in that part of the world except by means of political institutions identical with those of the states of the American continent,

and that the French-established monarchy was dangerous to the peace and happiness of the United States, as well as to its republican institutions.[30]

The French government did not interpret this as official resistance and continued its aggression. But in the same year, 1863, the Confederates were defeated at Gettysburg and at Vicksburg, and Federal authority was reëstablished in many of the states. Thereupon the North reaffirmed the principles of American tradition, and on April 4, 1864, the House of Representatives adopted this resolution:

The Congress of the United States does not by its silence intend to give the nations of the world the idea that it remains an indifferent spectator to the deplorable events which have actually taken place in Mexico. It deems it timely to declare that it is not suitable that the United States recognize a monarchical government, erected upon the ruins of a republican government in America, under the auspices of any European Power whatever.[31]

This resolution also was not taken seriously by the Napoleonic government, because consideration of it was postponed by the Senate. The *Moniteur* said,

It is known, moreover, that the Senate has indefinitely postponed consideration of that resolution, to which, in any case, the executive power would not give its consent.[32]

[29] Quoted in Beaumarchais, *op. cit.*, p. 83.
[30] Antokolets, p. 44.
[31] Lawrence, *op. cit.*, II. 365.
[32] *Archives Diplomatiques*, 1864, III. 78.

With the approaching end of the Civil War, the United States recompensed Juárez for his indomitable tenacity by recognizing his government, and in sending him arms and money, and the Senate ordained that correspondence to American consuls in Mexico should bear the insignia of the Mexican Republic. The surrender of the southern armies caused a veritable stupor among the Mexican imperialists. The world waited to see the United States act, and on May 22, 1865, Seward wrote to the American minister at Paris that attention would be immediately given to the matter of French status in Mexico.[33] This statement was followed by another on December 6, to the French minister at Washington, which clearly indicated the change in American attitude with the close of the war.[34]

The French government feigned not to understand the disguised menace in this note. It reiterated the free choice of Maximilian by the Mexican people, and tried to show that the United States was the real obstacle to Mexican freedom of action.[35] This was answered by the demand that French troops be recalled. There ensued a bitter controversy over the terms of evacuation, paralleled by unprincipled violence by both belligerents in Mexico. Finally, in the face of the most determined French opposition, Napoleon took steps to recall his forces, laying all the blame for the excesses in Mexico at the door of Maximilian. He no longer thought he had the same interest as three years earlier in making sacrifices to insure the Mexican crown to an Austrian prince. On January 22, 1866, Napoleon told the French chambers that "the only real object of the Powers had been to enforce the execution of the obligations contracted by that State (Mexico)".[36] This disinterested attitude found many incredulous, even in France. In December, 1866, Napoleon renounced a monarchical government and accepted a republic in Mexico, on the condition that the United States would maintain the government thus established. The

[33] Beaumarchais, op. cit., p. 88.

[34] Archives Diplomatiques, 1866, I. 394.

[35] Cf. the article by Keratry, "Le Mexique et les chances de salut du nouvel empire", in Revue des Deux Mondes, September 15, 1866.

[36] Petin, op. cit., p. 197.

last French troops were withdrawn March 13, 1867. Maximilian and his crumbling empire were left to their fate, and both soon perished.

A great discontent flamed up in France because of the hostile attitude of the United States and the ruinous expense of the expedition. This fiasco may be said to be at the bottom of the consistent opposition displayed by the French on subsequent occasions when the Doctrine was invoked, whether they were directly concerned or not. This attitude is well illustrated by the following quotation from the work of a recent French writer:

The Monroe Doctrine triumphed. The United States were going to place upon all independent America their heavy and arrogant hegemony. They were going to take the advantage for themselves of the deformed doctrine of 1823, for extorting, not more influence, but the sovereignty of Europe from her choicest colonies.[37]

The historian Beaumarchais says that with the Mexican episode the United States reached the parting of the ways. Before this time the American policy had been "America for Americans"; afterward it was "America for the United States"[38]; while Petin sums up the Doctrine under Roosevelt and his successors as "The world and America for the United States"![39]

HALFORD L. HOSKINS.

Tufts College, 1921.

[37] Barral-Montferrat, *De Monroë à Roosevelt, 1823–1905*, p. 100. *Cf.* in this connection, Lawrence, *op. cit.*, II. 361; and an article by Barclay in *Revue de Droit Internationale*, for June 2, 1866, 516 ff.

[38] *La Doctrine de Monroë*, p. 91.

[39] *Les États-Unis et la Doctrine de Monroë*, p. 445.

THE LIBERATION AND THE LIBERATORS OF SPANISH AMERICA

To understand something of that period of Spanish American history which is suggested by the subject of this paper, it will be necessary to journey back into the past some three hundred years and prepare a proper setting. We must turn back the scroll of history to that century of ocean chivalry in which bold buccaneers and care-free *conquistadores* sailed the Spanish Main and dared the cold and storm-tossed waters of far-off Cape Horn in order to unfurl on unknown shores the banners of their King. It was then that men followed the trail of the setting sun across the heaving bosom of untravelled seas in search of "El Dorado", the Golden Man,—of the mysterious regions of the far West.

It was an age in which the veins of men ran red wine and a mere handful of chosen spirits sufficed for the overthrow of a kingdom or for the subversion of an empire. Five hundred and fifty-three Spanish soldiers, with but fifteen muskets and thirty-two arquebuses among them, under Hernan Cortés overturned the mighty empire of Montezuma; and one hundred and sixty-four men of the same stern mold as the Spanish swineherd, Francisco Pizarro, enabled him to wrest from the vacillating hands of Atahualpa the sceptre over lands which the Inca chieftains had long ruled in utter disdain of those below them.

Balboa, Almagro, Cortés, Pizarro, and Valdivia were but the advance guard of a host of equally hardened and daring adventurers and, almost before the rest of the world had time to realize the trend of events, the colors of the king of Spain had been flung to the breeze from Cape Horn to the straits of Behring and the burdened galleons reeled homeward laden to the scuppers with the spoils of ruined and conquered empires.

But Spanish soldiers and Spanish priests remained behind to organize and hold the conquered dominions in the name of their king and pope. The history of the seventeenth and eighteenth centuries in Spanish America is the history of the establishing of the power of Spain along ten thousand miles of a surf-swept coast, practically from British Colombia to the Southern extremity of the continent, and from the Río de la Plata and the plains of Patagonia to the mouths of the Orinoco and Cape Gallinas.

Save for the territory of Brazil, which was a colony of Portugal, Spain ruled with undisputed authority in the southern half of the continent and disputed with other nations the hegemony of other lands to the north, even to the frozen shores of Behring.

For the purpose of governing and, in particular, of exploiting these rich territories, the dominions of the Spanish crown were divided into four viceroyalties, each governed by a viceroy appointed by the king.

The viceroyalty of Nueva España included the ancient Aztec empire, which embraced all territory from the southern borders of the present republic of Costa Rica to Florida; the republic of Mexico; the states of Texas, Nevada, Arizona, and California; the West Indies, and the Spanish East Indies.

That of Nueva Granada included the present republics of Colombia, Venezuela, Ecuador, and Panamá.

The viceroyalty of the Río de la Plata was formed by the territory now included in Argentina, Paraguay, Uruguay, and eastern Bolivia.

Peru, which was the most important of the viceroyalties, since it was the richest, included what were then known as Upper and Lower Peru,—now the republics of Peru and Bolivia—and the cold lands that stretched off to the south and were known as Chile.

All these colonies or viceroyalties were considered the personal property of the Spanish monarch, but the local or civil government was entrusted to the Council of the Indies which had its seat in the West Indies, at Habana, and which made the laws for the mainland. This council was the supreme judicial court of Spanish America and the East Indies. Of it, Bancroft, the American historian says:

Its jurisdiction extended to every department, civil, ecclesiastical and commercial, with particular attention to the welfare of the Indians, and, with the existing laws of Spain for guidance in forming *cedulas*, together with the royal decrees, formed the laws of Spanish America. By it viceroys and governors were made and unmade, also patriarchs and bishops, and even the pope had to submit to it for approval his bulls and briefs concerning the Indies.

The council was subject only to the sovereign, who conferred with the Council of Castile before sending to it his decrees. The representative of the council was the viceroy and, in practice, he often arrogated to himself powers that were not nominated in the bond. In each of the viceroyalties, the bounds of authority were ill-defined and this looseness and lack of cohesion, from the very beginning, gave rise to dissensions that boded ill for the continuance of Spanish power in America.

The great extent of the country, the want of moral cohesion, the admixture of races, the general corruption of manners, the absence of a common ideal, the lack of political and industrial activity, and the profound ignorance of the masses, all contributed to produce a state of semi-barbarism by the side of a weakly civilization and vitiated the entire social system. From this embryo was to spring a new republican world, the product of the germs latent within it.

As a former President of the Argentine Federation has expressed it in his description of the evolution of the Spanish-American republics:

The genii that surrounded the cradle of Washington were not the same that presided over the advent of the South American republics. The proud conquerors in iron mail who trod this part of America, with rare notions of liberty and right, with absolute faith in the effect of brute force and violence, were very different from those Puritans who disembarked at Plymouth with no arms but the Gospel, no other ambition than that of founding a new community under the law of love and equality. Hence, the Latin republics stand in need of greater perseverance, judgment, and energy to wash out their original stain and to assimilate virtues which they did not inherit.

Not only was the viceroyalty of Peru the most important of the four, because of its local wealth and prestige, but, in practice, it may be said to have ruled all Spanish America.   In all things the viceroy was supreme.   He was the presiding officer of the Audiencia that represented the authority of the monarch, the superintendent of finances, the protector of the Church, and the official head of the army.

The only organization through which the people might be heard was the *Cabildo,* or *Ayuntamiento*—a kind of municipal council—the members of which, in theory, at least, were elected by a free vote of the people.   But all powers were subordinate to that of the viceroy who lived as befited the representative of one of the greatest kings of his day.

García Calderón, the Peruvian historian, says of that official:

A luxurious court surrounded him, the flattery of courtiers intoxicated him and subornation had its sway with him.   Sometimes the viceroys represented the real aspirations of the people and were serious legislators—such as Francisco de Toledo, in Peru.   Or, they defended the colonists from the filibustering expeditions with such an energy that fiercely contested battles evoked the sentiment of nationality.   At other times they enriched themselves by the sale of posts and drained the treasury, or passed through their states like haughty overlords, surrounded by luxury and gold.

The viceroy, as the representative of the king, interested himself particularly in the material progress of the territory over which he ruled.   He was ably assisted by the representatives of the pope, who had charge of the ecclesiastical branch of the government of the colonies.   It was quite in accord with the spirit of the time that the ecclesiastical censorship of all publications was transferred to America, and that immense power was given into the hands of the religious and other ecclesiastics.   The principal branch of the Inquisition in the New World was established in Lima, the center of the power of the Church in America.   There it did service for almost two centuries and a half, from 1570 until its suppression in 1813.   During that time, to quote Ricardo Palma, the famous historian and librarian of Peru, sixty-eight persons were burned and four hundred and fifty-eight others suffered excommunication, exile, or loss of property. Of those burned, fifty-nine were burned alive, while nine had their bones disinterred and burned in the public square.

———

Such was the condition of the Spanish colonies at the beginning of the nineteenth century. The monarchic idea was supreme and was rigidly enforced by viceroys and papal delegates. The people had no rights. The only authority recognized was the *de facto* government, and intolerance was the watchword of that government. But, in many places, the fires of revolution burned and smoldered, and needed but the quickening of a sudden breeze to be fanned into a continent-wide conflagration. The seeds of liberty which had been dropped into the hearts of men, in ways and at times unknown to their rulers, were taking deep root and in due time blossomed into that group of nineteen republics that today occupy the territory that belonged to Spain.

CAUSES OF THE REVOLUTION

No doubt the underlying fundamental cause of the uprising against the power of Spain in the New World was the unusual, almost inexplicable, movement away from all things monarchical and toward republicanism that manifested itself in Europe and America at the end of the eighteenth century and at the beginning of the nineteenth. When this movement first made itself felt among the colonists of North America, there was but one republic in the world—that of Switzerland—excepting, of course, the un-important communities of Andorra and San Marino, which, under the name of republics, have existed for centuries but whose influence does not extend beyond their own very limited borders.

But the brief tenure of power by the Commonwealth in England in the seventeenth century had been sufficient to instil into the British heart a desire for liberty that had its full fruition only in the latter part of the following century. It was at that time that the English colonists of North America ex-

pressed their belief that "the inalienable rights of Englishmen
had been violated" and, in defense of those rights (in no country
more widely and thoroughly respected today than in Great
Britain itself), declared themselves to be a free and independent
people. This was at the beginning of the last quarter of the
eighteenth century. Before the end of that century, the spirit
of revolution had recrossed the wide Atlantic, and had swept
Louis and his queen from their throne and into the arms of
"Madame la Guillotine", thus paving the way for the coming
of the little Corsican who was to overshadow all Europe and
make his influence felt even to the furthest corners of the American colonies of Spain and Portugal.

The colonies of the Iberian nations felt, in particular, the
power of Napoleon. The Portuguese court fled to Brazil and,
soon after its return to Europe, that colony, having experienced
the thrill of liberty which had begun to sweep the continent,
declared itself independent of the mother country and set up an
independent empire that lasted until, by a bloodless revolution
which ended in the voluntary abdication of Dom Pedro II., in
1889, the present republic of Brazil was established.

The seating of Joseph Bonaparte on the throne of the Bourbons,
in 1807, proved two things to the expectant colonies. The first
was the debility of the mother country and, in particular, of the
reigning monarchy which had so weakly capitulated to the threats
and insinuations of Napoleon, and the second was the unwelcome
fact that they might, in the succession of events, suddenly find
themselves subject to another ruler even more despotic than
Charles IV., who had so servilely relinquished his throne, or
Ferdinand, the son and heir, who, in a state of seemingly complete ineptitude, had done nothing to avenge the *coup d'état of*
Napoleon. The sudden and unexpected overthrow of the Spanish
power in the Iberian Peninsula was but the precursor, the occasion, of the deathblow to that power in *ultramar*. From Neuva
España to Cape Horn the colonies were atremble with expectation, and the doctrine that, with the disappearance of the monarch, his sovereignty reverts to the people, was boldly and
eagerly proclaimed.

Starting from this point, it was easy to arrive at the conclusion that the people had a right to appoint *juntas* or local councils for their own security and that the colonists owed no allegiance to the government constituted in Madrid at the time of the French revolution, through the abdication of the king of the house of Bourbon. This doctrine was earnestly accepted, in particular, by those of the colonists who were of mixed blood; was the immediate cause of friction between these creoles and the people of pure Spanish race; and may be said to have been the cause of igniting the smoldering brands of the revolution.

The Spaniard still held loyally to the home government, although it was in eclipse for a time, while the creoles, born in the country and of only one half or even less pure Spanish blood, had little or no interest in, or affection for, the Spanish throne and frankly aspired to independent government. General Bartolomé Mitre has said:

When the revolution broke out in 1810, it was said that South America would become English or French. When the revolution triumphed, it was said that the continent would relapse into barbarism. By the will and work of the creole, it became American, republican, and civilized.

Consequently, it is well to note that it was through the efforts of the creole or half-breed population that Spanish America was finally able to shake off the fetters of the monarchical form of government and become independent.

The *gaucho*, who may be called the modern centaur, from the plains of Argentina, with the fatality of the Arab and the dash and impetuosity of the Cossack, gave a peculiar type to the revolution which distinguished it from La Plata to Chimborazo. The *llaneros*, or plainsmen from the reaches of the Amazon and the Orinoco, formed the famous flying squadrons of the north whose feats of daring were celebrated from Cape San Roque to Potosí. The Chilean *roto*, or ragged fellow, whose stolid Araucanian blood had been quickened by a generous dash of the sparkling vintage of sunny Spain joined the Argentine *cuyano* in the formation of fighting battalions that easily put to rout the trained soldiers of the Spanish lines who, but a short time before, had hurled from the peninsula the veteran troops of Napoleon.

FIRST ACTS OF THE REVOLUTION

One of the first acts of the revolution was the overthrow of constituted authority in Quito, now the capital of Ecuador but then a city of Colombia, and the naming of a new council which at once levied troops for its defense. The peoples of America were exhorted to follow the lead thus set and the announcement was made that "*Law has resumed authority under the Equator and the rights of men are, by the disappearance of despotism, no longer at the mercy of arbitrary power*".

In May, 1809, a new government was proclaimed in Upper Peru, and in July of the same year La Paz followed the example thus set. These local revolts were soon put down and the leaders died on the scaffold, with all the refinements of cruelty of which that age was capable, or on the field of battle fighting in defense of their ideals. One of those who perished on the gallows exclaimed as he went to his death, "*I have lighted a fire which shall never be quenched.*" His words were true. Before the heads and limbs of these early aspirants for liberty had rotted on the posts of the highways, to which they had been nailed as a warning to others, the fires of revolution were found to be burning in various centers of New Granada and Peru. And, although the movement was again suppressed, it was to cover the fire with ashes which but served to conserve the heat. Within a year, all the Spanish colonies, with a spontaneous unanimity that astounded the world, rose in rebellion against the government in Madrid as represented by the local viceroys.

Beginning at the furthermost limits of the far-flung line of Spanish dominion, one outpost after another gave the cry of liberty and it was but a matter of days until the swelling chorus reached the very centers of the power of the viceroys who must have trembled as they realized that the expected movement for the liberation of a continent had begun and that the enthusiastic shouts of the populace against an effete monarchy were their own death sentence. So united, so unanimous was the sentiment for liberty, so intimately did the movement satisfy the deepest and most sacred aspirations of the people, that it may be said that it had gained its end even before the first gun had been fired.

THE LIBERATORS OF SPANISH AMERICA

The story of the battles fought and of the varied and complex movements in this struggle for liberty in Spanish America can not be entered into in detail in this short sketch. Probably no better understanding of that struggle of a continent in demand of civil liberty could be given in short compass, than in an outline of the life and work of the leading spirits who took part in the revolution and led it to a successful conclusion. A great galaxy of sta 's appeared in the political firmament of the southern half of the western continent at the beginning of the eighteenth century. Some few were of unusual brightness, some were relatively dim, and others were almost lost in the surrounding gloom. But each of them contributed some little ray of light toward dispelling the darkness that had settled down over the colonies.

Belgrano and San Martín, in Argentina; Francia, in Paraguay; Artigas, in the Banda Oriental del Uruguay; Hidalgo and Iturbide, in Mexico; Morazán, in Central America; Carrera, O'Higgins, and Cochrane, in Chile; Dom Pedro I., in Brazil; Simón Bolívar, a Venezuelan by birth but the liberator of five republics: these were the best known of the liberators and each in his way and within his own sphere of influence aided in the liberation of his own and other territories from the power of monarchy across the seas. Of all these political luminaries, only two may be considered as of the first magnitude, namely, José de San Martín, born at Yapeyú, in Argentina, February 25, 1778, and Simón Bolívar, born in Caracas, Venezuela. July 14, 1783.

Coming from almost the two extremes of the dominions of the king of Spain in the New World, fighting for a common cause through twelve years of unusual vicissitudes and difficulties, gradually converging with their forces toward a common point in the strategy of war, these two heroes in the American conflict met but once. Under the equator, with the wide Pacific rolling to the west and the high Andes piled in snowy peaks to the east, at the moment of their greatest common triumph, these two statesmen-warriors met in the little port of Guayaquil. A first and last embrace was given, a few hurried hours of consultation snatched from the busy scenes that held them, and then they went their separate ways. One quietly embarked on his waiting ship and in the darkness of the night turned its prow toward his voluntary exile. The other as quietly and undemonstratively stepped into his place, the curtain was rung up once more and the play went on to the end. For twenty-five years no other person knew what subjects had been discussed by these sphinx-like men in their few hours of discussion, and no one even today, knows the full extent of the resolutions taken, nor the decisions made, that were so full of import for Spanish America.

Of these two men, San Martín and Bolívar, it is necessary that we should speak in greater detail, not only to gain a more exact knowledge of them, but, also, of the work and the movement which they, to an unusual degree, represented in their persons and in their official positions.

JOSÉ DE SAN MARTÍN

Born in the viceroyalty of Río de la Plata, the son of the lieutenant-governor of the province of Yapeyú, José de San Martín was accustomed to martial life and scenes from his earliest childhood. At eight years of age he was taken to Madrid and placed in the seminary of Nobles. But, before he had completed twelve years, he was entered as a cadet in the Military School and soon after received his baptism of fire in a campaign against the Moors, in Africa. He then took part in a war against the French and, on the conclusion of a treaty between the two countries, joined the Spanish navy and fought against Great Britain. He was soon found enrolled in one of the peninsular wars, in which Spain was engaged against Portugal, and finally fought on the side of Spain in the conflict with Napoleon.

It was about this time that he came into contact with the "Society of Lautaro", or the "Society of Rational Men", as it was called. The branch in Spain was affiliated with the central Society in London which had been founded by Francisco Miranda. The special object of the societies established by Miranda was the independence of the American colonies and every attempt was made, though in secret, as the order required, to enlist sympathy and members for the cause. Each member was obliged to recognize "no government in America as legitimate unless it was elected by the free and spontaneous will of the people, and to work for the foundation of the republican system". The declared object of the organization was

To work systematically for the independence and happiness of America, proceding with honor and justice. . . Membership was limited exclusively to men of American birth. By its constitution, if any member of the brotherhood was elected supreme ruler of a state, he could take no important step without consulting the lodge. He could not appoint a diplomatic agent, general-in-chief, governor of a province, judge of an upper court, high church dignitary, nor general officers, and could not punish any member of the brotherhood by his own authority. It was law of the society that all members should mutually assist each other in all the exigencies of civil life, that at the risk of life they should uphold the decrees of the lodge, and that they should inform it of anything which could influence public opinion or affect the public security. . .

A careful study of the acts of San Martín, in his after years, especially in his relations with his brother officers, shows the result of this affiliation. More than once he was compelled to forego just punishment of officers who were serving under him, and his own plans had to be approved by these same men before they could be put into execution.

It was during the last years that San Martín spent in Europe that he offered his services to Great Britain against the common foe, Napoleon. He had now won distinction on many a hard-fought battlefield, had served under some of the most distinguished generals of his time, and had reached that point in his career when he was considered the equal of any of his brother officers in daring and the superior of them all in strategy.

At this juncture, with the slow facilities of the age, word of the recent uprisings in the Spanish colonies reached the Old World and set aflame the martial spirits of the many seasoned officers and soldiers of the colonies who were serving in the armies of Europe. San Martín was an American by birth, by instinct a revolutionist, an ardent republican by education and training, and at once decided to return to Argentina, his native country.

Early in 1812, with a number of other officers, he embarked in London for Buenos Aires and, having reached the scene of the conflict at just the time when serious fighting had begun, he offered his services to the leaders of the revolution. He was immediately confirmed in his rank of Lieutenant-colonel of cavalry and at once began what was to be the great work of his life—the liberation of the Spanish colonies from the rule of the mother country.

In this paper it will be possible to give only the most meagre details of his notable career in the tremendous conflict that was just beginning. It has been said that he was not a man, but a mission, so great was his influence on the destinies of humanity. General Mitre says of him:

He was at once the arm and the head of the Argentine hegemony. He combined the evolutions of armies with those of nations, marking each evolution with some achievement either political or military, obtained great results with the least possible means and without waste of strength, and showed how a people may be redeemed without being opporessed. His character is even yet an historical enigma. . . The moral grandeur of San Martín consists in this: that nothing is known of the secret ambitions of his life, that he was in everything disinterested, that he confined himself strictly to his mission, and that he died in silence, showing neither weakness, pride, nor bitterness at seeing his work triumphant and his part in it forgotten.

Having enlisted in the army of the patriots, he at once took high standing among his fellow officers and in the estimation of the common soldier. He organized the famous *gaucho* regiments into flying squadrons of the most effective cavalry, and was soon ready to put to a test that master stroke in military strategy which changed the destinies of the New World and definitely assigned to San Martín a high place among the greatest strategists of whom there is a record in history. His plan in his own words was as follows:

To cross into Chile with a small well-disciplined army and, finishing off the Goths (Spaniards) who may be found in that country, put an end to anarchy, and then, uniting our forces with the patriot forces of Chile, go by sea to Lima. This is our course. There can be no other.

To understand the audacity of this plan, which, at first reading, may seem simple, especially in view of modern means and methods of mobilization, it must be remembered that the only passes of the Andes that give access to Chile, save in the far south, are from nine to twelve thousand feet above the sea, and that these passes are open only in the summer months.

No one in the royalist army in Chile believed that any attempt would be made to enter the country through the mountains, even during the most favorable months of the year, and all rumors of the invasion planned by San Martín were considered as subjects fit only for ridicule. The passes in many places are so narrow that only one soldier or one animal may advance at a time, there was no food nor forage available, and, in addition, the passes were held by hostile Indians in the pay of the royalists. These Indians, however, were won over by San Martín, who invited them to a great feast in the heights above Mendoza, and under the new influence they quickly and fully divulged the secrets of the royalists. They were led to believe that the Spaniards who held Chile were enemies of the red man and that the patriot armies had come to liberate the native races and restore to them their conquered territories.

But, understanding the treacherous nature of the Indian, San Martín did not reveal to them his own plans. They were led to believe that he expected to enter Chile through the low passes of the far south, and a part of his army did, in fact, choose the southern route, since as many as six passes were employed in the advance on Chile, the two most widely separated being thirteen hundred miles apart. His real plan, however, was to send the main division of his army through the Uspallata Pass, which leads into the Aconcagua valley, while the reserves crossed with him through the pass of Los Patos, which opens into the valley of the Putaendo, and under the command of General Bernardo O'Higgins. The former and shorter of these two passes lies to the south of snow-capped Aconcagua, which towers 23,096 feet above the sea, and is now used by the Transandean railway, while the other is on the northern flank of this mountain.

Having reached Chile by these two passes, his plan was to

unite his forces and strike for the capital. His army consisted
of 3,000 infantry, 250 artillery, and 1,200 cavalry. These
troops were well equipped and understood the serious work
ahead of them. Food and forage were accumulated for the
march and, with almost the precision of a machine, the two
divisions crossed the divide as planned, drove back the scattered
and startled royalists, and finally debouched into the plains on
the western side of the mountain wall. In spite of the terrible
cold and the indescribable sufferings from snow blindness,
hunger, and thirst, only a small number of men and animals
had been lost, and the troops reached Chile ready for action.

General Bartolomé Mitre, the Argentine historian, already
quoted in this paper, thus describes this daring feat of San
Martín and assigns it a high place in the history of military
strategy:

> The passage of the Andes by San Martín was a feat requiring greater
> strategy and skill than the passage of the Alps by Napoleon or Hannibal.
> It was not until Bolívar repeated the exploit on the equator that the
> feat was equalled. If compared with the former exploits of Hannibal
> and Napoleon, it is seen to be a much greater achievement than either
> of them, from its effects on the human race.
>
> In place of vengeance, greed, or ambition, San Martín was animated
> by the hope of giving liberty and independence to a new world. The
> passage of the Andes by Bolívar resulted in the battle of Boyacá; the
> passage by San Martín in the battle of Maipó. These were two decisive
> victories which liberated entire peoples from the slavery of foreign
> despotism. The passage of the Alps by Hannibal and Napoleon
> resulted only in the sterile victories of Trebia and Marengo.

Soon after entering Chile, near the junction of the Aconcagua
and Putaendo rivers, the army of the Andes fell like a thunder-
bolt on the Spanish forces, the battle of the heights of Chacabuco
was fought, and the resulting patriot victory opened the road to
the capital. This was entered in triumph on the 13th of August,
1817, and a proclamation was issued convoking the electors for
the appointment of a governor general. The first vote gave this
position to San Martín, but he refused to consider it since he

felt that his work in the field was not yet done and that he should carry out his original plan and proceed to the liberation of the viceroyalties of the north. The second vote gave the position of supreme Director of Chile to Bernardo O'Higgins, which was according to the wish of San Martín.

It might seem that the conquest of Chile by the patriot armies had now been completed. But the royalist forces had merely been scattered, through an inexplicable failure on the part of San Martín to follow up his victory, and the complete subjugation of the country cost four more years of almost continual fighting. However, the battle of Maipó, less than two months subsequent to the battle of Chacabuco, had crushed the hopes of the royalists and practically destroyed their power from Mexico to the Cape.

While the fighting had been going on by land, the first Chilean fleet had been formed and preparations were being made to carry the expeditionary forces to Peru, the strongest of the viceroyalties and the center of the power of Spain in the New World. Lord Cochrane, an ex-member of the British parliament, who had been compelled to leave his own land because of too rabid revolutionary sympathies—a brilliant, hot-tempered, ardent, patriot—had reached Chile and at once took over the command of the newly formed fleet. Blanco Encalada, the Chilean admiral, in order that the Britisher might hold the highest position, generously resigned his own commission and served under Cochrane.

San Martín, after seeing a stable government constituted and after due consultation with his brother officers, recrossed the mountains and returned to Buenos Aires for the purpose of recruiting forces for the expedition to Peru. He had accepted the rank of Brigadier-General in the Chilean Army and, having completed his mission in the capital of Argentina, made his final preparations for the last and greatest period of his life. The way to the north had, by this time, been opened by Cochrane and Blanco Encalada, but there arose new and unforeseen difficulties which had to be overcome before the expedition could set out. Among other troubles, he heard of the mutiny of some of his best troops in Argentina, and was even compelled to witness the breaking up of that confederation into a number of small fragments, each intent on forming itself into a republic with an aspiring chieftain at its head. Personal illness overtook him and he had to be carried about among his troops in a litter. There were also dissensions on the sea where the ambitious Cochrane aspired to the leadership of the expeditionary army, and even among his most trusted officers. Yet, with an infinite patience, these difficulties were met and overcome and the fleet set sail for Peru with San Martín on board as commander in chief of the expedition. On the eve of sailing he addressed a proclamation to his soldiers in which he said:

Whatever may be my lot in Peru, I shall prove that since my return to my native land her independence has occupied my every thought, and that I have never had any other ambition than to merit the hatred of the ungrateful and the esteem of the virtuous.

The expedition sailed from Valparaiso on the 20th of August, 1820, and in a little less than a year San Martín was able to proclaim himself protector of Peru. During that year a number of engagements had been fought on land and on sea, with victory generally on the side of the patriots, and Lima, the capital of the viceroy, was entered in triumph in July, 1821. San Martín soon after wrote to O'Higgins as follows:

At last, by patience, we have compelled the enemy to abandon the capital of the Pizarro; at last, our labors are crowned by seeing the independence of America secure. Peru is free. I now see before me the end of my public life and watch how I may leave this heavy burden in safe hands, so that I may retire into some quiet corner and live as a man should live.

SIMÓN BOLÍVAR, THE VENEZUELAN

It will be well, at this point, to leave San Martín, at the moment of his great success, and turn to the north, to New Granada, and to a review of the life and work of that other great man, the complement of San Martín in the liberation of Spanish America, Simón Bolívar, the hero of Boyacá. Like his great comrade in arms, he was educated in Europe, where he married the daughter of a fellow-countryman who was then living in France. His wife died not long after the marriage, in Venezuela, and he then returned to Europe.

It was on the occasion of this visit to the Old World that he saw Napoleon crowned king of Milan and, no doubt, formed his own opinion as to the danger to the world in the unchecked progress of that master of men across the stage of the nations. Returning to Venezuela, he retired for some time to his ancestral estates and led the life of the usual rich man of his day. In the midst of luxury and ease he seemed to the casual observer to take no interest in the gathering clouds that heralded the approaching storm, but gave himself up to ease and pleasure. But a state of anarchy was soon declared and every citizen had to declare his allegiance to the colors of Spain or take up arms against them. Now, there was no hesitation or weakness in the declarations of Bolívar. He went over, soul and body, to the cause of the patriots, although he knew that this meant the renunciation of future ease and the giving of himself to forwarding a doubtful cause and to almost certain death or exile. In a very short time he had distinguished himself among the other leaders because of his bravery and keen intellect. His personality was so attractive, there was such a complete poise and calm in his bearing, that he inspired all who met him with absolute confidence in himself and the cause which he had espoused.

He was an extremist, however, and so convinced of his own superior knowledge and skill that he found it difficult to submit to the discipline of his superior officers. His personal bravery was such that he carried all before him and soon came to be the ideal of the troops. At the head of fifteen hundred men he entered Caracas in triumph and was at once hailed as dictator. This early triumph was short-lived, however, and it was only after years of fighting and of the greatest privation and loss that Venezuela found itself definitely free from Spanish rule and Bolívar supreme and secure in his position of dictator.

Of all this infinite detail of battle, of defeat and victory, of exile and imprisonment that spelled the liberation of New

Granada, together with the triumph of Bolívar, we can not speak in this paper. But, once that important viceroyalty had been definitely liberated, Bolívar conceived the idea of crossing the Andes, as San Martín had done in the south, and proceeding to help in the final liberation of Peru and that part of Colombia which lay to the west of the high wall of the mountains. An army was prepared for the march and, after intense suffering, he found himself on the western side, with a greatly reduced force and compelled to face an enemy that was well equipped and knew thoroughly the ground over which it had to fight. By his brilliant strategy, in which he was probably the equal of San Martín, he was able to get his forces into a favorable position on the banks of the Boyacá and in a hard-fought battle completely defeated the royalist forces and definitely gave New Granada to the patriot army.

After a number of less important triumphs, by which he made his victory secure, he issued a proclamation to the people of Colombia in which he could say:

From the banks of the Orinoco to the Andes of Peru, the liberating army, marching from triumph to triumph, has covered with its protecting arms the whole of Colombia. Share with me the ocean of joy which bathes my heart and raise in your own hearts altars to this army which has conquered for you glory and peace and liberty.

The territory which is now occupied by the modern republics of Venezuela, Colombia, and Ecuador was now free of Spanish soldiers and the army of Bolívar was ready to effect its union with that of San Martín which was advancing from the south. It has been said that history "presents no other example of so vast a military combination, carried on with steady perseverance for twelve long years, ending in the concentration of the forces of an entire continent upon one strategic point, which concentration gave the final victory".

This final triumph of San Martín and Bolívar is all the more remarkable if we remember that they could not avail themselves of telegraph, telephone, or wireless; that between them lay the almost impenetrable, even unexplored, unknown uplands of the continent, inhabited by hostile Indians and wild beasts or garrisoned by the forces of the royalists, and the high cold wall of the Andes whose barrier was practically impassable save in the warmest months of the year, and then with great risk. The only possibility of communication was by means of messengers sent overland through these dangers, and the reception of a return message must have been, in many cases, a matter of many months, if not of years. Yet the campaign was carried on to its final conclusion and the two chieftains were now to meet, for the first time, in the port of Guayaquil, in what is now the republic of Ecuador, to discuss and decide their future plan of action. So far, all had gone well and each of them, supported by a strong and loyal army, felt secure in his own prowess and in the prestige of his triumphs. Only the final union of the conquered territories remained and this should have offered no difficulties.

It was about this time that San Martín discovered that a number of his highest officers had formed a cabal against him, the end of which was to deprive him of the command, by means of assassination should this be necessary, and, under another leader, prosecute more vigorously the campaign in Peru. Although the plan was revealed to San Martín by one of his officers who had refused to become a party to the plot, no drastic action was taken, probably because of the rules of the society already referred to which forbade any punishment in such cases save by order of the society itself. A historian of the epoch has said:

From that moment he took the definite and irrevocable determination of abandoning public life. His heart was torn by so many deceptions, treacheries, ingratitude, and vileness, and he could not bear to continue.

In the decree which he published at the time, delegating the command while he should be absent at the conference of Guayaquil, he says:

The cause of the American continent impels me to carry out a plan which I have treasured as one of my dearest hopes. I am going to meet the Liberator of Colombia, in Guayaquil. The general interests of

Peru and Colombia, the energetic termination of the war we are carrying on and the stability of that destiny which America is rapidly approaching make our interview necessary, inasmuch as the order of things has constituted us, in an unusual degree, the arbiters of the outcome of this sublime undertaking.

But there was to be an apple of discord in the final arrangements for peace and the consolidation of the conquered territories. In this case, the cause of discontent centered in Guayaquil, a great province lying along the sea, which had hesitated between accepting the authority of Bolívar or that of San Martín, but seemed inclined to favor the latter and thus become a part of the new republic of Peru. This was not in accord with the ambitions of Bolívar and, in preparing for the meeting, he took care to fill the little port with his own soldiers. The two met in the palace of the governor and after some hours of discussion and the fetes and military displays incident to such occasions, separated to meet no more.

It is the general conclusion that San Martín recognized the fiery, unrestrained character of Bolívar, his ambitions to be the head of the whole movement for the liberation of the continent, and that he was desirous of avoiding trouble. He was too high-minded to permit himself to be dragged into a personal quarrel over the liberated lands and preferred to retire from the field and leave all to his younger colleague who at the last, had proved to be his rival.

The reach of the ambitions of Bolívar may be judged from a toast given by him in a banquet which was tendered him in the city of Guayaquil, at which a number of the officers from the army of San Martín were present. He said:

To the day, not far distant, when I shall carry the flag of Colombia triumphant to the public square of Buenos Aires,

then, pausing to note the effect of his words on his hearers and having received no applause, he added,

in order that it may give an embrace of peace to those who have with such enthusiasm and valor maintained the rights of liberty, etc.

The difference in character of the two men may also be judged from other toasts proposed by them in the banquet which celebrated their interview in Guayaquil. Bolívar said:

To the two greatest men of South America—San Martín and myself!

San Martín proposed:

The speedy conclusion of the war, the organization of the different republics of the continent, and the health of the Liberator of Colombia!

From Guayaquil, San Martín returned to Peru and soon afterward left America. He made one brief visit to Argentina but in 1850 he died in France, poverty-stricken and humiliated by the lack of appreciation and gratitude shown him by the peoples whom he had liberated. Argentina, however, thirty years afterward, gallantly recognized its debt. His body was repatriated and now rests in the beautiful cathedral of Buenos Aires, the glory of that nation to redeem whose soil he had suffered so keenly and for so many years.

Bolívar, as San Martín evidently expected, continued his march to the south, made himself master of Peru, and was promptly elected dictator. The southern half of Peru in due time, took its place among free nations as the republic of Bolivia and Bolívar was named its permanent president.[1] His dream, evidently, was to unite all the republics of South America in a single great confederacy, modelled after the Delian League, with himself as its permanent head. But this dream was not to be realized. His wealth was gone, his popularity, due to his violent temper and soaring ambitions, was on the wane, and his body had been weakened by exposure and excesses. In 1830, twenty years before the death of San Martín, he offered the resignation of all the powers he held. This was accepted

---

[1] The republic of Bolivia has placed a plate near the mausoleum of Bolívar in the Pantheon of Caracas, which reads as follows: "Bolivia, to the posterity of America: You behold the giant sleeping. God and Liberty keep vigil over his couch. The Conqueror of Iberia, he triumphed over Oblivion and found the throne of Glory too strait for him. While there is a heart-beat on Earth, while a chord of sympathy vibrates in the human breast, men must bow low before this Man who gave me life and, dying, willed me his name."

and he was voted a liberal pension for life. He then retired
from public life, dissatisfied, soured because of what he es-
teemed a lack of gratitude on the part of the citizens of the
liberated countries, but still hoping that an opportunity might
present itself for him to return to power. This opportunity
came but a short time before his death. A revolution seemed
to offer what he desired, but he was defeated and ordered to
leave the country. He then retired to the little village of Santa
Marta, in the northeastern corner of what is now Colombia to
a little property which he still possessed, and there, like his
great prototype on Santa Helena, he died, alone, a tragic, abandoned figure.

In the vexation of his spirit he is said to have exclaimed, as
he gave up his power and retired to private life:

Those who have served the revolution have ploughed the sand. If
it were possible for a part of the earth to return to its primitive chaos,
such would be the last phase of America. There is no faith in America,
neither in individuals nor in nations. Their treaties are mere scraps
of paper, their constitutions paper and ink, their elections are battles,
liberty is anarchy and life a torment.

Yet, his thoughts, as he lay dying, seemed to be for the happiness of the people whom he had served, and his words indicate
the really great spirit that dominated the man—great, in spite
of his faults and vices. He said:

My wishes are for the happiness of my country. If my death weakens
the divisions and helps to consolidate union, I go to the tomb content.

Then he added:

Yes, to the tomb, to which I am sent by my fellow-countrymen.
But I forgive them. O that I could take with me the consolation of
knowing that they will keep united.

His last words are said to have been:

I believe that the two greatest buffoons of humanity have been Don
Quijote and I!

This was in 1830. In 1842 the government of Venezuela ordered the body of Bolívar brought back to Caracas and it now rests in the Pantheon of this, his natal city, in the site of honor among many illustrious dead of that nation.

Both San Martín and Bolívar were great men, so great, possibly, that no one continent could hold them both. Of the two, San Martín was, undoubtedly, the greater.[2] He was utterly unselfish in his devotion to the cause which he defended with his life. He sought no personal gain or advantage and, like the great Liberator of the north, laid aside his authority when he felt that his peculiar work was done and that a longer tenure of power on his part might engender strife and jeopardize the success of the movement toward liberation and the establishing of free communities. His respect for the rights of the individual nation made impossible his acceptance of the idea of Bolívar for the federation of all around one central power. Austere and unpretentious, even puritanical, by comparison, in his own life, he could have had no symptahy with the ideals and conduct of Bolívar who, at the height of his power in Peru, surrounded himself with the splendor and voluptuousness of an oriental prince.

Of the other liberators, each contributed to the extent of his ability to the success of the great enterprise which all defended with their blood. But no one of them can be compared in greatness with either of the two who have been described in greater detail.

Lord Cochrane stands preëminent among them all, but he was a foreigner. Before he came to America he had been sentenced

----

[2] This statement, of course, would be energetically combated in the countries that formed Nueva Granada, and as warmly applauded further south. This is to be expected, since each of these great men is a hero to his own people, who feel that his reputation must be enhanced at all costs, even belittling that of the other should this be necessary. Readers of Spanish will be interested in a little volume, *Simón Bolívar Intimo*, by Martínez, published by the "Casa Editorial Hispano-Americana", in Paris which throws much light on the private life of this really great man.

to the pillory by his indignant countrymen. After his death, so thoroughly had he purged the errors of his youth, he was given a resting place among the greatest of England's dead in the historic halls of Westminster.

The others, almost without exception, died in disgrace or by violence or treachery. Bernardo O'Higgins was banished from Chile and died in Lima. José Miguel de Carrera was shot in Mendoza, as a traitor, before a reprieve signed by San Martín could reach him. Francisco Miranda, the founder of the societies which played such an important part in the war for the liberation of the American colonies, died, alone and naked, in a military dungeon in Cádiz and his body was lost in the potter's field on the mud banks over which the waters of the Mediterranean ebb and flow before that city.[3] The curate, Miguel Hidalgo y Costilla, of Mexico, was executed as a common criminal. Agustín de Iturbide, the only one of the liberators who foolishly crowned himself emperor, died on the scaffold—a possible presage of the pitiful end of another emperor of Mexico whose corpse was sent back to Europe by the Indian Juárez as a discouragement to the imposition of monarchy on the free nations of America. Manuel Belgrano, the hero of Tucuman, was allowed to die in obscurity. Antonio José de Sucre, the hero of Ayacucho, one of the greatest battles of the revolution, was murdered by his own soldiers as they marched along a lonely road.[4] José Artigas, the liberator of the Banda Oriental del Uruguay, now the republic of that name, died, after thirty

[3] In the Pantheon of Caracas, where rest many of that country's illustrious dead, one may read the following reference to Francisco Miranda on a tablet which marks the cenotaph reserved for him: "Venezuela sorrows because of grief at not having been able to find the remains of General Miranda which have been lost in the potter's field of the prison in which this great martyr of American liberty passed away.

"The republic would treasure them, with all the honor due them, in this spot which has been set aside for that purpose by decree of the President, General Joaquín Crespo, under date of January 22, 1896".

[4] A monument to Sucre in the same city, has this legend: "He was present at the birth of the revolution of independence. At the battle of Ayacucho he made certain the liberty of America. Antonio José de Sucre. His native country, thankful, inconsolable for the loss of his ashes, dedicates to him this monument which was inaugurated during the administration of General Joaquín Crespo."

years of exile, in a lonely hut in Paraguay, a pensioner on the bounty of the stern dictator, José Gaspar Rodríguez de Francia.

Bernardino Rivadavia, the greatest civil genius of South America, who gave form to the existing constitutions, and of whom it has been said that "he stands in America second only to Washington as the representative statesman of a free people", died in exile. José María Morelos, the priest of the revolution was condemned by the Holy Office of the Inquisition as "a heretic and an abettor of heretics, a traitor to God, to the king and to the Pope, and a disturber of the ecclesiastical hierarchy", was turned over to the tender mercies of the secular arm of the law, and was finally shot in Mexico.

Both Simón Bolívar and José de San Martín died in banishment, although it was voluntary on the part of the latter.

WEBSTER E. BROWNING.

THE BOUNDARY OF NEW MEXICO AND THE GADSDEN TREATY

A dispute regarding the southern and western boundaries of New Mexico is likely to occupy a comparatively large portion of the completed narrative of the negotiations which ended in the Gadsden Treaty of December 30, 1853. The treaty of Guadalupe Hidalgo described a new boundary between the United States and Mexico and provided for its survey and location in the following language:

The boundary line between the two Republics shall commence in the Gulf of Mexico, three leagues from land, opposite the mouth of the Rio Grande, otherwise called the Rio Bravo del Norte, or opposite the mouth of its deepest branch, if it should have more than one branch emptying directly into the sea; from thence up the middle of that river following the deepest channel, where it has more than one, to the point where it strikes the southern boundary of New Mexico, thence westward, along the whole southern boundary of New Mexico (which runs north of the town called Paso) to its western termination; thence northward along the western line of New Mexico, until it intersects the first branch of the river Gila; (or if it should not intersect any branch of that river, then to the point on the said line nearest to sucn branch, and thence in a direct line to the same); thence down the middle of said branch and of the said river, until it empties into the Rio Colorado; thence across the Rio Colorado, following the division line between Upper and Lower California, to the Pacific Ocean.

The southern and western limits of New Mexico, mentioned in this article, are those laid down in the map entitles *"Map of the United States as organized and defined by various acts of the congress of said republic, and constructed according to the best authorities. Revised edition. Published at New York, in 1847, by J. Disturnell"*.

In order to designate the boundary line with due precision, upon authoritative maps, and to establish upon the ground landmarks which shall show the limits of both republics, as described in the present article, the two Governments shall each appoint a commissioner and a

715

surveyor, who, before the expiration of one year from the date of the exchange of ratifications of this treaty, shall meet at the port of San Diego, and proceed to run and mark said boundary in its whole course to the mouth of the Rio Bravo del Norte. . .[1]

Organization and Work of the First Commission.   The progress of the boundary survey was hampered from the beginning by partisan politics in the United States.   On July 6, 1848, two days after the proclamation of the Treaty of Guadalupe Hidalgo, Polk sent a special explanatory message to the House and asked for appropriations.   In this message he referred to the stipulation in the fifth article which required both countries to appoint a commissioner and a surveyor who should meet at San Diego within a year from the date of the ratification of the treaty.   He said it was necessary that *"provision be made by law"* for the appointment of a commissioner and surveyor on the part of the United States.[2] The Senate promptly passed a bill making such provision,[3] but it was introduced in the House just three days before the close of the session and died in the hands of the Committee on Foreign Affairs.[4]

The general appropriation bill passed by this session of congress provided, however, for $50,000 to be expended in defraying the expenses of the boundary commission.[5] Polk thereupon proceeded to make the necessary appointments. This he did either because he thought the stipulation in the appropriation bill warranted such action, or because he was anxious to fill the positions on the commission before the expiration of his term of office.   The Senate, which contained a membership of thirty-six democrats and twenty-two whigs, of course confirmed Polk's nominations.[6]

When the Senate bill providing for the organization of the commission was taken up in the House during the next session of Congress, the Whigs, who held a majority in this body, at-

---

[1] W. M. Malloy, *Treaties*, etc. (Washington, 1910), I. 1109-1110.
[2] *Globe*, 30 cong., 1 sess., pp. 901-902.
[3] *Ibid.*, pp. 1043-1052.
[4] *Ibid.*, p. 1064.
[5] 9 U. S. Stat. at Large, 301.
[6] *Sen. Ex. Journal*, VIII. 24.

tempted to nullify the action of Polk. They introduced amendments confining appointments to the boundary commission to members of the Topographical Corps, and providing that no part of the money appropriated then or thereafter be used to pay the salaries of any officers or persons connected with the boundary survey whose appointment had been made without authority of law. Both of these amendments passed the House, and their partisan nature is shown by the yeas and nays on the latter. Eighty-one Whigs and two Democrats voted for the measure, while forty-four Democrats and one lone Whig voted against it.[7] The Senate refused to accept the bill as amended by the House[8] and, consequently, the boundary commission was forced to proceed with limited funds and with uncertainty as to the amount of salary each member was to receive.

The joint commission from Mexico and the United States met at San Diego on July 6, 1849, only a few days after the time stipulated by the treaty. The American group was composed of John B. Weller, commissioner; Andrew B. Gray, surveyor; William H. Emory, astronomer; and John C. Cremony, interpreter. The Mexican government was represented by Pedro García Condé as commissioner, and José Salazar y Larregui as surveyor and astronomer.[9] Besides these, there were several assistants and a military escort for the commission of each government.[10]

On October 10, 1849, the initial point of the boundary was ascertained. A written statement in English and Spanish was placed in a bottle which, after being hermetically sealed, was deposited in the ground, and a temporary monument was erected upon the spot. The commission then proceeded to determine the point of junction of the Gila and the Colorado. In the following January, this point was agreed upon. All that now remained to be done, so far as this portion of the boundary was concerned, was to survey a straight line from the junction of

[7] *Globe*, 30 cong., 2 sess., pp. 617–624.
[8] *Ibid.*, pp. 667–668.
[9] *Sen. Ex. Doc.* No. 119, 32 cong., 1 sess. (ser. 626), pp. 59, 67.
[10] *Ibid., loc. cit.*

these two rivers to the initial point on the Pacific coast. Accordingly, engineers were appointed for this task, and the commission adjourned on February 15, 1850, to meet in El Paso on the first Monday in the following November.[11]

The Dismissal of Weller. But long before this part of the task had been completed the Whigs had decided to get Weller's scalp. Even prior to his arrival at San Diego, where he was to take up his work, his successor had been appointed. Weller reached San Diego on July 1, 1849,[12] but on June 26, John C. Fremont had been chosen to supersede him and had been given a letter from the Secretary of State to Weller informing him of his dismissal.[13] Fremont at first accepted the appointment, but he later changed his mind, having in the meantime decided to run for United States Senator from California.[14] The letter of June 26, apparently never reached Weller.[15] Soon afterwards the oversight of the boundary commission was transferred from the Department of State to that of Interior. On December 19, the secretary of the latter department addressed another letter of dismissal to Weller.[16] This dispatch the commissioner received, and he proceeded according to instructions to turn over the books, papers, and other paraphernalia to Major Emory. The letter of the Secretary of Interior accused Weller of carelessness in the management of the commission, and he later declared that' Weller had maltreated subordinate officials; but as all this occurred, if at all, after the decision to remove Weller had already been made, there was strong suspicion that the whole affair was a political move.[17]

The Second Commission. At any rate, Weller was removed and John Russell Bartlett was at length appointed in his stead on June 19, 1850.[18] A virtual reorganization of the commission

[11] *Ibid.*, pp. 60, 65; *Sen. ex. Doc.*, No. 34, 31 cong., 1 sess. (ser. 558), pp. 31–38.
[12] *Globe*, 31 cong., 2 sess., pp. 78–79.
[13] *Ibid.*, pp. 78–84; *Sen. Ex. Doc.*, No. 34, 31 cong. 1 sess. (ser. 558), pp. 9–10.
[14] William H. Emory, "Report", *House Ex. Doc.* No. 135, 34 cong., 1 sess. (ser. 861), p. 5.
[15] *Globe*, 31 cong., 2 sess., p. 80.
[16] *Sen. Ex. Doc.*, No. 34, 31 cong., 1 sess. (ser. 558), p. 15.
[17] *Globe*, 31 cong., 2 sess., pp. 80 ff.
[18] *Sen. Ex. Doc.*, No. 119, 32 cong. 1 sess. (ser. 626), p. 87.

then took place. Gray was retained as surveyor, but John McClellan was appointed as chief astronomer instead of Emory who had resigned.[19] Neither the American nor the Mexican group reached El Paso by the appointed time. The former, with the exception of Gray, arrived on November 13, and the latter put in their appearance December 1.[20]

Compromise Regarding the Initial Point on the Rio Grande. The first question to be decided was the initial point on the Rio Grande. According to Article V. of the treaty of 1848, the southern and western boundaries of New Mexico were to be those laid down in Disturnell's map, and the boundary of the United States was to extend up the middle of the Rio Grande "to the point where it strikes the southern boundary of New Mexico (which runs south of the town called Paso)". But it was soon found that there were errors in the Disturnell map. El Paso was not only located thirty minutes too far north, but both it and the Rio Grande were placed more than two degrees too far to the east. Again, according to this map the southern boundary of New Mexico was three degrees long and seven minutes north of El Paso. A dispute arose as to whether the actual position of El Paso and of the Rio Grande should be made the starting point and a line beginning seven minutes north of El Paso run westward for three degrees, or whether the points were to be located by parallels and meridians as laid down on Disturnell's map. The Mexican commissioner contended that the initial point should be fixed on the Rio Grande as actually situated, but at the parallel of thirty-two degrees and twenty-two minutes as it appeared on the Disturnell map; and that, moreover, the length of the southern boundary of New Mexico should be determined by subtracting the distance between the Rio Grande as actually situated and as it appeared upon this map, from three degrees (175.28 English miles), thus leaving this portion of the line about one-third its length as shown on the Disturnell map.[21]

[19] *Sen. Ex. Doc.*, No. 34, 31 cong., 1 sess. (ser. 558), pp. 12–13.
[20] J. R. Bartlett, *Personal Narrative* (New York, 1854), II. 145, 150.
[21] Bartlett, *Personal Narrative*, I. 201–203; *Sen. Ex. Doc.* No. 119, 32 cong., 1 sess. (ser. 626), pp. 289, *passim*.

The commissioner for the United States dissented from this view, and after a number of meetings, a compromise was reached, by the terms of which the southern boundary of New Mexico was to extend three degrees west of the Rio Grande as the river was actually situated, running along the parallel of thirty-two degrees and twenty-six minutes, or seven minutes north of El Paso as that city appeared upon the Disturnell map.[22] With this compromise Bartlett was well pleased, for he believed that Condé would never have consented to the extension of the boundary three degrees west of the Rio Grande had the American commissioner refused to fix the initial point thirty minutes further north than it would have fallen according to the relative actual positions of the southern boundary of New Mexico and the town of El Paso. He felt, also, that in consenting to such a compromise he had yielded land of no great value while gaining territory rich in gold and silver mines.[23] Moreover, the Secretary of the Interior and the Secretary of State approved Bartlett's action.

The agreement regarding the initial point was reached on December 25, 1850,[24] before Surveyor Gray put in his appearance. When he arrived late in July, 1851, he found the corner stone marking the spot already laid and a portion of the southern boundary of New Mexico already run.[25] He refused, however, to sign the agreement reached by Bartlett and Condé, and recalling Lieutenant Whipple, who had been acting as surveyor *ad interim*, from his work on this line, he sent him with two parties to the Gila.[26] Colonel Graham who was now the astronomer of the commission likewise disapproved, as did Whipple,

[22] *Sen. Ex. Doc.*, No. 119, pp. 391-394, 406-409, and accompanying maps. *See also*, H. H. Bancroft, *History of Arizona and New Mexico, 1530-1888* (San Francisco, 1889), p. 451.

[23] *Sen. Ex. Doc.* No. 119, pp. 145-148; *Sen. Ex. Doc.*, No. 131 (ser. 627), pp. 1-3.

[24] *Ibid.*, p. 391.

[25] Bartlett, *Personal Narrative*, I. 206-207; *Sen. Ex. Doc.* No. 119 (ser. 626), p. 298.

[26] The best statement of Gray's views is found in *Sen. Ex. Doc.* No. 55, 33 Cong., 2 sess. (ser. 752).

and later, Major Emory.[27] Owing to quarrels between the
American astronomer and surveyor, as well as between the
commissioner and his subordinates, operations proceeded slowly
on the Gila,[28] and both Gray and Graham were recalled before
the end of the year.[29] Their combined functions were then
conferred upon Emory, and better results were achieved. By
the fall of 1852, the survey was completed, so far as the United
States commission was concerned, from San Diego to the headwaters of the Gila, and from El Paso to Eagle Pass.[30] Notwithstanding the death of General Condé, the Mexican commission had completed by that time the entire survey west of
the Rio Grande, and had begun operations on that river.[31]
Bartlett now decided to send Whipple back to the boundary of
New Mexico to take up the work where he had left off, while
he and most of his men prepared to join Emory at Eagle Pass.[32]
But while en route, he received a communication from Washington which convinced him that further operations of the commission would be impossible.[33] It was accordingly disbanded,
and Bartlett and Emory set out for the capital.[34]

Congressional Action. Congress had in fact legislated the
commission out of existence. It will be recalled how slow that
body had been about taking the action necessary for its organization. In April, 1850, a bill had at length been passed fixing the
salaries of the commissioner, the surveyor, and the astronomer,
and providing for the termination of the commission three years

[27] For a statement of Graham's contentions, see *ibid*, No. 121, 32 cong., 1 sess.
(ser. 627). The most concise presentation of Bartlett's reasons for his course
of action is contained in *Sen. Ex. Doc.* No. 41, 32 cong., 2 sess. (ser. 665). It
would obviously not be pertinent to the main interest of this monograph to go into
the arguments for and against the line agreed upon by the commissioners. They
maintained that the boundary should have been established on a parallel thirty
minutes farther south than had been done by the compromise line.

[28] *Sen. Ex. Doc.* No. 119 (ser. 626), pp. 172 *passim*.

[29] *Ibid.*, pp. 442–443; also *Sen. Ex. Doc.*, No. 121, 32 cong., 1 sess. (ser. 627),
p. 49.

[30] *Ibid.*, No. 6, 33 cong., special sess. (ser. 688), pp. 18, 61–68, 117–119.

[31] *Sen. Ex. Doc.* No. 6, 33 cong., special sess. (ser. 688) pp. 18, 61–68, 117–119.

[32] *Ibid.*, pp. 71–74, 161.

[33] Bartlett, *Personal Narrative*, II. 514.

[34] *Ibid.*, 517 ff.

from January, 1850. In May and in September of the same year appropriations were made amounting to $185,000, while the general appropriation bill for the following year set apart another $100,000 for the boundary survey.[35]

But signs of an approaching storm were already visible. When news of Weller's dismissal reached Washington early in 1851, it occasioned vigorous protests on the part of the democratic element in the Senate.[36] Upon being released from the commission, Weller had remained in California where he made a successful race for the United States Senate. As soon as he obtained his seat in that body, he began to take active interest in the boundary survey. In March, 1852, he introduced a long resolution calling upon the Secretary of Interior to submit copies of all instructions given the commission, all correspondence relating to it, the number and names of persons employed, the amount of money spent, the manner of its disbursal, and an estimate of the amount necessary to complete the work. Weller also brought in a resolution asking information as to whether any charges had been filed in the War Department against the commission.[37]

The latter resolution had reference to charges preferred against Bartlett by Colonel McClellan whom he had discharged from the commission for drunkenness, efforts to destroy the authority of the commissioner, and conduct unbecoming a gentleman and an officer.[38] The chief complaints against Bartlett were the private use of transportation provided by the government for the boundary commission, unpardonable mismanagement of public interests and funds entrusted to him, and neglect of the health, comfort, and lives of individuals connected with the commission.[39] Into the details regarding the charges it is not necessary to go. They are mentioned here because they tend to cast discredit upon the commission and to delay the appro-

[35] Emory, "Report", *House Ex. Doc.*, No. 135, 34 cong., 1 sess. (ser. 861), p. 21; *Globe*, 31 cong., 1 sess., pp. 744, 745.

[36] *Globe*, 31 cong., 2 sess., pp. 78–84.

[37] *Ibid.*, 32 cong., 1 sess., p. 814.

[38] *Sen. Ex. Doc.*, No. 60, 32 cong., 1 sess. (ser. 620), pp. 10–17, 46–63.

[39] *Ibid.*, pp. 2–5, 23–46.

priations necessary to carry out its work, while, at the same time, they have some bearing upon the complaints of the Mexican government to be considered later.

More important than these charges, was the contention that Bartlett had departed from the treaty of 1848 in establishing the initial point on the Rio Grande. Rusk of Texas was the principal champion of this view. In May, 1852, he proposed, along with an amendment to the deficiency bill appropriating $80,000 for running the boundary, a proviso that nothing in the amendment should be construed so as to sanction a departure from the point on the Rio Grande north of the town called Paso designated in the treaty of Guadalupe Hidalgo.[40] In the following July, while speaking of the charges preferred against Bartlett, Rusk declared that he would do everything in his power to resist the appropriation of money until there was assurance that this treaty and not the agreement of the commissioners should settle the question of the initial point on the Rio Grande.[41] The $80,000 eventually appropriated for the boundary contained Rusk's proviso.[42]

Prominent among those who sided with Rusk was Mason of Virginia. In the latter part of August, 1852, when the expenses for running the boundary were being considered as an item in the general appropriation bill, he proposed "that no part of the appropriation should be used until it should be made to appear to the President of the United States that the southern boundary of New Mexico had not been established further north of El Paso than is laid down in the Disturnell Map".[43] Before the close of the month, the bill with the amendment received the approval of both houses and became a law.[44] Fillmore, in accordance with the provision, examined all the reports of the boundary commission, and, concluding that the money could not be used, ordered the Secretary of the Interior to discontinue

[40] *Globe*, 32 cong., 1 sess., p. 1404.
[41] *Ibid.*, p. 1660.
[42] *Ibid.*, p. 1404.
[43] *Ibid.*, pp. 2270-2271.
[44] *Ibid.*, p. 2407.

operations.[44]   In the following March, that part of the appropriation bill which applied to the Mexican boundary was so amended
as to permit the use of the funds necessary to complete the survey
of the Rio Grande.[45]   Work on the southern boundary of New
Mexico was not to be resumed, however, and the dispute was left
over for the incoming administration.

Factors Complicating the Situation.   There were two factors
which tended to lend gravity to the situation.   In the first
place, it was believed that the settlement agreed upon by the
commissioners involved the loss of the only practicable southern
route for a Pacific railway.   This was deemed a matter of considerable importance.   Major Emory had brought the subject
to Buchanan's notice while negotiations which resulted in the
Guadalupe Hidalgo treaty were in progress.[47]   A provision relating to the matter was embodied in that treaty as finally
drafted, Article VI. being made to provide for a joint agreement
between the contracting parties with reference to the construction
of a road, canal, or railway running "along the river Gila, or
upon its right or its left bank, within the space of one marine
league from either margin of the river".   In his instruction to
Weller, Buchanan had suggested that the "selection of individuals" for the boundary commission might be "made with
reference to the incidental collection of information relative to
the construction" of the proposed communication.[48]   In the
following February, the Secretary of State again called the subject to Weller's attention, declaring that the inquiry regarding
the route was one of "great importance to the country".[49]   The
instructions of Commissioner Bartlett made the investigations
regarding a railway of more than "incidental" importance.
Referring to Article VI. of the treaty of Guadalupe Hidalgo,
Secretary of Interior, wrote:

    [44] *Ibid.*, 32 cong., 2 sess., p. 10.
    [45] *Ibid.*, pp. 881, 1045, app. p. 331.
    [47] Emory, "Report", *House Ex. Doc.* No. 135, 34 cong., 1 sess. (ser. 861), pp.
50–51.
    [48] Buchanan to Weller, Jan. 24, 1849, *ibid.*, No. 34, 31 cong. 1 sess., (ser. 558),
pp. 2–3.
    [49] Same to same, Feb. 13, 1849, *ibid.*, 3–6.

As the examinations to be made and the information to be collected, agreeably to this article, are of very great importance, you will make such organization of parties, and assign to them such duties, as will be productive of the desired results.[50]

At least one member of the commission, Major Emory, was intensely interested in the matter. Writing from San Diego, California, April 2, 1849, he said:

By pushing the survey eastward, and looking for a branch of the Gila which shall fulfil the conditions of the treaty—the first to intersect the boundary of New Mexico—you will inevitably be made to strike that boundary far north of the parallel of the copper mines; because all the streams south of that parallel, having their sources in the Sierra Madre, running towards the Gila, disappear in the sands before they reach Gila, except in cases of unusual freshets. Working eastward their almost trackless beds must escape the notice of the keenest observer. Working from the 'Paso del Norte' northward, you strike the sources of the streams themselves; and although they may disappear many leagues before reaching the Gila, they may nevertheless be affluents of that river, and fulfil the conditions of that treaty.

Another view of the case may also be taken. The inaccuracy of the map upon which the treaty was made, and which thereby becomes a part of the treaty, is notorious. It is also known to all who have been much in the frontier States of Mexico, that the boundaries of those States have never been defined on the ground, and are unknown. This is particularly the case with the boundary betwixt New Mexico and Chihuahua. In this condition of things the commission must negotiate, and they may adopt the 32d parallel of latitude, until it strikes the San Pedro, or even a more southern parallel of latitude. This would give what good authority, combined with my own observations, authorises me to say is a practicable route for a railroad—I believe the only one from ocean to ocean within our territory.[51]

Speaking of this letter at a later date, Emory asserted that he had written it "in the hope that the United States commissioner might succeed in torturing the treaty of Guadalupe Hidalgo to

[50] Secretary of Interior to Bartlett, Aug. 1, 1850, Bartlett, *Personal Narrative*, II. 589.

[51] Emory, "Report", *House Ex. Doc.* No. 135, 34 cong. 1 sess. (ser. 861), pp. 20–21.

embrace a practicable route" for the proposed road.[52] But
Bartlett had agreed to the parallel of thirty-two degrees and
twenty-two minutes, and had thus, as some believed, surrendered
the line best adapted to the purpose.[53]

Attitude of the People and Authorities in the Disputed Section.
The second factor which tended to render the situation dangerous
was the attitude of the inhabitants and the officials living in and
near the territory in dispute. Of the area of some 5,950 square
miles in question—that is to say, the territory between the
compromise line and that claimed by Gray—all except a narrow
strip along the Rio Grande was considered barren and worthless.
This strip, called *La Mesilla*, was known to be very fertile.[54] As
to the motives leading to its settlement, and the political sentiments of the inhabitants, the authorities differ. Bartlett says
the Mexican element of Doña Ana, which had been exasperated
by the encroachments of the Anglo-Americans, sought new homes
there in the belief that it would fall within the limits of Mexico,
and that the Mexican government later encouraged Mexicans
from New Mexico to make homes there.[55] Reports sent to the
governors of New Mexico and forwarded by them to Washington
indicated that the settlers came there with the clear understanding that it was to be within the jurisdiction of the United States.[56]
At any rate the settlement of the valley began about 1849 or
1850, the region was in a flourishing condition,[57] and there were
differences of opinion in regard to the political desires of the
settlers. The Mexican officials contended that virtually all of
them were desirous of being annexed to Chihuahua,[58] and with
this view Bartlett was apparently in agreement, though he admitted that they may have been inveigled by wily land speculators

---

[52] *Ibid.*, p. 51.
[53] *Globe*, 32 cong., 1 sess., pp. 2402–2404, app., 776 ff.
[54] Bartlett, *Personal Narrative*, I. 188, 212.
[55] *Ibid.*, I. 213, II. 391. See also Bancroft, *Arizona and New Mexico*, p. 652.
[56] Houghton to Lane, September 1, 1853, and inclosures; Mansfield to Merriwether, October 25, 1853; Marcy to Merriwether, May 28, 1853. State Department, B.I.A.
[57] Bartlett, *op. et loc. cit.*
[58] Commissioners of Chihuahua to Lane, March 19, and Trias to Lane, March
28, 1853, State Department, B.I.A.

to petition for annexation to New Mexico.[59]   That a group of its inhabitants sent in a petition expressing vigorous opposition to annexation to Chihuahua is certain;[60] and Judge Hyde of El Paso declared that the American population and "many of the Mexicans" had organized. to resist any authorities Mexico might send, and were preparing to petition the governor of New Mexico to order elections for the civil officials of the district.[61] There was probably some truth in both statements, the Anglo-Saxon portion of the heterogeneous population being, in general, partial to New Mexico, while the majority of the Mexican element gave preference to Chihuahua.

A population thus divided served to render the situation more critical.   Soon after the boundary commission reached the compromise regarding the southern boundary of New Mexico, the chief executive of Chihuahua responded to the supposed desire of the people for the protecting arm of his government, and apparently showed little regard for the persons and property of those who refused to accept his benevolence.   The Americans, and those "favorable to American rights and privileges" naturally objected, not only petitioning the governor of New Mexico, but also asking that their complaints be laid before the federal government for redress.[62]

So far as the governor of New Mexico at the time was concerned, their efforts resulted in little more than calling forth from a dying man a wail because one more vexation had been added to a problem already difficult.[63]   Before the new governor, William Carr Lane, left the east, he was urged by the territorial delegate to congress from New Mexico to occupy the disputed ground by force.[64]   Lane took no action, however, until he learned that the federal congress had repudiated Bartlett's

[59] Bartlett, op. cit. II. 391–392.

[60] Citizens of Mesilla to Calhoun, August 25, 1851, James A. Calhoun, Official Correspondence (ed. A. H. Abel, Washington, 1915), pp. 404–405.

[61] Sen. Ex. Doc., No. 41, 32 cong., 2 sess. (ser. 665), p. 13.

[62] Calhoun, Official Correspondence, pp. 404–405.

[63] Ibid., pp. 424–425.

[64] Lane to Taylor, January 23, 1854, House Rep. No. 81, 33 cong. 2 sess. (ser. 806), pp. 1–2.

line. He then set out toward the disputed territory. When he arrived at Doña Ana, he issued a proclamation laying claim to jurisdiction over it,[65] justifying the step on the ground (1) that the section had been under the acknowledged jurisdiction of New Mexico from 1825 to 1851; (2) that the forcible annexation of the territory by Chihuahua at the latter date was illegal because the agreement of the commissioners did not constitute a final settlement; (3) that Chihuahua had signally failed not only to secure the inhabitants of the region in their rights of person, property, and conscience, but also to protect them from the depredations of the Indians; (4) that the revolutionary condition of Mexico precluded the hope of such protection being furnished in the future, (5) that a large portion of the inhabitants were claiming the protection of the United States and soliciting the re-annexation of that territory to New Mexico; (6) that during the year 1852 the United States had virtually asserted sovereignty over the region, and therefore it was his duty now to re-assert it.[66]

Lane mailed a copy of his proclamation to Angel Trias, the governor of Chihuahua, who responded with a counter declaration and prepared to resist Lane's claim by military force. Trias declared that the limits of Chihuahua had extended not only over the territory in question, but even farther northward; that, in regard to the disputed region, Mexico had in its favor the possession of the territory from time immemorial, its *pacific* occupation under the sight of the officials of the United States who were not accustomed to remain silent in cases where their rights were in doubt, its inclusion within the limits of Mexico by the joint boundary commission and the establishment of the immigrants who had chosen to leave the United States within it. Trias maintained, furthermore, that the inhabitants of the disputed section did not desire annexation to the United States, and, even if they did, this would not justify annexation; that in resorting to force, the governor of New Mexico would violate the

[65] *Ibid.*, pp. 3–4.
[66] Proclamation of March 13, 1853, State Department, B.I.A. A copy was printed in Spanish in *El Siglo XIX*, 10 de abril de 1853.

21st article of the Treaty of Guadalupe Hidalgo; and that it was not the prerogative of the governor to maintain the rights of the United States in a purely federal matter. In bringing his communication to a conclusion Trias sounded a note of warning regarding Lane's proposed occupation of the territory in dispute:

I shall use the means unquestionably necessary for its defense and conservation, in case it is attacked, and upon Your Excellency alone shall rest the responsibility for the consequences to which the procedure may give place."[87]

Prior to the arrival of this dispatch, Lane received a long communication from the so-called commissioners of Chihuahua who, endowed also with certain federal functions, were at that time upon the frontier. They set forth a line of argument similar to that of Trias, and the conclusion of their dispatch was no less bellicose:

Your Excellency will pardon my recommending that, in the interest of peace and neighborliness . . you will maturely reflect and abandon your present resolution; because, if you do not, it becomes my duty as a commissioner of the Mexican Government not to permit any occupation of territory which would be prejudicial to the national honor.[88]

To the commissioners Lane replied immediately, giving evidence designed to support the contentions of his proclamation, and declaring that neither he nor the people of the United States coveted any portion of Mexican territory. The tone of his reply, however, was by no means pacifying. He said:

They [the American people] do not covet any territory that justly belongs to you, and if they did, you well know how easy would be the acquisition. . . I came here in the spirit of peace, to perform a rightful and imperious duty, and had hoped to have found the authorities of Chihuahua reasonable and law-abiding; but instead thereof, I

[87] Trias to Lane, March 28, 1853, *El Siglo XIX*, 10 de abril de 1853; also in *El Universal*, 11 de abril de 1853 and in State Department, B.I.A.

[88] Dispatch dated March 19, 1853, *El Siglo XIX*, 10 de abril de 1853; also English translation published in Santa Fé *Gazette*, a clipping of which is in the State Department, B.I.A.

have been met with demonstrations of absurd and impotent hostility. . . . [69]

Before Lane found time to frame an answer to Trias, events occurred which modified the situation. In the first place, Colonel Sumner, the commander of the Department of New Mexico, refused to respond to his call for assistance in enforcing his proclamation; and although Texan and New Mexican volunteers offered to help him occupy the territory, he deemed it inadvisable under the circumstances to do so. Accordingly, he decided to lay the whole matter before the President.[70] Secondly, he received, on May 12, a letter from Alfred Conkling, the minister of the United States in Mexico, and another from Governor Trias. Conkling had been given by the Mexican Minister of Relations the proclamation of Lane and the reply of the commissioners of Chihuahua. His official duty would have been sufficiently discharged by forwarding the documents to Washington, but in view of the "extreme gravity" of the situation he decided to make known to Lane his opinion that nothing short of indubitable right and necessity could justify the occupation of the territory, and to advise him "gracefully" to change the attitude he had assumed.[71] The dispatch from Trias informed Lane that he had received a copy of the letter of Conkling to the governor of New Mexico, and expressed the confident hope that, in view of the advice of the Minister of the United States, Lane would do nothing to interrupt the amicable relations of the two countries.[72]

Lane's reply to Trias was therefore more conciliating. He declared that the authorities of Chihuahua had erred in attributing to him warlike measures. He had brought the subject to the attention of the cabinet in Washington, and he did not propose to move further until he received advices from that

[69] Dispatch of March 23, 1853, State Department, B.I.A.; also Spanish translation in *El Universal*, 15 de mayo de 1853.

[70] Lane to Taylor, January 23, 1854, *House Rep*. No. 81, 33 cong., 2 sess. (ser. 808), pp. 1–2.

[71] Dispatch of April 8, 1853, State Department, B.I.A.

[72] Dispatch of April 30, 1853, *ibid*.

source, "unless some unexpected contingency made further action indispensibly necessary".[73]

Attitude of the Government of the United States Regarding the Action of Lane. Instead of instructing Lane as to further procedure in the matter, the federal government, in apparent disapproval of his action, sent out David Merriwether to supersede him. Merriwether was given full information regarding the state of the boundary dispute. He was told that an "unaccountable blunder" had been made in the survey. The American commissioner had given his consent to

an initial point on the Rio Grande about thirty-two miles farther north than indicated by the map annexed to and made a part of the treaty. In consequence of this mistake the line proposed to be established would exclude a large and valuable tract of country, heretofore regarded as a part of New Mexico. . . This error in the yet unfinished labor of the boundary commission has [had] furnished a pretext to Mexico to assert a claim to this extensive tract.

For numerous reasons the United States could not admit this claim. What the Mexican government or the State of Chihuahua had done in relation to the occupancy of the country was not definitely known, but Merriwether was instructed to

abstain from taking forcible possession of the tract, even if on your [his] arrival in New Mexico you find [he found] it held adversely to the claim of the U. S. by Mexico or the authorities of Chihuahua.[74]

Colonel Sumner was likewise superseded by the appointment of Brevet Brigadier-General John Garland. The new commander was given a copy of Merriwether's instructions, and informed that they contained the views of the government in regard to the New Mexican boundary.

Your tried patriotism and known discretion [said the Secretary of War] give all needful assurance that you will, on every occasion, promptly and properly maintain the rights of your country and the

[73] Dispatch of May 15, 1853, *ibid.*
[74] Marcy to Merriwether, May 28, 1853, State Department, B.I.A.

honor of its flag; and in doing so, it is expected that you will avoid, as far as you consistently can, any collision with the troops or civil authorities of the Republic of Mexico or State of Chihuahua.[75]

At the same time Secretary of State Marcy wrote Conkling that the administration had no intention of departing from the path marked out by international law in such disagreements. He said:

Where a dispute as to territorial limits arises between two nations, the ordinary course is to leave the territory claimed by them, respectively, in the same condition in which it was when the difficulty first occurred until an arrangement can be made. . . It has not been the intention of the United States to deviate from this course, nor has any notice been given by Mexico that she proposed to assume jurisdiction over it. . .[69]

Governor Lane is justified in claiming the disputed territory as part of New Mexico and in denying that the acts of the boundary commission had in any manner effected a transfer of the territory from New Mexico to Chihuahua, but his proceeding to enter the territory and hold it by force of arms [!] is not approved and will not be, unless it shall appear that the authorities of Chihuahua had changed or were attempting to change the state of things in the disputed territory from the condition in which they were before the action of the boundary commission on that part of the line. The successor of Governor Lane will proceed without delay to New Mexico with instructions to pursue a course fair towards Mexico and usual in such cases.[76]

Alarm in Mexico. Such of this correspondence as came to light could hardly be calculated to allay the uneasiness and suspicion in Mexico. The Mexicans were especially apprehensive because of the aggressive attitude of the Anglo-Americans as revealed by the actions of the Tehuantepec company and the filibusters, and in the United States press. The Mexican commissioner had shown certain uneasiness almost from the beginning. On April 20, 1850, De la Rosa complained to Webster

[75] Davis to Garland, June 2, 1853, War Department.
[76] J. B. Moore, *History and Digest of International Law,* (Washington, 1906), I. 754.

of delay in the execution of the survey, concluding his note with the significant remark that he had called the matter to the attention of the United States government

in order that if in the future the unsettled state of the boundary between the two republics should unfortunately give rise to any unpleasant differences between them, no blame whatever may [might] be imputed to the government of Mexico.[77]

In the following year, after the reorganization of the commission of the United States, he objected to multiplicity of duties thrust upon the new body. He complained that it would require five years to complete the work at the previous rate of progress, and went on to call attention to the importance of the completion of the boundary survey to the preservation of the relations of friendship and good understanding between the two countries.[78] Again, in 1852, La Vega lodged with the Secretary of State a somewhat lengthy protest. He reminded Webster that, notwithstanding the fact that the joint commission had long since reached an agreement concerning the initial point of the boundary, its survey had been constantly delayed by the absence of the American surveyor, by numerous changes in the personnel of the United States commission, and by lack of harmony among its members. He implored the United States to organize the commission in permanent form, and declared that if the same method of confusion was continued, Mexico would not be responsible for the consequences.[79]

The news of Lane's proclamation not only caused the State of Chihuahua to take immediate action, but it led to some preparations on the part of the Mexican Federal government. On April 1, the former sent out circulars to the *jefe-politicos* instructing them to make effective the national guard. On the following day Trias was granted leave of absence for the purpose of proceeding to the frontier. He levied a forced loan,[80] collected

[77] *Sen. Ex. Doc.* No. 119, 32 cong., 1 sess. (ser. 626), pp. 2–4.
[78] De la Rosa to Webster, *Sen. Ex. Doc.* No. 120, 32 cong., 1 sess. (ser. 627), pp. 1–2.
[79] De la Vega to Webster, January, 1852, *loc. cit.*, pp. 2–4.
[80] *El Siglo XIX*, 23 de abril y 17 de mayo de 1853; *El Universal*, 20 de abril de 1853.

troops and supplies, and before the close of the month, arrived at El Paso with some 800 men.[81]   At the same time, he dispatched to Mexico City a commissioner who was to present the claims of Chihuahua to the supreme government.[82]   The action of Trias seems to have been approved.   According to reports, the central government ordered to Chihuahua two companies of the Battalion of the Line, the *cuerpos activos* of Aguas Calientes and Guanajuato, and three pieces of artillery.[83]   At the same time the governor of Durango was ordered to the aid of Chihuahua.   The chief executive of Zacatecas apparently had already dispatched 200 troops of the national guard to the frontier.[84]

The Mexican press showed considerable interest and uneasiness regarding the matter.   The two leading papers of Mexico City sought to arouse the patriotism of their countrymen.   On May 15, the editor of *El Universal* exhorted his readers to recall the "infinite offences" which their country had suffered with shameful resignation from the neighboring republic.   Seeking to stimulate confidence, he contended that Mexico's seven millions were not defeated in 1847 by Scott, but rather by the vicious federal political system which had created a perennial source of internal strife by placing the divided power into the hands of the selfish and ignorant.   Under such a system good men had been made the victims of unjust contumelies and atrocious persecutions, and had consequently lost all spirit and hope.   But all this had changed now.   The present government, based as it was upon fixed and sound principles, was capable of giving encouragement and creating patriotism.   If Governor Lane was judging Mexico in 1853 by Mexico in 1847 he was destined to have his eyes opened.   Mexico now had "magnificent prospects; *y un pueblo con estas esperanzas no las abandona facilmente, no se deja subyugar*".   On May 24, the same periodical reported the news that Lane's conduct had been disapproved by the cabinet at Washington.   But the editor was still uneasy.

Trias wrote Lane from El Paso on April 30.
El Universal, 11 de mayo de 1853.
El Siglo XIX, 23 de abril y 17 de mayo de 1853.
El Siglo XIX, 26 de abril de 1853.

This approval, if indeed it had occurred, might indicate that Pierce would respect Mexican rights, but his term would soon be over, and even during his administration "unexpected contingencies" might arise. On June 5, he came forth with an editorial urging the organization of a strong army, pointing out as the chief reason for this action the fact that the reported attitude of the Pierce government regarding Mesilla could not be taken as unfailing evidence that the United States would always be able to restrain the sentiment for unlimited expansion.

Statements coming from an organ which, like *El Universal*, was supporting Santa Anna and his centralist system, probably should be somewhat discounted. The threat of foreign invasion may have had something to do with his recall from exile,[44] and it could certainly be used to consolidate his power. But even *El Siglo XIX* gave evidence of considerable feeling and alarm. On June 5, the editor stated that indications pointed to the conclusion that the United States had not been responsible for Lane's action. It might be that war would not result. He hoped not. The Mexican people did not desire war, but they could not afford to allow their rights to be infringed upon. "If just because Mexico is weaker than the United States, we should submit to the most exaggerated pretensions, our country would be unworthy of the name nation."

News that the disapproval of Lane's action was probably the cause of his removal, and that the commander of the federal forces in New Mexico had refused to support the territorial executive, should have served to allay the disturbed state of mind at least temporarily, but certain factors tended to nullify the effect of these actions. Lane had been replaced, but what instructions had been given to Merriwether who superseded him? Sumner had refused to assist Lane in his proposed occupation of *Mesilla*, but he had now been transferred elsewhere, and the instructions and attitude of Garland who had been placed in command of the New Mexican department were matters for uneasy conjecture. Conkling had assumed a conservative and

[44] *El Universal*, 30 de marzo de 1853, and following; Bancroft, *History of Mexico* (San Francisco, 1883-1888), V. 634.

friendly attitude regarding the dispute, but what instructions would be given to Gadsden who was soon to succeed to his post?

In the absence of definite knowledge the Mexican public turned to the American newspaper. June 22, *El Universal* reported that the latest periodicals from the United States indicated the most interesting topic of discussion to be *La Mesilla*. The New Orleans *Picayune* had announced that the affair had taken on new complications. A number of troops had already received orders to proceed from Texas to New Mexico, among which were six companies of the eighth regiment of infantry. The two companies of light artillery already stationed in New Mexico were to receive fresh horses. Three hundred recruits were to leave Fort Leavenworth on the 20th for Santa Fé. Under the command of Garland, they were to form a sort of escort for Governor Merriwether. Although the administration did not think war would result, it had resolved to have forces in readiness upon the frontier. The *True Delta* of New Orleans declared that the United States meant to repel any Mexican force that appeared in the disputed region. The *True Delta* did not believe a serious break would occur, however, for Mexico surely must know that such a step would mean "the disappearance forever of its nationality". At the same time these periodicals, together with the Washington *Union* which was supposed to be the official organ, asserted that Gadsden was to proceed to Mexico with authority to purchase the Mesilla Valley and whatever other territory the government "desired" or was "compelled to have" for the purpose of a Pacific railway.

On June 29, the entire front page of *El Universal* was covered by an editorial treating of the recent news from the United States, and giving special attention to an article contained in a recent number of the *Union*. The editor remarked that although the first news from Washington had been gratifying, it now seemed that there had been a change. He was inclined to this opinion the more, because the news had been conveyed by official and semi-official channels. Moreover, Mexico need not be surprised to learn of the changed attitude, because the nation had already had occasion to be grieved by the iniquitous genius of the Republic of the North for advancing its material interests. The *Union* had produced arguments in support of the contention that *La Mesilla* belonged to the United States; but to a nation whose politics were based upon the brutal laws of force only one argument, that of self-interest, was necessary. Why not renounce the treaty of Guadalupe Hidalgo, renew the fight which it terminated, and require more territory as the price of peace?

President Polk invaded us because his country desired . . . more territory. To-day there exists the same desire. . . Why does not Mr. Pierce give pleasure to the democrats? Why does he not extend, as they say, the *area of liberty* so as to cause to participate in its benefits the people which they consider slaves? Ah! it would be worthy of the Model republic to *emancipate* the new world by the same system which it had employed in Texas, California, and New Mexico!

Finally, while the same organ, on July 25, denied the statement that hostilities had opened between the Mexican and American forces in the neighborhood of Mesilla, it reported in its number of September 8, news purporting to come from a reliable source that the United States had 10,000 troops on the Rio Grande and that a skirmish had occurred between Trias and an American detachment.

Once more it must be borne in mind that *El Universal* was a supporter of Santa Anna whose interest such alarm would serve. Nevertheless, these reports must have kept the public in a state of anxiety. Moreover, *El Siglo XIX*, continued to give alarming excerpts from the news of the United States relating to the dispute. The *Chronicle* of New York, for instance, was quoted as reporting that Merriwether had orders to resist the occupation of Mesilla by Mexican troops, while a clipping from the *Times* declared that Trias and Garland could not carry out their respective orders without "clash and bloodshed", and that the arms and munitions sent to the frontier were more than had been at the disposal of General Taylor during his campaign.[86]

[86] *El Siglo XIX*, 11 y 13 de julio de 1853.

Public Opinion in the United States. As the foregoing quotations have already indicated, a portion of the press in the United States assumed either a somewhat defiant or a patronizing attitude. The editor of the *Alta California* of May 25, said that Santa Anna knew better than to attack the United States, but on August 22, he declared that he was "by no means satisfied" that the matter would be settled without war. The order of General Garland to the valley with troops was "entirely without meaning" if he did not mean to take possession, and, if he did, war was "inevitable". In the following September, the same paper reported that news from Washington was "unpleasantly indicative of a renewal of hostilities". The editor considered the "gradual absorption or the violent dismemberment of Mexico" an event which was to be consummated within a few years. And yet, Santa Anna had shown more disposition to carry his point by diplomacy than by war. It might be, also, that the increased military force lately ordered to the Rio Grande by the government of the United States was "designated to defend the frontier from Indian invasion".[87]

The exciting rumors in the United States apparently reached their climax in August. At that time the journals of New York, New Orleans, and Baltimore reported that Mexico was throwing a large body of troops on the Rio Grande with hostile intent. Such statements at length led the Mexican legation in the United States to send to the papers of Washington an explanatory communication to the effect that the movement of Mexican troops had for its purpose the maintenance of order and the defense of the frontier against the Indians.[88]

The Mexican Version of the Gadsden Treaty. The rumors of a threatened outbreak of hostilities gave opportunity for Santa Anna and his party to frame a version of the Gadsden negotiations which placed his sale of Mexican territory before his constituency in a somewhat favorable light. When the news of the alienation of the national domain aroused a storm of protest, the dictator and his friends endeavored to excuse their action

[87] *Alta California*, September 8, 1853.
[88] *El Siglo XIX*, 11 de noviembre de 1853; *Harper's Monthly*, VIII. (November, 1853), 835.

by the allegation that the United States would have taken the territory by force had they not consented to its sale.[89] This story was not sufficiently convincing, however, to stem the tide of opposition which soon ended in Santa Anna's overthrow, and on two subsequent occasions he referred to the affair, along with other matters, in an attempt to restore himself to the good graces of the Mexican people. These two accounts, one contained in a *pronunciamiento* issued from his place of exile in 1858 and the other in his memoirs written some ten years later, agree in essentials. In the first, he said, in substance, that the government of the United States, with the view of stirring up trouble, had dispatched a considerable force to threaten the department of Chihuahua; that the Mexicans "had nothing with which to oppose the invaders arrogantly appearing along the frontier but the sad spectacle . . . of our [their] exceeding weakness"; that during the progress of the negotiations Gadsden gave the Mexican officials to understand that the territory in question was absolutely essential to the United States, and that Mexico had as well sell it for a reasonable price, since "imperious necessity" would at length compel the Washington government to take it anyway. In the second statment, Santa Anna asserted that the United States government, "with knife in hand, was still trying to cut another piece from the body it had just horribly mutilated"; and that "an American division was already treading the soil of the State of Chihuahua". He then proceeded to describe the diplomatic conferences in detail. Although in the first account Santa Anna had said that Gadsden made propositions regarding "Baja California, part of Chihuahua and Sonora", in the later version he added Sinaloa and part of Durango. He remarked here, also, that Gadsden's threat to the effect that his government would resort to force in case Mexico persisted in refusing to part with territory, was made at a moment when the envoy was angry at the tenacity with which the Mexican negotiators supported their contentions.[90]

[89] See *El Universal*, 25 de enero de 1853, *et seq.*; *El Siglo XIX*, 26 de enero de 1853, *et seq.*

[90] For an English translation of these statements of Santa Anna, see *The Southwestern Historical Quarterly*, XXIV. No. 3 (January, 1921), 235 ff.

Since this version of the negotiations has been accepted by some of the leading historians of Mexico,[91] the concluding paragraphs of this paper may appropriately be given to an examination tion of the matter in the light of the documents now available. It will be noted that, according to this view, two charges are preferred against the United States government: (1) it occupied the territory in dispute prior to Santa Anna's decision to sell the region in question, and (2), it concentrated forces on the Rio Grande with the purpose of intimidating Mexico and compelling a cession of territory. The whole truth will not be known, of course, until all the Gadsden correspondence has been revealed, as well as all of the orders issued to the military commanders on the southern frontier; but the evidence now available renders the first charge in this version of the matter highly improbable. Reference has already been made to Marcy's decision that the territory in dispute should remain just as it was prior to the occurrence of the disagreement. It has been seen, also, that the region in question had probably not been occupied before Lane's removal from office, that Merriwether was instructed not to take any steps toward occupying the territory, even if upon his arrival he should find Mexican troops on the ground; and that Garland, who superseded Sumner as commander of the forces of the United States in the region, was handed a copy of Merriwether's instructions for his guidance. These facts seem to indicate the absence of any intention on the part of the United States to occupy the disputed section; and apparently there was no change of purpose prior to the completion of the negotiations which resulted in the Gadsden treaty.

In the first letter written from his post of duty, Merriwether remarked that there were about thirty Mexican soliders in the disputed territory, and that rumor had it that there were many more on their way, but he made not the slightest reference

[91] See, for instance, Vicente Riva Palacio, *Mexico a través de los Siglos* (Barcelona, 1888-1889), IV. 812, 916; Niceto de Zamacois, *Historia de Méjico* (Mexico, 1877-1882), XIII. 663-664, 776; Francisco de Paula de Arrangois y Berzábal, *Mexico desde 1808 hasta 1867* (Madrid, 1871-1872), II. 344; Ignacio Álvarez, *Estudios sobre la Historia de Mexico* (Zacatecas, 1869-1877), VI. 75-76.

to United States troops being stationed there.[92] In his dispatch of August 31, he confirmed his previous view of the situation, but maintained the same significant silence regarding the forces of the United States.[93] Although no letter of Merriwether's written during September or October has been seen, the communication of Gadsden (dated October 8, 1853) to the military officer commanding in New Mexico, which informed him that an agreement to leave the territory in *statu quo* had been made but gave no directions as to the removal of troops, appears to be strong evidence that no news regarding an occupation on the part of United States forces had reached the American Minister up to this time.[94] Lastly a letter from Merriwether to Marcy, dated November 14, indicates that such action had not yet been taken. Merriwether asked for instructions regarding a criminal who had escaped to the disputed region. He said, he feared that if he asked the governor of Chihuahua for the culprit, his request might be construed into an acknowledgment of the possession of the section by that state, and that an attempt at forcible seizure might "precipitate matters more than it is [was] desirable to the government at Washington".[95] Since the report of subsequent occupation could hardly have reached Mexico City in time to effect the Gadsden negotiations, the conclusion seems warranted that the first charge preferred against the United States by Santa Anna is false.

The second charge, however, apparently rests upon a firmer basis. It may be at least a half truth; it seems pretty certain that the United States did increase its forces on the southwestern frontier. Moreover, this augmentation may have been designed to intimidate Mexico into a favorable settlement of the points at issue. The concluding paragraph of Merriwether's letter of November 14 gives some indication of such a purpose. He said:

At this time there is no military force in the disputed territory, the Mexicans having removed their small force some time since, and should

[92] Merriwether to Marcy, August 13, 1853, State Department, B.I.A.
[93] Same to same, *loc. cit.*
[94] State Department, B.I.A.
[95] State Department, B.I.A.

the general government desire to precipitate matters this will afford an opertunity [sic] of so doing.

The fact that troops were concentrated on the frontier would not, however, necessarily imply an intention on the part of the United States government to resort to force in order to settle the dispute; they could have been sent for the purpose of dealing with the Indian situation in New Mexico which was sufficiently grave to justify the step, or as a counter move against the reported concentration of Mexican troops on the northern frontier.

J. FRED RIPPY.

University of Chicago.

ROYAL ORDINANCES CONCERNING THE LAYING OUT OF NEW TOWNS

To those who, like the writer, have observed the uniformity of the plans of so many Hispano-American cities and enjoyed the beauty of their central plazas filled with trees and flowers and surrounded by public buildings, and their picturesque churches, the following ordinances concerning the laying out of towns in the New World, issued by King Philip II. from the Escorial in 1573 can not but be of interest.

These ordinances are contained in the voluminous royal decree entitled: "Ordinances concerning discoveries, settlements, and pacifications", which remarkable document I came across in the National Archives in Madrid in 1912. Being particularly impressed by the wisdom and foresight revealed in the set of ordinances relating to the choice of the sites and the laying out of new towns, I copied these for future reference and use and am now pleased to present to the readers of THE HISPANIC AMERICAN HISTORICAL REVIEW so interesting a legacy from the past.

It seems more than probable that these ordinances issued by the painstaking monarch were the outcome of long discussions with the group of the foremost architects, engineers, and learned men of his time whom he assembled about him at his court when the palace of the Escorial was in process of construction. It is obvious that the plan he prescribed was an ideal one which embodied all advantages from the various points of view of artists, churchmen, engineers, architects, strategists, meteorologists, and hygienists. No feature that could ensure the beauty, commodiousness, and salubrity of a town seems to have been overlooked.

On the one hand minute directions are given concerning the proportions and size of the main square which was to form the nucleus of every town; to furnish a plan of recreation for its

743

inhabitants; and to be surrounded by stately public buildings, shops, and commercial houses only lined with an arcade. Four main streets, also lined with arcades, were to extend from the middle of each of the sides of the square, while two minor streets were to converge at each of its corners. These were to face the cardinal points so that the main streets leading to the square should not be exposed to the four principal winds "which would cause much inconvenience". The parish church and monasteries were to occupy entire blocks, the only buildings permitted near them being such as would add to their ornamentation or commodiousness.

The site of the parish church of a coast town was to be chosen, preferably on an elevation, so that it would be visible to those who landed and could also serve as an additional means of defense for a port. On the other hand it is a surprising revelation to find that each town was to support two hospitals. One of these, for the poor suffering from non-contagious diseases was to be built within the cloister or enclosure of the church. The other, for those stricken with contagious diseases, was to be built, if possible, on elevated ground and so placed that the prevailing winds passing over it would not convey hurt to the inhabitants of the rest of the town.

Sea ports were to be oriented according to the prevailing winds. The sea was not to lie at their south or west. If possible they were not to be near lagoons and swamps in which venomous animals [mosquitoes?] breed and which corrupt the air and water.

All fisheries, slaughterhouses, tanneries, and other industries producing filthy refuse were to be relegated below the town to seashore or river bank where the refuse could be conveniently disposed of and where the prevailing wind would carry away the evil smells. A wise order, intended to ensure the comfort of their inhabitants, is one directing that while in cool climates streets were to be wide, in hot countries they were to be narrow so that they would always be shaded and cool.

When one considers the haphazard way most North American towns have sprung up without a thought being given to their future beauty or sightliness, commodiousness, salubrity, or growth, one can not but regretfully realize what opportunities have been lost, and what a benefit it would have been if, throughout the New World, King Philip's ordinances had been known and followed. As it is, they constitute what was probably the most remarkable attempt ever made to formulate principles of town planning and to impose their execution, *pro bono publico*, on the pioneers of a New World whose descendants to this day have good reason to be grateful to their authors, the Spanish king and his counselors.

ZELIA NUTTALL.

REAL ORDENANZAS PARA NUEVAS POBLAÇIONES, ETC.[1]

San Lorenzo, 3 de Julio 1573. Yo el Rey. Ordenanzas para descubrimientos, nuevas poblaçiones y pacificaciones.

110. . . . Aviendo hecho el descubrimiento elegido de la Provincia Comarca y tierra que se oviere de poblar y los sitios de los lugares adonde se han de hazer las nuebas poblaçiones y tomandose el assiento sobre ellos, los que fueren a cumplirlo executen en la forma siguiente = llegando al lugar donde se a de hazer la poblaçion el qual mandamos que sea de los que estuvieren vacantes y que por disposiçion fira se puede tomar sin perjuicio de los yndios y naturales, o con su libre consentimiento se haga la planta del lugar rrepartiendola por sus plaças calles y solares a cordel y rregla, començando desde la plaça mayor, y desde alli sacando las calles a las puertas y caminos principales y dexando tanto compas abierto que aunque la poblaçion vaya en crecimiento se pueda siempre prosseguir en la mesma forma, y auiendo dispusiçion en el sitio y lugar que se escogiere para poblar se haga la planta en la forma siguiente.

111. Auiendo Hecho la Eleçion del sitio adonde se ha de hazer la poblaçion que como esta dicho a de ser en lugares lebantados, a donde aya sanidad fortaleza fertilidad y copia de tierra de labor y pasto, leña y madera y materiales, aguas dulces, gente natural, comodidad, acarretos, entrada y salida, que este descubierto de viento norte, siendo en costa tengase consideraçion al puerto y que no tenga al mar al medio dia ni al poniente si fuere pussible no tenga cerca de si lagunas ni pantanos en que se crien animales venenossos y corrupçion de ayre y aguas.

[1] Pressmark: "MS. 3017. Bulas y Cedulas para el Gobierno de las Indias."

112. La Plaça mīor de donde se a de començar la poblaçion siendo en costa de mar se deue hazer al desembarcadero del puerto y siendo en lugar mediterraneo, en medio de la poblaçion.   La plaça sea en cuadro prolongado que por lo menos tenga de largo una vez y media de su ancho porque este tamaño es el mejor para las fiestas de a cavallo y qualesquier otras que se ayan de hazer.

113. La grandeza de la plaça sea proporcionada a la cantidad de los vezinos teniendo consideraçion que en las poblaçiones de yndios como son nuebas se van y es con yntento de que an de ir en augmento y anssi se hara la Eleçion de la plaça teniendo rrespecto a que la poblaçion puede crecer, no sea menor que de duçientos pies en ancho y treçientos en largo, ni mayor de ochocientos pies de largo y treinta y dos [sic] de ancho de mediana y de buena proporçion es de seysçientos pies de largo y quatroçientos de ancho.

114. De la plaça salgan quatro calles prinçipales una por medio de cada costado de la plaça y dos calles por cada esquina de la plaça, las quatro esquinas de la plaça miren a los quatro vientos principales, porque desta manera saliendo las calles de la plaça no estan expuestas a los quatro vientos principales que seria de mucho ynconveniente.

115. Toda la plaça a la rredonda y las quatro calles principales que dellas salen tengan portales, porque son de mucha comodidad para los tratantes que aqui suelen concurrir, las ocho calles que salen de la plaça por las quatro esquinas lleguen libres a la plaça sin encontrarse con los portales retrayendoles de manera que hagan azera derecha con la calle y plaça.

116. Las calles en lugares frios sean anchas y en los calientes sean angostas, pero para defenssa adonde ay cauallos son mexores anchas.

117. Las calles se prossigan desde la plaça mīor de manera que aunque la poblaçion venga en mucho crecimiento no venga a dar en algun ynconveniente que sea caussa de afear lo que se houiere reedificado o perjudique su defenssa y comodidad.

118. A trechos de la poblaçion se vayan formando plaças menores en buena proporçion adonde se an de edificar los templos de la yglesia mayor, parochias y monasterios de manera que todo se rreparta en buena proporçion por la dotrina.

119. Para el temple de la yglesia mīor siendo la poblaçion en costa se edifique en parte que en saliendo de la mar se vea y su fabrica que en parte sea como defenssa del mesmo puerto.

120. Para el templo de la yglesia mīor parochia o monasterio se señalen solares, los primeros despues de la plaça y calles y sean en ysla

entera de manera que ningun edificio se le arrime sino el perteneçiente a su comodidad y ornato.

121. Señalese luego sitio y lugar para la cassa Real de conçejo y cavildo y aduana y atarazana junto al mesmo templo y puerto de manera que en tiempo de neçessidad se puedan fauoreçer las unas a las otras. El ospital para pobres y enfermos de enfermedades que no sean contagiossas se ponga junto al templo y por claustro del, para los enfermos de enfermedades contagiossas se ponga el ospital en parte que ningun viento dañoso passando para el vaya a herir en la demas poblaçion, y si se edificare en lugar leuantado sera mejor.

122. El sitio y solares para carniçerias, pescaderias, tenerias y otras cossas que se caussan ynmundiçias se den en parte que con facilidad se puedan conserbar sin ellas.

123. Las poblaçiones que se hisieren fuera del puerto de mar en lugares mediterraneos si pudieren ser en ribera de rio navegable sera de mucha comodidad y procuresse que la ribera quede la parte del cierço y quede la parte del rrio y mar, baxa de la poblaçion se pongan todos los ofiçios que caussan ynmundiçias.

124. El templo en lugares mediterraneos no se ponga en la plaça sino distante della y en parte que este separado de edifiçio que a el se llegue que no sea tocante a el, y que de todas partes sea visto porque se puede ornar mejor y tenga mas authoridad, ase de procurar que sea algo leuantado del suelo de manera que se aya de entrar en el por gradas y çerca del entre la plaça mIor y se edifiquen las cassas rreales y del conçejo y cauildo aduana no de manera que den embaraço al templo sino que lo authorizen, el ospital de los pobres que no fueren de enfermedad o contagiossa a la parte del çierço con comodidad suya de manera que goze del medio dia.

125. La mesma planta se guarde en qualquier lugar mediterraneo en que no aya ribera con que se mire mucho que aya las demas comodidades que se Requieren y son menester.

126. En la Plaça no se den solares para particulares donde para fabrica de la yglessia y cassas Reales y propios de la çiudad y edifiquense tiendas y cassas para tratantes y sea lo primero que se edifique para lo qual contribuyan todos los pobladores y se ymponga algun moderado derecho sobre las mercaderias para que se edifiquen.

127. Los demas solares se rrepartan por suerte á los poladores continuandolos a los que dellos corresponden a la plaça mIor y los que restaren queden para nos para hazer mȓd. dellos a los que despues fueren a poblar, o, lo que la nȓa mȓd fuere, y para que se açierte mejor lleuase siempre hecha la planta de la poblacion que se ovieren de hazer.

128. Auiendo hecho la planta de la poblaçion y rrepartimiento de solares cada vno de los pobladores en el suyo assienten su toldo si lo tuuiere para lo qual los capitanes les persuadan que los lleuen y los que no los tuuieren hagan su rrancho de materiales que con façilidad puedan auer, adonde se puedan rrecoger y todos con la mayor presteza que pudieren hagan alguna paliçada o trinchea en çerco de la plaça de manera que no puedan rreçiuir daño de los yndios naturales.

129. Señalese a la poblaçion exido en tan competente cantidad que aunque la poblacion vaya en mucho crecimiento siempre quede bastante espacio adonde la gente se pueda salir a recrear y salir los ganados sin que hagan daño.

130. Confinando con los exidos se señalen dehessas para los buyes de labor y para los Cauallos y para los ganados de las carnicerias y para el numero ordinario de ganados que los pobladores por ordenança an de tener en alguna buena cantidad, mas para que se acojan para propios del conçejo y lo rrestante se señale en tierras de labor de que se hagan suertes en la cantidad que se ofreçiere de manera que sean tantas como los solares que puede auer en la poblaçion, y si ouiere tierras de regadio se haga dellas suertes y se repartan en la misma proporçion a los primeros pobladores por sus suertes y los demas queden para nos, para que hagamos mŕd a los que despues fueren a poblar.

131. En las tierras de labor repartidas luego ynmediatamente siembren los pobladores todas las semillas que llebaren y pudieren auer, para lo qual conviene que vayan muy proueydos y en la dehessa señaladamente todo el ganado que llebaren y pudieren juntar para que luego se comiençe a criar y multiplicar.

132. Auiendo sembrado los pobladores y acomodado el ganado en tanta cantidad y con tan buena diligencia de que esperen aver abundancia de comida comiençen con mucho cuydado y valor a fundar sus cassas y edificar de buenos cimientos y paredes, para lo qual vayan aperçibidos de Tapiales ó tablas para los Hazer y todas las otras herramientas para edificar con brebedad y a poca costa.

133. Dispongan los solares y edificios que en ellos hizieren de manera que en la habitaçion dellos se pueda gozar de los ayres de medio dia y del norte por ser los mejores disponganse los edifiçios de las cassas de toda la poblaçion generalmente, de manera que sirban de defenssa y fuerça contra los que quissieren estorbar ó ynfestar la poblaçion y cada cassa en particular la labren, de manera que en ella puedan tener sus cauallos y vestias de servicio con patios y corrales y con la mas anchura que fuere pussible para la salud y limpieza.

134. Procuren quanto fuere pussible que los edifiçios sean de vna forma por el ornato de la poblacion.

135. Tenga cuidado de andar viendo como esto se cumple, los fieles executores y alarifes y las perssonas que para esto diputare el gouernador, y que se den priessa en la labor y edificio para que se acabe con brebedad la poblaçion.

136. Si los naturales quissieren poner en defenssa de la poblacion se le de a entender como se quiere poblar alli no para hazerles algun mal ni tomarles sus haziendas sino para tomar amistad con ellos y enseñarlos a vivir politicamente y mostrarles a conocer á Dios y enseñarles su ley por lo qual se salbaran dandoselo á entender por medio de los religiossos y clerigos y perssonas que para ello diputaren gouernador y por buenas lenguas y procurando por todos los buenos medios pussibles que la poblacion se haga con su paz y consentimiento, y si todavia no lo consintieren auiendoles requerido por los muchos medios diverssas vezes los pobladores hagan su poblaçion sin tomar de lo que fuere particular de los yndios, y sin hazerles mas daño del que fuere menester para defenssa de los pobladores y para que la poblaçion [no] se estorbe.

137. Entretanto que la nueba poblaçion se acaua los pobladores en quanto fuere pussible procuren evitar la comunicaçion y trato con los yndios y de no yr a sus pueblos ni diuertirse ni derramarse por la tierra, ni que los yndios entren en el circuyto de la poblacion hasta tener hecha y puesta en defenssa y las cassas de manera que quando los yndios las vean les causse admiracion, y entiendan que los españoles pueblan alli de assiento y no de passo y los teman para no ossar ofender y rrespeten para dessear su amistad, y en començandose a hazer la poblaçion, el gouernador reparta alguna persona que se ocupe en sembrar y cultibar la tierra de pan y legumbres de que luego se puedan socorrer para sus mantenimientos y que los ganados que metieren se apaçienten donde esten seguros y no hagan daño en heredad ni cossa de los yndios para que assi mesmo de los susodichos ganados y sus crias se puedan serbir socorrer y sustentar la poblaçion. . . .

TRANSLATION

ROYAL ORDINANCES FOR NEW TOWNS, ETC.

San Lorenzo, July 3, 1573. I the King. Ordinances for discoveries, new settlements, and pacifications.

110. . . . Having made the chosen discovery of the province, district, and land which is to be settled, and the sites of the places where the new towns are to be made, and the agreement in regard to them having preceded, those who

go to execute this shall perform it in the following manner: On arriving at the place where the town is to be laid out (which we order to be one of those vacant and which by our ordinance may be taken without doing hurt to the indians and natives, or with their free consent), the plan of the place shall be determined, and its plazas, streets, and building lots laid out exactly, beginning with the main plaza. From thence the streets, gates, and principal roads, shall be laid out, always leaving a certain proportion of open space, so that although the town should continue to grow, it may always grow in the same manner. Having arranged the site and place that shall have been chosen for settlement, the foundation shall be made in the following manner.

111. Having chosen the place where the town is to be made, which as abovesaid must be located in an elevated place, where are to be found health, strength, fertility, and abundance of land for farming and pasturage, fuel and wood for building, materials, fresh water, a native people, commodiousness, supplies, entrance and departure open to the north wind. If the site lies along the coast, let consideration be had to the port and that the sea be not situated to the south or to the west. If possible, let there be no lagoons or marshes nearby in which are found venomous animals and corruption of air and water.

112. The main plaza whence a beginning is to be made, if the town is situated on the seacoast, should be made at the landing place of the port. If the town lies inland, the main plaza should be in the middle of the town. The plaza shall be of an oblong form, which shall have at the least a length equal to one and a half times the width, inasmuch as this size is the best for fiestas in which horses are used and for any other fiestas that shall be held.

113. The size of the plaza shall be proportioned to the number of the inhabitants, having consideration to the fact that in indian towns, inasmuch as they are new, the population will continue to increase, and it is the purpose that it shall increase. Consequently, the choice of a plaza shall be made with reference to the growth that the town may have. It shall be not less than two hundred feet wide and three hundred feet long, nor larger than eight hundred feet long and thirty two feet [sic] wide. A moderate and good proportion is six hundred feet long and four hundred feet wide.

114. From the plaza shall run four main streets, one from the middle of each side of the plaza; and two streets at each corner of the plaza. The four corners of the plaza shall face the four principal winds. For the streets running thus from the plaza, they will not be exposed to the four principal winds which cause much inconvenience.

115. The whole plaza round about, and the four streets running from the four sides shall have arcades, for these are of considerable convenience to the merchants who generally gather there. The eight streets running from the plaza at the four corners shall open on the plaza without any arcades and shall be so laid out that they may have sidewalks even with the street and plaza.

116. The streets in cold places shall be wide and in hot places narrow; but for purposes of defense, where horses are to be had, they are better wide.

117. The streets shall run from the main plaza in such wise that although the town increase considerably in size, no inconvenience may arise which may cause what may be rebuilt to become ugly or be prejudicial to its defense and commodiousness.

118. Here and there in the town smaller plazas shall be laid out, in good proportion, where are to be built the temples of the cathedral, the parish churches and the monasteries, such that everything may be distributed in good proportions for the instruction of religion.

119. As for the temple of the cathedral, if the town is situated on the coast, it shall be built in part so that it may be seen on leaving the sea, and in a place where its building may serve as a means of defense for the port itself.

120. For the temple of the cathedral, the parish church, or monastery, building lots shall be assigned, next after the plaza and streets and they shall be so completely isolated that no building shall be added there except one appertaining to its commodiousness and ornamentation.

121. After that a site and location shall be assigned for the royal council and cabildo house and for the custom house and arsenal near the temple and port itself so that in times of need the one may aid the other. The hospital for the poor and those sick of non-contagious diseases shall be built near the temple and its cloister; and that for those sick with contagious diseases shall be built in such a place that no harmful wind passing through it, may cause harm to the rest of the town. If the latter be built in an elevated place, so much the better.

122. The site and building lots for slaughter houses, fisheries, tanneries, and other things productive of filth shall be so placed that the filth can be easily disposed of.

123. It will be of considerable convenience if those towns which are laid out away from the port and inland be built if possible on the shores of a navigable river; and the attempt should be made to have the shore where it is reached by the cold north wind; and that all the trades that give rise to filth be placed on the side of the river and sea below the town.

124. The temple in inland towns shall not be placed on the plaza but distant from it and in such a place that it may be separated from any building which approaches it and which has no connection with it; and so that it may be seen from all parts. In order that it may be better embellished and have more authority, it must, if possible, be built somewhat elevated above the ground in order that steps will lead to its entrance. Nearby close to the main plaza shall be built the royal houses and the council and cabildo house, and the customs house so that they shall not cause any embarrassment to the temple but lend it authority. The hospital of the poor who shall be sick with non-contagious diseases, shall be built facing the cold north wind and so arranged that it may enjoy the south wind.

125. The same arrangement shall be observed in all inland places which have no shore provided that considerable care be given to providing the other conveniences which are required and which are necessary.

126. Building lots shall not be assigned to individual persons in the plaza where are placed the buildings of the church and royal houses and the public land of the city. Shops and houses shall be built for merchants and these shall be the first to be built and for this all the settlers of the town shall contribute, and a moderate tax shall be imposed on goods so that these buildings may be built.

127. The other building lots shall be distributed by lot to the settlers, those lots next to the main plaza being thus distributed and the lots which are left shall be held by us for assignment to those who shall later become settlers, or for the use which we may wish to make of them. And so that this may be done better, the town which is to be laid out should always be shown on a plan.

128. Having made the plan of the town and the assignment of building lots, each of the settlers shall set up his tent on his plot if he should have one. For this purpose the captains shall persuade them to carry tents. Those who do not possess tents shall build their huts of such materials that can be obtained easily, where they may have shelter. As soon as possible all settlers shall make some sort of a palisade or ditch about the plaza so that they may receive no harm from the indian natives.

129. A commons shall be assigned to the town of such size that although the town continues to grow, there may always be sufficient space for the people to go for recreation and for the cattle to be pastured without any danger.

130. Adjoining the commons there shall be assigned pastures for the work animals and for the horses as well as for the cattle belonging to the slaughter-houses and for the usual number of cattle which the settlers must have to some goodly number according to ordinance, and so that they may also be used as the common property of the council. The rest of the land shall be assigned as farm lands, of which lots shall be cast in proportion to the amount, so that there shall be as many farms as there are building lots in the town. And should there be irrigated lands, lots shall be cast for them, and they shall be distributed in the same proportion to the first settlers according to their lots. The rest shall remain for ourselves so that we may assign it to those who may become settlers.

131. The settlers shall immediately plant all the seeds they take with them and all that they can obtain on the farm lands after their distribution. For this purpose, it is advisable that they go well provided; and in the pastures especially all the cattle that they take with them and all that they can collect so that the cattle may begin to breed and multiply immediately.

132. The settlers having planted their seeds and made arrangements for the cattle to a goodly number, and with good diligence (from which they may hope to obtain abundance of food), shall commence with great care and activity to establish their houses and to build them with good foundations and walls. For that purpose they shall go provided with molds or planks for buildings them, and all the other tools for building quickly and at small cost.

133. They shall arrange the building lots and edifices placed thereon in such a manner that the rooms of the latter may enjoy the air of the south and north as these are the best. The buildings of the houses of the whole town generally shall be so arranged that they shall serve as a defense and fort against those who may try to disturb or invade the town. Each house in particular shall be so built that they may keep therein their horses and work animals, and shall have yards and corrals as large as possible for health and cleanliness.

134. They shall try so far as possible to have the buildings all of one form for the sake of the beauty of the town.

135. The faithful executors and architects and persons who may be deputed therefor by the governor shall be most careful in the performance of the above. They shall hurry the labor and building so that the town may be completed in a short time.

136. Should the natives care to place themselves under the defense of the town, they must be made to understand that it is desired to build a town there not in order to do them any harm nor to take their possessions from them, but to maintain friendship with them and to teach them to live in a civilised manner, to teach

them to know God, and to teach them His law, under which they shall be saved. This shall be imparted to them by the religious, ecclesiastical persons, and persons deputed therefor by the governor and by means of good interpreters. By means of all good methods possible, the attempt shall be made to have the town laid out with their goodwill and consent. However, should they not consent after having been summoned by various means on different occasions, the settlers shall lay out their town, but without taking anything that may belong in particular to the indians and without doing them other hurt than what may be necessary for the defense of the settlers and so that the town should [not] be molested.

137. Until the new town shall have been completed, the settlers shall try as much as possible to avoid communication and intercourse with the indians and shall not go to their towns and shall not amuse themselves nor give themselves up to sensual pleasures in the land. Neither shall the indians enter the precincts of the town until after it has been built and placd in a condition of defense, and the houses so built that when the indians see them they shall wonder and understand that the Spaniards settle there for good and not for the moment only; and so that they may fear them so much that they will not offend them and shall respect them so much as to desire their friendship. When they begin to build the town, the goveror shall assign some one person to take care of the sowing and cultivation of the land with wheat and vegetables of which the settlers may immediately make use for their maintenance. He shall also see that the cattle are put out to pasture where they shall be safe and where they shall cause no hurt to the cultivated land nor to anything belonging to the indians; and so that also the town may be served, aided, and sustained by the aforesaid cattle and their young. . . .

BOOK REVIEWS

Pan-Americanism: Its Beginnings. By JOSEPH BYRNE LOCKEY. (New York: The Macmillan Company, 1920. Pp. 503.)

From the year 1741 until 1825 the course of the idea of a great union of the different divisions of the New World is traced by this volume, and the fact that the sympathy of leading men of North America was given to that idea, and that less widely known North Americans gave material support to it, is made clear by a mass of evidence from official records and from different publications.

A hundred and eighty years ago a conspiracy that started in Peru had branches in Buenos Aires and in Chile, in New Granada and in Venezuela. Its purpose was to make all America independent of Spanish rule. It had the support of Creoles, of Spaniards, and of the Jesuits also. A similar blow for freedom was planned in Mexico at the same time. Great Britain was asked to help the movement, and steps were taken to lend aid. For some reason the project was laid aside.

A conspiracy to overthrow monarchy in Brazil existed in 1787, and in a letter one of the leading spirits wrote to Thomas Jefferson, then United States Minister at Paris, to ask for help from the young republic, "because it is necessary that the colony should obtain assistance from some power, and the United States alone could be looked to with propriety, 'because nature in making us inhabitants of the same continent has in some sort united us in the bonds of a common patriotism'."

In that letter Señor Maia may have given the first clear expression of the thought that the basic idea of all civilized peoples of America was in essence the same: equal opportunity for each people to live its own chosen way, so far as this would trespass upon no like right of others; freedom also from monarchial monopoly of privileges, of power or of riches.

In 1797 Francisco de Miranda was authorized, by a junta of Spanish Americans in Paris, to direct a general movement for the independence of Spanish America. He sought help of Great Britain and the United States. The latter showed, unofficially, sympathy with the movement, and its citizens helped form an expeditionary force, which sailed from this country in 1806. Miranda was captured in Venezuela in 1812, and sent to Spain to die in prison.

Fifty pages of Lockey's volume are devoted to early projects for continental union, and furnish evidence enough to show that the Pan-American idea had at all times the sympathy of the people of the United States, and usually material aid also from them. It seems obvious that credit for this idea of a union of all peoples of the New World may well be given to Hispanic Americans.

Lockey says of the meaning of the terms Pan-American and Pan-Americanism:

> The adjective, Pan-American, and the substantive, Pan-Americanism, were soon taken up and defined by the dictionaries; but the definitions are not satisfactory. The adjective is usually defined as including or pertaining to the whole of America, both North and South; which is inaccurate, as it pertains, by common usage, to the independent part of the continent only.

After quoting five or six dictionaries and encyclopedias he gives the definition from the second supplement of the *Diccionario Enciclopédico Hispano-Americano* as the

> Aspiration or tendency of the peoples of the New World to establish among themselves ties of union; to promote good understanding and fraternal harmony between all the states of the continent; and to act always in accord with a view to preventing the dominance or the influence of European powers in American territory.

Thirty-one pages of the work are given to this subject, and quote many statesmen to show what Pan-Americanism meant to them.

Other chapters tell of monarchial plots against America, before 1830; of the relations between Hispanic America and the United States; of international complications; of the attitude of Hispanic America toward the Monroe Doctrine; of British influence, of the Panama Congress of 1826, and of the attitudes of Argentina, Brazil, Chile, and the United States. Finally more than fifteen pages are filled by a list of sources, chiefly printed, from which data are taken for this valuable work. Altogether it should be very useful for those who would advocate the extension of Pan-Americanism.

EDWARD PERRY.

Simón Bolívar (el Libertador), patriot, warrior, statesman, father of five nations; a sketch of his life and work. By GUILLERMO A. SHERWELL. (Washington, D. C.; 1921. Pp. 233. Front., ports., plates, map.)

Dr. Sherwell, juristic expert of the International High Commission and a prominent educator, has in the above named work given us a very sympathetic sketch of the life works and remarkable personality

of the great Liberator.   With respect to the purpose and plan of his
work the author says:

> To follow a chronological order we have been guided by the beautiful biog-
> raphy written by Larrasábal, the man called by F. Lorain Petre 'the greatest
> flatterer of Bolívar'.   .   .   Petre's monograph contains apparent earmarks of
> impartiality, but in reality it is nothing but a bitter attack on the reputation of
> Bolívar.

The subject matter is arranged in 21 chapters, an introductory
chapter on the Spanish colonies in America and a concluding section
on the man and his work.   A most valuable feature of the work is the
inclusion of lengthy extracts from the addresses, or writings of Bolívar.
The illustrative matter, portraits, and map, add notably to its value.
The material available to English readers on Hispanic American
history and especially regarding the great political, military, and literary
leaders is, unfortunately, exceedingly limited.   From this point of
view, we have further reason for appreciating Dr. Sherwell's work
which he has written in English instead of increasing the extensive
bibliography of Bolívar by another monograph in Spanish.   The time
of its appearance, too, when attention is called to the work of the great
Venezuelan by the celebration in New York, is most opportune.

C. K. JONES.

*Documentos para la Historia Argentina.   Tomo XIII.   Communica-
ciones Oficiales y Confidenciales de Gobierno* (1820–1823).   Con advertencia de EMILIO RAVIGNANI.   Published by the History Section
of the Faculty of Philosophy and Letters of the University of Buenos
Aires.   (Buenos Aires; 1920.   Pp. XI, 371.   Indexes.   Paper.)

The Ministry of Foreign Relations of the Argentine Republic possesses valuable archives which, heretofore, have not been readily
accessible to the public.   In Volume XIII. of its series of Documents for
Argentine History, the Faculty of Philosophy and Letters of the National University of Buenos Aires has just published the contents of a
record book preserved in these archives.   It was facilitated by Sr.
Don Diego Luis Molinari, sub-secretary of Foreign Relations.   The
Faculty's History Section had determined upon the publication of
these documents under the directorship of Dr. Luis María Torres; it
has been carried into effect under his successor, Dr. Emilio Ravignani,
who, in a foreword, acknowledges Sr. Molinari's service in rendering
accessible the treasures of the Ministry's archives, a service to which

he is presently to add another in the study of the papers now published in Volume XIII., which study the History Section will include in its series of monographs. The documents of Volume XIII. concern domestic developments during the administration of Martín Rodríguez, from the year 1820—that is, forward from the crisis precipitated by the province of Buenos Aires in its insistence upon autonomy.

The appearance of this volume is of special interest, not only because of the value of the material for history which it puts into circulation, but also because of the successful progress it indicates in the Faculty's activities. Whereas the earlier publications of the Faculty concerned other matters, those of late years have had to do with the viceroyalty, that is, with the colonial era which preceded that of independence, and, apparently, it was the intention to continue along the single line of chronological order. When Sr. Molinari threw open the door of the archives of the Ministry of Foreign Relations the temptation became too great to resist, and it was desired also to contribute to that period which culminated in the constitution of 1853, and the Faculty has harked back to its three volumes, issued in 1911 and 1912, under the title of *Documentos relativos a la Organización Constitucional de la República Argentina*. The archives of the Ministry are to be levied upon for further contributions to the history of that formative period, and so also are the provincial archives of the Republic, which the Faculty has by no means overlooked in investigations which it has already made. Nevertheless, the colonial era of the viceroyalty is to be neither abandoned nor even neglected. Work there will continue, in evidence of which the Faculty announces, for instance, a *Relación descriptive de los Mapas, Planos*, etc., *del Virreinato de Buenos Aires existentes en el Archivo General de Indias*, second edition, prepared by Sr. Don Pedro Torres Lanzas, director of those archives, in Seville. Simultaneously, however, other work will now be carried on in later periods. Volumes are announced (Volume XIV., *Correspondencia General de la Provincia de Buenos Aires* relative to Foreign Relations, 1820–1823; Volume XV., The Federal Pact of January 4, 1831, and the Representative Commission) which will interlock with the earlier publications of the Faculty.

Here appears the value of possessing such a carefully considered, substantial plan for a large undertaking, as that to which the Faculty committed itself years past: since there is a definite plan, or pattern, a thread ("the organization of the Argentine Republic") dropped some time ago, can be picked up, and the design continued without difficulty or loss. Since there is such a definite plan, it can be attacked intelligently from more than one point, at the same time, without danger of duplication, derangement, or omission. This intensification of the Faculty's industry and increase in its output, announced by Dr. Ravignani in the introduction to Volume XIII., have been made possible by financial support which has just been voted by a national government which, evidently, appreciates the fact (especially patent to students of these matters) that the History Section's labors merit all possible support.

I. A. WRIGHT.

The Discovery of America and the Landfall of Columbus. The last Resting Place of Columbus. Two monographs based on personal investigations by RUDOLF CRONAU, with Reproduction of Maps, Inscriptions and Autographs, and of original Drawings by the Author; (New York: Published by R. Cronau, 140 East 198th Street, 1921. Pp. 89. Special edition of 300 copies. $5.00)

Has the age-long question as to the Landfall of Columbus in the new world been settled? The reader of the first essay in Mr. Cronau's book will incline to answer in the affirmative, if he accept the evidence adduced as trustworthy. The author's conclusions are based on personal investigations made for the purpose of studying this vexed question. Throughout he checks up his investigations with the journal of Columbus as preserved by Las Casas, and is quite satisfied that the island today known as Watling's Island is the island of Guanahani or San Salvador. He concludes that "if the beach under Riding Rock Point on the west coast be accepted as the landfall of Columbus, and if from that place we follow the track of the Admiral through the Bahamas to Cuba, the log-book of Columbus has no such contradictions or inexplicable passages as confronted all other scholars who tried to solve the Guanahani-Question. These difficulties were but natural, as it was impossible that the statements of the log-book could fit if the landing place was sought at a false spot. *The absolute conformity of the descriptions, as given by Columbus, with the still existing conditions and facts, proves that the Admiral in making the entries in his journal not only observed with great care, but very often went into details*". In his proof, the author relies somewhat on Juan de la Cosa's famous map, as well as other maps of the sixteenth and seventeenth centuries. He makes the common error of saying that Cosa's map was drawn on an oxhide,—an error to which Stevenson calls attention in the letterpress accompanying his reproduction of that map. Granted that Cosa's map represents fairly well the region under discussion, and the nomenclature of the period, the Agnese map proves nothing, as it is the product of professional map makers and not of explorers and is erroneous in more than one particular. The Ribero map of 1529, however, is a creditable map, but it is doubtful whether it or the other maps really prove anything in the present instance. In connection with this essay, the essay published in the February, 1919, issue of THE HISPANIC AMERICAN HISTORICAL REVIEW entitled "On the possibility of determining the first landfall of Columbus by archaeological research," and written by Theodoor de Booy, should be read.

The essay on the last resting place of Columbus describes the investigations made by the author in 1890 in the cathedral of the city of Santo Domingo, under credentials from the German government. He made there a complete examination, fully attested, of the coffin and remains said to be those of Columbus, and reproduces in his essay all the inscriptions, which he discusses at length. There appears to be no doubt that the real tomb of the great discoverer is in America and not in Seville under the costly mausoleum erected in the Cathedral of that city.

Both essays attest to the perennial interest that attaches to Columbus. The diction at times reveals that the native language of the author is not that in which the essays are printed. The maps and illustrations are clear.

JAMES ALEXANDER ROBERTSON.

Colección General de Documentos relativos a las Islas Filipinas existentes en el Archivo de Indias de Sevilla. Publicada por La Compañía General de Tabacos de Filipinos. Tomo IV (1522–1524). (Barcelona: Imprenta de la Viuda de Luis Tasso, 1921. Pp. viii, 380, (3). Paper 15 pesetas.)

The fourth volume of this carefully edited series maintains the high standard of excellence set by the three preceding volumes. According to the colophon, the printing of this volume was finished on May 21, 1921, which is considerably beyond the time when it should have appeared. The delay has been due, undoubtedly, to the disjointed times. Indeed, as intimated in the reviews of the preceding volumes, the publication of a series of this character has necessitated on the part of its publisher a vast amount of fortitude, for which the present reviewer can find only words of praise.

This contribution contains series documents nos. 127 to 194 inclusive. In general, it contains materials relative to the Magellan and Loaisa expeditions, the projected expedition of Esteban Gómez (who deserted Magellan in the Straits), to "Catayo Oriental", negotiations between Spain and Portugal with respect to the Moluccas and the Line of Demarcation, trade matters, and questions growing out of these. Here is found interesting and useful information bearing upon the early pilots, navigators, Spanish royal officials, the new problems of colonization appearing upon the Spanish horizon, and a multitude of other things that were combining to make of Spain the foremost nation of the day. Valuable biographical data are given, of special interest being the documents relating to that much execrated man, Esteban Gómez; to the famous and much discussed Sebastian Cabot; to Ruy Faleiro, who was to have accompanied Magellan as an equal, but who at the last moment was left behind as one demented; to Diego Díaz, factor of the powerful Cristóbal de Haro; to Bishop Fonseca, who exerted considerable influence on Spanish policy; to Diego Barbosa; and to others.

Side by side with expeditions, trade, political matters of high import, we are bidden to behold the arrangements for the marriage of King João of Portugal to the Spanish Infanta Doña Leonor, itself a part of a political game. In other documents, it is shown how the port of Coruña took on added importance as an outpost lying nearest to the new lands discovered or to be discovered within Spanish demarcation. The little frontier town of Badajoz comes into the limelight because of the Spanish-Portuguese negotiations carried on there in regard to the new lands. Throughout, we note in these documents the expanding world of the sixteenth century and the preparing of the stage for the present age. Very clearly do these valuable documents show us a Spain at its best—a nation bursting with energy, a people looking beyond the narrow confines of its home into a new world yet largely unknown, a country filled with ardent youths eager to venture themselves in the fascinating game of fame and fortune. We are in the midst here of a turmoil partly intellectual, that had grown greater with the years succeeding the voyage of Columbus.

Of the sixty-eight documents of this volume, only twenty-three have been previously published. Document 128 "Royal cedula stating the conditions for making contracts with those merchants who desire to have an interest in the Spicery fleets" (Valladolid, November 13, 1522), was published by Navarrete and Torres de Mendoza;

Doc. 132, "Anonymous undated memorial relative to the advisability of establishing the Spicery business at Coruña," by Navarrete; doc. 141, "Instructions issued by Carlos I. to his ambassadors relative to the proposals they are to make in his name to the king of Portugal about the Moluccas and the Spicery trade" (Valladolid, February 4, 1523), by Navarrete; doc. 147, "Letter of Ruy Faleiro to his majesty reciting that proposals have been made to him to return to Portugal, and petitioning that he be paid his salary and authorized to outfit a ship at his own expense" (Seville, March 22, 1523); by Medina; doc. 148, "Letter of Rodrigo Faleiro to his majesty indicating the advisability of annually sending fleets to the Indies, and petitioning that his salary be paid" (March 22, 1523), by Medina; doc. 149, "Contract made with the pilot Esteban Gómez for the discovery of East Cathay," (Valladolid, March 27, 1523); by Torres de Mendoza; doc. 156, "Evidence taken on petition of Simón de Burgos to prove that he was not a Portuguese but a citizen of Ciudad Rodrigo" (Coria, June 9, 1523), by Medina; doc. 162, "Letter of the emperor to D. Juan de Zúñiga, his ambassador in Portugal, informing him of negotiations with the envoys of that kingdom who came to Castilla to demand the ownership of the Moluccas" (Pamplona, December 18, 1523), by Navarrete; doc. 163, "Letter of Carlos I. to the king of Portugal, complaining that his ambassadors have not accepted the proposals made them with respect to the Moluccas" (Pamplona, December, 1523), by Navarrete; doc. 166, "Memorial addressed to the king by Diego Barbosa relative to certain events of the Magellan expedition and the means of carrying on the spice trade to the best profit" (1523), by Navarrete and Medina, as are all the following documents, except doc. 190, which was published by Navarrete alone, and doc. 194, by Medina alone; doc. 169, "Treaty of Victoria for the Junta of Badajoz" (Victoria, February 19, 1524); docs. 172, 173, and 174, royal cedulas appointing deputies and other officials to attend the Junta of Badajoz (Burgos, March 20 and 21, 1524); docs. 179, 180, and 181, royal cedulas giving directions to the deputies and other officials at the Junta of Badajoz (Burgos, April 10, 1524); doc. 185, "Signed opinion of Don Hernando Colón, with respect to the demarcation of the Ocean Sea" (Badajoz, April 13, 1524); doc. 186, "Opinion of Fray Tómas Durán, Sebastián Caboto, and Juan Vespucci, relative to the line of demarcation of the ocean sea" (Badajoz, April 15, 1524); doc. 190, a signed opinion by Hernando Colón on the same matter (Badajoz, April 27, 1524); docs. 190 and 193, royal cedulas addressed to the Spanish deputies and commissioners at the Junta of Badajoz (Burgos, May 7, 1524); and doc. 194, "Information educed at the request of Dr. Bernardino de Ribera to prove the right of the kings of Castile to the possession of the Moluccas (Badajoz, May 23, 1524). The editor states in his preliminary notes that an extract of docs. 141 and 162 were published (English translation) in Blair and Robertson, *The Philippine Islands*. He should have noted also that documents 169, 179, 180, 181, 185, 186, 190, and 193 are also reproduced in English translation in whole or in part in the same work.

The unpublished documents are naturally not of equal importance. Doc. 127, (Valladolid, November 6, 1522) consists of the "Instructions to Nicolás de Artieta, Diego de Cobarrubias, and Esteban Gómez for the preparation of the spicery fleet of which García de Loaisa went as captain". Other previously unpublished documents relative to the Loaisa expedition are nos. 136, 138, 142, 160, 165, and 167. The Magellan expedition and matters arising therefrom are treated in docs. 129, 130, 131, 135, 137, 139, 155, 156, and 164. The aspirations of Coruña to become a trade center are seen in docs. 133, 134, and 142. Doc. 140 is an authorization given by Carlos I. to Dr. Cabrero and Cristóbal Barroso to discuss matters relating to the Moluccas with the Portuguese monarch and to make arrangements for the marriage of the latter to Doña Leonors. Docs. 143 and 144 concern Ruy Faleiro or his kinsmen; docs. 145, 158, and 161, Sebastian Cabot; and docs. 146, 150–154, and 157, Esteban Gómez. Doc. 159 is a royal decree dated Valladolid, August 25, 1523, directing the officials of the house of trade to pay Juan de Aranda the sum of 19,000 maravedis annually for the needs of Juan Cermeño, an Indian from the Moluccas. The Junta de Badajoz forms the principal theme of docs. 168, 170, 175–178, 182–184, 187–189. Doc. 171, is a letter of March 10, 1524, from the royal officials of Santo Domingo relative to Gil González Dávila, who was to make a voyage for the discovery of the straits. Doc. 191, dated La Puebla, May 7, 1524, is a letter from Pedro Suárez de Castilla and Domingo de Ochandiano to the effect that the treaty between the kings of Spain and Portugal exists in Seville only in copies.

The volume is a creditable production. The notes which precede the documents are only explanatory of the documents and not historical or explanatory of subject matter. They show the care with which the editor has tried to locate all the documents in the Archivo de Indias of which others have spoken.

JAMES ALEXANDER ROBERTSON.

Moseteno Vocabulary and Treatises. By BENIGNO BIBOLOTI, Priest of the Franciscan Mission of Inmaculada Concepción de Covendo in Bolivia. From an Unpublished Manuscript in possession of Northwestern University Library. With an Introduction by Rudolph Schuller, formerly of the Museu Goeldi, Pará, Brazil. (Evanston and Chicago: Northwestern University, 1917. Pp. cxiii, 140, (1).)

Mr. Schuller, who has published a number of studies on early American subjects, and who has delved deeply into the early cartography of America, discovered the Biboloti Manuscript while arranging and collating the manuscripts acquired by Dr. Walter Lichtenstein, formerly librarian of Northwestern University and professor in the faculty of history of that institution. Recognizing its value as a contribution to the aboriginal languages of South America, Mr. Schuller recommended the publication of the manuscript. Mr. James A. Patten, president of the Board of Trustees of Northwestern University became interested in the vocabulary and treatises and furnished the funds necessary for their publication. However, the severance of diplomatic relations between this country and Austria made it necessary for Mr. Schuller to leave the United States before the task of editing the manuscript was completed. In taking up his work, the rough draft of the linguistic part of the introduction, was, in accordance with the advice of Professor Franz Boaz, of Columbia University, revised by Dr. Truman Mickelson of the Bureau of American Ethnology, while the historical part was revised by Dr. Lichtenstein and Professor George Edward. In the revision of Mr. Schuller's work, an English translation of the vocabulary of Father Biboloti made by Mr. Schuller, was omitted, and the author's errors which had been corrected by Mr. Schuller were restored, so that the published version corresponds to the manuscript.

Professor Boaz said of Dr. Schuller's work that although his grammar of the Moseteno tongue, as given in the introduction, is not complete, yet it is much more complete than any previously known. The Moseteno Indians of Bolivia, as explained by Mr. Schuller, have almost disappeared and the remnant is destined to become absorbed into other tribes by the process of amalgamation, due to the advance of modern civilization and the "fact that the primitive cis-Andine fishing and hunting tribes have little capacity for resistance". The introduction describes the manuscript, gives a sketch (as much as is known) of Father Biboloti, and shows the connection of the Moseteno Indians with the Franciscans. These are followed by a critical analysis of previous writings on the Moseteno language, by various vocabularies, and by the grammar, which form Mr. Schuller's special contribution. The introduction is concluded by three apendices, namely: Bresson's plagiarisms (1886) of Weddel" (1853)[1]; an "Estado eclesiástico del Arzobispado de la Plata" (1875); and a Bibliography of MSS. and of Printed Sources, consisting of six pages and forming a useful contribution.

The text of Biboloti's Manuscript follows the long introduction. The "Vocabulario Español-Musetano" [sic] consists of a list of Spanish words with their Moseteno equivalents. This is followed by phrases and treatises in the Moseteno language.

The volume is one for specialists and for that reason will appeal to a limited audience. The introduction is perhaps the most valuable part of the work, and is undoubtedly a contribution to American linguistics. Considerable credit is due to Dr. Lichtenstein, as well as to the other specialists who took up the work where Mr. Schuller left it, and who worked over his notes which had been left in a rather chaotic condition. No pains were spared in making this a presentable volume, and in its outward appearance, it is one in which the University and its special sponsor can take pride. Indeed, a business house could hardly afford to publish a volume of this nature with the hope of making it pay. It stands, however, as a tribute to pure scholarship, and will be referred to frequently by writers on the Indian language of South America.

JAMES ALEXANDER ROBERTSON.

The Italian Emigration of our Times. By ROBERT F. FOERSTER, Ph.D., Assistant Professor of Social Ethics in Harvard University (Cambridge: Harvard University Press; London: Humphrey Milford, Oxford University Press, 1919. Pp. xx, 558. $2.00)

A reviewer might well be excused for applying the term "magnificent" to this careful and scholarly work. Professor Foerster has given to sociologist, to economist, and to historian an illuminating

---

[1] Bresson's book above mentioned is entitled: *Bolivie. Sept Années d'explorations, de voyages et de séjours dans l'Amérique Australe*, Paris, 1886; and that of Weddel, *Voyage dans le Nord de la Bolivie et dans les parties voisins du Pérou ou visite au district aurifère de Tipuani*, Paris and London, 1853. The passages showing the similarity of Bresson to Weddel sufficiently prove the charge of plagiarism.

treatise on the most stupendous emigration of the nineteenth and twentieth centuries—an emigration, which, notwithstanding the temporary interruption caused by the European War and the present reconstruction period with its immigration laws, may be said to be yet in full swing. In making his study, the author has been actuated by a praiseworthy motive, as shown by the opening sentence of his preface; "A world engrossed as never before with defining the rights and obligations of nationalities and with mitigating the causes of national and international discord cannot afford to ignore the fertile field for study presented by the great migrations of the day". This is manifestly a modern work treated in a modern manner, and its findings are of value in the problems of various nations because of the presence in them of Italian immigrants.

The book is divided into four parts, namely: "Main currents", of two chapters; "Causes", of five chapters; "In foreign lands", of thirteen chapters; and "Italy among the nations", of four chapters. In the earlier and later chapters, the Italian national factors are well brought out—the social conditions of Italy, the need for emigration, the Italian government's recognition of that need, the effect on Italy of returned emigrants, and other factors. The third part discusses emigration to France, Germany, Switzerland, Austria-Hungary, other countries of Europe and North Africa, Argentina, Brazil, and the United States. Throughout these chapters, one is led to a comparison as to the effects of the immigration into the several countries. In each country, the part played by the Italian in its industrial upbuilding is shown, and everywhere, both the women and the men of that remarkable race, with their power of thrift and saving, and their uncomplaining attitude toward tasks and remuneration against which the people of almost every other race would protest, have made a record that has no counterpart among any other class of emigrant peoples. Occasionally the Italian emigrant has risen to fame and fortune, and more often to a competency, in his new home. On the other hand his health has often been jeopardized if not impaired, and his moral status has frequently suffered. Curiously enough, in the United States, Italian emigrants have not uncommonly turned away from their ancestral religion and embraced another faith.

Chapters thirteen and fourteen discuss Italian emigration to Argentina, and the new life there, and the following two chapters do the same for Brazil. No other Hispanic American country is discussed at length, although the emigration to Chile is mentioned briefly. It would have been desirable had the volume been made to include the last mentioned country, for Italian immigration there has not been unimportant. The four chapters form valuable contributions to the study of population in Argentina and Brazil, and can be used in the classroom.

In the former country, although some Italians had entered before 1860, the great influx came after that date. The immigration law of 1876, which was remarkably broad, stimulated Italian immigration as well as that of other peoples. In 1895, for instance, the foreign born (1,004,527) among the population of Argentina formed over a quarter of the inhabitants. In their new home, the Italians, who with their children and grandchildren, today number about 2,000,000, engaged in agriculture, and in trades and business, and sometimes in the professions, notably in the engineering profession. "The astonishing development of the broad agricultural provinces of Argentina has been mainly the achievement of Italian toil", declares the author, although the Italians were more often mere laborers following the several kinds of crops across the country and returning to Italy for the winter, a similar class who remained in Argentina, generally as unskilled laborers during the winter, those living on or near the fields cultivated, share cultivators, or renters; than proprietors. In general, it has been true that large fortunes have more often been made by Italians in trade and agriculture than in agriculture, but in many ways they have had an immense influence on the life and in the Prosperity of the country. Buenos Ayres, with its Italian population almost equal to that of Rome, presents much the same social problems as does New York with regard to its Italian population. After reading these chapters, we are ready for one of the conclusions of the author, namely, that

If Italian immigration were today wholly to cease, never to be revived, the Italian influence would forever count in Argentina, breathing a characteristic spirit into the political and social institutions of the land. Herein lies the great difference between an immigration of gold and an immigration of men. Some day the millions of English capital, so timely and so consequential when they came, may be withdrawn, just as still more millions have in the Great War been withdrawn from the United States; but the Italian contribution of blood to Argentina will remain.

In Brazil, the history of Italian immigration has been quite different from that of Argentina, but effects have been perhaps as striking and as lasting. Of it the author says; "Brazil cannot lose her Italian strain. It is too sturdily rooted". Before 1850, Italian immigration into Brazil was small. It gathered force about coincident with the period bounded by the laws regarding slavery in 1871 and the abolition of slavery in

1888, during which period over 200,000 Italian immigrants entered the country. Indeed, prior to the present century, actually more Italians entered Brazil than came to the United States. It was estimated in 1910 that the Italian population of Brazil was a million and a half. The Italian immigrants were destined to play a large part in the change of sugar cultivation to that of coffee as the great crop of Brazil with the consequent shifting of the economic center of the country from the north to the south. It was they who furnished hands for the coffee plantations and became agricultural laborers. More Italians, we are told, engaged in agricultural work in Brazil than in any other country to which Italians have emigrated. Of them, the author says:

When the best has been said, the experience of the immigrants on the fazendas has been one of broken hopes and vanished dreams. A great deal in production has been wrought, some planters—by no means all—have been enriched, but a narrow and stunted life, hedged about with worry, has been the reward of the mass of the cultivators.

In 1907, out of 57,000 landed estates, some 9 per cent belonged to Italians, and in some regions, it is true that the best farms are owned by Italians. But the majority have not arisen out of the more humble condition of workers, and culturally, existence has been, in general, on a humble scale.

In Brazil, as in other countries, Italians have worked at railway construction and at other work of a public nature, and as elsewhere have served to develop the country industrially. They have furnished also a merchant class, a competent artisan class, mill operatives, and workers at all the trades seen in a town or city.

The work throughout has been written in a readable style, which at times becomes eloquent. There are two indices, one bibliographical and one general, the conveniences of which may be questioned, although the first allows the author to avoid a bibliographical appendix on authorities cited.

JAMES ALEXANDER ROBERTSON.

Colombia. A Commercial and Industrial Handbook. By P. L. BELL, Trade Commissioner. Department of Commerce, Bureau of Foreign and Domestic Commerce, Special Agents Series, No. 206. (Washington: Government Printing Office, 1921. Pp. 423. Illustrations. Map of Colombia. Index. Cloth. 70 cents.)

The United States Government, through the Bureau of Foreign and Domestic Commerce, has undertaken to publish handbooks on

various countries as an aid to the foreign trade of the United States
These books are the result of personal investigation by trained observers.

The handbook on Colombia is an admirable work, and fills a real
need, for it gives in fairly brief compass, that economic information
that is desired by importers and exporters, engineers, capitalists, and
even teachers and students. To the last-named classes, indeed, it
will be found indispensable.

Mr. Bell, in his introduction treats of various incidental matters,
including the following: general economic position of Colombia, past
and present; European versus American trade with Colombia; language; currency, weights and measures; postage; and telegraphs, cables,
and wireless service. In succeeding sections, he discusses Geography,
topography, and climate; population and living conditions; government, education, and national finance; general conditions affecting
national industries; forest products; mining; petroleum; cattle raising; agriculture; domestic manufacturing; economic characteristics of
nine commercial districts; transportation; foreign trade; customs tariff
and import duties; trade-marks and patents; banks and banking;
practice of handling bills of exchange with Colombia; insurance; commercial practices and requirements; aliens—naturalization, immigration; and markets for specific classes of merchandise. In an appendix
sections are given on shipping, packing, commercial travelers, and
list of works published by the Bureau of Foreign and Domestic Commerce on Colombia. The map is reproduced by permission of Rand
McNally.

Mr. Bell probably knows Colombia as intimately as any other citizen
of the United States, and more intimately than most foreigners who
have traveled in that country. Throughout his work, he has used
discrimination as to what to include. The result has been a treatise
that is alive and of use.

JAMES ALEXANDER ROBERTSON.

Bolivia. A Commercial and Industrial Handbook. By WILLIAM LYTE
SCHURZ, Trade Commissioner. Department of Commerce, Bureau
of Foreign and Domestic Commerce, Special Agents Series,
No. 280. (Washington: Government Printing Office, 1921. Pp.
260. Illustrations. Map of Bolivia. Cloth. 65 cents.)

Dr. Schurz, whose handbook on Paraguay was noticed recently in this
REVIEW, has compiled in the present work the best treatise on Bolivia
yet written by a citizen of the United States. This is an authoritative work in which information never before collected in one single

volume, and much of which is absolutely new, is offered to those interested in the economic condition and development of Bolivia. Like the preceding work, the volume is the result of personal investigation.

In his introduction, the author covers briefly the subjects of geography; topography; climate; health conditions; population and living conditions; government, education, and intellectual life; and religion. In continuation, other topics treated are as follows; cities and towns; transportation and communications (external trade routes, railways, roads, lake and river navigation, and telegraphs); mining; petroleum; stockraising; agriculture; forest industries; manufactures; labor conditions; colonization, immigration, and land, trade; investments; banking and money; and public finance. The work is concluded by an appendix in which are discussed "Routes from United States to Bolivia", and "Accommodations for travelers in principal cities". There are twenty-three illustrations. The map, as in the preceding volume, is reproduced by permission of Rand McNally.

Although the volume has been compiled as an aid to foreign commerce, it will be found of use to many classes, including those engaged in the teaching profession. As is well known its author has had the advantage of a thorough training in historical investigation and has had actual academic experience as well, so that he has been able to plan his work with an understanding of values. The limitations imposed by the prime nature and purpose of the handbook has compelled a brevity of treatment in many instances which the teacher or student who makes use of it, will regret but excuse. The absence of an index is compensated for partly by an analytical table of contents. It would have been of service had the author appended a list of the best economic authorities of Bolivia. Dr. Schurz it should be noted, has been promoted to the position of Commercial Attaché and is stationed in Rio de Janeiro.

JAMES ALEXANDER ROBERTSON.

Africa and the discovery of America. Vol. 1. By LEO WIENER, Professor of Slavic Languages and Literatures at Harvard University. (Philadelphia: Innes & Sons, 1920. Pp. xix, (1), 290.)

The first thing that strikes the reader of this volume is its wonderful display of linguistic learning. The second is the daring with which the author invades the field of archaeologists and historians. Will the former relish being told that one of the conclusions of the eminent author is that "American archaeology was to a great extent built on sand"? And will the second receive with avidity the dogmatic manner with which the author settles historical points? It is believed not. The book is largely an attempt to prove by language the unreliability of early accounts of America, the foreign origin of certain plants supposedly American, and the early connection between Africa and America. Early civilization, such as it was in the western hemisphere, was largely influenced from Africa. This is the central theme of the volume. But it is not, strictly speaking, a unit. In successive chapters are discussed "The journal of the first voyage and the first letter of Columbus"; "The second voyage"; "Tobacco"; and "The bread roots". We are led far astray in the arguments and well nigh forget the purpose of the work in the discussion of the word roots which the author traces through many tongues.

In the preface, we are told that the study of words has convinced the author that tobacco, manioc, yams, sweet potatoes, and peanuts are not of American origin as is universally believed. Had he consulted the Standard Dictionary, he would have found a foreign origin ascribed to yams and apparently to manioc. It does not, moreover, appear that he has proven that tobacco is of foreign origin. His explanation of how the custom of tobacco smoking spread through the various tribes of American Indians is not convincing. Throughout the volume, there is a dogmatic tone that does not of itself lend credit to the author's assertions. The explanation of how certain readings came to be so in some of the old works is ingenious, but is, after all not good evidence, and in some instances appears far-fetched. On the other hand, the discussion relative to "ghost-words", will be followed with interest, although perhaps not with full credence. The discussion regarding the word "Guanahani", is probably the most interesting and may receive some serious consideration.

In writing the volume, Professor Wiener has consulted many authorities as is shown by the bibliographical list preceding the text. The volume, if not thrown aside after a brief examination, will prove stimulating, although perhaps, mainly in a negative way. A second volume is promised, in which the author will set forth his views regarding African fetichism, in which he proposes to show "by documentary evidence to what extraordinary extent the Indian medicine-man owes his evolution to the African medicine-man, who in his turn derives his wisdom from the popular Arabic medical science and religion". In the matter of Indian religion, everything is topsy-turvy, according to the author. Professor Wiener's work recalls to the reviewer a work written by an English clergyman some years ago wherein it is stated that all English history for some hundreds of years back has been misreported.

JAMES ALEXANDER ROBERTSON.

NOTES AND COMMENT

A PROBLEM AND ITS SOLUTION

[Published on request of The National Tuberculosis Association.]

On the basis of investigations made by the National Tuberculosis Association at Framingham, Mass., at least 1,000,000, of the population of the United States may be said to have active tuberculosis. In other words, there are a million consumptives at the present time in this country. Another one per cent has this disease in a relatively quiescent form, most of them arrested cases and probably never knowing that they have had the disease. Of the 1,000,000 active cases of tuberculosis according to the records of the United States Bureau of the Census, 132,000 have died during the past year.

To state the situation in another way, 120 deaths for every 100,000 population, according to the best available statistics, have been caused by tuberculosis during the last year. It has been estimated by comparing the present death rate with that of no longer than twenty years ago that a saving of approximately 75,000 lives annually has been effected. Hence, the present problem is: How may we best accelerate the decrease in the tuberculosis death toll?

So much for the problem—what of its solution? The National Tuberculosis Association has consistently contended that by education and proper organization the mortality and morbidity rates from tuberculosis may be constantly reduced.

Dr. Louis I. Dublin who is statistician for the Metropolitan Life Insurance Company has found that among its policy holders who represent all occupations there has been a decline of 42 per cent in the death rate from tuberculosis of the lungs among white persons during the period 1911 to 1919. In commenting upon this decline Dr. Dublin says: "This achievement we believe has resulted from the public health and educational work of communities generally during the past thirty years, and from the intensive health conservation work of this company on behalf of its policy holders".

In order to estimate the influence of tuberculosis upon the length of human life in this country the National Tuberculosis Association has prepared life tables with tuberculosis included and with tuberculosis excluded. On the basis of these results it is estimated that if tuberculosis could be eliminated as a cause of death in this country, two and one half years would be added to the life of every individual in the country. Capitalizing each individual life at $100 per year, the net saving to the country would be at least $25,000,000,000 and might run double that sum.

To provide the necessary health machinery to control tuberculosis would cost, according to experience gathered at Framingham and elsewhere, approximately $2.00 yearly per person in any average American community. This expenditure would undoubtedly have to be extended over a period of probably ten years at least. Applying these figures to the entire population we find that for an expenditure of approximately $2,000,000,000 the saving of $25,000,000,000 mentioned above could be secured, a net saving of $23,000,000,000.

The National Tuberculosis Association and its allied agencies are carrying on a winning fight against tuberculosis. The methods of the Association are proving effective. Their extension into every community of the United States will mean an increased saving of life and money.

The Tuberculosis Christmas Seal Sale to be held in December provides the "sinews of war" with which the national, state, and local tuberculosis associations can carry on their fight The sale of these seals offers not only an opportunity but a responsibility to every American citizen.

DEATH OF GENARO GARCÍA

After a painful illness of more than a year, during which he suffered from pernicious anemia, the distinguished Mexican historian, bibliographer, and publicist died on November 26th last. He was an intense intellectual worker for over thirty years, during which time he published nearly a hundred works, including documents and the fruits of his own researches. He was at the same time an educator of distinction, having served as Director of the National Preparatory School, Director of the National Museum, Professor in the National Conservatory of Music, and professor in the School of Jurisprudence. His arduous life service deserves the greatest recognition from the Mexican people, for he gave them the distinction of possessing a ripe scholar of international renown.

His best known works include the *Documentos inéditos o muy raros para la historia de México*, in thirty-seven volumes; his *Documentos históricos mexicanos*, in seven volumes; his edition of Bernal Diaz' *Verdadera historia de la conquista de la Nueva España*, in two volumes; the *Carácter de la conquista española en América y en México;* his *Plan de Independencia de 1808; Leona Vicario, Don Juan de Palafox, Derecho usual, Derecho constitucional,* his work on Gaston Raousset de Boulbon, his *Crónica oficial del primer; entenario de la Independencia;* his translations of Spencer's The *Ancient Mexicans* and *Ancient Yucatan;* his uncompleted work on Mexican Architecture, his *Dos antiguas relaciones de la Florida,* and his *Calendarios Mexicanos.*

He was fifty-three years old, having been born at Fresnillo, Zacatecas, on August 17, 1867. His father was Trinidad García, who served as secretary of Hacienda and of Gobernación under Díaz. He was admitted to the practice of the law in 1891, but never interested himself deeply in it, preferring his historical work. The Mexican Academy of History, of which Señor García was a member, will shortly publish his biography.

HERBERT I. PRIESTLEY.

A PLEA FOR COÖPERATION

No sharp line of demarcation exists between the two fields of Anthropology and History. Each supplements the other in gathering and sifting material in the borderlands. One of the most fruitful fields, where there is a wealth of unused material, lies in the unpublished manuscripts and unobtainable early books relating to the discovery and conquest of Hispanic America. There are numerous manuscripts of utmost importance yet unpublished and inaccessible to the public. Many of the early accounts written in Spanish, Portuguese, and Dutch are so rare that even the student conversant with the languages cannot obtain access to them.

The Cortes Society has been established for the purpose of selecting some of the more important documents and narratives either printed or in manuscript form and publishing English translations of them along with notes and elucidations by the editors. It is proposed in the case of unpublished and excessively rare printed material, to publish the document in the original language and in English translation.

Four volumes have already been published:

1. *A Narrative of Some Things of New Spain and the Great City of Temestitan, Mexico, by the Anonymous Conqueror, a Companion of Cortes,* translated and annotated by Marshall H. Saville.

2. *The Conquest of Peru, by Pedro Sancho, Secretary of Pizarro,* translated and annotated by Philip A. Means.

3. *The Itinerary of Grijalva, an account of the exploration of the coast of Yucatan,* translated by M. H. Saville. (In press.)

4. *The Relation of the Discovery and Conquest of the Kingdom of Peru,* by Pedro Pizarro, in two volumes, translated and annotated by Philip A. Means.

The Society is soon to publish the excessively rare work relating to Brazil entitled the *Historia da Provincia da Sancta Cruz,* by Pero de Magalaes de Gandavo, printed in Lisbon in 1576. The first volume will contain a facsmile of the Portuguese text as published, with a translation and notes by John B. Stetson, Jr.

Plans are being considered whereby it is hoped that the Society may be able to undertake for the first time the publication of a translation of what is undoubtedly the most important work falling within the scope of its activities. This is the great history of Oviedo y Valdes entitled *Historia General y Natural de las Indias, Islas y Tierra-Firme del Mar Oceano.*

There are no dues connected with membership in the Society, the only obligation being subscription to its publications. As the translators receive no compensation for their work, the only expenses are those of publication and delivery of the volumes. Hence the books will be delivered to members at practically the expense of production.

The cooperation of historians in this important undertaking is greatly desired and those who are interested in the Hispanic American field will be welcome to membership in the Society. Inquiries should be addressed to Marshall H. Saville, Museum of the American Indian, New York City.

WILLIAM CURTIS FARABEE,
President of the American Anthropological Association.

From a circular issued by the Society it is learned that the edition of the publications of the Society is limited to two hundred and fifty numbered copies, of which fifty will be held in reserve for future demands in Europe and America. Two hundred and forty copies constitute the regular edition, printed on Old Stratford paper, and ten larger paper copies are issued on a superior quality of hand-made paper. The general edition is uniformly bound in boards with buckram back. The price of the four volumes already issued is sixteen dollars. THE HISPANIC AMERICAN HISTORICAL REVIEW ventures to hope that many of its readers will take advantage of an opportunity that can not be open long.—J. A. R.

———————————

The following is a translation of an editorial that appeared in *La Nation*, Buenos Aires, June 20, 1921, and entitled, "Our Commercial Relations With The United States".

Any study of the general and particular reasons which at the present time are prejudicing the development of our commercial relations with the United States would not be complete without a consideration of certain phenomena which are actively operating in a similar way. Such a study is necessary for the reason that the strengthening of our commercial relations with the United States interests us not alone in the present but even more so insofar as the future is concerned. The development of our commercial relations with the United States is indispensable, because there are certain products whose best and most satisfactory source of supply is to be found in the industries of that country, so that it is by all means necessary to bring about some sort of an economic rapprochement, insofar as the respective products of the two countries are concerned, on the general principle that the imports of a country should pay for the greater part of its exports. Foreign trade cannot be maintained without strict reciprocity. Otherwise, the wealth of a country which is without a surplus for export and at the same time a large consumer of foreign products would be rapidly exhausted by the dissipation of its reserves, to the inevitable prejudice of its circulating and dynamic capital. The structure of a healthy national wealth for any national economic unit is based on the active mobilisation of its productive capital, assisted by the renewing and helpful influences of a reciprocal distribution of its surpluses, the result of which is the incorporation of new and foreign elements of which it has need for its development.

The presence of the United States commercially in our market as an important economic event is of comparatively recent date, with the exception of certain typical products of its industry. The participation of its industries was limited by two principal reasons: First, the defensive propaganda carried on here by the principal industrial countries of Europe, and the reluctance of the Argentine consumer to take advantage of the new source of supply. It may be said at the same time that the United States did not display any special activity for the reason that the surplus of its products available for export was insignificant. At that period, the industries of the United States were only able to produce a sufficient supply to take care of their domestic demand. The European war greatly changed that situation in two ways: it eliminated as a source of supply the European countries whose industries were concentrated on the production of war material, and, secondly, the great development in the industries of the United States, whose great production finally made necessary the search for new markets.

In previous articles we have analysed the reasons why the commercial conquest of Latin-America by the industries of the United States has been such a slow process and have referred to the remedies which its manufacturers might employ to correct it. It should be said, however, that there exist certain artificial causes which it would be possible to remove rapidly by the concerted action of the interested parties, that is to say, the American exporter and the Argentine consumer. We refer to the propaganda adverse to the commercial standing of the United States which has been carried on by its competitors and the existence of a prejudice on our part which makes such propaganda profitable. For many years past, and even up to the present time, there exists in Argentine the belief that the industries of the United States are imperfect and their products of an inferior nature as compared with those of other industrial nations.

In justice to all we cannot do other than qualify that supposition as a lamentable absurdity. Even without entering into a specific examination of the activities which are comprised in the productive powers of a country, a simple study of a phenomenon as a whole will show the condition of each one of the elements which go to make it up. The United States is without any doubt the most inspiring spectacle of the last fifty years. Its great increase in population, the submission of its national territory to creative action, the advanced standards of living, the incredible figures of its national and private wealth, the untiring spirit of progress of its inhabitants, their love of action and of work, their ability to respond even up to the point of sacrifice to the appeal of great moral causes of interest to all humanity, constitute a combination of virtues which must necessarily have its equivalent and complement in the other individual expressions of its national life. Its commerce and its industries, not alone as organizations purely material in their spirit and of wonderful power in the economic struggle of the world, but also as sources of energy which have need of a moral support, of a spirit of harmony, and even of an esthetic tendency, must progress and do progress in harmony with the most valued creations of modern civilization.

The products of the industries of the United States are as perfect as those of the most advanced industrial nations of the world, and this statement is made not only in reference to the potential capacity of its industrial establishment but also to the superiority of each individual product. To understand this assertion it will only be necessary to call attention to two facts: namely, its ability to supply all of its necessities with the products of its own industries, and, secondly, the demands, each day more varied and complex, which are the result of the habits of life of its people.

A country which has carried the expressions of its urban life to such extremes of convenience, hygiene, well being of its people, sumptuous magnificence and esthetic tastes, must necessarily have an industrial organization as powerful in its nature as it is subtle in its combinations, in order to supply such demands.

The Argentine consumers have not examined nor studied the problem in its real aspect, and, for this reason, it has been possible to spread a belief that the United States is only a great center of production, a sort of industrial phenomenon, characterized only by the great volume of its production. It is likely that one peculiar phase of United States industry has contributed to this belief as much as has the proselytizing influence of competitive nations. We refer to the dominant feature of its industrial life, that is, the "standardisation" which is the striking phenomenon of its manufacturing industries. This process whose industrial, economic, and ultimate advantages insofar as the employment of its output is concerned is the one which has run counter to the essentially individualistic temperament of the Latin, who expects to see in all the objects which surround him and in the things with which he has to do in his daily life an authentic and reflex expression of his own temperament. In his tailor-made clothes, his house built according to his own plans, his carriage of a certain design and color, his meals cooked especially to order, his own mixture of tobacco, and in many other ways, the exclusive tendency of our people protests against the levelling and gregarious spirit of modern social life which is daily becoming more pronounced and dominant. The question, then, may be summed up as the individualistic tendency of the consumer as opposed to the advantages of lower costs which are inherent in manufacturing processes on a large scale and on uniform standards.

If it for this reason that we have been in error as to the industrial flexibility of a country whose economic policy has directed its production along lines of ever increasing generalisation, and what was really a technical process of economic advantage we have qualified merely as an exaggerated expression of magnitude, without taking into account that in the enormous potential capacity of its industries there was nevertheless inherent the complete control of the delicate, the subtle and the artistic, in just the same way that the enormous mass of an elephant contains not alone the strength of its powerful structure but also an instrument adaptable to all forms of action, its trunk, which with the same facility can uproot a tree or pick up a needle.

These peculiarities of the industries of the United States should be well known and familiar in those countries whose commercial conquest its men of industry are interested in bringing about. It is a work of propaganda and of education, the ends of which will only be obtained by the unquestioned eloquence of actual facts. It will be a question of patient and demonstrative work on the part of its direct representatives. As a result of this work they shall attain not only the necessary compensation for their enormous industrial organisations but also the prestige so well merited by their modern conceptions of industry.

NEW FACTORS IN SOUTH AMERICA

There are not many visitors to South America who are not commercial travelers. Even our government representatives give most of their service to business interests. Their markets, their raw materials, their undeveloped natural resources have seemed to the people of South America the only thing we cared for.

It is true that a few men have gone to speak to them of our ideals. Mr. Root went as Secretary of State; Mr. Bryan went as a private citizen; Mr. Roosevelt as an ex-president; Mr. Colby again officially and to speak for a man whom they had come to admire as a great idealist, President Wilson.

All these men were heard gladly, if at times rather skeptically. The thinkers of South America were waiting to be shown. The war almost convinced them that we have ideals. Then came our peace slump, and they were more puzzled than ever. But they certainly are stirred. Our national efficiency was tremendously demonstrated. That is a thing they feel themselves deficient in, a fact that is beginning to disturb them.

Such is the background recently found by a non-commercial traveler who is interested in human values, on his third trip through South America. This traveler lectured before the University of Chile, the Paraguayan Institute, and several other prominent educational institutions. He had extended conferences with the editors of such prominent dailies as *La Nación* of Buenos Aires, *El Mercurio* of Santiago, and *El Comercio* of Chile, all of whom commented extensively on the significance of his visit. He was entertained by literary and political leaders in each country, and visited and discussed American problems at length with the presidents of three Republics. As typifying some of the significant changes that have come about during the seven years interval since his first visit, and some of the really important phases of human and moral values in South America today, he notes the following:

1. There is a new and very determined interest in North American education. During the war, Europe being inaccessible, Hispanic American students came to the United States. Heretofore the Hispanic States of America had looked to Europe, France especially, for educational leadership and standards. These returning students from the United States, and the tremendous surge of national unity and effectiveness which marked our participation in the war, are serving together to turn the attention of Hispanic educational leaders to this country. They begin to suspect that there is a whole realm of idealism and of intellectual evolution here upon which they have scarcely entered. They are even asking, "Is it not possible that an educational system freely developed in a free American state should have certain qualities that would fit it for the uses and needs of other free American states?" The question has suddenly become a fascinating one for them. What the results of their study of it are to be cannot be foretold, but they are undoubtedly studying it.

2. The revolt against political and social conservatism is marked. It has some extraordinary phases. As in China the students are finding themselves as a social and political factor. They are often foolish,

in aims and methods, often the manner of youth, but their influence is extraordinary. Lately they have taken to joining forces with the labor unions. As these are often decidedly radical, some of the results are startling. Both the students and the unions are compactly organized and usually they concentrate on some concrete and specific thing. The vigor of their organized movements is such that they are able to bring about compliance with their demands. In one or two of the South American republics the governments, local and general, are in open fear of what these new crusaders may do. Already the students are electing the faculties and laying out the courses of study for the schools. The labor unions, as in the case of Argentina and the stevedores, are able even to complicate foreign relations and to assert themselves against both their employers and the police.

3. Not unrelated to the radicalism of the students and labor people is the demand of the intellectuals and of the reading public generally for a fresh literature. They are weary of French fiction on the one hand and of standardized and rather antiquated types of literature on the other. Hispanic America has begun to demand its share of the best thought as expressed in books. Books that help to make it possible to accept modern views of science, of sociology, anthropology, ethics, physics and the rest, without surrendering the Christian faith, are coming to be in great demand. Finishing his tour with a visit to Spain, this traveler found the publishing houses there eager to meet these new demands and already busy in supplying the market created, mostly with translations from English, German, and French works.— GEORGE B. WINTON.

The Sub-Secretary of Public Instruction has recently issued a statement to the effect that Spain is considering a proposal made by the Belgian Government for the exchange of professors and students between Spain and Belgium. According to the proposed arrangement the Spanish and Belgian professors will continue to receive their salaries from their home Government and institutions, and will receive in addition a bonus from the respective Government to which they are sent. Arrangements are being considered also for a harmonization of the scholastic equivalents of the respective Belgian and Spanish universities in order that students may receive credit in their own institutions of learning for courses taken abroad. It is expected that the working out of this arrangement will strengthen the mutual national understandings of these two countries, equipping men of one country with the best elements offered by the other, bringing about in general better feeling and facilitating international co-operation. It is stated that only the final arrangements in this proceeding remain to be perfected and that, as a matter of fact, professors and students have already been appointed for the coming year. The Spanish Minister of Public Instruction has given orders for the immediate remission to Belgium of complete courses of study in Spanish institutions for the use of Belgian professors and students before their departure for Spain. Proper steps will be taken soon for the appointment of scholars and professors to be sent from Spain to Belgium during the coming year.

An administrative order issued on September 23 by the Minister of Public Instruction established an indefinite number of scholarships, valued at 1,250 pesetas each, to be conferred upon distinguished graduates of the general and technical institutes, *de segunda enseñanza.* The number of scholarships to be conferred will depend upon the number of students matriculated in each group and it will likewise depend upon the amount of money voted by the Cortes for this purpose. The assignment of these scholarships for candidates for the bachelor's degree will be made by a tribunal of professors constituted for this purpose and on consideration of the scholastic records of the students in question. Candidates will furthermore be called upon to pass special examinations for this purpose.

A popular subscription headed by the King of Spain is being raised to erect a memorial statue in Madrid to the famous Spanish author Juan Valera. Subscriptions are requested from those persons in the United States who may wish to be identified with this movement. Donations may be sent to the Instituto de las Españas, 419 West 117th Street, New York City.

The Rector of the University of Chile, Santiago, Chile, Sr. Dr. D. Domingo Amunátegui Solar, in a recent letter suggests that a bibliography of Anglo-American writers on Hispanic America would be most acceptable to students of Hispanic America. Such a bibliography should contain short resumés of each work. Dr. Amunátegui Solar points out that many Anglo-American writers have published volumes on the history or culture of Hispanic America and that the study of these works is of great value. To acquire all these books, however, or even the best of them, would require a considerable outlay which few students could manage, even if the books could be found. It is hoped that some student in the United States will be moved to undertake this work.

Professor Milledge L. Bonham, Jr., writes that Hamilton College for the first time in its history gave a course entirely on Hispanic America during the last semester of the past year. Various books were used for texts and considerable attention was paid to map work. The course also included lectures, oral reports, notebooks, etc. The need of a single good text was emphasized throughout the course. In the same institution, Professor Frank H. Wood in his course on political science, which was given during the same semester, used Latane's *The United States and Latin America* as a textbook for the first two months. Professor Bonham's course will be offered again in the spring of 1923, but Professor Wood's course is to be given annually.

Dr. N. Andrew N. Cleven, formerly of the University of Arkansas has accepted a call to the University of Pittsburgh, where he will have charge of the historical work on Hispanic America. A good class is registered for the present year.

The Brazilian Consul General in the United States, Senhor Helio Lobo, whose address is New York, is desirous of locating in the United States a portrait of Gonçalves Ledo, who took a prominent part in the events leading up to the independence of Brazil. It has been learned from an authoritative source that the only portrait of the above named gentleman was acquired in Brazil by a collector resident in the United States. Will any person having knowledge of such a portrait please communicate immediately with the above named Consul general.

Rev. John F. O'Hara, C. S. C., of the University of Notre Dame, reports that the interchange of students between that institution and South American institutions is working out well. During the summer seven undergraduates of Notre Dame made the trip to Buenos Aires and return, five of them working their way as ordinary seamen. There are about five hundred students in the school of commerce this year. Father O'Hara says:

We have made a new departure in the theory of commercial education. Last spring we arranged our programs of studies, giving the students a choice between the degree of Bachelor of Philosophy in Commerce or Bachelor of Commercial Science. The former degree requires a three years' course in philosophy and was intended as a protest against the common tendency to slight cultural courses in commercial programs. You may be surprised to hear that ninety-five per cent of the students have elected the philosophy programs. Although they have chosen a line of work for which vocational training is largely necessary, they seem to realise that the essentials of real college training are found best in a good groundwork of philosophy.

BIBLIOGRAPHICAL SECTION

HISPANIC AMERICAN BIBLIOGRAPHIES

Concluded

CRITICAL NOTES ON SOURCES BY JOSÉ TORIBIO MEDINA

The compiler feels that he is fortunate in being able, with the author's permission, to supplement this list with the critical notes on bibliographical sources of Señor José Toribio Medina, freely translated from his *Biblioteca Hispano-Americana (1493–1810)*.

It would be a work of supererogation in addressing bibliographers and students of Hispanic American history to outline the products of Señor Medina's fine scholarship and indefatigable labor in the fields of history, literature, and bibliography. This note is added simply as a tribute of homage, respect and appreciation, personal and collective, for the compiler well knows that every student of these subjects in this country is grateful to the distinguished Chilean scholar who has placed such indispensable bibliographical tools at his command.

Señor Medina's life, as his biographer, Señor Chiappa, has happily said, is portrayed in the catalogue of his works. Although he has spent many years in distinguished public service, his dominant interests have been those of scholarship, and his chosen field of research has been the colonial period of Spanish-American history and of the introduction and development of the press in the former colonies of Spain. In this field he has created for himself a position of distinguished authority. His contributions to the bibliography of Spanish America are comprehensive in character and equipped with full bibliographical descriptions and biographical and critical annotations. This remarkable and indispensable *corpus bibliographicum* in itself constitutes a monument more lasting than bronze and gives to the author the first place among those who devote themselves to these studies.

In the first part of this list the compiler has endeavored to note all of Señor Medina's works that deal more specifically with bibliography, biography, and literary history. A general list of his writings and compilations, presumably complete up to 1906, will be found in *Noticias acerca de la vida y obras de Don José Toribio Medina* by Víctor M. Chiappa, Santiago de Chile, 1907.

If we were to limit the bibliographical review which we have undertaken to the works of this character that refer exclusively to America the task would be both simple and brief. But, as is the truth in this case, Spanish American works and authors are found mentioned more or less fully in bibliographies of general character, in the chronicles of the religious orders, in monographs on the history of printing in many cities of Spain and in catalogues of public and private libraries and dealers lists, it has seemed that we should at least mention these works since from them we have had to take something even if no more than a reference.

We should commence, then, with the general bibliographies. In this class the post of honor belongs to Nicolás Antonio in recognition of his work, *Bibliotheca Hispana*, first printed in Rome in 1672 and of which a second edition was issued in Madrid during the years 1783–1788.[1]

In this work written in Latin are given notices of many American authors, considering the word American in its broadest sense. The titles of these works are given more or less abbreviated but always with exactness, and the place of publication, year, and size are added.

The author shows himself in his work to have been a scholarly man and so scrupulous in the notices he gives of works and authors that with the exception of a very few errors, the *Bibliotheca Hispana Nova* is a safe guide for the bibliographer. The Spanish edition is handsomely published and its copious indexes greatly facilitate its use, compensating for what seems to us an error of having adopted in the body of the work an arrangement by Christian instead of family names, a system long used by Spanish authors in their indexes.

Nicolás Antonio y Bernal was born in Seville, July 28, 1617. His early studies were carried on in the Colegio de Santo Tomás and in other schools of that city until 1636 when he was sent to the University of Salamanca. Here, three years later he was graduated as bachelor of laws, to which study he devoted himself under the guidance of the renowned jurist, Francisco Ramos del Manzano. In 1645, he went to Madrid to solicit the habit of the Order of Santiago, which he obtained. Here he remained until 1659, when Philip IV. sent him, now ordained as a priest, to Rome, it is thought in the capacity of procurador general

[1] The first two volumes of this edition, the *Hispana vetus*, were edited by Francisco Pérez Bayer; the second two, the *Hispana nova*, including authors who flourished since 1500, were edited by T. A. Sánchez, J. A. Pellicer, and R. C. Casalbón.—Cf. List, nos. 6–7.

of the kingdom. He lived in Rome until 1678 when he was recalled to Madrid to serve on the Consejo de Cruzada. This function he performed until his death which took place in 1684.

More comprehensive than Antonio's work, since according to the title at least, it embraces all the cities of the world, is that published in 1713 in two volumes by Rafael Savonarola under the pseudonym of Alfonso Lasor a Varea. This we have occasionally cited but it has but little value for the Americanist.

As a bibliographical monument, the *Biblioteca Lusitana* of Diego Barbosa Machado is, of course, infinitely superior and although, as may be inferred, it relates almost exclusively to Portuguese works, it treats when occasion offers of authors of interest to America.

The first volume of this work, really notable for its bio-bibliographical researches and printed with typographical elegance, was published in Lisbon in 1741 and was dedicated by the author to King John V. Despite this fact and for reasons not easy to explain the second volume was dedicated to the Bishop of Porto. This incongruity was brought to the author's attention and he afterwards had the title page and dedication removed for which reason copies of the original edition are today rare. The third volume is very rare. It is said that, irritated because it did not sell and because of the criticisms levelled at it, the author destroyed all the copies that remained in his possession. The fourth was published in 1759.

The Abbot Barbosa, says Silva, was a zealous and enthusiastic bibliophile—a necessary result of his studies. At the cost of many sacrifices and expenditures he was able to collect a select and extensive library which he offered King Joseph to replace the royal library destroyed by the earthquake of Lisbon in 1755. This was transferred to Brazil when King John VI. withdrew to that country and forms today a most important part of the National Library of Rio de Janeiro.

Barbosa Machado was born in Lisbon, May 31, 1682, the son of Captain Juan Barbosa Machado and Catalina Machado. He was abbot of the parochial church of San Adriano de Sever in Porto and one of the first forty academicians of the Royal Academy of History of Portugal. He died August 9, 1772.

Turning again to Spain, we must skip many years before finding a general bibliography. This delay, however, has a certain compensation in the character of the work which is presented—we refer to the *Ensayo de una biblioteca española de libros raros y curiosos*, the first volume of which was published in Madrid in 1863. It is so generally

THE HISPANIC AMERICAN HISTORICAL REVIEW

known that comment here seems unnecessary. This magnificent monument of Spanish bibliography, compiled by Remón Zarco del Valle and José Sancho Rayón on the basis of the notices of the learned and diligent investigator, Bartolomé José Gallardo, contains many titles of interest to the Americanist, the more interesting in that some are of extraordinary rarity and all are described by a master hand with all the details that the most exigent curiosity could demand.

But it will be easily understood that these general bibliographies, whatever be their merit, interest the student of American bibliography but indirectly in comparison with those wholly devoted to works dealing with the New World. And it is unfortunate that of these there have been so few even including works that treat but incidentally of this subject.

We have pointed out that the predecessor of León Pinelo in the office of historian of the Indias was Gil González Dávila, who, in his *Teatro eclesiástico de las Indias* had occasion to mention, though without bibliographical details, works written and published by the bishops whose biographies he was writing. It is unnecessary to say that from the point of view of the subject in hand his work hardly deserves mention.

Neither these bare citations nor those found in some chronicles relating to American authors of the different religious orders, of which we shall speak later, can be compared with the *Epítome* of León Pinelo—indeed taken together they are scarcely worth even a single title of that work which, notwithstanding all of its defects and despite the passing years continues to be a capital reference work for the bibliography of America.

It was left to a man of equal application to undertake the task of augmenting the bibliographical catalogue of the authors of the Indias. This was Andrés González de Barcía Carballido y Zúñiga, born in Madrid about 1673, the time when Nicolás Antonio was publishing in Rome his great *Bibliotheca Hispana*. Little is known of the life of this worthy *littérateur* and bibliographer, the result in part of the refusal of his descendants to furnish the author of his biography, Alvarez Baena, necessary information.[2] . . . .

González de Barcía was an indefatigable worker. He undertook to collect as many books and papers, printed and manuscript, relating to the Indias as possible, of which he published some of no inconsider-

---

[2] Alvares Baena Hijos de Madrid, v. l. p. 107.

able value. Becoming engaged in a new edition of the *Hechos de los Castellanos* of Antonio de Herrera he proposed to make as complete as possible the list of "authors printed and manuscript who have written concerning affairs of the West Indies" which appeared in the original edition. For the realization of this object, he undertook to discover the location of the complete work of León Pinelo, of which the *Epítome* was an extract. In this his efforts proved fruitless and in substitution he had to have recourse to his own valuable and comprehensive collection of American books, the result of years of effort. His basis in his task was always the work of his predecessor which he completed by adding the titles of works published or written since the appearance of the *Epítome* which he had before him, or which he took from compilations, Spanish and foreign, published up to that time. This was the origin of the *Biblioteca Oriental y Occidental* published in 1737.

We shall quote here the judgment of a notable bibliographer, which, unfortunately, is wholly exact: "Many of the errors which mar the utility of subsequent works can be traced to Barcía", says Harrisse.

As the latter took León Pineolo as a model for his work, so he in turn served as a model for Antonio de Alcedo, author of the notable *Diccionario histórico geográfico de las Indias Occidentales*, in compiling in 1807 his *Biblioteca americana; catálogo de los autores que han escrito de la América en diferentes idiomas y noticias de su vida y patria, años en que vivieron y obras que escribieron*, cited for the first time by Rich in his *Bibliotheca Americana nova*. The work consists of VI–1028 leaves in manuscript. . . . [3]

But whatever be the merits and defects of the work, the fact that it has never been published has caused no advance in bibliographical studies relating to America.

The *Biblioteca Mexicana* of Juan José de Eguiara y Eguren had a happier fate than the preceding work although not so happy as might have been desired. The first volume, embracing the letters A to C was published in Mexico in 1755. The manuscript extended to the letter J but the death of the author which occurred in 1753 prevented the completion of the work which was to contain bio-bibliographical notices of all authors born in New Spain (Mexico). Although in scope it did not include material relating to America in general, and although the fact of its being written in Latin (including titles of works) and

---

[3] Now in the John Carter Brown Library.

with a certain defective critical spirit on the part of the author, which led him to immerse himself in lengthy dissertations, caused it to lose in large part the merit to which, conceived on a better plan, it could have aspired, nevertheless the notices collected therein make it in some respects superior to the work which, with the same objective, José Marino Beristain de Sousa accomplished in his *Biblioteca hispano-americana septentrional*.[4] The author, who had spent twenty years in the compilation of this work, did not live to see it published.

The vast store of information it contains has not been surpassed by later bibliographers,[5] and despite its faults, the most serious of which we must agree with García Icazbalceta in considering the liberty taken in changing, abbreviating, and reconstructing titles to such a degree that some are unrecognizable, the work remains indispensable to the American bibliographer. In the course of our work we have had to refer to it more than to any other work of its kind.

The *Bibliothèque Américaine* of Henry Ternaux-Compans, published in Paris, 1837, is a work of more general character and specifically devoted to the bibliography of America. But its sole merit is that of having arranged in chronological order the books in this field published in all languages up to 1700. In the Spanish material the author was able to use his own collection of books and, for not a few titles, Pinelo-Barcía, but with so little care that sometimes the same work is cited with two or three different dates.

Titles to the number of 1153 are given in abbreviated form and are accompanied by a French translation and an occasional note of slight value. This bibliography was thus replete with errors and it has been a rich source for the transmission of these to many bibliographers who have followed it.

We now come to the true founder of modern American bibliography. We refer, as will have been divined, to Henry Harrisse, and to his work *Bibliotheca Americana Vetustissima*, the first volume of which

---

[4] The first edition was published in Mexico, 1816–1821. The fourth volume containing the anonyms which the author left in manuscript and some additions by others was published by Señor Medina in 1897 in a form similar to the edition of Amecameca of 1883. A biography of the author was included in this volume.

[5] García Icazbalceta himself in his incomparable *Bibliografía Mexicana del siglo XVI* was unable to see some of the works mentioned by Beristáin and Vicente de P. Andrade in his *Ensayo bibliográfico del siglo XVII* found himself under the necessity of simply mentioning many which the former apparently saw.

was published in 1866 with such typographical opulence in the facsimiles of the books it describes and in other external aspects that it
marked an unimagined progress in works of this character. But even
with this its appearance hardly corresponded to the careful work, the
wealth of descriptions, the profundity of research, and the knowledge
that the author prodigally furnishes on each page.

This first volume was followed in 1877 by another containing *Additions* to the titles previously described, the two volumes containing 304
plus 186 titles of works relative, or containing references, to America
printed in any country and language from 1493 to 1551.

Despite the intensive investigation and the exceptional opportunities
the author enjoyed in securing material for his work, he was not able
to include in it all that had been written on the subject—a matter, of
course, easily explained—nor did he fail to fall into some errors.

Of him Mr. Growell has said:

Henry Harrisse's name is connected with one of the most erudite bibliographies
ever published; indeed, according to Nicolas Trübner, Harrisse's *Bibliotheca
Americana Vetustissima* is a "work unrivalled in its extent, accuracy, and comprehensiveness." This is the more remarkable because Harrisse had no bibliographic training, and because the work in question was his first attempt in this
field. Before undertaking the work on the *Bibliotheca Americana*, he had devoted
himself exclusively to art, criticism, and the history of philosophy, translating
into English and annotating all the metaphysical works of Descartes. Being
unable to find a publisher in America for that class of books, he turned his attention to other subjects. At this time—about 1864–65—he made the acquaintance
of Samuel Latham Mitchell Barlow, the generous collector to whose munificence
bibliographical science is indebted for this splendid publication. Mr. Barlow
shortly before had bought the library of Colonel Aspinwall that was destroyed in
the fire which consumed the premises of Bangs, Merwin & Company, 696 Broadway, where the books were temporarily stored. Fortunately, Mr. Barlow, a
few days before this disaster, had removed to his house a number of the rarest
treasures in the collection. Harrisse was tempted, by the aid of Mr. Barlow's
rich mine of invaluable works, to write a history of the beginning, the decline,
and the fall of the Spanish Empire in the New World. In making his selections
among the many works, Harrisse naturally made a preliminary work of bibliography, and he began with Columbus. These notes were published in two instalments in the New York *Commercial Advertiser* under the title *Columbus in a
Nutshell*. Mr. Barlow, finding that these notes were eagerly demanded . . .
proposed that they be reprinted with some important additions. . . . These
studies were included in the following volume: *Notes on Columbus*. New York,
1866. (v, 2–227 p., 13 photographs.) . .

These researches inspired Harrisse to prepare a study of all the authentic
facts relating to the discovery, the conquest, and the history of America down
to the middle of the 16th century. The bibliographical data collected in the

course of these investigations became the nucleus of the *Bibliotheca Americana Vetustissima*. . . .

Harrisse was born in Paris in 1830. When quite young he came to the United States to join his family, and went south, where he taught modern languages to support himself while he was studying law. He received the degree of A. M. from the South Carolina College, read Blackstone with the Hon. W. W. Boyce, and prepared himself for the bar in the Law Department of the North Carolina University. The Hon. Stephen A. Douglas induced him to settle in Chicago; but after a few years of unrequited efforts as a lawyer, he removed to New York and entered the office of the late N. Dane Elingwood. . . . Thirty years ago he made Paris his home. Being discouraged at the treatment which his works, all written solely to promote a documentary and initial knowledge of the history of our country, received at the hands of the American public, Harrisse gave up Americana. At Mr. Barlow's request he returned to American subjects, toiling henceforth and unremittingly and gratuitously, as usual, at the task of clearing up obscurities that rest upon the period of American discovery, which includes the voyages of Columbus, Vespucci, the Cabots, and Cortereal. . . ".

A separate edition of 125 copies was issued of those pages of Harrisse's work which relate to the books printed in America from 1540 to 1600. The Spanish bibliographer Zarce del Valle and Sancho Rayón made a free translation of these pages adding notes, descriptions, and comments of their own and published it in Madrid, 1872, in a handsome volume of 59 pages with 3 leaves of facsimiles. This, due to the small edition, is now extremely rare.

During the years 1868 to 1892 there has been published in New York *A Dictionary of books relating to America from its discovery to the present time*, by Joseph Sabin. This reached the letter S, when the work was interrupted. In truth, few titles available for Spanish-American bibliography are found in it and these are transcribed usually from dealers' catalogues and without the indispensable bibliographical notices. It does not, therefore, in any degree. correspond to what one interested in this subject might expect from its title.

On the other hand, in the *Historia de la literatura de Nueva Granada*, of José María Vergara, Bogotá, 1867, a book of modest appearance but written with true critical spirit and no little scholarship, are found many data and references on Spanish-American books and authors not available elsewhere.

American languages have received special attention from bibliographers. We shall not discuss the work of Lorenzo Hervás, published in the dawn of the 19th century, the *Mithridates* of Adelung, the *Index alphabeticus* of Juan Severino Vater, the *Monographie* of Squier, the *Apuntes* of García Icazbalceta, nor many other works containing more or less extensive lists of writers in the native languages of America, in order to comment more fully on the work of Hermann E. Ludewig, of whom Harrisse has written a comprehensive biography. It is entitled *The Literature of American aboriginal languages*, London, 1868, "with additions and corrections by Professor Wm. W. Turner", and forms a valuable compend of the subject with references to authors who have incidentally worked in this field. Of course, it is not free from errors and omissions.

The value of the book, in its relation to Spanish bibliography, has, however, disappeared almost wholly with the publication of the *Bibliografiá española de lenguas indigenas de América*, by the Conde de Viñaza, Madrid, 1892. This, also, is not exempt from omissions but it is much superior to its predecessor in details and in the number of works described. "In it", says the author,

"we have collected all the grammars, vocabularies, lists of words and phrases, catechisms of Christian doctrine, and manuals for the administration of the Sacraments, sermons, pietistic books and all kinds of works, printed or manuscript, relating to the indigenous languages of America that have been written by Spaniards, Portuguese or citizens of Latin America from the 16th century to the present day. We have called the work, *Bibliografiá española* because the literature of those peoples who speak the language of Cervantes and Camoens will always be called Spanish as well as because Portugal and Latin America lived for a long space of time under the crown of our rulers, in the most glorious period of our history.

"There are included also some works written in our classical age by missionaries who, although born in Italy, Germany, or Flanders, passed the greater part of their lives among Spaniards, were Spaniards in truth, and acquired a greater facility and elegance in the use of Castilian than in their own."[4]

On the occasion of the fourth centennial of the discovery of America the Academy of History commissioned certain of its members to prepare a *Bibliografía Colombina*, that is to say, of the printed and manuscript documents, works of art, etc., that in some manner refer to the

[4] The Library of Congress, Washington, D. C., possesses a Bibliography of South-Central America, including Mexico, in manuscript, prepared by Dr. Rudolph R. Schuller. This contains some 7,000 titles, embracing history, geography, ethnology, linguistics, technology, etc. The entries are on sheets in the form and of the bibliographic fullness used by the same compiler in his Vocabulario araucano de 1642-1643, Santiago de Chile, 1907. Cf. Report of the Librarian of Congress, 1913, p. 34. In this connection should be mentioned José A. Rodríguez García's *Bibliografiá gramática y lexicografía castellanas*, Habana, 1903-13, 2 v. in folio, an important contribution by a Cuban scholar to the bibliography of the Spanish language.—TRANSLATOR.

discoverer of the New World, and there appeared in due time a quarto volume of about 700 pages. This comprehensive compilation, useful to the investigator on account of some of the material it contains, is exceedingly weak from every point of view in the real bibliographical part. This has justly brought upon it severe criticism both in Spain and abroad.

The catalogues of libraries, societies, and even of bookdealers, while of more modest appearance than bibliographies, are in some cases of greater practical value inasmuch as they contain titles of books whose existence is not affirmed by mere references.

No one, for instance, can overestimate the value to American bibliography possessed by the *Catálogo de la Biblioteca de Salvá*, prepared by Pedro Salvá y Mallén and published in Valencia in two bulky quarto volumes in 1872, with facsimiles, portraits, printers' devices, etc. In this work, without considering the numerous titles of interest, for some reason or other to the Americanist, there is an entire section devoted to books concerning the Indias described with a wealth of details and references to the various editions, all done with a commendable critical spirit.[7]

The catalogue of the Huth Library, London, 1880, in 5 volumes quarto, beautifully printed, also contains some titles worthy of the consideration of the American bibliographer.

Of the United States, where there are at least four important private collections of American books, we are acquainted with the *Catalogue of books relating to North and South America of John Carter Brown*, with notes by John Russell Bartlett published in 1866, which, in the opinion of a competent judge, "cannot fail to awaken the admiration of students and the envy of collectors".[8]

The publication in Seville of the *Catálogo de los libros impresos de la Biblioteca Colombina* was begun in 1888 with bibliographical notes by Simón de la Rosa y López, but with the issue in 1891 of the second volume, the publication was suspended. This is most regrettable for

[7] This notable library, acquired by Ricardo de Heredia, Count of Benahavis, was sold in Paris at public auction in 1891, with other books that formed the *Catalogue de la Bibliothèque*, 4 v., of that nobleman.

[8] Cf. Harrisse, *Bibl. Amer. Vetust.*, note on p. xxx.

The Lenox collection, now a part of the New York Public Library, should be mentioned in this connection, and also the Church collection, the catalogue of which, prepared by George Watson Cole, with a magnificent bio-bibliographical equipment, was published in New York, 1907, in 5 volumes (List, no. 38). TRANSLATOR.

although Harrisse[9] has described the past and present of that famous collection, it was necessary for us to know once for all what it contained. This, as was to be expected from the period of its collection, involves little of interest to the student of Americana.[10] Gabriel René Moreno published his *Biblioteca Boliviana* in Santiago de Chile, 1879, and more recently his *Biblioteca Peruana*, 1896, in which he has listed all the books on Peru found in the Library and in the National Institute. These are bibliographies in the true sense of the word, in which the learned Bolivian has described *de visu* all the titles catalogued, including occasionally pertinent observations in the style that is peculiar to him.

Recently the *Catálogo de la Biblioteca Museo de Ultramar* (Madrid, 1900) has been brought out, containing accurate transcriptions of many titles of American books, but it lacks, most regrettably, even the most essential bibliographical data.

Among dealers' catalogues should be noted those of Obadiah Rich, especially his *Bibliotheca Americana Nova*, London, 1835–1846, 2 v., which lists books relating to America printed between 1700 and 1844 in various languages; the *Bibliothèque Américaine redigé par Paul Trömel*, published by Brockhaus, Leipzig, 1861, which gives a detailed description of books relating to the New World issued up to 1700; and the *Bibliotheca Americana* which its author, Henry Stevens, called *Historical Nuggets*, published in London in 1861, and in which the most of the works are described with abundant details.

But of all the catalogues issued for the sale of American books, without doubt the best, on account of the number of titles contained as well as for the minute details and the biographical data regarding the authors, is that issued by Charles Leclerc, Paris, 1878.[11]

We have now to mention, even though but briefly, the Spanish bibliographies of special subjects and those of the provinces and cities of the Peninsula, which, although of little immediate interest to the Americanist, should be consulted, sometimes very profitably. We regret that limitations of space prevent a more exhaustive description of works and authors of which Spain may justly feel proud.

With respect to the special bibliographies, the first place must without doubt be conceded to the work of the Franciscan priest, Pedro de Alva y Astorga, entitled *Militia Immaculatæ Conceptionis Virginis*

[9] *Grandeur et décadence de la Colombine.* Paris, 1885.
[10] Since Señor Medina wrote the above, the publication has been resumed, 5 volumes having been published. Cf. List, no. 43.—TRANSLATOR.
[11] *Cf.* List, nos. 86–87.

Mariæ, printed in Louvain in 1663. In this work, which reveals immense work, Alva y Astorga has mentioned more than 5,000 authors, in whatever language they may have written, who occupied themselves with the subject he undertook to treat, citing the books with size, and date of publication.

But a century later, another special bibliography appeared in Spain which, for its minute format, forms a decided contrast to the one we have just mentioned, we refer to the *Bibliografía Militar Española* by Vicente García de la Huerta, published in Madrid, 1760, which contains a summary enumeration of the titles of books *de re militari*, among them many by American authors.

Six years later the Marqués de Alventos published in two volumes his *Historia del Colegio Mayor de San Bartolomé*, including in the second volume a list of authors of the six colleges, without bibliographical data and with some omissions of importance.

To overcome these deficiencies was the object of José de Rezábal y Ugarte, regent of the Royal Audiencia of Chile, in his *Biblioteca de los escritores que han sido individuos de los seis Colegios Mayores*, published in Madrid, in 1805. The author inserted his own autobiography in the work. On more than one occasion we have had recourse to this, for the information it contains relative to Spanish-American authors, especially regarding their native countries, public careers, and literary activities.

During the years 1842 to 1852 there was published in Madrid in seven volumes the *Historia bibliográfica de la medicina española*, a posthumous work of Antonio Hernández Morejón preceded by an historical and bibliographical eulogy of the author. In this work, notable from many points of view, titles are cited accurately with accompanying critical estimates and biographical data of the authors. These we have frequently been able to utilize.

Similar in character to the preceding, but naturally more modest in consideration of their scope are the bibliographical and biographical studies in Miguel Colmeiro's *La Botánica y los botánicos de la Peninsula hispano-lusitana*, Madrid, 1858.

Superior, of course, to both, in its value for American history is the *Biblioteca marítima española* of Martín Fernández de Navarrete, also a posthumous work, published in Madrid, in 1851, in two volumes.

Its value consists not only in the bio-bibliographical researches on books and authors mentioned but also in the documents that are cited at every step.

Of less value, but necessary for occasional consultation, is the *Diccionario bibliográfico-histórico de los antiguos reinos, provincias, ciudades, etc., de España* by Tomas Muñoz y Romero, which, like the work of Colmeiro was published in 1858, a prize volume of the National Library of Madrid and issued at its expense.

Special bibliographies of different kinds, also useful to the student of books and men relating to America are: *Catálogo del teatro antiguo español* of Barrera y Leirado, Madrid, 1860; *Apuntes para una Biblioteca española de libros, folletos, etc., relativos a las riquezas minerales concernientes a la Península y Ultramar* by Maffey y Rúa Figueroa, Madrid, 1871; *Bibliografía numismática española* by Rada y Delgado, Madrid, 1866; and *Biblioteca científica española del siglo XVI*, by Felipe Picatoste y Rodríguez, Madrid, 1891.

During the years 1785 to 1789, Juan Sempere y Guarinos brought out in six volumes his *Ensayo de una Biblioteca española de los mejores escritores del Reinado de Carlos III*, in which are found bio-bibliographical notices of not a few writers regarding American affairs.

Contemporaneously, Juan Antonio Pellicer y Saforcada published his *Ensayo de una Biblioteca de traductores españoles*, Madrid, 1788, in which also are found some data available for American bibliography.

Perhaps more important than the special bibliographies are those of regions and cities of the Peninsula which began to appear about the middle of the 17th Century. Thus, in 1747, José Rodríguez published his *Biblioteca Valentina*, and Vicente Ximeno issued his *Escritores del reino de Valencia*, in two volumes. These two works were completed by the publication in 1827 of the *Biblioteca Valenciana* of Justo Pastor Fuster.

Álvarez Baena's *Hijos ilustres de Madrid*, Madrid, 1789–1791, is of interest for the data it contains relative to our subject. In the preparation of the biographical part the author made many researches in the parochial registers of Madrid and in other sources not less worthy of confidence.

The *Biblioteca nueva de escritores aragoneses* of Félix Latassa follows in chronological order as the six volumes of which it consists were published from 1798 to 1802. This, as a continuation of the *Biblioteca antigua* published in 1796, includes authors who flourished from 1500 to the last date. Both works of the learned Aragonese, augmented and reedited in the form of a bio-bibliographical dictionary by Miguel Gómez Uriel, were reprinted in Zaragoza, 1884, in three volumes.

To this series of bibliographical works relating to the regions and provinces of Spain belong the *Catálogo de los libros, etc., que tratan de Extremadura*, published in 1865, by Vicente Barrantes, and ten years later the *Aparato bibliográfico para la historia de Extremadura* by the same author, both of interest, especially for data relating to Hernán Cortés, the Pizarros and other Extremadurans who participated in American affairs and whose deeds were subject matter for not a few authors.

To the same class of works belong the *Biblioteca del Bascófilo*, Madrid, 1887, by Angel Allende Salazar; the *Intento de un diccionario biográfico y bibliográfico de autores de la provincia de Burgos*, Madrid, 1890, by Manuel Martínez Añíbarro; the *Bibliografía española de Cerdeña*, Madrid, 1890, by Eduardo Todo y Güell; and the *Colección bibliográfico-biográfica de la provincia de Zamora*, Madrid, 1891, of the noted Americanist, Cesáreo Fernández Duro.

Similar to these is the *Catálogo razonado biográfico y bibliográfico de autores portugueses que escribieron en castellano*, Madrid, 1890, by Domingo Garcia Peres.

Of more distinctly bibliographical flavor and, for this reason, of greater value to the student of American books are the special works designed to catalogue the production of the press in some of the cities of the Peninsula. The first place in chronological order as well as in merit belongs to Cristóbal Pérez Pastor who in 1887 initiated this series with the publication of his *Imprenta en Toledo*, and who subsequently has enriched his country's literature by similar works on Medina del Campo and Madrid during the 16th century.

He has been closely followed by Juan Catalina García in the *Imprenta en Alcalá de Henares*, Madrid, 1889, and *Escritores de Guadalajara*, Madrid, 1899, and by José María Valdenebro y Cisneros in the *Imprenta en Córdoba*, Madrid, 1900. We must also mention Escudero y Perosso's *Tipografiá Hispalense*, a work of less value from every point of view, which will possibly delay for many years the publication of a worthy record of the products of the presses of that city.

It is regrettable that modern Spanish bibliographies—that of the Conde de Viñaza being an exception—have failed to refer to the authors who have previously mentioned the books that are described, and to give biographical information regarding the authors whose books are discussed.

To complete this review of the works we have been able to use in the preparation of the present Biblioteca,[12] we must give a brief review of

[12] *Biblioteca hispano-americana.* Cf. List no. 109.

the chronicles and bibliographies of the religious orders. In this we shall not occupy ourselves with those published in America because they refer almost wholly to books published there, nor with all of those published in Europe, because the bibliographical data are vague and of little value and their consideration would require more space than is available.

To the Jesuits, in our opinion, belongs the honor of having initiated the bibliography of the religious order with the publication by Pedro de Ribadeneira of Toledo of *Catalogus Scriptorum Religionis Societatis Jesu*, Antwerp, 1608. This was reprinted the following year and again in 1613, notices of American authors beginning to appear in the later edition. His work, brief as it necessarily was from the recent foundation of the order, served later as a basis for a much more extensive work, prepared by Felipe Alegambe, a native of Brussels, published also in Antwerp in 1643. This Nathan Southwell, born in Norfolk, England, increased by adding notices of authors who flourished up to 1675 and published under the same title in Rome, 1676, in a large volume of over 1000 pages.

During the 18th century the bibliography of the order, in so far as is of interest to our subject, was enriched, in an incidental manner, by two Mexican Jesuits, P. Clavigero in whose work published in 1780 are found two lists of American writers; and Juan Luis Maneiro who published his *De Vitis aliquot Mexicanorum*, in Bologna, 1791. In this are found interesting bibliographical notices.

The two *Supplementa Bibliothecae Scriptorum Societatis Jesu* by Raimundo Diosdado Caballero, published in Rome, 1814–1816 in two volumes were designed to study the lives and works of the Jesuits who were expelled from Spain and America and established themselves in Italy. In this work is found much of singular interest regarding these Jesuits in so precarious a time when so many concealed the fruits of their intelligence under anonymity.

In all of these works, however, notices of books are given very briefly with but the most indispensable data to distinguish them.

Both in this respect and in its comprehensiveness, the *Bibliothèque des écrivains de la Compagnie de Jésus* by Augustin and Alois de Backer surpassed all of these bibliographies. Its publication was begun in 1855 and completed in 1861.[13]

Inferior to this, notwithstanding the limitation of its scope to the historical part, is the work of Auguste Carayon, *Bibliographie historique*

[13] Nouv. édition par C. Sommervogel. Bruxelles, 1890–1909, 10 v. Cf. List. no. 16.

de la Compagnie de Jésus, Paris, 1864. To us, the most interesting section is chapter 4 of the third part which treats of the missions in America and contains nearly two hundred titles very briefly given.

The *Dictionnaire des ouvrages anonymes et pseudonymes* of authors belonging to the order, published by Carlos Sommervogel in Paris, is superior by reason of the research it shows. There is, however, little in it of value to the Americanist.

Much more useful and in part wholly reliable is *Los antiguos jesuitas del Perú* published in Lima in 1882 by Enrique Torres Saldamando, a most diligent and industrious author, who was able for the preparation of his book to consult the original documents of the order which were preserved in that city. The author gives us extensive biographical and bibliographical notices of 157 writers of the 16th and 17th centuries, and, according to his plan, which, for various reasons, he was unable to realize, these notices for completing the bibliography of the 17th and that of the 18th centuries, were to comprehend more than 300 authors. By the premature death of Torres Saldamando, American bibliography lost a worker of the highest character.

The Dominicans followed the Jesuits in publishing information concerning their authors. As early as 1611, Alonso Fernández in his *Historia eclesiástica de nuestros tiempos* published in Toledo, dedicated two chapters to books and authors of the New World, chapters which served León Pinelo in the compilation of his *Epítome.*

These notices, however, are insignificant in comparison with those found in the *Scriptores Ordinis Prædicatorum*· by the French authors Jacques Quétif and Jacques Echard, the second volume of which, published in Paris, 1721, and devoted to 16th and 17th century authors of the Order, forms a real monument of bio-bibliographical research, indispensable for consultation to one dealing with American books and authors.

Poor and inadequate in comparison is the *La Orden de Predicadores* which Ramón Martínez Vigil published in Madrid in 1884.

Tomás de Herrera initiated the bibliographical work of the Augustinians with his *Alphabetum Augustinianum,* printed in 1644, which contains some notices of American writers. Juan Martín Maldonado, however, in his *Breve Suma de la Provincia del Perú,* published in Rome in 1651, gave very full information concerning the authors of that part of America.

In the fourth volume of the *Chronica Espiritual Augustiniana,* written by Sebastián Portillo y Aguilar the same year that Maldonado brought out his work, but not published until 1732, there is found a catalogue of 983 authors of the Order. The data, however, are so brief that we might say that the bibliography of the Augustinians is yet to be done were it not for the *Catálogo de escritores agustinos españoles, portugueses y americanos* which Bonifacio Moral commenced to publish in 1882 in the review, *La Ciudad de Dios*, which meets, in some degree, this want. This work, which we believe, was not issued in the separate edition as prepared by the author, is worthy of commendation, particularly with respect to the Philippines.[14]

The Franciscans at an early date began the task of noting the productions of their authors. If we omit from consideration Francisco Gonzaga's *De Origine Seraphicae Religionis*, Rome, 1587, the fourth part of which, devoted to missions of America, contains an occasional bibliographical reference, and Lucas Wadding's *Scriptores Ordinis Minorum*, written in 1650, which contains the names of some American authors among the two thousand mentioned, we must come down to 1732 before finding the *Bibliotheca universa franciscana* by Juan de San Antonio of Salamanca. In this we find abundant and reliable information regarding American books and authors. Many, indeed are the names it contains and although titles are not catalogued and described *in extenso*, it possesses the advantage of indicating which books the author has personally handled, a valuable detail, especially for that period, which removes all doubt as to the existence of some that are now of the greatest rarity.

The Franciscans have also the *Saggio de bibliografia geografica storica etnografica sanfrancescana*, Prato, 1879, by Marcellino da Civezza, with titles copied literally, accompanied by compendious bibliographical descriptions and in some instances by transcriptions of passages which seemed of interest. It is, without doubt, a work of some value but very incomplete.

The Mercedarians possess the *Biblioteca Mercedaria* by José Antonio Garí y Siumell, published in Barcelona, 1875, which mentions 874 authors, including some Americans. But as the bibliographical part consists largely of a bare statement of the titles, it may be said to be wanting in adequate research.

Such, briefly indicated, are the principal sources of American bibliography.

C. K. JONES,
Translator.

[14] Cf. Santiago Vela, *Ensayo de una biblioteca ibero-americano de la Orden de San Agustín.* List, no. 148.—TRANSLATOR.

INDEX

Entries under countries, states, provinces, cities, etc. of Hispanic America are not given in the index; they will be found in the country divisions.

Abadiano, E., 753.
Abecía, V., 347.
Abel Rosales, J., 479.
Academia de historia de Cuba, 718.
Academia de la historia, Madrid, 1.
Academia guatemalteca, 740.
Academia nac. de medicina, 355.
Acevedo, L. de, 664.
Acosta, F. J., 754.
Acosta, J., 608a.
Acosta, N., 327.
Acosta de Samper, S., 609.
Acuña, M., 826.
Advielle, V., 1169.
Agreda y Sánchez., J. M. de, 822, 917.
Agriculture, 4.
Agüeros, V., 755, 783.
Aguilar y Santillán, R., 756-759.
Aguilera, R., 992, 993.
Ahumada Maturana, R., 480.
Alarcón, A., 328.
Albir, F. J., 747.
Album bibl. de Venezuela, 1139.
Album biográfico, 191.
Album nacional, 192.
Album patriótico., 1099.
Alcedo, A., 1a, 1b.
Alcover y Beltrán, A. M., 665.
Aldas, A., 193.
Alegambe, P., 142.
Alegre, F. J., 760, 809.
Almanak administrativo, 356.
Almanaque brasileiro, 357.
Almanaque del mensajero, 194.
Almanaque de "El Siglo," 1106.
Almeida Paes Leme, P. T. de, 358.
Almirante, J., 1a, 1c.
Alonso Criado, E., 195.
Altamirano, I. M., 761, 762, 826, 958.

Alva y Astorga, P. de., 2.
Alvares de Toledo, 595.
Alvares y Thomas, I., 257.
Amat di S. Filippo, P., 58.
Ambrosetti, J. B., 196.
Ameghino, F., 196, 244.
Amunátegui, M. L., 479, 481.
Amunátegui Solar, D., 482, 483.
Anales de la Univ. de Chile, 484-486.
Anderson, A. D., 763, 764.
Andrade, M. de J., 719, 765, 766.
Andrade, V. de P., 767-772.
Andrade Coello, A., 719a, 1192.
Andrés de San Nicolás, 3.
Añes, J., 610.
Angelis, P. de, 197.
Anglo-South Amer. handbook, 1244.
Angulo, D., 1018, 1019.
Alicante, 1223.
Annuaire général de médecins, 1193.
Annuario de Minas Geraes, 359.
Anonyms and pseudonyms, 21, 463, 739, 1236.
Anrique Reyes, N., 487-490, 720.
Anthropology, 399, 537, 565, 566, 569, 871, 1032.
Antioquia, 611.
Antología boliviana, 329.
Antón Ramírez, B., 4.
Antonio, N., 5-7.
Anuario bibl. de Argentina, 198.
Anuario bibl. nacional (Mexico), 773.
Anuario coahuilense, 774.
Anuario de la prensa argentina, 199.
Anuario de la prensa ecuatoriana, 721.
Anuario oficial (Argentina), 200.
Anzola, J., 1140.
Apuntes biog. contemporáneos, 201.
Arango Mejía, G., 611.

NOTES

American Consular agency at Chuquicamata, Chile, closed. No. 182, August 18.

American loan for Rio Grande do Sul, Brazil. No. 163, July 15.

American tire-repair materials used in Habana. *Id.*

American to direct new Brazilian Agricultural College. No. 202, August 30.

American trade with Bermuda. No. 172, July 26.

Amount of freight at Vera Cruz. No. 154, July 7.

Application of the Torrente law in Cuba. No. 163, July 15.

Argentine railway requests bids for quantity of hardware. No. 166, July 19.

Argentine sugar crop estimate for 1921. No. 174, July 28.

Argentine sugar statistics for 1920. No. 198, August 25.

Argentine trade and economic notes. Nos. 197 and 203, August 8 and 31.

Argentine-United States balance of trade for 1920–21. No. 180, August 4.

Bahia, Brazil, export trade for June quarter. No. 198, August 25.

The Banana trade industry in Tela, Honduras. No. 162, July 14.

Bids for supplying coal for Costa Rican railway. No. 175, July 29.

Bids invited for new hotel in Mexico City. No. 154, July 5.

Bolivian exports of tin concentrates for June. No. 175, July 29.

Brazilian budget for 1922. No. 186, August 11.

Brazilian economic notes. Nos. 166, and 198, July 19 and August 25.

Brazilian road and automobile notes. No. 176, July 30.

Brazilian state seeks American loan. No. 196, August 23.

Brazilian trade notes. Nos. 159, 161, 194, and 201, July 7, and 13, and August 20 and 29.

Brazil's 1921–22 coffee crop. No. 197, August 24.

Building operations in Guadalajara, Mexico. No. 156, July 7.

Business failures in Argentina. No. 180, August 4.

Cable rates to Brazil reduced. No. 165, July 18.

Campaign against hookworm in Paraguay. No. 153, July 2.

Cattle and beef industry in Rio Grande do Sul, Brazil. No. 172, July 26.

Changes in petroleum tax law of Ecuador. No. 185, August 10.

Chile opens a national pawn shop. No. 162, July 14.

Chilean conversion fund deposits. No. 173, July 27.

Chilean railways call for bids on coal. No. 162, July 14.

Chilean shoe industry. No. 168, July 21.

Chilean trade and economic notes. No. 172, July 26.

Coastwise steamship lines in Cuba. No. 168, July 21.

Coffee exports from Salina Cruz, Mexico. No. 179, August 3.

Colombia contracts a loan of 5,000,000 pesos. No. 199, August 26.

The Comodoro Rivadavia petroleum fields. No. 177, August 1.

Construction of national road in Panama. No. 171, July 25.

Construction work in foreign countries (Mexico). No 176, July 30.

Converter plant being installed by copper company in Mexico. No. 169, July 22.

Cost of living in Argentina. No. 196, August 23.

The cost of living in Lima, Peru. No. 185, August 10.

The cotton production of Lower California. No. 198, August 25.

Crop reports from British Guiana. No. 172, July 26.

Cuban customs duties for June and July. No. 184, August 9.

Cuban exports to the United States. No. 162, July 14.

Cultivation of foreign tobacco in Ecuador. No. 191, August 17.

Decline in Argentine export trade. No. 168, July 21.

Department of Commerce representative for Cuba. No. 193, August 19.

Details of Brazilan foreign trade. No. 153, July 2.

Development of petroleum deposits in Ecuador. No. 155, July 6.

Development projects in Baranquilla. No. 165, July 18.

Direct delivery of Argentine fuel oil. No. 200, August 27.

Dominican Republic imports and declared exports to the United States. No. 175, July 29.

Economic and trade notes on Chile. No. 191, August 17.

Economic situation in Guatemala. No. 202, August 30.

Ecuadorian school of aviation. No. 174, July 28.

Ecuadorian steamship and industrial project. No. 188, August 13.

Ecuadorian sugar plantation improved by American agricultural machinery. No. 196, August 23.

Exemption from taxation of Mexican real estate. No. 195, August 22.

Effect of drought on Mexican crops. No. 155, July 6.

Exhibition of dairy machinery in Argentina. No. 165, July 18.

Exportation of Uruguayan products. No. 193, August 19.

Exports from Isle of Pines, April–June, 1921. No. 170, July 23.

Exports of British Guiana products. No. 195, August 22.

Extension of Paraguayan moratorium. *Id.*

First International dairy exhibit in Argentina. *Id.*

First shipment of bananas from Tela, Honduras. No. 196, August 23.

The Foreign service of the Department of Commerce. No. 190, August 16.

Foreign tariff notes. No. 188, August 13. (Brazil, Costa Rica, and Mexico.)

Foreign tariffs. Argentina, nos. 164 and 183, July 16 and August 8; Bolivia, no. 164; British Honduras, no. 174, July 29; Chile, no. *id.*; Costa Rica, nos. 176, 180, and 183, July 30, and August 4 and 8; Ecuador, nos. 164 and 180; Haiti, no. 176; Mexico, nos. 164 and 176; Panama, no. 164; Salvador, no. 174; Trinidad, no. 180; Uruguay, no. 176.

Foreign trade of Brazil for first four months of 1921. No. 173, July 27.

Forwarding catalogues to Brazil. No. 188, August 13.

Free markets established in Rio de Janeiro. No. 164, July 16.

Freight conditions at Vera Cruz, Mexico. Nos. 159, 163, and 171, July 11, 15, and 25.

Gasoline imports into Brazil. No. 174, July 28.

Geological report on Pampa region of Argentina available. No. 197, August 24.

Government loan for British Guiana. No. 186, August 11.

Guatemalan Chamber of Commerce desires commercial literature. No. 160, July 12.

Initiation of new Japanese line to Para. No. 153, July 2.

Imports into Panama during May, 1921. No. 172, July 26.

Improved steamship service between Guatemala and New York. No. 162, July 14.

Increased number of automobiles, province of Santa Fe. No. 195, August 22.

Installation of water works in a Brazilian city. *Id.*

Jamaican steamship service. No. 174, July 28.

The Junta de Vigilancia makes a loan to the Peruvian government. No. 155, July 6.

Law regulating sale of drafts in Bolivia. No. 170, July 23.

List of English-speaking residents in Argentina. No. 174, July 28.

List of sugar plantations in Mexico available. No. 179, August 3.

Logwood industry in Jamaica. No. 198, August 25.

Low prices of coconuts exported from Panama. No. 152, July 1.

Magnesium and aluminium sulphates available (Chile). No. 180, August 4.

Manufacture of marine motors in Argentina. No. 169, July 22.

Market for construction materials in Brazil. No. 199, August 26.

Market for wheat flour in Colombia. No. 185, August 10.

Mexico Northwestern Railway to reopen line to Chihuahua, Mexico. No. 165, July 18.

Mexican trade in 1920. No. 176, July 30.

Mexican trade notes. No. 200, August 27.

Monthly cable service. Nos. 158 and 177, July 9 and August 1. (Argentina, Brazil, Chile, Mexico, and Peru.)

Motor vehicles and accessories in the Bahamas. No. 190, August 16.

Movement of petroleum from Tampico for July. No. 199, August 26.

National congress of engineers at Buenos Aires. No. 194, August 20.

New American company engages in lumbering in Nicaragua. No. 196, August 23.

New Brazilian insurance legislation. No. 165, July 18.

New Brazilian post regulations. No. 172, July 26.

New mining regulations in Peru. No. 193, August 19.

New Paraguayan meat-packing law. No. 196, August 23.

New regulatory commission for the henequen market. No. 199, August 28.

New steamship service for west coast of Mexico and Central America. No. 159, July 11.

New steamship service to Venezuela. No. 172, July 26.

No American Chamber of Commerce in Guatemala. No. 169, July 22.

Opportunity for sale of American pipe in Ecuador. No. 181, August 5.

Oil shipments from Tampico district. April, no. 160, July 12. May, no. 178, August 2. June, no. 185, August 10.

Packing plant for port of Guaymas, Mexico. No. 166, July 19.

Panama Canal traffic. Nos. 156 and 181, July 7 and August 5.

Paraguayan exchange fluctuating. No. 194, August 20.

Parcel post for Venezuela. No. 172, July 26.

Port of Iquitos, Peru, closed. No. 197, August 24.

Postponement of centennial ceremonies in Peru. No. 173, July 27.

Present position of Chilean nitrate industry. No. 184, August 9.

Production and export of petroleum in Mexico. No. 163, July 15.

Progress of Brazilian public construction projects. No. 159, July 11.

Proposed Brazilian-Paraguayan railway. No. 163, July 15.

Proposed remedies for Brazilian economic crisis. No. 202, August 30.

Proposed subway and tunnel for Habana, Cuba. No. 195, August 22.

Prospective output of oil in Mexico. No. 162, July 14.

Purchase of American locomotives by Mexican government. No. 193, August 19.

Purchase of Bolivian tin property by American company. No. 162, July 14.

Quality of German goods arriving in Chile. *Id.*

Recent developments of Tampico oil fields. No. 190, August 16.

Recent economic developments in Peru. No. 196, August 23.

Reduced postal rates from Honduras to United States. No. 184, August 9.

Removal of Cuban prohibition on the importation of rice. No. 159, July 11.

Report of the Bahia export trade for 1920. No. 169, July 22.

Report on Mexican situation available. No. 176, July 30.

Report on Mexican situation available. No. 198, August 25.

Restoration of certain export duties in Mexico. No. 175, July 29.

Revision of Commercial Travelers' Guide to Latin America. No. 177, August 1.

Rice industry in Rio Grande do Sul, Brazil. No. 166, July 19.

Roads in Venezuela. No. 185, August 10.

Rubber exported from Brazil and Peru during June, 1921. No. 182, August 6.

Santa Marta's declared exports for January–June. No. 179, August 3.

Silver exports from Chihuahua to United States. No. 186, August 11.

Steamship communications with Trinidad. No. 164, July 16.

Steamship liner service at Barbados. No. 162, July 14.

Stopping of oil shipments from Mexico. No. 155, July 6.

Sugar exports from United States from Nuevitas, Cuba. No. 176, July 30.

Sugar production in Colombia. No. 182, August 6.

Tenders requested for cast iron piping in Argentine. No. 199, August 26. *Id.*, for freights in Argentine. No. 192, August 18.

Terms of sale in Mexico. No. 156, July 7.

Tomato crop in the state of Sinaloa, Mexico. No. 179, August 3.

Trade and economic notes from Colombia. No. 198, August 25.

Trade figures for Santa Marta, Colombia. No. 173, July 27.
Trade notes from Ecuador. No. 153, July 2.
Trade notes from Guatemala. No. 154, July 5.
Trade notes from Mexico. Nos. 160 and 170, July 12 and 23.
Trade notes on Chile. No. 168, July 21.
Trade of British Guiana for first five months of 1921. No. 199.
   August 28.
Trade of Isle of Pines with United States. No. 172, July 26.
Withdrawal of National City Bank from Colombia. No. 188, August 13.
World wheat acreage and yield. No. 172, July 26.

Beginning with September, the format of *Commerce Reports* was changed, the publication being made harmonious in size with the *Congressional Record* and issued once a week instead of daily. The first number of the new publication appeared on September 5, and nos. 2, 3, and 4, on September 12, 19, and 26 respectively. Items on Hispanic America have appeared as follows:
Alteration in concession for electric railway in Peru. No. 4.
American competition in Brazilian coal trade. No. 3.
American secures contract to construct railroad in Peru. *Id.*
Argentine exports for the first half of 1921. No. 4.
Argentine law on refused shipments. No. 1.
Brazilian industrial notes. No. 3.
Brazilian market for codfish. No. 1.
Brazilian market for motor cars. No. 2.
Brazilian market for railway equipment. No. 3.
Brazilian markets for foodstuffs. *Id.*
Brazilian sales methods of British equipment manufacturers. No. 4.
Brazil's trade in leather and leather goods. *Id.*
Cable reports from Latin America. No. 1. (Argentina, Brazil, Chile, Mexico, and Peru.)
The Chilean coal market. No. 2.
The Chilean iodine industry. No. 4.
Coal needs in Argentina. No. 1.
Coffee shipments from Maracaibo, Venezuela. No. 4.
Congestion at Vera Cruz. *Id.*
Contract for lighthouse for Venezuelan coast. *Id.*
Cuban law on suspension of payments. No. 1.
Dominican Central Railway to use oil as fuel. No. 4.

Economic conditions in Mexico. No. 1.

Ecuadorian concern to build cement factory. No. 4.

Electric plants in the Rosario consular district, Argentina. No. 3.

Establishment of hydroelectric plants in Mexico. No. 1.

Factors affecting American trade with Brazil. No. 4.

Foreign customs tariffs. Argentina, no. 3; Barbados, no. 2; Brazil, no. 2; British Honduras, no. 3; Costa Rica, no. 1; Ecuador, no. 2; Mexico, nos. 2 and 3; Nicaragua, no. 1; Peru, no. 3; Salvador, nos. 1 and 2; Uruguay, no. 1.

Foreign markets for scientific apparatus. No. 4. (Argentina and Peru.)

Fuel oil in Tarapaca province, Chile. Id.

German competition in dyestuffs and chemicals in Mexico. Id.

German steamship lines touching at Pernambuco. No. 1.

Heavy taxes on Mexican crude petroleum. Id.

Immigration (1920) into Brazil. No. 4.

Low price of rubber affects Brazilian trade. No. 3.

Market for Pacific coast lumber in Mexico. No. 2.

Market for paints in Latin America. Id.

The Markets of Colombia, South America. No. 4.

Market possibilities in Brazil for agricultural machinery. No. 2.

Mexican trade and economic notes. Nos. 1, 3, and 4.

Movement of livestock through Laredo. No. 4.

New blast furnace in Jujuy, Argentina. Id.

New steamship service between American and Mexican ports. No. 3.

Paints and varnishes in Latin America. No. 1.

Petroleum explorations in Panama. No. 4.

Proposed anti-trust law in Argentina. No. 2.

Propagation of the Chilean Nitrate Railways concession. No. 4.

Portuguese financial agency at Rio de Janeiro reopened. Id.

Opportunities in Argentine oil fields. No. 1.

Railway project to connect Brazil and Paraguay. No. 2.

Railway project to connect Brazil and Paraguay. No. 3.

Recent port and shipping development in Mexico. No. 2.

Reported discovery of petroleum shale in Tarapaca, Chile. No. 4.

Rules for Brazilian exposition. No. 1.

Sale of medicinal drugs in Chile. No. 4.

Schurtz, William Lytle: Imports of electrical goods into Brazil. No. 2.

Sugar shipments from Pernambuco, Brazil, for six months. No. 1.

Tariff and trade regulations. No. 4. (Argentina, British Honduras, Costa Rica, and Mexico.)
Textile imports of Cuba. No. 2.
Water meters for San José, Costa Rica. No. 1.

The famous Mexicana collection of the late Genaro García has been acquired by the University of Texas. Dr. Charles W. Hackett, writing in the University of Texas Bulletin May 15, 1921, says:

The library is composed of printed books and manuscripts relating primarily to the history of Mexico. The printed works number over 20,000, including books and pamphlets; in addition there are about 2,000 volumes of Mexican newspapers and periodicals, many of which are unique, and the private archives of a number of prominent nineteenth century Mexican statesmen. The latter contain over 120,000 manuscript pages.

The largest collection in the library is that comprising the books on history and geography. In fact there hardly exists a known book concerning the history of Mexico which is not found in this section. It comprises books dealing with the prehistoric period, the Spanish conquest, the colonial period, and the national period down through the revolution which overthrew Carranza. There are between five and six thousand books alone covering the period since 1810.

While the core of the library is historical Mexico, the collection also comprises the following sections: general works, as bibliographies and encyclopedias, works of philosophy, of religion, of law, of indigenous linguistics and of Mexican *belles lettres*. The latter collection, containing over 2,000 volumes, is, it is claimed, more complete than the corresponding section of the National Library.

The value of such a collection can hardly be estimated or even appreciated. By the acquisition of this library the University of Texas undoubtedly takes first rank over all the institutions in the country in facilities for the study of Spanish North America from earliest to latest times and in practically all fields of investigation save that of religion. Only the University of California and Yale University can compare with the University of Texas in this respect. What the library will mean for graduate work and to scholars and investigators the world over it is only necessary to suggest.

The Sección de Historia of the Facultad de Filosofía y Letras of the University of Buenos Aires has published the following, many of which, as will be seen, are already exhausted:

Los Archivos de Paraná y Santa Fe.—Informe del Comisionado P. Antonio Larrouy. Buenos Aires, 1908. Pp. 24. (Exhausted.)
Los Archivos de Córdoba y Tucumán.—Informe del Comisionado P. Antonio Larrouy. Buenos Aires, 1909. Pp. 61.
Gobierno del Perú.—Obra escrita en el siglo XVI por el Licenciado don Juan Matienzo, Oidor de la Real Audiencia de Charcas. Buenos Aires, 1910. Pp. X, 219. (Exhausted.)

Documentos relativos a la Organización Constitucional de la República Argentina. 3 vols. Buenos Aires, 1911–1912. Indice alfabético de los tres tomos. Buenos Aires, 1914. (Vols. I. and III. exhausted.)

Documentos relativos a los antecedentes de la Independencia de la República Argentina. Buenos Aires, 1912. Pp. XII, 469. (Exhausted.)

Documentos relativos a los antecendentes de la Independencia de la República Argentina—Asuntos eclesiásticos (1809–1812). Buenos Aires, 1912. Pp. X, 230. Indice alfabético de los dos tomos. Buenos Aires, 1913. Pp. 43.

Documentos para la historia del Virreinato del Río de la Plata. 3 vols. Buenos Aires, 1912–1913. Indice alfabético de los tres tomos. Buenos Aires, 1913. Pp. 44. (Vol. III. exhausted.)

Documentos para la Historia Argentina. Vols. I–XIV. Buenos Aires, 1913–1921 (series being continued). (Vols. I.–IV. exhausted.)

MONOGRAFÍAS

I: La administración de Temporalidades en el Río de la Plata, por Luis María Torres. Buenos Aires, 1917. Pp. 24.

II: Constituciones del Real Colegio de San Carlos, por Emilio Ravignani. Buenos Aires, 1917. Pp. 18. (Exhausted.)

III: Valores aproximados de algunas monedas Hispano Americanas (1497–1771), por Juan Alvarez. Buenos Aires, 1917. Pp. 37. (Exhausted.)

IV: Los manuscritos del diario de Schmidel, pp. 10 and 6 plates, por Roberto Lehmann Nitsche. Buenos Aires, 1918.

V: Origen y Patria de Cristobal Colón, Crítica de sus fuentes históricas, por Rómulo D. Carbia, pp. 50 and 14 plates. (Exhausted.) Buenos Aires, 1918.

VI: La personalidad de Manuel Belgrano, ensayo conmemorativo, por Emilio Ravignani. Buenos Aires, 1920. Pp. 32.

VII: Relación descriptiva de los mapas, planos, etc. del Virreinato de Buenos Aires, existentes en el Archivo General de Indias, por Pedro Torres Lanzas. 2.ª edición, aumentada. Buenos Aires, 1921. Pp. 173 and 77 engravings.

EN PREPARACIÓN

La política portuguesa y la Infanta Carlota, en el Río de la Plata (1808–1809), por Diego Luis Molinari.

El período colonial a través de la historiografía argentina. Valoración de textos, por Rómulo D. Carbia.

Los Archivos de Catamarca y La Rioja, por el P. Antonio Larrouy.

Los Archivos de la ciudad de Buenos Aires, por Emilio Ravignani.

The University of California has issued an announcement catalogue of 27 pages in Spanish, under the title *La Universidad de California: su instalación, régimen, plan de estudios, etc., 1921.*

Doubleday, Page, & Co. began to publish in April, through its Spanish Book Department, a small catalogue entitled *La Revista de*

Libros, "a bibliographical guide for the use of teachers, students, and lovers of Spanish". This list "which will appear from time to time, will attempt to keep its readers informed of the current literary movement in Spain and the Spanish-American countries".

The Chile-American Association has issued a small pamphlet by the name of *Reciprocal resources of Chile and the United States* (New York, 1921, pp. 20). This gives various basic facts concerning Chile and the United States printed both in Spanish and in English. A brief introduction calls attention to the mutual interests of Chile and the United States, and to the work of the Chile-American Association in enlarging the knowledge of the United States in Chile.

Those wishing to study Spanish in Spain or to make well laid out trips in Spain, will find interesting the *Announcements* of the Ministerio de Instrucción Pública y Bellas Artes—Junta para Ampliación de Estudios, Centro de Estudios Históricos—Courses in Spanish language and Literature for foreigners in Madrid, 1921. With this is included a notice of the trips to Spain organized by the Spanish bureau of the Institute of International Education, with the cooperation of the Committee on Foreign Study and Travel of the American Association of Teachers of Spanish and the American Express Company. This can be obtained from the Institute of International Education, at 419 West 117th St., New York.

Miss Katherine Dreier, author of *Five Months in the Argentine from a Woman's Point of View*, donated 500 copies of her book to the Museum of Modern Art, Société Anonyme, Inc., 19 East 47th St., New York, to help meet the initial expenses of the undertaking.

D. Sturgis E. Leavitt of the University of North Carolina, who, when holding a Sheldon traveling fellowship from Harvard University, made extensive investigations in the libraries of Peru, Bolivia, Chile, Argentina and Uruguay, is arranging his bibliographical material for publication. The results of his researches will take the following form.

"A bibliography of Peruvian literature, 1821–1919". This is announced for publication by the *Romanic Review*. "It includes works actually consulted in the library of the University of San Marcos, the National Library, and in the private collection of Señor Javier Pardo y Ugarteche, rector of the University. . . . From the list are omitted books of a purely scientific nature".

A bibliography of Bolivian literature.   This is also to appear in the
Romanic Review.
"Chilean literature.   A bibliography of literary criticism, biography
and literary controversy".
"Argentine literature".
"Uruguyan literature."
Dr. Leavitt's work will form a valuable supplement to Coester's
Literary History of Spanish America, and a most useful aid to librarian
and student.   It is to be hoped that these bibliographical contribu-
tions may be published in collective form.—C. K. JONES.

Fred Wilbur Powell, Ph.D., has recently published through the
Stratford Co., of Boston, a needed volume entitled *The Railroads of
Mexico*.   The first part is concerned with the present condition in
Mexico and with the period following the Díaz regime.   The second
part contains a summary of the development of the great system of
land transportation which has so rapidly brought Mexico out of a long
economic stagnation.   The third part deals with conclusions which
are based on the two preceding parts.   Readers of this volume will
welcome the carefully worked out bibliography.   This work will be
discussed in a later issue of this REVIEW.

Mr. Alfred M. Tozzer, the first recipient of the traveling fellowship
in American archaeology of the Archaeological Institute of America,
has made an important contribution to American linguistics in the
publication of his *A Maya grammar with bibliography and appraisement of the works noted* (Cambridge, Mass., 1921, pp. xvi, 301) which
forms vol. 9 of the "Papers of the Peabody Museum of American Archaeology and Ethnology", Harvard University.   The bibliograpny
is notable.   In it "three are listed over 700 different works, not including
second editions, on or in the Maya language or referring to it in some
way.   It should be understood that the language in question is that
dialect spoken in the peninsula of Yucatan and not the Maya linguistic
stock which covers a far more extended area."   The author's appraisement of the works mentioned in the bibliography in which he discusses
with scholarly competency the relative value of the works listed, is a
most valuable feature.

A Bulletin no. 25, published by the Interamerican Division of International Conciliation, in June, 1921, was devoted to the recent Bolivar

celebration in New York. It contains a number of addresses given at the unveiling of the monument erected to Bolívar or in connection with that occasion, by the following persons: Beltrán Mathieu, Esteban Gil Borges, Santos A. Dominici, Rafael H. Alizalde, President Warren G. Harding, Mayor John Hylan, Governor Nathan L. Miller, and John Bassett Moore.

The second volume of *Anales de la Academia de la Historia* has at last been published. Although it bears the imprint, "Habana, 1919", it has issued from the press only during this year. In this volume, the excellent bibliographical articles begun in the first volume are continued, namely: "Elogio del doctor Ramón Meza y Suárez Inclán", and "Bibliografía de Enrique Píneyro". The "Centon Epistolario", and "Manuel de Quesada y Loynaz", the latter by Carlos Manuel de Céspedes y Quesada, are also continued.

Boletín del Centro de Estudios Americanistas, nos. 36–45 (two numbers to each issue) contains further instalments of Pedro Torres Lanzas's "Catálogo de Legajos del Archivo de Indias", and the same archivist's "Escudos de armas, títulos de ciudades y villas, fundaciones de pueblos, erección de obispados, etc". Nos. 36–37 contain: "Censos de la población del virreinato de Nueva España en el siglo XVI"; "Relaciones geográficas de Yucatán". Nos. 38–39: "Intervención tutelar de España en los problemas de límites de Hispano-América: II. Indeterminación de fronteras geográficas", by Germán Latorre; "Real Academia Hispano-Americano de Ciencias y Artes de Cádiz. Certamen artístico para conmemorar el día 12 de octubre". Nos. 40–41: "Intervención tutelar de España", by Germán Latorre; "Propuesta de Esteban Gómez, piloto, para establecer un dique en el arroyo Taguete, donde se junta con el Guadalquivir, 1533". Nos. 42–43: "Algunos documentos del Archivo de Indias sobre ciudades chilenas"; by Jesús Pabón and Luis Jiménez Placer y Ciaurrez; "En bien de Sevilla y del comercio sevillano", by Germán Latorre; and "Segundo congreso de Geografía e Historia Hispano-Americanas celebrado en Sevilla en conmeroración del centenario del viaje y descubrimientos de Fernando de Magallanes". Nos. 44–45: "II Congreso de Geografía e Historia Hispano-Americana celebrado en Sevilla en conmemoración del centenario del viaje y descubrimiento de Fernando de Magallanes"; "Documento parlamentario. Discurso pronunciado en el Senado en el día 2 de marzo de 1921, en la discusión del dictamen de contestación

al discurso al corona", by Luis Palmo; "Don José de Veitia Linaje y
su libro 'Norte de la Contratación de las Indias',"; and "Libro de
las longitudes . . . por Alonso de Santa Cruz" (continued).

Boletín de Historia y Antigüedades is the name of a pleasing review
published in the Imprenta Nacional de Bogotá. In various issues are
noted; June, 1919—"Academia de Historia del Magdalena"; "Aportaciones a la Bibliografía del precursor de la independencia suramericana, don Francisco de Miranda", by Juan M. Aguilar (concluded);
"Bases del certamen que abre la academia Nacional de la Historia de
Venezuela, para los ciudadanos de las repúblicas americanas, con motivo del centenario de la victoria de Bogota"; "Los Curas de Nóvita",
by Guillermo O. Hurtado; "Diario de las operaciones del ejército de don
Julio Arboleda, de marzo a agosto de 1862"; "Fundación de la
villa de Leiva", by Mateo Domínguez. July–August, 1919—"Ante
la tumba de Santander"; "Antonio Santos", by J. D. Monsalve;
"Anzoátegui", by Fabio Lozano y Lozano; "Centenario de la
batalla de Boyacá"; "Compañía de Nueva Granada"; "El Coronel
Fray Ignacio Mariño", by Nicolás García Samudio; "Cuarta función
del ejército libertador de la Nueva Granada, en Boyacá, el día 7 de
agosto de 1819"; "Después de Boyacá"; by Aníbal Galindo; "Discurso
pronunciado en el Parque de la Independencia", by Fabio Lozano T.;
"Discurso pronunciado en la sesión solemne de la Academia Nacional
de Historia, por su presidente", by Antonio Gómez Restrepo; "Elogio
de don José Manuel Restrepo en la Academia Nacional de Historia",
by Eduardo Zuleta; "Genealogía del general Santander", by José
María Restrepo Sáenz; "Informe del secretario perpetuo en la junta
pública extraordinaria del día 10 de agosto de 1919"; "José Concha",
by P. M. I.; "Juan José Reyes Patria", "Memorias de un oficial de
marina"; "Mito genealógico", by M. S. Sánchez; "Ocupación de la
ciudad de Tunja por el ejército libertador"; "Páginas inéditas sobre
Boyacá. Reminiscencias", by Andrés M. Gallo; "Palabras de Luis
Augusto Cuervos ante el cabildo de Tunja, en nombre de la municipalidad de Bogotá y de las Academias de Historia de Colombia y
Venezuela"; "Primer centenario del fusilamiento de Antonia Santos
en el Socorro"; "Tomás Manby", by Luis Augusto Cuervo; December
1919—the entire number is devoted to Pedro Maria Ibáñez.   January
1920—"Amores de Solís", by Raimundo Rivas; "Apostillas", by
E. Posada: "Cartas a Caldas sobre el doctor Mutís", by Lorenzo de
Laquérica"; "Discurso el 12 de octubre de 1919; al hacer entrega de

la presidencia de la Academia al doctor Raimundo Rivas", by Antonio Gómez Restrepo; "Epigrafía bogotana", by E. Posada; "Exposición hecha al virrey de Santafé sobre la necesidad de prevenir los progresos del mal de San Lázaro y de promover la destrucción de las plataneras dentro de las poblaciones como causa de las enfermedades endémicas que se padecen en la provincia del Socorro", by José Celestino Mutís; "Informe de un jurado de la Academia Nacional de Historia"; "Informe del bibliotecario de la Academia Nacional de Historia"; "Reglamentaria del secretario perpetuo de la Academia Nacional de Historia, doctor Pedro María Ibáñez, leido en la junta pública del 12 de octubre de 1919."

The *Bulletin de l'Amerique Latine* which has been published in Paris for eleven years will change its title in January, 1922, becoming the *Revue de l'Amérique Latine*. Each number will contain about 100 pages and the directors, one of whom is Señor Don Ventura García Calderón, propose to publish articles of general interest regarding Hispanic America by well known French and Hispanic American authors. Among the latter are Francisco García Calderón, Graça Aranha, Alfonso Reyes, Carlos A. Villanueva, Gonzalo Zaldumbide, Hugo D. Barbagelata, and others.—C. K. Jones.

The *Colombian Review* is a recent addition to the reviews published in New York which are devoted to Hispanic America. It is edited by Ernesto Ponce de León, chief of the Government Information Bureau of the Republic of Colombia in New York. The July, 1921, number (no. 8) contains: "A page of history (Initial diplomatic relations between Colombia and the United States of America following the signing of the declaration of independence, by Nicolás García Samudio; "Venezuelan historical documents at the Chicago Exposition"; "The Colombian berry, or giant blackberry of Colombia", by Wilson Popenol; "Colombian possibilities for the development of the calcium-carbide industry"; "Colombian custom house duties—law of 1913"; "Statistical data on the hide and leather industry in the Republic of Colombia, S. A."; "Republic of Colombia and its vegetable oils"; and "El Presidente Harding condena la tarifa sobre importación de petróleos".

The *Compass* (New York) publishes in recent issues articles as follows: January, 1921—"Business conditions today"; by James Brown; "Economic development of Brazil", by Carl Schafer. March—"Cuban sugar commission"; "Digest of Torrente Law (Cuba)"; "Exchange on Latin America"; "Fixed rate of exchange (Ecuador)"; "Post-war readjustment in Colombia"; "The Stock-raising industry of Venezuela"; by Alba A. Mohr. April—"Factors affecting Peruvian exchange", by Grosvenor M. Jones; "Financial situation in Brazil". May—"The Maracaibo oil basin," by C. H. Stewart; "Peruvian business and financial conditions", by Charles F. Hill; "Simón Bolívar honored". June—"American investment in the Argentine meat-packing industry", by Leslie Orear; "Argentine conditions and their effect on American trade", by F. J. Oehmichen; "Business and financial conditions in Peru", by C. F. Hill; "Colombian oil development", by Alba A. Mohr; "Conditions in Pernambuco, Brazil"; "Cuzco, Peru; The old Inca Capital"; "South American investments"; "Venadium in Peru".

Cuba Contemporánea, March, 1921, contains the following articles: "Bibliografía", by Enrique Gay Calbó; "Eça de Queiroz", by Manuel de la Cruz; "El Padre Las Casas y los conquistadores españoles en América", by Enrique A. Ortiz; "La Preponderancia de los Estados Unidos en el mar Caribe", by Raúl de Cárdenas; "Ramillete poético", by Enrique José Varona; "Reflexiones sobre la crisis económica", by André François-Poncet. In the August number appear "La Historia y los factores históricos", by Ramiro Guerra; "Páginas para la historia de Cuba", by Francisco G. del Valle; "La Pena de muerte en Cuba: su ejecución".

El Eco is the name of a useful paper published in Garden City, New York, by Doubleday, Page and Co., for the special use of teachers and students. This "Revista de la prensa española" is published twice each month for the eight months of October–May, or a total of 16 numbers annually. It is not published during the other four months of the year. The same company also publishes *Le Petit Journal* for those interested in French.

El Estudiante Latino-Americano publishes material as follows in various numbers: January, 1921—"Las Conferencias de Silver Bay", by Carlos Eduardo Monteverde; "Conferencias en el Lage Geneva"; "Cooperación en la América Latina"; "Estudante Brazileiro nos Estados Unidos. Suas primeiras impressões", by Antonio Ippolito; "La Federación de estudiantes del Perú y la Comisión de Relaciones Amistosas"; "A Literatura Brazileira nos Estados Unidos", by Gil-

berto Freyre; "Orientaciones, nordofobia y nordomania", by Jorge
Mañach; "Da Outra America. Tia Sam, mestre-escola do mundo.
O trabalho do triangulo Vermelho entre os estudantes estrangeiros",
by Gilberto Freyre. February—"A America Latina; sua nova situação", by Gilberto Freyre; "The Claims of starving European students
upon the students of America", by Charles D. Hurrey; "El Joven
Latino-Americano en los Estados Unidos", by Orestes Vera: "Message
to Latin-American students", by Leo S. Rowe; "El Progreso de la
educación femenil en el Perú", by J. Antonio Reyes; "O Que os estudantes devem levar para os seus paizes", by Milton Vianna; "Recent
conference on Pan-American education"; "Síntomas aleuladores de
amistad interamericana", by Samuel G. Inman; "La Sociedad Hispánica
de América", by Concha Romero. March—"Algo sobre la Argentina", by Santiago de Cuneo; "Galería de hombres célebres argentinos";
"Una Cuestión internacional. La actuación argentina en la Asamblea de Gineva", by Santiago de Cuneo; "O Dr. Oliveira Lima e a
República Argentina"; Embaixador intellectual do Brazil", by Gilberto Freyre; "Escalando los Andes", by E. Sola Torino; "Los Estudiantes argentinos en los Estados Unidos", by Bernardino L. Beckwith;
"Nuestra educación argentina", by E. L. Urteaga; "Un Saludo del
Embajador argentino", by Tomás A. Le Breton; "Sarmiento", by
José Ingenieros. April—"La Alianza con la tierra", by Jorge D.
Alberta; "Apresurarse lentamente", by Julio D. Sueldo; "Bolivia
intelectual", by Ernestina de Ayoroa; "Bolivia y los Estados Unidos",
by Andrés A. Sanz Guerrero; "La Educación del Indio", by George
McCutcheon McBride; "Los Estudiantes bolivianos en los Estados
Unidos", by C. Flavio Machicado; "Mr. Rockefeller y los estudiantes
latino-americanos", by Luis A. Buendía; "Discurso sobre a historia
politica do Brazil, na Universidade de Pennsylvania", by Helio Lobo;
"Nuestro deber", by Luis G. Bustamante; "Pedagogía nacional. Fragmento de un libro", by Franz Tamayo; "Saludo del Consul General
boliviano", by Carlos Gumucio. May—Aos Estudantes brazileiros",
by J. de Siqueira Coutinho; "Factos sobre o Brazil"; "A Grandeza
economica do Brazil futuro", by C. D. Ochoa; "Liga Panamericana de
Estudiantes", by William R. Shepherd; "O Lugar de estudantes estrangeiros nas universidades americanas", by Milton F. Vianna; "O Principe de Monaco e o Brazil", by Gilberto Freyre; "O Rio de Janeiro,
cidade federica"; "O Que eu fariasi fosse estudante brazileiro nos Estados
Unidos", by John C. Branner; "Saudação de embaixador", by A. de
Alencar; "Senhora Laura Oltoni". June—"Costa Rica", by Eduardo

Azuola; "Curiosidades de Rubén Darío"; "The Educational problem
in Central America", by Howard E. Jensen; "La Federación de Centro-
América", by Angel S. Sandoval; "La Liga Panamericana de Estudiantes"; "Palavras de Joaquim Nabuco"; "Los Progressos de la educación
en Centro-América", by G. L. Michaud; "Relaçães intellectuaes entre
o Brazil e os Estados Unidos", by M. B. Jones; "El Sur de los Estados
Unidos", by Oscar A. Gacitua; "Suscinta historia de los juegos florales
en el Salvador", by Abraham Ramírez Peña.

The Geographical Review (New York) contains the following articles
and items in April, 1921: "The coastal belt of Peru"; "The Colombia-Ecuador boundary"; "The distribution of population in Mexico",
by Sumner Cushing; "The natural regions of Mexico", by E. M. Sanders; "The relation of health to social capacity: the example of
Mexico", by Ellsworth Huntington. July: "An Exploration of the Río
de Oro, Colombia-Venezuela", by H. Case Willcox; "General Rondon's
work in the Brazilian wilderness"; "New Orleans at the time of the
Louisiana purchase", by Edna F. Campbell: "The Ratón mesas of
New Mexico and Colorado", by Willis T. Lee.

Hispania for March, 1921, contains "En defensa de la lengua española", by Julio Mercado, and for May, "Spanish in the High schools
of the middle west", by Grace E. Dalton; "Summer courses in Venezuela", "A summer vacation in Costa Rica", by Mina Weisinger.

The Universidad Nacional de la Plata, Argentina, has published the
first volume of a publication entitled *Humanidades*. This is issued
under the auspices of La Facultad de Ciencias de la Educación, under
the direction of the well known scholar Dr. Ricardo Levene (La Plata,
1921). This first volume (pp. 598) contains the following material:
"La educación de los adultos en Inglaterra", by Juan P. Ramos; "La
escuela normal, el maestro y la educación popular", by Pablo A. Piz-
zurno; "Papel de la educación física en la ética social", by E. Romero
Brest; "La función de la universidad", by Lidia Peradotto; "El problema de la educación estética en la enseñanza secundaria", by W.
Keiper; "La neuva conciencia histórica", by Saúl Taborda; "Introducción a la axiogenia", by Coriolano Alberini"; "Ideas para una
neuva teoria de la ciencia", by Benjamín Taborga and José Gabriel;
"El sistema de los problemas psicológicos", by Carlos Jesinghaus;
"El lenguaje interior", by Enrique Mouchet; "Logística", by Alfredo

Franceschi; "Una introducción a la historia de la psicología", by A. A. Jascalevich; "Luis Martín de la Plaza", by Arturo Marasso Rocca; "Acerca de la Shakespeare", by Rafael Alberto Arrieta; "De ilustribus scriptoribus latinis", by Juan Chiabra; "El origen de la tragedia", by Leopoldo Longhi: "La enseñanza del castellano", by Carmelo M. Bonet; "Al margen del ambiente literario", by Héctor Refia Alberdi; "El arcipreste", by E. L. Figueroa; "El dean Funes plagiario", by Rómulo D. Carbia; "Instrucciones de los diputados por Tucumán a la asamblea de 1813", by Alberto Padilla; "Juan de Solorzano y Pereyra", by Manuel Pinto; "La educación en la constitución alemana de 11 de agosto de 1919", by Eduardo de Bullrich; "El profesorado de enseñanza secundaria en matemáticas, en la Argentina", by Nicolás Besio Moreno; "La organización del trabajo escolar de acuerdo con nuevos principios," by José Rezzano; "La antropología en la enseñanza universitaria argentina", by R. Lehmann-Nitschi; "Estudio anamnésico del educando", by Alfredo D. Calcagno; "Enseñanza de niños anormales", by Luis Morzone; "Educación moderna", by Victorio M. Delfino"; "El dibujo", by León B. Glanzer; "Puntos de vista", by A. Isaac Bassani (hijo). There is also a section devoted to documents connected with the administration of the university, which are all signed · by Ricardo Levene. A note preceding these documents is to the effect that *Humanidades* is being published in order to show the problems of philosophy, history, ethics, and pedagogy. The publication will doubtless serve a very practical purpose. It should be known among institutions in this country and should be a means of drawing more tightly the intellectual bonds between the United States and Argentina.

The July, 1920, issue of *The Journal of International Relations* published the following: "American achievements in Santo Domingo, Haiti, and Virgin Islands", by George C. Thorpe; "The Caribbean policy of the United States", by William R. Shepherd; "Greetings to the world from the new liberal constitutional party in Mexico", by Manuel de la Pena; "The Mexican people", by Frederick Starr; "The present American intervention in Santo Domingo and Haiti", by Otto Schoenrich. October, 1920: "Are the Mexican people capable of governing themselves", by T. Esquivel Obregón; "The Central American Republics and their problem", by Webster E. Browning; "A Constructive policy for Mexico", by Roger W. Babson; "The Factor of Health on Mexican Character", by Ellsworth Huntington;

"How to restore peace in Mexico", by Henry Lane Wilson; "The Mexican Oil situation", by Frederic R. Kellogg; "The Present situation in the Caribbean", by Samuel Guy Inman; "The Railroad situation in Mexico", by A. W. Donly; "The United States and the nations of the Caribbean", by Jacinto López: and "Upon the Indian depends Mexico's future", by James Carson. January, 1921: "America's Mare 'Nostrum'", by Kirby Thomas; "Labor in Mexico", by James Lord; "Mexico and the present revolution", by John Vavasour Noel; "Porto Rico as a national problem", by Pedro Capó Rodríguez; "Recent conditions in Mexico", by Francis R. Taylor; "Reconstruction problems in Mexico", by E. D. Trowbridge; "The United States and Latin America", by John F. Moors. April: "The Colombian treaty—retrospect and prospect", by Isaac Joslin Cox.

Inter-America offers the following in various recent numbers: October, 1920—"The Bolívar doctrine", by J. L. Andara; "General Leonard Wood and public instruction in Cuba", by Aurelio Hevia; December—"Independence Day and Central American union", by Ramón Rosa. February, 1921—"The Belgian sovereigns in Brazil", by Anselmo Pagano (transl. from *Plus Ultra*, Buenos Aires, September, 1920); "Colonial life in Spanish America" (transl. from *Comercio Ecuatoriano*, Guayaquil, special no. 83); "The Founding of Tenochtitlan", by Heriberto Frias (transl. from *Atlántida*, Buenos Aires, August 19, 1920); "Impressions of Washington", by Enrique Molina (transl. from *Juventud*, Santiago, Chile, May, 1920); "The Law of vengeance", by Ramiro de Maeztú (transl. from *El Comercio*, Lima and *Cuasimodo*, Panamá, March, 1920): "Manuel Gálvez", by Manoel Gahisto (transl. from *Nosotros*, Buenos Aires, March, 1920); "The National Salon of Fine Arts", by José León Pagano (transl. from *El Hogar*, Buenos Aires, October 8, 1920); The "Natural sciences in Venezuela", by Diego Carbonell (transl. from *Cultura Venezolano*, Caracas, September, 1920); "Sarmiento", by Julio Noe (transl. from *Revista de Filosofía*, Buenos Aires, May, 1918; "Spaniards and Indians in early Peru", by Arturo Capdevila (transl. from *Nosotros*, Buenos Aires, October, 1920). April—"At the foot of Aconquija", by Santiago Fuster Castresoy (transl. from *Caras y Caretas*, Buenos Aires, August 14, 1920); "Brains and bulk", by Angel L. Sojo (transl. from *Fray Mucho*, Buenos Aires, November, 1920); "José S. Alvarez", by Mariano Joaquín Lorente (transl. from *Caras y Caretas*, August 21, 1920); "Mexican archaeology", by Hermann Beyer (transl. from

Revista de Revistas, Mexico, September 19, 1920 and June 9, 1921); "The Presidents of Argentina", (transl. from *Fray Mucho*, October 12, 1920); "Regarding realism", by Delfino Bunge de Gálvez (transl. from *Nosotros*, November, 1920); "Spain in America", by Mario Ribas (transl. from *Renacimiento*, Tegucigalpa, Honduras, October 15, 1920); "Supay-Chaca", by F. de Oliveira Cesar (transl. from *Atlántida*, December 9, 1920); "A Synopsis of the history of Argentine social ideas", by Raúl A. Orgaz (transl. from *Revista de Filosofía*, January, 1921); "With a great man of letters", by Julio Jiménez Rueda (transl. from *Revista de Revistas*, November 14, 1920). June—"American international law," by Federico S. de Tejada (transl. from *Centro-América*, Guatemala City, July-September, 1920); "Francisco de Goya y Lucientes", by Juan Bautista de Lavalle (transl. from *Studium*, Lima, October-November, 1920): "The Growth of Buenos Aires" (transl. from editorial in *La Argentina*, Barcelona, February, 1921); "In the wake of the *Mayflower*", by Helio Lobo (transl. from *La Nación* Buenos Aires, 1920); "The Preponderance of the United States on the Caribbean Sea", by Raúl de Cárdenas (transl. from *Cuba Contemporánea*, March, 1921); "Ripples on the surface of great themes," by Emilio J. Pasarell (transl. from *Puerto Rico*, San Juan December, 1920). August—"The Colonial city: its remote sources", by Laureano Vallenilla Sanz (transl. from *Cultura Venezolana*, September, 1920); "Florencio Sánchez: the man and the dramatist", by Vicente A. Salaverri (transl. from *Nosotros*, March, 1921); "The Formation of the Lake of Maracaibo", by Adolf Ernst (transl. from *Cultura Venezolana*, November, 1920); "The Glorification of Bolívar", by Benito Javier Pérez (transl. from *El Excelsior*, Mexico); "Liberty of utterance", by Enrique Gay Calbó (transl. from *Cuba Contemperánea*, April, 1921); "Modern Spanish literature in Puerto Rico", by S. Dalmau Canet (transl. from *Las Antillas*, Habana, September, 1920); "The Noble mission of the lawyer", by Alejandro Reyes (transl. from *Revista de Derecho y Legislación*, Caracas, November and December, 1920); "Our humiliating isolation", by Mario Ribas (transl. from *Renacimiento*, April 25, 1921); "La Doctrina Monroe como inteligencia continental", by Julius Klein (transl. from THE HISPANIC AMERICAN HISTORICAL REVIEW, May, 1921).

Mercurio Peruano for November, 1920, has the following: "Crónicas de Norteamérica", by Víctor Andrés Belaúnde (continued in following numbers); "La Universidad de Yale", by César Antonio Ugarte; "Régimen de la propiedad durante los Incas", by Carlos Valdez de la Torre: "Un Sacerdote de la cultura (a continued paper), by Edwin Elmore. December, 1920: "Lo Bello en la naturaleza", by Alejandro O. Deustua; "Las Interpretaciones del Quijote", by Jorge Mañach, January, 1921; "Lo Bello en la Arte", by Alejandro O. Deustua; "Cristóbal Colón", by Manuel I. Vegas; "Los poetas de la colonia", by Jorge Guillermo Leguia. February; "Los Copleros de la conquista", by Horacio H. Urteaga; "Don Francisco de Toledo", by Gérman Leguia y Martínez"; "La estética en la libertad", by Alejandro O. Duestua; "La guerra a muerte", by Fabio Lozano y Lozano; "Mariano Andrés Belaúnde", March-April: Carácteres de la crisis económica actual", by Carlos Ledgard; "Ciertos aspectos estéticos del arte antiguo del Perú", by Philip Ainsworth Means; "Cristóbal Colón", by Manuel I. Vegas; "La Profesión de hombre", by Juan A. Mackay. May: "A los Intelectuales y estudiantes de la América Latina. Mensaje de Anatole France y Henri Barbusse"; "El Ilusionismo", by Mariano Ibérico y Rodríguez; "La Ingeniería en la colonia", by Ricardo Tizón y Bueno; "Revista política (of various countries)", by Victor Andrés Belaúnde; "La Selección universitaria apropósito del Mensaje de France y Barbusse". June–July: "Las Ciencias biológicas", by Fortunato Quesada; "Las Ciencias matemáticas, físicas y técnicas", by Cristóbal Losada y Puga; "La Enseñanza en el Perú a traves de una centuria", by J. L. Madueño; "Estado económico del Peru", by J. M. Rodríguez;" Los Estudiantes de la arqueología del Peru", by Horacio H. Urteaga; "Evolución del Perú", by César Antonio Ugarte; "La Filosofía", by Mariano Ibérico y Rodríguez; "La Historia en el Perú", by Luis Alberto Sánchez; "El Sentido simpático de nuestra historia", by Arturo García.

México Moderno (Mexico City) in its issue for March, 1921, has an article on "Ramón Gómez de la Serna", by Alfonso Reyes. May, "Jesús Ureta", by Martín Luis Guzman; "and México-Tenoxtitlán", by Luis Castillo-Ledón. June: "Bibliografía Centro-Americana de 1920"; "La inmutabilidad del derecho de propiedad", by Fernando Gonsáles Roa; "Música y bailes criollos de la Argentina", by Julio Jiménez Rueda; "El Poder de las letras", by José López Portillo y Rojas; and "La Sombra de Karmídez", by José López Portillo y Rojas; and "la Sombra de Karmídez", by José Escobár.

A recent number of *Nueva Democracia*, which is published under the auspices of the Committee on Cooperation in Latin America has a very interesting article entitled "Turning friends against us in Latin America".

The *Pacific Review*, which is published quarterly by the University of Washington, at Seattle, is devoted largely to problems of the Pacific World. It treats of International relations, economics, history, art, and literature.

The Pan American Review publishes in recent issues articles and items as follows: December, 1920—"Aiding young Latin-Americans"; "Another trade conference (in Mexico)"; "Brazilian-American conference (in Mexico)"; "Brazilian-American conference"; "Carlos Valderrama, Peruvian composer-pianist", by Mary Siegrist; "Luncheon in honor of Dr. Victor Andrés Belaúnde"; "Report of the conference committee for the Dominican Republic"; "Unused tropical America and adverse exchange", by Fred A. G. Pape. March, 1921—"Gorgas memorial for Panama"; "A Great leader (Bolívar) honored": "The New York and Montevideo's mayors exchange greetings"; The real future of Pan Americanism"; "Report of the conference committee for Guatemala". April—"The Americas in accord"; "An Effective peace palace" (in Cartago, Costa Rica); "President Harding on Pan Americanism". May–June—"Closer ties between Spain and Latin America"; "Cooperative efforts for Latin America"; "A New era for Colombia", by Earl Harding. July—"A Latin league"; "Memory of Bartolomé Mitre", by James Carson; "Mexican banks classified", by John Claussen; "The New Pan Americanism", by Graham H. Stewart; "Our place in Latin-American commerce".

Razón y Fe (Madrid) for January, 1921, contains the following: "Los Españoles y Magallanes en la expedición del estrecho", by C. Bayle; "La Misión española en Chile". February: "El Año pedagógico hispano-americano". May: "Crónica de Cuba". June: "II. Congreso de Geografía y Historia Hispano-Americanas", by C. Bayle. August: "Crónica de Cuba"; and "Una Página de geografía añeja", by C. Bayle.

The April (1921) number of *La Reforma Social* contains a review and discussion of the boundary question between Panama and Costa Rica, by Jacinto López and "Antecedentes jurídicos de la controversia, Laudo Loubet, and the Convención Anderson-Porras". It contains also:

"Elecciones espurias en Cuba", by H. T. Spinden; "Una Fase más de las elecciones en Cuba", by Orestes Ferrara; "La Independencia de las Filipinas", by J. A. Frear; "La Justicia en los Estados Unidos", by Jacinto López.—C. K. JONES.

Revista Bimestre Cubana (Habana), of which the well-known Dr. Fernando Ortíz, is editor, has published much interesting material in recent issues.   In the issues for September-October, 1920 to May-July, 1921, continued papers appear as follows: "Catálogo de la Biblioteca de la Sociedad Económica de Amigos del País de la Habana"; "Cristóbal Colón y el descubrimiento del Nuevo Mundo", by Ricardo U. Rousset; "Datos históricos cubanos" (dealing with various matters); and "Un catauro de cubanismos (Mamotreto de 'Cubicherías' lexicográficas)".   "Apuntes históricos sobre la ciudad de San Felipe y Santiago de Bejucal", by Mercedes Herrera Reyes appeared in the issue for September–October, 1920; "Marcos de J. Melero" by Eduardo F. Plá, in that for November-December; and "Los Cabildos afrocubanos", by Fernando Ortíz, in that for January–February, 1921.

The *Revista Chilena de Historia y Geografía*, which is published in Santiago de Chile, is an excellent quarterly review.   Each number is a good sized volume of serious and on the whole well-written papers that will prove a mine for the student of Hispanic America.   In recent issues is found the following material: 3d quarter, 1920—"Biografía de Don Adolfo Ibáñez" (concluded), by Edulia Silva Salas; "Bosquejo histórico de la literatura chilena" (continued) by Domingo Amunátegui Solar; "Como y por qué se suprimió el castigo del 'guanti' en los colegios del estado", by Miguel Luis Amunátegui Reyes; "Cartas de don Bernardino Rivadavia a don Antonio Álvarez Jonte"; "Correspondencia de don Antonio Varas.   Candidatura presidencial de don Manuel Montt (1850–1851)" (continued in the following numbers described): "Estudios históricos.   Concepción a fines del siglo XVIII"; by Guillermo Feliú y Cruz; "Una Figura China encontrada en la Araucania", by Fray Gerónimo de Amberga: "El Liceo de la Serena", by Julio Zenteno Barros: "Noticias de Chile (1831–1832)" by William S. W. Buschenberger (continued in the succeeding numbers described); "Resena historico biográfica de los eclesiásticos en el descubrimientos y conquista de Chile", by Tomas Thayer Ojeda (continued in succeeding numbers); "Revista de crítica bibliografía" (continued in succeeding numbers); "El Servicio sanitario en el ejército

chileno durante la guerra del Pacífico, 1879–1884", by Rafael
Poblete M. (continued in following numbers); "Tradiciones, leyendas
y cuentos populares recogidos en Carahue", by Ramón A. Laval (continued in succeeding numbers); "Vida del Doctor Juan Martínez de
Rozas", by E. Montero Moore (continued in succeeding numbers),
4th quarter, 1920—"Actas de la Sociedad Chilena de Historia y Geografía"; "Un Alistamiento en 1915", by V. D. O.; "Las Biografías
de los dos 'Cristobales de Molina' publicadas por el escritor peruano
don Carlos A. Romero", by Tomás Thayer Ojeda; "Diario del viaje
efectuado por el doctor Aquinas Ried desde Valparaiso hasta el lago
Sanguihue, y de regreso (7 de Febrero de 1849 al 30 de junio del mismo
año)", by Aquinas Ried; "Los Brujas de Chillán en 1749", by Omer
Emeth; "Los Jesuitas en Chillán en el siglo XVIII", by Reinaldo
Muñoz Olave; "Manes, temblores y volcanes", by Fernando Montessus de Ballore; "Nomina de los socios de la Sociedad Chilena de
Historia y Geografía en 31 de diciembre de 1920"; "El Paraguay colonial y las provincias meridionales", by Fulgencio R. Moreno; "Séptima memoria que el secretario general de la Sociedad Chilena de
Historia y Geografía y director de la Revista presenta a la junta general
de socios celebrada el lunes 13 de diciembre de 1920"; "La Historia de
los grandes lagos del Altiplano boliviano y la relación que pueden tener
la fundacion y destrucción del primer Tiahuanacu y con la existencia
de los grandes mamiferos extintos de Ulloura", by Lorenzo Schmidt.
First quarter, 1921—"Actas de la Sociedad Chilena de Historia y
Geografía"; "Algunos datos sobre la geografía etnográfica, de parte
del Paraguay y del alto Perú", by Fulgencio R. Moreno"; "El Apellido Castro durante la colonia", by Guillermo Cuadra Gómez; "Derretero del viage de Magallanes y su paso por el estrecho", by Javier
Martín M.; "Episodio eclesiástico de la guerra del Pacífico", by Carlos
Silva Cotapos; "Don Joaquín Vicuña y Larraín. Sus ascendientes
y descendientes", by Santiago Marín Vicuña; "Los Indígenes de
Ecuador", by Joaquín Santa Cruz (continued in the following number);
"Límites entre las provincias de Atacama y Coquimbo", by Alberto
Edwards (concluded in the following number); "Servicio Médico en
las naos de Magallanes", by Vicente Daguine; "Sucinto paralelo entre
Colón y Magallanes (Discurso pronunciado en la sesión solemne cele-
brada por la Universidad de Chile el 29 de Noviembre de 1920 en conmemoración del 4° centenario del descubrimiento del estrecho de
Magallanes", by J. T. Medina; "El Valle longitudinal de Chile", by Fernando de Montessus de Ballore. 2nd quarter, 1921—"El Congreso

americano celebrado en Lima en 1864", by Miguel Varas Velásquez; "Guillermo Matta", by V. M. Valdivieso C.; "Historia del reino de Chile, situado en la América meridonal", by Fray Antonio Sors; "Liceo de la Serena", by Bernardo Ossandón: "La Junta de gobierno de 1810 y el consejo de Regencia y el virrey del Perú", by Enrique Matta Vial; "Noticia biográfica de Fray Antonio Sors", by J. T. Medina; "Las Primeras leyes electorales chilenas", by Juan B. Hernando E.; "Sobre una expedición a la Patagonia chilena", by Cristóbal M. Hicken; "Ventajas de la apertura del istmio de Ofqui", by Emilio De Vidts.

The *Revista de Ciencias sociales,* a new Mexican review under the direction of C. D. López, began publication in July of the current year. The following contributions are noted in the initial number: "La Capitalización interior", by Andrés Molina Enríquez; "Cuestiones sociales y económicas", by C. D. López; "La Deuda pública"; "La Evolución de la teoría de los impuestos según los economistas Seligman y Wagner", by Daniel R. Aguilar; "El Impuesto sobre las ganancias adoptado en toda la república", by Enrique Martínez Sobral; "Una Industria y una especulación," by Rafael Nieto; "Socialismo agrario y socialismo obrero en México", by José Covarrubias.—C. K. JONES.

Revista de Colegio Mayor de Nuestra Señora de Rosario (Bogotá), published on March 1 "Algo sobre Rodó", by José Echeverría; "Carta de Andrés Bello (1815) al gobierno de Cundinamarca sobre su estancia en Londres"; and "Don Víctor Mallarino", by R. M. C.

The *Revista de Costa Rica,* which is published in San José, Costa Rica, and now in its third year, is devoted to history, geography, geology, archaeology, natural history, ‹thnology, genealogy, etc. J. F. Trejos Quiros is its director general and it has a large staff of collaborators, among whom are scholars of international reputation. The first volume contains, among other things, the following; "Cartografía de Costa Rica", by Alejandre von Frantzius; "Viages a varias partes de la República de Costa Rica", by Bernardo Augusto Thiel; "El Mapa topográfico de Talamanca de Mr. William M. Gabb y la cartografía de Costa Rica en 1877", by Auguste Petermann; "Episodios coloniales." by Ricardo Fernández Guardia; "Nombres geográficos de Costa Rica", by Cleto González; "La Verdad histórica sobre la heroina dóna Rafaela de Herrera", by Ricardo Fernández Guardia; and "Costas suroccidentales de Costa Rica", by M. Obregón L. Recent issues contain articles as follows: February, 1921—"Acuerdo de la municipalidad de San José en la sesión del 24 de Julio de 1843"; "Contribución al estudio de las frutas de Costa Rica", by María Jiménez Luthmer; "Fray Rodrigo Pérez", by Pedro Pérez Zeledón; "Una piedra histórica" (the boundary stone near Santa Marta), by M. Gámez Monge. March—El Rincón de la Vieja", by Carlos Gagui; "Sobre la Unión de Centro-America", by Salomón de la Selva (transl. from THE HISPANIC AMERICAN HISTORICAL REVIEW, November, 1920). April-May—Ascensión al volcán Irazú, del Dr. Throlope", by Amelia M. Rohrmoser (transl. from the English); "Conflicto entre Panamá y Costa Rica" (reprinted from *Ibero Americana*, Madrid); "Demingo Jiménez", by Manuel J. Jiménez; "Nombres geográficos de Costa Rica", by Cleto González Víquez; "Primera contribución al estudio de los zancudos de Costa Rica", by Anastasio Álfaro. June—"Orígenes de los costarricenses", by Cleto González Víquez (continued in succeeding numbers); "La Subregión fitogeográfica costarricense", by Carlos Wercklé (continued in succeeding numbers); "Ujarráz", by Eladio Prado. July and August—"Curiosidades de Costa Rica" by M. Gámez Monge; "Los Microbios del latex. Interesante descubrimiento de un sabio costarricense", by Gustavo Michaud; "Notas sobre . . . vertebrado fosil . . . de Cartago", by J. Fidel Tristán; "San José en 1858", transl. from Anthony Trollope; "Unión Ibero-Americana. Concurso para 1922". September—"Los Fundadores de la República"; "La Independencia de Costa Rica"; "Pensamientos de los fundadores de la República".

The September, 1921 number of *Revista de Costa Rica* presents short biographies of the following "Fundadores de la República": Florencio del Castillo; Rafael Francisco Osejo; Manuel García Escalante; Juan de los Santos Madriz; Joaquín de Yglesias; José María de Peralta; Joaquín Bernardo Calvo; Ramón Jiménez; José Santos Lombardo; José Mercedes de Peralta; Victor de la Guardia; Juan Mora Fernández; Rafael G. Escalante; Manuel María de Peraeta; José Rafael de Gallegos; Antonio Pinto; Agustín Gutiérrez Hermenegildo Bonilla; Félix Fernández; José Francisco de Peralta; Rafael Barreta; Santiago Bonilla; Nicolás Carrillo; Manuel Alvarado; Joaquín Oreamuno; Mariano Montealegre; Eusebio Rodríguez; Narciso Esquivel; Gregorio José Ramírez; and Joaquín Estanislao Tarazo. Portraits are published of most of the above.

Gustave A. Frederking, in the July, 1921, number of *Revista de Economía Argentina*, which is published by Dr. Alejandro Bunge, has an article on "Carlos Alfredo Tornquist. Nuevo Académico de la Facultad de Ciencias Económicas". Other papers are as follows; "Desnivel internacional del poder de comprar de la moneda", by Alejandro E. Bunge; El "Doctor Adolfo Davila. Sus ideas y enseñanzas sobre los problemas económicos argentinos", by Carlos Alfredo Tornquist; "Expresión gráfica de hechos económicos".

Revista de Filosofía, for January, 1921, contains, among other articles, the following: "Hacia un nuevo derecho internacional", by Arturo Orzábal Quintana; "La personalidad de Urquiza", by Antonio Sagarna; "Psicología del conquistador español del siglo XVI", by R. Blanco-Fombona; "Sinopsis sobre la historia de las ideas sociales argentinas", by Raúl A. Orgaz.—C. K. JONES.

La Revista Mexicana, which was published in Washington under the auspices of the government of Mexico, suddenly suspended publication a few months ago. This periodical, although one of propaganda, contained much interesting material. Special mention should be made of the study that ran through many numbers, entitled "Mexican byways and Highways", by the editor, George F. Weeks. A section in each number was devoted to a discussion of the oilfields of Mexico and oil news. Some of the material appearing in the last few issues was as follows: "March, 1921—Bancos que operan hoy en México"; "High cost of living unknown (in Mexico)"; "Mexican children's congress"; "Mexican government most liberal"; "Mexican mining statistics", by Francisco Rivas; "Obregón urges needed reforms"; "The Pan American labor congress", by Samuel Gompers; "Progress of the state of Durango", by Alberto Terrones; "Reciprocity urged for two republics"; "The State of the Mexican Republic". April—Las Controversias entre México y los Estados Unidos"; "How about the Mexican", by Don H. Biggers; "Leniency to American lawbreakers"; "The Mexican petroleum question", by L. G. Ballesteros, Jr.; "Old banks to renew business"; "Revolutionary damage claims"; "The Stanford University Medal," by Percy Alvin Martin; "Through Tamaulipas and Nuevo Leon," by Catherine Vesta Sturgís. May—"The Actual situation in Porto Rico," by Santiago Iglesias; "Assistance to be given native colonists"; "Conclusion of the Benton case"; "The State of Sonora"; "The West coast of Mexico", by Leo Frederic Lynch;

"Education work in Mexico"; "Foreign trade of Mexico"; "Impecunious immigrants not wanted in Mexico". July—"Appeal for fair play to Mexico"; "Attitude of the United States toward Mexico as seen in Argentina"; "Fifty million bonds issued to pay for expropriated lands", "Interchange of students"; "Prehistoric Chinese in Mexico"; "Special commission to look after Mexican interests in the United States". August—"Report of national railway lines"; "Celebrating Mexico's independence day"; "Desarrollo del comercio Mexicano"; "The Interchange of scholarships", by Frank Bohn; "Mexican patriotic club organized in Mexico"; "Victoriano Huerta's debt", by Rafael Nieto.

The *Revista de la Universidad de Buenos Aires* is a dignified publication and is in all respects a review worthy of the great university which has given it name. The number for October–December, 1919, contains the following excellent material: "Un Auto del Cabildo de Lujan sobre instrucción primaria obligatoria. Año 1773", by Juan Probst; "Bibliografía de bibliografías argentinas", by Narciso Binayán; "Un Casamiento en 1805", by Carlos Correa Luna; La "Doctrina Drago", by Ernesto Quesada; "Las Inmigraciones de los Kilmes y la historia de los mismos", by S. A. Lafone; "Sobre la organización de la protección y asistencia de la infancia", by Gregorio Aráoz Alfaro; "Sobre la personalidad moral de San Martín. Nuevos documentos para su estudio", by Ricardo Levene; "La Universidad y la democracia", by F. Pedro Marotta. January–June, 1920: Bibliografía doctoral de la Universidad de Buenos Aires", by Marcial R. Candioti; "Metodología del estudio científico del castellano," by M. de Toro y Gómez; "Los perjuicios resultantes de las guerras para la población civil", by J. A. García.

In *The Southwestern Historical Quarterly* for January, 1921, appeared: "The Louisiana background of the colonization of Texas", 1763–1803", by Mattie Austin Hatcher; "A Ray of light on the Gadsden treaty", by J. Fred Rippy; and a further instalment of "Mirabeau Buonaparte Lamar", by A. K. Christian (also an instalment in the April number). April: "Donnelson's mission to Texas in behalf of annexation", by Annie Middleton: "Some precedents of the Pershing expedition into Mexico", by J. Fred Rippy. June: "The annexation of Texas and the Mississippi democrats", by James E. Winston; "Journal of Lewis Birdsal Harris, 1836–1842"; "The New régime in Mexico", by Charles W. Hackett; "The Texas convention of 1845", by Annie Middleton.

Zabala and Maurin, dealers in French and Spanish books and art, 135 West 49 St., New York, have recently issued an interesting catalogue, of 80 pages, entitled *Letras de España America*, which shows a comprehensive stock of books, both historical and literary, about Spain and Spanish America. The insertion of portraits of authors is a feature of special interest.—C. K. JONES.

Dr. Alberto Haas, in his "Psicología del pueblo argentino", an article in the September number of the *Revista de Filosofía* has made a valuable contribution to the study of the national character of the Argentine people. It is of special interest to North Americans students since it involves a comparison of the cultural and psychological characters of Anglo-Saxon and Hispanic America, in which respect it correlates with Rodo's study of the utilitarianism of puritan United States in his *Ariel*. Dr. Haas has arranged the material to the following sections:
1. Formación del coloniaje americano; 2. El criollo y los elementos de su origen; 3. Orientaciones ideológicas de la nacionalidad argentina; 4. Consecuencias económicas y políticas de la psicología argentina; 5. Causas y efectos de la inmigracion hasta la gran guerra; 6. Encauce de las nuevas corrientes inmigratorias.—C. K. JONES.

RECENT PUBLICATIONS

BOOKS

Acevedo Díaz, Eduardo: Geografía de América, física, política y económica. 3d ed. Buenos Aires, P. García, 1920. Pp. 390.

Adams, Rabdolph A.: Santo Domingo: a study in benevolent imperialism. Reprint from *The South Atlantic Quarterly*, January, 1921. Pp. 10–24.

Alcásar, Cayetano: Historia del correo en América (notas y documentos para su estudio). Madrid, Suc. de Rivadeneyra, 1920. Pp. 346.

Altamira y Crevea, Rafael: La política de España en América. Valencia, Editorial Edela, 1921. Pp. 230, (2).

Alsamóra, Isaac: La cuestión peruano-chilena. Paris, 1919.

Anales de economía, finansas, industria y comercio. México, 1921.

Araquistaín, Luis: La república de los soviets. San José, Costa Rica, Falcó y Borraso, 1920. Pp. 152.

Arenas B., Arturo: Bolivia en el Pacífico. La Pas, Imp. Casa Editora Mundial, 1920. Pp. XV, 210.

Asociación Española para el progreso de las ciencias. Congrese de Oporto, 26 junio–10 julio 1921. Junta directiva . . . . Madrid, Jiménes y Molina, 1921. Pp. 76.

Banchs, Enrique: Poemas selectas. Prólogo y selección de Francisco Monterde García Icasbalceta. México, Editorial México Moderno, 1921. (Cultura, tomo XIII).

Bayle, Constantino, S. J.: Magallanes. Madrid, Administración de *Rasón y Fe*, 1921. Pp. 94. (Grandesas Españolas.)

Beardsley, Wilfred Attwood: Infinitive constructions in old Spanish. New York, Columbia University Press, 1921. Pp. XIV, 279.

Bekker, L. J. de: The Plot against Mexico. New York, Alfred A. Knopf, 1919. Pp. (8), 295.

Bianco, José: La oligarquía universitaria. Buenos Aires, 1920.

Binayán, Narciso: El origen de la junta de historia y numismática americana. Buenos Aires, 1920.

Blakeslee, George H. (ed.): Mexico and the Caribbean. Clark University addresses. New York, G. E. Stechert & Co., 1920. Pp. x, 363.

Blanco, José M., S. J.: La antropometría y la ciencia. Buenos Aires, 1921. Pp. 185.

Bolton, Herbert E.: The Spanish borderlands: a chronicle of old Florida and the Southwest. New Haven, Yale University Press; Toronto, Glasgow, Brook & Co.; London, Humphrey Milford, Oxford University Press, 1921. Pp. xiv, 320. (Vol. 23, "The Chronicles of America" Series.)

Boman, Eric: Encore l'homme tertiaire dans l'Amérique du sud. (Extrait du *Journal des Americanistes de Paris*, 1919. Pp. 7.)

Bonilla, Policarpo: La unión de Centro América: conferencia dada en el Instituto de las Españas, Universidad de Colombia. el 24 de febrero de 1921. New York, De Laisne & Carranza, 1921. Pp. 20.

Boundary question between the Republic of Guatemala and the Republic of Honduras. New York, The Evening Post Job Printing Office, Inc., January, 1920. Pp. 108.

Breceda, Alfredo: México revolucionario (1913–1917), Vol. I. Madrid, Tip. Artística, [1920?]. Pp. 506.

Breitenbach, W.: Aus süd-Brasilien; erinnerungen und aufzeichnungen. Brackwede, I. W., W. Breitenbach, 1913. 2 vols. Pp. 251.

Bryce, James: Modern democracies. New York, Macmillan, 1921. ("The republics of Spanish America," vol. I., pp. 187–207.)

Bullrich, Eduardo J.: Asistencia social de menores. Buenos Aires, J. Menéndez, 1919. Pp. 427, vi. (Bibliografía general, pp. 13–26.)

Bulnes, M. Gonzalo: Chile and Peru. The causes of the war of 1879. Santiago de Chile, 1920.

Bustamante, A. S. de: Controversia de límites entre Panamá y Costa Rica. Panamá, 1921.

Bustamante, Daniel S.: Bolivia, su estructura y sus derechos en el Pacífico. La Paz, Arnó Hermanos, 1919. Pp. 377, vi.

Calderón Cirisinho, Adolfo: Short diplomatic history of the Chilean-Peruvian relations, 1819–1879. Santiago de Chile, 1920.

Carbio, Rómulo D.: Manuel de historia de la civilización argentina. Tomo I. Buenos Aires, Franzetti y Cía., 1917. Pp. 509.

Carrasco, José: Estudios constitucionales. La Paz, González y Medina, 1920. 4 vols.

Castañeda, Francisco: Nuevos estudios. San Salvador, Imprenta Nacional, 1919. 2 vols.

Carlos, M.: Ensaios de sociologia. Rio de Janeiro, 1920.

Castiglione, Antonio: Derecho civil argentino. Nulidad de los actos jurídicos. Buenos Aires, Librería Nacional de J. Lajouane, [1920 ?]. Pp. viii, 127.

Castro Nunes, José de: Do estado fiduado e sua organização municipal. Historia, doutrina, jurisprudencia, direito comparado. Rio de Janeiro, Leite Ribeiro, Maurillo. Pp. 575.

Catálogo de notariado de Porto Alegre. Por el Sr. Dr. Antonio Augusto Borges de Medeiros. Porto Alegre, 1918–1919. Vols. 1–5.

Celso Tindaro, Jorge: Amado Nervo. Acotaciones a su vida y a su obra. Buenos Aires, 1919.

Colín, Eduardo: Siete cabezas. Julio Laforgue; Emilio Verhaeren; Eça de Queiroz; Claudio Farrère; Miguel de Unamuno; Don Ramón del Valle Inclán; Azorín. [México, 1921.] Pp. CXVI.

Compañía General de Tabacos de Filipinas: Colección general de documentos referentes a las islas Filipinas existentes en el Archivo de Indias de Sevilla. Tomo. IV. (1522–1524.) Barcelona, Imprenta de la Viuda de Luis Tasso, 1921. Pp. VIII, 380.

Congresso Internacional de Historia da America. Promovido pelo Instituto Historico e Geographico Brazileiro para commemorar o centenario de independencia do Brazil, a 7 de setembro de 1922. Reglamento geral.

Theses da 15 secção, Historia do Brasil. Rio de Janeiro, Imprensa Nacional, 1921. Pp. 38.

Contreras, Francisco: Les écrivains contemporains de l'amérique espagnole. Le renaissance du livre. Paris, 1920. Pp. 184. (Bibliotheque Internationale de Critique.)

Cortijo Alahija, L.: Musicología latino-americana. La música popular y los músicos célebres de la América latina. Barcelona, Maucei, 1920. Pp. 443.

Crequi-Montfort and P. Rivet: Contribution a l'étude de l'archeologie et de la métallurgie colombiennes. Paris, 1919. Pp. 66.

Curtiss, John Somers: Handbook of Mexican properties and securities. El Paso, J. S. Curtiss & Co., 1920. Pp. 390.

Dark, Richard: The quest of the Indies. Oxford, B. Blackwell, 1920. Pp. XII, 241.

Destruge, Camelo: Biografía del general don León de Febres Cordero, procer de la independencia de Guayaquil. Guayaquil, Imp. Municipal, 1920. Pp. 98.

Desvernine, Raoul E.: Claims against Mexico. A brief study of the international law applicable to claims of citizens of the United States and other countries for losses sustained in Mexico during .the revolution of the last decade. With a foreword by Lindley M. Garrison. [New York], Private edition, 1921. Pp. iii, 149.

Díaz, José Virginio: Historia de Saravia. Montevideo, A. Barreiro y Ramos, 1920. Pp. 256.

Díaz Cisneros, César: La liga de las naciones y la actitud argentina. Buenos Aires, 1921.

La Diplomacia oriental en el Paraguay; correspondencia oficial y privada del doctor Juan José de Herrera, ministro de relaciones exteriores de los gobiernos de Berro ý Aguirre. Comentada por Luis Alberto de Herrera. Montevideo, 1919. Pp. 401.

Echagüe, Juan Pablo: Un teatro en formación. Buenos Aires, Imprenta Tragant, 1919. Pp. 404.

Elaúri, José: Correspondencia diplomática del doctor José Elaúri. (1839–1844.) Montevideo, A. Barreiro y Ramos, 1919. Pp. lxxv, 413, port.

Die Eröberung von Mexiko durch Ferdinand Cortes, mit den eigenhändigen berichten des Feldherrn an Kaiser Karl V. von 1520 und 1522. Hrsg. von Arthur Schurig. Leipzig, Insel-Verlag 1918. Pp. 499, front., map.

Fabella, Isidro: Los Estados Unidos contra la libertad. Estudios de historia diplomática americana. (Cuba, Filipinas, Panamá, Nicaragua, República Dominicana.) Barcelona, Talleres Gráficos Lux, 1921. Pp. 312.

Fernández Córdova, Miguel Angel: Cerebro y corazón. Guayaquil, Imp. Mercantil, 1919. Pp. 500, x.

Fernández Guardia, Ricardo: Crónicas coloniales. San Juan de Costa Rica, Imp. Trejos Hermanos, 1921. Pp. 318.

Fernández y Medina, B.: L'Uruguay et sa nouvelle constitution. Traduction de J. Sarrailt. Madrid, P. Orrier, [1920 ?]. Pp. 62.

Flores, Pastoriza: History of the boundary dispute between Ecuador and Peru. New York, 1921. Pp. 89. Map. (Doctoral dissertation, Columbia University.)

Franco, José R. del; La enseñanza de la historia y la solidaridad hispano-americana. Exposición y proyecto de revolución presentados a la consideración del II. Congreso de Historia y Geografía Hispano-Americanas. Córdoba, Bautista Cubas, 1921. Pp. 81.

García, Jacinto S.: San Martín, Bolívar, Gamarra, Santa Cruz, Castilla y las constituciones del Perú. Lima, 1920.

García Samudio, Nicolás: La reconquista de Boyacá en 1816. Tunja, Imprenta del Departamento, 1916. Pp. 142, II.

Garfías, Valentín R.: Principles governing Mexican taxation of petroleum. New York, 1921. Pp. 40. (From *Mining and Metallurgy*, February, 1921.)

Garry, L. S.: Textile markets of Brasil. Government Printing Office, 1920. Pp. 48. (Department of Commerce, Bureau of Foreign and Domestic Commerce. Special Agents Series, no. 203.)

Goding, Frederic Webster: A brief history of the American consulate general at Guayaquil, Ecuador. Livermore Falls, Maine, The Advertising Press, [1921]. Pp. 24.

Gonsáles, Joaquín V.: Patria y democracia. Buenos Aires, 1920. Pp. 174.

Gonsáles Lanusa, José A.: Discursos y trabajos del Dr. José A. Gonsáles Lanusa en la Cámara de Representantes, precedidos de su biografía. Habana, Imp. del Rambla, Bouza y Cía., 1921. Pp. VI, 975, port.

Hackett, Charles W.: The new regime in Mexico. Reprint from *The Southwestern Historical Quarterly*, June, 1921. Pp. 22.

Hand sketches of the Panama Canal. Panama City, I. L. Maduro, Jr., [1921 ?]. 24 engravings. No text.

Henao, Jesús María, and Gerardo Arrubla: Primer centenario de la batalla de Boyacá, 1819–1919. La campaña libertadora de 1819. Páginas de la historia de Colombia para la enseñanza secundaria. Bogotá, Escuela Tipografía Salesiana, 1919. Pp. 54.

Hernándes, Nicolás: La moral diplomática versus el cesarismo diplomático. San Juan, P. R., Tip. El Compas, 1921. Pp. 61.

Herrera, Gonsalo: Apreciaciones sobre la ley de matrimonio civil y divorcio. Lima, 1921.

Historia de la república del Ecuador. Tomo I (1809–1861). Quito, Prensa Católica, 1920. Pp. 470.

Humanidades. Publicación de la Facultad de Ciencias de la Educación. La Plata, 1921. Pp. 596.

Humbert, Jules: Histoire de la Colombie et du Venezuela des origines jusqu' à nos jours. Paris, F. Alcan, 1921. Pp. 216; port; map.

Ingeniero, José: La restauración. Buenos Aires, 1920.

J. L. R.: Historia de la república del Ecuador. I. 1809–1861. Quito, Tipografía y encuadernación de la Prensa Católica, 1920. Pp. 470.

Klein, Julius: The mesta. A study in Spanish economic history, 1273–1836. Cambridge, Harvard University Press, 1920. Pp. xviii, 444.

Laurencín, Marqués de: Discurse leído en la sesión inaugural del II. Congreso de Historia y Geografía Hispano-Americanas, celebrado en Sevilla en 1° de mayo de 1921. Madrid, Establecimiento tipografía de Jaime Ratés, 1921. Pp. 16.

León Suárez, José: Diplomacia universitaria americana, Argentina en el Brasil; ciclo de conferencias en las facultades de derecho, institutos de abogados e históricos y en otras instituciones de Rio de Janeiro, Bello Horizonte y San Paulo y en la Universidad de Montevideo. Buenos Aires, Imprenta Escoffier, Caracciolo y Cia., 1919. Pp. 616.

Levene, Ricardo: Facultad de humanidades y ciencias de la educación. La Plata, Imprenta Mercatali, 1921. Pp. 16. (Reprint from *Humanidades*, no. 1.)

Levillier, Roberto: Francisco de Aguirre y los orígenes del Tucumán (1550-1570). Madrid, J. Puyo, 1920.

The Liberator Simón Bolívar in New York. Addresses delivered on the occasion of the unveiling of the statue of the liberator Simón Bolívar presented to the city of New York by the government of Venezuela, Tuesday, April 19, 1921. (Bulletin no. 25, Interamerican Division, American Association for International Conciliation. June, 1921. Pp. 49.

Lira, Carmen: Los cuentos de mi tía Panchita. (Cuentos populares recogidos en Costa Rica.) San José, Costa Rica, García Monge y Cía., Editores, 1920. Pp. 159.

Maas, P. Otto, O. F. M.: Las órdenes religiosas de España y la colonización de América en la segunda parte del siglo XVIII. Estadísticas y otros documentos. Barcelona, Fidel Giró, 1918. Pp. 217.

Machado, José E.: Centón Lírico. Pasquinados y canciones, epigramas y corridos. Con notas históricas y geográficas, para la mejor comprensión del texto. Caracas, Tip. Americana, 1920. Pp. XXXV, 244.

Marín Vicuña, Santiago: La division comunal de la república. Finanzas municipales. Santiago, Imp. Universo, [1921 ?]. Pp. 210.

Markham, C. R.: The lands of silence: a history of Arctic and Antarctic exploration. Cambridge, The University Press, 1921. Pp. xxi, 539; maps; illustrations; bibliography; index.

Masferrer, Alberto: Pensamientos y formas; notas de viaje. San José, Costa Rica, Imprenta Alsina, 1921. Pp. 125.

Matienzo, José Nicolás: La jurisdicción sobre los ferrocarriles en el derecho constitucional argentino. Buenos Aires, 1920.

Means, Philip Ainsworth: Aspectos estético-cronológicos de las civilizaciones andinas. Quito, Tipografía y Encuadernación Salesiana, 1921. Pp. 32. (From *Boletín de la Academia Nacional de Historia*, vol. I, no. 2.

Mediation of the Honduran-Guatemalan boundary question held under the auspices of the Department of State, 1918-1919. Vol. I. Washington: Government Printing Office, 1919. Pp. 387.

Medina, José Toribio: Los romances basados en la Araucana con su texto y anotaciones. Santiago de Chile, Imprenta Elzeviriana, 1918. Pp. lxxvi, 52.

Mendoza del Solar, José A.: La evolución social y política en el antiguo Perú. Arequipa, Tipografía Cáceres, 1920. Pp. viii, 176.

Mejía, Manuel, S. J.: San Pedro Claver, de la Compañía de Jesús. Reseña histórica de su vida y de su culto. Cartagena, Colombia, Tipografía Mogollón, [1921 ?]. Pp. 124.

Meyers, William Starr: Mexican war diary of George B. McClellan. Princeton University Press, 1917. Pp. 97.

Molina, Enrique: Por las dos Américas. Notas y reflexiones. Santiago, Chile, Casa Editorial "Minerva", 1920. Pp. 219.

Montarroyos, E.: La cuestion du Pacifique devant le droit international; conférence donnée à la Sorbonne le 12 juin 1919. Paris, 1919. Pp. 78.

Moseley, William H.: Mexico today, as seen by our representative on a hurried trip completed October 30, 1920. New York, The American Exchange National Bank, [1920]. Pp. 26; map.

Navas U., José Buenaventura: Evolución social del obrero en Guayaquil, 1849-1920. Guayaquil, Imprenta Guayaquil, 1920. Pp. 163; illus., port.

Núñez, Enrique Bernardo: Después de Ayacucho. Caracas, 1920. Pp. 192. (Biblioteca Venezuela de "El Universal".)

Oliveira Lima, Manoel de: La evolución histórica de la América latina. Bosquejo comparativo. Transl. into Spanish by A. C. Rivas. Madrid, Editorial América [1918]. Pp. 280.

O'Leary, Daniel: Correspondencia de extranjeros notables con el libertador. Tomo I. Madrid, Editorial América, 1920. Pp. xvi, 123. (Biblioteca Ayacucho.)

Olmedo, Miguel Agustin: Un proyecto de camino de Quito a Guayaquil en el siglo XVIII. Quito, Ecuador, 1921.

Orgaz, Raúl A.: Notas sobre la religión colonial. Córdoba, 1920.

Oro Maini, Atilio dell': El impuesto sobre la renta y su aplicación en la República Argentina. Buenos Aires, 1920. Pp. 528.

Ors, Eugenio d': La filosofía del hombre que trabaja y que juega. Antología filosófica formada por R. Rucabado y J. Farran. Introducción de Manuel G. Morente. México, Editorial México Moderno, 1921. Pp. 181. (Cultura, tomo XIII, No. 5).

Ortiz, Fernando: Cuba en la paz de Versalles. Habana, Imprenta "La Universal", 1920. Pp. 30.

Ortiz Rubio, Pascual: Historia de Michoacán. Morelia, Tipografía Comercial, 1920. Pp. 43.

Orzábal Quintana, Arturo: El imperialismo yanqui en Santo Domingo. Buenos Aires, 1921.

Otero, José Pacífico: Nuestro nacionalismo. Buenos Aires, 1920.

Ots, José María: El derecho de familia y el derecho de sucessión en nuestra legislación de Indias. Madrid, Imprenta Helemen, 1921. Pp.220. (Publicaciones del Instituto.)

Peñuela, Cayo Leónidas: Album de Boyacá: publicación hecha bajo los auspicios del gobierno departamental. Bogotá, Arboleda y Valencia, 1919-. Vol. I. Illus.; map.

Pererya, Carlos: La obra de España en América. Madrid, [1920 ?]. Pp. 292. (Biblioteca Nueva.)

Pierce, Frank Cushman: Coloquial and idiomatic Mexican. Brownsville, Texas, 1921. Pp. 64.

Piñero, Norberto: La moneda, el crédito y los bancos en la Argentina. Buenos Aires, J. Ménendez, 1921. Pp. 400.

Planas Suárez, Simón: Condición legal de los extranjeros en Guatemala. Madrid, Imprenta de los Hijos de Reus, [1920 ?]. Pp. 62.

Ponciano Nieto, Asensio: Historia de la congregación de la misión en Méjico (1844-1884). Madrid, Asilo de Huérfanos, 1920. Pp. XII, 420.

Portocarrero, J. R.: El problema político-financiero social de Cuba. Sus causas y soluciones. Habana, 1921. Pp. 96.

Powell, Fred Wilbur: The railroads of Mexico. Boston, The Stratford Co., 1921. Pp. vii, 226; map.

Rabasa,——: La evolución histórica de México. México, 1921. Pp. 349.

Ravignani, Emilio: La personalidad de Manuel Belgrano. Buenos Aires, 1920.

Restrepo-Tirado, E.: Descubrimiento y Conquista de Colombia. Bogotá, Imprenta Nacional, 1919. Vol. II. Pp. 431.

Rey de Castro, Carlos: El artículo III del tratado de Ancón; sinopsis cronológica. Paris, 1919. Pp. 311.

Reyes, César: Los superhombres argentinos. La Rioja, 1920.

Rivet, P. P.: Bibliographie américaniste., 1914-1919. Paris, 1919. Pp. 64.

Rodríguez Codola, M.: Historia de España y de las pueblos hispanoamericanos hasta su independencia, Barcelona. 1919. Vol. I. Pp. 544.

Rolando, Carlos A.: Cronología del periodismo ecuatoriano. Pseudónimos del periodismo nacional. Guayaquil, Imprenta Monteverde y Velarde, 1920. Pp. 166.

Schmidt, Ernst Wilhelm: Die agrarische exportwirtschaft argentiniens. Jena, 1920. Pp. 296.

Sherwell, Guillermo A.: Simón Bolívar (el libertador): patriot, warrior, statesman, father of five nations. Washington, D. C., Press of Byron S. Adams, 1920. Pp. 233; map.

Sotela, Rogelio: Valores literarios de Costa Rica. San José, Costa Rica, 1920.

Spence, Lewis: Legends and romances of Spain. London, G. Harrap & Co., 1920. Pp. 404, front. Plates.

Stefanich, J.: Alberdi, la Argentina y el Paraguay. Asunción, 1920.

Suárez, Constantino: Vocabulario cubano. Habana, 1920.

Thompson, Wallace: Trading with Mexico. New York, Dodd, Mead & Co., 1921. Pp. xiv, 217.

Tozzer, Alfred M.: A Maya grammar with bibliography and appraisement of the books noted. Cambridge, Mass., 1921. Pp. xvi, 301. (Vol. 9, "Papers of Peabody Museum.")

Universidad Nacional de la Plata. Facultad de Ciencias de la educación: Programas (curso 1920-1921). La Plata, Talleres Gráficos Olivieri y Domínguez, 1921. Pp. 167.

Urien, Carlos María: Mitre.—Contribución al estudio de la vida pública del teniente general Bartolomé Mitre. Buenos Aires, Talleres Tipográficos de A. Molinaré, 1919. 2 vols. Pp. x, 462 and vii, 441.

Urrutia, F. J.: Los Estados Unidos de América y las repúblicas hispanoamericanas de 1810-1830. Bogotá, Imprenta Nacional, 1918.

Urtazún, Valentín: Historia diplomática de América. 1 pte. La emancipación de las colonias británicas. Tomo I. La alianza francesa. Pamplona, Higinio Coronas, 1920. Pp. xi, 560.

Valverde, Antonio L.: Exposición temática para explicar un curso de historia del comercio. Habana, 1921.

Vargas Vila, J. M.: Rubén Darío. Barcelona, R. Sopena, 1921. Pp. 247.

Vascones, Francisco, S. J.: Historia de la literatura ecuatoriana. Tomo I. Quito, Tipografía y Encuadernación de la Prensa Católica, 1919. Pp. 475.

Vega Toral, Tomás: La tomebamba de los Incas. Cuenca, Imprenta de la Universidad del Azeray, 1921. Pp. 21; plate.

Velasco Ceballos, R.: Se apoderá Estados Unidos de América de Baja California. (La invasión filibustera de 1911.) México, 1920. Pp. 198; plates.

Vera Estañol, Jorge: Carranza and his bolshevik regime. Los Angeles, [1920 ?].

La Vida colonial en Chile.—Colección de documentos históricos del Archivo del Arzobispado de Santiago. Tomo III. Cedulario, 1650–1699. Pp. VIII, 718. Santiago de Chile, Imprenta Cervantes, 1920.

Vincenzi, M.: Crítica transcendental. San José, Costa Rica, Imprenta María, Viuda de Lines, 1920. Pp. 160.

Wagemann, Ernst: Die deutschen Kolonisten im brasilienischen Staate Espirito Santo. München und Leipzig, Duncker & Humblot, 1915. Pp. 10, 151; plates; maps.

Watjen, Hermann: Das holländische Kolonialrecht in Brasilien. Haag, M. Nijhoff, 1921. Pp. xx, 348.

Wheless, Joseph (transl.): Civil code of Brasil. St. Louis, Thomas Law Book Co., [1920 ?]. Pp. xxxvi, 438.

Wilmart de Glymes, R.: El senado romano. El senado de los Estados Unidos. Buenos Aires, 1920.

Zeballos, E. S.: La república Argentina en la liga de las naciones. Buenos Aires, Publicaciones de "La Prensa", 1921. Pp. 100.

Zelaya, Ramón: Mea culpa centroamericana. San José, Imprenta Alsina, 1920. Pp. 60.

IN PERIODICALS

Abandoned wells. In *The Mexican Review*, August, 1921.

Academia de Historia del Magdalena. In *Boletín de Historia y Antigüedades* (Bogotá), June, 1919.

Actas de la Sociedad Chilena de Historia y Geografía. In *Revista Chilena de Historia y Geografía*, 4th quarter, 1920, and 1st quarter, 1921.

Acuerdo de la Academia Nacional de Historia. In *Boletín de Historia y Antigüedades*, December, 1919.

Acuerdo de la municipalidad de San José en la sesión del 24 de julio de 1843. In *Revista de Costa Rica* (San José), February, 1921.

Aguilar, Juan M.: Aportaciones a la bibliografía del precursor de la independencia suraméricana, don Francisco de Miranda (concluded). In *Boletín de Historia y Antigüedades*, June, 1919.

Aiding young Latin America. In *The Pan American Review*, December, 1920.

Alborta, Jorge D.: La Alianza con la tierra. In *El Estudiante Latino-Americano*, April, 1921.

Alfaro, Anastasio: Primera contribución al estudio de los Zancudos de Costa Rica. In *Revista de Costa Rica*, April and May, 1921.

Algunos documentos del Archivo de Indias sobre ciudades chilenas. In *Boletín del Centro de Estudios Americanistas*, Nos. 42 and 43, 1921.

Alleged religious restrictions in Mexico. In *The Mexican Review*, June, 1921.

Allende, José Domingo: Correspondencia sobre el Perú. In *Revista Chilena de Historia y Geografía*, 1st quarter, 1921.

Amberga, Fray Gerónimo de: Una figura china encontrada en la Araucanía. In *id.*, 3d quarter, 1920.

An American martyrology. In *Illinois Catholic Historical Review*, July, 1921.

American newspaper comment (on Mexico). In *The Mexican Review*, May, 1921.

The American Oil Association loses members. In *id.*, July, 1921.

The Americas in accord. In *The Pan-American Review*, April, 1921.

Amunátegui Reyes, Miguel Luis: Como y por qué se suprimió el castigo del "guanti" en los colegios del estado. In *Revista Chilena de Historia y Geografía*, 3d quarter, 1920.

Amunátegui Solar, Domingo: Bosquejo histórico de la literatura chilena (continued). In *id.*

Andara, J. L.: The Bolívar doctrine. In *Inter-America*, October, 1920.

Anderson, Chandler P.: The Costa Rica-Panama boundary dispute. In *American Journal of International Law*, April, 1921.

Andrew Carnegie and Pan-Americanism. In *The Pan American Review*, June, 1920.

Annual report of the National Railway lines. In *The Mexican Review*, August, 1921.

Another trade conference (in Mexico). In *The Pan American Review*, December, 1920.

Ante la tumba de Santander. In *Boletín de Historia y Antigüedades*, July–August, 1919.

Anti-Mexican propaganda denounced. In *The Mexican Review*, June, 1921.

Appeal for fair play to Mexico. In *id.*, July, 1921.

Aráoz Alfaro, Gregorio: Sobre la organización de la protección y asistencia de la infancia. In *Revista de la Universidad de Buenos Aires*, October–December, 1919.

La Argentina en la Liga de las Naciones. In *Revista Argentina de Ciencias Políticas*, December, 1920 and January, 1921.

Assistance to be given native colonists. In *The Mexican Review*, May, 1921.

Alencar, A. de: Saudação do ambaixador. In *El Estudiante Latino-Americano*, May, 1921.

Attitude of the United States toward Mexico as seen in Argentina. In *The Mexican Review*, July, 1921.

Ayoroa, Ernestina de: Bolivia intelectual. In *El Estudiante Latino-Americano*, April, 1921.

Asuola, Eduardo: Costa Rica. In *id.*, June, 1921.

Babson, Roger W.: A constructive policy for Mexico. In *The Journal of International Relations*, October, 1920.

Ballesteros, L. G., Jr.: The Mexican petroleum question. In *The Mexican Review*, April, 1921.

Bancos que operan hoy en México. In *id.*, March, 1921.

Barker, J. Ellis: The world's oil resources and the United States. In *Contemporary Review*, November, 1920.

Bases del certamen que abre la Academia Nacional de la Historia de Venezuela, para los ciudadanos de las repúblicas americanas, con motivo del centenario de la victoria de Boyacá. In *Boletín de Historia y Antigüedades*, June, 1919.

Bayle, C.: El Año pedagógico hispanoamericano. In *Razón y Fe* (Madrid), February, 1921.

II. Congreso de Geografía e Historia hispanoamerica. In *id.*, June, 1921.

Los Españoles y Magallanes en la expedición del estrecho. In *id.*, January, 1921.

Una página de geografía añeja. In *id.*, July and August, 1921.

Beckwith, Bernardino L.: Los Estudiantes argentinos en los Estados Unidos. In *El Estudiante Latino-Americano*, March, 1921.

Belaúnde, Víctor Andrés: Crónicas de Norteamérica. In *Mercurio Peruano* (Lima), November, 1920–February, 1921.

La Marcha del mundo. El nuevo presidente de los Estados Unidos. In *id.*, March and April, 1921.

Revista política [de varios países]. In *id.*, May, 1921.

Beltran Mathieu, — : Address at the unveiling of Bolívar's statue in New York. In Bulletin no. 25, Interamerican Division, *Internacional Conciliation*, June, 1921.

The neutrality of Chile during the European war. In *American Journal of International Law*, July, 1920.

Bewes, Wyndham A.: The new constitution of Peru. In *Journal of Comparative Legislation and International Law*, October, 1920.

Beyer, Hermann: Mexican archaeology. In *Inter-America*, April, 1921 (transl. from *Revista de Revistas*, Mexico, September 19, 1920 and January 9, 1921).

Bibliografía centro-americana de 1920. In *Mexico Moderno*, June 1, 1921.

Bibliografía de Enrique Piñeyro. Part 2. In *Anales de la Historia* (Habana), September-December, 1919.

Big growth of trade with Mexico. In *The Mexican Review*, July, 1921.

Biggers, Don H.: How about the Mexican? In *id.*, April, 1921 (reprinted from *Farm and Ranch*).

Binayán, Narciso: Bibliografía de bibliografías argentinas. In *Revista de la Universidad de Buenos Aires*, October–December, 1919.

Blackiston, A. Hooten: Appeal for fair play to Mexico. In *The Mexican Review*, June, 1921.

Blanco-Fombona, R.: Psicología del conquistador español del siglo XVI. In *Revista de Filosofía*, January, 1921.

Blásquez, Antonio: Libro de las longitudes . . . por Alonso de Santa Cruz (continued). In *Boletín del Centro de Estudios Americanistas*, Nos. 44 and 45, 1921.

Bogel, Felix: A South American Alsace-Lorraine. In *Living Age*, October 23, 1920.

Bohn, Frank: The Interchange of scholarships. In *The Mexican Review*, August, 1921.

Borges, Esteban Gil: Address at the unveiling of Bolívar's statue. In Bulletin no. 25 of the Interamerican Division of International Conciliation, June, 1921.

Bott, Ernesto J. J.: Los perjuicios resultantes de las guerras para la población civil. In *Revista de la Universidad de Buenos Aires*, January–June, 1920.

Branner, John C.: O que eu faria si fosse estudante brazileiro nos Estados Unidos. In *El Estudiante Latino-Americano*, May, 1921.

Brazilian-American conference. In *The Pan American Review*, December, 1921.

Bromfield, Helen: Mexico today. In *The Philippine Review*, February, 1921.

Brown, James: Business conditions today. In *The Compass*, January, 1921.

Browning, Webster E.: The Central American republics and their problems. In *Journal of International Relations*, October, 1920.

Buendía, Luis A.: Mr. Rockefeller y los estudiantes latino-americanos. In *El Estudiante Latino-Americano*, April, 1921.

Bunge, Alejandro E.: Desnivel internacional del poder de compra de la moneda. In *Revista de Economía Argentina*, July, 1921.

Bunge de Gálvez, Delfino: Regarding realism. In *Inter-America*, April, 1921 (transl. from *Nosotros*, Buenos Aires, November, 1920).

Bustamante, Luis G.: Nuestro deber. In *El Estudiante Latino-Americano*, April, 1921.

Campaña de Nueva Granada. In *Boletín de Historia y Antigüedades*, July-August, 1919.

Campbell, Edna T.: New Orleans at the time of the New Orleans purchase. In *The Geographical Review*, July, 1921.

Cancellation of Lower California concessions. In *The Mexican Review*, August, 1921.

Candioti, Marcial R.: Bibliografía doctoral de la Universidad de Buenos Aires. In *Revista de la Universidad de Buenos Aires*, January-July, 1920.

Capdevila, Arturo: Spaniards and Indians in early Peru. In *Inter-America*, February, 1921 (transl. from *Nosotros*, October, 1920).

Capó Rodríguez, Pedro: Porto Rico as a national problem. In *The Journal of International Relations*, January, 1921.

Carbonell, Diego: The national sciences in Venezuela. In *Inter-America*, February, 1921 (transl. from *Cultura Venezolano*, Caracas, September, 1920).

Cárdenas, Raúl de: The preponderance of the United States on the Caribbean Sea. In *id.*, June, 1921 (transl. from *Cuba Contemporánea*, March, 1921).

Carson, James: Memory of Bartolomé Mitre. In *The Pan American Review*, July, 1921.

Upon the Indian depends Mexico's future. In *The Journal of International Relations*, October, 1920.

Carta de Andrés Bello (1815) al gobierno de Cundinamarca sobre su estancia en Londrés. In *Revista del Colegio Mayor de Nuestra Sra. de Rosario* (Bogotá), March 1, 1921.

Cartas de Don Bernardino Rivadavia a Don Antonio Jonte. In *Revista Chilena de Historia y Geografía*, 3d quarter, 1920.

Castillo, Eduarto: Don Pedro María Ibáñez. In *Boletín de Historia y Antigüedades*, December, 1919.

Castillo-Ledón, Luis: México-Tenoxtitlán. In *México Moderno*, May 1, 1921.

Catálogo de la biblioteca de la Sociedad Económica de Amigos del Pais de la Habana. In *Revista Bimestre Cubana*, September-October, 1920 to May-June, 1921. (Continued.)

Celebrating Mexico's independence day. In *The Mexican Review*, August, 1921.

Censos de la población del virreinato de Nueva España en el siglo XVI. In *Boletín del Centro de Estudios Americanistas*, nos. 36 and 37, 1920.

Centenario de la batalla de Boyacá. In *Boletín de Historia y Antigüedades*, July and August, 1919.

Centón epistolario de Domingo del Monte. In *Anales de la Academia de la Historia* (Habana; continued), September–December, 1919.

Cespedes y Quesada, Carlos Manuel: Manuel de Quesada y Loynas. In *id.*

Chandler, Henry A.: Recent reform proposals concerning state taxation in Mexico. In *Bulletin of the National Tax Association*, October, 1920.

Chapman, Charles E.: The Chilean election. In *Nation*, October 20, 1920.

Christian, A. K.: In *The Southwestern Historical Quarterly*, January and April, 1921.

Clausen, John: Mexican banks classified. In *The Pan American Review*, July, 1921.

Clausen, John: The republic of Guatemala. Its commercial and financial possibilities. In *The Philippine Review*, November, 1920 (in English and Spanish).

Climatic and scenic attractions. In *The Mexican Review*, May, 1921.

Closer ties between Spain and Latin America. In *The Pan American Review*, May–June, 1921.

The coastal belt of Peru. In *The Geographical Review*, April, 1921.

Colliard, B.: Rumaging through old parish records. Historical sketch of the parish of Opelousas, Louisiana. In *St. Louis Catholic Historical Review*, January–April, 1921.

The Colombia-Ecuador boundary. In *The Geographical Review*, April, 1921.

Colombian possibilities for the development of the calcium-carbide industry. In *Colombian Review*, July, 1921.

The Colombian treaty. In *The Compass*, April, 1921.

Colonial life in Spanish America. In *Inter-America*, February, 1921 (transl. from *Comercio Ecuatoriano*, Guayaquil, special no. 83).

Conclusion of the Benton case. In *The Mexican Review*, May, 1921.

Conditions in Pernambuco, Brazil. In *The Compass*, June, 1921.

Conferencias en el Lago Geneva. In *El Estudiante Latino-Americano*, January, 1921.

Conflicto entre Panamá y Costa Rica. In *Revista de Costa Rica*, July and August, 1921 (reprinted from *Unión Ibero Americana* (Madrid), April, 1921.

II. Congreso de geografía e historia hispano-americana celebrado en Sevilla en conmemoración del contenario del viaje y descubrimientos de Fernando de Magallanes. In *Boletín del Centro de Estudios Americanistas*, nos. 42–43, 1921.

Cooperación en la América latina. In *El Estudiante Latino-Americano*, January, 1921.

Cooperative efforts for Latin America. In *The Pan American Review*, May–June, 1921.

Correa, Ramón: Ante el cadáver del doctor Pedro María Ibáñez. In *Boletín de Historia y Antigüedades*. December, 1919.

Correa Luna, Carlos: Un casamiento en 1805. In *Revista de la Universidad de la Buenos Aires*, October–December, 1919.

Correspondencia de don Antonio Varas. In *Revista Chilena de Historia y Geografía*, 3d and 4th quarters, 1920, and 1st and 2d quarters, 1921.

Cox, Isaac Joslin: The Colombian treaty. Retrospect and prospect. In *The Journal of International Relations*, April, 1921.

The Mexican problem; self-help or intervention. In *Political Science Quarterly*, June, 1921.

Crampton, Ethel N.: The legislative departments in the Latin-American constitutions. In *The Southwestern Political Science Quarterly*, September, 1921.

Crónica de Cuba. In *Razón y Fe*, May and August, 1921.

Cuadra Gormas, Guillermo: El apellido Castro durante la colonia. In *Revista Chilena de Historia y Geografía*, 1st quarter, 1921.

Cuarta pención de armas del ejército libertador de la Nueva Granada, en Boyacá, el día 7 de agoste de 1819. In *Boletín de Historia y Antigüedades*, July–August, 1919.

Cuban sugar commission. In *The Compass*, March, 1921.

Cuervo, Luis Augusto: In *Boletín de Historia y Antigüedades*, July–August, 1919.

Cuneo, Santiago de: Algo sobre la Argentina. In *El Estudiante Latino-Americano*, March, 1921.

Una Cuestión internacional. (La actuación Argentina en la asamblea de Gineva. In *id.*

Curiosidades de Rubén Darío. In *id.*

Cushing, Sumner: The distribution of population in Mexico. In *The Geographical Review*, April, 1921.

Cusco, Peru. The old Inca capital. In *The Compass*, June, 1921.

Dagnino, Vicente: Servicio Médico en las naos de Magallanes. In *Revista Chilena de Historia y Geografía*, 1st quarter, 1921.

Dalmau Canet, S.: Modern Spanish literature in Puerto Rico. In *Inter-America*, August, 1921 (transl. from *Las Antillas*, Habana, September, 1920).

Dalton, Grace E.: Spanish in the highschools of the middle west. In *Hispania*, May, 1921.

Datos históricos cubanos. In *Revista Bimestre Cubana*, November–December, 1920, to May–June, 1921 (continued).

Decreto número 2005, de 1919, sobre honores a la memoria del señor doctor don Pedro María Ibáñez. In *Boletín de Historia y Antigüedades*, December, 1919.

Delgado, Honorie F.: La selección universitaria a propositio del mensaje de France y Barbusse. In *Mercurio Peruano*, May, 1921.

Depuy, Henry F.: An early account of the establishment of Jesuit missions in America. In *Proceedings of the American Antiquarian Society*, April 14, 1920.

Desarrollo del comercio mexicano. In *The Mexican Review*, August, 1921.

El Descubrimiento de América. De interés para los enemigos de España. In *Plus Ultra*, June, 1920.

Deustua, Alejandro O.: Lo bello en el arte. In *Mercurio Peruano*, January, 1921. Lo bello en la naturaleza. In *id.*, December, 1920.

La estética de la libertad. In *id.*, February, 1921.

Developing oil on federal lands. In *The Mexican Review*, August, 1921.

De Vidts, Emilio: Ventajas de la apertura del istmo de Ofqui. In *Revista Chilena de Historia y Geografía*, 2d quarter, 1921.

Diario de las operaciones del ejército de don Julio Arboleda, de marzo a agosto, 1862. In *Boletín de Historia y Antigüedades*, June, 1919.

Digest of Torriente law (Cuba). In *The Compass*, March, 1921.

Discouraging bolshevism in Mexico. In *The Mexican Review*, July, 1921.

Discurso de don Raimundo Rivas, presidente de la Academia de Historia, en el acto de la inhumación del cadáver del doctor Pedro María Ibáñez. In *Boletín de Historia y Antigüedades*, December, 1919.

Dr. Oliveira Lima e a Republica Argentina. In *El Estudiante Latino-Americano*, March, 1921.

Domínguez, Mateo: Fundación de la villa de Leiva. In *Boletín de Historia y Antigüedades*, June, 1919.

Domínici, Santos A.: Address at the unveiling of Bolívar's statue in New York. In Bulletin no. 25, Interamerican Division, International Conciliation, June, 1921.

Donly, A. W.: The Railroad situation in Mexico. In *The Journal of International Relations*, October, 1920.

Echeverría, José Ignacio: Algo sobre Rodó. In *Revista del Colegio Mayor de Nuestra Sra. del Rosario* (Bogotá), March 1, 1921.

Educational work in Mexico. In *The Mexican Review*, June, 1921.

Edwards, Alberto: Límites entre las provincias de Atacama y Coquimbo. In *Revista Chilena de Historia y Geografía*, 1st and 2d quarter, 1921.

An Effective peace palace (in Cartago, Costa Rica). In *The Pan American Review*, April, 1921.

Elizalde, Rafael H.: Address at unveiling of Bolívar's statue. In Bulletin no. 25, Interamerican Division, International Conciliation, June, 1921.

Elmore, Edwin: Un sacerdote de Cultura. In *Mercurio Peruano*, November and December, 1921.

Emeth, Omer: Los brujas de Chillán en 1749. In *Revista Chilena de Historia y Geografía*, 4th quarter, 1920.

Encouraging financial conditions. In *The Mexican Review*, May, 1921.

Ernst, Adolf: The formation of the lake of Maracaibo. In *Inter-America*, August, 1921 (transl. from *Cultura Venezolana*, November, 1920).

Escobar, José U.: La Sombra del Karmidez. In *México Moderno*, June 1, 1921.

Escudos de armas, títulos de ciudades y villas, fundaciones de pueblos, erección de obispados, etc. In *Boletín del Centro de Estudios Americanistas*, nos. 38 and 39, 1920.

Esquivel Obregón, T.: "Are the Mexican people capable of governing themselves?" In *The Journal of International Relations*, October, 1920.

Exchange in Latin America. In *The Compass*, March, 1921.

Expresión geográfica de hechos económicos. In *Revista de Economía Argentina*, July, 1921.

Factos sobre o Brazil. In *El Estudiante Latino-Americano*, May, 1921.

La Federación de estudiantes del Perú y la comisión de relaciones amistosas. In *Id.* January, 1921.

Feliú y Cruz, Guillermo: Estudios históricos. Concepcion a fines del siglo XVIII. In *Revista Chilena de Historia y Geografía*, 3d quarter, 1920.

Fernández Peralta, R.: Combate del Jobo. In *Revista de Costa Rica*, July and August, 1921.

Ferrera, Orestes: Una fase más de las elecciones en Cuba. In *La Reforma Social*, April, 1921.

Fifty million bonds issued to pay for expropriated lands. In *The Mexican Review*, July, 1921.

Financial situation of Brazil. In *The Compass*, April, 1921.

Fixed rates of exchange (Ecuador). In *id.*, March, 1921.

Flóres, Benito: The writ of amparo under Mexican law. In *American Bar Association Journal*, August, 1921.

Flóres Álvarez, L.: Pedro María Ibáñez. In *Boletín de Historia y Antigüedades*, December, 1919.

Foreign trade of Mexico. In *The Mexican Review*, June, 1921.

Frankfurter, Felix: Haiti and intervention. In *New Republic*, December 15, 1920.

Frear, J. A.: La independencia de las Filipinas. In *La Reforma Social*, April, 1921.

Frederking, Gustavo A.: Carlos Alfredo Tornquist. Nuevo Académico de la facultad de ciencias económicas. In *Revista de Economía Argentina*, July, 1921.

French, Miriam Milner: Universal mother of the land. In *The Mexican Review*, April, 1921.

Freyre, Gilberto: A America Latina: Sua nova situação internacional. In *El Estudiante Latino-Americano*, February, 1921.

   Da outra America: Tio Sam, mestre-escola do mundo. O trabalho do triangulo vermelho entre os estudantes estrangeiros. In *id.*, January, 1921.

   O Embaixador intellectual do Brasil. In *id.*, March, 1921.

   A Literature brasileira nos Estados Unidos. In *id.*, January, 1921.

   O Principe de Monaco e o Brasil. In *id.*, May, 1921.

Frias, Heriberto: The founding of Tenochtitlán. In *Inter-America*, February, 1921 (transl. from *Atlántida*, Buenos Aires, August 19, 1920).

Los Fundadores de la república. In *Revista de Costa Rica*, September 15, 1921.

The Furniture making industry. In *The Mexican Review*, August, 1921.

Fuster Castresoy, Santiago: .At the foot of Aconquija. In *Inter-America*, April, 1921 (transl. from *Caras y Caretas*, Buenos Aires, August 14, 1920).

Gacitua, Oscar A.: El Sur de los Estados Unidos. In *El Estudiante Latino-Americano*, June, 1921.

Gagui, Carlos: El Rincón de la Vieja. In *Revista de Costa Rica*, March, 1921.

Gahisto, Manoel: Manuel Gálvez. In *Inter-America*, February, 1921 (transl. from *Nosotros*, March, 1920).

Galería de hombres célebres argentinos. In *El Estudiante Latino-Americano*, March, 1921.

Galindo, Aníbal: Después de Boyacá. In *Boletín de Historia y Antigüedades*, July–August, 1919.

Gallo, Andrés M.: Páginas inéditas sobre Boyacá. Reminiscencias. In *id.*

Gámez Monge, M.: Curiosidades de Costa Rica. In *Revista de Costa Rica*, July–August, 1921.

   Una Piedra histórica [boundary stone near Santa Marta]. In *id.*, February, 1921.

García, Arturo: El Sentido simpático de nuestra historia. In *Mercurio Peruano*, June–July, 1921.

García, J. A.: Rafael Obligado. In *Revista de la Universidad de Buenos Aires*, January–June, 1920.

García Samudo, Nicolás: El coronel fray Ignacio Mariño. In *Boletín de Historia y Antigüedades*, July–August, 1919.

Initial diplomatic relations between Colombia and the United States of America following the signing of the declaration of independence. In *Colombian Review*, July, 1921.

Gay Calbó, Enrique: Liberty of utterance. In *Inter-America*, August, 1921 (transl. from *Cuba Contemporánea*, April, 1921).

General Rondón's work in the Brazilian wilderness. In *The Geographical Review*, July, 1921.

El Gobierno [de España] concede tres becas a los estudiantes mejicanos. In *El Eco* (Garden City), March 26, 1921.

Gómez Restrepo, Antonio: Discurso el 12 de octubre de 1919, al hacer entrega de la presidencia de la academia al doctor Raimundo Rivas. In *Boletín de Historia y Antigüedades*, January, 1920.

Discurso pronunciado en la sesión solemne de la Academia Nacional de Historia, por su presidente. In *id.*, July–August, 1919.

Gompers, Samuel: The Pan-American Labor Congress. In *The Mexican Review*, March, 1921.

González Palenina, A.: Extracto del catálogo de los documentos del consejo de Indias conservados en la sección de consejos del Archivo Histórico Nacional. In *Revista de Archivos, Bibliotecas y Museos*, July, 1920.

González Roa, Fernando: La inmutabilidad del derecho de propiedad. In *México Moderno*, June, 1921.

González Víques, Cleto: Nombres geográficos de Costa Rica. In *Revista de Costa Rica*, April and May, 1921.

Orígenes de los Costarricenses (continued). In *id.*, June, July, and August, 1921.

Gorgas memorial for Panama. In *The Pan American Review*, March, 1921.

A Great leader [Bolívar] honored. In *id.*

The Growth of Buenos Aires. In *Inter-America*, June, 1921 (transl. from editorial in *La Argentina* (Barcelona), February, 1921).

Guerra, Ramiro: La Historia y los factores históricos. In *Cuba Contemporánea*, August, 1921.

Gumucio, Carlos: Saludo del Cónsul General boliviano. In *El Estudiante Latino-Americano*, April, 1921.

Gusmán, Martín Luis: Jesús Urueta. In *México Moderno*, May, 1921.

Haas, Alberto: Psicología social del pueblo argentino. In *Revista de Filosofía*, September, 1921.

Hackett, Charles W.: The new regime in Mexico. In *The Southwestern Political Science Quarterly*, June, 1921.

The Haitian memoir. In *Nation*, May 25, 1921.

Hanna, Paul: Mexico—1921. V. Relations with the United States. In *id.*, April 27, 1921.

Harding, Earl: A new era for Colombia. In *The Pan American Review*, May–June, 1921.

Harding, Warren G.: Address at the unveiling of Bolívar's statue in New York. In Bulletin no. 25, Interamerican Division, International Council, June, 1921.

Harcher, Mattie Austin: The Louisiana background of the colonization of Texas, 1763-1803. In *The Southwestern Historical Quarterly*, January, 1921.

Hayden, Ralston: The lesson of Haiti. In *Weekly Review*, December 8, 1920.

Hernández E., Juan B.: Las Primeras leyes electoriales chilenas. In *Revista Chilena de Historia y Geografía*, 2d quarter, 1921.

Herrera Reyes, Mercedes: Apuntes históricos sobre la ciudad de San Felipe y Santiago de Bejucat. In *Revista Bimestre Cubana*, September-October, 1920.

Hevia, Aurelio: General Leonard Wood and public instruction in Cuba. In *Inter-America*, October, 1920.

Hicken, Cristóbal M.: Sobre una expedición a la Patagonia chilena. In *Revista Chilena de Historia y Geografía*, 2d quarter, 1921.

High cost of living unknown. In *The Mexican Review*, March and April, 1921.

Hill, C. F.: Business and financial conditions in Peru. In *The Compass*, June, 1921.

Peruvian business and financial conditions. In *id.*, May, 1921.

Hill, Henry M.: Mexico and the United States. In *The Mexican Review*, June, 1921.

Holweck, F. G.: An American martyrology. In *The Catholic Historical Review*, January, 1921.

Homenaje a Mitre. In *Boletín del Museo Social Argentino* (Buenos Aires), July 10, 1921.

Las Huelgas en Buenos Aires en 1920. In *id.*

Huntington, Ellsworth: The factor of health in Mexican character. In *The Journal of International Relations*, October, 1920.

The relation of health to racial capacity. The example of Mexico. In *The Geographical Review*, April, 1921.

Hurrey, Charles D.: The claims of starving European students upon the students of America. In *El Estudiante Latino-Americano*, February, 1921.

Hurtado, Guillermo O.: Los curas de Novita. In *Boletín de Historia y Antigüedades*, June, 1919.

Hylan, John: Address at the unveiling of the statue of Bolívar in New York. In Bulletin no. 25, Interamerican Division, International Conciliation, June, 1921.

Ibáñez, Pedro María: Alejandro Prospero. In *Boletín de Historia y Antigüedades*, December, 1919.

Benedicto Domínguez. In *id.*

José Antonio de Plaza. In *id.*

Ibérico y Rodríguez, Mariano: La Filosofía. In *Mercurio Peruano*, June-July, 1921.

El Ilusionismo. In *id.*, May, 1921.

Iglesias, Santiago: The actual situation in Porto Rico. In *The Mexican Review*, May, 1921.

Impecunious immigrants not wanted in Mexico. In *id.*, June, 1921.

Important announcement by the government of Durango. In *id.*, May, 1921.

Impartial opinion on Mexican Railways. In *id.*, July, 1921.

In the field of Petroleum. In *id.*, March–July, 1921.

Independencia de América. In *El Eco*, May 14, 1921.

La Independencia de Costa Rica. In *Revista de Costa Rica*, September 15, 1921.

Informe de un jurado de la Academia Nacional de Historia. In *Boletín de Historia y Antigüedades*, January, 1920.

Informe de una comisión sobre el doctor don Pedro María Ibáñez. In *id.*, December, 1919.

Informe del bibliotecario sobre la biblioteca de la Academia Nacional de Historia. In *id.*, January, 1920.

Informe del secretario perpetuo en la junta pública extraordinaria del día 10 de agosto del 1919. In *id.*, July–August, 1919.

Informe reglamentaria del secretario perpetuo de la Academia Nacional de Historia, doctor don Pedro María Ibáñez, leido en la junta pública del 12 de octubre de 1919. In *id.*, January, 1920.

Ingenieros, José: Sarmiento. In *El Estudiante Latino-Americano*, March, 1921 (from *La Nueva Democracia*).

Inman, Samuel Guy: America's task in Santo Domingo and Haiti. In *Forum*, September–October, 1920.

    The present situation in the Caribbean. In *The Journal of International Relations*, October, 1920.

    Síntomas aleuladores de amistad interamericana. In *El Estudiante Latino-Americano*, February, 1921.

A los Intelectuales y estudiantes de la América Latina. Mensaje de Anatole France y Henri Barbusse. In *Mercurio Peruano*, May, 1921.

Interchange of Students. In *The Mexican Review*, July, 1921.

Ippolito, Antonio: Estudante Brazileiro nos Estados Unidos. Suas primeiras impressões. In *El Estudiante Latino-Americano*, January, 1921.

James, Herman G.: Constitutional tendencies in Latin America. In *Current History*, February, 1921.

Jensen, Howard E. The educational problem in Central America. In *El Estudiante Latino-Americano*, June, 1921.

Jiménez, Manuel J.: Domingo Jiménez. In *Revista de Costa Rica*. April and May 1921.

Jiménez Luthmer, María: Contribución al estudio de los frutos de Costa Rica. In *id.*, February, 1921.

Jiménez Rueda, Julio: Música y bailes criollos de la Argentina. In *México Moderno*, June 1, 1921.

    With a great man of letters. In *Inter-América*, April, 1921 (transl. from *Revista de Revistas*, Mexico, November 14, 1920).

Johnston, Charles: The two Mexicos. In *Atlantic Monthly*, November, 1920.

Jones, Grosvenor M.: Factors affecting Peruvian exchange. In *The Compass*, April, 1921.

Jones, Maro Beath: Relações intellectuales entre o Brasil e os Estados Unidos. In *El Estudiante Latino-Americano*, June, 1921.

Journal of Lewis Birdsall Harris, 1836–1842. In *The Southwestern Historical Quarterly*, July, 1921.

Juan José Reyes Patria. In *Boletín de Historia y Antigüedades*, July–August, 1921.

In justice to Mexico. In *The Mexican Review*, August, 1921 (from the *N. Y. World*).

Kellogg, Frederic R.: The Mexican oil situation. In *The Journal of International Relations*, October, 1920.

Kester, Harriet J.: The evolution of the Monroe doctrine. In *Constitutional Review*, April, 1921.

Klein, Julius: La doctrina de Monroe como inteligencia continental. In *Inter-America*, September, 1921 (transl. from THE HISPANIC AMERICAN HISTORICAL REVIEW, May, 1921).

Lafone Quevedo, S. A.: Las migraciones de los Kilmes y la historia de las mismas. In *Revista de la Universidad de Buenos Aires*, October–December, 1919.

Lannoy, Ch. de: La doctrine de Monroë et la pacte des nations. In *Revue de Droit International et Legislation comparative*. No. 3–4, 1920.

Latin America produces athletes. In *The Pan American Review*, June, 1920.

A Latin league. In *id.*, July, 1921.

Latorre, Germán: En bien de Sevilla y del comercio sevillano. In *Boletín del Centro de Estudios Americanistas*, nos. 42–43, 1921.
Intervención tutelar de España en los problemas de límites de Hispano-América. II. Indeterminación de fronteras geográficas. In *Boletín del Centro de Estudios Americanistas*, nos. 38 and 39, 1920, and nos. 40 and 41, 1921.

Laval. Ramón A.: Tradiciones, leyendas y cuentos populares recogidos en Carahue (continued). In *Revista Chilena de Historia y Geografía*, 3d and 4th quarters, 1920, and 1st and 2d quarters, 1921.

Lavalle, Juan Bautista de: Francisco de Goya y Lucientes. In *Inter-America*, June, 1921 (transl. from *Studium*, Lima, October–November, 1920).

Le Bretón, Tomás A.: Un saludo del embajador argentino. In *El Estudiante Latino-Americano*, March, 1921.

Ledgard, Carlos: Caracteres de la crisis económica actual. In *Mercurio Peruano*, March and April, 1921.

Lee, Willis T.: The Raton mesas of New Mexico and Colorado. In *The Geographical Review*, July, 1921.

Leguia, Jorge Guillermo: Los poetas de la colonia. In *Mercurio Peruano*, January, 1921.

Leguia y Martínez, Gérman: Don Francisco de Toledo. In *id.*, February, 1921.

Leniency to American law breakers. In *The Mexican Review*, April, 1921.

Lequerica, Lorenzo de: Carta a Caldas sobre el doctor Mutis. In *Boletín de Historia y Antigüedades*, January, 1920.

Levene, Ricardo: Sobre la personalidad moral de San Martín. Nuevos documentos para su estudio. In *Revista de la Universidad de Buenos Aires*, October–December, 1919.

Liévano, Roberto: Doctor Pedro María Ibáñez. In *Boletín de Historia y Antigüedades*, December, 1919.

La Liga panamericana de estudiantes. In *El Estudiante Latino-Americano*, June, 1921.

Lobo, Helio: In the wake of the Mayflower. In *Inter-America*, June, 1921
(transl. from *La Nación*, Buenos Aires, 1920).
Notavel conferencia sobre o Brazil. Discurso sobre a historia politica do
Brazil, na Universidade de Pennsylvania. In *El Estudiante Latino-Americano*, April, 1921.
López, Jacinto: La Justicia en los Estados Unidos. In *La Reforma Social*,
April, 1921.
The United States and the nations of the Caribbean. In *The Journal of International Relations*, October, 1920.
López Portillo y Rojas, José: El poder de las letras. In *México Moderno*, June
1, 1921.
Lord, James: Labor in Mexico. In *The Journal of International Relations*,
January, 1921.
Lorente, Mariano Joaquín: José S. Álvarez. In *Inter-America*, April, 1921
(transl. from *Caras y Caretas*, Buenos Aires, August 21, 1920).
Losada y Puga, Cristóbal: Las ciencias matemáticas, físicas y técnicas. In
Mercurio Peruano, June–July, 1921.
Lozano T., Fabio: Discurso pronunciado en el parque de la Independencia. In
Boletín de Historia y Antigüedades, July–August, 1919.
Lozano y Lozano, Fabio: Ansoátegui. In *id.*
La Guerra a muerte. In *Mercurio Peruano*, February, 1921.
Luncheon in honor of Dr. Víctor Andrés Belaúnde. In *The Pan American
Review*, December, 1920.
Lynch, Leo Frederic: Books—not bullets for Mexico. In *The Mexican Review*,
June, 1921.
McBride, George McCutcheon: La educación del Indio. In *El Estudiante Latino-Americano*, April, 1921.
McCormick, Medill: Our failure in Haiti. In *Nation*, December 1, 1920.
Machicado, C. Flavio: Los estudiantes bolivianos en los Estados Unidos. In
El Estudiante Latino-Americano, April, 1921.
Mackay, Juan A.: La profesión de hombre. In *Mercurio Peruano*, March and
April, 1921.
Madueño, J. L.: La enseñanza en el Perú a traves de una centuria. In *id.*,
June and July, 1921.
Maestú, Ramiro de: The law of vengeance. In *Inter-America*, February, 1921
(transl. from *El Comercio*, Lima; and *Cuasimodo*, Panamá, March, 1920).
Mañach, Jorge: Las interpretaciones del Quijote. In *Mercurio Peruano*, December, 1920.
Orientaciones. Nordofobia y Nordomania. In *El Estudiante Latino-Americano*, January, 1921.
Mariano Andrés Belaúnde. In *Mercurio Peruano*, February, 1921.
Marín Vicuña, Santiago: Don Joaquín Vicuña y Larraín. Sus ascendientes y
descendientes. In *Revista Chilena de Historia y Geografía*, 1st quarter,
1921.
Marotta, F. Pedro: La universidad y la democracia. In *Revista de la Universidad de Buenos Aires*, October–December, 1919.
Martin, Percy Alvin: O Brazil na segunda conferencia financeira pan-americana.
In *Revista do Brasil* (São Paulo), November, 1920.

The Stanford University medal. In *The Mexican Review*, April, 1921.

Martin M., Javier: Derretero del viaje de Magallanes y su paso por el estrecho. In *Revista Chilena de Historia y Geografía*, 1st quarter, 1921.

Matienzo, J. N.: La jurisdicción sobre los ferrocarriles en el derecho constitucional argentino. In *Revista de Derecho, Historia y Letras*, December, 1920.

Matta Vial, Enrique: La junta de gobierno de 1810 y el consejo de regencia y el virrey del Perú. In *Revista Chilena de Historia y Geografía*, 2d quarter, 1921.

Means, Philip Ainsworth: Ciertos aspectos estéticos del arte antiguo del Perú. In *Mercurio Peruano*, March–April, 1921.

Medina, J. T.: Noticia biográfica de fray Antonio Sors. In *Revista Chilena de Historia y Geografía*, 2d quarter, 1921.

Sucinto paralelo entre Colón y Magallanes. (Discurso pronunciado en la sesión solemne celebrada por la Universidad de Chile el 29 de noviembre de 1920 en conmemoración del 4.° centenario del descubrimiento del estrecho de Magallanes). In *id.*, 1st quarter, 1921.

Memorias de un oficial de marina. In *Boletín de Historia y Antigüedades*, July–August, 1919.

Mercado, Julio: En defensa de la lengua española. In *Hispania*, March, 1921.

Mexican-American relations. In *The Mexican Review*, August, 1921.

Mexican children's congress. In *id.*, March, 1921.

Mexican delegates welcomed. In *id.*, May, 1921.

Mexican government most liberal. In *id.*, March,1921.

The Mexican oil situation. In *id.*, April, 1921.

Mexican patriotic club organised in Texas. In *id.*, August, 1921.

Mexican products shown in California. In *id.*

Michaud, Gustavo: Los microbios del latex. Interesante descubrimiento de un sabio costarricense. In *Revista de Costa Rica*, July and August, 1921.

Michaud, G. L.: Los progresos de la educación en Centro América. In *El Estudiante Latino-Americano*, June, 1921.

Middleton, Annie: Donelson's mission to Texas in behalf of annexation. In *The Southwestern Historical Quarterly*, April, 1921.

The Texas convention of 1845. In *id.*, July, 1921.

Miller, Nathan L.: Address at the unveiling of Bolívar's statue, in New York. In Bulletin no. 25, Interamerican Division, International Conciliation. June, 1921.

La Misión española en Chile. In *Razón y Fe*, January, 1921.

Mohr, Alba A.: Colombian oil development. In *The Compass*, June, 1921.

The stock raising industry of Venezuela. In *id.*, March, 1921.

Molina, Enrique: Impressions of Washington. In *Inter-America*, February, 1921 (transl. from *Juventud*, Santiago, Chile, May, 1920).

Monsalve, J. D.: Antonia Santos. In *Boletín de Historia y Antigüedades*, July–August, 1919.

Montessus de Ballore, Fernando de: Manes, temblores y volcanes. In *Revista Chilena de Historia y Geografía*, 4th quarter, 1920.

El Valle longitudinal de Chile. In *id.*, 1st quarter, 1921.

Monteverde, Carlos Eduardo: Las conferencias de Silver Bay. In *El Estudiante Latino-Americano*, January, 1921.

Montoto, Santiago: Don José de Veitia Linaje y su libro "Norte de la Contratación de las Indias". In *Boletín del Centro de Estudios Americanistas*, Nos. 44 and 45, 1921.

Montt, Luis: Bibliografía chilena. In *Revista Chilena de Historia y Geografía*, 4th quarter, 1920, and 1st and 2d quarters, 1921.

Moore, John Bassett: Address at the unveiling of Bolívar's statue in NewYork. In Bulletin no. 25, Interamerican Division, International Conciliation, June, 1921.

Moors, Montero, E.: Vida del doctor Juan Martínez de Rozas (continued). In *Revista Chilena de Historia y Geografía*, 3d and 4th quarters, 1920, and 1st quarter, 1921.

Moore, John F.: The United States and Latin America. In *The Journal of International Relations*, January, 1921.

More light on the oil question. In *The Mexican Review*, August, 1921.

Moreno, Fulgencio R.: Algunos datos sobre la geografía etnográfica de parte del Paraguay y del alto Perú. In *Revista Chilena de Historia y Geografía*, 1st quarter, 1921.

El Paraguay colonial y las provincias meridionales. In *id.*, 4th quarter, 1920.

Muñoz Olave, Reinaldo: Los jesuitas en Chillán en el siglo XVIII. In *id.*, 4th quarter, 1920.

Mutis, José Celestine: Exposición hecha al virrey de Santafé sobre la necesidad de prevenir los progresos del mal de San Lázaro y de promover la destrucción de las plataneras dentro de las poblaciones, como causa de las enfermedades endémicas que se padecen en la provincia del Socorro. In *Boletín de Historia y Antigüedades*, January, 1920.

New oil tax decree. In *The Mexican Review*, August, 1921.

New rates of taxation on petroleum products. In *id.*, July, 1921.

The New York and Montevideo's mayors exchange greetings. In *The Pan American Review*, March, 1921.

Noé, Julio: Sarmiento the traveler. In *Inter-America*, February, 1921 (transl. from *Revista de Filosofía*, Buenos Aires, May, 1918).

Noel, John Vavasour: Mexico and the present revolution. In *The Journal of International Relations*, January, 1921.

Nomina de los socios de la Sociedad Chilena de Historia y Geografía en 31 de Diciembre de 1920. In *Revista Chilena de Historia y Geografía*, 4th quarter, 1920.

A Noteworthy organization (The American Chamber of Commerce in Mexico). In *The Mexican Review*, April, 1921.

Obregón, the man of the hour in Mexico. In *id.*, July, 1921.

Obregón urges needed reforms. In *id.*, March, 1921.

Ochoa, C. D.: A grandeza economica do Brazil futuro. In *El Estudiante Latino-Americano*, May, 1921.

Ocupación de la ciudad de Tunja por el ejército libertador. In *Boletín de Historia y Antigüedades*, July-August, 1919.

Oemichen, F. J.: Argentine conditions and their effect on American trade. In *The Compass*, June, 1921.

O'Hara, John F.: The league of Catholic women in Uruguay. In *Catholic World*, May, 1921.

Oil and Mexico. In *The Mexican Review*, July, 1921.

Oil land titles and oil taxation. In *id.*, June, 1921.

Oil profits in Mexico. In *id.*

Old banks to renew business. In *id.*, April, 1921.

Oliveira César, F. de: Supay-Chaca. In *Inter-America*, April, 1921 (transl. from *Atlántida*, December 9, 1920).

Orear, Leslie: American investment in the Argentine meat-packing industry. In *The Compass*, June, 1921.

Orgaz, Raúl A.: Sinopsis sobre la historia de las ideas sociales argentinas. In *Revista de Filosofía*, January, 1921.

A Synopsis of the history of Argentine social ideas. In *Inter-America*, April, 1921 (transl. from *Revista de Filosofía*, January, 1921).

Ortiz, Fernando: The Afro-Cuban festival of "The Day of the Kings". In *Inter-America*, June, 1921 (transl. from *La Reforma Social*, New York, August, 1920).

Los Cabildos Afro-Cubanos. In *Revista Bimestre Cubana*, January–February, 1921.

Un Cataure de cubanismos (Mamotreto de "Cubicheraís" lexicográficas). In *id.*, January–February, March–April, and May–June, 1921.

Orzábul Quintana, Arturo: Hacia un nuevo derecho internacional. In *Revista de Filosofía*, January, 1921.

Ossandón, Bernardo: Liceo de la Serena. (Recuerdos de un Ex-alumno. Decenio de 1862–1872). In *Revista Chilena de Historia y Geografía*, 2d quarter, 1921.

Otere D' Costa, E.: Pedro María Ibáñez. In *Boletín de Historia y Antigüedades*, December, 1919.

Our place in Latin-America commerce. In *The Pan American Review*, July, 1921.

Pabón, Jesús, and Luis Jiménez Placer y Ciaurrez: Algunos documentos del archivo de Indias sobre ciudades chilenas. In *Boletín del Centro de Estudios Americanistas*, nos. 42–43, 1921.

Pagano, Anselmo: The Belgian sovereigns in Brazil. In *Inter-America*, February, 1921 (transl. from *Plus Ultra*, Buenos Aires, September, 1920).

Pagano, José León: The national salon of fine arts. In *id.* (transl. from *El Hogar*, Buenos Aires, October 8, 1920).

Palabras de Amenábar. España e Hispano-América están identificadas por poseer ambas el alma común de nuestra raza. In *Plus Ultra* (New York), August, 1921.

Palabras de Luis Augusto Cuervo ante el Cabildo de la ciudad de Tunja, en nombre de la municipalidad de Bogotá y de las academias de Historia de Colombia y Venezuela. In *Boletín de Historia y Antigüedades*, July–August, 1919.

Palavicini, F. F.: Mexican editor makes a protest. In *The Mexican Review*, June, 1921.

Palavras de Joaquim Nabuco. In *El Estudiante Latino-Americano*, June, 1921.

Palmer, Thomas W.: A study of the mining law of Chile. In *Pennsylvania Labor Review*, November, 1920.

Palomó, Luis: Discurso pronunciado . . . en el día 2 de Marzo de 1921 en la discusión del dictamen de contestación al discurso de la corona. In *Boletín del Centro de Estudios Americanistas*, nos. 42 and 43, 1921.

Pape, Fred A. G.: Unused tropical American and adverse exchange. In *The Pan American Review*, December, 1920.

Pasarell, Emilio J.: Ripples on the surface of great themes. In *Inter-America*, June, 1921 (transl. from *Puerto Rico* (San Juan), December, 1920.

Pena, Manuel de la: Greetings to the world from the new liberal constitutional party in Mexico. In *The Journal of International Relations*, July, 1920.

La pena de muerte en Cuba: Su ejecución. In *Cuba Contemporánea*, August, 1921.

Pensamientos de los fundadores de la república. In *Revista de Costa Rica*, September, 15, 1921.

Pérez Díaz, Lucila L.: El hade del libertador. In *Cultura Venezolana*, February, 1921.

Pérez Verdía, Benito: The glorification of Bolívar. In *Inter-Amrica*, August, 1921 (transl. from *El Excelsior*, Mexico).

Pérez Zeledón, Pedro: Fray Rodrigo Péres. In *Revista de Costa Rica*, February, 1921.

Pesqueira, R. V.: Doheny's disclaimer refuted. In *The Mexican Review*, June, 1921.

Plá, Eduardo F.: Marcos de J. Melero. In *Revista Bimestre Cubana*, November-December, 1920.

P. M. I.: José Concha. In *Boletín de Historia y Antigüedades*, August, 1919.

Poblete M., Rafael: El servicio sanitario en el ejército de Chile durante la guerra del Pacífico, 1879–1884. In *Revista Chilena de Historia y Geografía*, 3d quarter, 1920, and 1st quarter, 1921.

Popernol, Wilson: The Colombian berry or the giant blackberry of Colombia. In *Colombian Review*, July, 1921.

Posada, E.: Apostillas. In *Boletín de Historia y Antigüedades*, January, 1920. Epigrafía bogotana. In *id*.

Post-war readjustment in Colombia. In *The Compass*, March, 1921.

Prado, Eladio: Ujarrás. In *Revista de Costa Rica*, June, 1921.

The Present Mexican situation. In *The Mexican Review*, May, 1921.

Prehistoric Chinese in Mexico. In *id*., July and August, 1921.

President Harding on Pan Americanism. In *The Pan American Review*, April, 1921.

President Obregón explains the position of Mexico before the world. In *The Mexican Review*, August, 1921.

President Obregón honors George Washington's memory. In *id*., April, 1921.

President Obregón makes a plain statement of the policy of the Mexican government. In *id*., May, 1921.

President Obregón makes a public statement. In *id*., July, 1921.

President Obregón talks to the press. In *id*., April, 1921.

El Presidente Harding condena la tarifa sobre importación de petróleos. In *Colombian Review*, July, 1920.

The presidents of Argentina. In *Inter-America*, April, 1921 (transl. from *Fray Mucho*, Buenos Aires, October 12, 1920).

Priestley, Herbert Ingram: Hope for Mexico. In *Cosmopolitan Student*, November, 1920.

Primer centenario del fusilamiento de Antonia Santos, en el Socorro. In *Boletín de Historia y Antigüedades*, July-August, 1919.

Probst, Juan: Un auto del cabildo de Luján sobre instrucción primaria obligatoria. Año 1773. In *Revista de la Universidad de Buenos Aires*, October-December, 1919.

Propuesta de Esteban Gómez, piloto, para establecer un dique en el arroyo Taguete, donde se junta con el Guadalquivir, 1553. In *Boletín del Centro de Estudios Americanistas*, nos. 40 and 41, 1921.

Protests against falsehoods regarding Mexican conditions. In *The Mexican Review*, May, 1921.

Quesada, Ernesto: La doctrina Drago. In *Revista de la Universidad de Buenos Aires*, October-December, 1919.

Quesada, Fortunato: Las ciencias biológicas. In *Mercurio Peruano*, June-July, 1921.

Ramírez, Mercedes (viuda de Ibáñez): Notas sobre su esposo. In *Boletín de Historia y Antigüedades*, December, 1919.

Ramírez Pena, Abraham: Suscinta historia de los juegos florales en El Salvador. In *El Estudiante Latino-Americano*, June, 1921.

Real Academia Hispano-Americana de Ciencias y Artes de Cádiz. Certamen artístico para conmemorar el día 12 de octubre. In *Boletín del Centro de Estudios Americanistas*, nos. 38 and 39, 1920.

The Real future of pan americanism. In *The Pan American Review*, March, 1921.

Recent conference on Pan American education. In *El Estudiante Latino Americano*, February, 1921.

Reciprocity urged for two republics. In *The Mexican Review*, March, 1921.

Relaciones geográficas de Yucatán. In *Boletín del Centro de Estudios Americanistas*, nos. 36 and 37, 1920.

Report of the conference committee for Argentina. In *The Pan American Review*, June, 1920.

Report of the conference committee for the Domincan Republic. In *id.*, December, 1920.

Report of the conference committee for Guatemala. In *id.*, March, 1921.

Republic of Colombia and its vegetable oils. In *Colombian Review*, July, 1921.

Restrepo Laverde, J.: Pedro María Ibáñez. In *Boletín de Historia y Antigüedades*, December, 1919.

Restrepo Sáenz, José María: Genealogía del General Santander. In *id.*, July-August, 1919.

Restrepo Tirado, Ernesto: El doctor Pedro María Ibáñes. In *id.*, December, 1919.

Revista de crítica y bibliografía. In *Revista Chilena de Historia y Geografía*, 3d and 4th quarters, 1920.

Revolutionary damage claims. In *The Mexican Review*, April, 1921.

Reyes, Alejandro: The noble mission of the lawyer. In *Inter-America*, August, 1921 (transl. from *Revista de Derecho y Legislación*, Caracas, November and December, 1920).

Reyes. Alfonso: Ramón Gómez de la Serna. In *México Moderno*, March 1, 1921.

Reyes, J. Antonio: El Progreso de la educación femenil en el Perú. In *El Estudiante Latino-Americano*, February, 1921.

Ribas, Mario: Our humiliating isolation. In *Inter-America*, August, 1921 (transl. from *Renacimiento*, Tegucigalpa, April 25, 1921).

Spain in America. In *id.*, April, 1921 (transl. from *id.*, October 15, 1920).

Ried, Aquinas: Diario del viaje efectuado por el doctor Aquinas Ried desde Valparaiso hasta el lago Hanquihue, y de regreso (7 de febrero de 1849 al 30 de junio del mismo año). In *Revista Chilena de Historia y Geografía*, 4th quarter, 1920.

O Rio de Janeiro, cidade feerica. In *El Estudiante Latino-Americano*, May, 1921.

Rippy, J. Fred: A Ray of light on the Gadsden treaty. In *The Southwestern Historical Quarterly*, January, 1921.

Some precedents of the Pershing expedition into Mexico. In *id.*, April, 1921.

Rivas, Francisco: Mexican mining statistics. In *The Mexican Review*, March, 1921.

Rivas, Raimundo: Amores de Solís. Lectura en la sesión solemne del 12 de octubre de 1919 de la Academia Nacional de Historia. In *Boletín de Historia y Antigüedades*, January, 1920.

R. M. C.: Don Víctor Mallarino. In *Revista del Colegio Mayor de Nuestra Señora del Rosario* (Bogotá), March 1, 1920.

Robledo, Eusebio: Discurso sobre el doctor don Pedro María Ibáñez. In *Boletín de Historia y Antigüedades*, December, 1919.

Rodríguez, J. M.: Estado económico del Perú. In *Mercurio Peruano*, June–July, 1921.

Rodríguez Lendián, Evelio: Elogio del doctor Ramón Meza y Suárez Inclán. Part II. In *Anales de la Academia de la Historia* (Cuba), September–December, 1919.

Rodríguez Triana, E.: Pedro María Ibáñez. In *Boletín de Historia y Antigüedades*, December, 1919.

Rohrmoser, Amelia M.: Ascensión del volcán. Irazú del Dr. Throllope. In *Revista de Costa Rica*, April and May, 1921 (transl. from the English).

Romero, Concha: La Sociedad Hispánica de América. In *El Estudiante Latino-Americano*, February, 1921.

Rosa, Ramón: Independence Day and Central American union. In *Inter-America*, December, 1920.

Rousset, Ricardo U.: Cristóbal Colón y el descubrimiento del nuevo mundo. In *Revista Bimestre Cubana*, September–October and November–December, 1920, and January–February, March–April, and May–June, 1921.

Rowe, Leo S.: Message to Latin American students. In *El Estudiante Latino-Americano*, February, 1921.

Ruschenberger, William S. W.: Noticias de Chile (1831–1832) por un oficial de la marina de los Estados Unidos de América. In *Revista Chilena de Historia y Geografía*, 2d, 3d, and 4th quarters, 1920, and 1st and 2d quarters, 1921.

Sagarna, Antonio: La personalidad de Urquiza. In *Revista de Filosofía*, January, 1921.

Salaverri, Vicente A.: Florencio Sánchez; the man and the dramatist. In *Inter-America*, August, 1921 (transl. from *Nosotros*, March, 1921).

Sanders, E. M.: The natural regions of Mexico. In *The Geographical Review*, April, 1921.

Sánchez, Luis Alberto: La historia en el Perú. In *Mercurio Peruano*, June–July, 1921.

Sánchez, M. S.: Mito genealógico. In *Boletín de Historia y Antigüedades*, July–August, 1919.

Sandoval, Angel A.: La federación de Centro-América. In *El Estudiante Latino-Americano*, June, 1921.

Santa Cruz, Joaquín: Los indígenas del Ecuador. In *Revista Chilena de Historia y Geografía*, 1st and 2d quarters, 1921.

Sanz Guerrero, Andrés A.: Bolivia y los Estados Unidos. In *El Estudiante Latino-Americano*, April, 1921.

Schafer, Carl: Economic development of Brazil. In *The Compass*, January, 1921.

Schoenrich, Otto: The present American intervention in Santo Domingo and Haiti. In *The Journal of International Relations*, July, 1920.

Secretary Pani addresses public. In *The Mexican Review*, April, 1921.

Segundo Congreso de Geografía e Historia Hispano-Americanas, celebrado en Sevilla en conmemoración del centenario del viaje y descubrimientos de Fernando de Magallanes. In *Boletín del Centro de Estudios Americanistas*, nos. 42–43, 1921.

Selva, Salomón de la: Sobre la unión de Centro-América. In *Revista de Costa Rica*, March, 1921 (transl. from THE HISPANIC AMERICAN HISTORICAL REVIEW, November, 1920).

Senhorita Laura Ottoni. In *El Estudiante Latino-Americano*, May, 1921.

Séptima memoria que el secretario general de la Sociedad Chilena de Historia y Geografía presenta a la junta general de socios celebrada el lunes 13 de diciembre de 1920. In *Revista Chilena de Historia y Geografía*, 4th quarter, 1920.

Sexton, Bernard: Education for all-America. In *The Pan American Review*, June, 1920.

Shaw, Albert: Porto Ricans as citizens. Some observations regarding their political future. In *Review of Reviews*, May, 1921.

Shepherd, William R.: The Caribbean policy of the United States. In *The Journal of International Relations*, July, 1920.
Liga panamericana de estudiantes. In *El Estudiante Latino-Americano*, May, 1921.

Ships for South America. In *The Pan American Review*, June, 1920.

Siegrist, Mary: Carlos Valderrama, Peruvian composer-pianist. In *id.*, December, 1920.

Silva Cotapos, Carlos: Episodio eclesiástico de la guerra del Pacífico. In *Revista Chilena de Historia y Geografía*, 1st quarter, 1921.

Silva Salas, Edulia: Biografía de don Adolfo Ibáñez. In *id.*, 3d quarter, 1920.

Simón Bolívar honored. In *The Compass*, May, 1921.

Siqueira Coutinho, J. de: Aos Estudantes brasileiros. In *El Estudiante Latino-Americano*, May, 1921.

Smidt, Lorenzo: La historia de los grandes lagos del altiplano boliviana y la relación que pueden tener la fundación y destrucción del primer Tiahuanacu y con la existencia de los grandes mamíferos extintos de Ulloura. In *Revista Chilena de Historia y Geografía*, 4th quarter, 1920.

Sojo, Angel L.: Brain and bulk. In *Inter-America*, April, 1921 (transl. from *Fray Mucho*, November, 1920).

Sola Torino, E.: Escalando los Andes. In *El Estudiante Latino-Americano*, March, 1921.

Some interesting petroleum statistics. In *The Mexican Review*, August, 1921.

Sors, Fray Antonio: Historia del reino de Chile, situado en la América Meridional. In *Revista Chilena de Historia y Geografía*, 2d quarter, 1921.

South American investments. In *The Compass*, June, 1921.

Special commission to look after Mexican interests in the United States. In *The Mexican Review*, July, 1921.

Spinden, H. T.: Elecciones espurias en Cuba. In *La Reforma Social*, April, 1921.

Starr, Frederick: The Mexican People. In *The Journal of International Relations*, July, 1920.

The State of Sonora. In *The Mexican Review*, May, 1921.

The States of the Mexican Republic. In *id.*, March, 1921.

Statistical data on the hide and leather industry in the Republic of Colombia, S. A. In *Colombian Review*, July, 1921.

Stewart, C. H.: The Maracaibo oil basin. In *The Compass*, May, 1921.

Stewart, Walter W.: Financing revolutions in Mexico. In *Journal of Political Economy*, October, 1920.

Stuart, Graham, H.: The new pan Americanism. In *The Pan American Review*, July, 1921.

Sturgis, Catherine Vesta: Through Tamaulipas and Nuevo León. In *The Mexican Review*, April, 1921.

Sueldo, Julio D.: Apresurarse lentamente. In *El Estudiante Latino-Americano*, April, 1921.

Summer courses in Venezuela. In *Hispania*, May, 1921.

Tamayo, Franz: Pedagogía nacional. Fragmentos de un libro. In *El Estudiante Latino-Americano*, April, 1921.

Taylor, Francis R.: Recent conditions in Mexico. In *The Journal of International Relations*, January, 1921.

Tejada, Frederico S. de: American international law. In *Inter-America*, June, 1921 (transl. from *Centro-America*, July, August, and September, 1920).

Terrones, Alberto: Progress of the State of Durango. In *The Mexican Review*, March, 1921.

Thayer Ojeda, Tomás: Las biografías de los dos "Cristóbales de Molina" publicadas por el escritor peruano don Carlos A. Romero. In *Revista Chilena de Historia y Geografía*, 4th quarter, 1920.

Reseña histórico-biográfica de los eclesiásticos en el descubrimiento y conquista de Chile. In *id.*, 3d and 4th quarters, 1920, and 1st and 2d quarters, 1921.

Thomas, Kirby: America's "Mare nostrum". In *The Journal of International Relations*, January, 1921.

Thorpe, George C.: American achievements in Santo Domingo, Haiti, and Virgin Islands. In *id.*, July, 1920.

Tizón y Bueno, Ricardo: La ingeniería en la colonia. In *Mercurio Peruano*, May, 1921.

Tornquist, Carlos Alfredo: El doctor Adolfo Dávila. Sus ideas y enseñanzas sobre las problemas económicas argentinas. In *Revista de Economía Argentina*, July, 1921.

Toro y Gómez, M. de: Metodología del estudio científico del castellano. In *Revista de la Universidad de Buenos Aires*, January-June, 1920.

Torres Lanzas, Pedro: Catálogo de legajos del Archivo General de Indias. In *Boletín del Centro de Estudios Americanistas*, nos. 38 and 39, 1920, and nos. 40-41, 42-43, 44-45, 1921.

Escudos de armas, títulos de ciudades, y villas, fundaciones de pueblos, erección de obispados. In *id.*, nos. 40-41, 1921.

Tricoche, G. N.: Batailles oubliées: les anglais à Buenos Aires, 8-9 juillet, 1807. In *Revue Historique*, July-August, 1920.

Tristan, J. Fid.: Apuntes sobre el volcán Rincón de la Vieja. In *Revista de Costa Rica*, February and March, 1921.

Notas sobre . . . un vertebrado fosil . . de Cartago. In *id.*, July and August, 1921.

Trollope, Anthony: San José in 1858. In *id.*

Trowbridge, E. D.: Reconstruction problems in Mexico. In *The Journal of International Relations*, January, 1921.

Ugarte, César Antonio: Evolución jurídica del Perú. In *Mercurio Peruano*, June-July, 1921.

La Universidad de Yale. In *id.*, November, 1920.

Underhand work continues. In *The Mexican Review*, April, 1921.

Unión Ibero Americana concurso para 1922. In *Revista de Costa Rica*, July and August, 1921.

La Unión Panamericana. In *El Eco* (Garden City), March 26, 1921.

Urteaga, E. L.: Nuestra educación argentina. In *El Estudiante Latino-Americano*, March, 1921.

Urteaga, Horacio H.: Los copleros de la conquista. In *Mercurio Peruano*, February, 1921.

Los estudios de la arqueología del Perú. In *id.*, June-July, 1921.

Valdivieso C., V. M.: Guillermo Matta. (Apuntes biográficos.) In *Revista Chilena de Historia y Geografía*, 2d quarter, 1921.

Váldes de la Torre, Carlos: Régimen de la propiedad durante los incas. In *Mercurio Peruano*, November, 1920.

Valle, Francisco G. del: Páginas para la historia de Cuba. Documentos para la biografía de José de la Luz y Caballero. III. In *Cuba Contemporánea*, August, 1921.

Vallenilla Lanz, Laureano: The colonial city: its remote sources. In *Inter-America*, August, 1921 (transl. from *Cultura Venezolana*, September, 1920).

Varas Velásques, Miguel: El congreso americano celebrado en Lima en 1864. In *Revista Chilena de Historia y Geografía*, 2d quarter, 1921.

V. D. O.: Un alistamiento en 1815. In *id.*, 4th quarter, 1920.

Vegas, Manuel I.: Cristóbal Colón: In *Mercurio Peruano*, January, and March and April, 1921.

Venadium in Peru. In *The Compass*, June, 1921.

Venezuelan historical documents at the Chicago exposition. In *Colombian Review*, July, 1921.

Vera, Orestes: El joven latino-americano en los Estados Unidos. In *El Estudiante Latino-Americano*, February, 1921.

Vianna, Milton F.: O Logar do estudante estrangeiro nas universidades americanas. In *id.*, May, 1921.

O Que os estudantes deven levar para os seus paizes. In *id.*, February, 1921.

Viñas Mey, C.: La legislación social en la recopilación de Indias. In *Revista de Archivos*, Bibliotecas y Museos, July, 1920.

To Warren G. Harding, Journalist. To Warren G. Harding, President. In *The Mexican Review*, April, 1921. (Reproduced from *El Universal*, Mexico.)

Weeks, George F.: Mexican byways and highways. In *id.*, January-June, 1921.

Weisinger, Nina: A summer vacation in Costa Rica. In *Hispania*, May, 1921.

Wercklé, Carlos: La subregión Fito Geográfica Costarricense. In *Revista de Costa Rica*, June, and July and August, 1921.

The West coast of Mexico. In *The Mexican Review*, May, 1921.

Will labor in harmony. In *id.*, March, 1921.

Willcox, H. Case: An explanation of the Rio de Oro, Colombia-Venezuela. In *The Geographical Review*, July, 1921.

Wilson, Henry Lane: How to restore peace in Mexico. In *The Journal of International Relations*, October, 1920.

Winston, James E.: The annexation of Texas and the Mississippi democrats. In *The Southwestern Historical Quarterly*, July, 1921.

Winter, G. B.: Los controversias entre México y los Estados Unidos. In *The Mexican Review*, April, 1921.

Zeballos, E. S.: United States diplomacy in South America. In *Living Age*, November 20, 1920.

Zenteno, Barros, Julio: El liceo de la Serena. In *Revista Chilena de Historia y Geografía*, 3d quarter, 1920.

Zuleta, Eduardo: Elogio de don José Manuel Restrepo en la Academia Nacional de Historia. In *Boletín de Historia y Antigüedades*, July-August, 1919.

THE HISPANIC AMERICAN HISTORICAL REVIEW

BOARD OF EDITORS

ISAAC J. COX   WILLIAM W. PIERSON, Jr.
WILLIAM R. MANNING   HERBERT INGRAM PRIESTLEY
PERCY ALVIN MARTIN   JAMES A. ROBERTSON

ADVISORY EDITORS

HERBERT E. BOLTON   WILLIAM R. SHEPHERD

JAMES A. ROBERTSON, Managing Editor
C. K. JONES, Bibliographer

Vol. IV   **FEBRUARY, 1921**   **No. 1**

CONTENTS

(For list of Book Reviews, see next page)

Published Quarterly by the Board of Editors of the Hispanic American
Historical Review

PUBLICITY AGENT: CHARLES LYON CHANDLER
Corn Exchange National Bank, Philadelphia, Pa.

BOOK REVIEWS

The annual subscription of the REVIEW is three dollars to all points within the United States of America and its possessions, the Dominion of Canada, Cuba, Mexico, and Panama; and three dollars and fifty cents to all other countries. Single numbers are one dollar each. Bound volumes may be supplied, within the limits of the edition, upon request.

All communications and manuscripts, and all books for review should be sent to the Williams & Wilkins Company, Mt. Royal and Guilford Avenues, Baltimore, Md., or Managing Editor, 1422 Irving Street N. E., Washington, D. C., and payments should be made to the latter address.

Delivery can not be guaranteed within any war zone.

THE HISPANIC AMERICAN HISTORICAL REVIEW

F3

Vol. IV   NOVEMBER, 1921   No. 4

CONTENTS

(For list of Book Reviews, see next page)

Published Quarterly by the Board of Editors of the Hispanic American
Historical Review

PUBLICITY AGENT: CHARLES LYON CHANDLER
Corn Exchange National Bank, Philadelphia, Pa.

WILLIAMS & WILKINS COMPANY
Baltimore. Md.. U. S. A.

BOOK REVIEWS

The annual subscription of the REVIEW is three dollars to all points
within the United States of America and its possessions, the Dominion
of Canada, Cuba, Mexico, and Panama; and three dollars and fifty
cents to all other countries. Single numbers are one dollar each.
Bound volumes may be supplied, within the limits of the edition, upon
request.

All communications and manuscripts, and all books for review should
be sent to the Williams & Wilkins Company, Mt. Royal and Guilford
Avenues, Baltimore, Md., or Managing Editor, 1422 Irving Street
N. E., Washington, D. C., and payments should be made to the latter
address.

Delivery can not be guaranteed within any war zone.